Solaris™ Internals
Second Edition

Solaris™ Internals
Second Edition

Solaris 10 and OpenSolaris Kernel Architecture

Richard McDougall
Jim Mauro

Sun Microsystems Press

PRENTICE HALL

Upper Saddle River, NJ • Boston • Indianapolis • San Francisco
New York • Toronto • Montreal • London • Munich • Paris • Madrid
Capetown • Sydney • Tokyo • Singapore • Mexico City

The publisher offers excellent discounts on this book when ordered in quantity for bulk purchases or special sales, which may include electronic versions and/or custom covers and content particular to your business, training goals, marketing focus, and branding interests. For more information, please contact: U.S. Corporate and Government Sales, (800) 382-3419, corpsales@pearsontechgroup.com.

For sales outside the U.S., please contact International Sales, international@pearsoned.com.

Visit us on the Web: www.prenhallprofessional.com

This Book Is Safari Enabled

The Safari® Enabled icon on the cover of your favorite technology book means the book is available through Safari Bookshelf. When you buy this book, you get free access to the online edition for 45 days.

Safari Bookshelf is an electronic reference library that lets you easily search thousands of technical books, find code samples, download chapters, and access technical information whenever and wherever you need it.

To gain 45-day Safari Enabled access to this book:

• Go to http://www.prenhallprofessional.com/safarienabled

• Complete the brief registration form

• Enter the coupon code BEDZ-RNDC-9RXN-6TCE-UJYI

If you have difficulty registering on Safari Bookshelf or accessing the online edition, please e-mail customer-service@safaribooksonline.com.

Library of Congress Cataloging-in-Publication Data
McDougall, Richard.
  Solaris internals : solaris 10 and OpenSolaris kernel architecture /
Richard McDougall, Jim Mauro.—2nd ed.
      p. cm.
  Mauro's name appears first on the earlier edition.
  Includes bibliographical references and index.
  ISBN 0-13-148209-2 (hardback : alk. paper)
  1. Operating systems (Computers) 2. Solaris (Computer file) I. Mauro,
Jim. II. Title.
  QA76.76.O63M37195 2006
  005.4'465—dc22
                                        2006015114

ISBN 0-13-148209-2
Text printed in the United States on recycled paper at Courier in Westford, Massachusetts.
Second printing, August 2006

For Traci, Madi, and Boston—
for your love, encouragement, and support . . .
                                    —Richard

Once again . . .
For Donna, Frank, and Dominick.
All my love, always . . .
                                    —Jim

Contents

PART THREE
Resource Management   **365**

PART SIX
Platform Specifics   **793**

Foreword

Over the past decade, a regrettable idea took hold: Operating systems, while interesting, were a finished, solved problem. The genesis of this idea is manifold, but the greatest contributing factor may simply be that operating systems were not understood; they were largely delivered not as transparent systems, but rather as proprietary black boxes, welded shut to even the merely curious. This is anathema to understanding; if something can't be taken apart—if its inner workings remain hidden—its intricacies can never be understood nor its engineering nuances appreciated. This is especially true of software systems, which can't even be taken apart in the traditional sense. Software is, despite the metaphors, information, not machine, and a closed software system is just about as resistant to understanding as an engineered system can be.

This was the state of Solaris circa 2000, and it was indeed not well understood. Its internals were publicly described only in arcane block comments or old USENIX papers, its behavior was opaque to existing tools, and its source code was cloistered in chambers unknown. Starting in 2000, this began to change (if slowly) —heralded in part by the first edition of the volume that you now hold in your hands: Jim Mauro and Richard McDougall's *Solaris™ Internals*. Jim and Richard had taken on an extraordinary challenge—to describe the inner workings of a system so complicated that no one person actually understands all of it. Over the course of working on their book, Jim and Richard presumably realized that no one book could contain it either. Despite scaling back their ambition to (for example) not include networking, the first edition of *Solaris™ Internals* still weighed in at over six hundred pages.

The publishing of *Solaris™ Internals* marked the beginning of change that accelerated through the first half of the decade, as the barriers to using and understanding Solaris were broken down. Solaris became free, its engineers began to talk about its implementation extensively through new media like blogs, and, most importantly, Solaris itself became open source in June 2005, becoming the first operating system to leap the chasm from proprietary to open. At the same time, the mechanics of Solaris became much more interesting as several revolutionary new technologies made their debut in Solaris 10. These technologies have swayed many a naysayer, and have proved that operating systems are alive after all. Furthermore, there are still hard, important problems to be solved.

If 2000 is viewed as the beginning of the changes in Solaris, 2005 may well be viewed as the end of the beginning. By the end of 2005, what was a seemingly finished, proprietary product had been transformed into an exciting, open source system, alive with potential and possibility. It is especially fitting that these changes are welcomed with this second edition of *Solaris™ Internals*. Faced with the impossible task of reflecting a half-decade of massive engineering change, Jim and Richard made an important decision—they enlisted the explicit help of the engineers that designed the subsystems and wrote the code. In several cases these engineers have wholly authored the chapter on their "baby." The result is a second edition that is both dramatically expanded and highly authoritative—and very much in keeping with the new Solaris zeitgeist of community development and authorship.

On a personal note, it has been rewarding to see Jim and Richard use DTrace, the technology that Mike Shapiro, Adam Leventhal, and I developed in Solaris 10. Mike, Adam, and I were all teaching assistants for our university operating systems course, and an unspoken goal of ours was to develop a pedagogical tool that would revolutionize the way that operating systems are taught. I therefore encourage you not just to read *Solaris™ Internals*, but to *download* Solaris, *run* it on your desktop or laptop or under a virtual machine, and *use* DTrace yourself to see the concepts that Jim and Richard describe—live, and on your own machine!

Be you student or professional, reading for a course, for work, or for curiosity, it is my pleasure to welcome you to your guides through the internals of Solaris. Enjoy your tour, and remember that Solaris is not a finished work, but rather a living, evolving technology. If you're interested in accelerating that evolution—or even if you just have questions on using or understanding Solaris—please join us in the many communities at `http://www.opensolaris.org`. Welcome!

Bryan Cantrill
San Francisco, California
June 2006

Preface

Welcome to the second edition of *Solaris™ Internals* and its companion volume, *Solaris™ Performance and Tools*. It has been almost five years since the release of the first edition, during which time we have had the opportunity to communicate with a great many Solaris users, software developers, system administrators, database administrators, performance analysts, and even the occasional kernel hacker. We are grateful for all the feedback, and we have made specific changes to the format and content of this edition based on reader input. Read on to learn what is different. We look forward to continued communication with the Solaris community.

About These Books

These books are about the internals of Sun's Solaris Operating System—specifically, the SunOS kernel. Other components of Solaris, such as windowing systems for desktops, are not covered. The first edition of *Solaris™ Internals* covered Solaris releases 2.5.1, 2.6, and Solaris 7. These volumes focus on Solaris 10, with updated information for Solaris 8 and 9.

In the first edition, we wanted not only to describe the internal components that make the Solaris kernel tick, but also to provide guidance on putting the information to practical use. These same goals apply to this work, with further emphasis on the use of bundled (and in some cases unbundled) tools and utilities that can be used to examine and probe a running system. Our ability to illustrate more of the kernel's inner workings with observability tools is facilitated in no small part by the inclusion of some revolutionary and innovative technology in Solaris 10— DTrace, a dynamic kernel tracing framework. DTrace is one of many new technologies in Solaris 10, and is used extensively throughout this text.

In working on the second edition, we enlisted the help of several friends and colleagues, many of whom are part of Solaris kernel engineering. Their expertise and guidance contributed significantly to the quality and content of these books. We also found ourselves expanding topics along the way, demonstrating the use of `dtrace(1)`, `mdb(1)`, `kstat(1)`, and other bundled tools. So much so that we decided early on that some specific coverage of these tools was necessary, and chapters were written to provide readers with the required background information on the tools and utilities. From this, an entire chapter on using the tools for performance and behavior analysis evolved.

As we neared completion of the work, and began building the entire manuscript, we ran into a bit of a problem—the size. The book had grown to over 1,500 pages. This, we discovered, presented some problems in the publishing and production of the book. After some discussion with the publisher, it was decided we should break the work up into two volumes.

Solaris™ Internals. This represents an update to the first edition, including a significant amount of new material. All major kernel subsystems are included: the virtual memory (VM) system, processes and threads, the kernel dispatcher and scheduling classes, file systems and the virtual file system (VFS) framework, and core kernel facilities. New Solaris facilities for resource management are covered as well, along with a new chapter on networking. New features in Solaris 8 and Solaris 9 are called out as appropriate throughout the text. Examples of Solaris utilities and tools for performance and analysis work, described in the companion volume, are used throughout the text.

Solaris™ Performance and Tools. This book contains chapters on the tools and utilities bundled with Solaris 10: `dtrace(1)`, `mdb(1)`, `kstat(1)`, etc. There are also extensive chapters on using the tools to analyze the performance and behavior of a Solaris system.

The two texts are designed as companion volumes, and can be used in conjunction with access to the Solaris source code on

`http://www.opensolaris.org`

Readers interested in specific releases before Solaris 8 should continue to use the first edition as a reference.

Intended Audience

We believe that these books will serve as a useful reference for a variety of technical staff members working with the Solaris Operating System.

Application developers can find information in these books about how Solaris OS implements functions behind the application programming interfaces. This information helps developers understand performance, scalability, and implementation specifics of each interface when they develop Solaris applications. The system overview section and sections on scheduling, interprocess communication, and file system behavior should be the most useful sections.

Device driver and kernel module developers of drivers, STREAMS modules, loadable system calls, etc., can find herein the general architecture and implementation theory of the Solaris OS. The Solaris kernel framework and facilities portions of the books (especially the locking and synchronization primitives chapters) are particularly relevant.

Systems administrators, systems analysts, database administrators, and Enterprise Resource Planning (ERP) managers responsible for performance tuning and capacity planning can learn about the behavioral characteristics of the major Solaris subsystems. The file system caching and memory management chapters provide a great deal of information about how Solaris behaves in real-world environments. The algorithms behind Solaris tunable parameters are covered in depth throughout the books.

Technical support staff responsible for the diagnosis, debugging, and support of Solaris will find a wealth of information about implementation details of Solaris. Major data structures and data flow diagrams are provided in each chapter to aid debugging and navigation of Solaris systems.

System users who just want to know more about how the Solaris kernel works will find high-level overviews at the start of each chapter.

Beyond the technical user community, those in academia studying operating systems will find that this text will work well as a reference. Solaris OS is a robust, feature-rich, volume production operating system, well suited to a variety of workloads, ranging from uniprocessor desktops to very large multiprocessor systems with large memory and input/output (I/O) configurations. The robustness and scalability of Solaris OS for commercial data processing, Web services, network applications, and scientific workloads is without peer in the industry. Much can be learned from studying such an operating system.

OpenSolaris

In June 2005, Sun Microsystems introduced OpenSolaris, a fully functional Solaris operating system release built from open source. As part of the OpenSolaris initiative, the Solaris kernel source was made generally available through an open license offering. This has some obvious benefits to this text. We can now include Solaris source directly in the text where appropriate, as well as refer to full source listings made available through the OpenSolaris initiative.

With OpenSolaris, a worldwide community of developers now has access to Solaris source code, and developers can contribute to whatever component of the operating system they find interesting. Source code accessibility allows us to structure the books such that we can cross-reference specific source files, right down to line numbers in the source tree.

OpenSolaris represents a significant milestone for technologists worldwide; a world-class, mature, robust, and feature-rich operating system is now easily accessible to anyone wishing to use Solaris, explore it, and contribute to its development.

Visit the Open Solaris Website to learn more about OpenSolaris:

```
http://www.opensolaris.org
```

The OpenSolaris source code is available at:

```
http://cvs.opensolaris.org/source
```

Source code references used throughout this text are relative to that starting location.

How the Books Are Organized

We organized the *Solaris™ Internals* volumes into several logical parts, each part grouping several chapters containing related information. Our goal was to provide a building block approach to the material by which later sections could build on information provided in earlier chapters. However, for readers familiar with particular aspects of operating systems design and implementation, the individual parts and chapters can stand on their own in terms of the subject matter they cover.

Volume 1: *Solaris™ Internals*

Updates and Related Material

To complement these books, we created a Web site at which we will place updated material, tools we refer to, and links to related material on the topics covered. We will regularly update the Web site (http://www.solarisinternals.com) with information about this text and future work on *Solaris™ Internals*. The Web site will be enhanced to provide a forum for Frequently Asked Questions (FAQs) related to the text, as well as general questions about Solaris internals, performance, and behavior. If bugs are discovered in the text, we will post errata on the Web site as well.

Notational Conventions

Table P.1 describes the typographic conventions used throughout these books, and Table P.2 shows the default system prompt for the utilities we describe.

Table P.1 Typographic Conventions

Typeface or Symbol	Meaning	Example
AaBbCc123	Command names, file names, and data structures.	The `vmstat` command. The `<sys/proc.h>` header file. The `proc` structure.
AaBbCc123()	Function names.	`page_create_va()`
AaBbCc123(2)	Manual pages.	Please see `vmstat(1M)`.

AaBbCc123	Commands you type within an example.	`$ vmstat`
		`r b w   swap  free  re  mf 0 0 0`
		`464440 18920   1   13`

AaBbCc123	New terms as they are introduced.	A *major page fault* occurs when…
MDB	The modular debuggers, including the user-mode debugger (mdb) and the kernel in-situ debugger (kmdb).	Examples that are applicable to both the user-mode and the in-situ kernel debugger.
mdb	The user-mode modular debugger.	Examples that are applicable the user-mode debugger.
kmdb	The in-situ debugger	Examples that are applicable to the in-situ kernel debugger.

Table P.2 Command Prompts

Shell	Prompt
Shell prompt	`minimum-osversion$`
Shell superuser prompt	`minimum-osversion#`
The mdb debugger prompt	`>`
The kmdb debugger prompt	`[cpu]>`

A Note from the Authors

Once again, a large investment in time and energy proved enormously rewarding for the authors. The support from Sun's Solaris kernel development group, the Solaris user community, and readers of the first edition has been extremely gratifying. We believe we have been able to achieve more with the second edition in terms of providing Solaris users with a valuable reference text. We certainly extended our knowledge in writing it, and we look forward to hearing from readers.

About the Authors

Had **Richard McDougall** lived 100 years ago, he would have had the hood open on the first four-stroke internal combustion-powered vehicle, exploring new techniques for making improvements. He would be looking for simple ways to solve complex problems and helping pioneering owners understand how the technology worked to get the most from their new experience. These days, Richard uses technology to satisfy his curiosity. He is a Distinguished Engineer at Sun Microsystems, specializing in operating systems technology and systems performance.

Jim Mauro is a Senior Staff Engineer in the Performance, Architecture, and Applications Engineering group at Sun Microsystems, where his most recent efforts have focused on Solaris performance on Opteron platforms, specifically in the area of file system and raw disk IO performance. Jim's interests include operating systems scheduling and thread support, threaded applications, file systems, and operating system tools for observability. Outside interests include reading and music—Jim proudly keeps his turntable in top working order, and still purchases and plays 12-inch vinyl LPs. He lives in New Jersey with his wife and two sons. When Jim's not writing or working, he's handling trouble tickets generated by his family on issues they're having with home networking and getting the printer to print.

Acknowledgments

The *Solaris™ Internals* Community Authors

Although there are only three names on the cover of these books, the effort was truly that of a community effort. Several of our friends went above and beyond the call of duty, and gave generously of their time, expertise, and energy by contributing material to the book. Their efforts significantly improved the content, allowing the books to cover a broader range of topics, as well as giving us a chance to hear from specific subject matter experts. Our sincerest thanks to the following.

Frank Batschulat. For help updating the UFS chapter. Frank has been a software engineer for 10 years and has worked at Sun Microsystems for a total of 7 years. At Sun he is a member of the Solaris File Systems Group primarily focused on UFS and the generic VFS/VNODE layer.

Russell Blaine. For x86 system call information. Russell Blaine has been juggling various parts of the kernel since joining Sun straight out of Princeton in 2000.

Joe Bonasera. For the x64 HAT description. Joe is an engineer in the Solaris kernel group, working mostly on core virtual memory support. Joe's background includes working on optimizing compilers and parallel database engines. His recent efforts have been around the AMD64 port, and porting OpenSolaris to run under the Xen virtualization software, specifically in the areas of virtual and physical memory management, and the boot process.

Jeff Bonwick. For a description of the vmem Allocator. Jeff is a Distinguished Engineer in Solaris kernel development. His many contributions include the original kernel memory slab allocator, and updated kernel vmem framework. Jeff's most recent work is the architecture, design, and implementation of the Zetabyte Filesystem, ZFS.

Peter Boothby. For the kstats overview. Peter Boothby worked at Sun for 11 years in a variety of roles: Systems Engineer; SAP Competence Centre manager for Australia and New Zealand; Sun's performance engineer and group manager at SAP in Germany; Staff Engineer in Scotland supporting European ISVs in their Solaris and Java development efforts. After a 2-year sabbatical skiing in France, racing yachts on Sydney Harbor, and sailing up and down the east coast of Australia, Peter returned to the Sun fold by founding a consulting firm that assists Sun Australia in large-scale consolidation and integration projects.

Rich Brown. For text on the file system interfaces as part of the File System chapters. Rich Brown has worked in the Solaris file system area for10 years. He is currently looking at ways to improve file system observability.

Bryan Cantrill. For the overview of the cyclics subsystem. Bryan is a Senior Software Engineer in Solaris kernel engineering. Among Bryan's many contributions are the cyclics subsystem, and interposing on the trap table to gather trap statistics. More recently, Bryan developed Solaris Dynamic Tracing, or DTrace.

Jonathan Chew. For help with the dispatcher NUMA and CMT sections. Jonathan Chew has been a software engineer in the Solaris kernel development group at Sun Microsystems since 1995. During that time, he has focused on Uniform Memory Access (NUMA) machines and chip multithreading. Prior to joining Sun, Jonathan was a research systems programmer in the Computer Systems Laboratory at Stanford University and the computer science department at Carnegie Mellon University.

Todd Clayton. For information on the large-page architectural changes. Todd is an engineer in Solaris kernel development, where he works on (among other things) the virtual memory code and AMD64 Solaris port.

Sankhyayan (Shawn) Debnath. For updating the UFS chapter with Sarah, Frank, Karen, and Dworkin. Sankhyayan Debnath is a student at Purdue University majoring in computer science and was an intern for the file systems group at Sun Microsystems. When not hacking away at code on the computer, you can find him racing his car at the local tracks or riding around town on his motorcycle.

Casper Dik. For material that was used to produce the process rights chapter. Casper is an engineer in Solaris kernel development, and has worked extensively in the areas of security and networking. Among Casper's many contributions are the design and implementation of the Solaris 10 Process Rights framework.

Andrei Dorofeev. For guidance on the dispatcher chapter. Andrei is a Staff Engineer in the Solaris Kernel Development group at Sun Microsystems. His interests include multiprocessor scheduling, chip multithreading architectures, resource management ,and performance. Andrei received an M.S. with honors in computer science from Novosibirsk State University in Russia.

Roger Faulkner. For suggestions about the process chapter. Roger is a Senior Staff Engineer in Solaris kernel development. Roger did the original implementation of the process file system for UNIX System V, and his numerous contributions include the threads implementation in Solaris, both past and current, and the unified process model.

Brendan Gregg. For significant review contributions and joint work on the performance and debugging volume. Brendan has been using Solaris for around a decade, and has worked as a programmer, a system administrator and a consultant. He is an OpenSolaris contributor, and has written software such as the DTrace toolkit. He teaches Solaris classes for Sun Microsystems.

Phil Harman. For the insights and suggestions to the process and thread model descriptions. Phil is an engineer in Solaris kernel development, where he focuses on Solaris kernel performance. Phil's numerous contributions include a generic framework for measuring system call performance called libMicro. Phil is an acknowledged expert on threads and developing multithreaded applications.

Jonathan Haslam. For the DTrace chapter. Jon is an engineer in Sun's performance group, and is an expert in application and system performance. Jon was a very early user of DTrace, and contributed significantly to identifying needed features and enhancements for the final implementation.

Stephen Hahn. For original material that is used in the projects, tasks, and resource control chapters. Stephen is an engineer in Solaris kernel development, and has made significant contributions to the kernel scheduling code and resource management implementation, among other things.

Sarah Jelinek. For 12 years of software engineering experience, 8 of these at Sun Microsystems. At Sun she has worked on systems management, file system management, and most recently in the file system kernel space in UFS. Sarah holds a B.S. in computer science and applied mathematics, and an M.S. in computer science, both from the University of Colorado, Colorado Springs.

Alexander Kolbasov. For the description of task queues. Alexander works in the Solaris Kernel Performance group. Interests include the scheduler, Solaris NUMA implementation, kernel observability, and scalability of algorithms.

Tariq Magdon-Ismail. For the updates to the SPARC section of the HAT chapter. Tariq is a Staff Engineer in the Performance, Availability and Architecture Engineering group with over 10 years of Solaris experience. His areas of contribution include large system performance, kernel scalability, and memory management architecture. Tariq was the recipient of the Sun Microsystems Quarterly Excellence Award for his work in the area of memory management. Tariq holds a B.S. with honors in computer science from the University of Maryland, College Park.

Stuart Maybee. For information on the file system mount table description. Stuart is an engineer in Sun's kernel development group.

Dworkin Muller. For information on the UFS on disk format. Dworkin was a UFS file system developer while at Sun.

David Powell. For the System V IPC update. Dave is an engineer in Solaris kernel development, and his many contributions include a rewrite of the System V IPC facility to use new resource management framework for setting thresholds, and contributing to the development of the Solaris 10 Service Management Facility (SMF).

Karen Rochford. For her contributions and diagrams for UFS logging. Karen Rochford has 15 years of software engineering experience, with her past 3 years being at Sun. Her focus has been in the area of I/O, including device drivers, SCSI, storage controller firmware, RAID, and most recently UFS and NFS. She holds a B.S. in computer science and mathematics from Baldwin-Wallace College in Berea, Ohio, and an M.S. in computer science from the University of Colorado, Colorado Springs. In her spare time, Karen can be found training her dogs, a briard and a bouvier, for obedience and agility competitions.

Eric Saxe. For contributions to the dispatcher, NUMA, and CMT chapters. Eric Saxe has been with Sun for 6 years and is a development engineer in the Solaris Kernel Performance Group. When Eric isn't at home with his family, he spends his time analyzing and enhancing the performance of the kernel's scheduling and virtual memory subsystems on NUMA, CMT, and otherwise large system architectures.

Eric Schrock. For the system calls appendix. Eric is an engineer in Solaris kernel development. His most recent efforts have been the development and implementation of the Zetabyte File System, ZFS.

Michael Shapiro. For contributions on kmem debugging and introductory text for MDB. Mike Shapiro is a Distinguished Engineer and architect for RAS features in Solaris kernel development. He led the effort to design and build the Sun architecture for Predictive Self-Healing, and is the cocreator of DTrace. Mike is the author of the DTrace compiler, D programming language, kernel panic subsystem, `fmd(1M)`, `mdb(1M)`, `dumpadm(1M)`, `pgrep(1)`, `pkill(1)`, and numerous enhancements to the `/proc` filesystem, core files, crash dumps, and hardware error handling. Mike has been a member of the Solaris kernel team for 9 years and holds an M.S. in computer science from Brown University.

Denis Sheahan. For information on Java in the tools chapter. Denis is a Senior Staff Engineer in the Sun Microsystems UltraSPARC T1 Architecture Group. During his 12 years at Sun, Denis has focused on application software and Solaris OS performance, with an emphasis on database, application server, and Java technology products. He is currently working on UltraSPARC T1 performance for current and future products. Denis holds a B.S. degree in computer science from Trinity College Dublin, Ireland. He received the Sun Chairman's Award for innovation in 2003.

Tony Shoumack. For contributions to the performance volume, and numerous reviews. Tony has been working with UNIX and Solaris for 12 years and he is an Engineer in Sun's Client Solutions organization where he specializes in commercial applications, databases and high-availability clustered systems.

Bart Smaalders. For numerous good ideas, and introductory text in the NUMA chapter. Bart is a Senior Staff Engineer in Solaris kernel development, and spends his time making Solaris faster.

Sunay Tripathi. For authoring the networking chapter. Sunay is the Senior Staff Engineer in Solaris Core Technology group. He has designed, developed and led major projects in Sun Solaris for the past 9 years in kernel/network environment to provide new functionality, performance, and scalability. Before coming to Sun, Sunay was a researcher at Indian Institute of Technology, Delhi, for 4 years and served a 2-year stint at Stanford where he was involved with Center of Design Research, creating smart agents and part of the Mosquito Net group experimenting with mobility in IP networks.

Andy Tucker. For the introductory text on zones. Andy has been a Principal Engineer at VMware since 2005, working on the VMware ESX product. Prior to that he spent 11 years at Sun Microsystems working in a variety of areas related to the Solaris Operating System, particularly scheduling, resource management, and virtualization. He received a Ph.D. in computer science from Stanford University in 1994.

The Reviewers

A special thanks to Dave Miller and Dominic Kay, copy-reviewer extraordinaires. Dave and Dominic meticulously reviewed vast amounts of material, and provided detailed feedback and commentary, through all phases of the book's development.

The following gave generously of their time and expertise reviewing the manuscripts. They found bugs, offered suggestions and comments that considerably improved the quality of the final work—Lori Alt, Roch Bourbonnais, Rich Brown, Alan Hargreaves, Ben Humphreys, Dominic Kay, Eric Lowe, Giri Mandalika, Jim Nissen, Anton Rang, Damian Reeves, Marc Strahl, Michael Schuster, Rich Teer, and Moriah Waterland.

Tony Shoumack and Allan Packer did an amazing eleventh-hour scramble to help complete the review process and apply several improvements.

Personal Acknowledgments from Richard

Without a doubt, this book has been a true team collaboration—when we look through the list, there are actually over 30 authors for this edition. I've enjoyed working with all of you, and now have the pleasure of thanking you for your help to bring these books to life.

First I'd like to thank my family, starting with my wife Traci, for your unbelievable support and patience throughout this multiyear project. You kept me focused on getting the job done, and during this time you gave me the wonderful gift of our new son, Boston. My 4-year-old daughter Madison is growing up so fast to be the most amazing little lady. I'm so proud of you—and that you've been so interested in this project, and for the artwork you so confidently drew for the cover pages. Yes, Madi, we can finally say the book's done!

For our friends and family who have been so patient while I've been somewhat absent. I owe you several years' worth of camping, dinners, and well, all the other social events I should have been at!

My co-conspirator in crime, Jim Mauro—hey, Jim, we did it! Thank you for being such a good friend and keeping me sane all the way through this effort!

Thanks, Phil Harman, for being the always-available buddy on the other side of IM to keep me company and bounce numerous ideas off. And of course for the many enjoyable photo-taking adventures.

I'd very much like to thank Brendan Gregg for joining in the fold and working jointly on the second volume on performance and tools. Your insights, thoughts, and tools make this volume something that it could not have been without your involvement.

Mary Lou Nohr, our copy editor, for whom I have the greatest respect—you had the patience to work with us as this project grew from 700 pages to 1600 and then from one book to two. For completing with incredible detail everything we sent your way, in record time. Without you this book would have not been what it is today.

Thank you to the Solaris development team, for the countless innovations that make writing about Solaris so much fun. Thanks to Bart Smaalders, Solaris Kernel performance lead, for the insights, comments, suggestions, and guidance along the way on this and many other projects.

To all the guest authors who helped, thanks for contributing—your insights and words bring a welcome completion to this Solaris story.

For my colleagues within the Sun Performance, Availability, and Architecture group in Sun. So much of the content of these books is owed to your hard efforts.

Thanks to my senior director, Ganesh Ramamurthy, for standing behind this project 100%, and giving us his full support and resources to get the job done.

Richard McDougall
Menlo Park, California
June 2006

Personal Acknowledgments from Jim

Thanks a million to Greg Doench, our Senior Editor at Prentice Hall, for waiting an extra two years for the updated edition, and jumping through hoops at the eleventh hour when we handed him two books instead of one.

Thanks to Mary Lou Nohr, our copy editor, for doing such an amazing job in record time.

My thanks to Brendan Gregg for a remarkable effort, making massive contributions to the performance book, while at the same time providing amazing feedback on the internals text.

Marc Strahl deserves special recognition. Marc was a key reviewer for the first edition of *Solaris™ Internals* (as well as the current edition). In a first edition eleventh-hour scramble, I somehow managed to get the wrong version of the acknowledgements copy in for the final typesetting, and Marc was left out. I truly appreciate his time and support on both editions.

Solaris Kernel Engineering. Everyone. All of you. The support and enthusiasm was simply overwhelming, and all while continuing to innovate and create the best operating system on the planet. Thanks a million.

My manager, Keng-Tai Ko, for his support, patience, and flexibility, and my senior director, Ganesh Ramamurthy, for incredible support.

My good friends Phil Harman and Bob Sneed, for a lot of listening, ideas, and opinions, and pulling me out of the burn-out doldrums many, many times.

My good mate Richard McDougall, for friendship, leadership, vision, and one hundred great meals and one thousand glasses of wine in the Bay Area. Looking forward to a lot more.

Lastly, my wife Donna, and my two sons, Frank and Dominick, for their love, support, encouragement, and putting up with two-plus years of—"I can't. I have to work on the book."

Jim Mauro
Green Brook, New Jersey
June 2006

PART ONE

Introduction to Solaris Internals

1

Introduction

The Solaris Operating System (Solaris OS) from Sun Microsystems has evolved steadily since the release of Solaris 2.0 in 1992. A combination of innovative features and newly designed implementations of core services have brought Solaris to the forefront as the industry's leading production operating system. Key areas of innovation and development include the following:

- **Reliability.** Development in fault and error detection, isolation and recovery, and service management combined with a strictly enforced rigorous set of standards for integrating new code into Solaris OS.
- **Performance and scalability.** Unsurpassed ability to run a wide variety of workloads on systems ranging from uniprocessor desktops and rack systems to high-end multiprocessor systems.
- **Manageability.** Tools and applications to handle the day-to-day administration and management of Solaris systems.
- **Observability.** Kernel features combined with user software to monitor and analyze the behavior and performance of applications and the Solaris kernel.
- **Resource management.** Management of available hardware resources to effectively meet performance requirements, enabling a variety of workloads to run within a Solaris system.

3

With the release of Solaris 10, the evolutionary progress of innovation in Solaris has taken a quantum leap. The new technology integrated into Solaris 10 in the areas of observability and debugging, reliability, performance, resource management, systems management, and software development sets new standards for operating systems technology. Throughout this book, the text and illustrations created to describe the core components of the Solaris 10 kernel are supplemented with examples of several of the tools and utilities integrated in Solaris 10. These examples not only demonstrate the use of the tool or utility, but also illustrate kernel behavior and the way in which it is observed.

In the remaining sections of this chapter, we describe the Solaris release model and summarize the key features of Solaris 8, 9, and 10. Finally, we take a broad look at the major subsystems as a warm-up to the detailed discussions that follow in the rest of the book.

1.1 Key Features of Solaris 10, Solaris 9, and Solaris 8

This section briefly summarizes the key features of the Solaris releases covered in this edition of *Solaris™ Internals*. It is not a complete or comprehensive list of every new feature. A detailed and complete listing of new features can be found in the *What's New* document, which is generated for each major Solaris release, as well as each update release. *What's New* documents are available publicly on http://docs.sun.com.

Remember, each release of Solaris is a proper superset of the previous release; thus, features found in Solaris 8 roll up into Solaris 9, and of course Solaris 10 incorporates features from Solaris 8 and 9. A feature initially introduced in an earlier release may be enhanced in a subsequent release. Examples here include UFS logging (introduced in Solaris 7, improved over time in Solaris 8 and Solaris 9), and Dynamic Intimate Shared Memory (DISM, introduced in Solaris 8 and improved in Solaris 9 and 10).

The notable exception to the inheritance rule is hardware support. Support for older hardware products may be dropped from a given Solaris release. For example, Solaris 10 does not support 32-bit SPARC processors or the UltraSPARC I processor (which was released in 1995). Solaris 10 is a 64-bit-only release for SPARC systems and will run on SPARC systems using UltraSPARC II, UltraSPARC III, and UltraSPARC IV processors, as well as on any new SPARC-based processors and products introduced from this point forward and through the life cycle of the release. Of course, 32-bit SPARC programs and applications are fully supported and work just fine on the 64-bit Solaris 10 kernel. Solaris 10 also supports systems based on 32-bit Intel x86 and 64-bit AMD Opteron technology.

1.1.1 Solaris 10

The list of new technologies integrated into Solaris 10 represents some of the most innovative work done in a volume production operating system.

- **Predictive self-healing.** The term *predictive self-healing* describes the benefits derived from the integration of the Solaris Fault Manager and Solaris Service Manager technologies. Predictive self-healing maximizes the availability of a Solaris system and the services it provides when hardware and software faults occur. Facilities for event detection, isolation, and dynamic deactivation of faulty components have been developed, along with improved messaging and services management.

- **Service Management Framework (SMF).** SMF affords a unified model in Solaris for the management and administration of services. A service is a program or set of programs that are managed by the system. These may be traditional services, such as remote login or file transfer (ftp), data services (NFS, database), or custom application services. The traditional method of managing these services is through the use of startup scripts and state/configuration information, typically in the form of an `/etc` file. SMF provides a set of commands, utilities, and documentation that facilitate the starting, stopping, and restarting of services, as well as defining service dependencies. The SMF framework is integrated with the predictive self-healing fault management facility described above, such that fault and error events specific to a service can be monitored and managed in a consistent and robust fashion.

- **Solaris Fault Manager.** This new software architecture for fault management incorporates several software components, including an event protocol for sending and recording error and fault information, a fault diagnosis engine, and a new set of programming interfaces that improve diagnosis, isolation, recovery, and dynamic deactivation of faulty hardware. A fault-centric software model correlates error reports into a binary telemetry flow (defined by the event protocol) and dispatches the telemetry stream to the appropriate diagnosis engine. Software can then diagnose the fault and generate specific information about the fault for use by systems maintenance personnel. If possible, corrective action (for example, offlining a faulty processor) is automatically taken.

- **Solaris Zones.** Zones is a software partitioning technology that enables the creation and management of multiple virtualized operating system execution environments within a single instance of the Solaris kernel. Each zone (virtualized environment) appears as a system to the processes, users, and administrators within the zone and is isolated from other zones running within the same kernel instance. The isolation provides security, since processes running in one zone are not visible to processes running in other zones in the same kernel instance. The only exception to this is the global zone, which is the primary zone that represents the Solaris kernel instance. All processes running in all zones in a kernel instance are visible to the global zone.

Zones also provide a resource management container, such that zones created to run specific applications (Web server, database server, etc.) can be configured to use a subset of the hardware resources available on the system.

See the *System Administration Guide: Solaris Containers, Resource Management and Solaris Zones* for information on creating, managing, and using Solaris Zones.

- **Dynamic resource pools (DRP).** Resource pools were introduced in Solaris 9. They provide a persistent configuration mechanism for assigning one or more processors to a specific application or set of applications. Additionally, resource pools allow for establishing a default scheduling class, such as the fair share or fixed-priority classes, for applications started within a resource pool. In Solaris 10, a new facility dynamically adjusts the assigned pool resources according to utilization, load, and properties. A new daemon, poold, is always active when DRPs are configured; it monitors system statistics, correlates statistics to pool configuration properties, and makes dynamic adjustments as needed. For example, if resource pool A is configured to run at a maximum of 80 percent utilization, and it exceeds that threshold for a sustained period, poold may assign additional CPU resources from another pool that is underutilized. All changes made by poold are logged, and the DRP framework provides a rich set of property definitions that include various constraints and objectives for the resource pools.

  See the *System Administration Guide: Solaris Containers, Resource Management and Solaris Zones* for information on creating, managing, and using dynamic resource pools.

- **Physical memory control.** With the project framework introduced in Solaris 9, limiting the amount of physical memory a process can use at any point is now possible. A resource-capping daemon, rcapd, was introduced in Solaris 10; it monitors the physical memory use of running processes at regular intervals and enforces physical memory caps if a process exceeds its configured limit. With rcapd, processes that consume more memory than allowed will effectively page against themselves and not consume additional physical memory at the expense of other processes running on the system.

  See the *System Administration Guide: Solaris Containers, Resource Management and Solaris Zones* for information on configuring memory resource caps, and monitoring memory usage.

- **Dynamic tracing facility (DTrace).** A comprehensive dynamic tracing facility that dynamically inserts probes into applications, user processes, and the Solaris kernel. To use DTrace, you program the probes to fire; when fired, each probe collects data at specified points in the execution path and makes that data available to you. DTrace probes are analogous to software sensors—imagine having thousands of programmable sensors that you can turn on and off dynamically, enabling you to record data throughout the entire execution path of your application or workload, from user-level processes through the entire kernel.

  DTrace provides all the information you need to understand system behavior, to analyze performance problems, to research areas for improved performance and efficiency in your application, and to uncover and root-cause aberrant behavior on your systems. A new utility, dtrace(1M), can be used from the command line to enable probes and collect data. Additionally, a new scripting language, called D, allows DTrace to be used by invocation of D language scripts, thus empowering users, administrators, developers, and performance analysts to collect, refine, and reuse scripts for system behavior and performance diagnosis.

  DTrace has been designed from the ground-up for use in critical production environments. DTrace is safe, having been implemented with rigorous security and error checking. When no DTrace probes are enabled, DTrace has a zero probe effect: It is just as if DTrace were not there. This is because DTrace instrumentation is dynamically inserted into the running system when a probe is enabled. DTrace literally inserts instructions in the appropriate location in the code path for a given probe (typically, the entry and return points of a function), then restores the instruction stream to its original state when the probe is disabled. This means that no DTrace code exists in the instruction stream at all when no probes are enabled. The actual probe effect of DTrace is commensurate with the number of probes enabled: Enabling a few probes will likely not induce a noticeable probe effect, whereas enabling thousands of probes on a busy system will likely induce some level of performance regression, but system integrity (availability and data integrity) is never at risk.

  DTrace is used extensively throughout this text to illustrate kernel behavior and code flow. See the *Solaris™ Performance and Tools* for information on using DTrace.

- **Process rights management.** Traditionally, superuser (root) privileges are required for performing specific tasks and using some features. However, providing superuser access to the user community at large imposes security risks, as well as threatening overall system integrity and availability. A simple mistake by a user running as root can have catastrophic consequences (for example, typing "rm -r *" in the root directory). Process rights management defines a set of privileges that can be assigned to specific users or roles or that can be enabled systemwide. A privilege is a bound and well-defined right to allow a process to perform a specific operation. Examples include these operations: using DTrace, changing file ownership, using high-resolution timers, setting processes to higher-priority levels, and using the real-time scheduling class.

See the *privileges(5)* and *ppriv(1)* man pages for additional information.

- **TCP/IP performance.** A significant amount of engineering went into improving TCP/IP performance in Solaris 10, with an emphasis on network throughput (data rate, typically expressed as number-of-bits or number-of-bytes per second), connection setup and teardown, first-byte latency, connection and CPU scalability (scale-up of the number of connections with more available CPUs), and efficiency (amount of CPU required to drive the network load). Several changes were implemented, including increased performance and efficiency of the code path by removal of the STREAMS infrastructure surrounding the TCP and IP protocol layers, implementation of a worker thread model to handle higher incoming packet rates, and improved use of hardware caches through improved instruction and data locality.

- **x64 architecture support.** Support for Intel x86 processors has been part of Solaris since Solaris 2.1. With the addition of servers based on the AMD Opteron processor added to Sun's hardware product, the same kind of support for the AMD64 architecture was a priority engineering effort during the development of Solaris 10. In addition to the basic porting work, significant effort went into optimization, tuning, and native support for a 64-bit kernel on Opteron processors. Solaris 10 supports both 32-bit Intel x86 processors and 32-bit and 64-bit Opteron processors. Of course, support for multiprocessor Opteron processors, with the exceptional scalability of Solaris OS is now available on both SPARC and AMD64 platforms.

This list is by no means a complete list of all the new features in Solaris 10. For a complete listing, see *What's New In Solaris 10* at:

```
http://docs.sun.com/app/docs/doc/817-0547
```

1.1.2 Solaris 9

Solaris 9 offers several new kernel features that widen the gap between Solaris and other commercial operating systems; these features include, memory performance enhancements, a new set of resource controls and facilities, and new scheduling classes.

- **Multiple page size support (MPSS).** Memory allocation is done in units called pages, which have a default size of 8 Kbytes. However, UltraSPARC hardware supports larger page sizes—up to 4 Mbytes. The MPSS set of command-line interfaces can be used to define larger page sizes for applications. The use of larger pages can provide substantial performance improvements for applications that require large physical memory allocations.

- **Memory placement optimization (MPO)** [Solaris 9 9/02]. Applications on Sun's high-end servers can benefit from allocation of physical memory pages in memory banks closest to the processors on which the application threads execute. This proximity of the executing threads to the memory they reference reduces latency on memory operations, thereby improving performance. MPO is tightly integrated into the Solaris dispatcher and memory allocation kernel code base, and it attempts to maintain proximity for physical memory allocations and the processors executing application threads.

- **Dynamic Intimate Shared Memory (DISM).** Intimate Shared Memory (ISM) was introduced in Solaris 2.6; it optimizes System V Shared Memory by allocating large memory pages for the shared segment, locking the pages in memory, and sharing low-level page translation information with all processes attaching to the shared memory segment. DISM dynamically resizes a shared segment, enabling use of dynamically added memory (using Sun's Dynamic Reconfiguration feature), and resizes database caches (implemented with System V shared memory segments) without the need to stop and restart the database instance. The original implementation of DISM (released in Solaris 8) did not include support for large pages. Solaris 9 9/02 adds large pages for DISM memory segments.

- **Resource Manager (RM).** Solaris 9 integrates resource management facilities, including resource pools for partitioning available hardware resources and the *projects* and *tasks* workload identifiers. Monitoring capabilities are integrated into bundled Solaris utilities (prstat(1M)), and the accounting subsystem is enhanced to provide extended accounting information based on workload identifiers and resource use.

- **Fair Share (FSS) and Fixed Priority (FX) scheduling classes.** In addition to the traditional Timeshare (TS), Real Time (RT), and Interactive (IA) scheduling classes, Solaris 9 adds the Fair Share (FSS) and Fixed Priority (FX) scheduling classes.The FSS class completely replaces the previous SHR class (Solaris Resource Manager 1.X); it allocates processor time to kernel threads based on user-defined allocations of shares of available processor resources. The FX class adds fixed-priority scheduling, by which the priority of threads in the FX class are not changed by the kernel during the thread's lifetime. The FSS class is an integral component of the Resource Manager facility, using resource pools to manage share allocation.

- **UNIX file system (UFS) enhancements.** UFS, the default file system in Solaris OS, improved performance in the areas of logging and direct I/O read/write concurrency.

- **Solaris Volume Manager (SVM).** Integrated into Solaris 9, SVM enables the creation of RAID 0, RAID 1, RAID 10, and RAID 5 storage volumes. Soft-partition support is also included, breaking the 7 partitions-per-volume barrier.

- **Threads library.** The threads library, `libthread.so`, boasts substantial performance improvements, and it transitions to a single-level threads model as default behavior for multithreaded applications.

1.1.3 Solaris 8

Solaris 8, first released in February 2000, contained a rich set of new features and underwent a series of continued improvements and enhancements over eight update releases.

- **Internet Protocol Version 6 (IPv6).** IPv6 extends IP addressing from 32 bits to 128 bits, resulting in a huge increase in the number of configurable nodes and networks. Other enhancements include a simplified IP header model, quality-of-service capabilities, and support for added authentication and privacy functionality. Solaris 8 allows configuration of a network interface card (NIC) with both an IPv4 and IPv6 address, and it supports network services, such as NIS and NFS, over IPv6.

- **IP Security Protocol for IPv4 (IPsec).** IPsec is a security protocol standard that secures data at the IP layer through encryption.

- **Native Lightweight Directory Access Protocol (LDAP).** LDAP support is integrated, so system administrators can easily adapt Solaris 8 systems into their LDAP environments or transition existing naming services to LDAP.

- **Core file management.** A new command, `coreadm(1M)`, empowers system administrators to configure a target directory for core files generated by user processes, as well as to define the naming convention used for the core files.

- **Role-Based Access Controls (RBAC).** With RBACs, system administrators can provide limited system administration capabilities to non-root users.

Execution profiles and roles are defined through configuration files, along with specific authorizations enabling the execution of tasks that otherwise require superuser (root) privileges.

- **Alternate threads library.** A new thread model replaces the original Solaris multilevel implementation with a 1-to-1, single-level thread model. This new model is made available in Solaris 8 through an alternative threads library, `libthread.so`, located in `/usr/lib/lwp`. (Note: This model became the default in Solaris 9.)

- **Dynamic Intimate Shared Memory (DISM).** Enhanced as described in the previous section, DISM was first introduced in Solaris 8.

- **UNIX file system (UFS).** UFS performance is improved in the areas of direct I/O, logging, concurrent direct I/O, and file system creation. Added features generate snapshots, and a new mount option defers access time updates.

- **Modular debugger.** A new kernel debugging facility, `mdb`, furnishes a rich set of utilities for examining kernel core files and a running system, as well as a development framework for building and integrating additional utilities (known as d commands) into the debugger. Note the `mdb(1)` 'd' commands are not to be confused with the DTrace 'D' scripting language.

- **Tools and utilities.** Some `/proc` tools are enhanced to work on core files. A new command, `prstat(1)`, examines running processes. The `apptrace(1)` tool traces library-level application calls. The new `pgrep(1)` command gets process IDs, based on process names; the new `pkill(1)` command sends signals from the command line. `truss(1)` now traces user-level function calls.

- **Hardware statistics utilities.** New utilities let you look at system performance with hardware-maintained counters. The `cpustat(1M)` command reads processor hardware counters that provide observability into cache hit rates, instructions per clock cycle, and other platform-specific statistics. `cputrack(1)` provides a similar set of data access as that provided by the `cpustat(1M)` command but has additional semantics for focusing on a specific process or group of processes. The `busstat(1M)` command lets you access statistics from the hardware counters maintained in the main system bus or interconnect.

- **Arbitrary resolution interval timers.** A new kernel facility, called `cyclics`, provides fine-grained arbitrary resolution interval timers. Previously, timer granularity was bound by the kernel clock interrupt mechanism. In Solaris 8 (and beyond) applications using interval timers can now program their timers to fire at arbitrary intervals and can achieve nanosecond granularity (the actual attainable granularity is hardware-dependent).

1.2 Key Differentiators

The continued development and integration of new technologies raises the bar for modern operating systems. With Solaris 10, new technologies combine to deliver on a common goal—reduced cost of ownership through the simplification of managing available system resources, handling fault and error events, and diagnosing application and system behavior. Here are some of the characteristics that makes Solaris OS stand out.

- **Reliability, availability, serviceability.** Solaris OS (SunOS 5.X) has been in development for almost twenty years, with millions of installations around the world running a wide variety of production workloads for well over a decade, on systems ranging from single-processor servers to high-end multiprocessor systems with massive memory and I/O configurations.

- **Scalable performance.** The Solaris kernel has been designed from the ground-up to support multiprocessor systems running a single, shared kernel instance. The kernel itself is multithreaded, using kernel threads to perform system tasks and services and manage regular events such as interrupts. Highly optimized, fine-grained locking primitives are implemented to provide high levels of concurrency on multiprocessor systems. Kernel-provided resources to support processes, threads, file I/O, etc., scale up dynamically with system size and load.

- **Observability.** No other operating system offers the wealth of tools and utilities available in Solaris OS for monitoring and analyzing system and application performance and behavior. In addition to the traditional "stat" tools (`vmstat`, `mpstat`, `iostat`, `netstat`), and `sar(1)`, Solaris OS includes the following: process-centric tools built on the `/proc` file system (the ptools); hardware statistics tools (`cpustat`, `busstat`); a powerful kernel and application debugger (`mdb`); `prstat(1M)` for dynamic systemwide process execution statistics; application execution tracing with `truss(1)` and `apptrace(1)`; and, of course, DTrace, which enables the dynamic insertion of thousands of software sensors in applications and the kernel.

- **Resource management.** Maximizing use of available hardware resources is critical to today's cost-conscious IT organizations, along with ensuring that business requirements and service levels are met and sustained. Combining multiple workloads on fewer systems to reduce overall server count is a common strategy. Solaris OS provides the tools and facilities necessary for effective management of these complex environments and delivery of required performance. With Solaris OS, you can partition processors and bind specific processes into processor sets, configure dynamic pools of processor sets with assigned scheduling classes, create multiple isolated, virtualized execution environments within a single Solaris instance, and limit physical memory use on a per-process basis.

- **Multiplatform support.** Solaris OS supports systems based on SPARC, Intel x86, and AMD Opteron processors. POSIX-compliant application programming interfaces (APIs) are consistent across the different platforms, as are the Solaris user and administration environments. A layered architecture means that over 90 percent of the Solaris source is platform-independent.

- **64-bit kernel and process address space.** A 64-bit kernel for 64-bit platforms delivers a LP64 execution environment. (LP64 refers to the data model: Long and pointer data types are 64 bits wide.) A 32-bit application environment is also available, allowing 32-bit binaries to execute on a 64-bit Solaris kernel alongside 64-bit applications. This is true for both SPARC and 64-bit AMD Opteron systems. Note that Solaris 10 no longer provides 32-bit kernel support on SPARC platforms. All Solaris 10 SPARC systems will boot and run as a 64-bit kernel only. This does not impact the support of 32-bit applications on Solaris 10 on SPARC: that is, 32-bit applications are fully supported.

- **Modular binary kernel.** The Solaris kernel uses dynamic linking and dynamic modules to divide the kernel into modular binaries, according to a well-defined directory hierarchy for the storage of different classes of kernel modules. A core kernel binary contains central facilities; device drivers, file systems, schedulers, and some system calls are implemented as dynamically loadable modules. Consequently, the Solaris kernel is delivered as a binary rather than source and object, and kernel compilations are not required upon a change of parameters or addition of new functionality.

- **Fully preemptable kernel.** The Solaris kernel is fully preemptable and does not require manipulation of hardware interrupt levels to protect critical data—locks synchronize access to kernel data. This means that threads needing to run can interrupt another, lower-priority, thread; hence, low latency scheduling and low latency interrupt dispatch is achieved. For example, a process waking up after sleeping for a disk I/O can be scheduled immediately, rather than waiting until the scheduler runs. Additionally, by not raising priority levels and blocking interrupts, the system need not periodically suspend activity during interrupt handling, so system resources are used more efficiently. The preemptable kernel is critical to providing support for real-time applications that require a bound, deterministic dispatch latency.

- **Multiple scheduler support.** Solaris provides a configurable scheduler environment. Multiple schedulers can operate concurrently, each with its own scheduling algorithms and priority levels. Schedulers are supplied as kernel modules and are dynamically loaded into the operating system. Solaris ships with a table-driven, usage-decayed timeshare scheduler (TS); an interactive scheduler (IA) optimized for the window system, a share-based scheduler (FSS), a fixed-priority scheduler (FX), and a real-time fixed priority scheduler (RT).

- **Multiple file system support.** In Solaris OS, a virtual file system (VFS) framework allows multiple file systems to be configured into the system. The framework implements several disk-based file systems (UNIX file system, MS-DOS file system, CD-ROM file system, etc.) and the network file system (NFS V2, V3, and V4). The virtual file system framework also implements pseudo file systems, including the process file system, `procfs`, a file system that abstracts processes as files. The virtual file system framework is integrated with the virtual memory system to provide dynamic file system caching that uses available free memory as a file system cache.

- **Demand-paged virtual memory system.** With this feature, systems can load applications on demand, rather than loading whole executables or library images into memory. Demand-paging speeds up application startup and potentially reduces memory footprint.

- **Modular virtual memory system.** The virtual memory system separates virtual memory functions into distinct layers; the address space layer, segment drivers, and hardware-specific components are consolidated into a hardware address translation (HAT) layer. Segment drivers can abstract memory as files, and files can be memory-mapped into an address space. Segment drivers enable different abstractions, including physical memory and devices, to appear in an address space.

- **Modular device I/O system.** Dynamically-loadable device and bus drivers allow a hierarchy of buses and devices to be installed and configured. A device driver interface (DDI) shields device drivers from platform-specific infrastructure, thus maximizing portability of device drivers. A Solaris system does not need to be rebooted when a device driver is added (or for most other loadable kernel modules).

- **Integrated networking.** With the data link provider interface (DLPI), multiple concurrent network interfaces can be configured, and a variety of different protocols—including Ethernet, X.25, SDLC, ISDN, FDDI, token bus, bi-sync, and other data-link-level protocols—can be configured.

- **Real-time architecture.** The Solaris kernel was designed and implemented to provide real-time capabilities. The combination of the preemptive kernel, kernel interrupts as threads, fixed-priority scheduling, high-resolution timers, and fine-grained processor control makes Solaris an ideal environment for real-time applications.

The differentiators listed above represent many innovative features integrated in the Solaris kernel. In the remaining chapters, we closely examine the core kernel modules and major subsystems.

1.3 Kernel Overview

The purpose of any operating system is to provide an execution environment for applications, managing and allocating the underlying hardware resources such that applications get execution time on processors, have their active address space segments resident in physical memory, are able to do I/O to files and devices, and can communicate over a network. The operating system must be able to execute multiple applications, support multiple users, effectively manage a wide range of hardware platforms, and provide facilities for managing (controlling) and observing (troubleshooting, diagnosing) the workloads running on the system. We refer to the core operating system components and subsystems as the kernel.

The primary functions of the kernel can be divided into two major categories: managing the hardware by allocating its resources among the programs running on it; and supplying a set of system services for those programs to use. The Solaris kernel, like other operating systems, provides a virtual machine environment that shields programs from the underlying hardware and allows multiple programs to execute concurrently on the hardware platform. Each program has its own virtual machine environment, with an execution context and state.

The basic unit of a program's environment is known as a *process*; it contains a virtual memory environment that is insulated from other processes on the system. Each Solaris process can have one or more *threads of execution* that share the virtual memory environment of the process, and each thread in effect executes independently within the process's environment. Think of the process as an execution container for one or more threads. The Solaris kernel scheduler manages the execution of these threads (as opposed to management by scheduling processes) by transparently time-slicing them onto one or more *processors*. The threads of execution start and stop executing as they are moved on and off the processors, but the user program is unaware of this. Each time a thread is moved off a processor, its complete execution environment (program counter, stack pointers, registers, etc.) is saved, so when it is later rescheduled onto a processor, its environment can be restored and execution can resume.

Mechanisms in the kernel can access operating system services, such as file I/O, networking, process and thread creation and termination, process control and signaling, process memory management, resource control and management, and interprocess communication. A process accesses these kernel services through the use of *system calls*. System calls are programming interfaces through which the operating system is entered so that the kernel can perform work on behalf of the calling thread.

1.3.1 Solaris Kernel Architecture

The Solaris kernel is grouped into several key components and is implemented in a modular fashion:

- **System call interface.** The system call interface allows user processes to access kernel facilities. The kernel then performs specific tasks on behalf of the calling process, such as reading or writing a file, or establishing a network connection. The system call layer consists of a common system call handler, which vectors execution into the appropriate kernel modules.

- **Process execution and scheduling.** Process management facilities enable process creation, execution, management, and termination. The scheduler implements the functions that divide the machine's processor resources among threads on the system. The scheduler allows different scheduling classes to be loaded for different behavior and scheduling requirements.

- **Memory management.** The virtual memory system manages mapping of physical memory to user processes and the kernel. The Solaris memory management layer is divided into two layers: the common memory management functions and the hardware-specific components. The hardware-specific components are located in the hardware address translation (HAT) layer.

- **Resource management.** The Solaris kernel contains the infrastructure and administrative framework for allocating specific system resources (processor, memory, network) to applications. Resource management can maximize the use of system hardware, handle multiple workloads within a single kernel instance, and support multiple, virtualized, isolated execution environments within a single kernel instance.

- **File systems.** Solaris OS implements a virtual file system framework, by which multiple types of file system can be configured into the Solaris kernel at the same time. Regular disk-based file systems, network file systems, and pseudo file systems are implemented in the file system layer.

- **I/O bus and device management.** The Solaris I/O framework implements bus nexus node drivers (bus-specific architectural dependencies, for example, a PCI bus) and device drivers (a specific device on a bus, for example, an Ethernet card) as a hierarchy of modules, reflecting the physical layout of the bus/device interconnect.

- **Kernel facilities (clocks, timers, etc.).** Central kernel facilities include regular clock interrupts, system timers, synchronization primitives, and loadable module support.

- **Networking.** The Solaris networking subsystem provides complete IPv4 and IPv6 support, socket-based interfaces for network programming, and the traditional STREAMS framework for insertion of custom modules in the protocol stack. The TCP/IP and UDP/IP implementation in Solaris 10 has been completely rewritten for optimal performance and efficiency. The STREAMS connections between TCP and IP, and UDP and IP, has been removed and the code core tightly integrated, leaving STREAMS in other areas of the networking infrastructure.

1.3.2 Modular Implementation

The Solaris kernel is implemented as a core set of operating system functions, with additional kernel subsystems and services linked in as dynamically loadable modules. This implementation is facilitated by a module loading and kernel runtime linker infrastructure, which allows kernel modules to be added to the operating system either during boot or on demand while the system is running.

The Solaris module framework supports seven types of loadable kernel modules: scheduling classes, file systems, loadable system calls, loaders for executable file formats, streams modules, bus or device drivers, and miscellaneous modules. Figure 1.1 shows the facilities contained in the core kernel and the various types of kernel modules that implement the remainder of the Solaris kernel.

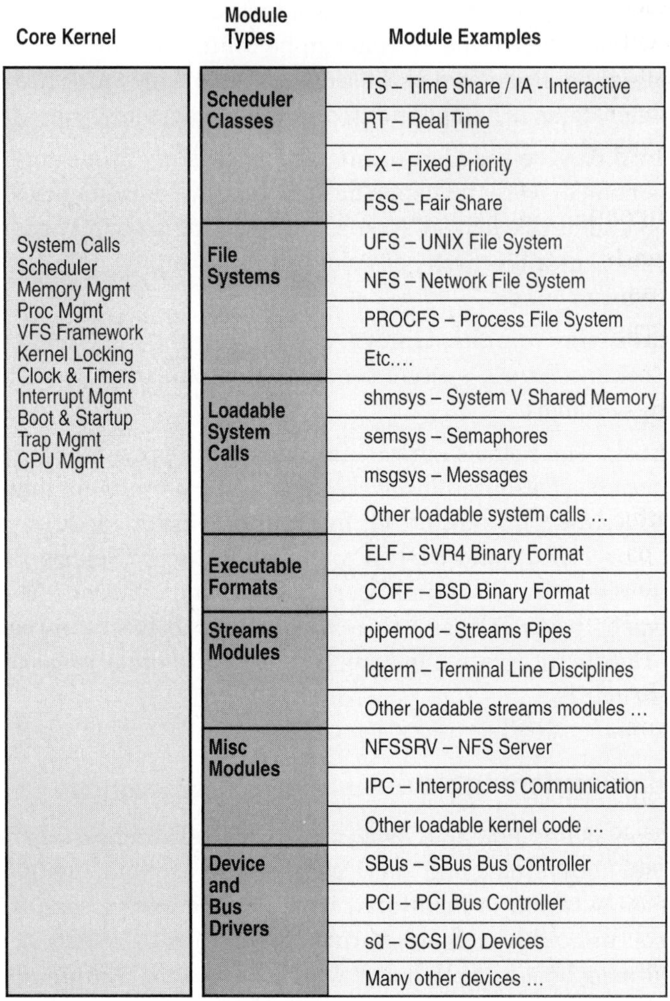

Core Kernel	Module Types	Module Examples
System Calls Scheduler Memory Mgmt Proc Mgmt VFS Framework Kernel Locking Clock & Timers Interrupt Mgmt Boot & Startup Trap Mgmt CPU Mgmt	Scheduler Classes	TS – Time Share / IA - Interactive
		RT – Real Time
		FX – Fixed Priority
		FSS – Fair Share
	File Systems	UFS – UNIX File System
		NFS – Network File System
		PROCFS – Process File System
		Etc....
	Loadable System Calls	shmsys – System V Shared Memory
		semsys – Semaphores
		msgsys – Messages
		Other loadable system calls ...
	Executable Formats	ELF – SVR4 Binary Format
		COFF – BSD Binary Format
	Streams Modules	pipemod – Streams Pipes
		ldterm – Terminal Line Disciplines
		Other loadable streams modules ...
	Misc Modules	NFSSRV – NFS Server
		IPC – Interprocess Communication
		Other loadable kernel code ...
	Device and Bus Drivers	SBus – SBus Bus Controller
		PCI – PCI Bus Controller
		sd – SCSI I/O Devices
		Many other devices ...

Figure 1.1 Core Kernel and Loadable Modules

1.4 Processes, Threads, and Scheduling

The Solaris kernel is multithreaded; that is, kernel services and tasks are executed as kernel threads. The kernel thread is the core unit of execution managed by the Solaris kernel. Kernel threads have an execution state and context that includes a global priority and scheduling class; kernel threads are the fundamental units that get scheduled, executed and context switched on and off processors. This same model applies to user level processes. The user process is a container that defines much of the execution context for its threads. Threads allow multiple streams of execution within a single virtual memory environment; consequently, switching execution between threads within the same process is inexpensive, since a virtual memory context switch is not required. The following objects form the nucleus of the Solaris kernel threads model and implementation.

- **Kernel threads.** The object that gets scheduled and executed on a processor.
- **User threads.** The user-level (non-kernel) thread state maintained within a user process.
- **Process.** The executable form of a program; the execution environment for a user program.
- **Lightweight process (LWP).** The kernel-visible execution context for a user thread.

Solaris executes kernel threads for kernel-related tasks, such as interrupt handling, memory page management, device drivers, etc. For user-process execution, kernel threads have a corresponding LWP; these kernel threads are scheduled for execution by the kernel on behalf of the user processes. Within the kernel, multiple threads of execution share the kernel's environment, primarily the kernel's address space. Processes also contain one or more threads, which share the virtual memory environment of the process as well as other components of the process context.

A process is an abstraction that contains the execution environment for a user program. It consists of a virtual memory environment (an address space), program resources such as an open file list, and at least one thread of execution. The virtual memory environment, open file list, and other components of the process environment are shared by all the threads within each process.

The LWP and its corresponding kernel thread define the virtual execution environment for a thread within a user process. Beginning in Solaris 9, there is a one-to-one relationship between user threads, LWPs, and kernel threads. That is, every thread in a user process is bound to an LWP, and each LWP has a kernel thread. The LWP allows each thread within a process to make system calls independently of other threads within the same process. Without an LWP, only one thread could enter the kernel at a time—only one thread at a time could make a system call. Each time a system call is made by a thread, its registers are placed on a stack within the LWP. Upon return from a system call, the system call return codes are made available to the LWP. Figure 1.2 shows the relationship among user threads, LWPs, kernel threads, and processes.

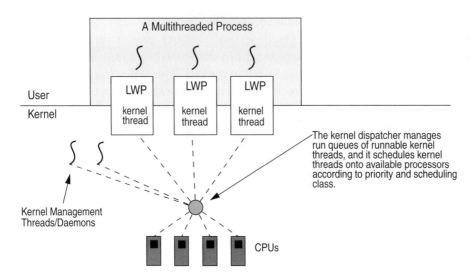

Figure 1.2 Kernel Threads, Processes, and Lightweight Processes

1.4.1 A New Threads Model

Solaris releases 2.2 through Solaris 8 implemented a two-level threads model, whereby user threads were multiplexed onto a potentially smaller pool of LWPs. The original design was intended to support hundreds or thousands of threads in a process, without the need to enter the kernel for many thread management tasks, such as creating and destroying threads. This model served us well for many years, but was not without its challenges. The multiplexing of user threads onto available LWPs required maintaining a runnable thread queue and user thread scheduler at the threads library level—separate and distinct from the kernel scheduler. A user thread needed to be bound to an LWP before the kernel could schedule it to run on a processor. Maintaining a library-level threads scheduler was enormously complex. Additionally, maintaining correct asynchronous signal behavior in the two-level model was quite challenging, since a user thread that is not masking a posted signal may not be on an LWP when the system attempts to deliver the signal. Finally, issues with concurrency management and scheduling latency could result in suboptimal performance for threaded applications. The scheduling latency was the effect of waiting for the threads library scheduler to link a user thread to an available LWP. The concurrency issue has to do with maintaining a sufficient number of LWPs such that the process does not have runnable user threads waiting for an execution resource (an LWP).

Beginning with Solaris 8, a new threads model was introduced: a single-level model. That is, when a user thread is created, an LWP and kernel thread are also created and linked to the user thread; the user thread is never without an LWP/kthread. This corresponds to what was referred to as bound threads in the two-level model. The threads programming interfaces provide a flag for the creation of bound threads; this flag has been available since the introduction of thread programming interfaces in Solaris. The new single-level model can be thought of as all bound threads, all the time. The new threads model was introduced in Solaris 8 through the distribution of an alternate threads library. By default, threaded applications link to `/usr/lib/libthread.so`, which in Solaris 8 delivers the original two-level model. An alternate `libthread.so` shared object library was placed in the `/usr/lib/lwp` directory. The new library is binary compatible with all existing threaded applications. You need not recompile to use the new threads library: simply set the runtime linker's path environmental variable to point to `/usr/lib/lwp`. The single-level threads library is the default library in Solaris 9 and Solaris 10, so setting the runtime linker path variable is not required in order to get the single-model behavior.

The new threads model offers several benefits over the original model:

- **Improved performance, scalability, and reliability.** The library source code was reduced substantially in size and complexity with the development of the single-level model. Internal library locks required for a library-level scheduler were done away with.

- **Reliable signal behavior.** Issues of sychronizing signal masks between the user thread and LWP no longer exist; asynchronous signal delivery is reliable and consistent.

- **Improved adaptive mutex lock implementation.** Mutual exclusion (mutex) locks are synchronization primitives used by threaded programs to protect data from concurrent access by multiple threads at the same time. Adaptive mutexes provide an optimization whereby a thread that wishes to acquire a lock that is being held will dynamically decide to spin waiting for the lock, or will sleep and rely on the wakeup mechanism to give it another shot at the lock when it is released. With the new model, the adaptive mutex implementation has been optimized.

- **User-level sleep queues for synchronization objects.** Synchronization objects, such as mutex locks, can be defined by the programmer to be intraprocess locks. This means that a lock will be shared only among threads within the process, not by threads in other processes. For these intraprocess locks, the code path for managing lock acquisition and release has been optimized to maintain threads waiting for a lock in a user-level sleep queue. There are fewer calls into the kernel for threads acquiring and releasing intraprocess locks.

These features, as well as other benefits derived from the new threads library, are discussed in more detail in Part Two.

1.4.2 Global Process Priorities and Scheduling

The Solaris kernel implements a global thread priority model for kernel threads. The kernel scheduler, or *dispatcher*, uses the model to select which kernel thread of potentially many runnable kernel threads executes next. The kernel supports the notion of *preemption*, allowing a higher-priority thread to preempt a running thread so that the higher-priority thread can execute. The kernel itself is preempt-able, an innovation providing for time-critical scheduling of high-priority threads.

There are 170 global priorities; numerically larger priority values correspond to better thread priorities. The priority name space is partitioned by different *scheduling classes* (see Figure 1.3). The Solaris dispatcher implements multiple scheduling classes that allow different scheduling policies to be applied to threads. The three primary scheduling classes are TS (IA is an enhanced TS), SYS, and RT. The scheduling classes are shown in Figure 1.3 and described below the figure.

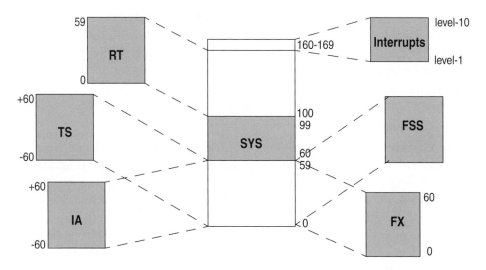

Figure 1.3 Global Thread Priorities

- **TS.** The timeshare scheduling class is the default class for processes and all the kernel threads within the process. It changes process priorities dynamically according to recent processor usage in an attempt to evenly allocate processor resources among the kernel threads in the system. Process priorities and time quantums are calculated according to a timeshare scheduling table at each clock tick or during wakeup after sleeping for an I/O. The TS class uses priority ranges 0 to 59.

- **IA.** The interactive class is an enhanced TS class used by the desktop windowing system to boost the priority of threads within the window under focus. The global priority range of IA class threads is also 0 to 59.

- **FSS.** The fair-share scheduling class is share-based, not priority-based; available CPU resources are allocated in units called shares, and threads are scheduled based on share allocation and processor utilitzation. The FSS class was introduced in Solaris 9, and is managed through the Solaris projects database.

- **FX.** The fixed-priority scheduling class. Threads in the FX class do not have their priority changed. The priority remains fixed throughout the lifetime of the thread. The FX class was introduced in Solaris 9.

- **SYS.** The system class is used by the kernel for kernel threads. Threads in the system class are bound threads; that is, there is no time quantum—they run until they block or complete. The system class uses priorities 60 to 99.

- **RT.** The real-time class implements fixed-priority, fixed-time-quantum scheduling. The real-time class uses priorities 100 to 159. Note that the priority of threads in the RT class is higher than that of kernel threads in the SYS class. RT class threads will preempt operating system kernel threads.

The interrupt priority levels shown in Figure 1.3 are not available for use by anything other than interrupt threads. Their positioning in the priority scheme is intended to guarantee that interrupt threads have priority over all other threads in the system.

The available scheduling classes, along with the user and administrator command set to observe and manage thread priorities and classes, furnish a rich environment in which any production workload, or combination of workloads, running within a single Solaris kernel instance can meet performance requirements and service levels.

1.5 Interprocess Communication

Processes communicate with one another by using one of several types of interprocess communication (IPC). With IPC, information transfer or synchronization occurs between processes. Solaris supports four different groups of interprocess communication: traditional (basic) IPC, System V IPC, POSIX IPC, and advanced Solaris IPC.

1.5.1 Traditional UNIX IPC

Solaris implements the traditional UNIX IPC facilities: pipes, named pipes, and UNIX domain sockets.

A pipe directly channels data flow between two related processes through an object that operates like a file. Data is inserted at one end of the pipe and travels to the receiving process in a first-in, first-out order. Data is read and written on a pipe with the standard file I/O system calls. Pipes are created with the `pipe(2)` system call.

Named pipes, also commonly known as FIFOs (which stands for first-in, first-out, the method of data movement in named pipes), are implemented as a file in the file system namespace. As such, it is easier to use FIFOs to connect processes that are not related. FIFOs are implemented with the `mkfifo(3C)` interface.

A socket is a file-like abstraction that provides a communication endpoint between processes. The communication can be over a network (a network domain socket) or a UNIX domain (local) socket. A local socket is a network-like connection using the `socket(2)` system call to directly connect two processes.

1.5.2 System V IPC

Three types of IPC originally developed for System V UNIX have become standard across all UNIX implementations: shared memory, message passing, and semaphores. These facilities provide the common IPC mechanism used by the majority of applications today.

- **System V Shared Memory.** Processes can create a segment of shared memory. Changes within the area of shared memory are immediately available to other processes that attach to the same shared memory segment.

- **System V Message Queues.** A message queue is a list of messages with a head and a tail. Messages are placed on the tail of the queue and are received on the head. Each messages contains a 32-bit type value, followed by a data payload.

- **System V Semaphores.** Semaphores are integer-valued objects that support two atomic operations: increment or decrement the value of the integer. Processes can sleep on semaphores that have a value of zero, then can be awakened when the value becomes greater than zero. Semaphores are really more a synchronization facility than an interprocess communication facility.

Setting kernel tunable parameters for System V IPC is extremely common in Solaris environments. It is rare to examine an `/etc/system` file on a Solaris system that does not have entries for System V IPC resource allocation. In Solaris 10, a significant amount of work went into reducing the need to tune IPC values, and the tuning method itself has changed. Most of the traditional tunable parameters are now obsolete, and those that remain have much larger default values. Should it be necessary to change a value from its default in Solaris 10, the method for changing these values involves the use of new resource control facilities. See Section 4.2 for information about using the `prctl(1)` and `rctladm(1)` commands for changing IPC values.

Other IPC tunable parameters not listed in the table are obsolete. Obsolete parameters in `/etc/system` are not always ignored.

1.5.3 POSIX IPC

The POSIX IPC facilities are similar in functionality to System V IPC but are very different in their implementation. Whereas the System V IPC facilities are kernel-maintained objects, POSIX IPC objects are abstracted on top of memory mapped files. The POSIX library routines are called by a program to create a new semaphore, shared memory segment, or message queue. Internally, Solaris file I/O system calls (`open(2)`, `read(2)`, `mmap(2)`, etc.) are used because the IPC objects exist as memory mapped files. The object type exported to the program through the POSIX interfaces is handled within the library routines.

1.5.4 Solaris Doors: Advanced Solaris IPC

Solaris Doors are a new, fast, lightweight mechanism for calling procedures between processes. Doors are a low latency method of invoking a procedure in a different process on the same system. A door server contains a thread that sleeps, waiting for an invocation from the door client. A client makes a call to the server through the door, along with a small (16-Kbyte) payload. When the call is made from a door client to a door server, scheduling control is passed directly to the thread in the door server. Once a door server has finished handling the request, it passes control and response back to the calling thread. The scheduling control allows ultra-low-latency turnaround because the client can complete the request without waiting for the server thread to be scheduled.

1.6 Signals

UNIX systems have provided a process signaling mechanism from the earliest implementations. The signal facility provides a method of interrupting a process or thread within a process as a result of a specific event. The events that trigger signals can be directly related to the current instruction stream. Such signals, referred to as synchronous signals, originate as hardware trap conditions arising from illegal address references (segmentation violation), illegal math operations (floating point exceptions), and the like.

The system also implements asynchronous signals, which result from an external event not necessarily related to the current instruction stream. Examples of asynchronous signals include job control signals and the sending of a signal from one process or thread to another. For example, sending a kill signal to terminate a process.

For each possible signal, a process can establish one of three possible signal dispositions that define what action, if any, will be taken when the signal is received. Most signals can be *ignored*; a signal can be *caught* and a process-specific signal handler invoked; or a process can permit the *default* action to be taken. Every signal has a predefined default action, for example, terminate the process. Solaris OS provides a set of programming interfaces that allow signals to be masked or a specific signal handler to be installed.

The traditional signal model was built on the concept of a process having a single execution stream at any time. The Solaris kernel's multithreaded process architecture accommodates multiple threads of execution within a process, meaning that a signal can be directed to a specific thread. The disposition and handlers for signals is the same for every thread in a multithreaded process. However, the Solaris model permits signals to be masked at the thread level, so different threads within the process can have different signals masked. (Masking is a means of blocking a signal from being delivered.)

1.7 Memory Management

Every object in the system is managed as a memory object in some form; data structures, kernel text, process address space segments, processes, threads, etc., all exist and are managed as objects in memory. Thus, the Solaris virtual memory (VM) system can be considered the core of the operating system—it manages the system's memory on behalf of the kernel and processes. The main task of the VM system is to manage efficient allocation of the system's physical memory to the processes and kernel subsystems running within the operating system. The VM system uses slower storage media (usually disk) to store data that does not fit within the physical memory of the system, thus accommodating programs larger than the size of physical memory. The VM system is what keeps the most frequently used portions within physical memory and the lesser-used portions on the slower secondary storage.

For processes, the VM system presents a simple linear range of memory, known as an *address space*. Each address space is broken into several *segments* that represent mappings of the executable; heap space (general-purpose, process-allocated memory), shared libraries, and a program stack. Each segment is divided into equal-sized pieces of virtual memory, known as *pages*, and a hardware memory management unit (MMU) manages the mapping of page-sized pieces of virtual memory to physical memory. Figure 1.4 shows the relationship between an address space, segments, the memory management unit, and physical memory.

The virtual memory system is implemented in a layered, modular fashion.The components that deal with physical memory management are mostly hardware-platform specific. The platform-dependent portions are implemented in the hardware address translation (HAT) layer.

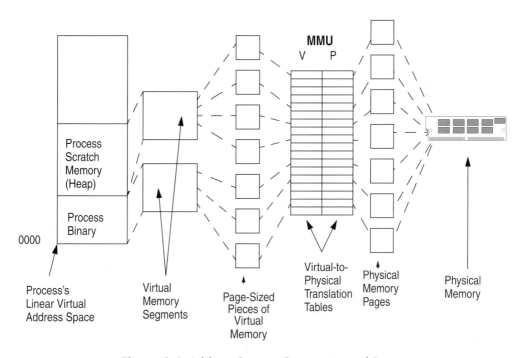

Figure 1.4 Address Spaces, Segments, and Pages

1.7.1 Global Memory Allocation

The VM system implements demand paging. Pages of memory are allocated on demand as they are referenced, and hence portions of an executable or shared library are allocated on demand. Loading pages of memory on demand dramatically lowers the memory footprint and the startup time of a process. When an area of virtual memory is accessed, the hardware MMU raises an event to tell the kernel that an access has occurred to an area of memory that does not have physical memory mapped to it. This event is a *page fault*. The heap of a process is similarly allocated. Initially, only virtual memory space is allocated to the process; when memory is first referenced, a page fault occurs and memory is allocated one page at a time.

The virtual memory system uses a global paging model that implements a single global policy to manage the allocation of memory between processes. A scanning algorithm calculates the least used portion of the physical memory. A kernel thread (the page scanner) scans memory in physical page order when the amount of free memory falls below a preconfigured threshold. Pages that have not been used recently are stolen and placed onto a free list for use by other processes.

1.7.2 The Cyclic Page Cache

All modern operating systems implement some form of file system caching, such that frequently referenced files have their contents in physical memory, providing significantly faster access. The virtual memory system and file system page cache have been tightly integrated in Solaris from the very beginning, originating in SunOS 4.0. In Solaris OS, all of free physical memory can be used to cache file system data.

The original page cache design implemented a special kernel address space segment, called segmap, to manage the mapping of files to physical memory. Since segmap is fixed in size (the actual size will vary based on Solaris release, hardware architecture, and physical memory size), a mechanism is required for handling workloads that exceed the size of segmap. In such situations, a page replacement algorithm is implemented, where least recently used pages are moved out of the segmap, making room for new pages to be cached. The moved pages may still be resident in physical memory, but a file I/O reference will require that the page be moved back into the segmap segment.

Before Solaris 8, pages moved out of segmap needed intervention by the page scanner in order to be available for use by other memory consumers. In Solaris 8, a new cyclic page cache was implemented; pages moved out of segmap are now placed on a cache list. Cache list pages appear to the VM system as free memory, available to other memory consumers. The page scanner is no longer required to reclaim memory in the form of pages that have been pushed out of segmap.

1.7.3 Kernel Memory Management

The Solaris kernel requires memory for kernel instructions, data structures, and caches. Most of the kernel's memory is not pageable; that is, it is allocated from physical memory that cannot be stolen by the page scanner. This characteristic avoids deadlocks that could occur within the kernel if a kernel memory management function caused a page fault while holding a lock for another critical resource. The kernel cannot rely on the global paging used by processes, so it implements its own memory allocation systems.

A core kernel memory allocator—the *slab allocator*—allocates memory for kernel data structures. As the name suggests, the allocator subdivides large contiguous areas of memory (slabs) into smaller chunks for data structures. Allocation pools are organized so that like-sized objects are allocated from the same continuous segments, thereby dramatically reducing fragmentation that could result from continuous allocation and deallocation.

The original slab allocator, integrated into Solaris 2.4, was significantly enhanced over time to keep pace with larger multiprocessor systems and to extend its use as a general-purpose kernel memory allocator. A new, per-processor caching scheme was introduced to provide scalable performance. A general-purpose resource allocator was added in the form of a virtual memory allocator, called *vmem*. The original slab allocator was designed to manage kernel heap memory allocations; the addition of the vmem layer extends the kernel memory allocator to much broader use as a general-purpose allocator of arbitrary-sized resources. Finally, the design, architecture, and algorithms used by the new kernel memory allocator were applied to a user-level memory allocator and implemented as a plug-in replacement for the `malloc(3C)` interface through a new library, `libumem`.

The new kernel memory allocator was implemented in Solaris 8. The user-level allocator, `libumem`, was introduced in Solaris 10.

1.8 Files and File Systems

Solaris provides a framework under which multiple file system types are implemented: the *virtual file system framework* (VFS). Earlier implementations of UNIX used a single file system type for all mounted file systems; typically, the UFS file system from BSD UNIX. The virtual file system framework, developed to enable the network file system (NFS) to coexist with the UFS file system in SunOS 2.0, became a standard part of System V in SVR4 and Solaris OS.

Each file system provides file abstractions in the standard hierarchical manner with file access interfaces even if the underlying file system implementation varies. The file system framework allows almost any objects to be abstracted as files and file systems. Some file systems store file data on storage-based media, whereas other implementations abstract objects other than storage as files. For example, the `procfs` file system abstracts the process tree, where each file in the file system represents a process in the process tree. We can categorize Solaris file systems into the following groups:

- **Storage-Based File Systems.** These are regular file systems that provide facilities for persistent storage and management of data. The Solaris UFS and PC/DOS file systems are examples.

- **Network File Systems.** These provide files that appear to be in a local directory structure but are stored on a remote network server. An example is the network file system (NFS).

- **Pseudo File Systems.** These present various abstractions as files in a file system. The /proc pseudo file system represents the address space of a process as a series of files.

The framework provides a single set of well-defined interfaces that are file system independent; the implementation details of each file system are hidden behind these interfaces. Two key objects represent these interfaces: the virtual file, or *vnode*, and the virtual file system, or *vfs* objects. The vnode interfaces implement file-related functions, and the vfs interfaces implement file system management functions. The vnode and vfs interfaces call appropriate file system functions depending on the type of file system being operated on. Figure 1.5 shows the file system layers. File-related functions are initiated through a system call or from another kernel subsystem and are directed to the appropriate file system via the vnode/vfs layer.

Table 1.1 summarizes some of the major file system types that are implemented in Solaris.

1.9 Resource Management

The hardware resources of a system are typically subdivided into four major categories: processors, memory, disk I/O, and network I/O. Resource management refers to the facilities and infrastructure available in the operating system to manage these hardware resources. Generically, the primary purpose of any operating system kernel is to manage available resources for applications and, generally, to allow multiple users, applications, and processes to share the resources effectively. Certainly, Solaris OS is no exception to that rule, and running a variety of workloads out of the box, without using additional resource management utilities to specifically allocate processors, memory, etc., works very well much of the time.

That said, there are some compelling reasons to implement and use resource allocation controls in today's IT environments:

- **Faster hardware**. Systems that ran at near or maximum capacity five years ago under load have room to spare today, thanks to more powerful proces-

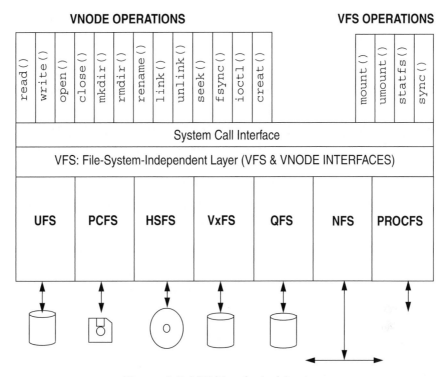

Figure 1.5 VFS/Vnode Architecture

Table 1.1 File Systems Available in Solaris File System Framework

File System	Type	Device	Description
ufs	Regular	Disk	UNIX Fast File system, default in Solaris
zfs	Regular	Disk	The new disk based file system in Solaris
qfs	Regular	Disk	High Bandwidth file system for Solaris, optionally with hierarchical storage management facilities
pcfs	Regular	Disk	MS-DOS file system
hsfs	Regular	Disk	High Sierra file system (CD-ROM)
tmpfs	Regular	Memory	Uses memory and swap
nfs	Network	Network	Network file system
cachefs	Pseudo	File system	Uses a local disk as cache for another NFS file system

continues

Table 1.1 File Systems Available in Solaris File System Framework (*continued*)

File System	Type	Device	Description
autofs	Pseudo	File system	Uses a dynamic layout to mount other file systems
specfs	Pseudo	Device Drivers	File system for the /dev devices
procfs	Pseudo	Kernel	/proc file system representing processes
sockfs	Pseudo	Network	File system of socket connections
fdfs	Pseudo	File Descriptors	Allows a process to see its open files in /dev/fd
fifofs	Pseudo	Files	FIFO file system

sors, increased physical memory, faster network interconnects, and storage subsystems.

- **Bigger hardware.** Large multiprocessor systems from Sun have enormous capacity in all dimensions—processors (up to 144), memory (up to 512 Gbytes), and I/O (up to 72 physical I/O channels for disk and network). All these resources can be managed within a single Solaris kernel instance.

- **Consolidation.** Consolidating production workloads onto a smaller number of physical servers reduces the total number of boxes that need to be managed.

- **Dynamic resource allocation.** Resources on Sun systems can be dynamically deallocated and reallocated, so workloads requiring additional CPU or memory can take advantage of dynamic reallocation and acquire these resources when needed. Resources can be reallocated according to a schedule, allocating (for example) maximum resources to online transaction processing during business hours and reallocating those resource to batch processing after hours.

Mixing multiple workloads within a single instance of Solaris OS can impose some risk when applications are not well-behaved or when usage patterns are unpredictable. In the default shared environment, an application with a memory leak or software bug that results in CPU-bound threads can consume an inordinate amount of resources at the expense of other applications, resulting in suboptimal performance. Setting effective resource management controls ensures that performance requirements and service levels are sustained.

1.9.1 Processor Controls and Domains

The introduction of resource management controls in Solaris OS has evolved over time, beginning with basic processor-binding capabilities (Solaris 2.4) through Solaris Containers (Solaris 10). Processor controls are bundled utilities that bind processes and threads to specific processors on the system, partition a processor, and manage interrupts.

- **Processor binding.** With this feature, a specific process can be bound to a processor in such a way that all the threads in the process will execute only on the designated processor. In Solaris 9, the addition of thread semantics allowed a thread (or group of threads) within a process to be specified for binding. The binding is not exclusive; that is, the kernel may schedule other threads from other processes on the processor targeted by the bind operation. Note that processor binding is stateless, meaning that bindings will not cross reboots.

  See the pbind(1M) and processor_bind(2) man pages.

- **Processor sets.** Introduced in Solaris 2.6, processor sets allow processors on a multiprocessor system to be partitioned into groups or sets, where each set has one or more physical processors assigned to it. Once a processor set has been created, the kernel will not schedule threads on the processors in the set. Explicit binding is required, where one or more processes (or threads) are bound to the processor set. Only those threads that have been bound will get scheduled. Since the kernel will not use processors in a set for operating system kernel threads, Solaris OS will not allow all available processors on a system to be configured into processor sets. At least one processor must remain available to run operating system kernel threads.

  Processor sets are dynamic: the creation and deletion of sets, adding and removing processors to and from sets, and process/thread binding are all done without requiring a system reboot. Processor sets in Solaris 8 and earlier are stateless. (In Solaris 9 onwards they can be managed by pools allowing processor set configurations and bindings to be persistent across reboots).

  See the psrset(1), pset_create(2) and pset_info(2) man pages.

- **Processor interrupt management.** Interrupts are asynchronous events that allow a device or software subsystem to notify a processor that it needs attention. An interrupt disrupts the execution flow of the thread running on the interrupted processor, so an interrupt service routine can be executed to handle the interrupt. Interrupts are a normal part of a busy system's activity, and Solaris OS distributes interrupts across available processors at boot time in an attempt to evenly distribute the interrupt load. This approach generally provides balanced system performance. However, some workloads and applications may require more effective interrupt management so that processors can be dedicated to running application threads without periodic interruptions. In extreme cases, a high rate of interrupts can disrupt thread execution enough to raise performance issues, not only because of the running thread being interrupted but also because of the cache effect of the processor running an interrupt thread. The text and data for the interrupt thread can displace data in the hardware cache lines that were part of the interrupted threads address space, thus causing cache misses when the interrupted thread resumes execution.

With Solaris OS, interrupt handling by a specific processor or processor set can be disabled. Placing a processor in no-interrupt mode causes any interrupts bound to the target processor to be redistributed to other processors that do not have interrupts disabled. Combining interrupt management with processor sets and processor set binding provides a powerful facility for CPU-bound workloads and real-time applications.

See the `psrset(1)`, `psrinfo(1)` and `psradm(1M)` man pages.

- **Dynamic system domains.** Domains are created by the physical partitioning of a server; each domain contains a subset of the total processors, memory, and I/O channels of the system. Each domain is configured with a dedicated boot disk, and each domain runs its own Solaris kernel instance, has a unique IP identity on the network, etc. A domain is effectively a stand-alone Solaris server that just happens to be a physically-partitioned piece of a larger physical system. In addition to providing resource control, domains provide a level of fault isolation where a failure in one domain should not impact the operation of other domains in the same system. The domain feature has a hardware dependency, and is available on a subset of Sun's server product line. Specifically, the UltraSPARC based Sun Fire 4800, 4900, 6800, 6900, 12K, 15K, E20K and E25K servers have domain capabilities.

Processor sets and bindings can, of course, be used in conjunction with dynamic system domains, by which one or more processor sets can be configured in the processors within a specific domain, thus allowing multiple levels of resource allocation and control.

Processors can also be taken offline entirely, meaning that the kernel scheduler will no longer use the processor for scheduling threads or handling interrupts. The `psradm(1M)` command manages a processor's operational state.

1.9.2 Solaris Resource Management

The naming convention for resource management changes after Solaris 8. For Solaris 8, an unbundled product called *Solaris Resource Manager*, or SRM, is available. In Solaris 9 and 10, resource management is integrated into the operating system. Generically speaking, resource management refers to specific software components and utilities used to manage hardware resources. Each release builds on the functions and features of the previous release; whereas Solaris 8 requires the installation of SRM for a share-based thread scheduler (SHR), a share-based scheduler is integrated into Solaris 9 (FSS), along with a new framework for managing resource allocations and limits. Solaris 9 also adds resource pools, which are further enhanced in Solaris 10 with the addition of dynamic resource pools. Finally, Solaris 10 adds virtualized execution environments, or Zones. Read on to learn more about these features.

1.9.2.1 Resource Management Framework

The Fair Share Scheduling class (FSS) is integrated into Solaris 9 (that is, it is not an unbundled add-on), along with a new framework for configuration and management. In addition to FSS, Solaris 9 introduces two new abstractions for defining resource allocations and limits; *projects* and *tasks*. Where the SHR scheduler in Solaris 8 used Inodes and UIDs for allocation and control, Solaris 9 (and 10) manage CPU shares through the projects database and administrative commands.

The projects framework provides a stateful namespace for binding users, processes, and applications to resource allocations and limits. The framework is hierarchically structured (see Figure 1.6); a project may have one or more tasks associated with it, and a task may have one or more processes associated with it.

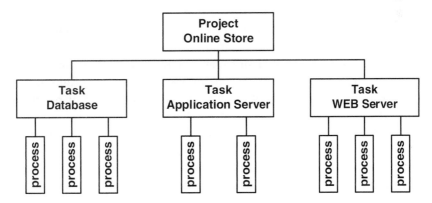

Figure 1.6 Projects and Tasks

The projects database and administrative interface allow groups of processes to be defined as a workload and configured opn the FSS scheduling class. Share allocation is done through attributes in the project definition file. In addition to allowing the allocation of CPU shares, the projects framework provides for setting resource limits at the project, task, and process level. For example, System V IPC resources for shared memory, semaphores, and message queues are defined at the project level. The maximum number of LWPs can be set either at the project or task level, and traditional UNIX resource limits are defined in the projects database on a per-process basis.

The projects framework enables another new feature to Solaris 9 resource management: *resource pools*. Resource pools are a persistent configuration mechanism for processor sets. Recall that processor sets managed with `psrset`(1M) have only in-memory state, meaning that a reboot requires a reconfiguration of the processor sets and bindings. Resource pools address this by using the project's database to store processor set configurations and bindings. Thus, a set of CPUs can be configured as a resource pool, with a specific project bound to the pool. All the tasks, processes, and LWPs associated with the project will be scheduled.

For physical memory control, the resource capping mechanism described previously has been added to the Solaris 9 12/03 release, and has been extended to use the project's database for establishing physical memory consumption limits at the project level.

See the *System Administration Guide: Resource Management and Network Services* for specific information on configuring and managing resources with projects in Solaris 9.

1.9.2.2 Enhancements to Resource Management in Solaris 10

Adding to the features introduced in Solaris 9, Solaris 10 contributes two significant features to Solaris resource management: *Dynamic Resource Pools* (DRPs) and *Zones*. Recall that resource pools in Solaris 9 give persistent process sets the option of binding a scheduling class as an attribute for threads that execute in the pool. Resource pools include a facility for dynamically adjusting the resources (number of CPUs) assigned to the pool in response to system load conditions. In Solaris 10, dynamic resource pools automatically adjust for utilization data and performance goals established in the configuration. A new Solaris daemon, *poold*, monitors system load and decides whether resource allocation adjustments are required.

Solaris 10 Zones provide multiple, virtualized, isolated execution environments for running multiple workloads or applications within a single kernel instance. When a zone is created, all the processes executing within the zone are isolated from processes running in other zones on the system. Think of zones as software partitions; kernel zone software sets the boundaries and isolation within each zone. By default, a global zone, which has visibility into all zones (see Figure 1.7), is the control point for systemwide zone configuration and management.

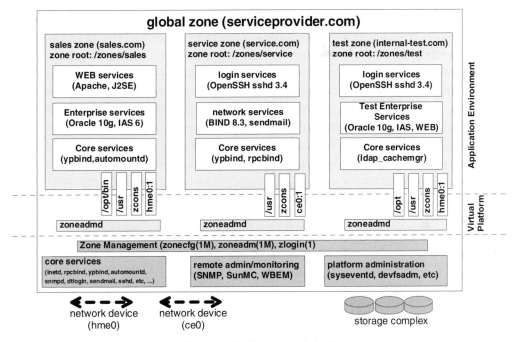

Figure 1.7 Zones in Solaris

Each nonglobal zone configured in a Solaris 10 system has at least one virtual network interface with its own network identity (address, hostname, domain). The network interface for each zone is channeled through one of the physical network interfaces on the system. The network traffic for a nonglobal zone is not visible to the other nonglobal zones on the system. Additionally, each nonglobal zone has its own root password and is only visible to a subset of the system's file system hierarchy, as defined when the zone is configured.

At the center of the zones design was consolidation: the ability to run multiple applications, including several instances of the same type of service (Web server, database server, etc.) in a contained and secure environment, with a simple management framework. Also, installing, configuring, and running applications in a zone must be no different than doing so on a stand-alone system. In other words, the zone must appear to the administrator as just another server running Solaris OS. No changes are required at the application level in order to install and run the software within a zone.

In Solaris 10, zones and resource pools have been integrated, such that a resource pool can be bound to specific zone. The combination of zones and resource pools is a powerful foundation for consolidating multiple applications and workloads within a single Solaris 10 instance; the environment is secure, manageable, flexible, and configurable to meet performance requirements and service levels for each application.

See the *System Administration Guide: Solaris Containers: Resource Management and Solaris Zones* for information on configuring and using zones, resource limits, processor sets, and resource pools.

1.9.3 Internet Protocol Quality of Service

Added to Solaris 9 9/02, the Internet Protocol Quality of Service (IPQoS) enabled administrators to manage resources for network services. Using IPQoS controls, administrators can allocate and regulate available network bandwidth for different classes of services and users through the use of filters configured in accordance with the following:

- Network services, such as email, ftp or WEB services
- Specific source and destination addresses, or port numbers
- User IDs
- Project IDs
- Protocol numbers

With IPQoS, administrators can prioritize, control, and gather statistics for the different service levels configured with the filter keys listed above. For information on configuring and monitoring IPQoS, see the *System Administration Guide: IP Services* for Solaris 10 and the *IPQoS Administration Guide* for Solaris 9.

1.9.4 Resource Management and Observability

Many of the bundled tools and utilities that ship with Solaris OS have been updated to improve the observability of a system running with configured processor sets, resource pools and zones. For example, CPU usage can be monitored with the prstat(1M) command on a per-processor set, per-project, or per-zone basis with the appropriate command-line flags. Commonly used commands, such as `ps(1)`, `ipcs(1)`, `pgrep(1)`, `proc(1)`, `sar(1)`, and others, now include the option to specify a zone ID on the command line to gather information about a specific zone. The `mpstat(1M)` command, when executed in a zone bound to a resource pool, displays information only about the processors in the configured pool. Memory consumption and `rcapd` daemon activity can be monitored with `rcapstat(1)`. Resource pool statistics on size and load can be viewed with `poolstat(1)`.

The bundled Solaris accounting subsystem has been updated to provide resource usage reporting on projects, tasks, and zones. Extended accounting, added to Solaris 9, includes a new accounting database and command set, along with a set of Perl interface modules with which scripts that access the extended accounting files can be developed in the Perl language.

Many other commands have been made aware of processor sets, resource pools, or zones. The key point here is the tight integration of these features into Solaris OS.

PART TWO

The Process Model

2

The Solaris Process Model

Contributions by Roger Faulkner, Phil Harman, and Rod Evans

T he process is one of the most basic and fundamental abstractions provided by an operating system. A process is an executable object, occupying pages of physical memory containing specific memory segments with instructions (text), stack space, data space, and other components necessary for execution.

Borrowing from the traditional definition, a process is the executable form of a program, and a program is simply a file (or collection of files) created to solve a problem or have the computer perform specific tasks. Users connect to a Solaris system and execute commands through interpreter processes called shells. Applications execute on Solaris as one or more processes. Bundled software that provides services for network connections, system resource management tasks, service monitoring, etc., all exist as processes. The Solaris kernel provides the necessary framework and infrastructure for the creation, execution, control, monitoring, and termination of processes. Solaris extends the traditional process model with integrated support for multithreaded processes or processes with multiple threads that can be scheduled and executed independently.

In this chapter, we examine the process model, the major data structures defined and maintained by the kernel, and the key components that define the execution environment. We discuss the Solaris threads model, why it changed, and how it is implemented in Solaris today. We cover the tools and methods available for observing process and thread behavior and the process file system. Finally, we look at the signal mechanism, followed by a summary of the life cycle of a process and thread in Solaris.

2.1 Components of a Process

The Solaris kernel supports an entity known as a *process* and maintains a system-wide *process table*, where each process is uniquely identified in the kernel by a positive integer called the process identification number, or PID. Solaris is a multiuser, multitasking operating system and as such supports the coexistence of many processes. On systems with sufficient hardware resources (processors, memory), several thousand processes may exist at any time and any number of them may have *multiple threads of execution*.

2.1.1 Thread Objects

Threaded execution, both within the kernel at large and user processes, is integrated into the core of the Solaris kernel. Solaris is a multithreaded operating system; tasks performed by the operating system are executed as *kernel threads*. For multithreaded processes, there are *user threads*, which are created with a *lightweight process (LWP)*—a kernel object that allows user threads to execute and enter the kernel independently of other threads in the same process. The unit of scheduling and execution in Solaris is the kernel thread; thus, user threads in processes must be linked to a kernel thread for execution. The relationship among these process objects is shown in Figure 2.1.

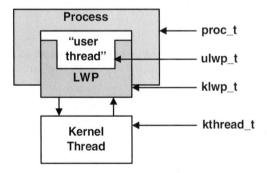

Figure 2.1 Process Objects

The names of the process objects, along with a definition, and location of the structure definition in the OpenSolaris source code, are shown in Table 2.1.

Table 2.1 defines a process as a state container for threads. Process state refers to all the bits of information contained within a process that the kernel needs to effectively manage the process. From a process perspective, the kernel abstracts

Table 2.1 Process Objects

Object	Definition	Name	Header File with Structure Definition
process	An execution environment—a state container for execution threads	`proc_t`	`uts/common/sys/proc.h`
user thread	A user-created unit of execution within a process	`ulwp_t`	`lib/libc/inc/thr_uberdata.h`
lightweight process (LWP)	An object that provides kernel state for a user thread	`klwp_t`	`uts/common/sys/klwp.h`
kernel thread	The fundamental unit of scheduling and execution in the kernel	`kthread_t`	`uts/common/sys/thread.h`

execution resources—a virtual machine for executing instructions. These are uncontended resources from the process perspective, since processes exist unaware of other processes running within the same instance of the operating system. It's a function of the kernel to manage the underlying hardware resources (processors, physical memory, I/O channels) and to provide each process the resources it requires: execution time on processors and allocation of physical memory, as well as to perform privileged services, such as network and disk IO. The kernel can impose constraints on how much of a given resource a process can consume, and Solaris includes a sophisticated resource management framework for allocating specific quantities of available resources (for example, processor cycles) and imposing thresholds or limits on how much of a particular resource a process can consume (see Section 2.5.1).

The kernel maintains a process structure (`proc_t`) for every process in the system; within a `proc_t`, process state data is maintained and referenced. `proc_t` itself resides in the kernel's address space, and as such is protected from access by user processes. Protection boundaries exist in the form of access modes and memory page-level protections such that user processes cannot directly read or write the kernel's address space, and the address space of user processes are protected from access by other processes in the system. Since the kernel exists as a layer of software between the hardware and user processes, direct access to hardware is protected and available to user processes only through a well-defined set of system services. These services are implemented as application programming interfaces

(APIs) that can be called from user programs to have the kernel perform a privileged task on behalf of the calling process, such as read or write a file, issue a control command to a device, create a new process or thread, allocate memory for the
process to use, etc. The set of APIs that exist directly between user processes and
the kernel are collectively known as system calls, documented in section two of the
man pages.

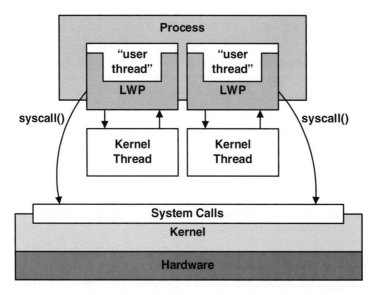

Figure 2.2 System Calls

Process information and control is available to users through a set of commands
that make use of the process file system, procfs. Procfs is a pseudo file system that
abstracts process information and control as a set of files and directories, rooted at
/proc (see Section 2.10). Commonly used commands, such as ps(1), prstat(1),
and the per-process utilities described in the proc(1) man page, are built on /proc.
As we move through this chapter, you'll see examples of these commands in action.

Just as every process in the kernel has a unique PID, so the other objects that
are part of the process model have an integer namespace; user threads and LWPs
have an LWP_ID, and kernel threads have a thread ID (TID). The process model in
Solaris 10 (which differs from previous releases) simplifies the namespace assignment. From a user-process perspective, the kernel thread ID is derived from the
LWP_ID (when a new thread is created, the LWP is created before the kernel
thread, but more on that in a bit). A full view of the process ID and LWP ID
namespace can be observed with the ps(1) and prstat(1) commands.

```
sol9$ prstat -Lc
   PID USERNAME  SIZE   RSS STATE  PRI NICE      TIME  CPU PROCESS/LWPID
     9 root      19M   15M sleep    59    0   6:29:58 1.2% svc.configd/12
     9 root      19M   15M sleep    54    0   1:34:36 0.2% svc.configd/13
   222 root     6608K 3144K sleep   44    0  13:20:22 0.2% inetd/1
   286 root     7664K 4088K sleep   59    0   7:21:14 0.1% automountd/1
 25092 root     8568K 4968K sleep   59    0   0:00:00 0.1% sshd/1
 25245 mauroj   4992K 4576K cpu8    49    0   0:00:00 0.1% prstat/1
 25295 allanp   1624K 1288K sleep   52    0   0:00:00 0.1% csh/1
 25301 allanp   1528K 1168K cpu1    34    0   0:00:00 0.1% csh/1
 25188 allanp   1640K 1304K sleep   59    0   0:00:00 0.0% csh/1
 25287 root     4072K 2312K sleep   52    0   0:00:00 0.0% in.rshd/1
     9 root      19M   15M sleep    59    0   1:01:20 0.0% svc.configd/7
 25187 root     4072K 2312K sleep   59    0   0:00:00 0.0% in.rshd/1
 25151 mauroj   8376K 2888K sleep   59    0   0:00:00 0.0% sshd/1
 14906 allanp   9400K 2752K sleep   60    0   0:00:01 0.0% cp/1
 23006 allanp   9400K 3936K sleep   60    0   0:00:00 0.0% cp/1
Total: 108 processes, 275 lwps, load averages: 0.52, 0.65, 0.90
```

The example above is the partial output of a `prstat -Lc` command and shows a small subset of the information maintained for all running processes. As we move through the chapter, we explore the fields displayed above, along with with tools and utilities available for observing and controlling processes.

2.1.2 Core Process Components

A process is represented internally in the kernel as a data structure, defined in `usr/src/uts/common/sys/proc.h`. We explore the various fields defined in the process structure in Section 2.4. Here, we provide a high-level view of the major components of a process in Solaris. These process components are shared by all the threads in a multithreaded process.

- **Address space.** The virtual and physical memory that comprise the process's various memory segments, which can be broadly categorized as follows. The text segment defines the memory pages containing the instruction stream the process executes when it runs. The stack segment defines memory space for the process stack (for processes with more than one thread, each thread has its own stack), and the data segment contains initialized data. All processes also have a heap segment, which defines the memory pages for uninitialized data.

- **Credentials.** The binding of a process to a user, group, and set of privileges. The credentials define the effective and real user identification (UID), group identification (GID), the list of privileges for the process, and project and zone information.

- **Process links.** A process will reside on several linked lists in the kernel. In addition to the process table, there are links for a process's family tree (parent, child and sibling processes, and orphans) and processes within the same process group. Process groups provide a mechanism for the kernel to take action on groups of processes, typically in the area of signal delivery as it relates to job control and terminal control functions.

- **CPU utilization.** Fields that track time spent by the process executing in user and kernel mode, as well as the cumulative time spent by all the child processes.

- **Signals.** Signal set fields for pending signals, signals to ignore, queued signals, etc.

- **Threads.** Various fields to track the number of LWPs in the process, LWP states, and a linked list of all the kernel threads in the process.

- **Microstate accounting.** Resource usage and microstate tracking for the process, including all the threads in the case of a multithreaded process.

- **User area.** An ancient UNIX abstraction, the user area (uarea), maintains various bits of information, such as the executable name and argument list, and links to the process open file list.

- **Procfs.** Support for integration with the process file system.

- **Resource management.** Support for resource controls, projects, tasks, and resource pools.

The items listed above offer a high-level description of the major components of a process in Solaris. An examination of `usr/src/uts/common/sys/proc.h` reveals a considerable number of `proc_t` structure members required to make it all work as well as it does. Many of these are will be examined more closely in subsequent sections.

2.2 Process Model Evolution

The multithreaded process model in Solaris underwent significant change in Solaris 10, but the evolution actually began in Solaris 8, with the introduction of an alternative threads library (`/usr/lib/lwp/libthread.so`). In Solaris 9, the new threads library became the default library for multithreaded applications. Additional changes were made in Solaris 10 with the Process Model Unification project, which integrated the threads library (`libthread.so`) into the standard C library (`libc.so`), creating a single process model for all processes in Solaris. In Solaris 10, threaded and nonthreaded processes have the same process objects and components. It is important to note that these changes, while involving significant work at the library and kernel level, are not visible to users and developers. Source and binary compatibility was maintained; running, developing, compiling, and using threaded applications in Solaris 10 is consistent with previous releases. The only difference worth noting is a simplification of writing and maintaining threaded applications in two specific areas: signal management and concurrency management. The complexity of maintaining and debugging threaded applications has been eased with the new model as well, since it is inherently much less complex.

2.2.1 Thread Model Evolution

The thread model in Solaris was originally a multilevel *MxN* model, in which a *user thread* was something separate and distinct from an LWP. User threads (*M*) were multiplexed onto a potentially smaller number of LWPs (*N*) by a user thread scheduler implemented in the thread library (`libthread.so`). There was not a one-to-one relationship between user threads and LWPs unless the developer explicitly created *bound threads*, an option available with the `thread_create()` API, or a settable attribute with `pthread_attribute_setscope()` when `pthread_create()` was used to create threads. The original MxN model worked well for many years, but some inherent difficulties in the implementation were extremely complex to overcome.

- **Signal behavior.** Delivery of asynchronous signals was problematic, since the thread targeted to receive the signal may not have been linked to an LWP when delivery was attempted.

- **Thread scheduling.** The threads library implemented a scheduler (not to be confused with the kernel scheduler). The threads library scheduler managed the scheduling of unbound user threads onto LWPs and maintained a library-level priority scheme. In some applications and workloads, the latency induced by this level of scheduling resulted in performance issues. Also, the scheduling lock maintained by the library could become a point of contention, impacting scalability. The expected level of concurrency was not always met, because concurrency was governed by the number of available LWPs.

- **Maintaining the LWP pool.** Keeping a sufficient number of LWPs available such that runnable user threads had the resources necessary to execute was a complex task performed by the threads library in the absence of specific hints from the application (the now obsolete `thr_setconcurrency()` API).

In addition to the issues listed above, the evolution of technology challenged some of the underlying assumptions that drove the original MxN implementation. First and foremost were processor performance and the cost of creating threads. The original model was intended to minimize the cost of creating threads by not requiring underlying kernel resources to be allocated and to facilitate the existence of hundreds or thousands of threads in a process without imposing undue overhead on the kernel. Processor performance has advanced to a point where this trade-off is no longer worth the cost in complexity in maintaining the old model. Thread creation with the new model, while more costly in absolute terms, is still a relatively fast operation.

Technology advances and issues with the original model, coupled with a desire to enhance specific features for threaded applications, led to the implementation of a new threads library. The new library was architected as a 1:1 model, in which every user thread is created with an LWP and associated kernel thread. For all intents and purposes, a user thread is an LWP in Solaris 10.

Note that the original threads model is discussed in detail in the first edition of Solaris Internals. A technical white paper, titled *Multithreading in the Solaris Operating Environment* and written by Sun Engineer Phil Harman, discusses the new threads library for Solaris 8 and Solaris 9 in detail. This white paper is available online at:

http://www.sun.com/software/whitepapers/solaris9/multithread.pdf

2.2.2 Unified Process Model

Before Solaris 10, two process models existed: single-threaded processes (not linked with libthread.so) and multithreaded processes (linked with libthread.so). The existence of two process models led to some fundamental problems.

- Libraries (like libnsl.so) that want to create helper threads have complex code to do one thing if the application to which libnsl.so is linked is single threaded and to do another if it is multithreaded.

- Some libraries use multithreading and satisfy their need for libthread.so by linking with it when the library is built. Such libraries can still be targeted for a dlopen(3C) call from an application. If a single-threaded application does call dlopen(), it becomes a multithreaded application, a condition for which it was not built and which is not necessarily expected by the developer.

- libc.so has become quite complex over time. It must operate in either process model and be prepared to switch to the multithreaded model whenever the application issues a dlopen(3C) on libthread.so. This induces enormous complexity into libc.so and can lead to performance issues.

- New developments in thread local storage (TLS), requiring cooperation between the compilers and the Solaris libraries, can only be accomplished in a multithreaded process model. The means that the Solaris libraries themselves cannot take advantage of TLS, since they must be prepared to operate with both single-threaded and multithreaded applications.

The list above represents the more salient issues with maintaining two process models. It was time to remove the complexity and confusion and implement a single process model in Solaris by integrating the code in `libthread` into `libc`. In Solaris 10, all thread APIs that were previously in `libthread` and `libpthread` are now in `libc`. `libthread` and `libpthread` are still provided with stubs for binaries that require resolving to `libthread` or `libpthread` as a result of library specifications in the build process. The actual thread's code is in `libc` and will ultimately be resolved from `libc`.

Unifying the process model required making another change in terms of the libraries shipped in Solaris: the removal of `libc.a`, an archive version of `libc` for creating statically linked binaries. The main problem with static `libc` and threading is that the static `libc` cannot contain multithreading interface functions. All multithreading interface functions require initialization before `main()` is called, and this initialization occurs through the init phase of dynamic linking and cannot occur with a static threading library. Thus, we cannot provide a static `libc` without special code in all the threads' API source files to suppress their contents when being compiled statically.

Also, statically linked programs cannot assume they are running in a multithreaded environment. This puts a constraint on all library code (at least libraries that are compiled for both static and dynamic linking). There must be conditional statements to take care of the two different possible process models. No library code can take advantage of the newly provided compiler-supported thread local storage. Also, unsolvable problems arise with binaries that are partially statically linked and that statically link to `libc.a`. If a partially statically linked binary loads a shared object through a `dlopen()` call, the dynamic version of `libc` is loaded into the binary. Much, but not all, of `libc` is already in the binary (as a result of the static linking), and the dynamic linker will resolve calls from the `libc` opened by `dlopen()` to those `libc` functions already in the binary. But the `libc` functions already in the binary were not compiled for multithreading. The process would suddenly become multithreaded, calls would be made from the dynamic `libc` into the application's copies of static components of `libc`, and chaos would ensue.

For these reasons, it was decided to stop shipping archive versions of bundled Solaris libraries. Note that for 64-bit Solaris, 64-bit versions of bundled archive libraries were not shipped, so 64-bit applications have been dynamically linking to `libc` and others for several years without incident.

The effect of no longer providing a `libc` for static linking required some changes in the root file system organization of Solaris, since several of the binaries that reside in /sbin were statically linked. With Solaris 10, many of the shared object libraries that historically shipped in /usr/lib are now part of the root file system, in /lib. All binaries in /sbin are now dynamically linked—moving the shared object libraries to /lib makes them available early on in the boot process, after root has been mounted but before /usr is mounted, for the binaries in /sbin that depend on them.

We can summarize as follows:

- The threads model has changed significantly in Solaris 10 and OpenSolaris. With the 1:1 model, all threads are LWPs and are immediately visible to the kernel scheduler.

- The process image is now consistent for threaded and nonthreaded processes. libthread and libpthread has been integrated into libc—threaded applications no longer need to link to libthread.

- The changes made with the new threads library and process model unification *did not impact source or binary compatibility.*

- Archive versions of bundled Solaris libraries are no longer available. Applications must dynamically link to libraries in /lib and /usr/lib.

2.3 Executable Objects

All processes originate as an executable file on disk. The process image defines what a process looks like when it is loaded in memory and ready for execution on a Solaris system. All processes begin life as programs, and programs are simply text files written in a computer programming language. The program is compiled and linked by the appropriate language-specific compiler. A successful compilation process results in the creation of an executable binary file on disk. This file becomes a process in the Solaris environment through invocation of the exec(2) system call, which is typically preceded by a fork(2) call. fork(2) creates a new process (a new proc_t), and exec(2) replaces the process image of the calling process with a new process image.

Once an executable object file is exec'd, the runtime linker, ld.so.1(1), is invoked to manage linking to other shared objects required for execution, typically a shared object library such as libc.so. This sequence of events is known as *dynamic linking*, whereby references in the program to shared object library functions (for example, printf(3), read(2)) are resolved at runtime by ld.so.1. It is possible to build *statically linked* executables through a compilation flag (-B static on the compile command line); this flag forces the inclusion of all referenced library functions in the executable object at build time. This technique requires that an archive version of the library be available (for example, libc.a for static linking and libc.so.1 for dynamic linking). However, as part of the merge of libthread into libc, archive libraries are no longer shipped in Solaris 10—/usr/lib/libc.a (among others) is no longer part of the distribution, so applications must dynamically link to system libraries.

A quick note on linkers is appropriate here before we continue. Two linkers are involved in the creation and execution of a process in Solaris: ld(1), which is commonly referred to as the link editor; and ld.so.1(1), which is the runtime linker. ld(1) is the link editor that executes as part of the compilation process. Specifically, it is called from the language-specific compiler (cc(1) for example, for compiling programs written in C) and is the last phase of the compilation process. ld(1) ultimately generates the executable file. Note that ld(1) can be executed as a standalone program for linking previously compiled object files to create an executable.

ld.so.1(1), the runtime linker, is invoked by the exec(2) system call when a new process image is loaded. The runtime linker takes over after exec(2), loads any required dependencies, and binds the associated objects together with the information generated by ld(1). The runtime linker can also be called upon by the application to load additional dependencies and to locate symbols.

Executable object files are generated in compliance with the industry-standard Executable and Linking Format (ELF). ELF is part of the System V application binary interface (ABI), which defines an operating system interface for compiled, executable programs. Since the ABI defines the binary interface for several implementations of UNIX System V across a variety of different hardware platforms, the ELF definition must be divided into two components: a platform-independent piece and a specification that is specific to a processor (for example, SPARC V8, SPARC V9, Intel 386, AMD64). Areas of the ABI that are processor specific include the definition of the function-calling sequence (system calls, stack management, etc.) and the operating system interface (signals, process initialization).

There are three different variations of ELF files: *executable*, *relocatable*, and *shared object* files. The type of ELF file generated depends on the options used during the compilation process. Relocatable files are generated by the compiler when the -c option is used (when the Sun Studio C compiler is used), and require further processing by the linker before executing (the -c option suppresses the running of the linker, ld(1)). Shared objects are created with the -G option and contain symbol information for the runtime linker, as well as executable code. Executable files are generated when the -G and -c flags are excluded from the compilation process, which includes running the link editor (ld(1)). Our focus for the remainder of this section is on the object file format, or ELF, as it applies to an *executable* file.

The ELF executable object file contains various sections, including an ELF header that provides specific information about the object file and a series of fields that describe the different components of the file. We use the elfdump(1) command to examine ELF object files.

```
sol10$ elfdump -e /bin/ls

ELF Header
  ei_magic:    { 0x7f, E, L, F }
  ei_class:    ELFCLASS32           ei_data:      ELFDATA2MSB
  e_machine:   EM_SPARC             e_version:    EV_CURRENT
  e_type:      ET_EXEC
  e_flags:                     0
  e_entry:              0x10e08   e_ehsize:     52  e_shstrndx:   21
  e_shoff:              0x66fc    e_shentsize:  40  e_shnum:      23
  e_phoff:               0x34     e_phentsize:  32  e_phnum:       6
```

The example above displays the ELF header for the ls(1) command. The fields in the header tell us it is a 32-bit SPARC executable and provide information about the two major sections of the file: the section header and program header. The section header is defined by a section header table, or SHT, and locates linkable sections of the executable. A program header table, or PHT, defines the program segments of the object file, which are segments of executable code. The ELF header provides the offsets into the file for the SHT (e_shoff) and PHT (e_phoff), as well as their respective sizes and the number of entries. Additional elfdump(1) flags dump an object's SHT and PHT.

```
sol10$ elfdump -c /bin/ls
. . .
Section Header[9]:  sh_name: .text
    sh_addr:       0x10e08       sh_flags:     [ SHF_ALLOC  SHF_EXECINSTR ]
    sh_size:       0x3484        sh_type:      [ SHT_PROGBITS ]
    sh_offset:     0xe08         sh_entsize: 0
    sh_link:       0             sh_info:      0
    sh_addralign: 0x8

Section Header[10]:  sh_name: .init
    sh_addr:       0x1428c       sh_flags:     [ SHF_ALLOC  SHF_EXECINSTR ]
    sh_size:       0xc           sh_type:      [ SHT_PROGBITS ]
    sh_offset:     0x428c        sh_entsize: 0
    sh_link:       0             sh_info:      0
    sh_addralign: 0x4
. . .
Section Header[17]:  sh_name: .data
    sh_addr:       0x26370       sh_flags:     [ SHF_WRITE  SHF_ALLOC ]
    sh_size:       0x154         sh_type:      [ SHT_PROGBITS ]
    sh_offset:     0x6370        sh_entsize: 0
    sh_link:       0             sh_info:      0
    sh_addralign: 0x8
. . .
Section Header[19]:  sh_name: .bss
    sh_addr:       0x26520       sh_flags:     [ SHF_WRITE  SHF_ALLOC ]
    sh_size:       0xbd0         sh_type:      [ SHT_NOBITS ]
    sh_offset:     0x6520        sh_entsize: 0
    sh_link:       0             sh_info:      0
    sh_addralign: 0x8
```

The section header listing for the ls(1) file is a partial listing, showing just a few of the sections with names that may sound familiar—the text section (.text), the initialization section (.init) and so on. The section header is a kind of road map used by exec(2) and the runtime linker to locate and load specific bits of the object file into memory for execution.

The runtime linker offers a wealth of features for understanding and debugging the linker operations and executable file shared object references. Using the LD_DEBUG environmental variable, the runtime linker reports symbol resolutions, search paths, files, bindings, etc. Try running:

```
sol10$ LD_DEBUG=help <my_exectuable>
```

Setting LD_DEBUG to "help" causes the runtime linker to display all the options available for LD_DEBUG. Multiple options can be specified, separated by commas. Be aware that, depending on which options are specified and how many shared objects are linked to the executable, the LD_DEBUG flags can generate voluminous amounts of output (try LD_DEBUG=all). You can easily save the output to a file (highly recommended) with the following command.

```
sol10$ LD_DEBUG=all LD_DEBUG_OUTPUT=/var/tmp/ld.out <executable_file>
```

The file name is the specified path and string, with the PID of the process appended to the end. For further information on ELF file formats and the use of the linker, refer to the *Linker and Libraries Guide*, available from http://docs.sun.com.

2.4 Process Structures

The objects that make up a process are defined as data structures and managed as such in the kernel. This includes not only kernel threads and LWPs but also many of the support objects linked to a process through pointers in the process structure. In this section, we examine the kernel data structures that define the major components of a process. For the record, not every member of every data structure is covered. The objective is to discuss the major components of the threaded process model in order to effectively cover key concepts. A great many subtleties are beyond the scope of our coverage in this text.

2.4.1 The `proc` Structure

The process structure, or *proc* structure, provides the framework for the creation and management of processes and threads in the Solaris environment. Like any kernel data structure, the members of the proc structure cover the full range of data types, including a great many pointers to support structures that, in total, make up the entire process picture in the Solaris environment.

Figure 2.3 provides the big picture.

The structure definition for a process can be found in `usr/src/uts/common/sys/proc.h`. As we take a closer look at the key fields, we will view segments of the process structure from the source along the way.

```
typedef struct proc {
    /*
     * Fields requiring no explicit locking
     */
    struct  vnode *p_exec;          /* pointer to a.out vnode */
    struct  as *p_as;               /* process address space pointer */
    struct  plock *p_lockp;         /* ptr to proc struct's mutex lock */
    kmutex_t p_crlock;              /* lock for p_cred */
    struct  cred    *p_cred;        /* process credentials */
. . .

                                    See usr/src/uts/common/sys/proc.h
```

- **p_exec.** A vnode pointer, referencing the executable on-disk file that was loaded (exec'd) to create this process image.

- **p_as.** Address space structure pointer. All of the memory pages mapped to a process make up that process's address space. The as structure, a kernel abstraction for managing the memory pages allocated to a process, defines the process's virtual address space. You can dump the address space mappings of a process by using the pmap(1) command.

```
sol10$ pmap -x 20636
20636:  ./ml
  Address  Kbytes     RSS    Anon  Locked Mode   Mapped File
 00010000       8       8       -       - r-x--  ml
 00020000       8       8       8       - rwx--  ml
 00022000    1528    1528    1528       - rwx--  [ heap ]
 FF280000     848     784       -       - r-x--  libc.so.1
 FF364000      32      32      32       - rwx--  libc.so.1
 FF36C000       8       8       8       - rwx--  libc.so.1
 FF3A0000      24      16      16       - rwx--  [ anon ]
 FF3B0000     176     176       -       - r-x--  ld.so.1
 FF3EC000       8       8       8       - rwx--  ld.so.1
 FF3EE000       8       8       8       - rwx--  ld.so.1
 FFBFE000       8       8       8       - rwx--  [ stack ]
 -------- ------- ------- ------- -------
 total Kb    2656    2584    1616       -
```

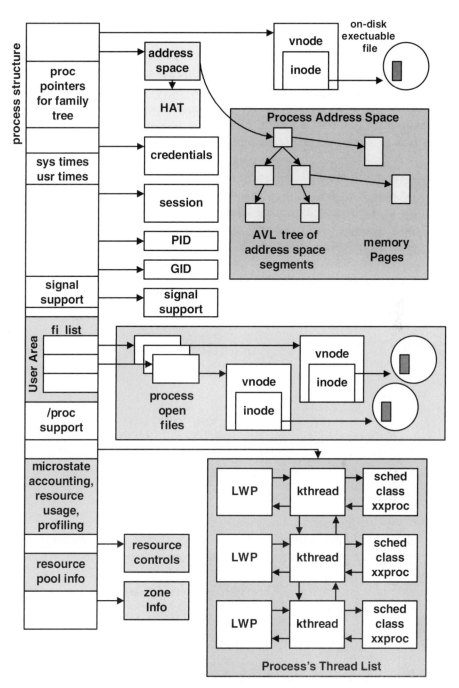

Figure 2.3 Process Structure

Above is sample output of the pmap(1) command (with the -x flag), which dumps all the segments that make up a process's virtual address space. The pmap(1) display provides the virtual address of the mapping (Address), the virtual address space size of the mapping (Kbytes), how much of the mapping is resident in physical memory (RSS), the number of memory pages of anonymous memory in the segment (Anon), number of pages locked (Locked), the segment permissions, and mapped file. Anon memory is reported for heap and stack segments, as well as copy-on-write (COW) pages (see Figure 9.2).

Note the permissions of the stack segment in the example. There is a security exposure to mapping stack pages with exec permissions. Buffer overflow attacks exploit executable stack segments by inserting rogue code on a process's stack, setting the program counter, and executing instructions. You can set an /etc/system variable, called noexec_user_stack, to prevent the mapping of stack pages with execute permissions. Note that this is necessary only for 32-bit executables because the SPARC V8 ABI specifies read/write/exec permissions for stack mappings. The ABI for 64-bit SPARC V9 binaries defines the stack as not executable (no exec). Here's the same test program recompiled as a 64-bit SPARC V9 binary.

```
sol10$ pmap -x 23727
23727:  ./ml
         Address    Kbytes       RSS       Anon    Locked  Mode   Mapped File
0000000100000000        8         8          -         -   r-x--  ml
0000000100100000        8         8          8         -   rwx--  ml
0000000100102000     1136      1136       1136         -   rwx--  [ heap ]
FFFFFFFF7F200000      896       616          -         -   r-x--  libc.so.1
FFFFFFFF7F3E0000       64        64         64         -   rwx--  libc.so.1
FFFFFFFF7F400000       24        16         16         -   rwx--  [ anon ]
FFFFFFFF7F500000        8         8          8         -   rwx--  [ anon ]
FFFFFFFF7F600000      176       176          -         -   r-x--  ld.so.1
FFFFFFFF7F72C000       16        16         16         -   rwx--  ld.so.1
FFFFFFFF7FFFE000        8         8          8         -   rw---  [ stack ]
                 ---------- ---------- ---------- ----------
       total Kb     2344      2056       1256         -
```

Note that the exec permission mode is not set on the stack segment. Also, we can easily tell this is a 64-bit binary by the Address column—the addresses are 64 bits wide.

Additional options to pmap(1) provide the memory page size for each segment and swap reservations.

- **p_lockp.** Process lock structure pointer. The p_lock is a kernel mutex (mutual exclusion) lock that synchronizes access to specific fields in the process structure. This level of granularity of the kernel lock increases parallelism because there is not a single lock on the entire process table. Instead, there is per-table entry locking, such that multiple kernel threads can concurrently access different process structures.

- **p_crlock.** Kernel mutex to synchronize access to the credentials structure.

- **p_cred.** Pointer to the credentials structure, which maintains the user credentials information such as user identification (UID) and group identification (GID), etc. Every user on a Solaris system has a unique UID as well as a primary GID, although a user can belong to multiple groups.

A user's UID and GID are established through fields in the /etc/passwd file when the user's account is set up. You can use the id(1M) command to see what your UID and GID are. Use the su(1) command to change user identities. Use the newgrp(1) command to change your real and effective GID. The UID and GID of the user that started the process have their credentials maintained here in the credentials structure, and *effective* UID and GID are maintained here as well.

Solaris supports the notion of *effective* UID and GID, which allow for the implementation of the setuid and setgid mode bits defined in a file's inode (remember, the process started life as an executable file on a file system). A process could have an effective UID that is different from the UID of the user that started the process.

A common example is a program that requires root (UID 0) privileges to do something, for example, the passwd(1) command, which writes to protected files (/etc/passwd and /etc/shadow). Such a program is owned by root (aka superuser), and with the setuid bit set on the file, the effective UID of the process is 0. During process execution, the kernel checks for effective UID and GID during permission checks, which will be the same as the UID and GID of the user if neither the setuid nor setgid mode bit has been set.

```
struct cred {
        uint_t          cr_ref;         /* reference count */
        uid_t           cr_uid;         /* effective user id */
        gid_t           cr_gid;         /* effective group id */
        uid_t           cr_ruid;        /* real user id */
        gid_t           cr_rgid;        /* real group id */
        uid_t           cr_suid;        /* "saved" user id (from exec) */
        gid_t           cr_sgid;        /* "saved" group id (from exec) */
        uint_t          cr_ngroups;     /* number of groups returned by */
                                        /* crgroups() */
        cred_priv_t     cr_priv;        /* privileges */
        projid_t        cr_projid;      /* project */
        struct zone     *cr_zone;       /* pointer to per-zone structure */
        gid_t           cr_groups[1];   /* cr_groups size not fixed */
                                        /* audit info is defined dynamically */
                                        /* and valid only when audit enabled */
        /* auditinfo_addr_t     cr_auinfo;      audit info */
};
                                        See usr/src/uts/common/sys/cred_impl.h
```

New features in Solaris 10 required some new fields in the credentials structure. Process privileges (see Chapter 5) allow processes to acquire specific privileges to perform operations that previously required root permissions.

```
struct priv_set {
        priv_chunk_t pbits[PRIV_SETSIZE];
};

typedef struct cred_priv_s {
        priv_set_t      crprivs[PRIV_NSET];    /* Priv sets */
        uint_t          crpriv_flags;          /* Privilege flags */
} cred_priv_t;
```
                                         See usr/src/uts/common/sys/priv_impl.h

For every process, there are four sets of privileges: the effective set, the inheritable set, the permitted set and the limit set. See the `privileges(5)` man page for a complete list of process privileges, and the `ppriv(1)` man page for information on setting process privileges.

Moving on to the next set of fields in `proc.h`, we arrive at the following:

```
. . .
int       p_swapcnt;        /* number of swapped out lwps */
char      p_stat;           /* status of process */
char      p_wcode;          /* current wait code */
ushort_t  p_pidflag;        /* flags protected only by pidlock */
int       p_wdata;          /* current wait return value */
pid_t     p_ppid;           /* process id of parent */
. . .
```
                                         See usr/src/uts/common/sys/proc.h

- **p_swapcnt.** Counter of process LWPs that have been swapped out. Under severe memory shortfalls, the memory scheduler (PID 0, the `sched` process) swaps out entire LWPs to free up some memory pages.

- **p_stat.** The process status, or state. The notion of process states in Solaris may be somewhat confusing, since the kernel thread, not the process, is the entity that gets scheduled, switched, put to sleep, etc. Kernel threads change state in the Solaris environment much more frequently than do processes. For a nonthreaded process, the process state is essentially whatever the state of the kthread is. For multithreaded processes, several kthreads that belong to the same process can be in different states (for example, running, sleeping, runnable, zombie, etc.). At the process level, several possible states are defined.

```
/* stat codes */

#define SSLEEP   1                /* awaiting an event */
#define SRUN     2                /* running */
#define SZOMB    3                /* process terminated but not waited for */
#define SSTOP    4                /* process stopped by debugger */
#define SIDL     5                /* intermediate state in process creation */
#define SONPROC  6                /* process is being run on a processor */
                                        See usr/src/uts/common/sys/proc.h
```

A few areas in the kernel operate on processes (as opposed to threads) where process state is set when a process is checked. In the fork() code, during process creation, the SIDL state is set, and later in fork, p_stat is set to SRUN—the process has been created and is runnable. In the exit() code, pstat is set to ZOMB when a process is terminated. The support code for process groups, process-to-CPU binding, and resource controls also checks process state at various points. Those areas aside, all other state changes during the lifetime of a process occur in the kthread and are reflected in the state field in the kthread structure. In fact, the state (S) column from the ps(1) command is derived from the kthread state field, not the process p_stat data. If a process has more than one LWP and the -L flag has not been specified on the ps(1) command line, then the state field is derived from a representative LWP, selected by the prchoose() kernel function when ps(1) is executed (the -L flag to ps(1) prints information about each LWP in each selected process).

- **p_wcode.** Defined as current wait code. A synchronization field that contains data to support SIGCLD (child signal) information. A process is sent a SIG-CLD signal when the status of one of its child processes has changed. The p_wcode holds a status bit that identifies the reason for the status change (for example, child has exited, stopped, coredumped, was killed, or has continued).

- **p_pidflag.** Another field used to support synchronization via signals. Status bits to indicate that a SIGCLD signal is pending or a SIGCLD was sent to notify the parent that the child process has continued (see Section 2.11).

- **p_wdata.** Also used for process synchronization with signals and used in conjunction with p_wcode; contains status bits that provide a reason for an event. For example, if a process is killed by a SIGKILL signal, the p_wcode indicates the child was killed and the p_wdata indicates a SIGKILL signal was the reason (see Section 2.11).

- **p_ppid.** The PID of the parent process.

The process model in the Solaris kernel maintains a lineage for all the processes running on the system. That is, every process has a parent process and may have child processes. The process creation model, in which a new process begins life as the result of an existing process issuing some variant of the `fork(2)` system call, means that, by definition, there will minimally be a parent process to the newly created process. Not only will a process have a parent, but it may also have siblings—processes that have been created by the same parent. Every process in the Solaris environment can reside on as many as a dozen or so linked lists maintained by the kernel; the `proc` structure stores the various pointers required.

```
struct  proc    *p_link;           /* forward link */
struct  proc    *p_parent;         /* ptr to parent process */
struct  proc    *p_child;          /* ptr to first child process */
struct  proc    *p_sibling;        /* ptr to next sibling proc on chain */
struct  proc    *p_psibling;       /* ptr to prev sibling proc on chain */
struct  proc    *p_sibling_ns;     /* prt to siblings with new state */
struct  proc    *p_child_ns;       /* prt to children with new state */
struct  proc    *p_next;           /* active chain link next */
struct  proc    *p_prev;           /* active chain link prev */
struct  proc    *p_nextofkin;      /* gets accounting info at exit */
struct  proc    *p_orphan;
struct  proc    *p_nextorph;
```
See usr/src/uts/common/sys/proc.h

We do not elaborate further on the process lineage pointers—they are generally self-explanatory.

The next set of pointers support process groups, session management, and PID information maintenance.

```
. . .
struct  proc    *p_pglink;         /* process group hash chain link next */
struct  proc    *p_ppglink;        /* process group hash chain link prev */
struct  sess    *p_sessp;          /* session information */
struct  pid     *p_pidp;           /* process ID info */
struct  pid     *p_pgidp;          /* process group ID info */
. . .
```
See usr/src/uts/common/sys/proc.h

- **p_pglink.** Process group link. Forward link to a hash chain of processes in the same process group. Processes are linked in a group when they are controlled by the same controlling terminal. See Section 2.12.

- **p_ppglink.** Previous process group link. Back link to a hash chain of processes in the same process group.

- **p_sessp.** Pointer to a session structure, which contains information for managing the process's control terminal. See Section 2.12.

- **p_pidp.** Pointer to a `pid` structure, for process ID (PID) information. The process's actual PID is stored in one of the fields in the `pid` structure (see Figure 2.4).

- **p_pgpidp.** Another `pid` structure pointer, for process group information (process group ID).

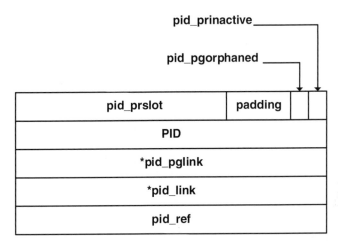

Figure 2.4 PID Structure

The PID structure stores 2 status bits, `pid_prinactive` and `pid_pgorphaned`, to flag the PID structure as being free (`prinactive`) and to mark the process as orphaned or not (`pgorphaned`—no parent process), followed by 6 pad bits (unused bits) and 24 bits to store the slot number of the `/proc` table entry for the process, `pid_prslot`. The PID is the actual process ID. The PID structure links to other PID structures in the kernel through `pid_link`, which maintains a hashed list of active PIDs in the kernel, and `pid_pglink`, which links back to the process structure.

Several condition variables are maintained in the `proc` structure. Condition variables in the Solaris environment implement sleep and wakeup. One such condition variable is *p_holdlwps*, a special condition variable for holding process LWPs. In a `fork()`, the LWPs must be suspended at some point so that their kernel stacks can be cloned for the new process. `p_lwpexit` is a condition variable used when a process's LWP is exiting so that the required process-level cleanup can be done and utilization fields updated.

The kernel maintains time totals that reflect the amount of user time and system time the process accumulated, as well as summations for all the child processes' system time and user time. The child information is summed when a child process exits. The `p_utime` and `p_stime` fields maintain the process's user and system time, respectively; the `p_cutime` and `p_cstime` fields maintain the child process's user and system time.

```
/*
 * Per-process lwp and kernel thread stuff
 */
id_t        p_lwpid;            /* most recently allocated lwpid */
int         p_lwpcnt;          /* number of lwps in this process */
int         p_lwprcnt;         /* number of not stopped lwps */
int         p_lwpdaemon;       /* number of TP_DAEMON lwps */
int         p_lwpwait;         /* number of lwps in lwp_wait() */
int         p_lwpdwait;        /* number of daemons in lwp_wait() */
int         p_zombcnt;         /* number of zombie lwps */
kthread_t  *p_tlist;           /* circular list of threads */
lwpdir_t   *p_lwpdir;          /* thread (lwp) directory */
lwpdir_t   *p_lwpfree;         /* p_lwpdir free list */
lwpdir_t  **p_tidhash;         /* tid (lwpid) lookup hash table */
uint_t      p_lwpdir_sz;       /* number of p_lwpdir[] entries */
uint_t      p_tidhash_sz;      /* number of p_tidhash[] entries */
uint64_t    p_lgrpset;         /* unprotected hint of set of lgrps */
                               /* on which process has threads */

. . .
                                       See usr/src/uts/common/sys/proc.h
```

The process maintains several bits of information on LWPs and kernel threads, including a total of all LWPs linked to the process (`p_lwpcnt`) and all LWPs created (`p_lwptotal`). Counters are maintained for the number of blocked LWPs (`p_lwpblocked`), runnable LWPs (`p_lwprcnt`), and zombie LWPs (`p_zombcnt`). A pointer rooted in the `proc` structure references a linked list of kernel threads (`p_tlist`) and a linked list of zombie threads (`p_zomblist`). A zombie process is a process that has exited but whose parent process did not issue a *wait* call to retrieve the exit status. Zombie processes appear as defunct in `ps(1)` output.

The remaining members of the process structure can be grouped into several categories. Per-process signal handling support involves linking to signal queue structures, supporting the signal mask and signal posting structures. The Solaris signal model has undergone significant work to support the multithreaded architecture and is discussed beginning on page 135. Support for the `/proc` file system requires the inclusion of various pointers and data types in the `proc` structure. Also, the Solaris kernel includes a facility called Doors, which provides a fast cross-process call interface for procedure calling.

Process-level resource usage and microstate accounting information are maintained within the process structure, as well as for each LWP. We discuss the details in Section 2.10.3.

Process profiling is supported by the inclusion of a `prof` structure (`p_prof`) and is enabled when the program is compiled (that is, before it becomes a "process").

During the execution of the process, process profiling gathers statistical data that tells the programmer which routines the process was spending time executing in and how much time was spent in each function relative to the total execution time of the process.

You can use the mdb(1) utility to examine the contents of a proc structure on a running system.

```
# ps
  PID TTY          TIME CMD
29487 pts/1        0:00 sh
 5995 pts/1        0:00 ps
# mdb -k
Loading modules: [ unix krtld genunix specfs dtrace ufs sd ip sctp usba fctl nca nfs
random sppp lofs crypto ptm ipc logindmux ]
> ::ps ! grep 29487
R  29487   9895  29487   9895     0 0x42004000 0000030009caf7d0 sh
R   6033  29487  29487   9895     0 0x42004000 0000030008c1aff0 mdb
R   6131   6033  29487   9895     0 0x42004000 0000030009cd6740 grep
> 0000030009caf7d0::print proc_t
{
    p_exec = 0x30001ca7dc0
    p_as = 0x30008555610
    p_lockp = 0x300016c3c80
    p_crlock = {
        _opaque = [ 0 ]
    }
    p_cred = 0x30c54cf6df8
. . .
> 0x30c54cf6df8::print cred_t
{
    cr_ref = 0xc1
    cr_uid = 0
    cr_gid = 0
    cr_ruid = 0
    cr_rgid = 0
    cr_suid = 0
    cr_sgid = 0
    cr_ngroups = 0xb
    cr_priv = {
        crprivs = [
            {
                pbits = [ 0x800e2, 0 ]
            }
            {
                pbits = [ 0x800e2, 0 ]
            }
            {
                pbits = [ 0x800e2, 0 ]
            }
            {
                pbits = [ 0xffffffff, 0xffffffff ]
            }
        ]
        crpriv_flags = 0
    }
    cr_projid = 0x1
    cr_zone = zone0
    cr_groups = [ 0 ]
}
```

In the above example, we used ps(1), determined the PID of our shell process, invoked mdb(1), used the ps dcmd to find the process of interest, grabbed the address of the proc structure, and displayed it. To further illustrate our ability to examine process information, we extracted and also printed the address of the credentials structure (the pbits fields represent the process privileges for each of the four privilege sets described earlier).

2.4.2 User Area

The role of the user area (traditionally referred to as the *uarea*), has changed somewhat in the Solaris environment when compared with traditional implementations of UNIX. The uarea was linked to the proc structure through a pointer and thus was a separate data structure. The uarea was swappable if the process was not executing and memory space was tight. Today, the uarea is embedded in the process structure. The process kernel stack, which was traditionally maintained in the uarea, is now implemented in the LWP (see Section 2.4.3).

```
typedef struct user {
        /*
         * These fields are initialized at process creation time and never
         * modified.  They can be accessed without acquiring locks.
         */
        struct execsw *u_execsw;           /* pointer to exec switch entry */
        auxv_t  u_auxv[__KERN_NAUXV_IMPL]; /* aux vector from exec */
        timestruc_t u_start;               /* hrestime at process start */
        clock_t u_ticks;                   /* lbolt at process start */
        char    u_comm[MAXCOMLEN + 1];     /* executable file name from exec */
        char    u_psargs[PSARGSZ];         /* arguments from exec */
        int     u_argc;                    /* value of argc passed to main() */
        uintptr_t u_argv;                  /* value of argv passed to main() */
        uintptr_t u_envp;                  /* value of envp passed to main() */
. . .

                                    See usr/src/uts/common/sys/user.h
```

The uarea fields shown above are self-explanatory and align with the standard application binary interface (ABI) in terms of maintaining objects set in the process image when loaded. These variables store the command, argument list from the command line, and the user's environmental variables—shell variables, such as PATH, TERM, HOME, etc.

The uarea is where process open file information is maintained, referenced through the uarea's u_finfo variable. This variable is a data structure, uf_info_t, which establishes the base for a list of open files in the process.

```
/*
 * Per-process file information.
 */
typedef struct uf_info {
        kmutex_t         fi_lock;         /* see below */
        kmutex_t         fi_pad;          /* unused -- remove in next release */
        int              fi_nfiles;       /* number of entries in fi_list[] */
        uf_entry_t *volatile fi_list;     /* current file list */
        uf_rlist_t       *fi_rlist;       /* retired file lists */
} uf_info_t;
```
                                                    See usr/src/uts/common/sys/user.h

The list of open files begins with `fi_list`, which is an array of file entry structures of the type `uf_entry_t`, and is indexed by the file descriptor—a numeric value returned from a successful `open(2)` system call.

```
typedef struct uf_entry {
        kmutex_t         uf_lock;         /* per-fd lock [never copied] */
        struct file      *uf_file;        /* file pointer [grow, fork] */
        struct fpollinfo *uf_fpollinfo;   /* poll state [grow] */
        int              uf_refcnt;       /* LWPs accessing this file [grow] */
        int              uf_alloc;        /* right subtree allocs [grow, fork] */
        short            uf_flag;         /* fcntl F_GETFD flags [grow, fork] */
        short            uf_busy;         /* file is allocated [grow, fork] */
        kcondvar_t       uf_wanted_cv;    /* waiting for setf() [never copied] */
        kcondvar_t       uf_closing_cv;   /* waiting for close() [never copied] */
        struct portfd    *uf_portfd;      /* associated with port [grow] */
        /* Avoid false sharing - pad to coherency granularity (64 bytes) */
        char             uf_pad[64 - sizeof (kmutex_t) - 2 * sizeof (void*) -
                2 * sizeof (int) - 2 * sizeof (short) -
                2 * sizeof (kcondvar_t) - sizeof (struct portfd *)];
} uf_entry_t;
```
                                                    See usr/src/uts/common/sys/user.h

The `uf_file` entry points to the file structure associated with the file.

```
typedef struct file {
        kmutex_t         f_tlock;         /* short term lock */
        ushort_t         f_flag;
        ushort_t         f_pad;           /* Explicit pad to 4-byte boundary */
        struct vnode     *f_vnode;        /* pointer to vnode structure */
        offset_t         f_offset;        /* read/write character pointer */
        struct cred      *f_cred;         /* credentials of user who opened it */
        struct f_audit_data    *f_audit_data;  /* file audit data */
        int              f_count;         /* reference count */
} file_t;
```
                                                    See usr/src/uts/common/sys/file.h

Within the file structure, we find a link to the vnode (`f_vnode`), which contains the file-system-specific object that defines the file. For example, for a file in UFS, the file's inode is found through the vnode and contains the information necessary to locate the body of the file (see Section 14.2 and Section 15.3 for further information).

The links to a process's open file list are shown in Figure 2.5.

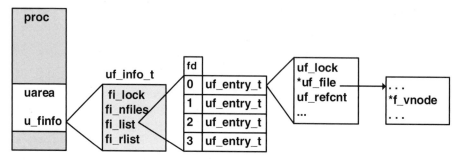

Figure 2.5 Process Open File List

The `fi_nfiles` value maintains the size of the `fi_list` array, which does not equate to the actual number of files the process has open. Rather, an initial number of file entries are created for a new process (7). As the process opens files, if the file list is full, a new set of `uf_entry_t` structures is allocated with `((fi_nfiles x 2) +1)` to determine how large to grow the file list. The actual number of files a process can have open is determined by a resource control, max-file-descriptor (see Section 2.6).

The `fi_rlist` is the retired file list. When the file list needs to grow, the new file list will be all the existing file entries, plus the new ones, appended to the end of the list. The old list becomes the process's retired file list. The old list is kept instead of being freed immediately, in case a reference (pointer) still exists to a structure in the old list. The kernel deals with such situations asynchronously—the cleanup of the old list can happen later and need not add time to the file open path.

To obtain a list of a process's open files, use the `pfiles(1)` command.

```
# pfiles 20208
20208:  cp /net/explo.east/proactive/rawdata/e5/82a81be5/explorer.82a81be5.abh
  Current rlimit: 256 file descriptors
   0: S_IFSOCK mode:0666 dev:276,0 ino:24852 uid:0 gid:0 size:0
      O_RDWR
        SOCK_STREAM
        SO_REUSEADDR,SO_KEEPALIVE,SO_LINGER(60),SO_SNDBUF(49152),SO_R
        sockname: AF_INET 129.154.54.9  port: 514
        peername: AF_INET 192.9.95.30  port: 829
   1: S_IFSOCK mode:0666 dev:276,0 ino:24852 uid:0 gid:0 size:0
      O_RDWR
        SOCK_STREAM
```

continues

```
          SO_REUSEADDR,SO_KEEPALIVE,SO_LINGER(60),SO_SNDBUF(49152),SO_R
          sockname: AF_INET 129.154.54.9  port: 514
          peername: AF_INET 192.9.95.30  port: 829
    2: S_IFIFO mode:0000 dev:277,0 ino:13720970 uid:0 gid:0 size:0
       O_RDWR
    3: S_IFREG mode:0644 dev:283,21917 ino:1439108 uid:1 gid:1 size:11755594
       O_RDONLY|O_LARGEFILE
       /net/explo.East/hanfs4/e5/82a81be5/
explorer.82a81be5.abh12bhi-2006.02.05.06.00-tar.gz
    4: S_IFREG mode:0600 dev:274,2 ino:757553547 uid:12115 gid:10 size:8388608
       O_WRONLY|O_CREAT|O_TRUNC|O_LARGEFILE
       /tmp/explorer.82a81be5.abh12bhi-2006.02.05.06.00-tar.gz
```

Note some new features in the output of pfiles(1). The target process in this case is cp(1), copying files over a network, so the first two file descriptors are TCP sockets. In addition to the original pfiles(1) data (file type, permissions, device, inode number, user and group ID), we see the local and remote address and port number for the socket connection and various socket attributes (SO_KEEPALIVE, etc).

Like the process structure, the uarea contains supporting data for signals, including an array that defines the disposition for each possible signal. The signal disposition tells the operating system what to do in the event of a signal: ignore it, catch it and invoke a user-defined signal handler, or take the default action. See Section 2.11.

2.4.3 Lightweight Processes (LWPs)

The threads model in Solaris 10 brings together the user thread, defined internally as a user LWP, and the kernel LWP. As implemented, the user LWP and kernel LWP are abstracted as two different data structures, but because they are so tightly integrated, along with the kernel thread, they should be thought of as a single execution entity.

The user LWP is defined in src/lib/libc/inc/thr_uberdata.h. The ulwp_t structure is implementation private and is not intended to be visible to callers of the interfaces (programs), although the structure members can be viewed under a debugger, such as mdb(1). The ulwp_t defines the user state for a thread of execution, which includes the user stack, thread-level scheduling policy and priority, synchronization primitive support (mutex locks, reader/writer locks, condition variables), signal support, and library-level sleep management.

Much of the data maintained at the library level and in the ulwp_t exists to support POSIX compliance and features for multithreaded programs. For the record, Solaris ships with two thread APIs: the Solaris and UNIX International (UI) APIs, and POSIX. The Solaris/UI APIs evolved in the very early days of Solaris, before the POSIX thread APIs were completed and standardized. At this point, the POSIX APIs have been stable for quite some time, and we recommend that developers use the POSIX interfaces for developing threaded applications. The underlying implementation in Solaris is the same, no matter which APIs are used.

For example, threads can be created with either `pthread_create(3C)` (POSIX) or `thr_create(3C)`. These interfaces take different arguments, and altering the attribute of a thread is done differently depending on which interfaces are used. The POSIX interface require an additional interface call to change the stack size of a thread, whereas the Solaris/UI interface has an optional stack size in the `thr_create(3C)` argument list. The interfaces in `libc.so` serve as wrappers, parsing and validating the argument list. Both create APIs that ultimately call the same library-internal routine for creating the thread.

The programmable thread attributes can establish the stack size, stack address, and the scheduling policy and priority. Multithreaded applications typically use synchronization primitives, mutex locks, reader/writer locks, and condition variables for protecting shared data, and POSIX defines settable attributes for these synchronization objects as well. A mutex lock can be defined as having visibility across multiple processes (interprocess) or only within threads in the same process (intraprocess). Refer to the appropriate man pages and the *Multithreaded Programming Guide* on `http://docs.sun.com` for a complete list of thread and lock attributes.

Another object used internally for user state is the `uberdata` structure, `uberdata_t`. There is one processwide uberdata object, which is used internally by the library support code for fast thread management and data access. The uberdata provides a globally visible view of the process's user threads and includes status flags, thread counts, and thread lists. By maintaining a processwide structure in the library, the support code does not have to enter the kernel to retrieve needed bits of information on user thread state. Also, performance optimizations can be made through the use of hash tables and linked lists rooted in the uberdata, allowing the library code to do fast searches and lookups of thread data.

The `uberdata` and `ulwp_t` data can be examined on running processes with `mdb(1)`.

```
sol10$ mdb -p 18304
Loading modules: [ ld.so.1 libc.so.1 ]
> ::uberdata
libc.so.1`_uberdata:
            &link_lock          &fork_lock          fork_owner
+0x0        0xff368bc0          0xff368c00          <NULL>
. . .
            queue_head          thr_hash_table      hash_size  hash_mask
+0x1088     0xff380000          0xff260000          1024       0x3ff
            ulwp_one            all_lwps            all_zombies
```

continues

```
+0x1098    0xff3a2000            0xff3a2000            <NULL>
           nthreads    nzombies  ndaemons    pid       sigacthandler
+0x10a4    25          0         0           18304     0xff331b20
           lwp_stacks            lwp_laststack         nfreestack  stk_cache
+0x10b8    <NULL>                <NULL>                0           10
           ulwp_freelist         ulwp_lastfree
+0x10c8    <NULL>                <NULL>
           ulwp_replace_free     ulwp_replace_last     atforklist
+0x10d0    <NULL>                <NULL>                0xff3a0080
  . . .
> 0xff3a2000::walk ulwps |::print ulwp_t ul_lwpid
ul_lwpid = 0x1
ul_lwpid = 0x2
ul_lwpid = 0x3
ul_lwpid = 0x4
ul_lwpid = 0x5
ul_lwpid = 0x6
ul_lwpid = 0x7
ul_lwpid = 0x8
ul_lwpid = 0x9
ul_lwpid = 0xa
ul_lwpid = 0xb
ul_lwpid = 0xc
ul_lwpid = 0xd
ul_lwpid = 0xe
ul_lwpid = 0xf
ul_lwpid = 0x10
ul_lwpid = 0x11
ul_lwpid = 0x12
ul_lwpid = 0x13
ul_lwpid = 0x14
ul_lwpid = 0x15
ul_lwpid = 0x16
ul_lwpid = 0x17
ul_lwpid = 0x18
ul_lwpid = 0x19
>
```

In the above example, mdb(1) is invoked with the -p flag, to grab a running process (PID 18304 is a threaded test process). Once in mdb(1), the uberdata dcmd is executed, and we can use the uberdata to learn a bit about the process (there are 25 threads, no daemon or zombie threads, etc). We can also use the uberdata pointers to look at the ulwp_t fields of interest. all_lwps is a pointer to the beginning of the linked list of all user threads (ulwp_ts). A ulwp walker in mdb(1) will walk the linked list. In this example, we examine one particular field of each ulwp_t in the process (the ID). The example demonstrates observability into the library-level data—uberdata and per-thread ulwp_t data. Note that these structures are implementation private and can change at any time, including with a patch or an update.

Where the ulwp_t maintains user statistics, the klwp_t, or kernel LWP, maintains the kernel state of a thread. Most of the above LWP structure members exist to support system calls and to maintain hardware context information. Remember, system calls are function calls into the kernel—a thread's way of asking the operating system to do something on its behalf (for example, open/read/write a file, get my PID, etc.). Since LWPs can be scheduled on processors (along with their corresponding kernel thread) independently of other LWPs in the same process, they need to be able to execute system calls on behalf of the thread they're bound to. An LWP blocked on a system call does not cause the entire process to block (as long as it's a multithreaded process).

Within each LWP, per-thread usage data is maintained, updated throughout the lifetime of the thread.

```
/*
 * Resource usage, per-lwp plus per-process (sum over defunct lwps).
 */
struct lrusage {
        u_longlong_t    minflt;         /* minor page faults */
        u_longlong_t    majflt;         /* major page faults */
        u_longlong_t    nswap;          /* swaps */
        u_longlong_t    inblock;        /* input blocks */
        u_longlong_t    oublock;        /* output blocks */
        u_longlong_t    msgsnd;         /* messages sent */
        u_longlong_t    msgrcv;         /* messages received */
        u_longlong_t    nsignals;       /* signals received */
        u_longlong_t    nvcsw;          /* voluntary context switches */
        u_longlong_t    nivcsw;         /* involuntary context switches */
        u_longlong_t    sysc;           /* system calls */
        u_longlong_t    ioch;           /* chars read and written */
};
                                        See usr/src/uts/common/sys/klwp.h
```

The usage data is reflected in procfs, accessible programmatically through /proc/<pid>/lusage and /proc/<pid>/lwp/<lwp_id>/lwpusage. Refer to the proc(4) man page for specifics, and see Section 2.10.

The LWP usage data can be observed with dtrace(1).

```
sol10$ dtrace -n 'profile-97hz / pid == 3015 / { @sc[tid]=sum(curthread->t_lwp->lwp_ru.sysc) }'
dtrace: description 'profile-97hz ' matched 1 probe
^C

            5        134302
            8        314840
           20        435048
            6        714194
           14        732452
            7        733875
            4        744547
            3        772063
           10        845876
           21        916301
           23       1625899
```

The above example uses the profile provider, set to fire 97 times per second and targeting a specific process (PID 3015). The sum() function tracks the system call counts per thread (TID key in the sum() aggregation). The output shows the thread ID in the left column and the system call count on the right.

Other important bits in the klwp_t support hardware context and state information, signal handling, and procfs support fields.

```
    struct pcb        lwp_pcb;              /* user regs save pcb */
    uintptr_t         lwp_oldcontext;       /* previous user context */

    /*
    * system-call interface
    */
    long     *lwp_ap;          /* pointer to arglist */
    int      lwp_errno;        /* error for current syscall (private) */
    /*
    * support for I/O
    */
    char     lwp_error;        /* return error code */
    char     lwp_eosys;        /* special action on end of syscall */
    char     lwp_argsaved;     /* are all args in lwp_arg */
    char     lwp_watchtrap;    /* lwp undergoing watchpoint single-step */
    long     lwp_arg[MAXSYSARGS];   /* args to current syscall */
    void     *lwp_regs;        /* pointer to saved regs on stack */
    void     *lwp_fpu;         /* pointer to fpu regs */
    label_t  lwp_qsav;         /* longjmp label for quits and interrupts */


    /*
    * signal handling and debugger (/proc) interface
    */
    uchar_t lwp_cursig;            /* current signal */
    uchar_t lwp_curflt;            /* current fault */
    uchar_t lwp_sysabort;          /* if set, abort syscall */
    uchar_t lwp_asleep;            /* lwp asleep in syscall */
    uchar_t lwp_extsig;            /* cursig sent from another contract */
    stack_t lwp_sigaltstack;       /* alternate signal stack */
    struct sigqueue *lwp_curinfo;  /* siginfo for current signal */
    k_siginfo_t     lwp_siginfo;   /* siginfo for stop-on-fault */
    k_sigset_t      lwp_sigoldmask; /* for sigsuspend */
                                  See usr/src/uts/common/sys/klwp.h
```

Recall that the kernel LWP allows user threads to execute system calls, enter the kernel, and (if necessary) block in the kernel, independently of other threads in the same process. Thus, we see syscall support (lwp_ap, lwp_errno, lwp_eosys, etc.), in addition to the execution state fields (lwp_pcb, lwp_oldcontext, lwp_regs, and lwp_fpu).

2.4.4 Kernel Threads

The kernel thread is the entity that actually gets put on a dispatch queue and scheduled. This fact is probably the most salient departure from traditional UNIX implementations, where processes maintain a priority and processes are put on run queues and scheduled. It's the kthread, not the process, that is assigned a scheduling class and priority. You can examine this on a running system by using the -L and -c flags to the ps(1) command. The columns in the ps(1) output below provide the process ID (PID), the LWP number within the process (LWP), the scheduling class the LWP is in (CLS), and the priority (PRI).

```
# ps -eLc
     PID   LWP  CLS PRI TTY         LTIME CMD
       0     1  SYS  96 ?            0:17 sched
       1     1  TS   59 ?          161:10 init
       2     1  SYS  98 ?            0:00 pageout
       3     1  SYS  60 ?          721:13 fsflush
     172     1  TS   59 ?            0:00 keyserv
     172     2  TS   59 ?            0:00 keyserv
     172     3  TS   59 ?            0:00 keyserv
       7     1  TS   59 ?            0:00 svc.star
  . . .
    6374     1  TS   59 ?            0:00 dol.2686
   16961     1  TS   59 ?            0:00 dol.2686
    6365     1  TS   59 ?            0:00 csh
   17513     1  TS   60 ?            0:00 cp
   17501     1  TS   59 ?            0:00 in.rshd
   14925     1  TS   59 ?            0:00 in.rshd
   13753     1  TS   60 ?            0:01 cp
   15771     1  TS   59 ?            0:00 dol.2686
   17851     1  TS   39 pts/1       0:00 ps
   13751     1  TS   59 ?            0:00 dol.2686
   13162     1  TS   59 ?            0:00 csh
    7387     1  TS   60 ?            0:02 cp
   11886     1  TS   60 ?            0:01 cp
   16963     1  TS   60 ?            0:00 cp
   10830     1  TS   49 ?            0:01 sshd
   17787     1  TS   59 ?            0:00 dol.2686
    3245     1  TS   59 ?            0:00 in.rshd
   15774     1  TS   60 ?            0:00 cp
   17789     1  TS   59 ?            0:00 cp
   17612     1  TS   59 ?            0:00 dol.2686
   10838     1  TS   59 pts/1       0:00 ksh
   17778     1  TS   59 ?            0:00 csh
  . . .
```

It is interesting to note that the output provides the LWP ID. In Solaris 10, the kernel thread and LWP ID have the same ID value.

The kernel thread structure is defined in usr/src/uts/common/sys/thread.h. The significant fields in the kthread include the following:

- **t_link.** Pointer to a kthread structure. Linked list support, links the kthread with other kthreads on the same queue: dispatch queue, sleep queue, and free queue.

- **t_stack.** Kernel stack pointer (address).

- **t_bound_cpu.** Pointer to a CPU structure. Data to manage binding to a processor, and data to support a processor set.

- **t_affinitycnt.** Maintains CPU affinity (loose coupling to a specific processor, a best effort to keep a thread on the same CPU).

- **t_bind_cpu.** User-specified CPU binding (that is, pbind(2)).

- **t_flag.** Thread flag bits. Thread flags provide the kernel with a method of setting and tracking necessary bits of information about the thread, such as whether the thread is an interrupt thread, whether it is blocking, whether its corresponding LWP is in a zombie state, etc.

- **t_proc_flag.** Additional thread flag bits. The distinction between these bits and the ones in t_flag above are locking requirements. Only the T_WAKEABLE flag in t_flag requires a synchronization lock for setting or checking since it must coincide with the thread state. The bits in t_proc_flag are set and checked under protection of the p_lock, the kernel mutex that synchronizes access to the proc structure.

- **t_schedflag.** Flags the dispatcher uses for scheduling. They indicate conditions such as the thread is in memory, the thread should not be swapped, or the thread is on a swap queue. The dispatcher also uses these flags to change the thread's state to runnable.

- **t_preempt.** Flag used to specify that a thread should not be preempted.

- **t_state.** Thread state. Any one of the following:

  - TS_FREE. Free thread structure.
  - TS_SLEEP. Sleeping on an event.
  - TS_RUN. Runnable, waiting for a processor.
  - TS_ONPROC. Thread is running on a processor.
  - TS_ZOMB. Thread has exited, but not yet been reaped.
  - TS_STOPPED. Thread is stopped. Initial thread state; possible through a debugger as well (or with pstop(1)).

The description of the process table showed that a process state field is maintained in the process structure along with the kernel thread. The kernel thread, not the process, changes during execution. There is, for the most part, a correlation between states defined for the process and kernel thread states, as shown in Table 2.2.

Thread state transitions are shown in Figure 2.6.

The IDL state is actually a process state, and PINNED is not technically a thread state but is shown because it represents a potentially common transition that kernel threads make during execution.

Table 2.2 Kernel Thread and Process States

Process	Kernel Thread	Description
SIDL		State during `fork(2)` (creation).
SRUN	TS_RUN	Runnable.
SONPROC	TS_ONPROC	Running on a processor.
SSLEEP	TS_SLEEP	Sleeping (blocked).
SSTOP	TS_STOPPED	Stopped.
SZOMB	TS_ZOMB	Kthread/process has terminated.
	TS_FREE	Thread is waiting to be reaped.

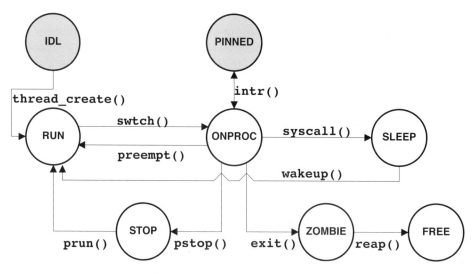

Figure 2.6 Kernel Thread States

The disparities in the state of a process and kernel thread have to do with process creation (process SIDL state) and the state of a kernel thread following termination (TS_FREE). We discuss this subject in Sections 2.7 and 2.9.

- **t_pri.** The thread's scheduling priority
- **t_epri.** The thread's inherited priority—used for the implementation of priority inheritance, which addresses the priority inversion problem
- **t_wchan0, t_wchan.** Wait channel—what the thread is blocking (sleeping) on

- **t_sobj_ops.** Pointer to a synchronization-object-specific operations (functions) vector
- **t_cid.** Scheduling class ID (for example, TS, RT)
- **t_cldata.** Pointer to a scheduling-class-specific data structure
- **t_clfuncs.** Pointer to scheduling-class operations vector
- **t_cpu.** Pointer to a CPU structure for the CPU that the thread last ran on
- **t_lpl.** Load average for the thread's home lgroup
- **t_tid.** Kthread/LWP ID
- **t_sigqueue**—Pointer to a siginfo structure—root pointer of siginfo queue
- **t_sig.** Signals pending to this thread
- **t_hold.** Signal hold bit mask
- **t_forw.** Kthread pointer, forward link for linked list, processwide
- **t_back.** Kthread pointer, backward pointer for above
- **t_lwp.** Pointer to the LWP structure
- **t_procp.** Pointer to the proc structure
- **t_next.** Forward pointer for systemwide linked list of kernel threads
- **t_prev.** Back pointer for above
- **t_cred.** Pointer to current credentials structure
- **t_sysnum.** System call number

The following kernel thread members are used by the dispatcher code for thread scheduling.

- **t_lockp.** Pointer to queue lock (dispatch queue or sleep queue)
- **t_oldspl.** The previous priority level
- **t_pre_sys.** Flag for system call preprocessing
- **t_disp_queue.** Pointer to the thread's dispatch queue
- **t_disp_time.** Last time this thread was running
- **t_kpri_req.** Kernel priority required for this thread

The next group of kthread members deals with post-system-call or post-trap handling. The kthread members are embedded in the kthread structure as a union. A bit set in any of these members prevents a direct return to user mode of the thread until the condition has been satisfied.

- **_t_astflag.** Flag to indicate post-trap processing required, such as signal handling or a preemption.

- **_t_sig_check.** Signal pending.

- **_t_post_syscall.** Some post-system-call processing is required.

- **_t_trapret.** Invokes the scheduling class-specific trap return code.

- **t_prioinv, t_ts.** Turnstile pointers. Turnstiles are sleep queues that support priority inheritance and are used for threads sleeping on synchronization primitives (mutex locks, reader/writer locks).

The thread structure(s) fields can be examined with mdb(1) or dtrace(1).

```
# dtrace -n 'profile-97hz / pid ==26195 / { @p[tid]=lquantize(curthread->t_pri,1,60,5);
}'
dtrace: description 'profile-97hz ' matched 1 probe
^C

    9
        value  ------------ Distribution ------------ count
            1 |                                         0
            6 |@@@@@@@@@@@@@@@                          15
           11 |                                         0
           16 |@@@@@@@@@@@@@                            13
           21 |                                         0
           26 |@@@@@@@                                  7
           31 |                                         0
           36 |@@@@                                     4
           41 |                                         0
           46 |@                                        1
           51 |                                         0

    6
        value  ------------ Distribution ------------ count
            1 |                                         0
            6 |@@@@@@@@@@@@@                            13
           11 |                                         0
           16 |@@@@@@@@@@@@@                            13
           21 |                                         0
           26 |@@@@@@                                   6
           31 |                                         0
           36 |@@@@                                     4
           41 |                                         0
           46 |@@@                                      3
           51 |                                         0
```

The example shown tracks the priority of all the threads in process PID 26195, using the lquantize aggregating function. lquantize is a good fit here because we know the range of values for the threads in this process (see Section 3.7.1), and lquantize allows us to specify the lower and upper bound for the range of values, as well as the incremental step value (5 in this case). The number at the upper left of each aggregation in the output is the TID, which we used as a key to the aggregation. The `value` column represents the thead's priority, and the `count` column represents the number of times during the sampling period the thread's priority fell within the range defined in the `value` column for that row. Using the `dtrace(1)` curthread built-in variable, we can track any field in the `kthread_t` structure (curthread is defined by `dtrace` as being a pointer to the kthread structure of the thread running on the CPU when the probe fires).

2.5 Kernel Process Table

Every process occupies a slot in the kernel process table, which maintains a process structure (commonly abbreviated as *proc structure*) for the process. The process structure is relatively large, and contains all the information the kernel needs to manage the process and schedule the LWPs and kthreads for execution. As processes are created, kernel memory space for the process table is allocated dynamically by the kmem cache allocation and management routines.

The kernel process objects are allocated from object-specific kernel memory (kmem) caches. A *process_cache*, *thread_cache*, and *lwp_cache* are created and initialized at boot time, and kernel memory for processes, threads, and LWPs is managed through each object's respective kmem cache. Statistics on these caches can be observed with the `mdb(1)` kmem_cache and kmastat dcmds, as well as the `kstat(1)` command.

```
# mdb -k
Loading modules: [ unix krtld genunix specfs dtrace ufs sd ip sctp usba fctl nca nfs
random sppp lofs crypto ptm ipc logindmux ]
> ::kmastat
cache                      buf    buf    buf    memory      alloc alloc
name                      size in use  total   in use    succeed  fail
------------------------- ------ ------ ------ ---------- --------- -----
kmem_magazine_1               16   7982   8064     131072      7982     0
kmem_magazine_3               32   6790   6804     221184      8809     0
. . .
thread_cache                 848    180    198     180224     12923     0
lwp_cache                   1408    180    192     294912       919     0
. . .
process_cache               3120     50     63     200704      1509     0
. . .
```

The most commonly requested information for memory statistics is memory used or consumed, which can be determined for each cache from the `memory in use` column in the example above (the value is in bytes).

The kstats for each cache are observed with the `kstat(1)` command:

```
# kstat -n process_cache
module: unix                              instance: 0
name:   process_cache                     class:      kmem_cache
        align                   8
        alloc                   1515
        alloc_fail              0
        buf_avail               22
        buf_constructed         14
        buf_inuse               50
        buf_max                 72
        buf_size                3120
        buf_total               72
        chunk_size              3120
        crtime                  246.452541137
        depot_alloc             46
        depot_contention        0
        depot_free              53
        empty_magazines         3
        free                    1472
        full_magazines          0
        hash_lookup_depth       0
        hash_rescale            0
        hash_size               64
        magazine_size           3
        slab_alloc              64
        slab_create             8
        slab_destroy            0
        slab_free               0
        slab_size               28672
        snaptime                284376.59969931
        vmem_source             23
```

The kstats maintained reflect the objects managed by the kmem allocator. See Section 11.2 for a description of the `buf`, `depot`, `magazine`, and `slab` objects that constitute a kmem cache. The same set of statistics is maintained for the thread_cache and lwp_cache. Actually, statistics are maintained for all kernel object kmem caches (try `kstat -c kmem_cache` on your Solaris 10 systems).

The fast, scalable kmem cache mechanism is a perfect fit for the kernel process objects. It quickly allocates and frees kernel memory as processes and threads are created and destroyed on a running system. It reuses uninitialized object structures for fast instantiation when a new process, thread, or LWP is created.

2.5.1 Process Limits

At system boot time, the kernel initializes the process_cache to begin the allocation of kernel memory for storing the process table. Initially, space is allocated for one `proc` structure. The table itself is implemented as a doubly linked list, such that each `proc` structure contains a pointer to the next process and previous processes on the list.

The maximum size of the process table is based on the amount of physical memory (RAM) in the system and is established at boot time. The system first sets an internal variable called `maxusers` (which has absolutely nothing to do with the maximum number of the users the system will support), using the following code.

```
#define MIN_DEFAULT_MAXUSERS    8u
#define MAX_DEFAULT_MAXUSERS    2048u
#define MAX_MAXUSERS            4096u

if (maxusers == 0) {
            pgcnt_t physmegs = physmem >> (20 - PAGESHIFT);
            pgcnt_t virtmegs = vmem_size(heap_arena, VMEM_FREE) >> 20;
            maxusers = MIN(MAX(MIN(physmegs, virtmegs),
                MIN_DEFAULT_MAXUSERS), MAX_DEFAULT_MAXUSERS);
}
if (maxusers > MAX_MAXUSERS) {
            maxusers = MAX_MAXUSERS;
            cmn_err(CE_NOTE, "maxusers limited to %d", MAX_MAXUSERS);
}
                                    See usr/src/uts/common/conf/param.c
```

The net effect of the code above is that `maxusers` is set according to memory size, with a ceiling value of `MAX_MAXUSERS` (4096). `maxusers` is subsequently used to set the kernel variables `max_nprocs` and `maxuprc`.

```
 /*
 * This allows platform-dependent code to constrain the maximum
 * number of processes allowed in case there are, e.g., VM limitations
 * with how many contexts are available.
 */
if (max_nprocs == 0)
            max_nprocs = (10 + 16 * maxusers);
if (platform_max_nprocs > 0 && max_nprocs > platform_max_nprocs)
            max_nprocs = platform_max_nprocs;
if (max_nprocs > maxpid)
            max_nprocs = maxpid;

if (maxuprc == 0)
            maxuprc = (max_nprocs - reserved_procs);
                                    See usr/src/uts/common/conf/param.c
```

The `max_nprocs` value is the maximum number of processes systemwide, and `maxuprc` determines the maximum number of processes a non-root user can have occupying a process table slot at any time. The system actually uses a data structure, the `var` structure, which holds generic system configuration information, to store these values in. There are three related values:

- **v_proc.** Set equal to `max_nprocs`.

- **v_maxupttl.** The maximum number of process slots that can be used by all non-root users on the system. It is set to max_nprocs minus some number of reserved process slots (currently reserved_procs is 5).

- **v_maxup.** The maximum number of process slots a non-root user can occupy. It is set to the maxuprc value. Note that v_maxup (an individual non-root user) and v_maxupttl (total of all non-root users on the system) end up being set to the same value, which is max_nprocs minus 5.

You can use mdb(1) to examine the values of maxusers, max_nprocs, and maxuprc on a running system.

```
# mdb -k
Loading modules: [ unix krtld genunix specfs dtrace ufs sd ip sctp usba fctl nca nfs
random sppp lofs crypto ptm ipc logindmux ]
> max_nprocs/D
max_nprocs:
max_nprocs:        30000
> maxuprc/D
maxuprc:
maxuprc:           29995
> maxusers/D
maxusers:
maxusers:          2048
>
```

You can also use mdb(1) to examine the system var structure.

```
> v::print "struct var"
{
    v_buf = 0x64
    v_call = 0
    v_proc = 0x7530
    v_maxupttl = 0x752b
    v_nglobpris = 0xaa
    v_maxsyspri = 0x63
    v_clist = 0
    v_maxup = 0x752b
    v_hbuf = 0x1000
    v_hmask = 0xfff
    v_pbuf = 0
    v_sptmap = 0
    v_maxpmem = 0
    v_autoup = 0x1e
    v_bufhwm = 0x14350
}
>0x7530=d
                30000
>
```

Note that the values are displayed in base 16 (hex). You can convert to decimal right in mdb(1), as shown at the bottom of the example.

Finally, sar(1M) with the -v flag gives you the maximum process table size and the current number of processes on the system.

```
$ sar -v 1 1

SunOS pae1 5.10 Generic sun4u    02/24/2006

20:09:52  proc-sz     ov  inod-sz      ov  file-sz    ov   lock-sz
20:09:53  118/30000    0  21719/129797  0  556/556     0    0/0
```

Under the proc-sz column, the 118/30000 values represent the current number of processes (118) and the maximum number of processes (30,000).

The kernel does impose a maximum value in case max_nprocs is set in /etc/system to something beyond what is reasonable, even for a large system. The maximum is 30,000, which is determined by the MAXPID macro in the param.h header file (available in /usr/include/sys).

In the kernel fork code, the current number of processes is checked against the v_proc parameter. If the limit is reached, the system produces an "out of processes" message on the console and increments the proc table overflow counter maintained in the cpu_sysinfo structure. This value is reflected in the ov column to the right of proc-sz in the sar(1M) output. For non-root users, a check is made against the v_maxup parameter, and an "out of per-user processes for uid (UID)" message is logged. In both cases, the calling program gets a -1 return value from fork(2), signifying an error.

The kernel maintains a /var/adm/utmp and /var/adm/wtmp file for the storage of user information used by the who(1), write(1), and login(1) commands (the accounting software and commands use utmp and wtmp as well). The PID data is maintained in a signed short data type, which has a maximum value of 32,000.

2.5.2 Thread Limits

Now that we've examined the limits the kernel imposes on the number of processes systemwide, let's look at the limits on the maximum number of LWP/kthread pairs that can exist in the system at any one time.

Each LWP has a kernel stack, allocated out of the segkp kernel address space segment. The size of the kernel segkp segment and the space allocated for LWP kernel stacks can vary according to the hardware platform. The stack itself is a default size of 24 Kbytes, and the default segkp size on both UltraSPARC and x64 platforms is 2 Gbytes. Thus, there is space for roughly (2GB ÷ 24K) 88,000 LWP stacks. This is a theoretical limit—other constraining factors, such as available physical memory, may well come into play before we reach 88,000 LWPs. Also, the segkp segment is used for other pageable components of the LWP, not just the stack. Even though segkp is a pageable kernel segment, the performance of a system actively paging LWP stacks in and out would likely be unacceptable.

You can determine the size of your system's segkp segment by using kstat(1).

```
sol10$ kstat -n segkp
module: vmem                                    instance: 34
name:   segkp                                   class:      vmem
        alloc                                   586432
        contains                                0
        contains_search                         0
        crtime                                  144.618836467
        fail                                    0
        free                                    586231
        lookup                                  170
        mem_import                              0
        mem_inuse                               26345472
        mem_total                               2147483648

. . .
```

The mem_total field indicates 2 Gbytes for segkp on this system (26 Mbytes are actually being used—mem_inuse field).

The maximum number of *user threads* is constrained by the process's address space size for 32-bit binaries. Each user thread has a user stack, and the default stack size is 1 Mbyte for a 32-bit process. Since a 32-bit process has a maximum address space of 4 Gbytes (this varies slightly for different platforms), the maximum number of threads would equate to roughly (4GB ÷ 1MB) or 4,000 threads. In practice, the number is less since a process's address space is consumed by other segments (text, heap, etc.). For 64-bit processes, the default thread stack size is 2 Mbytes.The address space of a 64-bit process is large enough that limits imposed by available address space for thread stacks are virtually nonexistent. A 64-bit process tends to be constrained by other resource issues (available physical memory, LWP limits, etc.).

2.6 Process Resource Attributes

Specific limits are imposed on how much of a given resource a process can consume. Traditionally, these limits were accessible with the shell limit(1) or ulimit(1) commands (depending on which shell was being used). Solaris 10 includes the plimit(1) command, which checks and sets process limits.

```
sol10$ plimit $$
13475:  -ksh
   resource              current          maximum
   time(seconds)         unlimited        unlimited
   file(blocks)          unlimited        unlimited
   data(kbytes)          unlimited        unlimited
   stack(kbytes)         8192             unlimited
   coredump(blocks)      unlimited        unlimited
   nofiles(descriptors)  256              65536
   vmemory(kbytes)       unlimited        unlimited
```

The resource limits displayed are defined as follows.

- **time (seconds).** Maximum CPU time in seconds. The clock interrupt handler tests for this limit and sends a SIGXCPU signal if the limit is reached.

- **file (blocks).** Maximum file size, in 512 byte blocks. The file system write code (the wrip() function in UFS) tests for this limit and sends a SIGXFSZ signal to the process if the limit is reached.

- **data (kbytes).** Maximum size of the process data segment. Hitting this limit can cause an ENOMEM error if a memory allocation routine (for example, malloc()) is called.

- **stack (kbytes).** Maximum size of the process stack segment.

- **coredump (blocks).** Maximum core file size. A value of 0 here prevents the creation of a core file.

- **nofiles (descriptors).** Maximum number of open files.

- **vmemory (kbytes).** Maximum address space. In reality, 4 Gbytes is the maximum virtual address space attainable for a 32-bit process. A 64-bit process has a theoretical limit of 18 exabytes. However, this varies according to implementation details of different processors. For example, early UltraSPARC processors had a 44-bit virtual address space, or a maximum of 16 terabytes.

Solaris 10 extends process resource attributes and controls, adding supporting commands to display and manage process resource allocation.

```
sol10$ prctl $$
process: 13475: -ksh
NAME       PRIVILEGE        VALUE    FLAG    ACTION            RECIPIENT
process.max-port-events
           privileged       65.5K      -     deny                      -
           system           2.15G    max     deny                      -
process.max-msg-messages
           privileged       8.19K      -     deny                      -
```

continues

```
        system          4.29G    max   deny                            -
process.max-msg-qbytes
        privileged      64.0KB     -   deny                            -
        system          16.0EB   max   deny                            -
process.max-sem-ops
        privileged        512      -   deny                            -
        system          2.15G    max   deny                            -
process.max-sem-nsems
        privileged        512      -   deny                            -
        system          32.8K    max   deny                            -
process.max-address-space
        privileged      16.0EB   max   deny                            -
        system          16.0EB   max   deny                            -
process.max-file-descriptor
        basic             256      -   deny                        13475
        privileged      65.5K      -   deny                            -
        system          2.15G    max   deny                            -
process.max-core-size
        privileged      8.00EB   max   deny                            -
        system          8.00EB   max   deny                            -
process.max-stack-size
        basic           8.00MB     -   deny                        13475
        privileged      8.00EB     -   deny                            -
        system          8.00EB   max   deny                            -
process.max-data-size
        privileged      16.0EB   max   deny                            -
        system          16.0EB   max   deny                            -
process.max-file-size
        privileged      8.00EB   max   deny,signal=XFSZ                -
        system          8.00EB   max   deny                            -
process.max-cpu-time
        privileged      18.4Es   inf   signal=XCPU                     -
        system          18.4Es   inf   none                            -
  . . .
```

The prctl(1) example lists the set of resource controls bound to a process. Other resource controls at the project, task, and zone level are not explored here (see Chapter 7). prctl(1) can also dynamically change the value of a resource where the applied change has scope for the life of the process. Note that the resources listed in the above example include the set of traditional thresholds discussed earlier (open files descriptors, stack size, etc.), along with a set of resources that apply to a process's use of the System V interprocess communication (IPC) facilities. The parameters for System V semaphores, shared memory, and message queues, which historically were set systemwide in the /etc/system file, have been integrated into process-level controls. The actual number of parameters that apply to System V IPC have also been reduced, and the default values are larger than in previous Solaris releases. See the *System Administration Guide: Solaris Containers—Resource Management and Zones* for specific information on setting and using these controls.

Each defined resource has a privilege level and action associated with it. The privilege levels are defined as follows:

- **Basic.** The resource control can be modified by the owner of the calling process.

- **Privileged.** The resource control can be modified only by privileged (super-user) callers.
- **System.** The resource scope is fixed for the duration of the operating system instance (until an OS reboot).

The action attribute specifies what happens when a resource threshold is reached. For local scope actions (the execution context of the process), a resource action attribute can be set to take no action (none), deny a request for the resource (deny), or send a signal when the resource threshold is reached. For the signal action, there are choices as to which signal should be generated.

The implementation is built on links in the proc_t.

```
    . . .
    struct rctl_set *p_rctls;       /* resource controls for this process */
    rlim64_t        p_stk_ctl;      /* currently enforced stack size */
    rlim64_t        p_fsz_ctl;      /* currently enforced file size */
    rlim64_t        p_vmem_ctl;     /* currently enforced addr-space size */
    rlim64_t        p_fno_ctl;      /* currently enforced file-desc limit */
    pid_t           p_ancpid;       /* ancestor pid, used by exacct */
    . . .
                                    See usr/src/uts/common/sys/proc.h
```

The resource controls, along with the attributes, are maintained in an rctl_set, linked to the process through the p_rctls link. Several process-level limits are maintained directly in the proc_t (p_stk_ctl, etc.) as a performance optimization—the values can be tested without traversal of additional links and structures.

rctl_set links to a hash table of resource control structures that provide the entity-level information. In this example, the process is the entity to which the resource information is bound. Other possible entities are projects, tasks, and zones. rctl_set also links to an rctl_dict_entry that defines the systemwide scope for the resource. Figure 2.7 illustrates the big picture.

At system initialization, a systemwide primary set of resource controls is instantiated. The resource management framework provides a registration facility by which kernel subsystems can register their resource controls. The per-entity resource controls are defined and managed by the kernel subsystem and code for the particular entity. For example, process resource controls are defined in the usr/src/uts/common/os/rctl_proc.c source file. An initialization function, rctlproc_init(), is called at boot time to register the process resource controls and add them to the systemwide dictionary, which is referenced through the rctl_dict hash table.

When a process is created with the fork(2) system call, the new (child) process inherits a duplicate copy of the parent's resource controls, which reflect the

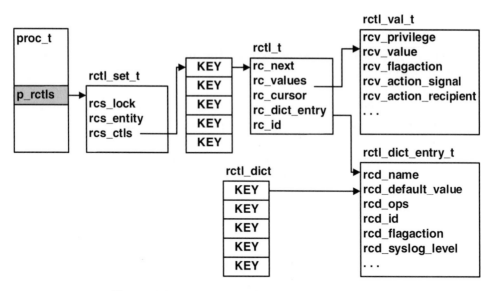

Figure 2.7 Process Resource Control Structures

default values and attributes if changes were not explicitly made with the administrative controls prctl(1) and rctladm(1). As the process executes and consumes resources—opening files, growing memory, using System V semaphores, etc.—each subsystem in the kernel that manages a controlled resources imposes a limit test to determine if the process request can be granted. If it cannot, the attribute for the resource defines what action to take (none, deny, or send a signal). The lookup for a specific resource is done dynamically for each process by hashing on the resource control ID and referencing the resource value and attributes through the per-resource rctl_val_t.

You can examine the system's resource control dictionary by using mdb(1).

```
> ::walk rctl_dict_list |::print rctl_dict_entry_t
{
    rcd_next = 0xffffffff80a2fbb0
    rcd_name = 0xfffffffffb8b1038 "process.max-port-events"
    rcd_default_value = 0xffffffff80a28b88
    rcd_ops = rctl_absolute_ops
    rcd_id = 0xc
    rcd_entity = 0 (RCENTITY_PROCESS)
    rcd_flagaction = 0x20100000
    rcd_syslog_level = 0
    rcd_strlog_flags = 0
    rcd_max_native = 0x7fffffff
    rcd_max_ilp32 = 0x7fffffff
}
```

continues

```
{
    rcd_next = 0xffffffff80a2fc00
    rcd_name = 0xfffffffffb8b1088 "process.max-msg-messages"
    rcd_default_value = 0xffffffff80a28c08
    rcd_ops = rctl_absolute_ops
    rcd_id = 0xb
    rcd_entity = 0 (RCENTITY_PROCESS)
    rcd_flagaction = 0x20100000
    rcd_syslog_level = 0
    rcd_strlog_flags = 0
    rcd_max_native = 0xffffffff
    rcd_max_ilp32 = 0xffffffff
. . .
```

2.7 Process Creation

The fork(2) system call creates a new process. The newly created process is assigned a unique process identification (PID) and is a child of the process that called fork(2); the calling process is the parent. The exec(2) system call overlays the new process with an executable specified as a path name in the first argument to the exec(2) call. The model, in pseudocode format, looks like this.

```
main(int argc, char *argv[], char *envp[])
{
        pid_t child_pid;
        child_pid = fork();
        if (child_pid == -1)
                perror("fork"); /* fork system call failed */
        else if (child_pid == 0)
                execv("/path/new_binary",argv); /* in the child, so exec */
        else
                wait()  /* pid > 0, weUre in the parent */
}
```

The pseudocode above calls fork(2) and checks the return value from fork(2) (PID). Remember, once fork(2) executes successfully, there are two processes: fork returns a value of 0 to the child process and returns the PID of the child to the parent process. In the example, we called exec(2) to execute new_binary once in the child. Back in the parent, we simply wait for the child to complete (we get back later to this notion of "waiting").

The default behavior of fork(2) has changed in Solaris 10. In prior releases, fork(2) replicated all the threads in the calling process unless the code was linked with the POSIX thread library (-lpthread), in which case, fork(2) created a new process with only the calling thread. Previous releases provided a fork1(2) interface for programs that needed to replicate only the calling thread in the new process and did not link with pthread.so. In Solaris 10, fork(2) replicates only the calling thread in the new process, and a forkall(2) interface replicates all threads in the new process if desired.

Finally, there's vfork(2), which is described as a "virtual memory efficient" version of fork. A call to vfork(2) results in the child process "borrowing" the address space of the parent, rather than the kernel duplicating the parent's address space for the child, as it does in fork(2) and fork1(2). The child's address space following a vfork(2) is the same address space as that of the parent. More precisely, the physical memory pages of the new process's (the child) address space are the same memory pages as for the parent. The implication here is that the child must not change any state while executing in the parent's address space until the child either exits or executes an exec(2) system call—once an exec(2) call is executed, the child gets its own address space. In fork(2) and fork1(2), the address space of the parent is copied for the child by means of the kernel address space duplicate routine.

Another addition to Solaris 10 on the process creation front is the posix_ spawn(3C) interface, which does fork/exec in one library call and does so in a memory efficient way (the vfork(2) style of not replicating the address space).

We can trace the entire code path through the kernel for process creation when fork(2) is called, using the following dtrace script.

```
#!/usr/sbin/dtrace -s

#pragma D option flowindent

syscall::fork1:entry
{
        self->trace=1;
}
fbt:::
/ self->trace /
{
}
syscall::fork1:return
{
        self->trace=0;
        exit(0);
}
```

The dtrace script sets a probe to fire at the entry point of the fork1() system call. The reason we're using fork1() here instead of fork() is an implementation detail that has to do with the new fork() behavior described previously. In order to maintain source and binary compatibility for applications that use fork1(), the interface is still in the library. fork(2) now does the same thing fork1(2) did, so we can implement fork(2) and fork1(2) with a single source file, as long as both interfaces resolve to the same code.

```
/*
 * fork() is fork1() for both POSIX threads and Solaris threads.
 * The forkall() interface exists for applications that require
 * the semantics of replicating all threads.
 */
#pragma weak fork = _fork1
#pragma weak _fork = _fork1
#pragma weak fork1 = _fork1
                                        See usr/src/lib/libc/port/threads/scalls.c
```

The #pragma binding directives associate fork and fork1. The dtrace system call provider cannot enable a fork:entry probe because, technically, the system call table does not contain a unique entry for fork(2). This is implemented in such a way as to be transparent to applications—fork(2) system call behaves exactly as expected when implemented in application code.

Running the dtrace script on a test program that issues a fork(2) generates over 2000 lines of kernel function-flow output. The text below is cut from the output, aggressively edited, including replacing the CPU column with a LINE column—this was done by postprocessing the output file; it is not a dtrace option.

```
LINE FUNCTION
  1  -> fork1
  2  -> cfork
  3    -> holdlwps
  4      -> schedctl_finish_sigblock
  5      -> pokelwps
  6    -> getproc
  7      -> pid_assign
  8      <- pid_assign
  9      -> crgetruid
 10      -> task_attach
 11        -> task_hold
 12        -> rctl_set_dup
 13      <- task_attach
 14    <- getproc
 15    -> as_dup
 16    -> forklwp
 17      -> flush_user_windows_to_stack
 18      -> save_syscall_args
 19        -> lwp_getsysent
 20          -> lwp_getdatamodel
 21      -> lwp_create
 22        -> segkp_cache_get
 23        -> thread_create
 24          -> lgrp_affinity_init
 25          -> lgrp_move_thread
 26        <- thread_create
 27        -> lwp_stk_init
 28        -> thread_load
 29        -> lgrp_choose
 30        -> lgrp_move_thread
 31      -> init_mstate
 32      -> ts_alloc
 33      -> ts_fork
 34        -> thread_lock
 35        -> disp_lock_exit
```

continues

```
36      <- ts_fork
37    <- forklwp
38    -> pgjoin
39    -> ts_forkret
40      -> continuelwps
41        -> setrun_locked
42          -> thread_transition
43            -> disp_lock_exit_high
44        -> ts_setrun
45        -> setbackdq
46          -> cpu_update_pct
47            -> cpu_decay
48              -> exp_x
49          -> cpu_choose
50          -> disp_lowpri_cpu
51            -> disp_lock_enter_high
52          -> cpu_resched
53  <= fork1
```

The kernel `cfork()` function is the common fork code that executes for any variant of `fork(2)`. After some preliminary checking, `holdlwps()` is called to suspend the calling LWP in the process so that it can be safely replicated on the new process or, in the case of `forkall()`, can suspend all the LWPs. `getproc()` (LINE 6) is where the new `proc_t` is created, allocated from the kmem process_cache. Once the `proc_t` is allocated, the state for the new process is set to `SIDL`, and a PID is assigned with the `pid_assign()` function, where a `pid_t` structure is allocated and initialized (see Figure 2.4).

The Solaris kernel implements an interesting throttle here in the event of a process forking out of control and thus consuming an inordinate amount of system resources. A failure by the kernel `pid_assign()` code or a lack of an available process table slot indicates a large amount of process creation activity. In this circumstance, the kernel implements a delay mechanism by which the process that issued the `fork` call is forced to sleep for an extra clock tick (a tick occurs every 10 milliseconds). By implementing this mechanism, the kernel ensures that no more than one fork can fail per CPU per clock tick.

The throttle also scales up, such that an increased rate of fork failures results in an increased delay before the code returns the failure and the issuing process can try again. In that situation, you'll see the console message "out of processes," and the `ov` (overflow) column in the `sar -v` output will have a non-zero value. You can also look at the kernel `fork_fail_pending` variable with `adb`. If this value is non-zero, the system has entered the fork throttle code segment. Below is an example of examining the `fork_fail_pending` kernel variable with `mdb(1)`.

```
# mdb -k
Loading modules: [ unix krtld genunix specfs dtrace uppc pcplusmp ufs ip sctp usba fcp
fctl nca md lofs zfs random nfs fcip cpc crypto logindmux ptm sppp ipc ]
> fork_fail_pending/D
fork_fail_pending:
fork_fail_pending:            0
```

Much of the remaining work in getproc() is the initialization of the fields in the new proc_t, which includes copying the parent's uarea, updating the open file pointers and reference counts, and copying the list of open files into the new process. Also, the resource controls of the parent process are replicated for the child using rctl_set_dup() (LINE 12).

Back in cfork(), the code tests to determine if a vfork() was issued, in which case the new (child) process's address space is set to the parent's address space. Otherwise, as_dup() is called to duplicate the parent's address space for the new process, looping through all of the parent's address space segments and duplicating each one to construct the address space for the child process. The next set of functions (LINES 16–37) created a new LWP and new kernel thread in the new process, which involves stack initialization and setting the home lgroup (see Section 3.2). With the LWP and thread work completed, pgjoin() sets up the process group links in the new process.

Depending on the scheduling class of the calling thread, the class-specific forkret() code sets up the scheduling class information and handles CPU selection for placing the kernel thread in the new process on a dispatch queue (see Section 3.3). At this point, the new process is created, initialized, and ready to run.

With a newly created process/LWP/kthread infrastructure in place, most applications invoke exec(2). The exec(2) system call overlays the calling program with a new executable image. (Not following a fork(2) with an exec(2) results in two processes executing the same code; the parent and child executes whatever code exists after the fork(2) call.)

There are several flavors of the exec(2) call; the basic differences are in what they take as arguments. The exec(2) calls vary in whether they take a path name or file name as the first argument (which specifies the new executable program to start), whether they require a comma-separated list of arguments or an argv[] array, and whether the existing environment is used or an envp[] array is passed.

Because Solaris supports the execution of several different file types, the kernel exec code is split into object file format-dependent and object file format-independent code segments. Most common is the previously discussed ELF format. Among other supported files is a.out, which is included to provide a degree of binary compatibility that enables executables created on a SunOS 4.X system to run on SunOS 5.X. Other inclusions are a format-specific exec routine for programs that run under an interpreter, such as shell scripts and awk programs, and support code for programs in the Java programming language with a Java-specific exec code segment.

Calls into the object-specific exec code are done through a switch table mechanism. During system startup, an execsw[] array is initialized with the magic number of the supported object file types. Magic numbers uniquely identify different object file types on UNIX systems. See /etc/magic and the magic(4) man page. Each array member is an execsw structure.

```
struct execsw {
        char    *exec_magic;
        int     exec_magoff;
        int     exec_maglen;
        int     (*exec_func)(struct vnode *vp, struct execa *uap,
                    struct uarg *args, struct intpdata *idata, int level,
                    long *execsz, int setid, caddr_t exec_file,
                    struct cred *cred);
        int     (*exec_core)(struct vnode *vp, struct proc *p,
                    struct cred *cred, rlim64_t rlimit, int sig,
                    core_content_t content);
        krwlock_t    *exec_lock;
};
                                        See usr/src/uts/common/sys/exec.h
```

- **exec_magic, exec_magoff, exec_maglen.** Support to locate and correctly read the magic number.

- **exec_func.** A function pointer; points to the exec function for the object file type.

- **exec_core.** A function pointer; points to the object-file-specific core dump routine.

- **exec_lock.** A pointer to a kernel read/write lock, to synchronize access to the exec switch array.

The object file exec code is implemented as dynamically loadable kernel modules, found in the /kernel/exec directory (aoutexec, elfexec, intpexec) and /usr/kernel/exec (javaexec). The elf and intp modules load through the normal boot process since these two modules are used minimally by the kernel startup processes and startup shell scripts. The a.out and java modules load automatically when needed as a result of exec'ing a SunOS 4.X binary or a Java program. When each module loads into RAM (kernel address space in memory), the mod_install() support code loads the execsw structure information into the execsw[] array.

You can examine the execsw[] array on your system by using mdb(1). Because execsw[] is an array of execsw structures, you need to calculate the address of each array entry based on the size of an execsw structure. Fortunately, mdb(1) offers a couple of nice features that make this relatively painless. In the following example, we use the sizeof dcmd to determine the array size and let mdb(1) do the math for us.

```
> execsw::print "struct execsw"
{
    exec_magic = elf32magicstr
    exec_magoff = 0
    exec_maglen = 0x5
    exec_func = elf32exec
    exec_core = elf32core
    exec_lock = 0xffffffff80132a18
}
>
> ::sizeof "struct execsw"
sizeof (struct execsw) = 0x28
> execsw+0x28::print "struct execsw"
{
    exec_magic = elf64magicstr
    exec_magoff = 0
    exec_maglen = 0x5
    exec_func = elfexec
    exec_core = elfcore
    exec_lock = 0xffffffff80132a10
}
> execsw+0x50::print "struct execsw"
{
    exec_magic = intpmagicstr "#!"
    exec_magoff = 0
    exec_maglen = 0x2
    exec_func = intpexec
    exec_core = 0
    exec_lock = 0xffffffff80132a08
}
> execsw+0x78::print "struct execsw"
{
    exec_magic = javamagicstr
    exec_magoff = 0
    exec_maglen = 0x4
    exec_func = 0
    exec_core = 0
    exec_lock = 0xffffffff80132a00
}
```

The first entry is examined with the execsw symbol in mdb(1), which represents the address of the beginning of the execsw[] array. After examining the first entry, we use sizeof to determine how large an execsw structure is, add that value to the base address of the array, and get the second array entry. By doing additional arithmetic based on the number of entries into the array we want to see, we can move down the array and examine each entry. We see that the array is initialized for 32-bit ELF files, 64-bit ELF files, interpreter files (shell, Perl, etc.) and Java programs.

Figure 2.8 illustrates the flow of exec for an ELF file.

All variants of the exec(2) system call resolve in the kernel to a common routine, exec_common(), where some initial processing is done. The path name for the executable file is retrieved, exitlwps() is called to force all but the calling LWP to exit, any POSIX4 interval timers in the process are cleared (p_itimer field in the proc structure), and the sysexec counter in the cpu_sysinfo structure is

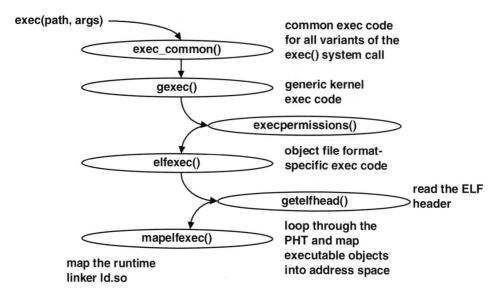

Figure 2.8 exec() Flow

incremented (counts exec system calls, readable with sar(1M)). If scheduler activations have been set up for the process, the door interface used for such purposes
is closed (that is, scheduler activations are not inherited), and any other doors that
exist within the process are closed. The SPREXEC flag is set in p_flags (proc
structure field), signifying that an exec is in the works for the process. The
SPREXEC flag blocks any subsequent process operations until exec() has completed, at which point the flag is cleared.

The kernel generic exec code, gexec(), is now called; here is where we switch to
the object-file-specific exec routine through the execsw[] array. The correct array
entry for the type of file being exec'd is determined by a call to the kernel vn_
rdwr() (vnode read/write) routine and a read of the first four bytes of the file,
which is where the file's magic number is stored. Once the magic number has been
retrieved, the code looks for a match in each entry in the execsw[] array by comparing the magic number of the exec'd file to the exec_magic field in each structure in the array. Before entering the exec switch table, the code checks
permissions against the credentials of the process and the permissions of the
object file being exec'd. If the object file is not executable or the caller does not
have execute permissions, exec fails with an EACCESS error. If the object file has
the setuid or setgid bits set, the effective UID or GID is set in the new process
credentials at this time.

Note separate execsw[] array entries for each data model supported: 32-bit ILP32
ELF files and 64-bit LP64 ELF files. Let's examine the flow of the elfexec()
function, since that is the most common type of executable run on Solaris systems.

Upon entry to the `elfexec()` code, the kernel reads the ELF header and program header (PHT) sections of the object file (see Section 2.3 for an overview of the ELF header and PHT). These two main header sections of the object file give the system the information it needs to proceed with mapping the binary to the address space of the newly forked process. The kernel next gets the argument and environment arrays from the `exec(2)` call and places both on the user stack of the process, using the `exec_args()` function. The arguments are also copied into the process `uarea`'s `u_psargs[]` array at this time (see Figure 2.9).

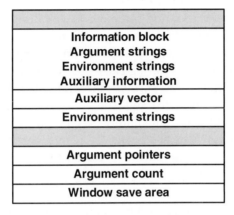

Figure 2.9 Initial Stack Frame

Before actually setting up the user stack with the `argv[]` and `envp[]` arrays, a 64-bit kernel must first determine if a 32-bit or 64-bit binary is being `exec`'d. A 32-bit Solaris 10 system can only run 32-bit binaries. On SPARC systems, Solaris 10 is 64-bit only, but on x64, a 32-bit or 64-bit kernel can be booted. The binary type information is maintained in the ELF header, where the system checks the `e_ident[]` array for either an `ELFCLASS32` or `ELFCLASS64` file identity. With the data model established, the kernel sets the initial size of the `exec` file sections to 4 Kbytes for the stack, 4 Kbytes for stack growth (stack increment), and 1 Mbyte for the argument list (ELF32) or 2-Mbyte argument list size for an ELF64.

Once the kernel has established the process user stack and argument list, it calls the `mapelfexec()` function to map the various program segments into the process address space. `mapelfexec()` walks through the program header table (PHT), and for each `PT_LOAD` type (a loadable segment), `mapelfexec()` maps the segment into the process's address space. `mapelfexec()` bases the mapping on the `p_filesz` and `p_memsz` sections of the header that define the segment, using the lower-level kernel address space support code. Once the program loadable segments have been mapped into the address space, the dynamic linker (for dynamically linked executables), referenced through the PHT, is also mapped into the process's address space. The `elfexec` code checks the process resource limit `RLIMIT_VMEM` (maximum virtual memory size) against the size required to map the object file and runtime linker. An `ENOMEM` error is returned in the event that an address space requirement exceeds the limit.

All that remains for `exec(2)` to complete is some additional housekeeping and structure initialization, which is done when the code returns to `gexec()`. This last part deals with clearing the signal stack and setting the signal disposition to default for any signals that have had a handler installed by the parent process. The `p_lwptotal` is set to 1 in the new process. Finally, all open files with the close-on-exec flag set are closed, and the `exec` is complete. A call made into procfs clears the `SPREXEC` flag and unlocks access to the process by means of `/proc`.

As you'll see in the next chapter, threads inherit their scheduling class and priority from the parent. Some scheduling-class-specific fork code executes at the tail end of the fork process that takes care of placement of the newly created kthread on a dispatch queue. This practice gets the child executing before the parent in anticipation that the child will immediately execute an `exec(2)` call to load in the new object file. In the case of a `vfork(2)`, where the child is mapped to the address space of the parent, the parent is forced to wait until the child executes and gets its own address space.

2.8 System Calls

System calls are the set of application programming interfaces (APIs) that allow programs to have the kernel perform a privileged service on their behalf. Common examples include memory allocation, file I/O, signal management, and interprocess communication. Standards define the names of the system calls, the arguments they take, the way they behave from the application's perspective, and the values they return to the calling program. System calls are described in section 2 of the man pages.

Because system calls are privileged operations that can only be done by the kernel, making a system call results in the calling process transitioning from operating in user mode to operating in kernel mode. With the process in kernel mode, there is visibility into the kernel's address space (among other things). The platform's trap mechanism manages the transition to kernel mode. That is, when a system call is executed, a trap (a vectored transfer of control to a trap handler) is taken, and the system call trap handler takes over.

Much of the system call entry and setup work depends on the process architecture. The main system call code—the actual system calls—are implemented in C language and can be found in `usr/src/uts/common/syscall`. The trap mechanism, however, is platform specific, and as such the mechanics of handling a system call trap and setting up the thread state and registers for system call execution are different for SPARC systems versus AMD64 systems. The following text walks through a system call on a SPARC system. Note that all the following text describes code written in SPARC assembly language. Some knowledge of SPARC assembly, along with register windows and general register use, is helpful, though not a requirement.

2.8.1 System Calls on SPARC Architectures

An application making a system call actually calls a `libc` wrapper function that performs any required posturing and then enters the kernel with a software trap instruction. This means that user code and compilers do not need to know the path into the kernel and that binaries can work on later versions of the OS where perhaps the path has been modified, system call numbers were newly overloaded, etc.

Solaris for SPARC supports three software traps for entering the kernel, as listed in Table 2.3.

Table 2.3 Software Traps for System Calls on SPARC Achitectures

Software Trap	Instruction	Description
0x0	`ta 0x0`	Used for system calls for binaries running in SunOS 4.x binary compatability mode
0x8	`ta 0x8`	32-bit (ILP32) binary running on 64-bit (ILP64) kernel
0x40	`ta 0x40`	64-bit (ILP64) binary running on 64-bit (ILP64) kernel

As of Solaris 10, Solaris no longer includes a 32-bit kernel, the ILP32 syscall on ILP32 kernel is no longer implemented.

In the wrapper function, the syscall arguments are rearranged if necessary. The kernel function implementing the syscall may expect the arguments in a different order from that of the syscall API, for example, or multiple related system calls may share a single system call number and select behavior based on an additional argument passed into the kernel. The kernel function then places the system call number in register %g1 and executes one of the above trap-always instructions (for example, the 32-bit `libc` library uses `ta 0x8`, and the 64-bit `libc` uses `ta 0x40`). There's a lot more activity and posturing in the wrapper functions than described here, but for our purposes we simply note that it all boils down to a `ta` instruction to enter the kernel.

2.8.1.1 Handling a System Call Trap

A SPARC trap instruction (`ta n`) executed in userland by the wrapper function results in a trap type `0x100 + n` being taken, and we move from trap-level 0 (TL0) (where all userland and most kernel code executes) to trap-level 1 (TL1) in nucleus context. Code that executes in nucleus context has to be hand-crafted in assembler since nucleus context does not comply with the ABI conventions and is generally much more restricted in what it can do. The task of the trap handler executing at TL1 is to provide the necessary glue in order to get us back to TL0 and running privileged (kernel) C code that implements the actual system call.

The trap table entries for the `sun4u` and `sun4v` architectures for these traps are identical. In the following examples, we explore the two primary syscall traps and ignore the SunOS 4.x trap. Note that a trap table handler has just eight instructions dedicated to it in the trap table; it must use these to do a little work and then branch elsewhere.

```
/*
 * SYSCALL is used for system calls on both ILP32 and LP64 kernels
 * depending on the "which" parameter (should be either syscall_trap
 * or syscall_trap32).
 */
#define SYSCALL(which)                          \
        TT_TRACE(trace_gen)              ;\
        set     (which), %g1             ;\
        ba,pt   %xcc, sys_trap           ;\
        sub     %g0, 1, %g4              ;\
        .align  32

...
...

trap_table:
scb:
trap_table0:
        /* hardware traps */
        ...

        ...
        /* user traps */
        GOTO(syscall_trap_4x);          /* 100  old system call */
        ...
        SYSCALL(syscall_trap32);        /* 108  ILP32 system call on LP64 */
        ...
        SYSCALL(syscall_trap)           /* 140  LP64 system call */
        ...
```

                                See usr/src/uts/sun4u/ml/trap_table.s

In both cases we branch to `sys_trap`, requesting TL0 handler of `syscall_trap32` for an ILP32 syscall and `syscall_trap` for a ILP64 syscall. In both cases, we request the processor interrupt level (PIL) to remain as it currently is (always 0 since we came from userland). The `sys_trap` code is generic glue that takes us from nucleus (TL > 0) context back to TL0 running a specified handler (address in

%g1, usually written in C) at a chosen PIL. The specified handler is called with arguments as given by registers %g2 and %g3 at the time we branch to sys_trap. The SYSCALL macro above does not move anything into these registers—no arguments to be passed to handler. sys_trap handlers are always called with a first argument pointing to a struct regs that provides access to all the register values at the time of branching to sys_trap; for syscalls these include the system call number in %g1 and arguments in output registers. Note that %g1 as prepared in the wrapper and %g1 as used in the SYSCALL macro for the trap table entry are not the same register. On a trap we move from regular global registers (as userland executes in) to alternate global registers, but the sys_trap glue collects all the correct user registers and makes them available in the struct regs it passes to the handler.

The sys_trap glue is also responsible for setting up our return linkage. When the TL0 handling is complete, the handler returns, restoring the stack pointer and program counter as constructed in sys_trap. Since we trapped from userland, user_rtt is interposed as the glue into which TL0 handling code returns, which gets us back out of the kernel and into userland again when the system call completes.

2.8.2 A Tour through a System Call

We follow the ILP32 syscall route; the route for ILP64 is analogous with trivial differences in terms of not having to clear the upper 32 bits of arguments and deal with other items related to the data width. The syscall_trap code runs at TL0 as a sys_trap handler, so it could be written in C. However, for performance it is coded in assembler. Our task is to look up and call the nominated system call handler and perform the required housekeeping along the way.

```
syscall_trap32(struct regs *rp);

ENTRY_NP(syscall_trap32)
ldx     [THREAD_REG + T_CPU], %g1        ! get cpu pointer
mov     %o7, %l0                         ! save return addr
```

See usr/src/uts/sparc/v9/ml/syscall_trap.s

First note that we do not obtain a new register window here—we stay within the window that sys_trap crafted for itself. Normally, this would mean that we would have to live within the output registers, but by agreement, handlers called through sys_trap are permitted to use registers %l0 through %l3.

We begin by loading a pointer to the CPU on which this thread is executing into %g1 and saving the return PC (as constructed by sys_trap) in %o7.

```
!
! If the trapping thread has the address mask bit clear, then it's
!   a 64-bit process, and has no business calling 32-bit syscalls.
!
ldx     [%o0 + TSTATE_OFF], %l1        ! saved %tstate.am is that
andcc   %l1, TSTATE_AM, %l1           !  of the trapping proc
be,pn   %xcc, _syscall_ill32         !
mov     %o0, %l1                      ! save reg pointer
```

See usr/src/uts/sparc/v9/ml/syscall_trap.s

The comment says it all. The AM bit in the PSTATE register at the time we trapped executed the ta instruction and is available in the %tstate register after the trap—sys_trap preserved that for us before it could be modified by further traps in the regs structure. Assuming we're not a 64-bit process making a 32-bit syscall, here's what happens.

```
srl     %i0, 0, %o0                   ! copy 1st arg, clear high bits
srl     %i1, 0, %o1                   ! copy 2nd arg, clear high bits
ldx     [%g1 + CPU_STATS_SYS_SYSCALL], %g2
inc     %g2                           ! cpu_stats.sys.syscall++
stx     %g2, [%g1 + CPU_STATS_SYS_SYSCALL]
```

See usr/src/uts/sparc/v9/ml/syscall_trap.s

The libc wrapper placed up to the first 6 arguments in %o0 through %o5, with the rest, if any, on stack. During sys_trap, a SAVE instruction obtained a new register window, so those arguments are now available in the corresponding input registers, despite our not performing a save in syscall_trap32 itself. We're going to call the real handler, so we prepare the arguments in our outputs, which we're sharing with sys_trap, but outputs are understood to be volatile across calls. The shift-right-logical by 0 bits is a 32-bit operation (that is, not srlx) so it performs no shifting, but it does clear the uppermost 32-bits of the arguments. We also increment the statistic counting the number of system calls made by this CPU; this statistic is in the cpu_t, and the offset is generated by the genasym tool.

```
!
! Set new state for LWP
!
ldx     [THREAD_REG + T_LWP], %l2
mov     LWP_SYS, %g3
srl     %i2, 0, %o2                   ! copy 3rd arg, clear high bits
stb     %g3, [%l2 + LWP_STATE]
srl     %i3, 0, %o3                   ! copy 4th arg, clear high bits
ldx     [%l2 + LWP_RU_SYSC], %g2      ! pesky statistics
```

continues

```
srl     %i4, 0, %o4                    ! copy 5th arg, clear high bits
addx    %g2, 1, %g2
stx     %g2, [%l2 + LWP_RU_SYSC]
srl     %i5, 0, %o5                    ! copy 6th arg, clear high bits
! args for direct syscalls now set up
```

See usr/src/uts/sparc/v9/ml/syscall_trap.s

We continue preparing arguments as above. Interleaved with these instructions we change the `lwp_state` member of the associated LWP structure to signify that it is running in-kernel (`LWP_SYS`, would have been `LWP_USER` before this update) and increment the count of the number of syscall made by this particular LWP.

Next we write a TRAPTRACE entry—only on DEBUG kernels, which are visible with the MDB's `::traptrace` dcmd.

```
!
! Test for pre-system-call handling
!
ldub    [THREAD_REG + T_PRE_SYS], %g3   ! pre-syscall proc?
YSCALLTRACE
sethi   %hi(syscalltrace), %g4
ld      [%g4 + %lo(syscalltrace)], %g4
orcc    %g3, %g4, %g0                   ! pre_syscall OR syscalltrace?

tst     %g3                            ! is pre_syscall flag set?
* SYSCALLTRACE */
bnz,pn  %icc, _syscall_pre32           ! yes - pre_syscall needed
  nop

! Fast path invocation of new_mstate
mov     LMS_USER, %o0
call    syscall_mstate
mov     LMS_SYSTEM, %o1

lduw    [%l1 + O0_OFF + 4], %o0        ! reload 32-bit args
lduw    [%l1 + O1_OFF + 4], %o1
lduw    [%l1 + O2_OFF + 4], %o2
lduw    [%l1 + O3_OFF + 4], %o3
lduw    [%l1 + O4_OFF + 4], %o4
lduw    [%l1 + O5_OFF + 4], %o5

! lwp_arg now set up
3:
```

See usr/src/uts/sparc/v9/ml/syscall_trap.s

If the `curthread->t_pre_sys` flag is set, then we branch to `_syscall_pre32` to call `pre_syscall`. If that action does not abort the call, then `pre_syscall` reloads the outputs with the args (they were lost on the call to `_syscall_pre32`), using `lduw` instructions from the `regs` area and loading from just the lower 32-bit word of the args, and branches back to label 3 above. If we don't have pre-syscall work to perform, then we call `syscall_mstate(LMS_USER, LMS_SYSTEM)` to record the transition from user to system state for microstate accounting. Microstate accounting is always performed in Solaris 10 (in previous releases, it needed to be explicitly enabled).

After the unconditional call to `syscall_mstate`, we reload the arguments from the `regs` struct into the output registers (as after the pre-syscall work). Evidently our earlier `srl` work in the args is a complete waste of time (although not expensive) since we always end up loading the args from the passed `regs` structure. This is a holdover from days when microstate accounting was not always enabled.

```
!
! Call the handler.  The %o's have been set up.
!
lduw     [%l1 + G1_OFF + 4], %g1            ! get 32-bit code
set      sysent32, %g3                     ! load address of vector table
cmp      %g1, NSYSCALL                     ! check range
sth      %g1, [THREAD_REG + T_SYSNUM]      ! save syscall code
bgeu,pn %ncc, _syscall_ill32
  sll    %g1, SYSENT_SHIFT, %g4            ! delay - get index
add      %g3, %g4, %g5                     ! g5 = addr of sysentry
ldx      [%g5 + SY_CALLC], %g3             ! load system call handler

brnz,a,pt %g1, 4f                          ! check for indir()
mov      %g5, %14                          ! save addr of sysentry
!
! Yuck.  If %g1 is zero, that means we're doing a syscall() via the
! indirect system call.  That means we have to check the
! flags of the targeted system call, not the indirect system call
! itself.  See return value handling code below.
!
set      sysent32, %14                     ! load address of vector table
cmp      %o0, NSYSCALL                     ! check range
bgeu,pn %ncc, 4f                           ! out of range, let C handle it
  sll    %o0, SYSENT_SHIFT, %g4            ! delay - get index
add      %g4, %14, %14                     ! compute & save addr of sysent

call     %g3                               ! call system call handler
nop
4:
```

See usr/src/uts/sparc/v9/ml/syscall_trap.s

We load the nominated syscall number into `%g1`, sanity-check it for range, and look up the entry at that index in the `sysent32` table of 32-bit system calls, and extract the registered handler (the real implementation). Ignoring the indirect syscall work, we call the handler and the real work of the syscall is executed.

```
!
! If handler returns long long, then we need to split the 64 bit
! return value in %o0 into %o0 and %o1 for ILP32 clients.
!
lduh    [%14 + SY_FLAGS], %g4              ! load sy_flags
andcc   %g4, SE_64RVAL | SE_32RVAL2, %g0  ! check for 64-bit return
bz,a,pt %xcc, 5f
  srl   %o0, 0, %o0                        ! 32-bit only
srl     %o0, 0, %o1                        ! lower 32 bits into %o1
srlx    %o0, 32, %o0                       ! upper 32 bits into %o0
```

See usr/src/uts/sparc/v9/ml/syscall_trap.s

Once the system call executes, we set up the return value. For ILP32 clients we need to massage 64-bit return types into two adjacent and paired registers.

```
!
! Check for post-syscall processing.
! This tests all members of the union containing t_astflag, t_post_sys,
! and t_sig_check with one test.
!
ld      [THREAD_REG + T_POST_SYS_AST], %g1
tst     %g1                          ! need post-processing?
bnz,pn  %icc, _syscall_post32        ! yes - post_syscall or AST set
mov     LWP_USER, %g1
stb     %g1, [%12 + LWP_STATE]       ! set lwp_state
stx     %o0, [%11 + O0_OFF]          ! set rp->r_o0
stx     %o1, [%11 + O1_OFF]          ! set rp->r_o1
clrh    [THREAD_REG + T_SYSNUM]      ! clear syscall code
ldx     [%11 + TSTATE_OFF], %g1      ! get saved tstate
ldx     [%11 + nPC_OFF], %g2         ! get saved npc (new pc)
mov     CCR_IC, %g3
sllx    %g3, TSTATE_CCR_SHIFT, %g3
add     %g2, 4, %g4                  ! calc new npc
andn    %g1, %g3, %g1                ! clear carry bit for no error
stx     %g2, [%11 + PC_OFF]
stx     %g4, [%11 + nPC_OFF]
stx     %g1, [%11 + TSTATE_OFF]
```

See usr/src/uts/sparc/v9/ml/syscall_trap.s

If post-syscall processing is required, the code branches to _syscall_post32, which calls post_syscall, and then "returns" by jumping to the return address passed by sys_trap (which is always user_rtt for syscalls). If post-syscall processing is not required, then the code changes the lwp_state back to LWP_USER and saves the return value (possibly in two registers as above) in the regs structure, clears the curthread->t_sysnum since a system call is no longer executing, and steps the PC and nPC values so that the RETRY instruction at the end of user_rtt, to which the code is about to "return," does not simply reexecute the ta instruction.

```
! fast path outbound microstate accounting call
mov     LMS_SYSTEM, %o0
call    syscall_mstate
mov     LMS_USER, %o1

jmp     %l0 + 8
nop
```

See usr/src/uts/sparc/v9/ml/syscall_trap.s

The code then captures the transition of the thread state from system to user for microstate accounting and returns through `user_rtt` as arranged by `sys_trap`. `user_rtt`'s task is to get us back out of the kernel to resume at the instruction indicated in `%tstate` (for which the PC and nPC were stepped) and continue execution in userland.

Once a system call has completed, a value is returned to the calling program. The programmer must ensure that return values are checked before execution continues. System calls generally return a minus one (-1) value if they could not complete for some reason and set a system-defined error number (`errno`) that provides additional information about why the system call failed.

The equivalent code for system calls on x64 platforms can be found in `usr/src/uts/i86pc/ml`. The source files `syscall_asm.s` and `syscall_asm_amd64.s` contain the assembly language code that handles the system call entry point, register setup, state transition, etc. The code is actually fairly well documented by comments. However, as with SPARC code, some knowledge of x64 assembler and hardware register use will help.

2.9 Process Termination

The termination of a process results from one of three possible events. First, the process explicitly calling `exit(2)` or `_exit(2)` causes all the threads in a multithreaded process to exit. The threads libraries include `thr_exit(3T)` and `pthread_exit(3T)` interfaces for programmatically terminating an individual user thread without causing the entire process to exit. Second, the process simply completes execution and falls through to the end of the `main()` function—which is essentially an implicit exit. Third, a signal is delivered, and the disposition for the signal is to terminate the process. This disposition is the default for some signals (see Section 2.11). One other possibility is that a process can explicitly call the `abort(3C)` function and cause a `SIGABRT` signal to be sent to the process. The default disposition for `SIGABRT` is to terminate the process and create a core file.

Regardless of which event causes the process to terminate, the kernel exit function is ultimately executed, freeing whatever resources have been allocated to the process, such as the address space mappings, open files, etc., and setting the process state to SZOMB, or the *zombie* state. A zombie process is one that has exited and that requires the parent process to issue a wait(2) system call to gather the exit status. The only kernel resource that a process in the zombie state is holding is the process table slot. Successful execution of a wait(2) call frees the process table slot. Orphaned processes are inherited by the init process solely for this purpose.

An exception to the above scenario is possible if a parent process uses the sigaction(2) system call to establish a signal handler for the SIGCLD signal and sets the SA_NOCLDWAIT flag (no child wait) in the sa_flags field of the sigaction structure. A process is sent a SIGCLD signal by the kernel when one of its child processes terminates. If a process installs a SIGCLD handler as described, the kernel sets the SNOWAIT bit in the calling (parent) process's p_flag field, signifying that the parent process is not interested in obtaining status information on child processes that have exited. The actual mechanics happen in two places: when the signal handler is installed and when the kernel gets ready to post a SIGCLD signal.

First, when the sigaction() call is executed and the handler is installed, if SA_NOCLDWAIT is true, then SNOWAIT is set in p_flags and the code loops through the child process list, looking for child processes in the zombie state. For each such child process found, the kernel freeproc() function is called to release the process table entry. (The kernel exit code, described below, will have already executed, since the process must have terminated—otherwise, it would not be in the zombie state.) In the second occurrence, the kernel calls its internal sigcld() function to post a SIGCLD signal to a process that has had a child terminate. The sigcld() code calls freeproc() instead of posting the signal if SNOWAIT is set in the parent's p_flags field.

Having jumped ahead there for a second, let's turn our attention back to the kernel exit() function, starting with a summary of the actions performed.

```
exit()
        Exit all but 1 LWP (exitlwps())
        Clean up any doors created by the process
        Clean up any pending async I/Os
        Clean up any realtime timers
        Flush signal information (set ignore for all signals, clear posted signals)
        Set process LWP count to zero (p_lwpcnt = 0)
        NULL-terminate the process kernel thread linked list
        Set process termination time (p_mterm)
        Close all open file descriptors
        if (process is a session leader)
                Release control terminal
        Clean up any semaphore resources being held
        Release the process's address space
        Reassign orphan processes to next-of-kin
```

continues

```
Reassign child processes to init
Set process state to zombie
Set process p_wdata and p_wcode for parent to interrogate
Call kernel sigcld() function to send SIGCLD to parent
        if (SNOWAIT flag is set in parent)
                freeproc() /* free the proc table slot - no zombie */
        else
                post the signal to the parent
```

The sequence of events outlined above is reasonably straightforward. It's a matter of walking through the process structure, cleaning up resources that the process may be holding, and reassigning child and orphan processes. Child processes are handed over to init, and orphan processes are linked to the next-of-kin process, which is typically the parent. Still, we can point out a few interesting things about process termination and the LWP/kthread model as implemented in Solaris.

2.9.1 LWP and Kernel Thread Exit

The exitlwps() code is called immediately upon entry to the kernel exit() function, which, as the name implies, is responsible for terminating all but one LWP in the process. If the number of LWPs in the process is 1 (the p_lwpcnt field in the proc structure) and there are no zombie LWPs (p_zombcnt is 0), then exitlwps() simply turns off the SIGWAITING signal and returns. SIGWAITING creates more LWPs in the process if runnable user threads are waiting for a resource. We certainly do not want to catch SIGWAITING signals and create LWPs when we're terminating.

If the process has more than one LWP, the LWPs must be stopped (quiesced) so that they are not actively changing state or attempting to grab resources (file opens, stack/address space growth, etc.). Essentially what happens is this:

1. The kernel loops through the list of LWP/kthreads in the process, setting the t_astflag in the kernel thread. If the LWP/kthread is running on a processor, the processor is forced to enter the kernel through the cross-call interrupt mechanism.

2. Inside the trap handler, which is entered as a result of the cross-call, the kernel tests the t_astflag (which is set) and tests for what condition it is that requires post-trap processing. The t_astflag specifically instructs the kernel that some additional processing is required following a trap.

3. The trap handler tests the process HOLDFORK flag and if it is set in p_flags (which it is in this case), calls a holdlwp() function that, under different circumstances, would suspend the LWP/kthread.

4. During an exit, with `EXITLWPS` set in `p_flags`, the `lwp_exit()` function is called to terminate the LWP. If the LWP/kthread is in a sleep or stopped state, then it is set to run so that it can ultimately be quiesced as described.

The kernel `lwp_exit()` function does per-LWP/kthread cleanup, such as timers, doors, signals, and scheduler activations. Finally, the LWP/kthread is placed on the process's linked list of zombie LWPs, `p_zomblist`. Once all but one of the LWP/kthreads in the process have been terminated and placed on the process zombie list, the `exit()` code executes the functions summarized on the previous page. The pseudocode below summarizes the `exitlwps()` function.

```
exitlwps()
        if (process LWP count == 1)
                nuke SIGWAITING
                return
        else
                for (each LWP/kthread on the process linked list)
                        if (LWP/kthread is sleeping or stopped)
                                make it runnable
                        if (LWP/kthread is running on a processor)
                                t_astflag = 1;
                                poke_cpu() /* cross-call, to trap into the kernel */
                                        holdlwp()
                                                lwp_exit()
                                                place kthread/LWP on zombie list
                done (loop)
        place zombie threads on deathrow
        return to kernel exit()
```

Once the `exit()` code has completed, the process is in a zombie state, occupying only a process table entry and PID structure. When a `wait()` call is issued on the zombie, the kernel `freeproc()` function is called to free the process and PID structures.

2.9.2 Deathrow List

`exitlwps()` does one last bit of work before it returns to `exit()`. It places a zombie's kernel threads on *deathrow*.

The kernel maintains a list, called deathrow, of LWPs and kernel threads that have exited, in order to reap a terminated LWP/kthread when a new one needs to be created (`fork()`). If an LWP/kthread is available on the list of zombies, the kernel does not need to allocate the data structures and stack for a new kthread; it simply uses the structures and stack from the zombie kthread and links the kthread to the process that issued the `fork(2)` (or `thread_create()`) command.

In the process creation flow, when the `forklwp()` code calls `lwp_create()`, `lwp_create()` first looks on deathrow for a zombie thread. If one exists, the LWP, kthread, and stack are linked to the process, and the kernel is spared the need to allocate a new kthread, an LWP, and stack space during the `fork()` process. The kernel simply grabs the structures from the deathrow list, links the pointers appropriately, and moves on. `thread_create()` (kernel thread create, not the user thread API), called from `lwp_create()` is passed the LWP data and stack and thus avoids doing any kernel memory allocations.

A kernel thread, `thread_reaper()`, runs periodically and cleans up zombie threads that are sitting on deathrow. The list of zombie threads on deathrow is not allowed to grow without bounds (no more than 32 zombies), and the zombies are not left on deathrow forever.

2.10 The Process File System

The process file system, procfs, is a pseudo file system. Pseudo file systems provide file-like abstractions and file I/O interfaces to something that is not a file in the traditional sense. Procfs abstracts the Solaris kernel's process architecture such that all processes running on the system appear in the root directory name space under the `/proc` directory; every process in the system exists as a file under `/proc`, with the process's PID serving as the file name. The PID file name under `/proc` is actually a directory containing other files and subdirectories that, combined, make up the complete `/proc` directory space. The many kernel data structures that provide process data and control points appear as files within the `/proc/<pid>` directory hierarchy, and multithreaded processes have a subdirectory for each LWP in the process. Per-LWP data and control structures exist as files under the `/proc/<pid>/lwp/<lwp_id>`. The objects that appear under `/proc` are not on-disk files; they are objects that exist in kernel memory. When a user executes an `ls(1)` command in `/proc` or any `/proc` subdirectory, the system reads kernel memory.

This file-like abstraction for processes provides a simple and elegant means of extracting information about processes, their execution environment, and their kernel resource utilization. Simple things, such as opening a `/proc` file object to read bits of information about a process, are relatively easy to do with procfs. Process control is powerful and relatively straightforward; processes can be stopped and started, and event-driven stops can be established for things like signals, traps, and system calls. In general, process management and debugging is greatly simplified. It is worth noting that the original design goal of procfs was to provide a set of interfaces for writing debuggers; procfs has evolved considerably since the original implementation.

The Solaris system ships with several commands that implement `/proc` for extracting information and issuing control directives. These commands are described in the proc(1) manual page. We use some of these commands through-out the book to provide examples of different kernel abstractions, such as opened files or a process's address space. Process information commands, ps(1) and prstat(1), are built on top of the procfs interfaces.

The control and informational data made available through the /proc file system is maintained in a hierarchy of files and subdirectories. The files and subdirectories implemented in /proc are listed below. See the proc(4) manual page for additional information on these files and their uses.

- **/proc.** Top-level directory for procfs.

- **/proc/<pid>.** Top-level directory for a specific process, where the process's PID is the directory name.

- **/proc/<pid>/as.** The process's address space, as defined by the p_as link to an address space structure (struct as) in the process's proc structure. In other words, the process's address space as represented by the /proc/<pid>/as file is not a /proc-specific representation of the address space. Rather, /proc provides a path to address space mappings through the proc structure's p_as pointer.

- **/proc/<pid>/auxv.** Array of auxv (auxiliary vector, defined in /usr/include/sys/auxv.h) structures, with the initial values as passed to the dynamic linker when the process was exec'd.

- **/proc/<pid>/contracts.** Directory containing references to the contracts held by the process. Each entry is a symbolic link to the contract's directory under /system/contract.

- **/proc/<pid>/cred.** Process credentials, as described in the prcred structure (/usr/include/sys/procfs.h).

- **/proc/<pid>/ctl.** A process control file. Can be opened for write-only, and can be used to send control messages to a process to initiate a specific event or to enable a particular behavior. Examples include stopping or starting a process, setting stops on specific events, or turning on microstate accounting.

- **/proc/<pid>/cwd.** Symbolic link to the process's current working directory.

- **/proc/<pid>/fd.** Directory that contains references to the process's open files.

- **/proc/<pid>/fd/nn.** The process's open file descriptors. Directory files are represented as symbolic links.

- **/proc/<pid>/lpsinfo.** Per-LWP ps(1) information.

- **/proc/<pid>/lstatus.** Array of lwpstatus structures, one for each LWP in the process.

- **/proc/<pid>/lusage.** Array of LWP resource usage data. See Section 2.10.2.

- **/proc/<pid>/lwp.** Subdirectory containing files that represent all the LWPs in the process.

- **/proc/<pid>/map.** Address space map information. The data displayed by the pmap(1) command.

- **/proc/<pid>/object.** Subdirectory containing binary shared object files the process is linked to.

- **/proc/<pid>/object/nn.** Binary object files. The process's executable binary (a.out), along with shared object files the process is linked to.

- **/proc/<pid>/pagedata.** Another representation of the process's address space. Provides page-level reference and modification tracking.

- **/proc/<pid>/path.** Subdirectory containing symbolic links of file objects (open files, executable image location, root directory, shared object libraries).

- **/proc/<pid>/priv.** Description of the privileges associated with the process, described by a prpriv_t structure.

- **/proc/<pid>/psinfo.** Process information as provided by the ps(1) command. Similar to the status data as described above, in that a representative LWP is included with an embedded lwpsinfo structure.

- **/proc/<pid>/rmap.** Reserved address space segments of the process.

- **/proc/<pid>/root.** Symbolic link to the process's root directory.

- **/proc/<pid>/sigact.** Array of sigaction structures, each representing the signal disposition for all signals associated with the process.

- **/proc/<pid>/status.** General state and status information about the process. The specific contents are defined in the pstatus structure, defined in /usr/include/sys/procfs.h. pstatus is also described in proc(4).

- **/proc/<pid>/usage.** Process resource usage data. See Section 2.10.2.

- **/proc/<pid>/watch.** Array of prwatch structures (defined in /usr/include/sys/procfs.h), as created when the kernel sets a PCWATCH operation by writing to the control file. Allows for monitoring (watching) one or more address space ranges, such that a trap is generated when a memory reference is made to a watched page.

- **/proc/<pid>/xmap.** Extended address space map information. The data displayed when the pmap(1) command is run with the -x flag.

The LWP subdirectories contain per-lwp information.

- **/proc/<pid>/lwp/<lwpid>/asrs.** This file exists only for 64-bit SPARC V9 processes. It contains an `asrset_t` structure, defined in `<sys/regset.h>`, containing the values of the LWP's platform-dependent ancillary state registers. If the LWP is not stopped, all register values are undefined.

- **/proc/<pid>/lwp/<lwpid>/gwindows.** General register windows. This file exists only on SPARC-based systems and represents the general register set of the LWP (part of the hardware context), as defined in the `gwindows` structure in `/usr/include/sys/regset.h`.

- **/proc/<pid>/lwp/<lwpid>/lwpctl.** Control file for issuing control operations for each LWP.

- **/proc/<pid>/lwp/<lwpid>/lwpsinfo.** LWP `ps(1)` command information, as defined in `lwpsinfo`, also in `/usr/include/sys/procfs.h`.

- **/proc/<pid>/lwp/<lwpid>/lwpstatus.** LWP state and status information, as defined in the `lwpstatus` structure in `/usr/include/sys/procfs.h`.

- **/proc/<pid>/lwp/<lwpid>/lwpusage.** LWP resource usage data. See Section 2.10.2.

- **/proc/<pid>/lwp/<lwpid>/templates.** A directory that contains references to the active templates for the lwp, named by the contract type. See `contract(4)`.

- **/proc/<pid>/lwp/<lwpid>/xregs.** Extra general state registers; this file is processor-architecture specific and may not be present on some platforms. On SPARC-based systems, the data contained in this file is defined in the `prxregset` structure, in `/usr/include/sys/procfs_isa.h`.

Refer to the `proc(4)` manual page for more detailed information on the various files in `/proc` and for a complete description of the control messages available.

2.10.1 Procfs Implementation

Procfs is implemented as a dynamically loadable kernel module, `/kernel/fs/procfs`, and is loaded automatically by the system at boot time. `/proc` is mounted during system startup by virtue of the default `/proc` entry in the `/etc/vfstab` file. The mount phase causes the invocation of the procfs `prinit()` (initialize) and `prmount()` file-system-specific functions, which initialize the `vfs` structure for procfs and create and initialize a `vnode` for the top-level directory file, `/proc`.

The kernel memory space for the /proc files is, for the most part, allocated dynamically, with an initial static allocation for the number of directory slots required to support the maximum number of processes the system is configured to support (see Section 2.5).

A kernel procdir (procfs directory) pointer is initialized as a pointer to an array of procent (procfs directory entry) structures. The size of this array is derived from the v.v_proc variable established at boot time, representing the maximum number of processes the system can support. The entry in procdir maintains a pointer to the process structure and maintains a link to the next entry in the array. The procdir array is indexed through the pr_slot field in the process's pid structure. The procdir slot is allocated to the process from the array and initialized at process creation time (fork()) (see Figure 2.4).

The specific format of the procfs directory entries is described in the procfs kernel code. It is modeled after a typical on-disk file system: Each directory entry in the kernel is described with a directory name, offset into the directory, a length field, and an inode number. The inode number for a /proc file object is derived internally from the file object type and process PID. Note that /proc directory entries are not cached in the directory name lookup cache (dnlc); by definition they are already in physical memory.

Because procfs is a file system, it is built on the virtual file system (VFS) and vnode framework. In Solaris, an instance of a file system is described by a vfs object, and the underlying files are each described by a vnode. Procfs builds the vfs and vnode structures, which are used to reference the file-system-specific functions for operations on the file systems (for example, mount, unmount), and file-system-specific functions on the /proc directories and file objects (for example, open, read, write).

Beyond the vfs and vnode structures, the procfs implementation defines two primary data structures that describe file objects in the /proc file system. The first, prnode, is the file-system-specific data linked to the vnode. Just as the kernel UFS implementation defines an inode as a file-system-specific structure that describes a UFS file, procfs defines a prnode to describe a procfs file. Every file in the /proc directory has a vnode and prnode.

```
typedef struct prnode {
        vnode_t          *pr_next;       /* list of all vnodes for process */
        uint_t           pr_flags;       /* private flags */
        kmutex_t         pr_mutex;       /* locks pr_files and child pr_flags */
        prnodetype_t     pr_type;        /* node type */
        mode_t           pr_mode;        /* file mode */
        ino_t            pr_ino;         /* node id (for stat(2)) */
        uint_t           pr_hatid;       /* hat layer id for page data files */
        prcommon_t       *pr_common;     /* common data structure */
```

continues

```
        prcommon_t      *pr_pcommon;   /* process common data structure */
        vnode_t         *pr_parent;    /* parent directory */
        vnode_t         **pr_files;    /* contained files array (directory) */
        uint_t          pr_index;      /* position within parent */
        vnode_t         *pr_pidfile;   /* substitute vnode for old /proc */
        vnode_t         *pr_realvp;    /* real vnode, file in object,fd dirs */
        proc_t          *pr_owner;     /* the process that created this node */
        vnode_t         *pr_vnode;     /* pointer to vnode */
        struct contract *pr_contract;  /* contract pointer */
        int             pr_cttype;     /* active template type */
} prnode_t;
```

See usr/src/uts/common/fs/proc/prdata.h

The second structure, prcommon, resides at the directory level for /proc directory files. That is, the /proc/<pid> and /proc/<pid>/lwp/<lwpid> directories each link to a prcommon structure. The underlying nondirectory file objects within /proc/<pid> and /proc/<pid>/lwp/<lwpid> do not have an associated prcommon structure. The reason is that prcommon's function is the synchronization of access to the file objects associated with a process or an LWP within a process.

```
/*
 * Common file object to which all /proc vnodes for a specific process
 * or lwp refer.  One for the process, one for each lwp.
 */
typedef struct prcommon {
        kmutex_t        prc_mutex;     /* to wait for the proc/lwp to stop */
        kcondvar_t      prc_wait;      /* to wait for the proc/lwp to stop */
        ushort_t        prc_flags;     /* flags */
        uint_t          prc_writers;   /* number of write opens of prnodes */
        uint_t          prc_selfopens; /* number of write opens by self */
        pid_t           prc_pid;       /* process id */
        model_t         prc_datamodel; /* data model of the process */
        proc_t          *prc_proc;     /* process being traced */
        kthread_t       *prc_thread;   /* thread (lwp) being traced */
        int             prc_slot;      /* procdir slot number */
        id_t            prc_tid;       /* thread (lwp) id */
        int             prc_tslot;     /* lwpdir slot number, -1 if reaped */
        int             prc_refcnt;    /* this structure's reference count */
        struct pollhead prc_pollhead;  /* list of all pollers */
} prcommon_t;
```

See usr/src/uts/common/fs/proc/prdata.h

The prcommon structure provides procfs clients with a common file abstraction of the underlying data files within a specific directory.

Structure linkage is maintained at the proc structure and LWP level, which reference their respective /proc file vnodes. Every process links to its primary /proc vnode (that is, the vnode that represents the /proc/<pid> file), and maintains an LWP directory list reference to the per-LWP /proc entries.

```
/*
 * An lwp directory entry.
 * If le_thread != NULL, this is an active lwp.
 * If le_thread == NULL, this is an unreaped zombie lwp.
 */
typedef struct lwpent {
        kthread_t       *le_thread;     /* the active lwp, NULL if zombie */
        id_t            le_lwpid;       /* its lwpid (t->t_tid) */
        uint16_t        le_waiters;     /* total number of lwp_wait()ers */
        uint16_t        le_dwaiters;    /* number that are daemons */
        clock_t         le_start;       /* start time of this lwp */
        struct vnode    *le_trace;      /* pointer to /proc lwp vnode */
} lwpent_t;

/*
 * Elements of the lwp directory, p->p_lwpdir[].
 *
 * We allocate lwp directory entries separately from lwp directory
 * elements because the lwp directory must be allocated as an array.
 * The number of lwps can grow quite large and we want to keep the
 * size of the kmem_alloc()d directory as small as possible.
 *
 * If ld_entry == NULL, the entry is free and is on the free list,
 * p->p_lwpfree, linked through ld_next.  If ld_entry != NULL, the
 * entry is used and ld_next is the thread-id hash link pointer.
 */
typedef struct lwpdir {
        struct lwpdir   *ld_next;       /* hash chain or free list */
        struct lwpent   *ld_entry;      /* lwp directory entry */
} lwpdir_t;
. . .
struct proc {
. . .
        kthread_t *p_tlist;             /* circular list of threads */
        lwpdir_t *p_lwpdir;             /* thread (lwp) directory */
        lwpdir_t *p_lwpfree;            /* p_lwpdir free list */
        lwpdir_t **p_tidhash;           /* tid (lwpid) lookup hash table */
        uint_t   p_lwpdir_sz;           /* number of p_lwpdir[] entries */
        uint_t   p_tidhash_sz;          /* number of p_tidhash[] entries */
. . .
        struct vnode *p_trace;          /* pointer to primary /proc vnode */
        struct vnode *p_plist;          /* list of /proc vnodes for process */
. . .
```

See usr/src/uts/common/sys/proc.h

Indexing of the process `p_lwpdir` is based on the `/proc` directory entry slot for the target LWP. The `lwpent_t` references the vnode for an LWP's `/proc/<pid>/lwp/<lwpid>/` through the `vnode` and `prnode_t`, as illustrated in Figure 2.10.

Figure 2.10 shows a single process with two LWPs that link to the underlying procfs objects. Each LWP in the process links to its procfs `prnode` through the `lwpent_t` vnode path shown. The LWP's `prnode` links back to the process's `prnode` through the `pr_pcommon` pointer. The connection to the `/proc` directory slot is through the process's `pid_t pr_slot` link (not shown in Figure 2.10; see Figure 2.4). `/proc/<pid>/lwp/<lwpid>` slots are linked for each LWP in their respective `prc_tslot` field.

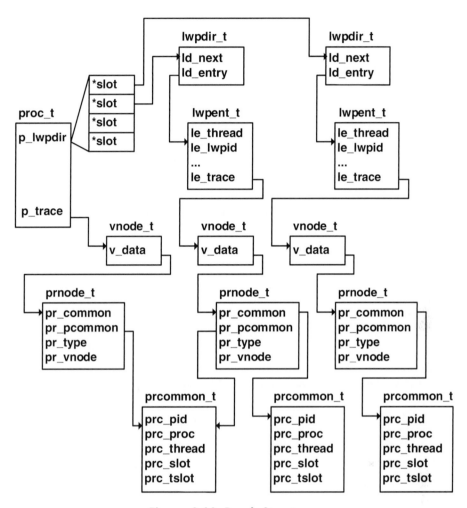

Figure 2.10 Procfs Structures

When a reference is made to a procfs directory and underlying file object, the kernel dynamically creates the necessary structures to service a client request for file I/O. More succinctly, the procfs structures and links are created and torn down dynamically. They are not created when the process is created (aside from the procdir procfs directory entry and directory slot allocation). They appear to be always present because the files are available whenever an open(2) request is made or a lookup is done on a procfs directory or data file object. (It is something like the light in your refrigerator—it's always on when you look, but off when the door is closed).

The data made available through procfs is, of course, always present in the kernel proc structures and other data structures that, combined, form the complete process model in the Solaris kernel. By hiding the low-level details of the kernel process model and abstracting the interesting information and control channels in a relatively generic way, procfs provides a service to client programs interested in extracting bits of data about a process or somehow controlling the execution flow. The abstractions are created when requested and are maintained as long as necessary to support file access and manipulation requests for a particular file.

File I/O operations through procfs follow the conventional methods of first opening a file to obtain a file descriptor, then performing subsequent read/write operations, and closing the file when the operation is completed. The creation and initialization of the prnode and prcommon structures occur when the procfs-specific vnode operations are entered through the vnode switch table mechanism as a result of a client (application program) request. The actual procfs vnode operations have specific functions for the lookup and read operations on the directory and data files within the /proc directory.

The implementation in procfs of lookup and read requests through an array of function pointers that resolve to the procfs file-type-specific routine is accomplished through the use of a lookup table and corresponding lookup functions. The file type is maintained at two levels. At the vnode level, procfs files are defined as VPROC file types (v_type field in the vnode). The prnode includes a type field (pr_type) that defines the specific procfs file type being described by the pnode.

```
/*
 * Node types for /proc files (directories and files contained therein).
 */
typedef enum prnodetype {
        PR_PROCDIR,             /* /proc                         */
        PR_SELF,                /* /proc/self                    */
        PR_PIDDIR,              /* /proc/<pid>                   */
        PR_AS,                  /* /proc/<pid>/as                */
        PR_CTL,                 /* /proc/<pid>/ctl               */
        PR_STATUS,              /* /proc/<pid>/status            */
        PR_LSTATUS,             /* /proc/<pid>/lstatus           */
        PR_PSINFO,              /* /proc/<pid>/psinfo            */
. . .

                                See usr/src/uts/common/fs/proc/prdata.h
```

The procfs file types correspond directly to the description of /proc files and directories that are listed at the beginning of this section (and in the proc(2) man page).

The vnode kernel layer is entered (vn_open()), and a series of lookups is performed to construct the full path name of the desired /proc file. Macros in the

vnode layer invoke file-system-specific operations. In this example, VOP_LOOKUP()
resolves to the procfs pr_lookup() function. pr_lookup() checks access permissions and vectors to the procfs function appropriate for the directory file type, for
example, pr_lookup_piddir() to perform a lookup on a /proc/<pid> directory. Each of the pr_lookup_xxx() directory lookup functions does some direc-
tory-type-specific work and calls prgetnode() to fetch the prnode.

prgetnode() creates the prnode for the /proc file and initializes several of
the prnode and vnode fields. For /proc PID and LWPID directories (/proc/
<pid>, /proc/<pid>/lwp/<lwpid>), the prcommon structure is created, linked
to the prnode, and partially initialized. Note that for /proc directory files, the
vnode type is changed from VPROC (set initially) to VDIR, to correctly reflect the
file type as a directory (it is a procfs directory, but a directory file nonetheless).

Once the path name is fully constructed, the VOP_OPEN() macro invokes the
file-system-specific open() function. The procfs propen() code does some additional prnode and vnode field initialization and file access testing for specific file
types. Once propen() completes, control is returned to vn_open() and ultimately a file descriptor representing a procfs file is returned to the caller.

The reading of a procfs data file object is similar in flow to the open scenario, in
which the execution of a read system call on a procfs file ultimately causes the
code to enter the procfs prread() function. For each available file object (data
structure), the procfs implementation defines a specific read function: pr_read_
psinfo(), pr_read_pstatus(), pr_read_lwpsinfo(), etc. The specific function is entered from prread() through an array of function pointers indexed by
the file type—the same method employed for the previously described lookup operations.

The Solaris 10 implementation of procfs, in which both 32-bit and 64-bit binary
executables can run on a 64-bit kernel, provides 32-bit versions of the data files
available in the /proc hierarchy. For each data structure that describes the contents of a /proc file object, a 32-bit equivalent is available in a 64-bit Solaris kernel (for example, lwpstatus and lwpstatus32, psinfo and psinfo32). In
addition to the 32-bit structure definitions, each of the pr_read_xxx() functions
has a 32-bit equivalent in the procfs kernel module—a function that deals specifically with the 32-bit data model of the calling program. Procfs users are not
exposed to the multiple data model implementation in the 64-bit kernel. When
prread() is entered, it checks the data model of the calling program and invokes
the correct function as required by the data model of the caller. An exception to
this is a read of the address space (/proc/<pid>/as) file; the caller must be the
same data model. A 32-bit binary cannot read the as file of a 64-bit process. A
32-bit process can read the as file of another 32-bit process running on a 64-bit
kernel.

The pr_read_xxx() functions essentially read the data from its original source in the kernel and write the data to the corresponding procfs data structure fields, thereby making the requested data available to the caller. For example, pr_read_ psinfo() reads data from the targeted process's proc structure, credentials structure, and address space (as) structure and writes it to the corresponding fields in the psinfo structure. Access to the kernel data required to satisfy the client requests is synchronized with the proc structure's mutex lock, plock. This approach protects the per-process or LWP kernel data from being accessed by more than one client thread at a time.

Writes to procfs files are much less frequent. Aside from writing to the directories to create data files on command, writes are predominantly to the process or LWP control file (ctl) to issue control messages. Control messages (documented in proc(1)) include stop/start messages, signal tracing and control, fault management, execution control (for example, system call entry and exit stops), and address space monitoring.

> **Note:** We've discussed I/O operations on procfs files in terms of standard system calls because currently those calls are the only way to access the /proc files from developer-written code. However, a set of interfaces specific to procfs is used by the proc(1) commands that ship with Solaris. These interfaces are bundled into a libproc.so library and are not currently documented or available for public use. The libproc.so library is included in the /usr/lib distribution in Solaris 10, but the interfaces are evolving and not yet documented. Plans are under way to document these libproc.so interfaces and make them available as a standard part of the Solaris APIs.

The diagram in Figure 2.11 shows more than one path into the procfs kernel routines. Typical developer-written code makes use of the shorter system call path, passing through the vnode layer as previously described. The proc(1) command is built largely on the libproc.so interfaces. The need for a set of library-level interfaces specific to procfs is twofold: An easy-to-use set of routines for code development reduces the complexity of using a powerful kernel facility; the complexity

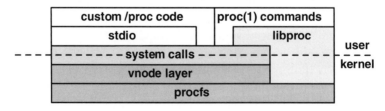

Figure 2.11 libproc and procfs

in controlling the execution of a process, especially a multithreaded process, requires a layer of code that really belongs at the application programming interface (as opposed to kernel) level.

The developer controls a process by writing an operation code and (optional) operand to the first 8 bytes of the control file (or 16 bytes if it's an LP64 kernel). The control file write path is also through the vnode layer and ultimately enters the procfs `prwritectl()` function. The implementation allows multiple control messages (operations and operands) to be sent to the control file in a single write. The `prwritectl()` code breaks multiple messages into distinct operation/operand pairs and passes them to the kernel `pr_control()` function, where the appropriate flags are set at the process or LWP level as a notification that a control mechanism (for example, a stop on an event) has been injected.

Table 2.4 lists the possible control messages (operations) that are currently implemented. We include them here to provide context for the subsequent descriptions of control functions, as well as to illustrate the power of procfs. See also the proc(1) manual page and `/usr/include/sys/procfs.h`.

Table 2.4 Procfs Control Messages

Control Message	Operand (arg)	Description
PCSTOP	n/a	Requests process or LWP to stop; waits for stop.
PCDSTOP	n/a	Requests process or LWP to stop.
PCWSTOP	n/a	Waits for the process or LWP to stop. No timeout implemented.
PCTWSTOP	timeout value	Waits for stop, with millisecond timeout arg.
PCRUN	long	Sets process or LWP runnable. The long arg can specify clearing of signals or faults, setting single step mode, etc.
PCCSIG	n/a	Clears current signal from LWP.
PCCFAULT	n/a	Clears current fault from LWP.
PCSSIG	siginfo_t	Sets current signal from siginfo_t.
PCKILL	long	Posts a signal to process or LWP.
PCUNKILL	long	Deletes a pending signal from the process or LWP.
PCSHOLD	sigset_t	Sets LWP signal mask from arg.
PCSTRACE	sigset_t	Sets traced signal set from arg.
PCSFAULT	fltset_t	Sets traced fault set from arg.

continues

Table 2.4 Procfs Control Messages (*continued*)

Control Message	Operand (arg)	Description
PCSENTRY	sysset_t	Sets tracing of system calls (on entry) from arg.
PCSEXIT	sysset_t	Sets tracing of system calls (on exit) from arg.
PCSET	long	Sets mode(s) in process/LWP.
PCUNSET	long	Clears mode(s) in process/LWP.
PCSREG	prgregset_t	Sets LWP's general registers from arg.
PCSFPREG	prfpregset_t	Sets LWP's floating-point registers from arg.
PCSXREG	prxregset_t	Sets LWP's extra registers from arg.
PCNICE	long	Sets nice value from arg.
PCSVADDR	long	Sets PC (program counter) to virtual address in arg.
PCWATCH	prwatch_t	Sets or clears watched memory area from arg.
PCAGENT	prgregset_t	Creates agent LWP with register values from arg.
PCREAD	priovec_t	Reads from the process address space through arg.
PCWRITE	priovec_t	Writes to process address space through arg.
PCSCRED	prcred_t	Sets process credentials from arg.
PCSASRS	asrset_t	Sets ancillary state registers from arg.

As you can see from the variety of control messages provided, the implementation of process/LWP control is tightly integrated with the kernel process/LWP subsystem. Various fields in the process, user (uarea), LWP, and kernel thread structures facilitate process management and control with procfs. Establishing process control involves setting flags and bit mask fields to track events that cause a process or thread to enter or exit the kernel. These events are signals, system calls, and fault conditions. The entry and exit points for these events are well defined and thus provide a natural inflection point for control mechanisms.

The system calls, signals, and faults are set through the use of a *set* data type, where sigset_t, sysset_t, and fltset_t operands have values set by the calling (controlling) program to specify the signal, system call, or fault condition of interest. A stop on a system call entry occurs when the kernel is first entered (the system call trap), before the argument list for the system call is read from the process. System call exit stops have the process stop after the return value from the system call has been saved. Fault stops also occur when the kernel is first entered; fault conditions generate traps, which force the code into a kernel trap handler. Signal stops are tested for at all the points where a signal is detected, on a return from a system call or trap, and on a wakeup (see Section 2.11).

Address space watch directives allow a controlling process to specify a virtual address, range (in bytes), and access type (for example, read or write access) for a segment of a process's virtual address space. When a watched event occurs, a watchpoint trap is generated, which typically causes the process or LWP to stop, either through a trace of a FLTWATCH fault or by an unblocked SIGTRAP signal.

In some cases, the extraction of process information and process control requires the controlling process to have the target process perform specific instructions on its behalf. For example, the pfiles(1) command, which lists the open files of a process and provides information about each opened file, requires the target process to issue a stat(2) system call on each of its open file descriptors. Since the typical process running on a Solaris system spends a fair amount of its time blocking on a system call (not related to procfs), getting control of the target process to perform a specific task requires grabbing the process while it is blocked and preserving the system call state so that it can be restored and resume properly when the controlling process has had its request satisfied.

Procfs implements an agent LWP for this purpose. Rather than complicating state preservation and restoration by using an existing LWP in the target process, procfs provides a facility for creating an agent LWP (note the PCAGENT control message). When an agent LWP is created, it remains the only runnable LWP in the process for the duration of its existence. The agent LWP controls the execution of the target process as required to satisfy the controlling process's request (for example, execute system calls within the target process). When completed, the agent LWP is destroyed and the process/LWP state is restored. The proc structure maintains a pointer, p_agenttp, that is linked to the agent LWP when one is created. A test on this pointer in various areas of the kernel determines whether an agent LWP exists for the process.

The finer details of the process control directives, their use, and the subtleties of the behavior they create are well documented in the proc(4) man page.

Among its many benefits, procfs enables us to track and extract information about process resource utilization and state changes—the subject of the next section.

2.10.2 Process Resource Usage

The kernel supports the gathering of relatively fine-grained resource-utilization information in the process framework. Resource usage data is a collection of counters embedded in a structure called lrusage. A process contains two lrusage structures—p_ru, which is the total for all completed LWPs; and p_cru, which tallies usage for child processes. Each LWP contains an lrusage (lwp_ru in klwp_t) structure that is updated during the execution life cycle of the LWP. When an LWP terminates, the lrusage data is copied from the LWP to the process-level lrusage structure. Thus, the data reflected at the process level represents the

Table 2.5 `lrusage` Fields

Field	Description
`minflt`	Minor page faults (a page fault resolved without a disk I/O).
`majflt`	Major page faults (disk I/O required). Incremented in the kernel block I/O `pageio_setup()` routine, which sets up a `buf` struct for a page.
`nswap`	Number of times the LWP was swapped out. Incremented in the LWP `swapout()` code.
`inblock`	Number of input blocks. Incremented in the kernel block I/O subsystem (`bio.c`) for block device reads, bread_common() and breada().
`oublock`	Number of output blocks. As above, incremented in `bio.c` for block device writes, bwrite_common().
`msgsnd`	STREAMS messages sent. Incremented in the STREAMS common code for `putmsg()`.
`msgrcv`	STREAMS messages received. Incremented in the STREAMS common code for `getmsg()`.
`nsignals`	Number of signals received. Incremented in the kernel `psig()` code, where the LWP is set up to run the signal handler.
`nvcsw`	Number of voluntary context switches. Incremented when an LWP blocks (is put to sleep), waiting for an I/O or synchronization primitive.
`nivcsw`	Number of involuntary context switches. Incremented when an LWP is context-switched because it uses up its allotted time quantum or is preempted by a higher-priority kthread.
`sysc`	Number of system calls. Incremented in the system call trap handler.
`ioch`	Characters read and written. Incremented in the read/write system call code.

sum total for all the LWPs in the process. Table 2.5 describes the `lrusage` counters.

The resource utilization counters do not require microstate accounting enabling for the process or LWP. The counters are accessible through the usage structure maintained by procfs, where `/proc/<pid>/usage` represents the process-level usage and `/proc/<pid>/lwp/<lwp_id>/lwpusage` represents the per-LWP usage data.

Within the process, the operating system maintains a high-resolution time-stamp that marks process start and terminate times. A `p_mstart` field, the process start time, is set in the kernel `fork()` code when the process is created, and the process termination time, `p_mterm`, is set in the kernel `exit()` code. Start and termination times are also maintained in the LWP when microstate accounting is enabled. The associated process's `p_mlreal` field contains a sum of the LWP's elapsed time, as derived from the start and terminate times.

The system uses an internal `gethrtime()` routine, `get_high_resolution_time` (there is an equivalent `gethrtime(3C)` API). When `get_high_resolution_time` is called, it returns a 64-bit value expressed in nanoseconds. The value is not related to current time and thus is only useful when used in conjunction with a subsequent call to `gethrtime()`. In that case, the difference in the return values from the first call and the second call yields a high-resolution measurement of elapsed time in nanoseconds. This is precisely how it is used when microstate accounting is enabled. For example, the difference between the value of `p_mstart`, which is set during process creation, and `p_mterm`, which is set when the process terminates, yields the elapsed time of the process. `p_mlreal` is the sum total elapsed time, taken in a similar fashion, for the process's LWPs. The fine-grained, nanosecond-level values are derived from a hardware register in the processor that maintains a count of CPU clock cycles (on UltraSPARC processors, it's the `TICK` register). Processor-specific conversion routines convert the register value to nanoseconds, based on processor clock speeds.

2.10.3 Microstate Accounting

The kernel also supports the notion of microstate accounting, that is, the timing of low-level processing states. Microstate accounting is the fine-grained retrieval of time values taken during one of several possible state changes that can occur during the lifetime of a typical LWP. The timestamps are maintained in arrays at the LWP and process level. As was the case with resource utilization, the LWP microstates are recorded during execution, and the array in the process is updated when the LWP terminates. The microstate accounting (and resource usage) structures for the process and LWP are shown below.

```
/*
 * Microstate accounting, resource usage, and real-time profiling
 */
hrtime_t p_mstart;              /* hi-res process start time */
hrtime_t p_mterm;              /* hi-res process termination time */
hrtime_t p_mlreal;            /* elapsed time sum over defunct lwps */
hrtime_t p_acct[NMSTATES];    /* microstate sum over defunct lwps */
hrtime_t p_cacct[NMSTATES];   /* microstate sum over child procs */
struct lrusage p_ru;          /* lrusage sum over defunct lwps */
struct lrusage p_cru;         /* lrusage sum over child procs */
...
                                    See usr/src/uts/common/sys/proc.h
```

continues

```
        /*
         * Microstate accounting.  Timestamps are made at the start and the
         * end of each microstate (see <sys/msacct.h> for state definitions)
         * and the corresponding accounting info is updated.  The current
         * microstate is kept in the thread struct, since there are cases
         * when one thread must update another thread's state (a no-no
         * for an lwp since it may be swapped/paged out).  The rest of the
         * microstate stuff is kept here to avoid wasting space on things
         * like kernel threads that don't have an associated lwp.
         */
        struct mstate {
                int ms_prev;                    /* previous running mstate */
                hrtime_t ms_start;              /* lwp creation time */
                hrtime_t ms_term;               /* lwp termination time */
                hrtime_t ms_state_start;        /* start time of this mstate */
                hrtime_t ms_acct[NMSTATES];     /* per mstate accounting */
        } lwp_mstate;
```

See usr/src/uts/common/sys/klwp.h

Microstate accounting is enabled by default in Solaris 10 (it was disabled by default in previous Solaris releases). Microstate accounting enabled is reflected in a flag at the process level (SMSACCT in the proc structure's p_flag field) and at the LWP/kthread level (TP_MSACCT in the t_proc_flag field). The kernel lwp_create() code tests the process-level SMSACCT flag to determine if microstate accounting has been enabled. If it has, then lwp_create() sets the TP_MSACCT flag in the kernel thread. lwp_create() also initializes the microstate accounting structure, lwp_mstate, regardless of the state of the SMSACCT flag. This allows the kernel to set the start time (ms_start in the LWP's lwp_mstate structure) and initialize the ms_acct[] array.

The kernel implementation of microstate accounting requires only four kernel functions:

- The initialization function init_mstate()
- An update function, new_mstate(), called during state changes
- The term_mstate() function, to update the process-level data when an LWP terminates
- The restore_mstate() function, called from the dispatcher code when an LWP/kthread has been selected for execution

At various points, the kernel code tests the TP_MSACCT flag to determine if microstate accounting is enabled; if it is, the code updates the current microstate by a call into the new_mstate() function, which is passed as an argument flag indicating the new microstate. The actual microstates are shown below.

```
/* LWP microstates */
#define LMS_USER         0    /* running in user mode */
#define LMS_SYSTEM       1    /* running in sys call or page fault */
#define LMS_TRAP         2    /* running in other trap */
#define LMS_TFAULT       3    /* asleep in user text page fault */
#define LMS_DFAULT       4    /* asleep in user data page fault */
#define LMS_KFAULT       5    /* asleep in kernel page fault */
#define LMS_USER_LOCK    6    /* asleep waiting for user-mode lock */
#define LMS_SLEEP        7    /* asleep for any other reason */
#define LMS_WAIT_CPU     8    /* waiting for CPU (latency) */
#define LMS_STOPPED      9    /* stopped (/proc, jobcontrol, lwp_suspend) */
. . .
```
                                    See usr/src/uts/common/sys/msacct.h

The microstate measurements are taken as follows: `init_mstate()` initializes the microstate date of a new LWP/kthread when the LWP/kthread is created. The `init_mstate()` function performs the following actions (see the previous page).

- Set the previous microstate, `ms_prev`, to `LMS_SYSTEM`.
- Set `ms_start` to return the value of the `gethrtime()` call.
- Set `ms_state_start` to return the value of `gethrtime()` call.
- Set `t_mstate` in the kernel thread to `LMS_STOPPED`.
- Set `t_waitrq` in the kernel thread to zero.
- Zero the `msacct[]` array.

The LWP/kthread microstate data is thus initialized before executing for the first time. The above initialization steps show two additional microstate-related fields not yet discussed. In the kernel thread structure, the current microstate is maintained in `t_mstate`, and `t_waitrq` calculates CPU wait time. You will see where this comes into play in a moment.

During execution, if `TP_MSACCT` is set, calls are made to the `new_mstate()` routine when a state transition occurs. The caller passes `new_mstate()` a state flag (`LMS_USER`, `LMS_SYSTEM`, etc.) that stipulates the new state. The system calculates the time spent in the previous state by finding the difference between the current return value of `gethrtime()` and the `ms_state_start` field, which was set during initialization and is reset on every pass through `new_mstate()`, marking the start time for a new state transition. The `ms_acct[]` array location that corresponds to the previous microstate is updated to reflect elapsed time in that state. Since the time values are summed, the current value in the `ms_acct[]` location is added to the new elapsed time just calculated. Thus, the `ms_acct[]` array contains the elapsed time in the various microstates, updated dynamically when state changes occur. Lastly, the kernel thread's `t_mstate` is set to reflect the new microstate.

The calls into `new_mstate()` for the tracked microstates come from several areas in the kernel. Table 2.6 lists the kernel functions that call `new_mstate()` for specific state changes.

Table 2.6 Microstate Changes

New State	Called From
LMS_USER	System call handler, on return from system call
LMS_SYSTEM	System call handler, when a system call is entered
LMS_TRAP	Trap handler, when a trap occurs
LMS_TFAULT	Text page fault trap handler
LMS_DFAULT	Data page fault trap handler
LMS_KFAULT	Kernel page fault trap handler
LMS_USER_LOCK	LWP support code, when a user-level synchronization primitive is handled
LMS_SLEEP	Sleep queue code, when an LWP is about to block
LMS_WAIT_CPU	Dispatcher code. Not updated with `new_mstate()`; updated with `restore_mstate()`
LMS_STOPPED	Signal code, when a stop signal is sent

The last function to discuss apropos of microstate accounting is `restore_mstate()`, which is called from a few places in the dispatcher code to restore the microstate of an LWP just selected for execution. `restore_mstate()` calculates the microstate time value spent in the previous state (typically, a sleep) by using the same basic algorithm described for the `new_mstate()` function; the previous state is restored from the `ms_prev` field (`lwp_mstate` structure).

When LWP/kthreads terminate, the microstate accounting data in the `ms_acct[]` array and the resource usage counters are added to the values in the corresponding locations in the `proc` structure. Again, the process level resource counters and microstate accounting data reflect all LWP/kthreads in the process.

Tracking LWP microstates in Solaris 10 is a snap with `prstat(1)`. Use the `-mL` flags, which provide microstate columns for each LWP (thread) in the process.

The `prstat(1)` output shows the percentage of time spent in a given microstate over the last sampling period (default is 5 seconds), beginning with the USR column, up to and including the LAT column. The values in the columns USR through LAT should total 100, accounting for 100% of the threads time for the last sampling period. See the `prstat(1)` man page.

```
sol9$ prstat -mL
   PID USERNAME USR SYS TRP TFL DFL LCK SLP LAT VCX ICX SCL SIG PROCESS/LWPID
   985 mauroj   22 0.0 0.0 0.0 0.0  11 0.0  66  21 103  31   0 tds/3
   985 mauroj   17 0.0 0.0 0.0 0.0 7.9 0.0  75  19  79  27   0 tds/2
   985 mauroj   13 0.0 0.0 0.0 0.0  34 0.0  52  14  58  21   0 tds/6
   985 mauroj   10 0.0 0.0 0.0 0.0  56 0.0  33  21  44  28   0 tds/4
   985 mauroj  9.9 0.0 0.0 0.0 0.0  51 0.0  39  18  63  26   0 tds/9
   985 mauroj  9.4 0.0 0.0 0.0 0.0  48 0.0  43  19  41  29   0 tds/5
   985 mauroj  9.1 0.0 0.0 0.0 0.0  69 0.0  22  15  42  18   0 tds/8
   985 mauroj  7.7 0.0 0.0 0.0 0.0  46 0.0  46  20  36  27   0 tds/7
   986 mauroj  0.0 0.1 0.0 0.0 0.0 0.0 100 0.0  41   0 287   0 prstat/1
   689 mauroj  0.0 0.1 0.0 0.0 0.0 0.0 100 0.1 112   0 632   0 java/11
   664 mauroj  0.0 0.0 0.0 0.0 0.0 0.0 100 0.1  25   0  64   0 gnome-netsta/1
   689 mauroj  0.0 0.0 0.0 0.0 0.0 0.0 100 0.3 130   0 214   0 java/33
   704 mauroj  0.0 0.0 0.0 0.0 0.0 0.0 100 0.1  21   0  44   0 gnome-termin/1
   689 mauroj  0.0 0.0 0.0 0.0 0.0 0.0 100 0.3 142   0  89   0 java/8
   473 mauroj  0.0 0.0 0.0 0.0 0.0 0.0 100 0.0  20   0  80  10 Xorg/1
 . . .
Total: 71 processes, 210 lwps, load averages: 1.20, 0.27, 0.09
```

2.11 Signals

Signals are a means by which a process or thread can be notified of a particular event. Signals are often compared with hardware interrupts, when a hardware subsystem, such as a disk I/O interface (for example, a SCSI host adapter), generates an interrupt to a processor when an I/O is completed. The interrupt causes the processor to enter an interrupt handler, so subsequent processing, based on the source and cause of the interrupt, can be done in the operating system. The hardware interrupt analogy is close to what signals are all about. Similarly, when a signal is sent to a process or thread, a signal handler may be entered (depending on the current *disposition* of the signal), analogous to the system entering an interrupt handler as the result of receiving an interrupt.

The occurrence of a signal may be *synchronous* or *asynchronous* to the process or thread, depending on the source of the signal and the underlying reason or cause. Synchronous signals occur as a direct result of the executing instruction stream, where an unrecoverable error such as an illegal instruction or illegal address reference requires an immediate termination of the process. Such signals are directed to the thread whose execution stream caused the error. Because an error of this type causes a trap into a kernel trap handler, synchronous signals are sometimes referred to as traps.

Asynchronous signals are, as the term implies, external (and in some cases unrelated) to the current execution context. An obvious example is a process or thread sending a signal to another process by means of a kill(2), _lwp_kill(2), or sigsend(2) system call or by invocation of the thr_kill(3T), pthread_kill(3T), or sigqueue(3R) interfaces. Asynchronous signals are also referred to as interrupts.

Every signal has a unique signal name: an abbreviation that begins with `SIG`, such as `SIGINT` (interrupt signal), `SIGILL` (illegal instruction signal), etc., and a corresponding signal number. For all possible signals, the system defines four possible default *dispositions*, or an action to take, when a signal occurs:

- **Exit.** Terminate the process.
- **Core.** Create a core image of the process and terminate.
- **Stop.** Suspend process execution (typically, job control or debug).
- **Ignore.** Discard the signal and take no action, even if the signal is blocked.

A signal's disposition within a process's context defines what action the system will take on behalf of the process when a signal is delivered. All threads and LWPs within a process share the signal disposition—it is processwide and cannot be unique among threads within the same process. The process `uarea` maintains a `u_signal[MAXSIG]` array, with an entry for every possible signal that defines the signal's disposition for the process. The array contains a 0, indicating a default disposition; a 1, which means ignore the signal; or a function pointer, if a user-defined handler has been installed. Table 2.7 describes all signals and their default action.

Table 2.7 Signals

Name	Number	Default Action	Description
SIGHUP	1	Exit	Hang up (see `termio(7)`)
SIGINT	2	Exit	Interrupt (see `termio(7)`)
SIGQUIT	3	Core	Quit (see `termio(7)`)
SIGILL	4	Core	Illegal instruction
SIGTRAP	5	Core	Trace or breakpoint trap
SIGABRT	6	Core	Abort
SIGEMT	7	Core	Emulation trap
SIGFPE	8	Core	Floating-point arithmetic exception
SIGKILL	9	Exit	Kill. Cannot be caught or ignored
SIGBUS	10	Core	Bus error; misaligned address error
SIGSEGV	11	Core	Segmentation fault—typically, a reference to an illegal memory address
SIGSYS	12	Core	Bad system call

continues

Table 2.7 Signals *(continued)*

Name	Number	Default Action	Description
SIGPIPE	13	Exit	Broken pipe
SIGALRM	14	Exit	Alarm clock (`setitimer(2)`, `alarm(2)`)
SIGTERM	15	Exit	Termination
SIGUSR1	16	Exit	User-defined signal 1
SIGUSR2	17	Exit	User-defined signal 2
SIGCHLD	18	Ignore	Child process status change
SIGPWR	19	Ignore	Power fail or restart
SIGWINCH	20	Ignore	Window size change
SIGURG	21	Ignore	Urgent socket condition
SIGPOLL	22	Exit	Pollable event (see `streamio(7)`)
SIGIO	22	Exit	`aioread/aiowrite` completion
SIGSTOP	23	Stop	Stop (cannot be caught or ignored)
SIGTSTP	24	Stop	Stop (job control)
SIGCONT	25	Ignore	Continue
SIGTTIN	26	Stop	Stopped—tty input (see `termio(7)`)
SIGTTOU	27	Stop	Stopped—tty output (see `termio(7)`)
SIGVTALRM	28	Exit	Alarm clock—`setitimer(2)` ITIMER_VIRTUAL alarm
SIGPROF	29	Exit	Profiling alarm—`setitimer(2)` ITIMER_PROF, ITIMER_REALPROF
SIGXCPU	30	Core	CPU time limit exceeded
SIGXFSZ	31	Core	File size limit exceeded
SIGWAIT-ING	32	Ignore	Concurrency signal, used by the thread's library before Solaris 10
SIGLWP	33	Ignore	Inter-LWP signal used by the thread's library before Solaris 10
SIGFREEZE	34	Ignore	Checkpoint suspend
SIGTHAW	35	Ignore	Checkpoint resume
SIGCANCEL	36	Ignore	Cancellation
SIGLOST	37	Ignore	Resource lost
SIGRTMIN	38	Exit	Lowest-priority real-time signal
SIGRTMAX	45	Exit	Highest-priority real-time signal

The SIGWAITING and SIGLWP signals were implemented in the original thread model for managing concurrency and are no longer used in Solaris 10. SIGPOLL and SIGIO are both defined as signal number 22. SIGIO is generated as a result of a process issuing an asynchronous read or write through aioread(3) or aiowrite(3) (or the POSIX equivalent aio_read(3R) or aio_write(3R)), to notify the process that the I/O completed or that an error occurred. SIGPOLL is a more generic indicator that a pollable event has occurred.

The disposition of a signal can be changed from its default, and a process can arrange to catch a signal and invoke a signal handling routine of its own or can ignore a signal that may not have a default disposition of ignore. The only exceptions to this are SIGKILL and SIGSTOP—the default disposition of these two signals cannot be changed. The interfaces for defining and changing signal disposition are the signal(3C) and sigset(3C) libraries and the sigaction(2) system call.

Signals can also be blocked, which means that the process or thread has temporarily prevented delivery of a signal. The generation of a signal that has been blocked results in the signal remaining pending to the process until it is explicitly unblocked or until the disposition is changed to ignore. Signal masks for blocking signals exist within the kernel thread. The sigprocmask(2) system call sets or gets a signal mask for a thread within a process—each thread has its own signal masks, and different threads in the same process can mask different signals (though all threads share the disposition). A call to sigprocmask(2) affects the signal mask of the calling thread, providing the same behavior as a call to pthread_sigmask(3C).

The psig(1) command lists the signal actions for a process. The example below dumps the signal actions for our ksh process.

```
sol10$ psig $$
1097:    -ksh
HUP      blocked,caught   sig_sh_done      RESTART
INT      blocked,caught   sh_fault         RESTART
QUIT     blocked,caught   sh_fault         RESTART
ILL      blocked,caught   sig_sh_done      RESTART
TRAP     blocked,caught   sig_sh_done      RESTART
ABRT     blocked,caught   sig_sh_done      RESTART
EMT      blocked,caught   sig_sh_done      RESTART
FPE      blocked,caught   sig_sh_done      RESTART
KILL     default
BUS      blocked,caught   sig_sh_done      RESTART
SEGV     blocked,default
SYS      blocked,caught   sig_sh_done      RESTART
PIPE     blocked,caught   sig_sh_done      RESTART
ALRM     blocked,caught   sh_fault         RESTART
TERM     blocked,ignored
USR1     blocked,caught   sig_sh_done      RESTART
USR2     blocked,caught   sig_sh_done      RESTART
```

continues

```
CLD      blocked,caught  sh_fault        NOCLDSTOP
PWR      blocked,default
WINCH    blocked,default
URG      blocked,default
POLL     blocked,default
STOP     default
. . .
```

Recall that a signal can originate from several different places, for a variety of reasons. SIGHUP, SIGINT, and SIGQUIT, are typically generated by a keyboard entry from the controlling terminal (SIGINT and SIGQUIT) or if the control terminal is disconnected, which generates a SIGHUP. Note that use of the nohup(1) command makes processes "immune" from hangups by setting the disposition of SIGHUP to ignore. Other terminal I/O-related signals are SIGSTOP, SIGTTIN, SIGTTOU, and SIGTSTP. For those signals that originate from a keyboard command, the actual key sequence that results in the generation of these signals is defined within the parameters of the terminal session, typically, by stty(1). For example, ^c [Control-C] is usually the interrupt key sequence and results in a SIGINT being sent to a process, which has a default disposition of forcing the process to exit.

Signals generated as a direct result of an error encountered during instruction execution start with a hardware trap on the system. Different processor architectures define various traps that result in an immediate vectored transfer of control to a kernel trap-handling function. The Solaris kernel builds a trap table and inserts trap handling routines in the appropriate locations, based on the architecture specification of the processors that the Solaris environment supports. In Intel parlance the routines are called interrupt descriptor tables, or IDTs. On SPARC, they are called trap tables. The kernel-installed trap handler ultimately generates a signal to the thread that caused the trap. The signals that result from hardware traps are SIGILL, SIGFPE, SIGSEGV, SIGTRAP, SIGBUS, and SIGEMT. Table 2.8 lists traps and signals for UltraSPARC.

Signals can originate from sources other than terminal I/O and error trap conditions; process-induced (for example, SIGXFSZ) and external events (kill()) can also generate signals. Examples include the following:

- Applications can create user-defined signals as a somewhat crude form of interprocess communication by defining handlers for SIGUSR1 or SIGUSR2 and sending those signals between processes.

- The kernel sends SIGXCPU if a process exceeds its processor time resource limit or sends SIGXFSZ if a file write exceeds the file size resource limit.

- A SIGABRT is sent as a result of an invocation of the abort(3C) library.

Table 2.8 UltraSPARC Traps and Resulting Signals

Trap Name	Signal
instruction_access_exception	SIGSEGV, SIGBUS
instruction_access_MMU_miss	SIGSEGV
instruction_access_error	SIGBUS
illegal_instruction	SIGILL
privileged_opcode	SIGILL
fp_disabled	SIGILL
fp_exception_ieee_754	SIGFPE
fp_exception_other	SIGFPE
tag_overflow	SIGEMT
division_by_zero	SIGFPE
data_access_exception	SIGSEGV, SIGBUS
data_access_MMU_miss	SIGSEGV
data_access_error	SIGBUS
data_access_protection	SIGSEGV
mem_address_not_aligned	SIGBUS
privileged_action	SIGILL
async_data_error	SIGBUS

- If a process is writing to a pipe and the reader has terminated, SIGPIPE is generated.

- kill(2), sigsend(2), or pthread_kill(3C) does an explicit, programmatic send.

- The kill(1) command sends a signal to a process from the command line.

- sigsend(2) and sigsendset(2) programmatically send signals to processes or groups of processes.

- The kernel notifies parent processes of a status change in a child process by SIGCHLD.

- The alarm(2) system call sends a SIGALRM when the timer expires.

These are just a few examples of how and where signals may originate. Refer to the *Solaris Software Developer Collection* on http://docs.sun.com for additional information on signal types and managing signals in software.

2.11.1 Signals Implementation

A signal is represented as a bit (binary digit) in a data structure (several data structures actually, as you'll see shortly). More precisely, the posting of a signal by the kernel results in a bit getting set in a structure member at either the process or thread level. Because each signal has a unique signal number, we use a structure member of sufficient width, such that we can represent every signal by simply setting the bit that corresponds to the signal number of the signal we want to post. For example, set the 17th bit to post signal 17, SIGUSR1 (which is actually bit number 16 because the bit numbers start with 0 and the signal numbers start with 1).

Signals traditionally go through two well-defined stages: *generation* and *delivery*. Signal *generation* is the point of origin of the signal—the sending phase. A signal is said to be *delivered* when whatever disposition has been established for the signal is invoked, even if it is to be ignored. If a signal is being blocked, thus postponing delivery, it is considered *pending*.

Signal disposition in Solaris is processwide, but each thread has its own *signal mask*. Threads can choose to block signals independently of other threads executing in the same process; thus, different threads may be available to take delivery of different signals at various times during process execution. An interface, pthread_sigmask(3C), establishes per-thread signal masks. Since the disposition and handlers for all signals are shared by all threads in a process, a SIGINT (for example) with the default disposition in place causes the entire process to exit. Synchronous signals, generated as a result of a trap (SIGFPE, SIGILL, etc.) are sent to the thread that caused the trap. Asynchronous signals, which are all signals not defined as traps, are delivered to the first thread that is found not blocking the signal.

Before we delve into the mechanics of signal delivery, let's look at the data types that support signals in the processes and threads.

The primary data fields at the process and thread level are the *signal set fields*, and the *siginfo* structure.

```
typedef struct {                    /* signal set type */
        unsigned int    __sigbits[4];
} sigset_t;
. . .
typedef struct {
        unsigned int    __sigbits[2];
} k_sigset_t;
                                       See usr/src/uts/common/sys/signal.h
```

The sigset_t field is 128 bits wide; the k_sigset_t field is 64 bits wide. Fewer than 50 signals are defined, so a 64-bit-wide field is sufficient. However, the System V application binary interface (ABI) specification defines a 128-bit-wide field for signals, so the signal fields in the user thread (`ulwp_t`) must comply, and they use the `sigset_t`. In the kernel, `k_sigset_t` is used.

A `siginfo` structure stores various bits of information for many different types of signals. The `siginfo` structure fields are summarized in Table 2.9. The source code for the structure can be found in `usr/src/uts/common/sys/siginfo.h`. The structure definition includes several unions—a data union with nested unions, meaning the actual datum will vary according to the variable references in the source code. Table 2.9 shows all possible variables.

Table 2.9 `siginfo` Structure

struct or union	Variable Name	Data Type	Description
siginfo	si_signo	integer	Signal number
	si_code	integer	Code from signal
	si_errno	integer	Error number from `sys/errno.h`
_proc			proc union instantiated in `kill(2)`, `SIGCLD`, and `sigqueue()`
	pid	pid_t	PID
	ctid	ctid_t	Contact ID
	zoneid	zoneid_T	Zone ID
_kill			Data for `SIGKILL`
	uid	uid_t	UID
	value	sigval	Signal value (check this)
_cld	utime	clock_t	Child process user time
	stime	clock_t	Child process system time
	status	int	Child process exit status
_fault			Fault union for `SIGSEGV`, `SIGBUS`, `SIGILL`, `SIGTRAP`, `SIGFPE`
	addr	void *	Fault address
	trapno	int	Illegal trap number
	pc	caddr_t	Program counter—address of faulting instruction
_file			File union for `SIGPOLL` and `SIGXFZ`
	fs	int	File descriptor
	band	long	

continues

Table 2.9 `siginfo` Structure *(continued)*

struct or union	Variable Name	Data Type	Description
_prof			Profiling (SIGPROF) signal information
	faddr	caddr_t	Last fault address
	tstamp	timestruct	Timestamp
	syscall	short	Current system call
	nsysarg	char	Number of arguments
	fault	char	Last fault type
	sysarg	long[]	Array of system call arguments
	mstate	int[]	Array of microstates
_rctl			Resource control information
	entity	int32_t	Resource type exceeded

References in the code to specific fields of a target `siginfo` structure can be tricky to read given the number, and nesting, of unions. A set of preprocessor definitions in `siginfo.h` makes it a little easier and also illustrates the union and variable relationship in a `siginfo_t`.

```
siginfo structure members

#define si_pid        __data.__proc.__pid
#define si_ctid       __data.__proc.__ctid
#define si_zoneid     __data.__proc.__zoneid
#define si_status     __data.__proc.__pdata.__cld.__status
#define si_stime      __data.__proc.__pdata.__cld.__stime
#define si_utime      __data.__proc.__pdata.__cld.__utime
#define si_uid        __data.__proc.__pdata.__kill.__uid
#define si_value      __data.__proc.__pdata.__kill.__value
#define si_addr       __data.__fault.__addr
#define si_trapno     __data.__fault.__trapno
#define si_trapafter  __data.__fault.__trapno
#define si_pc         __data.__fault.__pc
#define si_fd         __data.__file.__fd
#define si_band       __data.__file.__band
#define si_tstamp     __data.__prof.__tstamp
#define si_syscall    __data.__prof.__syscall
#define si_nsysarg    __data.__prof.__nsysarg
#define si_sysarg     __data.__prof.__sysarg
#define si_fault      __data.__prof.__fault
#define si_faddr      __data.__prof.__faddr
#define si_mstate     __data.__prof.__mstate
#define si_entity     __data.__rctl.__entity
```

See usr/src/uts/common/sys/siginfo.h

The `siginfo` data is available to programs that need to know more about the reason a signal was generated. The `sigaction(2)` system call programmatically provides this information. An optional `SA_SIGINFO` flag (in the `sa_flags` field of the `sigaction` structure) results in two additional arguments being passed to the signal handler (assuming of course that the signal disposition has been set up to be caught). The first argument is always the signal number. A non-`NULL` second argument is a pointer to a `siginfo` structure (described in Table 2.9), and a third argument is a pointer to a `ucontext_t` data structure that contains hardware context information (stack pointer, signal mask, and general register contents) about the receiving process when the signal was delivered. The `siginfo` data can be useful for debugging when a trap signal is generated; for example, in the case of a `SIGILL` or `SIGFPE`, more specific information about the underlying reason for the trap can be gleaned from the data the kernel plugs into `siginfo` when getting ready to send a signal. See the `sigaction(2)`, `siginfo(5)`, `ucontext(5)`, and `siginfo.h(3HEAD)` man pages for more information on using `siginfo` data.

The threads model in Solaris requires per-thread signal masks and signal support at several points in the objects that make up the process model.

```
ulwp_t
. . .
sigset_t        ul_sigmask;       /* thread's current signal mask */
sigset_t        ul_tmpmask;       /* signal mask for sigsuspend/pollsys */
siginfo_t       ul_siginfo;       /* deferred siginfo */
. . .
                                  See usr/src/lib/libc/inc/thr_uberdata.h
klwp_t
. . .


/*
 * signal handling and debugger (/proc) interface
 */
uchar_t lwp_cursig;                /* current signal */
uchar_t lwp_curflt;                /* current fault */
uchar_t lwp_sysabort;              /* if set, abort syscall */
uchar_t lwp_asleep;                /* lwp asleep in syscall */
uchar_t lwp_extsig;                /* cursig sent from another contract */
stack_t lwp_sigaltstack;           /* alternate signal stack */
struct sigqueue *lwp_curinfo;      /* siginfo for current signal */
k_siginfo_t     lwp_siginfo;       /* siginfo for stop-on-fault */
k_sigset_t      lwp_sigoldmask;    /* for sigsuspend */
. . .
                                  See usr/src/uts/common/sys/klwp.h
kthread_t
. . .
struct sigqueue *t_sigqueue;       /* queue of siginfo structs */
k_sigset_t      t_sig;             /* signals pending to this process */
k_sigset_t      t_extsig;          /* signals sent from another contract */
k_sigset_t      t_hold;            /* hold signal bit mask */
. . .
                                  See usr/src/uts/common/sys/thread.h
proc_t
. . .
```

continues

```
k_sigset_t p_sig;              /* signals pending to this process */
k_sigset_t p_extsig;           /* signals sent from another contract */
k_sigset_t p_ignore;           /* ignore when generated */
k_sigset_t p_siginfo;          /* gets signal info with signal */
struct sigqueue *p_sigqueue;   /* queued siginfo structures */
struct sigqhdr *p_sigqhdr;     /* hdr to sigqueue structure pool */
struct sigqhdr *p_signhdr;     /* hdr to signotify structure pool */
uchar_t p_stopsig;             /* jobcontrol stop signal */
. . .
                                         See usr/src/uts/common/sys/proc.h

uarea in proc_t

k_sysset_t u_entrymask;        /* /proc syscall stop-on-entry mask */
k_sysset_t u_exitmask;         /* /proc syscall stop-on-exit mask */
k_sigset_t u_signodefer;       /* signals deferred when caught */
k_sigset_t u_sigonstack;       /* signals taken on alternate stack */
k_sigset_t u_sigresethand;     /* signals reset when caught */
k_sigset_t u_sigrestart;       /* signals that restart system calls */
k_sigset_t u_sigmask[MAXSIG];  /* signals held while in catcher */
void    (*u_signal[MAXSIG])(); /* Disposition of signals */
. . .
                                         See usr/src/uts/common/sys/user.h
```

The `ulwp_t`, which represents the user component of a thread, maintains a signal mask for per-thread pending signals. A signal is deferred if it cannot be delivered because the target thread is in a critical code section; `ul_siginfo` stores the `siginfo_t` if signal delivery needs to be deferred. The kernel LWP stores the current signal in `lwp_cursig` and stores a pointer to a `sigqueue` struct with the `siginfo` data for the current signal in `lwp_curinfo`, which is used in the signal delivery phase. Other fields include a stack pointer if an alternative signal stack, `lwp_sigaltstack`, is set up by a call to `sigaltstack(2)`. It is sometimes desirable for programs that do their own stack management to handle signals on an alternative stack, as opposed to the default use of the thread's runtime stack (`SA_ONSTACK` through `sigaction(2)` when the handler is set). The kernel thread maintains two `k_sigset_t` members: `t_sig` and `t_hold`. `t_sig` has the same meaning as `p_sig` at the process level, that is, a mask of pending signals; `t_hold` is a bit mask of signals to block.

In addition, `t_sigqueue` points to a `sigqueue` for `siginfo` data. A signal's `siginfo` structure will be placed either on the process `p_sigqueue` or the kthread's `t_sigqueue`. The kthread `t_sigqueue` is used when a non-NULL kthread pointer has been passed in the kernel signal code, indicating a directed signal targeting a specific thread.

In the embedded `uarea`, several bit maps are maintained for flagging various signal-related events or forcing a particular behavior, settable by the `sigaction(2)` system call. An array of pointers signals dispositions: `u_signal[MAXSIG]`, which contains one array entry per signal. The entries in the array may indicate the signal is to be ignored (`SIG_IGN`) or the default action is set (`SIG_DEF`). If the signal is to be caught, with a handler installed by `signal(3C)` or `sigaction(2)`, the array location for the signal points to the function to be invoked when the signal is delivered. The other uarea signal fields are described in the following list. The described behavior occurs when a signal corresponding to a bit that is set in the field is posted.

- **u_sigonstack.** Flags an alternative signal stack for handling the signal. Assumes sigaltstack(2) has been called to set up an alternative stack. If one has not been set up, the signal is handled on the default stack. Set by sigaction(2) with the SA_ONSTACK flag in sa_flags field of the sigaction structure.

- **u_sigresethand.** Resets the disposition to default (SIG_DEF) when the handler is entered for the signal. The signal is not blocked when the handler is entered. As above, set by SA_RESETHAND in sa_flags.

- **u_sigrestart.** If inside a system call when the signal is received, restarts the system call. This behavior does not work for all system calls, only those that are potentially "slow" (for example, I/O-oriented system calls—read(2), write(2)). Interrupted system calls typically result in an error, with the errno being set to EINTR. Set by SA_RESTART in sa_flags.

- **u_signodefer.** Does not block subsequent occurrences of the signal when it is caught. Normally, a signal is blocked when it has been delivered and a handler is executed. Set by SA_NODEFER in sa_flags.

- **u_sigmask[].** Signals that have been caught and are being held while a handler is executing.

- **u_signal[].** Signal dispositions.

Clearly, there appears to be more than a little redundancy in the signal support structure members spread throughout the various entities that exist within the context of a process. This redundancy is due to the requirements for support of the multithreaded model and the fact that different signals get posted to different places, depending on the signal itself and the source. Earlier in the discussion, we provided several examples of why some signals are sent and where they originate. Asynchronous signals could originate from a user or from various places in the kernel. Signals that are sent from userland (for example, kill(1), kill(2), sigqueue(2)) are sent to the process. Some signals that originate in the kernel are directed to a particular thread. For example, the kernel clock interrupt handler may send a SIGPROF or SIGVTALRM directly to a thread. The pthread_kill(3C) and thr_kill(3C) library interfaces provide for sending asynchronous signals to a specific thread. The STREAMS subsystem sends SIGPOLL and SIGURG to the process when appropriate (for example, a polled event occurs or an urgent out-of-band message is received).

2.11.1.1 Synchronous Signals

Synchronous signals, or trap signals, originate from within the kernel trap handler. When an executing instruction stream causes one of the events described in (missingCRef), the event is detected by hardware and execution is redirected to a kernel trap handler. The trap handler code populates a `siginfo` structure with the appropriate information about the trap and invokes the `trap_cleanup()` function, which determines whether to stop the thread because of a debugger "stop on fault" flag. The entry point into the kernel signal subsystem is through the `trapsig()` function, which is executed next. If the signal is masked or if the disposition has been set to ignore, then `trapsig()` unmasks the signal and sets the disposition to default. The `siginfo` structure is placed on the kthread's `t_sigqueue` list, and `sigtoproc()` is called to post the signal.

The kernel `sigtoproc()` function takes three arguments: a process pointer, a kernel thread pointer, and the signal number. Signals that should be directed to the thread call `sigtoproc()` with a valid kthread pointer. A NULL kthread pointer signifies that the signal should be posted to the process. Let's look at the code flow of `sigtoproc()`.

```
/*
 * Post a signal.
 * If a non-null thread pointer is passed, then post the signal
 * to the thread/lwp, otherwise post the signal to the process.
 */
void
sigtoproc(proc_t *p, kthread_t *t, int sig)
. . .
if (signal == SIGKILL)
        post it to proc
else if (signal == SIGCONT) /* job control continue */
        remove SIGSTOP, SIGTSTP, SIGTTOU, SIGTTIN from signal queue
        clear p_stopsig
        if (process is multithreaded)
                remove SIGSTOP, SIGTSTP, SIGTTOU, SIGTTIN from each thread
                start all stopped threads
else if (signal is SIGSTOP | SIGTDTP | SIGTTOU | SIGTTIN)
        clear SIGCONT in process and threads
if (signal is discardable)
        return
if (signal is directed to a thread)
        add the signal to t_sig in the kthread
        eat_signal()
else if (process is threaded, but signal is not directed)
        find a thread to take the signal
                                        See usr/src/uts/common/os/sig.c
```

A lot of the up-front work in `sigtoproc()` deals with job control and the terminal I/O signals. In compliance with the POSIX specifications, this behavior is documented in the `signal(5)` man page, which we summarize here: Any pending SIGCONT signals are discarded upon receipt of a SIGSTOP, SIGTSTP, SIGTTIN, or

SIGTTOU signal, regardless of the disposition. The inverse is also true; if any of
those four signals are pending when a SIGCONT is received, they are discarded,
again regardless of the disposition.

Two areas in the signal-posting pseudocode above require expanding: discard-
able signals and eat_signal. The kernel sig_discardable() function determines whether a signal can be discarded.

```
/*
 * Return true if the signal can safely be discarded on generation.
 * That is, if there is no need for the signal on the receiving end.
 * The answer is true if the process is a zombie or
 * if all of these conditions are true:
 *      the signal is being ignored
 *      the process is single-threaded
 *      the signal is not being traced by /proc
 *      the signal is not blocked by the process
 */
```
                                                   See usr/src/uts/common/os/sig.c

eat_signal() ensures that the thread is not blocking the signal by testing two
fields in the kernel thread: the t_hold field and a scheduler control field that can
be set to signify that the thread is blocking all signals. A sleeping thread is made
runnable, taken off the sleep queue, and put on a dispatch queue, and the t_astflag
in the kthread structure is set.

The t_astflag forces the thread to check for a signal when execution resumes.
With the signal now posted, sigtoproc() is done and the code returns to trap_
cleanup(). The cleanup code invokes the ISSIG_PENDING macro, which determines from the bit set in the t_sig field that a signal has been posted. Once the
macro establishes the presence of the signal, it invokes the kernel psig() function to handle actual delivery.

```
trap_cleanup()
. . .
if (ISSIG_PENDING(curthread, lwp, p)) {
                    if (issig(FORREAL))
                            psig();
                    curthread->t_sig_check = 1;
        }
. . .
```
                                                   See usr/src/uts/sun4/os/trap.c

ISSIG_PENDING is one of several macros the system defines for speeding up the
examination of the process p_sig and kthread t_sig fields for the presence of a
posted signal.

```
/* Macro to reduce unnecessary calls to issig() */

#define ISSIG(t, why)   ISSIG_FAST(t, ttolwp(t), ttoproc(t), why)

/*
 * Fast version of ISSIG.
 *      1. uses register pointers to lwp and proc instead of reloading them.
 *      2. uses bit-wise OR of tests, since the usual case is that none of them
 *         are true; this saves orcc's and branches.
 *      3. loads the signal flags instead of using sigisempty() macro which does
 *         a branch to convert to boolean.
 */
#define ISSIG_FAST(t, lwp, p, why)              \
        (ISSIG_PENDING(t, lwp, p) && issig(why))

#define ISSIG_PENDING(t, lwp, p)                \
        ((lwp)->lwp_cursig |                    \
            sigcheck((p), (t)) |               \
            (p)->p_stopsig |                   \
            (t)->t_dtrace_stop |              \
            (t)->t_dtrace_sig |               \
            ((t)->t_proc_flag & (TP_PRSTOP|TP_HOLDLWP|TP_CHKPT|TP_PAUSE)) | \
            ((p)->p_flag & (SEXITLWPS|SKILLED|SHOLDFORK1|SHOLDWATCH)))
                                    See usr/src/uts/common/sys/proc.h
```

ISSIG and ISSIG_FAST resolve to ISSIG_PENDING, which performs a logical OR on the p_sig and t_sig fields (through sigcheck()), logically ANDing that result with the return value of issig(why).

The issig() function is the last bit of work the kernel does before actual signal delivery. The "why" argument passed to issig is one of JUSTLOOKING or FORREAL. The JUSTLOOKING flag causes issig() to return if a signal is pending, but the flag does not stop the process if a debugger requests a stop. In the case of a trap signal, issig() is passed FORREAL, which causes the process to be stopped if a stop has been requested or a traced signal is pending. Assuming no special debugger flags or signal tracing, the kernel invokes the psig() signal-delivery function to carry out the delivery phase according to the current disposition of the signal.

Once a signal has been posted, the existence of a signal must be made known to the process/thread so that action can be taken. When you consider that a signal is represented by the setting of a bit in a data structure, it seems intuitive that the kernel must periodically check for set bits (that is, pending signals). This is, in fact, precisely how delivery is done. The kernel checks for posted signals at several points during the typical execution flow of a process:

- Return from a system call
- Return from a trap
- Wake up from a sleep

In essence, the determination of the existence of a signal is a polling process by which the signal fields in the process p_sig and kthread t_sig fields are examined frequently for the presence of a set bit. Once it is determined that a signal is posted, the kernel can take appropriate action, based on the signal's current disposition in the context of the process that received it. In this instance (synchronous signals), a trap event occurred, and with the signal posted, the detection of the posted signal will happen on the return to trap_cleanup() (shown on the previous page). The kernel psig() code takes over to continue signal delivery.

When psig() is entered, the signal bit set when the signal was posted has been cleared, lwp_cursig contains the current signal number, and lwp_curinfo points to the siginfo structure for the signal. psig() does some checking to ensure that things have not changed since the signal was posted, and sets an internal variable, func, to the disposition of the signal from the process u_signal[] array. psig() also does some additional testing, to determine if the signal disposition has changed since the signal was posted or if the signal has been deferred, and updates various fields in the process object according to the signal type. psig() handles all cases in which the signal is ignored, or the default signal disposition is set, which typically involves the process exiting, exiting with a core file, stopping the process (job control), or ignoring the signal (see Table 2.7). psig() also increments the LWP resource usage nsignal counter. If a user signal handler has been defined, the kernel sendsig() function is called to set up the thread for running the user's signal handler.

Because sendsig() requires intimate knowledge of the process and thread internal organization, which vary according to processor type (SPARC or x64), sendsig() is defined in the platform-specific directories of the source tree. sendsig() essentially hand-crafts the execution environment for the user's signal handler, setting up the thread state such that control is passed to the signal handler when the execution context changes from kernel back up to user. sendsig() handles the setting up of an alternative thread stack if that option has been specified and manages the low-level hardware context setup (registers) for handler execution. When the thread context returns through the kernel call stack back to user mode, the point of execution is the user's installed signal handler.

The event flow for synchronous signals can be summarized as follows:

- An executing thread generates a fault condition as a direct result of the current instruction stream.

- The fault condition is detected and a system trap occurs. A trap is a vectored transfer of control to a kernel trap handler.

- The kernel trap handler determines the type of fault, gathers some information based on the fault type, and calls sigtoproc() to post a signal to the target thread.

- The thread is set up to check for signals, and, with a signal posted, `psig()` is called to complete signal delivery.

- `psig()` handles default signal dispositions. If a user-defined signal handler has been installed, `sendsig()` is called.

- `sendsig()` constructs the execution environment for the user's signal handler in the thread.

- When the thread returns to user mode, the user's signal handler executes.

2.11.1.2 Asynchronous Signals

Asynchronously generated (interrupt) signals can originate from a user command, program, or from somewhere inside the kernel. The `kill(1)` command can send a signal to a target process, the `kill(2)` system call or `pthread_kill(3C)` interface can send signals programatically, and signals can come from keyboard events for process termination (Control-C), job control (Control-Z), etc. When an asynchronous signal is generated, it is delivered to the first thread the kernel finds that is not masking the signal.

Using `dtrace(1)`, we can trace the execution flow through the kernel when a `kill(2)` system call is executed. The D script to do this is very simple.

```
#!/usr/sbin/dtrace -s
#pragma D option flowindent
syscall::kill:entry
/ pid == $target /
{
        self->t = 1;
}
fbt:::
/ self->t /
{
}
syscall::kill:return
/ self->t /
{
        self->t = 0;
        exit(0);
}
```

The D script uses a predicate on the `kill:entry` probe—we run our `kill(1)` command under control of this `dtrace` script, which sets the `$target` variable used in the predicate. Running a target process in the background, we execute the kill command,

```
sol10$ ./kill.d -c "kill -USR1 2667"
```

where `kill.d` is the D script name, and `2667` is the PID of a target process that was previously started and that has a signal handler installed for a `SIGUSR1`. Once the script is executed, we get a trace of the code path through the kernel to complete sending the signal.

```
CPU FUNCTION
  0   -> kill
  0     -> sigqkill
  0       -> prfind
  0         -> prfind_zone
  0           -> pid_lookup
  0           <- pid_lookup
  0         <- prfind_zone
  0       <- prfind
  0       -> sigsendproc
  0         -> prochasprocperm
  0           -> secpolicy_basic_proc
  0             -> priv_policy
  0             <- priv_policy
  0           <- secpolicy_basic_proc
  0           -> hasprocperm
  0           <- hasprocperm
  0         <- prochasprocperm
  0         -> getzoneid
  0         <- getzoneid
  0         -> crgetruid
  0         <- crgetruid
  0         -> sigaddq
  0           -> sig_discardable
  0           <- sig_discardable
  0           -> kmem_alloc
  0             -> kmem_cache_alloc
  0             <- kmem_cache_alloc
  0           <- kmem_alloc
  0           -> sigaddqins
  0           <- sigaddqins
  0           -> sigtoproc
  0             -> sig_discardable
  0             <- sig_discardable
  0             -> thread_lock
  0               -> uppc_setspl
  0               <- uppc_setspl
  0             <- thread_lock
  0             -> eat_signal
  0               -> signal_is_blocked
  0                 -> schedctl_sigblock
  0                 <- schedctl_sigblock
  0               <- signal_is_blocked
  0             <- eat_signal
  0             -> disp_lock_exit
  0               -> uppc_setspl
  0               <- uppc_setspl
  0             <- disp_lock_exit
  0           <- sigtoproc
  0         <- sigaddq
  0       <- sigsendproc
  0     <- sigqkill
  0   <- kill
```

kill(2) simply sets up a sigsend_t structure, setting the signal number and code value to signify that the signal originated from a user.

```
int
kill(pid_t pid, int sig)
{
        sigsend_t v;

        bzero(&v, sizeof (v));
        v.sig = sig;
        v.checkperm = 1;
        v.sicode = SI_USER;

        return (sigqkill(pid, sig, &v));
}
static int sigqkill(pid_t pid, int signo, sigsend_t *sigsend)
{
        register proc_t *p;
        int error;

        if (signo < 0 || signo >= NSIG)
                return (set_errno(EINVAL));

        if (pid == -1) {
                procset_t set;

                setprocset(&set, POP_AND, P_ALL, P_MYID, P_ALL, P_MYID);
                error = sigsendset(&set, sigsend);
        } else if (pid > 0) {
                mutex_enter(&pidlock);
                if ((p = prfind(pid)) == NULL || p->p_stat == SIDL)
                        error = ESRCH;
                else {
                        error = sigsendproc(p, sigsend);
                        if (error == 0 && sigsend->perm == 0)
                                error = EPERM;
                }
                mutex_exit(&pidlock);
. . .
```

See usr/src/uts/common/syscall/sigqueue.c

sigqkill() is called from kill(2) and does some basic checking for a valid signal number, does a lookup on the PID, and calls sigsendproc(); which checks credentials, updates the siginfo structure fields, and calls sigaddq(); which allocates a signal queue structure and calls sigaddqins(); which inserts the signal information into the queue. When sigaddqins() returns, sigtoproc() is called to post the signal.

We looked at sigtoproc() in the previous section. For a directed signal, the signal is posted to the target thread. Otherwise, the code loops through the list of threads in the process and posts the signal to the first thread that is not blocking it.

The eat_signal() function connects the dots between an external source (like the kill(1) command) posting a signal and forcing the target process (or thread)

to do one of two things—acknowledge the signal and execute the handler or take
the default disposition if a handler has not been installed.

```
eat_signal(kthread_t *t, int sig)
. . .
/*
        * Do not do anything if the target thread has the signal blocked.
        */
    if (!signal_is_blocked(t, sig)) {
            t->t_sig_check = 1;       /* have thread do an issig */
            if (t->t_state == TS_SLEEP && (t->t_flag & T_WAKEABLE)) {
                    setrun_locked(t);
                    rval = 1;
            } else if (t->t_state == TS_STOPPED && sig == SIGKILL) {
                    ttoproc(t)->p_stopsig = 0;
                    t->t_dtrace_stop = 0;
                    t->t_schedflag |= TS_XSTART | TS_PSTART;
                    setrun_locked(t);
            } else if (t != curthread && t->t_state == TS_ONPROC) {
                    if ((t != curthread) && (t->t_cpu != CPU))
                            poke_cpu(t->t_cpu->cpu_id);
                    rval = 1;
            } else if (t->t_state == TS_RUN) {
                    rval = 1;
            }

    }
. . .
```
                                                   See usr/src/uts/common/os/sig.c

    The target thread's t_sig_check flag is set, which forces the thread to run
issig(). If the target thread is sleeping, setrun_locked() forces a wakeup; the
thread checks for a signal on wakeup and enters psig() for delivery and handling of the signal. A stopped thread receiving a SIGKILL signal also gets nudged
with setrun_locked(). If the thread is currently running (TS_ONPROC), poke_
cpu() interrupts the processor the thread is running on, and the subsequent handler falls through the trap code where the thread checks for a signal and enters
psig(). Finally, if the thread is runnable (TS_RUN), eat_signal() returns to
sigtoproc(). If the t_sig_check bit is set in the thread, then when the thread
is selected by the dispatcher to run, it returns from the kernel, sees the t_sig_
check flag is set, and calls psig().

2.11.2 Observing Signal Activity

For the adventurous among you, using the dtrace fbt provider and tracking the
various signal-related functions in the kernel is always an option for drilling down
on signal support. All Solaris 10 systems ship with a wonderful set of dtrace
scripts in /usr/demo/dtrace, and the sig.d script tracks signal senders, recipi-
ents, signal types, and counts.

```
# dtrace -s ./sig.d
^C
                SENDER          RECIPIENT        SIG COUNT
                   ksh              mysig        16 1
                  sshd             dtrace         2 1
                  sshd                 sh         2 1
                 sched               Xorg        14 67
```

See /usr/demo/dtrace/sig.d

The output of sig.d is self-explanatory, and of course the script can be modified to focus on a specific process or thread.

The prstat(1) command can track the number of signals received for processes and threads.

```
PID USERNAME USR SYS TRP TFL DFL LCK SLP LAT VCX ICX SCL SIG PROCESS/NLWP
2883 mauroj  0.0 0.1 0.0 0.0 0.0 0.0 100 0.0  43   0 242   0 prstat/1
 664 mauroj  0.0 0.0 0.0 0.0 0.0 0.0 100 0.0  25   0  63   0 gnome-netsta/1
 473 mauroj  0.0 0.0 0.0 0.0 0.0 0.0 100 0.0  20   0  80  10 Xorg/1
 704 mauroj  0.0 0.0 0.0 0.0 0.0 0.0 100 0.0  21   0  51   0 gnome-termin/2
 . . .
```

The SIG column represents a count of the number of signals received in the last sampling period (5 seconds, by default).

2.11.3 Summary

Signals are a process and thread-notification mechanism, providing a framework used by the kernel when an executing thread generates a fault condition stemming from its instruction flow (synchronous signals) or from allowing external events to force a process or thread into a specific routine (asynchronous signals). Signals are commonly used in application code, wherein custom signal handlers are developed to manage events that may occur during the execution of the application code. Signals also provide the infrastructure for process control (start/stop), and various job control functions available in the system command-line interpreters (shells).

The implementation of signals in the kernel and support libraries is nontrivial, especially with support of multiple threads within a single process. Signal management is a delicate dance—a significant number of conditional tests and operations throughout the code are left unexplored in this text. A line-by-line exploration is an exercise for the reader.

On a related note, the signal flow explains why zombie processes cannot be killed (any horror movie fan knows you can't kill a zombie). A process must be executing in order to take delivery of a signal. A zombie process is, by definition, a process that has terminated. It exists only as a process table entry, with all of its execution state having been freed by the kernel (see `preap(1)` for cleaning up zombie processes).

2.12 Sessions and Process Groups

The kernel creates several groupings of processes representing different abstractions by which it manages various aspects of process control. In addition to the family hierarchy of process parent/child, the kernel implements *process groups* and links processes associated with the same terminal *session*. Both sessions and process groups are collections of one or more processes that have a common relationship or ancestry. The two abstractions, sessions and process groups, are intimately related to each other and tied closely to the signal and terminal (tty) subsystems.

Historically, process groups and sessions arose from the desire to increase the power and flexibility available to UNIX users: developers, systems administrators, and end users. The groups and sessions enable users to run multiple, concurrent jobs from a single login session, to place jobs in the background, bring them into the foreground, suspend and continue jobs, and toggle which job is actively connected to the control terminal (the foreground job).

The kernel maintains process groups and session links to establish an event notification chain in support of job control shells. The signal facility starts and stops processes (or *jobs* in this context), puts processes in the background, and brings them into the foreground. Using the process group linkage makes signal delivery to multiple, related processes much easier to implement. Adding the sessions abstraction puts a boundary between the process group jobs and the interactive login session.

Every process belongs to a process group, identified by the `p_pgidp` pointer in the process structure, and is established in the kernel fork code when the process is created. Thus, processes in the same parent/child/sibling chain, by default belong to the same process group. The process group ID (PGID) is the process PID of the process group leader. That is, every process group has a process group leader whose PID and PGID are the same. Sibling processes are assigned the PGID of the parent process; thus, the PGID of siblings will be the PID of the process group leader.

When a stand-alone process is started from a shell, it is placed in its own process group with the `setpgid(2)` system call, invoked from the shell code after the process is created with `fork(2)`. Processes grouped on a command line (for example, a pipeline) are all part of the same process group. The first process created becomes the process group leader of the new process group, and subsequent processes in the pipeline are added to the group. Here's a quick example.

```
ksh> cat report_file | sort -1 +2 | lp &
```

The shell in the above example is the Korn shell. Three processes are created, one each for cat(1), sort(1), and lp(1), and all are placed in the same process group. That group is put in the background, where the above *job* crunches away while an interactive user session continues. In this context, a job refers to processes in the same process group working toward a common goal and connected by pipes. The proper job control keystrokes (Control-Z in /bin/ksh) could stop all the processes in the group, sending a SIGTSTP signal to all the processes in the process group. The setpgid(2) system call places the processes in the same process group. Although process groups are most commonly created from the user's shell, an application program can use the setpgid(2) or setpgrp(2) system calls to create new process groups.

Process groups can be in the foreground or the background. The foreground process group is the process group that has access to the controlling terminal, meaning that input characters are sent to the foreground process group and output characters (writes to stdout and stderr) are sent to the controlling terminal. Background process groups cannot read from or write to the controlling terminal. An attempt to read from or write to the controlling terminal by a process in a background process group results in a SIGTTIN (read) or SIGTTOU (write) signal from the kernel to the processes in the background process group. The default disposition for these signals is to stop the processes.

Processes belonging to the same process group are linked on a doubly linked list by pointers in the process structure: p_pglink (points to the next process in the process group) and p_ppglink (points to the previous process). Figure 2.12 illustrates the process group links and the ID name space links (pointers to the PID structures).

Figure 2.12 illustrates a process as the only member of a process group (upper diagram), and three processes in the same process group (lower diagram). The processes in the lower diagram that are not the process group leader obtain their PGID by linking to the PID structure of the process group leader.

Process groups are a subset of *sessions*; a session has one or more process groups associated with it. A session abstracts a process and the process's control terminal and extends the abstraction to include process groups. All the process groups within a session have a common controlling terminal. Thus, all processes belong to a process group and are associated with a session. Sessions are

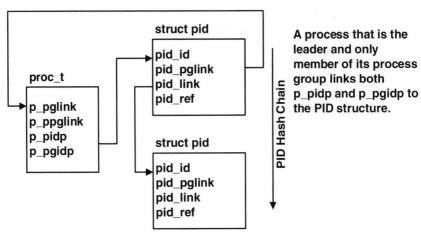

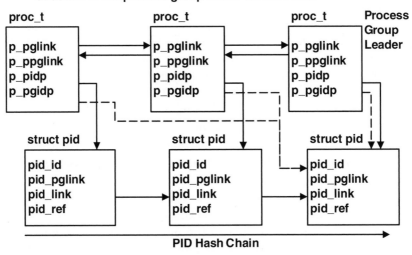

Figure 2.12 Process Groups

abstracted by the session data structure, which the process links to through its `p_sessp` pointer. As with process groups, sessions are inherited through the `fork()` code.

The control terminal is typically the login terminal the user connects to when logging in to a Solaris system. The phrase *control terminal* is more an abstraction these days (as opposed to an actual, physical terminal) because most login sessions are network based and the *terminal* is a window on the screen of a workstation, implemented by one of many terminal emulation utilities (xterm, dtterm, shelltool, cmdtool, etc.). Network logins (rlogin(1), telnet(1), etc.) are supported by pseudoterminals, which are software abstractions that provide terminal I/O semantics over a network link or through a window manager running under the X Window System. (X Windows is the network-transparent windowing system that virtually all UNIX vendors on the planet use for their graphical user interface (GUI)-based workstation environments.)

A control terminal is associated with a session, and a session can have only one control terminal associated with it. A control terminal can be associated with only one session. We sometimes refer to a session leader, which is the foreground process or process group that has established a connection to the control terminal. The session leader is usually the login shell of the user. The session leader directs certain input sequences (job control keystrokes and commands) from the control terminal to generate signals to process groups in the session associated with the controlling terminal. Every session has a session ID, which is the PGID of the session leader.

The session abstraction is implemented as a data structure, the session structure, and some support code in the kernel for creating sessions and managing the control terminal. The session structure includes the following:

- The device number of the control terminal device special file
- A pointer to the vnode for the control terminal device, which links to the snode, since it's a device
- UID and GID of the process that initiated the session
- A pointer to a credentials structure that describes the credentials of the process that initiated the session
- A reference count
- A link to a PID structure

The session ID is derived in the same way as the PGID for a process. That is, the session structure links to the PID structure of the process that is attached to the control terminal, the login shell in most cases. Note that daemon processes, which do not have a control terminal, have a NULL vnode pointer in the session structure. All processes thus link to a session structure, but processes without control terminals do not have the vnode link; that is, they have no connection to a control device driver.

Figure 2.13 illustrates a broad view, encapsulating a login session (a session) with a shell process in its own process group, plus three additional process groups. One process group is in the foreground, thus attached to the control terminal, receiving characters typed and able to write to the terminal screen. Job control

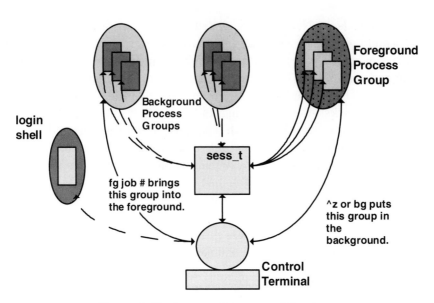

Figure 2.13 Process Groups and Sessions

shells use a ^Z (Control-Z) key sequence to place a foreground process/process group in the background. A SIGTSTP signal is sent to all the processes in the group, and the processes are stopped. If a process sets up a signal handler and catches SIGTSTP, the handler is invoked and governs the process behavior.

Figure 2.14 shows some details of the data structures and links for a simple case of a login session with two process groups. One process group has only one process, the login shell. The other process group has three processes. They all link to the session structure, which connects to the device and device driver through the s_vp vnode pointer. The session leader is the login shell, and the session ID is the PID of the login shell.

The session leader (for example, the shell) handles the communication link to the control terminal by using library calls that translate to ioctl() routines into the STREAMS subsystem. (The character device drivers in Solaris for serial terminals and pseudoterminals are STREAMS based.) The standard C library includes tcsetpgrp(3) and tcgetpgrp(3) interfaces for setting and getting the process group ID for a control terminal.

When processes or process groups are moved from the background into the foreground, the session leader issues a tcsetpgrp(3) call to direct the control terminal to the new foreground process. The tcsetpgrp(3) call results in an ioctl() call into the tty/pty driver code with the TIOCSPGRP flag, which in turn enters the STREAMS subsystem, calling the strsetpgrp() function (STREAM set process

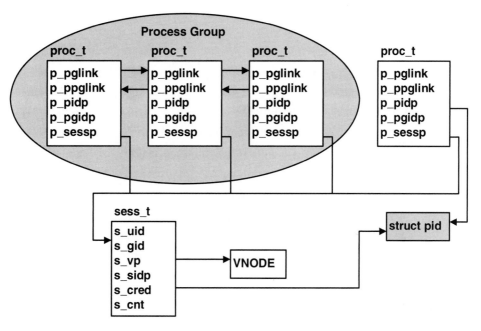

Figure 2.14 Process Group and Session Links

group). The data structures associated with the control terminal include a STREAM header structure, `stdata`, which contains a pointer to a PID structure for the foreground process group. When a new process or process group is placed into the foreground, the `sd_pgidp` pointer is set to reference the PID structure of the process group leader in the new foreground process group. In this way, the control terminal is dynamically attached to different process groups running under the same session.

The signal mechanism in the kernel that delivers signals to groups of processes is the same code used for other signal delivery. A `pgsignal()` (process group signal) interface is implemented in the kernel. The function follows the pointers that link processes in a process group and calls the generic `sigtoproc()` function in each pass through the loop, causing the signal to be posted to each process in the process group.

2.13 MDB Reference

Table 2.10 MDB Reference for Processes

dcmd or walker	Description
contract	Display a contract
ctid	Convert id to a contract pointer
mappings	Print address space mappings
nm	Print symbols
nmadd	Add name to private symbol table
nmdel	Remove name from private symbol table
objects	Print load objects information
pfiles	Print process file information
pgrep	Pattern match against all processes
pid2proc	Convert PID to proc_t address
pmap	Print process memory map
ps	List processes (and associated thr, lwp)
ptree	Print process tree
rctl	Print a rctl_t, only if it matches the handle
rctl_dict	Print systemwide default rctl definitions
rctl_list	Print rctls for the given proc
rctl_validate	Test resource control value sequence
seg	Print address space segment
thread	Display a summarized kthread_t
threadlist	Display threads and associated C stack traces
tsd	Print tsd[key-1] for this thread
tsdtot	Find thread with this tsd

Scheduling Classes and the Dispatcher

Contributions by Jonathan Chew, Eric Saxe, and Andrei Dorofeev

One of the core functions of any modern multitasking operating system is the management and scheduling of runnable threads onto available processors. The kernel's primary goal is to maintain fairness: allowing all threads to get processor cycles while ensuring that critical work, such as interrupt handling, gets done as needed. This is the function of the kernel dispatcher—selecting threads and dispatching them to available system processors. The threads will be in one of several possible scheduling classes, by which the thread's priority is established relative to all other threads on the system. Multiple scheduling classes provide a powerful and flexible mechanism for managing various workloads with different scheduling requirements and making efficient use of the system's processors.

In this chapter, we look in detail at the kernel dispatcher, examining run queue management, thread selection, and several other functions performed by the dispatcher. We discuss the supported scheduling classes and describe the scheduling algorithms and how they differ across the various scheduling classes and where they fit in the systemwide global priority scheme. The thread sleep and wakeup mechanism is an integral part of the scheduling management subsystem, and we cover it in this chapter as well.

3.1 Fundamentals

The kernel dispatcher is the code that places runnable threads on a dispatch queue (run queue), selects the next thread to run on a processor, and manages the switching of threads on and off processors. A thread's priority determines how soon it will run, and the kernel implements a global priority scheme that selects the highest-priority runnable thread from all other runnable threads at any time. Every thread is in one of several possible scheduling classes; this arrangement determines the range of priorities for the thread, as well as which class-specific scheduling algorithms will be applied as the thread goes through its state transitions.

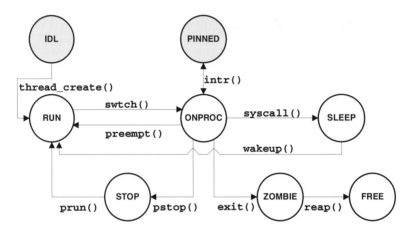

Figure 3.1 Thread States

By and large, the life cycle of a thread is typically spent in the ready-to-run (RUN) state, running (ONPROC) state, and waiting-for-an-event (SLEEP) state. A thread's transition between these states in managed largely by the dispatcher. The PINNED and IDL states in the figure are represented in shaded circles because they are not technically thread states. The states are defined as follows.

```
/*
 * Values that t_state may assume. Note that t_state cannot have more
 * than one of these flags set at a time.
 */
#define TS_FREE      0x00   /* Thread at loose ends */
#define TS_SLEEP     0x01   /* Awaiting an event */
#define TS_RUN       0x02   /* Runnable, but not yet on a processor */
#define TS_ONPROC    0x04   /* Thread is being run on a processor */
#define TS_ZOMB      0x08   /* Thread has died but hasn't been reaped */
#define TS_STOPPED   0x10   /* Stopped, initial state */

                    See usr/src/uts/common/sys/thread.h
```

IDL is a *process state* set when a *process* is created. A thread that is in the ONPROC state is *pinned* when the processor on which the thread is executing fields an interrupt. The processor switches to running an interrupt thread, temporarily moving aside (pinning) the thread that was running. This is discussed in Section 3.11.

As Figure 3.1 suggests, the core of the dispatcher's work can be described as a queue management system. All threads in the RUN state reside on dispatch queues, and all threads in the SLEEP state reside on a sleep queue. The available processors on the system can also be thought of as a queue of resources (execution resources in this case). Thus, we can summarize the core functions of the dispatcher as follows:

- **Queue management.** Insert and remove threads from the dispatch queues.
- **Thread selection.** Determine which thread among all runnable threads will next execute on a processor.
- **Processor selection.** Choose the processor on which a thread will run. In some instances, the dispatcher may need to do this.
- **Context switching.** Place a thread on a processor in preparation for execution (switch on) or the removal of a thread from a processor (switch off). This is referred to as a context switch because the processor sees one thread leave and another arrive, so the execution context changes.

Scheduling decisions and actions taken by the dispatcher code are either *time based* or *event based*. That is, some dispatcher functions occur synchronously at regular intervals, while others are asynchronous, originating at random times while the system is running.

The time-based work is through the kernel clock interrupt mechanism and callout facility. By default, a clock interrupt occurs 100 times per second (every 10 milliseconds). The clock interrupt handler processes the running threads and determines their time quantum expiration. Also in the kernel callout queue are dispatcher kernel threads that execute at regular intervals.

Events of interest to the dispatcher originate from many places: the creation of a new thread, thread wakeups, etc. Such events may require a thread preemption, which forces the dispatcher to remove a thread running on a processor to make the processor available to run a higher-priority thread.

A detailed look at the time-based and event-based work performed by the dispatcher is just around the corner, so stay with us.

Different workloads have different scheduling and execution requirements. By default, a Solaris system prioritizes and runs threads on a time-share basis, attempting to maintain an even distribution of processor resources among the threads. A Solaris desktop system—a workstation or notebook computer running a windowing system—runs threads on a time-share basis as well but accords an extra priority boost for threads bound to active windows on the user's computer. This is done with the interactive *scheduling class.*

Solaris implements several scheduling classes that constitute a powerful and flexible infrastructure for managing a variety of workloads by establishing the range of priorities a thread will be assigned, as well as which set of scheduling rules will apply. The following scheduling classes are integrated into Solaris 10:

- **Timeshare (TS).** Priority adjustments are made based on the time a thread spends waiting for processor resources or consuming processor resources, and the thread's time quantum (the maximum amount of time the thread can execute on the processor) varies according to its priority.

- **Interactive (IA).** IA is the same as timeshare, with the addition of a mechanism that boosts the priority of a thread connected to the active window on a desktop.

- **Fair Share (FSS).** Available processor cycles are divided into units called shares, and administrative tools allocate shares to processes using the Solaris projects and tasks framework. A thread in the FSS class has its priority adjusted according to its share allocation, recent utilization, and shares consumed by other threads in the FSS class.

- **Fixed Priority (FX).** The assigned priority is not changed or adjusted over the lifetime of the thread.

- **Real Time (RT).** Real-time threads occupy the highest range of assignable priorities. Real-time scheduling provides the fastest possible dispatch latency—the elapsed time between an RT thread becoming runnable and getting scheduled onto a processor.

- **System (SYS).** The kernel uses this class for the execution of operating system threads. The priority range occupied by the SYS class is higher than all other scheduling classes, with the exception of the real-time class.

For the dispatcher to make the appropriate scheduling decisions with thousands of threads at different priorities and scheduling classes, a global priority scheme is required. Every thread has a global priority, allowing the dispatcher to determine its position relative to all other threads on the system.

In addition to priority, other conditions and configuration parameters factor into dispatcher scheduling decisions. These can be broadly categorized as resource management parameters and system architecture.

Resource management refers to a set of technologies integrated into Solaris that provide the framework, tools, and utilities for allocating and managing different amounts of hardware resources. From the kernel dispatcher perspective, the effects on scheduling decisions have to do with some form of binding or affinity between processors and threads. The specific resource controls are listed below.

- **Processor binding.** Binds processes to processors. The dispatcher would naturally need to honor a user-defined binding and ensure that bound processes have their threads scheduled onto the designated processor.
- **Processor sets.** Enables the creation of one or more user-defined processor sets, comprising some subset of the total number of installed processors (introduced in Solaris 2.6). Use of processor sets requires explicit binding of processes to the set.
- **Resource Pools.** Are essentially stateful processor sets (introduced in Solaris 9). The dispatcher accounts for resource pools and process bindings when it schedules threads.
- **Zones.** Provides a virtualized execution environment. Solaris can bind a resource pool to a zone; thus, the dispatcher needs to honor such bindings when making scheduling decisions about threads running in a zone.

The second category, system architecture, refers to enhancements and optimizations made to the dispatcher code to account for the architectural nuances of the system. A good example of this is Memory Placement Optimization (MPO). MPO was introduced in Solaris 9; it mitigates the effects of systems with nonuniform memory access times by scheduling threads onto processors that are close to the thread's allocated physical memory. MPO is described in *Kernel Support for NUMA* and *CMT Hardware*.

A second, and more recent, architectural consideration is chip technology. Specifically the implementation of chip multithreading (CMT) processors, which integrate multiple execution pipelines (cores) and multiple hardware threads per core on a single piece of silicon. Sun's UltraSPARC T1 processor is a CMT design, with eight execution pipelines and four hardware threads per pipeline. To the Solaris kernel, a single UltraSPARC T1 chip appears as 32 processors (8 cores times 4 hardware threads per core—each hardware thread is viewed as a processor by the kernel dispatcher). The dispatcher has been modified to accommodate certain implementation details of the hardware design, such as the level of sharing of hardware resources among the cores (caches, data paths, etc.) to minimize contention, while at the same time maintaining cache warmth through judicious assignments of threads to cores. CMT is discussed in Chapter 16.

The idea of placing unbound threads on the processor on which they last executed is not new. The kernel dispatcher implemented *warm affinity* as early as Solaris 2.5. The idea again is that a thread placed back on the same processor has a better probability of finding a *warm cache*—a hardware cache that has some of the thread's instructions and data, thus reducing pipeline stalls for memory references.

As we move through the remainder of this chapter, we explore the topics introduced here in greater detail:

- Processor abstractions and groupings in the kernel
- Organization of the dispatcher queues and queue management
- Core kernel dispatcher functions for selecting threads
- Variables and parameters involved in scheduling decisions
- Global priority scheme
- Scheduling classes—priorities and algorithms
- Sleep and wakeup queues and queue management

3.2 Processor Abstractions

The kernel dispatcher primarily manages two types of objects: threads and processors. Threads were discussed in the previous chapter. Before we probe the internals of the dispatcher, we need a clear view of how hardware processors (CPUs) are abstracted and a definition of what specific groupings of processors are maintained in the kernel.

Previous releases of Solaris defined a cpu structure (cpu_t), and a one-to-one mapping existed between physical processors and instantiated cpu_t structures in the kernel. The cpu_t maintains information required by the dispatcher and kernel-at-large for thread scheduling, interrupt handling, CPU state transitions, utilization and accounting, processor groupings, and administrative controls (psradm(1M)). Processor resource control facilities—processor sets and resource pools—are implemented through abstractions in the kernel that define groups of processors. Multicore processor technology and multiprocessor system designs introduced architectural considerations that require visibility by the kernel; thus, some new abstractions were needed for the kernel to take full advantage of new processors and systems.

The following processor-related abstractions are defined and maintained in the kernel:

- **cpu_t.** A processor abstraction. Each cpu_t instantiated in the kernel is viewed by the dispatcher as an execution resource for a thread.
- **chip_t.** The kernel representation of a physical processor chip. Chips with multiple execution cores have a cpu_t for each core. One or more cpu_t

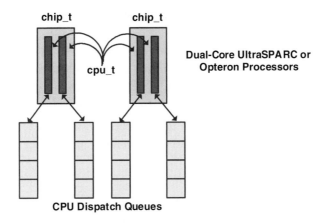

Figure 3.2 Chips and CPUs

structures are linked to the `chip_t`, affording the kernel a view of which CPUs are associated with which chip. The `chip_t` was originally implemented to make the kernel aware of which `cpu_t`s share physical processors. With the introduction of multithreaded, multicore processors, the `chip_t` use was extended to track load and facilitate load balancing across groups of `cpu_t`s sharing processing cores. Chips with multiple cores and multiple hardware threads per core (for example, UltraSPARC T1) will have a `chip_t` per core and a `cpu_t` for each hardware thread per core. A Sun Fire T2000 system with an 8-core UltraSPARC T1 chip will have eight `chip_t` structures and four `cpu_t` structures per `chip_t`, so the kernel view is 32 (8 × 4) logical CPUs on which threads can be scheduled.

The `chip_t` object provides various structure members used by the dispatcher for load balancing, assigning chips into latency groups (lgroups—more on that in a minute), maintaining per-chip statistics, and identifying an enumerated chip type that can be used to make scheduling decisions based on the shared resources implemented in the chip, for example, shared hardware caches. The chip types are enumerated below.

```
typedef enum chip_type {
        CHIP_DEFAULT,             /* Default, non CMT processor */
        CHIP_SMT,                 /* SMT, single core */
        CHIP_CMP_SPLIT_CACHE,     /* CMP with split caches */
        CHIP_CMP_SHARED_CACHE,    /* CMP with shared caches */
        CHIP_NUM_TYPES
} chip_type_t;

                                 See usr/src/uts/common/sys/chip.h
```

- **CHIP_DEFAULT.** A traditional processor chip with one execution core and one thread per core.

- **CHIP_SMT.** A symmetric multithread chip—a chip with more than one execution core, where each core is visible to the kernel as a logical processor (a cpu_t). The logical processors on an SMT chip share an execution pipeline and typically share instruction and data caches and other chip resources.

- **CHIP_CMP_SPLIT_CACHE.** A chip multiprocessor, where each CMP chip contains multiple execution cores, and each core is represented by a cpu_t and is visible to the kernel as a logical CPU. For CMP designs with some level of dedicated (nonshared) cache per core.

- **CHIP_CMP_SHARED_CACHE.** As above, but a CMP design with shared hardware caches. The UltraSPARC T1 processor is an example of this type.

You can determine the kernel's defined chip type for your system by using mdb(1).

```
An UltraSPARC II-based system:

# mdb -k
> ::walk cpu |::print cpu_t cpu_chip |::print chip_t chip_type
chip_type = 0 (CHIP_DEFAULT)
chip_type = 0 (CHIP_DEFAULT)
. . .
chip_type = 0 (CHIP_DEFAULT)

# prtdiag | more
System Configuration:  Sun Microsystems   sun4u 8-slot Sun Enterprise 4000/5000
System clock frequency: 84 MHz
Memory size: 4096Mb

========================= CPUs =========================

                    Run    Ecache    CPU     CPU
Brd   CPU   Module  MHz      MB     Impl.   Mask
---   ---   ------  ----   ------   ------  ----
 0     0      0     336     4.0     US-II    2.0
 0     1      1     336     4.0     US-II    2.0
 . . .

A T2000 UltraSPARC T1 based system:
# mdb -k
> ::walk cpu |::print cpu_t cpu_chip |::print chip_t chip_type
chip_type = 3 (CHIP_CMP_SHARED_CACHE)
chip_type = 3 (CHIP_CMP_SHARED_CACHE)
chip_type = 3 (CHIP_CMP_SHARED_CACHE)
 . . .

# prtdiag | more
System Configuration:  Sun Microsystems   sun4v Sun Fire T200
System clock frequency: 200 MHz
Memory size: 32760 Megabytes
```

continues

```
========================= CPUs ==================================================

                              CPU                   CPU
Location      CPU    Freq     Implementation        Mask
------------  -----  -------- -------------------   -----
MB/CMP0/P0      0 1200 MHz    SUNW,UltraSPARC-T1
MB/CMP0/P1      1 1200 MHz    SUNW,UltraSPARC-T1
. . .
```

A CPU will belong to one of the CPU groupings listed here:

- **CPU partitions.** A kernel abstraction consisting of a set of CPUs and partition-wide kernel preempt (kp) dispatch queue. At system initialization (boot) time, all CPUs belong to the default (system) partition. The system partition is not visible to users.

- **Processor sets.** A user-level abstraction of a set of one or more processors. Processor sets are implemented internally as CPU partitions. Currently, there is a 1-to-1 mapping between processor sets and CPU partitions, with the exception of the default partition. Processor sets are created and managed with the psrset(1) command.

- **Resource pools.** A resource pool is essentially a stateful processor set. Processor sets created with psrset(1) are stateless—the kernel does not create or maintain nonvolatile state for processor sets; thus, created sets and process/thread bindings are lost if the system is restarted. Resource pools, introduced in Solaris 9, address this by maintaining on-disk state, as well as by adding additional features, such as the ability to bind a scheduling class to a resource pool. In the kernel, the CPU grouping configured as a resource pool's processor set is, in fact, a CPU partition. Simply put, internally, processor sets created with psrset(1) and processor sets assigned to a resource pool are both instantiated as CPU partitions. A resource pool may also assigned to a Solaris 10 Zone.

- **Locality groups (lgroups).** Solaris 9 included a feature called memory placement optimization (MPO). The goal of MPO is to mitigate the performance effects of systems with nonuniform memory access (NUMA) times. The kernel needs to know which CPUs and memory banks are close to each other so that it can optimize for locality—keep threads on CPUs close to the thread's memory. The implementation of MPO is through the kernel locality group abstraction. An lgroup is an object in the kernel that presents a grouping of processors and memory that exist within a bound latency to each other.
    Lgroups are organized into a hierarchy or topology that represents the latency topology of the machine. There is always at least a root lgroup in the system. It represents all the hardware resources in the machine at a latency

large enough that any hardware resource can at least access any other hardware resource within that latency. A Uniform Memory Access (UMA) machine is represented with one lgroup (the root). In contrast, a NUMA machine is represented at least by the root lgroup and some number of leaf lgroups, where the leaf lgroups contain the hardware resources within the least latency of each other, and the root lgroup still contains all the resources in the machine.

CPUs are assigned to lgroups at system initialization time according to platform-specific code that creates the lgroups as the architectural characteristics of the system dictate. As an example, a high-end Sun Fire server is configured with one or more system boards, where each system board is populated with CPUs and memory. Such systems will create an lgroup for each system board.

The kernel uses the lgroup abstraction to know how to allocate resources near a given process/thread. At `fork()` and `lwp/thread_create()` time, a "home" lgroup is chosen for a thread. The kernel dispatcher does this by picking the lgroup with the lowest load average. Binding to a processor or processor set changes the home lgroup for a thread. The scheduler has been modified to try to dispatch a thread on a CPU in its home lgroup. Physical memory allocation is lgroup aware, so memory is allocated from the current thread's home lgroup if possible. If the desired resources are not available, the kernel traverses the lgroup hierarchy, going to the parent lgroup to find resources at the next level of locality until it reaches the root lgroup.

The `cpu_t` structure in the kernel maintains several linked lists to locate all the CPUs in a processor set or lgroup.

```
/*
 * Per-CPU data.
 */
typedef struct cpu {
        processorid_t   cpu_id;                 /* CPU number */
...

        /*
         * Links to other CPUs.  It is safe to walk these lists if
         * one of the following is true:
         *      - cpu_lock held
         *      - preemption disabled via kpreempt_disable
         *      - PIL >= DISP_LEVEL
         *      - acting thread is an interrupt thread
         *      - all other CPUs are paused
         */
        struct cpu      *cpu_next;              /* next existing CPU */
        struct cpu      *cpu_prev;              /* prev existing CPU */
        struct cpu      *cpu_next_onln;         /* next online (enabled) CPU */
        struct cpu      *cpu_prev_onln;         /* prev online (enabled) CPU */
        struct cpu      *cpu_next_part;         /* next CPU in partition */
        struct cpu      *cpu_prev_part;         /* prev CPU in partition */
```

continues

```
          struct cpu      *cpu_next_lgrp;      /* next CPU in latency group */
          struct cpu      *cpu_prev_lgrp;      /* prev CPU in latency group */
          struct cpu      *cpu_next_chip;      /* next CPU on chip */
          struct cpu      *cpu_prev_chip;      /* prev CPU on chip */
          struct cpu      *cpu_next_lpl;       /* next CPU in lgrp partition */
          struct cpu      *cpu_prev_lpl;
   ...
   }
                                            See usr/src/uts/common/sys/cpuvar.h
```

Note two sets of lgroup-related pointers, `cpu_next_lgrp` and `cpu_next_lpl` (and their respective prev pointers). An lgroup can be partitioned when the CPUs in the lgroup reside in different CPU partitions (processor sets). An lgroup partition partition represents the intersection of an lgroup and processor set, as shown in Figure 3.3. The scheduling implications of dealing with lgroup partitions is discussed in Section 3.9

In Figure 3.3, CPUs 2, 4, 6, and 8 are in a user-created processor set spanning two lgroups. CPUs 2 and 4 would be on one `cpu_[next|prev]_lpl list`, and CPUs 6 and 8 on another. CPUs 2, 4, 6 and 8 would be linked togther on each `cpu_[next|prev]_part` list. CPUs 1, 2, 3, and 4 would be linked in the `cpu_[next|prev]_lgrp` pointer chain (as would CPUs 4, 5, 6, and 7). Maintaining multiple linked lists that reflect different group abstractions (partitions, lgroups, and lgroup partitions) simplifies operations from the dispatcher and the kernel-at-

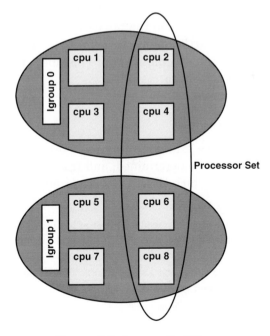

Figure 3.3 Lgroup Partitions

large that target a CPU group abstraction, such as determining the size and membership of a specific grouping of interest. For example, the dispatcher uses these lists to determine on what CPUs in a given lgroup a thread bound to a particular processor set could be legally scheduled to run on.

The `chip_t` objects are also linked in several useful ways.

```
typedef struct chip {
        chipid_t        chip_id;            /* chip's "id" */
        chipid_t        chip_seqid;         /* sequential id */
        struct chip     *chip_prev;         /* previous chip on list */
        struct chip     *chip_next;         /* next chip on list */
        struct chip     *chip_prev_lgrp;    /* prev chip in lgroup */
        struct chip     *chip_next_lgrp;    /* next chip in lgroup */
        chip_type_t     chip_type;          /* type of chip */
        uint16_t        chip_ncpu;          /* number of active cpus */
        uint16_t        chip_ref;           /* chip's reference count */
        struct cpu      *chip_cpus;         /* per chip cpu list */
        struct lgrp     *chip_lgrp;         /* chip lives in this lgroup */
...

                                        See usr/src/uts/common/sys/chip.h
```

A CPU can belong to only one partition and lgroup at any time. CPUs in the same lgroup can be part of different partitions (such as a user-defined processor set or resource pool). All the CPUs in a `chip_t` belong to the same lgroup as the chip. In Section 3.9, we walk through the process of selecting which CPU's dispatch queue a thread will be inserted on, given configured partitions and lgroups and the possibility of user-defined thread-to-CPU bindings.

At the thread level, several fields in the `thread_t` structure maintain information on CPU bindings, the partition that contains the thread, and the thread's lgroup affinity. We examine the specific structure members in Section 3.9 as we go through the CPU selection algorithm.

3.2.1 Processor Observability

In the next few pages we have examples of lgroup observability[1]—how the CPUs and lgroup configurations can be determined, and tracking the execution of all the threads in a target—showing which CPUs in which lgroups execute the threads.

---

1. Solaris kernel engineering has created a wonderful set of tools targeting lgroup observability and control, including an lgroup-aware Perl module. You can find the tools, along with detailed descriptions of their use, on the OpenSolaris Web site:

    `http://www.opensolaris.org/os/community/performance/numa/observability/`

    The tool set includes some very useful DTrace scripts:

    `http://www.opensolaris.org/os/community/performance/numa/observability/dtrace/`

    We encourage you to spend time on this site and to download and use the tools provided.

Using `mdb(1)`, we can examine a running system and determine which CPUs are members of which lgroups and partitions.

```
Example from a Sun v40Z 4-way Opteron based system:

> ::walk cpu |::print cpu_t cpu_lpl |::print lgrp_t lgrp_id
lgrp_id = 0x1
lgrp_id = 0x2
lgrp_id = 0x3
lgrp_id = 0x4

Example from a Sun Fire T2000 8-core UltraSPARC T1 based system:

> ::walk cpu |::print cpu_t cpu_lpl |::print lgrp_t lgrp_id
lgrp_id = 0
lgrp_id = 0
...
lgrp_id = 0
lgrp_id = 0
```

Note in the Sun Fire T2000 example, most of the lines were cut for brevity. All 32 virtual CPUs are in the same lgroup (0) because the T2000 has a uniform memory access architecture.

Here's a handy script created by Jon Haslam (author of the DTrace chapter in *Solaris™ Performance and Tools*) that reports the lgroup of a particular process and dumps the CPUs and lgroups configured on the system.

```
# cat getlgrp
/usr/ucb/echo -n "PID $1 lgrp = "
echo "0t$1::pid2proc | ::walk thread | ::print -t kthread_t t_lpl | \
::print struct lgrp_ld lpl_lgrpid" | mdb -k

echo
echo "CPUs on system"
echo "cpus::list cpu_t cpu_next | ::print cpu_t cpu_id" | mdb -k

echo
echo "... and their lgrps"
echo "cpus::list cpu_t cpu_next | ::print -t struct cpu cpu_lpl | \
::print -t struct lgrp_ld lpl_lgrpid" | mdb -k

# ./getlgrp $$
PID 3321 lgrp = lpl_lgrpid = 0x1

CPUs on system
cpu_id = 0
cpu_id = 0x1
cpu_id = 0x2
cpu_id = 0x3

... and their lgrps
lgrp_id_t lpl_lgrpid = 0x1
lgrp_id_t lpl_lgrpid = 0x2
lgrp_id_t lpl_lgrpid = 0x3
lgrp_id_t lpl_lgrpid = 0x4
```

The kernel maintains statistics on lgroups through the kstats framework, and these can be examined on a running system to track load, migrations (number of times a thread was migrated to the lgroup), and memory events.

```
# kstat -m lgrp -n lgrp4
module: lgrp                            instance: 4
name:   lgrp4                           class:    misc
        alloc fail                      2
        cpus                            1
        crtime                          252.646499713
        default policy                  0
        load average                    65516
        lwp migrations                  44
        next-touch policy               119290
        pages avail                     2097152
        pages failed to mark            0
        pages failed to migrate from    0
        pages failed to migrate to      0
        pages free                      2078708
        pages installed                 2097152
        pages marked for migration      0
        pages migrated from             0
        pages migrated to               0
        random policy                   15584
        round robin policy              0
        snaptime                        679637.602945989
        span process policy             0
        span psrset policy              0
```

And, of course, we can use DTrace to track which CPUs and lgrps the thread was scheduled on:

```
#!/usr/sbin/dtrace -qs

sched:::on-cpu
/ pid == $1/
{
        self->lgrp = curthread->t_cpu->cpu_chip->chip_lgrp->lgrp_id;
        @[tid,self->lgrp,cpu]=count();
}
END
{
        printf("Threads CPUs and lgrps for PID %d\n",pid);
        printf("%-8s %-8s %-8s %-8s\n","TID","LGRP","CPUID","COUNT");
        printf("==================================\n");
        printa("%-8d %-8d %-8d %-@8d\n",@);
}

# ./lgrp.d 3416
^C
Threads CPUs and lgrps for PID 3416
TID      LGRP     CPUID    COUNT
==================================
1        2        1        1
2        2        1        1014
5        3        2        1149
```

continues

```
4          3          2        1193
3          2          1        1313
3          1          0        1460
3          3          2        1465
5          4          3        1820
2          1          0        1898
  . . .
```

The D script above was saved in a file called `lgrp.d` and executed to track process 3416. The aggregation shows the number of times (COUNT) a given thread (TID) executed on a particular CPU and lgroup. We can see from the output that each thread is getting a respectable number of runs on a given CPU, but some migration is also happening, likely the result of load balancing by the dispatcher.

3.3 Dispatcher Queues, Structures, and Variables

Dispatcher queues, or run queues, are linked lists of runnable kernel threads (threads in the RUN state), waiting to be selected by the dispatcher for execution on a processor. Solaris implements per-processor dispatch queues; that is, every processor on a Solaris system is initialized with its own set of dispatcher queues. The queues are organized as an array of queues, where a separate linked list of threads is maintained for each global priority. The per-processor queue arrangement improves scalability, eliminating the potential for a highly contended mutex lock that would be required for a global, systemwide queue. Additionally, per-processor queues simplify managing affinity and binding of threads to processors, since bound threads are simply placed on the dispatch queue of the processor to which they are bound.

Processors with more than one execution core per processor, such as Sun's UltraSPARC IV+, which has two cores per processor chip, have a dispatch queue per core. That is, the kernel configures each execution core as a processor. Sun's Sun Fire T1000 and T2000 servers, based on the UltraSPARC T1, are configured such that each hardware thread is a processor to the kernel dispatcher. For the typical configuration of a fully loaded T1000 or T2000, with eight execution cores, each with four hardware threads per core, Solaris will configure (8 × 4) 32 processors, each with its own set of dispatch queues.

These per-processor queues are used for threads in all scheduling classes, with the exception of real-time threads. The real-time scheduling class offers a unique set of features for applications with specific requirements. For optimal support for real-time, real-time threads are placed on a special set of dispatcher queues, called kernel preemption queues, or *kp queues*. Whenever a real-time thread is placed on a kp queue, a kernel preemption is generated, forcing the processor to enter the scheduler (see Section 3.9).

3.3.1 Dispatcher Structures

The dispatcher uses several data structures and per-structure variables to perform the tasks of thread management, queue management, and scheduling. These tasks are quite complex, especially on systems with multiple processors running workloads with hundreds or thousands of active threads. Resource management facilities for pools of processors and binding, dynamic reconfiguration capabilities, and processor state changes (offline, online) all combine to make dispatcher functions a delicate dance that required some brilliant engineering to maintain correctness while providing excellent performance and scalability.

The dispatcher uses the following data structures and variables:

- **cpu_t.** There is a cpu_t structure for every processor in a system. In addition to several dispatcher-specific variables within the cpu_t structure itself, the cpu_t links to a disp_t structure that maintains additional per-processor dispatcher information, as well as a link to the processor's actual dispatch queues.

```
/*
 * Scheduling variables.
 */
disp_t          *cpu_disp;              /* dispatch queue data */
/*
 * Note that cpu_disp is set before the CPU is added to the system
 * and is never modified.  Hence, no additional locking is needed
 * beyond what's necessary to access the cpu_t structure.
 */
char            cpu_runrun;     /* scheduling flag - set to preempt */
char            cpu_kprunrun;          /* force kernel preemption */
pri_t           cpu_chosen_level;      /* priority at which cpu */
                                       /* was chosen for scheduling */
kthread_t       *cpu_dispthread; /* thread selected for dispatch */
disp_lock_t     cpu_thread_lock; /* dispatcher lock on current thread */
uint8_t         cpu_disp_flags; /* flags used by dispatcher */
/*
 * The following field is updated whenever the cpu_dispthread
 * changes. Also in places, where the current thread(cpu_dispthread)
 * priority changes. This is used in disp_lowpri_cpu()
 */
pri_t           cpu_dispatch_pri; /* priority of cpu_dispthread */
clock_t         cpu_last_swtch; /* last time switched to new thread */

                        See usr/src/uts/common/sys/cpuvar.h
```

- **cpupart_t.** This structure is part of the framework for processor partitions, which is how processor sets are defined internally. Processor sets are a facility for grouping one or more processors on a multiprocessor system into a user-defined processor set. Processes and threads can be explicitly bound to the processors in the set, providing a means of partitioning processor resources for applications and workloads.

```
typedef struct cpupart {
        disp_t          cp_kp_queue;    /* partition-wide kpreempt queue */
        cpupartid_t     cp_id;          /* partition ID */
        int             cp_ncpus;       /* number of online processors */
        struct cpupart  *cp_next;       /* next partition in list */
        struct cpupart  *cp_prev;       /* previous partition in list */
        struct cpu      *cp_cpulist;    /* processor list */
        struct kstat    *cp_kstat;      /* per-partition statistics */

        /*
         * cp_nrunnable and cp_nrunning are used to calculate load average.
         */
        uint_t          cp_nrunnable;   /* current # of runnable threads */
        uint_t          cp_nrunning;    /* current # of running threads */

        /*
         * cp_updates, cp_nrunnable_cum, cp_nwaiting_cum, and cp_hp_avenrun
         * are used to generate kstat information on an as-needed basis.
         */
        uint64_t        cp_updates;         /* number of statistics updates */
        uint64_t        cp_nrunnable_cum;   /* cum. # of runnable threads */
        uint64_t        cp_nwaiting_cum;    /* cum. # of waiting threads */

        struct loadavg_s cp_loadavg;        /* cpupart loadavg */

        klgrpset_t      cp_lgrpset;     /* set of lgroups on which this */
                                        /*     partition has cpus */
        lpl_t           cp_lgrploads[NLGRPS_MAX];
                                        /* table of load averages for this  */
                                        /*     partition, indexed by lgrp ID */
        uint64_t        cp_hp_avenrun[3]; /* high-precision load average */
        uint_t          cp_attr;        /* bitmask of attributes */
        lgrp_gen_t      cp_gen;         /* generation number */
#if defined(_MACHDEP)
        /*
         * These guarded members must reside at the end of the structure
         */
        cpuset_t        cp_haltset;     /* bitmask of halted cpus */
        chip_set_t      cp_chipset;     /* set of chips spanned by this part */
#endif   /* _MACHDEP */
} cpupart_t;
                                        See usr/src/uts/common/sys/cpupart.h
```

- **dispq_t.** A dispatch queue, linking to the first and last thread in the queue, along with counting the runnable threads on the queue.

```
* The following is the format of a dispatcher queue entry.
*/
typedef struct dispq {
kthread_t       *dq_first;      /* first thread on queue or NULL */
kthread_t       *dq_last;       /* last thread on queue or NULL */
int             dq_sruncnt;     /* number of loaded, runnable */
                                /*     threads on queue */

} dispq_t;

                                See usr/src/uts/common/sys/disp.h
```

- **disp_t.** Per-processor variables on the state of the processor's dispatch queues, including a link to the dispatch queue.

```
typedef struct _disp {
disp_lock_t      disp_lock;       /* protects dispatching fields */
pri_t            disp_npri;       /* # of priority levels in queue */
dispq_t          *disp_q;         /* the dispatch queue */
dispq_t          *disp_q_limit;   /* ptr past end of dispatch queue */
ulong_t          *disp_qactmap;   /* bitmap of active dispatch queues */

/*
 * Priorities:
 *      disp_maxrunpri is the maximum run priority of runnable threads
 *      on this queue.  It is -1 if nothing is runnable.
 *
 *      disp_max_unbound_pri is the maximum run priority of threads on
 *      this dispatch queue but runnable by any CPU.  This may be left
 *      artificially high, then corrected when some CPU tries to take
 *      an unbound thread.  It is -1 if nothing is runnable.
 */
pri_t            disp_maxrunpri; /* maximum run priority */
pri_t            disp_max_unbound_pri;   /* max pri of unbound threads */

volatile int     disp_nrunnable; /* runnable threads in cpu dispq */

struct cpu       *disp_cpu;       /* cpu owning this queue or NULL */
} disp_t;
```

See usr/src/uts/common/sys/disp.h

- **disp_queue_info.** There is one queue info structure per processor. The variables in queue info provide temporary placeholders for queue data that will change during the normal flow of dispatcher events. The disp_queue_info structures are maintained in an array, referenced in the kernel through the disp_mem pointer.

```
/* Dispatch queue allocation structure and functions */
struct disp_queue_info {
          disp_t *dp;
          dispq_t *olddispq;
          dispq_t *newdispq;
          ulong_t *olddqactmap;
          ulong_t *newdqactmap;
          int     oldnglobpris;
};
```

See usr/src/uts/common/disp/disp.c

- **kthread_t.** This structure defines a kernel thread. The kthread_t maintains, among other things, the thread's assigned and inherited priority, a link to a scheduling-class-specific structure (xxproc_t), and timestamps for tracking execution and wait times.

```
typedef struct _kthread {
...
        pri_t   t_pri;          /* assigned thread priority */
        pri_t   t_epri;         /* inherited thread priority */
...
        struct thread_ops *t_clfuncs;   /* scheduling class ops vector */
        void    *t_cldata;      /* per scheduling class specific data */
...
                                        See usr/src/uts/common/sys/thread.h
```

- **xxproc_t,** where *xx* is one of either **ts**, **ia**, **rt**, **fx**, or **fss**, corresponding to the scheduling class of the kernel thread (for example, a kernel thread in the timeshare (TS) class will link to a tsproc_t structure, a kernel thread in the fair-share (FSS) class will link to a fssproc_t structure, and so forth). These structures maintain time quantum information and other class-specific data. The example below is the timeshare class structure.

```
/*
 * time-sharing class specific thread structure
 */
typedef struct tsproc {
        int             ts_timeleft;    /* time remaining in procs quantum */
        uint_t          ts_dispwait;    /* wall clock seconds since start */
                                        /* of quantum (not reset upon preemption */
        pri_t   ts_cpupri;      /* system controlled component of ts_umdpri */
        pri_t   ts_uprilim;     /* user priority limit */
        pri_t   ts_upri;        /* user priority */
        pri_t   ts_umdpri;      /* user mode priority within ts class */
        char    ts_nice;        /* nice value for compatibility */
        char    ts_boost;       /* interactive priority offset */
        unsigned char ts_flags; /* flags defined below */
        kthread_t *ts_tp;       /* pointer to thread */
        struct tsproc *ts_next; /* link to next tsproc on list */
        struct tsproc *ts_prev; /* link to previous tsproc on list */
} tsproc_t;
                                        See usr/src/uts/common/sys/ts.h
```

3.3.2 Dispatcher Structure Linkage

Specific details on how and where the structure variables are used by the dispatcher are discussed in the following sections. First, let's look at how the structure pieces fits together in Figure 3.4. For clarity, the class-specific data that is linked to a kernel thread's t_cldata pointer is not shown in the figure.

The diagram in Figure 3.4 shows the organization of the per-processor dispatcher queues, used for queueing all runnable threads except those in the real-time scheduling class. There is a dispq_t for every global priority, ordered numerically in descending order. That is, the first dispq_t is the root of all threads at the highest (best) global priority (either 109 or 169. See Section 3.6 for the particulars), the next one down links threads at next lowest priority, and so on.

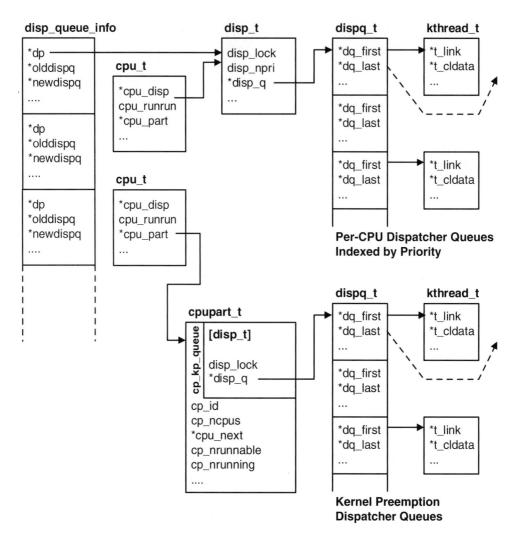

Figure 3.4 Dispatcher Queue Structures

Dispatcher queues for real-time threads (kp queues) are managed in a slightly different way. The per-priority queue arrangement is the same (60 queues for real-time priorities 0–59), but the number of actual queues is not per-processor, but rather per-processor partition or processor set. By default, on a Solaris system that has not had any user-defined processor sets created, there will be one systemwide kp_preempt queue for real-time threads. If processor sets are created, then the number of kp_queues will equal the number of configured processor sets plus 1.

That is, one kp_queue per processor set, plus one for the default (system) set. Note also that the `disp_t` structure is embedded in the `cpupart_t` structure, as opposed to a pointer link.

The dispatcher structures are created and initialized at boot time in accordance with the number of processors installed on the system. Initialization functions can also be called while the system is up and running in order to support the dynamic reconfiguration capabilities of some of Sun's server systems. For example, adding a system board to a high-end server will change the number of available processors, requiring to kernel to allocate and initialize structures for the additional processors. Also, scheduling classes are implemented as dynamically loadable kernel modules; the loading of a scheduling class requires calling dispatcher initialization functions.

3.3.3 Examining Dispatcher Structures

Let's quickly look at how we can examine these structures on a running system and thus determine the values of the structure variables of interest. We use the system debugger, `mdb(1)`, as well as `dtrace(1)`.

```
# mdb -k
> ::cpuinfo
 ID ADDR        FLG NRUN BSPL PRI RNRN KRNRN SWITCH THREAD       PROC
  0 0000180c000 1b     0    0  17  no  t-2     300022f7660 threads
  1 30001b50000 1b     0    0  17  no   no t-0  30002def920 threads
  4 30001b52000 1b     1    0  51  no   no t-0  30003c1e640 tar
  5 30001bf2000 1b     0    0  59  no   no t-0  300065a3320 mdb
  8 30001bf0000 1b     0    0  59  no   no t-0  300063d2cc0 sshd
  9 30001be6000 1b     1    0  32  no   no t-0  300065a29c0 tar
 12 30001be0000 1b     0    0  17  no   no t-1  300061c9c80 threads
 13 30001bdc000 1b     0    0  17  no   no t-2  3000230b960 threads
```

The `mdb ::cpuinfo` dcmd provides a tabular summary for every CPU on the system. In this example, we have eight CPUs. The `cpuinfo` output provides several interesting bits of information used by the dispatcher. We can see the name of the process the CPU is executing (if it's running a process thread at the time the command is executed), the address of the thread structure (THREAD), the priority of the running thread (PRI), and the number of runnable threads on the CPU's dispatch queues (NRUN). The ADDR column is the kernel virtual address of the processor's `cpu_t` structure. The RNRN and KRNRN fields represent the CPU's `cpu_runrun` and `cpu_kprunrun` flags, respectively. These flags trigger a preemption. A preemption is initiated by the operating system when an event occurs that requires a processor's attention, such as a thread insertion on a CPU's dispatch queue that is of a higher priority than the CPU's current highest-priority thread. Solaris defines user preemptions, triggered by cpu_runrun, and kernel preemptions, triggered by cpu_kprunrun. See Section 3.9.

Displaying the entire cpu_t for a CPU is a simple matter of grabbing the address (ADDR) of the desired CPU and using the mdb(1) print command.

```
> 30001be0000::print cpu_t
{
    cpu_id = 0xc
    cpu_seqid = 0x6
    cpu_flags = 0x1b
    cpu_self = 0x30001be0000
    cpu_thread = 0x30003b909e0
...
    cpu_disp = 0x30001b2ecd8
    cpu_runrun = '\0'
    cpu_kprunrun = '\0'
    cpu_chosen_level = 0xffff
    cpu_dispthread = 0x300061c9640
    cpu_thread_lock = 0
    cpu_disp_flags = 0
    cpu_dispatch_pri = 0x31

...
```

The output from the above command is quite large; we snipped most of it for this example. This gives us another view of some of the per-CPU data displayed by the cpuinfo dcmd, such as the CPU preemption flags (runrun), the address of the thread structure running on the CPU, the CPU's current priority, and the like.

The cpu_disp field provides the address of the CPU's dispatcher (disp_t) structure.

```
> 30001b2ecd8::print disp_t
{
    disp_lock = 0
    disp_npri = 0x6e
    disp_q = 0x30001be4a80
    disp_q_limit = 0x30001be54d0
    disp_qactmap = 0x30001b73a58
    disp_maxrunpri = 0xffff
    disp_max_unbound_pri = 0xffff
    disp_nrunnable = 0
    disp_cpu = 0x30001be0000
}
```

The disp_t fields include a dispatcher lock (see Section 3.4), the number of global priorities on the system (0x6E = 110 decimal. Section 3.7.1 explains this value). The disp_maxrunpri value of 0xffff equates to –1, which means the CPU is not currently running a thread (the CPU is idle). Other variables in the structure and others we have examined are described in the following sections that cover the execution of key dispatcher functions.

Be aware that examining this data on a running system is a moving target. Many of these fields change hundreds or thousands of times per second. That is why certain variables, such as thread address and priority, appear different as we move through the examples.

Pipelines of mdb(1) dcmds can be grouped to provide a more direct path to data of interest. Below is a snapshot of the priority of the thread running on a CPU, for all CPUs.

```
> ::walk cpu |::print cpu_t cpu_thread |::print kthread_t t_pri
t_pri = 0x11
t_pri = 0xffff
t_pri = 0x1d
t_pri = 0xffff
t_pri = 0x1d
t_pri = 0x11
t_pri = 0x11
t_pri = 0x11
>
```

Here we see that of the eight CPUs, two are idle (t_pri = 0xffff), four are running threads at priority 17 (0x11 = 17 decimal), and two are running threads at priority 29 (0x1d = 29 decimal).

Having a look at the kp_queue requires dumping the cpupart_t structure linked to a CPU of interest. In this example, a user-defined processor set has not been created, so we have the default set, which is all the processors on the system. For referencing the default (system) kp_queue, a kernel variable, cp_default, is set in the dispatcher code for quick reference to the default partition data. On systems that have not had processor sets or resource pools configured, there will be one kp_preempt queue for the entire system.

```
> cp_default::print cpupart_t
{
    cp_kp_queue = {
        disp_lock = 0
        disp_npri = 0xaa
        disp_q = 0xd2e84800
        disp_q_limit = 0xd2e84ff8
        disp_qactmap = 0xd2cee158
        disp_maxrunpri = 0xffff
        disp_max_unbound_pri = 0xffff
        disp_nrunnable = 0
        disp_cpu = 0
    }
    cp_id = 0
    cp_ncpus = 0x1
....
```

Note that the embedded `disp_t` is properly formatted as part of the `cpupart_t` formatted structure output. For systems with configured processor sets or resource pools, use the `cpu_part` pointer in a CPU that is a member of the set of interest. You can use a simple but powerful command pipeline to format and dump the `cpupart_t`, as shown in the next example.

```
> ::cpuinfo
 ID ADDR          FLG NRUN BSPL PRI RNRN KRNRN SWITCH THREAD        PROC
  0 0000180c000   1b    0    0  -1  no    no  t-1    2a10001fcc0  (idle)
  1 30001bcc000   1b    0    0 120  no    no  t-44   30002c37300  cpuhog
  4 30001bce000   1b    0    0  -1  no    no  t-6    2a10038fcc0  (idle)
  5 30001c6e000   1b    0    0 120  no    no  t-39   300029c15e0  cpuhog
  8 30001c6c000   1b    0    0  -1  no    no  t-1    2a100501cc0  (idle)
  9 30001c62000   1b    0    0 120  no    no  t-41   300022ca040  cpuhog
 12 30001c5c000   1b    0    0 120  no    no  t-36   300028aa680  cpuhog
 13 30001c58000   1b    0    0  59  no    no  t-1    30002a49920  mdb

> 30001bcc000::print cpu_t cpu_part |::print cpupart_t
{
    cp_kp_queue = {
        disp_lock = 0
        disp_npri = 0xaa
        disp_q = 0x30002901000
        disp_q_limit = 0x30002901ff0
        disp_qactmap = 0x3000622f398
        disp_maxrunpri = 0xffff
        disp_max_unbound_pri = 0xffff
        disp_nrunnable = 0
        disp_cpu = 0
    }
    cp_id = 0
    cp_ncpus = 0x8
    cp_next = cp_default
    cp_prev = cp_default
    cp_cpulist = cpu0
    cp_kstat = kstat_initial+0xb1a0
    cp_nrunnable = 0x1
    cp_nrunning = 0x8
    cp_updates = 0x31868d
    cp_nrunnable_cum = 0x1058
    cp_nwaiting_cum = 0
    cp_loadavg = {
        lg_cur = 0x7
        lg_len = 0xb
        lg_total = 0
        lg_loads = [ 0x10edc5006, 0xf84cace8, 0xd9dcafcb, 0xce1366e8, 0x1103a83ac,
0xb9e7b718, 0x943a762f
, 0xf5eb8825, 0xa56f5481, 0x135dd9a10, 0x984b5f3c ]
    }
    cp_lgrpset = 0x1
    cp_lgrploads = cp_default_lpls
    cp_nlgrploads = 0x5
    cp_hp_avenrun = [ 0x3e292, 0x3e268, 0x3ada9 ]
    cp_attr = 0x1
    cp_gen = 0
}
>
```

DTrace can also be used to examine dispatcher events of interest on a running system. For example, we may wish to monitor the number of runnable threads on a per-CPU basis, as well as RT-class threads on the kp_queue. The following dtrace script uses the dtrace FBT provider and segues nicely into a description of the dispatcher queue management functions since we enable probes in the queue insertion functions to track run queue depth.

For non-RT-class threads, the kernel inserts a thread on either the front or back of the target dispatch queue, using either setfrontdq() or setbackdq(), so we instrument the entry points for these functions and grab the disp_nrunnable value when these probes fire. Insertions onto the kp_queue are done with the setkpdq() kernel function, so the D script enables a probe at the entry point of that function and grabs the nrunnable value for the queue. The aggregation keys are the CPU ID for the per-CPU queues and the partition ID for the kp_queues, so we get queue depth for all CPUs and queue depth for all kp_queues. Here is the dtrace D script.

```
#!/usr/sbin/dtrace -qs

long dq_enters;
long kpdq_enters;

fbt::setfrontdq:entry, fbt::setbackdq:entry
{
        dq_enters++;
        cpu_id = args[0]->t_cpu->cpu_id;
        dqcnt  = args[0]->t_cpu->cpu_disp->disp_nrunnable;
        @nrt[cpu_id] = quantize(dqcnt);
}

fbt::setkpdq:entry
{
        kpdq_enters++;
        part_id = args[0]->t_cpu->cpu_part->cp_id;
        kpqcnt  = args[0]->t_cpu->cpu_part->cp_kp_queue.disp_nrunnable;
        @rt[part_id] = quantize(kpqcnt);
}

tick-5sec
{
        printf("Non RT Class Threads, by CPU (%ld enters)\n",dq_enters);
        printa(@nrt);

        printf("\nRT Class Threads, by Partition ID (%ld enters)\n",kpdq_enters);
        printa(@rt);

        trunc(@nrt);
        trunc(@rt);
        dq_enters = 0; kpdq_enters = 0;

        printf("\n\n");
}
```

Here is sample output from running the script for a few seconds on a four-processor system. A processor set has been created on the system, with CPU 1 the only CPU in the set. A multithreaded process was bound to the processor set and put in the real-time scheduling class. A second multithreaded process is running across the remaining three CPUs in the default (system) set.

```
# ./rqcc.d
Non RT Class Threads, by CPU (48669 enters)

     1
         value ------------- Distribution ------------- count
             0 |                                               0
             1 |@@@@@@@@@@@@@@@@@@@@@@@@@@@@@@@@@@@@@@@@@@ 106
             2 |                                               1
             4 |                                               0

     2
         value ------------- Distribution ------------- count
            -1 |                                               0
             0 |@@@@@@@@@@@@                                 1559
             1 |@@@@@@@@@@@@@@@@@                            2153
             2 |@@@@@@@@@                                   1128
             4 |                                              12
             8 |                                               0

     3
         value ------------- Distribution ------------- count
            -1 |                                               0
             0 |@@@@@@@@@@@@                                 6354
             1 |@@@@@@@@@@@@@@@@@@                           9557
             2 |@@@@@@@@@                                   4515
             4 |                                              69
             8 |                                               0

     0
         value ------------- Distribution ------------- count
            -1 |                                               0
             0 |@@@@@@@@@@                                   5505
             1 |@@@@@@@@@@@@@@@@@@@@                        11081
             2 |@@@@@@@@@@@@                                 6949
             4 |@                                            306
             8 |                                               0

RT Class Threads, by Partition ID (1146 enters)

     0
         value ------------- Distribution ------------- count
            -1 |                                               0
             0 |@@@@@@@@@@@@@@@@@@@@@@@@@@@@@@@@@@@@@@@@@@ 1062
             1 |                                               0

     1
         value ------------- Distribution ------------- count
             4 |                                               0
             8 |@@@@@@@@@@@@@@@@@@@@@@@@@@@@@@@@@@@@@@@@@@ 106
            16 |                                               0
```

Referencing the sample output on the previous page, the "RT Class threads, by Partition ID" data shows two aggregations since there are two partitions (the default, and the one we created). The default partition (ID 0) also has a zero value for the count of runnable threads, which is expected since we ran the RT-class threads on the user-defined set (partition 1), which shows a varying number of runnable threads on the kp_queue.

The "Non-RT Class Threads, by CPU" shows a queue depth of various sizes over the source of the sampling period for each CPU.

The output data is in the form of aggregations; the result of the dtrace quantize aggregating function, which takes a scalar value as an argument and aggregates according to the value into a power-of-two distribution. The left column, value, represents a range of values of the aggregated data (the number of runnable threads on the queue in the case). The right column, count, represents the number of times the aggregated data fell within the corresponding value range. For example, looking at the CPU 0 distribution, the nrrunnable value was 0 for 5505 occurrences of the probe firing. The value was 1 for 11081 occurrences of the probe firing. The value was not less than 2 and not greater than 4 (that is, 2 or 3) for 6949 occurrences of the probe firing, and the value was not less than 4 and not greater than 8 for 306 occurrences of the probe firing.

3.4 Dispatcher Locks

The kernel implements several types of synchronization primitives to facilitate support for hardware platforms with more than one processor. The most common is the mutual exclusion lock, or mutex lock. Other locking mechanisms used by the kernel include reader/writer locks and, in some cases, semaphores. These are discussed in Chapter 17.

These locking mechanisms provide fast and scalable methods of synchronizing activity among many kernel threads and maintain coherency for the various bits of kernel data and state they protect. However, mutex locks, by design, can require calling threads to enter the dispatcher for sleep, wakeup, and associated context switch operations. Also, interrupt activity requires dispatcher functions for managing the pinning of a running thread and putting an interrupt thread on a processor for execution. In some cases, interrupt threads may block, requiring the dispatcher code to manage changing the state of the interrupt thread from ONPROC to SLEEP, placing it on a sleep queue, and setting up the interrupted thread to resume execution.

Specific areas of the dispatcher code must be allowed to execute safely, without risk of an event or branch in the code that would reenter the dispatcher from another source. It is in these areas of the kernel that dispatcher locks are used. Simply put, a dispatcher lock is an implementation of a spin lock that runs at a high-priority level, blocking all but the highest-priority interrupts. A spin lock, as the name implies, causes the calling thread to enter a spin loop if the lock the thread is attempting to acquire is not free. If the target lock is free, the processor executing the thread that takes ownership of the dispatcher lock has its priority interrupt level (PIL) elevated to block low-level interrupts.

The exact priority level is shown in the header file below.

```
/*
 * The definitions of the symbolic interrupt levels:
 *
 *    CLOCK_LEVEL =>  The level at which one must be to block the clock.
 *
 *    LOCK_LEVEL  =>  The highest level at which one may block (and thus the
 *                    highest level at which one may acquire adaptive locks)
 *                    Also the highest level at which one may be preempted.
 *
 *    DISP_LEVEL  =>  The level at which one must be to perform dispatcher
 *                    operations.
 *
 * The constraints on the platform:
 *
 *    - CLOCK_LEVEL must be less than or equal to LOCK_LEVEL
 *    - LOCK_LEVEL must be less than DISP_LEVEL
 *    - DISP_LEVEL should be as close to LOCK_LEVEL as possible
 *
 * Note that LOCK_LEVEL and CLOCK_LEVEL have historically always been equal;
 * changing this relationship is probably possible but not advised.
 *
 */
#define CLOCK_LEVEL      10
#define LOCK_LEVEL       10
#define DISP_LEVEL       (LOCK_LEVEL + 1)

#define HIGH_LEVELS      (PIL_MAX - LOCK_LEVEL)

#define PIL_MAX          15
```
                                        See usr/src/uts/sparc/sys/machlock.h

Several symbolic constants represent key interrupt levels. On both SPARC and Intel architectures, there are 15 interrupt priority levels, with interrupt levels 11 through 15 defined as high-priority interrupts. Interrupts are discussed in Section 3.11, but for this discussion, there is one key point to be aware of regarding high-priority interrupts: The interrupt handler for high-priority interrupts cannot block—doing so would violate a critical constraint that kernel programmers must comply with when writing high PIL interrupt handlers.

The constraint exists because dispatcher locks are held at interrupt level 11 (DISP_LEVEL); thus, a processor executing a thread that acquires a dispatcher lock is blocking interrupts at and below 11—only level 12 interrupts and higher cause the processor to stop what it's doing and allow the interrupt to be handled. This means that it's possible to interrupt a thread holding a dispatcher lock. Entering the dispatcher while executing in high-level interrupt context on the processor that was already in the dispatcher and holding a dispatcher lock would be disastrous and would most certainly either hang or panic the kernel. This is why mutex locks are not used for most dispatcher functions—the adaptive behavior of kernel mutex locks can require entering the dispatcher to put the calling thread to sleep.

To elaborate a bit on this complex topic, when a dispatcher lock is held, the CPU is at DISP_LEVEL (PIL 11)—all interrupts at DISP_LEVEL and below are blocked. This raises the question as to why DISP_LEVEL and LOCK_LEVEL are not the same. They used to be, prior to Solaris 7—DISP_LEVEL did not exist, and the dispatcher operated at PIL 10, the same as CLOCK_LEVEL. The problem with this arrangement was that, on one hand, we can not preempt a thread holding a dispatcher lock (remember, at PIL 10), but on the other hand, if the clock interrupt thread, which operates at PIL 10, were to block, leaving the CPU at PIL 10, later, when the clock thread becomes runnable, we must preempt the non-interrupt thread running on the CPU, which is still at PIL 10. So with the dispatcher lock and clock thread running at the same PIL, we could not tell (given a CPU at PIL 10) whether a dispatcher lock is held (in which case we can not preempt), or if the clock was blocked and we need to preempt the thread that is now running on the CPU. In order to address this issue, DISP_LEVEL was introduced, and it was mandated that the dispatcher run at PIL 11. This way, we know we can preempt anything at PIL 10, and anything at PIL 11 is illegal.

Thus, we have well-defined constraints for coding high-level interrupt handlers; don't block, and make it fast. High-priority interrupt handlers are reserved for critical system events, such as hardware faults, which is why DISP_LEVEL is not 15; even in a critical section, we do not want to mask notification of important system events.

The actual dispatcher locks are embedded in the disp_t structure, (disp_lock), one of which exists for each per-processor dispatch queue. There is also a disp_t (and associated disp_lock) for the kernel preempt (kp) queues (see Figure 3.4). Last, several locks that are defined in the dispatcher code are not directly associated with a dispatch queue but are part of the dispatcher subsystem—the swapped_lock, which manages the thread swap queue, and the shuttle_lock, which protects shuttle objects, are examples of dispatcher locks not directly bound to a dispatch queue. Dispatcher locks are simply an unsigned char data type (1 byte in size) that is set to zero when the lock is initialized.

3.4.1 Dispatcher Lock Functions

The kernel implements functions for initializing, acquiring, releasing, and destroying dispatcher locks.

```
/*
 * Dispatcher lock type, macros and routines.
 *
 * disp_lock_t is defined in machlock.h
 */
extern   void     disp_lock_enter(disp_lock_t *);
extern   void     disp_lock_exit(disp_lock_t *);
extern   void     disp_lock_exit_nopreempt(disp_lock_t *);
extern   void     disp_lock_enter_high(disp_lock_t *);
extern   void     disp_lock_exit_high(disp_lock_t *);
extern   void     disp_lock_init(disp_lock_t *lp, char *name);
extern   void     disp_lock_destroy(disp_lock_t *lp);
                                            See usr/src/uts/common/sys/t_lock.h
```

Dispatcher locks are acquired with `disp_lock_enter()` or `disp_lock_enter_high()` and released by calls to `disp_lock_exit()` or `disp_lock_exit_high()`. The `disp_lock_enter_high()` code acquires the specified dispatcher lock (passed as an argument) without explicitly elevating the processor's PIL. It is called when the processor's PIL is already at PIL. `disp_lock_enter()` elevates the processor's PIL to `DISP_LEVEL`, then attempts to acquire the lock. The required PIL manipulation aside, the general flow for both lock enter functions is similar:

1. Enter assembly code and test if lock is free.
2. If the lock is free, take ownership and return.
3. If the lock is not free (owned), enter spin loop.
4. In each pass through the loop, test to see if the lock is held. If it is not held, retry step 1 to take ownership of the lock.

The mechanism is fast and simple by design, allowing a lock to be acquired in just a couple of assembly language instructions if the lock is free. One added point on the spin loop: The `lock_set_spl_spin()` code does not execute the spin loop at an elevated PIL (`DISP_LOCK`). Inside the spin loop, the processor's PIL is lowered to the PIL value the processor was operating in when the `disp_lock_enter()` function was called. Since the thread is not holding a dispatcher lock inside the spin loop, we need not block low-level interrupts within the loop.

When it's time to free the lock, `disp_lock_exit_high()` causes the lock to be cleared and return. `disp_lock_enter()` is used when it's safe to test for a kernel preemption on lock release. Recall that with `disp_lock_enter_high()`, the processor is already at an elevated PIL (`DISP_LOCK`), and as such, `disp_lock_exit_high()` does not allow for a kernel preemption on freeing the lock—it is not safe to allow a kernel preemption with the processor at a high PIL. `disp_lock_exit()` tests to determine if a kernel preemption is pending and if that condition is true, clears the lock and enters the preempt code. Otherwise, it just clears the lock.

3.4.2 Thread Locks

Thread locks are per-thread dispatcher locks that protect a thread's dispatch queue and critical thread state information. Where a dispatcher lock protects a dispatch queue to maintain consistency for various dispatcher functions, a thread lock provides a mechanism for protecting the dispatch queue specific to a kernel thread, along with the thread's state. Thread locks are implemented specifically to provide a fast synchronization mechanism. Rather than require kernel code to make two lock calls (one to get a dispatcher lock and one to get a lock to protect thread state), the kernel can quickly protect both the target thread and the dispatch queue it is linked to with a single lock call to acquire the thread lock. Put another way, acquiring the thread lock locks the thread and its dispatch queue.

The lock itself is a member of the kernel thread structure and is defined as a pointer to a dispatcher lock data type.

```
/*
 * Pointer to the dispatcher lock protecting t_state and state-related
 * flags.  This pointer can change during waits on the lock, so
 * it should be grabbed only by thread_lock().
 */
disp_lock_t     *t_lockp;        /* pointer to the dispatcher lock */
```
See usr/src/uts/common/thread.h

A kernel thread's `t_lockp` is set to point to the dispatcher lock of the dispatch queue onto which the thread is inserted in the queue insertion functions, using the `THREAD_SET_STATE` macro.

```
#define THREAD_SET_STATE(tp, state, lp) \
            ((tp)->t_state = state, (tp)->t_lockp = lp)
```
See usr/src/uts/common/sys/thread.h

The macro is passed the thread pointer, the state to set the thread to (for example, `TS_RUN`), and a pointer to the dispatcher lock.

The actual lock backing the thread lock depends on the thread's state. A thread in TS_ONPROC state has its lock in the CPU on which it is running. A TS_RUN thread's lock is in the dispatch queue the thread is on, and a TS_SLEEP thread's lock resides in the corresponding sleep queue. Setting the thread state with THREAD_SET_STATE sets the thread's thread lock to the appropriate place based on the new state.

A kernel thread's t_lockp may also reference the *transition_lock*, the *stop_lock*, or a sleep queue lock. The lock names give us a good indication of their use; a thread's t_lockp is set to the transition lock when the thread's state is changing. The transition lock is necessary because thread state changes often result in changes to the thread's t_lockp. For example, when a thread transitions from running (TS_ONPROC) to sleep (TS_SLEEP), the t_lockp is set to the lock associated with the sleep queue on which the thread is placed. If a thread is migrated to another processor, the address of the dispatcher lock changes (since dispatch queues are per-processor), resulting in a change to the thread's t_lockp. The transition lock provides a simple and safe mechanism for protecting thread state during such transitions.

The stop lock is used when a thread is being created, which is the initial state of a thread. Threads can also be stopped when executed under the control of a debugger.

3.4.3 Thread Lock Functions

The functions called to acquire and release thread locks are similar to the dispatcher lock code. thread_lock() and thread_lock_high() both attempt to acquire the thread lock and enter a spin loop, checking for lock availability in each pass through the loop. Like dispatcher locks, thread locks are held with the processor at an elevated interrupt level. If the spin loop is entered (the lock is not free), the processor's interrupt priority level is lowered to the level it was running at when the thread_lock() function was entered and raised to DISP_LEVEL when the lock is acquired. thread_lock_high() is called when the processor is already running at DISP_LEVEL.

```
void     thread_transition(kthread_t *); /* move to transition lock */
void     thread_stop(kthread_t *);       /* move to stop lock */
void     thread_lock(kthread_t *);       /* lock thread and its queue */
void     thread_lock_high(kthread_t *);  /* lock thread and its queue */
void     thread_onproc(kthread_t *, struct cpu *); /* set onproc state lock */

#define thread_unlock(t)              disp_lock_exit((t)->t_lockp)
#define thread_unlock_high(t)         disp_lock_exit_high((t)->t_lockp)
#define thread_unlock_nopreempt(t)    disp_lock_exit_nopreempt((t)->t_lockp)

                                    See usr/src/uts/common/sys/thread.h
```

The lock release (unlock) functions are substituted with the dispatcher lock release functions by the C language #define directive (shown above): The disp_ `lock_exit()`, etc., functions are actually called to release thread locks. When a lock is freed, a test is made to determine if a kernel preemption is pending. If it is, the lock is freed, the processor's interrupt priority level is restored to its previous value, and the kernel preemption function is called (see Section 3.9). A no-preempt release function is used when the dispatcher is in the process of selecting the best priority thread to run (the kernel `disp_getbest()` function) and preparing to context-switch the selected thread onto a processor for execution. Since this specific code segment is doing priority-based thread selection, a real-time thread would be selected for execution if one was runnable; and recall that it is real-time threads that generate kernel preemptions.

3.4.4 Lock Statistics

Statistics on dispatcher locks and thread locks are available through the `lockstat(1)` command (which is a `dtrace` consumer), or the lock functions can be instrumented through the use of the `dtrace` FBT provider. `lockstat(1)` can be invoked with an event list that specifies reporting only on spin locks and thread locks (events 2 and 3), as in the following.

```
# lockstat -e2,3 sleep 10

Spin lock spin: 129 events in 10.119 seconds (13 events/sec)

Count indv cuml rcnt     spin Lock                    Caller
-------------------------------------------------------------------------------
   11   9%   9% 0.00        5 0x30001bacd08           setfrontdq+0x158
    9   7%  16% 0.00        4 0x30001bacc18           setfrontdq+0x158
    8   6%  22% 0.00        5 0x30001bacc78           disp+0x84
    8   6%  28% 0.00        4 0x30001baccd8           setfrontdq+0x158
    7   5%  33% 0.00       43 0x30001bacd08           disp+0x84
    7   5%  39% 0.00        5 0x30001bacc78           setfrontdq+0x158
    6   5%  43% 0.00        5 0x30001baccd8           setbackdq+0x2d0
    5   4%  47% 0.00        2 0x30001bacd08           setbackdq+0x2d0
 . . .
    1   1% 100% 0.00        4 0x30001bacbe8           setbackdq+0x2d0
-------------------------------------------------------------------------------

Thread lock spin: 40 events in 10.119 seconds (4 events/sec)

Count indv cuml rcnt     spin Lock                    Caller
-------------------------------------------------------------------------------
    7  18%  18% 0.00       87 cpu[12]+0xf8            ts_tick+0x8
    6  15%  32% 0.00       75 cpu[5]+0xf8             ts_tick+0x8
    4  10%  42% 0.00       29 cpu[5]+0xf8             cv_wait_sig_swap_core+0x54
    4  10%  52% 0.00       87 cpu[4]+0xf8             ts_tick+0x8
 . . .
    1   2%  90% 0.00       22 cpu[1]+0xf8             preempt+0x1c
    1   2%  92% 0.00       29 cpu[4]+0xf8             cv_wait_sig_swap_core+0x54
    1   2%  95% 0.00      471 transition_lock         ts_update_list+0x68
    1   2%  98% 0.00       67 sleepq_head+0x4b8       ts_tick+0x8
    1   2% 100% 0.00   135475 0x30001bacbe8           ts_update_list+0x68
-------------------------------------------------------------------------------
```

The example above reports 129 spin lock events on dispatcher locks and 40 occurrences of a thread lock spin. The values in the example here are pretty tame—the values reported in the Count and spin columns are relatively small, suggesting that this system is not burning significant time in lock spin loops, nor is there any indication of a hot lock (a lock that is highly contended).

3.5 Dispatcher Initialization

Dispatcher initialization begins at boot time, when the core operating system startup code calls dispinit(). Among the basic initialization tasks performed by dispinit() are the setup of the default CPU partition (cpupart_initialize_ default()) and calls into the scheduler-class-specific init functions for all the pre-loaded scheduling classes. disp_setup() is called to establish the actual dispatch queues and initialize the queue variables. Table 3.1 described the initialization functions.

Table 3.1 Dispatcher Initialization Functions

Function	Description
disp_setup()	Allocate dispatcher structures and variables
dispinit()	Initialize loaded scheduling classes and the dispatcher framework
disp_add()	Initialize a newly loaded scheduling class
cpu_dispalloc()	Allocate per-processor dispatch queues
disp_dq_alloc()	Allocate the kernel memory for the queues and set the pointers; support function for cpu_dispalloc()
disp_dq_assign()	Assign priorities to dispatch queues
disp_dq_free()	Free dispatch queue resources (kernel memory)
disp_cpu_init()	Initialize a dispatch queue for a processor
disp_kp_alloc()	Allocate a kernel preempt (kp) queue
disp_kp_free()	Free a previously allocated kp queue

The initialization sequence and flow is illustrated below.

The cpupart_initialize_default() function is part of the CPU partition support code. A CPU partition is the kernel abstraction for user-defined processor

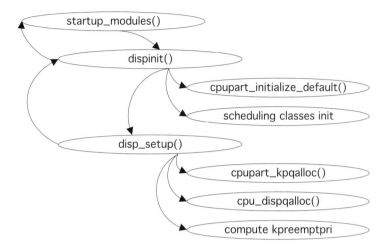

Figure 3.5 Dispatcher Initialization Functions

sets (processor sets are created with psrset(1M)). Processor sets and CPU partitions are different but related abstractions. Users create processor sets and explicitly bind threads to the set, and the kernel guarantees that only threads bound to
the set are executed on the processors in the set. Within the kernel, a processor
partition has been defined; this partition represents a grouping of one or more processors, with a global dispatch queue. The kp queue for real-time threads is global
for the partition: Each processor in the partition still has a per-processor set of dispatch queues for threads in other scheduling classes. As part of the dispatcher initialization process, the default CPU partition is created and initialized.

Each scheduling class has a class-specific initialization function that gets called for
each loaded scheduling class. The scheduling class initialization functions are relatively simple, establishing priority limit variables, setting up list arrays that maintain linked lists of threads in each class, and initializing class-specific parameters.

The dispatch queue setup code allocates the kernel memory and sets up the
linked lists, pointers and structure variables for the per-CPU dispatch queues and
the kp queue. When the dispatch queue initialization is complete, the last step is
to compute the global base priority for interrupt threads, based on the number of
global priorities (see Figure 3.8). The number of global priorities and the base priority of interrupt threads are determined by the presence or absence of the real-
time scheduling class. If the real-time class is not loaded (default), there are 100
global priorities (0–99) for noninterrupt threads and the interrupt thread priorities are 100–109. If real-time is loaded, the number of global priorities is increased
to 160 (0–159) and interrupt threads occupy priorities 160–169.

3.6 Scheduling Classes

Before diving into the specifics of dispatcher thread selection and operations, we need to discuss thread priorities and the individual scheduling classes implemented in the kernel. The core dispatcher code and scheduling-class specific code are tightly integrated, and a thorough explanation of the CPU and thread selection and scheduling process requires a background in the priority scheme and the functions managed by the scheduling-class specific code.

The dispatcher subsystem can be decomposed into the core dispatcher functions and the scheduling-class specific functions. While core dispatcher code and scheduling class functions are tightly integrated and are maintained in the same source directory—usr/src/uts/common/disp—the architecture allows for a single instance of the dispatcher to support multiple scheduling classes. The different scheduling classes determine the priority range for threads and vary in terms of the algorithms applied to thread-specific functions.

Solaris provides six bundled scheduling classes:

- **Timeshare (TS).** Priority adjustments are based on the time a thread spends waiting for processor resources or consuming processor resources. The thread's time quantum—the maximum amount of time the thread can execute on the processor—varies according to its priority.

- **Interactive (IA).** The same as timeshare, with the addition of a mechanism that boosts the priority of a thread connected to the active window on a desktop. IA class threads exist only in a laptop/desktop environment when a window manager is started (you won't see IA class threads on a server).

- **Fair Share (FSS).** Available processor cycles are divided into units called shares, and administrative tools allocate shares to processes using the Solaris projects and tasks framework. A thread in the FSS class has its priority adjusted according to its share allocation, recent utilization, and shares consumed by other threads in the FSS class.

- **Fixed Priority (FX).** The assigned priority is not changed or adjusted by the kernel over the lifetime of the thread.

- **Real Time (RT).** Real-time threads occupy the highest range of assignable priorities. Real-time scheduling provides the fastest possible dispatch latency—the elapsed time between an RT thread becoming runnable and getting scheduled onto a processor.

- **System (SYS).** The kernel uses this class for the execution of operating system threads. The priority range occupied by the SYS class is higher than all other scheduling classes, with the exception of the real-time class.

The default scheduling class out of the box is the TS class or the IA class for desktops and laptops for threads started by the user under a window manager. User and administrative commands exist for placing threads in other classes. priocntl(1) can change the scheduling class and priority of a thread or process; note that improving priorities and using the RT class requires a privileged account). Using the FSS class requires a little more administrative work to do the share allocation. See *System Administration Guide: Solaris Containers—Resource Management and Solaris Zones* (http://docs.sun.com) for specifics.

3.6.1 Scheduling Class Data

Each scheduling class has a unique data structure referenced through a kernel thread's t_cldata pointer. The structures take the name of *xxproc*, where *xx* is *ts, rt, fss, fx* or *ia*. As an example, the tsproc_t object is shown below. The class-specific structures for the other scheduling classes are similar in terms of the structure members and their use.

```
/*
 * time-sharing class specific thread structure
 */
typedef struct tsproc {
        int             ts_timeleft;    /* time remaining in procs quantum */
        uint_t          ts_dispwait;    /* wall clock seconds since start */
                                        /*   of quantum (not reset upon preemption */
        pri_t   ts_cpupri;      /* system controlled component of ts_umdpri */
        pri_t   ts_uprilim;     /* user priority limit */
        pri_t   ts_upri;        /* user priority */
        pri_t   ts_umdpri;      /* user mode priority within ts class */
        pri_t   ts_scpri;       /* remembered priority, for schedctl */
        char    ts_nice;        /* nice value for compatibility */
        char    ts_boost;       /* interactive priority offset */
        uchar_t ts_flags;       /* flags defined below */
        kthread_t *ts_tp;       /* pointer to thread */
        struct tsproc *ts_next; /* link to next tsproc on list */
        struct tsproc *ts_prev; /* link to previous tsproc on list */
} tsproc_t;
                                        See usr/src/uts/common/sys/ts.h
```

The kernel maintains doubly linked lists of the class-specific structures—separate lists for each class, with the exception of IA class threads. Threads in the IA class link to a tsproc structure, and most of the class-supporting code for interactive threads is handled by the TS routines. IA threads are distinguished from TS threads by a flag in the ts_flags field, the TSIA flag.

Maintaining the linked lists for the class structures greatly simplifies the dispatcher-supporting code that updates different fields, such as time quantum, in the structures during the clock-driven dispatcher housekeeping functions.

For the TS/IA, FX, and FSS classes, the kernel builds an array of 16 xxproc structure pointers that anchor up to 16 doubly linked lists of the xxproc structures,

systemwide. The code implements a hash function, based on the thread pointer, to
determine which list to place a thread on, and each list is protected by its own kernel mutex, implemented as a listlock array, once for each class. Implementing multiple linked lists in this way makes for faster traversal of all the xxproc structures
for a given scheduling class in a running system, and the use of a lock per list
allows for concurrency—multiple kernel threads can traverse the lists. Here's the
implementation for the FSS class.

```
/*
 * The fssproc_t structures are kept in an array of circular doubly linked
 * lists.  A hash on the thread pointer is used to determine which list each
 * thread should be placed in.  Each list has a dummy "head" which is never
 * removed, so the list is never empty.  fss_update traverses these lists to
 * update the priorities of threads that have been waiting on the run queue.
 */
#define FSS_LISTS               16 /* number of lists, must be power of 2 */
#define FSS_LIST_HASH(t)        (((uintptr_t)(t) >> 9) & (FSS_LISTS - 1))
#define FSS_LIST_NEXT(i)        (((i) + 1) & (FSS_LISTS - 1))

#define FSS_LIST_INSERT(fssproc)                                        \
{                                                                       \
        int index = FSS_LIST_HASH(fssproc->fss_tp);                     \
        kmutex_t *lockp = &fss_listlock[index];                         \
        fssproc_t *headp = &fss_listhead[index];                        \
. . .

#define FSS_LIST_DELETE(fssproc)                                        \
{                                                                       \
        int index = FSS_LIST_HASH(fssproc->fss_tp);                     \
        kmutex_t *lockp = &fss_listlock[index];                         \
. . .
static fssproc_t fss_listhead[FSS_LISTS];
static kmutex_t fss_listlock[FSS_LISTS];
```
                                                  See usr/src/uts/common/disp/fss.c

The fss_listhead[] array represents the beginning of the 16 lists of
fssproc_t structures, each with a corresponding lock in fss_listlock[]. The
lists for the other classes are implemented in much the same fashion, with the
exception of the RT list, which is implemented as a single list.

The kernel framework for scheduling classes begins with the sclass array of
sclass_t structures.

```
extern struct sclass sclass[];   /* the class table */
typedef struct sclass {
        char            *cl_name;       /* class name */
        /* class specific initialization function */
        pri_t           (*cl_init)(id_t, int, classfuncs_t **);
        classfuncs_t    *cl_funcs;      /* pointer to classfuncs structure */
        krwlock_t       *cl_lock;       /* class structure read/write lock */
        int             cl_count;       /* # of threads trying to load class */
} sclass_t;
```
                                                  See usr/src/uts/common/sys/class.h

For each loaded scheduling class, the sclass array is initialized with the members listed above and indexed with the class ID (cid) kernel variable.

```
# mdb -k
Loading modules: [ unix krtld genunix specfs dtrace uppc pcplusmp ufs ip sctp usba uhci
s1394 fctl nca lofs zfs random nfs audiosup cpc fcip crypto ptm sppp ipc ]
> ::class
SLOT NAME           INIT FCN                      CLASS FCN
   0 SYS            sys_init                      sys_classfuncs
   1 TS             ts_init                       ts_classfuncs
   2 FX             fx_init                       fx_classfuncs
   3 IA             ia_init                       ia_classfuncs
   4 RT             rt_init                       rt_classfuncs
   5                0                             0
   6                0                             0
. . .
```

The example above uses the mdb(1) class dcmd to dump the sclass array. The cid is displayed in the SLOT column. Note that the FSS class is not loaded in the example. The kernel loaded required classes at boot time (SYS, TS)—other classes get loaded dynamically as needed (as a result of placing a thread in a particular class) or through administrative commands (modload(1)). Part of the scheduling class loading and initializing process is the instantiation of the sclass_t object and entry in the sclass array.

Part of each scheduling class is a set of pointers to the functions within the class, referenced with the cl_funcs pointer in the sclass_t. Scheduling class functions are subdivided into two categories—thread operations and class operations. As the names suggest, the thread operations are the class functions that act on a kernel thread, and the class operations are administrative and management functions.

```
typedef struct classfuncs {
        class_ops_t      sclass;
        thread_ops_t     thread;
} classfuncs_t;

typedef struct sclass {
        char            *cl_name;       /* class name */
        /* class specific initialization function */
        pri_t           (*cl_init)(id_t, int, classfuncs_t **);
        classfuncs_t    *cl_funcs;      /* pointer to classfuncs structure */
        krwlock_t       *cl_lock;       /* class structure read/write lock */
        int             cl_count;       /* # of threads trying to load class */
} sclass_t;
                                        See usr/src/uts/common/sys/class.h
```

The class functions are embedded in a sclass_t object, which is also linked to kernel threads (based of course on the scheduling class of the thread). Figure 3.6 illustrates the big picture:

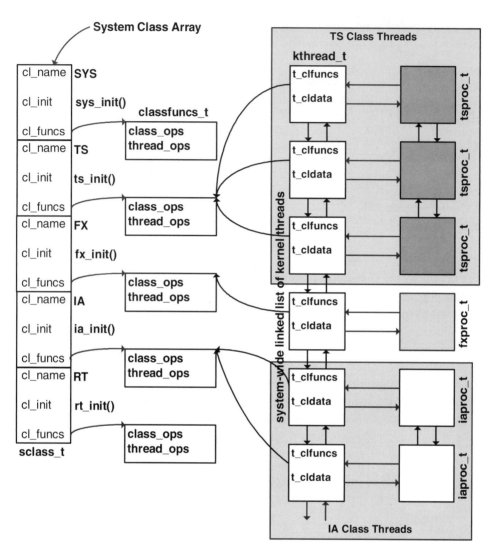

Figure 3.6 Scheduling Class Framework

For space and readability, the FSS class framework is shown separately in Figure 3.6. The framework is similar for FSS, with the addition of several FSS-specific objects linked off fssproc_t. The FSS class is unique since it implements a share-based scheduling policy that requires administrative input for share allocation and (optionally) processor sets. Additional support structures, the fssproj_t (project interface) and fsspset_t (processor set interface) are linked to the fssproc_t. There is also a fsszone_t to manage FSS threads running in zones.

Figure 3.7 shows three FSS class threads that are all part of the same project—each thread's fssproc_t references the same fssproj_t project structure. The kernel's internal project structure, kproject_t, maintains the share value allocated to the project and various project-level resource controls. Data on the CPU set allocated to the project is maintained in the fsspset_t, which links to a CPU partition structure (cpupart_t). The fsszone_t object is defined and instantiated by the kernel when a zone is created and shares are allocated. This behavior supports Solaris Zones and the ability to allocate a given number of CPU shares to a zone.

Getting back to Figure 3.6, the scheduling class operations vector (the function pointers in the class_t object) is at the center of the framework, referenced by the kernel through the system class array and by individual kernel threads

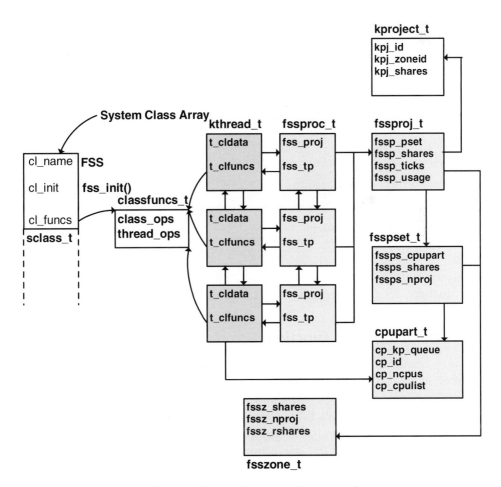

Figure 3.7 FSS Structure Framework

through the thread's `t_clfuncs` pointer. The class and thread operations function prototypes can be found in the `class.h` header file.

```
typedef struct class_ops {
        int     (*cl_admin)(caddr_t, cred_t *);
        int     (*cl_getclinfo)(void *);
        int     (*cl_parmsin)(void *);
        int     (*cl_parmsout)(void *, pc_vaparms_t *);
        int     (*cl_vaparmsin)(void *, pc_vaparms_t *);
        int     (*cl_vaparmsout)(void *, pc_vaparms_t *);
        int     (*cl_getclpri)(pcpri_t *);
        int     (*cl_alloc)(void **, int);
        void    (*cl_free)(void *);
} class_ops_t;

typedef struct thread_ops {
        int     (*cl_enterclass)(kthread_id_t, id_t, void *, cred_t *, void *);
        void    (*cl_exitclass)(void *);
        int     (*cl_canexit)(kthread_id_t, cred_t *);
        int     (*cl_fork)(kthread_id_t, kthread_id_t, void *);
        void    (*cl_forkret)(kthread_id_t, kthread_id_t);
        void    (*cl_parmsget)(kthread_id_t, void *);
        int     (*cl_parmsset)(kthread_id_t, void *, id_t, cred_t *);
        void    (*cl_stop)(kthread_id_t, int, int);
        void    (*cl_exit)(kthread_id_t);
        void    (*cl_active)(kthread_id_t);
        void    (*cl_inactive)(kthread_id_t);
        pri_t   (*cl_swapin)(kthread_id_t, int);
        pri_t   (*cl_swapout)(kthread_id_t, int);
        void    (*cl_trapret)(kthread_id_t);
        void    (*cl_preempt)(kthread_id_t);
        void    (*cl_setrun)(kthread_id_t);
        void    (*cl_sleep)(kthread_id_t);
        void    (*cl_tick)(kthread_id_t);
        void    (*cl_wakeup)(kthread_id_t);
        int     (*cl_donice)(kthread_id_t, cred_t *, int, int *);
        pri_t   (*cl_globpri)(kthread_id_t);
        void    (*cl_set_process_group)(pid_t, pid_t, pid_t);
        void    (*cl_yield)(kthread_id_t);
} thread_ops_t;
```
                                                    See usr/src/uts/common/sys/class.h

The functions are described in the next section.

3.6.2 Scheduling Class Functions

Below is a complete list of the kernel scheduling-class-specific routines and a description of what they do. More details on many of the functions described below follow in the subsequent discussions on thread priorities and the dispatcher algorithms. The first nine functions fall into the class management category and, in general, support the `priocntl(2)` system call, which is invoked from the `priocntl(1)` and `dispadmin(1M)` commands. `priocntl(2)` can, of course, be called from an application program as well.

- **cl_admin.** Retrieve or alter values in the dispatch table for the class.
- **cl_getclinfo.** Get information about the scheduling class. Currently, only the max user priority (*xx_maxupri*) value is returned.
- **cl_parmsin.** Validate user-supplied priority values to ensure that they fall within range. Also check permissions of caller to ensure that the requested operation is allowed. For the TS, IA, FX, and FSS classes, do a limit check against the max user priority (maxupri). For the RT class, the notion of a user priority does not exist, so make a range check against the max RT priority. The function supports the PC_SETPARMS command in priocntl(2).
- **cl_parmsout.** Support PC_GETPARMS command in priocntl(2). Retrieve the class-specific scheduling parameters.
- **cl_vaparmsin, cl_vaparmsout.** Are a variant of the parmsin/parmsout functions and take an addition argument with a variable parameter list.
- **cl_getclpri.** Get class priority ranges. For each scheduling class, return the minimum (lowest) and maximum (highest) global priority.
- **cl_alloc, cl_free.** Allocate or free a class-specific structure (xxproc_t).

The following functions support and manage threads.

- **cl_enterclass.** Allocate the resources needed for a thread to enter a scheduling class—the xxproc_t structure. Initialize the fields and links. The class cl_enterclass functions are discussed in their respective sections.
- **cl_exitclass.** Remove the class-specific data structure (xxproc_t) from the linked list and free it.
- **cl_canexit.** For FSS class threads, ensure that the thread's credentials permit the thread to exit (requires the PRIV_PROC_PRIOCNTL privilege. See (Chapter 5 and privileges(1)).
- **cl_fork.** Process fork support code. Allocate a class-specific data structure (tsproc or rtproc), initialize it with values from the parent thread, and add it to the linked list. Called from the lwpcreate() and lwpfork() kernel functions as part of the fork(2) system call.
- **cl_forkret.** Support a fork(2) system call. It is called from the kernel cfork() (common fork) code and is the last thing done before the fork(2) returns to the calling parent and the newly created child process. The *xx_forkret* functions resolve the run order of the parent and child, since it is desired that the child run first so the new object can be exec'd and can set up its own address space mappings to prevent the kernel from needlessly duplicating copy-on-write pages. The child is placed at the back of the dispatch queue and the parent gives up the processor.

- **cl_parmsget.** Get the current user priority and max user priority for a thread.

- **cl_parmsset.** Set the priority of a thread on the basis of passed input arguments. A user parameter data structure, *xxparms*, is defined for each scheduling class.

- **cl_stop.** Prepare a thread for a transition to the stop state.

- **cl_exit.** Handle an exiting thread. For FSS class threads, the project's framework needs to be updated, such as freeing shares that have been allocated to the exiting thread. For FX class threads, any registered callback functions are nulled and the callback list entry is deleted.

- **cl_active, cl_inactive.** Track active projects in a processor set. These functions are implemented only by the FSS scheduler and are called when an FSS class thread sleeps or wakes up.

- **cl_swapin.** Calculate the effective priority of a thread to determine the eligibility of its associated LWP for swapping in.

- **cl_swapout.** Calculate the effective priority of a thread for swapping out its LWP. Called by the memory scheduler (sched(), the swap-out function is passed a pointer to a kthread and a flag to indicate whether the memory scheduler is in hardswap or softswap mode (called from a similar loop in sched(), as described above). Softswap means avefree < desfree, (average free memory is less than desired free), so only threads sleeping longer than maxslp (20) seconds are marked for swap-out. Hard swap mode means that avefree has been less than minfree and desfree for an extended period of time (30 seconds), an average of two runnable threads are on the dispatch queues, and the paging (pagein + pageout) rate is high. (See Section 10.3.6.)

  The code is relatively simple; if in softswap mode, set effective priority to 0. If in hardswap mode, calculate an effective priority in a similar fashion as for swap-in, such that threads with a small address space that have been in memory for a relatively long amount of time are swapped out first. A time field, t_stime, in the kthread structure is set by the swapper when a thread is marked for swap-out as well as swap-in.

- **cl_trapret.** Readjust the thread's priority. Trap return code, called on return to user mode from a system call or trap.

- **cl_preempt.** Preempt a kernel thread and place it on a dispatch queue. Threads interrupted in kernel mode are given a SYS class priority so that they return to execution quickly. Preemption is discussed in Section 3.9.

- **cl_setrun.** Set a kernel thread runnable, typically called when a thread is removed from a sleep queue. Place the thread on a dispatch queue. For most threads, readjust the global dispatch priority if the thread has been waiting (sleeping) an inordinate amount time.

- **cl_sleep.** Prepare a thread for sleep. Set the thread's priority on the basis of wait time or if a kernel priority is requested (the kernel thread's t_kpri_req flag). A kernel priority (SYS class priority) is set if the thread is holding an exclusive lock on a memory page or an RW write lock.

- **cl_tick.** Process ticks for the thread. Called from the clock interrupt handler (see Section 19.1). Class-specific tick processing is discussed in the class-specific sections (beginning in Section 3.7.3.2).

- **cl_wakeup.** Move a thread from a sleep to a dispatch queue and reset several thread and class structure values.

- **cl_donice.** Adjust the priority according to the nice value for the target thread. Called when a nice(1) command is issued on the thread to alter the priority. nice(1) is not supported for RT and SYS class threads; the kernel functions for SYS and RT return an invalid operation error. The nice(1) command exists in Solaris for compatibility. Thread priority adjustments should be done with priocntl(1).

- **cl_globpri.** Return the global dispatch priority that a thread would be assigned for a given user-mode priority. The calculation of the actual dispatch priority of a thread is based on several factors, including the notion of a user priority. See Section 3.7 for details.

- **cl_set_process_group.** Establish the process group associated with the window session for IA class threads.

- **cl_yield.** Cause a thread to surrender the processor. Called from the yield(2) system call. The kernel thread is placed at the back of a dispatch queue.

The dispatcher and the kernel-at-large call the appropriate routine for a specific scheduling class, using essentially the same method used in the VFS/Vnode subsystem. A set of macros resolve to the class-specific function by indexing through either the current kernel thread pointer or the system class array. Certain functions exist in support of setting up a thread for a scheduling class; as such, the links will not yet be in place in the thread to locate a function in the class operations array, so calls are resolved through the system class array.

```
#define CL_ENTERCLASS(t, cid, clparmsp, credp, bufp) \
        (sclass[cid].cl_funcs->thread.cl_enterclass) (t, cid, \
            (void *)clparmsp, credp, bufp)

#define CL_EXITCLASS(cid, clprocp)\
        (sclass[cid].cl_funcs->thread.cl_exitclass) ((void *)clprocp)

#define CL_CANEXIT(t, cr)        (*(t)->t_clfuncs->cl_canexit)(t, cr)

#define CL_FORK(tp, ct, bufp)    (*(tp)->t_clfuncs->cl_fork)(tp, ct, bufp)

#define CL_FORKRET(t, ct)        (*(t)->t_clfuncs->cl_forkret)(t, ct)

#define CL_GETCLINFO(clp, clinfop) \
        (*(clp)->cl_funcs->sclass.cl_getclinfo)((void *)clinfop)
. . .
```
                                    See usr/src/uts/common/sys/class.h

CL_ENTERCLASS, for example, is entered through the system class array, indexed with the class ID (cid). CL_CANEXIT, CL_FORK, etc., are entered through the thread's t_clfuncs pointer. For a complete list of the class operations macros, see usr/src/uts/common/sys/class.h.

3.6.3 Scheduling Class Dispatcher Tables

Threads execute on a CPU until they block (sleep—issue a blocking system call), are preempted (a higher-priority thread becomes runnable), or they use their time quantum. A time quantum is the maximum execution time allotted to a thread before it gets forced off the CPU and must wait for its turn to come around again. The allotted time quantum varies according to the scheduling class and, in some cases, the priority of the thread. Solaris maintains time quanta for each scheduling class in an object called a dispatch table. The row and columns in a table vary across the different scheduling classes, but they all provide the user interface to adjusting time quanta.

You can examine the dispatch table for a given scheduling class by using dispadmin(1):

```
# dispadmin -g -c FSS

#
# Fair Share Scheduler Configuration
#
RES=1000
#
# Time Quantum
#
QUANTUM=110
```

The -c flag in the command line is followed by the scheduling class we're inter-ested in, FSS in this example. The QUANTUM unit of time is based on a resolu-tion value (reported as RES in the output). The unit of time is a reciprocal of the resolution; thus, a resolution value of 1000 equates to a unit of time of millisec-onds (1/1000 = 0.001), meaning the time quantum shown for FSS threads is 110 milliseconds for FSS threads at any priority.

The FX and RT classes allocate different time quanta according to the priority of the thread:

```
# Real Time Dispatcher Configuration
RES=1000

# TIME QUANTUM                    PRIORITY
# (rt_quantum)                    LEVEL
     1000                #            0
. . .
      800                #           10
. . .
      600                #           20
. . .
      400                #           30
. . .
      200                #           40
. . .
      100                #           50
. . .
      100                #           59
```

The RT table above lists quantum values for every one of 60 (0–59) possible pri-orities. Starting with a quantum of 1 second (1000 milliseconds) for the lowest-priority RT threads (priorities 0–9), the quantum is reduced as the priorities get better, pro-viding a balance: Higher-priority threads can consume fewer CPU cycles, and lower-priority threads, which tend to wait longer for CPU time, get a larger time quantum. The dispatch table for the FX class is similar, in that the table has two columns, assigning different time quanta for different priority threads—the actual time quantum values are different.

The SYS class is not implemented with a dispatch table, since SYS class threads are not subject to time limits when they execute. A SYS class thread runs until it completes, is preempted, or voluntarily releases the processor.

The TS/IA table has several additional columns for managing the priority of TS/ IA class threads based on different events and conditions. The example below shows the default values for a selected group of timeshare/interactive priorities. In the interest of space and readability, we don't list all 60 (0–59) priorities since we only need a representative sample for this discussion.

```
# Time Sharing Dispatcher Configuration
RES=1000

# ts_quantum  ts_tqexp  ts_slpret  ts_maxwait  ts_lwait  PRIORITY LEVEL
       200        0        50          0          50        #      0
. . .
       160        0        51          0          51        #     10
. . .
       120       10        52          0          52        #     20
. . .
        80       20        53          0          53        #     30
. . .
        40       30        55          0          55        #     40
. . .
        20       49        59      32000          59        #     59
```

Each entry in the TS/IA dispatch table (each row) is defined by the tsdpent (time-share dispatch entry) data structure.

```
/*
 * time-sharing dispatcher parameter table entry
 */
typedef struct tsdpent {
        pri_t   ts_globpri;     /* global (class independent) priority */
        int     ts_quantum;     /* time quantum given to procs at this level */
        pri_t   ts_tqexp;       /* ts_umdpri assigned when proc at this level */
                                /*   exceeds its time quantum */
        pri_t   ts_slpret;      /* ts_umdpri assigned when proc at this level */
                                /* returns to user mode after sleeping */
        short   ts_maxwait;     /* bumped to ts_lwait if more than ts_maxwait */
                                /* secs elapse before receiving full quantum */
        short   ts_lwait;       /* ts_umdpri assigned if ts_dispwait exceeds  */
                                /* ts_maxwait */
} tsdpent_t;
```
See usr/src/uts/common/sys/ts.h

RES and the PRIORITY LEVEL column are not defined in tsdpent. Those fields, along with the defined members in the structure table, are described below.

- **RES (resolution value).** Defines the unit of time for the ts_quantum column.

- **PRIORITY LEVEL.** The class-dependent priority, not the systemwide global priority. The PRIORITY LEVEL column is derived as the row number in the dispatch table. Every row corresponds to a unique priority level within the TS/IA) class, and each column in the row contains values that determine the priority adjustments made on the thread running at that particular priority. This is not the same as ts_globpri.

- **ts_globpri.** The only table parameter (tsdpent structure member) that is not displayed in the output of the dispadmin(1M) command, and also the only value that is not tuneable. ts_globpri is the class-independent global priority that corresponds to the timeshare priority (column farthest to the right). Refer to Figure 3.8 for a list of global priorities when all the bundled scheduling classes are loaded. Since TS/IA is the lowest class, the kernel global priorities 0–59 correspond to the TS/IA class priorities 0–59.

- **ts_quantum.** The time quantum; the amount of time that a thread at this priority is allowed to run before it must relinquish the processor, have its priority reset, and be assigned a new time quantum. Be aware that the ts_dptbl(4) man page, as well as other references, indicates that the value in the ts_quantum field is in ticks. A tick is a unit of time that can vary from platform to platform. In Solaris, there are 100 ticks per second, so a tick occurs every 10 milliseconds. The value in ts_quantum is in ticks only if RES is 100. If RES is any other value, including the default value of 1000, then ts_quantum represents some fraction of a second, the fractional value determined by the reciprocal value of RES. With a default value of RES = 1000, the reciprocal of 1000 is .001 (milliseconds).

We can change the RES value by using the -r flag with dispadmin(1M).

```
# dispadmin -g -c TS -r 100

# Time Sharing Dispatcher Configuration
RES=100

# ts_quantum  ts_tqexp  ts_slpret  ts_maxwait  ts_lwait  PRIORITY LEVEL
          20         0         50           0         50      #         0
          20         0         50           0         50      #         1
 . . .
```

This command causes the values in the ts_quantum column to change but does not change the actual quantum allocation. For example, at priority 0, instead of a quantum value of 200 with a RES of 1000, we have a quantum value of 20 with a RES of 100. The fractional unit is different. Instead of 200 milliseconds with a RES value of 1000, we get 20 tenths-of-a-second, which is the same amount of time, just represented differently [20 × .010 = 200 × .001]. In general, it makes sense to simply leave the RES value at the default of 1000, which makes it easy to interpret the ts_quantum field as milliseconds.

- **ts_tqexp.** Time quantum expired. The new priority a thread is set to when it has exceeded its time quantum. From the default values in the TS dispatch table, threads at priorities 0–10 have their priority set to 0 if they burn through their allotted time quantum. As another example, threads at priority 50 have a 40-millisecond time quantum and have their priority set to 40 if they use up their time.

- **ts_slpret.** The sleep return priority value. A thread that has been sleeping has its priority set to this value when it is woken up. These are set such that the thread will be placed at a higher priority (in some cases, substantially higher) so that the thread gets some processor time after having slept (waited for an event, which typically is a disk or network I/O).

- **ts_maxwait, ts_lwait.** These parameters compensate threads that have been preempted and have waited a relatively long time before using up their time quantum—it's a starvation avoidance mechanism that improves the priority of threads that have been sitting on a dispatch queue for an inordinate amount of time. ts_maxwait is the time threshold, and ts_lwait is the new priority for a thread that has waited longer than ts_maxwait.

   A thread's ts_dispwait variable is reset to zero when the thread is inserted on a dispatch queue, following a time-quantum expiration or a wakeup; note that preemption by a higher-priority thread does not result in ts_dispwait getting reset to zero. ts_dispwait is incremented once per second for every thread on a dispatch queue and sleep queue. When a thread's ts_dispwait exceeds ts_maxwait, the thread's priority is boosted to the corresponding priority value in the ts_lwait column.

   The priority boost for threads on sleep queues reflects a change that was introduced in Solaris 9, as a result of a thread starvation scenario that surfaced with certain workloads. The ts_dispwait field previously resulted only in a priority boost for threads in the TS_RUN state (runnable); threads on a sleep queue (TS_SLEEP state) did not get a priority change, so threads blocked on a synchronization object would continue to sleep with their priority unchanged. For certain types of synchronization, particularly where threads are woken one by one in priority order such as when acquiring an rwlock as a writer, threads that block at a low priority can be starved. For this reason, we added a change that bumps the priority of threads in sleep state as well as those in run state. This change is enabled with the ts_ sleep_promote parameter, which is set to 1 by default.

   Interesting to note is that the default values in the TS/IA dispatch table inject a 0 value in ts_maxwait for every priority except the highest priority (59). So just one increment in the ts_dispwait field causes the thread priority to be readjusted to ts_lwait, except for priority 59 threads. The net effect is that all but the highest-priority (59) timeshare threads have their priority bumped to the 50–59 range (ts_lwait) every second.

   This process has the desirable effect of not penalizing a thread that is CPU bound for an extended period of time. Threads that are CPU intensive will, over time, end up in the low 0–9 priority range as they keep using up their time quantum, because of priority readjustments by `ts_tqexp`. Once a second, they could get bumped back up to the 50–59 range and will only migrate back down if they sustain their CPU-bound behavior.

Priority 59 threads are handled differently. These threads are already at the maximum (best) priority for a timeshare thread, so there's no way to bump their priority with `ts_maxwait` and make it better. The `ts_update()` routine is the kernel code segment that increments the `ts_dispwait` value and readjusts thread priorities by means of `ts_lwait`. `ts_update()` reorders the linked list of threads on the dispatch queues after adjusting the priority. The reordering after the priority adjustment puts threads at the front of their new dispatch queue for that priority. The threads on the priority 59 linked list would end up reordered but still at the same priority.

You can apply user-supplied values to the dispatch tables by using the `dispadmin(1M)` command or by compiling a new `/kernel/sched/TS_DPTBL` loadable module and replacing the default module. The `ts_dptbl(4)` man page provides the source and the instructions for doing this. Either way, any changes to the dispatch tables should be done with extreme caution and tested extensively before going into production.

3.7 Thread Priorities

In Solaris, two types of priorities are involved in scheduling activity: *global* priorities and *user* priorities. The latter are often referred to as user-mode priorities, implemented in the TS/IA, FSS, and FX classes; SYS and RT do not implement user priorities. Global priorities are the systemwide range of priorities used by the dispatcher to determine which thread gets to run next on a CPU. User-mode priorities are a range of user-settable priorities that allow users to alter a thread's priority, that is, to make it better or worse. For you who are familiar with the traditional UNIX `nice(1)` command: User-mode priorities are the modern implementation of `nice(1)`; the command-line interface for setting user priorities is `priocntl(1)`.

Figure 3.8 illustrates the global priority range and per-scheduling class user-priority range.

We should note that it is not required (or even recommended) that users, administrators, and developers apply user priorities as they put Solaris to work. The implementation supports them, but the dispatcher and underlying infrastructure are designed to work optimally without user-defined priorities being explicitly set.

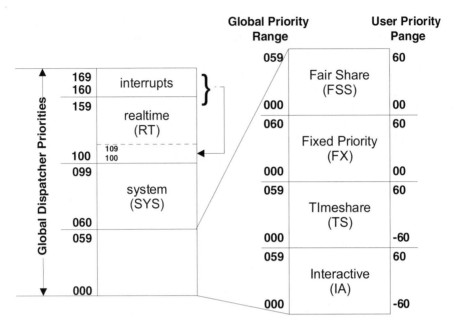

Figure 3.8 Dispatcher Global Priorities

3.7.1 Global Priorities

Global priorities refer to the numeric priority value assigned to every kernel thread on the system (t_pri variable in the kthread_t); they are initially-derived from the scheduling class of the thread issuing the thread_create() call. The global attribute means the priority value falls within a valid range of systemwide values, providing a scheme by which the highest-priority thread on the system can be determined simply by locating the thread with the highest numeric priority value relative to all other runnable threads on the system. In Solaris, larger values are better priorities.

The per-processor dispatch queues are arranged in a priority-ordered fashion, with a separate queue for each global priority on the system. We see from Figure 3.2 that there is one dispq_t for each priority. All threads at the same priority are placed on the same queue, implemented as a linked list of kernel threads. Threads are selected from the front of the per-priority queue but can be inserted at the front or back of the queue.

There are 170 global priorities: 0–169, with 0 being the lowest priority, and 169 the highest (or best) priority. Priorities 160–169 are not actually scheduling priorities, but rather priority levels reserved exclusively for interrupt threads. However, if an interrupt thread blocks, it becomes a real, schedulable thread, where its priority is 159 + PIL. If the clock thread blocks (for example), it becomes a (159 + PIL 10) priority 169 thread.

Priorities 100–159 are used exclusively by the real-time (RT) scheduling class. Priorities 60–99 are used exclusively for SYS class threads; core operating system kernel threads run in the SYS class. Last, priorities 0–59 are the global priority range shared by all the threads in the Timeshare (TS), Fixed (FX), Fair Share (FSS) and Interactive (IA) scheduling classes. This is shown in Figure 3.3.

The actual number of global priorities changes according to the presence or absence of the real-time scheduling class in the running system. By default, if a process or thread is not explicitly placed in the real-time class, the real-time class will not load into the kernel at boot time. If the real-time class is not loaded, the range is 0–109, with interrupts occupying the top ten priority levels, 100–109. Since the real-time class has a range of 60 priorities, once loaded, global priorities span 0–169. Interrupts remain the highest-priority scheduling events on the system, moving to 160–169 when the real-time class is loaded.

The global priority of a thread typically changes frequently over time (with the exception of FX class threads, and FSS class threads with 0 shares allocated), and a global priority change requires a change in the thread's position on a dispatch queue. As such, the priority change functions handle both the calculation and storage on the thread's new priority (the kthread_t t_pri field) and insert the thread into a new position on the dispatch queues.

3.7.2 User Priorities

User priorities warrant coverage here because they factor into the calculation of a thread's global priority every time a thread's priority is changed. Each scheduling class that supports user priorities has a predefined priority range, viewable with the priocntl(1) command.

```
# priocntl -l

CONFIGURED CLASSES
==================

SYS (System Class)

TS (Time Sharing)
        Configured TS User Priority Range: -60 through 60

FX (Fixed priority)
        Configured FX User Priority Range: 0 through 60

RT (Real Time)
        Maximum Configured RT Priority: 59

FSS (Fair Share)
        Configured FSS User Priority Range: -60 through 60
```

The intent is to provide users some level of control over the priority of their processes and threads, without allowing a user to directly set the global priority. The setting of a user priority has the net effect of changing the global priority of the target thread (or process), making it either better or worse, depending on the user value specified. Think of user priorities as a priority control knob that allows users to turn the priority up or down (better or worse). Here's a quick example.

```
# ps -Lc
    PID   LWP  CLS PRI TTY         LTIME CMD
  23359    1   TS  59 pts/2        0:00 sh
  23374    1   TS  59 pts/2        0:00 ps

# priocntl -s -c TS -i pid -p 0 $$

# ps -Lc
    PID   LWP  CLS PRI TTY         LTIME CMD
  23359    1   TS  49 pts/2        0:00 sh
  23376    1   TS  59 pts/2        0:00 ps

# priocntl -s -c TS -i pid -p -60 $$

# ps -Lc
    PID   LWP  CLS PRI TTY         LTIME CMD
  23359    1   TS   0 pts/2        0:00 sh
  23378    1   TS   0 pts/2        0:00 ps

# priocntl -s -c TS -i pid -p 60 $$

# ps -Lc
    PID   LWP  CLS PRI TTY         LTIME CMD
  23359    1   TS  59 pts/2        0:00 sh
  23380    1   TS  59 pts/2        0:00 ps
```

The example above uses priocntl(1) to tweak the priority of the shell process. It's a TS class process, at priority 59—the best global priority for TS class threads. We set the user priority to 0, which is in the middle of the TS range of –60 to 60. This command results in the shell's global priority getting slightly worse, going to 49 (from 59). We then turn the knob all the way down, setting the user priority to –60, the lowest possible value, which has the effect of dragging the shell's global priority down to 0, the lowest possible global priority for TS class threads. Last, we turn the priority knob in the other direction, setting a user-priority value of 60. This results in a large global priority boost for the target process, bringing the global priority from 0 to 59.

The key point here is that user priorities do not map directly to global priorities; note that the changed global priority in the example was not the same absolute value specified on the priocntl(1) command line. User priorities serve as an advice/request mechanism to the dispatcher to make the priority of the target thread or process either better or worse. The actual effect will not always be as extreme as the example. Note also that nonprivileged users cannot improve a priority; they can only move it in a negative (worse) direction. The ability to improve priority requires either root or the process-level `PRIV_PROC_PRIOCNTL` privilege (see `privileges(5)`).

3.7.3 Setting Thread Priorities

Thread priorities can change as a result of *event-driven* or *time-interval-driven* events. Event-driven changes are asynchronous in nature; they include state transitions as a result of a blocking system call, a wakeup from sleep, a preemption, or expiration of the allotted time quantum. A user can generate a priority change event by changing a thread's user priority, its scheduling class, or both. Time-driven tick and update functions execute at regular intervals and typically result in changing the priority of threads. Changing a thread's priority varies in complexity depending on the scheduling class, with some substantial differences in implementation. There's a common component in the dispatch queue insertion functions, which happens (typically) as the last operation in a priority change. Figure 3.9 illustrates the flow.

A thread's global priority is stored in the thread's `kthread_t t_pri` field. Kernel support for user priorities exists within the class-specific structures (*xxproc_t*), which includes a `upri` field to store the user-specified priority value and a `umdpri` variable to store the derived user-mode priority for a thread (`ts_umdpri`, `fss_umdpri`, and `ia_umdpri` for their respective scheduling classes). The implementation details differ across the different scheduling classes in terms of how user priority determines how the `umdpri` field is set and how `umdpri` determines the global priority of the thread.

3.7.3.1 Time-Based Class Functions

Two class-specific operations get called at regular time intervals—tick processing and update processing. Tick processing is handled through the class *xx_tick()* function and is called from the kernel clock interrupt handler, which executes 100 times a second, based on the default `hz` value of 100 (100 Hz = 1/100 = .010 seconds or 10 milliseconds). Update processing is done for TS/IA and FSS class threads and is called through the kernel callout mechanism (`timeout(9f)`), using the class *xx_update()* code (the SYS, FX, and RT classes do not implement an update function).

The tick and update functions perform very different tasks. Tick processing operates on all threads that are executing on a CPU (TS_ONPROC state) and handles updating the tick counter in the thread's *xxproc_t* structure to track execution time. Update processing operates on threads that are either sitting on a dispatch queue (TS_RUN) or sitting on a sleep queue (TS_SLEEP). The intention of

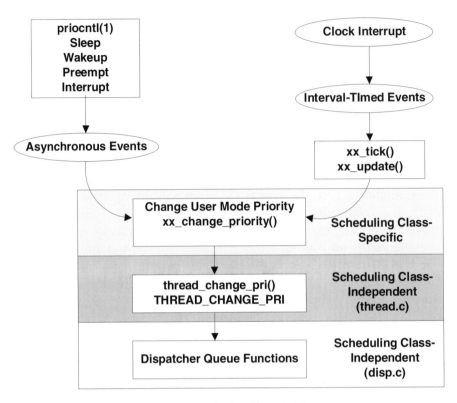

Figure 3.9 Priority Change Flow

the update function for TS/IA class threads is to track threads that have spent an inordinate amount of time on a queue and could use a priority boost to more quickly get back on a CPU. Priority adjustments are made if needed. Essentially, TS/IA update is a starvation avoidance mechanism. The update function for FSS has a very different role. Time spent waiting for a CPU is not tracked for FSS threads. It's not necessary since fair-share scheduling, by definition, ensures that threads get the CPU resources allocated to them. Update for FSS manages the adjustment and normalization of share usage and resets thread priorities accordingly.

Tick Processing.   Tick processing is done for all threads, except those in the SYS class since the rules of CPU usage and time quanta do not apply to threads running at a kernel priority. Tick processing begins in the clock interrupt handler (common/os/clock.c), which includes code that executes a loop, checking every CPU on the system. The interesting part of the loop code that may call clock_tick() is shown here.

```
 * If we haven't done tick processing for this
 * lwp, then do it now. Since we don't hold the
 * lwp down on a CPU it can migrate and show up
 * more than once, hence the lbolt check.
 *
 * Also, make sure that it's okay to perform the
 * tick processing before calling clock_tick.
 * Setting thread_away to a TRUE value (ie. not 0)
 * results in tick processing not being performed for
 * that thread.  Or, in other words, keeps the thread
 * away from clock_tick processing.
 */
thread_away = ((cp->cpu_flags & CPU_QUIESCED) ||
    CPU_ON_INTR(cp) || intr ||
    (cp->cpu_dispthread == cp->cpu_idle_thread) || exiting);

if ((!thread_away) && (lbolt - t->t_lbolt != 0)) {
        t->t_lbolt = lbolt;
        clock_tick(t);
}
```

See usr/src/uts/common/os/clock.c

The `clock_tick()` function is called if the thread is *due* for tick processing, the CPU *is not* executing the idle thread, and the CPU *is online* (not quiesced) and *not executing* an interrupt thread. The class-specific tick function is called out of `clock_tick()` through the `CL_TICK(t)` macro. The work performed by the class-specific tick handler is to charge the thread with another tick of CPU time, check to see if the thread has used its time quantum, and, if it has, reprioritize the thread and force it to surrender the CPU. The details are covered in the per-class sections that follow. The following pseudocode is a generic representation of thread tick processing.

```
xx_tick()
      get threadlock
      get thread's fssproc_t structure
      increment thread's tick count
      if (the thread is not at a SYS priority)
            decrement thread's timeleft variable
            if (timeleft <= 0) /* no time left - quantum used */
                  if (thread has preemption control enabled)
                        let it run unless it's been a while
                        return
                  set a new priority for the thread
                  reestablish the thread's position on a disp queue or sleep queue

            else (if the thread has not used its time quantum)
            if (thread's priority <  disp queue's highest priority thread)
                  set the thread's flag to be placed on the back of the disp queue
                  surrender the CPU
      release the threadlock
```

Once the class-specific tick processing is completed, the code returns to `clock_tick()`, which performs a few additional tasks:

- Updates user or system time used at the process and task level
- Updates user-defined interval timers, if they exist, and send a signal to the process if a timer has expired
- Tests resource control limits on allocated CPU time at the process and task level
- Updates memory usage for the currently running process

Once `clock_tick()` completes, it returns to the main loop in `clock.c`. Each CPU in the system has tick processing done on the CPU's thread unless the conditions described at the beginning of this section are not met, in which case the CPU is passed over and the next CPU is checked.

Update Processing.   While tick processing is driven directly out of clock interrupts, update functions are driven indirectly out of clock interrupts, through the kernel's callout mechanism. Each scheduling class uses the kernel `timeout(9F)` function to place its update function on the kernel callout queue, resulting in `ts_update()` and `fss_update()` executing once per second. Callout queue processing is done in the clock interrupt handler (the `callout_schedule()` function).

Only the TS/IA and FSS classes implement update functions, and the two class-specific functions differ significantly in implementation. For TS/IA class threads, the amount of time a thread waits to use its time quantum is tracked through the `ts_diswait` field in `tsproc_t`. The `ts_update()` function increments the dispwait field for threads that are runnable (TS_RUN) or sleeping (TS_SLEEP) and will boost priorities as needed.

The FSS update function has a very different role, which is to update share usage and change priorities accordingly. The FSS class is significantly more complex due to the inherent nature of fair-share scheduling and the administrative framework required to implement the allocation of shares.

The implementation details are discussed in the following sections for the individual scheduling classes.

3.7.3.2 Timeshare Thread Priorities

This section covers both TS and IA class threads, since the majority of IA class work is done in the TS code. We start by covering user-priority setting, then get into setting the global priority.

The TS/IA class uses the kernel TS_NEWUMDPRI macro to set a user-mode priority.

```
#define TS_NEWUMDPRI(tspp) \
{ \
        pri_t pri; \
        pri = (tspp)->ts_cpupri + (tspp)->ts_upri + (tspp)->ts_boost; \
        if (pri > ts_maxumdpri) \
                (tspp)->ts_umdpri = ts_maxumdpri; \
        else if (pri < 0) \
                (tspp)->ts_umdpri = 0; \
        else \
                (tspp)->ts_umdpri = pri; \
        ASSERT((tspp)->ts_umdpri >= 0 && (tspp)->ts_umdpri <= ts_maxumdpri); \
}
```

                                                  See usr/src/uts/common/disp/ts.c

Three components are involved in setting the `ts_umdpri` value: `ts_cpupri`, `ts_upri`, and `ts_boost`. `ts_cpupri` is the system- (kernel-) controlled component of the user-mode priority, `ts_upri` stores the actual user-specified value (from the `priocntl(1)` command line), and `ts_boost` is an IA-class specific variable for priority-boosting threads attached to active windows on desktops.

The `TS_NEWUMDPRI` code is executed in many places throughout the TS functions: essentially whenever a priority change is required. As an example here, we assume that a user triggered an event by issuing a `priocntl(1)` command on a TS class thread to change the user priority. The `ts_parmsset()` function handles setting a user priority when a `priocntl(1)` command is issued. After permission and boundary testing, the interesting code is as shown below.

```
ts_parmsset()
. . .
        * Set ts_nice to the nice value corresponding to the user
        * priority we are setting.  Note that setting the nice field
        * of the parameter struct won't affect upri or nice.
        */
       nice = NZERO - (reqtsupri * NZERO) / ts_maxupri;
       if (nice >= 2 * NZERO)
               nice = 2 * NZERO - 1;

       thread_lock(tx);

       tspp->ts_uprilim = reqtsuprilim;
       tspp->ts_upri = reqtsupri;
       TS_NEWUMDPRI(tspp);
       tspp->ts_nice = nice;

       if ((tspp->ts_flags & TSKPRI) != 0) {
               thread_unlock(tx);
               return (0);
       }

       tspp->ts_dispwait = 0;
       ts_change_priority(tx, tspp);
. . .
```

                                                  See usr/src/uts/common/disp/ts.c

A nice value is derived from the requested user priority, `ts_uprilim` (user-priority limit) and `ts_upri` are set according to command-line values, and `TS_NEWUMDPRI()` is executed to set `ts_umdpri`.

Setting the new `ts_umdpri` value is pretty clear—sum the three component values and ensure that the new value falls within the maximum and minimum value boundaries. The `ts_umdpri` value is used subsequently when the thread's global priority is changed. Note that the default for these values is zero when a thread enters the `TS` class, unless user-defined values have been specified. On a thread create, the values are inherited from the parent thread.

Getting from a user priority to a new thread global priority is handled in `ts_change_priority()`.

```
ts_change_priority()
new_pri = ts_dptbl[tspp->ts_umdpri].ts_globpri;
        ASSERT(new_pri >= 0 && new_pri <= ts_maxglobpri);
        if (t == curthread || t->t_state == TS_ONPROC) {
                /* curthread is always onproc */
                cpu_t   *cp = t->t_disp_queue->disp_cpu;
                THREAD_CHANGE_PRI(t, new_pri);
                                        See usr/src/uts/common/disp/ts.c
```

If the thread is running (`TS_ONPROC`), the new global priority is derived from the `ts_globpri` column of the `TS` dispatcher table, as indexed with `ts_umdpri` and set with the `THREAD_CHANGE_PRI` macro. Otherwise, the class-independent `thread_change_pri()` function is called.

```
thread_change_pri(kthread_t *t, pri_t disp_pri, int front)
{
        state = t->t_state;
        /*
         * If it's not on a queue, change the priority with
         * impunity.
         */
        if ((state & (TS_SLEEP | TS_RUN)) == 0) {
                t->t_pri = disp_pri;
                if (state == TS_ONPROC) {
                        cpu_t *cp = t->t_disp_queue->disp_cpu;
                        if (t == cp->cpu_dispthread)
                                cp->cpu_dispatch_pri = DISP_PRIO(t);
                }
                return (0);
        }
                                        See usr/src/uts/common/disp/thread.c
```

The code does another test on the thread state, and if the thread is not on a queue, sets the thread's `t_pri` directly.

The bottom half of the function handles thread's on a run queue or a sleep queue.

```
thread_change_pri(kthread_t *t, pri_t disp_pri, int front)
. . .
        * It's either on a sleep queue or a run queue.
        */
       if (state == TS_SLEEP) {
               /*
                * If the priority has changed, take the thread out of
                * its sleep queue and change the priority.
                * Re-enqueue the thread.
                * Each synchronization object exports a function
                * to do this in an appropriate manner.
                */
               if (disp_pri != t->t_pri)
                       SOBJ_CHANGE_PRI(t->t_sobj_ops, t, disp_pri);
       } else {
               /*
                * The thread is on a run queue.
                * Note: setbackdq() may not put the thread
                * back on the same run queue where it originally
                * resided.
                *
                * We still requeue the thread even if the priority
                * is unchanged to preserve round-robin (and other)
                * effects between threads of the same priority.
                */
               on_rq = dispdeq(t);
               ASSERT(on_rq);
               t->t_pri = disp_pri;
               if (front) {
                       setfrontdq(t);
               } else {
                       setbackdq(t);
               }
```

See usr/src/uts/common/disp/thread.c

For threads on a sleep queue, invoke the synchronization object-specific change priority macro (SOBJ_CHANGE_PRI) to handle changing the priority and managing the thread's position on a sleep queue. If the thread is on a run queue, dequeue the thread, set the priority, and queue the thread (with a different priority, the thread's queue position will change).

TS Tick Processing. ts_tick() tracks thread execution time with the ts_timeleft variable in tsproc_t. ts_timeleft is set to the time quantum (from the dispatch table) when the thread is switched on a CPU to begin execution. It is decremented in ts_tick(), and if ts_timeleft has reached zero, the thread's priority is reset from the dispatch table (the ts_tqexp value), and the CPU's user preemption flag (cp_runrun) is set to force a preemption. If the thread has been assigned a short-term SYS priority (the TSKPRI flag is set in ts_flags), the tick processing is not done on the thread (a thread will be assigned a SYS priority when the thread is holding a critical resource, such as a reader/writer lock or a memory page lock).

In the case in which the thread has used its time quantum, the ts_tick() code tests to see if a *scheduler activation* has been turned on for the thread, in the form of *preemption control* (see the paragraph beginning "It is in the dispatcher queue insertion code" on page 262).

If preemption control has been turned on for the thread, it is allowed an extra couple of clock ticks to execute, no priority tweaks are done, and `ts_tick()` is finished with the thread. There is a limit to how many additional clock ticks a kthread with preemption control turned on will be given. If that limit has been exceeded, the kernel sets a flag such that the thread gets one more time slice and on the next pass through `ts_tick()`, the preemption control test fails and normal tick processing is done. In this way, the kernel does not allow the scheduler activation to keep the thread running indefinitely.

A thread priority adjustment from TS tick processing does a couple of extra steps in setting new values from the TS dispatch table. `ts_cpupri` is used as an index into the TS dispatch table and is assigned a new value that is based on `ts_tqexp` from the indexed location. The user-mode priority is calculated, `ts_dispwait` is set to 0, and a new dispatcher priority is derived from the TS/IA dispatch table. The new priority is based on the global priority value in the table row corresponding to `ts_umdpri`, which is used as the dispatch table array index. A call to `thread_change_pri()` follows. A change in a thread's priority may warrant a change in its position on a queue; `thread_change_pri()` handles such a case. In the fork return, we are dealing with a new thread that has not yet been on a queue, so it's not an issue.

> **TS Update Processing.**   The work of `ts_update()` is well documented in the source code:

```
/*
 * Update the ts_dispwait values of all time sharing threads that
 * are currently runnable at a user mode priority and bump the priority
 * if ts_dispwait exceeds ts_maxwait.  Called once per second via
 * timeout which we reset here.
 *
 * There are several lists of time sharing threads broken up by a hash on
 * the thread pointer.  Each list has its own lock.  This avoids blocking
 * all ts_enterclass, ts_fork, and ts_exitclass operations while ts_update
 * runs.  ts_update traverses each list in turn.
 *
 * If multiple threads have their priorities updated to the same value,
 * the system implicitly favors the one that is updated first (since it
 * winds up first on the run queue).  To avoid this unfairness, the
 * traversal of threads starts at the list indicated by a marker.  When
 * threads in more than one list have their priorities updated, the marker
 * is moved.  This changes the order the threads will be placed on the run
 * queue the next time ts_update is called and preserves fairness over the
 * long run.  The marker doesn't need to be protected by a lock since it's
 * only accessed by ts_update, which is inherently single-threaded (only
 * one instance can be running at a time).
 */
```

See usr/src/uts/common/disp/ts.c

The actual priority tweaks are done in ts_update_list(), which is called by ts_update() to update a list of threads. The basic algorithm implemented in ts_update_list() is represented in the pseudocode flow below.

```
ts_update()
        set list from ts_plisthead[] /* lists of tsproc structures */
        ts_update_list()
                while (not at the end of the current list)
                        if (thread is not in TS or IA class)
                                bail out
                        incremement thread's dispwait
                        if (thread is at a SYS priority)
                                bail out
                        if (thread has preemption control turned on)
                                bail out
                        if (thread is not TS_RUN)
                                AND
                           (thread is not TS_SLEEP) OR (ts_sleep_promote is disabled)
                                        set thread flags for post trap processing
                                        bail out
                        kthread->tsproc.ts_cpupri = ts_dptbl[ts_cpupri].ts_lwait
                        TS_NEWUMDPRI
                        kthread->tsproc.ts_dispwait = 0
                        if (the thread's priority global priority changed)
                                ts_change_priority()
                end loop
```

The actual priority change is handled with the same code previously described: TS_NEWUMDPRI to set the user-mode priority, and ts_change_priority() if the global priority is different.

3.7.3.3 Fair-Share Thread Priorities

The FSS class also implements a user-mode priority, fss_umdpri, that is an integral part of establishing a thread's global priority. The use of fss_umdpri as a knob available to users to make priority adjustments is consistent with its use in the TS/IA class as well. Unlike the TS class, the FSS class does not have a specific code path just for setting fss_umdpri. Rather, fss_umdpri updates are done through fss_newpri(), a function used whenever an FSS priority change is required. By default, when a thread is placed in the FSS class, fss_umdpri is set to 29 (fss_maxumdpri / 2), and when a thread is created from an FSS-class thread, the fss_umdpri and fss_upri are inherited from the parent thread.

FSS Tick Processing.   FSS class tick processing does a bit more work than we saw in the TS example. That's due to the share-based priority mechanism and the integration with the Projects and Zones frameworks, which are required as the administrative model for share allocation. Threads in the FSS class are associated with a project, through the projects database (/etc/project), and the execution time of FSS class threads needs to get charged to the project the thread belongs to, in addition to the actual thread. This is accomplish this by increment-ing `fssp_ticks` in the project structure, in addition to the per-thread tick count (`fss_ticks`—see Figure 3.7). Aside from the project update, the work done in `fss_tick()` is essentially the same as with the other classes. If the target thread has used its time quantum, a new priority is set with `fss_newpri()`, which is covered in the next section.

FSS Update Processing. The `fss_update()` work sets the stage for discussion of our next two topics: the concept of fair-share scheduling and the implementation of usage and shares management with respect to how it effects priority changes. A substantial amount of code and complexity in share decay usage processing awaits us, but first we need to lay a foundation.

FSS is based on shares, but the dispatcher schedules threads based on their glo-bal priority (see `FSS(7)`), and the allocation of CPU shares is at the project or zone level, not the process or thread (by the `project.cpu-shares` or `zone.cpu-shares` resource controls). Additionally, one or more projects can be configured within a zone. A project may have just one single-threaded process in it, or it may have many multithreaded processes. The actual number of processes and threads within a project does not factor into the usage measurement or adjustment mechanism. Thus, the FSS code must factor in the number of shares allocated and recent CPU utilization (shares consumed) within projects and zones in order to establish a FSS thread's new priority. Figure 3.10 provides the big picture.

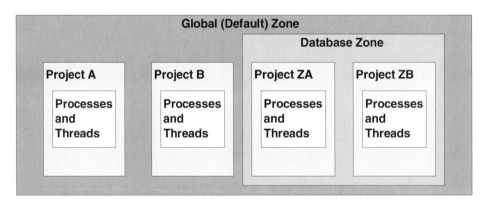

Figure 3.10 Zones and Projects

A few points on Figure 3.10. First, the projects framework includes an abstrac-tion called tasks, which are a subset of projects and a superset of processes and threads—a project can contain one or more tasks, and each task can encapsulate one or more processes. In the interest of space and simplicity, tasks are not shown (also, FSS share allocation is not done at the task level). Second, the objects shown in the figure may have resource allocations for CPU shares, and the shares may be charged to specific processor set configurations. That is, Projects A and B (for example) may both exist in a processor set, and the share allocation is based on the processors in the set, not on all the processors systemwide. These facilities are well documented in the *System Administration Guide: Solaris Containers—Resource Management and Solaris Zones* guide (http://docs.sun.com). The figure sets the context for the current discussion. A brief summary of what the premise of fair-share scheduling is drawn from and what the decay usage component needs to accomplish will also help.

The FSS scheduler provides two levels of scheduling. At the top level, zones that compete with each other for the same CPU resources (that is, within the same processor set) are allocated CPU cycles based on the ratio between their shares and the total amount of zone shares. So, the actual number of shares assigned to each zone is not important, but the ratio between them is. If one zone has 5 shares and the only other zone has 10 shares, the first zone will receive 5/15th (or 1/3rd) of the CPU cycles, and the second would receive 10/15th (or 2/3rds). More importantly, assigning two zones 5 and 10 shares each will have the same effect if they were assigned 10 and 20 shares instead.

At the level below that, projects are allocated their CPU cycles according to the ratio of their assigned shares to the total amount of project shares within each zone. CPU cycles that were assigned to the zone at the top level get distributed between different projects in it if they all compete for the same CPU resources again. Note that if there is only one project in a zone, then the number of shares assigned to that project doesn't matter—it will get all the CPU cycles that were allocated to the zone. Similarly, if there is only one zone on the system, it will get all available CPU cycles no matter how many shares were assigned to it.

It is important to understand that shares only start to impact CPU allocation when projects or zones actually compete for the same CPU resources. For example, imagine two CPU-bound threads running in projects with different amounts of shares on a two-processor system. Since each thread can only run on one CPU at the time, these two threads would not actually compete for CPU cycles, and therefore the number of shares allocated to each of their projects does not matter here. CPU shares are not reservations. A project or a zone without actively running threads does not affect other projects or zones. When the total number of shares is calculated for each zone running on each processor set, only shares of zones and projects that have at least one actively running thread are counted.

The fair-share scheduler must implement a model by which usage can be tracked and decayed at regular time intervals. The term *decay* here means normalize usage according to recent activity and allocated shares, keeping in mind that share allocation can change dynamically (some project, for example, can have its allocation increased from 20 to 50 shares between sampling periods). Simply put, the scheduler needs to calculate share usage over time, factoring actual usage with allocated shares and other share consumption in the project and zone.

In `fss_decay_usage()`, the usage adjustment is done according to the following formula:

$$shusage_{project} = usage \times \frac{activeshares^2_{pset}}{shares^2_{project}} \times \frac{zoneactiveshares^2_{pset}}{zoneallocatedshares^2}$$

where the share usage (shusage) is derived from the decayed actual usage, factored with the active shares in the processor set and total shares in the project. If we're calculating zone usage, the zone's active and allocated shares are factored in.

Getting back to `fss_update()`, the first step in the update process is a call to `fss_usage_decay()`, which manages usage updates for all projects. Before stepping through the actual code, we need to refer to some constants used in the calculations.

```
/*
 * Decay rate percentages are based on n/128 rather than n/100 so that
 * calculations can avoid having to do an integer divide by 100 (divide
 * by FSS_DECAY_BASE == 128 optimizes to an arithmetic shift).
 *
 * FSS_DECAY_MIN        =  83/128 ~= 65%
 * FSS_DECAY_MAX        = 108/128 ~= 85%
 * FSS_DECAY_USG        =  96/128 ~= 75%
 */
#define FSS_DECAY_MIN    83      /* fsspri decay pct for threads w/ nice -20 */
#define FSS_DECAY_MAX    108     /* fsspri decay pct for threads w/ nice +19 */
#define FSS_DECAY_USG    96      /* fssusage decay pct for projects */
#define FSS_DECAY_BASE   128     /* base for decay percentages above */

#define FSS_NICE_MIN     0
#define FSS_NICE_MAX     (2 * NZERO - 1)
#define FSS_NICE_RANGE   (FSS_NICE_MAX - FSS_NICE_MIN + 1)

static int       fss_nice_tick[FSS_NICE_RANGE];
static int       fss_nice_decay[FSS_NICE_RANGE];
                                  See usr/src/uts/common/disp/fss.c
```

The `FSS_DECAY_MIN` and `FSS_DECAY_MAX` constants are used when the FSS class is first initialized, to seed values in the `fss_nice_tick[]` and `fss_nice_delay[]` arrays (more on these arrays in a moment). `FSS_DECAY_USG` is used in the usage decay function to calculate the decayed usage.

First, let's take a look at how the decayed usage is derived.

```
* Decay usage for each project running on
                       * this cpu partition.
                       */
                      fssproj->fssp_usage =
                          (fssproj->fssp_usage * FSS_DECAY_USG) /
                          FSS_DECAY_BASE + fssproj->fssp_ticks;
                      fssproj->fssp_ticks = 0;
                                          See usr/src/uts/common/disp/fss.c
```

The project's `fssp_usage` decay is based on its current value, the decay constants (rate of 75%), and the number of ticks used by the project, that is, the actual CPU ticks used—see page 212) Even though `fssp_usage` is stored as a 64-bit value, decaying is necessary to avoid possible integer overflows and to keep track of CPU usage history over a short time. The speed of decay determines the length of such a period. Floating-point operations generally are not permitted to be used by the kernel (mostly for performance), so the scheduler is using large integer values (note that the project's `fssp_ticks` gets charged by almost 1000 points for each clock tick) to get reasonable precision at a very low cost. To further increase the performance of this code, integer divisions used for decaying are optimized by the compiler into simple arithmetic shifts due to the carefully chosen decay base— `FSS_DECAY_BASE` is set to 128.

The next step is to determine the number of actual shares allocated, in case it changed.

```
/*

                      * Readjust our number of shares if it has
                      * changed since we checked it last time.
                      */
                     kpj_shares = fssproj->fssp_proj->kpj_shares;
                     if ((fssproj->fssp_shares != kpj_shares) &&
                         (fssproj->fssp_runnable != 0)) {
                             fsszone->fssz_shares -=
                                 fssproj->fssp_shares;
                             fssproj->fssp_shares = kpj_shares;
                             fsszone->fssz_shares += kpj_shares;
                     }
                                         See usr/src/uts/common/disp/fss.c
```

In the above code segment, the current share allocation is saved (`kpj_shares`: from the `kproject_t`, which is linked to `fssproj_t`). If the share allocation changed and there are runnable threads in the project (meaning it's active), adjust the share values at the zone and project level. Note that a similar code segment follows in the source that does the same algorithm. The first case covers projects in a zone; the second case covers a zone with no projects.

With the decayed usage and share calculations done, the normalized share usage can be completed.

```
fssproj->fssp_shusage =
        (fssproj->fssp_usage *
        fsspset->fssps_shares *
        fsspset->fssps_shares *
        fsszone->fssz_shares *
        fsszone->fssz_shares) /
        (kpj_shares * kpj_shares *
        zone_shares * zone_shares);
```
                                        See usr/src/uts/common/disp/fss.c

The code segment above is the implementation of the formula shown previously; doing the math with sample values is left as an exercise for the reader.

The `fss_decay_usage()` algorithm is summarized in the pseudocode below.

```
fss_decay_usage()
    for (every CPU)
        fsspset = pset /* set the pset for the CPU */
        if (there's a partition)
            if (there are projects)
                decay the max FSS priority for the partition
            for (every project in the partition)
                decay project usage based on accumulated project ticks
                reset project tick count to zero
                set the zone object pointers
                set the allocated share value (in case it changed)
                if (project allocated shares changed) AND (runnable threads in the proj)
                    readjust the number of shares
                if (zone allocated shares changed) AND (runnable threads in zone)
                    readjust number of shares in the zone
                calculate normalized share value to be used for fsspri increments
```

`fss_decay_usage()` returns to the update function after completing the task of looping through all CPUs, partitions, and zones and updating share usage accordingly. The remaining work required in the update function is to make the actual thread priority adjustments, which happens in `fss_update_list()`. Looping through a partial list (similar to `ts_upate()`), the code runs the same tests to ensure that the thread is in the FSS class and not currently a SYS priority. Assuming a non-zero number of shares, the fsspri (priority) value is decayed. If the thread does not have a preemption control enabled and is in the TS_RUN state, `fss_newpri()` is called to set the thread's new priority.

All the dots get connected in `fss_newpri()` or `fss_change_priority()`—the decayed `fsspri` and the normalized share usage all come together as part of the priority calculation process. The decayed `fsspri` value set in `fss_update_list()` is the `fss_fsspri` variable in the thread's `fssproc_t` and represents the internal FSS priority, not the thread's actual CPU priority, which is `t_pri` in the thread structure. In `fss_newpri()`, the `fsspri` value is readjusted according to the normalized share usage (`shusage`), the number of runnable threads in the project, and the current tick value of the thread.

```
/*
        * fsspri += shusage * nrunnable * ticks
        */
    ticks = fssproc->fss_ticks;
    fssproc->fss_ticks = 0;
    fsspri = fssproc->fss_fsspri;
    fsspri += fssproj->fssp_shusage * fssproj->fssp_runnable * ticks;
    fssproc->fss_fsspri = fsspri;
                                            See usr/src/uts/common/disp/fss.c
```

With an updated `fsspri` value, a new user-mode priority, `fss_umdpri` is set by the code segment below.

```
    /*
     * The general priority formula:
     *
     *                          (fsspri * umdprirange)
     *   pri = maxumdpri - ------------------------
     *                              maxfsspri
     *
     * If this thread's fsspri is greater than the previous largest
     * fsspri, then record it as the new high and priority for this
     * thread will be one (the lowest priority assigned to a thread
     * that has non-zero shares).
     * Note that this formula cannot produce out of bounds priority
     * values; if it is changed, additional checks may need to be
     * added.
     */
    maxfsspri = fsspset->fssps_maxfsspri;
    if (fsspri >= maxfsspri) {
            fsspset->fssps_maxfsspri = fsspri;
            disp_lock_exit_high(&fsspset->fssps_displock);
            fssproc->fss_umdpri = 1;
    } else {
            disp_lock_exit_high(&fsspset->fssps_displock);
            invpri = (fsspri * (fss_maxumdpri - 1)) / maxfsspri;
            fssproc->fss_umdpri = fss_maxumdpri - invpri;
    }
                                            See usr/src/uts/common/disp/fss.c
```

Note that the real dispatcher priority of the thread t_pri is calculated by reverse-quantizing of the internal FSS priority, fss_fsspri to one in the range from 1 to fss_maxumdpri. The quantization works such that the lower values of fss_fsspri map to higher dispatcher priorities, and vice versa. The lowest dispatcher priority of 0 is reserved for threads that run in zones and projects with zero shares. This allows administrators to easily have some noncritical jobs run in the background when other projects or zones with non-zero shares are not using all the available CPU cycles.

The code resets the maximum FSS priority, maxfsspri, if the new value is larger than the previous value, and finally sets the user-mode priority in the thread's fssproc_t. With the user-mode priority set, the code returns to fss_update_list() and calls fss_change_priority(), shown here.

```
fss_change_priority(kthread_t *t, fssproc_t *fssproc)
{
        pri_t new_pri;

        ASSERT(THREAD_LOCK_HELD(t));
        new_pri = fssproc->fss_umdpri;
        ASSERT(new_pri >= 0 && new_pri <= fss_maxglobpri);

        fssproc->fss_flags &= ~FSSRESTORE;
        if (t == curthread || t->t_state == TS_ONPROC) {
                /*
                 * curthread is always onproc
                 */
                cpu_t *cp = t->t_disp_queue->disp_cpu;
                THREAD_CHANGE_PRI(t, new_pri);
                if (t == cp->cpu_dispthread)
                        cp->cpu_dispatch_pri = DISP_PRIO(t);
                if (DISP_MUST_SURRENDER(t)) {
                        fssproc->fss_flags |= FSSBACKQ;
                        cpu_surrender(t);
                } else {
                        fssproc->fss_timeleft = fss_quantum;
                }
        } else {
                /*
                 * When the priority of a thread is changed, it may be
                 * necessary to adjust its position on a sleep queue or
                 * dispatch queue.  The function thread_change_pri accomplishes
                 * this.
                 */
                if (thread_change_pri(t, new_pri, 0)) {
                        /*
                         * The thread was on a run queue.
                         */
                        fssproc->fss_timeleft = fss_quantum;
                } else {
                        fssproc->fss_flags |= FSSBACKQ;
                }
        }
}
```

See usr/src/uts/common/disp/fss.c

Algorithmically very similar to the TS class equivalent, the procedure is that if the thread is running, use THREAD_CHANGE_PRI to set the new t_pri value; otherwise, call thread_change_pri() and reset the time quantum if the thread was on a dispatch queue. If the thread was on a sleep queue, set the flag to instruct the dispatcher queue function to insert the thread at the back of the appropriate queue.

3.7.3.4 Fixed-Priority Thread Priorities

The FX class is a convenient class to use when you want to keep a process or thread at the same priority throughout its execution and not have the system change the priority over time. The FX priority range is somewhat unique in that it defines 61 priority levels (0–60), as opposed to the other classes (except SYS), that define 60 priority levels (0–59). As such, an FX class thread can be placed at global priority 60, while remaining in the FX class; typically, a thread at priority 60 has been promoted to SYS class for a short duration. Here's a snapshot of the FX dispatch table with most of the lines deleted for space.

```
# Fixed Priority Dispatcher Configuration
RES=1000

# TIME QUANTUM                        PRIORITY
# (fx_quantum)                         LEVEL
        200                    #          0
. . .
        160                    #         10
. . .
        120                    #         20
. . .
         80                    #         30
. . .
         40                    #         40
. . .
         40                    #         50
. . .
         20                    #         59
         20                    #         60
```

The default table implements a descending quantum allocation scheme, in which the time quantum goes down as the priority of the thread goes up. Threads at priority 0–9 get a 200 millisecond quantum, which drops to 160 milliseconds for priorities 10–19, and so on, down to 20 milliseconds for the highest-priority threads. Note the presence of 61 priority levels (0–60).

The FX priority implements user-mode priorities differently than we've seen in the previous examples. The fxproc_t does not include a fx_umdpri variable; the fx_pri field is used to store user priorities, and these translate directory to global priorities. That is, using `priocntl(1)` to set a process or thread to FX priority 30 (for example) results in a global priority of 30. And because this is a fixed-priority class, the priority remains 30 throughout the execution of the thread unless it is explicitly changed by a user.

A quick note for readers that will be reading the Solaris source code or taking advantage of OpenSolaris and developing kernel software. The FX source and header files include a callback mechanism. The FX callback functionality was added to support a specific OEM some time ago. It is not used by any bundled Solaris software, and use of the callback feature requires a header file that is not included in the standard Solaris distribution. We plan to remove the FX callback framework in the near future. We do not discuss the callback framework here.

FX Tick Processing.   Tick processing for FX class threads is consistent with our previous examples: Decrement the counter for the active thread, charging it for another tick of CPU use. If the thread has used its time quantum, force the thread off the CPU and queue on the appropriate dispatcher queue. A check for an enables preemption control is also done in `fx_tick()`.

```
fx_tick()
. . .
            new_pri = fx_dptbl[fxpp->fx_pri].fx_globpri;
            ASSERT(new_pri >= 0 && new_pri <= fx_maxglobpri);
            /*
             * When the priority of a thread is changed,
             * it may be necessary to adjust its position
             * on a sleep queue or dispatch queue. Even
             * when the priority is not changed, we need
             * to preserve round robin on dispatch queue.
             * The function thread_change_pri accomplishes
             * this.
             */
            if (thread_change_pri(t, new_pri, 0)) {
                    fxpp->fx_timeleft = fxpp->fx_pquantum;
            } else {
                    fxpp->fx_flags |= FXBACKQ;
                    cpu_surrender(t);
            }
        } else if (t->t_pri < t->t_disp_queue->disp_maxrunpri) {
            fxpp->fx_flags |= FXBACKQ;
            cpu_surrender(t);
        }
. . .
                                    See usr/src/uts/common/disp/fx.c
```

If the thread has used its time quantum, a `new_pri` value is set from the FX dispatch table, with the `fxproc_t fx_pri` value used as an index. With the FX class, priorities are not changed by the system—the `fx_pri` value equates to the thread's global priority, `t_pri`, and the new global priority from the dispatch table is the same as the existing priority, as long as a user has not explicitly changed the priority. If a user issued a priority change, the `fx_pri` field reflects the user input value, indexing into a different row in the dispatch table, resulting in a priority change. `thread_change_pri()` sets the thread's `t_pri` field and calls into the appropriate subsystem to queue the thread if it's on a run queue or sleep queue.

The FX class does not implement an update function.

3.7.3.5 Real-Time Thread Priorities

Real-time applications require a system that can provide a dispatch latency that is fast, bound, and consistent. Dispatch latency refers to the amount of time that elapses from when a thread becomes runnable to when it is context-switched onto a processor—from runnable to running. Solaris enables rapid context switching for real-time threads through several features.

- **Global priority placement.** Real-time threads are the highest-priority threads on the system. Only interrupt threads have priority of real time. Processor control mechanisms can be enabled to keep interrupt threads off processors running real-time threads.

- **Kernel preempt dispatch queue.** Real-time threads are managed on a separate dispatch queue from other class threads.

- **Kernel preemption.** When a real-time thread becomes runnable, a kernel preemption is triggered, forcing the CPU to switch off its current thread and switch on the real-time thread (see Section 3.9).

Real-time class threads run at one of 60 priorities, 0–59, which translate to global priorities 100–159. Like the FX class, the real-time class does not implement a rt_umdpri variable in support of user-mode priorities. The `rt_pri` field in `rtproc_t` stores a user-defined priority, which is used as an index into the RT dispatch table to set the global priority. A user-supplied RT priority of 0 results in a global priority of 100, user priority 1 yields global priority 101, and so on. Like FX, RT is a fixed priority class—the kernel will not change the priority of a real-time thread over time, unless initiated by a user event, such as a `priocntl(1)` command or a `priocntl(2)` system call.

Real-Time Tick Processing.   Tick processing for real-time threads is consistent with previous examples. The implementation is much simpler because it is not necessary to test for preemption controls or a SYS priority. Real-time is already a higher priority than SYS, and preemption controls would be superfluous in real-time since real-time threads get the processor and keep it unless a higher-priority real-time thread comes along, or an interrupt needs to be processed.

```
/*
 * Check for time slice expiration (unless thread has infinite time
 * slice).  If time slice has expired arrange for thread to be preempted
 * and placed on back of queue.
 */
static void
rt_tick(kthread_t *t)
{
        rtproc_t *rtpp = (rtproc_t *)(t->t_cldata);

        ASSERT(MUTEX_HELD(&(ttoproc(t))->p_lock));

        thread_lock(t);
        if ((rtpp->rt_pquantum != RT_TQINF && --rtpp->rt_timeleft == 0) ||
            (DISP_MUST_SURRENDER(t))) {
                if (rtpp->rt_timeleft == 0 && rtpp->rt_tqsignal) {
                        thread_unlock(t);
                        sigtoproc(ttoproc(t), t, rtpp->rt_tqsignal);
                        thread_lock(t);
                }
                rtpp->rt_flags |= RTBACKQ;
                cpu_surrender(t);
        }
        thread_unlock(t);
}
```

See usr/src/uts/common/disp/rt.c

The code tests for an infinite time quantum, defined as RT_TQINF. The RT dispatch table can be modified to establish infinite time quantums if required. The FX class provides this capability as well. Also, the priocntl(1) command and system call let us set the time quantum of an RT or FX class thread. The specifier RT_TQINF—or FX_TQINF for FX class threads—establishes an infinite time quantum. If the RT thread does not have an infinite quantum and has used its allotted quantum after decrementing rt_timeleft, DISP_MUST_SURRENDER() code runs. Let's quickly look at what this macro expands to.

```
#define DISP_MUST_SURRENDER(t)                                  \
        ((DISP_MAXRUNPRI(t) > DISP_PRIO(t)) ||                  \
        (CP_MAXRUNPRI(t->t_cpupart) > DISP_PRIO(t)))
. . .
#define CP_MAXRUNPRI(cp)                ((cp)->cp_kp_queue.disp_maxrunpri)
. . .
/*
 * Macro for use by scheduling classes to decide whether the thread is about
 * to be scheduled or not.  This returns the maximum run priority.
 */
#define DISP_MAXRUNPRI(t)               ((t)->t_disp_queue->disp_maxrunpri)
. . .
/* The dispatch priority of a thread */
#define DISP_PRIO(t) ((t)->t_epri > (t)->t_pri ? (t)->t_epri : (t)->t_pri)
```

See usr/src/uts/common/sys/cpupart.h, thread.h, disp.h

The code segment shows the embedded macros as well, to facilitate walking through DISP_MUST_SURRENDER(). The purpose here is to determine if there is a higher-priority thread runnable, which would force the current thread to yield the CPU. This requires testing the thread's priority (DISP_PRIO) against the maxrunpri of the thread's current queue (DISP_MAXRUNPRI) and the CPU partition's kp_queue maxrunpri (CP_MAXRUNPRI).

Getting back to rt_tick(), if a higher-priority thread is runnable or one of the other conditions previously described is true, then another test is performed to determine if a signal was set for RT time quantum expiration. This feature is unique to the RT class, where it may be desirable for an application to be notified if its RT threads are using their time quanta. priocntl(1) implements a -t flag that can be used on the command line with RT class threads to set a signal number, which is stored in the rt_tqsignal field in rtproc_t. If a signal has been set, the kernel sigtoproc() function sends the signal. If a signal number has not been set, the code simply sets the rt_flag to instruct the dispatcher to queue this thread at the back of the queue, and cpu_surrender() is called. The cpu_surrender() code is discussed in Section 3.8.

The RT class does not implement an update function.

3.7.3.6 Monitoring Thread Priorities

The easiest way to monitor thread priorities is with the prstat(1) command, which by default displays the priority in the PRI column. prstat(1) with the -L flag provides a row for every thread in each process. To determine the scheduling class, use the ps(1) command with the -c flag. A ps -ec command lists all the processes on the system with a CLS and PRI column, displaying the scheduling class and priority, respectively.

To track the various priority-related fields of a thread, run the following DTrace script, which takes a process name as a command-line argument and displays various priority fields for the active thread.

```
#!/usr/sbin/dtrace -qs

profile-5sec
/ execname == $$1 /
{
        self->cid   = curthread->t_cid;
        self->pri   = curthread->t_pri;
        self->epri  = curthread->t_epri;
        self->cpupri = ((tsproc_t *)curthread->t_cldata)->ts_cpupri;
        self->upril  = ((tsproc_t *)curthread->t_cldata)->ts_uprilim;
        self->upri   = ((tsproc_t *)curthread->t_cldata)->ts_upri;
        self->umdpri = ((tsproc_t *)curthread->t_cldata)->ts_umdpri;
        self->nice   = ((tsproc_t *)curthread->t_cldata)->ts_nice;
        printf("PID: %d, TID: %d, CID: %d, PRI: %d CPUPRI: %d UMDPRI: %d UPRI: %d\n",
                pid,tid,self->cid,self->pri,self->cpupri,self->umdpri,self->upri);
}
```

Here is an example—running the script on a process called `threads`:

```
# ./pri.d threads
PID: 5053, TID: 218149, CID: 1, PRI: 47, CPUPRI: 59, UMDPRI: 47
PID: 5053, TID: 218670, CID: 1, PRI: 47, CPUPRI: 59, UMDPRI: 47
PID: 5053, TID: 219148, CID: 1, PRI: 47, CPUPRI: 59, UMDPRI: 47
```

Most of the script output is (hopefully!) clear at this point. The CID is the scheduling class ID; 1 is the TS class.

DTrace implements a sched provider that manages several probes for tracking dispatcher activity. Several `change-pri` probes are implemented in the various scheduling-class-specific functions that initiate a priority change (yield, sleep, wakeup, preempt, and setrun).

```
# dtrace -l -n change-pri
   ID    PROVIDER          MODULE                          FUNCTION NAME
 1834      sched          genunix               thread_change_pri change-pri
 1876      sched          TS                   ts_change_priority change-pri
 1877      sched          TS                             ts_yield change-pri
 1878      sched          TS                            ts_wakeup change-pri
 1879      sched          TS                           ts_trapret change-pri
 1880      sched          TS                             ts_sleep change-pri
 1881      sched          TS                            ts_setrun change-pri
 1882      sched          TS                           ts_preempt change-pri
 2554      sched          FX                   fx_change_priority change-pri
 2555      sched          FX                             fx_yield change-pri
 2556      sched          FX                            fx_wakeup change-pri
 2557      sched          FX                           fx_preempt change-pri
 2578      sched          RT                   rt_change_priority change-pri
 2583      sched          FSS                           fss_wakeup change-pri
 2584      sched          FSS                            fss_sleep change-pri
 2585      sched          FSS                           fss_setrun change-pri
 2586      sched          FSS                          fss_preempt change-pri
 2587      sched          FSS                          fss_trapret change-pri
 2588      sched          FSS                 fss_change_priority change-pri
```

Here's a simple script that enables all the `change-pri` probes, uses the `count()` aggregating function, and keys the aggregation on the probe function name, the name of the executable, the thread ID, and the thread priority.

```
#!/usr/sbin/dtrace -qs

change-pri
{
        @[probefunc,execname,tid,curthread->t_pri] = count();
}
END
{
```

continues

```
            printf("%-16s %-16s %-8s %-8s %-8s\n","FUNC","EXEC","TID","PRI","CNT");
            printa("%-16s %-16s %-8d %-8d %-@8d\n",@);
}
solaris10> ./cpri.d
^C
FUNC               EXEC              TID      PRI      CNT
ts_preempt         threads           34923    47       1
. . .
ts_preempt         threads           35347    37       283
ts_yield           threads           35347    59       283
ts_preempt         threads           35343    37       294
ts_yield           threads           35343    59       294
ts_preempt         threads           35339    37       303
ts_yield           threads           35339    59       303
ts_preempt         threads           35357    37       338
ts_yield           threads           35357    59       338
ts_preempt         threads           35355    37       427
ts_yield           threads           35355    59       427
thread_change_pri  sched             0        169      433
```

In this example, our handy threads program is active and having its priorities changed through preempt and yield functions. Using the probe function makes it easy to see the scheduling class of the threads running when the probe fires. Since we see a lot of preemptions here, it will be interesting to see which threads are getting preempted and which are causing the preemptions. As it happens, /usr/demo/dtrace/whopreempt.d gives us exactly this information.

```
# dtrace -s ./whopreempt.d
^C
                   PREEMPTOR PRI                  PREEMPTED PRI      #
                        Xorg  59                    threads  27      1
                        Xorg  59                    threads  59      1
. . .
                       sched  99                    threads  47      92
                        Xorg  59                    threads  47      107
                       sched  99                    threads  37      150
                     threads  47                    threads  27      166
                     threads  47             xscreensaver-loc  32      7615
                     threads  47                    threads  37      9638
                     threads  47             xscreensaver-loc  42      13287
                     threads  37             xscreensaver-loc  32      13599
```

Based on the DTrace output, we can see that the process generating the most preemptions is our threads workload. The PRI columns show the higher priority of the preemptor threads over the threads getting preempted, so we see user preemption in action. If the PRI of the preemption thread falls in the 100–159 range, we know that it's a real-time thread and that it caused a kernel preemption.

These examples barely scratch the surface of what can be observed and understood regarding dispatcher behavior with the sched provider. We encourage you to explore the endless possibilities DTrace offers.

3.8 Dispatcher Functions

The dispatcher's primary functions are to decide which runnable thread gets executed next, to manage the context switching of threads on and off processors, and to provide a mechanism for inserting into a dispatch queue kthreads that become runnable. Other dispatcher functions handle initialization and scheduling class loading, the lock functions previously discussed, preemption, and support for user and administrative commands, such as `dispadmin(1M)` and `priocntl(1)`, that monitor or change dispatcher-related behavior.

The main entry point into the dispatcher is through a call to `swtch()`, which finds the highest-priority runnable thread and context-switches it onto the target CPU. Several areas of the dispatcher subsystem, as well as the kernel at large, enter the dispatcher through `swtch()` to initiate a thread switch. Much of the work is performed by the core `disp()` code, which is called from `swtch()`. Queue insertion is handled by the `setfrontdq()` and `setbackdq()` functions for the per-processor dispatch queues, and `setkpdq()` for kernel preempt (kp) queues. These functions place a thread on a dispatch queue according to the thread's priority. Whether the thread is placed at the front or the back of the queue is determined before the queue insertion function is called. We first look at the queue insertion functions and then examine `swtch()`.

3.8.1 Dispatcher Queue Management

The dispatcher queue functions insert and remove threads from the appropriate dispatch queue.

Table 3.2 Dispatch Queue Management Functions

Function	Description
`setbackdq()`	Insert a thread at the back of a dispatch queue
`setfrontdq()`	Insert a thread at the front of a dispatch queue
`setkpdq()`	Insert a real-time thread on the kernel preempt (kp) queue
`dispdeq()`	Remove a thread from its dispatch queue

The queue insertion functions are entered from various places in the dispatcher, but the majority of thread queue insertions are initiated from the following events:

- **Thread creation.** The first time a thread is assigned to and inserted onto a dispatch queue is when it is created. The thread's scheduling class is inherited from the thread issuing the `thread_create()` call, and a class-specific `setrun()` function is entered after the thread's priority (which is also inherited) is set. Newly created threads inherit the current CPU. That is, the new thread's `t_cpu` is set to the CPU on which the `thread_create()` code is executing.

- **Thread sleep.** A thread issuing a blocking system call is voluntarily switched off a CPU and inserted into a sleep queue.

- **Thread wake-up.** On wake-up, the scheduling-class-specific wakeup functions call into the dispatcher to insert a newly awakened thread, moving it from a sleep queue to a dispatch queue.

- **Thread preemption.** A preempted thread is context-switched off its CPU and inserted on a dispatch queue.

- **Thread priority change.** Typically, a thread's priority changes frequently over its lifetime, and a priority change means a dispatcher queue change (since the queues are organized by CPU and priority).

Figure 3.11 illustrates the execution phases of a typical kernel thread as it is moved to and from dispatch queues and sleep queues.

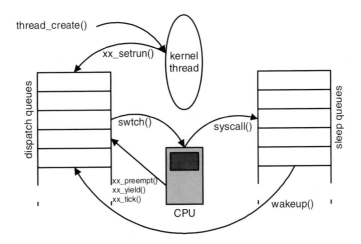

Figure 3.11 Kernel Thread Queue Insertion

The function calls with the *xx*_prefix are scheduling-class-specific functions. The thread yield (*xx*_yield) scenario occurs only when a yield call is issued programmatically in application code through `thr_yield(3T)`. Preemption means that a thread is involuntarily context-switched off a processor in favor of a higher-priority thread or that the executing thread used its time quantum—*time-quantum expiration uses the preempt mechanism to force the context switch.*

The queue insertion functions select a CPU for the thread to run on next. Which CPU's dispatch queue wins is driven by several factors:

- The priority of the thread
- The home lgroup of the thread
- Whether or not the thread is bound (processor set or `pbind`)
- Dynamic load balancing by the dispatcher code

We look at the queue insertion functions, then summarize the algorithms that we implemented.

Here's a comment from the top of `setbackdq()`, along with several constants used in the function for load balancing.

```
/*
 * setbackdq() keeps runqs balanced such that the difference in length
 * between the chosen runq and the next one is no more than RUNQ_MAX_DIFF.
 * For threads with priorities below RUNQ_MATCH_PRI levels, the runq's lengths
 * must match.  When per-thread TS_RUNQMATCH flag is set, setbackdq() will
 * try to keep runqs perfectly balanced regardless of the thread priority.
 */
#define RUNQ_MATCH_PRI  16      /* pri below which queue lengths must match */
#define RUNQ_MAX_DIFF   2       /* maximum runq length difference */
#define RUNQ_LEN(cp, pri)       ((cp)->cpu_disp->disp_q[pri].dq_sruncnt)
```

See usr/src/uts/common/disp/disp.c

`setbackdq()` is passed a pointer to the thread to be queued. If the thread is not bound to a CPU or processor set, the `cpu_choose()` function is called to select a CPU for the thread; if the thread is bound, CPU selection is easy.

```
/*
 * Select a CPU for this thread to run on.  Choose t->t_cpu unless:
 *      - t->t_cpu is not in this thread's assigned lgrp
 *      - the time since the thread last came off t->t_cpu exceeds the
 *        rechoose time for this cpu (ignore this if t is curthread in
 *        which case it's on CPU and t->t_disp_time is inaccurate)
 *      - t->t_cpu is presently the target of an offline or partition move
 *        request
 */
static cpu_t *
cpu_choose(kthread_t *t, pri_t tpri)
{
        ASSERT(tpri < kpqpri);
```

continues

```
    if ((((lbolt - t->t_disp_time) > t->t_cpu->cpu_rechoose) &&
         t != curthread) || t->t_cpu == cpu_inmotion) {
             return (disp_lowpri_cpu(t->t_cpu, t->t_lpl, tpri, NULL));
    }

    /*
     * Take a trip through disp_lowpri_cpu() if the thread was
     * running outside its home lgroup
     */
    if (!klgrpset_ismember(t->t_lpl->lpl_lgrp->lgrp_set[LGRP_RSRC_CPU],
         t->t_cpu->cpu_lpl->lpl_lgrpid)) {
             return (disp_lowpri_cpu(t->t_cpu, t->t_lpl, tpri,
                 (t == curthread) ? t->t_cpu : NULL));
    }
    return (t->t_cpu);
}
```
                                              See usr/src/uts/common/disp/disp.c

The first conditional test in the code determines if the thread has been waiting longer than the `cpu_rechoose` value. Rechoose is a warm affinity mechanism that places threads back on the CPU they last ran on, thus potentially benefiting from a warm hardware cache. If too many cycles have passed since the thread last ran, the likelihood of finding a warm cache is diminished, so `cpu_rechoose` just selects the next best CPU. The original systemwide `rechoose_interval` tuneable still exists, but as part of the evolving CMT chip support, a per-CPU rechoose value, `cpu_rechoose` in the `cpu_t`, has been created. This value can be adjusted according to a per-chip rechoose adjustment value. Currently, `cpu_rechoose` is set to the `rechoose_interval` default value of 3.

If the thread's time on a dispatcher queue exceeds the CPU's rechoose value (3 ticks), then `disp_lowpri_cpu()` shall find a CPU for the thread. Otherwise (moving down to the next conditional statement), if the thread is not a member of its home lgroup, then `disp_lowpri_cpu()` find a CPU for the thread. `cpu_choose()` selects the thread's current `t_cpu` if the previous conditional statements are not true. Specifically, if the thread was waiting less than `cpu_rechoose` (warm affinity is still good) and the thread is a member of its home lgroup, the CPU the thread was on last is the best CPU.

`disp_lowpri_cpu()` looks for the CPU running the lowest-priority thread. One of the arguments passed is the thread's current `t_cpu` pointer (the last CPU the thread ran on), which provides the starting point for the search. The thread's lgroup and priority are used to select a CPU. The code favors locality over priority for placement. `disp_lowpri_cpu()` walks the CPUs in the thread's partition in lgroup distance order, testing CPUs in the thread's home lgroup first, than the next furthest set of CPUs, and so on until all the CPUs in the partition are considered. Within each lgroup, the best (lowest priority) CPU is determined. When we find a CPU where the thread could immediately run—the thread's priority is higher than the running thread and the highest priority thread on the CPU's queue, the loop is terminated and the CPU is selected.

Note the algorithm described in the previous paragraph applies to hierarchical lgroups, which were introduced in Solaris 10 1/06 (update 1) and OpenSolaris build 8. Prior to hierarchical lgroups, the `disp_lowpri_cpu()` loop walked the partitions CPU list, keeping track of the best local and remote CPUs. At the end of the loop, if the thread had a high enough priority to run immediately in the home lgroup, the best CPU was chosen from the home lgroup. Otherwise, the best CPU in the remote lgroup was selected.

Back in `setbackdq()`, a CPU has been selected, so it's time to see if some load balancing is required. The dispatcher code attempts to keep the length of the run queues closely balanced so that no one CPU has an inordinate number of threads on its queue relative to the other CPUs. Also, the dispatcher determines if it should load-balance across chips that have multiple execution cores and the system has NUMA properties (more than one lgroup). The following macro tests for the need to balance across chips.

```
/*
 * Balancing is possible if multiple chips exist in the lgroup
 * but only necessary if the chip has multiple online logical CPUs
 */
#define CHIP_SHOULD_BALANCE(chp)                        \
        (((chp)->chip_ncpu > 1) && ((chp)->chip_next_lgrp != (chp)))
```

See usr/src/uts/common/sys/chip.h

The rationale here is this: If a chip has one core (one CPU), the extra load balancing is not necessary—one CPU that's idle is OK to run on. Contrast with a two-core chip, where even if only one of the two cores (CPUs) is busy, it's still better to try to find a chip where both CPUs are idle. Otherwise, we could end up having a chip with two busy cores and another chip on the same system with two idle cores. More succinctly, for systems with multicore chips, try to load-balance across physical chips, spreading the workload across CPUs on physical chips rather than filling up CPUs on chip 0, then the CPUs on chip 1, and so on.

In `setbackdq()`, if the thread's partition is not the same as the partition of the selected CPU, call `disp_lowpri_cpu()` again and move the thread to a different CPU, and place it on that queue. Otherwise, if the thread's CPU partition is the same as that of the selected CPU (from `cpu_choose()`), CHIP_SHOULD_BALANCE runs. If the chip has multiple CPUs and there's another chip in the lgroup to balance against, `chip_balance()` is called and determines, based on load (number of threads, number of CPUs on the chips), whether balancing is necessary. If load balancing is necessary, a lesser-loaded CPU is found; otherwise, we use the same CPU that was selected by `cpu_choose()`.

Next is the run queue length balance test, which uses the RUNQ constants shown earlier. If it is determined that run queue length is out of balance, then a CPU in the next partition is selected.

Once the CPU is selected, it's a matter of inserting the thread at the end of the selected CPU's queue, according to the thread's priority, and updating the appropriate `disp_t` structure variables (run count, queue occupancy bitmap, etc.). The last step is setting the thread's state to `TS_RUN` and determining if the newly inserted thread has a higher priority than the thread the CPU is running. If the new thread has a higher priority, `cpu_resched()` is called to initiate the preemption process. `cpu_resched()` checks the priority of the thread currently executing on the processor against the priority of the thread just inserted onto the processor dispatch queue and also tests for a user or kernel preemption. A user preemption means the thread has a greater priority than the currently running thread, but not greater than `kpreemptpri`. More succinctly, if the thread's priority is less than 100 but greater than that of the currently running thread, the code sets up a user preemption. A kernel preemption is the result of the thread having a priority greater than the currently running thread and greater than `kpreemptpri`, which means it's an RT class thread. For a user preemption, the `cpu_runrun` flag is set. For a kernel preemption, `cpu_kprunrun` is set. The last step is to call `poke_cpu()`, which executes a cross-call (CPU-to-CPU interrupt), forcing the CPU into a trap handler. The runrun flags are tested in the trap handler, and the CPU executes the preemption as needed. The `cpu_resched()` function is shown below.

```
cpu_resched()
{
        int     call_poke_cpu = 0;
        pri_t   cpupri = cp->cpu_dispatch_pri;

        if (!CPU_IDLING(cpupri) && (cpupri < tpri)) {
                TRACE_2(TR_FAC_DISP, TR_CPU_RESCHED,
                    "CPU_RESCHED:Tpri %d Cpupri %d", tpri, cpupri);
                if (tpri >= upreemptpri && cp->cpu_runrun == 0) {
                        cp->cpu_runrun = 1;
                        aston(cp->cpu_dispthread);
                        if (tpri < kpreemptpri && cp != CPU)
                                call_poke_cpu = 1;
                }
                if (tpri >= kpreemptpri && cp->cpu_kprunrun == 0) {
                        cp->cpu_kprunrun = 1;
                        if (cp != CPU)
                                call_poke_cpu = 1;
                }
        }

        /*
         * Propagate cpu_runrun, and cpu_kprunrun to global visibility.
         */
        membar_enter();

        if (call_poke_cpu)
                poke_cpu(cp->cpu_id);
}
```

The `setfrontdq()` code implements basically the same algorithm as `setbackdq()`, with the exception of the load balancing component. Inserting at the front of the queue is analogous to stepping in front of a line—the depth of the line doesn't really matter. In this case, the depth of the queue doesn't really matter, since the newly inserted thread is going to run next.

The decision as to whether `setfrontdq()` or `setbackdq()` is called from the various points in the kernel where queue insertion is called is driven by factors such as how long a thread has been waiting to run, whether or not the thread is in the IA class, and similar concerns. IA class threads are put at the front of a dispatch queue for an additional edge on getting scheduled. A preempted thread with a scheduler activation is always placed at the front of a queue. RT class threads are always placed at the back of the kernel preempt queue. Threads that have waited awhile (relatively speaking) to run (as determined by the thread's `t_disp_time` value) are placed at the front of a queue.

For threads in the RT class, a partition-wide kp_queue is used. The kp_queue insertion process is done with `setkpdq()`. The thread's dispatch queue is derived from the `t_cpupart->cp_kp_queue` pointer, the queue's `nrunnable` count is incremented, and the specific queue pointer is set according to the thread's RT priority. If the queue has more than one runnable thread on it, the thread is placed at the back of the queue. Otherwise, if this is the only thread that will be on the run queue, it is simply inserted in the queue. The remaining `disp_t` fields (the bitmap of occupied queues and the `maxrunpri` fields) are updated. After the thread is inserted on a queue, the kp_queue process ensures that the thread's partition didn't change. If it did, a CPU is selected from the thread's partition (based on the thread's `t_cpupart->cp_cpulist`).

The selected CPU at this point is considered a top contender for running this thread next, and as such is passed to the `disp_lowpri_cpu()`, which may or may not change the selected CPU, depending on the criteria used by that function (described previously). With the final selection done, `cpu_resched()` is called to initiate a kernel preemption, since an RT class thread is runnable.

To summarize, the queue insertion functions are responsible for selecting which CPU a thread will run on next. The functions factor in thread bindings, thread priority, partitions, lgroups, and load balancing. Here's how the queue insertions functions select the CPU for non-RT class threads.

- A newly created thread has its CPU set to the CPU running the thread create code, unless that CPU is not in the default partition, in which case, `disp_lowpri_cpu()` selects the new thread's CPU.

- If the thread is bound (for example, to a processor set by `psrset(1)`), select a CPU in the processor set (partition).

- If the thread has been waiting 3 ticks or less (warm affinity threshold through `rechoose_interval`), use the thread's `t_cpu` (last CPU it ran on).

- If warm affinity expired, but the thread is in its home lgroup, use `t_cpu`.

- Otherwise, look for a CPU running at a lower priority in the local lgroup. If one is not found, look in the remote lgroup. If all CPUs are at a higher priority, select a CPU from the local lgroup.

- After a CPU has been selected, check chip load balancing; if load balancing is necessary, select a CPU on a chip with less load.

- After a CPU has been selected, check run queue depth balancing. If the difference in run queue sizes is greater than 2, select a CPU with a smaller run queue length.

3.8.1.1 Monitoring Queue Activity

The DTrace `sched` provider manages several probes that enable us to observe dispatcher queue insertion (and removal). The `enqueue` probe fires immediately before a thread is inserted on a queue, and the argument arrays extract information on the thread, process, and CPU. The args[3] value is a boolean set to 0 if the thread will be placed at the back of the queue, and 1 if insertion is at the front of the queue. And of course the `setfrontdq()`, `setbackdq()`, `setkpdq()`, and related functions can be instrumented directly with the DTrace FBT provider.

The `/usr/demo/dtrace` directory in all Solaris 10 distributions contains several excellent D scripts for monitoring dispatcher queues. `qlen.d` monitors the queue length for each CPU.

```
# dtrace -s ./qlen.d
dtrace: script './qlen.d' matched 5 probes
^C
        9
        value  ------------- Distribution ------------- count
          < 0 |                                         0
            0 |@@@@@@@@@@@@@@@@@@@@@@@@@@@@@@@@@@@@@@     14106
            1 |@@@@@                                    2070
            2 |@                                        249
            3 |                                         15
            4 |                                         1
            5 |                                         0


. . .
        0
        value  ------------- Distribution ------------- count
          < 0 |                                         0
            0 |@@@@@@@@@@@@@@@@@@@@@@@@@@@@@@@@@@@@@@     14811
            1 |@@@@@@                                   2427
            2 |@                                        268
            3 |                                         14
            4 |                                         1
            5 |                                         0
```

continues

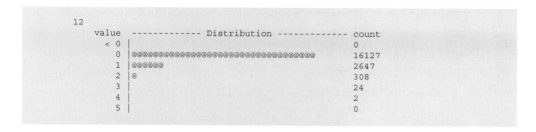

```
   12
        value ------------- Distribution ------------ count
          < 0 |                                                     0
            0 |@@@@@@@@@@@@@@@@@@@@@@@@@@@@@@@@@@@@@@@      16127
            1 |@@@@@@                                            2647
            2 |@                                                 308
            3 |                                                  24
            4 |                                                  2
            5 |                                                  0
```

qlen.d was executed on an 8-CPU system, but we cut the output for all but three CPUs for space. We can see that, during the qlen.d collection, the dispatcher queue length balancing works quite well; no one CPU's queue length was significantly different in size from the others.

This is just one example. Please try out /usr/demo/dtrace/qtime.d and /usr/demo/dtrace/whoqueue.d to further observe dispatch queue activity (and check out the sched provider in the *Solaris Dynamic Tracing Guide*).

3.8.2 The Heart of the Dispatcher: swtch()

The kernel swtch() routine initiates the context switching of a thread off a processor, figures out which thread should run next, and context-switches the selected thread onto a processor for execution. It's called from many places within the operating system: in the class-fork-return function (a thread has just been created), from the idle thread (executed by processors if there are no runnable threads on a dispatch queue), by interrupt and trap handlers (to reenter the dispatcher), for thread sleep management, in kernel synchronization support code (mutexes, reader/writer locks, condition variables, etc.), and, of course, from the preempt() function. The various entry points to swtch() are listed in Table 3.3.

Entering the swtch() routine causes the cpu_sysinfo.pswtch counter to be incremented, as reported in mpstat(1M) in the csw column, and reflects the number of context switches per second for each processor. The swtch() function first checks to see if the current thread is an interrupt thread. When interrupts happen, the thread stack is switched from the linked list of interrupt threads in the processor's cpu structure to the thread stack of an interrupt thread. If swtch() was entered with an interrupt thread as the current thread, the kernel must restore the interrupted thread's state so it can be resumed. The interrupted thread is unpinned (a thread that has been preempted for an interrupt is considered pinned), and the kernel resume_from_interrupt() assembly routine is called to restore the state of the interrupted thread.

If the current thread is *not* an interrupt thread, swtch() calls the disp() function, which is the code segment that looks for the highest-priority thread to run,

Table 3.3 Sources of Calls to `swtch()`

Kernel Subsystem	Kernel Function	Description
Dispatcher	`idle`	Per-processor idle thread
	`preempt`	Last phase of a preemption
Kthread	`release_interrupt`	Called from an interrupt thread
TS/IA class	`ts_forkret`	After kthread is created
Sleep/wakeup	`cv_xxxx`	Various conditional variable functions
CPU	`force_migrate`	Thread migration to another processor
	`cpu_pause`	Processor state change to pause
Mutex	`mutex_vector_enter`	Mutex lock acquisition
RWlock	`rw_enter_sleep`	RW lock acquisition
Memory scheduler	`sched`	PID 0
Semaphore	`sema_p`	Semaphore "p" operation
Signal	`stop`	Thread stop function
Sleep/wakeup	`slp_cv_wait`	Thread to sleep state
Interrupt	`intr_thread_exit`	Exit of an interrupt handler

sets the thread's state to running (TS_ONPROC), and arranges for it to be switched onto the current processor. At a high level, the disp() function searches the dispatch queues for the best-priority kernel thread, starting with the kernel preempt queue and then searching the queue of the current processor—that is, the processor executing the disp() code. If those searches come up blank, then the code searches the dispatch queues of other processors on a multiprocessor system, looking for a runnable kernel thread. If no threads are found on the dispatch queues, the processor executes its idle thread, which executes a tight loop, testing for runnable threads on each pass through the loop and entering swtch() if the run count is greater than 0.

The search for the highest-priority thread begins with the kernel preempt queue, as referenced by the current processor through its cpu_part structure, where the preempt queue is linked to cp_kp_queue. In this case, on a system with multiple processor partitions, the preempt queue for the processor partition that the executing processor belongs to is searched first. The cp_kp_queue search is represented in the following pseudocode.

```
kpq = pointer to kernel preempt queue
dq = pointer to processor's dispatch queue
while ( priority = kpq->dispmaxrunpri >= 0 ) AND
                ( priority >= dq->dispmaxrunpri) AND
                ( the current CPU is NOT offline) AND
                ( thread_pointer = disp_getbest(kpq) != NULL )
                        if (disp_ratify(thread_pointer, kpq) != NULL)
                                return(thread_pointer)
```

The preceding queue search loop validates the priority value according to the queue's `disp_maxrunpri`, which reflects the highest-priority thread sitting on the queue, makes sure the current processor is not offline, and calls the dispatcher `disp_getbest()` code to fetch the best-priority thread from the kernel preempt queue. `disp_getbest()` finds the highest-priority unbound thread, calls `dispdeq()` to have the thread removed from the dispatch queue, and returns the thread pointer back to `disp()`. If nothing is found, NULL is returned.

```
disp_getbest()
        dpq = dispatch queue pointer (cp_kp_queue in this example)
        priority = dpq->disp_max_unbound_pri
        if (priority == -1)
                return(NULL)
        queue = dpq->disp_q[pri];
        thread_pointer = queue->dq_first;
        loop through linked list of threads on queue, skip bound threads
        if (no unbound threads)
                return NULL
        else
                thread_pointer = thread found
        dispdeq(thread_pointer)
        set thread t_disp_queue, processorUs cpu_dispthread, thread state to ONPROC
        return (thread_pointer)
```

If an unbound thread is found in `disp_getbest()`, the thread is dequeued with `dispdeq()`, the thread's `t_disp_queue` pointer is set to reference the processor's `cpu` structure `cpu_disp` queue pointer, the processor's `cpu_dispthread` pointer is set to the selected thread pointer, and the thread state is set to ONPROC.

`dispdeq()` deals with updating the dispatch queue data structures with the selected thread removed from the queue. It decrements `disp_nrunnable`, which is the total count for all the queues, and `dq_sruncnt`, which maintains the count of runnable threads at the same priority. If the per-priority queue count, `dq_sruncnt`, is 0, then the queue bitmap is updated to reflect an empty queue. The `disp_qactmap` bitmap uses a set bit to reflect the presence of runnable threads on a per-priority queue; thus, the bit that corresponds to the zeroed queue is cleared. The `disp_maxrunpri` and `disp_max_unbound_pri` fields are also updated to reflect the new highest-priority thread on the queue if it is different from the thread that has just been removed from the queue.

Once the thread selection has been made and the thread dequeued, the code returns to `disp()`, which calls `disp_ratify()` to ensure that the selected thread was, in fact, the best candidate to run next. The fine-grained locking used within the dispatcher routines allows for simultaneous changes to be made to the queues and the queue state by potentially many processors. For this reason, a *select-and-ratify* algorithm was chosen for implementation.

Now that the select phase of the algorithm is completed, `disp_ratify()` is entered to complete the ratify phase. The ratify code simply compares the priority of the selected thread to the `disp_maxrunpri` values of the processor and kernel preempt queue. If the selected thread priority is greater than `maxrunpri`, the selection is ratified and the context switch is done. If not, the code loop is reentered to find the best runnable thread. More precisely, if a higher-priority thread appears on the queue when `disp_ratify()` executes, the selected thread is placed back on the dispatch queue with a call to `setfrontdq()`, and `disp_ratify()` returns NULL to `disp()`.

If a thread is not found on the kernel preempt queue, then the per-processor queue `disp_maxrunpri` is tested. A value of –1 means that nothing is on the queue. In that case, the code searches the queues of the other processors on the system, beginning with the `disp_getwork()` code, which finds a processor with the highest-priority thread. Then, the code uses the `disp_getbest()` and `disp_ratify()` functions previously described.

If the current processor's `disp_maxrunpri` indicates runnable threads, the first thread from the highest-priority queue is removed, the queue data is updated (`disp_nrunnable`, `dq_nruncnt`, `disp_qactmap`, `disp_max_unbound_pri`, and `disp_maxrunpri`), the selection is ratified, and `disp()` returns the thread pointer to `swtch()`.

If no work is found on any of the dispatch queues, `disp_getwork()` selects the processor's idle thread by setting the thread pointer to the `cpu_idle_thread`, referenced from the processor's `cpu` structure. The pointer to the idle thread is returned to the `swtch()` code.

Back in `swtch()`, with a thread pointer for the selected thread (or idle thread), the kernel `resume()` code is called to handle the switching of the thread on the processor. `resume()` is implemented in assembly language because the process of context switching requires low-level contact with processor hardware, to save the hardware context of the thread being switched off, and to set up the hardware registers and other context information so that the new thread can begin execution.

3.9 Preemption

We mentioned preemption several times in the preceding text. First, a quick review of what preemption is.

The kernel preempts a thread running on a processor when a higher-priority thread is inserted onto a dispatch queue. The thread is effectively forced to reschedule itself and surrender the processor before having used up its time quantum. Two types of preemption conditions are implemented—a *user* preemption and a *kernel* preemption—distinguished by the priority level of the preempted thread, which drives how quickly the preemption will take place.

A user preemption occurs if a thread is placed on a dispatch queue and the thread has a higher priority than the thread currently running on the processor associated with the queue but has a lower priority than the minimum required for a kernel preemption. A kernel preemption occurs when a thread is placed on a dispatch queue with a priority higher than kpreemptpri, which is set to 100, representing the lowest global dispatch priority for an RT class thread. RT and interrupt threads have global priorities greater than kpreemptpri.

User preemption enables higher-priority threads to get processor time expediently. Kernel preemption is necessary for support of real-time threads. Traditional real-time support in UNIX systems was built on a kernel with various preemption points, allowing a real-time thread to displace the kernel at a few well-defined preemptable places. The Solaris implementation goes the next step and implements a *preemptable* kernel with a few *non-preemption* points. In critical code paths, Solaris temporarily disables kernel preemption for a short period and enables it when the critical path has completed. Kernel preemption is disabled for very short periods in the thread_create() code during the pause_cpus() routine and in a few memory management (MMU) code paths, such as when a hardware address translation (HAT) is being set up.

Preemptions are flagged through fields in the per-processor cpu structure: cpu_runrun and cpu_kprunrun. cpu_runrun flags a user preemption; it is set when a thread inserted into a dispatch queue is a higher priority than the one running but a lower priority than kpreemptpri. cpu_kprunrun flags a kernel preemption. We saw in the cpu_resched() code one example of where these flags get set. The runrun flags can also get set in the following kernel routines.

- **cpupart_move_cpu().** When a processor set configuration is changed and a processor is moved from a processor set, the runrun flags are set to force a preemption so the threads running on the processor being moved can be moved to another processor in the set they've been bound to. Note that if only one processor is left in the set and there are bound threads, the processor set cannot be destroyed until any bound threads are first unbound.

- **`cpu_surrender()`.** A thread is surrendering the processor it's running on. Recall from the section on thread priorities that `cpu_surrender()` is called following a thread's priority change and a test to determine if preemption conditions exist. Entering `cpu_surrender()` means a preemption condition has been detected and is the first step in a kthread giving up a processor in favor of a higher-priority thread.

  Two other areas of the kernel that potentially call `cpu_surrender()` are the priority inheritance code and the processor support code that handles the binding of a thread to a processor. The conditions under which the priority inheritance code calls `cpu_surrender()` are the same as previously described, that is, a priority test determined that a preemption is warranted. The thread binding code forces a preemption through `cpu_surrender()` when a thread is bound to a processor in a processor set and the processor the thread is currently executing on is not part of the processor set the thread was just bound to. This is the only case in which a preemption that is not the result of a priority test is forced.

  `cpu_surrender()` sets the `cpu_runrun` flag and sets `cpu_kprunrun` if the preemption priority is greater than `kpreemptpri`. On a multiprocessor system, if the processor executing the `cpu_surrender()` code is different from the processor that needs to preempt its thread, then a cross-call is sent to the processor that needs to be preempted, forcing it into a trap handler. At that point the runrun flags are tested. The other possible condition is one in which the processor executing the `cpu_surrender()` code is the same processor that must preempt the current thread, in which case it will test the runrun flags before returning to user mode; thus, the cross-call is not needed. In other words, the processor is already in the kernel because it is running the `cpu_surrender()` kernel routine, so a cross-call would be superfluous.

Once the preemption condition has been detected and the appropriate runrun flag has been set in the processor's CPU structure, the kernel must enter a code path that tests the runrun flags before the actual preemption occurs. This happens in different areas of the kernel for user versus kernel preemptions. User preemptions are tested for `cpu_runrun` when the kernel returns from a trap or interrupt handler. Kernel preemptions are also tested for `cpu_kprunrun` when a dispatcher lock is released.

The trap code that executes after the main trap or interrupt handler has completed tests `cpu_runrun`, and if it is set, calls the kernel `preempt()` function. `preempt()` tests two conditions initially. If the thread is not running on a processor (thread state is not `ONPROC`) *or* if the thread's dispatch queue pointer is referencing a queue for a processor other than the processor currently executing, then no preemption is necessary and the code falls through and simply clears a dispatcher lock.

Consider the two test conditions. If the thread is not running (the first test), then obviously it does not need to be preempted. If the thread's `t_disp_queue` pointer is referencing a dispatch queue for a different processor (different from the processor currently executing the `preempt()` code), then clearly the thread has already been placed on another processor's queue, so that condition also obviates the need for a preemption.

If the conditions just described are not true, `preempt()` increments the LWP's `lrusage` structure `nicsw` counter, which counts the number of involuntary context switches. The processor's `inv_switch` counter is also incremented in the `cpu_sysinfo` structure, which counts involuntary context switches processor-wide, and the scheduling-class-specific preempt code is called. The per-processor counters are available with `mpstat(1M)`, reflected in the `icsw` column.

The class-specific code for threads prepares the thread for placement on a dispatch queue and calls either `setfrontdq()` or `setbackdq()` for actual queue insertion. *xx*_`preempt()` checks whether the thread is in kernel mode and whether the kernel-priority-requested flag (`t_kpri_req`) in the thread structure is set. If it is set, the thread's priority is set to the lowest `SYS` class priority (typically 60). The `t_trapret` and `t_astflag` kthread flags are set, causing the *xx*_`trapret()` function to run when the thread returns to user mode (from kernel mode). At that point, the thread's priority is set back to something in the thread's priority range. *xx*_`preempt()` tests for a scheduler activation on the thread. If an activation has been enabled *and* the thread has not avoided preemption beyond the threshold of two clock ticks *and* the thread is not in kernel mode, then the thread's priority is set to the highest user-mode priority (59) and is placed at the front of a dispatch queue with `setfrontdq()`.

If the thread's *XXBACKQ* flag is set, signifying that the thread should be placed at the back of a dispatch queue with `setbackdq()`, the thread preemption is due to time-slice expiration. (Recall that *xx*_`tick()` will call `cpu_surrender()`.) The thread's `t_dispwait` field is zeroed, and a new time quantum is set in *xx*_`timeleft` from the dispatch table before `setbackdq()` is called. Otherwise, if *XXBACKQ* is not set, a real preemption occurred (higher-priority thread became runnable) and the thread is placed at the front of a dispatch queue.

The `rt_preempt()` code is less complex. If `RTBACKQ` is true, the preemption was due to a time quantum expiration (as was the case previously) and `setbackdq()` is called to place the thread at the back of a queue after setting the `rt_timeleft` value from `rt_pquantum`. Otherwise, the thread is placed at the front of a dispatch queue with `setfrontdq()`.

The class-specific preempt code, once completed, returns to the generic `preempt()` routine, which then enters the dispatcher by calling `swtch()`. We look at the `swtch()` code in the next section.

Recall that kernel preemption is detected when a dispatcher lock is released. It is also tested for in kpreempt_enable(), which reenables kernel preemption after kpreempt_disable() blocked preemptions for a short time. The goal is to have kernel preemptions detected and handled more expediently (with less latency) than user preemptions.

Because the test, cpu_kprunrun, for a kernel preemption is put in the disp_lock_exit() code, the detection happens synchronously with respect to other thread scheduling and queue activity. The dispatcher locks are acquired and freed at various points in the dispatcher code, either directly through the dispatcher lock interfaces or indirectly through macro calls. For example, each kernel thread maintains a pointer to a dispatcher lock, which serves to lock the thread *and* the queue during dispatcher functions. The THREAD_LOCK and THREAD_UNLOCK macros use the dispatcher lock entry and exit functions. The key point is that a kernel preemption will be detected before a processor running a thread flagged for preemption completes a pass through the dispatcher.

When disp_lock_exit() is entered, it tests whether cpu_kprunrun is set; if so, then disp_lock_exit() calls kpreempt(). A clear cpu_kprunrun flag indicates that a kernel preemption is not pending, so there is no need to call kpreempt(). Kernel preemptions are handled by the kpreempt() code, represented here in pseudocode.

```
kpreempt()
        if (current_thread->t_preempt)
                do statistics
                return
        if (current_thread NOT running) OR (current_thread NOT on this CPUs queue)
                return
        if (current PIL >= LOCK_LEVEL)
                return
        block kernel preemption (increment current_thread->t_preempt)
        call preempt()
        enable kernel preemption (decrement current_thread->t_preempt)
```

The preceding pseudocode summarizes at a high level what happens in kpreempt(). Kernel threads have a t_preempt flag, which, if set, signifies that the thread is not to be preempted. This flag is set in some privileged threads, such as a processor's idle and interrupt threads. Kernel preemption is disabled by incrementing t_preempt in the current thread and is reenabled by decrementing t_preempt. kpreempt() tests t_preempt in the current thread; if t_preempt is set, kpreempt() increments some statistics counters and returns. If t_preempt is set, the code does not perform a kernel preemption.

The second test is similar in logic to what happens in the `preempt()` code previously described. If the thread is not running or is not on the current processor's dispatch queue, there's no need to preempt.

The third test checks the priority level of the processor. If we're running at a high PIL, we cannot preempt the thread, since it may be holding a spin lock. Preempting a thread holding a dispatcher spin lock could result in a deadlock situation.

Any of the first three test conditions evaluating `true` causes `kpreempt()` to return without actually doing a preemption. Assuming the kernel goes ahead with the preemption, kernel preemptions are disabled (to prevent nested kernel preemptions) and the `preempt()` function is called. Once `preempt()` completes, kernel preemption is enabled and `kpreempt()` is done.

Kernel statistical data is maintained for kernel preemption events in the form of a `kpreempt_cnts` structure.

```
struct kpreempt_cnts {  /* kernel preemption statistics */
        int     kpc_idle;        /* executing idle thread */
        int     kpc_intr;        /* executing interrupt thread */
        int     kpc_clock;       /* executing clock thread */
        int     kpc_blocked;     /* thread has blocked preemption (t_preempt) */
        int     kpc_notonproc;   /* thread is surrendering processor */
        int     kpc_inswtch;     /* thread has ratified scheduling decision */
        int     kpc_prilevel;    /* processor interrupt level is too high */
        int     kpc_apreempt;    /* asynchronous preemption */
        int     kpc_spreempt;    /* synchronous preemption */
}       kpreempt_cnts;
                      See usr/src/uts/sun4/os/trap.c or usr/src/uts/i86pc/os/trap.c
```

The `kpreempt_cnts` data is not accessible with a currently available Solaris command, but can be read with `mdb(1)`.

```
# mdb -k
> ::nm -x !grep kpreempt_cnts
0xfffffffffbc2e7d0|0x0000000000000024|OBJT |GLOB |0x0  |16      |kpreempt_cnts
> 0xfffffffffbc2e7d0::print -d struct kpreempt_cnts
{
    kpc_idle = 0
    kpc_intr = 0t1668
    kpc_clock = 0
    kpc_blocked = 0t12
    kpc_notonproc = 0
    kpc_inswtch = 0
    kpc_prilevel = 0
    kpc_apreempt = 0t1595
    kpc_spreempt = 0t128
}
```

Most of the `kpreempt_cnts` counter descriptions are well described in the source code listing. The last two counters, asynchronous preemption and synchronous preemption, count each of the possible methods of kernel preemption. The `kpreempt()` function is passed one argument, `asyncspl`. For asynchronous preempts, `asyncspl` is a priority-level argument, and the `kpreempt()` code raises the PIL, as dictated by the value passed. Synchronous preempts pass a –1 argument and do not change the processor's priority level. In the case of both user and kernel preemption, the code ultimately executes the `preempt()` function, which as a last step, enters the dispatcher `swtch()` routine.

DTrace also provides several probes for tracking preempt activity. We saw one example in Section 3.7.3.6, where we tracked which thread was preempted and which thread initiated the preemption. The DTrace FBT provider manages probes and the entry and return points for the class-specific preempt functions, and the sched provider manages a preempt probe, which fires immediately before the current thread is preempted. Here's a simple example.

```
# dtrace -qn 'sched:unix:preempt:preempt { @s[execname,tid]=count() }'
^C

  thrds-sp                              89269                    1
  thrds-sp                                  1                    1
  dtrace                                    1                    1
  . . .
  thrds-sp                              89246                    4
  thrds-sp                              89260                    4
  . . .
  thrds-sp                              89256                    5
  thrds-sp                              89264                    5
```

Using a simple dtrace command-line command with the count aggregation, we can get a snapshot on which threads in which process are getting preempted.

A final note about preemptions and context switching. The system tracks two categories of context switches; voluntary and involuntary. A voluntary context switch occurs when a thread issues a blocking system call and goes to sleep. An involuntary context switch occurs when a thread has been preempted. The issue is that a thread may be preempted for one of two reasons: a higher-priority thread came along or the running thread used its time quantum. Time quantum expiration uses the preempt mechanism to nudge a thread off the CPU. These context switch rates can be tracked with `mpstat(1)`, watching the `csw` and `icsw` columns. If `icsw` rates are high (involuntary), it's interesting to know the how many relate to time-quantum expiration versus the advent of a higher-priority thread. Here's a DTrace script that decomposes involuntary context switches.

```
#!/usr/sbin/dtrace -Zqs

long inv_cnt;    /* all invountary context switches */
long tqe_cnt;    /* time quantum expiration count    */
long hpp_cnt;    /* higher-priority preempt count    */
long csw_cnt;    /* total number context switches    */

dtrace:::BEGIN
{
        inv_cnt = 0; tqe_cnt = 0; hpp_cnt = 0; csw_cnt = 0;

        printf("%-16s %-16s %-16s %-16s\n","TOTAL CSW","ALL INV","TQE_INV","HPP_INV");
        printf("=====================================================\n");
}

sysinfo:unix:preempt:inv_swtch
{
        inv_cnt += arg0;
}
sysinfo:unix::pswitch
{
        csw_cnt += arg0;
}

fbt:TS:ts_preempt:entry
/ ((tsproc_t *)args[0]->t_cldata)->ts_timeleft <= 1 /
{
        tqe_cnt++;
}

fbt:TS:ts_preempt:entry
/ ((tsproc_t *)args[0]->t_cldata)->ts_timeleft > 1 /
{
        hpp_cnt++;
}

fbt:RT:rt_preempt:entry
/ ((rtproc_t *)args[0]->t_cldata)->rt_timeleft <= 1 /
{
        tqe_cnt++;
}

fbt:RT:rt_preempt:entry
/ ((rtproc_t *)args[0]->t_cldata)->rt_timeleft > 1 /
{
        hpp_cnt++;
}

tick-1sec
{
        printf("%-16d %-16d %-16d %-16d\n",csw_cnt,inv_cnt,tqe_cnt,hpp_cnt);

        inv_cnt = 0; tqe_cnt = 0; hpp_cnt = 0; csw_cnt = 0;
}
```

Note that the script enables probes at the class-specific preempt functions. If you have active FX and/or FSS class threads, you need to add those probes, along with the correct predicate and the appropriate structure name. The script provides per-second counters.

```
solaris10> ./c.d
TOTAL CSW          ALL INV          TQE_INV          HPP_INV
====================================================================
  6147             1294             233              1066
  9199             1193             141              1055
  9886              846             186               661
  4940              658             128               531
  7359              702             149               553
  4892              874             134               742
  5504              846             152               699
  6994              972             183               790
 11835             1041             210               837
  7507             1018             209               815
 . . .
```

In this example, the number of involuntary switches was much less than voluntary (TOTAL CSW, ALL INV); of the involuntary switches, most are due to a higher-priority thread. If we had a high rate of time quantum expirations (TQE_INV), we could consider increasing time quanta by using the dispatch tables for the appropriate scheduling class.

3.10 The Kernel Sleep/Wakeup Facility

The typical lifetime of a thread includes not only execution time on a processor but also time spent waiting for requested resources to become available. An obvious example is a read or write from disk, when the thread issues the read(2) or write(2) system call, then sleeps so another thread can make use of the processor while the I/O is being processed by the kernel. Once the I/O has been completed, the kernel wakes up the thread so it can continue its work.

Threads that are runnable and waiting for a processor reside on dispatch queues. Threads that must block, waiting for an event or resource, are placed on sleep queues. A thread is placed on a sleep queue when it needs to sleep, awaiting availability of a resource (for example, a mutex lock, reader/writer lock, etc.) or awaiting some service by the kernel (for example, a system call). A few sleep queues implemented in the kernel vary somewhat, although they all use the same underlying sleep queue structures. Turnstiles are implemented with sleep queues and are used specifically for sleep/wakeup support in the context of priority inheritance, mutex locks, and reader/writer locks. Threads put to sleep for something other than a mutex or reader/writer lock are placed on the system's sleep queues.

3.10.1 Condition Variables

The underlying synchronization primitive used for sleep/wakeup in Solaris is the *condition variable*. Condition variables are always used in conjunction with mutex locks. A condition variable call is issued according to whether a specific condition is either true or false. The mutex ensures that the tested condition cannot be altered during the test and maintains state while the kernel thread is being set up to block on the condition. Once the condition variable code is entered and the thread is safely on a sleep queue, the mutex can be released. This is why all entry points to the condition variable code are passed the address of the condition variable and the address of the associated mutex lock.

In implementation, condition variables are data structures that identify an event or a resource for which a kernel thread may need to block and are used in many places around the operating system.

```
/*
 * Condition variables.
 */

typedef struct _condvar_impl {
        ushort_t        cv_waiters;
} condvar_impl_t;

#define CV_HAS_WAITERS(cvp)      (((condvar_impl_t *)(cvp))->cv_waiters != 0)
```

See usr/src/uts/common/sys/condvar_impl.h

The condition variable itself is simply a 2-byte (16-bit) data type with one defined field, `cv_waiters`, that stores the number of threads waiting on the specific resource the condition variable has been initialized for. The implementation is such that the various kernel subsystems that use condition variables declare a condition variable data type with a unique name either as a stand-alone data item or embedded in a data structure. Try doing a `grep(1)` command on `kcondvar_t` in the `/usr/include/sys` directory, and you'll see dozens of examples of condition variables. A generic kernel `cv_init()` function sets the condition variable to all zeros during the initialization phase of a kernel module. Other kernel-level condition variable interfaces are defined and called by different areas of the operating system to set up a thread to block a particular event and to insert the kernel thread on a sleep queue.

At a high level, the sleep/wakeup facility works as follows. At various points in the operating system code, conditional tests are performed to determine if a specific resource is available. If it is not, the code calls any one of several condition variable interfaces, such as `cv_wait()`, `cv_wait_sig()`, `cv_timedwait()`, `cv_wait_stop()`, etc., passing a pointer to the condition variable and mutex. This sequence is represented in the following small pseudocode segment.

```
kernel_function()
        mutex_init(resource_mutex);
        cv_init(resource_cv);
        mutex_enter(resource_mutex);
        if (resource is not available)
                cv_wait(&resource_cv, &resource_mutex);
        consume resource
        mutex_exit(resource_mutex);
```

These interfaces provide some flexibility in altering behavior as determined by the condition the kernel thread must wait for. Ultimately, the `cv_block()` interface is called; the interface is the kernel routine that actually sets the `t_wchan` value in the kernel thread and calls `sleepq_insert()` to place the thread on a sleep queue. The `t_wchan`, or *wait channel*, contains the address of the conditional variable that the thread is blocking on. This address is listed in the WCHAN column in the output of a `ps -efl` command.

The notion of a wait channel or wchan is something that's familiar to folks that have been around UNIX for a while. Traditional implementations of UNIX maintained a wchan field in the process structure, and it was always related to an event or resource the process was waiting for (why the process was sleeping). Naturally, in the Solaris multithreaded model, we moved the wait channel into the kernel thread, since kernel threads execute independently of other kernel threads in the same process and can execute system calls and block.

When the event or resource that the thread was sleeping on is made available, the kernel uses the condition variable facility to alert the sleeping thread (or threads) and to initiate a wakeup, a process that moves the thread from a sleep queue to a processor's dispatch queue.

Figure 3.12 illustrates the sleep/wake process.

3.10.2 Sleep Queues

Sleep queues are organized as a linked list of kernel threads, each linked list rooted in an array referenced through a `sleepq_head` kernel pointer, which references a doubly linked sublist of threads at the same priority. A hashing function indexes the `sleepq_head` array, hashing on the address of the condition variable. The singly linked list that establishes the beginning of the doubly linked sublists of kthreads at the same priority is also in ascending order of priority. The sublist is implemented by `t_priforw` (forward pointer) and `t_priback` (previous pointer) in the kernel thread. Also, a `t_sleepq` pointer points back to the array entry in `sleepq_head`, identifying which sleep queue the thread is on and also affording a quick method to determine if a thread is on a sleep queue at all. (If `t_sleepq ==` NULL, the thread is not on a sleep queue).

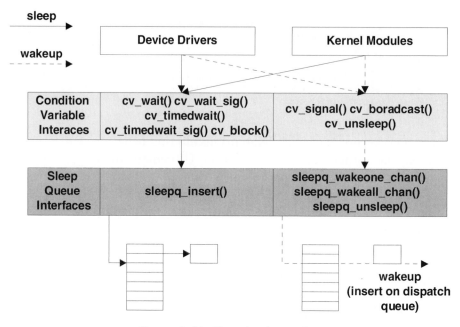

Figure 3.12 Sleep/Wakeup Flow

The number of kernel interfaces to the sleep queue facility is minimal. Only a few operations are performed on sleep queues: inserting a kernel thread on a sleep queue (putting a thread to sleep), removing a thread from a sleep queue (waking a thread up), and traversing the sleep queue in search of a kernel thread. There are interfaces that let us wake one thread only or all threads sleeping on the same condition variable.

Insertion of a thread simply involves indexing into the sleepq_head array to find the appropriate sleep queue specified by the condition variable address, then traversing the list, checking thread priorities along the way to determine the proper insertion point. Once the appropriate sublist has been found (at least one kernel thread at the same priority) or it has been determined that no other threads on the sleep queue have the same priority, a new sublist is started, the kernel thread is inserted, and the pointers are set up properly.

The removal of a kthread involves either searching for and removing a specific thread that has been specified by the code calling into sleepq_dequeue() or sleepq_unsleep(), or waking up all the threads blocking on a particular condition variable. Waking up all threads or a specified thread is relatively straightforward: the code hashes into the sleepq_head array specified by the address of the condition variable, and walks the list, either waking up each thread or searching for a particular thread and waking the targeted thread. In case a single, unspeci-

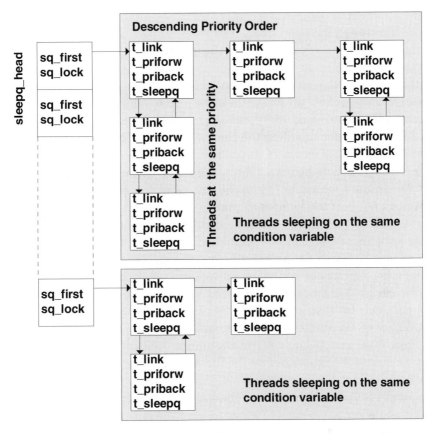

Figure 3.13 Sleep Queues

fied thread needs to be removed, the code implements the list as a FIFO (First In, First Out), so the kthread that has been sleeping the longest on a condition variable is selected for wakeup first.

3.10.3 The Sleep Process

Now that we've introduced condition variables and sleep queues, let's tie them together to form the complete sleep/wakeup picture in Solaris. The interfaces to the sleep queue (sleepq_insert(), etc.) are, for the most part, called only from the condition variables and turnstiles subsystems.

The process of putting a thread to sleep begins with a call into the condition variable code wait functions, one of cv_wait(), cv_wait_sig(), cv_wait_sig_swap(), cv_timedwait(), or cv_timedwait_sig(). Each of these functions is passed the condition variable and a mutex lock. They all ultimately call `cv_block()` to prepare the thread for sleep queue insertion. `cv_wait()` is the simplest condition variable sleep interface; it grabs the dispatcher lock for the kthread and invokes the class-specific sleep routine (for example, `ts_sleep()`). The *timed* variants of the `cv_wait()` routines take an additional time argument, ensuring that the thread will be woken up when the time value expires if it has not yet been removed from the sleep queue. `cv_timedwait()` and `cv_timedwait_sig()` use the kernel callout facility for handling the timer expiration. The `realtime_timeout()` interface is used and places a high-priority timeout on the kernel callout queue. The `setrun()` function is placed on the callout queue, along with the kernel thread address and time value. When the timer expires, `setrun()`, followed by the class-specific `setrun` function (for example, `rt_setrun()`), executes on the sleeping thread, making it runnable and placing it on a dispatch queue.

The *sig* variants of the condition variable code, `cv_wait_sig()`, `cv_timedwait_sig()`, etc., are designed for potentially longer-term waits, when it is desirable to test for pending signals before the actual wakeup event. These variants return 0 to the caller if a signal has been posted to the kthread. The swap variant, `cv_wait_sig_swap()`, can be used if it is safe to swap out the sleeping thread while it's sleeping. The various condition variable routines are summarized below. Note that all functions described below release the mutex lock after `cv_block()` returns, and they reacquire the mutex before the function itself returns.

- **cv_wait().** Calls `cv_block()`. Then, `cv_wait()` enters the dispatcher with `swtch()` when `cv_block()` returns.

- **cv_wait_sig().** Checks for `SC_BLOCK` scheduler activation (last LWP in the process is blocking). If `false`, `cv_wait_sig()` calls `cv_block_sig()`. On return from `cv_block_sig()`, it tests for a pending signal. If a signal is pending, `cv_wait_sig()` calls `setrun()`; otherwise, it calls `swtch()`. If an `SC_BLOCK` activation is `true`, `cv_wait_sig()` removes the thread timeout and returns –1 unless a signal is pending; then, it returns 0.

- **cv_wait_sig_swap().** Essentially the same as `cv_wait_sig()` but flags the thread as swappable.

- **cv_timedwait().** Tests for timer expiration on entry. If the timer has expired, `cv_timedwait()` returns –1. It calls `realtime_timeout()` to set a callout queue entry, calls `cv_block()`, and checks the timer on return from `cv_block()`. If the timer has expired, `cv_timedwait()` calls `setrun()`; otherwise, it calls `swtch()`.

- **cv_timedwait_sig().** Tests for time expiration. If the timer has expired, `cv_timedwait_sig()` returns –1 unless a signal is pending; then, it returns 0. If neither condition is `true`, then `cv_timedwait_sig()` calls `realtime_` `timeout()` to set the callout queue entry and tests for an `SC_BLOCK` activation. If `false`, `cv_timedwait_sig()` calls `cv_block_sig()`. On return from `cv_block_sig()`, it tests for a pending signal. If a signal is pending, `cv_timedwait_sig()` calls `setrun()`; otherwise, it calls `swtch()`. If an `SC_BLOCK` activation is `true`, `cv_timedwait_sig()` removes the thread timeout and returns –1 unless a signal is pending; then, it returns 0.

All of the above entry points into the condition variable code call `cv_block()` or `cv_block_sig()`, which just sets the `T_WAKEABLE` flag in the kernel thread and then calls `cv_block()`. `cv_block()` does some additional checking of various state flags and invokes the scheduling-class-specific sleep function through the `CL_SLEEP()` macro, which resolves to `ts_sleep()` for a TS/IA class thread. The intention of the `ts_sleep()` code is to boost the priority of the sleeping thread to a SYS priority if such a boost is flagged. As a result, the kthread is placed in an optimal position on the sleep queue for early wakeup and quick rescheduling when the wakeup occurs. Otherwise, the priority is reset according to how long the thread has been waiting to run. The `ts_sleep()` function is the most complex of all the class *xx*_sleep() routines, so we start with `ts_sleep()`.

The assignment of a SYS priority to the kernel thread is not guaranteed every time `ts_sleep()` is entered. Flags in the kthread structure, along with the kthread's class-specific data (`ts_data` in the case of a TS class thread), specify whether a kernel mode (SYS) priority is required. A SYS class priority is flagged if the thread is holding either a reader/writer lock or a page lock on a memory page. For most other cases, a SYS class priority is not required and thus will not be assigned to the thread. RT class threads do not have a class sleep routine; because they are fixed-priority threads, there's no priority adjustment work to do. The `ts_sleep()` function is represented in the following pseudocode.

```
ts_sleep()
        if (SYS priority requested) /* t)_kpri_req flag */
                set TSKPRI flag in kthread
                set t_pri to requested SYS priority /* tpri = ts_kmdpris[arg] */
                set kthread trap return flag /* t_trapret */
                set thread ast flag      /* t_astflag */
        else if (ts_dispwait > ts_maxwait) /* has the thread been waiting long */
                calculate new user mode priority
                set ts_timeleft = ts_dptbl[ts_cpupri].ts_quantum
                set ts_dispwait = 0
                set new global priority in thread (t_pri)
                if (thread priority < max priority on dispatch queue)
                        call cpu_surrender() /* preemption time */
        else if (thread is already at a SYS priority)
                set thread priority to TS class priority
                clear TSKPRI flag in kthread
                if (thread priority < max priority on dispatch queue)
                        call cpu_surrender() /* preemption time */
```

The thread priority setting in `ts_sleep()` in the second code segment above is entered if the thread has been waiting an inordinate amount of time to run, as determined by `ts_dispwait` in the `ts_data` structure and by the `ts_maxwait` value from the dispatch table, as indexed by the current user-mode priority, `ts_umdpri`.

The code returns to `cv_block()` from `ts_sleep()`, where the thread's `t_wchan` is set to the address of the condition variable and the thread's `t_sobj_ops` is set to the address of the condition variable's operations structure.

```
/*
 * Type-number definitions for the various synchronization
 * objects defined for the system. The numeric values
 * assigned to the various definitions begin with zero, since
 * the synch-object mapping array depends on these values.
 */
#define SOBJ_NONE       0       /* undefined synchronization object */
#define SOBJ_MUTEX      1       /* mutex synchronization object */
#define SOBJ_RWLOCK     2       /* readers/writer synchronization object */
#define SOBJ_CV         3       /* cond. variable synchronization object */
#define SOBJ_SEMA       4       /* semaphore synchronization object */
#define SOBJ_USER       5       /* user-level synchronization object */
#define SOBJ_USER_PI    6       /* user-level sobj having Prio Inheritance */
#define SOBJ_SHUTTLE    7       /* shuttle synchronization object */

/*
 * The following data structure is used to map
 * synchronization object type numbers to the
 * synchronization object's sleep queue number
 * or the synch. object's owner function.
 */
typedef struct _sobj_ops {
        int             sobj_type;
        kthread_t       *(*sobj_owner)();
        void            (*sobj_unsleep)(kthread_t *);
        void            (*sobj_change_pri)(kthread_t *, pri_t, pri_t *);
} sobj_ops_t;
```
                                              See usr/src/uts/common/sys/sobject.h

This is a generic structure that is used for all types of synchronization objects supported by the operating system. Note the types in the header file; they describe mutex locks, reader/writer locks, semaphores, condition variables, etc. Essentially, this object provides a placeholder for a few routines that are specific to the synchronization object and that may require invocation while the kernel thread is sleeping. In the case of condition variables (our example), the `sobj_ops` structure is populated with the address of the `cv_owner()`, `cv_unsleep()`, and `cv_change_pri()` functions, with the `sobj_type` field set to `SOBJ_CV`. The address of this structure is what the kthread's `t_sobj_ops` field is set to in the `cv_block()` code.

With the kthread's wait channel and synchronization object operations pointers set appropriately, the correct sleep queue is located by use of the hashing function on the condition variable address to index into the `sleepq_head` array. Next, the `cv_waiters` field in the condition variable is incremented to reflect another kernel thread blocking on the object, and the thread state is set to `TS_SLEEP`. Finally, the `sleepq_insert()` function is called to insert the kernel thread into the correct position (based on priority) in the sleep queue. The kthread is now on a sleep queue in a `TS_SLEEP` state, waiting for a wakeup.

The remaining *xx_sleep()* functions are actually quite simple. For `FSS` class threads, a `SYS` priority is set if `t_kpri_req` was true or the `FSSKPRI` flag was set in `fss_flags` (which would happen for the same reason as the TS/IA case—a RW lock or memory page lock is being held by the thread). Otherwise, the function just sets the thread's `t_stime` field (sleep time) and returns. The `FX` class is much the same. The `RT` class does not implement a sleep function; since `RT` class threads are already at a priority higher than the `SYS` class, so there's no reason to request a `SYS` class priority for an `RT` thread.

3.10.4 The Wakeup Mechanism

For every `cv_wait()` (or variant) call on a condition variable, a corresponding wakeup call uses `cv_signal()`, `cv_broadcast()`, or `cv_unsleep()`. `cv_signal()` wakes up one thread, and `cv_broadcast()` wakes up all threads sleeping on the same condition variable. Here is the sequence of wakeup events.

- The `cv_broadcast()` function simply locates the address of the sleep queue by invoking the hash function on the address of the condition variable, which was passed to `cv_broadcast()` as an argument, clears the `cv_waiters` field in the condition variable (all the threads are getting a wakeup, so the condition variable should reflect zero threads waiting on the condition variable), and calls `sleepq_wakeall_chan()`.

- `sleepq_wakeall_chan()` traverses the linked list of kernel threads waiting on that particular condition variable and, for each kthread, calls `sleepq_unlink()`. `sleepq_unlink()` removes the thread from the sleep queue linked list, adjusts the pointers (the `t_priforw` and `t_priback` pointers), and returns to `sleepq_wakeall_chan()`.

- On the return to `sleepq_wakeall_chan()`, the thread's `t_wchan` and `t_sobj_ops` fields are cleared, and the scheduling-class-specific wakeup code is called (`CL_WAKEUP()`).

The `ts_wakeup()` code puts the kernel thread back on a dispatch queue so that it can be scheduled for execution on a processor. Threads that have a kernel mode priority (as indicated by the `TSKPRI` flag in the class-specific data structure, which is set in `ts_sleep()` if a `SYS` priority is assigned) are placed at the front of the appropriate dispatch queue. IA class threads also result in setfrontdq() being called; otherwise, setbackdq() is called to place the kernel thread at the back of the dispatch queue.

Threads that are not at a SYS priority are tested to see if their wait for a shot at getting scheduled is longer than the time value set in the ts_maxwait field in the dispatch table for the thread's priority level.

If the thread has been waiting an inordinate amount of time to run (if dispwait > dispatch_table[priority]dispwait), then the thread's priority is recalculated with the ts_slpret value from the dispatch table. This is essentially the same logic used in ts_sleep() and gives a priority boost to threads that have spent an inordinate amount of time on the sleep queue.

For RT and FX class threads, the class wakeup function is very simple—we just reset the time quantum for the thread and call setbackdq() to insert the thread at the back of a dispatch queue.

The fss_wakeup() code is also relatively simple. If the thread already has a SYS priority, we call setbackdq(). If the thread has a kernel priority request flag (t_kpri_req), we boost the thread's priority to a SYS priority, and call setbackdq(). Otherwise, we just recalculate the priority and call setbackdq().

It is in the dispatcher queue insertion code (setfrontdq(), setbackdq()) that the thread state is switched from TS_SLEEP to TS_RUN. It's also in these functions that we determine if the thread we just placed on a queue is of a higher priority than the currently running thread and if so, force a preemption. At this point, the kthread has been woken up and is sitting on a dispatch queue, ready to get context-switched onto a processor when the dispatcher swtch() function runs again and the newly inserted thread is selected for execution.

For monitoring sleep events, have a look at /usr/demo/dtrace/whatfor.d, which uses the sched provider's off-CPU probe to track when a thread is going to sleep, and aggregates on the type of synchronization object, so we get an idea of how much time per-synchronization object was spent sleeping.

3.11 Interrupts

Understanding interrupts and what happens when an interrupt is generated are important components of the big dispatcher picture. A running thread gets pinned for a short period when the CPU on which it is running fields an interrupt. Additionally, the dispatcher code contains many conditional tests to determine whether a CPU is running an interrupt thread and takes a different code path depending on whether that condition is true.

An interrupt is the mechanism that a hardware device or a component of the kernel-at-large (through software interrupts) can use to interrupt the current execution flow and force a CPU into running an interrupt handler. The hardware device interrupt scenario is generally well known—a host bus adapter (HBA) for disk I/O generates interrupts on I/O completion, or a network interface card (NIC) generates interrupts for incoming network packets. The Solaris kernel programs an internal clock to generate an interrupt every 10 milliseconds to enter a clock interrupt handler and perform some housekeeping chores in the kernel. An interrupt can be initiated by software as well. A common use on Solaris multiprocessor systems is the cross-call mechanism, a facility whereby one CPU can send an interrupt to one or more of the other CPUs on the system (or to all of them) to force the CPU into a handler to take a specific action. The preemption mechanism uses cross-calls to force a CPU out of its current flow of execution so that the thread can be preempted.

Interrupts are directed to specific processors, and on reception, a processor stops executing the current thread (see Figure 3.14). The current thread is pinned, and the interrupt thread allowed to execute. When the interrupt thread completes, the interrupted thread is unpinned and resumes exection. This allows interrupts to be processed quickly, since a full context switch is not required. If the interrupt thread blocks, it is given full thread state and placed on a sleep queue, and the

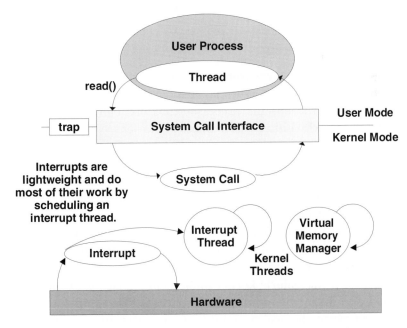

Figure 3.14 Process, Interrupt, and Kernel Threads

interrupted thread will be unpinned. Kernel threads handle all but high-priority interrupts. Consequently, the kernel can minimize the amount of time spent holding critical resources, thus providing better scalability of interrupt code and lower overall interrupt response time.

3.11.1 Interrupt Priorities

Solaris assigns priorities to interrupts to allow overlapping interrupts to be handled with the correct precedence; for example, a network interrupt can be configured to have a higher priority than a disk interrupt.

The kernel implements 15 interrupt priority levels: level 1 through level 15, where level 15 is the highest priority level. On each processor, the kernel can mask interrupts below a given priority level by setting the processor's interrupt level. Setting the interrupt level blocks all interrupts at the specified level and lower. That way, when the processor is executing a level 9 interrupt handler, it does not receive interrupts at level 9 or below; it handles only higher-priority interrupts.

Interrupts that occur with a priority level at or lower than the processor's interrupt level are temporarily ignored. An interrupt is not acknowledged by a processor until the processor's interrupt level is less than the level of the pending interrupt. More important interrupts have a higher-priority level to give them a better chance to be serviced than lower-priority interrupts.

Figure 3.15 illustrates interrupt priority levels.

3.11.2 Interrupts as Threads

Interrupt priority levels can synchronize access to critical sections used by interrupt handlers. By raising the interrupt level, a handler can ensure exclusive access to data structures for the specific processor that has elevated its priority level. This is in fact what early, uniprocessor implementations of UNIX systems did for synchronization.

But masking out interrupts to ensure exclusive access is expensive; it blocks other interrupt handlers from running for a potentially long time, which could lead to data loss if interrupts are lost because of overrun. (An overrun condition is one in which the volume of interrupts awaiting service exceeds the system's ability to queue the interrupts.) In addition, interrupt handlers using priority levels alone cannot block, since a deadlock could occur if they are waiting on a resource held by a lower-priority interrupt.

For these reasons, the Solaris kernel implements most interrupts as asynchronously created and dispatched high-priority threads. This implementation allows the kernel to overcome the scaling limitations imposed by interrupt blocking for synchronizing data access and thus provides low-latency interrupt response times.

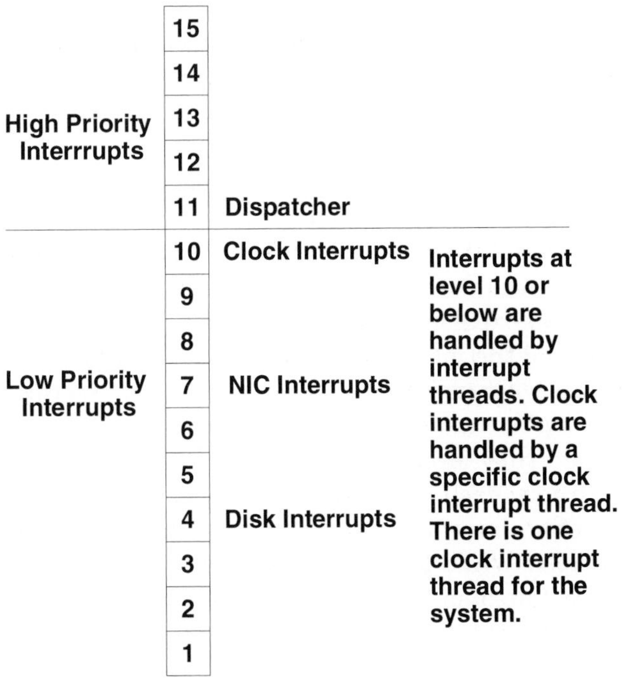

	15	
	14	
High Priority Interrrupts	**13**	
	12	
	11	**Dispatcher**
	10	**Clock Interrupts**
	9	
	8	
Low Priority Interrupts	**7**	**NIC Interrupts**
	6	
	5	
	4	**Disk Interrupts**
	3	
	2	
	1	

Interrupts at level 10 or below are handled by interrupt threads. Clock interrupts are handled by a specific clock interrupt thread. There is one clock interrupt thread for the system.

Figure 3.15 Interrupt Priority Levels

Interrupts at priority 10 and below are handled by Solaris threads. These interrupt handlers can then block if necessary, using regular synchronization primitives such as mutex locks. Interrupts, however, must be efficient, and it is too expensive to create a new thread each time an interrupt is received. For this reason, each processor maintains a pool of partially initialized interrupt threads, one for each of the lower 9 priority levels plus a systemwide thread for the clock interrupt. When an interrupt is taken, the interrupt uses the interrupt thread's stack, and only if it blocks on a synchronization object is the thread completely initialized. This approach, allows simple, fast allocation of threads at the time of interrupt dispatch.

A typical scenario: An interrupt with priority 9 or less occurs (level 10 clock interrupts are handled slightly differently). When an interrupt occurs, the interrupt level is raised to the level of the interrupt to block subsequent interrupts at this level (and lower levels). The currently executing thread is interrupted and *pinned* to the processor. A thread for the priority level of the interrupt is taken from the pool of interrupt threads for the processor and is context-switched in to handle the interrupt.

The term *pinned* refers to a mechanism employed by the kernel that avoids context-switching out the interrupted thread. The executing thread is pinned under the interrupt thread. The interrupt thread "borrows" the LWP from the executing thread. While the interrupt handler is running, the interrupted thread is pinned to avoid the overhead of having to completely save its context; it cannot run on any processor until the interrupt handler completes or blocks on a synchronization object. Once the handler is complete, the original thread is unpinned and rescheduled.

If the interrupt handler thread blocks on a synchronization object (for example, a mutex or condition variable) while handling the interrupt, it is converted into a complete kernel thread capable of being scheduled. Control is passed back to the interrupted thread, and the interrupt thread remains blocked on the synchronization object. When the synchronization object is unblocked, the thread becomes runnable and may preempt lower-priority threads to be rescheduled.

The processor interrupt level remains at the level of the interrupt, blocking lower-priority interrupts, even while the interrupt handler thread is blocked. This prevents lower-priority interrupt threads from interrupting the processing of higher-level interrupts. While interrupt threads are blocked, they are pinned to the processor they initiated on, guaranteeing that each processor will always have an interrupt thread available for incoming interrupts.

Level 10 clock interrupts are handled similarly, but since there is only one source of clock interrupt, there is a single, systemwide clock thread. Clock interrupts are discussed further in Section 19.1.

3.11.3 Interrupt Thread Priorities

Interrupts that are scheduled as threads share global dispatcher priorities with other threads. Interrupt threads use the top ten global dispatcher priorities, 160 to 169. Figure 3.8 shows the relationship of the interrupt dispatcher priorities to the other scheduling classes.

3.11.4 High-Priority Interrupts

Interrupts above priority 10 block out all lower-priority interrupts until they complete. For this reason, high-priority interrupts need to have an extremely short code path to prevent them from affecting the latency of other interrupt handlers and the performance and scalability of the system.

High-priority interrupt threads also cannot block; they can use only the spin variety of synchronization objects. This is due to the priority level the dispatcher uses for synchronization. Since the dispatcher runs at level 11, code running at higher interrupt levels cannot enter the dispatcher.

High-priority threads typically service the minimal requirements of the hardware device (the source of the interrupt), then post down a lower-priority software interrupt to complete the required processing.

3.11.5 Interrupt Management

For some workloads, it may be desirable to partition the system such that application threads are isolated from CPUs handling interrupt traffic. Network-intensive applications, for example, can result in high interrupt rates to the CPU(s) handling the NIC interrupts. Application threads running on a such a CPU may frequently be pinned, which can degrade performance, especially if the pinned threads are holding a critical resource such as a lock.

Using processor sets (psrset(1)), we can partition off interrupt loading by creating a processor set for the application processes and using the psrset -f flag to disable interrupts to all the CPUs in the set. This forces the kernel to rebind the device interrupts to the remaining CPUs (not in the user-defined set). With the application processes bound to the user-defined set, they will execute on CPUs not fielding interrupts. This method should of course be tested before being applied to a production workload.

3.11.6 Interrupt Monitoring

You can use the mpstat(1M) and vmstat(1M) commands to monitor interrupt activity on a Solaris system. mpstat(1M) provides interrupts-per-second for each CPU in the intr column and interrupts handled on an interrupt thread (low-level interrupts) in the ithr column.

Solaris 10 added an intrstat(1) command, which displays interrupt-to-CPU bindings, interrupt rates, and time spent handling interrupts. For example, looking at mpstat(1), we can observe interrupt rates to CPUs.

```
# mpstat 1
CPU minf mjf xcal   intr  ithr   csw icsw migr smtx  srw syscl  usr sys  wt idl
  0    0   0    0    557   217   621    0    3    0    0   475    0   1   0  99
  1    0   0    0  12971 12962 25457    0    3    0    0 25459    2   8   0  90
  2    8   0    0     15     0    24    0    0    0    0    57    0   0   0 100
  3    0   0    0      2     1     0    0    0    0    0     0    0   0   0 100
CPU minf mjf xcal   intr  ithr   csw icsw migr smtx  srw syscl  usr sys  wt idl
  0    0   0    0    442   216   394    1    6    0    0   255    0   0   0 100
  1    0   0    0  13031 13023 25807    0    3    1    0 25792    1   8   0  91
  2    0   0    0      7     0    11    0    0    0    0    28    0   2   0  98
  3    0   0    0      1     0     0    0    0    0    0     0    0   0   0 100
```

In this example, CPU 1 is taking the highest rate of interrupts, which means it is likely that CPU 1 has device interrupt bindings. Using `intrstat(1)`, we see

```
# intrstat

      device |   cpu0 %tim      cpu1 %tim      cpu2 %tim      cpu3 %tim
-------------+-------------------------------------------------------------
      ata#1 |      0  0.0         4  0.0         0  0.0         0  0.0
      bge#0 |      1  0.0         0  0.0         0  0.0         0  0.0
      mpt#0 |      0  0.0     12661  4.8         0  0.0         0  0.0

      device |   cpu0 %tim      cpu1 %tim      cpu2 %tim      cpu3 %tim
-------------+-------------------------------------------------------------
      ata#1 |      0  0.0         0  0.0         0  0.0         0  0.0
      bge#0 |      6  0.0         0  0.0         0  0.0         0  0.0
      mpt#0 |      0  0.0     12630  4.7         0  0.0         0  0.0
```

The `intrstat(1)` data shows us that device mpt#0 (mpt is the device nomenclature, #0 refers to instance 0 of the device) is generating interrupts to CPU 1, which is spending about 5% of its time handling mpt interrupts. If you're not sure what an mpt device is, a good place to start is finding a match in the kernel module description.

```
# modinfo | grep mpt
 29 fffffffffbb4a3d0  2f948 169   1  mpt (MPT HBA Driver v1.49)
 #
```

Here we determined the mpt device is our Host Bus Adapter (HBA), which is a disk interface. In this example, we clearly have a respectable rate of disk I/O traffic. We would use `iostat(1)` in conjunction with the DTrace io provider to determine precisely which processes are generating the I/O and which files are receiving the I/O traffic.

3.11.7 Interprocessor Interrupts and Cross-Calls

The kernel can send an interrupt or trap to another processor when it requires another processor to do some immediate work on its behalf. Interprocessor interrupts are delivered through the `poke_cpu()` function; they are used for the following purposes:

- **Preempting the dispatcher.** A thread may need to signal a thread running on another processor to enter kernel mode when a preemption is required (initiated by a clock or timer event) or when a synchronization object is released. Preemption is discussed in detail in Section 3.9.

- **Delivering a signal.** The delivery of a signal may require interrupting a thread on another processor.
- **Starting/stopping /proc threads.** The /proc infrastructure uses interprocessor interrupts to start and stop threads on different processors.

Using a similar mechanism, the kernel can also instruct a processor to execute a specific low-level function by issuing a processor-to-processor *cross-call*. Cross-calls are typically part of the processor-dependent implementation. UltraSPARC kernels use cross-calls for two purposes:

- **Implementing interprocessor interrupts.** As discussed above.
- **Maintaining virtual memory translation consistency.** Implementing cache consistency on SMP platforms requires the translation entries to be removed from the MMU of each CPU that a thread has run on when a virtual address is unmapped. On UltraSPARC, user processes issuing an unmap operation make a cross-call to each CPU on which the thread has run, to remove the TLB entries from each processor's MMU. Address space unmap operations within the kernel address space make a cross-call to *all* processors for each unmap operation.

Both cross-calls and interprocessor interrupts are reported by mpstat(1M) in the xcal column as cross-calls per second.

```
# mpstat 3
CPU minf mjf xcal  intr ithr  csw icsw migr smtx  srw syscl  usr sys  wt idl
  0    0   0    6   607  246 1100  174   82   84    0  2907   28   5   0  66
  1    0   0    2   218    0 1037  212   83   80    0  3438   33   4   0  62
```

High numbers of reported cross-calls can result from either of the activities mentioned in the preceding section—most commonly, from kernel address space unmap activity caused by file system activity.

Once again, we can use DTrace to root out the source of cross-calls.

```
# dtrace -n 'xcalls { @[stack()]=count()}'
dtrace: description 'xcalls ' matched 3 probes
^C
. . .
              SUNW,UltraSPARC-II`send_one_mondo+0x20
              SUNW,UltraSPARC-II`send_mondo_set+0x1c
              unix`xt_some+0xc4
              unix`xt_sync+0x3c
              unix`hat_unload_callback+0x808
```

continues

```
         unix`bp_mapout+0x74
         genunix`biowait+0xb0
         ufs`ufs_putapage+0x400
         ufs`ufs_putpages+0x2a4
         genunix`segmap_release+0x300
         ufs`ufs_diraddentry+0x2e4
         ufs`ufs_direnter_cm+0x2a8
         ufs`ufs_create+0x254
         genunix`fop_create+0x38
         genunix`vn_createat+0x550
         genunix`vn_openat+0x130
         genunix`copen+0x260
         unix`syscall_trap+0xac
       15848
```

In the example, we cut all but the last kernel stack frame, since the DTrace count aggregating function nicely generates output in ascending order, the last entry is the aggregation key (in this case, the kernel stack) that occurred most frequently during the sampling period. The kernel stack shown indicates a lot of cross-call traffic from the UFS I/O code path, which uses segmap for page caching. We can see segmap_release on the stack, followed by a hat_mapout and hat_unload_callback function. Without digressing into too many details, the cross-calls are due to segmap activity and the need to push pages out. This requires unmapping the page (handled by the HAT layer), and generating cross-call activity (xt_sync, xt_some on the stack) to maintain MMU-level coherence across the processors.

3.12 Summary

The dispatcher is one of the more complex subsystems in the kernel, made all the more so with changes to system and chip architectures and new features implemented in Solaris for resource management and control. The implementation of a core dispatcher with support for multiple scheduling classes provides a flexible environment for running a variety of workloads. The per-CPU run queue implementation provides speed and scalability on multiprocessor platforms. The wealth of observability tools in Solaris (prstat(1), mpstat(1), dtrace(1), etc.) makes understanding your workload and your systems behavior an attainable goal.

One final note: With the availability of the source code on www.opensolaris.com, it is expected that some readers will read the source listings as they use this text for reference. The text does not describe every function and every line of source code in the dispatcher. Such a text would be onerous to read, to say the least. The goal here was to describe how things work with some level of detail. Areas of the code that are not mentioned or included in the text are not an accidental omission, but rather the result of a conscious decision by the writers to maintain a balance between including what's important and excluding what are nonessential, subtle details.

3.13 MDB Reference

Table 3.4 MDB Reference for the Dispatcher and Classes

walker	Description
callout	Print callout table
class	Print process scheduler classes
cpuinfo	Print CPUs and runnable threads
cpupart	Print cpu partition info
lgrp	Display an lgrp
lnode	Print lnode structure(s)
lnode2dev	Print vfs_dev given lnode
sobj2ts	Perform turnstile lookup on synch object
turnstile	Display a turnstile
wchaninfo	Dump condition variable

4

Interprocess Communication

Interprocess communication (IPC) is the sharing of data and synchronization of events among processes. Contrast IPC with networking-based facilities, such as sockets and RPC interfaces, which enable communication over a network link between distributed systems. Early IPC facilities originated in AT&T UNIX System V, which added support for shared memory, semaphores, and message queues around 1983. This original set of three IPC facilities is generally known as System V IPC. Over time, a similar set of IPC features evolved from the POSIX standards, and we now have POSIX semaphores, shared memory, and message queues. The System V and POSIX IPCs use different APIs and are implemented differently in the kernel, although for applications they provide similar functionality.

Other facilities for interprocess communication include memory mapped files (mmap(2)), named pipes (also known as FIFOs), UNIX domain sockets, and the recently added Solaris Doors, which provide an RPC-like facility for threads running on the same system. Each method by which an application can do interprocess communication offers specific features and functionality which may or may not be useful for a given application. It's up to the application developer to determine what the requirements are and which method best meets those requirements.

Our goal here is not to provide a tutorial on programming with these interfaces, although some mention of the APIs is necessary when we describe a feature or functional component. Several texts discuss programming and interprocess communication, most notably, *Solaris Systems Programming* by Rich Teer and *UNIX Network Programming—Interprocess Communication, Second Edition, Volume 2*, by W. Richard Stevens.

4.1 The System V IPC Framework

The System V interprocess communication (IPC) facilities provide three services—message queues, semaphore arrays, and shared memory segments—which are managed by file-system-like namespaces. Unlike a file system, these namespaces aren't mounted and accessible via a path. Instead, a special API interacts with the different facilities (nothing precludes a VFS-based interface, but the standards require the special APIs). Furthermore, these special APIs don't use file descriptors, nor do they have an equivalent. This means that every operation which acts on an object needs to perform the equivalent of a lookup, which in turn means that every operation can fail if the specified object doesn't exist in the facility's namespace.

4.1.1 IPC Objects

Each object in a namespace has a unique ID, which the system assigns and uses to identify the object when performing operations on it. An object can also have a key, which is selected by the user at allocation time and is used as a primitive rendezvous mechanism. An object without a key is said to have a "private" key.

To perform an operation on an object given its key, you first perform a lookup and obtain its ID. The ID is then used to identify the object when the operation is performed. If the object has a private key, the ID must be known or obtained by other means.

Each object in the namespace has a creator UID and GID, as well as an owner UID and GID. Both are initialized with the RUID and RGID of the process that created the object. The creator or current owner can change the owner of the object. Each object in the namespace has a set of file-like permissions, which, in conjunction with the creator and owner UID and GID, control read and write access to the object (execute is ignored). Each object also has a creator project, which accounts for the object's resource usage.

All three facilities have five operations in common: GET, SET, STAT, RMID, and IDS:

- GET, like open, allocates a new object or obtains an existing one (using its key). It takes a key, a set of flags and mode bits, and, optionally, facility-specific arguments. If the key is IPC_PRIVATE, a new object with the requested mode bits and facility-specific attributes is created. If the key isn't IPC_PRIVATE, the GET attempts to look up the specified key and either returns that or creates a new key, depending on the state of the IPC_CREAT and `IPC_EXCL` flags, much like `open`. If `GET` needs to allocate an object, it can fail if there is insufficient space in the namespace (the maximum number of IDs for the facility has been exceeded) or if the facility-specific initialization fails. If `GET` finds an object it can return, it can still fail if that object's permissions or facility-specific attributes are less than those.

- `SET` adjusts facility-specific parameters of an object, in addition to the owner UID and GID and mode bits. It can fail if the caller isn't the creator or owner.

- `STAT` obtains information about an object, including the general attributes as well as facility-specific information. It can fail if the caller doesn't have read permission.

- `RMID` removes an object from the namespace. Subsequent operations using the object's ID or key will fail (until another object is created with the same key or ID). Since an `RMID` can be performed asynchronously with other operations, it is possible that other threads or processes will have references to the object. While a facility may have actions that need to be performed at `RMID` time, only when all references are dropped can the object be destroyed. `RMID` fails if the caller isn't the creator or owner.

- `IDS` obtains a list of all IDs in a facility's namespace. There are no facility-specific behaviors of `IDS`.

4.1.2 IPC Framework Design

Because some IPC facilities provide services whose operations must scale, a mechanism that allows fast, concurrent access to individual objects is needed. Of primary importance is object lookup based on ID (`SET`, `STAT`, others). Allocation (`GET`), deallocation (`RMID`), ID enumeration (`IDS`), and key lookups (`GET`) are lesser concerns but should be implemented in such a way that ID lookup isn't affected (at least not in the common case).

Starting from the bottom up, each object is represented by a structure, the first member of which must be a `kipc_perm_t`. The `kipc_perm_t` contains the information described above in Section 4.1.1, a reference count (since the object may continue to exist after it has been removed from the namespace), as well as some additional metadata that manages data structure membership. These objects are dynamically allocated.

Above the objects is a power-of-2 sized table of ID slots. Each slot contains a pointer to an object, a sequence number, and a lock. An object's ID is a function of its slot's index in the table and its slot's sequence number. Every time a slot is released (by `RMID`), its sequence number is increased. Strictly speaking, the sequence number is unnecessary. However, checking the sequence number after a lookup provides a certain degree of robustness against the use of stale IDs (useful since nothing else does). When the table fills up, it is resized (see Section 4.1.3).

Of an ID's 31 bits (an ID is, as defined by the standards, a signed int) the top IPC_SEQ_BITS are used for the sequence number with the remainder holding the index into the table. The size of the table is therefore bounded at 2 ^ (31 – IPC_SEQ_BITS) slots.

Managing this table is the ipc_service structure. It contains a pointer to the dynamically allocated ID table, a namespace-global lock, an id_space for managing the free space in the table, and sundry other metadata necessary for the maintenance of the namespace. An AVL tree of all keyed objects in the table (sorted by key) is used for key lookups. An unordered doubly linked list of all objects in the namespace (keyed or not) is maintained to facilitate ID enumeration.

To help visualize these relationships, Figure 4.1 illustrates a namespace with a table of size 8 containing three objects (IPC_SEQ_BITS = 28).

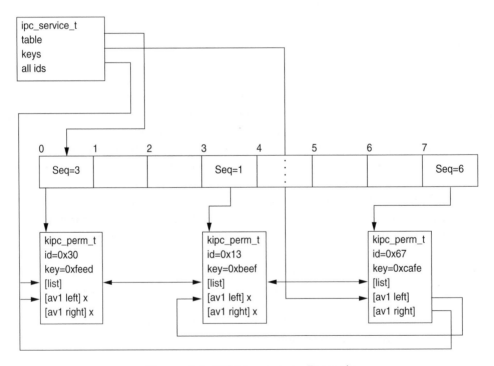

Figure 4.1 IPC Namespace Example

4.1.3 Locking

Three locks (or sets of locks) ensure correctness: the slot locks, the namespace lock, and p_lock (needed when checking resource controls). Their ordering is

```
namespace lock -> slot lock 0 -> ... -> slot lock t -> p_lock
```

Generally, the namespace lock protects allocation and removal from the namespace, ID enumeration, and resizing the ID table. Specifically,

- Write access to all fields of the `ipc_service` structure; read access to all variable fields of `ipc_service` except `ipcs_tabsz` (table size) and `ipcs_table` (the table pointer)
- Read/write access to `ipc_avl`, `ipc_list` in visible objects' `kipc_perm` structures (that is, objects that have been removed from the namespace don't have this restriction); write access to `ipct_seq` and `ipct_data` in the table entries

A slot lock by itself is meaningless (except when resizing). Of greater interest conceptually is the notion of an ID lock—a "virtual lock" that refers to whichever slot lock an object's ID currently hashes to.

An ID lock protects all objects with that ID. Normally, there will only be one such object: the one pointed to by the locked slot. However, if an object is removed from the namespace but retains references (for example, an attached shared memory segment that has been RMID'd), it continues to use the lock associated with its original ID. While this can result in increased contention, operations that require taking the ID lock of removed objects are infrequent.

Specifically, an ID lock protects the contents of an object's structure, including the contents of the embedded `kipc_perm` structure (but excluding those fields protected by the namespace lock). It also protects the `ipct_seq` and `ipct_data` fields in its slot (it is really a slot lock, after all).

Recall that the table is resizable. To avoid requiring every ID lookup to take a global lock, we employed a scheme much like that employed for file descriptors (see Section 14.2.1) is used. Note that the sequence number and data pointer are protected by both the namespace lock and their slot lock. When the table is resized, the following operations take place:

1. A new table is allocated.
2. The global lock is taken.

3. All old slots are locked, in order.

4. The first half of the new slots are locked.

5. All table entries are copied to the new table and cleared from the old table.

6. The `ipc_service` structure is updated to point to the new table.

7. The `ipc_service` structure is updated with the new table size.

8. All slot locks (old and new) are dropped.

Because the slot locks are embedded in the table, ID lookups and other operations that require taking a slot lock need to verify that the lock taken wasn't part of a stale table. To verify that, we check the table size before and after dereferencing the table pointer and taking the lock: if the size changes, the lock must be dropped and reacquired. It is this additional work that distinguishes an ID lock from a slot lock.

Because we can't guarantee that threads aren't accessing the old tables' locks, they are never deallocated. To prevent spurious reports of memory leaks, a pointer to the discarded table is stored in the new one in step 5. (Theoretically, `ipcs_destroy` will delete the discarded tables, but it is only ever called from a failed `_init` invocation; that is, when there aren't any.)

The following interfaces are provided by the `ipc` module for use by the individual IPC facilities.

```
int ipcperm_access(kipc_perm_t *, int, cred_t *);
```

Given an object and a cred structure, determines if the requested access type is
allowed.

```
int ipcperm_set(ipc_service_t *, struct cred *, kipc_perm_t *, struct ipc_perm *,
                model_t);
int ipcperm_set64(ipc_service_t *, struct cred *, kipc_perm_t *, ipc_perm64_t *);
void ipcperm_stat(struct ipc_perm *, kipc_perm_t *, model_t);
void ipcperm_stat64(ipc_perm64_t *, kipc_perm_t *);
```

Performs the common portion of an STAT or SET operation. All (except stat and stat64)
can fail, so they should be called before any facility-specific non-reversible changes
are made to an object. Similarly, the set operations have side effects, so they should
only be called once the possibility of a facility-specific failure is eliminated.

```
ipc_service_t *ipcs_create(const char *, rctl_hndl_t, size_t, ipc_func_t *,
                           ipc_func_t *, int, size_t);
```

Creates an IPC namespace for use by an IPC facility.

```
void ipcs_destroy(ipc_service_t *);
```

Destroys an IPC namespace.

```
void ipcs_lock(ipc_service_t *);
void ipcs_unlock(ipc_service_t *);
```

continues

Takes the namespace lock. Ideally such access wouldn't be necessary, but there may be facility-specific data protected by this lock (e.g. project-wide resource consumption). ipc_lock

`kmutex_t *ipc_lock(ipc_service_t *, int);`

Takes the lock associated with an ID. Can't fail.

`kmutex_t *ipc_relock(ipc_service_t *, int, kmutex_t *);`

Like ipc_lock, but takes a pointer to a held lock. Drops the lock unless it is the one that would have been returned by ipc_lock. Used after calls to cv_wait.

`kmutex_t *ipc_lookup(ipc_service_t *, int, kipc_perm_t **);`

Performs an ID lookup, returns with the ID lock held. Fails if the ID doesn't exist in the namespace.

`void ipc_hold(ipc_service_t *, kipc_perm_t *);`

Takes a reference on an object.

`void ipc_rele(ipc_service_t *, kipc_perm_t *);`

Releases a reference on an object, and drops the object's lock.
Calls the object's destructor if last reference is being released.

`void ipc_rele_locked(ipc_service_t *, kipc_perm_t *);`

Releases a reference on an object. Doesn't drop lock, and may only be called when there is more than one reference to the object.

`int ipc_get(ipc_service_t *, key_t, int, kipc_perm_t **, kmutex_t **);`
`int ipc_commit_begin(ipc_service_t *, key_t, int, kipc_perm_t *);`
`kmutex_t *ipc_commit_end(ipc_service_t *, kipc_perm_t *);`
`void ipc_cleanup(ipc_service_t *, kipc_perm_t *);`

Components of a GET operation. ipc_get performs a key lookup, allocating an object if the key isn't found (returning with the namespace lock and p_lock held), and returning the existing object if it is (with the object lock held). ipc_get doesn't modify the namespace.

ipc_commit_begin begins the process of inserting an object allocated by ipc_get into the namespace and can fail. If successful, it returns with the namespace lock and p_lock held. ipc_commit_end completes the process of inserting an object into the namespace and can't fail. The facility can call ipc_cleanup at any time following a successful ipc_get and before ipc_commit_end or a failed ipc_commit_begin to fail the allocation. Pseudocode for the suggested GET implementation:

```
top:

        ipc_get

        if failure
                return

        if found {

                if object meets criteria
                        unlock object and return success
                unlock object and return failure
```

continues

```
        } else {

                perform resource control tests
                drop namespace lock, p_lock
                if failure
                        ipc_cleanup

                perform facility-specific initialization
                if failure {
                        facility-specific cleanup
                        ipc_cleanup
                }

                ( At this point the object should be destructible using the
                  destructor given to ipcs_create )

                ipc_commit_begin
                if retry
                        goto top
                else if failure
                        return

                perform facility-specific resource control tests/allocations
                if failure
                        ipc_cleanup
                ipc_commit_end

                perform any infallible post-creation actions, unlock, and return
        }
int ipc_rmid(ipc_service_t *, int, cred_t *);

Performs the common portion of an RMID operation -- looks up an ID removes it, and calls
the a facility-specific function to do RMID-time cleanup on the private portions of the
object.

int ipc_ids(ipc_service_t *, int *, uint_t, uint_t *);

Performs the common portion of an IDS operation.
```

4.1.4 Module Creation

The System V IPC kernel modules are implemented as dynamically loadable modules. Each facility has a corresponding loadable module in the /kernel/sys directory (shmsys, semsys, and msgsys). In addition, all three methods of IPC require loading of the /kernel/misc/ipc module, which provides two low-level routines shared by all three facilities. The ipcperm_access() routine verifies access permissions to a particular IPC resource, for example, a shared memory segment, a semaphore, or a message queue. The ipcget() code fetches a data structure associated with a particular IPC resource that generated the call, based on a *key* value that is passed as an argument in the shmget(2), msgget(2), and semget(2) system calls.

When an IPC resource is initially created, a positive integer, known as an *identifier*, is assigned to identify the IPC object. The identifier is derived from a *key* value. The kernel IPC *xxx*get(2) system call will return the same identifier to processes or threads, using the same key value, which is how different processes can be sure to access the desired message queue, semaphore or shared memory segment. An ftok(3C), or file-to-key interface, is the most common method of having different processes obtain the correct key before they call one of the IPC *xxx*get() routines.

Associated with each IPC resource is an *id* data structure, which the kernel allocates and initializes the first time an *xxx*get(2) system call is invoked with the appropriate flags set. The *xxx*get(2) system call for each facility returns the identifier to the calling application, again based on arguments passed in the call and permissions. The structures are similar in name and are defined in the header file for each facility (see Table 4.1).

The number of *xxx*id_ds structures available is capped by each facility's project.max-*xxx*-ids resource control limit (see Chapter 7), that is, max-shm-ids, max-sem-ids, and max-msg-ids determine the maximum number of msgid_ds, semid_ds, and shmid_ds structures available, respectively.

Table 4.1 IPC ID Structure Names

Facility Type	xxxget(2)	ID Structure Name
semaphores	semget(2)	semid_ds
shared memory	shmget(2)	shmid_ds
message queues	msgget(2)	msgid_ds

Most fields in the ID structures are unique for each IPC type, but they all include as the first structure member a pointer to an ipc_perm data structure, which defines the access permissions for that resource, much as access to files is defined by permissions maintained in each file's inode. The ipc_perm structure is defined as follows.

```
/* Common IPC access structure */

struct ipc_perm {
        uid_t           uid;    /* owner's user id */
        gid_t           gid;    /* owner's group id */
        uid_t           cuid;   /* creator's user id */
        gid_t           cgid;   /* creator's group id */
        mode_t          mode;   /* access modes */
        uint_t          seq;    /* slot usage sequence number */
        key_t           key;    /* key */
#if !defined(_LP64)
        int             pad[4]; /* reserve area */
#endif
};
                                                See /usr/include/sys/ipc.h
```

For each IPC resource, the UID and GID of the owner and creator will be the same. Ownership could subsequently be changed through a control system call, but the creator's IDs never change. The access mode bits are similar to file access modes, differing in that there is no execute mode for IPC objects; thus, the mode bits define read/write permissions for the owner, group, and all others. The `seq` field, described as the slot usage sequence number, is used by the kernel to establish the unique identifier of the IPC resource when it is first created.

4.2 System V IPC Resource Controls

Traditionally, the behavior of the System V IPC facilities (shared memory, message queues, and semaphores) was influenced through a large set of `/etc/system` tuneables. While some of the tuneables allowed you to set meaningful administrative limits (for example, maximum shared memory segment size), many simply exposed implementation details (for example, the number of undo entries in an undo structure). There were many limitations with the traditional implementation:

- Relying on `/etc/system` as an administrative mechanism meant that reconfiguration required a reboot.

- Many parameters were used to size data structures allocated at boot (or module load) time. There was a penalty for sizing the parameters larger than was needed.

    There were a large variety of parameters to change, many of which were implementation specific and didn't align well with public interface boundaries. Yet they were necessary to configure the system for different workloads.

- The tuneables, named by combining a three-character facility abbreviation with a three-character parameter abbreviation, were a veritable alphabet soup. It was very easy for an administrator to misconfigure the system (see 4381822).

- The algorithms used by the traditional implementation assumed statically sized data structures. Changing many of the tuneables at runtime wouldn't have been possible, even if an interface were available to let you do so.

- There was no way to allocate additional resources to one user without allowing all users those resources. Since the amount of resources was always fixed, one user could have trivially prevented another from performing its desired allocations.

- There was no good way to observe the values of the parameters.

- Additionally, a perpetual complaint was that the default values for these tuneables were too small.

4.2.1 The Solution

In Solaris 10, we removed these limitations by reworking much of the System V IPC implementation to not require as much administrative hand-holding (removing unnecessary tuneables), and by using task-based resource controls to limit users' access to the System V IPC facilities (replacing the remaining tuneables). At the same time, we raised the default values for those limits that remained to more reasonable values. Last, for compatibility, the legacy tuneables are interpreted and used to initialize the default privileged limit for the new resource controls. The new resource controls are shown in Table 4.2.

Table 4.2 New Resource Controls

Resource Control	Similar Tuneable	Old Default	New Default	Max Value
project.max-shm-ids	shminfo_shmmni	100	128	1<<24
project.max-msg-ids	msginfo_msgmni	50	128	1<<24
project.max-sem-ids	seminfo_semmni	10	128	1<<24
project.max-shm-memory	shminfo_shmmax	512k	1/4 physical	UINT64_MAX
process.max-sem-nsems	seminfo_semmsl	25	512	SHRT_MAX
process.max-sem-ops	seminfo_semopm	10	512	INT_MAX
process.max-msg-qbytes	msginfo_msgmnb	4096	65536	ULONG_MAX
process.max-msg-messages	msginfo_msgtql	40	8192	UINT_MAX

The following tuneables no longer have any effect: semsys:seminfo_semmns, semsys:seminfo_semvmx, semsys:seminfo_semmnu, semsys:seminfo_semaem, semsys:seminfo_semume, semsys:seminfo_semusz, semsys:seminfo_semmap, shmsys:shminfo_shmseg, shmsys:shminfo_shmmin, msgsys:msginfo_msgmap, msgsys:msginfo_msgseg, msgsys:msginfo_msgssz, and msgsys:msginfo_msgmax.

The specific improvements are these:

- It is now possible to limit use of the System V IPC facilities on a per-process or per-project basis (depending on the resource being limited) without rebooting the system.

- None of these limits affect allocation directly; they can be made as large as possible without any immediate effect on the system. (Note that doing so would allow a user to allocate resources without bound, which would have an effect on the system.)

- Implementation internals are no longer exposed to the administrator, greatly simplifying configuration.

- The resource controls are fewer and are more verbosely and intuitively named than the tuneables.

- Limit settings can be observed with the common resource control interfaces, such as `prctl(1)` and `getrctl(2)`.

- Shared memory is limited in accordance with the total amount allocated per project, not a per-segment limit. This means that an administrator can permit a user to allocate a lot of segments and large segments, without having to permit the user to create a lot of large segments.

Because resource controls are the administrative mechanism, this configuration can be persistent across reboots by use of `project(4)`, as well as through a network service. See Chapter 7 for more information on how to set resource controls.

The following major implementation changes were made (for all the details, see the changes made to `os/ipc.c`, `os/msg.c`, `os/shm.c`, `syscall/sem.c`):

- Message headers are allocated dynamically. Previously, all message headers were allocated at module load time, linked into a global freelist, and allocated from there. (The locking on this list also caused a scalability problem.)

- Semaphore arrays are allocated dynamically. Previously semaphore arrays were allocated from a `seminfo_semmns`-sized vmem arena, which meant that allocations could fail because of fragmentation.

- Semaphore undo structures are allocated dynamically, and are per-process and per-semaphore array. They are unlimited in number and are always as large as the semaphore array they correspond to. Previously, the number of per-process undo structures was limited and allocated at module load time. Furthermore, the undo structures each had the same fixed size. It was possible for a process to not be able to allocate an undo structure or for the process's undo structure to be full.

- Semaphore undo structures maintain their undo values as signed integers, so no semaphore value is too large to be undone.

- All facilities formerly allocated objects from a fixed-size namespace, allocated at module load time. All facility namespaces are now resizable and will grow as demand increases.

4.3 Configuring IPC Tuneables on Solaris 10

The new framework enables us to dynamically configure IPC tuneable parameters by using the resource control framework. Ideally, we want these to be statically defined for our applications. We can also put these definitions within a network database (LDAP), to remove any per-machine settings.

The following example shows how to observe the System V Shared memory max parameter for a given login instance by using the `prctl` command.

```
sol10$ id -p
uid=0(root) gid=0(root) projid=3(default)
sol10# prctl -n project.max-shm-memory -i project 3
project: 3: default
NAME    PRIVILEGE       VALUE    FLAG   ACTION                  RECIPIENT
project.max-shm-memory
        privileged      246MB     -     deny                         -
        system          16.0EB   max    deny                         -
```

The shared memory maximum for this login has defaulted to 246 Mbytes. The following example shows how we can dynamically raise the shared memory limit.

```
sol10# prctl -n project.max-shm-memory -r -v 500mb -i project 3
sol10# prctl -n project.max-shm-memory -i project 3
project: 3: default
NAME    PRIVILEGE       VALUE    FLAG   ACTION                  RECIPIENT
project.max-shm-memory
        privileged      500MB     -     deny                         -
        system          16.0EB   max    deny                         -
```

To make this permanent, we would create a project entry for the user or project in question.

```
sol10# projadd -c "My database" -U oracle user.oracle
sol10# projmod -sK "project.max-shm-memory=(privileged,64G,deny)" user.oracle
sol10# su - oracle
oracle$ prctl -n project.max-shm-memory -i project user.oracle
project: 101: user.oracle
NAME    PRIVILEGE       VALUE    FLAG   ACTION                  RECIPIENT
project.max-shm-memory
        privileged      64.0GB    -     deny                         -
        system          16.0EB   max    deny                         -
```

4.4 System V Shared Memory

Shared memory affords an extremely efficient means of sharing data among multiple processes on a Solaris system since the data need not actually be moved from one process's address space to another. As the name implies, shared memory is exactly that: the sharing of the same physical memory (RAM) pages by multiple processes, such that each process has mappings to the same physical pages and can access the memory through pointer dereferencing in code. The use of shared memory in an application requires implementation of just a few interfaces bundled into the standard 3C language library, as listed in Table 4.3. Consult the manual pages for more detailed information. In the following sections, we examine what these interfaces do from a kernel implementation standpoint.

Table 4.3 Shared Memory APIs

System Call	Arguments Passed	Returns	Description
shmget(2)	key, size, flags	Identifier	Creates a shared segment if one with a matching key does not exist, or locates an existing segment based on the key.
shmat(2)	Identifier, address, flags	Pointer	Attaches shared segment to processes address space.
shmdt(2)	Address	0 or 1	Detaches a shared segment from a process's address space.
shmctl(2)	Identifier, command, status structure	0 or 1 (success or failure)	Control call—gets/sets permissions, gets stats, destroys identifier, etc.

The shared memory kernel module is not loaded automatically by Solaris at boot time; none of the System V IPC facilities are. The kernel will dynamically load a required module when a call that requires the module is made. Thus, if the shmsys and ipc modules are not loaded, then the first time an application makes a shared memory system call (for example, shmget(2)), the kernel loads the module and executes the system call. The module remains loaded until it is explicitly unloaded by the modunload(1M) command or until the system reboots.

The kernel maintains certain resources for the implementation of shared memory. Specifically, a shared memory identifier, shmid, is initialized and maintained by the operating system whenever a shmget(2) system call is executed successfully. The shmid identifies a shared segment that has two components: the actual shared RAM pages and a data structure that maintains information about the shared segment, the shmid_ds data structure, detailed in Table 4.4.

Table 4.4 shmid_ds Data Structure

Name	Data Type	Corresponding ipcs(1M) Column	Description
shm_perm	struct	*See ipc perm table.*	Embedded ipc_perm structure. Generic structure for IPC facilities that maintains permission information
shm_segsz	unsigned int	SEGSZ	Size in bytes of the shared segment
shm_amp	pointer	none	Pointer to corresponding anon map structure (see Section 9.6)
shm_lkcnt	unsigned short	none	Lock count; number of locks on the shared segment
shm_lpid	long	LPID	Last PID; PID of last process to do a shared memory operation on the segment
shm_cpid	long	CPID	Creator PID; PID of the process that created the shared segment
shm_nattch	unsigned long	NATTCH	Number of attaches to the shared segment
shm_cnattch	unsigned long	none	Number of ISM attaches to the shared segment
shm_atime	long	ATIME	Time of last attach
shm_dtime	long	DTIME	Time of last detach
shm_ctime	long	CTIME	Time of last change to shmid_ds structure

Since Solaris 10, only two tuneable parameters are associated with shared memory. They are described in Table 4.5.

Table 4.5 Shared Memory Resource Controls

Name	Default Value	Maximum Value	Description
`project.max-shm-memory`	1/4 physical	16EB	Maximum size in bytes of a shared memory segment
`project.max-shm-ids`	128	1<<24	Maximum number of `shmid_ds` structures, systemwide

They are defined quite simply.

- **max-shm-memory.** Total amount of shared memory allowed a project. When `shmget()` allocates a shared memory segment, the segment's size is allocated against this limit. If the space allocation doesn't succeed, `shmget()` fails and errno is set to `EINVAL` (currently returned when "The size argument is less than the system-imposed minimum or greater than the system-imposed maximum."). The size is deallocated once the last process has detached the segment and `shmctl(, IPC_RMID)` has been successfully executed on the segment.

- **max-shm-ids.** Maximum number of shared memory IDs allowed a project. When `shmget()` allocates a shared memory segment, one ID is allocated. If the ID allocation doesn't succeed, `shmget()` fails and errno is set to `ENOSPC` (previously returned when "The system-imposed limit on the maximum number of allowed shared memory identifiers systemwide would be exceeded"). Upon successful execution of `shmctl(, IPC_RMID)`, the ID is deallocated.

4.4.1 Shared Memory Kernel Implementation

In this section we look at the flow of kernel code that executes when the shared memory system calls are called.

Applications first call `shmget(2)` to get a shared memory identifier. The kernel uses a key value passed in the call to locate (or create) a shared segment.

```
[application code]
shmget(key, size, flags [PRIVATE or CREATE])

[kernel]
shmget()
        ipcget() /* get an identifier - shmid_ds */
        if (new shared segment)
                check size against min and max tunables
                get anon_map and anon array structures
                initialize anon structures
                initialize shmid_ds structure
        else /* existing segment */
                check size against existing segment size
        return shmid (or error) back to application
ipcget()
        if (key == IPC_PRIVATE)
                loop through shmid_ds structures, looking for a free one
                        if (found)
                                goto init
                        else
                                return ENOSPC /* tough cookies */
        else /* key is NOT IPC_PRIVATE */
                loop through shmid_ds structures, for each one
                if (structure is allocated)
                        if (the key matches)
                                if (CREATE or EXCLUSIVE flags set as passed args)
                                        return EEXIST error /* segment with matching key
exists */
                                if (permissions do NOT allow access)
                                        return EACCESS error
                        set status
                        set base address of shmid_ds
                        return 0 /* that's a good thing */

        set base address of shmid_ds /* if we reach this, we have an unallocated shmid_
ds structure */
        if (do not CREATE)
                return ENOENT error /*we're through them all, and didn't match keys */
        if (CREATE and no space)
                return ENOSPC error
        do init
        return 0 /* goodness */
```

shmget(), when entered, calls ipcget() to fetch the shmid_ds data structure.
Remember, all possible shmid_ds structures are allocated up-front when /kernel/
sys/shmsys loads, so we need to either find an existing one that matches the key
value or initialize an unallocated one if the flags indicate we should and a structure is available. The final init phase of ipcget() sets the mode bits, creator UID,
and creator GID. When ipcget() returns to shmget(), the anon page mappings
are initialized for a new segment or a simple size check is done. (The size argument
is the argument passed in the shmget(2) call, not the size of the existing segment.)

Once a shmget(2) call returns success to an application, the code has a valid
shared memory identifier. The program must call shmat(2) to create the mappings (attach) to the shared segment.

```
[application]
shmat(shmid, address, flags)

[kernel]
shmat()
        ipc_access() /* check permissions */
        /* ipc_access() will return EACCESS if permission tests fail */
        /* and cause shmat() to bail out */
        if (kernel has ISM disabled)
                clear SHM_SHARE_MMU flag
        if (ISM and SHM_SHARE_MMU flag)
                calculate number pages
                find a range of pages in the address space and set address
                if (user-supplied address)
                        check alignment and range
                map segment to address
                create shared mapping tables
        if (NOT ISM)
                if (no user-supplied address)
                        find a range of pages in the address space and set address
                else
                        check alignment and range
        return pointer to shared segment, or error
```

Much of the work done in `shmat()` requires calls into the lower-level address space support code and related memory management routines. The details on a process's address space mappings are covered in Chapter 9. Remember, attaching to a shared memory segment is essentially just another extension to a process's address space mappings.

At this point, applications have a pointer to the shared segment they use in their code to read or write data. The `shmdt(2)` interface allows a process to unmap the shared pages from its address space (detach itself). Unmapping does not cause the system to remove the shared segment, even if all attached processes have detached themselves. A shared segment must be explicitly removed by the `shmctl(2)` call with the `IPC_RMID` flag set or from the command line with the `ipcrm(1)` command. Obviously, permissions must allow for the removal of the shared segment.

We should point out that the kernel makes no attempt at coordinating concurrent access to shared segments. The software developer must coordinate this access by using shared memory to prevent multiple processes attached to the same shared pages from writing to the same locations at the same time. Coordination can be done in several ways, the most common of which is the use of another IPC facility, semaphores, or mutex locks.

The `shmctl(2)` interface can also be used to get information about the shared segment (returns a populated `shmid_ds` structure), to set permissions, and to lock the segment in memory (processes attempting to lock shared pages must have sufficient process privileges; see Chapter 5).

You can use the `ipcs(1)` command to look at active IPC facilities in the system. When shared segments are created, the system maintains permission flags similar to the permission bits used by the file system. They determine who can read and write the shared segment, as specified by the user ID (UID) and group ID (GID) of the process attempting the operation. You can see extended information on the shared segment by using the `-a` flag with the `ipcs(1)` command. The information is fairly intuitive and is documented in the `ipcs(1)` manual page. We also listed in Table 4.4 the members of the `shmid_ds` structures that are displayed by `ipcs(1)` output and the corresponding column name. The permissions (mode) and key data for the shared structure are maintained in the `ipc_perm` data structure, which is embedded in (a member of) the `shmid_ds` structure and described in Table 4.2.

4.4.2 Intimate Shared Memory (ISM)

Many applications, and especially databases, use shared memory to cache frequently used data (the buffer cache) and to facilitate interprocess communication. Solaris provides an optimized shared memory capability known as Intimate Shared Memory (ISM), and all major databases take advantage of it. ISM offers a number of benefits: The shared memory is automatically locked by the kernel when the segment is created. This not only ensures that the memory cannot be paged out but also allows the kernel to use a fast locking mechanism when doing I/O into or out of the shared memory segment, thereby saving significant CPU time. Kernel virtual-to-physical memory address translation structures are shared between processes that attach to the shared memory, saving kernel memory and CPU time. Large pages, supported by the UltraSPARC Memory Management Unit (MMU), are automatically allocated for ISM segments (as of Solaris 2.6). The Solaris page size is currently 8 Kbytes; large MMU pages can be up to 4 Mbytes in size, so large pages can reduce the number of memory pointers by a factor of 512. This reduction in complexity translates into noticeable performance improvements, especially on systems with large amounts of memory. Since the memory is locked, it is not necessary to provide swap space to back it, thereby saving disk space.

Intimate shared memory (ISM) is an optimization introduced first in Solaris 2.2. It allows for the sharing of the low-level kernel data and structures involved in the virtual-to-physical address translation for shared memory pages, as opposed to just sharing the actual physical memory pages. Typically, non-ISM systems maintain per-process mapping information for the shared memory pages. With many processes attaching to shared memory, this scheme creates a lot of redundant mapping information to the same physical pages that the kernel must maintain.

Figure 4.2 illustrates the difference between ISM and non-ISM shared segments.

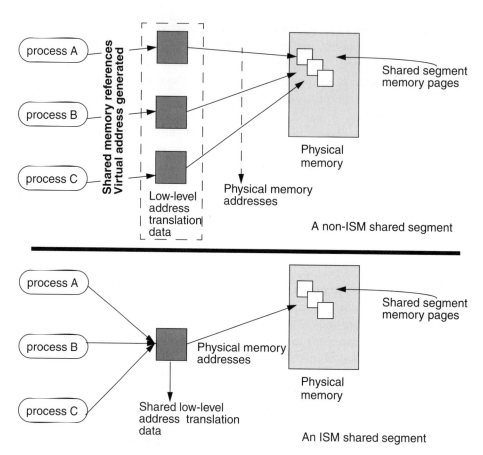

Figure 4.2 Comparison of ISM and Non-ISM Shared Segments

The actual mapping structures differ across processors. That is, the low-level address translation structures and functions are part of the hardware-specific kernel code, known as the Hardware Address Translation (HAT) layer. The HAT layer is coded for a specific processor's Memory Management Unit (MMU), which is an integral part of the processor design and responsible for translating virtual addresses generated by running processes to physical addresses generated by the system hardware to fetch the memory data.

In addition to the translation data sharing, ISM provides another useful feature: When ISM is used, the shared pages are locked down in memory and will never be paged out. This feature was added for the RDBMS vendors. As we said earlier, shared memory is used extensively by commercial RDBMS systems to cache data (among other things, such as stored procedures). Non-ISM implementations treat shared memory just like any other chunk of anonymous memory—it gets backing store allocated from the swap device, and the pages themselves are fair game to be paged out if memory contention becomes an issue. The effects of paging out shared memory pages that are part of a database cache would be disastrous from a performance standpoint—RAM shortages are never good for performance. Since a vast majority of customers that purchase Sun servers use them for database applications and since database applications make extensive use of shared memory, addressing this issue with ISM was an easy decision.

Solaris implements memory page locking by setting some bits in the memory page's page structure. Every page of memory has a corresponding page structure that contains information about the memory page. Page sizes vary across different hardware platforms. UltraSPARC-based systems implement an 8-Kbyte memory page size, which means that 8 Kbytes is the smallest unit of memory that can be allocated and mapped to a process's address space.

The page structure contains several fields, among which are two fields called p_cowcnt and p_lckcnt, that is, page copy-on-write count and page lock count. Copy-on-write tells the system that this page can be shared as long as it's being read, but once a write to the page is executed, the system should make a copy of the page and map it to the process that is doing the write. Lock count maintains a count of how many times page locking was done for this page. Since many processes can share mappings to the same physical page, the page can be locked from several sources. The system maintains a count to ensure that processes that complete and exit do not result in the unlocking of a page that has mappings from other processes. The system's pageout code, which runs if free memory gets low, checks the status to the page's p_cowcnt and p_lckcnt fields. If either of these fields is nonzero, the page is considered locked in memory and thus not marked as a candidate for freeing. Shared memory pages using the ISM facility do not use the copy-on-write lock (that would make for a nonshared page after a write). Pages locked through ISM implement the p_lckcnt page structure field.

ISM locks pages in memory so that they'll never be paged out; swap is not allocated for ISM pages. The net effect is that allocation of shared segments by ISM requires sufficient available unlocked RAM for the allocation to succeed. Using ISM requires setting a flag in the shmat(2) system call. Specifically, the SHM_ SHARE_MMU flag must be set in the shmflg argument passed in the shmat(2) call to instruct the system to set up the shared segment as intimate shared memory. Otherwise, the system will create the shared segment as a non-ISM shared segment.

In Solaris 9 onward, we can use the pmap utility to check whether allocations are using ISM shared memory. In the example below, we start a program called maps, which creates several mappings, including creating and attaching two 8-Mbyte shared segments, and we use a key value of 2 and 3. Looking at the address space listing, we can see that at the address of the shared segment, 0A000000, we have a shared memory segment created with ISM.

```
sol9$ pmap -x 15492
15492:  ./maps
 Address  Kbytes     RSS    Anon  Locked Mode   Mapped File
00010000       8       8       -       - r-x--  maps
00020000       8       8       8       - rwx--  maps
00022000   20344   16248   16248       - rwx--    [ heap ]
03000000    1024    1024       -       - rw-s-  dev:0,2 ino:4628487
04000000    1024    1024     512       - rw---  dev:0,2 ino:4628487
05000000    1024    1024     512       - rw--R  dev:0,2 ino:4628487
06000000    1024    1024    1024       - rw---    [ anon ]
07000000     512     512     512       - rw--R    [ anon ]
08000000    8192    8192       -    8192 rwxs-    [ dism shmid=0x5]
09000000    8192    4096       -       - rwxs-    [ dism shmid=0x4]
0A000000    8192    8192       -    8192 rwxsR    [ ism shmid=0x2 ]
0B000000    8192    8192       -    8192 rwxsR    [ ism shmid=0x3 ]
FF280000     680     672       -       - r-x--  libc.so.1
FF33A000      32      32      32       - rwx--  libc.so.1
FF390000       8       8       -       - r-x--  libc_psr.so.1
FF3A0000       8       8       -       - r-x--  libdl.so.1
FF3B0000       8       8       8       - rwx--    [ anon ]
FF3C0000     152     152       -       - r-x--  ld.so.1
FF3F6000       8       8       8       - rwx--  ld.so.1
FFBFA000      24      24      24       - rwx--    [ stack ]
-------- ------- ------- ------- -------
total Kb   50464   42264   18888   16384
```

See Section 12.2.5 for more detail on the SPARC implementation of ISM.

4.4.3 Dynamic ISM Shared Memory

Dynamic Intimate Shared Memory (DISM) was introduced in the 1/01 release of
Solaris 8 (Update 3) to supply applications with ISM shared memory that is
dynamically resizable. The first major application to support DISM was Oracle9*i*.
Oracle9*i* uses DISM for its newly introduced dynamic System Global Area (SGA)
capability.

With regular ISM, it is not possible to change the size of an ISM segment once it
has been created. To change the size of database buffer caches, databases must be
shut down and restarted (or designed to use a variable number of shared memory
segments—a more complicated alternative). This limitation has a negative impact
on system availability. For example, if memory is to be removed from a system
because of a dynamic reconfiguration event, one or more database instances may
first have to be shut down. DISM was designed to overcome this limitation. A large
DISM segment can be created when the database boots, and sections of it can be
selectively locked or unlocked as memory requirements change. Instead of the kernel automatically locking DISM memory, though, locking and unlocking is done by
the application (for example, Oracle), providing the flexibility to make adjustments dynamically.

DISM is like ISM except that it isn't automatically locked. The application, not
the kernel does the locking is done by using `mlock()`. Kernel virtual-to-physical

memory address translation structures are shared among processes that attach to the DISM segment, saving kernel memory and CPU time.

4.4.3.1 DISM Performance

Tests have shown that, as of this release, DISM and ISM performance are equivalent. This is an important development, since it means that the availability benefits of DISM can be realized without compromising performance in any way.

4.4.3.2 DISM Implementation

As with ISM, `shmget(2)` creates the segment. The `shmget()` size specified is the total size for the segment, that is, the maximum size. The size of the segment can be larger than physical memory. If the segment size is larger than physical memory, then enough of disk swap should be available to cover maximum possible DISM size.

The DISM segment is attached to a process through the `shmat(2)` interface. A new `shmat(2)` flag, `SHM_DYNAMIC`, tells `shmat(2)` to create Dynamic ISM. Physical memory is allocated on demand (ZFOD) page by access or by locking within DISM virtual area.

4.5 System V Semaphores

A semaphore, as defined in the dictionary, is a mechanical signaling device or a means of doing visual signaling. The analogy typically used is the railroad mechanism of signaling trains: mechanical arms would swing down to block a train from a section of track that another train was currently using; when the track was free, the arm would swing up and the waiting train could then proceed.

The notion of using semaphores as a means of synchronization in computer software was originated by a Dutch mathematician, E. W. Dijkstra, in 1965. Dijkstra's original work defined two semaphore operations, wait and signal (which correlate nicely with the railroad example). The operations were referred to as P and V operations. The P operation was the wait, which decremented the value of the semaphore if it was greater than zero, and the V operation was the signal, which incremented the semaphore value. The terms P and V originate from the Dutch terms for try and increase. P is from *Probeer,* which means *try* or *attempt*, and V is from *Verhoog*, which means *increase*. P(robeer) decreases the semaphore count and V(erhoog) increases the count. (Thanks to henk-jan_van_scherpenseel@stratus.com for sharing that bit of trivia with us.)

Semaphores provide a method of synchronizing access to a sharable resource by multiple processes. They can be used as a binary lock for exclusive access or as a counter; they manage access to a finite number of shared resources, where the semaphore value is initialized to the number of shared resources. Each time a process needs a resource, the semaphore value is decremented. When the process is done with the resource, the semaphore value is incremented. A zero semaphore value conveys to the calling process that no resources are currently available, and the calling process blocks until another process finishes using the resource and frees it.

The semaphore implementation in Solaris (System V semaphores) allows for semaphore sets, meaning that a unique semaphore identifier can contain multiple semaphores. Whether a semaphore identifier contains one semaphore or a set of semaphores is determined when the semget(2) system call creates the semaphore. The second argument to semget(2) determines the number of semaphores that will be associated with the semaphore identifier returned by semget(2). The semaphore system calls allow for some operations on the semaphore set, such that the programmer can make one semctl(2) or semop(2) system call and touch all the semaphores in the semaphore set. This approach makes dealing with semaphore sets programmatically a little easier.

4.5.1 Semaphore Kernel Resources

The tuneable kernel parameters that apply to semaphores are summarized in Table 4.6.

Table 4.6 Semaphore Kernel Tuneables

Name	Default Value	Maximum Value	Description
project.max-sem-ids	128	1<<24	Number of semaphore identifiers
process.max-sem-nsems	512	65536	Maximum number semaphores per identifier
process.max-sem-ops	512	2 billion	Maximum operations per semop(2) call

We next take a closer look at each one and discuss how kernel resources are allocated.

- **project.max-sem-ids.** Maximum number of semaphore IDs allowed a project. When semget() allocates a semaphore set, one ID is allocated. If the ID allocation doesn't succeed, semget() fails and errno is set to ENOSPC (previously returned when "The system-imposed limit on the maximum number of allowed semaphores or semaphore identifiers systemwide would be exceeded"). Upon successful `semctl(, IPC_RMID)`, the ID is deallocated.

- **process.max-sem-nsems.** Maximum number of semaphores allowed per semaphore set. When `semget()` allocates a semaphore set, the size of the set is compared with this limit. If the number of semaphores exceeds the limit, `semget()` fails and errno is set to `EINVAL` (previously returned when "The nsems argument is ... greater than the system-imposed limit").

- **process.max-sem-ops.** Maximum number of semaphore operations allowed per semop call. When `semget()` successfully allocates a semaphore set, the minimum enforced value of this limit is used to initialize the "system-imposed maximum" number of operations a `semop()` call for this set can perform.

4.5.2 Kernel Implementation of System V Semaphores

During initialization of the semaphore code, when `/kernel/sys/semsys` is first loaded, the value of `semmni` is checked to ensure that it is not greater than the maximum allowable value of 65536 (64 Kbytes). If it is, it gets set to 65536 and prints a console message stating that the value of `semmni` was too large. Following that, the tuneable parameters, with the exception of `semusz`, from the `/etc/system` file are plugged into the internal `seminfo` data structure.

4.5.3 Semaphore Operations

The creation of a semaphore set by an application requires a call to `semget(2)`. Every semaphore set in the system is described by a `semds_id` data structure, which contains the following elements.

```
/*
 * Structure Definitions.
 */

struct semid_ds {
        struct ipc_perm sem_perm;       /* operation permission struct */
        struct sem      *sem_base;      /* ptr to first semaphore in set */
        ushort_t        sem_nsems;      /* # of semaphores in set */
#if defined(_LP64)
        time_t          sem_otime;      /* last semop time */
        time_t          sem_ctime;      /* last change time */
#else   /* _LP64 */
        time_t          sem_otime;      /* last semop time */
        int32_t         sem_pad1;       /* reserved for time_t expansion */
        time_t          sem_ctime;      /* last change time */
        int32_t         sem_pad2;       /* time_t expansion */
#endif  /* _LP64 */
        int             sem_binary;     /* flag indicating semaphore type */
        long            sem_pad3[3];    /* reserve area */
};
                                                            See sys/sem.h
```

The system checks to see if a semaphore already exists by looking at the key value passed to semget(2) and checks permissions by using the IPC support routine, ipcperm_access(). Semaphore permissions differ slightly from permission modes we're used to seeing in things like Solaris files. They're defined as READ and ALTER, such that processes can either read the current semaphore value or alter it (increment/decrement). Permissions are established with arguments passed to the semget(2) call, following the owner, group, and other conventions used for Solaris file permissions.

Assuming a new semaphore, space is allocated from the resource map pool as needed for the number of semaphores in the set requested, and the elements in the semid_ds data structure are initialized, with the sem_base pointer being set to point to the first semaphore in the set.

Once the semaphore is created, typically the next step is initializing the semaphore values. Initialization is done with the semctl(2) call, using either SETVAL to set the value of each semaphore in the set one at a time (or if there is but one semaphore in the set) or SETALL to set the value of all the semaphores in the set in one operation. The actual kernel flow is relatively straightforward, with the expected permission and value checks against the maximum allowable values and the setting of the user-defined values if everything checks out.

Actual semaphore use by application code involves the semop(2) system call. semop(2) takes the semaphore ID (returned by semget(2)), a pointer to a sembuf structure, and the number of semaphore operations as call arguments. The sembuf structure contains the following elements.

```
/*
 * User semaphore template for semop system calls.
 */
struct sembuf {
        ushort_t        sem_num;        /* semaphore # */
        short           sem_op;         /* semaphore operation */
        short           sem_flg;        /* operation flags */
};
```
                                                              See sys/sem.h

The programmer must create and initialize the sembuf structure, setting the semaphore number (specifying which semaphore in the set), the operation (more on that in a minute), and the flag. The value of sem_op determines whether the semaphore operation will alter or read the value of a semaphore. A non-zero sem_op value either negatively or positively alters the semaphore value. A zero sem_op value simply reads the current semaphore value.

The semop(2) manual page contains a fairly detailed flow in the DESCRIPTION section on what the operation is for a given sem_op value and a given flag value.

4.6 System V Message Queues

Message queues provide a means for processes to send and receive messages of various sizes in an asynchronous fashion on a Solaris system. As with the other IPC facilities, the initial call when message queues are used is an `ipcget` call, in this case, `msgget(2)`. The `msgget(2)` system call takes a key value and some flags as arguments and returns an identifier for the message queue. Once the message queue has been established, it's simply a matter of sending and receiving messages. Applications use `msgsnd(2)` and `msgrcv(2)` for those purposes. The sender simply constructs the message, assigns a message type, and calls `msgsnd(2)`. The system places the message on the appropriate message queue until a `msgrcv(2)` is successfully executed. Sent messages are placed at the back of the queue, and messages are received from the front of the queue; thus, the queue is implemented as a FIFO (First In, First Out).

The message queue facility implements a message type field, which is defined by the user (programmer). So programmers have some flexibility, since the kernel has no embedded or predefined knowledge of different message types. Programmers typically use the `type` field for priority messaging or directing a message to a particular recipient.

Last, applications use the `msgctl(2)` system call to get or set permissions on the message queue and to remove the message queue from the system when the application is finished with it. For example, `msgct(2)` offers a clean way to implement an application shutdown procedure because the system will not remove an empty and unused message queue unless it is explicitly instructed to do so or the system is rebooted.

4.6.1 Kernel Resources for Message Queues

Like the IPC facilities previously discussed, the message queue facility comes in the form of a dynamically loadable kernel module, `/kernel/sys/msgsys`, and depends on the IPC support module, `/kernel/misc/ipc`, to be loaded in memory.

The number of resources that the kernel allocates for message queues is tuneable. Values for various message queue tuneable parameters can be increased from their default values so that more resources are made available for systems running applications that make heavy use of message queues. Table 4.7 summarizes the tuneable parameters and lists their default and maximum values.

- **`project.max-msg-ids`.** Maximum number of message queue IDs allowed a project. When `msgget()` is used to allocate a message queue, one ID is

Table 4.7 Message Queue Resource Limits

Name	Default	Max	Description
`project.max-msg-ids`	50	1<<24	Maximum number of message queue identifiers
`process.max-msg-qbytes`	4096	Unlimited	Maximum number of bytes on a message queue
`process.max-msg-messages`	40	2B	Maximum number of message headers

allocated. If the ID allocation doesn't succeed, `msgget()` fails and errno is set to `ENOSPC` (previously returned when "The system-imposed limit on the maximum number of allowed message queue identifiers systemwide would be exceeded"). Upon successful `msgctl(, IPC_RMID)`, the ID is deallocated.

- **process.max-msg-qbytes.** Maximum number of bytes of messages on a message queue. When `msgget()` successfully allocates a message queue, the minimum enforced value of this limit is used to initialize `msg_qbytes` (which was previously "set to the system limit").

    If an application attempts to put a new message on a message queue that will result in the total bytes being greater then `max-msg-qbytes`, then either the `msgsnd(2)` call returns an error or the process blocks, waiting for the message to be pulled off the queue, depending on whether the `IPC_WAIT` flag is `true`.

- **process.max-msg-messages.** Maximum number of messages on a message queue. When `msgget()` successfully allocates a message queue, the minimum enforced value of this limit is used to initialize a per-queue limit on the number of messages.

When the `/kernel/sys/msgsys` module is first loaded, an initialization routine executes. The routine does much the same sort of work that is done for shared memory and semaphore initialization.

The kernel data structure that describes each message queue is the `msqid_ds` structure.

```
struct msg;
struct msqid_ds {
        struct ipc_perm msg_perm;       /* operation permission struct */
        struct msg      *msg_first;     /* ptr to first message on q */
        struct msg      *msg_last;      /* ptr to last message on q */
        msglen_t        msg_cbytes;     /* current # bytes on q */
        msgqnum_t       msg_qnum;       /* # of messages on q */
        msglen_t        msg_qbytes;     /* max # of bytes on q */
        pid_t           msg_lspid;      /* pid of last msgsnd */
        pid_t           msg_lrpid;      /* pid of last msgrcv */
#if defined(_LP64)
        time_t          msg_stime;      /* last msgsnd time */
        time_t          msg_rtime;      /* last msgrcv time */
        time_t          msg_ctime;      /* last change time */
#else
        time_t          msg_stime;      /* last msgsnd time */
        int32_t         msg_pad1;       /* reserved for time_t expansion */
        time_t          msg_rtime;      /* last msgrcv time */
        int32_t         msg_pad2;       /* time_t expansion */
        time_t          msg_ctime;      /* last change time */
        int32_t         msg_pad3;       /* time_t expansion */
#endif
        short           msg_cv;
        short           msg_qnum_cv;
        long            msg_pad4[3];    /* reserve area */
};
                                                              See sys/msg.h
```

4.6.2 Kernel Implementation of Message Queues

Let's walk through the kernel flow involved in the creation of a message queue and the sending and receiving of messages, since these represent the vast majority of message queue activities.

1. The creation of a message on behalf of an application calling the msgget(2) system call starts with a call to the kernel ipc_get() routine. An ipc_perm structure is available for every message queue identifier.

2. Once a structure has been allocated, the system initializes the structure members as specified by the UID and GID of the calling process and the permission mode bits passed by the calling code, then sets the IPC_ALLOC bit to signify the ipc_perm structure has been allocated. (The ipc_get() code is covered in Section 4.1.)

   If ipc_get() returns successfully, the application code has a valid message queue identifier, can send and receive messages, and can run message control (msgctl(2)) operations.

A message send (msgsnd(2)) call requires the application to construct a message, setting a message type field and creating the body of the message (for example, a text message).

1. The code copies the message from the user address space to a designated area in the kernel.

2. Next, we do general housekeeping—such as incrementing the processor statistics to announce a message queue system call is being executed. The `cpu_sysinfo` structure maintains an `msg` counter that reflects the total number of message queue system calls executed.

3. The code verifies the calling process's access permissions.

4. The rest of the message send flow is best represented in pseudocode.

```
copy message data from user space to kernel space (map area)

lookup a message id via ipc_lookup()

if (message queue no longer exists)
        return EIDRM error

if (current bytes on queue + bytes in new msg > msgmax)
        if (IPC_NOWAIT is set)
                return EAGAIN
        else
                increment the message's msg_snd_cnt

        /* on wakeup, code will validate msqid and set EDIRM if it has been removed */

        /* sleep waiting for space */
        call cv_wait_sig()

        /*
         * Once the wakeup is issued, the necessary resources are available for
         * putting the message on the queue
         */
        increment msg_qnum
        msg_cbytes += new message size
        mds_lspid = PID of caller
        msg_stime = current time

        insert onto message queue (msg_list)

        if (messages are available)
                /* wakeup waiters */
                cv_broadcast()

return success to calling program
```

The `msgrcv` support code is a little less painful, since now we're looking for a message on the queue (as opposed to putting one on the queue). Kernel resources do not need to be allocated for a `msgrcv`. The general flow of the kernel code path for receiving messages involves checking permissions for operation in a loop through all the messages on the queue.

1. If the requested message type matches a message on the queue, the code copies the message type to the user-supplied location and copies the message data to the user-supplied location.

2. Next, the code updates the `msqid_ds` structure fields, subtracts the message size from `msg_cbytes`, sets the PID in `msg_lrpid`, sets time in `msg_rtime`, frees the message resources, frees the message header (`msg` structure), and frees the resource map entry.

   If the code looped through all messages and found no matching type, it returns a No Message error.

   When the sequence is completed, the application code has the message type and data in a buffer area supplied in the `msgrcv(2)` system call. The only remaining callable routine for applications to use is the `msgctl(2)` system call. The control functions are straightforward; they typically involve either retrieving or setting values in a message queue's `ipc_perm` structure.

3. When `msgctl(2)` is invoked with the `IPC_RMID` flag, meaning the caller wants to remove the message queue from the system, the kernel walks the linked list of messages on the queue, freeing up the kernel resources associated with each message.

4. The kernel sends a wakeup signal to processes (threads) sleeping on the message queue. The processes ultimately end up with an `EIDRM` error (ID removed).

5. The system simply marks the `msqid_ds` structure as being available, and returns.

4.7 POSIX IPC

The evolution of the POSIX standard and associated application programming interfaces (APIs) resulted in a set of industry-standard interfaces that provide the same types of facilities as the System V IPC set: shared memory, semaphores, and message queues. They are quite similar in form and function to their System V equivalents but very different in implementation.

The POSIX implementation of all three IPC facilities is built in userland libraries on top of existing IPC facilities. It uses the notion of POSIX IPC names, which essentially look like file names but need not be actual files in a file system. This POSIX name convention provides the necessary abstraction, a file descriptor, to use the Solaris file memory mapping interface, `mmap(2)`, on which all the POSIX IPC mechanisms are built. This is very different from the System V IPC functions, for which a key value was required to fetch the proper identifier of the desired IPC resource. In System V IPC, a common method used for generating key values was the `ftok(3C)` (file-to-key) function, whereby a key value was generated, based on the path name of a file. POSIX eliminates the use of the key, and processes acquire the desired resource by using a file name convention.

No kernel tuneable parameters are required (or available) for the POSIX IPC code. The per-process limits of the number of open files and memory address space are the only potentially limiting factors in POSIX IPC.

Table 4.8 lists the POSIX APIs for the three IPC facilities.

Table 4.8 POSIX IPC Interfaces

Semaphores	Message Queues	Shared Memory
sem_open	mq_open	shm_open
sem_close	mq_close	shm_unlink
sem_unlink	mq_unlink	
sem_init	mq_getattr	
sem_destroy	mq_setattr	
sem_wait	mq_send	
sem_trywait	mq_receive	
sem_post	mq_notify	
sem_getvalue	mq_getvalue	

All the POSIX IPC functions are either directly or indirectly based on memory mapped files. The message queue and semaphore functions make direct calls to mmap(2), creating a memory mapped file, based on the file descriptor returned from the xx_open(3R) call. Using POSIX shared memory requires the programmer to make the mmap(2) call explicitly from the application code.

The details of mmap(2) and memory mapped files are covered in subsequent chapters, but, briefly, the mmap(2) system call maps a file or some other named object into a process's address space, as shown in Figure 4.3. The address space mapping created by mmap(2) can be private or shared. It is the shared mapping capability that the POSIX IPC implementation relies on.

4.7.1 POSIX Shared Memory

The POSIX shared memory interfaces provide an API for support of the POSIX IPC name abstraction. The interfaces shm_open(3R) and shm_unlink(3R) do not allocate or map memory into a calling process's address space. The programmer using POSIX shared memory must create the address space mapping with an explicit call to mmap(2). Different processes that must access the same shared segment can execute shm_open(2) on the same object, for example, shm_open("seg1",...,), and then execute mmap(2) on the file descriptor returned

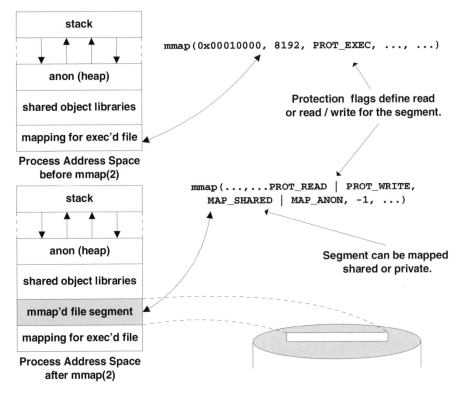

Figure 4.3 Process Address Space with `mmap(2)`

from `shm_open(3R)`. Any writes to the shared segment are directed to an underlying file and thus made visible to processes that run `mmap(2)` on the same file descriptor or, in this case, POSIX object name.

Under the covers, the `shm_open(3R)` call invokes `open()` to open the named object (file). `shm_unlink(3R)` also uses the `unlink(2)` system call to remove the directory entry. That is, the file (object) is removed.

4.7.2 POSIX Semaphores

The POSIX specification provides for two types of semaphores that can be used for the same purposes as System V semaphores but that are implemented differently. POSIX *named* semaphores follow the POSIX IPC name convention discussed earlier and are created with the `sem_open(3R)` call. POSIX also defines *unnamed* semaphores, which do not have a name in the file system space and are memory based. Additionally, a set of semaphore interfaces that are part of the Solaris threads library provides the same level of functionality as POSIX unnamed semaphores

Table 4.9 Solaris Semaphore APIs

Origin or Type	Interfaces	Library	Manual Section
System V	`semget()`, `semctl()`, `semop()`	`libc`	Section (2)
POSIX named	`sem_open()`, `sem_close()`, `sem_unlink()`, `sem_wait()`, `sem_try-wait()`, `sem_post()`, `sem_getvalue()`	`libposix4`	Section (3R)
POSIX unnamed	`sem_init()`, `sem_destroy()`, `sem_wait()`, `sem_try-wait()`, `sem_post()`, `sem_getvalue()`	`libposix4`	Section (3R)
Solaris threads	`sema_init()`, `sema_destroy()`, `sema_wait()`, `sema_try-wait()`, `sema_post()`	`libthread`	Section (3T)

but uses a different API. Table 4.9 lists the different semaphore interfaces that currently ship with Solaris.

Note the common functions for named and unnamed POSIX semaphores: The actual semaphore operations—sem_wait(3R), sem_trywait(3R), sem_post(3R) and sem_getvalue(3R)—are used for both types of semaphores. The creation and destruction interfaces are different. The Solaris implementation of the POSIX sem_init(3R), sem_destroy(3R), sem_wait(3R), sem_trywait(3R), and sem_post(3R) functions actually invokes the Solaris threads library functions of the same name through a jump-table mechanism in the Solaris POSIX library. The jump table is a data structure that contains function pointers to semaphore routines in the Solaris threads library, libthread.so.1.

The use of POSIX named semaphores begins with a call to sem_open(3R), which returns a pointer to an object defined in the /usr/include/semaphore.h header file, sem_t. The sem_t structure defines what a POSIX semaphore looks like, and subsequent semaphore operations reference the sem_t object. The fields in the sem_t structure include a count (sem_count), a semaphore type (sem_type), and magic number (sem_magic). sem_count reflects the actual semaphore value. sem_type defines the scope or visibility of the semaphore, either USYNC_THREAD, which means the semaphore is visible only to other threads in the same process, or USYNC_PROCESS, which means the semaphore is visible to other processes running on the same system. sem_magic is simply a value that uniquely identifies the synchronization object type as a semaphore rather than a condition variable, mutex lock, or reader/writer lock (see /usr/include/synch.h).

Semaphores within the same process are maintained by the POSIX library code on a linked list of semaddr structures. The structure fields and linkage are illustrated in Figure 4.4.

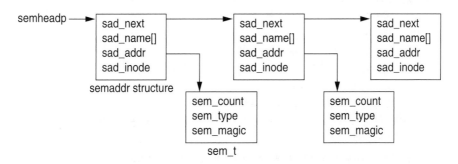

Figure 4.4 POSIX Named Semaphores

The linked list exists within the process's address space, not in the kernel. semheadp points to the first semaddr structure on the list, and sad_next provides the pointer for support of a singly linked list. The character array sad_name[] holds the object name (file name), sad_addr points to the actual semaphore, and sad_inode contains the inode number of the file that was passed in the sem_open(3R) call. Here is the sequence of events.

1. When entered, sem_open(3R) obtains a file lock on the passed file argument, using the pos4obj_lock() internal interface.

2. Once the lock is acquired, pos4obj_open() and underlying routines open the file and return a file descriptor.

3. If this is a new semaphore, the file is truncated with `ftruncate(3C)` to the size of a `sem_t` structure (it does not need to be any larger than that).

4. If it's not a new semaphore and the process is opening an existing semaphore, then the linked list is searched, beginning at `semheadp`, until the inode number of the file argument to `sem_open(3R)` matches the `sad_inode` field of one of the `semaddr` structures, which means the code found the desired semaphore.

5. Once the semaphore is found, the code returns `sad_addr`, a pointer to the semaphore, to the calling program.

The POSIX semaphore code uses the `/tmp` file system for the creation and storage of the files that the code memory maps according to the name argument passed in the `sem_open(3R)` call. For each semaphore, a lock file and a data file are created in `/tmp`, with the file name prefix of `.SEML` for the lock file, and `.SEMD` for the data file. The full file name is prefix plus the strings passed as an argument to `sem_open(3R)`, without the leading slash character. For example, if a `sem_open(3R)` call was issued with "`/sem1`" and the first argument, the resulting file names in `/tmp` would be `.SEMLsem1` and `.SEMDsem1`. This file name convention is used in the message queue code as well, as we'll see shortly.

If a new semaphore is being created, the following events occur.

1. Memory for a `semaddr` structure is `malloc`'d, the passed file descriptor is `mmap`'d, the semaphore (`sem_t`) fields and `semaddr` fields are initialized, and the file descriptor is closed.

    Part of the initialization process is done with the jump table and a call to `sema_init()`. (`sema_init()` is used for semaphore calls from the Solaris threads library, `libthread`, and also used for POSIX unnamed semaphores.) `sema_init()` is passed a pointer to a `sem_t` (either from the user code or when invoked from `sem_open(3R)`, as is the case here), an initial semaphore value, and a type.

2. The fields in `sem_t` are set according to the passed arguments, and the code returns. If a type is not specified, the type is set to `USYNC_PROCESS`.

The `sem_t` structure contains two additional fields not shown in the diagram. In `semaphore.h`, they are initialized as extra space in the structure (padding). The space stores a mutex lock and condition variable used by the library code to synchronize access to the semaphore and to manage blocking on a semaphore that's not available to a calling thread.

The remaining semaphore operations follow the expected, documented behavior for using semaphores in code.

3. `sema_close(3R)` frees the allocated space for the `semaddr` structure and unmaps the `mmap`'d file.

   Once closed, the semaphore is no longer accessible to the process, but it still exists in the system—similar to what happens in a file.

4. close. `sem_unlink(3R)` removes the semaphore from the system.

4.7.3 POSIX Message Queues

POSIX message queues are constructed on a linked list built by the internal `libposix4` library code. Several data structures are defined in the implementation, as shown in Figure 4.5. We opted not to show every member of the message queue structure, in the interests of space and readability.

The essential interfaces for using message queues are `mq_open(3R)` which opens, or creates and opens, a queue, making it available to the calling process, `mq_send(3R)` and `mq_receive(3R)` for sending and receiving messages. Other interfaces (see Table 4.8) manage queues and set attributes, but our discussion focusses on the message queue infrastructure, built on the open, send, and receive functions.

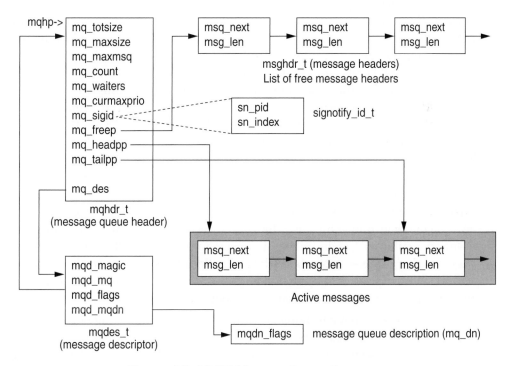

Figure 4.5 POSIX Message Queue Structures

A POSIX message queue is described by a message queue header, a data structure created and initialized when the message queue is first created. The message queue header contains information on the queue, such as the total size in bytes (mq_totsize), maximum size of each message (mq_maxsz), maximum number of messages allowed on the queue (mq_maxmsq), current number of messages (mq_current), current number of threads waiting to receive messages (mq_waiters), and the current maximum message priority (mq_curmaxprio).

Some attributes are tuneable with mq_setattr(3R). The library code sets default values of 128 for the maximum number of messages, 1024 for the maximum size of a single message, and 32 for maximum number of message priorities. If necessary, you can increase the message size and number of messages by using msg_setattr(3R), or you can increase them initially when the queue is created, by populating an attributes structure and passing it on the mq_open(3R) call.

The message pointers, mq_headpp and mq_tailpp, in the header do not point directly to the messages on the linked list. That is, they do not contain the address of the message headers. Since the shared mapping can result in the different processes referencing the message queue so that each has a different virtual address within their address space for the mapping, mq_headpp and mq_tailpp are implemented as offsets into the shared region.

A message descriptor maintains additional information about the queue, such as the file permission flags (read-only or read/write) and the magic number identifying the type of POSIX named object. A second structure (mq_dn) maintains per-process flags on the message, allowing different processes to specify either blocking or nonblocking behavior on the message queue files. This is analogous to regular file flags, for which a file descriptor for an open file is maintained at the process level, and different processes can have different flags set on the same file. (For example, one process could have the file opened for read/write and another process could have the same file opened read-only.)

With the big picture in place (Figure 4.5), let's look at what happens when a message queue is created and opened.

1. When mq_open() is entered, it creates the lock file and acquires a file lock. All the message queue files use the /tmp directory and follow a file name convention similar to that described in the semaphore section. That is, file names begin with a prefix—.MQD (data file), .MQL (lock file), .MQP (permission file), or .MQN (description file)—and end with the appended file name passed as an argument to mq_open(3R) minus the slash character.

2. If a new message queue is being created, the maximum message size and messages per-queue sizes are set, either with the default values or from a passed attributes structure in the mq_open(3R) call.

3. The permission file is opened, permissions are verified, and the file is closed.

4. The total amount of space needed for messages, based on the limits and structure size, is calculated, and the data file is created, opened, and set to the appropriate size with `ftruncate(3C)`.

5. If a new message queue is not being created, then an existing queue is being opened, in which case the permission test is done and the queue data file is tested to ensure the queue has been initialized.

The steps described next apply to a new or existing message queue; the latter case is a queue being opened by another process.

6. Space for a message queue descriptor is malloc'd (`mqdes_t`), and the data file is mmap'd into a shared address space, setting the `mqhp` pointer (Figure 4.5) as the return address from the `mmap(2)` call.

7. The message queue descriptor file is created, opened, mmap'd (also into a shared address space), and closed.

8. For new message queues, the `mq_init()` function (not part of the API) is called to complete the initialization process. Each message queue header has several semaphores (not shown in Figure 4.5) that used to synchronize access to the messages, the header structure, and other areas of the queue infrastructure.

   `mq_init()` initializes the semaphores with calls to `sem_init()`, which is part of the `libposix4.so` library.

9. The queue head (`mq_headpp`), tail (`mq_tailpp`), and free (`mq_freep`) pointers are set on the message header structure, and `mq_init()` returns to `mq_open()`, completing the open process.

Once a queue is established, processes insert and remove messages by using `mq_send(3R)` and `mq_receive(3R)`.

10. `mq_send(3R)` does some up-front tests on the file type (`mqd_magic`) and tests the `mq_notfull` semaphore for space on the queue.

11. If the process's queue flag is set for nonblocking mode, `sem_trywait()` is called and returns to the process if the semaphore is not available, meaning there's no space on the queue.

12. Otherwise, `sem_wait()` is called, causing the process to block until space is available.

13. Once space is available, `sem_wait()` is called to acquire the `mq_exclusive` mutex, which protects the queue during message insertions and removals.

POSIX message queues offer an interesting feature that is not available with System V message queues: automatic notification to a process or thread when a message has been added to a queue. An `mq_notify(3R)` interface can be issued by a process that needs to be notified of the arrival of a signal. To continue with the sequence for the next code segment:

14. `mq_send()` checks to determine if a notification has been set up by testing the `mq_sigid` structure's `sn_pid` field. If it is non-NULL, the process has requested notification, and a notification signal is sent if no other processes are already blocked, waiting for a message.

15. Finally, the library's internal `mq_putmsg()` function is called to locate the next free message block of the free list (`mq_freep`) and to place the message on the queue.

For receiving messages

1. `mq_receive()` issues a `sem_trywait()` call on the `mq_notempty` semaphore.

2. If the queue is empty and the descriptor has been set to nonblock, `sem_trywait()` returns with an EAGAIN error to the caller.

3. Otherwise, the `mq_rblocked` semaphore is incremented (`sem_post`), and `sem_wait()` is called.

4. Once a message shows up on the queue, the `mq_exclusive` semaphore is acquired, and the internal `mq_getmsg()` function is called.

5. The next message is pulled off the head of the queue, and the pointers are appropriately adjusted.

Our description omits some subtle details, mostly around the priority mechanism available for POSIX message queues. A message priority can be specified in the `mq_send(3R)` and `mq_receive(3R)` calls. Messages with better priorities (larger numeric values) are inserted into the queue before messages of lower priority, so higher-priority messages are kept at the front of the queue and are removed first.

4.8 Solaris Doors

Doors provide a facility for processes to issue procedure calls to functions in other processes running on the same system. Using the APIs, a process can become a door server, exporting a function through a door it creates with the `door_create(3X)` interface. Other processes can then invoke the procedure by issuing `door_call(3X)`, specifying the correct door descriptor. Our goal here is not to provide a programmer's guide to doors but rather to focus on the kernel implementation, data structures, and algorithms. Some discussion of the APIs is, of course, necessary to keep things in context, but we suggest that you refer to the manual pages and to Steven's book [35] to understand how to develop applications with doors.

The door APIs were first available in Solaris 2.6. The Solaris kernel ships with a shared object library, `libdoor.so`, that must be linked to applications using the doors APIs. Table 4.10 describes the door APIs available in Solaris. During the course of our coverage of doors, we refer to the interfaces as necessary for clarity.

Table 4.10 Solaris Doors Interfaces

Interface	Description
`door_create(3X)`	Creates a door. Called from a door server to associate a procedure within the program with a door descriptor. The door descriptor, returned by `door_create(3X)`, is used by client programs that need to invoke the procedure.
`door_revoke(3X)`	Revokes client access to the door. Can only be called by the server.
`door_call(3X)`	Invokes a function exported as a door. Called from a client process.
`door_return(3X)`	Returns from a door function. Typically used as the last function call in a routine exported as a door.
`door_info(3X)`	Fetches information about a door.
`door_server_create(3X)`	Specifies a door thread create function.
`door_cred(3X)`	Fetches client credential information.
`door_bind(3X)`	Associates the calling thread with a door thread pool.
`door_unbind(3X)`	Removes current thread from door pool.

4.8.1 Doors Overview

Figure 4.6 illustrates broadly how doors provide an interprocess communication mechanism. The file abstraction used by doors is the means by which client kernel threads retrieve the proper door handle required to issue a `door_call(3X)`. It is similar to the methodology employed when POSIX IPC facilities are used; a path name in the file system namespace is opened, and the returned file descriptor is

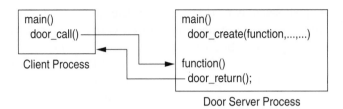

Figure 4.6 Solaris Doors

passed as an argument in the door_call(3X) to call into the desired door. An argument structure, door_arg_t, is declared by the client code and used for passing arguments to the door server function being called. The address of the door_arg_t structure is passed as the second argument by the client in door_call(3X).

On the server side, a function defined in the process can be made available to external client processes by creation of a door (door_create(3X)). The server must also bind the door to a file in the file system namespace. This is done with fattach(3C), which binds a STREAMS-based or door file descriptor to a file system path name. Once the binding has been established, a client can issue an open to the path name and use the returned file descriptor in door_call(3X).

4.8.2 Doors Implementation

Doors are implemented in the kernel as a pseudo file system, doorfs, which is loaded from the /kernel/sys directory during boot. Within a process, a door is referenced through its door descriptor, which is similar in form and function to a file descriptor, and, in fact, the allocation of a door descriptor in a process uses an available file descriptor slot.

The major data structures required for doors support are illustrated in Figure 4.7.

The two main structures are door_node, linked to the process structure with the p_door_list pointer, and door_data, linked to the door_node with the door_data pointer. A process can be a door server for multiple functions (multiple doors). Each call to door_create(3X) creates another door_node, which links to an existing door_node (if one already exists) through the door_list. door_data is created as part of the setup of a server thread during the create process, which we're about to walk through. door_data includes a door_arg structure that manages the argument list passed in door_call(3X), and a link to a door descriptor (door_desc) that passes door descriptors when a door function is called.

To continue: A call to door_create(3X) enters the libdoor.so library door_create() entry point (as is the case with any library call). The kernel door_create() is invoked from the library and performs the following actions.

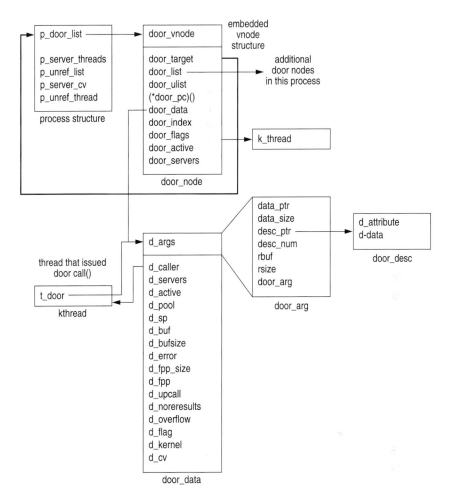

Figure 4.7 Solaris Doors Structures

1. Allocates kernel memory for door_node and initializes several fields of door_node and the door vnode (part of the door_node structure).

2. Links the door_target field to the process structure of the calling kernel thread.

3. Sets door_pc, a function pointer, to the address of the function being served by the door (the code that will execute when a client calls door_call(3X)).

4. Sets door_flags as directed by the attributes passed by the caller.

5. Initializes the vnode mutex lock (v_lock) and condition variable (v_cv). Initializes several other fields in the vnode to specify the vnode type (VDOOR)

and references to the vnode operations and virtual file system (VFS) switch table entries of the doorfs file system.

6.   Adds the door_node to the process's door list (p_door_list) and allocates a file descriptor for the door descriptor by means of the kernel falloc() function, which allocates a file structure and user file descriptor.

7.   The kernel door_create() now completed, the code returns to the libdoor.so door_create() code.

8.   The library code makes sure that the calling process has been linked with the Solaris threads library, libthread.so and returns an error if the link has not been made.

   A door server requires linking with libthread.so because the door code uses the threads library interfaces to create and manage a pool of door server threads.

9.   The last thing the library-level door_create() code does is call thr_create(3T) to create a server thread for the door server, as an execution resource for calls into the function being exported by the door server.

10.   thr_create(3T) creates a detached, bound thread that executes the library door_create_func() routine, which disables cancellation of the current thread (pthread_setcancelstate(3T)) and enters the kernel door_return() code.

   door_return(3X) is part of the doors API and is typically called at the end of the function being exported by the door_create(3X) call.

11.   door_return(3X) returns processor control to the thread that issued door_call(3X) and causes the server thread to sleep, waiting for another invocation of the door function.

   When entered (remember, we're in the kernel now, not in the doors library), door_return() allocates a door_data structure for the calling thread and links it to the kernel thread's t_door pointer.

   This sequence is done if the current thread's t_door pointer is NULL, signifying a door_data structure has not yet been allocated.

   The next bit of code in door_return() applies to argument handling, return data, and other conditions that need to be dealt with when a kernel thread issues door_call(3X). We're still in the door create phase, so a bit later we'll revisit what happens in door_return() as a result of door_call(3X).

   Continuing with the door create in the door_return() kernel function:

12.   The kernel door_release_server() code is called to place the current thread on the list of threads available to execute on behalf of door calls into the server.

13. The kernel thread is linked to the process's `p_server_thread` link, and `cv_broadcast()` is done on the door condition variable, `door_cv`, causing any threads blocked in `door_call(3X)` to wake up.

    At this point, the door create is essentially completed.

14. A call into the shuttle code to place the kernel thread to sleep on a shuttle synchronization object is made (`shuttle_swtch()`); the thread is thus placed in a sleep state and enters the dispatcher through `swtch()`.

We now digress slightly to explain shuttle synchronization objects. Typically, execution control flow is managed by the kernel dispatcher (see Chapter 5), using condition variables and sleep queues. Other synchronization primitives, mutex locks, and reader/writer locks are managed by turnstiles, an implementation of sleep queues that provides a priority inheritance mechanism.

Shuttle objects are a relatively new (introduced in Solaris 2.5, when doors first shipped) synchronization object that essentially allows very fast transfer of control of a processor from one kernel thread to another without incurring the overhead of the dispatcher queue searching and normal kernel thread processing. In the case of a `door_call()`, control can be transferred directly from the caller (or client in this case), to a thread in the door server pool, which executes the door function on behalf of the caller. When the door function has completed, control is transferred directly back to the client (caller), all using the kernel shuttle interfaces to set thread state and to enter the dispatcher at the appropriate places. This direct transfer of processor control contributes significantly to the IPC performance attainable with doors. Shuttle objects are currently used only by the doors subsystem in Solaris.

Kernel threads sleeping on shuttle objects have a 0 value in their wait channel field (`t_wchan`) and a value of 1 in `t_wchan0`. The thread's `t_sobj_ops` (synchronization object operations table) pointer is set to the shuttle object's operations structure (`shuttle_sops`); the thread's state is, of course, `TS_SLEEP`, and the thread's `T_WAKEABLE` flag is set.

Getting back to door creation, we see the following.

15. A default of one server thread is created unless there are concurrent invocations, in which case a thread will be created for each door call. The API allows for programs creating their own separate, private pool of door threads that have different characteristics than the default thread properties.

16. The doors library creates a bound, detached thread with the default thread stack size and signal disposition by default.

This completes the creation of a door server. A server thread in the door pool is left sleeping on a shuttle object (the call to `shuttle_swtch()`), ready to execute the door function.

Application code that creates a door to a function (becomes a door server) typically creates a file in the file system to which the door descriptor can be attached, using the standard open(2) and fattach(3C) APIs, to make the door more easily accessible to other processes.

The fattach(3C) API has traditionally been used for STREAMS code, where it is desirable to associate a STREAM or STREAMS-based pipe with a file in the file system namespace, for precisely the same reason one would associate a door descriptor with a file name: that is, to make the descriptor easily accessible to other processes on the system so application software can take advantage of the IPC mechanism. The door code can build from the fact that the binding of an object to a file name, when that object does not meet the traditional definition of what a file is, has already been solved.

fattach(3C) is implemented with a pseudo file system called namefs, the name file system. namefs allows the mounting of file systems on nondirectory mount points, as opposed to the traditional mounting of a file system that requires the selected mount point to be a directory file. Currently, fattach(3C) is the only client application of namefs; it calls the mount(2) system call, passing namefs as the file system name character string and a pointer to a namefs file descriptor. The mount(2) system call enters the VFS switch table through the VFS_MOUNT macro and enters the namefs mount code, nm_mount().

With the door server in place, client processes are free to issue a door_call(3X) to invoke the exported server function.

1. The kernel door_call() code (nothing happens at the doors library level in door_call()) allocates a door_data structure from kernel memory and links it to the t_door pointer in the calling kernel thread.

2. If a pointer to an argument structure (door_arg) was passed in the door_call(3X), the arguments are copied from the passed structure in user space to the door_arg structure embedded in door_data.

3. If no arguments were passed, the door_arg fields are zeroed and the d_noresults flag in door_data is set to specify that no results can be returned.

    The door_call(3X) API defines that a NULL argument pointer means no results can be returned. A lookup is performed on the passed door descriptor and returns a pointer to the door_node. Typically, file descriptor lookups return a vnode pointer. In this case, the vnode pointer and the door_node pointer are one and the same because the vnode is embedded in the door_node, located at the top of the structure.

4. The kernel door_get_server() function retrieves a server kernel thread from the pool to execute the function.

5. The thread is removed from the list of available server threads (p_server_
threads) and changed from TS_SLEEP to TS_ONPROC state (this kernel
thread was sleeping on a shuttle object, not sitting on a sleep queue).

6. The arguments from the caller are copied to the server thread returned from
door_get_server(). The door_active counter in the door_node is incremented, the calling (client) thread's d_error field (in door_data) is set to
DOOR_WAIT, the door server thread's d_caller field (door_data structure
for the server thread) is set to the client (caller), and a pointer to the door_
node is set in the server thread's door_data d_active field.

   With the necessary data fields set up, control can now be transferred to the
server thread; this transfer is done with a call to shuttle_resume().

7. shuttle_resume() is passed a pointer to the server thread removed from
the door pool.

 Just to get back to the forest for a moment (in case you're lost among the trees),
we're into shuttle_resume() as a result of a kernel thread issuing door_
call(3X). The door_call() kernel code up to this point essentially allocated or
initialized the necessary data structures for the server thread to have the exported
function executed on behalf of the caller. The shuttle_resume() function is
entered from door_call(), so the kernel thread now executing in shuttle_
resume() is the door client. So, what needs to happen is really pretty simple (relatively speaking)—the server thread, which was passed to shuttle_resume() as
an argument, needs to get control of the processor, and the current thread executing the shuttle_resume() code needs to be put to sleep on a shuttle object, since
the current thread and the door client thread are one and the same.

8. shuttle_resume() sets up the current thread to sleep on a shuttle object in
the same manner described previously (t_wchan0 set to 1, state set to TS_
SLEEP, etc.); the server thread has its T_WAKEABLE flag, t_wchan0 field, and
t_sobj_ops field cleared.

9. The code tests for any interesting events that may require attention, such as
a hold condition on the thread, and checks for posted signals. If any signals
are posted, setrun() is called with the current (client) thread.

10. The dispatcher swtch_to() function is called and is passed the server
thread address. swtch_to() updates the per-processor context-switch
counter in the cpu_sysinfo structure (pswitch) and calls resume() to
have the server thread context-switched onto the processor. The general flow
is illustrated in Figure 4.8.

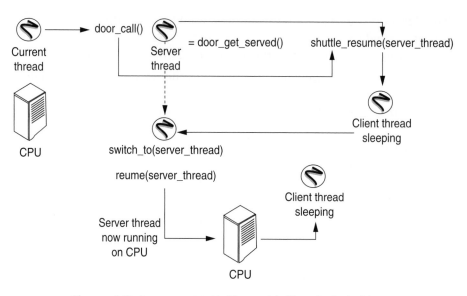

Figure 4.8 `door_call()` Flow with Shuttle Switching

11. The server thread executes the function associated with the `door_node`, as specified by the first argument passed when the server executed `door_create(3X)`.

12. The last call made by the server function is `door_return(3X)`, which returns results and control to the calling thread (client) and blocks in the server, waiting for another `door_call(3X)`.

13. The kernel `door_return()` code copies the return data back to the caller and places the server thread back in the door server pool. The calling (client) thread, which we left in a sleep state back in `door_call()`, is set back to an `T_ONPROC` state, and the shuttle code (`shuttle_resume()`) is called to give the processor back to the caller and have it resume execution.

Some final points to make regarding doors. There's a fair amount of code in the kernel `doorfs` module designed to deal with error conditions and the premature termination of the calling thread or server thread. In general, if the calling thread is awakened early, that is, before `door_call()` has completed, the code figures out why the wakeup occurred (signal, exit call, etc.) and sends a cancel signal (`SIGCANCEL`) to the server thread. If a server thread is interrupted because of a signal, exit, error condition, etc., the `door_call()` code bails out. In the client, an `EINTR` (interrupted system call) error is set, signifying that `door_call()` terminated prematurely.

4.9 MDB Reference

Table 4.11 MDB Reference for IPC

dcmd or walker	Description
dcmd id2msq	convert message queue ID to pointer
dcmd id2sem	convert semaphore ID to pointer
dcmd id2shm	convert shared memory ID to pointer
dcmd ipcid	perform an IPC id lookup
dcmd ipckey	perform an IPC key lookup
dcmd ipcperm	display an IPC perm structure
dcmd ipcs	display System V IPC information
dcmd kmsqid	display a struct kmsqid
dcmd ksemid	display a struct ksemid
dcmd kshmid	display a struct kshmid
dcmd msg	display contents of a message
walk ipcsvc	walk a System V IPC service
walk msgqueue	walk messages on a message queue
walk msq	walk the active msqid_ds structures
walk sem	walk the active semid_ds structures
walk shm	walk the active shmid_ds structures

5

Process Rights Management

This chapter is based on original material by Casper Dik.

This chapter describes the introduction of process privileges in Solaris. Process privileges serve one main purpose: restricting processes to the privileges required to perform the task at hand and no more.

5.1 Then and Now

The traditional UNIX privilege model associates all privileges with the effective uid 0. The basic flaw of that model is the all-or-nothing approach. An application that needs a single special privilege, such as a Web server binding to the reserved port 80, a program running in the real-time scheduling class, a server to keep the clock synchronized, the NFS server, all need to run or start as root.

This traditional approach has a number of shortcomings:

- It is not possible to restrict a process to a limited set of privileged operations.
- Each privileged process has complete reign over the system; all vulnerable privileged processes can be leveraged to full access to the system.
- It is not possible to extend an ordinary user's capabilities with a restricted set of privileges.
- It is often unclear exactly what privileged functionality a process requires access to.

Many operating systems, such as VMS, Trusted Solaris, and Windows NT, have addressed these shortcomings by introducing process privileges of some sort. Process privileges allow the implementation of what is known as the Principle of Least Privilege, that is, running applications with the least privilege required to perform a certain task. This is generally considered to be a better security model.

In Solaris, the various privileged operations inside the kernel are grouped under appropriate privileges. The process model is extended with privilege sets each containing zero or more privileges. Each process has one *Effective set,* which contains the privileges that are currently in effect; a *Permitted set,* which contains privileges that can be made effective; an *Inheritable set,* which is made effective at exec(2)*;* and a Limit set, which is an upper bound on all future effective sets for a process and its offspring. The project also strives to maintain maximum compatibility with uid 0.

System and library calls are introduced to examine and change the privilege sets; the existing user_attr(4), prof_attr(4), and exec_attr(4) and associated utilities are extended to support privileges for role-based access control (RBAC) profiles and users. Added utilities inspect and manipulate process privileges, assign privileges required to open devices, and define additional privileges.

The consumers of this facility fall into several categories; Solaris proper can use this facility to restrict the privileges of daemons now running under uid 0. This allows us to lessen the risk that comes with enabling such daemons.

Over the past years, new functionality, which was considered too risky to use for ordinary users, has been introduced in Solaris: settaskid(2), RT scheduling class, CLOCK HIRES timers. By associating a specific privilege with each of these, local administrators can allow ordinary users access to these facilities without having to resort to set-uid wrappers, which are notoriously difficult to get right.

5.2 Least Privilege in Solaris

In this section we discuss the privilege models found in Solaris, some background that was considered when moving Least Privilege to Solaris, and the model that exists in Solaris today. In Section 5.3 we give the complete formal definition of our model and the additional features. The details of the data structure changes in the kernel, new data structures, and interfaces presented to programs and users can be found in Section 5.5.

Throughout this chapter we use the following notation:

$\lor$ logical OR
$\land$ logical AND
$\in$ element of

∪	setwise union
∩	setwise intersection
⊂	is a subset of
⊆	is a subset or equal
∅	the empty set
B	the set of basic privileges
P	the set of all privileges
←	assignment

5.3 Process Privilege Models

The Least Privilege model in Solaris followed a simple set of guidelines:

- The new model should be completely transparent to legacy applications.

- Applications expecting the old and new model should be able to coexist in the same Solaris instance.

- It should be possible to restrict a process and its offspring to a certain set of privileges.

The Solaris Least Privilege implementation provides full backward compatibility while still allowing use of the new functionality in the system at all times. If the functionality were such that it could be turned off, Solaris itself would not be able to use it and we could not apply the principle of Least Privilege to Solaris system daemons. Acceptance by software vendors would also be impacted. The functionality would not be guaranteed to be configured on. Conversely, if traditional Solaris applications couldn't work in the new environment, we would need ugly knobs to turn the functionality off.

The third requirement follows naturally from the traditional UNIX capability of set-uid applications: applications that gain elevated privileges merely by being executed. By limiting the extent of privileges a process can gain even in the face of set-uid applications, we further our goal of improving overall system security. For example, one can imagine a system in which the privileges needed to configure network interfaces can only be obtained when logging in on the console. By extending privileges to cover actions that are not privileged at this time, we could disallow all outgoing network activity for sessions originating from the network, making it impossible to use a system as a stepping stone.

Compatibility, coexistence, and containment are the three guiding principles. In the remainder of this section, we continue with a high-level description of the current Solaris superuser model and the new Solaris privilege model, followed by an in-depth discussion of the Solaris privilege implementation.

5.3.1 The Traditional Solaris Superuser Model

The traditional Solaris Security model has seen only minor revisions since the first UNIX days.

Each process has a credential associated with it; the credential consists of an effective, saved, and real user and group IDs as well as a supplementary group list. With a few exceptions, a process is considered privileged if and only if the effective uid is 0. This test is generally performed in two kernel routines, the DDI-compliant interface `drv_priv(9f)` and the traditional UNIX kernel function `suser()`, although some code checks the credential against uid 0 directly.

The three uids fare usually exactly the same. When they differ, they allow a coarse-grained swapping between different privilege states.

In the context of our discussion, we define C, the process credential; C', the credential resulting from an operation; and X, the properties of an executable. The following are items of interest for our discussion:

- **$C.e$.** Effective uid of a process
- **$C.r$.** Real uid of a process
- **$C.s$.** Saved uid of a process
- **$X.u$.** uid of the user owning an executable

Both `suser()` and `drv_priv()` are essentially defined as $C.e = 0$.
There are several times at which uids can change:

- When a non-set-uid program is executed, the saved uid is made equal to the effective uid. Typically, this doesn't cause a change to the process credential.
$$C'.s \leftarrow C.e$$

- When a set-uid program is executed, the saved and effective uid are set to the uid of the program.
$$C'.s \leftarrow C'.e \leftarrow X.u$$

- When a process manipulates uids by using any of the `setuid(2)` family of system calls.
  - `setuid(u)` —Change $C.e, r, s$ if we're superuser, else change $C.e$.
  $$suser(C) \Rightarrow C'.s \leftarrow u, C'.e \leftarrow u, C'.r \leftarrow u$$
  $$C.r = u \vee C.s = u \Rightarrow C'.e \leftarrow u$$
  - `seteuid(u)` —Change $C'.e$.
  $$C.r = u \vee C.s = u \vee suser(C) \Rightarrow C'.e \leftarrow u$$

- setreuid(r, e)—Change *C.e*, *C.r*, update *C.s* if *C.r* changes and the new *C.e* is not equal to the new *C.r*.

$$e \neq \text{-}1 \wedge (C.s = e \vee suser(C)) \Rightarrow C'.e \leftarrow e$$
$$r \neq -1 \wedge (C.e = \rho \vee suser(C)) \Rightarrow C'.r \leftarrow r$$
$$r \neq -1 \wedge C'.e \neq C'.r \Rightarrow C'.s \leftarrow C'.e$$

In the Solaris kernel, the superuser policy is enforced with the following checks, in decreasing frequency of use:

- Direct comparison of `cr->cr_uid` (the effective uid)
- The traditional kernel function call `suser(cred_t *)`
- The DDI-compliant function call `drv_priv(cred_t *)`
- Direct comparison of `cr->cr_ruid` (the real uid, used in some resource limit situations)

Additionally, files and device nodes on the system are protected by file ownership and permissions bits, also known as discretionary access control (DAC).

5.3.2 Extending Solaris with Process Privileges

One of the major features of Solaris is continued backward binary compatibility, allowing applications to live on in binary form without change, hopefully forever.

Moving from the suser model to an exclusively fine-grained, privilege-based model would have broken quite a few application or deployment scenarios. Applications assuming they have powers with uid 0 and set-uid root binaries would suddenly break. The new Solaris model is one by which ordinary user IDs can have additional privileges and in which the user with uid 0 is no longer all-powerful. This means that we now check against the privilege sets rather than simply checking whether the uid is 0.

The implementation uses four privilege sets:

- **C.I.** The Inheritable set
- **C.P.** The Permitted set
- **C.E.** The Effective set
- **C.L.** The Limit set

The traditional components of C behave as in Solaris. The Effective set contains the privileges that are currently in effect; the Permitted set contains privileges that the process can put in the Effective set at will. The Inheritable set contains those privileges that are inherited across `exec(2)`. The Limit set (L) is the upper bound of privileges that a process and its offspring can inherit. The Limit set is enforced only at exec time, allowing a process to drop privileges on exec, while still using them until that time. L can be seen as carrying A with a process; all executables will appear to have L as the allowed set for that particular process.

A process can manipulate the privilege sets E, P, and I in a restricted fashion by using the setppriv(2) system call, such that the following conditions are always met:

$$C'.I \subseteq C.I \cup C.P$$
$$C'.P \subseteq C.P$$
$$C'.E \subseteq C'.P$$
$$C'.S \subseteq C'.P$$

A process can add privileges from P to I and E; a process can remove privileges from I, P, and E, noting that when privileges are removed from P they are automatically removed from E as well but they are not removed from I. When a program X is executed, the following transformations take place:

$$C'.I \leftarrow C.I \cap C.L$$
$$C'.P \leftarrow C'.I$$
$$C'.E \leftarrow C'.P$$
$$C'.L \leftarrow C.L$$

The uids follow the same rules as in Solaris before Least Privilege.

In the Solaris kernel, the kernel policy is enforced by checking whether the required privilege p is a member of the Effective set, C E:

$$p \in C.E$$

As we have chosen to implement security policy enforcement solely based on the effective privileges of a process, superuser compatibility would appear to be a daunting task.

5.3.3 How the Solaris 10 Least Privilege Model Was Chosen

A wide range of options was available when we were enhancing Solaris with Least Privilege capability. The following were the primary driving reasons for selecting the current model:

- **Simplicity.** Complexity is the enemy of security and usability; we want fewer privilege sets and few operations with unexpected or unintended side effects.
- **Compatibility.** We want full compatibility for existing software, including programs customers are known to replace, such as daemons like telnetd(1m) and sshd(1m) and programs like login(1) and sendmail(1m). Installing

an older version of Solaris user code on a privilege-aware kernel should work as it did before.

- **Least surprise.** Compatibility features should not get in the way of programs using Least Privilege. It should be possible to completely separate user ID and privilege manipulation.

- **Permitted set bounding.** The Permitted set should not gain privileges except when set-uid root.

- **Forward compatibility.**

5.3.3.1 Trusted Solaris

Trusted Solaris was not developed with compatibility as an absolute goal; it assigns no special meaning to uid 0, and it is therefore incompatible with the Solaris superuser model.

5.3.3.2 Root Set

The Root Set proposal added a systemwide set R. This set would be added into P and E when executing a set-uid program. If a program performed the system call `setuid(0)`, R could be added to I; once a process made all of its uids non-zero, R was subtracted from all privilege sets except L, or, in another variant, the other privilege sets were recovered from I. R suffers from several drawbacks: precarious privilege set manipulations were needed in order to retain privileges while getting rid of uid 0; adding R was easy enough, but removing R would be destructive; a single privilege awarded to a process could not survive any uid 0 transitions.

Privilege manipulations on transition from or to an effective uid of 0 were needed, but they made it impossible to run a process in a mode that only cared about privileges and not about uids.

Full compatibility wasn't achieved. While it might have gotten there, that would certainly have pushed the model's complexity to an unacceptable level. The Root Set model also included the future possibility of removing privileges from R to end up with an empty R in the far future.

Variants that used R as E when euid 0 were also discussed; such models disallow running a uid 0 process without privileges except with the help of L; that was considered too limiting for certain applications.

5.3.3.3 As Many Sets as It Takes

Extend the model with as many sets as necessary to achieve the desired result was also tried.

- $\mathbf{E_R}$. The effective set if $C.e = 0$
- $\boldsymbol{P_R}$. The permitted set if $C.e = 0 \vee C.s = 0 \vee C.r = 0$ (any of the process's uids is 0)

With E_R P_R P, this does give full compatibility, but E_R and P_R are visible to applications. When an application needs to have its privileges independent from uid manipulations, it must make sure that $E_R = E$ and $P_R = P$. More complicated is the behavior on exec, especially in the light of set-uid root applications: Should E_R and P_R be inherited, or are they reset to either L or a systemwide R on exec?

The main problem with this model is the fact that the application needs to be aware that uid manipulations affect E and P and that the application needs to manipulate both in order to achieve uid independence. Another is the counterintuitive behavior that a process can have fewer privileges when the effective uid is 0 than when it is non-zero. The different privilege sets might also need to be manipulated directly, which would require changes to applications if we were to adopt a privilege-only model in future. Or there would need to be a mode bit to indicate that the sets for uid 0 and non-0 are now connected.

5.3.3.4 Privilege Awareness

The final compatibility model is the Privilege Awareness model; the privilege state of the program is extended with a privilege-aware state (pas), which can take the values *PA* (privilege aware) and *NPA* (not privilege aware). We also introduce the notion of observed Effective and Permitted sets, E^O and P^O, respectively. These are the E and P as observed by the code that enforces the kernel security policy, the process itself, and other processes.

A process running in *NPA* mode behaves almost exactly like a traditional process. It may have privileges in E and P, and the kernel will honor those. But if the process set its effective uid to 0, the upper bound of that process's privileges, L, is used as the Effective set instead. Similarly, if any of the process's uids become 0, L is used as the observed P. An observer will see E follow the transition of the effective uid and will see P revert when all of the process's uids are no longer 0. In contrast, the implementation sets P^I and E^I remain unchanged during uid manipulations. The observer will not see E and P change when a process in *PA* mode changes its uids around.

Summarizing, the observer sees E and P behave as follows:

$$C.E^O = C.e \neq 0 \lor C.pas = PA \; ? \; C.E^I : C.L$$
$$C.P^O = (C.e \neq 0 \land C.s \neq 0 \land C.r \neq 0) \lor C.pas = PA \; ? \; C.P^I : C.L$$

Changing pas is mostly automatic and restricted; a process that manipulates E or P automatically becomes privilege aware because E^O and P^O must be decoupled from L; similarly, if L is changed, E^O and P^O must remain unchanged, which can only be achieved by a change to *PA*. A change to I only has effect after the subsequent exec(2) and does not affect pas until that time. A process can only become *NPA* if E, P can be adjusted in a manner that keeps E^O and P^O unchanged and when such a change cannot lead to the process leveraging uid 0 into full privileges.

While we admit that a state bit such as pas doesn't deserve any credit toward the software-engineering-of-the-month award, it has some benefits over the other proposals:

- It is immediately obvious that a process is fully backward compatible with the Solaris superuser model when it is *NPA*; that is, unless an application chooses to be incompatible, it will not notice the existence of privileges.

- It is immediately obvious that when a process is *PA*, no manipulation of uids will ever affect the privilege sets.

- There is no need to keep and administer alternative copies of *E* or other sets with all the possible resynchronization trouble that brings.

Some or most of the shortcomings of the other models could also be addressed with a pure privilege state bit. We believe, however, that this model offers best compatibility; the ability to switch to a pure privilege model on a per-process basis; easy extensibility with the ability to force all processes to be privilege aware, which allows, for example, for a Trusted Solaris implementation; and relatively easy understandability.

5.3.4 Other UNIX Implementations

A long time ago, a POSIX standard, 1003.1e, was in development. The standard was abandoned for various reasons. Some blame lack of interest by the industry at the time. Others blame the scope: POSIX 1003.1e tried to standardize mandatory access controls, access control lists, information labels, security auditing, and capabilities. It was abandoned in January 1998.

Even though the defunct draft standard uses the term *privileges* throughout the document, the term *capabilities* was substituted for most uses of privileges in the standard shortly before the standard floundered. The rationale given for this was that "It has been pointed out that the term privilege has been commonly used for a mechanism that achieves the above stated goals. However, the term privilege is also commonly used in the international community to mean something else entirely. It is felt that the confusion that would result from using the term privilege would not serve this standard well."

It's not well understood what this confusion is about. Moreover, the term capability is already well established in computer science and has a completely different meaning. The choice of terminology has made the documentation more confusing, because capabilities and privileges are used almost interchangeably but are not quite the same.

Various drafts of the POSIX standard are being used in various forms in both IRIX and Linux. The IRIX implementation appears to allow developers to hard-code fixed-size bit sets in executables. Both implementations make numerical capability values visible as manifest constants. Differences exist in the precise rules for process inheritance. Linux appears to have started with draft 17; IRIX capabilities have their roots in draft 16.

Each process and each executable file have associated capabilities; each capability has three flags associated with it, named Inheritable, Permitted, and Effective. We can think of this in terms of three sets of capabilities associated with each executable and process.

The `exec(2)` rules are defined as follows in Linux, with the restriction that $X.E$ is either $\varnothing$ or P:

$$C'.I \leftarrow C.I$$
$$C'.P \leftarrow X.P \cup C.P\,(X.I \cap C.I\,)$$
$$C'.E \leftarrow C'.P \cap X.E$$

and as follows in SGI IRIX:

$$C'.I \leftarrow C.I \; \cap \; X.I$$
$$C'.P \leftarrow X.P \cup (X.I \cap C.P\,)$$
$$C'.E \leftarrow C'.P \cap X.E$$

and different again in POS I X 1003.1e, draft 17:

$$C'.I \leftarrow C.I$$
$$C'.P \leftarrow (X.P \cap XX) \cup (X.I \cap C.I\,)$$
$$C'.E \leftarrow C'.P \cap X.E$$

where XX is an additional implementation-specific restriction. The last definition is much like our privilege sets: $C.I$ remains constant, $X.I$ is virtually identical to the Allowed set, and $X.P$ behaves like our Forced set. $X.E$ should contain all privileges for applications not aware of privileges and none for those applications that know how to turn privileges on. XX fits our Limit set.

IRIX 6.5 can be configured either to use capabilities exclusively or to also allow uid 0 to be honored. IRIX has support for capabilities in the file system, as long as you use XFS.

Linux 2.4.16 has various settings; the default assigns all capabilities to uid 0 and removes them on `set*uid(2)` calls that do away with the effective uid. The system supports a per-process flag that lets you keep privileges when getting rid of uid 0; Linux supports a global flag that causes uid juggling not to affect privileges at all.

But it was found that such solutions are problematic. It was, therefore, no surprise that the direction experimental Linux patches take is making sets and uids orthogonal, introducing a per-process flag that determines whether uid 0 is special or not. Unprivileged processes, however, cannot affect this state and it must be changed explicitly. A further set-uid 0 not allowed flag exists. Both flags are inherited.

Additionally, patches add basic privileges to Linux. In the first Linux model these patches need to be special-cased on all points where uid 0 causes capability sets to be changed.

Analogous to the Solaris per-process Limit set, Linux has a systemwide capability bound. Later patches have made the bound per-process, though strangely not part of the capability state proper. It is unclear to us why the flags and per-process capability bound are not part of the capability state.

The main reason Solaris did not go with an implementation based on the POSIX 1003.1e draft is that not only is it an unapproved standard, it is even withdrawn. What exists in implementation space is very much a moving target. Some of the features now found in Linux and in our proposal did not exist when we started our project. The standard took more than 10 years to develop and then failed. The terminology chosen is often confusing; all known implementations use some form of sets, but the standard tries hard not to speak of three capability sets. Using the same three sets for executables and processes doesn't do wonders for clarity either. The Linux capability FAQ[1] explains this as follows: "Now to make sense of the equations think of $X.P$ as the Forced set of the executable, and $X.I$ as the Allowed set of the executable."

The current Linux implementation is very much in flux; it has gone through several iterations trying to achieve sufficient uid 0 compatibility.

By choosing a completely separate namespace, PRIV over CAP, Solaris keeps open the option of implementing 1003.1e-compatible interfaces on top of the existing implementation in future, once those are sufficiently established.

Both the IRIX and Linux implementation address few of our forward binary compatibility constraints by externalizing numerical constants and binary representation in file systems.

IRIX appears to make the size of a capability set a first-class citizen for much of the code, whereas Linux appears to limit the visibility of the data structure to the kernel. Since binary device drivers are a necessity for Solaris, we cannot use numeric constants or bit test macros outside the core kernel.

Linux device access is arranged ad hoc inside the kernel. Support for capabilities in the file system is only available as an experimental patch at the time of this writing (2005).

---

1. `http://www.kernel.org/pub/linux/libs/security/linux-privs/kernel-2.4/` `capfaq-0.2.txt`

5.4 Privilege Awareness: The Details

In this section we present the precise semantics and describe the various features of our privilege model.

5.4.1 Per-Process State

We extend the per-process state from Section 5.3.2 with the privilege awareness property, pas, and the semantically void[2] privilege debugging flag, db, and get

- **C.I.** The Inheritable set
- **C.P.** The Permitted set
- **C.E.** The Effective set
- **C.L.** The Limit set
- **C.pas.** The privilege-awareness property
- **C.db.** The privilege debugging flag

The notion of observed Effective and Permitted set is used only in those cases in which we need to distinguish between the implementation sets E^I and P^I and the observed sets E^O and P^O. When talking about the semantics and the user-visible behavior, we use E and P for E^O and P^O. These are also the values returned by getppriv(2) and as shown by ppriv(1). For reference, these are the observation rules:

$$C.E^O \ = C.e \ \neq 0 \ \vee \ C.pas = PA \ ? C.E^I : C.L$$
$$C.P^O \ = (C.e \ \neq 0 \wedge \ C.s \ \neq 0 \ \wedge C.r \ \neq 0) \ \vee \ C.pas = PA \ ? \ C.P^I : C.L$$

The initial process init starts off with $E^I = P^I = I = I^O$ and $L = P$. I^O is the set of basic privileges and can be empty. This default process credential behaves exactly like the superuser model: When the effective uid is non-zero, the process has the default privileges; when the effective uid is 0, the process has all privileges.

5.4.2 Privilege Awareness State Transitions

In this section we describe the transitions between being privilege aware and not being privilege aware. This can only happen if the observed set invariance condi-

---

2. In Trusted Solaris, privilege debugging is a systemwide property that requires a reboot to switch on or off. It then allows applications in the Trusted Path to manipulate the privilege debugging flag for certain applications; those applications will then have all privilege checks succeed. This privilege debugging property is not semantically void.

tion is met. That is, when a process transitions between *PA* and *NPA*, no changes to E and P are observed.

5.4.2.1 Becoming Privilege Aware

There are no restrictions on becoming privilege aware. Assuming *pas* = *NPA*, the following changes to the credential take place when transitioning to *PA*:

$$C'.pas \leftarrow PA$$
$$C'.E^I \leftarrow C.e \neq 0 \ ? \ C.E^I : C.L$$
$$C'.P^I = C.e \neq 0 \wedge C.s \neq 0 \wedge C.r \neq 0 \ ? \ C.P^I : C.L$$

E^O and P^O are constant under this operation. This mechanism converts a uid 0 process that appears to follow the superuser model to a fully privileged process for which uid manipulations no longer have an effect on the privilege status.

5.4.2.2 Losing Privilege Awareness

There are several times when a process may want to lose the privilege awareness, for example, on `exec(2)`. Several restrictions apply since not all combinations of privilege sets can successfully and safely be converted to an equivalent *NPA* process. We derived the following rules from the observed set invariance property:

- If any of the uids is 0, P^I must be equal to L.
- If the effective uid is 0, E^I must be equal to L.
- If none of the uids is 0, there are no restrictions.

The last rule tells us that in a process without any 0 uids, `pas` can be changed at will.

When the conditions are met and a process transitions to *NPA*, *C.pas* is set to *NPA* and the implementation sets are conditionally changed as follows:

$$C.e = 0 \ \vee \ C.s = 0 \ \vee \ C.r = 0 \Rightarrow C'.P^I \leftarrow C.I \cap C.L$$
$$C.e = 0 \ \Rightarrow \ C'.E^I \leftarrow C.I \cap C.L$$

Again note that E^O and P^O are unchanged under these operations.

5.4.3 Privilege State Manipulation

The per-process state changes at various times, either as a result of explicit actions or as a side effect of other actions. In some cases the changes are merely observed and not reflected in the underlying data structures.

5.4.3.1 What Happens When User IDs Change?

In all circumstances, the actual implementation sets remain unchanged, but we can distinguish several cases. In privilege-aware processes, no changes are observed.

In processes not having any uids set to 0, no changes are observed, even if privileges are used to obtain uid 0.

In non-privilege-aware processes, E^O alternates between L and E^I depending on the value of the effective uid. P^O appears as L until the last uid is set to non-zero; it then reverts to P^I.

5.4.3.2 What Happens When a Process Is Created?

When a process is created by any of `fork(2)`, `vfork(2)`, or `fork1(2)`, the full privilege state is inherited by the child process.

5.4.3.3 What Happens When a Program Is Exec'd?

When any of members of the `exec(2)` family is called, the following rules apply:

$$C'.I \leftarrow C.I \cap C.L$$
$$C'.P \leftarrow (C'.I \cup X.F) \cap X.A$$
$$C'.E \leftarrow C'.P$$
$$C'.L \leftarrow C.L$$

We include $X.A$ and $X.F$ in these equations both for use in future implementations and to keep open the option of per-mount point allowed sets and some form of forced privilege emulation.

At one stage the prototype emulated a single forced privilege by using the setgid bit. A single privilege appears to be sufficient for many Solaris applications; for example, commands using `rcmd(3socket)`, such as `rsh(1)` and `rlogin(1)` as well as applications using raw sockets, such as `ping(1m)` and `traceroute(1m)`.

The `db` property is inherited across `exec(2)`; `pas` is adjusted according to the following rules:

- If a process is *NPA*, it becomes *PA* only in the presence of forced privileges, taking the following rule into consideration.

- If a process is *PA*, the privileges are examined before exec and a process becomes *NPA* if possible, according to the rules outlined in Chapter 3. If the process remains *PA*, a second attempt at reverting to *NPA* is attempted directly after the exec.

The changes to the implementation sets E^I and P^I are defined in such a way that the observed sets E^O and P^O remain the same. As a consequence of these rules, it is not always possible for *PA* processes to gain privileges by executing a set-uid root executable. It is possible to gain privileges in that way for *NPA* processes.

In addition to the current practice of marking a process NOCD | SUGID[3] if the real and effective IDs do not match, we add the marker if the permitted set of the process calling exec(2) is not a superset of the inheritable set. That is, when the child process runs with more privileges, it is awarded additional protection.

An implementation of Trusted Solaris might force most or all processes to *PA*.

5.4.3.4 Manipulating Privileges Directly

This project adds a system call family, setppriv(2), that allows a process to manipulate its privileges directly.

The function setppriv() takes three arguments: the operation to perform, which is one of PRIV_OFF, PRIV_ON, or PRIV_SET; the privilege set name; and a privilege set with privileges to switch off or on, or which can completely replace the current set.

The Effective set is most useful to perform privilege bracketing. In the superuser world, privilege bracketing looks like this:

```
/* program start */
uid = getuid();
seteuid(uid);

/* privilege bracketing */
seteuid(0);

/* code requiring super-user privileges */
....
seteuid(uid);

/* ordinary code */
....

/* Permanently giving up root */
setreuid(uid, uid);
```

---

3. We introduced the NOCD flag when we realized that the current credentials of a process do not properly reflect the capability status of a process. That is, if a process has opened a restricted file or device or has acquired some other capability and afterwards dropped its extra privileges, the process still has some capabilities or data that should be restricted. The name originates from NO Core Dump but was later extended to deny process inspection through /proc and to restrict the use of certain environment variables in libraries. The SUGID flag is set when a process results from the exec of a set-uid or set-gid executable.

With process privileges, the code (simplified) becomes

```
/* program start */
getppriv(PRIV_PERMITTED, pset);
setppriv(PRIV_SET, PRIV_EFFECTIVE, emptyset);

/* privilege bracketing */
setppriv(PRIV_SET, PRIV_EFFECTIVE, pset);
/* code requiring privileges */
....
setppriv(PRIV_SET, PRIV_EFFECTIVE, emptyset);

/* ordinary code */
....

/* Permanently giving up privileges */
setppriv(PRIV_SET, PRIV_PERMITTED, emptyset);
```

The added advantage is that this manipulation can be done at the level of single privileges. For this purpose, a single convenience function, `priv_set(3c)`, is provided. Removing privileges from E is not restricted; only privileges in P can be added to E. A process manipulating E needs to be PA; it will transition to PA following the rules in Section 5.4.2, if necessary. The permitted set can only be shrunk; a process should shrink its Permitted set if it does not have any future need for the privileges. Privileges removed from P are automatically removed from E, enforcing $E \subseteq P$. Processes manipulating P will automatically transition to PA.

The Inheritable set can be added to and removed from; privileges from P can be added freely to I. Privileges can be removed from I without restriction. Because changing I does not influence E^O or P^O, a process does not need to transition to PA when manipulating I but might transition to PA on subsequent `exec(2)`. I is allowed to be a superset of P, that is, removing privileges from P does not affect I.

The Limit set cannot be added to by any mechanism. Privileges can be removed from the Limit set, but not without peril. Applications running under uid 0 usually assume full privileges on the OS; this often leads to no error checking for privileged operations or, worse, different behavior of certain operations whether you are privileged or not. For example, setuid(non-0) will reset all uids to non-0 if the effective uid is 0 but will only change the effective uid if a process is not privileged but can swap uids because of the value of the saved uid.

It was discovered[4] that removing selected privileges from a further privileged process could render it insecure. To rectify the problem, we defined the set of unsafe privileges, the privileges without which it is too risky to allow privilege ele-

---

4. Linux capabilities introduce a similar feature: Unrestricted use triggered a problem in sendmail(1m) mailer. See http://www.sendmail.org/sendmail.8.10.1.LINUX-SECURITY.txt

vation. A process that does not have in L all privileges from the unsafe set, currently PRIV_PROC_SETID, PRIV_SYS_RESOURCE, and PRIV_PROC_AUDIT, will fail to execute set-uid 0 processes.

Changing the limit set would influence P^O and E^O, so a process needs to transition to *PA* when it changes L.

A process that manipulates its privileges is marked NOCD, which awards the process additional protection.

5.4.3.5 Manipulating pas Directly

Using getpflags(2) and setpflags(2) processes can query and change pas. The latter function enforces the rules outlined in Section 5.4.2.

5.4.3.6 Manipulating Privileges through proc(4)

The proc(4) interface is extended to allow inspecting and changing privileges through the /proc file system. The modifications through this interface are severely restricted:

- A process can only attach to a target process when all the uids and gids of the target process are equal to its effective uid and gid, respectively, and when the process does not have the NOCD flag set or when the process has the PRIV_PROC_OWNER privilege. The attaching process must also have all the privileges available in the target process in its E, and its Limit set must be a superset of the target's L. That is, $C_T P \subseteq C_A.E \ \land \ C_T I \subseteq C_A.E \ \land \ C_T L \subseteq C_A.L$. This prevents the attaching process from gaining privileges directly or after exec(2).

- $C_T L$ cannot be grown, only shrunk (following the rules in Section 5.4.3.4).

- Only privileges in E of the attaching process can be added to the other sets of the target process.

- A process that has its privileges manipulated directly becomes *PA* unless it can swap to *NPA* mode following the rules in Section 5.4.2.

In addition, if a process can modify the state of a process, it can always switch db on or off.

The above rules help enforce the fact that the special privilege PRIV_PROC_OWNER is not sufficient to gain control over a process when such control can lead to escalation of privileges.

In the special case in which any of the user IDs in the target process is zero, the full set of privileges is required. The privilege does give unrestricted read access.

5.4.4 Privilege Escalation Prevention

The privilege escalation is defined as the process whereby a subject can obtain one or more privileges by performing an action that does not require those privileges if that action is not specifically allowed by the security policy.

One of the often recognized problems with privilege implementation is that some privileges provide back doors to others. We can think of many cases where this can happen:

- A privilege to modify all processes privileges would allow a process to obtain all privileges by modifying its own privileges.

- A privilege sufficient to attach to all processes is equivalent to obtaining the superset of all privileges currently in permitted sets.

- A privilege sufficient to modify the system or administration files could allow a process to assign all privileges to a user.

- A privilege to write directly to `/dev/kmem` allows a process to change its own credentials, so this is equivalent to having all privileges.

- A privilege to write directly to `/dev/dsk/*` allows a process full access over all file contents, so this is equivalent to having all the file * privileges or even all privileges if the disks in question contain system configuration files or allow set-uid execution.

While L could make certain that such privileges aren't accorded to ordinary users, such restrictions on L may preclude perfectly valid, controlled uses of such privileges by privileged programs, so we feel that we should put extra hurdles whenever we find a place where certain privileges can be leveraged to more privileges. Where we can identify such cases of privilege escalation, we require a process to either possess as many privileges as it would be able to obtain with the specific action or, in the specific instance of a process P_S granting privileges to a process P_O, we require that those privileges do not exceed $P_S.E \cap P_O.L$.

5.4.5 The Trouble with uid 0

The superuser's user ID is used not only for privilege checks but also for discretionary access control on files and devices, because the superuser owns most files and devices on the system. Even without any of the `PRIV_FILE_DAC*` discretionary access overrides, a process with uid 0 still has near complete reign of the system. It therefore stands to reason that we run as few system processes with uid 0 as possible. Rather, we run the daemons that need privileges as user daemon with some privileges rather than as root with most privileges removed.

When we look at the privileges (for the complete set used in our implementation see `privileges(5)`), we find that many privileges are potentially too powerful—they make no distinction between objects owned by root and objects owned by ordinary users, and without such distinction, they can switch to just any uid or to root.

In that situation, MAC labeling would really help. In keeping with our Prevention of Privilege Escalation policy, we will require the full set of privileges if the effective uid of a process is not 0 when that process needs a privilege to modify an object owned by uid 0 or wants to control a process with any of its uids 0. If a process switches from any uid to 0 and none of its other uids is 0, it will also require all privileges.

Ordinary file, directory, and other permissions still apply to root-owned objects; it is not until a privilege is needed that the additional requirement comes into force. For all other intents and purposes, root-owned objects behave exactly the same as ordinary objects.

The more interesting applications of process privileges will be the use in processes not running with uid 0. Our implementation runs a few daemons with a very restricted set of privileges. We can run daemons under different uids, and we document which privileges we actually use at the same time. The daemons themselves have been changed to drop the excess privileges and run under a different uid.

```
# ppriv `pgrep rpcbind` `pgrep statd` `pgrep nfsd` `pgrep lockd`
170: /usr/sbin/rpcbind
flags = 0x2
        E: net_privaddr,proc_fork,sys_nfs
        I: none
        P: net_privaddr,proc_fork,sys_nfs
        L: all
328: /usr/lib/nfs/statd
flags = 0x2
        E: proc_fork
        I: none
        P: proc_fork
        L: all
335: /usr/lib/nfs/nfsd
flags = 0x2
        E: sys_nfs
        I: none
        P: sys_nfs
        L: all
330: /usr/lib/nfs/lockd
flags = 0x2
        E: sys_nfs
        I: none
        P: sys_nfs
```

5.4.6 Basic Privileges

In certain situations, you may think that the standard Solaris user has too many
privileges enabled by default. Or you might want to enable unrestricted chown(2)
for just a handful of users. Or make sure that a process never forks or execs, a feature that can be used to make any editor safe for use in a restricted menu environment. If you are using quotas, you may sometimes want to prevent users from
creating hard links to files they do not own. To facilitate such features, we have
implemented what we call basic privileges. Basic privileges are just like ordinary
privileges except that the default I contains all basic privileges.

Administrators can assign different privileges to users or withdraw the basic
privileges away from specific users. The initial set of privileges, I^0, is assigned the
full set of basic privileges, B. This initial set is inherited by all processes and also
determines the privileges associated with ordinary users authenticated to the kernel services using a form of RPC, such as NFS.

The system(4) variable rstchown determines whether the privilege file_
chown_self is present in I^0; the ability to change ownership of files owned by the
current effective uid is now per-process and can be awarded user by user.

The set of basic privileges is part of the information the kernel supplies about
its configuration; it is, therefore, easy to determine whether a process runs with
more than the basic set of privileges.

So that more standard functionality can migrate into the set of basic privileges,
the functions that convert privilege sets to strings expand the basic privileges into
the string "basic" by default. If one or more privileges from B are missing from a
set, the expansion will read "basic,!basic missing1,!basic missing2", thus preserving the privileges the set conveys over future expansions of B. Options change the
default behavior for those cases in which the literal privilege set is required or in
which the shortest output form is wanted.

To write a process or daemon that uses privileges that need to be ported forward, programmers must take care that the process or daemon requires B in addition to the other privileges they may need. Individual basic privileges that are
known not to be required can be removed from P. For example, if we were to make
open(..., O *WR*) a basic privilege, such a daemon would retain that privilege
simply by retaining the basic privilege set at startup. In the OS release with the
additional basic privilege, the process or daemon would automatically get that
additional privilege.

5.4.7 Privileges and the Runtime Environment

The Solaris runtime environment, consisting of the runtime linker and the runtime libraries, is user configurable to a considerable degree, mostly with environ-

ment variables. The runtime environment restricts the configurability for processes that are set-uid or set-gid.

Applications that completely assume different identities in subprocesses, for example, `su(1m)` and `sendmail(1m)`, clean the environment before executing subprocesses that cannot determine that they run under an assumed uid, for example, because the effective and real uid are now identical.

The runtime environment does not impose restrictions on privileged processes merely because they are privileged; rather, it does so only when it knows that the privileged processes derive from unprivileged processes, for example, through set-uid.

In Solaris, this mechanism remains largely unchanged; it remains the responsibility of applications to vet the environment if privileges are moved to I. The kernel will take care of those cases in which extra privileges are gained through set-uid or, in the future, forced privileges. In Solaris, this responsibility is handled by extending `issetugid(2)`. In the initial implementation, this solution is unnecessary, since the only way to gain privileges is through set-uid 0 executables and those are already caught by the current mechanism.

The interface between the runtime linker and kernel is slightly changed; the kernel has better knowledge about how the process transitioned and how it was started; a new aux vector, `AT_SUN_AUXFLAGS`, is passed to the runtime linker. Its value is a bit mask for which we define a single bit, `AF_SUN_SETUGID`, which, when set, indicates that the runtime linker can trust only secure directories.

5.4.8 Privileges and NFS

The network file system, NFS, authorizes operations on files according to network credentials. In the insecure, default mode of operation, the NFS client sends the identity of the caller directly with each request, without giving the server any way to verify the credentials of the process on the NFS client. Proper authorizations schemes have been developed, but all of them focus on the "user" for granularity of access control. But because proper authorization is not widespread, NFS servers typically map requests by the superuser to a guest or nobody credential. Allowing privileged operations over NFS is atypical.

There is one use of NFS for which this approach is not fine: the use for diskless clients, including the case of network installation. Diskless clients are slightly more complicated because root write access is also required.

In both of the above cases, the NFS file systems are exported with full root access. We achieve compatibility by still having our system and install processes run as root; this gives those systems full file system access for those insecure exports. In those cases in which daemons are converted to run as a uid other than root, the appropriate ownership or permission changes are made.

In the future we can think of client-verified (for example, digitally signed) additional credentials that hold the effective privileges of a process. However, we believe that allowing clients to wield privileges on NFS servers is generally ill-advised.

It is NFS that prevents us from replacing the kernel tunable `rstchown` with the privilege `PRIV_FILE_CHOWN_SELF`.

Several kernel RPC functions had their implementation changed: the NFS-specific privilege check was moved to the `nfssys` system call because it was out of place in the RPC layer.

The NFS system generates kernel credentials from network credentials in several locations; we changed the code that generates credentials and the functions to generate full credentials. This changes the signatures of certain kernel `rpc` functions. The function `authdes_getucred` is renamed as `kauthdes_getucred` because the former also exists in the `rpc` libraries. The signature of `sec_svc_getcred` just changes.

```
/* Old signatures */
int sec_svc_getcred(struct svc_req *req, uid_t *uid, gid_t *gid,
                    short *ngroups, gid_t *groups, caddr_t *principal, int *secmod)
int authdes_getucred(const struct authdes_cred *, uid_t *, gid_t *, short *,
                    gid_t *);

/* New signatures */
int sec_svc_getcred(struct svc_req *req, cred_t *cr, caddr_t *principal,
                    int *secmod);

int kauthdes_getucred(const struct authdes_cred *adc, cred_t *cr);
```

5.4.9 Privileges and Third-Party File Systems

There are no changes to the file system interfaces, so preexisting file systems will continue to work unless they reference the `cr_groups` field directly. But unmodified file systems will not honor privileges; they most likely will still require uid 0 for privileged operations until they are converted to using the Least Privilege file system policy routines.

5.5 Least Privilege Interfaces

In this section we describe the details of how the implementation of process privileges is layered in the kernel and the interfaces offered between various subsystems.

5.5.1 The Conspiracy of Bit Sets and Constants

The most convenient data structure for privileges and privilege sets are integers and bit sets.

A few words of memory are indexed by bit and a privilege number as an index. This is how the implementation in Trusted Solaris works as well as most implementations that are based on the defunct POS I X draft P1003.2c capabilities.

It was clear to the design team that bit sets with implementation visible sizes and manifest constants will soon be an impediment to future expansion and interoperability. Either memory is wasted by picking a likely upper bound for privilege sets sizes or, more likely, a number that is too small is picked.

For efficiency, the core kernel still operates with fixed-size bit sets and manifest constants. But the constants and set sizes are not visible to user applications or DDI-compliant kernel modules at compile time. The data structures exported by the kernel are all self-describing; they contain a header with a field that denotes the size of the header as well as the size of additional data following the header.

The kernel publishes all relevant information to user processes in that fashion. The following parameters of the system are not fixed in any of the kernel/userland or kernel/kernel interfaces:

- Number of privilege sets
- Size of the privilege sets
- Names of the privilege sets
- Number of privileges
- Name-to-number mapping of privileges

These parameters are then used to configure the library interfaces to the privilege system and should not be directly used by user programs.

Applications use privilege names and privilege set names as strings, and the library takes care of name/number mappings in most cases; in general, applications do not need to convert individual privileges to numbers.

The current implementation does fix all these values in the kernel, but they could be made fully dynamic. For example, if we choose to allow kernel modules to allocate preposterous numbers of privileges, we could introduce a kernel parameter that would grow privilege sets to a specific size at boot.

The privilege names are not localized; the conversion of privileges and privilege sets to and from strings is locale neutral.

The library routine `priv_gettext(3C)`, which maps privileges to a descriptive text, is localized. It obtains the textual description from `/etc/security/priv` names in the C locale and uses an algorithm similar to the one for `magic(4)` to find a localized version of the text messages.

Another important outcome of the early design reviews was that privilege sets as bits should not exist in a permanent form anywhere, except when accompanied by information sufficient for interpretation of the bits. We use this in one place, process core dumps.

5.5.2 Privilege Names and Constants

The privileges used in Solaris are described in `privileges(5)`. The privileges are part of the interface specification in several ways. They are available as manifest integer constants for use in the core kernel; they are available as manifest string constants as a public interface.

The names of privileges are looked up in tables maintained by the kernel; there is an obvious mapping between the manifest constants and the actual privilege names. The manifest constants are upper case and prefixed with `PRIV`. The strings themselves are lower case without the prefix. The name lookup routines are case insensitive; they also accept the "priv" prefix which is stripped before doing the actual lookup.

Some of the privileges are very specific; we believe they should be classified as stable. Some privileges are evolving because they are too generic (`PRIV_SYS_CONFIG`) or might be made obsolete (`PRIV_SYS_SUSER_COMPAT`). The privilege constants are all classified as stable.

Privileges are logically grouped according to the scope of the privilege.

- FILE privileges operate on file system objects. The subgroup `FILE_DAC` overrides discretionary access control on files.
- IPC privileges override IPC object access controls.
- NET privileges give access to specific network functionality.
- PROC privileges allow processes to modify restricted properties of the process itself and give access to features with a process scope, such as high resolution timers, locked memory, etc.
- The SYS family gives processes unrestricted access to various system properties.

5.5.3 Kernel Data Structures

The privilege sets are in one place: `cred_t`. That data structure currently carries the information about process privileges; it is also the data structure available at those locations where we need to test for privileges. In Solaris 10, accessor functions are provided to access and manipulate the `cred_t`; `<sys/cred.h>` is essentially reduced to this:

```
typedef struct cred cred_t;

int prochasprocperm(struct proc *, struct proc *, const cred_t *);
int supgroupmember(gid_t, const cred_t *);
uint_t crgetref(const cred_t *);
uid_t crgetuid(const cred_t *);
uid_t crgetruid(const cred_t *);
uid_t crgetsuid(const cred_t *);
gid_t crgetgid(const cred_t *);
gid_t crgetrgid(const cred_t *);
gid_t crgetsgid(const cred_t *);
const gid_t *crgetgroups(const cred_t *);
int crgetngroups(const cred_t *);
int crsetresuid(cred_t *, uid_t, uid_t, uid_t);
int crsetresgid(cred_t *, gid_t, gid_t, gid_t);
int crsetugid(cred_t *, uid_t, gid_t);
int crsetgroups(cred_t *, int, gid_t *);
```

For the most part, these are the obvious accessor functions; they should have a classification of Public, Evolving and should be made part of the Solaris specific DDI/DKI. The function `crgetref()`, an implementation artifact, and the `crset*()` functions are Consolidation Private.

The new function `prochasprocperm()` behaves like the original `hasprocperm()` but takes two processes as argument. This allows the function to check for identical processes, session IDs, and so on.

The function `supgroupmember()` behaves like `groupmember()` but checks only the supplemental groups and not the effective group ID. The existing interface did not allow `exec(2)` to correctly determine whether a process was set-gid.

By making `cred_t` an incomplete type, we guarantee that all code that declares objects of type `cred_t` and all code that dereferences `cred_t` breaks on the first recompile, requiring further investigation by the developer. Note that such uses were suspect already since `cred_t` is a dynamically sized structure. The intention is that this further investigation leads to the use of the proper interfaces as defined in `<sys/cred.h>`.

A second reason that `cred_t` is opaque is that we want the implementation to evolve. Inside the kernel, process privileges are carried around as bit sets for efficiency. Although we don't want to fix privilege numbers, the size of privilege sets, or even the number of privilege sets, we do want to carry them all directly in `cred_t`. We also like to enable other Solaris projects, to extend the credential with data types of their choosing, and to allow certain data structures that logically belong in `cred_t` to be moved there.

The full `cred_t` is defined in `<sys/cred_impl.h>`.

```
struct cred {
        uint_t          cr_ref;           /* reference count */
        uid_t           cr_uid;           /* effective user id */
        gid_t           cr_gid;           /* effective group id */
        uid_t           cr_ruid;          /* real user id */
        gid_t           cr_rgid;          /* real group id */
        uid_t           cr_suid;          /* "saved" user id (from exec) */
        gid_t           cr_sgid;          /* "saved" group id (from exec) */
        uint_t          cr_ngroups;       /* number of groups returned by */
                                          /* crgroups() */
        cred_priv_t     cr_priv;          /* privileges */
        projid_t        cr_projid;        /* project */
        struct zone     *cr_zone;         /* pointer to per-zone structure */
        gid_t           cr_groups[1];     /* cr_groups size not fixed */
                                          /* audit info is defined dynamically */
                                          /* and valid only when audit enabled */
        /* auditinfo_addr_t     cr_auinfo;     audit info */
};

extern int ngroups_max;
```

This new definition is not binary compatible because the `cr_groups` field was moved down.

The privilege sets are defined in `<sys/priv_impl.h>`.

```
typedef uint32_t priv_chunk_t;

/*
 * priv_set_t is a structure holding a set of privileges
 */

struct priv_set {
        priv_chunk_t pbits[PRIV_SETSIZE];
};

typedef struct cred_priv_s {
        priv_set_t      crprivs[PRIV_NSET];     /* Priv sets */
        uint_t          crpriv_flags;           /* Privilege flags */
} cred_priv_t;
```

The manifest constants `PRIV_SETSIZE` and `PRIV_NSET` are generated at kernel compile time and sized according to the number of actually defined privileges and sets. For all privileges, a manifest constant is generated as well; all privilege manifest constants are Consolidation Private. They are included in the generated header file `<sys/priv_const.h>`, which is shipped to allow kernel browsers to continue to compile.

Another existing kernel data structure, the STREAMS data block `dblk_t`, is changed; the `db_uid` field is replaced by a `db_credp` field, allowing us to base security policy decisions on the sender of the message, rather than on the credentials of the process opening the devices. This lets us return to BSD socket semantics and use the privileges at `bind(3socket)` time rather than the privileges at `socket(3socket)` time to determine whether a `bind()` command to a privileged port can succeed. This makes Solaris more compatible with other UNIX socket implementations.

By reclaiming an unused field, dropping `db_uid`, and slightly rearranging the nonpublic fields of `dblk_t`, we succeeded in shrinking `dblk_t` by 8 bytes. Macros were defined to access the field, and new functions were defined to allocate `mblk_t` with data blocks initialized either with a credential or from a template message block.

5.5.4 Kernel Interfaces

At the heart of the privilege code are the `priv_policy*` routines. These routines are passed a credential, a privilege to check, and possibly some additional information for debugging. The functions handle auditing, logging, and debugging, and also take care of the antiquated ASU flag for `acct(2)` accounting. On failure, the missing privilege is recorded in the `lwp` structure.

```
int priv_policy(const cred_t *, int, int, const char *);
boolean_t priv_policy_only(const cred_t *, int);
boolean_t priv_policy_choice(const cred_t *, int);
```

These functions are generally not called directly from kernel modules, because they require inlining privilege constants. Additional functions, `secpolicy_name`, are now used instead of direct calls. Most of the functions map directly onto a single privilege, but in an N-to-M and not a one-to-one mapping. The `secpolicy_vnode_setattr()` function moves all policy decisions typically found in VOP_SETATTR to a single function. The side effect of these changes is that all file systems using these new interfaces will make identical policy decisions. The functions are defined in `<sys/policy.h>`.

```
int secpolicy_acct(const cred_t *);
int secpolicy_allow_setid(const cred_t *, uid_t, boolean_t);
int secpolicy_audit_config(const cred_t *);
int secpolicy_audit_getattr(const cred_t *);
int secpolicy_audit_modify(const cred_t *);
int secpolicy_chroot(const cred_t *);
int secpolicy_clock_highres(const cred_t *);
int secpolicy_console(const cred_t *);
int secpolicy_coreadm(const cred_t *);
int secpolicy_dispadm(const cred_t *);
int secpolicy_excl_open(const cred_t *);
int secpolicy_fs_config(const cred_t *);
int secpolicy_fs_linkdir(const cred_t *);
int secpolicy_fs_minfree(const cred_t *);
```

continues

```
int secpolicy_fs_mount(const cred_t *, vnode_t *);
int secpolicy_fs_quota(const cred_t *);
int secpolicy_ipc_access(const cred_t *, const struct kipc_perm *, mode_t);
int secpolicy_ipc_config(const cred_t *);
int secpolicy_ipc_owner(const cred_t *, const struct kipc_perm *);
int secpolicy_lock_memory(const cred_t *);
int secpolicy_modctl(const cred_t *, int);
int secpolicy_net(const cred_t *, int, boolean_t);
int secpolicy_net_config(const cred_t *, boolean_t);
int secpolicy_net_privaddr(const cred_t *, in_port_t);
int secpolicy_net_rawaccess(const cred_t *);
int secpolicy_newproc(const cred_t *);
int secpolicy_nfs(const cred_t *);
int secpolicy_pcfs_modify_bootpartition(const cred_t *);
int secpolicy_ponline(const cred_t *);
int secpolicy_power_mgmt(const cred_t *);
int secpolicy_proc_access(const cred_t *);
int secpolicy_proc_excl_open(const cred_t *);
int secpolicy_proc_owner(const cred_t *, const cred_t *, int);
int secpolicy_pset(const cred_t *);
int secpolicy_rctlsys(const cred_t *);
int secpolicy_resource(const cred_t *);
int secpolicy_rpcmod_open(const cred_t *);
int secpolicy_rsm_access(const cred_t *, uid_t, mode_t);
int secpolicy_setpriority(const cred_t *);
int secpolicy_settime(const cred_t *);
int secpolicy_spec_open(const cred_t *, struct snode *, int, vtype_t);
int secpolicy_sti(const cred_t *cr);
int secpolicy_sys_config(const cred_t *, boolean_t);
int secpolicy_sys_devices(const cred_t *);
int secpolicy_tasksys(const cred_t *);
int secpolicy_vnode_access(const cred_t *, vnode_t *, uid_t, mode_t);
int secpolicy_vnode_create_gid(const cred_t *);
int secpolicy_vnode_owner(const cred_t *, uid_t);
int secpolicy_vnode_remove(const cred_t *);
int secpolicy_vnode_setdac(const cred_t *);
int secpolicy_vnode_setid_retain(const cred_t *, boolean_t);
int secpolicy_vnode_setids_setgids(const cred_t *, gid_t);
int secpolicy_vnode_stky_modify(const cred_t *cr);
int secpolicy_basic_exec(const cred_t *);
int secpolicy_basic_fork(const cred_t *);
int secpolicy_basic_proc(const cred_t *);
int secpolicy_basic_link(const cred_t *);
int secpolicy_vnode_setattr(const cred_t *, struct vnode *, struct vattr *,
const struct vattr *, int, int iaccess(/* void *, int, cred_t **/), void *);
```

The privilege checks in the kernel are all replaced with calls to the appropriate `secpolicy*()` functions, to which are passed sufficient arguments, always including the current process credential and often more information, such as a pointer to the object on which the operation is performed. Different security policy functions may map to a check for the presence of the same privilege.

Privilege numbers, privilege set numbers, and set sizes are Consolidation Private. Other components must call the kernel policy functions; if a driver needs to obtain the number of a specific privilege, the driver can look up its number by using `priv_getbyname(9f)`.

The function `priv_getbyname(9f)` also enables kernel modules to allocate new privileges by specifying `PRIV_ALLOC` as a flags argument. Privileges allocated with this function are limited in size to `PRIVNAME_MAX(32)` characters and can only contain alphanumeric characters and underscores. Privilege names are case insensitive but case preserving. The number of slots for allocating new privileges is limited both by the number of unaccounted bits in the bit sets and by the amount of memory reserved for the additional privilege names. While we advise an algorithm to pick unique names, nonunique privilege names will not cause fatal clashes of any kind; the "clashing" privilege allows a process to perform both restricted operations, adding just a little bit to the "Least" in Least Privilege.

At this time, the `secpolicy` functions are a private implementation detail, and the interface is unstable. The `priv_policy` functions are intended for public consumption.

5.5.5 System Call Interfaces

The privilege system defines a number of new system calls; `getprivinfo(2)` returns a self-describing data structure that contains the parameters of the privilege implementation on the currently running kernel. These parameters include the number of privilege sets, the names of the privilege sets, the size of each privilege set, the names of all privileges, and other systemwide information. The privilege set size is specified in units of `priv_chunk_t`, and the virtual privilege state definition looks like this:

```
priv_chunk_t privs[info.priv_nsets][info.priv_setsize]
```

Even though additional privileges can be allocated later, the data structure returned has a fixed size. That way, it can be kept at the same location by `libc`, thus obviating the need for locking out accesses to those parts of the structure that are fixed by the implementation, that is, all characteristics of the implementation except for the number of privileges and the names of the privileges added later.

The system include file `<sys/priv.h>` defines the main data structures used. The `priv_impl_info` objects can be extended by one or more objects with a priv info header that contains length and size. The basic type used throughout is `uint32_t`, which is a convenient type with the same size in each compilation environment. This approach relieves the implementation of most of the 32- and 64-bit conversion chores.

```
typedef struct priv_impl_info {
        uint32_t        priv_headersize;      /* sizeof (priv_impl_info) */
        uint32_t        priv_flags;           /* additional flags */
        uint32_t        priv_nsets;           /* number of priv sets */
        uint32_t        priv_setsize;         /* size in priv_chunk_t */
        uint32_t        priv_max;             /* highest actual valid priv */
        uint32_t        priv_infosize;        /* Per proc. additional info */
        uint32_t        priv_globalinfosize;  /* Per system info */
} priv_impl_info_t;

/*
 * Header of the privilege info data structure; multiple structures can
 * follow the privilege sets and priv_impl_info structures.
 */
typedef struct priv_info {
        uint32_t        priv_info_type;
        uint32_t        priv_info_size;
} priv_info_t;

typedef struct priv_info_uint {
        priv_info_t     info;
        uint_t          val;
} priv_info_uint_t;

/*
 * Global privilege set information item; the actual size of the array is
 * {priv_setsize}.
 */
typedef struct priv_info_set {
        priv_info_t     info;
        priv_chunk_t    set[1];
} priv_info_set_t;

/*
 * names[1] is a place holder which can contain multiple NUL terminated,
 * non-empty strings.
 */

typedef struct priv_info_names {
        priv_info_t     info;
        int             cnt;          /* number of strings */
        char            names[1];     /* "string1\0string2\0 ..stringN\0" */
} priv_info_names_t;

/*
 * Privilege information types.
 */
#define PRIV_INFO_SETNAMES          0x0001
#define PRIV_INFO_PRIVNAMES         0x0002
#define PRIV_INFO_BASICPRIVS        0x0003
#define PRIV_INFO_FLAGS             0x0004
```

The system calls setppriv(2) and getppriv(2) allow a process to change and inspect its privilege sets. The system calls setpflags(2) and getpflags(2) allow a process to change and inspect the process flags such as *pas* and *db*. The system call modctl() is extended with a number of subcodes to allow the device configuration command devfsadm(1m) to install the device policy and to allow the allocation of additional privileges. It, too, is subject to escalation of privilege prevention in that only processes with all privileges asserted can change the device policy.

5.5.6 Library Interfaces

In this section we describe two different sets of interfaces: one set of interfaces for manipulating privilege set and a second set of interfaces that abstracts the kernel credentials (cred_t) into an opaque user credential (ucred_t) with a functional interface.

5.5.6.1 Privilege Specific Library Interfaces

The library interfaces are primarily for manipulating privilege sets and converting from privilege names to numbers and back. Since the implementation protects the programmer from the details of the implementation in the currently running kernel, functions are available to allocate sufficient memory for privilege sets as well as for functions that take privileges and privilege sets and do computations.

The library loads the privilege implementation details the first time it is required. These details are kept around for future calls to the library. When library calls query any part of the structure that may have been changed, the library checks with the kernel and updates the internal information if necessary. An application will learn about privileges added after it first caused the implementation details to be loaded by the C library. A Consolidation Private secondary set of functions that accepts the implementation details as arguments is provided for use by libproc(4) and other programs inspecting core dumps.

The manifest constants, defined by including <priv.h> in user code, map to strings only.

The manifest constants are present for early detection of typos in privilege names. The constants are cast to (const char *) to allow compilers to merge identical strings and to prevent accidental string concatenation.

```
#define PRIV_IPC_DAC_READ ((const char *)"ipc_dac_read")
#define PRIV_IPC_DAC_WRITE ((const char *)"ipc_dac_write")
#define PRIV_IPC_OWNER ((const char *)"ipc_owner")
#define PRIV_SYS_IPC_CONFIG ((const char *)"sys_ipc_config")
```

The privilege sets are represented as opaque pointers; applications should only declare pointers to priv_set_t and should allocate, free, and manipulate them by using appropriate functions, keeping the actual structure hidden from view. Utility functions that parse strings representing privilege sets and convert privilege sets back to strings are provided both for pretty printing, ease of input, and permanent storage of privilege sets. The strings can contain those privileges currently defined in the kernel and can also contain special tokens such as all for P, basic for B, none for no privileges. A single dash "-" or exclamation mark "!" preceding a privilege negates its presence, allowing shorthand notation for all privileges except. . . . The implementation prefers "!" as the negation character on output but will use "-" if the exclamation mark is specified as separator. Both can be used on input; the exclamation mark looks nicer but needs to be escaped by certain shells; the dash can be more convenient in such cases.

The special token `all` represents the set of all bits set, not just those privileges defined in the system. Similarly, tests against the full set and the set comparison and manipulation functions always take all bits of the underlying implementation into account, even those that do not represent valid privileges.

A full set of functions to manipulate sets in user code is contained in `<priv.h>`, including a number of functions that allow easy manipulation of individual privileges.

```
int setppriv(priv_op_t, priv_ptype_t, const priv_set_t *);
int getppriv(priv_ptype_t, priv_set_t *);
int setpflags(uint_t, uint_t);
uint_t getpflags(uint_t);
const priv_impl_info_t *getprivimplinfo(void);

int priv_set(priv_op_t, priv_ptype_t, ...);
boolean_t priv_ineffect(const char *);
priv_set_t *priv_str_to_set(const char *, const char *, const char **);
char *priv_set_to_str(const priv_set_t *, char, int);

int priv_getbyname(const char *);
const char *priv_getbynum(int);
int priv_getsetbyname(const char *);
const char *priv_getsetbynum(int);
char *priv_gettext(const char *);

priv_set_t *priv_allocset(void);
void priv_freeset(priv_set_t *);

void priv_emptyset(priv_set_t *);
void priv_fillset(priv_set_t *);
boolean_t priv_isemptyset(const priv_set_t *);
boolean_t priv_isfullset(const priv_set_t *);
boolean_t priv_isequalset(const priv_set_t *, const priv_set_t *);
boolean_t priv_issubset(const priv_set_t *, const priv_set_t *);
void priv_intersect(const priv_set_t *, priv_set_t *);
void priv_union(const priv_set_t *, priv_set_t *);
void priv_inverse(priv_set_t *);
int priv_addset(priv_set_t *, const char *);
void priv_copyset(const priv_set_t *, priv_set_t *);
int priv_delset(priv_set_t *, const char *);
boolean_t priv_ismember(const priv_set_t *, const char *);
```

The mapping functions for name-to-number and back are included for completeness but they are not generally useful. The other interfaces discourage the use of privileges and sets as numbers; no function takes privileges or sets as numbers except the mapping functions. The actual size of privilege sets can only be determined with `getprivimplinfo(3c)`; writing privilege sets to files as bits requires getting the set and obtaining the system-specific set size. The interface to convert a privilege set to a string is more convenient. The shorthand privilege bracketing functions let you switch privileges on or off without having to manually do the set allocation and other tedious work with variable argument functions with NULL as terminator.

```
priv_set(PRIV_ON, PRIV_EFFECTIVE, PRIV_NET_PRIVADDR, NULL);

bind(... reserved port ...);

priv_set(PRIV_OFF, PRIV_EFFECTIVE, PRIV_NET_PRIVADDR, NULL);

/* Permanently giving up our privilege */
priv_set(PRIV_OFF, PRIV_PERMITTED, PRIV_NET_PRIVADDR, NULL);
```

5.5.6.2 User Credential Library Interfaces

Certain types of IPCs need the daemon handling the request of the client to establish the client's credentials. Several mechanisms have been tried. Mechanisms such as reserved ports whereby the client had to be a privileged process were discarded long ago. One newer mechanism used trusted kernel mechanisms, such as door_cred(3door), to forward an ad hoc subset of the kernel credential of the client process to the server process. Another method used private interfaces such as rpc_get_local_uid(), which was soon replaced with a more complete but still inextensible rpc_get_local_cred().

As with the extensions to the kernel credential, the userland representation of the kernel credential is made extensible. For obtain maximum flexibility, an opaque type ucred_t is defined, size unknown, and the only way to retrieve information from this opaque type is by using access functions as defined in <ucred.h>. The functions may return −1 or NULL if the underlying user credential is incomplete, since underlying interfaces may not provide a complete user credential. For completeness, a function ucred_get(3c) is available to retrieve the complete user credential from any process through /proc.

The old_door_cred(3door) interface is implemented on top of these new interfaces and mark it obsolete. The rpc functions are not extended; not only are they private, the rpc credentials include only user and group IDs across the board.

```
typedef struct ucred_s ucred_t;

ucred_t *ucred_get(pid_t pid);

void ucred_free(ucred_t *);

uid_t ucred_geteuid(const ucred_t *);
uid_t ucred_getruid(const ucred_t *);
```

continues

```
uid_t ucred_getsuid(const ucred_t *);
gid_t ucred_getegid(const ucred_t *);
gid_t ucred_getrgid(const ucred_t *);
gid_t ucred_getsgid(const ucred_t *);
int ucred_getgroups(const ucred_t *, const gid_t **);

const priv_set_t *ucred_getprivset(const ucred_t *, priv_ptype_t);
uint_t ucred_getpflags(const ucred_t *, uint_t);

pid_t ucred_getpid(const ucred_t *);
```

5.5.6.3 Private Daemon and Set-uid Interfaces

To get a higher return on the initial Least Privilege implementation, we added two private utility interfaces, `init_daemon_priv()` and `init_suid_priv()`. These interfaces allow daemons to specify which privileges they need on top of B. The library calls put those privileges in *P* and *E* and reset the effective uid for set-uid applications or set a specific daemon uid and clear the group list for a daemon. If requested, the library routine also clears *I* and *L* or sets *I* equal to *P*. The basic set is preserved insofar as present in the inheritable set so that code changes are not required for every basic privilege added. Utilities and daemons can revoke those basic privileges that existed at the time the code was written and aren't needed by the program.

In the following example, the set-uid program never needs to call `fork(2)` or `exec(2)`, so it rescinds those privileges. The added benefit is that when the program is exploited, the exploit code will need to run in the original executable because execing a shell is not possible. The function is a no-op when run by a process that otherwise possesses all privileges, for example, processes started by the superuser.

The special-purpose function `priv_bracket()` switches on and off the privileges requested by the initial call to `init_suid_priv()` by adding them to *E* or removing them from *E*, depending on the argument; `priv_relinquish()` gives up the requested privileges permanently by removing them from *P*.

By making judicious use of `priv_bracket()` in the `rcmd(3socket)` implementation, set-uid root programs that need to use those functions can be adapted with ease: Add one call to `init_suid_priv()` and remove all the application's uid juggling code.

```
/* Returns with the required privilege in P but not in E */
__init_suid_priv(PRIVUTIL_CLEARLIMIT, PRIV_NET_RAWACCESS, NULL);

/* Basic privileges not needed by this program */
priv_set(PRIV_OFF, PRIV_ALLSETS, PRIV_PROC_EXEC, PRIV_PROC_FORK, NULL);
....
/* Need privilege for raw socket, adds it to E */
__priv_bracket(PRIV_ON);
```

continues

```
s = socket(AF_INET, SOCK_RAW, IPPROTO_ICMP);

/* Don't need it for a while, remove it from E */
__priv_bracket(PRIV_OFF);

/* or don't need the privilege ever again, remove it from P and E */
__priv_relinquish();
```

Similarly, this daemon runs with as few privileges as required. A possible exploit also needs to run in the context of this process; it cannot escape and run a different executable.

```
/* NFS server: needs NFS privilege and access to the FX scheduler */

__init_daemon_priv(PRIVUTIL_CLEARLIMIT, DAEMON_UID, DAEMON_GID,
                   PRIV_SYS_NFS, PRIV_PROC_PRIOCNTL, NULL);

/* Basic privileges I do not need */
priv_set(PRIV_OFF, PRIV_ALLSETS, PRIV_PROC_EXEC, PRIV_PROC_FORK,
         PRIV_PROC_SESSION, NULL);
```

5.5.7 Using Privileges with Role-Based Access Control

The RBAC framework allows administrators to define profiles for users and roles as well as attributes for executables when running as part of a profile. We extend the exec_attr(4) database with a new attribute as part of our project. The attribute specifies I for the program to run with; some existing entries can make immediate use of this feature.

```
Object Access Management:solaris:cmd:::/usr/bin/chmod:privs=file_setdac
Object Access Management:solaris:cmd:::/usr/bin/chgrp:privs=file_chown
Object Access Management:solaris:cmd:::/usr/bin/setfacl:privs=file_setdac
Object Access Management:solaris:cmd:::/usr/bin/chown:privs=file_chown
```

In addition, we renamed the current Solaris default policy from suser, which reflects the old world, to solaris, which reflects the new world. The new world has only one model, the Solaris model, which can evolve and incorporate new security attributes over time. This change is derived from Trusted Solaris, with the difference that we allow only symbolic and not numeric privileges. Old suser entries are kept on upgrade in case the file is used as a source for a name service supporting multiple Solaris releases; new solaris entries are added for commands that run correctly with a few privileges supplied. When matching an entry, the code first looks for a solaris entry; if none is found, the code tries suser instead. This approach also supports sharing information between old and new systems.

The project team found that the current procedures for upgrading the RBAC files are defunct; it is not possible to remove entries or attributes on upgrade, and the output appears in random order in the file, making it difficult to edit. We improved this situation by sorting the output in all cases.

A new feature, specifically added for the benefit of those privileges with which you might trust some, but not all users, are privilege specifications in user_attr(4). The two keywords are limitpriv, L for the user's processes; and defaultpriv, the inheritable privileges the user logs in with by default. The default for defaultpriv is I^0, and the default for limitpriv is P. Special care must be taken to document limitpriv; overeager restrictions may cause certain programs such as dtsession(1) to fail to unlock a user's terminal.

Additionally, privileges can be assigned to profiles in prof_attr(4); users can exercise the privileges granted to their profiles by using pfexec(1).

```
Real Time:::User with real time privileges:\
        privs=proc_priocntl,sys_cpu_config,proc_clock_highres
```

These attributes can be manipulated with a single new option to the commands useradd(1m), usermod(1m), roleadd(1m), and rolemod(1m), as well as with the Solaris Management Console GUI tools and with the smuser(1m) and smrole(1m) commands.

We extend policy.conf(4) with two new keywords: PRIV_LIMIT and PRIV_DEFAULT. These specify the defaults for the two new user attr keywords (limitpriv and defaultpriv).

This example allows user casper to use high-resolution timers. But it disallows all sessions originating from his logins to use the PRIV_SYS_LINKDIR privilege; that is, he cannot make hard links to directories or unlink directories, even after executing su(1m) to root. The first example shows how linking and unlinking can be achieved with usermod(1m). The second example is the resulting user_attr(4) entry, with lines wrapped for ease of reading.

```
sol10# usermod -K defaultpriv=basic,proc_clock_highres \
          -K limitpriv=all,!sys_linkdir
```

```
casper casper::::type=normal;defaultpriv=basic,proc_clock_highres;\
        limitpriv=all,!sys_linkdir
```

It can be argued that some privileges should not be in the default Limit set. A prime candidate would be sys_linkdir: There is no reason to make hard links to directories.

It is noted in the manual page that `limitprivs` is a useful but dangerous piece of rope handed to the system administrator. As long as B is preserved, all processes running with an effective uid not equal to 0 will run properly; processes that need to run with euid 0 may experience difficulties. The system administrator may very well intend for this to happen, but in some cases the side effects can be unintended. Looking over the set-uid root applications shipped with Solaris, we find that most applications require either simple single privileges such as `PRIV_NET_ PRIVADDR` or require access to root-owned files for which the effective uid of 0 suffices still.

It becomes more important for set-uid root applications to do proper error checking; in those specific cases in which lack of error detection could result in either missing audit records or failure to give up privileges in the traditional way, we prevent the execution of set-uid 0 executables.

5.5.8 Using Privileges with Role-Based Access Control

The Solaris Service Management Facility has the capability to start applications with customized privilege sets. The following is an example from the manifest configuration file for the DNS server, `/var/svc/manifest/network/dns/server.xml`:

```
<exec_method
        type='method'
        name='start'
        exec='/usr/sbin/named'
        timeout_seconds='60' >
        <method_context>
        <!--
            privileges: file_dac_read, file_dac_search
            privileges are necessary for reading the
            configuration file even it is restricted by
            the file permission. sys_resource privilege
            is for setting the resource limits (eg. stack
            size)
        -->
        <method_credential
                user='root'
                group='root'
                privileges='basic,!proc_session,!proc_info,
                            !file_link_any,net_privaddr,
                            file_dac_read,file_dac_search,
                            sys_resource' />
        </method_context>
</exec_method>
```

This runs the DNS server with fewer privileges so that is hardened against some attacks. Although the DNS server runs as root, it is given the "basic" set rather than "all," and has some privileges removed and some added. `NET_PRIVADDR` is added so that the server can listen on a privileged port (53).

5.5.9 Using DTrace for Tracking Privileges

DTrace provides probes that allow us to trace privilege checks and privilege errors, which allow us to monitor privilege events in our own scriptable way.[5] The probes are

```
# dtrace -ln 'sdt:::priv*'
   ID    PROVIDER         MODULE                              FUNCTION NAME
 9206       sdt          genunix             priv_policy_only priv-ok
 9207       sdt          genunix           priv_policy_choice priv-ok
 9208       sdt          genunix                  priv_policy priv-ok
 9209       sdt          genunix             priv_policy_only priv-err
 9210       sdt          genunix           priv_policy_choice priv-err
 9211       sdt          genunix              priv_policy_err priv-err
```

5.5.10 Enhancements to `proc(4)` and Core Dumps

The process privileges and flags are made visible as a new entry in the /proc/<pid> directory, priv. A new utility, ppriv(1) examines and sets process privileges. The same information is made available in the ELF note section of core dumps. Additionally, core dumps contain the annotated information returned by getprivimplinfo(3c) in order to allow ppriv(1) and debuggers to interpret the privilege set information included in core dumps.

Two new ELF notes are introduced, NT_PRPRIV and NT_PRPRIVINFO, and gcore(1) and the kernel are enhanced to add these notes to core dumps. This allows ppriv and other utilities to show the appropriate number of properly sized sets and to correctly map the bits in the bit sets to privilege names. Private interfaces in libc allow libproc to leverage the libc privilege set conversion routines for core dumps. The data structure used for PCSPRI V is another example of a self-describing data structure; the header expresses some fixed quantities from which the header size can be derived and the size of the multiple instances of priv information that can follow it.

```
#define PCSPRIV 29L /* set process privileges from prpriv_t argument */
/*
 * Process privileges.  PCSPRIV and /proc/<pid>/priv
 */
typedef struct prpriv {
        uint32_t        pr_nsets;               /* number of privilege set */
        uint32_t        pr_setsize;             /* size of privilege set */
        uint32_t        pr_infosize;            /* size of supplementary data */
        priv_chunk_t    pr_sets[1];             /* array of sets */
} prpriv_t;
```

---

5. A tool is available to demonstrate tracing privilege events from dtrace, called privdebug. It is available from http://www.opensolaris.org/os/community/security/projects/privdebug

Since standards dictate that we cannot change error codes returned in errno, those codes remain the same. But the lwpstatus t structure defined in <sys/procfs.h>, which is used by truss(1) to report system call return values, can be extended. We added a pr_errpriv field in place of one of the filler fields. It is set to PRIV_NONE if there are no missing privileges, to the missing privilege if there is only one, to PRIV_ALL when all privileges are required, or to PRIV_MULTIPLE when more than one privilege is required.

5.5.11 Privilege Debugging

Process privileges radically change the way in which privileged operations work. While we plan on keeping just slap uid 0 working for the time being, it is important to be able to determine exactly which privileges are missing when we try to minimize the set of privileges for a new application. Privilege debugging can also be used to determine exactly what privileges specific Solaris utilities need for specific tasks. During the development of our prototype, we found that logging of failures alone was sufficient to compute the set of privileges needed for something as complex as a nightly build.

We have therefore introduced a per-process flag, PRIV_DEBUG, which causes kernel_printf() to log privilege failures. These messages then appear on the terminal associated with the process. PRIV_DEBUG can be set and unset with setpflags(2). We have also introduced a global kernel tunable, priv_debug, settable through system(4) or with mdb(1), which uses cmn_err(9f) to turn on privilege failure logging for all applications, thus capturing privilege debugging information in the system logs.

The ppriv(1) utility lets us set and unset the per-process flag and run processes with the flag set. We can use this feature both to determine exactly which privileges are required for certain actions or which privileges are actually used by certain set-uid applications by running them as plain executables.

```
sol10$ cat /etc/shadow
cat: cannot open /etc/shadow
sol10$ ppriv -e -D cat /etc/shadow
cat[12341]: missing privilege "file_dac_read" (euid = 21782), needed at
ufs_iaccess+0xfc
cat: cannot open /etc/shadow

sol10$ cp /usr/sbin/ping /tmp
sol10$ /tmp/ping localhost
/tmp/ping: socket Permission denied
sol10$ ppriv -e -D /tmp/ping localhost
ping[12373]: missing privilege "proc_setid" (euid = 21782), needed at
seteuid+0x76
ping[12373]: missing privilege "net_rawaccess" (euid = 21782), needed at
icmp_open+0xd
/tmp/ping: socket Permission denied
```

The `seteuid(2)` failure can directly be attributed to old-style privilege bracketing done by `ping(1m)`; the return value is obviously not checked. To make privilege failures more obvious for the uninitiated users of Solaris enhanced with privileges, we use our extended `/proc` interfaces and report the missing privilege after the error code in `truss` output.

```
sol10$ truss -t open cat /etc/shadow
open("/var/ld/ld.config", O_RDONLY) Err#2 ENOENT
open("/usr/lib/libc.so.1", O_RDONLY) = 3
open("/usr/lib/libdl.so.1", O_RDONLY) = 3
open("/usr/lib/locale/en_US/en_US.so.2", O_RDONLY) = 3
open64("/etc/shadow", O_RDONLY) Err#13 EACCES [file_dac_read]
cat: cannot open /etc/shadow

sol10$ truss -t so_socket /tmp/ping localhost
so_socket(PF_INET6, SOCK_DGRAM, IPPROTO_IP, "", SOV_XPG4_2) = 5
so_socket(PF_INET6, SOCK_RAW, IPPROTO_ICMPV6, "", SOV_XPG4_2)
Err#13 EACCES [net_rawaccess]
/tmp/ping: socket Permission denied
```

5.5.12 Privilege Auditing

The project introduces a system call that needs auditing, `setppriv(2)`; it also adds two new opcodes to `modctl()` that need auditing too. Three new audit events, `AUE_SETPPRIV`, `AUE_MODALLOCPRIV`, and `AUE_MODDEVPLCY` are generated for changing privilege sets, adding a privilege from outside the kernel, and changing the device policy, respectively.

Solaris keeps track of whether `suser()` was called and whether it was called successfully and recorded its information in the audit trail. Many "privilege checks," such as `drv_priv(9f)`, turned out to be direct comparisons of the effective uid to zero, which are not recorded in the audit trail.

The Least Privilege implementation takes a cue from Trusted Solaris and records the privileges the process used or failed to use in the audit trail. The privileges are recorded in their textual representation. The successful use of basic privileges is not audited. The attempt to use a basic privilege that is missing is audited because it can be considered an event that should not have taken place. The already defined audit modifier tokens `AUT_PRIV` and `AUT_UPRIV` are used for that purpose.

5.5.13 Device Protection

Several of the restricted system interfaces are currently protected with discretionary access control on the `/dev/*` entries. In a privilege scenario, this has several shortcomings: Privileges that override DAC might give full access to all of the system. File permissions still influence who can use raw sockets and such.

We define an additional level of access control, configured with devfsadm(1m) and in file /etc/security/device policy. This is loosely modeled after Trusted Solaris device policy(4).

With this new interface, we can bind privilege sets with the open for reading or writing of devices. For example, in the case of /dev/ip, we change the file permission to mode 0666 but we require the net_rawaccess privilege to open the device. The intention is that the device policy replaces the current hard-coded checks in the open routines of device drivers. Administrators thus have more flexibility in granting users permission to open devices than in the current situation in which file permissions are sometimes amended with hard-coded superuser checks in the device open routine. In the particular case of /dev/ip, this happens at the expense of users in group sys; they are no longer allowed to open the device, for example, to read MIB2 information.

We believe that our change is the correct change to make because those users can currently send raw IP packets circumventing the implied security policy, which presumes that only the superuser can send such packets. Applications that need MIB2 information typically open /dev/ip and push the arp, tcp, and udp STREAMs modules. The applications should open /dev/arp and push only tcp and udp instead. This requires no privileges.

Access to a number of devices is currently restricted to the superuser. Where such access could lead to escalation of privileges, we added access controls requiring those privileges that can be gained; typically, that would be all privileges for writing and discretionary access control for reading. For example, when opening any of the kernel memory devices for writing, the default device policy would require the process performing the open(2) to have all privileges.

The add_drv(1m), rem_drv(1m), and update_drv(1m) commands are enhanced to allow the addition and removal of device policy entries and driver-specific privileges, either for the device policy or for the driver proper, when a device driver is installed, removed, or updated.

The getdevpolicy(1m) command allows users and administrators to query the system device policy and the device policy in effect for specific devices.

When the system boots, access to all devices is restricted until devfsadm(1m) is run for the first time during the boot sequence and the default policy is relaxed. The initial policy is designed to be fail-safe. The upgrade routines relax the device permissions on a number of devices to allow for privilege-only access controls. With the initial policy made as strict as possible, a missing devpolicy file will not allow all users to send out unrestricted IP packets. Rather, it will prevent all users except the superuser from initiating connections.

This failure mode is similar to the situation that arose when we introduced soconfig(1m); the failure is obvious and needs to be corrected. This approach is vastly preferred over a failure mode in which users have the run of the system with nobody noticing that anything is amiss for some time.

PART THREE

Resource Management

Zones

Contributions by John Beck, David Comay, Ozgur Leonard, Daniel
Price, Andy Tucker, Andrew Gabriel, and Blaise Sanovillet of the
Solaris Resource Management Group

In this chapter, we introduce Solaris Zones (zones), a solution for server consolidation projects in the Solaris environment.

6.1 Introduction

Zones provides a means of virtualizing operating system services, allowing one or more processes to run in isolation from other activity on the system. This isolation prevents processes running within a given zone from monitoring or affecting processes running in other zones. A zone is a "sandbox" within which one or more applications can run without affecting or interacting with the rest of the system. It also provides an abstraction layer that separates applications from physical attributes of the machine on which they are deployed, such as physical device paths and network interface names.

Zones features include the following:

- **Security.** Network services can be run in a zone, limiting the damage possible in the event of a security violation. An intruder who successfully exploits a security hole in software running within a zone is limited to the restricted set of actions possible within that zone. For example, an application running within most zones cannot load customized kernel modules, modify kernel memory, or create device nodes. The set of privileges available within a zone are a subset of those available in the system as a whole.

- **Isolation.** Zones allow the deployment of multiple applications on the same machine, even where those applications operate in different trust domains, require exclusive access to a global resource, or present difficulties with global configurations. For example, multiple applications running in different zones (but on the same system) can bind to the same network port by using the distinct IP addresses associated with each zone. The applications are also prevented from monitoring or intercepting one another's network traffic, file system data, process activity, etc.

- **Virtualization.** Zones provide a virtualized environment that can hide such details as physical devices and the system's primary IP address and host name from the application. This can be useful to support rapid deployment (and redeployment) of applications, since the same application environment can be maintained on different physical machines. The virtualized environment can be rich enough to allow separate administration of each zone; one could "give out the root password" to a zone administrator, knowing that any actions taken by that administrator would not affect the rest of the system. Such a facility is of interest to service providers who are looking for more granular ways to subdivide systems among customers (both internal and external).

- **Granularity.** Unlike physical partitioning technologies (such as domains or LPARs), zones can provide isolation at almost arbitrary granularity. A zone does not require a dedicated CPU, physical device, or chunk of physical memory; those resources can either be multiplexed across a number of zones running within a single domain or system, or allocated per zone with the resource management features available in the operating system. The result is that even a small uniprocessor system can support a number of zones running simultaneously; the primary restriction (aside from the performance requirements of the applications running within each zone) is the disk space to hold the files that are unique within each zone.

- **Transparency.** One of the basic design principles of Zones is to avoid changing the environment in which applications are executing, except as necessary to achieve the goals of security and isolation. Zones does not present a new API or ABI to which applications must be "ported"; instead, it provides the standard Solaris interfaces and application environment, with some restrictions. The restrictions primarily affect applications attempting to perform privileged operations, as discussed in Section 6.4.

6.1.1 Zone Basics

Figure 6.1 shows a system with four zones. Zones blue, foo, and beck are each running a disjoint workload in a sample consolidated environment. They are enclosed within a global zone.

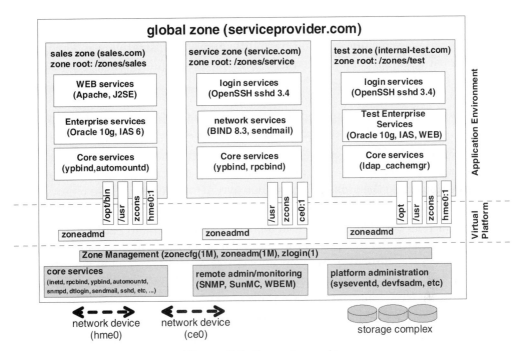

Figure 6.1 Zones Example

This example demonstrates that different versions of the same application can run without negative consequence in different zones, to match the consolidation requirements. Each zone can provide an almost arbitrarily rich and customized set of services.

Basic process isolation is also demonstrated. Each zone is given access to at least one logical network interface; applications running in distinct zones cannot observe the network traffic of the other, even though their respective streams of packets travel through the same physical interface. Finally, each zone is provided a portion of the file system hierarchy. Because each zone is confined to its subtree of the file system hierarchy, the workloads cannot access one another's on-disk data.

Enclosing the previously mentioned zones is the global zone. Processes running in this zone have (by and large) the same set of privileges available on a pre-zone Solaris system—they may load kernel modules, access physical devices, etc. An administrator logged in to the global zone can monitor and control the system as a whole (including the physical devices and network interface that are hidden from the other zones). The global zone always exists and acts as the "default" zone in which all processes run if no zones have been explicitly created by the administrator.

6.1.2 Zone Principles

Zones advantages include isolation, visibility, and administrative complexity. The following list contains some of the basic principles that guide the design priorities of Zones, grouped according to general area.

- The kernel exports a number of distinct objects that can be associated with a particular zone. These include processes, file system mounts, network interfaces, and System V IPC objects.

- No zone (other than the global zone) can access objects belonging to another zone (including the global zone), either to control or modify those objects in some way or to simply monitor or read them.

- As much as possible, processes in a non-global zone should not be able to interfere with the execution of processes in other zones in the system. Although it is difficult to prevent all possible active denial-of-service attacks, however unlikely, by privileged processes in non-global zones, accidental and relatively trivial interference are prevented.

- Appropriately privileged processes in the global zone can access objects associated with other zones. As much as possible, the zone with which each such object is associated can be administratively and programmatically identified.

- Cross-zone communication may occur over the network (which is actually looped back inside IP, as with any traffic routed between logical interfaces in the same system) but not through other mechanisms without the participation of the global zone.

6.1.2.1 Compatibility

- Applications in the global zone can run without modification, whether or not additional zones are configured.

- With the exception of certain privilege limitations (discussed in Section 6.4.2) and a reduced object namespace, applications within a (non-global) zone can run unmodified.

6.1.2.2 Administration

- Administration of the system infrastructure (physical devices, routing, DR, etc.) is only possible in the global zone.

- Administration of software services executing within a non-global zone is possible within the zone itself.

6.1.2.3 Security

- Privileged processes in non-global zones are prevented from performing operations that can have systemwide impact, whether that impact would have performance, security, or availability consequences.

- Even unprivileged processes in the global zone may perform operations not allowed to privileged processes in a non-global zone. For example, ordinary users in the global zone can see information about every process in the system. In environments where this is a significant concern, access to the global zone should be restricted.

6.1.2.4 Resource Management

The Zones infrastructure provides administrative support for aligning individual zones with resource allocation boundaries. However, resource management features are treated as orthogonal from a design standpoint. This is discussed further in Section 6.10.

6.2 Zone Runtime

This section explains the overall structure of the zone runtime, including the `zoneadmd(1M)` daemon. Most of this information is knowledge that global administrators will need to understand before deploying zones; zone administrators are not required to understand these topics.

6.2.1 Zone State Model

The administrative tasks mentioned in the chapter introduction are managed as transitions in a finite state machine. This section describes the states that form the state machine abstraction. See Figure 6.2 for a graphical representation of this model. A zone can be in one of six states:

- **Configured.** A zone's configuration has been completely specified and committed to stable storage.
- **Installed.** A zone's configuration has been instantiated on the system; Packages have been installed under the zone's root path. In this state, the zone has no associated virtual platform.
- **Ready.** At this stage, the virtual platform for the zone has been established: The kernel has created the `zsched` process, network interfaces have been plumbed, file systems have been mounted, devices have been configured, but no processes associated with the zone have been started.

- **Running.** User processes associated with the zone application environment are running. The zone enters the running state as soon as the first user process associated with the application environment (init) has been created.

- **Shutting_down and down.** These transitional states are visible while the zone is being halted. The zone may become stuck in one of these states if it is unable to tear down application environment state (such as mounted file systems) or if some portion of the virtual platform cannot be destroyed. In such cases, operator intervention is required.

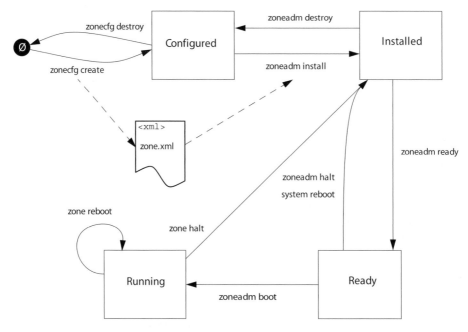

Figure 6.2 Zones State Diagram

The following section shows how to use the zoneadm(1M) command to initiate transitions between these states.

6.2.2 Zone Names and Numeric IDs

Each zone, including the global zone, is assigned a zone name. The rules for a valid zone name are similar to those for host names: They must start with an alphanumeric character, and all remaining characters must consist of alphanumerics plus "-" and "_". The name "global" is reserved for the global zone; also reserved is any name beginning with "SUNW".

Each zone is dynamically assigned a unique numeric zone identifier (or zoneid) when the zone is made ready; this ID uniquely identifies the zone on a given system while the zone is in the ready or running state.

The global zone always has the name "global", is always mapped to ID 0, and is always reported as running. Zone names and IDs are generally of little interest within non-global zones. The `zonename(1)` command can be useful for distinguishing between zones.

It is worth noting that each zone also has a node name (that is, returned by `uname -n` in the zone). Unlike the zone name, the node name for each zone is under the control of the zone administrator and generally of little interest to other zones. The node name is completely independent of the zone name.

6.2.3 Zone Runtime Support

To manage the virtual platform and the application environment, two new processes are used by the zone runtime. `zoneadmd` manages most of the resources associated with the zone. `zsched` is a system process (like `sched`) that tracks kernel resources associated with the zone.

6.2.3.1 `zoneadmd(1M)`

`zoneadmd(1M)` is the primary process responsible for managing the zone's virtual platform. It is also responsible for setup and teardown of the application environment. There is one `zoneadmd` running for each active (ready, running, shutting_down) zone on the system.

The `zoneadmd` command is responsible for consulting the zone configuration and then setting up the zone as directed. This entails the following:

- Calling the `zone_create(2)` system call; this allocates a zone ID and starts the `zsched` (see Section 6.2.3.2) system process.
- Setting zonewide resource controls.
- Registering the zone with `devfsadmd(1M)`.
- Plumbing virtual network interfaces.
- Mounting loopback and conventional file systems.
- Instantiating and initializing the zone console device.

`zoneadmd` is automatically started by `zoneadm(1M)` if not already running and can be contacted by userland applications (such as `zoneadm` in the global zone) and the kernel (as part of `uadmin(2)` calls from the managed zone).

An example of `zoneadmd` in action is as follows:

```
# dtrace -qn 'proc:::exec-success { printf("%-14s %s\n",
curthread->t_procp->p_parent->p_user.u_comm, curpsinfo->pr_psargs); }'
bash            zoneadm -z demozone boot
zoneadm         zoneadmd -z demozone
zoneadmd        mount -o zonedevfs /zones/demozone/dev /zones/demozone/root/dev
zoneadmd        mount -o ro,nosub,nodevices /lib /zones/demozone/root/lib
zoneadmd        mount -o ro,nosub,nodevices /platform /zones/demozone/root/platform
zoneadmd        mount -o ro,nosub,nodevices /sbin /zones/demozone/root/sbin
zoneadmd        mount -o ro,nosub,nodevices /usr /zones/demozone/root/usr
zoneadmd        devfsadm -z demozone
zsched          /sbin/init
init            INITSH -c exec /lib/svc/bin/svc.startd   >/dev/msglog 2<>/dev/msglog </
dev/consol
init            /lib/svc/bin/svc.startd
svc.startd      /lib/svc/bin/svc.configd
svc.startd      /sbin/sh -c exec /lib/svc/method/fs-root
svc.startd      /sbin/sh /lib/svc/method/fs-root
fs-root         /sbin/zonename
fs-root         /usr/bin/moe -32 /usr/lib/libc/$HWCAP
fs-root         egrep -s ^/lib/libc.so.1 on
egrep           /usr/sbin/mount
fs-root         /usr/sbin/mount -O -F lofs /usr/lib/libc/libc_hwcap1.so.1 /lib/libc.so.1
fs-root         mount -O /usr/lib/libc/libc_hwcap1.so.1 /lib/libc.so.1
svc.startd      /sbin/sh -c exec /lib/svc/method/net-physical
svc.startd      /sbin/sh /lib/svc/method/net-physical
net-physical    /sbin/zonename
...
```

6.2.3.2 zsched

Every active (ready through shutting_down) zone has an associated kernel process, `zsched`. Kernel threads doing work on behalf of the zone are owned by `zsched`. It exists largely to enable the zones subsystem to keep track of per-zone kernel threads.

6.2.4 Listing Zone Information

Pulling together the concepts presented in this chapter thus far, we can employ the `zoneadm(1M)` command to observe zones on the system. `zoneadm` is the primary tool used to manage zones once they have been configured. This command can be used to list zones.

```
global# zoneadm list -cv
    ID NAME            STATE          PATH
     0 global          running        /
     - my-zone         configured     /aux0/my-zone
     - fun             installed      /aux0/fun
    15 nofun           ready          /aux1/nofun
     7 lucky           running        /aux0/lucky
    13 unlucky         shutting_down  /aux1/unlucky
```

continues

```
global# pgrep -lf zoneadmd
100819 zoneadmd nofun
100227 zoneadmd lucky
100304 zoneadmd unlucky
```

The -c flag lists all zones (even those not yet installed) instead of the default of all running zones; the -v flag specifies a verbose listing. It is useful to note that, as expected, zones that are configured or installed have no associated numeric ID.

6.3 Booting Zones

Although the virtualization that zones provides is spread throughout the source code, the primary implementation in the kernel can be found in zone.c. As with many Solaris frameworks, there is a big block comment at the start of the file which is very useful for understanding the lay of the land with respect to the code. Besides describing the data structures and locking strategy used for zones, there is a description of the states a zone can be in from the kernel's perspective and at what points a zone may transition from one state to another. For brevity, only the states covered during a zone boot are listed here:

```
 *
 *   Zone States:
 *
 *   The states in which a zone may be in and the transitions are as
 *   follows:
 *
 *   ZONE_IS_UNINITIALIZED: primordial state for a zone. The partially
 *   initialized zone is added to the list of active zones on the system but
 *   isn't accessible.
 *
 *   ZONE_IS_READY: zsched (the kernel dummy process for a zone) is
 *   ready.  The zone is made visible after the ZSD constructor callbacks are
 *   executed.  A zone remains in this state until it transitions into
 *   the ZONE_IS_BOOTING state as a result of a call to zone_boot().
 *
 *   ZONE_IS_BOOTING: in this shortlived-state, zsched attempts to start
 *   init.  Should that fail, the zone proceeds to the ZONE_IS_SHUTTING_DOWN
 *   state.
 *
 *   ZONE_IS_RUNNING: The zone is open for business: zsched has
 *   successfully started init.  A zone remains in this state until
 *   zone_shutdown() is called.
                                                                See os/zone.c
```

It is important to note here that there are a number of zone states not represented here—those are for zones which do not (yet) have a kernel context. An example of such a state is for a zone that is in the process of being installed. These states are defined in libzonecfg.h.

One of the players in the zone boot dance is the zoneadmd process which runs in
the global zone and performs a number of critical tasks. Although much of the virtualization for a zone is implemented in the kernel, `zoneadmd` manages a great
deal of a zone's infrastructure as outlined in zoneadmd.c:

```
/*
 * zoneadmd manages zones; one zoneadmd process is launched for each
 * non-global zone on the system.  This daemon juggles four jobs:
 *
 * - Implement setup and teardown of the zone "virtual platform": mount and
 *   unmount filesystems; create and destroy network interfaces; communicate
 *   with devfsadmd to lay out devices for the zone; instantiate the zone
 *   console device; configure process runtime attributes such as resource
 *   controls, pool bindings, fine-grained privileges.
 *
 * - Launch the zone's init(1M) process.
 *
 * - Implement a door server; clients (like zoneadm) connect to the door
 *   server and request zone state changes.  The kernel is also a client of
 *   this door server.  A request to halt or reboot the zone which originates
 *   *inside* the zone results in a door upcall from the kernel into zoneadmd.
 *
 *   One minor problem is that messages emitted by zoneadmd need to be passed
 *   back to the zoneadm process making the request.  These messages need to
 *   be rendered in the client's locale; so, this is passed in as part of the
 *   request.  The exception is the kernel upcall to zoneadmd, in which case
 *   messages are syslog'd.
 *
 *   To make all of this work, the Makefile adds -a to xgettext to extract *all*
 *   strings, and an exclusion file (zoneadmd.xcl) is used to exclude those
 *   strings which do not need to be translated.
 *
 * - Act as a console server for zlogin -C processes; see comments in zcons.c
 *   for more information about the zone console architecture.
 *
 * DESIGN NOTES
 *
 * Restart:
 *   A chief design constraint of zoneadmd is that it should be restartable in
 *   the case that the administrator kills it off, or it suffers a fatal error,
 *   without the running zone being impacted; this is akin to being able to
 *   reboot the service processor of a server without affecting the OS instance.
 */
```

See zoneadmd.c

When a user wishes to boot a zone, `zoneadm` will attempt to contact `zoneadmd`
via a door that is used by all three components for a number of things including
coordinating zone state changes. If for some reason `zoneadmd` is not running, an
attempt will be made to start it. Once that has completed, zoneadm tells zoneadmd
to boot the zone by supplying the appropriate `zone_cmd_arg_t` request via a door
call. It is worth noting that the same door is used by zoneadmd to return messages back to the user executing `zoneadm` and also as a way for `zoneadm` to indicate to `zoneadmd` the locale of the user executing the boot command so that
messages are localized appropriately.

Looking at the door server that `zoneadmd` implements, there is some straight-forward sanity checking that takes place on the argument passed via the door call as well as the use of some of the technology that came in with the introduction of process privileges in Solaris 10 (see Chapter 5).

```
if (door_ucred(&uc) != 0) {
        zerror(&logsys, B_TRUE, "door_ucred");
        goto out;
        }
        eset = ucred_getprivset(uc, PRIV_EFFECTIVE);
        if (ucred_getzoneid(uc) != GLOBAL_ZONEID ||
            (eset != NULL ? !priv_ismember(eset, PRIV_SYS_CONFIG) :
            ucred_geteuid(uc) != 0)) {
        zerror(&logsys, B_FALSE, "insufficient privileges");
        goto out;
        }

        kernelcall = ucred_getpid(uc) == 0;

        /*
         * This is safe because we only use a zlog_t throughout the
         * duration of a door call; i.e., by the time the pointer
         * might become invalid, the door call would be over.
         */
        zlog.locale = kernelcall ? DEFAULT_LOCALE : zargp->locale;
```

Using `door_ucred`, the user credential can be checked to determine whether the request originated in the global zone,[1] whether the user making the request had sufficient privilege to do so[2] and whether the request was a result of an upcall from the kernel. That last piece of information is used, among other things, to determine whether or not messages should be localized by `localize_msg`.

It is within the door server implemented by zoneadmd that transitions from one state to another take place. There are two states from which a zone boot is permissible, installed and ready. From the installed state, zone_ready is used to create and bring up the zone's virtual platform that consists of the zone's kernel context (created using zone_create) as well as the zone's specific file systems (including the root file system) and logical networking interfaces. If a zone is supposed to be bound to a non-default resource pool, then that also takes place as part of this state transition.

---

1. This is a bit of defensive programming since unless the global zone administrator were to make the door in question available through the non-global zone's own file system, there would be no way for a privileged user in a non-global zone to actually access door used by `zoneadmd`.
2. `zoneadm` itself checks that the user attempting to boot a zone has the necessary privilege but it's possible some other privileged process in the global zone might have access to the door but lack the necessary `PRIV_SYS_CONFIG` privilege.

When a zone's kernel context is created using zone_create, a `zone_t` structure is allocated and initialized. At this time, the status of the zone is set to `ZONE_IS_UNINITIALIZED`. Some of the initialization that takes place is in order to set up the security boundary which isolates processes running inside a zone. For example, the `vnode_t` of the zone's root file system, the zone's kernel credentials and the privilege sets of the zone's future processes are all initialized here.

Before returning back to the `zoneadmd` command, zone_create adds the primordial zone to a doubly-linked list and two hash tables[3],one hashed by zone name and the other by zone ID. These data structures are protected by the `zonehash_lock` mutex which is then dropped after the zone has been added. Finally a new kernel process is then created, `zsched`, which is where kernel threads for this zone are parented. After calling `newproc` to create this kernel process, `zone_create` will wait using `zone_status_wait` until the zsched kernel process has completed initializing the zone and has set its status to `ZONE_IS_READY`.

Since the user structure of the process initialization has not been completed, the first thing the new `zsched` process does is finish that initialization along with reparenting itself to PID 1 (the global zone's init, process). And since the future processes to be run within the new zone may be subject to resource controls, that initialization takes place here in the context of zsched.

After grabbing the `zone_status_lock` mutex in order to set the status to `ZONE_IS_READY`, zsched will then suspend itself, waiting for the zone's status to been changed to `ZONE_IS_BOOTING`.

Once the zone is in the ready state, `zone_create` returns control back to `zoneadmd` and the door server continues the boot process by calling zone_bootup This initializes the zone's console device, mounts some of the standard Solaris file systems like `/proc` and `/etc/mnttab` and then uses the `zone_boot` system call to attempt to boot the zone.

As the comment that introduces `zone_boot` points out, most of the heavy lifting has already been done either by zoneadmd or by the work the kernel has done through `zone_create`. As this point, zone_boot saves the requested boot arguments after grabbing the `zonehash_lock` mutex and then further grabs the `zone_status_lock` mutex in order to set the zone status to `ZONE_IS_BOOTING`. After dropping both locks, it is zone_boot that suspends itself waiting for the zone status is be set to `ZONE_IS_RUNNING`.

Since the zone's status has now been set to `ZONE_IS_BOOTING`, `zsched` now continues where it left off after it has suspended itself with its call to `zone_status_wait_cpr` After checking that the current zone status is indeed `ZONE_IS_BOOTING`, a new kernel process is created in order to run init in the zone. This

---

3. Both of these are worth examining in the Solaris source base.

process calls `zone_icode`, which is analogous to the traditional `icode` function that is used to start init in the global zone and in traditional UNIX environments. After doing some zone-specific initialization, each of the `icode` functions end up calling `exec_init` to actually exec the init process after copying out the path to the executable, `/sbin/init`, and the boot arguments. If the exec is successful, `zone_icode` will set the zone's status to `ZONE_IS_RUNNING` and in the process, `zone_boot` will pick up where it had been suspended. At this point, the value of `zone_boot_err` indicates whether the zone boot was successful or not and is used to set the global `errno` value for `zoneadmd`.

There are two additional things to note with the zone's transition to the running state. First of all, `audit_put_record` is called to generate an event for the Solaris auditing system so that it's known which user executed which command to boot a zone. In addition, there is an internal `zoneadmd` event generated to indicate on the zone's console device that the zone is booting. This internal stream of events is sent by the door server to the zone console subsystem for all state transitions, so that the console user can see which state the zone is transitioning to.

6.4 Security

One of the basic tenets of the zone design is that no process running within a (non-global) zone, even one with superuser credentials (running with an effective user ID of 0), is allowed to view or affect activity in other zones. This implies that any operation initiated from within a zone must have an effect that is local to that zone. For example, the following activities are not allowed within a non-global zone:

- Loading custom kernel modules (those not installed in the system's module search path)
- Rebooting or shutting down the system as a whole
- Accessing kernel memory through `/dev/kmem`
- Accessing physical devices (other than those that may be assigned to the zone for its exclusive use)
- Configuring physical network interfaces or network infrastructure (for example, routing tables)

The security model requires that only a subset of the operations normally restricted to superuser will be allowed within a zone, since many of those operations have a global impact. Operations that are not allowed include halting or rebooting the system, creating device nodes, and controlling allocation of global system resources. Processes running in the global zone still have the full set of privileges, allowing them to affect activity in any zone of the system. Effectively, the zone in which a process is running becomes part of its credential information, restricting its capabilities beyond those of processes with identical effective user and group IDs running in other zones.

The following example shows the available privileges for the global and local zones.

```
global# ppriv -S $$
19876:  bash
flags = <none>
        E: all
        I: basic
        P: all
        L: all

global# zlogin demozone
[Connected to zone 'demozone' pts/2]
Last login: Sat Feb 18 14:03:34 on pts/2
Sun Microsystems Inc.   SunOS 5.10      Generic January 2005

myzone# id
uid=0(root) gid=0(root)

myzone# ppriv -S $$
23829:  -sh
flags = <none>
        E: zone
        I: basic
        P: zone
        L: zone
```

6.4.1 Credential Handling

Zones adds to the `cred_t` structure in the kernel, adding a `cr_zone` field pointing to the zone structure associated with the credential. This field is set for any process entering a zone and is inherited by the credentials used by all descendent processes within the zone. The `cr_zone` field is examined during privilege checks that use credential information, such as `priv_policy(9F)`, `drv_priv(9F)`, and `hasprocperm`. The kernel interface `crgetzoneid(9F)` accesses the zone ID without directly dereferencing the `cred_t` structure.

6.4.2 Fine-Grained Privileges

The Process Rights Management infrastructure (see Chapter 5) added a facility for breaking up the privileges that the kernel previously granted to processes with an effective uid of 0. The notion of "superuser privilege" is replaced by a set of specific privileges, such as the privilege to perform a mount or manipulate processor sets. This means that processes can perform certain privileged operations, but not others.

6.4.2.1 Safe Privileges

The privilege framework allows the restrictions on activity within a non-global zone to be expressed as a subset of privileges that are considered "safe" from a zone standpoint—that is, those privileges that do not allow the exercising process to violate the security restrictions on a zone. Table 6.1 shows this list, and Table 6.2 shows the list of unsafe privileges that will normally only be available within the global zone. Note that the brief descriptions of privileges here are meant to be illustrative, not comprehensive; see the `privileges(5)` man page for the full descriptions.

Table 6.1 Safe Privileges Allowed within a Zone

Privilege	Description
PRIV_FILE_CHOWN	Allows process to change file ownership.
PRIV_FILE_CHOWN_SELF	Allows process to give away files it owns.
PRIV_FILE_DAC_EXECUTE	Allows process to override execute permissions.
PRIV_FILE_DAC_READ	Allows process to override read permissions.
PRIV_FILE_DAC_SEARCH	Allows process to override directory search permissions.
PRIV_FILE_DAC_WRITE	Allows process to override write permissions.
PRIV_FILE_LINK_ANY	Allows process to create hard links to files owned by someone else [basic].
PRIV_FILE_OWNER	Allows nonowning process to modify file in various ways.
PRIV_FILE_SETDAC	Allows nonowning process to modify permissions.
PRIV_FILE_SETID	Allows process to set setuid/setgid bits.
PRIV_IPC_DAC_READ	Allows process to override read permissions for System V IPC.
PRIV_IPC_DAC_WRITE	Allows process to override write permissions for System V IPC.
PRIV_IPC_OWNER	Allows process to control System V IPC objects.
PRIV_NET_ICMPACCESS	Allows process to create an IPPROTO_ICMP or IPPROTO_ICMP6 socket.
PRIV_NET_PRIVADDR	Allows process to bind to privileged port.
PRIV_PROC_AUDIT	Allows process to generate audit records.
PRIV_PROC_CHROOT	Allows process to change root directory.
PRIV_PROC_EXEC	Allows process to exec [basic].
PRIV_PROC_FORK	Allows process to fork [basic].

continues

Table 6.1 Safe Privileges Allowed within a Zone (*continued*)

Privilege	Description
PRIV_PROC_OWNER	Allows process to control/signal other processes with different effective uids.
PRIV_PROC_SESSION	Allows process to send signals outside of session [basic].
PRIV_PROC_SETID	Allows process to set its uids.
PRIV_PROC_TASKID	Allows process to enter a new task.
PRIV_SYS_ACCT	Allows process to configure accounting.
PRIV_SYS_ADMIN	Allows the process to set the domain and node names and coreadm and nscd settings.
PRIV_SYS_MOUNT	Allows process to mount and unmount file systems.
PRIV_SYS_NFS	Allows process to perform operations needed for NFS.
PRIV_SYS_RESOURCE	Allows process to configure privileged resource controls. Privileged per-zone resource controls cannot be modified from within a non-global zone even with this privilege.

Table 6.2 Unsafe Privileges Restricted to the Global Zone

Privilege	Description
PRIV_NET_RAWACCESS	Allows a process to have direct access to the network layer.
PRIV_PROC_CLOCK_HIGHRES	Allows process to create high-resolution timers.
PRIV_PROC_LOCK_MEMORY	Allows process to lock pages in physical memory.
PRIV_PROC_PRIOCNTL	Allows process to change scheduling priority or class.
PRIV_PROC_ZONE	Allows process to control/signal other processes in different zones.
PRIV_SYS_AUDIT	Allows process to manage auditing.
PRIV_SYS_CONFIG	Allows a variety of operations related to the hardware platform.
PRIV_SYS_DEVICES	Allows process to create device nodes.
PRIV_SYS_IPC_CONFIG	Allows process to increase size of System V IPC message queue buffer.
PRIV_SYS_LINKDIR	Allows process to create hard links to directories.
PRIV_SYS_NET_CONFIG	Allows process to configure network interfaces.

continues

Table 6.2 Unsafe Privileges Restricted to the Global Zone (*continued*)

Privilege	Description
PRIV_SYS_RES_CONFIG	Allows process to configure system resources.
PRIV_SYS_SUSER_COMPAT	Allows process to successfully call third-party kernel modules that use suser().
PRIV_SYS_TIME	Allows process to set system time.

6.4.2.2 Zone Privilege Limits

To enable the restriction of privileges within a zone, the zone_create(2) system call includes an argument to specify the zone's privilege limit. This is the set of privileges that is used as a mask for all processes entering the zone, including the process that initiates booting the zone.

Note that the limit on privileges available within a zone does not eliminate the need for restrictions on the objects a zone can access. Privileges can determine whether a process can perform a given operation, but if the operation is allowed, they do not restrict the objects to which that operation can be applied. (A special case involves objects with an effective user ID of 0, as described below, but the general rule holds.) For example, the PRIV_PROC_MOUNT privilege allows a process to mount file systems; if the process has that privilege, it can mount file systems anywhere in the file system namespace. Zones, on the other hand, primarily restrict the namespace and objects to which operations (even unprivileged operations) can be applied; it is only when such restrictions are not possible that the privileges available within a zone must be limited. In short, privileges and zones are complementary technologies.

At present, the set of privileges available within a zone is fixed (to the "safe" set) and cannot be modified by an administrator.

The ppriv(1) command has been extended to include an option to report the privileges available within the current zone, and the zone token can be used in strings passed to priv_str_to_set(3c) to refer to the zone's privilege set. The following example shows the output of the new ppriv option.

```
my_zone# ppriv -z
file_chown
file_chown_self
file_dac_execute
file_dac_read
file_dac_search
file_dac_write
file_link_any
```

continues

```
file_owner
file_setdac
file_setid
ipc_dac_read
ipc_dac_write
ipc_owner
net_privaddr
net_icmpaccess
proc_chroot
proc_audit
proc_exec
proc_fork
proc_owner
proc_session
proc_setid
proc_taskid
sys_acct
sys_admin
sys_mount
sys_nfs
sys_resource
```

This option can also be combined with -v for more verbose output describing each privilege.

6.4.2.3 Privilege Escalation

The problem of privilege escalation represents an additional complication. To prevent a process with a subset of privileges from being able to use those privileges to acquire additional privileges, a number of operations involving root-owned system objects require that the calling process have all privileges. For example, write access to root-owned files by a non-root process requires all privileges, as does establishing control over a process with an effective uid of 0. The intent is to prevent non-root processes with some but not all privileges from using the special treatment of root to escalate privileges; for example, if a non-root process with the PRIV_FILE_DAC_WRITE privilege is allowed to modify the text of kernel modules, it can cause a module to be loaded that awards it all privileges.

Since no process in a non-global zone will have all privileges, the requirement of all privileges for operations involving root-owned objects presents a problem. On the other hand, since even root within a zone has a restricted set of privileges, no privilege escalation is possible beyond the set of zone's privilege limit; thus, it seems appropriate to change the restriction to be the privilege limit for the zone (or all privileges in the global zone).

Note that certain other operations (for example, loading kernel modules) require all privileges because they can be used to control the entire system. These operations should continue to require all privileges, regardless of the zone in which the process is running.

6.4.3 Role-Based Access Control

Like privileges, the role-based access control (RBAC) facility provides a way of making the superuser model more granular. With RBAC, an administrator can give particular users (or "roles"—identities that can be assumed by existing users through su(1M) but cannot be used for external login) the right to perform operations that would otherwise require superuser privileges. These operations are expressed as authorizations; as rights explicitly checked by applications (usually running setuid root); or with profiles, lists of commands that can be executed with pfexec(1) or the "profile shells" (pfsh(1), pfcsh(1), pfksh(1)). Authorizations differ from privileges in that authorizations are enforced by user-level applications (including the profile shells), rather than the kernel. Like privileges, though, they provide fine-grained control over the set of operations a given process can perform, but not over the objects that those operations can affect. As with privileges, this control complements the restrictions imposed by zones.

The zone administration commands requiring privilege (zoneadm(1M), zonecfg(1M), and zlogin(1)) use a new "Zone Management" rights profile.

6.4.4 `chroot` Interactions

The functionality made available by chroot(2) is similar in some ways to zones, in that both provide ways to restrict the part of the file system hierarchy that a process and its descendants can access. chroot, however, has a number of problems from a security perspective. In particular, any process that is given superuser privileges can easily escape a chroot restriction. The problem is that chroot calls don't "nest" safely. A process inside a chrooted environment can call chroot to change its working directory to something "below" the current working directory, then make successive chdir("..") calls until it reaches the real root directory for the system. This works because the check to determine whether a process is escaping its chroot restriction works by processing a path name and comparing the directory being traversed in each component with the root directory that has been set for the process; if the process has access to a directory "above" its root directory, the check is bypassed.[4]

This issue is addressed for zones in two ways. One is that a process inside a zone (other than the global zone) cannot enter another zone; this prevents a process running as superuser in a zone from escaping the zone's root directory restriction in a manner similar to what is possible with chroot. The other is that the

---

4. Even if we were to somehow fix this problem, a process with superuser privileges inside a chroot restriction could still escape by using mknod(2) to create a /dev/kmem device node and writing to the appropriate kernel data structure.

zone's root directory (represented by the `zone_rootvp` field in the kernel's `zone_t` structure) is distinct from the root directory set by `chroot` for processes within a zone (represented by the `u_rdir` field in the kernel's `user_t`) structure). Both restrictions are checked when traversing path-name components; this means that `chroot` can be used within a zone, but a process that escapes from its chroot restriction will still be unable to escape the zone restriction.

6.5 Process Model

As described in Section 6.4, processes within one zone (other than the global zone) must not be able to affect the activity of processes running within another zone. This also extends to visibility; processes within one (non-global) zone should not even be able to see processes outside that zone.[5] We enforce this by restricting the process ID space exposed through /proc accesses and process-specific system calls (`kill(2)`, `priocntl(2)`, etc.). If the calling process is running within a non-global zone, it can only see or affect processes running within the same zone; applying the operations to any other process IDs returns an error.

Note that the intent here is not to try to prevent all possible covert channels from passing information between zones. Given the deterministic algorithm for assigning process IDs, it would be possible to transmit information between two zones on an otherwise idle system by forking processes periodically and monitoring the assigned process IDs. The intent is to prevent unintentional information flow from one zone to another, not to block intentionally constructed (from both sides) low-bandwidth channels of information.

6.5.1 Signals and Process Control

As mentioned above, processes in one zone cannot affect the activity of those in other zones (with the exception that processes in the global zone can affect the activity of other processes). This is the case even if the acting process has an effective user ID of 0 or is executing within an RBAC profile. As a result, attempts to signal or control (through /proc or other mechanisms) processes in other zones fail. Such attempts fail with an error code of ESRCH (or ENOENT for /proc accesses), rather than EPERM; this avoids revealing the fact that the selected process ID exists in another zone. More importantly, it ensures that an application running in a zone sees a consistent view of system objects; there aren't objects that are visible through some means (for example, when probing the process ID space using `kill(2)`) but not others (for example, /proc).

---

5. With the exception of sched and init, as noted in Section 6.5.3.

6.5.2 Global Zone Visibility and Access

The dual role of the global zone, acting as both the default zone for the system and as a zone for systemwide administrative control, can cause certain problems. Since applications within the zone have access to processes and other system objects in other zones, the effect of administrative actions may be wider than expected. For example, service shutdown scripts often use pkill(1) to signal processes of a given name to exit. When run from the global zone, all such processes in the system, regardless of zone, will be signaled.

On the other hand, the systemwide scope is often quite desirable. For example, an administrator who wants to monitor the systemwide resource usage might want to look at process statistics for the whole system. A view of just global zone activity would miss relevant information from other zones in the system that may be sharing some or all of the system resources. Such a view is particularly important when the use of relevant system resources (CPU, memory, swap, I/O) is not strictly partitioned by resource management facilities.

Zones solve this problem by allowing any processes in the global zone to observe processes and other objects in non-global zones. This allows such processes to have systemwide observability. The ability to control or send signals to processes in other zones, however, is restricted by a new privilege, PRIV_PROC_ZONE. The privilege is similar to PRIV_PROC_OWNER in that it allows processes to override the restrictions placed on unprivileged processes; in this case, the restriction is that unprivileged processes in the global zone cannot signal or control processes in other zones. This is true even in cases in which the user IDs of the processes match or the acting process has the PRIV_PROC_OWNER privilege. Also, the PRIV_PROC_ZONE privilege can be removed from otherwise privileged processes to restrict possibly destructive actions to the global zone.

6.5.3 /proc

The /proc file system (or procfs) implements the process visibility and access restrictions mentioned above and information about the zone association of processes. The process access restrictions are based on a mount option, -o zone=<zoneid>, that specifies that the instance of procfs being mounted will only contain processes associated with the specified zone. The mount point for that instance will generally be the "proc" subdirectory of the corresponding zone root directory; this allows processes running within the zone to access /proc just as they would previously, except that they only see processes running within the same zone. If the /proc mount is issued from inside a non-global zone, the -o zone=<zoneid> option is implicit. If the /proc file system is mounted from within the global zone and no -o zone option is specified, then the file system will contain all processes in the system.

The `procfs` entries (when `-o zone` is used) are further altered to prevent leakage of process information from the global zone and to provide a consistent process tree within the zone. In particular, processes 0 (`sched`) and 1 (`init`) are visible within every zone; any process whose parent does not belong to the zone appears to be parented by process 1. This allows tools like `ptree(1)` that expect a tree of processes (rather than a forest) to continue to work without modification. (We could fix `ptree`, but assume that other applications have similar expectations.) It also prevents exposure of the real parent process IDs (belonging to the global zone) within the zone.

Another approach to limiting access to certain processes within an instance of `procfs` would be to filter in accordance with the zone context of the opening process, rather than through use of a mount option. That would mean that, when a process in the global zone opened a `procfs` instance associated with another zone, it would actually see all processes in the system rather than just the ones associated with that zone. This was thought to be more confusing than the mount option approach, whereby a given `procfs` instance will export the same processes regardless of the context of the reader.

The files exported by `procfs` include data about the zone with which each process is associated. In particular, a zone ID is added to the `pstatus` and `psinfo` structures (available by reading the corresponding files in `procfs`). The zone ID replaces a `pad` field in each structure, so it will not affect binary compatibility. This addition allows processes in the global zone to determine the zone associations of processes they are observing or controlling.

The following example shows `/proc` viewed from the global zone and a nonglobal zone.

```
global# zoneadm list -v
    ID NAME            STATE          PATH
     0 global          running        /
   100 my-zone         running        /aux0/my-zone
global# ps -e -o pid,zoneid,comm
     0     0 sched
     1     0 /etc/init
   ...
100180     0 /usr/lib/netsvc/yp/ypbind
100228     0 /usr/lib/autofs/automountd
100248     0 /usr/sbin/nscd
103152   100 /usr/sbin/inetd
   ...
103148   100 /usr/lib/autofs/automountd
103141   100 /usr/lib/netsvc/yp/ypbind
global# zlogin my-zone ps -e -o pid,zoneid,comm
   PID ZONEID COMMAND
     0     0 sched
     1     0 /etc/init
103148   100 /usr/lib/autofs/automountd
103141   100 /usr/lib/netsvc/yp/ypbind
103152   100 /usr/sbin/inetd
103139   100 /usr/sbin/rpcbind
103143   100 /usr/sbin/nscd
```

6.5.4 Core Files

Since the zone in which a process is running defines a part of its environment and since knowledge of that environment is often critical for postmortem debugging, it is desirable to have a way to determine the zone in which a process was running from the core file saved after a process crash. Although the `pstatus` and `psinfo` structures from /proc are saved in the core file and can be used to determine the zone ID of the process, the zone ID will not be very useful (and can even be misleading) if the zone is no longer running or has been rebooted. Thus, we have added a new note type to the core file: the NT_ZONENAME contains the name of the zone in which the process was running.

6.6 File Systems

Virtualization of storage in a zone is achieved by means of a restricted root, similar to the `chroot(2)` environment at the file system level. Processes running within a zone are limited to files and file systems that can be accessed from the restricted root. Unlike chroot, a zone is not escapable; once a process enters a zone, it and all of its children will be restricted to that zone and associated root.

The loopback file system (`lofs`) provides a useful tool for constructing a file system namespace for a zone. This is used to mount segments of a file system in multiple places within the namespace; for example, /usr could also be mounted underneath a zone root.

6.6.1 Configuration

Generally speaking, the set of file systems mounted in a zone is the set of the file systems mounted when the virtual platform is initialized plus the set of file systems mounted from within the application environment itself (for instance, the file systems specified in a zone's /etc/vfstab, as well as `autofs` and `autofs`-triggered mounts and mounts explicitly performed by zone administrator). Certain restrictions are placed on mounts performed from within the application environment to prevent the zone administrator from denying service to the rest of the system or otherwise negatively impacting other zones.

6.6.1.1 `zonecfg` File System Configuration

The global administrator can specify a number of mounts to be performed when the virtual platform is set up. Shown below is the interface for specifying that /dev/dsk/c0t0d0s7 in the global zone is to be mounted as /var/tmp in zone my-zone and that the file system type to use should be UFS, mounted with logging enabled.

```
zonecfg:newzone> add fs
zonecfg:newzone:fs> set dir=/var/tmp
zonecfg:newzone:fs> set special=/dev/dsk/c0t0d0s7
zonecfg:newzone:fs> set raw=/dev/rdsk/c0t0d0s7
zonecfg:newzone:fs> set type=ufs
zonecfg:newzone:fs> set options=noatime
zonecfg:newzone:fs> end
zonecfg:newzone> info fs dir=/var/tmp
fs:
        dir: /var/tmp
        special: /dev/dsk/c0t0d0s7
        raw: /dev/rdsk/c0t0d0s7
        type: ufs
        options: [noatime]
```

File systems loopback-mounted (via `lofs`) into a zone must be mounted with the `-o nodevices` option to prevent `dev_t` proliferation.

6.6.2 Size Restrictions

The Zones infrastructure does not attempt to provide limits, through zone-wide quotas or otherwise, on how much disk space can be consumed by a zone. The global administrator is responsible for space restriction. Administrators interested in this functionality have a number of options, including the following:

- **lofi.** A global administrator may place the zone on a `lofi(7D)`-mounted partition, limiting the amount of space consumable by the zone to that of the file used by `lofi`.

- **Soft partitions.** Disk slices or logical volumes can be divided into up to 8192 partitions. A global administrator can use these partitions as zone roots, and thus limit per-zone disk consumption.

- **ZFS.** A virtually unlimited number of file systems can be created from a storage pool; this is also an option for global administrators.

6.6.3 File System-Specific Issues

There are certain security restrictions on mounting certain file systems from within a zone, while other file systems exhibit special behavior when mounted in a zone. The modified file systems are summarized below.

- **autofs.** Each zone runs its own copy of `automountd`, with the automaps and timeouts under the zone administrator's control. Since the zone's file system namespace is really only a subset of that of the global zone, the global zone could possibly create automaps that reference the non-global zone or traverse into non-global zones and attempt to trigger mounts. This would cause a number of complications, which we circumvent by saying that triggering a mount in another zone (that is, crossing an `autofs` mount point for a non-global zone from the global zone) is disallowed and that the lookup request fails. Note that such situations cannot arise without the participation of the global zone.

Certain `autofs` mounts are created in the kernel when another mount is triggered. For example, the `autofs` mount /net/rankine/export1 is created in the kernel when the NFS mount /net/rankine is triggered. Such mounts cannot be removed with the regular `umount(2)` interface since they must be mounted or unmounted as a group to preserve semantics. A kernel thread periodically wakes up and attempts to communicate with `automountd` in order to remove such mounts, but no interface explicitly attempts to remove such mount points. Zones implements a private kernel interface to provide this functionality, which is necessary for zone shutdown.

- **mntfs.** mntfs is modified such that the set of file systems visible via `mnttab(4)` from within a non-global zone is the set of file systems mounted in the zone, plus an entry for "/". Mount points with a "special device" (that is, /dev/rdsk/c0t0d0s0) not accessible from within the zone have their special device set to the same as the mount point. `mntfs` takes a zone argument similar to what is described for `procfs` in Section 6.5.3. All mounts in the system are visible from the global zone's `mnttab`.

  When mounted from within a zone, mntfs file systems behave as though mounted with "-o zone='zonename'".

- **NFS.** mounts from within a zone behave (implicitly) as though mounted with the -o nodevices option.

- **procfs.** See Section 6.5.3 for a full description of /proc modifications. When mounted from within a zone, `procfs` file systems behave as though mounted with -o zone='zonename'.

- **tmpfs.** Although a "virtual" file system, `tmpfs` could be used by a malicious zone administrator to consume all available swap on the system.

  In addition to consuming all of swap and thus causing a denial of service, a zone may consume a lot of physical memory on the machine by creating many small files, exploiting the fact that inodes on a `tmpfs` file system are always kept in core. This is actually a problem in stock Solaris as well, although certain threshold values in the kernel prevent `tmpfs` from using all of physical memory. In the absence of explicit per-zone limits, one zone would be able to cause `tmpfs` file creations in another zone to fail.

- **lofs.** Read-only `lofs` mounts traditionally did not prevent read-write access to files. An enhancement allows zones to take advantage of `lofs` during zone installation.

  Note that the scope of what can be mounted via `lofs` is limited to the portion of the file system visible to the zone. Hence, there are no restrictions on `lofs` mounts in a zone.

- **UFS, `hsfs`, `pcfs`.** These are file system types that (due to bad metadata or other problems with the backing physical device) may cause the system as a whole to fail and hence cannot safely be mounted from within a zone. They may, however be mounted in a zone if an appropriate block device is exported to the zone. Hence, for such file systems to exist within a zone they must either be mounted directly by or with the explicit consent (expressed in the zone configuration profile) of the global zone administrator.

6.6.4 File System Traversal Issues

Recall that a zone's file system namespace is a subset of that accessible from the global zone. Global zone processes accessing a zone's file system namespace can open up a host of problems on the system.

Unprivileged processes in the global zone are prevented from traversing a non-global zone's file system hierarchy by insisting on the zone root's parent directory being owned, readable, writable, and executable by root only, and restricting access to directories exported by `/proc` (see Section 6.5.3).

The following are highlighted as potential issues that are avoided by restricted access into the zone's file system namespace but that should be taken into account by the global administrator.

- **Security.** Since zone administrators can set the setuid bit on executables, an unprivileged process in the global zone could coordinate with a privileged process in a non-global zone, effectively giving the process in the global zone all privileges.

- **Zone startup and shutdown.** Cross-zone file accesses may cause certain complications during zone shutdown. As described in Section 6.5.3, all file systems mounted in the zone's namespace must unmounted before the zone can be fully shut down. While certain file systems (such as NFS) support forcible unmounts, many do not. File systems with files open because of access from the global zone will not be able to be unmounted; hence, cross-zone access can interfere with zone rebooting or shutting down.

  Furthermore, it is not possible to boot a zone if preestablished mounts would end up visible from within the zone.

 ▪ **autofs.** As noted earlier in Section 6.6.3, attempting to access `autofs` nodes
   mounted for another zone will fail. The global administrator should thus take
   care to not have automaps that descend into other zones.

The following example illustrates the per-zone `mnttab`.

```
global# zoneadm list -v
     ID NAME           STATE           PATH
      0 global         running         /
    100 my-zone        running         /aux0/my-zone

global# cat /etc/mnttab
/dev/dsk/c0t0d0s0       /       ufs rw,intr,largefiles,logging,xattr,oner-
ror=panic,suid,dev=800000 1028243575
/devices        /devices        devfs   dev=9cbc0000    1028243566
/proc   /proc   proc    dev=9cc00000    1028243572
mnttab  /etc/mnttab     mntfs   dev=9ccc0000    1028243572
fd      /dev/fd fd      rw,suid,dev=9cd00001    1028243575
swap    /var/run        tmpfs   xattr,dev=1     1028243596
swap    /tmp    tmpfs   xattr,dev=2     1028243598
proc    /aux0/my-zone/proc      proc    zone=my-zone,dev=9cc00000 1028570870
fd      /aux0/my-zone/dev/fd    fd      rw,suid,dev=9cd00004 1028570870
/opt    /aux0/my-zone/opt       lofs    rw,suid,dev=800000 1028570870
/sbin   /aux0/my-zone/sbin      lofs    rw,suid,dev=800000 1028570870
swap    /aux0/my-zone/tmp       tmpfs   xattr,dev=7     1028570870
swap    /aux0/my-zone/var/run   tmpfs   xattr,dev=8     1028570870
mnttab  /aux0/my-zone/etc/mnttab mntfs  zone=my-zone,dev=9ccc0000 1028570870
taxman.eng:/web /aux0/my-zone/net/taxman.eng/web nfs
intr,nosuid,grpid,xattr,dev=9cec0020    1028572145
jurassic.eng:/export/home14/ozgur       /home/ozgur     nfs
intr,nosuid,noquota,xattr,dev=9cec0043  1028939560

global# cat /aux0/my-zone/etc/mnttab
/       /       ufs     rw,intr,largefiles,logging,xattr,onerror=panic,suid,dev=800000
1028243575
/usr    /usr    lofs    rw,suid,dev=800000      1028243598
proc    /proc   proc    zone=my-zone,dev=9cc00000       1028570870
fd      /dev/fd fd      rw,suid,dev=9cd00004    1028570870
/opt    /opt    lofs    rw,suid,dev=800000      1028570870
/sbin   /sbin   lofs    rw,suid,dev=800000      1028570870
swap    /tmp    tmpfs   xattr,dev=7     1028570870
swap    /var/run        tmpfs   xattr,dev=8     1028570870
mnttab  /etc/mnttab     mntfs   zone=my-zone,dev=9ccc0000       1028570870
taxman.eng:/web /net/taxman.eng/web     nfs intr,nosuid,grpid,xattr,dev=9cec0020 145
```

6.7 Networking

Consider a server that contains several zones as a result of a server consolidation
program. Externally over the network, it will appear to be a multihomed server that
has inherited all the IP addresses of the original servers. However, internally it will
look quite different from a traditional multihomed server. The IP stack must partition the networking between the zones in much the same way it would have been
partitioned between separate servers. While the original servers could potentially

all communicate with each other over the network, they could also all run the same services such as sendmail(1M), apache(1M), etc. The same features are provided by zones—the zones can all communicate with one another just as though they were still linked by a network, but they also all have separate bindings such they can all run their own server daemons, and these can be the same as those running in another zone listening on the same port numbers without any conflict. The IP stack resolves these conflicts by considering the IP addresses for which incoming connections are destined; the addresses identify the original server and now the zone the connection is considered to be in.

6.7.1 Partitioning

The IP stack in a system supporting zones implements the separation of network traffic between zones. Each logical interface on the system belongs to a specific zone (the global zone by default). Likewise, each stream or connection belongs to the zone of the process that opened it.

Bindings (connections) between upper-layer streams and logical interfaces are restricted such that a stream can establish bindings only to logical interfaces in the same zone. Likewise, packets from a logical interface can only be passed to upper-layer streams in the same zone as the logical interface. Applications that bind to INADDR_ANY for receiving IP traffic are silently restricted to receiving traffic from the same zone. Each zone conceptually has a separate set of binds (mainly used for listens), so that each zone can be running the same application listening on the same port number without binds failing because the address is already in use. Thus, each zone can, for example, run its own inetd(1M) with a full configuration file, sendmail(1M), apache(1M), and the like.

Each zone conceptually has its own loopback interface, and bindings to the loopback address are kept partitioned within a zone. An exception is the case in which a stream in one zone attempts to access the IP address of an interface in another zone—such bindings are established through the pseudo loopback interface, as is currently the case in Solaris systems before zone support. Since there is currently no mechanism to prevent such cross-zone bindings, existing Solaris firewalling products will not be able to filter or otherwise act on cross-zone traffic, because it is handled entirely within IP and is not visible to any underlying firewalling products. In the future as part of another project, an option might be provided to prevent such cross-zone bindings.

Sending and receiving broadcast and multicast packets is supported in all zones. Interzone broadcast and multicast is implemented by replication of outgoing and incoming packets as necessary so that each zone that should receive a broadcast packet or has joined a particular multicast group receives the appropriate data.

Zones (other than the global zone) get restricted access to the network. The standard TCP/UDP transport interfaces are available, but some lower-level interfaces are not. These restrictions are in place to ensure that a zone cannot gain uncontrolled access to the network, such that it might be able to behave in undesirable ways (for example, masquerade as a different zone, interfere with the network structure or operation, or obtain from the network some data that does not relate to itself).

The if_tcp(7P) SIOCTMYADDR ioctl tests whether a specified address belongs to this node. The uses of this ioctl identified so far require a "node" to be interpreted as a zone.

6.7.2 Interfaces

Each zone that requires network connectivity has one or more dedicated IP addresses. These addresses are associated with logical network interfaces that can be placed in a zone by ifconfig(1M) using a new zone argument. Zone interfaces configured by zonecfg(1M) are automatically plumbed and placed in the zone when it is booted, although ifconfig(1M) can add or remove logical interfaces once the zone is running. A new if_tcp(7P) ioctl is provided to place a logical interface into a zone, SIOCSLIFZONE (along with the corresponding SIOCGLIFZONE to read back the value). Interfaces can only be configured from within the global zone; zone administrators are not permitted to change the configuration of their network interfaces.

Within a local zone, only that zone's interfaces are visible to ifconfig(1M). In the global zone, ifconfig(1M) can be run with a new -Z flag, which restricts the command to global zone interfaces, but by default, all interfaces are shown, and those not in the global zone are indicated. The example below shows interfaces in all zones. The existing if_tcp(7p) ioctls, SIOCGLIFCONF and SIOCGLIFNUM, return interfaces only in the caller's zone (for both global and local zones). The struct lifconf used by SIOCGLIFCONF and the struct lifnum used by SIOCGLIFNUM include a new flag, LIFC_ALLZONES, which requests that interfaces in all zones be returned in the response. This flag is ignored if the requester is not in the global zone.

```
global# ifconfig -a
lo0: flags=1000849<UP,LOOPBACK,RUNNING,MULTICAST,IPv4> mtu 8232 index 1
        inet 127.0.0.1 netmask ff000000
lo0:1: flags=1000849<UP,LOOPBACK,RUNNING,MULTICAST,IPv4> mtu 8232 index 1
        zone my-zone
        inet 127.0.0.1 netmask ff000000
hme0: flags=1000843<UP,BROADCAST,RUNNING,MULTICAST,IPv4> mtu 1500 index 2
        inet 129.146.126.89 netmask ffffff00 broadcast 129.146.126.255
        ether 8:0:20:b9:37:ff
```

continues

```
hme0:1: flags=1000843<UP,BROADCAST,RUNNING,MULTICAST,IPv4> mtu 1500 index 2
        zone my-zone
        inet 129.146.126.203 netmask ffffff00 broadcast 129.146.126.255

global# ifconfig -aZ
lo0: flags=1000849<UP,LOOPBACK,RUNNING,MULTICAST,IPv4> mtu 8232 index 1
        inet 127.0.0.1 netmask ff000000
hme0: flags=1000843<UP,BROADCAST,RUNNING,MULTICAST,IPv4> mtu 1500 index 2
        inet 129.146.126.89 netmask ffffff00 broadcast 129.146.126.255
        ether 8:0:20:b9:37:ff

global# zlogin my-zone ifconfig -a
lo0:1: flags=1000849<UP,LOOPBACK,RUNNING,MULTICAST,IPv4> mtu 8232 index 1
        inet 127.0.0.1 netmask ff000000
hme0:1: flags=1000843<UP,BROADCAST,RUNNING,MULTICAST,IPv4> mtu 1500 index 2
        inet 129.146.126.203 netmask ffffff00 broadcast 129.146.126.255
```

To efficiently remove all the logical interfaces associated with a particular non-global zone, a new ioctl, SIOCREMZONEIFS, will be introduced for use when shutting down such a zone.

6.7.3 IPv6

As with IPv4, the use of IPv6 within a zone can be supported by logical interfaces placed in the zone. IPv6, however, does include a number of unique features (such as address autoconfiguration), that require special consideration when they are configured for use with zones. These features are discussed below.

At the time of this writing, you can use IPv6 within non-global zones only by manually configuring addresses and assigning them to zones, using zonecfg(1M) or ifconfig(1M). Support for address autoconfiguration and default address selection will be part of future Solaris releases.

6.7.3.1 Address Autoconfiguration

Unlike IPv4 in which where the global administrator assigns addresses to a zone, the use of the address autoconfiguration feature of IPv6 provides a useful mechanism to generate unique addresses for the zone. Since typically the system's IEEE 802 48-bit MAC address is used to generate unique addresses for the global zone, a different mechanism is required for each of the local zones so that each has a unique EUI-64 interface identifier as described in RFC 2373. The existing IPv6 address token mechanism is extended to permit multiple tokens to be assigned to a physical interface, each tied to an associated zone (in the existing system, only a single token is permitted for a physical interface), and a per-zone token can be one of the properties that can be set for a network resource that has been assigned to a zone. When in.ndpd(1M) (which runs within the global zone) performs address autoconfiguration, it can use the list of tokens assigned to a physical interface and the prefixes being advertised on that interface to plumb logical interfaces and assign them to their respective zones. It may also be possible to automate the generation of the interface identifier by combining part of the system's MAC address with the zoneid itself.

6.7.3.2 Address Selection

The IPv6 Default Address Selection facility introduced a mechanism for a global administrator to select which source and destination IPv6 addresses should be used when sending datagrams in the case for which multiple addresses are available.

6.7.4 IPsec

IPsec configuration applies systemwide, but zone-specific configuration can be created by specifying a zone's IP address as the `laddr` field in a ruleset. Tunnels, just like physical interfaces, can be placed into non-global zones by means of logical interfaces and used with IPsec. Multiple logical interfaces are required with the 0th logical interface in the global zone, and further logical interfaces are required in those zones that need access to the tunnel. Appropriate IPsec configuration can block traffic to or from the global zone's logical interface through its IP address, where access from the global zone needs to be explicitly excluded.

IPsec operation between zones is the same as that currently operated over the loopback interface—some performance gains are made here on the basis that the traffic is not exposed on any external interfaces.

IPsec can be configured only from the global zone.

6.7.5 Raw IP Socket Access

General raw IP socket access is not available in a non-global zone. Such access gives a privileged user in the zone the uncontrolled ability to fabricate and receive packets contrary to the network partitioning between zones.

One special case of raw socket access is supported for the `ICMP` protocol since this is required by the `ping(1M)` command. However, the `IPPROTO_IP`-level option `IP_HDRINCL` option is not allowed. To this end, a new privilege, `PRIV_NET_ICMPACCESS`, is introduced and granted to all zones by default. The device policy now allows processes with this privilege to open `/dev/icmp`, `/dev/icmp6`, `/dev/rawip`, and `/dev/rawip6` read-write and read-only.

The `/dev/ip` device node is not provided within a zone because of the difficulty of ensuring that it could not be used to circumvent the Raw IP Socket Access restrictions. Some applications use `/dev/ip` to access network statistics, but this can be done with `/dev/arp` and those applications will be modified appropriately.

6.7.6 DLPI Access

DLPI access provides the raw interface to the network drivers on Solaris.

6.7.7 Routing

Routing remains a systemwide feature, just as it is today on Solaris systems before zone support. Since routing changes affect the whole system, routing changes are allowed only from the global zone. Views of the routing table from within zones are restricted to routes relevant to that zone.

6.7.8 TCP Connection Teardown

The ioctl `TCP_IOC_ABORT_CONN` can abort existing TCP connections and unconnected TCP endpoints without waiting for a timeout. It is used by the Sun Cluster and Netra High Availability (HA) Suite products to allow quick failover of IP addresses from one node to another. The `tcp_ic_abort_conn_t` structure has been extended to include a zone ID, allowing all connections associated with a given zone to be terminated; this is used internally as part of zone shutdown. You can preserve the previous behavior by setting the zone ID field (`ac_zoneid`) to `ALL_ZONES`.

6.8 Devices

All applications make use of devices; however, the great majority of applications interact directly only with pseudo-devices, which makes the task of providing a zoned device environment feasible. These are the key goals for providing devices in a zone:

- **Security.** Users interacting with devices appearing in a zone must not be able to use those devices to compromise another zone or the system as a whole.

- **Virtualization.** Some devices must be modified to provide namespace or resource isolation for operation in a zone.

- **Administration.** It must be easy to place a default, safe collection of devices in a zone; warnings must occur when an administrator attempts to place unsafe devices into a zone; it must be possible for a knowledgeable administrator to assign physical devices to zones when needed.

- **Automatic Operation.** With the advent of `devfsadm(1M)`, device file system management in Solaris became largely automated. Zones should not require administrator intervention to create dynamically managed device nodes.

This section begins by classifying devices according to their virtualization and security characteristics. Discussions of the `/devices` namespace, device privilege and permission, device administration tools, and the special handling required to support pseudo-terminals follow.

6.8.1 Device Categories

Treatment of devices with respect to zones must of necessity vary depending on the type of device. For this discussion, we divide devices into the following categories:

1. **Unsafe.** Devices that cannot be safely used within a zone.
2. **Fully virtual.** Devices that reference no global state and may safely appear in any zone.
3. **Sharable-virtual.** Devices that reference global state, but may safely be shared across zones, possibly as the result of modification made by the zones project.
4. **Exclusive.** Devices that can be safely assigned to and used exclusively by a single zone.

6.8.1.1 Unsafe Devices

Examples of unsafe devices include those devices that expose global system state, such as:

- `/dev/kmem`
- `/dev/cpc` (`cpc(3CPC)`)
- `/dev/trapstat` (`trapstat(1M)`)
- `/dev/lockstat` (`lockstat(7D)`)

There is no way to allow use of such devices from a zone without violating the security principles of zones. Note that this is not restricted to control operations; for example, read access to `/dev/kmem` will allow a zone to snoop on activity within other zones (by looking at data stored in kernel memory).

This category includes most physical device instances present on the platform, including bus nexus devices, platform support drivers, and devices in support of the device administration infrastructure. All these devices are central to the operation of the platform as a whole and are not appropriate to expose for monitoring or control by the lower-privilege environment inside a nonglobal zone.

6.8.1.2 Fully Virtual Devices

A few of the system's pseudo-devices are "fully virtualized"; these are device instances that reference no global system state and may safely appear in any zone. An excellent example is /dev/tty (tty(7D)), which references only the controlling terminal of the process in whose context it executes.

Other fully virtual devices include

- /dev/null (null(7D)) and /dev/zero (zero(7D)).
- /dev/poll (poll(7D))
- /dev/logindmux, used to link two streams in support of applications including telnet(1).

6.8.1.3 Sharable Virtual Devices

Those device instances that reference some sort of global state but may be modified to be zone-compatible are said to be sharable virtual devices. Some examples:

- /dev/kstat (kstat(7D))
- /dev/ptmx (ptm(7D)), the pty master device. See the "Pseudo-Terminals" discussion in Section 6.8.5.1.

A principal example of such a device is the random(7D) driver, which exports the /dev/random and /dev/urandom minor nodes. In this case, the global state is the kernel's entropy pool, from which it provides a stream of cryptographic-quality random bytes.

6.8.2 /dev and /devices Namespace

The devfs(7FS) file system is used by Solaris to manage /devices. Each element in this namespace represents the physical path to a hardware device, pseudo-device, or nexus device; it is a reflection of the device tree. As such, the file system is populated by a hierarchy of directories and device special files.

The /dev file hierarchy, which is today part of the / (root) file system, consists of symbolic links (logical paths) to the physical paths present in /devices. /dev is managed by a complex system comprising devfsadm(1M), syseventd(1M), the devinfo(7D) driver, libdevinfo(3lib), and RCM.

Few end-user applications reference /devices. Instead, applications reference the logical path to a device, presented in /dev. So, while the system's /devices file system is important to a few system administration applications, it was decided that /devices would not appear within a zone.

6.8.3 Device Management: Zone Configuration

An interface indicates which devices should appear in a particular zone; this functionality is provided by the zonecfg(1M) infrastructure according to a flexible rule-matching system. Devices matching one of the rules are included in the zone's /dev file system.

To include an additional device in the zone, the administrator can specify it by adding an additional rule:

```
zonecfg:demozone> add device
zonecfg:demozone:device> set match=/dev/scsi/scanner/c3t4*
zonecfg:demozone:device> end
zonecfg:demozone> info device
device
        match: /dev/scsi/scanner/c3t4*
```

With this syntax, a device can be specified in one of three ways.

6.8.4 Device Management: Zone Runtime

Zones adds new interfaces and capabilities to the devfsadm daemon; the system's single instance of devfsadmd is part of the virtual platform layer for each zone. The changes are somewhat obscure and are enumerated below.

1. When the daemon starts up, it discovers which zones on the system are ready or running; it is assumed that such zones have a valid /dev file hierarchy. devfsadmd retains a list of said zones; it also loads the zone's configuration database in order to know the <device> matching rules.

2. When the virtual platform is set up, the zoneadmd(1M) invokes the devfsadm command (not the daemon) and passes arguments to it indicating which zone's /dev directory should be populated. Additionally, the zone is registered with the devfsadmd daemon by a door call to a new door, /dev/.zone_reg_door.

3. When a zone is discovered by (1) or (2) above, devfsadmd creates a file under the zone's root directory at /dev/.devfsadm_synch_door and attaches the appropriate door to it. It also loads the zone's configuration database in order to know applicable <device> matching rules. If the zone being registered is already registered, its configuration is reread, and its door file is recreated.

4. When the virtual platform is destroyed, the zone is unregistered from devfsadmd, which then frees associated resources and ceases to manage the zone.

5. When a device-related event occurs (for example, in response to a hotplug event), a device entry in /dev may need to be created. When this occurs, the devfsadmd link-generator module calls the devfsadm_mklink() routine.

     This routine first services the global zone, establishing the device symbolic link requested by the link-generator. Next, the routine iterates across all registered zones. Instead of creating links, however, the routine creates device nodes with mknod(2); node creation is subject to the filtering rules for the zone's configuration.

6.8.4.1 Read-Only Mount of /dev

A significant problem with this approach is that devfsadmd must "reach into" zones in order to execute mknod, create, delete and symlink on files. This violates zone file system principles outlined in Section 6.6, and there is a distinct danger of buffer-overrun and symlink attacks.

To solve this problem, the /dev file system is loopback-mounted into the zone by means of a read-only mount. Device nodes can be freely accessed (opened O_RDWR, for example) by zone processes, but other file operations (creation, unlink, symlink, link, etc.) are prevented.

A risk is associated with this change; some applications may expect to be able to manipulate /dev entries. However, such applications are generally not zone-appropriate, so we believe this risk is minimal.

6.8.4.2 Device Privilege Enforcement

In Solaris, privileges held by applications interact with device drivers in a complex way. File system permissions, device policy (see getdevpolicy(1M)), and driver-based privilege checks (drv_priv(9F) and priv_policy(9F)) may all come into effect during a call to open(2). This section discusses issues related to driver privileges.

6.8.5 Zone Console Design

Figure 6.1 demonstrates that zones export a virtualized console. More generally, the system's console is an important and widely referenced notion; as seen in previous examples, the zone console is a natural and familiar extension of the system for administrators.

While zone consoles are similar to the traditional system console, they are not identical. In general, the notion of a system console has the following properties:

- Applications may open and write data to the console device.
- The console remains accessible when other methods of login (such as telnet(1)) fail.

- The system administrator uses the system console to interact with the system when no other system services are running.

- The console captures messages issued at boot-up.

- The console remains available even when the operating system has failed or shut down; that is, you can remain "on console" of systems that are powered down or rebooted, even though no I/O may be possible.

- The console need not have a process consuming data written to it in order to drain its contents.

- Windowing systems make use of the SRIOCSREDIR ioctl and the redirmod STREAMS module to redirect console output to a designated terminal in the window system.

- The console can be configured such that console messages are copied to auxiliary hardware devices like terminals or serial lines by the consadm(1M) command.

The zone console design implements the most crucial subset of these; future projects could enable additional functionality as customer needs demand. The zone console is implemented by the zcons(7D) driver. As in a normal Solaris instance, a non-global zone's console I/O (including zone boot messages) are directed to this device.

Within a non-global zone, /dev/console, /dev/msglog, /dev/syscon, /dev/sysmsg, and /dev/systty are all symbolic links to the /dev/zconsole device.

The auxiliary console facilities provided by consadm(1M) are not supported for zone consoles; additionally, the SRIOCSREDIR ioctl is not supported.

A zone's console is available for login once the zone has reached the ready state and can last across halt/boot cycles.

6.8.5.1 Pseudo-Terminals

Solaris's pseudo-terminal support consists of a pair of drivers, ptm(7D), and pts(7D); several STREAMS modules, including ptem(7M) (terminal emulator), ldterm(7D) (line discipline), and ttcompat(7M) (V7, 4BSD and XENIX compatibility); and userland support code in libc and /usr/lib/pt_chmod.

The ptm and pts drivers are enhanced such that an open of a pts device can occur only in the zone that opened the master side for the corresponding instance (the ptm driver is self-cloning).

In the case of the zlogin(1) command, it is necessary to allocate a pty in the global zone and to then "push" that pty into a particular zone. To accomplish this, a private zonept(3C) library call is introduced. zonept issues the ZONEPT ioctl to the master device requesting that the current terminal be assigned the supplied zone owner.

The number of pts devices may grow without bound.[6] This dynamic growth is triggered when the number of ptys must grow beyond the current limit (for example, when allocating the 17th pty). This must function even when the application opening /dev/ptmx is unprivileged. This functionality (provided in libc) relies on a door call to devfsadmd, which is wrapped by the di_devlink_init() interface. The code can also start devfsadmd as needed.

To solve this problem in the zone, we place the appropriate door to the global zone's devfsadmd into the non-global zone. This allows the zone to demand that the global zone install the appropriate /dev/pts/ device nodes as needed. There is some risk of denial-of-service attack against devfsadmd here. A future enhancement may be to allow the zoneadmd(1M) process (see Section 6.2.3.1) to act as a "proxy server" for such door calls; zoneadmd would simply turn the zone's request for devlink creation into a call to di_devlink_init(), which would in turn start devfsadmd if it was not running. zoneadmd could throttle requests as needed.

A final issue is that the global administrator should be able to limit the number of pseudo-terminal devices available to each zone. One possibility is to implement a zone-scoped resource control (See Section 6.10) for pty creation.

6.8.6 ftpd

Solaris provides the ftpconfig(1M) command to set up anonymous FTP environments. Anonymous FTP allows users to remotely log on to the FTP server by specifying the user name "ftp" or "anonymous" and the user's email address as password; anonymous FTP environments are run in a chroot'd environment, and ftpconfig uses cpio(1) to propagate device special files from /dev to the chroot area as follows:

```
cpio -pduL "$home_dir" >/dev/null 2>&1 <<-EOF
        /dev/conslog
        /dev/null
        /dev/udp
        /dev/udp6
        /dev/zero
        EOF
```

The zone application environment lacks the SYS_DEVICES privilege, so this will fail. Chroot environments that require device special files cannot be created from within a zone. The global zone administrator can, however, cooperate with the zone administrator to set up such an environment.

---

6. In practice, the number of pts devices on the system is limited by the size of the minor number space in the operating system.

6.9 Interprocess Communication

Local interprocess communication (IPC) represents a particular problem for zones, since processes in different (non-global) zones should normally only be able to communicate through network APIs, as would be the case with processes running on separate machines. It might be possible for a process in the global zone to construct a way for processes in other zones to communicate, but this should not be possible without the participation of the global zone. In this section, we look at the different forms of IPC and how this issue is handled for each.

6.9.1 Pipes, STREAMS, and Sockets

IPC mechanisms that use the file system as a rendezvous, for example, pipes (through `fifofs`), STREAMS (through `namefs`), and UNIX domain sockets (through `sockfs`), fit naturally into the zone model without modification since processes in one zone will not have access to file system locations associated with other zones. Since the file system hierarchy is partitioned, there is no way to achieve the rendezvous without the involvement of the global zone (which has access to the entire hierarchy). If processes in different zones are able to communicate, the `getpeerucred(3c)` interface can determine the credentials (including zone ID) of processes on the other end of the connection.

6.9.2 Doors

Doors also use the file system as a rendezvous (through `namefs`), so potential door clients will normally only be able to call servers within the same zone. Doors, however, also provide a way of safely supporting cross-zone communication, since the server can retrieve the credentials of the caller by using `door_ucred(3door)`. We have extended the private data structure returned by `door_ucred` to include a zone ID and have added a `cred_getzoneid(3c)` interface to retrieve the zone ID from the structure. This allows the creation of truly global door servers if desired; a door server from the global zone could be mounted in each zone, and the server could check whether the caller is authorized to perform a given operation based on its zone ID as well as other credential information. The door-server approach provides a means for doing efficient cross-zone communication with doors when necessary (although we think that most such services should be written with networking interfaces for optimal flexibility and portability). In fact, this functionality is used to implement the per-zone device node creation described in Section 6.8 (allowing processes in each zone to contact the global `devfsadmd` daemon).

6.9.3 Loopback Transport Providers

The loopback transport providers—`ticlts`, `ticots`, and `ticotsord`—provide yet another mechanism for IPC. These transports, like traditional network transports such as UDP or TCP, can be accessed through standard transport-independent TLI/XTI interfaces. However, the loopback transports are limited to communication among processes on the same machine and are implemented as pseudo-devices without involving the kernel networking stack. The transport providers support "flex addresses," which are arbitrary sequences of octets of length greater than 0. When zones are in use, the flex address space is partitioned to prevent communication among processes in different zones. In other words, each zone has its own flex address namespace. This is done by internally (within the `tl` driver) associating zone IDs with transport endpoints, based on the zone ID of the process performing the `bind(3socket)` call. This means that a process calling `connect(3socket)` connects only to the endpoint with a matching address associated with the caller's zone. In addition, multiple processes can bind to the same address as long as they are in different zones; this means that multiple applications can use the same address without conflict if they are running in different zones, thereby avoiding the need for cross-zone coordination in address selection.

6.9.4 System V IPC

The System V IPC interfaces allow applications to create persistent objects (shared memory segments, semaphores, and message queues) for communication and synchronization among processes on the same system. The objects are dynamically assigned numeric identifiers that can be associated with user-defined keys, allowing use of a single object in unrelated processes. Objects are also associated with an owner (based on the effective user ID of the creating process unless explicitly changed) and permission flags that can be set to restrict access when desired.

To prevent sharing (intentional or unintentional) among processes in different zones, a zone ID is associated with each object, based on the zone in which the creating process was running at time of creation. Processes running in a zone other than the global zone can only access or control objects associated with the same zone. There are no new restrictions for processes running in the global zone (though the existing user ID-based restrictions will be honored); this allows an administrator in the global zone to manage IPC objects throughout the system without needing to enter each zone. The key namespace is per-zone, which avoids the possibility of key collisions between zones.

The administrative commands, `ipcs(1)` and `ipcrm(1)`, have been updated with zone-specific options for use when run in the global zone. By default, `ipcs` reports objects from the current zone. When run in the global zone, however, the `-z zone` option reports objects from the specified zone, and the -Z option reports objects from all zones, with the zone association of each identified. These options can be used to disambiguate between objects that may have identical keys but are in different zones and in general to provide better observability into the usage of IPC objects within zones.

The ipcrm command similarly operates on objects in the current zone, unless run in the global zone and given the -z zone option. This option removes objects in other zones.

In the past, the System V IPC implementation in Solaris included a number of static systemwide limits on the number of objects that can be created, as well as various details of those objects (maximum size of shared memory segments, maximum depth of message queues, etc.). In a system with zones, this would lead to an obvious problem with processes in one zone exhausting all the available objects. Fortunately, this implementation was recently revised to eliminate the need for these limits (see Section 4.2); the only tunable parameters in the new code are per-project and per-process resource controls, which require no adaptation to work in a zone environment.

6.9.5 POSIX IPC

The POSIX IPC interfaces implemented in librt, unlike the System V interfaces, use files to rendezvous between processes. This means that they fall into the same category as pipes, sockets, and streams, in that no changes are necessary to enforce per-zone isolation and object key namespaces.

6.10 Resource Management and Observability

Most of the discussion in this chapter has described the ways in which zones can be used to isolate applications in terms of configuration, namespace, security, and administration. Another important aspect of isolation is ensuring that each application receives an appropriate proportion of the system resources: CPU, memory, and swap space. Without such a capability, one application can either intentionally or unintentionally starve other applications of resources.

In addition, there may be reasons to prioritize some applications over others or to adjust resources depending on dynamic conditions. For example, a financial company might want to give a stock trading application high priority while the trading floor is open, even if it means taking resources away from an application analyzing overall market trends.

The zones facility is tightly integrated with existing resource management controls available in Solaris. These controls come in three flavors: entitlements, which ensure a minimum level of service; limits, which bound resource consumption; and partitions, which allow physical resources to be exclusively dedicated to specific consumers. Each of these types of controls can be applied to zones. For example, a fair-share CPU scheduler can be configured to guarantee a certain share of CPU capacity for a zone. In addition, an administrator within a zone can configure CPU shares for individual applications running within that zone; these shares determine how to carve up the portion of CPU allocated to the zone. Likewise, resource limits can be established on either a per-zone basis (limiting the consumption of the entire zone) or a more granular basis (individual applications or users within the zone). In each case, the global zone administrator is responsible for configuring per-zone resource controls and limits, while the administrator of a particular non-global zone can configure resource controls within that zone.

Figure 6.3 shows how the fair-share CPU scheduler can divide CPU resources among zones. In the figure, the system is divided into four zones, each of which is assigned a certain number of CPU shares. If all four zones contain processes that are actively using the CPU, then the CPU is divided according to the shares; that is, the red zone receives 1/7 of the CPU (since a total of 7 shares is outstanding), the neutral zone receives 2/7, etc. In addition, the lisa zone has been further subdivided into five projects, each of which represents a workload running within that zone. The 2/7 of the CPU assigned to the lisa zone (based on the per-zone shares) is further subdivided among the projects within that zone according to the specified shares.

Resource partitioning is supported through a mechanism called resource pools, which allows an administrator to specify a collection of resources that will be

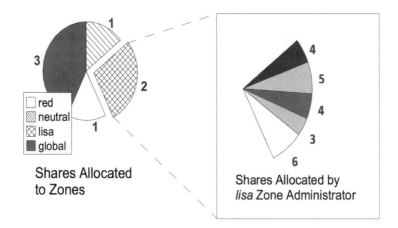

Figure 6.3 Zones and the Fair-Share Scheduler

exclusively used by some set of processes. Although the only resources initially supported are CPUs, this is planned to later encompass other system resources such as physical memory and swap space. A zone can be "bound" to a resource pool, which means that the zone runs only on the resources associated with the pool. Unlike the resource entitlements and limits described above, this approach allows applications in different zones to be completely isolated in terms of resource usage; the activity within one zone has no effect on other zones. This isolation is furthered by restricting the resource visibility. Applications or users running within a zone bound to a pool see only resources associated with that pool. For example, a command that lists the processors on the system lists only the ones belonging to the pool to which the zone is bound. Note that the mapping of zones to pools can be one-to-one, or many-to-one; in the latter case, multiple zones share the resources of the pool, and features like the fair-share scheduler can control the manner in which they are shared.

Figure 6.4 shows the use of the resource pool facility to partition CPUs among zones. Note that processes in the global zone can actually be bound to more than one pool; a special case allows the use of resource pools to partition workloads even without zones. Non-global zones, however, can be bound to only one pool (that is, all processes within a non-global zone must be bound to the same pool).

6.10.1 Performance

One of the advantages of technologies like zones that virtualize the operating system environment over a traditional virtual machine implementation is the minimal

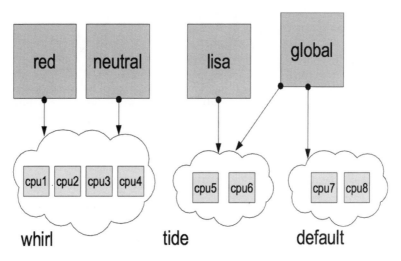

Figure 6.4 Zones and Resource Pools

performance overhead. To substantiate this, we measured the performance of a variety of workloads when running in a non-global zone compared to the same workloads running without zones (or in the global zone). This data is shown in Table 6.3 (in each case, higher numbers represent a faster run).

Table 6.3 Performance Impact of Running in a Zone

Workload	Base	Zone	Diff (%)
Java	38.45	38.29	99.6
Time-sharing	23332.58	22406.51	96.0
Networking	283.30	284.24	100.3
Database	38767.62	37928.70	97.8

The final column shows the percentage degradation (or improvement) of the zone run versus the run in the global zone. As can be seen, the impact of running an application in a zone is minimal. The 4% degradation in the time-sharing workload is primarily due to the overhead associated with accessing commands and libraries through lofs.

We also measured the performance of running multiple applications on the system at the same time in different zones, partitioning CPUs either with resource pools or the fair-share scheduler. In each case, the performance when zones were used was equivalent to, and in some cases better than, the performance when each application was run on separate systems.

Since all zones on a system are part of the same operating system instance, processes in different zones can actually share virtual memory pages. This is particularly true for text pages, which are rarely modified. For example, although each zone has its own init process, each of those processes can share a single copy of the text for the executable, libraries, etc. This can result in substantial memory savings for commonly used executables and libraries such as libc. Similarly, other parts of the operating system infrastructure, such as the directory name lookup cache (or DNLC), can be shared among zones to minimize overheads.

6.10.2 Solaris Resource Management Interactions

The resource management features in Solaris and their interactions with zones are summarized below.

6.10.2.1 Accounting

The traditional accounting system uses a fixed record size and cannot be extended to differentiate between a process running in the global zone and a non-global zone. We have modified the system such that accounting records generated in any (including the global) zone contain only records pertinent to the zone in which the process executed.

The extended accounting subsystem is virtualized to permit different accounting settings and files on a per-zone basis for process- and task-based accounting. Since `exacct` records are extensible, they can be tagged with a zone name (`EXD_PROC_ZONENAME` and `EXD_TASK_ZONENAME`, for processes and tasks, respectively), allowing the global administrator to determine resource consumption per-zone. Accounting records are written to the global zone's accounting files as well as to their per-zone counterparts. The `EXD_TASK_HOSTNAME`, `EXD_PROC_HOSTNAME`, and `EXD_HOSTNAME` records contain the `uname -n` value for the zone in which the process/task executed,[7] rather than the global zone's node name.

6.10.2.2 Projects, Resource Controls, and the Fair-Share Scheduler

Projects are abstracted such that different zones may use separate `project(4)` databases, each with its own set of defined projects and resource controls. Projects running in different zones with the same project ID are considered distinct by the kernel, eliminating the possibility of cross-zone interference and allowing projects running in different zones (with the same project ID) to have different resource controls.

To prevent processes in a zone from monopolizing the system, zonewide limits for applicable resources limit the total resource usage of all process entities within a zone (regardless of project). The global administrator can specify these limits in the zonecfg configuration file.[8] Privileged zone-wide rctls can be set only by superuser in the global zone.

Some of the zonewide rctls include `zone.cpu-shares`, which is the top-level number of FSS shares allocated to the zone. CPU shares are thus first allocated to zones, and then further subdivided among projects within the zone (based on the zone's `project(4)` database). In other words, `project.cpu-shares` is now relative to the zone's `zone.cpu-shares`. Projects in a zone multiplex the shares allocated to the zone; in this way, FSS share allocation in a zone can be thought of as a two-level hierarchy.

---

7. Tasks may not span zones.
8. The exact interface for specifying the limits has not yet been determined.

6.10.2.3 Resource Pools

Resource pools are controlled by an attribute in the zone configuration, `zone.pool`, similar to `project.pool`. The zone as a whole is bound to this pool upon creation, and it can enforce this binding in the kernel, as well as limit the visibility of resources not in the resource pool.

Non-global zones must be bound to resource pools in their entirety; that is, attempting to bind individual processes, tasks, or projects in a non-global zone to a resource pool will fail. This allows the virtualization of pools such that the pool device only reports information about the particular pool that the zone is bound to.

`poolstat(1M)` will thus reveal information only about the resources with which the zone's pool is associated.

6.10.3 Kstats

The kstat framework is used extensively for applications monitoring the system's performance including `mpstat(1M)`, `vmstat(1M)`, `iostat(1M)`, and `kstat(1M)`. Unlike traditional Solaris systems, the values reported in a particular kstat may not be relevant (or accurate) in non-global zones.

When executing in a zone and if the pools facility is active, `mpstat(1M)` will only provide information for those processors which are a member of the processor set of the pool to which the zone is bound.

The `vmstat`, `mpstat` style commands show you activity for the whole system, unless you are using pools and processor sets for the zones, in which case these kstat commands will provide some zone specific information. This is because kstat isn't zone aware yet, but it is CPU aware.

Statistics fall into one of the following categories as far as zones are concerned:

- Those that report information on the system as a whole and should be exported to all zones. Most kstats currently fall under this category. Examples include `kmem_cache` statistics.

- Those that should be virtualized. These kstats have the same module: instance:name:class but export different values depending on which zone is viewing them. Examples include `unix:0:rpc_client` and a number of other kstats consumed by `nfsstat(1M)` that should report virtualized statistics since the subsystems they represent have been virtualized.

- Those that "belong" to a particular zone and should only be exported to the zone to which they belong (and in some cases, the global zone as well). `nfs:*:mntinfo` is a good example of this category since zone A should not be exported information about the NFS mounts in zone B.

The kstat framework has been extended with new interfaces to specify (at creation time) which of the above classes a particular statistic belongs to.

6.10.3.1 Zone Observability via `prstat -Z`

The -Z option of `prstat` provides a summary per Zone.If run from the global zone, a summary of all zones is visible.

```
$ prstat -Z
   PID USERNAME  SIZE   RSS STATE  PRI NICE      TIME  CPU PROCESS/NLWP
 21132 root     2952K 2692K cpu0    49    0   0:00:00 0.1% prstat/1
 21109 root     7856K 2052K sleep   59    0   0:00:00 0.0% sshd/1
  2179 root     4952K 2480K sleep   59    0   0:00:21 0.0% automountd/3
 21111 root     1200K  952K sleep   49    0   0:00:00 0.0% ksh/1
  2236 root     4852K 2368K sleep   59    0   0:00:06 0.0% automountd/3
  2028 root     4912K 2428K sleep   59    0   0:00:10 0.0% automountd/3
   118 root     3372K 2372K sleep   59    0   0:00:06 0.0% nscd/24

ZONEID    NPROC  SIZE   RSS MEMORY      TIME  CPU ZONE
     0       47  177M  104M    11%   0:00:31 0.1% global
     5       33  302M  244M    25%   0:01:12 0.0% gallery
     3       40  161M   91M   9.2%   0:00:40 0.0% nakos
     4       43  171M   94M   9.5%   0:00:44 0.0% mcdougallfamily
     2       30   96M   56M   5.6%   0:00:23 0.0% shared
     1       32  113M   60M   6.0%   0:00:45 0.0% packer
     7       43  203M   87M   8.7%   0:00:55 0.0% si
Total: 336 processes, 1202 lwps, load averages: 0.02, 0.01, 0.01
```

6.10.3.2 DTrace

DTrace has special variables that can provide zone context. In the following example, we can easily discover which zone is causing the most page faults to occur.

```
# dtrace -n 'vminfo:::as_fault {@[zonename]=count()}'
dtrace: description 'vminfo:::as_fault' matched 1 probe
^C
global 4303
lisa 29867

global# dtrace -qn 'proc:::exec-success { printf("%-16s %s\n", zonename, curpsinfo->pr_
psargs); }'
global           zlogin myzone init 0
myzone           /usr/bin/su root -c init 0
myzone           sh -c init 0
myzone           init 0
myzone           sh -c /usr/sbin/audit -t
myzone           /usr/sbin/audit -t
myzone           /sbin/sh /sbin/rc0 stop
myzone           /usr/bin/who -r
myzone           /usr/bin/uname -a
myzone           /lib/svc/bin/lsvcrun /etc/rc0.d/K03samba stop
myzone           /bin/sh /etc/rc0.d/K03samba stop
myzone           pkill smbd
myzone           pkill nmbd
```

continues

```
myzone          /lib/svc/bin/lsvcrun /etc/rc0.d/K05appserv stop
myzone          /bin/sh /etc/rc0.d/K05appserv stop
myzone          /lib/svc/bin/lsvcrun /etc/rc0.d/K05volmgt stop
myzone          /bin/sh /etc/rc0.d/K05volmgt stop
myzone          /sbin/zonename
...
```

For an example of how the zonename can be used, see zvmstat from the DTrace-Toolkit (see Section 6.3.3 in *Solaris™ Performance and Tools*).

6.11 MDB Reference

Table 6.4 MDB Reference for Zones

dcmd or walker	Description
dcmd zone	Display kernel zone(s)
dcmd zsd	Lookup zsd value from a key
walk zone	Walk a list of kernel zones
walk zsd	Walk list of zsd entries for a zone

Projects, Tasks, and Resource Controls

Contributions by Stephen Hahn

T his chapter introduces concepts new to Solaris: projects and tasks, which are used to manage workloads.

7.1 Projects and Tasks Framework

In this section, we describe the central administration objects that are used for resource management, observability and accounting in Solaris.

7.1.1 Introduction

The *project* and *task* entities are used in Solaris to describe workloads, which consist of a set of related processes. Processes are grouped into tasks, tasks are a member of a project. Projects and tasks are used to control and observe the resources of a workload. Some of the key uses for the Project and Tasks in Solaris are:

- They provide an attachment point in the basic administrative model for controlling resources. Various system facilities including the Solaris resource manager fair share scheduler (See Section 3.7.3.3), the IP Quality of Service (IPQOS) and the Resource Pools infrastucture. This provides a unification of implementation aspects of the various forms resource management within the Solaris operating environment. For example, if want to limit a workload consisting of a group of processes to be entitled to at least 50% of the CPU resources on the system, we would define a project for that workload, and then configure the resource manager allow the specified resource entitlement within that project.

- As an entity to observe and record the resource consumption of a workload. For example, we wanted to report the total CPU consumption of all of the proceses in a workload, we could use prstat to display resource utilization on a per-project basis, using `prstat -J`.

- To meter and enforce resource limits across sub-components or all of a workload. For example, if we wanted to limit the maximum amount of shared memory resources that a workload can allocate, then we could set a per-project *resource limit* on that resource.

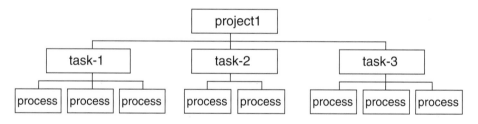

Figure 7.1 Projects and Tasks Hierarchy

7.1.2 Projects

The *project* participates in the administrative model at a level equivalent to a user or group ID. A user who is a member of more than one project can run processes in multiple projects at the same time. All processes that are started by a process inherit the project of the parent process. When you switch to a new project in a startup script, all child processes run in the new project.

An executing user process has an associated user identity (uid), group identity (gid), and project identity (projid). Process attributes and abilities are inherited from the user, group, and project identities to form the execution context for a task.

7.1.3 Tasks

A *task* is a group of related processes associated with a project. Processes inherit their project and task identifiers across fork(2) and exec(2); a new task is created when a new project identifier is bound to a process. Resource consumption by a task is charged to a project. The resources tracked by the accounting system are configurable systemwide.

The project acts as a source of resources to be made available to that same collection of related work, allowing resource controls and limits to be set for each task. Section 7.5.

Tasks are formally distinct from sessions (see `setsid(2)`) so as to avoid unnecessarily contaminating the semantics of tasks with the semantics of terminals. A new task is created for each login session when the user's project is bound to the user's login shell. Within a login session, the project ID can be changed with the `newtask(1)` utility. This command can also be used to run applications against different projects in the same session while preserving full shell task control semantics for the invoking shell.

7.1.4 Why We Added Tasks to Solaris

The basic requirements for tasks stem from the associated accounting capabilities: the actions of a task must be accountable, and the set of actions must be equivalent to the typical actions performed during an interactive login or a queue submission. Furthermore, an interactive user must be able to switch projects during his login session. There were two viable process aggregates in standard UNIX implementations: process groups and sessions:

- Process groups are not a valid solution, since every pipeline forms a new process group. Tasks include pipelines as well as other commands in a given sequence, so process groups aren't semantically large enough to accommodate the definition of a task.

- The POSIX session is large enough to contain the accountability attributes of a task, but its additional property of an associated controlling terminal prevents it from supporting the ability to switch projects (or charge codes) during an interactive login. The following limitations on a session-based approach:
  - Multiple sessions cannot share a terminal without an intermediary.
  - `newtask`, as an intermediary, would need to pass through all task control signals, including SIGKILL, to its children.
  - `newtask` cannot protect stdin and stdout from the other competing sessions. More succinctly, a controlling terminal cannot sensibly be shared by two sessions.

For these reasons, and to avoid any compatibility complications from changes to the POSIX session definition, the task is introduced as an unencumbered entity to represent a distinct family of related processes in Solaris.

7.2 The Project Database

The /etc/project project file is the heart of workload hierarchy. The project database is maintained on a system through the /etc/project file or over the network through a naming service, such as NIS or LDAP.

The /etc/project file contains five standard projects:

Table 7.1 Standard Projects in /etc/project

Project	Description
system	This project is used for all system processes and daemons.
user.root	All root processes run in the user.root project.
noproject	This special project is for IPQoS.
default	A default project is assigned to every user.
group.staff	This project is used for all users in the group staff.

The /etc/projects file is represented by the following structure:

```
struct project {
        char    *pj_name;        /* name of the project */
        projid_t pj_projid;      /* numerical project id */
        char    *pj_comment;     /* project description */
        char    **pj_users;      /* vector of pointers to project user names */
        char    **pj_groups;     /* vector of pointers to project group names */
        char    *pj_attr;        /* project attributes string */
};
                                                            See project.h
```

The project structure members include the following:

- **pj_name.** Name of the project.
- **pj_projid.** Project ID.
- **pj_comment.** User-supplied project description.
- **pj_users.** Pointers to project user members.
- **pj_groups.** Pointers to project group members.
- **pj_attr.** Project attributes. Use these attributes to set values for resource controls and project pools.

Through project attributes, the resource usage can be controlled. Four prefixes are used to group the types of resource control attributes:

- **`project.*`**. This prefix denotes attributes that are used to control projects. For example, project.max-device-locked-memory indicates the total amount of locked memory allowed, expressed as a number of bytes. The project.pool attributes binds a project to a resource pool.

- **`task.*`**. This prefix is used for attributes that are applied to tasks. For example, the task.max-cpu-time attribute sets the maximum CPU time that is available to this task's processes, expressed as a number of seconds.

- **`process.*`**. This prefix is used for process controls. For example, the process.max-file-size control sets the maximum file offset that is available for writing by this process, expressed as a number of bytes.

- **`zone.*`**. The zone.* prefix is applied to projects, tasks, and processes in a zone. For example, zone.max-lwps prevents too many LWPs in one zone from affecting other zones. A zone's total LWPs can be further subdivided among projects within the zone within the zone by using project.max-lwps entries.

A full list of resource controls can be found in `resource_controls(5)`.

7.3 Project and Task APIs

7.3.1 Interfaces for Projects and Tasks

In this section, we discuss them and then look at those kernel components that must be modified to support the new model. We then discuss the project database and the `libexacct` accounting file library. Finally, we consider new commands to access the new functionality, and modifications to existing commands to support it. The following functions are provided to interface with projects. The functions use entries that describe user projects in the project database.

Table 7.2 Interfaces for Projects and Tasks

Interface Name	Description
`endprojent(3PROJECT)`	Close the project database and deallocate resources when processing is complete.
`fgetprojent(3PROJECT)`	Returns a pointer to a structure containing an entry in the project database. Rather than using nsswitch.conf, fgetprojent() reads a line from a stream.

continues

Table 7.2 Interfaces for Projects and Tasks (*continued*)

Interface Name	Description
getdefaultproj(3PROJECT)	Check the validity of the project keyword, look up the project, and return a pointer to the project structure if found.
getprojbyid(3PROJECT)	Search the project database for an entry with the number that specifies the project ID.
getprojbyname(3PROJECT)	Search the project database for an entry with the string that specifies project name.
getprojent(3PROJECT)	Returns a pointer to a structure containing an entry in the project database.
inproj(3PROJECT)	Check whether the specified user is permitted to use the specified project.
setproject(3PROJECT)	Add a user process to a project.
setprojent(3PROJECT)	Rewind the project database to allow repeated searches.

7.4 Kernel Infrastructure for Projects and Tasks

Several new data types and system calls were added for projects and tasks.

7.4.0.1 Project and Task System Calls

New id_t equivalent types distinguish task and project associations within the kernel as well as interfaces that can determine these attributes for a process.

```
typedef id_t    taskid_t;
typedef id_t    projid_t;

/*
 *      The following defines the values for an identifier type.  It
 *      specifies the interpretation of an id value.  An idtype and
 *      id together define a simple set of processes.
 */
typedef enum {
        P_PID,          /* A process identifier.                 */
        P_PPID,         /* A parent process identifier.          */
        P_PGID,         /* A process group (job control group)   */
...
        P_TASKID,       /* A task identifier.                    */
        P_PROJID,       /* A project identifier.                 */
...
} idtype_t;

                                                     See sys/procset.h
```

The `settaskid(2)` system call causes the calling process to be associated with the project identifier `projid`. The new task identifier that results from a successful change of project is returned to the caller. The task identifier returned is allocated from an ID space independently of the space used for process identifiers. You can issue `settaskid()` with the `TASK_FINAL`.

The `getprojid(2)` system call returns the project ID associated with the current process. The `gettaskid(2)` system call returns the task ID associated with the current process.

7.4.1 System Call Interaction with Projects

Certain system calls have additional code that implement the new administrative model. The `fork(2)` and `exec(2)` family of routines ensure that the `task_id` and `project_id` are inherited across these operations. The `exit(2)` system call writes extended process accounting records, as well as to update the task accounting information on process termination. Extensions to the implementation of `sigsend(2)` and `sigsendset(2)` allow signals to be sent to tasks; no additional privilege is granted over that available for existing processes to execute `kill(2)` on one another.

Extensions to the implementation of `priocntl(2)`, `pset_bind(2)`, and `processor_bind(2)` allow the `idtype` argument to be set to `P_TASKID` so that the function applies to all lightweight processes (LWPs) currently associated with processes in the specified task.

7.4.2 `proc(4)`

The `task_id` and project memberships are visible through the `proc(4)` file system, via the the `psinfo` file. It can be read without any special permission, as with the other identifiers for the process: the parent process ID, the process group leader, the session ID, etc. This allows allow `ps(1)` to report a process's task membership while remaining an unprivileged executable.

7.4.3 In-Kernel Project Data Structures

A dictionary of all active projects is maintained by the kernel so that we may track project usage and limits. (By an active project, we mean a project associated with one or more tasks, and therefore with one or more processes.) The dictionary is built on top of the mod_hash facility, based on the assumption that project additions and deletions are relatively rare events. An integer-to-pointer mapping is maintained within the hash, representing the map from project id to project structure. All projects, including the primordial "project 0", are allocated via the `project_hold_by_id()` interface.

```
typedef struct kproject_data {          /* Datum protected by: */
        rctl_qty_t      kpd_shmmax;      /* shm's ipcs_lock */
        rctl_qty_t      kpd_shmmni;      /* shm's ipcs_lock */
        rctl_qty_t      kpd_semmni;      /* sem's ipcs_lock */
        rctl_qty_t      kpd_msgmni;      /* msg's ipcs_lock */
        rctl_qty_t      kpd_devlockmem; /* umem_devlockmem_rctl_lock */
        rctl_qty_t      kpd_contract;    /* contract_lock */
        rctl_qty_t      kpd_crypto_mem; /* crypto_rctl_lock */
} kproject_data_t;

/*
 * The first two fields of this structure must not be reordered.
 */
typedef struct kproject {
        projid_t        kpj_id;          /* project ID          */
        zoneid_t        kpj_zoneid;      /* zone ID             */
        uint_t          kpj_count;       /* reference counter   */
        uint32_t        kpj_shares;      /* number of shares    */
        rctl_set_t      *kpj_rctls;      /* resource control set */
        struct kproject *kpj_prev;       /* previous project    */
        struct kproject *kpj_next;       /* next project        */
        kproject_data_t kpj_data;        /* subsystem-specfic data */
        kmutex_t        kpj_poolbind;    /* synch. with pools   */
        rctl_qty_t      kpj_nlwps;       /* protected by project's zone's */
                                         /* zone_nlwps_lock */
        rctl_qty_t      kpj_nlwps_ctl;  /* protected by kpj_rctls->rcs_lock */
        rctl_qty_t      kpj_ntasks;      /* protected by project's zone's */
                                         /* zone_nlwps_lock */
        rctl_qty_t      kpj_ntasks_ctl; /* protected by kpj_rctls->rcs_lock */
} kproject_t;
```

See sys/project.h

Currently, the project contains a reference count; the project ID, which is examined by the extended accounting subsystem as well as /proc; a resource control set, which contains the allowable values (and actions on exceeding those values) for controlled project-level resources on the system; and a number of CPU shares, which is used by the fair share scheduling class (FSS) to support its proportion-based scheduling algorithm.

There is a mdb(1) dcmd and walker for projects:

```
> ::project
    ADDR PROJID ZONEID REFCNT
d9ada680      0      0    455
d5b2fa00      0      1    167
d5b2f380      0      2    150
d692fec0      0      3    163
d692fe40      0      4    175
d5b2f680      0      5    175
d5b2f600      0      6    176
d5b2f580      0      7    183
d5b2f500      0      8    197
d87a3840     10      7      4
d8bc17c0      1      1      5
dc6a4bc0     10      3      5
db34c040      3      0      5
```

continues

```
> ::walk projects
d9ada680
d5b2fa00
d5b2f380
d692fec0
d692fe40
d5b2f680
d5b2f600
d5b2f580
d5b2f500
d87a3840
d8bc17c0
dc6a4bc0
db34c040
```

7.4.3.1 Reference Counting Convention

The dictionary entry does not itself count as a reference--only references outside of the subsystem are tallied. At the drop of the final external reference, the project entry is removed. The reference counter keeps track of the number of threads *and* tasks within a project.

7.4.3.2 Locking

Walking the doubly-linked project list must be done while holding projects_list_ lock. Thus, any dereference of `kpj_next` or `kpj_prev` must be under `projects_ list_lock`.

If both the hash lock, `project_hash_lock`, and the list lock are to be acquired, the hash lock is to be acquired first.

7.5 Resource Controls

This section describes the extensible resource control framework, first introduced in Solaris 9. It leverages the project database introduced in Section 7.1 allowing the implementation of a network-wide static resource policy. Several new interfaces are introduced to enumerate, set, and get controls on processes, tasks, and projects; these interfaces could potentially be applied to other system entities. Additional interfaces simplify interaction with active projects.

We discuss the facility for resource controls, including the ability to control the number of LWPs in a task. The policy source for the various controls of a given process, task, or project shall reside in the project database introduced by Projects and Tasks, although a new API allows subsequent modification of those controls on the current OS instance. (The primordial policy source, in the absence of attribute definitions in the project database, is the set of operating system defaults.)

7.5.1 Introduction to Resource Controls

The resource controls framework permits applications to set the values of resource controls advertised by various kernel subsystems. Invalid control settings are ignored, with an error code returned. The controls framework—called `rctl`—is designed to be flexible. It is applied here to the existing process `rlimit`. It is able to encapsulate the apparently defunct POSIX draft standard for process and session limits if that draft is reactivated. (As the task is a Solaris-specific extension, no existing task limit standards are known or anticipated.)

Initially, a small set of resource controls are implemented:

- CPU seconds per task
- number of LWPs per task

The existing process limits are made available through the `rctl` interface:

- CPU seconds per process
- Maximum file size
- Data size for this process
- Stack size for this process
- Core file size for this process
- Number of file descriptors per process
- Maximum mapped memory per process

Many other Solaris facilities leverage the resource control infrastructure, including these:

- The fair-share scheduler (FSS), which also uses a set of project-based resource controls associating some number of CPU shares with a project
- The System V message parameters
- Event ports
- The Cryptographic framework

7.5.2 What Is an `rctl`?

The resource control framework generalizes the `rlimit`-process relationship to a resource control-entity relationship. In this sense, a resource control is some amount of information associated with the entity pertinent to resource management operations. The kernel subsystem publishing the resource control can associate default actions to be taken at various thresholds of the resource usage; these actions can be modified or new actions (on new thresholds) can be introduced by the user process or by the administrator.

Resource controls are an extension of the basic rlimit concept. Infinite values are supported by a separate flag bit and do not contaminate the numeric values available for a resource. The hard/soft limit approach is also extended, to distinguish an administratively established maximum from absolute constraint from the operating system. And, as noted earlier, resource controls could potentially be applied to abstractions other than the process—in this document, resource limits are attached to tasks and projects.

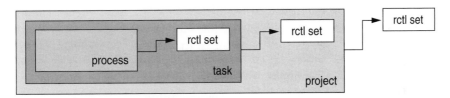

Figure 7.2 Process Collectives and Resource Control Sets

Resource controls are flexible, in that controls for which the subsystem associates no actions act as subsystem-specific attributes. The subsystem has then associated one or more named integers with the entity and offers no operations other than set or get operations on the value of the integer. An example resource control used primarily as an attribute would be the number of CPU shares associated with a project, or a priority associated with a task (for arbitration between two tasks contesting over a finite resource). Because of implementation restrictions, certain resource controls may not support all possible actions offered by the framework. In particular, the legacy rlimits may have restrictions on available actions. These limitations are usually expressed through the global flag values on a resource control.

Multiple resource controls can exist on a resource, one at each container level in the process model. For instance, CPU time limits are enforced on both the process and the task. The general statement of enforcement, in the case that resource controls on the same resource would be active with a resource allocation, is that the smallest container's control is enforced first. Thus, `process.max-cpu-time`'s action would be taken before `task.max-cpu-time`'s action if they were simultaneously encountered. (In the case of signals, this behavior may not be realized at the recipient process if the signal's implementation reorders the delivery of the resultant signals.)

7.5.3 Numeric Values of Resource Controls

Although resource controls represent an opportunity to associate arbitrary data with one or more kernel entities, we strongly restrict that to 64-bit unsigned integer data (in the form of an `rctl_qty_t`). In particular, we exclude floating-point data out of hand and discourage use of percentages as values within the resource management framework. Infinite values (those not being enforced) are marked by a flag bit, keeping the infinity concept separate from the range of valid values.

7.5.4 Resource Control Definitions

The resource controls facility provides a reasonably rich interface to describe controlled quantities. Implementation restrictions prevent all controls from having identical properties and, as a result, we require descriptive constants to distinguish the various restrictions and properties on controls and control values. Table 7.3 summarizes the key constant values; more complete specifications are given in the manual pages and in relevant parts of the technical discussion. A summary of defined constants for resource control facility is shown in Table 7.4 and Table 7.6.

Table 7.3 Privilege Levels of Resource Control Values

Privilege Name	Description
RCPRIV_BASIC	Can be modified by the owner of the calling process.
RCPRIV_PRIVILEGED	Value requires privilege to modify action; value can be lowered if global flag is set RCPRIV_SYSTEM.
RCPRIV_SYSTEM	Value cannot be modified.

Table 7.4 Operational Flags for `setrctl(2)` and `getrctl(2)`

Operational Flag	Description
RCTL_DELETE	Passed to `setrctl(2)` to remove given resource control value.
RCTL_FIRST	Passed to `getrctl(2)` to retrieve first defined value on given resource control.
RCTL_INSERT	Passed to `setrctl(2)` to insert given resource control value in value sequence.

continues

Table 7.4 Operational Flags for `setrctl(2)` and `getrctl(2)` (*continued*)

Operational Flag	Description
RCTL_NEXT	Passed to `getrctl(2)` to retrieve next defined value in value sequence following the given resource control value.
RCTL_REPLACE	Passed to `setrctl(2)` to replace the first given resource value with the second given resource control value.
RCTL_USAGE	Passed to `getrctl(2)` to get current usage of the specific resource control by the calling process.

Table 7.5 Global Resource Control Properties and Actions

Global Resource Control	Description
RCTL_GLOBAL_DENY_ALWAYS	The action taken when a control value is exceeded on this control will always include denial of the resource.
RCTL_GLOBAL_DENY_NEVER	The action taken when a control value is exceeded on this control will always exclude denial of the resource; the resource will always be granted, although other actions may also be taken.
RCTL_GLOBAL_CPU_TIME	The valid signals available as local actions include the `SIGXCPU` signal.
RCTL_GLOBAL_FILE_SIZE	The valid signals available as local actions include the `SIGXFSZ` signal.
RCTL_GLOBAL_INFINITE	This resource control supports the concept of an unlimited value; generally true only of accumulation-oriented resources such as CPU time.
RCTL_GLOBAL_LOWERABLE	Nonprivileged callers are able to lower the value of privileged resource control values on this control.
RCTL_GLOBAL_NOACTION	No global action will be taken when a resource control value is exceeded on this control.
RCTL_GLOBAL_NOBASIC	No values with the `RCPRIV_BASIC` privilege are permitted on this control.
RCTL_GLOBAL_NOLOCALACTION	No local actions (deny or signals, presently) are permitted on this control.

continues

Table 7.5 Global Resource Control Properties and Actions (*continued*)

Global Resource Control	Description
RCTL_GLOBAL_SYSLOG	The defined message will be logged by the `syslog` facility when any resource control value on a sequence associated with this control is exceeded.
RCTL_GLOBAL_UNOBSERVABLE	The resource control (generally on a task- or project-related control) does not support observational control values: as `RCPRIV_BASIC` privileged control value placed by a process on the task or process will only generate an action if the value is exceeded by that process.

Table 7.6 Local (Value-Specific) Resource Control Properties and Actions

Local Resource Control	Description
RCTL_LOCAL_DENY	When this resource control value is encountered, the request for the resource will be denied. Set on all values if `RCTL_GLOBAL_DENY_ALWAYS` is set for this control; cleared on all values if `RCTL_GLOBAL_DENY_NEVER` is set for this control.
RCTL_LOCAL_MAXIMAL	This resource control value represents a request for the maximal amount of resource for this control; in the case that `RCTL_GLOBAL_INFINITE` is set for this resource control, then `RCTL_LOCAL_MAXIMAL` indicates an unlimited resource control value-one that will never be exceeded.
RCTL_LOCAL_NOACTION	No local action will be taken when this resource control value is exceeded.
RCTL_LOCAL_SIGNAL	The specified signal, set with `rctlblk_set_local_action(3C)`, will be sent to the process that placed this resource control value in the value sequence.

7.5.5 Policy

The resource controls facility enables one aspect of simple resource management policy: static controls on process model abstractions. Furthermore, it is a natural mechanism for placing importance or priority attributes on these abstractions—these attributes can then be used to implement more dynamic resource management policies (which can usually be viewed as scheduling algorithms). These forms of policies can be contrasted with those involving system-level abstractions, such as processor set sizes or interrupt binding assignments (which can also be made statically or dynamically). Aspects of this facility help provide an interface between the process model abstractions and those of the system.

The policy simplification that this framework affords is that administrative concentration of some resource management constraints can now be seated in a networkwide name service. Furthermore, the `rctl` facility enables both systemwide and entity-specific monitoring of events related to increasing resource usage, which is meant to assist the administrator in estimating capacity requirements and workload sizes.

As with the CPU second variance noted in Section 7.5.3, machine-specific attributes probably should not be resource controls nor should they appear in a name-service database akin to the project, since these databases provide replies indiscriminate of the machine making the request. There is a further need for a name service capable of distinct replies to distinguishable machines; the grammar for the project attributes does not preclude a node-specific enhancement if a standard name service of this kind does not emerge.

7.5.6 Consequences of Exceeding an `rctl`

The use of a given resource by a given entity can be evaluated at the time of a request for additional units of that resource (a synchronous test) or at an arbitrary time (an asynchronous test). In the case of a synchronous test, the resource request can be denied or permitted; in both cases, a signal can be sent to the violating process (or a process that is a member of the violating entity) or a system message can be logged.

That is, there is a set of actions that resource limit violation can result in:

- A signal sent to triggered or monitoring process, set with the `setrctl(2)` system call
- A message through `syslogd(1M)`, activated or deactivated with the `rctladm(1M)` command.

A self-monitoring process can use the delivered signal to trigger garbage collection, or some other release of resources, and then reattempt the potentially failed operation as necessary. External daemons can then monitor syslog output or express explicit interest in individual tasks.

A control with the `RCTL_LOCAL_DENY` flag set, in addition to any action taken, will refuse the resource to the requesting process when the implementation permits it. (For instance, in the current implementation, a CPU second cannot be denied, in that its use is evaluated after the period of its grant.) Thus, a resource control value with RCTL_LOCAL_DENY set will be activated each time a request for the controlled resource is made.

Although local and global actions are currently simply signals or syslog messages, respectively, as the system event interfaces mature, we expect supporting standard system events on both a local and global basis for exceeded rctls. System events, with their well-defined structure, forthcoming subscription model, and support for multiple channels, will provide a much richer event vocabulary to management applications using resource controls for workload monitoring.

7.5.7 Signal and `siginfo` Semantics for Exceeded Controls

Many of the signals in the UNIX environment have precise semantics; we cannot offer a framework that allows any signal to be sent on the occasion of a resource control being exceeded. Certain signals are reserved very specifically to one behavior; the behavior associated with others is more open to interpretation. We simplify by allowing only the signals listed below.

- SIGABRT
- SIGHUP
- SIGSTOP
- SIGTERM
- SIGKILL

The new signal SIGXRES is used specifically within the resource control framework, with the clear semantic that "a resource control value has been exceeded." Additional information will be available from the siginfo code and accompanying structure, as discussed below.

Two global flags are defined to enable certain controls to use the historical resource limit signals SIGXFSZ and SIGXCPU. In particular, task.max-cpu-time and process.max-cpu-time will have RCTL_GLOBAL_CPU_TIME set, while process.max-file-size will have the global flag RCTL_GLOBAL_FILE_SIZE set.

The second issue is that we cannot easily distinguish between two resource control values sending identical signals. We provide the rctlblk_get_firing_time(3C) function, which allows the ultimate discrimination of all values across the resource controls associated with process and those of the task and project of which the process is a member. However, we can simplify this determination considerably if we can identify whether the triggering value was associated with the process or with its containers. For this purpose, a new siginfo code, SI_RCTL and a new union within the siginfo make this identification directly. Two members for

this union, si entity, contain the container type holding this resource control as an
`rctl_entity_t`, as defined below.

```
typedef enum {
        RCENTITY_PROCESS,
        RCENTITY_TASK,
        RCENTITY_PROJECT,
        RCENTITY_ZONE
} rctl_entity_t;
```

With the firing time identifying the most recent tripped value, the received signal, and the entity type, resolution of which exact control and control value were
triggered is straightforward.

7.5.8 Generalizing Hard and Soft Limits

The hard/soft `rlimit` interface implies a simple capability model on rlimits: a nonprivileged user can modify the soft limit up to the value defined by the hard limit
and can lower the hard limit. Only a root-privileged user can raise the hard limit.

The capability matrix defined by rlimits is not complete: not all hard limit settings are actually sustainable by the operating system. (For instance, the current
file descriptor limit cannot be set to INT64_MAX.) Thus, one further extension, to
allow the description of an operating system limit, is needed. This framework
includes three classes of limit:

- **Basic.** Writable by an unprivileged application
- **Privileged.** Writable only by a privileged application
- **System.** Established by the operating system instance and is not writable

The quantity for a given system value can be a calculated value for the given
system size, but is more likely to be a theoretical maximum from the underlying
implementation or the defining type. System limits cannot be changed. Because
multiple basic limits can be placed on rctls associated with process collectives (by
monitoring processes), the only ordering statement that can be made is that all
limits on an `rctl` must be less than the system limit on that `rctl`.

7.5.9 Resource Controls and the Task

Resource controls provide enforceable limits on each task. These task limits are
defined in the project database, although they can also be set explicitly. In general,
task limits are available for fewer attributes than process limits, since not all process
attributes are sensible over the entire task. (Limiting aggregate stack size, for instance,

does not seem particularly useful.) The enforced limit for each resource is the smallest of the set of `rctl` values not yet encountered on that resource, although signal delivery is only to the observing process in the case of controls on collectives.

The current behavior of resource control values being exceeded on the task or on any process collective is that the resource control values on the task of type `RCPRIV_PRIVILEGED` or `RCPRIV_SYSTEM` deliver their local action to the violating process, whereas `RCPRIV_BASIC` type values deliver their local action to the process placing the resource control value on the task.

7.5.10 Visibility through `/proc`; Privileges and Ownership

The principle behind the representation of the process model via `/proc` is that the entirety of the process state is retrievable by a debugger. This principle can be satisfied for the process's local state, such as heap data or library static data, from accessing the appropriate parts of the process's address space in the as file. For kernel state, you can obtain the state visible to the process by forcing the victim process to execute the appropriate system call or calls through the agent LWP. With these two mechanisms, `/proc` and `libproc` present the entire environment of the process to a debugger.

The decision to provide a file entry in `/proc` is generally made for performance reasons—the series of calls into `libproc` to make the victim yield the desired information is measured to be too expensive for a specific, frequent operation.

Thus, and analogous to rlimits, the resource controls do not explicitly appear in a separate file in `/proc`. Furthermore, since we are trying to keep the properties of the resource control abstract, a `/proc` realization would present a conflicting technical requirement (in that the file would contain structural representations).

Three privilege levels are available for resource controls: `RCPRIV_BASIC`, `RCPRIV_PRIVILEGED`, and `RCPRIV_SYSTEM`. `RCPRIV_BASIC`, the properties of which are modifiable by any calling process, is analogous to the soft limit of resource limits. The hard limit is encapsulated by the `RCPRIV_PRIVILEGED`, which requires root privilege to insert, delete, or modify. The final privilege level for a resource control is `RCPRIV_SYSTEM`, which is not changeable by any process, privileged or otherwise.

7.6 Interfaces for Resource Controls

We first examine the project database entries required to support the resource control functionality for login (or project binding in general). Additionally, we give a grammar for the attribute field of the project database. We then define the new system calls required to support the `rctls` functionality.

7.6.1 Project Name-Service Attributes

The final field of the project database is defined as part of the projects and tasks infrastructure as an open-ended series of delimited name-value pairs. The resource control framework defines a collection of name-value pairs and defines rules for future attribute names in this space. The following collection of examples illustrate the convention.

The names of a name-value pair are restricted to letters, digits, the underscore, and the period, which is used as a separator between the categories and subcategories of the `rctl`. The first character of an attribute name must be a letter. The attribute name is case sensitive, following standard UNIX conventions.

The right-hand side of the assignment, being the value, can be structured with commas and parentheses (for precedence). Since a semicolon separates name-value pairs, it is not legal within a value definition. And since a colon separates project fields, it too is not legal within a value definition.

```
entity.structured.attr=alpha,(beta,gamma)
```

7.6.2 Attributes Originating within Solaris

The attribute namespace uses the form [*entity*] . [*control name*] to encode these limits. Valid entities are task, process, and project.

Solaris facilities using `rctls` must acquire valid control names from a governance body, which will own the `rctl` namespace. A listing of the valid resource controls available with the base operating system is presented in the manual page for `rctladm(1M)`.

7.6.3 Grammar for Attributes

A grammar restricting the attribute namespace is given below.

```
attribute list : attribute [ ; attribute list ]
attribute : name [ = structured value list ]
name : [ stock symbol , ] symbol character sequence
structured value list : value, structured value list
value : valid character sequence -- ( structured value list )
```

7.6.4 Interpretation of `rctl` Attributes

By default, the specification of a resource control in the project database as a simple key-value pair defines the privileged resource control and local action for the entity being constructed (through login/PAM or `setproject`). Thus,

```
task.max.lwps=(PRIVILEGED,32,signal=SIGXRES)
```

translates to a call of the form

```
rctlblk.t *blk = malloc(rctlblk.size());

...

rctlblk.set.privilege(blk, RCPRIV.PRIVILEGED);
rctlblk.set.local.action(blk, RCTL.LOCAL.SIGNAL, SIGXRES);
rctlblk.set.value(blk, 32);
if (setrctl("task.max.lwps", NULL, blk, RCTL.REPLACE) == -1 && errno == ESRCH) {
        if (setrctl("task.max-lwps", NULL, blk, RCTL.INSERT) == -1)
                /* log error message */
}
```

(If the SIGXRES specification and the parentheses were omitted, then the local action would be set to RCTL_LOCAL_NOACTION.)

To specify more general attributes, the project database allows the setting of a series of resource control values by connecting a set of triplets in a comma-separated list:

```
task.max-lwps=(BASIC,24,none),(PRIVILEGED,32,signal=SIGXRES,deny)
```

which translates to a call sequence of the form

```
/* allocate blk and blk2 */
rctlblk.set.privilege(blk, RCPRIV.BASIC);
rctlblk.set.local.action(blk, RCTL.LOCAL.NOACTION, 0);
rctlblk.set.value(blk, 24);
rctlblk.set.privilege(blk2, RCPRIV.PRIVILEGED);
rctlblk.set.local.action(blk2, RCTL.LOCAL.DENY -- RCTL.LOCAL.SIGNAL, SIGXRES);
rctlblk.set.value(blk2, 32);
if (setrctl("task.max.lwps", NULL, blk, RCTL.REPLACE) == -1 && errno == ESRCH) {

        if (setrctl("task.max-lwps", NULL, blk, RCTL.INSERT) == -1)

                /* log error message */
                ...

if (setrctl("task.max.lwps", NULL, blk2, RCTL.REPLACE) == -1 &&
                        errno == ESRCH) {

                if (setrctl("task.max-lwps", NULL, blk2, RCTL.INSERT) == -1)

                /* log error message */
                ...
```

The following is an example of a series of resource controls for `process.max-cpu-time`:

```
process.max-cpu-time=(PRIVILEGED,30,signal=SIGXCPU),
(PRIVILEGED,40,signal=SIGTERM),(PRIVILEGED,50,signal=SIGKILL)
```

In this example, the resource value is seconds of CPU time. By configuring three actions in this way, when a process exceeds 30 seconds of CPU time it is sent a SIGXCPU. If the process ignores that and continues to run, then after exceeding 40 seconds of CPU time it is sent a SIGTERM. At this point any sensible process should terminate. If it does continue to run, we resort to a SIGKILL after 50 seconds of CPU time.

```
# projadd -K 'process.max-cpu-time=(privileged,30,signal=SIGXCPU),'\
> '(privileged,40,signal=SIGTERM),(privileged,50,signal=SIGKILL)' cpulimit

# newtask -p cpulimit sh

# trap 'echo "got XCPU: \c"; date' XCPU

# trap 'echo "got TERM: \c"; date' TERM

# echo "Started : \c"; date; while :; do :; done
Started : Sat Feb 18 18:27:19 EST 2006
got XCPU: Sat Feb 18 18:27:49 EST 2006
got TERM: Sat Feb 18 18:27:59 EST 2006
Killed
```

7.6.5 An Example `/etc/project`

A simple example of a files-based project database is given below. Given the `/etc/group` file

```
sol9$ grep beatles /etc/group beatles::1000:paul,george,ringo
```

we can define a simple set of projects.

```
system:0::::
user.root:1::::
noproject:2::::
group.beatles:1000::::task.max-lwps=256
user.paul:2000::::task.max-lwps=512;process.max-core-size=0
user.george:2002::::process.max-cpu-seconds=1000
user.ringo:2003::::task.max-cpu-seconds=3000
```

Note that the absence of the default project prevents any of the defined users from escaping their default group or `group.beatles` to a project with greater resources.

7.6.6 System Calls and Private Kernel Interfaces

The `setrctl(2)`, `getrctl(2)`, `setrctl(2)`, and `getrctl(2)` system calls allow the values on rctls for various entities in the system to be established or retrieved. Because of the variable number of resource control values, these system calls use an opaque structure, the resource control block whose members are set with the `rctlblk` routines of "rctlblk Manipulation Routines" on the next page and provide an iteration-based interface.

Private subcodes on the `rctlsys` system call will enable the `rctladm(1M)` command and the `rctl_walk(3C)` library function described below. A similar private subcode on the task or project system call enables the `project_walk(3PROJECT)` function. All the `rctl` registration and implementation functions internal to the kernel are Consolidation Private.

7.6.7 Library Functions

Five library functions are described in this section: `setproject`, `project_walk`, `rctl_walk`, `getproject`, and `rctlblk_size`.

Table 7.7 Library Functions for `rctls`

Interface	Description
setproject(3PROJECT)	setproject() provides a simplified interface to bind the current process to the specified project with all pertinent rctl settings as recorded in the project database. Invocation of setproject() includes a call to settaskid(2), implying that the calling process must possess root privilege for the operation to succeed.
project_walk(3PROJECT)	The project_walk() function provides a mechanism for an application to visit, with a callback function provided by the application, each project active on the system.
rctl_walk(3C)	The rctl_walk() function allows the application to have a callback function invoked for each active resource control on the system.

continues

Table 7.7 Library Functions for `rctls` (*continued*)

Interface	Description
The `getproject()` Derived Family of Library Calls	The following calls already support the attributes field of the project database: • `getproject(3PROJECT)` • `fgetproject(3PROJECT)` • `getprojbyname(3PROJECT)` • `getprojbyid(3PROJECT)` • `getdefaultproj(3PROJECT)` The key-value pair management functions of `libsecdb(3LIB)` can be used to manipulate the field after a project entry is retrieved. The name service calls themselves are not modified by this project.
`rctlblk` Manipulation Routines	These interfaces are provided to keep the contents and layout of the resource control block opaque. A sizing routine, `rctlblk_size(3C)`, is provided so that applications will maintain binary compatibility in the face of enhancements to the resource control block.

7.7 Kernel Interfaces for Resource Controls

The `rctl` subsystem provides a mechanism for kernel components to register their individual resource controls with the system as a whole, such that those controls can subscribe to specific actions while being associated with the various process-model entities provided by the kernel: process, task, project, and zone. (In principle, only minor modifications would be required to connect the resource control functionality to non-process-model entities associated with the system.)

Subsystems register their rctls with `rctl_register()`. Subsystems also wishing to provide additional limits on a given `rctl` can modify them once they have the `rctl` handle. Each subsystem should store the handle to its `rctl` for direct access.

A primary dictionary, `rctl_dict`, contains a hash of the ID to the default control definition for each controlled resource-entity pair on the system. The `::rctl_dict` dcmd can be used to walk the resource dictionary.

```
> ::rctl_dict
ID NAME                      ADDR     TYPE GLOBAL_FLAGS
12 process.max-port-events   d9911c80 process 0x20100000
11 process.max-msg-messages  d9911cb8 process 0x20100000
10 process.max-msg-qbytes    d9911cf0 process 0x20400000
 9 process.max-sem-ops       d9911d28 process 0x20100000
```

continues

```
 8 process.max-sem-nsems       d9911d60 process 0x20100000
 7 process.max-address-space   d9911d98 process 0x62400000
 6 process.max-file-descriptor d9911dd0 process 0x60100000
 5 process.max-core-size       d9911e08 process 0x62400000
 4 process.max-stack-size      d9911e40 process 0x62400000
 3 process.max-data-size       d9911e78 process 0x62400000
 2 process.max-file-size       d9911eb0 process 0x68400000
 1 process.max-cpu-time        d9911ee8 process 0x55200000
27 task.max-cpu-time           d9911938    task 0x15a00000
26 task.max-lwps               d9911970    task 0x00100000
23 project.max-contracts       d9911a18 project 0x20100000
22 project.max-device-locked-memory d9911a50 project 0xa0400000
21 project.max-port-ids        d9911a88 project 0xa0100000
20 project.max-shm-memory      d9911ac0 project 0xa0400000
19 project.max-shm-ids         d9911af8 project 0xa0100000
18 project.max-msg-ids         d9911b30 project 0xa0100000
17 project.max-sem-ids         d9911b68 project 0xa0100000
16 project.max-crypto-memory   d9911ba0 project 0xa0400000
15 project.max-tasks           d9911bd8 project 0x80100000
14 project.max-lwps            d9911c10 project 0x80100000
13 project.cpu-shares          d9911c48 project 0x92100000
25 zone.max-lwps               d99119a8    zone 0x80100000
24 zone.cpu-shares             d99119e0    zone 0x92100000
```

A secondary dictionary, `rctl_dict_by_name`, contains a hash of name to resource control handles. The resource control handles are distributed by the `rctl_ids` ID space. The handles are private and not to be advertised to userland; all userland interactions are through the `rctl` names.

Entities inherit their rctls from their predecessor. Since projects have no ancestor, they inherit their rctls from the `rctl` dictionary for project rctls. It is expected that project controls will be set to their appropriate values shortly after project creation, presumably from a policy source such as the project database.

7.7.1 Data Structures

The `rctl_set_t` attached to each of the process model entities is a simple hash table keyed on the `rctl` handle assigned at registration. The entries in the hash table are `rctl_ts`, whose relationship with the active control values on that resource and with the global state of the resource we illustrate in Figure 7.3.

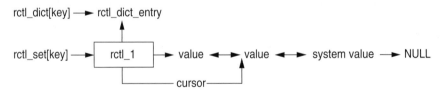

Figure 7.3 `rctl` Entry Relationships

That is, the `rctl` contains a back pointer to the global resource control state for this resource, which is also available in the `rctl_dict` hash table mentioned earlier. The `rctl` contains two pointers to resource control values: `values` indicates the entire sequence of control values and `cursor` indicates the currently active control value—the next value to be enforced. The value list itself is an open, doubly linked list, the last non-NULL member of which is the system value for that resource (being the theoretical or conventional maximum allowable value for the resource on this OS instance). The `::rctl_list` dcmd can be used to walk a processes rctl list.

```
> d847f420::rctl_list
d862f3f8        8 : process.max-sem-nsems
        (cur) 0x200               privileged    flags=<DENY>
              0x7fff                  system    flags=<DENY,MAX>
d862f3e0        1 : process.max-cpu-time
        (cur) 0xffffffffffffffff privileged    flags=<SIGNAL,MAX>
              0xffffffffffffffff      system    flags=<MAX>
d862f3c8        9 : process.max-sem-ops
        (cur) 0x200               privileged    flags=<DENY>
              0x7fffffff              system    flags=<DENY,MAX>
```

7.7.2 Operations Vector

The ops vector contains methods to perform set, test, and actions.

```
/*
 * Default resource control callback functions.
 */

typedef struct rctl_ops {
        void          (*rco_action)(struct rctl *, struct proc *,
            rctl_entity_p_t *);
        rctl_qty_t    (*rco_get_usage)(struct rctl *, struct proc *);
        int           (*rco_set)(struct rctl *, struct proc *,
            rctl_entity_p_t *, rctl_qty_t);
        int           (*rco_test)(struct rctl *, struct proc *,
            rctl_entity_p_t *, rctl_val_t *, rctl_qty_t, uint_t);
} rctl_ops_t;

#define RCTLOP_ACTION(r, p, e) (r->rc_dict_entry->rcd_ops->rco_action(r, p, e))
#define RCTLOP_GET_USAGE(r, p) (r->rc_dict_entry->rcd_ops->rco_get_usage(r, p))
#define RCTLOP_SET(r, p, e, v) (r->rc_dict_entry->rcd_ops->rco_set(r, p, e, v))
#define RCTLOP_TEST(r, p, e, v, i, f) \
        (r->rc_dict_entry->rcd_ops->rco_test(r, p, e, v, i, f))
```
                                                              See sys/rctl.h

Subsystems publishing rctls need not provide instances of all of the functions specified by the `ops` vector. In particular, if general `rctl_*()` entry points are not being called, certain functions can be omitted. These align as follows.

```
rco_set()
```

You may wish to provide a set callback if locking circumstances prevent it or if the performance cost of requesting the enforced value from the resource control is prohibitively expensive. For instance, the currently enforced file size limit is stored on the process in the p_fsz_ctl to maintain read()/write() performance.

```
int rco_test(rctl_hndl_t, rctl_set_t *, struct proc *, rctl_qty_t, uint_t);
```

You must provide a test callback if you are using the rctl_test() interface. An action callback is optional.

```
rco_action()
```

You may wish to provide an action callback.

7.7.3 Interface Overview

The commonly used resource control interfaces are listed in Table 7.8.

Table 7.8 Commonly Used `rctl` Kernel Interfaces

Interface	Description
rctl_register()	Registers a new rctl with the subsystem. New resource controls can be added to a running instance by loaded modules via registration. (The current implementation does not support unloadable modules; this functionality can be added if needed, through an activation/deactivation interface involving the manipulation of the ops vector for the resource control(s) needing to support unloading.)
rctl_test()	Increment the resource associated with the given handle, return an error if limits exceeded.
rctl_add_default_limit()	Add a new default limit for the resource control.
rctl_enforced_value()	Get the enforced value of the resource control.
rctl_action()	Ask the rctl subsystem to enforce the registered action for the rctl. Typically used for nonmanaged resources where rctl_test isn't used; e.g., maximum file size.
rctl_add_legacy_limit()	Add a limit with a named legacy /etc/system tuneable (used for System V tuneables, etc.)

7.7.4 Interface Definitions

```
rctl_hndl_t rctl_register(const char *, rctl_entity_t, int, rlim64_t,
                          rlim64_t, rctl_ops_t *)
```

Overview
rctl_register() performs a look-up in the dictionary of rctls
active on the system; if a rctl of that name is absent, an entry is
made into the dictionary. The rctl is returned with its reference
count incremented by one. If the rctl name already exists, we panic.
(Were the resource control system to support dynamic loading and unloading,
which it is structured for, duplicate registration should lead to load
failure instead of panicking.)

Each registered rctl has a requirement that a RCPRIV_SYSTEM limit be
defined. This limit contains the highest possible value for this quantity
on the system. Furthermore, the registered control must provide infinite
values for all applicable address space models supported by the operating
system. Attempts to set resource control values beyond the system limit
will fail.

Return values
The rctl's ID.

Caller's context
Caller must be in a context suitable for KM_SLEEP allocations.

```
int rctl_test(rctl_hndl_t, rctl_set_t *, struct proc *, rctl_qty_t, uint_t)
```

Overview
Increment the resource associated with the given handle, returning zero if
the incremented value does not exceed the threshold for the current limit
on the resource.

Return values
Actions taken, according to the rctl_test bitmask.

Caller's context
p_lock held by caller.

```
void rctl_add_default_limit(const char *name, rctl_qty_t value,
  rctl_priv_t privilege, uint_t action)
```

Overview
Create a default limit with specified value, privilege, and action.

Return value
No value returned.

```
rlim64_t rctl_enforced_value(rctl_hndl_t, rctl_set_t *, struct proc *)
```

Overview
Given a process, get the next enforced value on the rctl of the specified handle.

Return value
The enforced value.

Caller's context
For controls on process collectives, p->p_lock must be held across the operation.

See os/rctl.c

```
int rctl_action(rctl_hndl_t, rctl_set_t *, struct proc *, uint_t)

Overview
Take the action associated with the enforced value (as defined by
rctl_get_enforced_value()) being exceeded or encountered.  Possibly perform
a restricted subset of the available actions, if circumstances dictate that
we cannot safely allocate memory (for a sigqueue_t) or guarantee process
persistence across the duration of the function (an asynchronous action).

Return values
Actions taken, according to the rctl_test bitmask.

Caller's context
Safe to acquire rcs_lock.

void rctl_add_default_limit(const char *name, rctl_qty_t value,
  rctl_priv_t privilege, uint_t action)

Overview
Create a default limit with specified value, privilege, and action.

Return value
No value returned.
```
See os/rctl.c

7.7.5 An Example Resource Control

You can see an example of a resource control in the System V shared memory
implementation. The System V shared memory implements a maximum size for
share memory allocations, in bytes. Historically, this was implemented as a systemwide parameter, tuneable only through /etc/system. In Solaris 10, this limit
is implemented with a resource control within the scope of a project. This allows
the limit to be set dynamically (unlink the set and reboot required with the old
model). It also allows the parameter to be set within the scope of a project, which
permits multiple application configurations within the same kernel instance. For
example, two database applications might be run, each within its own project ID,
fitting within its own administrable shared memory limits.

We register the shared memory resource controls in project.c by setting up a
rctl ops template and then performing the registration with rctl_register().

```
static rctl_ops_t project_shmmax_ops = {
        rcop_no_action,
        rcop_no_usage,
        rcop_no_set,
        project_shmmax_test
};

/*ARGSUSED*/
static int
project_shmmax_test(struct rctl *rctl, struct proc *p, rctl_entity_p_t *e,
    rctl_val_t *rval, rctl_qty_t inc, uint_t flags)
```

continues

```
{
        rctl_qty_t v;
        ASSERT(MUTEX_HELD(&p->p_lock));
        ASSERT(e->rcep_t == RCENTITY_PROJECT);
        v = e->rcep_p.proj->kpj_data.kpd_shmmax + inc;
        if (v > rval->rcv_value)
                return (1);

        return (0);
}

project_init()
{
...

        rc_project_shmmax = rctl_register("project.max-shm-memory",
            RCENTITY_PROJECT, RCTL_GLOBAL_DENY_ALWAYS | RCTL_GLOBAL_NOBASIC |
            RCTL_GLOBAL_BYTES, UINT64_MAX, UINT64_MAX, &project_shmmax_ops);


        rctl_add_default_limit("project.max-shm-memory", qty,
            RCPRIV_PRIVILEGED, RCTL_LOCAL_DENY);
```

See common/os/project.c

Once registered, the IPC subsystem can update and check the resource against the limits administered by the users of the system.

```
sol10$ prctl  -n project.max-shm-memory $$
process: 3053: ksh
NAME       PRIVILEGE        VALUE    FLAG   ACTION                          RECIPIENT
project.max-shm-memory
        privileged        246MB      -     deny                                -
        system            16.0EB     max   deny                                -
```

The resource limits are checked and enforced in the IPC implementation. Each call to `shmget()` tests and decrements the available share memory, through `rctl_test()`.

```
extern rctl_hndl_t rc_project_shmmax;

shmget()
{
..
                /*
                 * Check rsize and the per-project limit on shared
                 * memory.  Checking rsize handles both the size == 0
                 * case and the size < ULONG_MAX & PAGEMASK case (i.e.
                 * rounding up wraps a size_t).
                 */
                if (rsize == 0 || (rctl_test(rc_project_shmmax,
                    pp->p_task->tk_proj->kpj_rctls, pp, rsize,
```

continues

```
            RCA_SAFE) & RCT_DENY)) {
                mutex_exit(&pp->p_lock);
                mutex_exit(lock);
                ipc_cleanup(shm_svc, (kipc_perm_t *)sp);
                return (EINVAL);
        }
    ..
    }
```

See common/os/project.c

PART FOUR

Memory

8

Introduction to Solaris Memory

The virtual memory sub-system can be considered the core of a Solaris instance, and the implementation of Solaris virtual memory affects just about every other subsystem in the operating system. In this chapter, we look at some of the memory management basics. In the next chapter, we discuss practical techniques for analyzing and monitoring memory. In the subsequent chapters we analyze in more detail how Solaris *implements* virtual memory management.

8.1 Virtual Memory Primer

A virtual memory (VM) system offers the following benefits:

- It presents a simple memory programming model to applications so that application developers need not know how the underlying memory hardware is arranged.
- It allows processes to see linear ranges of bytes in their address space, regardless of the physical layout or fragmentation of the real memory.
- It affords a programming model with a larger memory size than that of available physical storage (e.g., RAM) and enables the use of slower but larger secondary storage (e.g., disk) as a backing store to hold the pieces of memory that don't fit in physical memory.

8.2 Two Levels of Memory

A virtual view of memory storage, known as an *address space*, is presented to the application while the VM system transparently manages the virtual storage between RAM and secondary storage. Because RAM is significantly faster than disk (100 ns versus 10 ms, or approximately 100,000 times faster), the job of the VM system is to keep the most frequently referenced portions of memory in the faster primary storage. In the event of a RAM shortage, the VM system is required to free RAM by transferring infrequently used memory out to the backing store. By so doing, the VM system optimizes performance and removes the need for users to manage the allocation of their own memory requirements.

8.3 Memory Sharing and Protection

Multiple users' processes can share memory within the VM system. In a multiuser environment, multiple processes can be running the same process executable binaries; in older UNIX implementations, each process had its own copy of the binary—a vast waste of memory resources. The Solaris virtual memory system optimizes memory use by sharing program binaries and application data among processes, so memory is not wasted when multiple instances of a process are executed. The Solaris kernel extended this concept further when it introduced dynamically linked libraries in SunOS, allowing C libraries to be shared among processes.

To properly support multiple users, the VM system implements memory protection. For example, a user's process must not be able to access the memory of another process; otherwise, security could be compromised or a program fault in one program could cause another program (or the entire operating system) to fail. Hardware facilities in the memory management unit perform the memory protection function by preventing a process from accessing memory outside its legal address space (except for memory that is explicitly shared among processes).

8.4 Pages: Basic Units of Physical Memory

Physical memory (RAM) is divided into fixed-sized pieces called *pages*. The size of a page can vary across different platforms; the common size for a page of memory on an UltraSPARC Solaris system is 8 Kbytes. Each page of physical memory is associated with a file and offset; the file and offset identify the *backing store* for the page. The backing store is the location to which the physical page contents will be migrated (known as a *page-out*) should the page need to be taken for another use; it's also the location from which the file will be read back if it's migrated in (known as a *page-in*). Pages used for regular process heap and stack, known as *anonymous memory,* have the swap file as their backing store. A page can also be a cache of a page-size piece of a regular file. In that case, the backing store is simply the file it's caching—this is how the Solaris OS uses the memory system to cache files.

If the virtual memory system needs to take a *dirty* page (a page that has had its contents modified), its contents are migrated to the backing store. Anonymous memory is paged out to the swap device when the page is freed. If a file page needs to be freed and the page-size piece of the file hasn't been modified, then the page can simply be freed; if the piece has been modified, then it is first written back out to the file (the backing store in this case), then freed.

8.5 Virtual-to-Physical Translation

Rather than managing every byte of memory, we use page-size pieces of memory to minimize the amount of work the virtual memory system has to do to maintain virtual-to-physical memory mappings. Figure 8.1 shows how the management and

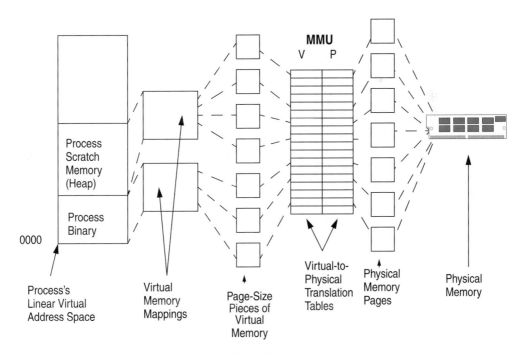

Figure 8.1 Solaris Virtual-to-Physical Memory Management

translation of the virtual view of memory (the address space) to physical memory is performed by hardware known as the *virtual memory management unit* (MMU).

The Solaris kernel breaks up the linear virtual address space into *mappings*, one for each type of memory area in the address space. For example, a simple process has a memory mapping for the process binary and one for the scratch memory (known as *heap space*). Each mapping manages the spanned virtual address range and converts that mapping into MMU pages. The hardware MMU maps those pages into physical memory by using a platform-specific set of translation tables. Each entry in the table has the physical address of the page of memory in RAM so that memory accesses can be converted on-the-fly in hardware. We cover more on how the MMU works later in this Part when we discuss the platform-specific implementations of memory management.

8.6 Physical Memory Management: Paging and Swapping

It is possible to have more virtual address space than physical address space because the operating system can overflow memory onto a slower medium, such as a disk. The slower medium in UNIX is known as *swap space*. Two basic types of memory management manage the allocation and migration of physical pages of memory to and from swap space: *swapping* and *demand paging*.

The swapping algorithm for memory management uses a user process as the basic unit for managing memory. If there is a shortage of memory, then all of the pages of memory of the least-active processes are swapped out to the swap device, freeing memory for other processes. This method is easy to implement, but performance suffers badly during a memory shortage because a process cannot resume execution until all of its pages have been brought back from secondary storage. The demand-paged model uses a *page* as the granularity for memory management. Rather than swapping out a whole process, the memory system just swaps out small, least-used chunks, allowing processes to continue while an inactive part of the process is swapped out.

The Solaris kernel uses a combined demand-paged and swapping model. Demand paging is used under normal circumstances, and swapping is used only as a last resort when the system is desperate for memory. We cover swapping and paging in more detail in Section 10.3.

8.7 Virtual Memory as a File System Cache

The Solaris VM system implements many more functions than just management of application memory. In fact, the Solaris virtual memory system is responsible for managing most objects related to I/O and memory, including the kernel, user applications, shared libraries, and file systems. This strategy differs significantly from other operating systems like earlier versions of System V UNIX, where file system I/O used a separate disk cache.

One of the major advantages of using the VM system to manage file system caching is that all free memory in the system is available as a cache, providing significant performance improvements for applications that use the file system and removing the need for manual tuning of the size of the cache. The VM system can allocate all free memory for file system cache, meaning that on a typical system with file system I/O, almost all of the physical memory will be advantageously used.

In summary, the Solaris VM system performs these major functions:

- It manages virtual-to-physical mapping of memory.
- It manages the swapping of memory between primary and secondary storage to optimize performance.
- It handles requirements of shared images between multiple users and processes.
- It acts as an integrated file cache.

8.8 New Features of the Virtual Memory Implementation

The Solaris virtual memory system was originally derived from BSD UNIX. From there, the significant major architectural changes have been the union of files and virtual memory to provide a unified cache and the object layering of VM into modules, maximizing the commonality of the code across multiple platforms and devices.

During the development of Solaris, there have been many unique features added to the virtual memory system, building upon the underlying framework:

- **File system cache scalability improvements.** Historically, the file system cache could be quite intrusive on application performance, by virtue of paging pressure caused by filesystem reads and writes. Beginning with Solaris 8, the file system cache was lowered in priority and made cyclic, such that file system reads and writes consume the available free memory and pages against itself.

  A new page mapping facility minimizes the overhead of accessing pages during file system I/O. By using the 64-bit address space (on SPARC and x64 architectures), the kernel creates a permenant mapping of all physical pages into its address space (SEGKPM), eliminating the need to map/unmap for each I/O.

- **Utilization of large MMU pages.** As Moore's law marches on, memory sizes have effectively doubled every 18 months. The virtual memory has scaled from an original design center of around one megabyte to one terabyte today. To enable performance to scale, MMU's typically support more than one page size, and the largest page size has scaled approximately with physical memory size. MMU sizes on the first SPARC processors were 4Kbytes, and the largest available now is 256MBytes.

  The kernel text and some data is placed on a large MMU page, when possible. Beginning with Solaris 2.6 some types of shared memory (specifically ISM used by Oracle, Sybase etc) is configured to use large pages when available. A generic framework—Multiple Page Size Selection (MPSS) was introduced in Solaris 9 to allow applications leverage different MMU page sizes.

- **Support for non-uniform (NUMA) architectures.** Many high end systems now have federated non-uniform memory locality groups. By definition, all processors in an SMP system need shared access to the system memory, however as SMP systems grow to larger processor counts, their memory system often has to reflect higher memory latencies, giving good system throughput at the expense of lowering per-processor performance. Alternatively, the memory system can be broken into clusters of processors and memory with fast access to memory "close" to the processor, and slower access to memory that resides in another group. This approach is the basis for NUMA architectures.

  The Solaris virtual memory system beginning with Solaris 9, introduces Memory Placement Optimization (MPO) with the concept of locality groups (Lgroups), which allows the kernel to optimally place memory allocations closer to the processors which are likely to use them. Applications are able to provide hints to the kernel about the intended relationship between memory and threads, which is used to optimize scheduling and page allocation accordingly.

- **Dynamic reconfiguration.** Added to allow hardware components (including physical memory boards) to added and removed from the system whilst online. The virtual memory system has been enhanced to optimize itself to maximize the amount of memory that can be added and removed from the system.

  Memory can be added dynamically, resulting in new pages being added to the system's free list for immediate consumption by other applications. To facilite dynamic removal of memory, the kernel has facilities for dynamically freeing or relocating pages if they are being used by applications. Kernel pages are restricted into a "kernel cage," since they are sometimes non-relocatable, allowing all but one board to be dynamically removed from the system. Beginning with Solaris 10, all but a small component of the kernel is restricted to the cage.

Event hooks are also provided to pre-notify applications of physical memory capacity changes. These hooks are provided by the resource configuration manager (RCM) and provide a scriptable interface to notify interested applications. At the time of writing, Oracle 9 is one such application. Using Oracle's dynamic SGA feature, Oracle can be configured to automatically grow and shrink according to memory capacity changes.

- **Modern memory allocators.** Have been added to the kernel. Beginning with Solaris 2.4, the allocator was replaced with the "Slab Allocator." The new allocator provides efficient allocation of memory objects with minimal fragmentation. The allocator optimizes for SMPs by providing distinct re-use caches for each processor in the system, minimizing the amount of cross-processor memory sharing traffic. Beginning with Solaris 8, the kernel also uses a universal resource allocator (vmem). The vmem allocator manages allocations of arbitrary resources, represented by sets of integers. It replaces the older resource map allocators, as well as servering as a backend to the slab allocator to managed kernel virtual memory.

9

Virtual Memory

In this section we take a tour through the implementation of the virtual memory layer of Solaris—the virtual address management, anonymous memory, and swap layers are covered.

9.1 Design Overview

Early SunOS versions (SunOS 3 and earlier) were based on the old BSD-style memory system, which was not modularized, and thus it was difficult to move the memory system to different platforms. The virtual memory system was completely redesigned at that time, with the new memory system targeted at SunOS 4.0. The new SunOS 4.0 virtual memory system was built with the following goals in mind:

- Use of a new object-oriented memory management framework
- Support for shared and private memory (copy-on-write)
- Page-based virtual memory management

The VM system that resulted from these design goals provides an open framework that now supports many different memory objects. The most important objects of the memory system are segments, vnodes, and pages. For example, all of the following have been implemented as abstractions of the new memory objects:

- Physical memory, in chunks called pages
- A new virtual file object, known as the vnode
- File systems as hierarchies of vnodes
- Process address spaces as segments of mapped vnodes
- Kernel address space as segments of mapped vnodes
- Mapped hardware devices, such as frame buffers, as segments of hardware-mapped pages

The Solaris virtual memory system we use today is implemented according to the framework of the SunOS 4.0 rewrite. It has been significantly enhanced to provide scalable performance on multiprocessor platforms and has been ported to many platforms. Figure 9.1 shows the layers of the Solaris virtual memory implementation.

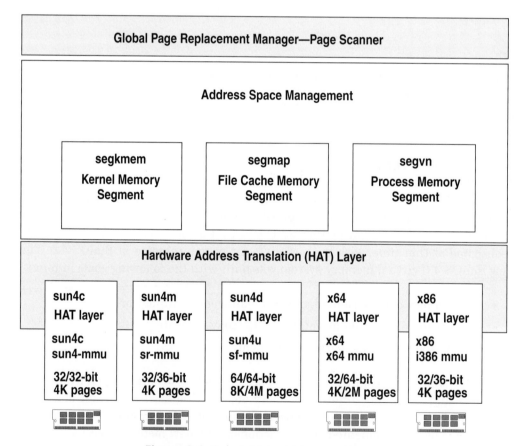

Figure 9.1 Solaris Virtual Memory Layers

Physical memory management is done by the hardware MMU and a hardware-specific address translation layer known as the *Hardware Address Translation (HAT) layer*. Each memory management type has its own specific HAT implementation. Thus, we can separate the common machine-independent memory management layers from the hardware-specific components to minimize the amount of platform-specific code that must be written for each new platform.

The next layer is the address space management layer. Address spaces are mappings of segments, which are created with segment device drivers. Each segment driver manages the mapping of a linear virtual address space into memory pages for different device types (for example, a device such as a graphics frame buffer can be mapped into an address space). The segment layers manage virtual memory as an abstraction of a file. The segment drivers call into the HAT layer to create the translations between the address space they are managing and the underlying physical pages.

9.2 Virtual Address Spaces

The virtual address space of a process is the range of memory addresses that are presented to the process as its environment; some addresses are mapped to physical memory, some are not. A process's virtual address space skeleton is created by the kernel at the time the `fork()` system call creates the process. (See Section 2.7.) The virtual address layout within a process is set up by the dynamic linker and sometimes varies across different hardware platforms. As we can see in Figure 9.2, virtual address spaces are assembled from a series of memory mappings. Each process has at least four mappings:

- **Executable text.** The executable instructions in the binary reside in the text mapping. The text mapping is mapped from the on-disk binary and is mapped read-only, with execute permissions.
- **Executable data.** The initialized variables in the executable reside in the data mapping. The data mapping is mapped from the on-disk binary and is mapped read/write/private. The private mapping ensures that changes made to memory within this mapping are not reflected out to the file or to other processes mapping the same executable.
- **Heap space.** Scratch, or memory allocated by `malloc()`, is allocated from anonymous memory and is mapped read/write.
- **Process stack.** The stack is allocated from anonymous memory and is mapped read/write.

Figure 9.2 illustrates a process's virtual address space.

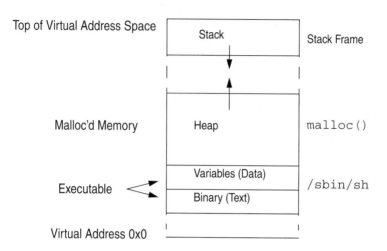

Figure 9.2 Process Virtual Address Space

The figure shows how the /sbin/sh process has its executable mapped in near the bottom address, with the heap adjoining it, the stack at the top, and a hole between the heap and the stack. The heap grows upward as more memory is allocated through malloc(), and the stack grows downward as more frames are placed on the stack. Not all of the virtual address space within a process is mapped, and the process can legally access memory only within the areas with valid mappings; a process's attempt to access memory outside of the mappings causes a page fault. A more sophisticated process may have more mappings; those that make use of shared libraries or mapped files will have additional mappings between the heap and stack.

9.2.1 Sharing Executables and Libraries

The Solaris kernel supports sharing of memory, files, libraries, and executables. For example, the Solaris kernel shares libraries by dynamically mapping the library file into the address space during program startup. The libraries are mapped into the address space between the stack and the heap, at different positions on different platforms.

When a shared library object is mapped into a process's address space, it can be mapped *shared* so that all processes share the same physical memory pages. Executable text and data are shared in the same manner, by simply mapping the same executable file into every address space.

We see more about how mapping of files and sharing of memory occur when we explore the vnode segment driver, which is responsible for mapping files into address spaces.

9.2.2 Address Spaces on SPARC Systems

The process address space on SPARC systems varies across different SPARC platforms according to the MMU on that platform. SPARC has three different address space layouts:

- The SPARC V7 combined 32-bit kernel and process address space, found on sun4c, sun4d, and sun4m machines. Note that support for SPARC V7 exists only in Solaris 9 and earlier.
- The SPARC V9 32-bit separated kernel and process address space model, found on sun4u machines
- The SPARC V9 64-bit separated kernel and process address space model, found on sun4u machines

The SPARC V7 systems use a shared address space between the kernel and process and use the processor's privilege levels to prevent user processes from accessing the kernel's address space. The kernel occupies the top virtual memory addresses, and the process occupies the lower memory addresses. This means that part of the virtual address space available to the process is consumed by the kernel, limiting the size of usable process virtual memory to between 3.5 and 3.75 Gbytes, depending on the size of the kernel's virtual address space. This also means that the kernel has a limited size, ranging between 128 and 512 Mbytes. The SPARC V7 combined 32-bit kernel and process address space is shown in Figure 9.3.

The SPARC V9 (UltraSPARC, sun4u) microprocessor allows the kernel to operate in an address space separate from user processes, so the process can use almost all of the 32-bit address space (a tiny bit is reserved at the top for the Open Boot PROM) and also allows the kernel to have a similar, large address space. This design removes the 512-Mbyte limit for kernel address space, which was a major problem for large machines such as the older SPARCcenter 2000 machines. The process address space looks similar to the shared kernel/process address space, except that the kernel area is missing and the stack and libraries are moved to the top of memory.

The UltraSPARC processor also supports the SPARC V9 64-bit mode, which allows a process to have a virtual address space that spans 64 bits. The UltraSPARC-I and -II implementations, however, support only 44 bits of the address space, which means that there is a virtual address space hole in the middle of the address space. This area of memory creates a special type of UltraSPARC trap when accessed. Some future generations of SPARC V9 processors will not have the same hole in the address space. The UltraSPARC V9 32-bit and 64-bit address spaces are shown in Figure 9.4.

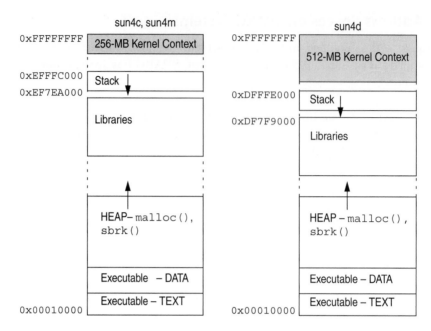

Figure 9.3 SPARC 32-Bit Shared Kernel/Process Address Space

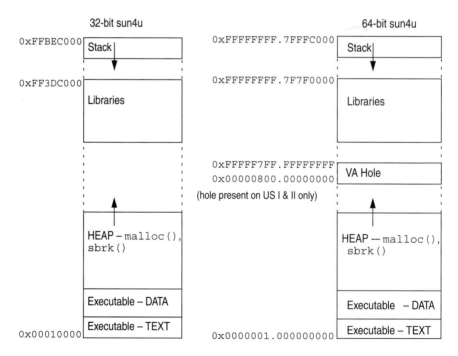

Figure 9.4 SPARC sun4u 32- and 64-Bit Process Address Space

On all SPARC platforms, the bottom of the virtual address space is not mapped. Null pointer references cause a segmentation fault rather than return spurious contents of whatever was at the bottom of the address space.

9.2.3 x86 and x64 Address Space Layout

The Intel x86 32-bit user address space also includes a mapping of the kernel. The main difference with the Intel address space is that the space is reserved at the top of the address space for the kernel and the stack is mapped underneath the executable binary, growing down toward the bottom. The x64 address space is a closer representation of the SPARC 64-bit address space. The x86 and x64 address spaces are shown in Figure 9.5.

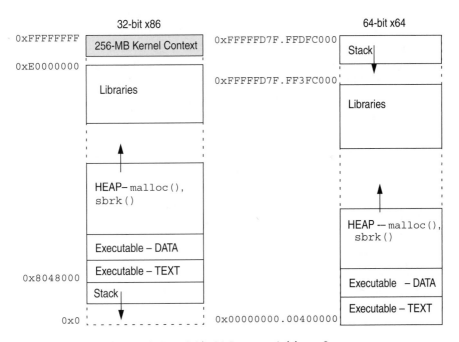

Figure 9.5 x86/x64 Process Address Spaces

9.2.4 Growing the Heap

Process virtual memory for user data structures is allocated from the heap mapping, which resides above the executable data mapping. The heap starts out small and then grows as virtual memory is allocated. The heap grows in units of pages; it is simply a large area of virtual memory available for reading and writing. A single, large, virtual memory area is difficult to program to, so a general-purpose memory allocator manages the heap area; thus, arbitrarily sized memory objects can be allocated and freed. The general-purpose memory allocator is implemented with `malloc()` and related library calls.

A process grows its heap space by making the `sbrk()` system call. The `sbrk()` system call grows the heap mapping by the amount requested each time it is called. A user program does not need to call `sbrk()` directly because the `malloc()` library calls `sbrk()` when it needs more space to allocate from. The `sbrk()` system call is shown below.

```
void *sbrk(intptr_t incr);
```

The heap mapping is virtual memory, so requesting memory with `malloc` and `sbrk` does not allocate physical memory; it merely allocates the virtual address space. Only when the first reference is made to a page within the allocated virtual memory is physical memory allocated, one page at a time. The memory system transparently achieves this "zero fill on demand" allocation because a page fault occurs the first time a page is referenced in the heap, and the segment driver then recognizes the first memory access and simply creates a page at that location on-the-fly.

Memory pages are allocated to the process heap by zero-fill-on-demand and then remain in the heap mapping until the process exits or until they are stolen by the page scanner. Calls to the memory allocator `free()` function do not return physical memory to the free memory pool; `free()` simply marks the area within the heap space as free for later use. For this reason, the amount of physical memory allocated to a process typically grows, but unless there is a memory shortage, it will not shrink, even if `free()` has been called.

The heap can grow until it collides with the memory area occupied by the shared libraries. The maximum size of the heap depends on the platform virtual memory layout and differs on each platform. In addition, on 64-bit platforms, processes may execute in either 32- or 64-bit mode. As shown in Figure 9.4, the size of the heap can be much larger in processes executing in 64-bit mode. Table 9.1 shows the maximum heap sizes and the operating system requirements that affect the maximum size.

9.2.5 The Stack

The process stack is mapped into the address space with an initial allocation and then grows downward. The stack, like the heap, grows on demand, but no library grows the stack; instead, a different mechanism triggers this growth.

Table 9.1 Maximum Heap Sizes

Solaris Version	Maximum Heap Size	Notes
Solaris x86 32-bit mode	2 Gbytes by default	Boot option kernel base can be moved to allow larger process address space.
Solaris x64 64-bit mode	16 Ebytes	Virtually unlimited.
SPARC 32-bit mode	3.75 Gbytes 3.90 Gbytes	(Non-sun4u platform). (sun4u platforms).
SPARC 64-bit mode	16 Tbytes onUltraSPARC I and II 16 Ebytes on UltraSPARC III onwards.	Virtually unlimited.

Initially, a single page is allocated for the stack, and as the process executes and calls functions, it pushes the program counter, arguments, and local variables onto the stack. When the stack grows larger than one page, the process causes a page fault, and the kernel notices that this is a stack-mapping page fault and grows the stack mapping.

9.2.5.1 Memory Mapped Files

The address space mapping architecture makes it easy for one or more processes to map the same file into their address space. When files are mapped into one or more processes, seg_vn mappings are created in each process that points to the same vnode. Each process has its own virtual memory mapping to the file, but they all share the same physical memory pages for the files. The first mapping to cause a page fault reads a page into physical memory, and then the second and subsequent mappings simply create a reference to the existing physical memory page—as *attaching*.

Figure 9.6 shows how two processes can map the same file. Each process creates its own mapping object, but both mappings point to the same file and are mapped to the same physical pages. Notice that the second process need not have all the pages attached to the mapping, even if both mappings map the same parts of the file. In this case, the second process would *attach* to these pages when they are referenced. A minor fault is used to describe this event. You can see minor faults by using vmstat.

Several options govern how a file is shared when it is mapped between two or more processes. These options control how changes are propagated across the shared file. For example, if one process wants to modify one of the pages mapped into the process, should the other process see exactly the same change or should

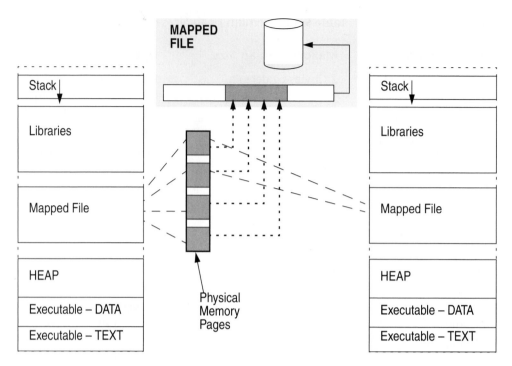

Figure 9.6 Shared Mapped Files

the change remain private to the process that made the change? The options allow
you to choose which behavior you desire. The options are those that can be passed
to the protection and flags argument of mmap() when the file is mapped. The
behavior for the different flags is listed in Table 9.2.

Table 9.2 mmap Shared Mapped File Flags

Flag	Protection Mode	Result
MAP_SHARED	PROT_READ | PROT_WRITE	Modifications are reflected among all processes sharing the mapping.
MAP_PRIVATE	PROT_READ | PROT_WRITE	Modifications are seen only by the process mapping the file. The copy-on-write process creates a page of anonymous memory and gives a private copy to the process.

9.2.6 Using `pmap` to Look at Mappings

Use the `pmap` command to inspect the mappings for a process. One line of output is shown for each mapping, along with descriptive data.

```
sol9$ pmap 102905
102905:    sh
00010000    192K r-x--  /usr/bin/ksh                          [ Text Mapping ]
00040000      8K rwx--  /usr/bin/ksh                          [ Data Mapping ]
00042000     40K rwx--    [ heap ]                            [ Heap]
FF180000    664K r-x--  /usr/lib/libc.so.1                    [ C Library Text ]
FF236000     24K rwx--  /usr/lib/libc.so.1                    [ C Library Data ]
FF23C000      8K rwx--  /usr/lib/libc.so.1                    [ C Library Data ctd... ]
FF250000      8K rwx--    [ anon ]                            [ Misc anon mapping ]
FF260000     16K r-x--  /usr/lib/en_US.ISO8859-1.so.2         [ Library mappings con-
tunue..]
FF272000     16K rwx--  /usr/lib/en_US.ISO8859-1.so.2
FF280000    560K r-x--  /usr/lib/libnsl.so.1
FF31C000     32K rwx--  /usr/lib/libnsl.so.1
FF324000     32K rwx--  /usr/lib/libnsl.so.1
FF340000     16K r-x--  /usr/lib/libc_psr.so.1
FF350000     16K r-x--  /usr/lib/libmp.so.2
FF364000      8K rwx--  /usr/lib/libmp.so.2
FF380000     40K r-x--  /usr/lib/libsocket.so.1
FF39A000      8K rwx--  /usr/lib/libsocket.so.1
FF3A0000      8K r-x--  /usr/lib/libdl.so.1
FF3B0000      8K rwx--    [ anon ]
FF3C0000    152K r-x--  /usr/lib/ld.so.1
FF3F6000      8K rwx--  /usr/lib/ld.so.1
FFBFC000     16K rw---    [ stack ]                           [ Stack ]
 total      188
```

As shown in the example, the program's address space comprises several mappings. At the top is the program's binary, mapped as a read-only text mapping followed by a writable data mapping, continuing through to the process stack. Without any further options, `pmap` simply shows the starting address, the virtual address size, protection modes, and a description of each mapping. The columns are explained as follows:

- **Starting address.** The starting virtual address of the mapping.
- **Size.** The size of the virtual address mapping. This is typically the size between the start and end of the mappings.
- **Flags.** One or more of the allowable permissions or flags are shown for the mapping:
  - r. The mapping may be read by the process.
  - w. The mapping may be written by the process.
  - x. Instructions that reside within the mapping may be executed by the process.

- s. The mapping is shared such that changes made in the observed address space are committed to the mapped file and are visible from all other processes sharing the mapping.

- R. Swap space is not reserved for this mapping. Mappings created with MAP_NORESERVE and System V ISM shared memory mappings do not reserve swap space.

9.3 Tracing the VM System

There are only a few DTrace probes in the VM system at the time of writing—specifically those via the `sysinfo` provider and those in the `page_create()` code-path. It is, however, possible to trace a larger portion of the VM, using the fbt provider.

```
sol10# ./gvm.sh >vm.d
sol10# ./vm.d <pid>
sol10# more vm.d

:::BEGIN
{
        start = timestamp;
}

syscall:::
/$target == pid/
{
        trace((timestamp - start) / 1000);
}

::add_physmem:,
::sptcreate:,
...
::sptdestroy:,
::va_to_pfn:
/$target == pid/
{
        trace((timestamp - start) / 1000);
}
```

Running the VM trace script on a target process allows you to observe the VM level tasks of a target process. A simple example might be to trace the entire code path for a specific VM operation, however this often results in too many probes, creating significant probe effect. A simple script allows us to instrument just the VM system, by converting the function prototypes from the VM header files and auto-generating a DTrace script. This technique instruments just the perimeters of the VM modules we care about—address spaces, segments, and page level interfaces.

```
0   => munmap                                              3194
0    -> as_unmap                                           3199
0     -> as_findseg                                        3206
0     <- as_findseg                                        3209
0     -> segvn_unmap                                       3211
0      -> segvn_lockop                                     3217
0      <- segvn_lockop                                     3219
0      -> hat_unload_callback                              3221
0       -> page_get_pagesize                               3236
0       <- page_get_pagesize                               3237
0       -> hat_page_setattr                                3239
0       <- hat_page_setattr                                3240
0       -> free_vp_pages                                   3247
0        -> page_share_cnt                                 3252
0         -> hat_page_getshare                             3255
0         <- hat_page_getshare                             3256
0        <- page_share_cnt                                 3258
0       <- free_vp_pages                                   3259
0      <- hat_unload_callback                              3261
0      -> seg_free                                         3263
0       -> as_removeseg                                    3265
0       <- as_removeseg                                    3270
0       -> segvn_free                                      3272
0        -> segvn_lockop                                   3273
0        <- segvn_lockop                                   3274
0       <- segvn_free                                      3279
0      <- seg_free                                         3281
0     <- segvn_unmap                                       3282
0    <- as_unmap                                           3284
0   <= munmap                                              3286
```

In this example, we can see the munmap() system call's implementation—a munmap() request calls into the AS layer to locate a mapping for a given address, which searches the AVL tree for the target address space, locating all the mappings within the specified addresses. For each mapping, the AS layer calls the appropriate segment driver, which contains the majority of the unmap implementation for this address range. In this example, the seg_vn driver calls into the HAT to unload the MMU mappings for each of the pages within the supplied addresses.

9.4 Virtual Address Space Management

A virtual address space is a container for a set of mappings. There is one address space for each process within the system, and one for the kernel. The address space layers manage setup and teardown changes to the address spaces on behalf of a process or the kernel, and MMU faults within.

9.4.1 Address Space Management

The Solaris kernel is implemented with a central address management subsystem that other parts of the kernel call into. The address space module is a wrapper around the segment drivers, so that subsystems need not know what segment driver is used for a memory range. The address space object shown in Figure 9.7 is linked from the process's address space and contains pointers to the segments that constitute the address space.

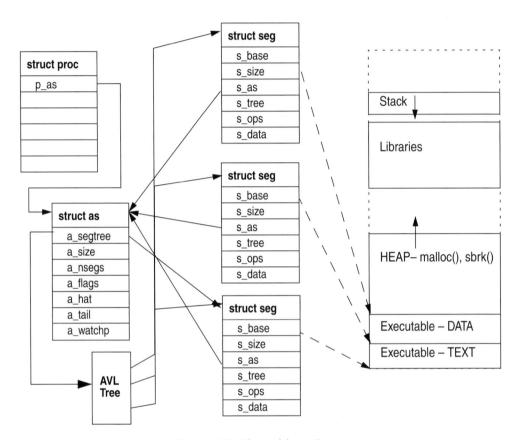

Figure 9.7 The Address Space

The address space subsystem manages the following functions:

- Duplication of address spaces, for fork()
- Destruction of address spaces, for exit()
- Creation of new segments within an address space
- Removal of segments from an address space
- Setting and management of page protection for an address space

- Page fault routing for an address space
- Page locking and advice for an address space
- Management of watchpoints for an address space

Recall that the process and kernel subsystems call into the address space subsystem to manage their address spaces. The address space subsystem consists of a series of functions, grouped to perform the functions listed above. Although the subsystem has a lot of entry points, the implementation is fairly simple because most of the functions simply look up which segment the operation needs to operate on and then route the request to the appropriate segment driver.

A call to the `as_alloc()` function creates an address space, but `as_alloc()` is invoked only once—when the system boots and the init process is created. After the init process is created, all address spaces are created by duplication of the init process's address space with `fork()`. The `fork()` system call in turn calls the `as_dup()` function to duplicate the address space of the current process as it creates a new process, and the entire address space configuration, including the stack and heap, is replicated at this point.

The behavior of `vfork()` at this point is somewhat different. Rather than calling `as_dup()` to replicate the address space, `vfork()` creates a new process by borrowing the parent's existing address space. The `vfork` function is useful if the fork is going to call `exec()` since it saves all the effort of duplicating the address space that would otherwise have been discarded once `exec()` is called. The parent process is suspended while the child is using its address space, until `exec()` is called. Once the process is created, the address space object is allocated and set up. The Solaris 10 data structure for the address space object is shown below.

```
struct as {
        kmutex_t a_contents;    /* protect certain fields in the structure */
        uchar_t  a_flags;       /* as attributes */
        uchar_t  a_vbits;       /* used for collecting statistics */
        kcondvar_t a_cv;        /* used by as_rangelock */
        struct  hat *a_hat;     /* hat structure */
        struct  hrmstat *a_hrm; /* ref and mod bits */
        caddr_t a_userlimit;    /* highest allowable address in this as */
        struct seg *a_seglast;  /* last segment hit on the addr space */
        krwlock_t a_lock;       /* protects segment related fields */
        size_t  a_size;         /* size of address space */
        struct seg *a_lastgap;  /* last seg found by as_gap() w/ AS_HI (mmap) */
        avl_tree_t a_segtree;   /* segments in this address space. (AVL tree) */
        struct watched_page *a_wpage;   /* list of watched pages (procfs) */
        int     a_nwpage;       /* number of watched pages */
        uchar_t a_updatedir;    /* mappings changed, rebuild a_objectdir */
        vnode_t **a_objectdir;  /* object directory (procfs) */
        size_t  a_sizedir;      /* size of object directory */
        struct as_callback *a_callbacks; /* callback list */
};
                                                                See vm/as.h
```

The following output from the DTrace `vm.d` script shows the path through the virtual memory layers as a process allocates more memory via `brk()`:

```
0   => brk                                            13076
0    -> as_rangelock                                  13077
0    <- as_rangelock                                  13078
0    -> as_map                                        13082
0     -> seg_alloc                                    13087
0      -> seg_attach                                  13091
0       -> as_addseg                                  13093
0       <- as_addseg                                  13101
0      <- seg_attach                                  13102
0     <- seg_alloc                                    13104
0     -> segvn_create                                 13106
0      -> anon_resvmem                                13108
0      <- anon_resvmem                                13110
0      -> anon_grow                                   13117
0      <- anon_grow                                   13123
0      -> seg_free                                    13125
0       -> as_removeseg                               13127
0       <- as_removeseg                               13132
0      <- seg_free                                    13134
0     <- segvn_create                                 13137
0     -> as_setwatch                                  13139
0     <- as_setwatch                                  13141
0    <- as_map                                        13143
0    -> as_rangeunlock                                13144
0    <- as_rangeunlock                                13146
0   <= brk                                            13147
```

Address space fault handling is performed in the address space subsystem; some of the faults are handled by the common address space code, and others are redirected to the segment handlers. When a page fault occurs, the Solaris trap handlers call the `as_fault()` function, which looks to see what segment the page fault occurred in by calling the `as_setat()` function. If the fault does not lie in any of the address space's segments, then `as_fault()` sends a `SIGSEGV` signal to the process. If the fault does lie within one of the segments, then the segment's fault method is called and the segment handles the page fault.

Table 9.3 lists the segment functions in alphabetical order.

Table 9.3 Solaris 10 Address Space Functions

Method	Description
as_add_callback()	Register a callback for certain events from clients of the address space.
as_addseg()	Creates a new segment and links it into the address space.

continues

Table 9.3 Solaris 10 Address Space Functions (*continued*)

Method	Description
as_alloc()	Creates a new address space object (only called from the kernel for the init process).
as_clearwatch()	Clears all watch points for the address space.
as_ctl()	Sends memory advice to an address range for the address space.
as_delete_callback()	Delete a callback.
as_dup()	Duplicates the entire address space.
as_exec()	Is a special code for exec to move the stack segment from its interim place in the old address space to the right place in the new address space.
as_fault()	Handles a page fault in the address space.
as_findseg()	Finds a segment containing the supplied virtual address.
as_free()	Destroys the address space object; called by exit().
as_gap()	Finds a hole of at least the specified size within [*base, base + len*). If the flag supplied specifies AH_HI, the hole will have the highest possible address in the range. Otherwise, it will have the lowest possible address. If the flag supplied specifies AH_CONTAIN, the hole will contain the address *addr*. If an adequate hole is found, *base* and *len* are set to reflect the part of the hole that is within range, and 0 is returned. Otherwise, −1 is returned.
as_getmemid()	Calls the segment driver containing the supplied address to find a unique ID for this segment.
as_getprot()	Gets the current protection settings for the supplied address.
as_incore()	Determine whether data from the mappings in interval [addr, addr + size) are in the primary memory.
as_map()	Maps a file into the address space.
as_memory()	Returns the next range within [*base, base + len*) that is backed with "real memory."
as_pagelock()	Locks a page within an address space by calling the segment page lock function.
as_pagereclaim()	Retrieves a page from the free list for the address supplied.
as_pageunlock()	Unlocks a page within the address space.

continues

Table 9.3 Solaris 10 Address Space Functions (*continued*)

Method	Description
as_purge()	Delete all segments in the address space marked with S_PURGE (for non-faulting segments).
as_rangebroadcast()	Wakes up all threads waiting on the address space condition variable.
as_rangelock()	Locks the pages for the supplied address range.
as_rangeunlock()	Unlocks the pages for the supplied address range.
as_rangewait()	Waits for virtual addresses to become available in the specified address space. AS_CLAIMGAP must be held by the caller and is reacquired before returning to the caller.
as_setat()	Finds a segment containing the supplied address.
as_setpagesize()	Set the page size advice for the range of supplied addresses.
as_setprot()	Sets the virtual mapping for the interval from [*addr* : *addr* + *size*) in address space as to have the specified protection.
as_setwatch()	Sets a watchpoint for the address. On a system without watchpoint support, does nothing.
as_swapout()	Swaps the pages associated with the address space to secondary storage, returning the number of bytes actually swapped.
as_unmap()	Unmaps a segment from the address space.

9.4.2 Address Space Callbacks

An address space callback is a facility which supports the ability to inform clients of specific events pertaining to address space management. An example of such an event is an address space unmap request—to prevent holding the address space's lock (a_lock) for a large amount of time during an unmap (which can cause ps(1) and other tools to hang), the unmap is performed as a callback without holding the a_lock. As one example, we use this facility to prevent an NFS server timeout from hanging ps.

A client calls as_add_callback() to register an address space callback for a range of pages, specifying the events that need to occur. When as_do_callbacks() is called and finds a matching entry, the callback is called once, and the callback function MUST call as_delete_callback() when all callback activities are complete. The thread calling as_do_callbacks() blocks until the as_delete_callback() is called. This allows for asynchronous events to subside before the as_do_callbacks() thread continues. An example of the need for this is a driver which has done long-term locking of memory. Address space management operations (events) such as `as_free()`, `as_unmap()`, and `as_setprot()` will block indefinitely until the pertinent memory is unlocked. The callback mechanism provides the way to inform the driver of the event so that the driver may do the necessary unlocking.

9.4.3 Virtual Memory Protection Modes

We break each process into segments so that we can treat each part of the address space differently. For example, the kernel maps the machine code portion of the executable binary into the process as read-only to prevent the process from modifying its machine code instructions. The virtual memory subsystem does this by taking advantage of the hardware MMU's virtual memory protection capabilities. Solaris relies on the MMU having the following protection modes:

- **Read.** The mapping is allowed to be read from.
- **Write.** The mapping is allowed to be written to.
- **Executable.** The mapping is allowed to have machine codes executed within its address range.

The implementation of protection modes is done in the segment and HAT layers.

9.4.4 Page Faults in Address Spaces

The Solaris virtual memory system uses the hardware MMU's memory management capabilities. MMU-generated exceptions tell the operating system when a memory access cannot continue without the kernel's intervention, by interrupting the executing process with a trap and then invoking the appropriate piece of memory management code. Three major types of memory-related hardware exceptions can occur: *major page faults*, *minor page faults*, and *protection faults*.

A *major page fault* occurs when an attempt to access a virtual memory location that is mapped by a segment does not have a physical page of memory mapped to it and the page does not exist in physical memory. The page fault allows the virtual memory system to hide the management of physical memory allocation from the process. The virtual memory system traps accesses to memory that the process believes is accessible and arranges to have either a new page created for that address (in the case of the first access) or copies in the page from the swap device. Once the memory system places a real page behind the memory address, the process can continue normal execution. If a reference is made to a memory address that is not mapped by any segment, then a segmentation violation signal (`SIGSEGV`) is sent to the process. The signal is sent as a result of a hardware exception caught by the processor and translated to a signal by the address space layer.

A *minor page fault* occurs when an attempt is made to access a virtual memory location that resides within a segment and the page is in physical memory, but no current MMU translation is established to the physical page from the address space that caused the fault. For example, a process maps in the `libc.so` library and makes a reference to a page within it. A page fault occurs, but the physical page of memory is already present and the process simply needs to establish a mapping to the existing physical page. Minor faults are also referred to as *attaches*.

A *page protection fault* occurs when a program attempts to access a memory address in a manner that violates the preconfigured access protection for a memory segment. Protection modes can enable any of read, write, or execute access. For example, the text portion of a binary is mapped read-only, and if we attempt to write to any memory address within that segment, we will cause a memory protection fault. The memory protection fault is also initiated by the hardware MMU as a trap that is then handled by the segment page fault handling routine.

Figure 9.8 shows the relationship between a virtual address space, its segments, and the hardware MMU.

In the figure, we see what happens when a process accesses a memory location within its heap space that does not have physical memory mapped to it. This has most likely occurred because the page of physical memory has previously been stolen by the page scanner as a result of a memory shortage. In the numbered events in the figures we see:

1. A reference is made to a memory address that does not map to a physical page of memory. In this example, the page has been paged out and now resides on the swap device.

2. When the process accesses the address with no physical memory behind it, the MMU detects the invalid reference and causes a trap to occur on the processor executing the code of the running thread. The fault handler recognizes this as a memory page fault and establishes which segment the fault occurred in by comparing the address of the fault to the addresses mapped by each segment.

3. The address space `as_fault()` routine compares the address of the fault with the addresses mapped by each segment and then calls the `page_fault` routine of the segment driver for this segment (in this case, the `vnode` segment driver).

4. The segment driver allocates and maps the page of memory by calling into the HAT layer and then copies the contents of the page from the swap device.

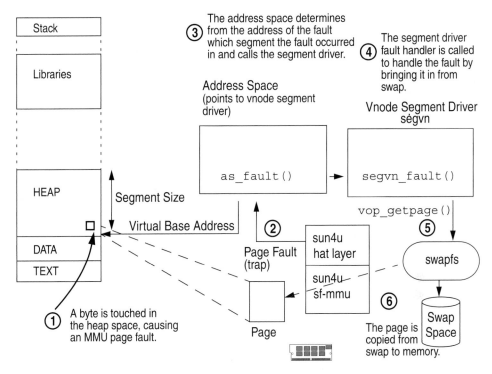

Figure 9.8 Virtual Address Space Page Fault Example

5. The segment driver then reads the page in from the backing store by calling the getpage() function of the backing store's vnode.

6. The backing store for this segment is the swap device, so the swap device getpage() function is called to read in the page from the swap device.

Once this process is completed, the process can continue execution. The following example using the DTrace vm.d script shows the logical flow for a zero-fill on demand page fault.

```
0   -> as_fault                          4210
0   | as_fault:as_fault                  4210
0    -> as_segat                         4211
0    <- as_segat                         4212
0    -> segvn_fault                      4213
0      -> anonmap_alloc                  4216
0        -> anon_create                  4219
0        <- anon_create                  4224
0      <- anonmap_alloc                  4225
0      -> anon_array_enter               4227
```

continues

```
0              -> page_get_pagecnt                    4228
0              <- page_get_pagecnt                    4229
0              -> anon_get_slot                       4230
0              <- anon_get_slot                       4231
0          <- anon_array_enter                        4232
0          -> anon_zero                               4234
0              -> anon_alloc                          4236
0              <- anon_alloc                          4240
0              -> page_lookup                         4243
0                -> page_lookup_create                4244
0                <- page_lookup_create                4245
0              <- page_lookup                         4246
0              -> page_create_va                      4248
0                -> page_get_freelist                 4251
0                  -> page_trylock                    4258
0                  <- page_trylock                    4259
0                  -> page_sub                        4261
0                  <- page_sub                        4262
0                <- page_get_freelist                 4266
0                -> page_hashin                       4268
0                <- page_hashin                       4270
0                -> page_io_lock                      4272
0                <- page_io_lock                      4273
0                -> page_add                          4275
0                <- page_add                          4276
0              <- page_create_va                      4278
0              -> pvn_plist_init                      4279
0                -> page_sub                          4280
0                <- page_sub                          4281
0                -> page_io_unlock                    4283
0                <- page_io_unlock                    4285
0              <- pvn_plist_init                      4286
0              -> pagezero                            4289
0              <- pagezero                            4294
0              -> page_downgrade                      4296
0              <- page_downgrade                      4297
0            | anon_zero:zfod                         4298
0              -> hat_page_setattr                    4299
0              <- hat_page_setattr                    4301
0          <- anon_zero                               4302
0          -> anon_set_ptr                            4303
0          <- anon_set_ptr                            4305
0          -> hat_memload                             4306
0          <- hat_memload                             4316
0          -> page_unlock                             4317
0          <- page_unlock                             4318
0          -> anon_array_exit                         4319
0          <- anon_array_exit                         4320
0        <- segvn_fault                               4321
0    <- as_fault                                      4322
```

9.5 Segment Drivers

Another example of the object-oriented approach to memory management is the memory "segment" object. Memory segments manage the mapping of a linear range of virtual memory into an address space. The mapping is between the address space and some type of device. The objective of the memory segment is to allow both memory and devices to be mapped into an address space. Traditionally, this required hard-coding memory and device information into the address space handlers for each device. The object architecture allows different behaviors for different segments.

For example, one segment might be a mapping of a file into an address space (with mmap()), and another segment might be the mapping of a hardware device into the process's address space (a graphics framebuffer). In this case, the segment driver provides a similar view of linear address space, even though the file mapping operation with mmap() uses pages of memory to cache the file data, whereas the framebuffer device maps the hardware device into the address space.

The flexibility of the segment object allows us to use virtually any abstraction to represent a linear address space that is visible to a process, regardless of the real facilities behind the scenes.

```
struct seg {
        caddr_t s_base;                 /* base virtual address */
        size_t  s_size;                 /* size in bytes */
        uint_t  s_szc;                  /* max page size code */
        uint_t  s_flags;                /* flags for segment, see below */
        struct as *s_as;                /* containing address space */
        avl_node_t s_tree;              /* AVL tree links to segs in this as */
        struct  seg_ops *s_ops;         /* ops vector: see below */
        void *s_data;                   /* private data for instance */
};
                                                                  See vm/seg.h
```

To implement an address space, a segment driver implementation is required to provide at least the following: functions to create a mapping for a linear address range, page fault handling routines to deal with machine exceptions within that linear address range, and a function to destroy the mapping. These functions are packaged together into a *segment driver*, which is an instantiation of the segment object interface. Figure 9.9 illustrates the relationship between an address space and a segment and shows a segment mapping the heap space of a process.

A segment driver implements a subset of the methods described in Table 9.5, as well as a constructor function to create the first instance of the object. Functions in the segment operations structure, s_ops, point to functions within the vnode segment driver and are prefixed with segvn. A segment object is created when another subsystem wants to create a mapping by calling as_map() to create a mapping at a specific address. The segment's create routine is passed as an argument to as_map(), a segment object is created, and a segment object pointer is returned. Once the segment is created, other parts of the virtual memory system can call into the segment for different address space operations without knowing what the underlying segment driver is using the segment method operations for.

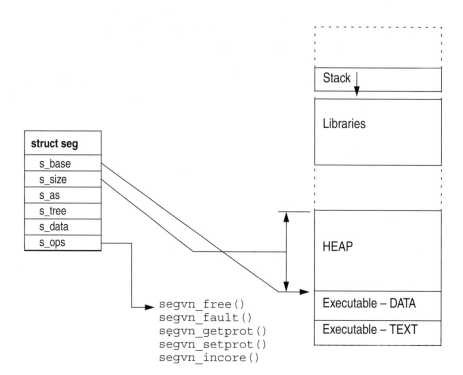

Figure 9.9 Segment Interface

For example, when a file is mapped into an address space with mmap(), the address space map routine as_map() is called with segvn_create() (the vnode segment driver constructor) as an argument, which in turn calls into the seg_vn segment driver to create the mapping. The segment object is created and inserted into the segment list for the address space (struct as), and from that point on, the address space can perform operations on the mapping without knowing what the underlying segment is.

The address space routines can operate on the segment without knowing what type of segment is underlying by calling the segment operation macros. For example, if the address space layer wants to call the fault handler for a segment, it calls SEGOP_FAULT(), which invokes the segment-specific page fault method, as shown below.

```
#define SEGOP_FAULT(h, s, a, l, t, rw) \
            (*(s)->s_ops->fault)((h), (s), (a), (l), (t), (rw))
                                                    See vm/seg.h
```

The Solaris kernel is implemented with a range of segment drivers for various functions. The different types of drivers are shown in Table 9.4. Most of the process address space mapping—including executable text, data, heap, stack and memory-mapped files—is performed with the vnode segment driver, seg_vn. Other types of mappings that don't have vnodes associated with them require different segment drivers. The other segment drivers are typically associated with kernel memory mappings or hardware devices, such as graphics adapters.

Table 9.5 describes segment driver methods implemented in Solaris 10.

Table 9.4 Solaris 10 Segment Drivers

Segment	Function
seg_vn	The vnode mappings into process address spaces are managed with the seg_vn device driver. Executable text and data, shared libraries, mapped files, heap and stack (heap and stack are anonymous memory) are all mapped with seg_vn.
seg_kmem	The segment from which the bulk of nonpageable kernel memory is allocated. (See Chapter 11.)
seg_kp	The segment from which pageable kernel memory is allocated. Only a very small amount of the kernel is pageable; kernel thread stacks and TNF buffers are the main consumers of pageable kernel memory.
seg_kpm	A mapping of all physical memory into the kernel's address space on 64-bit systems—to facilitate fast mapping of pages. The file systems use this facility to read and write to pages to avoid excessive map/unmap operations.
seg_spt	Shared page table segment driver. Fast System V shared memory is mapped into process address space from this segment driver. Memory allocated from this driver is also known as Intimate Shared Memory (ISM).
seg_map	The kernel uses the seg_map driver to map files (vnodes) into the kernel's address space, to implement file system caching.
seg_dev	Mapped hardware devices.
seg_mapdev	Mapping support for mapped hardware devices, through the ddi_mapdev(9F) interface.
seg_lock	Mapping support for hardware graphics devices that are mapped between user and kernel address space.
seg_drv	Mapping support for mapped hardware graphics devices.
seg_nf	Nonfaulting kernel memory driver.

Table 9.5 Solaris Segment Driver Methods

Method	Description
advise()	Provides a hint to optimize memory accesses to this segment. For example, sequential advice given to mapped files causes read-ahead to occur.
checkprot()	Checks that the requested access type (read, write, exec) is allowed within the protection level of the pages within the segment.
dump()	Dumps the segment to the dump device; used for crash dumps.
dup()	Duplicates the current memory segment, including all of the page mapping entries to the new segment pointer provided.
fault()	Handles a page fault for a segment. The arguments describe the segment, the virtual address of the page fault, and the type of fault.
faulta()	Starts a page fault on a segment and address asynchronously. Used for read-ahead or prefaulting of data as a performance optimization for I/O.
free()	Destroys a segment.
getmemid()	Gets a unique identifier for the memory segment.
getoffset()	Queries the segment driver for the offset into the underlying device for the mapping. (Not meaningful on all segment drivers.)
getpolicy()	Get the MPO Lgroup Policy for the supplied address
getprot()	Asks the segment driver for the protection levels for the memory range.
gettype()	Queries the driver for the sharing modes of the mapping.
getvp()	Gets the vnode pointer for the vnode, if there is one, behind this mapping.
incore()	Queries to find out how many pages are in physical memory for a segment.
kluster()	Asks the segment driver if it is OK to cluster I/O operations for pages within this segment.
lockop()	Locks or unlocks the pages for a range of memory mapped by a segment.
pagelock()	Locks a single page within the segment.
setpagesize()	Advises the page size for the address range

continues

Table 9.5 Solaris Segment Driver Methods (*continued*)

Method	Description
setprot()	Sets the protection level of the pages within the address range supplied.
swapout()	Attempts to swap out as many pages to secondary storage as possible.
sync()	Syncs up any dirty pages within the segment to the backing store.
unmap()	Unmaps the address space range within a segment.

9.5.1 The vnode Segment: seg_vn

The most widely used segment driver is the vnode segment driver, seg_vn. The seg_vn driver maps files (or vnodes) into a process address space, using physical memory as a cache. The seg_vn segment driver also creates anonymous memory within the process address space for the heap and stack and provides support for System V (non ISM) shared memory. (See Section 4.4.)

The seg_vn segment driver manages the following mappings into process address space:

- Executable text
- Executable data
- Heap and stack (anonymous memory)
- Shared libraries
- Mapped files

9.5.1.1 Memory Mapped Files

We can map a file into a process's address space with the mmap system call. (See mmap(2).) When we map a file into our address space, we call into the address space routines to create a new segment, a vnode segment. A vnode segment handles memory address translation and page faults for the memory range requested in the mmap system call, and the new segment is added to the list of segments in the process's address space. When the segment is created, the seg_vn driver initializes the segment structure with the address and length of the mapping, then creates a seg_vn-specific data structure within the segment structure's s_data field. The seg_vn-specific data structure holds all of the information the seg_vn driver needs to handle the address mappings for the segment.

The seg_vn-specific data structure (struct segvn_data) contains pointers to the vnode that is mapped and to any anonymous memory that has been allocated for this segment. The file system does most of the work of mapped files once the mapping is created. As a result, the seg_vn driver is fairly simple—most of the seg_vn work is done during creation and deletion of the mapping.

The more complex part of the seg_vn driver implementation is its handling of anonymous memory pages within the segment, which we discuss in the sections that follow. When we create a file mapping, we put the vnode and offset of the file being mapped into the segvn_data structure members, vp and offset. The seg_vn data structure is shown below; Figure 9.10 illustrates the seg_vn segment driver vnode relationship.

```
typedef struct  segvn_data {
        krwlock_t lock;              /* protect segvn_data and vpage array */
        kmutex_t segp_slock;         /* serialize insertions into seg_pcache */
        uchar_t pageprot;            /* true if per page protections present */
        uchar_t prot;                /* current segment prot if pageprot == 0 */
        uchar_t maxprot;             /* maximum segment protections */
        uchar_t type;                /* type of sharing done */
        u_offset_t offset;           /* starting offset of vnode for mapping */
        struct  vnode *vp;           /* vnode that segment mapping is to */
        ulong_t anon_index;          /* starting index into anon_map anon array */
        struct  anon_map *amp;       /* pointer to anon share structure, if needed */
        struct  vpage *vpage;        /* per-page information, if needed */
        struct  cred *cred;          /* mapping credentials */
        size_t  swresv;              /* swap space reserved for this segment */
        uchar_t advice;              /* madvise flags for segment */
        uchar_t pageadvice;          /* true if per page advice set */
        ushort_t flags;              /* flags - from sys/mman.h */
        ssize_t softlockcnt;         /* # of pages SOFTLOCKED in seg */
        lgrp_mem_policy_info_t policy_info; /* memory allocation policy */
} segvn_data_t;
```
                                                                        See vm/seg_vn.h

Creating a mapping for a file is done with the mmap() system call, which calls the map method for the file system that contains the file. For example, calling mmap() for a file on a UFS file system will call ufs_map(), which in turn calls into the seg_vn driver to create a mapped file segment in the address space with the segvn_create() function.

At this point we create an actual virtual memory mapping by talking to the hardware through the hardware address translation functions by using the hat_map() function. The hat_map() function is the central function for creating address space mappings. It calls into the hardware-specific memory implementation for the platform to program the hardware MMU, so that memory address references within the supplied address range will trigger the page fault handler in the segment driver until a valid physical memory page has been placed at the accessed location. Once the hardware MMU mapping is established, the seg_vn driver can begin handling page faults within that segment.

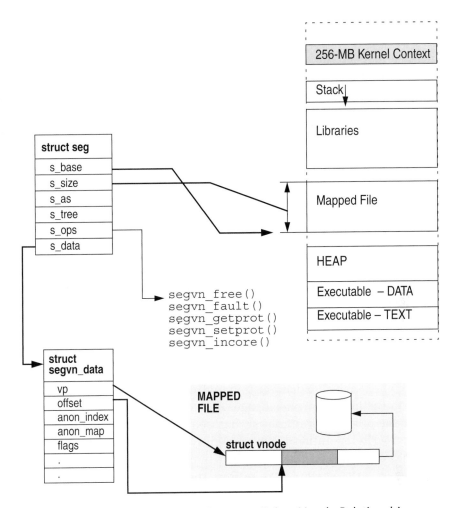

Figure 9.10 The seg_vn Segment Driver Vnode Relationship

Having established a valid hardware mapping for our file, we can look at how our mapped file is effectively read into the address space. The hardware MMU can generate traps for memory accesses to the memory within that segment. These traps will be routed to our seg_vn driver through the as_fault() routine. (See Section 9.4.4.) The first time we access a memory location within our segment, the segvn_fault() page fault handling routine is called. This fault handler recognizes our segment as a mapped file (by looking in the segvn_data structure) and simply calls into the vnode's file system (in this case, with ufs_getpage()) to read in a page-sized chunk from the file system. The subsequent access to memory that is now backed by physical memory simply results in a normal memory access.

It's not until a page is stolen from behind the segment (the page scanner can do this) that a page fault will occur again.

Writing to a mapped file is done by updating the contents of memory within the mapped segment. The file is not updated instantly, since there is no software- or hardware-initiated event to trigger any such write. Updates occur when the file system flush daemon finds that the page of memory has been modified and then pushes the page to the file system with the file systems `putpage` routine, in this case, `ufs_putpage()`.

9.5.2 Copy-on-Write

The copy-on-write process occurs when a process writes to a page that is mapped with `MAP_PRIVATE`. This process prevents other mappings to the page from seeing changes that are made. `seg_vn` implements a copy-on-write by setting the hardware MMU permissions of a segment to read-only and setting the segment permissions to read-write. When a process attempts to write to a mapping that is configured this way, the MMU generates an exception and causes a page fault on the page in question. The page fault handler in `seg_vn` looks at the protection mode for the segment; if it is mapped private and read-write, then the handler initiates a copy-on-write.

The copy-on-write unmaps the shared `vnode` page where the fault occurred, creates a page of anonymous memory at that address, and then copies the contents of the old page to the new anonymous page. All of this happens in the context of the page fault, so the process never knows what's happening underneath it.

The copy-on-write operation behaves slightly differently under different memory conditions. When memory is low, rather than creating a new physical memory page, the copy-on-write steals the page from the offset of the file underneath and renames it to be the new anonymous page. This only occurs when free memory is lower than the system parameter `minfree`.

9.5.3 Page Protection and Advice

The `seg_vn` segment supports memory protection modes on either the whole segment or individual pages within a segment. Whole segment protection is implemented by the `segvn_data` structure member, `prot`; its enablement depends on the boolean switch, `pageprot`, in the `segvn_data` structure. If `pageprot` is equal to zero, then the entire segment's protection mode is set by `prot`; otherwise, page-level protection is enabled.

Page-level protection is implemented by an array of page descriptors pointed to by the `vpage` structure, shown below. If page-level protection is enabled, then `vpage` points to an array of `vpage` structures. Every possible page in the address space has one array entry, which means that the number of `vpage` members is the segment virtual address space size divided by the fundamental page size for the segment (8 Kbytes on UltraSPARC).

```
struct vpage {
        uchar_t nvp_prot;       /* see <sys/mman.h> prot flags */
        uchar_t nvp_advice;     /* pplock & <sys/mman.h> madvise flags */
};
                                                            See vm/page.h
```

The vpage entry for each page uses the standard memory protection bits (see mmap(2)). The per-page vpage structures are also used to implement memory advice for memory-mapped files in the seg_vn segment.

9.6 Anonymous Memory

At many points we have mentioned *anonymous memory*. Anonymous memory refers to pages that are not directly associated with a vnode. Such pages are used for a process's heap space, its stack, and copy-on-write pages. In the Solaris kernel, two subsystems are dedicated to managing anonymous memory: the anon layer and the swapfs file system.

The anonymous memory allocated to the heap of a process is a result of a zero-fill-on-demand operation (ZFOD). The ZFOD operation is how we allocate new pages. A ZFOD occurs when we touch a memory address for the first time, and a new page of memory is dynamically allocated at that address. ZFOD is the allocation method used for the heap space and segments created as a map of /dev/zero with segment protection of MAP_PRIVATE. A page fault on a segment of this type will be recognized as ZFOD, and a new zeroed anonymous memory page is created at the fault location. The seg_vn segment fault handler, segvn_fault, handles the fault and creates ZFOD pages.

The seg_vn segment driver allocates anonymous memory to the segment by calling into the anonymous memory layer interfaces and attaching anonymous maps to the amp (anonymous map pointer) member in the segvn_data structure. Figure 9.11 shows a seg_vn segment with the anonymous map structures allocated to it.

Every allocated page-sized piece of virtual memory in the segment is assigned an anonymous map slot. For example, when a segment is first created, there are no anonymous map slots allocated, but the first time a zero fill-on-demand page fault occurs, a slot is allocated for a page, corresponding to the address within the segment where the fault occurred. At that time, a physical page is attached to the slot. Later, the page may be stolen and no page is associated anymore, but an empty slot remains.

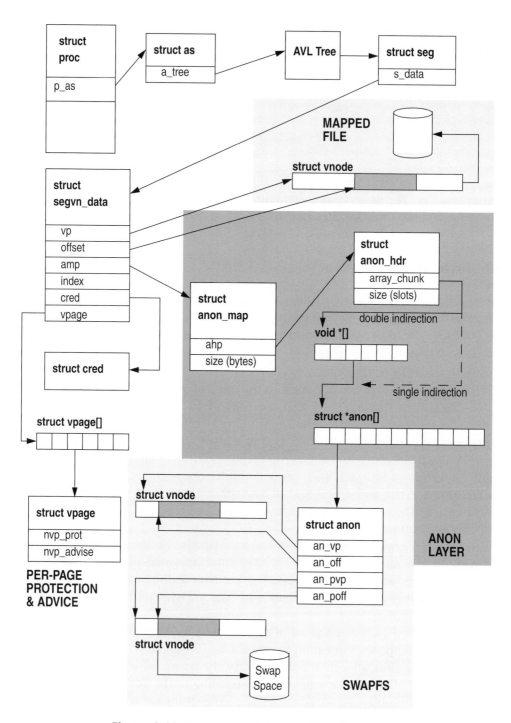

Figure 9.11 Anonymous Memory Data Structures

9.7 The Anonymous Memory Layer

Anonymous pages are created through the `anon` layer interfaces. The first time a segment receives a page fault, it allocates an `anon` map structure (which describes where to find the `anon` header) and puts a pointer to the `anon` header into the `ahp` field of the anonymous map. It then allocates the slot array, big enough to hold the number of potential pages in the segment. The slot array is either a single or double indirection list, depending on how many slots are required.

32-bit systems require double indirection for segments larger than 16 Mbytes; 64-bit systems, because of larger pointer sizes, require double indirection for segments larger than 8 Mbytes. When we use single indirection, the `anon` header `array_chunk` directly references the anon slot array. When we use double indirection, the array is broken into chunks: 2,048 slot chunks for 32-bit systems and 1,024 slot chunks for 64-bit systems. An additional array of pointers is referenced by the `array_chunk` field pointing to each chunk. Figure 9.11 shows the single and double indirection arrays. This allocation process is handled by the `anon` layer interface, `anon_create`. The anon slot is shown below.

```
struct anon {
        struct vnode *an_vp;     /* vnode of anon page */
        struct vnode *an_pvp;    /* vnode of physical backing store */
        anoff_t an_off;          /* offset of anon page */
        anoff_t an_poff;         /* offset in vnode */
        struct anon *an_hash;    /* hash table of anon slots */
        int an_refcnt;           /* # of people sharing slot */
};
                                                         See vm/anon.h
```

Each `anon` slot points to an `anon` structure, which describes the virtual page of memory corresponding to the page-sized area in the address space. SVR4 implementations simply had a page structure for each slot that had a physical page associated with it, or NULL if there was no physical page in memory. However, the Solaris implementation does things differently. Recall that all physical pages have a vnode and offset. The Solaris kernel identifies that physical page, which points to the swap vnode, and offset assigned to the page. Note that this is not the swap device *actual* vnode and offset; rather, it's a vnode and offset *pointing to* the `swapfs` file system (which we'll discuss shortly). The `anon` structure also contains space for other information of interest to `swapfs`.

The `anon` layer functions are listed alphabetically in Table 9.6.

Table 9.6 Anon Layer Functions

Function	Description
anon_alloc()	Allocates an anon slot and returns it with the lock held.
anon_copy_ptr()	Copies anon array into a given new anon array.
anon_create()	Creates the array of pointers.
anon_decref()	Decrements the reference count of an anon page. If the reference count goes to zero, frees it and its associated page (if any).
anon_dup()	Duplicates references to *size* bytes worth of anon pages. Used when duplicating a segment that contains private anon pages.
anon_free()	Frees a group of *size* anon pages, *size* in bytes, and clears the pointers to the anon entries.
anon_get_next_ptr()	Returns the anon pointer for the first valid entry in the anon list, starting from the given index.
anon_getpage()	Returns the kept page(s) and protections to the segment driver.
anon_get_ptr()	Returns the pointer from the list for a specified anon index.
anon_pages()	Returns a count of the number of existing anon pages in the anon array in the range.
anon_private()	Turns a reference to an object or shared anon page into a private page with a copy of the data from the original page.
anon_release()	Frees the array of pointers.
anon_resvmem()	Reserves anon space.
anon_set_ptr()	Sets list entry with a given pointer for a specified offset.
anon_unresv()	Gives back an anon reservation.
anon_zero()	Allocates a private zero-filled anon page.
anonmap_alloc()	Allocates and initializes an anon_map structure for segment associating the given swap reservation with the new anon_map.
anonmap_free()	Frees an anon map structure.
anon_map_getpages()	Allocates array of private zero-filled anon pages for empty slots and kept pages for nonempty slots within given range.
non_anon()	Returns true if the array has some empty slots.
set_anoninfo()	Is called from clock handler to sync ani_free value.

9.8 The `swapfs` Layer

Each physical page of memory is identified by its vnode and offset. The vnode and offset identify a backing store that tells where to find the page when it's not in physical memory. For a regular file, the physical page caching the file has a vnode and offset that are simply the file's vnode and offset. Swap space is used as a backing store for anonymous pages of memory, so that when we are short of memory, we can copy a page out to disk and free up a page of memory.

Because swap space is used as the backing store for anonymous memory, we need to ensure we have enough swap space for the pages we may need to swap out. We do that by reserving space upfront when we create writable mappings backed by anonymous memory for heap space, stack, and writable mapped files with MAP_PRIVATE set.

The Solaris kernel allows us to allocate anonymous memory without reserving physical swap space when sufficient memory is available to hold the virtual contents of a process. This means that under some circumstances a system can run with little or no swap.

Traditional UNIX implementations need a page-sized unit of swap space for every page-sized unit of writable virtual memory. For example, a `malloc` request of 8 Mbytes on a traditional UNIX system would require us to reserve 8 Mbytes of swap disk space, even if that space was never used. This requirement led to the old rule of swap space = 2 × memory size—the rough assumption was that processes would, on average, have a virtual size about twice that of the physical pages they consumed. The `swapfs` layer allows Solaris to be much more conservative; you only need swap space for the amount of virtual memory that is larger than the pageable physical memory available in the machine.

The Solaris swap implementation uses `swapfs` to implement space-efficient swap allocation. The `swapfs` file system is a pseudo file system between the anon layer and the physical swap devices. The `swapfs` file system acts as if there is real swap space behind the page, even if no physical swap space was allocated.

9.8.1 `swapfs` Implementation

The `swapfs` file system uses a system global variable, `availrmem`, to keep track of the available pageable physical memory in the system and adds it to the total amount of swap space available. When we reserve virtual swap, we simply decrement the amount of virtual memory available from the pool. As long as enough memory and physical swap space are available, then the swap allocations succeed. It's not until later that physical swap space is assigned.

When we create a private segment, we reserve swap and allocate anon structures. At this stage, that's all that happens until a real memory page is created as
a result of a ZFOD or copy-on-write (COW). When a physical page is faulted in, it is
identified by vnode/offset, which for anonymous memory is the virtual swap device
for the page.

Anonymous pages in Solaris are assigned a swapfs vnode and offsets when the
segment driver calls anon_alloc() to get a new anonymous page. The anon_
alloc() function calls into swapfs through swapfs_getvp() and then calls
swapfs_getpage() to create a new page with swapfs vnode/offset. The anon
structure members, an_vp and an_off, which identify the backing store for this
page, are initialized to reference the vnode and offset within the swapfs virtual
swap device.

Figure 9.12 shows how the anon slot points into swapfs. At this stage, we still
don't need any physical swap space—the amount of virtual swap space available
was decremented when the segment reserved virtual swap space—but because we
haven't had to swap the pages out to physical swap, no physical swap space has
been allocated.

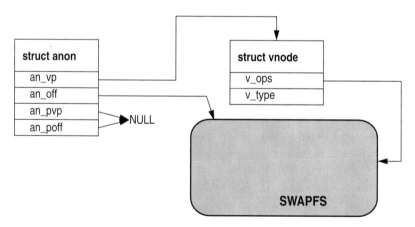

Figure 9.12 Anon Slot Initialized to Virtual Swap before Page-Out

It's not until the first page-out request occurs—because the page scanner must
want to push a page to swap—that real swap is assigned. At this time, the page
scanner looks up the vnode for the page and then calls its putpage() method.
The page's vnode is a swapfs vnode, and hence swapfs_putpage() is called to
swap this page out to the swap device. The swapfs_putpage() routine allocates a

page-sized block of physical swap and then sets the physical vnode an_pvp and an_poff fields in the anon slot to point to the physical swap device. The page is pushed to the swap device. At this point we allocate physical swap space. Figure 9.13 shows the anon slot *after* the page has been swapped out.

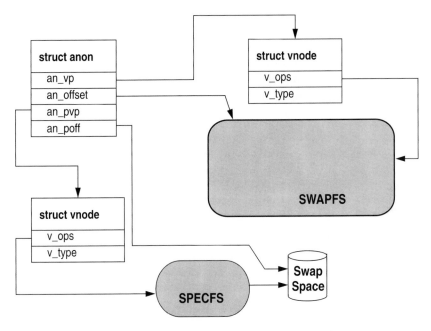

Figure 9.13 Physical Swap after a Page-Out Occurs

When we exhaust physical swap space, we simply ignore the putpage() request for a page, resulting in memory performance problems that are very hard to analyze. A failure does not occur when physical swap space fills; during reservation, we ensured that we had sufficient available virtual swap space, comprising both physical memory and physical swap space. In this case, the swapfs_ putpage() simply leaves the page in memory and does not push a page to physical swap. This means that once physical swap is 100 percent allocated, we begin effectively locking down the remaining pages in physical memory. For this reason, it's often a bad idea to run with 100 percent physical swap allocation (swap −1 shows 0 blocks free) because we might start locking down the wrong pages in memory and our working set might not correctly match the pages we really want in memory.

9.9 Virtual Memory Watchpoints

The Solaris kernel implements virtual memory watchpoints within address spaces. A watchpoint is similar to a breakpoint, except that a watchpoint stops execution when an address location is read or modified, whereas a breakpoint stops execution when an instruction is executed at a specified location. Watchpoints also provide the ability to implement breakpoints through the watchpoint interface.

You set and clear watchpoints through the /proc file system interface, by opening the control file for a process and then sending a PCWATCH command. The PCWATCH command is accompanied by a prwatch structure, which contains the address, the length of the area to be affected, and the type of watchpoint.

```
typedef struct prwatch {
        uintptr_t pr_vaddr;  /* virtual address of watched area */
        size_t   pr_size;    /* size of watched area in bytes */
        int  pr_wflags;      /* watch type flags */
} prwatch_t;
                                                    See sys/watchpoint.h
```

The pr_vaddr field specifies the virtual address of an area of memory to be watched in the controlled process; pr_size specifies the size of the area, in bytes, and pr_wflags specifies the type of memory access to be monitored as a bit-mask of the flags shown in Table 9.7.

Table 9.7 Watchpoint Flags

Flag	Description
WA_READ	Read access
WA_WRITE	Write access
WA_EXEC	Execution access
WA_TRAPAFTER	Trap after the instruction completes

If pr_wflags is nonzero, then a watched area is established for the virtual address range specified by pr_vaddr and pr_size. If pr_wflags is zero, then any previously established watched area starting at the specified virtual address is cleared; pr_size is ignored.

A watchpoint is triggered when an LWP in the traced process makes a memory reference that covers at least one byte of a watched area and the memory reference is as specified in pr_wflags. When an LWP triggers a watchpoint, it incurs a watchpoint trap. If FLTWATCH is being traced, the LWP stops; otherwise, it is sent a SIGTRAP signal. If SIGTRAP is being traced and is not blocked, then the LWP stops.

The watchpoint trap occurs before the instruction completes unless WA_TRAPAFTER was specified, in which case it occurs after the instruction completes. If the trap occurs before completion, the memory is not modified. If it occurs after completion, the memory is modified (if the access is a write access). A minimal example of how a watchpoint is established is shown below. The program creates a watchpoint for read and write access to the bytes occupied by the integer, test.

```
#include <sys/types.h>
#include <sys/fcntl.h>
#include <procfs.h>

typedef struct {
        long cmd;
        prwatch_t prwatch;
} ctl_t;

main(int argc, char **argv)
{
        int ctlfd;
        ctl_t ctl;
        int test;

        if ((ctlfd = open("/proc/self/ctl", O_WRONLY)) < 0) {
                perror("open /proc");
                exit (1);
        }

        ctl.cmd = PCWATCH;
        ctl.prwatch.pr_vaddr = (uintptr_t)&test;
        ctl.prwatch.pr_size = sizeof(int);
        ctl.prwatch.pr_wflags = WA_READ|WA_WRITE;

        if (write(ctlfd, &ctl, sizeof (ctl)) != sizeof (ctl)) {
                perror("Set PCWATCH");
                exit (1);
        }

        test = 0;
}
```

When we attempt to write to the integer test, we trigger a watchpoint and, by default, the process core dumps.

```
sol8$ ./watchpoint
Trace/Breakpoint Trap(coredump)
```

The /proc process information file, prinfo, contains information pertinent to the watchpoint trap and can be read into a struct pr_info. In particular, the si_addr field contains the virtual address of the memory reference that triggered the watchpoint, and the `si_code` field contains one of `TRAP_RWATCH`, `TRAP_WWATCH`, or `TRAP_XWATCH`, indicating read, write, or execute access, respectively. The `si_trapafter` field is zero unless `WA_TRAPAFTER` is in effect for this watched area; nonzero indicates that the current instruction is not the instruction that incurred the watchpoint trap. The `si_pc` field contains the virtual address of the instruction that incurred the trap. Figure 9.14 illustrates watchpoint data structures.

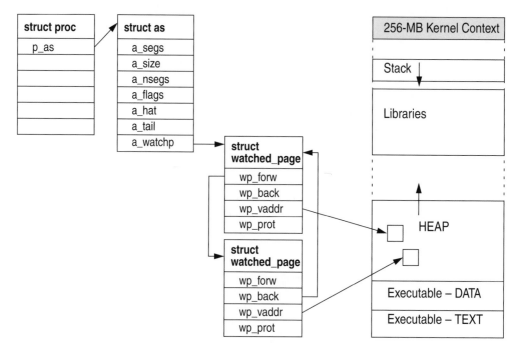

Figure 9.14 Watchpoint Data Structures

9.10 Changes to Support Large Pages

Solaris provides support for large MMU pages, as part of the Multiple Page Sizes for Solaris (MPSS) infrastructure. In this section, we discuss enhancements to page allocation and segment drivers.

9.10.1 System View of a Large Page

Solaris implements large pages in way that localizes changes to to only a few layer of the virtual memory system, and that does not slow down operations and applications not using large pages. The file systems and I/O layers need no knowledge of large pages. The only exception to this is the swap file system (swapfs), which is explained in more detail later.

Solaris 9 added a `p_szc` field to the `page_t` structure. This field used to exist in the sun4u version of the `machpage_t` structure. Since support for multiple page sizes above the HAT and platform layers is generic, the representation of large page sizes is also generic. As in Solaris 2.6, a large page is represented as a physically contiguous range of the kernel's minimum pagesize (`PAGESIZE`) pages that are physically aligned on the large-page-size boundary. For example, a 64-Kbyte page is represented by eight `page_t` structures, each with its `p_szc` field set to 1 and the physical address of the first `page_t` on a 64-Kbyte boundary. The size codes for 8-Kbyte, 64-Kbyte, 512-Kbyte, and 4-Mbyte pages, respectively, are (0, 1, 2, 3).

Most large page operations loop across the large page, performing operations in `PAGESIZE` increments. Another advantage of representing a large page as a group of `PAGESIZE` `page_t` structures is that `page_lookup()` operations are not slowed down. If the implementation had rather represented a large page with a single, variable-size `page_t`, it would have meant repeatedly rehashing inside `page_lookup()` on misses across all supported page sizes. The implementation allows us to do one lookup on the `page_t` and check its `p_szc` field. At this point, it's easy to compute the index of the base `page_t` (first constituent page of the large page). As long as any one of the constituent pages of a large page is locked, the size of the large page cannot change. The constituent pages must be exclusively locked to change their size.

9.10.2 Free List Organization

The page free list consists of two logical free lists: the cache list and the free list. The cache list contains free pages that still have identity. That is, they contain valid data. The free list contains pages without identity. In Solaris 2.6, the free list was subdivided into free lists per page size for large-page ISM support. The cache list supports only `PAGESIZE` pages since we do not support large pages for mapped files.

Each free list and the cache list is subdivided into bin lists for each page color. UltraSPARC uses direct-mapped, physically indexed external caches. Page color in this context means the size of the external cache divided by the page size. There is a group of these lists for each memory node on the machine for NUMA.

9.10.3 Large-Page Faulting

In this section we describe the following aspects of large-page faulting:

- How a large page is created on first access.
- How a large page is paged in from the swap device.

- How we handle COW (copy-on-write) faults.

- How we do locking for I/O.

9.10.3.1 Page Size-Up/Size-Down Policy

A page-size code field (s_szc) in the segment structure provides information about the preferred page size to lower levels of the virtual memory system. The segment driver attempts to allocate pages in accordance with this page size. This field normally is set with SEGOP_SETPAGESIZE() (e.g., memcntl(2)) or at creation time in segvn_create(). The latter is based on two kernel variables: mpss_brkpgszsel and mpss_stkkpgszsel. These kernel variables determine the default page size for heaps and stacks at exec time. They are passed to segvn_create() through the exec code. They could be used to set default heap and stack page size for all processes in the system.

These kernel variables are also useful for MPSS stress testing. If the variable is set to –1, a random page size is selected, on the basis of the value of the tick register, and passed into segvn_create(). At fault time, if the page is not found in the system, segvn allocates a page of the size specified in the segment size code field s_szc. If the correct size for a large page cannot be allocated, segvn_create() immediately tries to allocate a smaller one. This approach is better than blocking until a large page becomes available. At this point the choice is between the next size down and just trying PAGESIZE pages. For processors that have fully associative TLBs, it makes more sense to keep trying the next size down until successful.

9.10.3.2 Page-In

MAP_PRIVATE anonymous pages are allocated in swapfs. At fault time, if the ANON layer cannot find the page in the system, it invokes the swapfs VOP_GETPAGE() interface to create the page. If the contents are on backing store, it is brought in by swapfs to fill the newly allocated page.

The page identity (vnode, offset) naming rules for anonymous pages made it impossible to handle large pages with a single call to the current VOP_GETPAGE() interface for swapfs. It was designed to deal only with PAGESIZE pages. The ANON layer allocates an anon slot for each anonymous page.

```
struct anon {
        struct vnode *an_vp;    /* vnode of anon page */
        struct vnode *an_pvp;   /* vnode of physical backing store */
        anoff_t       an_off;   /* offset of anon page */
        anoff_t       an_poff;  /* offset in vnode */
        struct anon  *an_hash;  /* hash table of anon slots */
        int           an_refcnt; /* # sharing slot */
};
                                                              See vm/anon.h
```

The ANON layer then calls into swapfs to assign a unique identity to the anonymous page (vnode, offset). This identity will later be used by the ANON layer and swapfs for page lookup and creations for the life of the anonymous page. To generate a unique vnode and offset, swapfs simply splits the virtual address of the anon slot into two portions for generating a vnode index and offset. swapfs maintains a pool of fake vnodes identified by their vnode index. Since the address of the anon slot in the system is unique, the vnode offset page name generated from it will also be unique. VOP_GETPAGE() takes a vnode, offset, and length as part of its arguments. To make a single call through this interface for handling a large page would mean that the vnode would have to be the same for all constituent pages of the large page.

The vnode offset for the base constituent page should be aligned on the large-page-size boundary with each successive constituent page's offset increasing in PAGESIZE increments. With the current naming scheme, a large page can actually have different vnodes for its constituent pages with improperly aligned offsets.

A simplified solution to this problem is used—for a large page, the ANON layer first preallocates the large page. It then loops across the large page in PAGESIZE increments invoking swapfs's VOP_GETPAGE() interface to insert the page in the system and fill in the contents from backing store if necessary. Each constituent page of the preallocated large page is passed down to swapfs by a new pointer (t_vmdata) we added to the thread structure. If swapfs sees that a preallocated constituent page is passed down, it knows it's handling a large page. It first checks to see if a page already exists in the system. If a page of the same size or larger is found, that page's constituent page is returned and the preallocated large page is freed. If a smaller page is found, swapfs relocates the constituent page of the smaller page into the constituent page of the preallocated page and frees the old one. This is done in PAGESIZE steps as the ANON layer loops across the range of the large page.

9.10.3.3 Copy-on-Write Faults

New functions in the ANON layer help segvn deal with large pages. Copy-on-write (COW) faults for MAP_PRIVATE anonymous large pages are handled in a way similar to that for PAGESIZE pages. The anon structure keeps a reference count, to know when the last reference to a page has been removed before it can be freed. A large page is made up of PAGESIZE constituent pages. Therefore, each constituent page of the large page also has an anon slot associated with it.

When we handle a COW fault for a large page, we need to make sure we do not partially share a large page. That is, from the ANON layer's point of view we do not allow partial sharing of a subrange of anon slots representing a large page. This restriction greatly simplifies the freeing of large pages since we can only free them when the reference counts for all `anon` slots for each constituent page is zero. While handling a COW fault in the ANON layer, if we find that a large page cannot be allocated, we allocate enough smaller pages (equal to a large-page size) to satisfy the COW. This guarantees that our reference counts stay consistent across all the `anon` slots in the large page region, even if we fail to allocate a large page.

9.10.3.4 Page Locking for IO

In Solaris 2.6, a fast path was added for locking pages during IO and for caching the page list. The caching was an improvement over the old method, `as_fault(F_SOFTLOCK)`, for locking the pages and their MMU translations during IO setup. The MMU translations had to be locked so that the nexus driver could call into the HAT and build a list of page frame numbers for DMA. Later, when the IO completed the translations, the pages were unlocked. For IO-intensive applications, the overhead of repetitively locking the same pages and their MMU translations, calling into the HAT for the page frame list, and then unlocking was expensive.

The new fast path locks the pages once, inserts the list into a segment page cache, and then passes the page list (shadow list) down to the nexus driver through the `buf(9S)` framework. With the fast path we no longer need to lock the MMU translations, since we already have the page list. When the IO completes, the shadow list can be left in the segment page cache, which means the pages remain locked. If the IOs continue to come in, are of at a short enough duration, and keep using the same buffer in the user address space, then the `as_pagelock()` fast path will probably find the shadow list in the segment page cache with an inexpensive lookup. It then passes the shadow list down to the nexus driver, thereby reducing relock/unlock overhead.

When we insert a shadow list into the segment page cache with `segvn_pagelock()`, we need to decrement `availrmem` by the number of the pages in the shadow list. For I/O with large pages, holding the shared/exclusive lock of one or more constituent pages in a large page has the effect of locking the entire large page. The reason is that a large page cannot be freed or demoted unless we first lock all constituent pages exclusively. Therefore, in `segvn_pagelock()`, for large pages we adjust the pagelock region, the address, and the length to include the entire large page(s) and decrement `availrmem` according to the new size.

We do not want to just decrement `availrem` by the large-page size without also adjusting the address and length of the request. If we did not resize the request, we could end up decrementing `availrmem` by large-page amounts for every constituent page locked by a new `as_pagelock()` request. So resizing has the advantage of coalescing multiple requests within the large page(s) into a single segment page cache entry and decrementing `availrmem` by the correct amount.

9.10.4 Large-Page Freeing

Large pages are handled mostly as with regular pages—they are returned to the freelist when no longer needed. There are however the following differences:

- **Dirty page cleanup with page-out and `msync(3C)`.** When memory pressure becomes high, the page-out code will try to clean dirty pages by writing them out to their backing store so that they can possibly be freed. And applications themselves can synchronize the contents of their dirty pages with their backing store through `msync(3C)`. In both cases, this synchronization involves the use of `VOP_PUTPAGE()` to write out the dirty page. As we explained earlier with anonymous page naming, you cannot use the VOP interface for swapfs to operate across a large page in a single call.

  For both page-out and `msync(3C)`, we simply try to demote the large page to `PAGESIZE` pages. To demote a large page, we try to exclusively lock each constituent page of the large page. If successful, we can unload the mappings and safely reset the `p_szc` to 0 for each constituent page. This allows us to handle the old large page as `PAGESIZE` pages are handled today.

- **Placement of freed large pages.** Large pages are placed back on the free list, not on the cache list, as large pages only when they are being destroyed; for example, when a process exits or unmaps a segment and there is no low-level sharing of the large page because of `fork(2)`.

- **User page locking `mlock(3c)`.** Using `mlock(3C)` for large pages is no different from using it for `PAGESIZES` pages. If an application wants to lock a large page in memory, it must lock the entire range of the large-page mapping. If the application locks only a subrange of a large-page mapping, the system is still free to demote the page and take away the unlocked portions if free memory is low and pressure is high.

9.10.5 Operations That Interfere with Large Pages

The implementation adds support for large pages as transparently as possible. Two operations that can destroy large pages however are unaligned requests for changing memory protections and unloading mappings.

Consider the example of a process using 512-Kbyte pages for a `MAP_PRIVATE` `/dev/zero` mapping in its address space. It then attempts to execute `munmap(2)` or `mprotect(2)` on an 8-Kbyte range in the middle of the mapping. The segment driver, `segvn`, will detect this and demote the range affected by the operation to `PAGESIZE` pages and return an internal retry return value (`IE_RETRY`) back up to the Address Space (AS) layer. The AS layer will then drop the address space lock, take it back, and restart the operation. Page size is a property of a segment.

So, demoting a range in the address space, as in the example above, can involve splitting existing segments to accommodate the unaligned request. Manipulating the seg list in an address space requires that the address space lock be held as a writer. Today, this requirement is already met for the case of SEGOP_UNMAP() but not for SEGOP_SETPROT(). Since large pages can now involve the manipulation of the seg lists for possible demote operations, we now also lock the as writer for SEGOP_SETPROT() operations. This locking is not a performance problem, since SETPROTs are relatively rare.

Also, the watchpoint facility in /proc works by changing protections at PAGESIZE granularity. The implications for large pages are the same as above. The process may end up losing some or all of its large pages if it had any.

9.10.6 HAT Support

The Solaris sfmmu, UltraSPARC HAT, has always supported large pages. Prior to MPSS, on the user side, only large (4-, 32- or 256-Mbyte) pages for ISM are optimally supported. Only 8-Kbyte and 4-Mbyte pages are supported in the TSB (translation storage buffer). This means the trap handler for user dTLB misses will probe the TSB for both 4-Mbyte and 8-Kbyte pages. If both miss, the trap handler searches the hardware mapping entry (HME) hash for the correct translation table entry (TTE). Since ISM is optimized to use 4-Mbyte pages, the trap handler first does a hash search for the 4-Mbyte TTE. If the search fails, the trap handler rehashes and searches again for an 8-Kbyte TTE.

For MPSS we generalized large-page support for any kind of user data TLB miss. Today, the HAT probes the TSB at most twice on user data TLB misses. That is, we use the 8-Kbyte pointer generated in hardware, and if that fails, we recalculate a 4-Mbyte pointer and reprobe. Although we could use the 64-Kbyte pointer generated by hardware and calculate a 512-Kbyte pointer in software, the expense of the extra TSB lookups would degrade performance of all applications. So, for 64-Kbyte and 512-Kbyte pages, we simply replicate from the 8-Kbyte pointer.

For example, a 64-Kbyte TTE can occupy 8 TSB entries, and a 512-Kbyte TTE can occupy 64 entries. This situation has two disadvantages. First, it means the TSB reach is the same for 64-Kbyte and 512-Kbyte pages as it is for 8-Kbyte pages. Second, it takes longer to warm up the TSB with the replicated TTEs and demap TTEs of these two page sizes. The performance of handling TSB misses is critical. For that reason we wanted to handle TSB misses for any page size in the trap handler and not at C code ($tl = 0$). To that end, that HAT now keeps accurate per-mapping-size TTE counts. This information helps the TSB miss handler determine whether a particular mapping size even exists for the current context and saves on rehashes for a process not using large pages or rehashing on a particular page size if not in use.

9.10.7 `procfs` Changes

The `procfs(1)` `xmap` file exported page mapping size information. The `prxmap` structure adds a new HAT page size mapping field.

9.11 MDB Reference

Table 9.8 MDB Reference for Virtual Memory

`dcmd` or `walker`	Description
dcmd addr2smap	Translate address to smap
dcmd as2proc	Convert as to proc_t address
dcmd kgrep	Search kernel as for a pointer
dcmd memstat	Display memory usage summary
dcmd pmap	Print process memory map
dcmd seg	Print address space segment
dcmd swapinfo	Display a struct swapinfo
walk anon	Given an amp, list of anon structures
walk anon_cache	Walk the anon_cache cache
walk anonmap_cache	Walk the anonmap_cache cache
walk as_cache	Walk the as_cache cache
walk avl	Given any avl_tree_t *, forward walk all entries in tree
walk leak	Given a leaked bufctl or vmem_seg, find leaks w/ same stack trace
walk leakbuf	Given a leaked bufctl or vmem_seg, walk buffers for leaks w/ same stack trace
walk seg	Given an as, list of segments
walk seg_cache	Walk the seg_cache cache
walk segvn_cache	Walk the segvn_cache cache
walk swapinfo	Walk swapinfo structures
walk vn_cache	Walk the vn_cache cache

Physical Memory

Physical memory is managed globally in Solaris via a central free pool and a system daemon to manage the use of physical memory. In this section, we discuss the life cycle of memory as it is consumed and the policies used to manage allocation between the consumers within the system.

10.1 Physical Memory Allocation

Solaris uses the system's RAM as a central pool of physical memory for many different consumers within the system. Physical memory is distributed through the central pool at allocation time and returned to the pool when it is no longer needed. A system daemon (the page scanner) proactively manages memory allocations when there is a systemwide shortage of memory. The flow of memory allocations is shown in Figure 10.1.

10.1.1 The Allocation Cycle of Physical Memory

The most significant central pool physical memory is the *freelist*. Physical memory is placed on the freelist in page-size chunks when the system is first booted and then consumed as required. Three major types of allocations occur from the freelist, as shown in Figure 10.1.

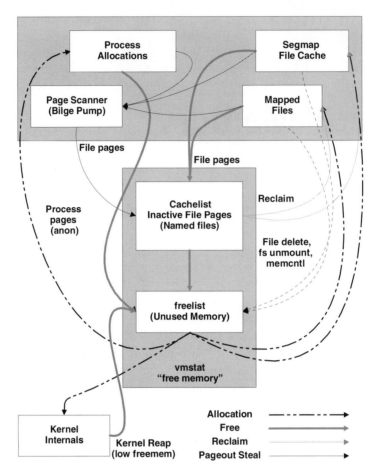

Figure 10.1 Life Cycle of Physical Memory

- **Anonymous/process allocations.** Anonymous memory, the most common
  form of allocation from the freelist, is used for most of a process's memory
  allocation, including heap and stack. Anonymous memory also fulfills shared
  memory mappings allocations. A small amount of anonymous memory is also
  used in the kernel for items such as thread stacks. Anonymous memory is
  pageable and is returned to the freelist when it is unmapped or if it is stolen
  by the page scanner daemon.

- **File system "page cache."** The page cache is used for caching of file data
  for file systems other than the ZFS file system. The file system page cache
  grows on demand to consume available physical memory as a file cache and

caches file data in page-size chunks. Pages are consumed from the freelist as files are read into memory. The pages then reside in one of three places: the *segmap* cache, a process's address space to which they are mapped, or on the *cachelist*.

The cachelist is the heart of the page cache. All unmapped file pages reside on the cachelist. Working in conjunction with the cache list are mapped files and the `segmap` cache.

Think of the `segmap` file cache as the fast first level file system read/write cache. `segmap` is a cache that holds file data read and written through the read and write system calls. Memory is allocated from the freelist to satisfy a read of a new file page, which then resides in the `segmap` file cache. File pages are eventually moved from the `segmap` cache to the cachelist to make room for more pages in the `segmap` cache.

The cachelist is typically 12% of the physical memory size on SPARC systems. The `segmap` cache works in conjunction with the system cachelist to cache file data. When files are accessed through the read and write system calls, up to 12% of the physical memory file data resides in the segmap cache and the remainder is on the cache list.

Memory mapped files also allocate memory from the freelist and remain allocated in memory for the duration of the mapping or unless a global memory shortage occurs. When a file is unmapped (explicitly or with `madvise`), file pages are returned to the cache list.

The cachelist operates as part of the freelist. When the freelist is depleted, allocations are made from the oldest pages in the cachelist. This allows the file system page cache to grow to consume all available memory and to dynamically shrink as memory is required for other purposes.

- **Kernel allocations.** The kernel uses memory to manage information about internal system state; for example, memory used to hold the list of processes in the system. The kernel allocates memory from the freelist for these purposes with its own allocators: `vmem` and `slab`. However, unlike process and file allocations, the kernel seldom returns memory to the freelist; memory is allocated and freed between kernel subsystems and the kernel allocators. Memory is consumed from the freelist only when the total kernel allocation grows.

    Memory allocated to the kernel is mostly nonpageable and so cannot be managed by the system page scanner daemon. Memory is returned to the system freelist proactively by the kernel's allocators when a global memory shortage occurs.

10.2 Pages: The Basic Unit of Solaris Memory

Pages are the fundamental unit of physical memory in the Solaris memory management subsystem. In this section, we discuss how pages are structured, how they are located, and how free lists manage pools of pages within the system.

Physical memory is divided into pages. Every active (not free) page in the Solaris kernel is a mapping between a file (vnode) and memory; the page can be identified with a vnode pointer and the page size offset within that vnode. A page's identity is its vnode/offset pair. The vnode/offset pair is the backing store for the page and represents the file and offset that the page is mapping. The page structure and associated lists are shown in Figure 10.2.

The hardware address translation (HAT) and address space layers manage the mapping between a physical page and its virtual address space (which is described in Chapter 12). The key property of the vnode/offset pair is reusability; that is, we can reuse each physical page for another task by simply synchronizing its contents in RAM with its backing store (the vnode and offset) before the page is reused.

For example, we can reuse a page of heap memory from a process by simply copying the contents to its vnode and offset, which in this case will copy the contents to the swap device. The same mechanism is used for caching files, and we simply use the vnode/offset pair to reference the file that the page is caching. If we were to reuse a page of memory that was caching a regular file, then we simply synchronize the page with its backing store (if the page has been modified) or just reuse the page if it is not modified and does not need resyncing with its backing store.

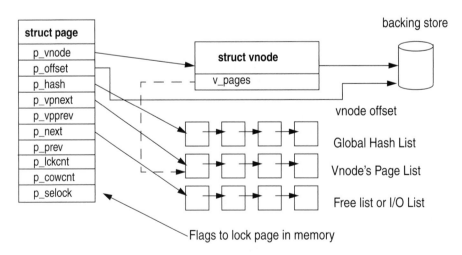

Figure 10.2 The Page Structure

10.2.1 The Page Hash List

The VM system hashes pages with identity (a valid vnode/offset pair) onto a global hash list so that they can be located by vnode and offset. Three page functions search the global page hash list: page_find(), page_lookup(), and page_lookup_nowait(). These functions take a vnode and offset as arguments and return a pointer to a page structure if found.

The global hash list is an array of pointers to linked lists of pages. The functions use a hash to index into the page_hash array to locate the list of pages that contains the page with the matching vnode/offset pair. Figure 10.3 shows how the page_find() function indexes into the page_hash array to locate a page matching a given vnode/offset.

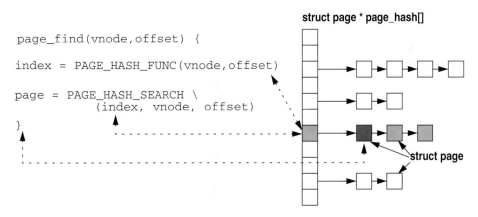

Figure 10.3 Locating Pages by Their Vnode/Offset Identity

page_find() locates a page as follows:

1. It calculates the slot in the page_hash array containing a list of potential pages by using the PAGE_HASH_FUNC macro, shown below.

```
#define PAGE_HASHSZ        page_hashsz
#define PAGE_HASHAVELEN         4
#define PAGE_HASH_FUNC(vp, off) \
        ((((uintptr_t)(off) >> PAGESHIFT) + \
            ((uintptr_t)(off) >> (PAGESHIFT + PH_SHIFT_SIZE)) + \
            ((uintptr_t)(vp) >> 3) + \
            ((uintptr_t)(vp) >> (3 + PH_SHIFT_SIZE)) + \
            ((uintptr_t)(vp) >> (3 + 2 * PH_SHIFT_SIZE))) & \
            (PAGE_HASHSZ - 1))
```

See vm/page.h

2. It uses the `PAGE_HASH_SEARCH` macro, shown below, to search the list refer-
    enced by the slot for a page matching vnode/offset. The macro traverses the
    linked list of pages until it finds such a page.

```
#define PAGE_HASH_SEARCH(index, pp, vp, off) { \
        for ((pp) = page_hash[(index)]; (pp); (pp) = (pp)->p_hash) { \
                if ((pp)->p_vnode == (vp) && (pp)->p_offset == (off)) \
                        break; \
        } \
```
See vm/vm_page.h

10.2.2 Page Structures

The page structure is as follows:

```
typedef struct page {
        u_offset_t      p_offset;       /* offset into vnode for this page */
        struct vnode    *p_vnode;       /* vnode that this page is named by */
        selock_t        p_selock;       /* shared/exclusive lock on the page */
#if defined(_LP64)
        int             p_selockpad;    /* pad for growing selock */
#endif
        struct page     *p_hash;        /* hash by [vnode, offset] */
        struct page     *p_vpnext;      /* next page in vnode list */
        struct page     *p_vpprev;      /* prev page in vnode list */
        struct page     *p_next;        /* next page in free/intrans lists */
        struct page     *p_prev;        /* prev page in free/intrans lists */
        ushort_t        p_lckcnt;       /* number of locks on page data */
        ushort_t        p_cowcnt;       /* number of copy on write lock */
        kcondvar_t      p_cv;           /* page struct's condition var */
        kcondvar_t      p_io_cv;        /* for iolock */
        uchar_t         p_iolock_state; /* replaces p_iolock */
        uchar_t         p_szc;          /* page size code */
        uchar_t         p_fsdata;       /* file system dependent byte */
        uchar_t         p_state;        /* p_free, p_noreloc */
        uchar_t         p_nrm;          /* non-cache, ref, mod readonly bits */
#if defined(__sparc)
        uchar_t         p_vcolor;       /* virtual color */
#else
        uchar_t         p_embed;        /* x86 - changes p_mapping & p_index */
#endif
        uchar_t         p_index;        /* MPSS mapping info. Not used on x86 */
        uchar_t         p_toxic;        /* page has an unrecoverable error */
        void            *p_mapping;     /* hat specific translation info */
        pfn_t           p_pagenum;      /* physical page number */

        uint_t          p_share;        /* number of translations */
#if defined(_LP64)
        uint_t          p_sharepad;     /* pad for growing p_share */
#endif
        uint_t          p_msresv_1;     /* reserved for future use */
#if defined(__sparc)
        uint_t          p_kpmref;       /* number of kpm mapping sharers */
        struct kpme     *p_kpmelist;    /* kpm specific mapping info */
#else
```

continues

```
        /* index of entry in p_map when p_embed is set */
        uint_t          p_mlentry;
#endif
        uint64_t        p_msresv_2;     /* page allocation debugging */
} page_t;
```
See vm/page.h

The stored information includes bits that indicate whether the page has been referenced or modified, for use in the page scanner (covered later in the chapter). The page structure also contains a pointer to the HAT-specific mapping information, p_mapping, which points to a machine-specific hat structure.

10.2.3 Free List and Cache List

The free list and the cache list hold pages that are not mapped into any address space and that have been freed by page_free(). The sum of these lists is reported in the *free* column in vmstat. Even though vmstat reports these pages as free, they can still contain a valid page from a vnode/offset and hence are still part of the global page cache. Memory on the cache list is not really free, it is a valid cache of a page from a file. However, pages will be moved from the cache list to the free list and their contents discarded if the free list becomes exhausted. The cache list exemplifies how the file systems use memory as a file system cache.

The free list contains pages that no longer have a vnode and offset associated with them—which can only occur if the page has been destroyed and removed from a vnode's hash list. The free list is generally very small, since most pages that are no longer used by a process or the kernel still keep their vnode/offset information intact. Pages are put on the free list when a process exits, at which point all of the anonymous memory pages (heap, stack, and copy-on-write pages) are freed.

The cache list is a hashed list of pages that still have mappings to valid vnode and offset. Recall that pages can be obtained from the cache list by the page_lookup() routine. This function accepts a vnode and offset as the argument and returns a page structure. If the page is found on the cache list, then the page is removed from the cache list and returned to the caller. When we find and remove pages from the cache list, we are *reclaiming* a page. Page reclaims are reported by vmstat in the "re" column.

10.2.4 Physical Page "memseg" Lists

The Solaris kernel uses a segmented global physical page list, consisting of segments of contiguous physical memory. (Many hardware platforms now present memory in noncontiguous groups.) Contiguous physical memory segments are

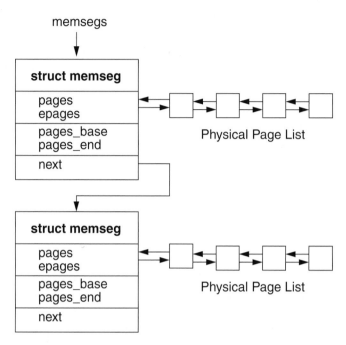

Figure 10.4 Contiguous Physical Memory Segments

added during system boot. They are also added and deleted dynamically when physical memory is added and removed while the system is running. Figure 10.4 shows the arrangement of the physical page lists into contiguous segments.

10.2.5 The Page-Level Interfaces

The Solaris virtual memory system implementation has grouped page management and manipulation into a central group of functions. These functions are used by the segment drivers and file systems to create, delete, and modify pages. The major page-level interfaces are shown in Table 10.1.

The `page_create_va()` function allocates pages. It takes the number of pages to allocate as an argument and returns a page list linked with the pages that have been taken from the free list. `page_create_va()` also takes a virtual address as an argument so that it can implement page coloring (discussed in Section 10.2.7). The new `page_create_va()` function subsumes the older `page_create()` function and should be used by all newly developed subsystems because `page_create()` may not correctly color the allocated pages.

Table 10.1 Solaris 10 Page Level Interfaces

Method	Description
page_create()	Creates pages. Page coloring is based on a hash of the vnode offset. page_create() is provided for backward compatibility only. Don't use it if you don't have to. Instead, use the page_create_va() function so that pages are correctly colored.
page_create_va()	Creates pages, taking into account the virtual address they will be mapped to. The address is used to calculate page coloring.
page_exists()	Tests that a page for vnode/offset exists.
page_find()	Searches the hash list for a page with the specified vnode and offset that is known to exist and is already locked.
page_first()	Finds the first page on the global page hash list.
page_free()	Frees a page. Pages with vnode/offset go onto the cache list; other pages go onto the free list.
page_isfree()	Checks whether a page is on the free list.
page_ismod()	Checks whether a page is modified. This function checks only the software bit in the page structure. To sync the MMU bits with the page structure, you may need to call hat_pagesync() before calling page_ismod().
page_isref()	Checks whether a page has been referenced; checks only the software bit in the page structure. To sync the MMU bits with the page structure, you may need to call hat_pagesync() before calling page_isref().
page_isshared()	Checks whether a page is shared across more than one address space.
page_lookup()	Finds a page representing the specified vnode/offset. If the page is found on a free list, then it will be removed from the free list.
page_lookup_nowait()	Finds a page representing the specified vnode/offset that is not locked or on the free list.
page_needfree()	Informs the VM system we need some pages freed up. Calls to page_needfree( ) must be symmetric; that is, they must be followed by another page_needfree( ) with the same amount of memory multiplied by -1, after the task is complete.
page_next()	Finds the next page on the global page hash list.

continues

Table 10.1 Solaris 10 Page Level Interfaces (*continued*)

Method	Description
page_lock()	Lock a page structure either exclusively or shared.
page_unlock()	Unlock a page structure.
page_release()	Unlock a page structure after unmapping it, and place it back on the cachelist if appropriate. This allows the file systems to recycle the page cache though the cachelist, rather than waiting for the page scanner to garbage collect it later.

10.2.6 The Page Throttle

Solaris implements a page creation throttle so a small core of memory is available for consumption by critical parts of the kernel. The page throttle, implemented in the page_create() and page_create_va() functions, causes page creates to block when the PG_WAIT flag is specified. That is, when available memory is less than the system global, throttlefree. By default, the system global parameter, throttlefree, is set to the same value as the system global parameter minfree. By default, memory allocated through the kernel memory allocator specifies PG_WAIT and is subject to the page-create   throttle. (See Section 11.2 for more information on kernel memory allocation.)

10.2.7 Page Coloring

Some interesting effects result from the organization of pages within the processor caches, and as a result, the page placement policy within these caches can dramatically affect processor performance. When pages overlay other pages in the cache, they can displace cache data that we might not want overlaid, resulting in less cache utilization and "hot spots."

The optimal placement of pages in the cache often depends on the memory access patterns of the application; that is, is the application accessing memory in a random order, or is it doing some sort of strided ordered access? Several different algorithms can be selected in the Solaris kernel to implement page placement; the default attempts to provide the best overall performance.

To understand how page placement can affect performance, let's look at the cache configuration and see when page overlaying and displacement can occur. The UltraSPARC-I and -II implementations use virtually addressed L1 caches and physically addressed L2 caches. The L2 cache is arranged in lines of 64 bytes, and transfers are done to and from physical memory in 64-byte units. Figure 12.2 shows the architecture of the UltraSPARC-I and -II CPU modules with their caches. The L1 cache is 16 Kbytes, and the L2 (external) cache can vary between 512 Kbytes and 8 Mbytes. We can query the operating system with adb to see the size of the caches reported to the operating system. The L1 cache sizes are recorded in the `vac_size` parameter, and the L2 cache size is recorded in the `ecache_size` parameter.

```
# mdb -k
> vac_size/D
vac_size:       16384
> ecache_size/D
ecache_size:    1048576
```

We'll start by using the L2 cache as an example of how page placement can affect performance. The physical addressing of the L2 cache means that the cache is organized in page-sized multiples of the physical address space, which means that the cache effectively has only a limited number of page-aligned slots. The number of effective page slots in the cache is the cache size divided by the page size. To simplify our examples, let's assume we have a 32-Kbyte L2 cache (much smaller than reality), which means that if we have a page size of 8 Kbytes, there are four page-sized slots on the L2 cache. The cache does not necessarily read and write 8-Kbyte units from memory; it does that in 64-byte chunks, so in reality our 32-Kbyte cache has 512 addressable slots. Figure 10.5 shows how our cache would look if we laid it out linearly.

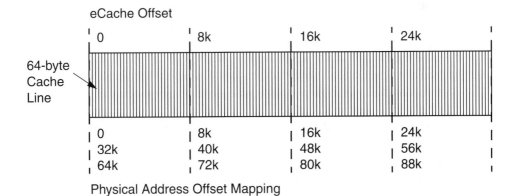

Figure 10.5 Physical Page Mapping into a 32-Kbyte Physical Cache

The L2 cache is direct-mapped from physical memory. If we were to access physical addresses on a 32-Kbyte boundary, for example, offsets 0 and 32678, then both memory locations would map to the same cache line. If we were now to access these two addresses, we cause the cache lines for the offset 0 address to be read, then flushed (cleared), the cache line for the offset 32768 address to be read in, and then flushed, then the first reloaded, etc. This ping-pong effect in the cache is known as cache flushing (or cache ping-ponging), and it effectively reduces our performance to that of real-memory speed, rather than cache speed. By accessing memory on our 32-Kbyte cache-size boundary, we have effectively used only 64 bytes of the cache (a cache line size), rather than the full cache size. Memory is often up to 10–20 times slower than cache and so can have a dramatic effect on performance.

Our simple example was based on the assumption that we were accessing physical memory in a regular pattern, but we don't program to physical memory; rather, we program to virtual memory. Therefore, the operating system must provide a sensible mapping between virtual memory and physical memory; otherwise, effects such as our example can occur.

By default, physical pages are assigned to an address space from the order in which they appear in the free list. In general, the first time a machine boots, the free list may have physical memory in a linear order, and we may end up with the behavior described in our "ping pong" example. Once a machine has been running, the physical page free list will become randomly ordered, and subsequent reruns of an identical application could get very different physical page placement and, as a result, very different performance. On early Solaris implementations, this is exactly what customers saw—differing performance for identical runs, as much as 30 percent difference.

To provide better and consistent performance, the Solaris kernel uses a page coloring algorithm when pages are allocated to a virtual address space. Rather than being randomly allocated, the pages are allocated with a specific predetermined relationship between the virtual address to which they are being mapped and their underlying physical address. The virtual-to-physical relationship is predetermined as follows: The free list of physical pages is organized into specifically colored bins, one color bin for each slot in the physical cache; the number of color bins is determined by the ecache size divided by the page size. (In our example, there would be exactly four colored bins.)

When a page is put on the free list, the `page_free()` algorithms assign it to a color bin corresponding to its physical address. When a page is consumed from the free list, the virtual-to-physical algorithm takes the page from a physical color bin, chosen as a function of the virtual address to which the page will be mapped. The algorithm requires that when allocating pages from the free list, the page create function must know the virtual address to which a page will be mapped.

New pages are allocated by calling the `page_create_va()` function[1]. The `page_create_va()` function accepts the virtual address of the location to which the page is going to be mapped as an argument; then, the virtual-to-physical color bin algorithm can decide which color bin to take physical pages from. The `page_create_va()` function is described with the page management functions in Table 10.1.

No one algorithm suits all applications because different applications have different memory access patterns. Over time, the page coloring algorithms used in the Solaris kernel have been refined as a result of extensive simulation, benchmarks, and customer feedback. The kernel supports a default algorithm and two optional algorithms. The default algorithm was chosen according to the following criteria:

- Fairly consistent, repeatable results
- Good overall performance for the majority of applications
- Acceptable performance across a wide range of applications

The default algorithm uses a hashing algorithm to distribute pages as evenly as possible throughout the cache. The default and other available page coloring algorithms are shown in Table 10.2.

You can change the default algorithm by setting the system parameter `consistent_coloring`, either on-the-fly with mdb or permanently in /etc/system.

```
# mdb -kw
> consistent_coloring/D
consistent_coloring:            0
> consistent_coloring/W 1
consistent_coloring:            0x0              =       0x1
```

So, which algorithm is best? Well, your mileage will vary, depending on your application. Page coloring usually only makes a difference on memory-intensive scientific applications, and the defaults are usually fine for commercial or database systems. If you have a time-critical scientific application, then we recommend that you experiment with the different algorithms and see which is best.

---

1. The `page_create_va()` function deprecates the older `page_create()` function. We chose to add a new function rather than adding an additional argument to the existing `page_create()` function so that existing third-party loadable kernel modules which call `page_create()` remain functional. However, because `page_create()` does not know about virtual addresses, it has to pick a color at random—which can cause significant performance degradation. The `page_create_va()` function should always be used for new code.

Table 10.2 Solaris Page Coloring Algorithms

Algorithm		
No.	Name	Description
0	Hashed VA	The physical page color bin is chosen based on a hashed algorithm to ensure even distribution of virtual addresses across the cache. A skew using a hash of the process address is included, to ensure a different address range is used for each process. This prevents pathological cache conflicts when many similar processes are running.
1	P. Addr = V. Addr	The physical page color is chosen so that physical addresses map directly to the virtual addresses (as in our example).
2	Bin Hopping	Physical pages are allocated with a round-robin method.

Remember that some algorithms will produce different results for each run, so aggregate as many runs as possible.

10.3 The Page Scanner

The page scanner is the memory management daemon that manages systemwide physical memory. The page scanner and the virtual memory page fault mechanism are the core of the demand-paged memory allocation system used to manage Solaris memory. When there is a memory shortage, the page scanner runs to steal memory from address spaces by taking pages that haven't been used recently, syncing them up with their backing store (swap space if they are anonymous pages), and freeing them. If paged-out virtual memory is required again by an address space, then a memory page fault occurs when the virtual address is referenced and the pages are recreated and copied back from their backing store.

The balancing of page stealing and page faults determines which parts of virtual memory will be backed by real physical memory and which will be moved out to swap. The page scanner does not understand the memory usage patterns or working sets of processes; it only knows reference information on a physical page-by-page basis. This policy is often referred to as *global page replacement*; the alternative process-based page management is known as *local page replacement*.

The subtleties of which pages are stolen govern the memory allocation policies and can affect different workloads in different ways. During the life of the Solaris kernel, only two significant changes in memory replacement policies have occurred:

- Enhancements to minimize page stealing from extensively shared libraries and executables

- Enhancements to allow auto-tuning of the `fastscan` and `handspread` parameters

We discuss these changes in more detail when we describe page scanner implementation.

10.3.1 Page Scanner Operation

The page scanner tracks page usage by reading a per-page hardware bit from the hardware MMU for each page. Two bits are kept for each page; they indicate whether the page has been modified or referenced since the bits were last cleared. The page scanner uses the bits as the fundamental data to decide which pages of memory have been used recently and which have not.

The page scanner is a kernel thread, which is awakened when the amount of memory on the free-page list falls below a system threshold, typically 1/64th of total physical memory. The page scanner scans through pages in physical page order, looking for pages that haven't been used recently to page out to the swap device and free. The algorithm that determines whether pages have been used resembles a clock face and is known as the two-handed clock algorithm. This algorithm views the entire physical page list as a circular list, where the last physical page wraps around to the first. Two hands sweep through the physical page list, as shown in Figure 10.6.

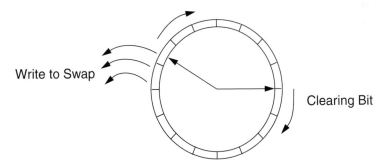

Figure 10.6 Two-Handed Clock Algorithm

The two hands, the front hand and back hand, rotate clockwise in page order around the list. The front hand rotates ahead of the back hand, clearing the referenced and modified bits for each page. The trailing back hand then inspects the referenced and modified bits some time later. Pages that have not been referenced or modified are swapped out and freed. The rate at which the hands rotate around the page list is controlled by the amount of free memory on the system, and the gap between the front hand and back hand is fixed by a dynamically calculated value, `handspreadpages`.

10.3.2 Page-Out Algorithm and Parameters

The page-out algorithm is controlled by several parameters, some of which are calculated at system startup by the amount of memory in the system, and some of which are calculated dynamically based on memory allocation and paging activity.

The parameters that control the clock hands do two things: They control the rate at which the scanner scans through pages, and they control the time (or distance) between the front hand and the back hand.

Starting with Solaris 9, a new maximum clamp is calculated for the page scanner, based on number of pages the scanner could scan in one second at its maximum rate. This number is calculated based on a simple experiment when the scanner first starts, and is stored in the dynamic variable `pageout_new_spread`. We can check the calculated value with `mdb`:

```
# mdb -k
> pageout_new_spread/E
pageout_new_spread:
pageout_new_spread:            127678
```

The distance between the back hand and the front hand is `handspreadpages` and is expressed in units of pages. The maximum distance between the front hand and backhand is calculated based on the scanner's performance (`pageout_new_spread`).

10.3.2.1 Scan Rate Parameters

The scanner starts scanning when free memory is lower than `lotsfree` number of pages free plus a small buffer factor, `deficit`. The scanner starts scanning at a rate of `slowscan` pages per second at this point and gets faster as the amount of free memory approaches zero. The system parameter `lotsfree` is calculated at startup as 1/64th memory, and the parameter `deficit` is either zero or a small number of pages—set by the page allocator at times of large memory allocation to let the scanner free a few more pages above `lotsfree` in anticipation of more memory requests.

Figure 10.7 shows the rate at which the scanner scans increases linearly as free memory ranges between `lotsfree` and zero. The scanner starts scanning at the

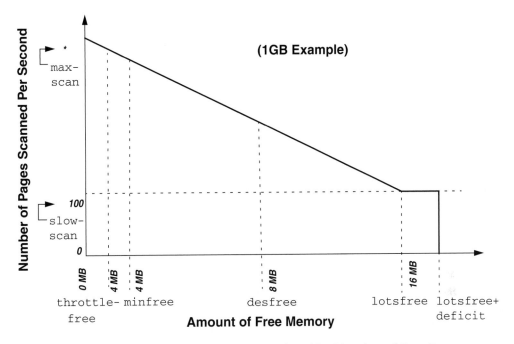

Figure 10.7 Page Scanner Rate, Interpolated by Number of Free Pages

minimum rate set by `slowscan` when memory falls below `lotsfree` and then increases to `calculated` maximum if memory falls low enough. The maximum scan rate is set to the value of `pageout_new_spread` and stored in the global variable `fastscan`, based on the maximum number of pages the scanner can scan per second.

The number of pages scanned increases from the slowest rate (set by `slowscan` when `lotsfree` pages are free) to a maximum determined by the dynamic variable `fastscan`. Free memory never actually reaches zero, but for simplicity the algorithm calculates the maximum interpolated rate against the free memory ranging between `lotsfree` and zero. In our example system with 1 Gbyte of physical memory (shown in Figure 10.7), we can see that the scanner starts scanning when free memory falls to 16 Mbytes plus the short-term memory deficit.

For this example, we'll assume that the deficit is zero. When free memory falls to 16 Mbytes, the scanner will wake up and start examining 100 pages per second, according to the system parameter `slowscan`. The `slowscan` parameter is 100 by default on Solaris systems, and `fastscan` is dynamically calculated. If free memory falls to 12 Mbytes (1,536 8K-byte pages), the scanner scans at a higher rate, according to the page scanner interpolation shown in the following equation:

$$scanrate = \left(\frac{lotsfree - freememory}{lotsfree} \times fastscan\right) + \left(slowscan \times \frac{freemem}{lotsfree}\right)$$

We can read the calculated value for fastscan via `mdb`:

```
# mdb -k
> fastscan/E
fastscan:
fastscan:          127678
```

If we convert free memory and `lotsfree` to numbers of pages (free memory of 12 Mbytes is 1,536 pages, and `lotsfree` is set to 16 Mbytes, or 2,048 pages), then we scan at 31,994 pages per second.

$$scanrate = \left(\frac{2048 - 1536}{2048} \times 127678\right) + \left(100 \times \frac{1536}{2048}\right) = 31994$$

By default, the scanner is run four times per second when there is a memory shortage. If the amount of free memory falls below the system parameter `minfree`, the scanner is awoken by the page allocator for each page-create request. This scheme helps the scanner try to keep at least `minfree` pages on the free list.

10.3.2.2 Not-Recently-Used Time

The time between the front hand and back hand varies according to the number of pages between the front hand and back hand and the rate at which the scanner is scanning. The time between the front hand clearing the reference bit and the back hand checking the reference bit is a significant factor that affects the behavior of the scanner because it controls the amount of time that a page can be left alone before it is potentially stolen by the page scanner. A short time between the reference bit being cleared and checked means that only the most active pages remain intact; a long time means that only the largely unused pages are stolen. The ideal behavior is the latter because we want only the least recently used pages stolen, which means we want a long time between the front and back hands.

The time between clearing and checking of the reference bit can vary from just a few seconds to several hours, depending on the scan rate.

10.3.3 Shared Library Optimizations

A subtle optimization added to the page scanner prevents it from stealing pages from extensively shared libraries. The page scanner looks at the share reference count for each page; if the page is shared more than a certain amount, then it is skipped during the page scan operation. An internal parameter, po_share, sets the threshold for the amount of shares a page can have before it is skipped. If the page has more than po_share mappings (i.e., it's shared by more than po_share processes), then it is skipped. By default, po_share starts at 8; each time around, it is decremented unless the scan around the clock does not find any page to free, in which case po_share is incremented. The po_share parameter can float between 8 and 134217728.

10.3.3.1 Page Scanner CPU Utilization Clamp

A CPU utilization clamp on the scan rate prevents the page-out daemon from using too much processor time. Two internal limits govern the desired and maximum CPU time that the scanner should use. Two parameters, min_percent_cpu and max_percent_cpu, govern the amount of CPU that the scanner can use. Like the scan rate, the actual amount of CPU that can be used at any given time is interpolated by the amount of free memory. It ranges from min_percent_cpu when free memory is at lotsfree (cachefree with priority paging enabled) to max_percent_cpu if free memory were to fall to zero. The defaults for min_percent_cpu and max_percent_cpu are 4% and 80% of a single CPU, respectively (the scanner is single threaded).

10.3.4 Parameters That Limit Pages Paged Out

Another parameter, maxpgio, limits the rate at which I/O is queued to the swap devices. It is set low to prevent saturation of the swap devices. The parameter defaults to 40 I/Os per second on x86 architectures and to 60 I/Os per second on SPARC.

Because the page-out daemon also pages out dirty file system pages that it finds during scanning, this parameter can also indirectly limit file system throughput. File system I/O requests are normally queued and written by user processes and hence are not subject to maxpgio. However, when a lot of file system write activity is going on and many dirty file system pages are in memory, the page-out scanner trips over these and queues these I/Os; as a result, the maxpgio limit can sometimes affect file system write throughput.

10.3.4.1 Summary of Page Scanner Parameters

Table 10.3 describes the parameters that control the page-out process in the current Solaris and patch releases.

Table 10.3 Page Scanner Parameters

Parameter	Description	Min	Default
lotsfree	The scanner starts stealing anonymous memory pages when free memory falls below lotsfree.	512K	1/64th of memory
desfree	If free memory falls below desfree, then the page-out scanner is started 100 times/second.	minfree	lotsfree/2
minfree	If free memory falls below minfree, then the page scanner is signaled to start every time a new page is created.		desfree/2
throttlefree	The number at which point the page_create routines make the caller wait until free pages are available.	—	minfree
slowscan	The rate of pages scanned per second when free memory = lotsfree.	—	100
maxpgio	A throttle for the maximum number of pages per second that the swap device can handle.	~60	60 or 90 pages/s

10.3.5 Page Scanner Implementation

The page scanner is implemented as two kernel threads, both of which use process number 2, "pageout." One thread scans pages, and the other thread pushes the dirty pages queued for I/O to the swap device. In addition, the kernel callout mechanism wakes the page scanner thread when memory is insufficient. (The kernel callout scheduling mechanism is discussed in detail in Section 19.2.)

The scanner schedpaging() function is called four times per second by a callout placed in the callout table. The schedpaging() function checks whether free memory is below the threshold (lotsfree or cachefree) and, if required, triggers the scanner thread. The page scanner is not only awakened by the callout thread, it is also triggered by the page allocator if memory falls below throttlefree. Figure 10.8 illustrates how the page scanner works.

When called, the schedpaging routine calculates two setup parameters for the page scanner thread: the number of pages to scan and the number of CPU ticks that the scanner thread can consume while doing so. The number of pages and cpu

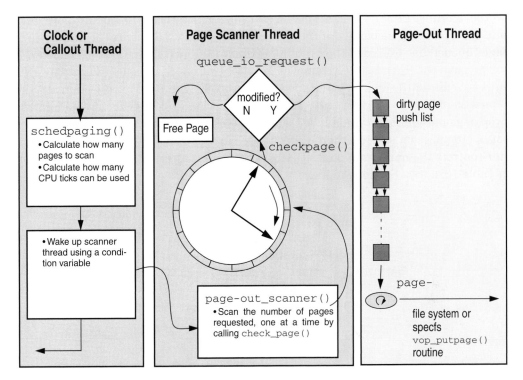

Figure 10.8 Page Scanner Architecture

ticks are calculated according to the equations shown in Section 10.3.2.1 and Section 10.3.3.1. Once the scanning parameters have been calculated, schedpaging triggers the page scanner through a condition variable wakeup.

The page scanner thread cycles through the physical page list, progressing by the number of pages requested each time it is woken up. The front hand and the back hand each have a page pointer. The front hand is incremented first so that it can clear the referenced and modified bits for the page currently pointed to by the front hand. The back hand is then incremented, and the status of the page pointed to by the back hand is checked by the check_page() function. At this point, if the page has been modified, it is placed in the dirty page queue for processing by the page-out thread. If the page was not referenced (it's clean!), then it is simply freed.

Dirty pages are placed onto a queue so that a separate thread, the page-out thread, can write them out to their backing store. We use another thread so that a deadlock can't occur while the system is waiting to swap a page out. The page-out thread uses a preinitialized list of async buffer headers as the queue for I/O requests. The list is initialized with 256 entries, which means the queue can contain at most 256 entries. The number of entries preconfigured on the list is controlled by the `async_request_size` system parameter. Requests to queue more I/Os onto the queue will be blocked if the entire queue is full (256 entries) or if the rate of pages queued has exceeded the system maximum set by the `maxpgio` parameter.

The page-out thread simply removes I/O entries from the queue and initiates I/O on it by calling the `vnode putpage()` function for the page in question. In the Solaris kernel, this function calls the `swapfs_putpage()` function to initiate the swap page-out via the `swapfs` layer. The `swapfs` layer delays and gathers together pages (16 pages on sun4u), then writes these out together. The `klustsize` parameter controls the number of pages that `swapfs` will cluster; the defaults are shown in Table 10.4. (See Section 9.8.)

Table 10.4 `swapfs` Cluster Sizes

Platform	Number of Clustered Pages (set by klustsize)
sun4u	16 (128k)
i86	14 (56k)

10.3.6 The Memory Scheduler

In addition to the page-out process, the CPU scheduler/dispatcher can swap out entire processes to conserve memory. This operation is separate from page-out. Swapping out a process involves removing all of a process's thread structures and private pages from memory, and setting flags in the process table to indicate that this process has been swapped out. This is an inexpensive way to conserve memory, but it dramatically affects a process's performance and hence is used only when paging fails to free enough memory consistently.

The memory scheduler is launched at boot time and does nothing unless memory is consistently less than `desfree` memory (30 second average). At this point, the memory scheduler starts looking for processes that it can completely swap out. The memory scheduler will soft-swap out processes if the shortage is minimal or hard-swap out processes in the case of a larger memory shortage.

10.3.6.1 Soft Swapping

Soft swapping takes place when the 30-second average for free memory is below `desfree`. Then, the memory scheduler looks for processes that have been inactive for at least `maxslp` seconds. When the memory scheduler finds a process that has been sleeping for `maxslp` seconds, it swaps out the thread structures for each thread, then pages out all of the private pages of memory for that process.

10.3.6.2 Hard Swapping

Hard swapping takes place when all of the following are true:

- More than two processes are on the run queue, waiting for CPU.
- The average free memory over 30 seconds is consistently less than desfree.
- Excessive paging (determined to be true if page-out + page-in > maxpgio) is going on.

When hard swapping is invoked, a much more aggressive approach is used to find memory. First, the kernel is requested to unload all modules and cache memory that are not currently active, then processes are sequentially swapped out until the desired amount of free memory is returned. Parameters that affect the Memory Scheduler are shown in Table 10.5.

Table 10.5 Memory Scheduler Parameters

Parameter	Effect on Memory Scheduler
desfree	If the average amount of free memory falls below desfree for 30 seconds, then the memory scheduler is invoked.
maxslp	When soft-swapping, the memory scheduler starts swapping processes that have slept for at least maxslp seconds. The default for maxslp is 20 seconds and is tunable.
maxpgio	When the run queue is greater than 2, free memory is below desfree, and the paging rate is greater than maxpgio, then hard swapping occurs, unloading kernel modules and process memory.

10.4 MDB Reference

Table 10.6 MDB Reference for Physical Memory

dcmd or walker	Description
dcmd memlist	Display a struct memlist
dcmd memseg_list	Show memseg list
dcmd memstat	Display memory usage summary

continues

Table 10.6 MDB Reference for Physical Memory (*continued*)

dcmd or walker	Description
dcmd page	Display a summarized page_t
dcmd whatis	Given an address, return information
walk memlist	Walk specified memlist
walk memseg	Walk the memseg structures
walk page	Walk all pages, or those from the specified vnode
walk vn_cache	Walk the vn_cache cache

11

Kernel Memory

$\mathbf{I}$n the last chapter, we looked mostly at process address space and process memory, but the kernel also needs memory to run the operating system. Kernel memory is required for the kernel text, kernel data, and kernel data structures. In this chapter, we look at what kernel memory is used for, what the kernel virtual address space looks like, and how kernel memory is allocated and managed.

11.1 Kernel Virtual Memory Layout

The kernel, just like a process, uses virtual memory and uses the memory management unit (MMU) to translate its virtual memory addresses into physical pages. The kernel has its own address space and corresponding virtual memory layout. The kernel's address space is constructed of address space segments, using the standard Solaris memory architecture framework.

Most of the kernel's memory is nonpageable, or "wired down." The reason is that the kernel requires its memory to complete operating system tasks that could affect other memory-related data structures and, if the kernel had to take a page fault while performing a memory management task (or any other task that affected pages of memory), a deadlock could occur. Solaris does, however, allow some deadlock-safe parts of the Solaris kernel to be allocated from pageable memory, which is used mostly for the lightweight process thread stacks.

Kernel memory consists of a variety of mappings from physical memory (physical memory pages) to the kernel's virtual address space, and memory is allocated by a layered series of kernel memory allocators. Two segment drivers handle the creation and management of the majority of kernel mappings. Nonpageable kernel memory is mapped with the segkmem kernel segment driver and pageable kernel memory with the segkp segment driver. On platforms that support it, the critical and frequently used portions of the kernel are mapped from large (4-Mbyte) pages to maximize the efficiency of the hardware TLB.

11.1.1 Kernel Address Space

The kernel virtual memory layout differs from platform to platform, mostly based on the platform's MMU architecture. On x86, and platforms earlier than the sun4u, the kernel uses the top 256 Mbytes or 512 Mbytes of a common virtual address space, shared by the process and kernel (see Section 9.4). Sharing the kernel address space with the process address space limits the amount of usable kernel virtual address space to 256 Mbytes and 512 Mbytes, respectively, which is a substantial limitation on some of the older platforms (e.g., the SPARCcenter 2000). On sun4u platforms, the kernel has its own virtual address space context and consequently can be much larger. The sun4u kernel address space is 4 Gbytes on 32-bit kernels and spans the full 64-bit address range on 64-bit kernels.

The kernel virtual address space contains the following major mappings:

- The kernel text and data (mappings of the kernel binary)
- The kernel 64-bit heap (data structures, caches, etc.)
- A 32-bit heap, for module text and data (64-bit kernels only)
- The trap table (SPARC)
- Critical virtual memory data structures (TSB, etc.)
- A place for mapping the file system cache (segmap)

The layout of the kernel's virtual memory address space is mostly platform specific, and as a result, the placement of each mapping is different on each platform. For reference, we show the sun4u 64-bit kernel address space map in Figure 11.1.

11.1.2 Kernel Text and Data Segments

The kernel text and data segments are created when the kernel core is loaded and executed. The text segments contain the instructions, and the data segment contains the initialized variables from the kernel/unix image file, which is loaded at boot time by the kernel bootstrap loader.

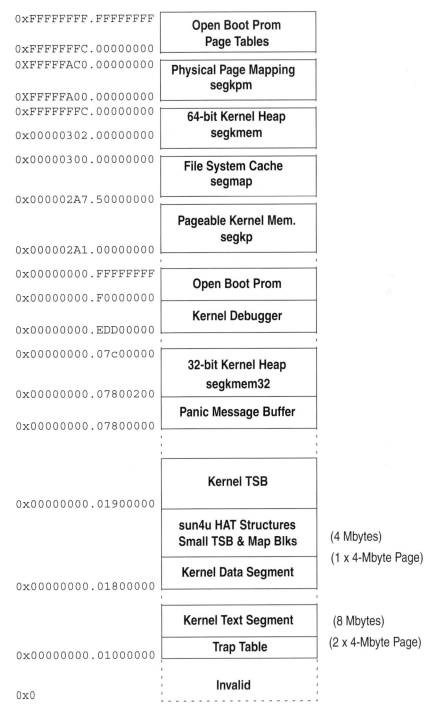

Figure 11.1 Solaris 10 sun4u 64-Bit Kernel Address Space

The kernel text and data are mapped into the kernel address space by the Open Boot PROM, before general startup of the kernel, to allow the base kernel code to be loaded and executed. Shortly after the kernel loads, the kernel creates the kernel address space and the segkmem kernel memory driver creates segments for kernel text and kernel data.

On systems that support large pages, the kernel creates a large translation mapping for the first 4 megabytes of the kernel text and data segments and then locks that mapping into the MMU's TLB. Mapping the kernel into large pages greatly reduces the number of TLB entries required for the kernel's working set and has a dramatic impact on general system performance. Performance was increased by as much as 10 percent, for two reasons:

1. The time spent in TLB miss handlers for kernel code was reduced to almost zero.

2. The number of TLB entries used by the kernel was dramatically reduced, leaving more TLB entries for user code and reducing the amount of time spent in TLB miss handlers for user code.

On SPARC platforms, we also put the trap table at the start of the kernel text (which resides on one large page).

11.1.3 Virtual Memory Data Structures

The kernel keeps most of the virtual memory data structures required for the platform's HAT implementation in a portion of the kernel data segment and a separate memory segment. The data structures and allocation location are typically those summarized in Table 11.1.

Table 11.1 Virtual Memory Data Structures

Platform	Data Structures	Location
sun4u	The Translation Storage Buffer (TSB). The HAT mapping blocks (HME), one for every page-sized virtual address mapping. (See Section 12.2.)	Allocated initially from the kernel data-segment large page, and overflows into another large-page, mapped segment, just above the kernel data segment.
amd64	Page Tables, Page Structures	Allocated in the kernel data-segment large page.
x86	Page Tables, Page Structures	Allocated from a separate VM data structure's segment.

11.1.4 UltraSPARC Kernel Nucleus

Required on sun4u kernel implementations is a core area of memory that can be accessed without missing in the TLB. This memory area is necessary because the sun4u SPARC implementation uses a software TLB replacement mechanism to fill the TLB, and hence we require all the TLB miss handler data structures to be available during a TLB miss. As we discuss in Section 12.2, the TLB is filled from a software buffer, known as the translation storage buffer (TSB), of the TLB entries; all the data structures needed to handle a TLB miss and to fill the TLB from the TSB must be available with wired-down TLB mappings. To accommodate this requirement, SPARC V8 and SPARC V9 implement a special core of memory, known as the nucleus. On sun4u systems, the nucleus is the kernel text, kernel data, and the additional "large TSB" area, all of which are allocated from large pages.

11.1.5 Loadable Kernel Module Text and Data

The kernel loadable modules require memory for their executable text and data. On sun4u, up to 256 Kbytes of module text and data are allocated from the same segment as the kernel text and data, after which the module text and data are loaded from the general kernel allocation area: the kernel map segment. The location of kernel module text and data is shown in Table 11.2.

Table 11.2 Kernel Loadable Module Allocation

Platform	Module Kernel and Text Allocation
sun4u 64 bit	Up to 256 Kbytes of kernel module are loaded from the same large pages as the kernel text and data. The remainder are loaded from the 32-bit kernel map segment, a segment that is specifically for module text and data.
amd64	Up to 256 Kbytes of kernel module are loaded from the same large pages as the kernel text and data. The remainder are loaded from an additional segment, shared by HAT data structures and module text/data.
x86	Up to 256 Kbytes of kernel module are loaded from the same large pages as the kernel text and data. The remainder are loaded from an additional segment, shared by HAT data structures and module text/data.

We can see which modules fit into the kernel text and data by looking at the module load addresses with the `modinfo` command.

```
# modinfo
 Id Loadaddr    Size Info Rev Module Name
  5 1010c000    4b63    1   1 specfs (filesystem for specfs)
  7 10111654    3724    1   1 TS (time sharing sched class)
  8 1011416c     5c0    -   1 TS_DPTBL (Time sharing dispatch table)
  9 101141c0   29680    2   1 ufs (filesystem for ufs)
                  .
                  .
                  .

                  .
 97 10309b38    28e0   52   1 shmsys (System V shared memory)
 97 10309b38    28e0   52   1 shmsys (32-bit System V shared memory)
 98 1030bc90     43c    -   1 ipc (common ipc code)
 99 78096000    3723   18   1 ffb (ffb.c 6.42 Aug 11 1998 11:20:45)
100 7809c000    f5ee    -   1 xfb (xfb driver 1.2 Aug 11 1998 11:2)
102 780c2000    1eca    -   1 bootdev (bootdev misc module)
```

Using the modinfo command, we can see on a sun4u system that the initial modules are loaded from the kernel-text large page. (Address 0x1030bc90 lies within the kernel-text large page, which starts at 0x10000000.)

On 64-bit platforms, we have an additional segment for the spillover kernel text and data. The reason for having the segment is that the address at which the module text is loaded must be within a 32-bit offset from the kernel text. That's because the 64-bit kernel is compiled with the ABS32 flag so that the kernel can fit all instruction addresses within a 32-bit register. The ABS32 instruction mode provides a significant performance increase and allows the 64-bit kernel to provide similar performance to the 32-bit kernel. Because of that, a separate kernel heap mapping (segkmem32) within a 32-bit offset of the kernel text is used for spillover module text and data.

Solaris does allow some portions of the kernel to be allocated from pageable memory. That way, data structures directly related to process context can be swapped out with the process during a process swap-out operation. Pageable memory is restricted to those structures that are not required by the kernel when the process is swapped out:

- Lightweight process stacks
- The TNF Trace buffers
- Special pages, such as the page of memory that is shared between user and kernel for scheduler preemption control

Pageable memory is allocated and swapped by the seg_kp segment and is only swapped out to its backing store when the memory scheduler (swapper) is activated. (See Section 10.3.6.)

11.1.6 The Kernel Address Space and Segments

The kernel address space is represented by the address space pointed to by the system object, `kas`. The segment drivers manage the manipulation of the segments within the kernel address space (see Figure 11.2).

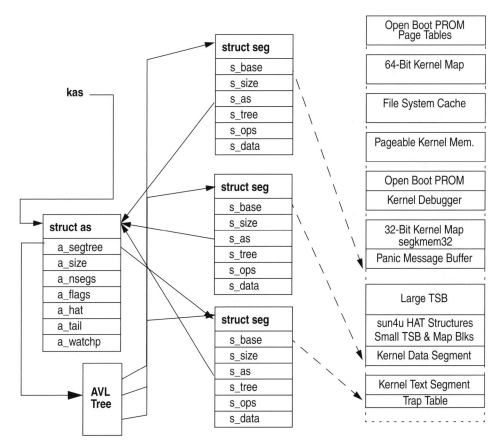

Figure 11.2 Kernel Address Space

The full list of segment drivers the kernel uses to create and manage kernel mappings is shown in Table 11.3. The majority of the kernel segments are manually calculated and placed for each platform, with the base address and offset hard-coded into a platform-specific header file. See Appendix A for a complete reference of platform-specific kernel allocation and address maps.

Table 11.3 Solaris Kernel Memory Segment Drivers

Segment	Function
seg_kmem	Allocates and maps nonpageable kernel memory pages.
seg_kp	Allocates, maps, and handles page faults for pageable kernel memory.
seg_nf	Nonfaulting kernel memory driver.
seg_map	Maps the file system cache into the kernel address space.
seg_kpm	Maps physical memory into the kernel address space, on 64-bit platforms. Allows fast access to file system page cache.

11.2 Kernel Memory Allocation

Kernel memory is allocated at different levels, depending on the desired allocation characteristics. At the lowest level is the page allocator, which allocates unmapped pages from the free lists so that the pages can then be mapped into the kernel's address space for use by the kernel.

Allocating memory in pages works well for memory allocations that require page-sized chunks, but there are many places where we need memory allocations smaller than one page; for example, an in-kernel inode requires only a few hundred bytes per inode, and allocating one whole page (8 Kbytes) would be wasteful. For this reason, in addition to the page-level allocator, Solaris has an object-level kernel memory allocator, which is stacked on top of the page-level allocator, to allocate arbitrarily sized requests. The kernel also needs to manage where pages are mapped, a function that is provided by the resource map allocator. The high-level interaction between the allocators is shown in Figure 11.3.

11.2.1 The Kernel Heap

We access memory in the kernel by acquiring a section of the kernel's virtual address space and then mapping physical pages to that address. We can acquire the physical pages one at a time from the page allocator by calling page_create_va(), but to use these pages, we first need to map them into our address space. A section of the kernel's address space, known as the *kernel heap*, is set aside for general-purpose mappings. (See Figure 11.1 for the location of the sun4u kernel heap; see also Appendix A for kernel heaps on other platforms.)

The kernel heap is a separate kernel memory segment containing a large area of virtual address space that is available to kernel consumers that require virtual address space for their mappings. Each time a consumer uses a piece of the kernel heap, we must record some information about which parts of the kernel map are

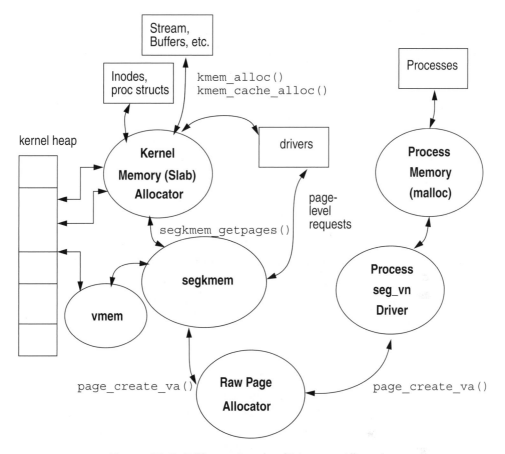

Figure 11.3 Different Levels of Memory Allocation

free and which parts are allocated so that we know where to satisfy new requests. To record the information, we use a general-purpose allocator to keep track of the start and length of the mappings that are allocated from the kernel map area. The allocator we use is the vmem allocator, which is used extensively for managing the kernel heap virtual address space, but since vmem is a universal resource allocator, it is also used for managing other resources (such as task, resource, and zone IDs).

We discuss the vmem allocator in detail in Section 11.3.

11.2.2 The Kernel Memory Segment Driver

The segkmem segment driver performs two major functions. It manages the creation of general-purpose memory segments in the kernel address space, and it also provides functions that implement a page-level memory allocator by using one of those segments—the kernel map segment.

The `segkmem` segment driver implements the segment driver methods described in Section 9.5, to create general-purpose, nonpageable memory segments in the kernel address space. The segment driver does little more than implement the `segkmem_create` method to simply link segments into the kernel's address space. It also implements protection manipulation methods, which load the correct protection modes via the HAT layer for `segkmem` segments. The set of methods implemented by the `segkmem` driver is shown in Table 11.4.

Table 11.4 Solaris `segkmem` Segment Driver Methods

Function	Description
segkmem_create()	Creates a new kernel memory segment.
segkmem_setprot()	Sets the protection mode for the supplied segment.
segkmem_checkprot()	Checks the protection mode for the supplied segment.
segkmem_getprot()	Gets the protection mode for the current segment.

The second function of the `segkmem` driver is to implement a page-level memory allocator by combined use of the resource map allocator and page allocator. The page-level memory allocator within the `segkmem` driver is implemented with the function `kmem_getpages()`. The `kmem_getpages()` function is the kernel's central allocator for wired-down, page-sized memory requests. Its main client is the second-level memory allocator, the *slab* allocator, which uses large memory areas allocated from the page-level allocator to allocate arbitrarily sized memory objects. We cover more on the slab allocator later in this chapter.

The `kmem_getpages()` function allocates page-sized chunks of virtual address space from the `kernelmap` segment. The `kernelmap` segment is only one of many segments created by the `segkmem` driver, but it is the only one from which the `segkmem` driver allocates memory.

The vmem allocator allocates portions of virtual address space within the `kernelmap` segment but on its own does not allocate any physical memory resources. It is used together with the page allocator, `page_create_va()`, and the `hat_memload()` functions to allocate physical mapped memory. The vmem allocator allocates some virtual address space, the page allocator allocates pages, and the `hat_memload()` function maps those pages into the virtual address space provided by vmem. A client of the `segkmem` memory allocator can acquire pages with `kmem_getpages` and then return them to the heap with `kmem_freepages`, as shown in Table 11.5.

Table 11.5 Solaris Kernel Page-Level Memory Allocator

Function	Description
`kmem_getpages()`	Allocates *npages* pages worth of system virtual address space and allocates wired-down page frames to back them.
	If *flag* is KM_SLEEP, blocks until address space and page frames are available.
`kmem_freepages()`	Frees *npages* (MMU) pages allocated with `kmem_getpages()`.

Pages allocated through `kmem_getpages` are not pageable and are one of the few exceptions in the Solaris environment where a mapped page has no logically associated vnode. To accommodate that case, a special vnode, `kvp`, is used. All pages created through the `segkmem` segment have `kvp` as the vnode in their identity—this allows the kernel to identify wired-down kernel pages.

11.2.3 The Kernel Memory Slab Allocator

In this section, we introduce the general-purpose memory allocator, known as the slab allocator. We begin with a quick walk-through of the slab allocator features, then look at how the allocator implements object caching, and follow up with a more detailed discussion on the internal implementation.

11.2.3.1 Slab Allocator Overview

Solaris provides a general-purpose memory allocator that provides arbitrarily sized memory allocations. We refer to this allocator as the slab allocator because it consumes large slabs of memory and then allocates smaller requests with portions of each slab. We use the slab allocator for memory requests that are

- Smaller than a page size
- Not an even multiple of a page size
- Frequently going to be allocated and *freed*, so would otherwise fragment the kernel map

The slab allocator was introduced in Solaris 2.4, replacing the *buddy* allocator that was part of the original SVR4 UNIX. The reasons for introducing the slab allocator were as follows:

- The SVR4 allocator was slow to satisfy allocation requests.
- Significant fragmentation problems arose with use of the SVR4 allocator.

- The allocator footprint was large, wasting a lot of memory.
- With no clean interfaces for memory allocation, code was duplicated in many places.

The slab allocator solves those problems and dramatically reduces overall system complexity. In fact, when the slab allocator was integrated into Solaris, it resulted in a net reduction of 3,000 lines of code because we could centralize a great deal of the memory allocation code and could remove a lot of the duplicated memory allocator functions from the clients of the memory allocator.

The slab allocator is significantly faster than the SVR4 allocator it replaced. Table 11.6 shows some of the performance measurements that were made when the slab allocator was first introduced.

Table 11.6 Performance Comparison of the Slab Allocator

Operation	SVR4	Slab
Average time to allocate and free	9.4 μs	3.8 μs
Total fragmentation (wasted memory)	46%	14%
Kenbus benchmark performance (number of scripts executed per second)	199	233

The slab allocator provides substantial additional functionality, including the following:

- General-purpose, variable-sized memory object allocation
- A central interface for memory allocation, which simplifies clients of the allocator and reduces duplicated allocation code
- Very fast allocation and deallocation of objects
- Low fragmentation and small allocator footprint
- Full debugging and auditing capability
- Coloring to optimize use of CPU caches
- Per-processor caching of memory objects to reduce contention
- A configurable backend memory allocator to allocate objects other than regular wired-down memory

The slab allocator uses the term *object* to describe a single memory allocation unit, *cache* to refer to a pool of like objects, and *slab* to refer to a group of objects that reside within the cache. Each object type has one cache, which is constructed from one or more slabs. Figure 11.4 shows the relationship between objects, slabs, and the cache. The example shows 3-Kbyte memory objects within a cache, backed by 8-Kbyte pages.

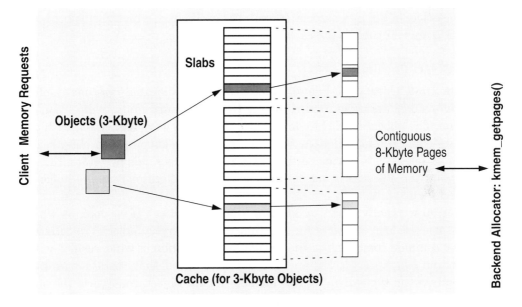

Figure 11.4 Objects, Caches, Slabs, and Pages of Memory

The slab allocator solves many of the fragmentation issues by grouping different-sized memory objects into separate caches, where each object cache has its own object size and characteristics. Grouping the memory objects into caches of similar size allows the allocator to minimize the amount of free space within each cache by neatly packing objects into slabs, where each slab in the cache represents a contiguous group of pages. Since we have one cache per object type, we would expect to see many caches active at once in the Solaris kernel. For example, we should expect to see one cache with 440 byte objects for UFS inodes, another cache of 56 byte objects for file structures, another cache of 872 bytes for LWP structures, and several other caches.

The allocator has a logical front end and back end. Objects are allocated from the front end, and slabs are allocated from pages supplied by the backend page allocator. This approach allows the slab allocator to be used for more than regular wired-down memory; in fact, the allocator can allocate almost any type of memory object. The allocator is, however, primarily used to allocate memory objects from physical pages by using kmem_getpages as the backend allocator.

Caches are created with `kmem_cache_create()`, once for each type of memory object. Caches are generally created during subsystem initialization, for example, in the `init` routine of a loadable driver. Similarly, caches are destroyed with the `kmem_cache_destroy()` function. Caches are named by a string provided as an argument, to allow friendlier statistics and tags for debugging. Once a cache is created, objects can be created within the cache with `kmem_cache_alloc()`, which creates one object of the size associated with the cache from which the object is created. Objects are returned to the cache with `kmem_cache_free()`.

11.2.3.2 Object Caching

Most of the time, objects are heavily allocated and deallocated, and many of the slab allocator's benefits arise from resolving the issues surrounding allocation and deallocation. The allocator tries to defer most of the real work associated with allocation and deallocation until it is really necessary, by keeping the objects alive until memory needs to be returned to the back end. It does this by telling the slab allocator what the object is being used for so that the allocator remains in control of the object's true state.

So, what do we really mean by keeping the object *alive*? If we look at what a subsystem uses memory objects for, we find that a memory object typically consists of two common components: the header, or description of what resides within the object and associated locks; and the actual payload that resides within the object. A subsystem typically allocates memory for the object, constructs the object in some way (writes a header inside the object or adds it to a list), and then creates any locks required to synchronize access to the object. The subsystem then uses the object. When finished with the object, the subsystem must deconstruct the object, release locks, and then return the memory to the allocator. In short, a subsystem typically allocates, constructs, uses, deallocates, and then frees the object.

If the object is being created and destroyed often, then a great deal of work is expended constructing and deconstructing the object. The slab allocator does away with this extra work by caching the object in its constructed form. When the client asks for a new object, the allocator simply creates a new one or finds an available constructed object. When the client returns an object, the allocator does nothing other than mark the object as free, leaving all the constructed data (header information and locks) intact. The object can be reused by the client subsystem without the allocator needing to construct or deconstruct—the construction and deconstruction is only done when the cache needs to grow or shrink. Deconstruction is deferred until the allocator needs to free memory back to the backend allocator.

To allow the slab allocator to take ownership of constructing and deconstructing objects, the client subsystem must provide a constructor and destructor method.

This service allows the allocator to construct new objects as required and then to deconstruct objects later asynchronously to the client's memory requests. The `kmem_cache_create()` interface supports this feature by providing a constructor and destructor function as part of the create request.

The slab allocator also allows slab caches to be created with no constructor or destructor, to allow simple allocation and deallocation of simple raw memory objects.

The slab allocator moves a lot of the complexity out of the clients and centralizes memory allocation and deallocation policies. At some points, the allocator may need to shrink a cache as a result of being notified of a memory shortage by the VM system. At this time, the allocator can free all unused objects by calling the destructor for each object that is marked free and then returning unused slabs to the backend allocator. A further callback interface is provided in each cache so that the allocator can let the client subsystem know about the memory pressure. This callback is optionally supplied when the cache is created and is simply a function that the client implements to return, by means of `kmem_cache_free()`, as many objects to the cache as possible.

A good example is a file system, which uses objects to store the inodes. The slab allocator manages inode objects; the cache management, construction, and deconstruction of inodes are handed over to the slab allocator. The file system simply asks the slab allocator for a "new inode" each time it requires one. For example, a file system could call the slab allocator to create a slab cache, as shown below.

```
inode_cache = kmem_cache_create("inode_cache",
            sizeof (struct inode), 0, inode_cache_constructor,
            inode_cache_destructor, inode_cache_reclaim,
            NULL, NULL, 0);

struct inode *inode = kmem_cache_alloc(inode_cache, 0);
```

The example shows that we create a cache named `inode_cache`, with objects of the size of an inode, no alignment enforcement, a constructor and a destructor function, and a reclaim function. The backend memory allocator is specified as `NULL`, which by default allocates physical pages from the `segkmem` page allocator.

We can see from the statistics exported by the slab allocator that the UFS file system uses a similar mechanism to allocate its inodes. We use the `kstat` command to dump the statistics. (We discuss allocator statistics in more detail in Section 11.2.3.9.)

```
sol8# kstat -n ufs_inode_cache
module: unix                            instance: 0
name:   ufs_inode_cache                 class:    kmem_cache
```

continues

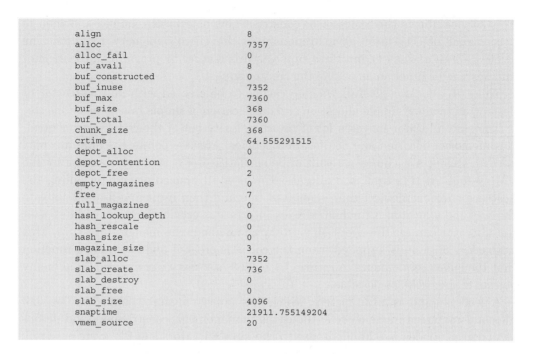

```
align                         8
alloc                         7357
alloc_fail                    0
buf_avail                     8
buf_constructed               0
buf_inuse                     7352
buf_max                       7360
buf_size                      368
buf_total                     7360
chunk_size                    368
crtime                        64.555291515
depot_alloc                   0
depot_contention              0
depot_free                    2
empty_magazines               0
free                          7
full_magazines                0
hash_lookup_depth             0
hash_rescale                  0
hash_size                     0
magazine_size                 3
slab_alloc                    7352
slab_create                   736
slab_destroy                  0
slab_free                     0
slab_size                     4096
snaptime                      21911.755149204
vmem_source                   20
```

The allocator interfaces are shown in Table 11.7.

Table 11.7 Solaris 10 Slab Allocator Interfaces from `<sys/kmem.h>`

Function	Description
kmem_cache_create()	Creates a new slab cache with the supplied *name*, aligning objects on the boundary supplied with alignment. The constructor, destructor, and reclaim functions are optional and can be supplied as NULL. An argument can be provided to the constructor with *arg*.
	The backend memory allocator can also be specified or supplied as NULL. If a NULL backend allocator is supplied, then the default allocator, kmem_getpages(), is used.
	Flags can supplied as KMC_NOTOUCH, KMC_NODEBUG, KMC_NOMAGAZINE, KMC_NOHASH, KMC_QCACHE, KMC_KMEM_ALLOC, and KMC_IDENTIFIER.
kmem_cache_destroy()	Destroys the cache referenced by *cp*.

continues

Table 11.7 Solaris 10 Slab Allocator Interfaces from `<sys/kmem.h>` (*continued*)

Function	Description
`kmem_cache_alloc()`	Allocates one object from the cache referenced by *cp*. Flags can be supplied as either `KM_SLEEP` or `KM_NOSLEEP`.
`kmem_cache_free()`	Returns the buffer *buf* to the cache referenced by *cp*.
`kmem_cache_stat()`	Returns a named statistic about a particular cache that matches the string name. Finds a name by looking at the `kstat` slab cache names, as also seen with `kstat -l -n kmem_cache`.

Caches are created with the `kmem_cache_create()` function, which can optionally supply callbacks for construction, destruction, and cache reclaim notifications. The callback functions are described in Table 11.8.

Table 11.8 Slab Allocator Callback Interfaces from `<sys/kmem.h>`

Function	Description
`constructor()`	Initializes the object *buf*. The arguments *arg* and *flag* are those provided during `kmem_cache_create()`.
`destructor()`	Destroys the object *buf*. The argument *arg* is that provided during `kmem_cache_create()`.
`reclaim()`	Where possible, returns objects to the cache. The argument is that provided during `kmem_cache_create()`.

11.2.3.3 General-Purpose Allocations

In addition to object-based memory allocation, the slab allocator provides backward-compatible, general-purpose memory allocation routines. These routines allocate arbitrary-length memory by providing a method to `malloc()`. The slab allocator maintains a list of various-sized caches to accommodate `kmem_alloc()` requests and simply converts the `kmem_alloc()` request into a request for an object from the nearest-sized cache. The sizes of the caches used for `kmem_alloc()` are named `kmem_alloc_n`, where *n* is the size of the objects within the cache (see Section 11.2.3.9). The functions are shown in Table 11.9.

Table 11.9 General-Purpose Memory Allocation

Function	Description
kmem_alloc()	Allocates *size* bytes of memory. Flags can be either KM_SLEEP or KM_NOSLEEP.
kmem_zalloc()	Allocates *size* bytes of zeroed memory. Flags can be either KM_SLEEP or KM_NOSLEEP.
kmem_free()	Returns to the allocator the buffer pointed to by *buf* and *size*.

11.2.3.4 Slab Allocator Implementation

The slab allocator implements the allocation and management of objects to the front-end clients, using memory provided by the backend allocator. In our introduction to the slab allocator, we discussed in some detail the virtual allocation units: the object and the slab. The slab allocator implements several internal layers to provide efficient allocation of objects from slabs. The extra internal layers reduce the amount of contention between allocation requests from multiple threads, which ultimately allows the allocator to provide good scalability on large SMP systems.

Figure 11.5 shows the internal layers of the slab allocator. The additional layers provide a cache of allocated objects for each CPU, so a thread can allocate an object from a local per-CPU object cache without having to hold a lock on the global slab cache. For example, if two threads both want to allocate an inode object from the inode cache, then the first thread's allocation request would hold a lock on the inode cache and would block the second thread until the first thread has its object allocated. The per-CPU cache layers overcome this blocking with an object cache per CPU to try to avoid the contention between two concurrent requests. Each CPU has its own short-term cache of objects, which reduces the amount of time that each request needs to go down into the global slab cache.

The layers shown in Figure 11.5 are separated into the slab layer, the depot layer, and the CPU layer. The upper two layers (which together are known as the magazine layer) are caches of allocated groups of objects and use a military analogy of allocating rifle rounds from magazines. Each per-CPU cache has magazines of allocated objects and can allocate objects (rounds) from its own magazines without having to bother the lower layers. The CPU layer needs to allocate objects from the lower (depot) layer only when its magazines are empty. The depot layer refills magazines from the slab layer by assembling objects, which may reside in many different slabs, into full magazines.

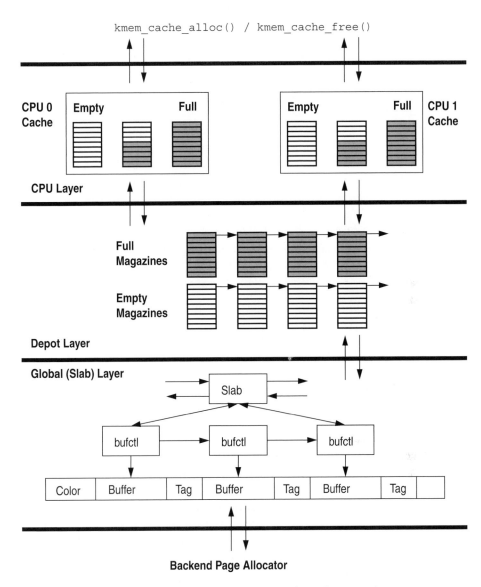

Figure 11.5 Slab Allocator Internal Implementation

11.2.3.5 The CPU Layer

The CPU layer caches groups of objects to minimize the number of times that an allocation will need to go down to the lower layers. This means that we can satisfy the majority of allocation requests without having to hold any global locks, thus dramatically improving the scalability of the allocator.

Continuing the military analogy: Three magazines of objects are kept in the CPU layer to satisfy allocation and deallocation requests—a full, a half-allocated, and an empty magazine are on hand. Objects are allocated from the half-empty magazine, and until the magazine is empty, all allocations are simply satisfied from the magazine. When the magazine empties, an empty magazine is returned to the magazine layer, and objects are allocated from the full magazine that was already available at the CPU layer. The CPU layer keeps the empty and full magazine on hand to prevent the magazine layer from having to construct and deconstruct magazines when on a full or empty magazine boundary. If a client rapidly allocates and deallocates objects when the magazine is on a boundary, then the CPU layer can simply use its full and empty magazines to service the requests, rather than having the magazine layer deconstruct and reconstruct new magazines at each request. The magazine model allows the allocator to guarantee that it can satisfy at least a magazine size of rounds without having to go to the depot layer.

11.2.3.6 The Depot Layer

The depot layer assembles groups of objects into magazines. Unlike a slab, a magazine's objects are not necessarily allocated from contiguous memory; rather, a magazine contains a series of pointers to objects within slabs.

The number of rounds per magazine for each cache changes dynamically, depending on the amount of contention that occurs at the depot layer. The more rounds per magazine, the lower the depot contention, but more memory is consumed. Each range of object sizes has an upper and lower magazine size. Table 11.10 shows the magazine size range for each object size.

Table 11.10 Solaris 10 Magazine Sizes

Object Size Range	Minimum Magazine Size	Maximum Magazine Size
1–64	15	143
65–256	7	143
257–512	3	143
513–1024	3	95
1025–2048	3	63
2049–3200	3	63
3201–4096	1	47
4097–8192	1	15
8193–16384	1	7
16385–32768	1	3
32769–	1	1

A slab allocator maintenance thread is scheduled every 15 seconds (controlled by the tunable `kmem_reap_interval`) to recalculate the magazine sizes. If significant contention has occurred at the depot level, then the magazine size is bumped up. Refer to Table 11.11 for the parameters that control magazine resizing.

11.2.3.7 The Global (Slab) Layer

The global slab layer allocates slabs of objects from contiguous pages of physical memory and hands them up to the magazine layer for allocation. The global slab layer is used only when the upper layers need to allocate or deallocate entire slabs of objects to refill their magazines.

The slab is the primary unit of allocation in the slab layer. When the allocator needs to grow a cache, it acquires an entire slab of objects. When the allocator wants to shrink a cache, it returns unused memory to the back end by deallocating a complete slab. A slab consists of one or more pages of virtually contiguous memory carved up into equal-sized chunks, with a reference count indicating how many of those chunks have been allocated.

The contents of each slab are managed by a `kmem_slab` data structure that maintains the slab's linkage in the cache, its reference count, and its list of free buffers. In turn, each buffer in the slab is managed by a `kmem_bufctl` structure that holds the free list linkage, the buffer address, and a back-pointer to the controlling slab.

For objects smaller than 1/8th of a page, the slab allocator builds a slab by allocating a page, placing the slab data at the end, and dividing the rest into equal-sized buffers. Each buffer serves as its own `kmem_bufctl` while on the free list. Only the linkage is actually needed, since everything else is computable. These are essential optimizations for small buffers; otherwise, we would end up allocating almost as much memory for `kmem_bufctl` as for the buffers themselves. The free list linkage resides at the end of the buffer, rather than the beginning, to facilitate debugging. This location is driven by the empirical observation that the beginning of a data structure is typically more active than the end. If a buffer is modified after being freed, the problem is easier to diagnose if the heap structure (free list linkage) is still intact. The allocator reserves an additional word for constructed objects so that the linkage does not overwrite any constructed state.

For objects greater than 1/8th of a page, a different scheme is used. Allocating objects from within a page-sized slab is efficient for small objects but not for large ones. The reason for the inefficiency of large-object allocation is that we could fit only one 4-Kbyte buffer on an 8-Kbyte page—the embedded slab control data takes up a few bytes, and two 4-Kbyte buffers would need just over 8 Kbytes. For large objects, we allocate a separate slab management structure from a separate pool of memory (another slab allocator cache, the `kmem_slab_cache`). We also allocate a buffer control structure for each page in the cache from another cache, the `kmem_bufctl_cache`. The `slab/bufctl/buffer` structures are shown in the slab layer in Figure 11.5.

The slab layer solves another common memory allocation problem by implementing slab coloring. If memory objects all start at a common offset (e.g., at 512-byte boundaries), then accessing data at the start of each object could result in the same cache line being used for all of the objects. The issues are similar to those discussed in Section 10.2.7. To overcome the cache line problem, the allocator applies an offset to the start of each slab so that buffers within the slab start at a different offset. This approach is also shown in Figure 11.5 by the color offset segment that resides at the start of each memory allocation unit before the actual buffer. Slab coloring results in much better cache utilization and more evenly balanced memory loading.

11.2.3.8 Slab Cache Parameters

The slab allocator parameters are shown in Table 11.11 for reference only. We recommend that none of these values be changed.

Table 11.11 Kernel Memory Allocator Parameters

Parameter	Description	S10 Default
`kmem_reap_interval`	This is the number of ticks after which the slab allocator update thread will run.	1500 (15s)
`kmem_depot_contention`	If the number of times depot contention occurred since the last time the update thread ran is greater than this value, then the magazine size is increased.	3
`kmem_reapahead`	If the amount of free memory falls below `cachefree + kmem_reapahead`, then the slab allocator will give back as many slabs as possible to the backend page allocator.	0

11.2.3.9 Slab Allocator Statistics

Two forms of slab allocator statistics are available: global statistics and per-cache statistics. The global statistics are available through the `mdb` debugger and display a summary of the entire cache list managed by the allocator.

```
# mdb -k
Loading modules: [ unix krtld genunix specfs dtrace ufs ip sctp usba s1394 fcp fctl nca
lofs nfs audiosup sppp random crypto logindmux ptm fcip md cpc zpool ]
> ::memstat
^C
> ::kmastat
cache                        buf    buf    buf    memory     alloc     alloc
name                        size in use  total  in use    succeed     fail
--------------------------- ----- ------ ------ --------- --------- -----
kmem_magazine_1               16  10410  21672    352256   1170957     0
kmem_magazine_3               32   5712   7560    245760    512141     0
kmem_magazine_7               64   5677  11214    729088    682328     0
kmem_magazine_15             128   7098  13237   1748992    666480     0
kmem_magazine_31             256    607    660    180224     27736     0
kmem_magazine_47             384     65    110     45056     21842     0
kmem_magazine_63             512    143    217    126976      8941     0
kmem_magazine_95             768      0     25     20480      4595     0
kmem_magazine_143           1152     15     33     45056      2829     0
kmem_slab_cache               56  45443 146880   8355840    723032     0
kmem_bufctl_cache             24 308453 787416  19197952   2575391     0
kmem_bufctl_audit_cache      192      0      0         0         0     0
kmem_va_4096                4096  48978 174080 713031680    973680     0
kmem_va_8192                8192   1500   3568  29229056    232825     0
             .
             .
zio_buf_131072            131072   9210   9605 1258946560   2333601      0
dmu_buf_impl_t               432  83995 105003  47788032   4994346     0
dnode_t                      768   5742  12255  10039296   1361264     0
zfs_znode_cache              168   4592  13488   2301952   1453000     0
zil_dobj_cache                40      0    101      4096  11692545     0
zil_itx_cache                136      7   9309   1314816  10550304     0
zil_lwb_cache                120      1     66      8192       188     0
zfs_acl_cache                 40      0      0         0         0     0
--------------------------- ----- ------ ------ --------- --------- -----
Total [hat_memload]                                1687552   1364579     0
Total [kmem_msb]                                  31047680   6396644     0
Total [kmem_va]                                  873070592   1361767     0
Total [kmem_default]                            1753763840 1290871216      0
Total [kmem_io_2G]                                 8429568      2103     0
Total [kmem_io_16M]                                  12288     30454     0
Total [bp_map]                                     1310720  10327220     0
Total [id32]                                          4096        21     0
Total [segkp]                                       393216      1613     0
Total [ip_minor_arena]                                 256     10768     0
Total [spdsock]                                         64         1     0
Total [namefs_inodes]                                   64        44     0
--------------------------- ----- ------ ------ --------- --------- -----
```

The ::kmastat dcmd shows summary information for each statistic and a systemwide summary at the end. The columns are shown in Table 11.12.

Table 11.12 kmastat Columns

Column	Description
Cache name	The name of the cache, as supplied during kmem_cache_ create().
buf_size	The size of each object within the cache in bytes.
buf_avail	The number of free objects in the cache.
buf_total	The total number of objects in the cache.
Memory in use	The amount of physical memory consumed by the cache in bytes.
Allocations succeeded	The number of allocations that succeeded.
Allocations failed	The number of allocations that failed. These are likely to be allocations that specified KM_NOSLEEP during memory pressure.

A more detailed version of the per-cache statistics is exported by the kstat mechanism. You can use the kstat command to display the cache statistics, which are described in Table 11.13.

```
sol8# kstat -n ufs_inode_cache
module: unix                         instance: 0
name:   ufs_inode_cache              class:    kmem_cache
           align                     8
           alloc                     7357
           alloc_fail                0
           buf_avail                 8
           buf_constructed           0
           buf_inuse                 7352
           buf_max                   7360
           buf_size                  368
           buf_total                 7360
           chunk_size                368
           crtime                    64.555291515
           depot_alloc               0
           depot_contention          0
           depot_free                2
           empty_magazines           0
           free                      7
           full_magazines            0
           hash_lookup_depth         0
           hash_rescale              0
           hash_size                 0
           magazine_size             3
           slab_alloc                7352
           slab_create               736
           slab_destroy              0
           slab_free                 0
           slab_size                 4096
           snaptime                  21911.755149204
           vmem_source               20
```

Table 11.13 Slab Allocator Per-Cache Statistics

Statistic	Description
align	The alignment boundary for objects within the cache.
alloc	The number of object allocations that succeeded.
alloc_fail	The number of object allocations that failed. (Should be zero!)
alloc_from_cpu*N*	Object allocations from CPU *N*.
buf_avail	The number of free objects in the cache.
buf_avail_cpu*N*	Objects available to CPU *N*.
buf_constructed	Zero or the same as buf_avail.
buf_inuse	The number of objects used by the client.
buf_max	The maximum number of objects the cache has reached.
buf_size	The size of each object within the cache in bytes.
buf_total	The total number of objects in the cache.
chunk_size	The allocation unit for the cache in bytes.
depot_alloc	The number of times a magazine was allocated in the depot layer.
depot_contention	The number of times a depot layer allocation was blocked because another thread was in the depot layer.
depot_free	The number of times a magazine was freed to the depot layer.
empty_magazines	The number of empty magazines.
free	The number of objects that were freed.
free_to_cpu*N*	Objects freed to CPU *N*.
full_magazines	The number of full magazines.
global_alloc	The number of times an allocation was made at the global layer.
global_free	The number of times an allocation was freed at the global layer.
hash_lookup_depth	Buffer hash lookup statistics.
hash_rescale	Buffer hash lookup statistics.
hash_size	Buffer hash lookup statistics.
magazine_size	The size of the magazine in entries.
memory_class	The ID of the backend memory allocator.
slab_create	The number of slabs created.
slab_destroy	The number of slabs destroyed.
slab_size	The size of each slab within the cache in bytes.

11.3 The Vmem Allocator

The kmem allocator relies on two lower-level system services to create slabs: a virtual address allocator to provide kernel virtual addresses, and VM routines to back those addresses with physical pages and establish virtual-to-physical translations. The scalability of large systems was limited by the old virtual address allocator (the resource map allocator). It tended to fragment the address space badly over time, its latency was linear in the number of fragments, and the whole thing was single-threaded.

Virtual address allocation is, however, just one example of the more general problem of *resource allocation*. For our purposes, a *resource* is anything that can be described by a set of integers. For example: virtual addresses are subsets of the 64-bit integers; process IDs are subsets of the integers [0, 30000]; and minor device numbers are subsets of the 32-bit integers.

In this section we describe the new general-purpose resource allocator, *vmem*, which provides guaranteed constant-time performance with low fragmentation. Vmem appears to be the first resource allocator that can do this.

We begin by providing background on the current state of the art. We then lay out the objectives of vmem, describe the vmem interfaces, explain the implementation in detail, and discuss vmem's performance (fragmentation, latency, and scalability) under both benchmarks and real-world conditions.

11.3.1 Background

Almost all versions of UNIX have a resource map allocator called `rmalloc()` [45]. A resource map can be any set of integers, though it's most often an address range like [0xe0000000, 0xf0000000). The interface is simple: `rmalloc(map, size)` allocates a segment of the specified size from map, and `rmfree(map, size, addr)` gives it back.

The old allocator suffered from serious flaws in both design and implementation:

- **Linear-time performance.** Previous allocators maintain a list of free segments, sorted in address order so the allocator can detect when coalescing is possible. If segments [a, b) and [b, c) are both free, they can be merged into a single free segment [a, c) to reduce fragmentation. The allocation code performs a linear search to find a segment large enough to satisfy the allocation. The free code uses insertion sort (also a linear algorithm) to return a segment to the free segment list. It can take several milliseconds to allocate or free a segment once the resource becomes fragmented.

- **Implementation exposure.** A resource allocator needs data structures to keep information about its free segments. In various ways, previous allocators make this the consumer of the allocator's problem. For example, the old resource map allocator requires the creator of the resource map to specify the maximum possible number of free segments at map creation time. If the map ever gets more fragmented than that, the allocator throws away resources in `rmfree()` because it has nowhere to put them.

11.3.2 Vmem Objectives

A good resource allocator should have the following properties:

- A powerful interface that can cleanly express the most common resource allocation problems
- Constant-time performance, regardless of the size of the request or the degree of fragmentation
- Linear scalability to any number of CPUs
- Low fragmentation, even if the operating system runs at full throttle for years

We begin by discussing the vmem interface considerations, then drill down to the implementation details.

11.3.3 Interface Description

The vmem interfaces do three basic things: create and destroy arenas to describe resources, allocate and free resources, and allow arenas to dynamically import new resources. This section describes the key concepts and the rationale behind them. The complete vmem interface specification is shown on the following page.

11.3.3.1 Creating Arenas

The first thing we need is the ability to define a resource collection, or arena. An arena is simply a set of integers. Vmem arenas most often represent virtual memory addresses (hence the name vmem), but in fact they can represent any integer resource, from virtual addresses to minor device numbers to process IDs.

The integers in an arena can usually be described as a single contiguous range, or span, such as [100, 500), so we specify this initial span to `vmem_create()`. For noncontiguous resources we can use `vmem_add()` to piece together the arena one span at a time.

```
vmem_t *vmem_create(
        char *name,                     /* descriptive name */
        void *base,                             /* start of initial span */
        size_t size,                            /* size of initial span */
        size_t quantum,                 /* unit of currency */
        void *(*afunc)(vmem_t *, size_t, int),  /* import alloc function */
        void (*ffunc)(vmem_t *, void *, size_t), /* import free function */
        vmem_t *source,                         /* import source arena */
        size_t qcache_max,                      /* maximum size to cache */
        int vmflag);                            /* VM_SLEEP or VM_NOSLEEP */
```

Creates a vmem arena called name whose initial span is [base, base + size). The arena's
natural unit of currency is quantum, so vmem_alloc() guarantees quantum's aligned
results. The arena may import new spans by invoking afunc on source, and may return
those spans by invoking ffunc on source. Small allocations are common, so the arena provides high-performance caching for each integer multiple of quantum up to qcache_max.
vmflag is either VM_SLEEP or VM_NOSLEEP depending on whether the caller is willing to
wait for memory to create the arena. vmem_create() returns an opaque pointer to the
arena.

void vmem_destroy(vmem_t *vmp);

Destroys arena vmp.

void *vmem_alloc(vmem_t *vmp, size_t size, int vmflag);

Allocates size bytes from vmp. Returns the allocated address on success, NULL on failure. vmem_alloc() fails only if vmflag specifies VM_NOSLEEP and no resources are currently available. vmflag may also specify an allocation policy (VM_BESTFIT, VM_
INSTANTFIT, or VM_NEXTFIT) as described in 4.3.2. If no policy is specified, the default
is VM_INSTANTFIT, which provides a good approximation to best-fit in guaranteed constant time.

void vmem_free(vmem_t *vmp, void *addr, size_t size);

Frees size bytes at addr to arena vmp.

**void *vmem_xalloc(vmem_t *vmp, size_t size, size_t align, size_t phase,
        size_t nocross, void *minaddr, void *maxaddr, int vmflag);**

Allocates size bytes at offset phase from an align boundary such that the resulting segment [addr, addr + size) is a subset of [minaddr, maxaddr) that does not straddle a
nocross-aligned boundary. vmflag is as above. One performance caveat: if either minaddr
or maxaddr is non-NULL, vmem may not be able to satisfy the allocation in constant time.
If allocations within a given [minaddr, maxaddr) range are common, it is more efficient
to declare that range to be its own arena and use unconstrained allocations on the new
arena.

void vmem_xfree(vmem_t *vmp, void *addr, size_t size);

Frees size bytes at addr, where addr was a constrained allocation. vmem_xfree() must be
used if the original allocation was a vmem_xalloc() because both routines bypass the
quantum caches.

void *vmem_add(vmem_t *vmp, void *addr, size_t size, int vmflag);

Adds the span [addr, addr + size) to arena vmp. Returns addr on success, NULL on failure. vmem_add() will fail only if vmflag is VM_NOSLEEP and no resources are currently
available.

For example, to create an arena to represent the integers in the range [100, 500) we can say:

```
foo = vmem_create("foo", 100, 400, ...);
vmem_add(foo, 600, 200, VM_SLEEP);
```

(Note: 100 is the start, 400 is the size.) If we want foo to represent the integers [600, 800) as well, we can add the span [600, 800) by using vmem_add().

The vmem_create() function specifies the arena's natural unit of currency, or qu, which is typically either 1 (for single integers like process IDs) or PAGESIZE (for virtual addresses). Vmem rounds all sizes to quantum multiples and guarantees quantum-aligned allocations.

11.3.3.2 Allocating and Freeing Resources

The primary interfaces to allocate and free resources are simple: vmem_ alloc(vmp, size, vmflag) allocates a segment of size bytes from arena vmp, and vmem_free(vmp, addr, size) gives it back.

We also provide a vmem_xalloc() interface that can specify common allocation constraints: alignment, phase (offset from the alignment), address range, and boundary-crossing restrictions (e.g., "don't cross a page boundary"). vmem_xalloc() is useful for things like kernel DMA code, which allocates kernel virtual addresses, using the phase and alignment constraints to ensure correct cache coloring.

For example, to allocate a 20-byte segment whose address is 8 bytes away from a 64-byte boundary and which lies in the range [200, 300), we can say

```
addr = vmem_xalloc(foo, 20, 64, 8, 0, 200, 300, VM_SLEEP);
```

In this example, addr will be 262: It is 8 bytes away from a 64-byte boundary (262 mod 64 = 8), and the segment [262, 282) lies within [200, 300).

Each vmem_[x]alloc() can specify one of three allocation policies through its vmflag argument:

- **VM_BESTFIT.** Directs vmem to use the smallest free segment that can satisfy the allocation. This policy tends to minimize fragmentation of very small, precious resources.

- **VM_INSTANTFIT.** Directs vmem to provide a good approximation to best-fit in guaranteed constant time. This is the default allocation policy.

- **VM_NEXTFIT.** Directs vmem to use the next free segment after the one previously allocated. This is useful for things like process IDs, when we want to cycle through all the IDs before reusing them.

We also offer an arena-wide allocation policy called quantum caching. The idea is that most allocations are for just a few quanta (e.g., one or two pages of heap or one minor device number), so we employ high-performance caching for each multiple of the quantum up to qcache_max, specified in vmem_create(). We make the caching threshold explicit so that each arena can request the amount of caching appropriate for the resource it manages. Quantum caches provide perfect-fit, very low latency, and linear scalability for the most common allocation sizes.

11.3.3.3 Importing from Another Arena

Vmem allows one arena to import its resources from another. vmem_create() specifies the source arena and the functions to allocate and free from that source. The arena imports new spans as needed and gives them back when all their segments have been freed.

The power of importing lies in the side effects of the import functions and is best understood by example. In Solaris, the function segkmem_alloc() invokes vmem_alloc() to get a virtual address and then backs it with physical pages. Therefore, we can create an arena of mapped pages by simply importing from an arena of virtual addresses, using segkmem_alloc() and segkmem_free().

11.3.4 Vmem Implementation

In this section we describe how vmem actually works. Figure 11.6 illustrates the overall structure of an arena.

11.3.4.1 Keeping Track of Segments

> "Apparently, too few researchers realized the full significance of Knuth's invention of boundary tags."
>
> —Paul R. Wilson, et al. [49]

Most implementations of malloc() prepend a small amount of space to each buffer to hold information for the allocator. These boundary tags, invented by Knuth in 1962 [18], solve two major problems:

- They make it easy for free() to determine how large the buffer is, because malloc() can store the size in the boundary tag.
- They make coalescing trivial. Boundary tags link all segments in address order, so free() can simply look both ways and coalesce if either neighbor is free.

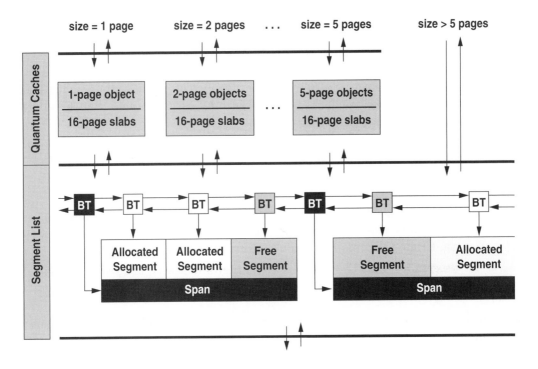

Figure 11.6 Structure of a Vmem Arena

Unfortunately, resource allocators can't use traditional boundary tags because the resource they're managing may not be memory (and therefore may not be able to hold information). In vmem we address this by using external boundary tags. For each segment in the arena we allocate a boundary tag to manage it, as shown in Figure 11.6. We'll see shortly that external boundary tags enable constant-time performance.

11.3.4.2 Allocating and Freeing Segments

Each arena has a segment list that links all of its segments in address order, as shown in Figure 11.6. Every segment also belongs to either a free list or an allocation hash chain, as described below. (The arena's segment list also includes span markers to keep track of span boundaries, so we can easily tell when an imported span can be returned to its source.)

We keep all free segments on power-of-two free lists; that is, free list[n] contains all free segments whose sizes are in the range [2n, 2n+1). To allocate a segment we search the appropriate free list for a segment large enough to satisfy the allocation. This approach, called segregated fit, actually approximates best-fit because any segment on the chosen free list is a good fit [49]. (Indeed, with power-of-two free lists, a segregated fit is necessarily within 2x of a perfect fit.) Approximations to best-fit are appealing because they exhibit low fragmentation in practice for a wide variety of workloads [15].

The algorithm for selecting a free segment depends on the allocation policy specified in the flags to `vmem_alloc()` as follows (in all cases, assume that the allocation size lies in the range [2n, 2n+1)):

- **VM_BESTFIT.** Search for the smallest segment on free list[n] that can satisfy the allocation.

- **VM_INSTANTFIT.** If the size is exactly 2n, take the first segment on free list[n]. Otherwise, take the first segment on free list[n+1]. Any segment on this free list is necessarily large enough to satisfy the allocation, so we get constant-time performance with a reasonably good fit.[1]

- **VM_NEXTFIT.** Ignore the free lists altogether and search the arena for the next free segment after the one previously allocated.

Once we've selected a segment, we remove it from its free list. If the segment is not an exact fit, we split the segment, create a boundary tag for the remainder, and put the remainder on the appropriate free list. We then add the boundary tag of our newly allocated segment to a hash table so that `vmem_free()` can find it quickly.

`vmem_free()` is straightforward: It looks up the segment's boundary tag in the allocated-segment hash table, removes it from the hash table, tries to coalesce the segment with its neighbors, and puts it on the appropriate free list. All operations are constant-time. Note that the hash lookup also provides a cheap and effective sanity check: The freed address must be in the hash table, and the freed size must match the segment size. This helps catch bugs such as duplicate frees.

The key feature of the algorithm described above is that its performance is independent of both transaction size and arena fragmentation. Vmem appears to be the first resource allocator that performs allocations and frees of any size in guaranteed constant-time.

---

1. We like instant-fit because it guarantees constant-time performance, provides low fragmentation in practice, and is easy to implement. There are many other techniques for choosing a suitable free segment in reasonable (e.g., logarithmic) time, such as keeping all free segments in a size-sorted tree; see [49] for a thorough survey. Any of these techniques could be used for a vmem implementation.

11.3.4.3 Locking Strategy

For simplicity, we protect each arena's segment list, free lists, and hash table with a global lock. We rely on the fact that large allocations are relatively rare and allow the arena's quantum caches to provide linear scalability for all the common allocation sizes.

11.3.4.4 Quantum Caching

The slab allocator can provide object caching for any vmem arena, so vmem's quantum caches are actually implemented as object caches. For each small integer multiple of the arena's quantum we create an object cache to service requests of that size. vmem_alloc() and vmem_free() simply convert each small request (size ≤ qcache_max) into a kmem_cache_alloc() or kmem_cache_free() on the appropriate cache, as illustrated in Figure 11.6. Because it is based on object caching, quantum caching provides very low latency and linear scalability for the most common allocation sizes.

> **Example.**   Assume the arena shown in Figure 11.6. A 3-page allocation would proceed as follows: vmem_alloc(foo, 3 * PAGESIZE) would call kmem_cache_alloc(foo->vm_qcache[2]). In most cases the cache's magazine layer would satisfy the allocation, and we would be done. If the cache needed to create a new slab it would call vmem_alloc(foo, 16 * PAGESIZE), which would be satisfied from the arena's segment list. The slab allocator would then divide its 16-page slab into five 3-page objects and use one of them to satisfy the original allocation.

When we create an arena's quantum caches we pass to kmem_cache_create() a flag, KMC_QCACHE, that directs the slab allocator to use a particular slab size: the next power of 2 above 3 * qcache_max. We use this particular value for three reasons. (1) The slab size must be larger than qcache_max to prevent infinite recursion. (2) By numerical luck, this slab size provides near-perfect slab packing (e.g., five 3-page objects fill 15/16 of a 16-page slab). (3) We see below that using a common slab size for all quantum caches helps to reduce overall arena fragmentation.

11.3.4.5 Fragmentation

> "A waste is a terrible thing to mind."
> —Anonymous

Fragmentation is the disintegration of a resource into unusably small, noncontiguous segments. To see how this can happen, imagine allocating a 1-Gbyte resource one byte at a time, then freeing only the even-numbered bytes. The arena would then have 500 Mbytes free, yet it could not even satisfy a 2-byte allocation.

We observe that it is the combination of different allocation sizes and different segment lifetimes that causes persistent fragmentation. If all allocations are the same size, then any freed segment can obviously satisfy another allocation of the same size. If all allocations are transient, the fragmentation is transient.

We have no control over segment lifetime, but quantum caching offers some control over allocation size—namely, all quantum caches have the same slab size, so most allocations from the arena's segment list occur in slab-sized chunks.

At first it may appear that all we've done is move the problem: The segment list won't fragment as much, but now the quantum caches themselves can suffer fragmentation in the form of partially used slabs. The critical difference is that the free objects in a quantum cache are of a size that's known to be useful, whereas the segment list can disintegrate into useless pieces under hostile workloads. Moreover, prior allocation is a good predictor of future allocation [48], so free objects are likely to be used again.

It is impossible to prove that prior allocation helps,[2] but it seems to work well in practice. We have never had a report of severe fragmentation since vmem's introduction (we had many such reports with the old resource map allocator), and Solaris systems often stay up for years.

11.3.5 Vmem Performance

Several performance studies were performed to validate Vmem's design.

11.3.5.1 Microbenchmark Performance

We've stated that vmem_alloc() and vmem_free() are constant-time operations regardless of arena fragmentation, whereas rmalloc() and rmfree() are linear-time. We measured alloc/free latency as a function of fragmentation to verify this. Figure 11.7 illustrates the results.

rmalloc() has a slight performance edge at very low fragmentation because the algorithm is so naïve. At zero fragmentation, vmem's latency without quantum caching was 1560 ns, vs. 715 ns for rmalloc(). Quantum caching reduces vmem's latency to just 482 ns, so for allocations that go to the quantum caches (the common case) vmem is faster than rmalloc() even at very low fragmentation.

11.3.5.2 System-Level Performance

Vmem's low latency and linear scaling remedied serious pathologies in the performance of kernel virtual address allocation under rmalloc(), yielding dramatic improvements in system-level performance.

---

2. In fact, it has been proved that "there is no reliable algorithm for ensuring efficient memory usage, *and none is possible*." [49].

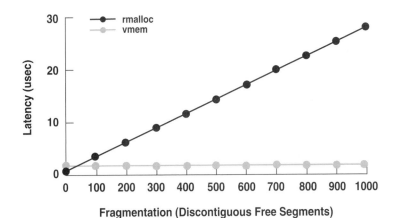

Figure 11.7 Latency vs. Fragmentation

LADDIS. Veritas reported a 50% improvement in LADDIS peak throughput with the new virtual memory allocator [40].

Web Service. On a large Starfire system running 2700 Netscape servers under the fair-share scheduler, vmem reduced system time from 60% to 10%, roughly doubling system capacity [37].

I/O Bandwidth. An internal I/O benchmark on a 64-CPU Starfire generated such heavy contention on the old rmalloc() lock that the system was essentially useless. Contention was exacerbated by very long hold times due to rmalloc()'s linear search of the increasingly fragmented kernel heap. lockstat(1M) revealed that threads were spinning for an average of 48 milliseconds to acquire the rmalloc() lock, thus limiting I/O bandwidth to just 1000/48 = 21 I/O operations per second per CPU. With vmem, the problem completely disappeared and performance improved by several orders of magnitude.

11.3.6 Summary

The vmem interface supports both simple and highly constrained allocations, and its importing mechanism can build complex resources from simple components. The interface is sufficiently general that we've been able to eliminate over 30 special-purpose allocators in Solaris since vmem's introduction.

The vmem implementation has proven to be very fast and scalable, improving performance on system-level benchmarks by 50% or more. It has also proven to be very robust against fragmentation in practice.

Vmem's instant-fit policy and external boundary tags appear to be new concepts. They guarantee constant-time performance regardless of allocation size or arena fragmentation.

Vmem's quantum caches provide very low latency and linear scalability for the most common allocations. They also present a particularly friendly workload to the arena's segment list, which helps to reduce overall arena fragmentation.

11.4 Kernel Memory Allocator Tracing

The slab allocator includes a general-purpose allocation tracing facility that tracks the allocation history of objects. The facility is switched off by default and can be enabled by setting the system variable kmem_flags. The tracing facility captures the stack and history of allocations into a slab cache, named as the name of the cache being traced, with .DEBUG appended to it. Audit tracing can be enabled by the following:

- Setting kmem_flags to indicate the type of tracing desired, usually 0x1F to indicate all tracing
- Booting the system with kadb -d and setting kmem_flags before startup

11.4.1 Enabling KMA DEBUG Flags

The following simple example shows how to trace a cache that is created on a large system, after the flags have been set. To enable tracing on all caches, the system must be booted with kmdb and the kmem_flags variable set. The steps for such booting are shown below.

```
ok boot kmdb -d
Loading kmdb...

Welcome to kmdb
[0]> kmem_flags/D
kmem_flags:
kmem_flags:        0
[0]> kmem_flags/W 0x1f
kmem_flags:        0x0                =        0x1f
[0]> :c

SunOS Release 5.10 Version gate:2004-10-18 32-bit
Copyright 1983-2004 Sun Microsystems, Inc.  All rights reserved.
Use is subject to license terms.
Loaded modules: [ ufs unix krtld genunix specfs ]
...
```

If instead, you're doing this with a system where GRUB is used to boot Solaris, you add the -kd to the "kernel" line in the GRUB menu entry (you can edit GRUB menu entries for this boot by using the GRUB menu interface, and the "e" (for edit) key).

Note that the total number of allocations traced will be limited by the size of the audit cache parameters, shown in Table 11.14. Table 11.14 shows the parameters that control kernel memory debugging.

Table 11.14 Kernel Memory Debugging Parameters

Parameter	Description	s10 Default
kmem_flags	Set this to select the mode of kernel memory debugging. Set to 0x1F to enable all debugging, or set the logical OR of the following: 0x1 transaction auditing 0x2 deadbeef checking 0x4 red-zone checking 0x8 freed buffer content logging	0
kmem_log_size	Specify the maximum amount of memory to use for slab allocator audit tracing.	2% of mem.
kmem_content_maxsave	Specify the maximum number of bytes to log in each entry.	256

11.4.2 Examining Kernel Memory Allocations with MDB

Recall from Section 11.2.3.9 how we can use the `::kmastat` dcmd to view the kmem caches. Another way to list the various kmem caches is with the `::kmem_cache` command.

```
# mdb -k
> ::kmem_cache
ADDR               NAME                      FLAG  CFLAG   BUFSIZE  BUFTOTL
ffffffff80021008   kmem_magazine_1           0000  080000       16    18900
ffffffff80021748   kmem_magazine_3           0000  080000       32     5922
ffffffff80022008   kmem_magazine_7           0000  080000       64     7497
...
ffffffff80025748   kmem_slab_cache           0000  080000       56   150912
ffffffff80026008   kmem_bufctl_cache         0000  080000       24   895608
ffffffff80026748   kmem_bufctl_audit_cache   0000  080000      192        0
ffffffff80027008   kmem_va_4096              0200  110000     4096   204640
ffffffff80027748   kmem_va_8192              0200  110000     8192     4880
ffffffff80029008   kmem_va_12288             0200  110000    12288      930
...
```

continues

```
ffffffff8002c008 kmem_alloc_8             0000 200000        8    55045
ffffffff8002c748 kmem_alloc_16            0000 200000       16    11340
ffffffff8002d008 kmem_alloc_24            0000 200000       24     7896
ffffffff8002d748 kmem_alloc_32            0000 200000       32    15120
ffffffff8002e008 kmem_alloc_40            0000 200000       40    15150
ffffffff8002e748 kmem_alloc_48            0000 200000       48    54936
...
```

This command is useful because it maps cache names to addresses and provides the debugging flags for each cache in the FLAG column. It is important to understand that the allocator's selection of debugging features is derived on a per-cache basis from this set of flags. These are set in conjunction with the global kmem_flags variable at cache creation time. Setting kmem_flags while the system is running has no effect on the debugging behavior, except for subsequently created caches (which is rare after boot-up).

Next, walk the list of kmem caches directly by using MDB's kmem_cache walker.

```
> ::walk kmem_cache
ffffffff80021008
ffffffff80021748
ffffffff80022008
ffffffff80022748
ffffffff80023008
ffffffff80023748
...
```

This produces a list of pointers that correspond to each kmem cache in the kernel. To find out about a specific cache, apply the kmem_cache dcmd.

```
> ffffffff80021008::kmem_cache
ADDR              NAME                    FLAG  CFLAG  BUFSIZE  BUFTOTL
ffffffff80021008  kmem_magazine_1         0000 080000      16    18900
```

Important fields for debugging include bufsize, flags, and name. The name of the kmem_cache (in this case, kmem_alloc_24) indicates its purpose in the system. bufsize gives the size of each buffer in this cache; in this case, the cache is used for allocations of size 24 and smaller. flags tells what debugging features are turned on for this cache. You can find the debugging flags listed in sys/kmem_impl.h. In this case, flags is 0x20f, which is KMF_AUDIT | KMF_DEADBEEF | KMF_REDZONE | KMF_CONTENTS | KMF_HASH. The debugging features are explained in subsequent sections.

When you are interested in looking at buffers in a particular cache, you can walk the allocated and freed buffers in that cache directly.

```
> ffffffff80021008::walk kmem
fffffe810c652000
fffffe810c652010
fffffe810c652020
fffffe810c652030
...
```

MDB provides a shortcut to supplying the cache address to the kmem walker: a specific walker is provided for each kmem cache, and its name is the same as the name of the cache. For example:

```
> ::walk kmem_alloc_24
ffffffff80120008
ffffffff80120020
ffffffff80120038
ffffffff80120050
ffffffff80120068
...
> ::walk thread_cache
ffffffff82f60120
ffffffff81f00140
ffffffff85320500
ffffffff852e0580
ffffffff81f004a0
ffffffff82f607e0
...
```

Now you know how to iterate over the kernel memory allocator's internal data structures and examine the most important members of the kmem_cache data structure.

11.4.3 Detecting Memory Corruption

One of the primary debugging features of the allocator is the inclusion of algorithms for quick recognition of data corruption. When corruption is detected, the allocator immediately panics the system.

This section describes how the allocator recognizes data corruption; you must understand this process to be able to debug these problems. Memory abuse typically falls into one of the following categories:

- Writing past the end of a buffer
- Accessing uninitialized data

- Continuing to use a freed buffer
- Corrupting kernel memory

Keep these problems in mind as you read the next three sections. They will help you understand the allocator's design and enable you to diagnose problems more efficiently.

11.4.4 Checking a Freed Buffer: 0xdeadbeef

When the KMF_DEADBEEF (0x2) bit is set in the flags field of a kmem_cache, the allocator tries to make memory corruption easy to detect by writing a special pattern into all freed buffers. This pattern is 0xdeadbeef. Since a typical region of memory contains both allocated and freed memory, sections of each kind of block will be interspersed; here is an example from the kmem_alloc_24 cache.

```
0x70a9add8:      deadbeef        deadbeef
0x70a9ade0:      deadbeef        deadbeef
0x70a9ade8:      deadbeef        deadbeef
0x70a9adf0:      feedface        feedface
0x70a9adf8:      70ae3260        8440c68e
0x70a9ae00:      5               4ef83
0x70a9ae08:      0               0
0x70a9ae10:      1               bbddcafe
0x70a9ae18:      feedface        139d
0x70a9ae20:      70ae3200        d1befaed
0x70a9ae28:      deadbeef        deadbeef
0x70a9ae30:      deadbeef        deadbeef
0x70a9ae38:      deadbeef        deadbeef
0x70a9ae40:      feedface        feedface
0x70a9ae48:      70ae31a0        8440c54e
```

The buffer beginning at 0x70a9add8 is filled with the 0xdeadbeef pattern, which is an immediate indication that the buffer is currently free. At 0x70a9ae28 another free buffer begins; at 0x70a9ae00 an allocated buffer is located between them.

Note: You might have observed that there are some holes in this picture. Three 24-byte regions should occupy only 72 bytes of memory, instead of the 120 bytes shown here. This discrepancy is explained in the next section.

11.4.5 Debugging with the Redzone Indicator: 0xfeedface

The pattern 0xfeedface appears frequently in the buffer above. This pattern is known as the "redzone" indicator. It enables the allocator (and a programmer debugging a problem) to determine if the boundaries of a buffer have been violated by "buggy" code. Following the redzone is some additional information. The contents of that data depend on other factors (see Section 11.4.8). The redzone and its suffix are collectively called the buftag region. Figure 11.8 summarizes this information.

Figure 11.8 The Redzone

The buftag is appended to each buffer in a cache when any of the KMF_AUDIT, KMF_DEADBEEF, or KMF_REDZONE flags are set in that buffer's cache. The contents of the buftag depend on whether KMF_AUDIT is set.

Decomposing the memory region presented above into distinct buffers is now simple.

```
0x70a9add8:     deadbeef        deadbeef  \
0x70a9ade0:     deadbeef        deadbeef  +- User Data (free)
0x70a9ade8:     deadbeef        deadbeef  /
0x70a9adf0:     feedface        feedface  -- REDZONE
0x70a9adf8:     70ae3260        8440c68e  -- Debugging Data

0x70a9ae00:     5               4ef83     \
0x70a9ae08:     0               0         +- User Data (allocated)
0x70a9ae10:     1               bbddcafe  /
0x70a9ae18:     feedface        139d      -- REDZONE
0x70a9ae20:     70ae3200        d1befaed  -- Debugging Data

0x70a9ae28:     deadbeef        deadbeef  \
0x70a9ae30:     deadbeef        deadbeef  +- User Data (free)
0x70a9ae38:     deadbeef        deadbeef  /
0x70a9ae40:     feedface        feedface  -- REDZONE
0x70a9ae48:     70ae31a0        8440c54e  -- Debugging Data
```

In the free buffers at 0x70a9add8 and 0x70a9ae28, the redzone is filled with 0xfeedfacefeedface. This a convenient way of determining that a buffer is free.

In the allocated buffer beginning at 0x70a9ae00, the situation is different. There are two allocation types:

1. The client requested memory by using kmem_cache_alloc(), in which case the size of the requested buffer is equal to the bufsize of the cache.

2. The client requested memory by using kmem_alloc(9F), in which case the size of the requested buffer is less than or equal to the bufsize of the cache.

For example, a request for 20 bytes will be fulfilled from the `kmem_alloc_24` cache. The allocator enforces the buffer boundary by placing a marker, the redzone byte, immediately following the client data.

```
0x70a9ae00:    5              4ef83     \
0x70a9ae08:    0              0          +- User Data (allocated)
0x70a9ae10:    1              bbddcafe  /
0x70a9ae18:    feedface       139d     -- REDZONE
0x70a9ae20:    70ae3200       d1befaed -- Debugging Data
```

0xfeedface at 0x70a9ae18 is followed by a 32-bit word containing what seems to be a random value. This number is actually an encoded[3] representation of the size of the buffer. To decode this number and find the size of the allocated buffer, use the following formula:

size = redzone_value / 251

So, in this example,

size = 0x139d / 251 = 20 bytes.

This result shows that the buffer requested was of size 20 bytes. The allocator performs this decoding operation and finds that the redzone byte should be at offset 20. The redzone byte is the hex pattern 0xbb, which is present at 0x729084e4 (0x729084d0 + 0t20) as expected (Figure 11.9).

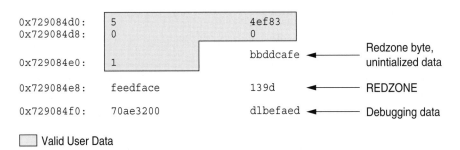

Figure 11.9 Sample `kmem_alloc(9F)` Buffer

---

3. Why is the allocation size encoded this way? To encode the size, the allocator uses the formula *(251 * size + 1)*. When the size decode occurs, the integer division discards the remainder of +1. However, the addition of 1 is valuable because the allocator can check whether the size is valid by testing whether *(size % 251 == 1)*. In this way, the allocator defends against corruption of the redzone byte index.

Figure 11.10 shows the general form of this memory layout.

Figure 11.10 Redzone Byte

If the allocation size is the same as the `bufsize` of the cache, the redzone byte overwrites the first byte of the redzone itself, as shown in Figure 11.11.

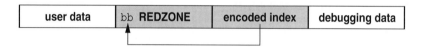

Figure 11.11 Redzone Byte at the Beginning of the Redzone

This overwriting results in the first 32-bit word of the redzone being 0xbbedface or 0xfeedfabb, depending on the endianness of the hardware on which the system is running.

11.4.6 Detecting Uninitialized Data: 0xbaddcafe

You might be wondering what the suspicious 0xbbddcafe at address 0x729084d4 was before the redzone byte got placed over the first byte in the word. It was 0xbaddcafe. When the KMF_DEADBEEF flag is set in the cache, allocated but uninitialized memory is filled with the 0xbaddcafe pattern. When the allocator performs an allocation, it loops across the words of the buffer and verifies that each word contains 0xdeadbeef, then fills that word with 0xbaddcafe.

A system can panic with a message such as the following:

```
panic[cpu1]/thread=e1979420: BAD TRAP: type=e (Page Fault)
rp=ef641e88 addr=baddcafe occurred in module "unix" due to an
illegal access to a user address
```

In this case, the address that caused the fault was 0xbaddcafe: The panicking thread has accessed some data that was never initialized.

11.4.7 Associating Panic Messages with Failures

The kernel memory allocator emits panic messages corresponding to the failure modes described earlier. For example, a system can panic with a message like this:

```
kernel memory allocator: buffer modified after being freed
modification occurred at offset 0x30
```

The allocator was able to detect this case because it tried to validate that the buffer in question was filled with 0xdeadbeef. At offset 0x30, this condition was not met. Since this condition indicates memory corruption, the allocator panicked the system.

Another example failure message is

```
kernel memory allocator: redzone violation: write past end of buffer
```

The allocator was able to detect this case because it tried to validate that the redzone byte (0xbb) was in the location it determined from the redzone size encoding. It failed to find the signature byte in the correct location. Since this circumstance indicates memory corruption, the allocator panicked the system. Other allocator panic messages are discussed later.

11.4.8 Memory Allocation Logging

This section explains the logging features of the kernel memory allocator and describes how you can employ them to debug system crashes.

11.4.8.1 Buftag Data Integrity

As explained earlier, the second half of each buftag contains extra information about the corresponding buffer. Some of this data is debugging information, and some is data private to the allocator. While this auxiliary data can take several different forms, it is collectively known as "Buffer Control" or `bufctl` data.

However, the allocator needs to know whether a buffer's `bufctl` pointer is valid since this pointer might also have been corrupted by malfunctioning code. The allocator confirms the integrity of its auxiliary pointer by storing the pointer and an encoded version of that pointer and then cross-checking the two versions.

As shown in Figure 11.12, these pointers are the `bcp` (buffer control pointer) and `bxstat` (buffer control XOR status). The allocator arranges `bcp` and `bxstat` so that the expression `bcp` XOR `bxstat` equals a well-known value.

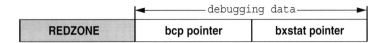

Figure 11.12 Extra Debugging Data in the Buftag

In the event that one or both of these pointers become corrupted, the allocator can easily detect such corruption and panic the system. When a buffer is allocated, bcp XOR bxstat = 0xa110c8ed ("allocated"). When a buffer is free, bcp XOR bxstat = 0xf4eef4ee ("freefree").

Note: You might find it helpful to reexamine the example provided in Section 11.4.4 in order to confirm that the buftag pointers shown there are consistent.

In the event that the allocator finds a corrupt buftag, it panics the system and produces a message similar to the following:

```
kernel memory allocator: boundary tag corrupted
    bcp ^ bxstat = 0xffeef4ee, should be f4eef4ee
```

Remember, if bcp is corrupt, it is still possible to retrieve its value by taking the value of bxstat XOR 0xf4eef4ee or bxstat XOR 0xa110c8ed, depending on whether the buffer is allocated or free.

11.4.8.2 The `bufctl` Pointer

The buffer control (bufctl) pointer contained in the buftag region can have different meanings, depending on the cache's kmem_flags. The behavior toggled by the KMF_AUDIT flag is of particular interest: When the KMF_AUDIT flag is not set, the kernel memory allocator allocates a kmem_bufctl_t structure for each buffer. This structure contains some minimal accounting information about each buffer. When the KMF_AUDIT flag is set, the allocator instead allocates a kmem_bufctl_audit_t structure, an extended version of the kmem_bufctl_t structure.

This section presumes the KMF_AUDIT flag is set. For caches that do not have this bit set, the amount of available debugging information is reduced.

The kmem_bufctl_audit_t structure (bufctl_audit for short) contains additional information about the last transaction that occurred on this buffer. The following example shows how to apply the bufctl_audit macro to examine an audit record. The buffer shown is the example buffer used in Section 11.4.4.

```
> 0x70a9ae00,5/KKn
0x70a9ae00:      5                    4ef83
                 0                    0
                 1                    bbddcafe
                 feedface             139d
                 70ae3200             d1befaed
```

With the techniques presented above, it is easy to see that 0x70ae3200 points to the bufctl_audit record: It is the first pointer following the redzone. To examine the bufctl_audit record it points to, apply the bufctl_audit macro.

```
> 0x70ae3200$<bufctl_audit
0x70ae3200:      next                 addr                 slab
                 70378000             70a9ae00             707c86a0
0x70ae320c:      cache                timestamp            thread
                 70039928             e1bd0e26afe          70aac4e0
0x70ae321c:      lastlog              contents             stackdepth
                 7011c7c0             7018a0b0             4
0x70ae3228:
                 kmem_zalloc+0x30
                 pid_assign+8
                 getproc+0x68
                 cfork+0x60
```

The addr field is the address of the buffer corresponding to this bufctl_audit record. This is the original address: 0x70a9ae00. The cache field points at the kmem_cache that allocated this buffer. You can use the ::kmem_cache dcmd to examine it.

```
> 0x70039928::kmem_cache
ADDR       NAME                      FLAG  CFLAG   BUFSIZE  BUFTOTL
70039928 kmem_alloc_24               020f  000000       24      612
```

The timestamp field represents the time this transaction occurred. This time is expressed in the same manner as gethrtime(3C).

thread is a pointer to the thread that performed the last transaction on this buffer.

The lastlog and contents pointers point to locations in the allocator's transaction logs. These logs are discussed in detail in Section 11.4.11.

Typically, the most useful piece of information provided by bufctl_audit is the stack trace recorded at the point at which the transaction took place. In this case, the transaction was an allocation called as part of executing fork(2).

11.4.9 Analyzing Memory with Advanced Techniques

This section describes facilities for performing advanced memory analysis, including locating memory leaks and sources of data corruption.

11.4.9.1 Finding Memory Leaks

The `::findleaks` dcmd provides powerful and efficient detection of memory leaks in kernel crash dumps for which the full set of kmem debug features has been enabled. The first execution of `::findleaks` processes the dump for memory leaks (this can take a few minutes), and then coalesces the leaks by the allocation stack trace. The `findleaks` report shows a `bufctl` address and the topmost stack frame for each memory leak that was identified.

```
> ::findleaks
CACHE       LEAKED     BUFCTL  CALLER
70039ba8         1   703746c0  pm_autoconfig+0x708
70039ba8         1   703748a0  pm_autoconfig+0x708
7003a028         1   70d3b1a0  sigaddq+0x108
7003c7a8         1   70515200  pm_ioctl+0x187c
------------------------------------------------------------
   Total         4 buffers, 376 bytes
```

Using the `bufctl` pointers, you can obtain the complete stack backtrace of the allocation by applying the `bufctl_audit` macro.

```
> 70d3b1a0$<bufctl_audit
0x70d3b1a0:    next            addr            slab
               70a049c0        70d03b28        70bb7480
0x70d3b1ac:    cache           timestamp       thread
               7003a028        13f7cf63b3      70b38380
0x70d3b1bc:    lastlog         contents        stackdepth
               700d6e60        0               5
0x70d3b1c8:
               kmem_alloc+0x30
               sigaddq+0x108
               sigsendproc+0x210
               sigqkill+0x90
               kill+0x28
```

You can usually use the `bufctl_audit` information and the allocation stack trace to quickly track down the code path that leaks the given buffer.

11.4.9.2 Finding References to Data

When trying to diagnose a memory corruption problem, you should know what other kernel entities hold a copy of a particular pointer. This is important because it can reveal which thread accessed a data structure after it was freed. It can also make it easier to understand what kernel entities are sharing knowledge of a particular (valid) data item. You use the ::whatis and ::kgrep dcmds to answer these questions. You can apply ::whatis to a value of interest.

```
> 0x705d8640::whatis
705d8640 is 705d8640+0, allocated from streams_mblk
```

In this case, 0x705d8640 is revealed to be a pointer to a STREAMS mblk structure. To see the entire allocation tree, use ::whatis -a instead.

```
> 0x705d8640::whatis -a
705d8640 is 705d8640+0, allocated from streams_mblk
705d8640 is 705d8000+640, allocated from kmem_va_8192
705d8640 is 705d8000+640 from kmem_default vmem arena
705d8640 is 705d2000+2640 from kmem_va vmem arena
705d8640 is 705d2000+2640 from heap vmem arena
```

This command reveals that the allocation also appears in the kmem_va_8192 cache—a kmem cache that is fronting the kmem_va vmem arena. It also shows the full stack of vmem allocations.

The complete list of kmem caches and vmem arenas is displayed by the ::kmastat dcmd. You can use ::kgrep to locate other kernel addresses that contain a pointer to this mblk. This approach illustrates the hierarchical nature of memory allocations in the system; in general, you can determine the type of object referred to by the given address from the name of the most specific kmem cache.

```
> 0x705d8640::kgrep
400a3720
70580d24
7069d7f0
706a37ec
706add34
```

And you can investigate them by applying ::whatis again.

```
> 400a3720::whatis
400a3720 is in thread 7095b240's stack
> 706add34::whatis
706add34 is 706add20+14, allocated from streams_dblk_120
```

Here, one pointer is located on the stack of a known kernel thread, and another is the mblk pointer inside of the corresponding STREAMS dblk structure.

11.4.10 Finding Corrupt Buffers with `::kmem_verify`

The MDB `::kmem_verify` dcmd implements most of the same checks that the kmem allocator does at runtime. `::kmem_verify` can be invoked in order to scan every kmem cache with appropriate `kmem_flags` or to examine a particular cache.

Here is an example of using `::kmem_verify` to isolate a problem.

```
> ::kmem_verify
Cache Name                       Addr      Cache Integrity
kmem_alloc_8                     70039428  clean
kmem_alloc_16                    700396a8  clean
kmem_alloc_24                    70039928  1 corrupt buffer
kmem_alloc_32                    70039ba8  clean
kmem_alloc_40                    7003a028  clean
kmem_alloc_48                    7003a2a8  clean
...
```

It is easy to see here that the `kmem_alloc_24` cache contains what `::kmem_verify` believes to be a problem. With an explicit cache argument, the `::kmem_verify` dcmd provides more detailed information about the problem.

```
> 70039928::kmem_verify
Summary for cache 'kmem_alloc_24'
  buffer 702babc0 (free) seems corrupted, at 702babc0
```

The next step is to examine the buffer that `::kmem_verify` believes to be corrupt.

```
> 0x702babc0,5/KKn
0x702babc0:    0            deadbeef
               deadbeef     deadbeef
               deadbeef     deadbeef
               feedface     feedface
               703785a0     84d9714e
```

The reason that `::kmem_verify` flagged this buffer is now clear: The first word in the buffer (at 0x702babc0) should probably be filled with the 0xdeadbeef pattern, not with a 0. At this point, examining the `bufctl_audit` for this buffer might yield clues about what code recently wrote to the buffer, indicating where and when it was freed.

Another useful technique in this situation is to use `::kgrep` to search the address space for references to address 0x702babc0, in order to discover what threads or data structures are still holding references to this freed data.

11.4.11 Using the Allocator Logging Facility

When KMF_AUDIT is set for a cache, the kernel memory allocator maintains a log that records the recent history of its activity. This transaction log records bufctl_audit records. If the KMF_AUDIT and the KMF_CONTENTS flags are both set, the allocator generates a contents log that records portions of the actual contents of allocated and freed buffers. The structure and use of the contents log is outside the scope of this book. The transaction log is discussed in this section.

MDB provides several facilities for displaying the transaction log. The simplest is ::walk kmem_log, which prints out the transaction in the log as a series of bufctl_audit_t pointers.

```
> ::walk kmem_log
70128340
701282e0
70128280
70128220
701281c0
...
> 70128340$<bufctl_audit
0x70128340:      next             addr             slab
                 70ac1d40         70bc4ea8         70bb7c00
0x7012834c:      cache            timestamp        thread
                 70039428         e1bd7abe721      70aacde0
0x7012835c:      lastlog          contents         stackdepth
                 701282e0         7018f340         4
0x70128368:
                 kmem_cache_free+0x24
                 nfs3_sync+0x3c
                 vfs_sync+0x84
                 syssync+4
```

A more elegant way to view the entire transaction log is by using the ::kmem_log command.

```
> ::kmem_log
CPU ADDR       BUFADDR        TIMESTAMP  THREAD
  0 70128340  70bc4ea8       e1bd7abe721 70aacde0
  0 701282e0  70bc4ea8       e1bd7aa86fa 70aacde0
  0 70128280  70bc4ea8       e1bd7aa27dd 70aacde0
  0 70128220  70bc4ea8       e1bd7a98a6e 70aacde0
  0 701281c0  70d03738       e1bd7a8e3e0 70aacde0

  ...
  0 70127140  70cf78a0       e1bd78035ad 70aacde0
  0 701270e0  709cf6c0       e1bd6d2573a 40033e60
  0 70127080  70cedf20       e1bd6d1e984 40033e60
  0 70127020  70b09578       e1bd5fc1791 40033e60
  0 70126fc0  70cf78a0       e1bd5fb6b5a 40033e60
  0 70126f60  705ed388       e1bd5fb080d 40033e60
  0 70126f00  705ed388       e1bd551ff73 70aacde0
  ...
```

The output of ::kmem_log is sorted in descending order by timestamp. The ADDR column is the bufctl_audit structure corresponding to that transaction; BUFADDR points to the actual buffer.

These figures represent transactions on buffers (both allocations and frees). When a particular buffer is corrupted, it can be helpful to locate that buffer in the transaction log, then determine in which other transactions the transacting thread was involved. This can help you assemble a picture of the sequence of events that occurred before and after the allocation (or free) of a buffer.

You can employ the ::bufctl command to filter the output of walking the transaction log. The ::bufctl -a command filters the buffers in the transaction log by buffer address. This example filters on buffer 0x70b09578.

```
> ::walk kmem_log | ::bufctl -a 0x70b09578
ADDR      BUFADDR    TIMESTAMP   THREAD   CALLER
70127020  70b09578   e1bd5fc1791 40033e60 biodone+0x108
70126e40  70b09578   e1bd55062da 70aacde0 pageio_setup+0x268
70126de0  70b09578   e1bd52b2317 40033e60 biodone+0x108
70126c00  70b09578   e1bd497ee8e 70aacde0 pageio_setup+0x268
70120480  70b09578   e1bd21c5e2a 70aacde0 elfexec+0x9f0
70120060  70b09578   e1bd20f5ab5 70aacde0 getelfhead+0x100
7011ef20  70b09578   e1bd1e9a1dd 70aacde0 ufs_getpage_miss+0x354
7011d720  70b09578   e1bd1170dc4 70aacde0 pageio_setup+0x268
70117d80  70b09578   e1bcff6ff27 70bc2480 elfexec+0x9f0
70117960  70b09578   e1bcfea4a9f 70bc2480 getelfhead+0x100
...
```

This example illustrates that a particular buffer can be used in numerous transactions.

Note: Remember that the kmem transaction log is an incomplete record of the transactions made by the kernel memory allocator. Older entries in the log are evicted as needed to keep the size of the log constant.

The ::allocdby and ::freedby dcmds provide a convenient way to summarize transactions associated with a particular thread. Here is an example of listing the recent allocations performed by thread 0x70aacde0.

```
> 0x70aacde0::allocdby
BUFCTL     TIMESTAMP CALLER
70d4d8c0   e1edb14511a allocb+0x88
70d4e8a0   e1edb142472 dblk_constructor+0xc
70d4a240   e1edb13dd4f allocb+0x88
70d4e840   e1edb13aeec dblk_constructor+0xc
70d4d860   e1ed8344071 allocb+0x88
70d4e7e0   e1ed8342536 dblk_constructor+0xc
70d4a1e0   e1ed82b3a3c allocb+0x88
70a53f80   e1ed82b0b91 dblk_constructor+0xc
70d4d800   e1e9b663b92 allocb+0x88
```

By examining bufctl_audit records, you can understand the recent activities of a particular thread.

11.5 MDB Reference

Table 11.15 MDB Reference for Kernel Memory

`dcmd` or `walker`	Description
`dcmd allocdby`	Given a thread, print its allocated buffers
`dcmd freedby`	Given a thread, print its freed buffers
`dcmd kmalog`	Display kmem transaction log and stack traces
`dcmd kmastat`	Kernel memory allocator stats
`dcmd kmausers`	Current medium and large users of the kmem allocator
`dcmd kmem_cache`	Print kernel memory caches
`dcmd kmem_debug`	Toggle kmem dcmd/walk debugging
`dcmd kmem_log`	Dump kmem transaction log
`dcmd kmem_verify`	Check integrity of kmem-managed memory
`dcmd vmem`	Print a vmem_t
`dcmd vmem_seg`	Print or filter a vmem_seg
`walk allocdby`	Given a thread, walk its allocated bufctls
`walk freectl`	Walk a kmem cache's free bufctls
`walk freectl_constructed`	Walk a kmem cache's constructed free bufctls
`walk freedby`	Given a thread, walk its freed bufctls
`walk freemem`	Walk a kmem cache's free memory
`walk freemem_constructed`	Walk a kmem cache's constructed free memory
`walk kmem`	Walk a kmem cache
`walk kmem_bufctl_audit_cache`	Walk the kmem_bufctl_audit_cache cache
`walk kmem_bufctl_cache`	Walk the kmem_bufctl_cache cache
`walk kmem_cache`	Walk list of kmem caches
`walk kmem_cpu_cache`	Given a kmem cache, walk its per-CPU caches
`walk kmem_hash`	Given a kmem cache, walk its allocated hash table
`walk kmem_log`	Walk the kmem transaction log
`walk kmem_slab`	Given a kmem cache, walk its slabs
`walk kmem_slab_cache`	Walk the kmem_slab_cache cache

continues

Table 11.15 MDB Reference for Kernel Memory (*continued*)

dcmd or walker	Description
walk kmem_slab_partial	Given a kmem cache, walk its partially allocated slabs
walk vmem	Walk vmem structures in pre-fix, depth-first order
walk vmem_alloc	Given a vmem_t, walk its allocated vmem_segs
walk vmem_free	Given a vmem_t, walk its free vmem_segs
walk vmem_postfix	Walk vmem structures in post-fix, depth-first order
walk vmem_seg	Given a vmem_t, walk all of its vmem_segs
walk vmem_span	Given a vmem_t, walk its spanning vmem_segs

12

Hardware Address Translation

The hardware address translation (HAT) layer controls the hardware that manages mapping of virtual memory to physical memory. The HAT layer interfaces implement the creation and destruction of mappings between virtual and physical memory and probe and control the MMU. The HAT layer also implements all the low-level trap handlers to manage page faults and memory exceptions. Figure 12.1 shows the logical demarcation between elements of the HAT layer.

12.1 HAT Overview

The HAT implementation is different for each type of hardware MMU, and hence there are several different HAT implementations. The HAT layer hides the platform-specific implementation and is used by the segment drivers to implement the segment driver's view of virtual-to-physical translation. The HAT uses the struct hat data structure to hold the top-level translation information for an address space. The hat structure is platform specific and is referenced by the address space structure (see Figure 12.1). HAT-specific data structures existing in every page represent the translation information at a page level.

The HAT layer is called when the segment drivers want to manipulate the hardware MMU. For example, when a segment driver wants to create or destroy an address space mapping, it calls the HAT functions specifying the address range

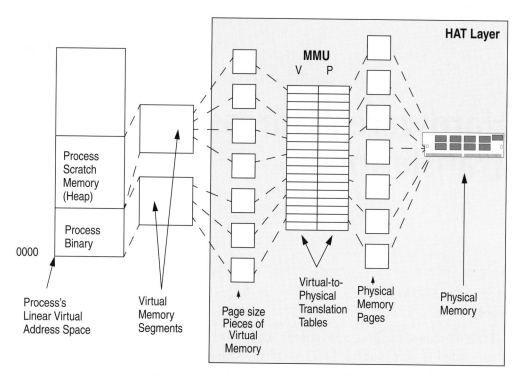

Figure 12.1 Role of the HAT Layer in Virtual-to-Physical Translation

and the action to be taken. We can call the HAT functions without knowing anything about the underlying MMU implementation; the arguments to the HAT
functions are machine independent and usually consist of virtual addresses,
lengths, page pointers, and protection modes.

Table 12.1 summarizes HAT functions.

Table 12.1 Machine-Independent HAT Functions

Function	Description
hat_alloc()	Allocates a HAT structure in the address space.
hat_chgattr()	Changes the protections for the supplied virtual address range.
hat_clrattr()	Clears the protections for the supplied virtual address range.
hat_free_end()	Informs the HAT layer that a process has exited.

continues

Table 12.1 Machine-Independent HAT Functions *(continued)*

Function	Description
`hat_free_start()`	Informs the HAT layer that a process is exiting.
`hat_get_mapped_size()`	Returns the number of bytes that have valid mappings.
`hat_getattr()`	Gets the protections for the supplied virtual address range.
`hat_memload()`	Creates a mapping for the supplied page at the supplied virtual address. Used to create mappings.
`hat_setattr()`	Sets the protections for the supplied virtual address range.
`hat_stats_disable()`	Finishes collecting statistics on an address space.
`hat_stats_enable()`	Starts collecting page reference and modification statistics on an address space.
`hat_swapin()`	Allocates resources for a process that is about to be swapped in.
`hat_swapout()`	Frees resources for a process that is about to be swapped out.
`hat_sync()`	Synchronizes the `struct_page` software referenced and modified bits with the hardware MMU.
`hat_unload()`	Unloads a mapping for the given page at the given address.

12.2 The UltraSPARC HAT Layer

In this section, we discuss the implementation of the Solaris HAT layer as implemented on UltraSPARC processors.

12.2.1 Introduction

As shown in Figure 12.2, UltraSPARC processors use a memory management unit in the microprocessor to convert virtual addresses to physical addresses on-the-fly. The MMU uses a table known as the *translation lookaside buffer* (TLB) to manage these translations. The HAT layer programs the microprocessor's TLB with entries identifying the relationship of the virtual and physical addresses.

Since the size of the TLB is limited by hardware, the TLB is typically supplemented by a larger (but slower) in-memory table of virtual-to-physical translations. On UltraSPARC processors, this table is known as the *translation storage*

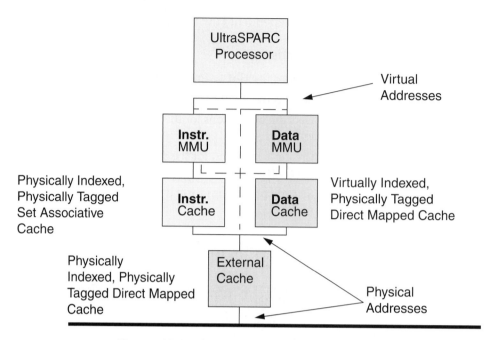

Figure 12.2 UltraSPARC-I–IV MMU Topology

buffer (TSB); on most other architectures, it is known as the *page table*. When the microprocessor needs to convert a virtual address into a physical address, it first searches the TLB (a hardware search), and if a physical address is not found (that is, hardware encountered a *TLB miss*), the microprocessor searches the larger in-memory table. The relationship of these components is shown in Figure 12.3.

UltraSPARC microprocessors use a *software TLB replacement strategy*: When a TLB miss occurs, software is invoked to search the in-memory table (the TSB) for the required translation entry.

Let's walk through a simple example. Suppose a process allocates some memory within its heap by calling `malloc()`, and further suppose that `malloc()` returns to the program a virtual address of the requested memory. When that memory is first referenced, the virtual memory layer requests a physical memory page from the system's free lists. This newly acquired page is an associated physical address within physical memory. The virtual memory system then constructs in software a translation entry containing the virtual address (the start of the page returned by `malloc`) and the physical address of the new page. This newly created translation entry is then inserted into the TSB and programmed into an available slot in the microprocessor's TLB. The entry is also kept in software, linked to the address space of the process to which it belongs. Later, the program reads from the virtual address, and if the new TLB entry still resides in the TLB (it may have been

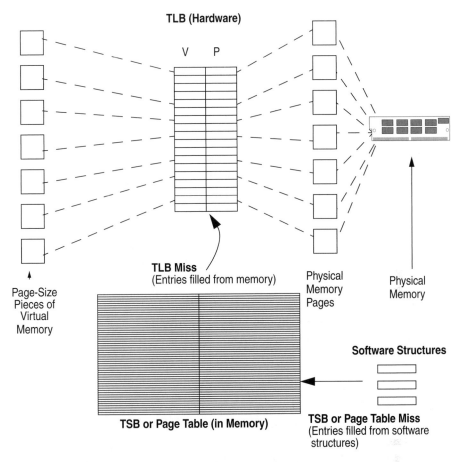

TLB (Hardware)

V   P

TLB Miss
(Entries filled from memory)

Page-Size
Pieces of
Virtual
Memory

Physical
Memory
Pages

Physical
Memory

Software Structures

TSB or Page Table (in Memory)

TSB or Page Table Miss
(Entries filled from software
structures)

Figure 12.3 Virtual Address Translation Hardware and Software

ousted by other activity), the virtual-to-physical address is translated on-the-fly. If the TLB entry had been evicted, a TLB miss occurs, a hardware exception occurs, and the translation entry is looked up in the larger TSB.

The TSB is also limited in size, and in extreme circumstances a TSB miss can occur, requiring a lengthy search of the software structures linked to the process.

12.2.2 struct hat

The UltraSPARC hat structure is responsible for anchoring all HAT layer information and structures relating to a single process address space. These include the process' context ID (also known as the context number); a pointer to its as structure and TSBs; and various flags and status bits to name a few. Lets look at an example of how we obtain the contents of the `hat` structure for a running process on the system:

```
# ps
   PID TTY         TIME CMD
  5152 pts/6       0:00 sh
  5153 pts/6       0:00 bash
  5162 pts/6       0:00 ps
```

To get to the `hat` structure associated with `sh` we first need to find the address of its `proc` structure. We can do this in `mdb` using the PID we obtained from above:

```
> 0t5152::pid2proc
30eb1c840b8
```

Alternatively, we could have just used the `::ps` dcmd which lists the `proc` address as part of its output:

```
> ::ps ! grep 5152
R   5152    5140    5152    5140      0 0x00004000 0000030eb1c840b8 sh
R   5153    5152    5153    5140      0 0x00014000 0000030077a64020 bash
```

Having obtained the `proc` address we can walk the link chain as illustrated in Figure 12.4 to get to the `hat` structure. Note that the `proc` structure is also known as `proc_t`:

```
> 30eb1c840b8::print proc_t p_as
p_as = 0x32b8832da68
> 0x32b8832da68::print struct as a_hat
a_hat = 0x32b8831dea8
> 0x32b8831dea8::print -t struct hat
{
    void *sfmmu_xhat_provider = 0
    cpuset_t sfmmu_cpusran = {
        ulong_t [9] cpub = [ 0x10, 0, 0, 0, 0, 0, 0, 0, 0 ]
    }
    struct as *sfmmu_as = 0x32b8832da68
    ulong_t [4] sfmmu_ttecnt = [ 0x26, 0, 0, 0 ]
    ulong_t [4] sfmmu_ismttecnt = [ 0, 0, 0, 0 ]
    union _h_un h_un = {
        ism_blk_t *sfmmu_iblkp = 0
        ism_ment_t *sfmmu_imentp = 0
    }
    unsigned sfmmu_free = 0
    unsigned sfmmu_ismhat = 0
    unsigned sfmmu_ctxflushed = 1
    uchar_t sfmmu_rmstat = 0
    uchar_t sfmmu_clrstart = 0xac
    ushort_t sfmmu_clrbin = 0xac
```

continues

```
short sfmmu_cnum = 0xbf7
uchar_t sfmmu_cext = 0
uchar_t sfmmu_flags = 0
struct tsb_info *sfmmu_tsb = 0x30004c92270
uint64_t sfmmu_ismblkpa = 0xffffffffffffffff
kcondvar_t sfmmu_tsb_cv = {
    ushort_t _opaque = 0
}
uint8_t [4] sfmmu_pgsz = [ 0, 0, 0, 0 ]
```

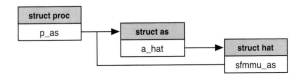

Figure 12.4 Linkage from the `proc` Structure to the `hat` Structure

The `hat` structure fields are as follows:

- **sfmmu_xhat_provider.** This is used by XHAT—an extension to the Solaris HAT layer which allows a device with a Memory Management Unit (MMUs) to share virtual address space with processes and kernel. It is set to NULL for "regular" CPU `hat` structures.

- **sfmmu_cpusran.** CPU bit-mask used for efficient cross-calling.

- **sfmmu_as.** Pointer to the `as` this `hat` provides mapping for.

- **sfmmu_ttecnt[].** Array of per-pagesize TTE counts.

- **sfmmu_ismttecnt[].** Array of per-page-size ISM TTE counts (estimated).

- **sfmmu_iblkp.** Pointer to ISM mapping block. See Section 12.2.5.

- **sfmmu_imentp.** Used by the ISM `hat` to point to its mapping list. See Section 12.2.5.

- **sfmmu_free.** A bit, if set, indicates that this `hat` is in the process of being freed. It is set by `as_free()` when an address space is being torn down.

- **sfmmu_ismhat.** A bit, if set, indicates that this is a dummy ISM `hat`. See Section 12.2.5.

- **sfmmu_ctxflushed.** A bit, if set, indicates that the ctx has been flushed.

- **sfmmu_rmstat.** Refmod stats reference count.

- **sfmmu_clrstart.** Start color bin for page coloring.

- **sfmmu_clrbin.** Per `as` physical page coloring bin.

- **sfmmu_cnum.** Context number (a.k.a. context ID).

- **sfmmu_flags.** hat disposition flags.

- **sfmmu_tsb.** List of per as TSBs.

- **sfmmu_ismblkpa.** PA of ISM mapping block. If there are no ISM mappings this is set to −1.

- **sfmmu_tsb_cv.** Signals TSB swap-in or relocation.

- **sfmmu_cext.** Encoding of large page sizes used to program the TLBs.

- **sfmmu_mflags.** MMU-specific page size exclusivity. The UltraSPARC IV+ MMU supports the use of either 32-Mbyte or 256-Mbyte TTEs but not both, on a per context basis. This field is used to flag the exclusive page size used by the process.

- **sfmmu_mcnt.** Keeps track of the number of segments using the exclusive page size.

- **sfmmu_pgsz[].** Preferred page size ranking for programming the TLBs.

12.2.3 The Translation Table

There are many ways to implement translation tables or page tables. The older SPARC (sun4m and sun4d) architectures employ a three-level page table as described in the *SPARC Reference MMU* (SRMMU) specification. The first-level page table consists of 256 entries that point to 256 second-level tables. In turn, each second-level table points to 64 third-level tables that contain the actual page table entries.

The problem with multilevel page tables in general is that they are inefficient in terms of space when sparse address spaces are mapped. This is because space for nonmapped pages needs to be allocated in the table. A 32-bit address space mapped with 4-Kbyte pages will require a total of $2^{32} \div 4096 = 1,048,576$ entries in the lowest-level page tables per context. With 32-bit page table entries this translates to 4 Mbytes of memory. So, if a process uses just 12 Kbytes (three 4-Kbyte pages) to map in its text, data, and stack segments, it would need at least 4 Mbytes for its page table.

Multilevel page tables don't scale in terms of space with larger address spaces either. If we were to map a 64-bit virtual address space using 8-Kbyte pages we would need more than 2 quadrillion entries alone in the lowest-level table per context! Of course we could reduce the number of entries needed by increasing the page size. But this wastes memory because it increases the allocation granularity.

So, as we have seen, page tables do not scale to sparse 64-bit address spaces. One possible solution, pioneered in the IBM System/38, for such an address space is the *inverted page table* (IPT). Inverted page tables have entries for each physical page of memory only, and hence their size does not depend on the size of the virtual address space.

The `sun4u` architecture employes an improvement over IPTs called *hashed page tables* (HPT). In general, HPTs use a hash of the virtual address to index into a hash table. The resulting hash bucket points to the head of a list of data nodes containing table entries that are searched for a matching virtual address and context.

Solaris implements a translation table based on the `hme_blk` and its associated data structures which are used to keep track of active mappings. There are two tables: one for kernel mappings and another for user mappings. Figure 12.5 illustrates the relationship between the different structures which perform a similar function to page tables in the `sun4m` architecture. The `hme_blk` structures each define virtual to physical mappings for a particular address space and virtual address range. They are organized into a series of hash buckets based on an address space identifier, the virtual address and the page size used. In the event of a TSB miss a hash of these elements is used to obtain the correct hash bucket and then a linear search of the list is made to find the corresponding `hme_blk` for the mapping.

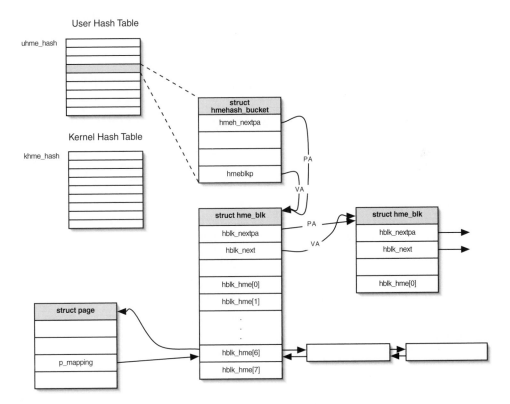

Figure 12.5 Hash Table Data Structures

In the following sections we will describe the data structures and functions associated with the hash table in detail.

12.2.3.1 The Translation Table Entry

Each entry of the TLB consists of a *Translation Table Entry* (TTE), which describes the mapping and provides details of its associated properties. The TTE may be thought of as corresponding to a page table entry, or PTE, in the `sun4m` architecture. A TTE is made up of two components, the tag and the translation data, each of length 64 bits. The TTE tag contains the encoded virtual address and context ID (Figure 12.7), and the TTE data contains the corresponding physical address together with various properties associated with the translation (Figure 12.6). The context ID is a 13-bit quantity which is used to distinguish between different address spaces, so that the same virtual addresses in different address spaces can coexist in the TLB. One of the most significant properties of the mapping is its size. Each TTE maps a contiguous area of memory, which can be 8 Kbytes, 64 Kbytes, 512 Kbytes or 4 Mbytes in size (and additionally 32 Mbytes and 256 Mbytes on UltraSPARC V+). Note that this mapping size is not directly related to the underlying virtual page size, which remains at 8 Kbytes (see Section 9.10.1). Other prop-

TTE Data:

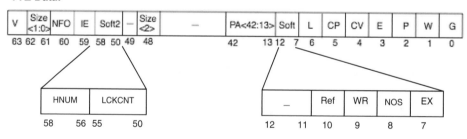

CP: Cache in physically indexed cache
CV: Cache in virtually indexed cache
E: Side effect
EX: Execute permission bit
G: Global bit
HNUM: Number of sf_hments in hme_blk
IE: Invert endianness bit
INV: TSB entry invalid bit
L: Lock in TLB
LCK: TSB entry locked bit
LCKCNT: TTE lock reference count
NFO: No-fault access only

NOS: No sync bit
P: Privileged bit
Ref: Reference bit
Size: Page size
Soft: Software defined fields
V: Valid bit
W: Writeable bit
WR: Write permission bit

Note: On UltraSPARCI/II TTE Data bits <49:41> are used for diagnostic access.

Figure 12.6 TTE Data Fields

erties of the mapping include the write and execute permissions and cacheability in the physically-indexed and virtually-indexed caches.

A TLB hit occurs if both the virtual address and context supplied to the TLB correspond to those of a particular TTE entry, loaded in the TLB. The comparison is based on the MMU TTE tag field. Address aliasing is permitted and so multiple TLB entries with the same physical address but different virtual addresses may exist. However, the reverse situation of multiple entries, with the same virtual address but different physical addresses, produces undefined results. In the event of a TLB miss trap, the TSB, provides a software managed, directly mapped cache, which is used to reload the TLB.

In Solaris 9 and prior versions, the `sun4u` kernel implemented TSBs that could be shared amongst many contexts just like the TLB, so the TTE tag used in the TSB contained the context ID. However, with the introduction of the per-process dynamic TSB framework in Solaris 10, TSBs are now private to a process and hence the context ID is no longer required in the TSB TTE tag (see Figure 12.7 for a description of the TSB TTE tag fields). A TSB hit occurs if the virtual address supplied corresponds to the tag of a particular entry in the faulting process's TSB.

MMU TTE Tag:

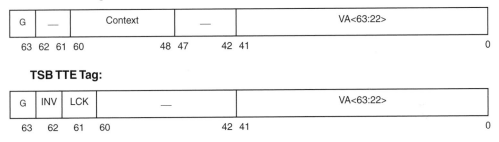

G: Copy of TTE Data Global bit
INV: TSB entry invalid bit
LCK: TSB entry locked bit

Figure 12.7 Hardware and Software Representations of the TTE Tag

12.2.3.2 `sf_hment` Structure

The HAT layer uses a *HAT mapping entry* (HME) structure to keep track of virtual-to-physical address translations. On the `sun4u` kernel architecture, this is called the `sf_hment` structure and it contains the TTE for a particular mapping.

```
struct sf_hment {
        tte_t hme_tte;                          /* tte for this hment */

        union {
                struct page *page;      /* what page this maps */
                struct pa_hment *data;  /* pa_hment */
        } sf_hment_un;

        struct  sf_hment *hme_next;     /* next hment */
        struct  sf_hment *hme_prev;     /* prev hment */
};
```

See sfmmu/vm/hat_sfmmu.h

The `sf_hment` structure points to the physical page it maps through the `page` pointer. There is a one-to-one correspondence between `sf_hment` structures and TTEs. The `hme_next` and `hme_prev` pointers form a chain that links all the virtual mappings for this physical page. Since a single physical page can be mapped into multiple address spaces at differing virtual addresses, one physical address can be referred to by many virtual addresses *(virtual address aliasing)*, meaning that one page can be pointed to by many `sf_hment` structures. Therefore, to speed up the search for mappings of a particular page, we put related `sf_hment` structures on a null-terminated, doubly linked list.

Let's dig into the instances of an example `bash` process running on a particular system.

```
> ::ps ! grep bash
R    4147    4145    4147    4147   75447 0x4a014000 000006000b255828 bash
R    4160    4159    4160    4147       0 0x4a014000 0000060002518010 bash
R    4112    4110    4112    4112   75447 0x4a014000 000006000b2587a8 bash
R    4126    4125    4126    4112       0 0x4a014000 000006000ba4c418 bash
R    4053    4051    4053    4053   75447 0x4a014000 000006000a43bb90 bash
```

The `::ps` mdb dcmd lists five running instances of `bash` with the 8th column of the output being the address of the process's `proc` structure. As an illustration, let's attempt to find the mapping for the virtual address `0x10028` belonging to the first reported process. The dcmd that will help us is `::sfmmu_vtop`, which prints the virtual-to-physical mapping of a given address. But before we can use it, we first need to get the address space belonging to the process from the `proc`.

```
> 000006000b255828::print proc_t p_as
p_as = 0x6000a96a2b8
> 0x10028::sfmmu_vtop -v -a 0x6000a96a2b8
sfmmup=6000b3a5c40 hmebp=70001cb8820 hmeblkp=3000493f7d8
tte=800000000b4906a1 pfn=5a48 pp=70002aa2400
address space 6000a96a2b8: virtual 10028 mapped to physical b490028
```

We found it! Virtual address `0x10028` is mapped to physical address `0xb490028`. Following are the other values reported by `::sfmmu_vtop` when the `-v` flag is used:

- **sfmmup.** Address of `hat` structure for this `as`
- **hmebp.** Pointer to the HME hash table entry this virtual address maps to (see Section 12.2.3.6)
- **hmeblkp.** Pointer to the `hme_blk` the contains this mapping (see Section 12.2.3.3)
- **tte.** TTE for this mapping
- **pfn.** Page frame number
- **pp.** Pointer to the `page` structure

Let's look at the `page` this virtual address belongs to.

```
> 70002aa2400::print struct page
{
    p_offset = 0
    p_vnode = 0x60014fe90c0
...
    p_mapping = 0x3000f0c8f10
    p_pagenum = 0x5a48
    p_share = 0x5
...
}
```

As a point of validation, notice that the `p_pagenum` field and the PFN reported by `::sfmmu_vtop` agree with each other, so we are in fact looking at the correct page. The `p_share` field is 5, indicating that this physical page is being mapped by five TTEs. Remember that five `bash` processes were reported by `::ps`. It so happens that the virtual address of `0x10028` that we picked for our example falls on a text page and so is shared among all the instances of the `bash` binary. The `sf_hment` structures containing these related TTEs are linked through the page's `p_mapping` list. We can use the `::list` dcmd to help us traverse the list.

```
> 0x3000f0c8f10::list struct sf_hment hme_next
3000f0c8f10
3000493f810
3000f0d2a90
300053d3b10
300049eba20
> 0x3000f0c8f10::list struct sf_hment hme_next|::print struct sf_hment sf_hment_un.page
sf_hment_un.page = 0x70002aa2400
sf_hment_un.page = 0x70002aa2400
sf_hment_un.page = 0x70002aa2400
sf_hment_un.page = 0x70002aa2400
sf_hment_un.page = 0x70002aa2400
```

The second command in the above example prints the page each `sf_hment` is pointing to. As expected, they all refer to the same page.

12.2.3.3 `hme_blk`

Solaris uses the `hme_blk` structures to keep track of active virtual-to-physical address mappings. Each `hme_blk` represents a contiguous area of mapped virtual memory for a particular address space, defined by a base page address and a span.

```
struct hme_blk_misc {
        ushort_t locked_cnt;    /* HAT_LOAD_LOCK ref cnt */
        uint_t  notused:10;
        uint_t  xhat_bit:1;     /* set for an xhat hme_blk */
        uint_t  shadow_bit:1;   /* set for a shadow hme_blk */
        uint_t  nucleus_bit:1;  /* set for a nucleus hme_blk */
        uint_t  ttesize:3;      /* contains ttesz of hmeblk */
};

struct hme_blk {
        uint64_t        hblk_nextpa;    /* physical address for hash list */

        hmeblk_tag      hblk_tag;       /* tag used to obtain an hmeblk match */

        struct hme_blk  *hblk_next;     /* on free list or on hash list */
                                        /* protected by hash lock */

        struct hme_blk  *hblk_shadow;   /* pts to shadow hblk */
                                        /* protected by hash lock */
        uint_t          hblk_span;      /* span of memory hmeblk maps */

        struct hme_blk_misc    hblk_misc;

        union {
                struct {
                        ushort_t hblk_hmecount; /* hment on mlists counter */
                        ushort_t hblk_validcnt; /* valid tte reference count */
                } hblk_counts;
                uint_t          hblk_shadow_mask;
        } hblk_un;

#ifdef  HBLK_TRACE
        kmutex_t        hblk_audit_lock;        /* lock to protect index */
        uint_t          hblk_audit_index;       /* index into audit_cache */
        struct  hblk_lockcnt_audit hblk_audit_cache[HBLK_AUDIT_CACHE_SIZE];
#endif  /* HBLK_AUDIT */

        struct sf_hment hblk_hme[1];    /* hment array */
};

#define hblk_lckcnt     hblk_misc.locked_cnt
#define hblk_xhat_bit   hblk_misc.xhat_bit
#define hblk_shw_bit    hblk_misc.shadow_bit
#define hblk_nuc_bit    hblk_misc.nucleus_bit
#define hblk_ttesz      hblk_misc.ttesize
#define hblk_hmecnt     hblk_un.hblk_counts.hblk_hmecount
#define hblk_vcnt       hblk_un.hblk_counts.hblk_validcnt
#define hblk_shw_mask   hblk_un.hblk_shadow_mask
```

See sfmmu/vm/hat_sfmmu.h

An `hme_blk` can have two different sizes, depending on the number of `sf_hment` elements it implicitly contains. When dealing with 64-Kbyte, 512-Kbyte, or 4-Mbyte `sf_hment` structures, we have one `sf_hment` for each `hme_blk`. When dealing with 8-Kbyte `sf_hment` structures, we allocate an `hme_blk` plus an additional seven `sf_hment` structures to give us a total of eight (NHMENTS) `sf_hment` structures that can be referenced through an `hme_blk`.

In the following example, the `hme_blk` at address `0x3000722a750` contains four `sf_hment` structures in its `hblk_hme[]`.

```
> 3000722a750::print struct hme_blk hblk_un.hblk_counts.hblk_hmecount
hblk_un.hblk_counts.hblk_hmecount = 0x4
```

Using the `::array` dcmd, we can then list the address of each `sf_hment` in `hblk_hme[]`.

```
> ::offsetof struct hme_blk hblk_hme
offsetof (struct hme_blk, hblk_hme) = 0x38
> 3000722a750+0x38::array struct sf_hment 4
3000722a788
3000722a7a8
3000722a7c8
3000722a7e8
```

The `hme_blk` structure contains two TTE reference counters that determine if it is all right to free the HME block. Both counters must be zero for the HME block to be freed. The counters are protected by `cas`. `hblk_hmecnt` is the number of `sf_hment` structures present on page mapping lists. `hblk_vcnt` reflects the number of `sf_hment` elements with valid TTEs in the `hme_blk`. The `hme_blk` also has per-TTE lock counts protected by `cas`. This is required because physio currently requires us to lock the page in memory since the driver will need to get to the page frame number (PFN). If we have multiple threads using the same buffer for physio, they will all lock that page, causing the lock count to be larger than the number of bits available in the TTE `lckcnt` field.

The `hmeblk_tag` structure that obtains a match on a `hme_blk` is shown below.

```
typedef union {
        struct {
                uint64_t        hblk_basepg: 51, /* hme_blk base pg # */
                                hblk_rehash: 13; /* rehash number */
                sfmmu_t         *sfmmup;
        } hblk_tag_un;
        uint64_t                htag_tag[2];
} hmeblk_tag;
```

See sfmmu/vm/hat_sfmmu.h

- **hblk_basepg.** Bits 63..13 of the virtual address.
- **hblk_rehash.** rehash number. This is actually only 3 bits encoding the span/ mapping size of the hme_blk as shown in Table 12.2. When we search the hash table to find the translation for a VA we usually do not know the page size in advance so, we start by looking for a 64-Kbyte mapping block (which may contain either a matching 8-Kbyte or 64-Kbyte TTE). If we do not find a match we re-hash with the next mapping size up. The cycle continues until we find a match or have exhausted all possible mapping sizes. We require hblk_rehash because we don't want to get a false hit on a 512-Kbyte or larger page rehash with a base address corresponding to an 8-Kbyte or 64-Kbyte HME block.

Table 12.2 HME Block Rehash Values

Rehash Number	Mapping Size
1	64-Kbyte (1x64-Kbyte TTE or 8x8-Kbyte TTEs)
2	512-Kbyte
3	4-Mbyte
4	32-Mbyte
5	256-Mbyte

A number of macros provided to build fields of the hmeblk_tag are listed below.

```
#define HME_HASH_SHIFT(ttesz)                                        \
        ((ttesz == TTE8K)? HBLK_RANGE_SHIFT : TTE_PAGE_SHIFT(ttesz)) \

#define HME_HASH_ADDR(vaddr, hmeshift)                               \
        ((caddr_t)(((uintptr_t)(vaddr) >> (hmeshift)) << (hmeshift)))

#define HME_HASH_BSPAGE(vaddr, hmeshift)                             \
        (((uintptr_t)(vaddr) >> (hmeshift)) << ((hmeshift) - MMU_PAGESHIFT))

#define HME_HASH_REHASH(ttesz)                                       \
        (((ttesz) < TTE512K)? 1 : (ttesz))

                                          See sfmmu/vm/hat_sfmmu.h
```

The advantage of the hme_blk structures is that much less memory is consumed when large address spaces that are only sparsely populated with translations are handled. A problem arises, however, when an entire user address space is unmapped. The obvious way to unmap that address space is to search the hash chains for each `hme_blk` associated with the process address space, iterating through the entire process virtual address range and searching for the mapping size equal to the range of one `hme_blk`. With a large user address space and given that with 8-Kbyte pages an `hme_blk` can only map 64 Kbytes, this approach would be time consuming and inefficient. To speed up this process, we introduced the *shadow* `hme_blk`.

12.2.3.4 Shadow HME Blocks

Each HME block allocated for a process has additional, larger, shadow `hme_blk` structures associated with it up to a span 4 Mbytes (256 Mbytes on UltraSPARC V+). These are dummy `hme_blk` structures which have the shadow flag set. For example, on pre-UltraSPARC IV+ platforms, when a 64-Kbyte HME block is allocated it is associated with a 512-Kbyte shadow HME block. That shadow HME block is in turn associated with its own 4-Mbyte shadow HME block. Each shadow HME block maintains a bit-mask in, `hblk_shw_mask`, of which of its constituent virtual address subranges are mapped by the next mapping size down. In the previous example, the 4-Mbyte shadow HME block would maintain a bit-mask of which of the 8 x 512-Kbyte VA sub-ranges within its VA range have 512-Kbyte have HME blocks associated with them; each of those may be a mapping using a 512-Kbyte TTE, or itself a 512-Kbyte shadow block. The 512-Kbyte shadow HME blocks in turn record which of the their 8 x 64-Kbyte VA sub-ranges have HME blocks allocated (those may be hblk1 structures with 64-Kbyte TTEs or hblk8 structures with 8-Kbyte TTEs). Note that since each shadow `hme_blk` spans 8 times as much as the size below it we only need to use bits <7:0> of `hblk_shw_mask`.

The strategy for unmapping an address range, is to walk through it using 4 Mbyte/256 Mbyte aligned VA strides, searching the hash chains for mappings. If no HME block (either "regular" or shadow) is found for a particular VA then we can be assured that there are no mappings for that 4/256 Mbyte range, even if the VA is not mapped with a 4/256-Mbyte TTE. However, if we do find a shadow HME block then we know that there might be a mapping, though we are not guaranteed of finding one because as we drill down on the HME blocks we may find that all the mappings in them have been invalidated without the block being freed.

In an address space sparsely populated with mappings the usual case is that no mapping exists for this range and so no shadow HME block will be found and that address range can be skipped. If, however, a shadow `hme_blk` is found then there must be at least one, smaller, real mapping so now we step through the address range mapped by the shadow `hme_blk` looking for the real mappings.

In summary, shadow HME blocks allow us to probe through a VA segment at a stride of 4/256 Mbytes and only drill down to smaller page sizes for those subranges that likely do contain mappings. But even this algorithm proves to be too slow when probing very large address spaces. In these situations, more precisely if the number of 4-Mbyte probes required is > UHMEHASH_SZ, the HAT layer resorts to a brute force search of the HME hash chains. The HAT layer loops through the entire uhme_hash table searching the hash chains for matching HME blocks.

12.2.3.5 HME Block Allocation

The sfmmu_hblk_alloc() routine allocates kernel and user HME blocks. It also allocates any required shadow HME blocks for a user address space by calling sfmmu_shadow_hcreate(). Under normal circumstances, sfmmu_hblk_alloc() dynamically allocates hblk8s and hblk1s from the sfmmu8_cache and the sfmmu1_cache kmem caches respectively. For the kernel kmem_cache_alloc() is called with KM_NOSLEEP allocations while for user allocations kmem_cache_alloc() is called with KM_SLEEP. The sfmmu8_cache kmem cache allocates its memory from the hat_memload_arena vmem arena while sfmmu1_cache draws on the kmem_default_arena vmem arena. During boot, however, hme_blk structures are used out of a static pool of pre-allocated blocks until segkmem is ready to allocate memory. The kernel allocates this static pool of *nucleus hme_blk structures* early on in the boot process by calling sfmmu_init_nucleus_hblks().

The HAT layer also maintains a reserve pool of free hblk8s pointed to by freehblkp. When sfmmu_hblk_alloc() successfully allocates a hblk8 for a user mapping from the sfmmu8_cache kmem cache it checks to see if the reserve pool is full. If it is not, sfmmu_hblk_alloc() adds the hblk8 to it and a new hblk8 is allocated. The free pool is rechecked and if it is still not full the cycle repeats.

If HME block allocations from the kmem caches fail due to resource constraints a hme_blk is "stolen" by sfmmu_hblk_steal(), which searches for an unused or unlocked hme_blk in the user hash table. If it finds a used HME block, it is stolen from the address space using it. In the worst case that a block could not be found in the user hash table, the kernel hash table is searched for a free HME block. If, in the most extreme case, a suitable block could still not be found, sfmmu_hblk_steal() retries the search looping indefinitely until it finds one. However we should never reach this case, since enough hme_blks were allocated at startup (nucleus hme_blks) and also since hme_blks were added dynamically.

Just before initializing and returning an allocated HME block, sfmmu_hblk_alloc() goes through a verification step that checks for a suitable HME block that already exists in the HME hash table that can be used. If it finds one, it frees the allocated HME block and if the HME block found is not a hblk_reserve (see below), it is initialized and returned for use. If the current thread is mapping into user space the allocated block is freed by first trying to put it into the free pool. If the free pool is full it is freed back to segkmem. On the other hand, if the current thread is mapping into kernel space the hblk8 is added to the free pool even if it is full so that we avoid freeing it to segkmem. This will prevent stack overflow due to possible recursion since `kmem_cache_free()` might require the creation of a slab which in turn needs an `hme_blk` to map that slab. We don't need to worry about freeing hblk1s to `segkmem` since they don't map any `kmem` slabs.

When we attempt to allocate an hblk8 from the `sfmmu8_cache` it is possible that the `kmem` cache itself needs to map in memory and so the HAT layer needs to take steps to prevent infinite recursion. If an `hme_blk` is being requested for a `sfmmu8_cache` slab `sfmmu_hblk_alloc()` tries to allocate it from the free pool. If the free pool is empty a specially reserved, pre-allocated `hme_blk`, the *hblk_reserve*, is returned with the current thread set to be its owner and the `hblk_reserve_lock` held to prevent another thread from attempting to use the reserved HME block. With this scheme, there is a possibility that a recursive condition could arise where a thread owning `hblk_reserve` tries to allocate another hblk8. In anticipation of this kind of scenario, the HAT layer specifically sets aside HBLK_RESERVE_MIN number of HME blocks in the reserve pool to be used exclusively by an owner of `hblk_reserve`. If these reserves are exhausted the system panics.

When the thread holding `hblk_reserve` successfully allocates an hblk8 from the `sfmmu8_cache` on a successive call to `sfmmu_hblk_alloc()` it atomically swaps the new `hme_blk` with `hblk_reserve` and tries to allocate another new HME block to satisfy the pending request.

During the verification step if `sfmmu_hblk_alloc()` finds a HME block in the HME hash table that is a `hblk_reserve` and the current thread is not the owner, `sfmmu_hblk_alloc()` blocks waiting for the `hblk_reserve_lock` to be released before re-trying the entire allocation process. But, if the thread is the owner, `hblk_reserve` is released since it is no longer needed, and the new HME block is used.

12.2.3.6 `hme_blk` Hash Tables

The `sun4u` kernel maintains two hashed tables of `hme_blk` structures: one for the kernel address space and one for all user address spaces. The kernel table is pointed to by the kernel variable `khme_hash`, and the user table is pointed to by `uhme_hash`. These tables are represented as an array of `hmehash_bucket` structures. The number of buckets in the user hash is defined by the variable `uhmehash_num`; the number of buckets in the kernel hash is defined by `khmehash_num`.

```
struct hmehash_bucket {
        kmutex_t          hmehash_mutex;
        uint64_t          hmeh_nextpa;    /* physical address for hash list */
        struct hme_blk *hmeblkp;
        uint_t            hmeh_listlock;
};
```
                                                              See sfmmu/vm/hat_sfmmu.h

There are two locks in the `hmehash_bucket`. The `hmehash_mutex` is a regular mutex that ensures that operations on a hash link are only done by one thread. Any operation that comes into the HAT with a <virtual address, as> will grab the `hmehash_mutex`. Normally, we would expect the TSB miss handlers to grab the hash lock to make sure the hash list is consistent while we traverse it. Unfortunately, this can lead to deadlocks or recursive mutex enters since someone holding the lock could take a TLB/TSB miss. To solve this problem, we added the `hmehash_listlock`. This lock is only grabbed by the TSB miss handlers and `sfmmu_vatopfn()` and while adding/removing an `hme_blk` from the hash list. The code is written to guarantee we won't take a TLB miss while holding this lock.

The number of buckets in the user hash table, `uhmehash_num`, is a power-of-2 based on a function of physical memory multiplied by a predefined overmapping factor (`HMEHASH_FACTOR`), such that the average hash chain length is `HMENT_HASHAVELEN`. To place an upper limit on how much kernel memory is required for the user hash table, we capped `uhmehash_num` at `MAX_UHME_BUCKETS`. Unlike the user hash table, the kernel hash table, `khmehash_num`, has its number of buckets set at a power-of-2 based on a function of physical memory, such that it maintains an average chain length of 1. The kernel table is capped to `MAX_KHME_BUCKETS`. However, a minimum size is also defined on the kernel hash table as `MIN_KHME_BUCKETS`. Table 12.3 shows the values of the HME hash table constants.

Table 12.3 HME Hash Table Constants

Name	Value
HMENT_HASHAVELEN	4
HMEHASH_FACTOR	16
MAX_UHME_BUCKETS	2M
MAX_KHME_BUCKETS	2M
MIN_KHME_BUCKETS	2K
MAX_NUCUHME_BUCKETS	16K
MAX_NUCKHME_BUCKETS	8K

The hash tables are allocated during system startup in the function `startup_memlist()`. `startup_memlist()` calls `ndata_alloc_hat()` to allocate the hash tables out of the nucleus data area. Depending on the amount of physical memory available on a 64-bit platform, the size of either the kernel hash table or the user hash table could exceed the maximum size permitted to be allocated off the kernel nucleus, controlled by the variables `max_nucuhme_buckets` and `max_nuckhme_buckets`, respectively. In this case `ndata_alloc_hat()` does not create the tables. Instead, `startup_memlist()` calls `alloc_hme_buckets()` to allocate the hash tables from the kernel's 64-bit heap (`kemem64`).

Indexing into the hme hash table is by means of the `HME_HASH_FUNCTION` macro shown below. (`HMEHASH_FUNC_ASM` is an assembly version of `HME_HASH_FUNCTION`.) The hashing function is based on the address of the HAT structure (`hatid`), virtual address, and size of the mapping.

```
#define HME_HASH_FUNCTION(hatid, vaddr, shift)                          \
        ((hatid != KHATID)?                                             \
        (&uhme_hash[ (((uintptr_t)(hatid) ^ ((uintptr_t)vaddr >> (shift))) \
                & UHMEHASH_SZ) ]):                                      \
        (&khme_hash[ (((uintptr_t)(hatid) ^ ((uintptr_t)vaddr >> (shift))) \
                & KHMEHASH_SZ) ]))
                                              See sfmmu/vm/hat_sfmmu.h
```

The algorithm to find an `hme_blk` is as follows.

1. Create a tag for the `hme_blk` structure being searched for.
2. Find the `hmehash_bucket` structure in the hme hash table by using the `HME_HASH_FUNCTION` macro.
3. Linearly search the hme hash chain associated with the `hmehash_bucket` for an element with a matching `hmeblk_tag`.

Three macros help perform the linear search:

- `HME_HASH_SEARCH`, which removes empty `hme_blk` structures from the linked list as it traverses the hme hash chain
- `HME_HASH_SEARCH_PREV`, which is identical to `HME_HASH_SEARCH` but additionally returns pointers to the previous `hme_blk` to the one found
- `HME_HASH_FAST_SEARCH`, which simply searches the list

Searching for an `hme_blk` in `mdb` is implemented by the `::sfmmu_vtop -v` dcmd. See the example on page 592.

12.2.4 The Translation Storage Buffer (TSB)

Since searching the HME hash chains for a translation on every TLB miss would be very expensive, Solaris caches the TTE's in a software-controlled cache (the

TSB). In Solaris 10 a process can have up to two TSBs that are allocated, grown, and shrunk on demand. Each TSB in the system is represented by its own `tsb_info` structure, and the HAT maintains a list of `tsb_info` structures for TSBs used by a process.

Let's look at an actual TSB. We can get the list of `tsb_info` structures from the `hat` structure by examining the `sfmmu_tsb` field.

```
> 0x300001d5d18::print struct hat sfmmu_tsb
sfmmu_tsb = 0x3000435ff88
> 0x3000435ff88::print -t struct tsb_info
{
    caddr_t tsb_va = 0x50000000000
    uint64_t tsb_pa = 0x3fe000000
    struct tsb_info *tsb_next = 0
    uint16_t tsb_szc = 0
    uint16_t tsb_flags = 0
    uint_t tsb_ttesz_mask = 0x7
    tte_t tsb_tte = {
...
    }
    sfmmu_t *tsb_sfmmu = 0x300001d5d18
    kmem_cache_t *tsb_cache = 0x3000083a008
    vmem_t *tsb_vmp = 0
}
```

- **tsb_va.** Base virtual address of TSB
- **tsb_pa.** Base physical address of TSB
- **tsb_next.** Pointer to next TSB, if any, used by this process
- **tsb_szc.** TSB size code; possible values range from 0 (8 Kbytes) to `tsb_max_growsize`
- **tsb_flags.** Flags giving the disposition of this TSB; defined as `TSB_*` in `hat_sfmmu.h`
- **tsb_ttesz_mask.** Bit mask of page sizes cached in TSB
- **tsb_tte.** TTE of TSB itself that is locked in the dTLB
- **tsb_sfmmu.** Pointer to process `hat` structure
- **tsb_cache.** Pointer to the `kmem` cache from which TSB memory is allocated
- **tsb_vmp.** Pointer to the `vmem` arena from which TSB memory is allocated

The `::tsbinfo` dcmd prints information on a TSB and its contents. The following example lists every entry in the TSB associated with the `tsb_info` structure at address `0x3000435ff88`.

```
> 0x3000435ff88::tsbinfo -l -a
TSBINFO            TSB                 SIZE      FLAGS              TTE SIZES
000003000435ff88 0000050000000000 8K        -                  8K,64K,512K
TSB @ 50000000000 (512 entries)
                   TAG                 TTE
ADDR               G I L VA 63:22      V S N I H LC PA 42:13 R W N X L P V E P W G
0000050000000000 1 1 1 3fffffffff 0 0 0 0 0  00000000 0 0 0 0 0 0 0 0 0 0
0000050000000010 1 1 1 3fffffffff 0 0 0 0 0  00000000 0 0 0 0 0 0 0 0 0 0
0000050000000020 1 1 1 3fffffffff 0 0 0 0 0  00000000 0 0 0 0 0 0 0 0 0 0
0000050000000030 1 1 1 3fffffffff 0 0 0 0 0  00000000 0 0 0 0 0 0 0 0 0 0
0000050000000040 0 0 0 000000003fc 1 0 0 0 4 0  001e5c44 1 1 0 1 0 1 1 0 0 1 0
0000050000000050 1 1 1 3fffffffff 0 0 0 0 0  00000000 0 0 0 0 0 0 0 0 0 0
0000050000000060 1 1 1 3fffffffff 0 0 0 0 0  00000000 0 0 0 0 0 0 0 0 0 0
0000050000000070 1 1 1 3fffffffff 0 0 0 0 0  00000000 0 0 0 0 0 0 0 0 0 0
0000050000000080 0 0 0 000000003fc 1 0 0 0 0 0  001fb5cc 1 0 0 1 0 1 1 0 0 0 0
0000050000000090 0 0 0 00000000000 1 0 0 0 1 0  001fec03 1 0 0 1 0 1 1 0 0 0 0
00000500000000a0 0 0 0 00000000000 1 0 0 0 2 0  001fe00a 1 0 0 1 0 1 1 0 0 0 0
00000500000000b0 0 0 0 00000000000 1 0 0 0 3 0  001fe00b 1 0 0 1 0 1 1 0 0 0 0
00000500000000c0 0 0 0 00000000000 1 0 0 0 4 0  001fe00c 1 0 0 1 0 1 1 0 0 0 0
...
```

When a process is created, it starts out with an 8-Kbyte TSB, and a second TSB can be added later. The size of the TSB here relates to the total number of entries that can be cached in the TSB and not to the page size being mapped.

When an address space is first created, hat_alloc() calls tsb_alloc() to create and initialize the tsb_info structure. At this point, memory for the TSB itself is not allocated. When the first MMU miss occurs, the miss handler enters sfmmu_tsbmiss_exception(), which then places another call to tsb_alloc() to actually allocate the TSB. TSBs by definition are always physically contiguous and size aligned in order to allow the following:

- Use of hardware-generated TSB pointers to access the TSB
- Physical addressing of the TSB on platforms that support it
- Hardware TSB walks on platforms that support it

After performing a mapping operation, the HAT looks at the number of TTEs for each page size. Based on the page sizes that are cached in each TSB, the number of mappings is compared to the number of entries in the TSB. If the number of TTEs exceeds the capacity of the TSB (which is a multiple of tsb_rss_factor, depending on the TSB size), the TSB is grown synchronously. The default TSB RSS factor is 0.75 times the number of entries in an 8-Kbyte TSB, so the TSB is actually grown before the entire capacity of the TSB is reached since some conflicts (mapping of multiple addresses to the same TSB entry) are anticipated. If the TSB needs to be grown but the system is low on memory (that is, freemem ≤ desfree) or TSB memory usage has reached the limit set by tsb_alloc_hiwater, the resize request is denied. Should the program attempt to map more memory later, the grow procedure will be reattempted.

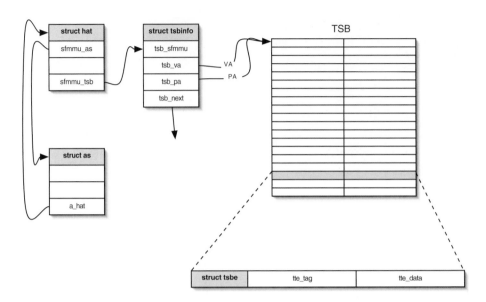

Figure 12.8 TSB Data Structures

In cases where system is under memory pressures or TSB memory usage is more than `tsb_alloc_hiwater`, TSB memory may be reclaimed when pages are unmapped. If a process unmaps part of its address space and the resulting address space resident size × 2 falls below the `tsb_rss_factor`, the TSB will be reduced in size. The resident set size is doubled to prevent thrashing (for example, growing the TSB very soon after shrinking it) and to avoid the overhead of throwing away all mappings in the TSB (unless the whole system can potentially benefit from the cleanup).

If the number of 4-Mbyte mappings residing in a process reaches `tsb_sectsb_threshold`, a second TSB is allocated to the process to cache 4-Mbyte mappings. Setting `tsb_sectsb_threshold` very high essentially disables the TSB for 4-Mbyte mappings and causes all 4-Mbyte mappings to be retrieved from the hash.

The maximum user TSB size is limited by `tsb_max_growsize` to the maximum supported by hardware (currently 1 Mbyte). The system's choice can be overridden by setting a different value for this variable in `/etc/system` if deemed necessary; however, the overriding value must not exceed `tsb_slab_size`. For kernel TSBs we may go beyond the hardware-supported sizes and implement larger TSBs in software.

To prevent TSBs using up too much physical memory, `tsb_alloc_hiwater` imposes a resource limit that defaults to 1/32 of physical memory. Once the high-water mark is reached or if `freemem` falls below `desfree`, the TSB memory allocation algorithms start throttling. The value of `tsb_alloc_hiwater` may be updated following DR events, in which case the value of `physmem`/`tsb_alloc_hiwaterfactor` is used to compute the new value. Note that `swapfs_minfree` and `segspt_minfree` must be kept considerably larger than `tsb_alloc_hiwater` to prevent system hangs under system stress, so exercise care when tuning this limit. You can safely decrease it, however.

12.2.4.1 TSB Memory Allocation

Where and how TSBs are allocated is based on how the size of the TSB compares to the base page size and what memory conditions dictate according to the following algorithm in `sfmmu_init_tsbinfo()`.

```
If allocating a "large" TSB (> 8 Kbytes)
        Allocate from the kmem_tsb_default_arena vmem arena with VM_NOSLEEP
else if low on memory or TSB_FORCEALLOC flag is set
        Allocate from kernel heap via sfmmu_tsb8k_cache with KM_SLEEP (never fails)
else
        Allocate from sfmmu_tsb_cache with KM_NOSLEEP
endif
```

Note that we always do nonblocking allocations from the TSB arena since we don't want memory fragmentation to cause processes to block indefinitely waiting for memory while the kernel algorithms coalesce large pages.

The `sfmmu_tsb_cache`, which is used by default, draws its memory from the `kmem_tsb_default_arena` vmem arena. The `sfmmu_tsb8k_cache` draws its memory from the kernel heap in 8-Kbyte chunks rather than from the large TSB slabs, and it is created without magazines (see Section 11.2.3.6) so that the memory is returned to the system as quickly as possible when the process terminates or calls `exec()`.

Since TSBs larger than 8 Kbytes in size are allocated a lot less frequently than their smaller counterparts, large TSBs are all allocated directly (with a best-fit algorithm) from the `kmem_tsb_default_arena`.

The `kmem_tsb_default_arena` vmem arena allocates large physical memory slabs and maps them to the virtual memory space it has allocated from the `kmem_tsb_arena`, which is its vmem source. The source for the `kmem_tsb_arena` is the `heap_arena`, which provides the virtual addresses for the TSBs. The intermediate layer of the `kmem_tsb_arena` at first glance seems superfluous, but it enforces slab-sized alignment on the allocated virtual memory, which vmem cannot do by default.

Regardless of whether the TSB is allocated from the `kmem_tsb_default_arena` or one of the `kmem` caches, the remainder of the allocation process is the same. The virtual and physical address of the TSB is added to a new `tsbinfo` structure, and relocation callbacks are registered with the HAT layer since the TSB has special relocation requirements.

12.2.4.2 Large Kernel Page Support

The quantum size for the `kmem_tsb_default_arena` is chosen to be a large page size in order to minimize external memory fragmentation and to reduce the number of TLB misses encountered by the kernel while accessing large user TSBs. On `sun4u` systems, this quantum will usually be 4 Mbytes, stored in the variable `tsb_slab_size`. This value must be a supported MMU mapping size, but otherwise has no restrictions. For memory conservation, small memory machines (for example, 1 Gbyte of memory or less) set the slab size at 512 Kbytes during startup since the largest TSB required to map that much of a resident set size is 512 Kbytes or smaller.

Currently, there is no generic framework for the dynamic allocation of large kernel pages, so physical memory for the `kmem_tsb_default_arena` must be acquired through special large-page-allocation routines, summarized in Table 12.4.

Table 12.4 Large Kernel Page Allocation Routines

Function	Description
`sfmmu_tsb_page_create()`	Counterpart of `segkmem_page_create()`. This function acquires a large, physical page of memory from the page free lists. It does some setup and calls `page_create_va_large()`.
`sfmmu_tsb_xalloc()`	This function reserves physical memory being allocated into the `kmem_tsb_arena`. It calls `sfmmu_tsb_page_create()`, takes care of handling any appropriate locking necessary, and establishes a kernel virtual mapping for the new TSB slab page before it is placed into `kmem_tsb_default_arena`.
`sfmmu_tsb_segkmem_alloc()`	This wrapper around `sfmmu_tsb_xalloc()` specifies additional parameters required for TSB allocations.
`sfmmu_tsb_segkmem_free()`	This function unmaps a TSB slab page from the kernel virtual address space, frees the physical page of memory, and returns the freed virtual memory to `kmem_tsb_arena`.
`page_create_va_large()`	Large-page counterpart of `page_create_va()`.

This limited support provides mappings backed by large pages. All allocations must be page-sized and page-aligned for the underlying platform, so this interface is unstable and not suitable for general-purpose kernel memory allocations.

12.2.4.3 TSB Page Relocation

Since TSB memory can be allocated from outside the kernel cage, we must be able to relocate TSBs during dynamic reconfiguration events or cage expansion—these events are asynchronous with respect to process execution. Upon a request to relocate a page that contains a TSB, `page_relocate()` invokes the kernel memory relocation framework. This framework is necessary since we need to prevent processes from accessing the TSB using a cached physical address while it is being relocated. It is all right to try to access the TSB through a virtual address since the access just faults on that virtual address once the mapping has been suspended.

For proper notification of relocations, at allocation time a callback is registered with the HAT layer before the `tsb_pa` or `tsb_tte` fields of the `tsbinfo` structure are updated. When a relocation is initiated, `hat_page_relocate()` invokes the pre-relocation callback with the `tsbinfo` pointer prior to the memory being locked so that accesses to the TSB can be quiesced. It then relocates the page and calls the post-relocation callback to complete the move of the TSB page. Moving the TSB around in physical memory requires updating the locked TTE used to access the TSB from the trap handlers while preventing accesses to it.

The pre-relocation and post-relocation callbacks for TSB pages are `sfmmu_tsb_pre_relocator()` and `sfmmu_tsb_post_relocator()`. The `sfmmu_tsb_pre_relocator()` routine acquires the `hat_lock` and sets the `TSB_RELOC_FLAG` flag in the `tsbinfo` structure, signifying that the TSB is being relocated. This relocation state is required because another thread (such as one destroying an ISM segment) may need to unmap a TTE from the TSB while data is being copied from the original location to the new location; without the flag, TTEs might be unmapped from the old location after they have been copied to the new location, resulting in data corruption. The `sfmmu_tsb_post_relocator()` routine acquires the `hat_lock`, updates `tsb_pa` and `tsb_tte`, checks whether a flush is required, and clears the `TSB_RELOC_FLAG` before releasing the `hat_lock`.

12.2.4.4 TSB Replacement

Whether a process is first starting to run, swapping in from disk, or growing or shrinking its TSB, the Solaris 10 HAT layer treats all four as being equivalent. The specifics of the TSB replacement algorithm are covered in this section.

When a TSB is replaced, the `tsbinfo` structure and the TSB must be completely replaced. The reason is that TSB relocation or growth should not need to pause all CPUs to prevent a race with `resume()`, which may be traversing the process's TSB list since it cannot acquire locks.

The general algorithm to replace a TSB is as follows:

1. Allocate a new TSB info/TSB pair.
2. Prevent further updates to the current TSB.
3. Temporarily set the process's context to invalid context.
4. Remap entries from the old TSB to the new one, if necessary.
5. Atomically update the pointers to the new `tsbinfo` structure.
6. Cross-call all CPUs running the process to reload the TSB base register and locked TTE.
7. Restore the old context.
8. Resume updates to the TSB.
9. Discard the old TSB and `tsbinfo` structure.

The first step in replacing a TSB is to allocate the new `tsbinfo`/TSB pair of the appropriate size. This allocation needs to be done while no locks are held, in order to avoid deadlock scenarios as discussed in Section 12.2.6.

Since we will be updating the HAT's `tsbinfo` list, we need to grab the appropriate `hat_lock`. This prevents any other threads from walking the list while it is being updated, and it also prevents any other threads from inserting or removing mappings into this process's TSB from kernel context until we release the lock. To prevent a thread executing in `resume()` during this window and actually accessing its TSB, we temporarily set the context to `INVALID_CONTEXT` in the `hat` structure. This generates a TSB exception should the process try to access the TSB before we are finished replacing it.

Depending on the type of replacement that is occurring, we can remap the entries in the old TSB into the new TSB at this point. If the TSB is growing from a small TSB to a larger TSB and the value of the kernel tuneable `tsb_remap_ttes` is non-zero, we remap the old entries into the new TSB since we expect those entries to be reused. The default value of this tuneable is zero; most workloads grow the TSB only during their warm-up phase and hence would realize little benefit from remapping. If a TSB is shrinking, there will be no copying of TSB entries since a simple one-to-one mapping cannot be done.

Next, we modify the process's `sfmmu_tsb` linked list to contain the new `tsbinfo`. From this point, any new threads that start to run pick up the new `tsbinfo` and thus program their TSB base register(s) and locked TTEs with the new TSB pointer rather than the old one. So we issue a barrier instruction to guarantee this and then store the value of the `hat` structure's `sfmmu_cpusran` field.

To handle those threads that may be on-processor and running with the old TSB, we execute an `xt_some()` call that causes those CPUs to update their TSB base registers if they are currently using the old TSB. This same logic is executed on the CPU that is currently relocating the TSB, to make sure that it is using the new TSB as needed. Following the cross-call and restoration of the context, there can be no further references to the old TSB, so we can drop the `hat_lock` and free the old `tsbinfo`/TSB pair.

12.2.4.5 TLB Miss Handling

The CPU generates a trap when the MMU is unable to find a translation for a virtual memory operation. For a data load or store, the CPU generates a `fast_data_access_MMU_miss`, and for an instruction fetch, a `fast_instruction_access_MMU_miss`, which are handled by the `DTLB_MISS()` and `ITLB_MISS()` handlers, respectively.

`DTLB_MISS()` loads the MMU TLB Tag Access register and TSB 8-Kbyte Pointer register into temporary registers. The ID of the faulting context is extracted from the Tag Access register and checked to see if it is less than or equal to `INVALID_CONTEXT`. If the condition is true, it means the MMU miss was within the kernel or invalid context and the handler branches to the kernel's TLB miss handler, `sfmmu_kdtlb_miss()`. The kernel's miss handler handles faults within the invalid context as a special case since processes may not actually have a TSB when running in invalid context.

For a user process, `DTLB_MISS()` checks whether the most significant bit of the TSB 8-Kbyte Pointer register is set, and if it is (signifying that there is more than one TSB), branches to `sfmmu_udtlb_slowpath()`. Otherwise, the TSB entry, which contains the TSB tag and corresponding TTE, is atomically loaded from the TSB and the TSB tag is compared to bits 63..22 of the virtual address held in the Tag Access register. If they are the same, a TSB hit has occurred and the TTE is loaded into the dTLB and a retry instruction is issued. In the event of a TSB miss, the handler branches to the `sfmmu_tsb_miss()` routine.

`ITLB_MISS()` works in the same way but with a few exceptions:

- Kernel and invalid context misses are handled by `sfmmu_kitlb_miss()`.
- If a TTE is found, execute permission on the page is checked. If the execute bit is not set in the TTE, `exec_fault()` is called and the program is ultimately terminated.
- The TTE is programmed into the iTLB.
- A TSB miss results in a branch to `sfmmu_uitlb_slowpath()`.

Kernel TLB Miss Handling.   The kernel dTLB miss handler `sfmmu_` `kdtlb_miss()` starts by probing the first TSB, using the 8-Kbyte virtual page as the index and looks for an 8-Kbyte/64-Kbyte/512-Kbyte mapping. The second TSB is probed only under one of two conditions:

1. The 64-bit kernel physical mapping segment (`segkpm`) is mapped with large pages.

2. The missing virtual address is below `0x80000000.00000000`. This optimization is possible since in this case `segkpm` is using small pages and we know no large kernel mappings will be located above `kpm_vbase`, which is at least `0x80000000.00000000`.

If we miss in the TSBs while searching for a `segkpm` address, we branch to `sfmmu_kpm_dtsb_miss_small()` or `sfmmu_kpm_dtsb_miss()`, depending on whether `segkpm` is mapped with small or large pages. Otherwise, the TSB miss is handled by `sfmmu_tsb_miss()`.

Since the non-nucleus (TLB unlocked) instruction pages are mapped with 8-Kbyte pages, the kernel iTLB handler `sfmmu_kitlb_miss()` probes only the first TSB. If there is a TSB hit, execute permissions are checked and the TTE is programmed into the iTLB. Otherwise, the handler branches to the `sfmmu_tsb_` `miss()` routine.

Multiple TSB Probes.   In Solaris 10, each process can have up to two TSBs. On `sun4u` architectures, the first TSB caches 8-Kbyte page-size entries replicating the 64-Kbyte and 512-Kbyte entries from the TSB 8-Kbyte pointer. The second TSB holds 4-Mbyte entries. With UltraSPARC IV+, the 32-Mbyte and 256-Mbyte entries are replicated with the 4-Mbyte pointer. Since the hardware-generated pointer is used for the first probe, the first TSB is limited to 1 Mbyte in size on `sun4u` systems for now, though in the future another case could be added to `sfmmu_udtlb_slowpath()` to support larger TSB sizes purely in software.

In the fast path of the TLB trap vectors, the most significant bit of the TSB 8-Kbyte Pointer register determines if a second TSB exists. In the usual case where it does not, the 8-Kbyte Pointer register contents can be used without modification to probe the only TSB. If the second TSB does exist, the miss handler branches to `sfmmu_udtlb_slowpath()` or `fmmu_idtlb_slowpath()` and the `GET_1ST_TSBE_PTR()` and `GET_2ND_TSBE_PTR()` macros generate pointers into the first and second TSBs. The slow-path handlers probe the first TSB for a TTE, and if no match is found, probe the second. If a matching TTE is not yet found, a TSB miss results and a branch is made to `sfmmu_tsb_miss()`.

For 64-bit processes, Solaris attempts to map all ISM segments above the 8-Gbyte boundary in the virtual address space. If the faulting address lies beyond 8 Gbytes but does not have the upper bit set (which would indicate mapped libraries or stack), the dTLB miss is predicted to be an ISM page. In this case, Since ISM is optimized to use 4-Mbyte pages, `sfmmu_udtlb_slowpath()` starts by probing the second TSB looking for a 4-Mbyte mapping. Only if that probe fails is the first TSB searched before a branch to `sfmmu_tsb_miss()`.

12.2.4.6 TSB Miss Handling

The TSB miss handler `sfmmu_tsb_miss()` searches the page tables for virtual-to-physical translations that are not cached in either the TLB or TSB and partially handles protection faults and page faults. It also handles TLB misses that occur in invalid context.

In resolving a TSB miss, `sfmmu_tsb_miss()` uses per-CPU `tsbmiss` areas to avoid cache misses. Each CPU's `tsbmiss` area contains a `tsbmiss` structure that duplicates some information needed for TSB miss handling and provides scratch space for temporary variable storage. The search for a TTE in the hash tables is performed by the `GET_TTE()` macro, whose parameters are described in Table 12.5.

Table 12.5 `GET_TTE()` Parameters

Parameter	Description
`tagacc`	Tag Access register containing the faulting virtual address and context ID. In the case of ISM, the virtual address used is offset into the ISM segment (clobbered).
`hatid`	`sfmmu` pointer (clobbered).
`tte`	TTE for TLB miss if found, otherwise clobbered (return value).
`hmeblkpa`	Physical address of the `hment` if found; otherwise, clobbered (return value).
`hmeblkva`	Virtual address of `hment` if found; otherwise, clobbered (return value).
`tsbarea`	Pointer to the CPU `tsbmiss` area.
`hmentoff`	Temporarily stores `hment` offset (clobbered).
`hmeshift`	Constant/register to shift virtual address to obtain the virtual page number for page size being searched.
`hashno`	Constant/register hash number. The coded page-size value used to form the hash tag.
`label`	Temporary label for branching within macro.
`foundlabel`	Label to jump to when TTE is found.
`exitlabel`	Label to jump to when TTE is not found. The `hmebp` lock is still held at this time.

If the virtual address that caused the miss is not in an ISM segment for the process, GET_TTE() is called with hatid set to the HAT address loaded from the tsbmiss area and hashno set to TTE64K to specify a search for 8-Kbyte or 64-Kbyte pages. If a mapping is not found in the HME hash chains, then GET_TTE() is called with hashno set to TTE512K to search for a 512-Kbyte page.

As a user TSB miss handling optimization, the sfmmu HAT flags stored in the tsbmiss area are checked to see if any 512-Kbyte pages have been mapped into the process's address space, and GET_TTE() is called only if any such pages are found. If no 512-Kbyte mapping is found, the search is continued for every other valid page size supported on the platform, as above (Note: the sun4u kernel is only mapped with page sizes up to 4 Mbytes).

If the TSB miss is for an ISM segment, GET_TTE() is called with hatid set to the ISM hatid and the virtual address of tagacc set to the offset within the segment. As an optimization in this case, sfmmu_tsb_miss() searches for the largest page size down to the smallest.

If a valid mapping is found, it is loaded into a TSB by the TSB_UPDATE_TL() routine. In the case of page sizes less than 4 Mbytes, the first TSB is used. For 4-Mbyte pages and larger, the second TSB is used if it exists. Finally, the translation is programmed into the appropriate TLB and program execution resumes.

The UltraSPARC IV+ iTLB miss handler code simulates 32-Mbyte and 256-Mbyte page sizes with 4-Mbyte pages, to provide support for programs, for example, Java programs, that may copy instructions into a 32-Mbyte or 256-Mbyte data page and then execute them. The code generates the 4-Mbyte PFN bits and saves them in the modified 32-Mbyte/256-Mbyte TTEs in the TSB by calling TSB_UPDATE_TL_PN(). If the TTE is stored in the dTLB to map a 32-Mbyte/256-Mbyte page, the 4-Mbyte PFN offset bits are ignored by hardware.

If no mapping is found in the HME hash chain search, then the behavior depends on the trap level at which that the handler was called. Both the DTLB_MISS() and ITLB_MISS() handlers are common to trap level 0 and trap level > 0 portions of the trap table.

In the case of a kernel TLB miss, if the current trap level is ≤ 1, a page fault has occurred in the kernel on a kernel address and the sfmmu_pagefault() routine is called. If CPU_DTRACE_NOFAULT is set in the cpuc_dtrace_flags, we don't actually want to call sfmmu_pagefault(). Instead, we note that a fault has occurred by setting CPU_DTRACE_BADADDR and issuing a done (instead of a retry) instruction. This steps over the faulting instruction. On the other hand, if the trap level is > 1, the kernel panics with a call to ptl1_panic(). Also, if the fault occurs on the same page as the stack pointer, then we know the stack is bad and the trap handler will fail, so we call the ptl1_panic() routine.

In the case of a user TLB miss, if the current trap level is > 1, the `sfmmu_window_trap()` routine is called. This deals with the case of a dTLB miss when handling a register window overflow or underflow trap. If the trap level is 1, a branch is made to `sfmmu_pagefault()`.

12.2.5 Intimate Shared Memory (ISM)

Every process that attaches a particular shared memory segment to its address space creates its own page table structures to map its virtual pages to the shared physical pages. That is, it maintains its own private `hme_blk` and `sf_hment` structures even though the `sf_hment` structures contain the same mappings across the different processes sharing the memory segment. For very large shared memory segments being shared by a large number of processes, as is typical of many commercial database installations, this practice can waste kernel memory. To overcome this drawback, Solaris implements a form of shared memory known as *Intimate Shared Memory* (ISM), whereby the page table structures are shared among each attaching process. We discussed more about ISM primitives in Section 4.4.2.

To share `hme_blk` structures across different address spaces, we need to be able to construct identical tags for the HME hash chain search. But recall that the `hmeblk_tag` is formed from the `hatid`, virtual address, and page size. Since each address space can map the shared segment at any virtual address, only the page size is guaranteed to be in common. To solve this problem, Solaris represents each ISM segment on the system with a separate dummy `hat` structure and uses the virtual address offset with the ISM segment to create the `hmeblk_tag`.

Each mapping of an ISM segment into a process address space is represented by the `ism_ment` structure and is used to link all the process `hat` structures sharing an ISM `hat`. This is similar in function to a page's `p_mapping` list of `sf_hment` structures. If a process uses ISM, the `hat` structure points to an ISM mapping block, `ism_blk[]`, an array of map entries that maintain information for each ISM segment attached to the process.

Two Solaris segment drivers support ISM: the `segspt` and `segspt_shm` drivers. Each instance of an ISM segment attached to a user address space has one `segspt_shm` segment. And each ISM segment on the system has one `segspt` segment. Therefore, in the simplest case, if two processes share an ISM segment, each process having a single mapping to it, then there will be two `segspt_shm` segments, one in each process's address space segment list. These will both point to a single common `segspt` segment that describes the memory and swap space allocated for the ISM mapping. Following is the sequence of events involved in the creation of these segments.

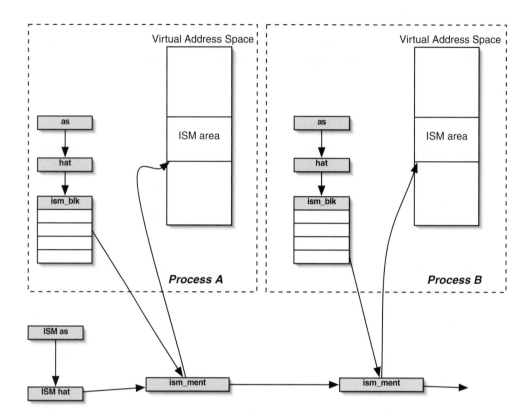

Figure 12.9 ISM Data Structures

```
-> shmat                              Entry point from shmat(2)
  -> ipc_lookup                       Look up the id created by shmget(2)
  <- ipc_lookup
  -> sptcreate                        Create the ISM segment
    -> as_alloc                       Allocate an ISM as and hat
    <- as_alloc
    -> as_map                         Create a segspt segment in the ISM as
      -> segspt_create                Get physical pages for segment
        -> anon_swap_adjust           Move reserved phys swap into memory swap
        <- anon_swap_adjust
        -> anon_map_createpages       Allocate physical pages
        <- anon_map_createpages
        -> hat_memload_array          Add hme_blks to hme hash chains
        <- hat_memload_array
      <- segspt_create
    <- as_map
  <- sptcreate
  -> as_map                           Create process's segspt_shm segment
    -> segspt_shmattach               Attach ISM segment
      -> hat_share                    Add ism_ment to ism_blk
      <- hat_share
    <- segspt_shmattach
  <- as_map
<- shmat                              All done
```

In more detail, the `shmat()` routine checks whether the `segspt` segment for the ISM has been created; if it has not, then `sptcreate()` is called. `sptcreate()` calls `as_alloc()` to allocate the common ISM `as` and `hat` structures and then calls `as_map()` to create the `segspt` segment and attach it to the ISM address space at virtual address `SEGSPTADDR`, which is `0x0`. The `segspt_create()` routine allocates a `vnode` and calls `anon_map_createpages()` to allocate physical pages for the ISM area.

The `anon_map_createpages()` routine allocates anonymous pages, allocating the largest page size possible for the given the virtual address and range. The `segspt_create()` routine then calls `hat_memload_array()` to create the mapping of the physical pages allocated for the ISM address space to the virtual address `SEGSPTADDR`. `hat_memload_array()` adds the appropriate `hme_blks` to the `hme` hash chains to created the mappings. Two flags are passed to `hat_memload_array()`: The `HAT_LOAD_LOCK` flag causes the routine to increment the lock field in the `hme_blk` structure, `hblk_lckcnt`; the `HAT_LOAD_SHARE` flag causes the routine to try to use the largest page size possible that is not disabled for ISM.

Large pages for ISM are disabled with the `disable_ism_large_pages` flag. A value of 1 disables all large pages. Bits 1 through 5, if set, disable 64-Kbyte, 512-Kbyte, 4-Mbyte, 32-Mbyte and 512-Mbyte pages, respectively. 512-Kbyte pages must be disabled for ISM; otherwise, a process would page fault indefinitely if it tried to access a 512-Kbyte page.

The `shmat()` routine then creates the `segspt_shm` segment and attaches it to the current process's address space by passing the user-specified attach address and the routine `segspt_shmattach()` to `as_map()`. The `segspt_shmattach()` routine creates and initializes the segment private `sptshm_data` area and then calls `hat_share()`, which allocates the `ism_blk` structures and links them to the process `hat` structure. If the user-specified address is 0, then `shmat()` picks a suitable address. In a 64-bit address space, it tries to put ISM segments between `PREDISM_BASE` and `PREDISM_BOUND`. The HAT can use these constants to predict that a virtual is contained within the ISM segment, a capability that may optimize translation. The range is treated as advisory; ISM segments may fall outside the range, and non-ISM segments may be contained within the range. To avoid collision between ISM addresses with, say, process heap addresses, `shmat()` tries to put ISM segments above `PREDISM_1T_BASE`. The HAT still expects that any virtual address larger than `PREDISM_BASE` may belong to ISM.

The `segspt` driver can allocate memory up to `availrrmem`—`segspt_minfree`. `segspt_minfree` is the memory left for the system after the ISM pages have been created; it is set up to 5% of `availrmem` in `sptcreate()` when ISM is created. ISM should not use more than around 90% of `availrmem`; if it does, then the performance of the system may decrease. Machines with large memories may be able to use more memory for ISM, so we set the default `segspt_minfree` to 5% (which gives ISM a maximum of 95% of `availrmem`. If kernel programmers want even more memory for ISM (risking hanging the system), they can patch the `segspt_minfree` to a smaller number.

12.2.6 Synchronization in the HAT Layer

The HAT layer needs to do a considerable amount of synchronization in order to function properly. Some of the synchronization includes waiting for the TLB to be flushed before acquiring a new context, protecting the list of available contexts, preventing a TSB from being removed from a process while handlers are accessing that TSB, or waiting for a TSB's physical memory to be relocated by another thread.

The locking scheme used in the Solaris 10 HAT layer has been significantly improved over that of previous OS versions. The new scheme decreases complexity while increasing scalability and minimizing bottlenecks. Table 12.6 describes the HAT locks.

Table 12.6 Summary of HAT Locks

Lock Variable	Description
`hat_lock`	New to Solaris 10, this is an array of adaptive mutex locks hashed on the `hatid`. This replaces the old `ctx_lock` to synchronize context acquisition as well as TLB and TSB flushing.
`ctx_rwlock`	This is a reimplementation of the obsolete, halfword reader-writer spinlock, `ctx_refcnt` lock in `struct ctx` as a true kernel reader-writer lock. It exists solely to protect the context from being stolen.
`ctx_list_lock`	New to Solaris 10, this lock protects access to the `ctxfree` and `ctxdirty` lists.
`ism_mlist_lock`	This is a global adaptive mutex, protecting access to an ISM `hat` structures mapping list.
`mml_table`	This is an array of adaptive mutex locks hashed on the address of the `page` structure protecting a page's `p_mapping` list and `p_nrm` field. These locks are also referred to as *mapping list locks*.
`p_selock`	This lock (a.k.a. the *page lock*) is a shared/exclusive lock in the `page` structure that synchronizes page manipulations.

12.2.6.1 `hat_lock`

The `hat_lock` is an array of `kmutex_t` adaptive mutex locks hashed on the `hatid` of the process address space. When a context needs to be acquired or entries need to be flushed from the TLB or TSB, the lock corresponding to the HAT's bucket is acquired. The `hat_lock`, when combined with the new `sfmmu_flags`, replaces the uses of the old `sfmmu_mutex` lock.

The `hat_lock` protects the `tsbinfo` list within each HAT from changing. This is convenient since TSB map and unmap operations need to access TSBs without fear that the TSB will be relocated during the operation, and map and unmap operations need to be synchronized with TSB flushing operations to prevent data corruption.

The `hat_lock` is acquired within the HAT through the utility function `sfmmu_hat_enter()` and is dropped by a call to `sfmmu_hat_exit()` with the `hatlock_t` that was returned from the `sfmmu_hat_enter()` call.

Note that in the case of a virtual address cache flush, such as for setting up of temporary noncacheable entries (TNC), it is not known which address spaces are affected ahead of time. Because of locking order constraints, the `hat_lock` must be acquired before the lower-level routines that have this information are entered. As with the `ctx_lock`, all the elements of the `hat_lock` array must be acquired. A set of utility functions are provided for this purpose (`sfmmu_hat_[un]lock_all()`).

To prevent a process from becoming bottlenecked on the `hat_lock`, operations that will take some time to complete (such as relocating a TSB's physical memory) are guarded by new flags in the `hat` and `tsbinfo` structures. Table 12.7 describes the flags.

To synchronize between processes mapping or unmapping shared segments, a new locking primitive, called `sfmmu_ismhat_enter()`, was built on top of the `hat_lock`. This primitive controls access to an `sfmmu_flags` flag with priority inheritance to provide mutual exclusion without introducing unnecessary lock contention, since ISM unmap operations can take a long time to complete.

Table 12.7 HAT Flags

Function	Description
HAT_SWAPPED	This process is swapped out, and all virtual memory translation resources have been freed.
HAT_SWAPIN	This process is being swapped in.
HAT_BUSY	The `tsbinfo` list of this `hat` structure is being changed because of TSB resizing.

continues

Table 12.7 HAT Flags (*continued*)

Function	Description
HAT_ISMBUSY	ISM mappings are being mapped or unmapped by this process. Use of this flag is restricted to the locking primitives sfmmu_ismhat_enter() and sfmmu_ismhat_exit().
HAT_64K_FLAG	This process does or might use 64-Kbyte mappings.
HAT_512K_FLAG	This process does or might use 512-Kbyte mappings.
HAT_4M_FLAG	This process does or might use 4-Kbyte mappings.
HAT_32M_FLAG	This process does or might use 32-Mbyte mappings.
HAT_256M_FLAG	This process does or might use 256-Mbyte mappings.

12.2.6.2 Locking Order

The order of lock acquisition is shown in Figure 12.10. One important note about the locking order is that the mapping list lock is acquired before many of the HAT operations that need to acquire the hat_lock are called. Thus, attempting to allocate kernel memory while hat_lock is held can result in deadlock. All memory allocations are therefore done without the hat_lock.

Attempting to acquire the hat_lock for the kernel's HAT is a no-op, so there is no chance of recursively trying to take the same lock while holding the hat_lock on behalf of the current process.

12.2.6.3 TSB Consistency

In older versions of Solaris, where multiple contexts could share a TSB when a context was stolen from a process, the TSB associated with that context needed to be flushed of all TTEs matching that context. Because of this, individual TSB entries did not need to be unmapped if the context was the invalid context.

With per-address space TSBs in Solaris 10, the context is no longer associated with the TSB, so flushing the TSB "per context" is no longer a supported operation and no unmapping is done if a context is stolen from a process. Instead, the process faults, acquires a new context, and continues using TTEs cached earlier in its TSB. This results in significant savings should a process's context be stolen. The trade-off, albeit a small one, is that now individual TSB entries must always be unmapped, regardless of the active context. However, the TLB flush is still skipped in this case, since the invalid context is never allowed to have TTEs in the TLB, and we know that the TLB will be flushed of the last context before it is reused on a given CPU.

In the new implementation, TTEs are unmapped from the TSB in the following instances:

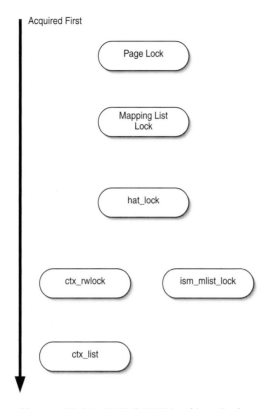

Figure 12.10 SPARC HAT Locking Order

- Address range unmap.
- Temporary noncacheable (TNC) entries due to virtual address cache (VAC) conflict with a new mapping.
- A change in protections of an existing mapping.
- A thread dilemma: It needs to unmap an entry in a process's TSB but could not acquire exclusive access to it because the TSB was being relocated in physical memory.

The entire TSB is flushed of all mappings in the following instances:

- ISM shared address range unmap
- Initial TSB memory allocation

Of note is that in the new implementation, `sfmmu_inv_tsb()` has been completely rewritten to use block store VIS instructions. This has the desired side effect of invalidating any data in level-1 caches that will be stale when the TSB is updated with its physical address, while simultaneously providing a tremendous boost in the rate at which TSBs may be flushed. Although the TSB is still flushed on an ISM address range unmap or when a TSB is first allocated, it is no longer flushed when an address space is freed and so conserves valuable CPU time when processes terminate or call `exec()`.

12.2.7 SPARC HAT Layer Kernel Tunables

Table 12.8 TSB Related Tunables

Tunable	Description
`default_tsb_size`	Selects size of initial TSB allocated to all processes. Default is 8K (size code 0). It's OK to tune this, but a value that is too large may waste kernel memory. In any case the default TSB size may never exceed the value of TSB slab size or the system will panic. The possible values are as follows:
	0—8 KBytes 1—16 KBytes 2—32 KBytes 3—64 KBytes 4—128 KBytes 5—256 KBytes 6—512 KBytes 7—1 MByte
`enable_tsb_rss_sizing`	When set to 1 (the default), TSBs may be resized per the RSS sizing algorithm discussed on page 603. When set to 0, TSBs will remain at `default_tsb_size`.
`tsb_remap_ttes`	When set to 1 (which is the default), TTEs will be remapped when a TSB is grown to a larger size. This saves the overhead of faulting on those mappings and repopulating the TSB, at the expense of doing the copy with the locks held (blocking all threads from running that process for the duration of the copy).
`tsb_rss_factor`	The value of `tsb_rss_factor` / 512 gives the percentage of the TSB that must be used before the TSB is grown to a larger size. 75% is chosen as the default value, since some virtual addresses are expected to map to the same slot (conflict) in the TSB.

continues

Table 12.8 TSB Related Tunables (*continued*)

Tunable	Description
tsb_alloc_hiwater_factor	The factor of physical memory used to determine the value to establish for tsb_alloc_hiwater, below. Defaults to 1/32 of physical memory (32).
tsb_alloc_hiwater	The limit of TSB memory usage, in bytes, beyond which TSBs will no longer be grown and may be shrunken as described in page 603. Care should be exercised when increasing this value, as it must be lower than other kernel values such as swapfs_minfree to prevent system hangs. It is always safe to set this value smaller than the default, which is 1/tsb_alloc_ hiwater factor of physical memory installed at boot time or during a DR reconfiguration event.
tsb_sectsb_threshold	The number of 4-Mbyte mappings a process must have resident before a second TSB is allocated to the process to cache 4-Mbyte mappings. The default value varies depending on the TLB characteristics of the machine. Setting it very high will essentially disable the TSB for 4-Mbyte mappings and will cause all 4-Mbyte mappings to be retrieved from the hash.

12.2.8 SPARC Hat Layer kstats

The sfmmu_global_stat kstats (described in Table 12.9) keep track of general HAT layer statistics while sfmmu_tsbsize_stat kstats provide information on TSB size allocations:

```
$ kstat -n sfmmu_tsbsize_stat
module: unix                        instance: 0
name:   sfmmu_tsbsize_stat          class:      hat
crtime                     799.82297424
        sf_tsbsz_128k               275
        sf_tsbsz_16k                3891
        sf_tsbsz_1m                 0
        sf_tsbsz_256k               75
        sf_tsbsz_2m                 0
        sf_tsbsz_32k                3721
        sf_tsbsz_4m                 0
        sf_tsbsz_512k               0
        sf_tsbsz_64k                371
        sf_tsbsz_8k                 228875
        snaptime           2081123.44794904
```

Table 12.9 HAT Layer Kstats from `unix:hat:sfmmu_global_stat`.

Statistic	Description
sf_tsb_exceptions	The number of calls to `sfmmu_tsbmiss_exception()`.
sf_tsb_raise_exception	The number of TSB exceptions raised to synchronize MMU state or update the TSB base register and TTE after the TSB replacement.
sf_pagefaults	Pagefaults.
sf_uhash_searches	User hash searches.
sf_uhash_links	User hash links.
sf_khash_searches	Kernel hash searches.
sf_khash_links	Kernel hash links.
sf_swapout	The number of times process TSBs were swapped out.
sf_ctxfree	The count of contexts allocated from free list.
sf_ctxdirty	The count of contexts allocated from dirty list.
sf_ctxsteal	The number of contexts allocated by stealing it away from another process.
sf_tsb_alloc	Number of TSB allocations.
sf_tsb_allocfail	The number of times TSB allocations failed due to resource exhaustion.
sf_tsb_sectsb_create	The number of times a second TSB was allocated for a process.
sf_tteload8k	The number of calls to `sfmmu_tteload_addentry()` to add a 8-Kbyte TTE to an `hme_blk`.
sf_tteload64k	The number of calls to `sfmmu_tteload_addentry()` to add a 64-Kbyte TTE to an `hme_blk`.
sf_tteload512k	The number of calls to `sfmmu_tteload_addentry()` to add a 512-Kbyte TTE to an `hme_blk`.
sf_tteload4m	The number of calls to `sfmmu_tteload_addentry()` to add a 4-Mbyte TTE to an `hme_blk`.
sf_tteload32m	The number of calls to `sfmmu_tteload_addentry()` to add a 32-Mbyte TTE to an `hme_blk`.
sf_tteload256m	The number of calls to `sfmmu_tteload_addentry()` to add a 256-Mbyte TTE to an `hme_blk`.

continues

Table 12.9 HAT Layer Kstats from `unix:hat:sfmmu_global_stat`. (*continued*)

Statistic	Description
`sf_tsb_load8k`	The number of times a TTE was pre-loaded into the 8-Kbyte indexed TSB at map time.
`sf_tsb_load4m`	Count of the number of times a TTE was pre-loaded into the 4-Mbyte indexed TSB at map time.
`sf_hblk_hit`	The number of times an `hme_blk` was found to add a TTE to.
`sf_hblk8_ncreate`	The number of static nucleus hblk8 structures created at startup.
`sf_hblk8_nalloc`	The number of hblk8 structures allocated from the static nucleus pool during startup.
`sf_hblk1_ncreate`	The number of static hblk1 structures created at startup.
`sf_hblk1_nalloc`	The number of `hblk1` structures allocated from the static nucleus pool during startup.
`sf_hblk_slab_cnt`	The number of `sfmmu8_cache` slabs created.
`sf_hblk_reserve_cnt`	The `hblk_reserve` usage count. This is the number of times we could not get an `hme_blk` to map a `sfmmu8_cache` slab from the reserve pool and had to use `hblk_reserve`.
`sf_hblk_recurse_cnt`	The count of recursive `hblk_reserve` owner requests. This is the condition where we already own `hblk_reserve` but need another `hblk8`.
`sf_hblk_reserve_hit`	The number of `hblk_reserve` hash hits. This is the number of times we encountered a `hblk_reserve` in the HME hash chains.
`sf_get_free_success`	The number of times we found an `hme_blk` in the reserve pool.
`sf_get_free_throttle`	The number of times we failed to obtain an `hme_blk` from the reserve pool due to throttling. Reserve pool allocations are throttled when the number of HME blocks in the pool reaches `HBLK_RESERVE_MIN`.
`sf_get_free_fail`	The number of times the reserve pool was empty when we went to grab a `hme_blk`.

continues

Table 12.9 HAT Layer Kstats from `unix:hat:sfmmu_global_stat`. (*continued*)

Statistic	Description
sf_put_free_success	The number of times a `hme_blk` was freed by adding it to the reserve pool.
sf_put_free_fail	The number of times a `hme_blk` could not be freed to the reserve pool because it was full.
sf_pgcolor_conflict	The number of times a virtual address cache (VAC) conflict was encountered while loading a mapping.
sf_uncache_conflict	The number of mappings made temporarily uncacheable (TNC) to resolve VAC conflicts. This happens in the case of a conflict within an existing large page (in which case all constituent mappings are uncached) or with a locked 8-Kbyte page.
sf_unload_conflict	The number of 8-Kbyte page mappings unloaded to resolve a VAC conflict.
sf_ism_uncache	The ISM mappings made TNC to resolve VAC conflicts.
sf_ism_recache	The ISM mappings previously uncached that were re-cached after the VAC conflict has passed.
sf_recache	The number of mappings previously uncached that were recached after the VAC conflict has passed.
sf_steal_count	The number of HME blocks stolen when we failed to allocate a new one.
sf_pagesync	The number of times `sfmmu_pagesync()` was called to syncronize a page structure's hardware dependent attributes.
sf_clrwrt	The number of times write permission was removed from a mapping to a page, so that we can detect the next modification of it
sf_pagesync_invalid	pagesync with invalid TTE
sf_kernel_xcalls	The count of kernel cross-calls.
sf_user_xcalls	The count of user cross-calls.
sf_tsb_grow	The number of times process TSBs were successfully increased in size.
sf_tsb_shrink	The number of times process TSBs were successfully decreased in size on unmap to free up memory.

continues

Table 12.9 HAT Layer Kstats from `unix:hat:sfmmu_global_stat`. (*continued*)

Statistic	Description
`sf_tsb_resize_failures`	The number of times a process TSB resize was attempted but could not succeed due to an allocation failure.
`sf_tsb_reloc`	The number of times a TSB was relocated.
`sf_user_vtop`	The number of `sfmmu_uvatopfn()` calls to translate a user VA into a PFN.
`sf_ctx_swap`	The number of times a process context was changed to serialize ISM demap with the trap handlers.
`sf_tlbflush_all`	The number of times all TLBs were flushed.
`sf_tlbflush_ctx`	The number of times a context was flushed from the TLBs.
`sf_tlbflush_deferred`	The number of times a TLB context flush was not immediately performed. As a performance optimization on platforms that support the TLB demap-all operation, requests to flush a context are deferred until a context is allocated. At that time if the context free list is empty, a context is allocated from the dirty list, a TLB demap-all is issued, and the dirty list is moved to the free list.
`sf_tlb_reprog_pgsz`	The number of times the TLBs were reprogrammed with new page sizes.

12.3 The x64 HAT Layer

12.3.1 MMU Configuration

Modern x64 processors provide both segmentation and paging mechanisms to assist an operating system in memory management. In general, Solaris uses a "flat" model that ignores the x64 segmentation mechanisms as a means of protection (isolating applications and kernel memory) in favor of a pure page table model. The base page size for memory management is always 4096 bytes (4 KB). Once paging mode is activated, all addresses that reference memory by kernel or application instructions are translated from virtual addresses to physical addresses by the processor through the interpretation of page tables. The processor control register (CR3) holds the physical memory address of a top-level page table. Various bits from a virtual address interpret the page tables to derive a physical address. Figure 12.11 shows how it works for 64-bit mode.

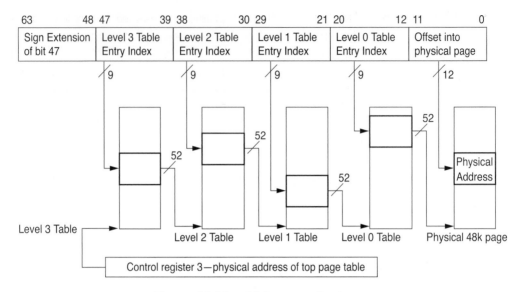

Figure 12.11 x64 Segment Registers

Note that bits 48..63 of every 64-bit virtual address must be either all 0s or all 1s on all current x64 processor implementations. This means that every 64-bit virtual address space has a "hole" of unusable addresses; however, we still have many terabytes of virtual address space.

The exact features and configuration used by Solaris for virtual memory management vary by processor type and operating mode.

- **32-bit non-PAE.** Two levels of page tables with 1024 entries, 4 bytes per entry. Used when there is less than 4 gigabytes of physical memory. Large pages if supported by the processor are 4 megabytes.

- **32-bit PAE.** Three levels of page tables. The top table has 4 entries, and other levels have 512 entries, 8 bytes per entry. Used when there are 4 or more gigabytes of memory or the processor supports the NX bit in page table entries. Large pages if supported by the processor are 2 megabytes.

- **64 bit.** Four levels of page tables of 512 entries, 8 bytes per entry. Used in 64-bit Solaris. Large pages if supported by the processor are 2 megabytes.

Note that Solaris source code ignores the architectural names Intel and AMD used for the page tables at different levels; instead, they are always just referred to by using their level number: 0 (Page Table), 1 (Page Directory), 2 (Page Directory Pointer), or 3 (Page Map Level-4).

12.3.2 `struct mmu` Variable

In Solaris, a single variable (`struct mmu`) is filled in during startup to hold the
configuration of the MMU. Here is what it typically contains in 64-bit kernel running on an AMD Opteron processor.

```
/*
 * HAT/MMU parameters that depend on kernel mode and/or processor type
 */
struct htable;
struct hat_mmu_info {
        x86pte_t pt_nx;            /* either 0 or PT_NX */
        x86pte_t pt_global;       /* either 0 or PT_GLOBAL */

        pfn_t highest_pfn;

        uint_t num_level;         /* number of page table levels in use */
        uint_t max_level;         /* just num_level - 1 */
        uint_t max_page_level;    /* maximum level at which we can map a page */
        uint_t ptes_per_table;    /* # of entries in lower level page tables */
        uint_t top_level_count;   /* # of entries in top most level page table */

        uint_t hash_cnt;          /* cnt of entries in htable_hash_cache */
        uint_t vlp_hash_cnt;      /* cnt of entries in vlp htable_hash_cache */

        uint_t pae_hat;           /* either 0 or 1 */

        uintptr_t hole_start;     /* start of VA hole (or -1 if none) */
        uintptr_t hole_end;       /* end of VA hole (or 0 if none) */

        struct htable **kmap_htables; /* htables for segmap + 32 bit heap */
        x86pte_t *kmap_ptes;      /* mapping of pagetables that map kmap */
        uintptr_t kmap_addr;      /* start addr of kmap */
        uintptr_t kmap_eaddr;     /* end addr of kmap */

        uint_t pte_size;          /* either 4 or 8 */
        uint_t pte_size_shift;    /* either 2 or 3 */
        x86pte_t ptp_bits[MAX_NUM_LEVEL];       /* bits set for interior PTP */
        x86pte_t pte_bits[MAX_NUM_LEVEL];       /* bits set for leaf PTE */

        /*
         * The following tables are equivalent to PAGEXXXXX at different levels
         * in the page table hierarchy.
         */
        uint_t level_shift[MAX_NUM_LEVEL];      /* PAGESHIFT for given level */
        uintptr_t level_size[MAX_NUM_LEVEL];    /* PAGESIZE for given level */
        uintptr_t level_offset[MAX_NUM_LEVEL];  /* PAGEOFFSET for given level */
        uintptr_t level_mask[MAX_NUM_LEVEL];    /* PAGEMASK for given level */

        uint_t tlb_entries[MAX_NUM_LEVEL];      /* tlb entries per pagesize */
};
```

See i86pc/vm/hat_pte.h

The structure members are as follows:

- **pt_nx.** Indicates if and where the processor supports the NX (No eXecute) bit
  in page table entries.

- **pt_global.** Indicates if and where the processor supports the Global Page bit in page table entries.
- **highest_pfn.** highest_pfn × 4K is the highest physical address the processor can access.
- **num_level.** Number of page table levels in use.
- **max_level.** num_level − 1.
- **max_page_level.** Indicates the highest-level page table that supports a large page. The 1 here indicates that the processor supports large (2 Mbyte) pages.
- **ptes_per_table.** Number of entries in each page table except the top level.
- **top_level_count.** Number of entries in top-level page table.
- **pae_hat.** Indicates we are using PAE mode (8 bytes / PTE).
- **hole_start and hole_end.** Give the boundaries (if any) of a virtual address hole.
- **pte_size.** Number of bytes in each page table entry.
- **pte_size_shift.** Log (base 2) of pte_size.
- **level_size[1].** Indexed by level, tells the page size that an entry at that page table level covers.
- **level_shift[1].** Log (base 2) of level_size.; that is, 1 << level_shift[1] == level_size[1].
- **level_offset[1].** level_size − 1.
- **level_mask[1].** Same as ~level_offset[1].

12.3.3 Virtual Address Space Layout

On x64 platforms, the Solaris kernel shares the virtual address space with applications by initializing the top few entries in every application's top-level page tables to the same values used in the kernel's page tables. A bit in each page table entry control prevents user mode access to kernel memory. Additionally, if the processor supports the global page bit in PTEs, then all kernel mappings are marked global. This prevents kernel TLB entries from being lost when context-switching between applications.

In the 32-bit kernel, the dividing line between kernel and user virtual addresses is lower if the system has large amounts of physical memory installed to allow enough kernel memory for struct pages.

To deal with the AMD64 addressing modes, the 64-bit kernel has a "core heap" area in which to ensure that all loadable kernel modules reside within 2 Gbytes of the kernel text and data.

The 64-bit kernel also reserves a 1 Gbyte region at `toxic_addr` in which to map I/O device control registers. This makes it possible to use `::kgrep` to search kernel memory without adverse results from memory mapped device control registers. Since the 32-bit kernel has stricter virtual address limitations, it maintains a bitmap (1 bit per 4-Kbyte page) to indicate which kernel virtual addresses are mapped to I/O devices.

```
(64 bit)
> ::print toxic_addr
> ::print toxic_size
(32 bit)
> ::print toxic_bit_map
> ::print toxic_bit_map_len (in bits)
```

On the 64-bit kernel, the `segkpm` segment provides immutable virtual mappings to all physical memory on the system. When the 64-bit kernel needs to briefly access memory in any given physical page, it can add the physical address to the value given in `kpm_vbase` and directly use that virtual address. The `seg-kpm` mappings are established with the largest possible page size to reduce the number of page tables needed. Again, because of virtual addressing limitations, `seg_kpm` is not available in the 32-bit kernel, so the 32-bit kernel must modify its page tables to establish a temporary mapping to the physical page.

12.3.4 64-Bit Address Space Layout

The kernel text and data are the first two things loaded into memory. Early kernel startup code allocates the initial `page_t` structures, as well as other data structures required by the kernel's memory allocator, immediately below the kernel text. The Core Heap is used for loadable kernel modules (all kernel text needs to live in the same 2-Gbyte region for the AMD64 memory address model we use). The layout of address space was chosen to allow maximal usable virtual memory to 64 applications while providing Solaris enough memory to map all physical memory in `segkpm` and to have a large kernel heap. (See Figure 12.12.)

12.3.5 32-Bit Address Space Layout

Unlike the case in Linux, the kernel text and data live at the top of the virtual address range. This allows the value of `kernelbase` on machines with large physical memory to be automatically adjusted downward to accommodate additional `page_t` structures without relinking the kernel image.

```
                    +-----------------------+
                    | Kernel Debugger (kmdb)|  (optionally loaded module)
0xFFFFFFFF.FF800000 |-----------------------|- SEGDEBUGBASE
                    |   Kernel Data / BSS   |
0xFFFFFFFF.FBC00000 |-----------------------|
                    |     Kernel Text       |
0xFFFFFFFF.FB800000 |-----------------------|- KERNEL_TEXT
                    |      Core Heap        |  (used for loadable modules)
0xFFFFFFFF.C0000000 |-----------------------|- core_base
                    |   initial page_t's    |
                    |   memsegs, memlists,  |  (allocated during early startup)
                    |   page hash, etc.     |
  ---               |-----------------------|- valloc_base / ekernelheap
                    | Kernel Dynamic Heap   |
0xFFFFFXXX.XXX00000 |-----------------------|- kernelheap (floating)
                    |        seg_map        |
0xFFFFFXXX.XXX00000 |-----------------------|- segkmap_start (floating)
                    | Mem Mapped Devices    |
0xFFFFFXXX.XXX00000 |-----------------------|- toxic_addr (floating)
                    |        segkp          |
  ---               |-----------------------|- segkp_base
                    |        segkpm         |
0xFFFFFE00.00000000 |-----------------------|
                    |///////Red Zone////////|
0xFFFFFD80.00000000 |-----------------------|- KERNELBASE
                    |     User Stack        |- User space memory
                    |                       |
                    | shared objects, etc   |   (grows downward)
                    :                       :
0xFFFF8000.00000000 |-----------------------|
                    |///////////////////////|
                    |    Virt. Addr. Hole   |
                    |///////////////////////|
0x00008000.00000000 |-----------------------|
                    :                       :
                    |      User Heap        |   (grows upward)
                    |-----------------------|
                    |     User Data/BSS     |
                    |-----------------------|
                    |      User Text        |
0x00000000.04000000 |-----------------------|
                    |       Invalid         |VA==0 not mapped to catch NULL ptr refs
0x00000000.00000000 +-----------------------+
```

Figure 12.12 Solaris 64-Bit Address Space Layout (with 64-Bit Application)

Although not shown, when a 32-bit application is run on the 64-bit kernel, the application uses all virtual memory below 0xFE000000; on a few very early x64 processors, though, this is reduced to 0xC0000000 to work around a processor erratum. This means that 32-bit applications on the 64-bit kernel can use almost 1 gigabyte more memory. (See Figure 12.13.)

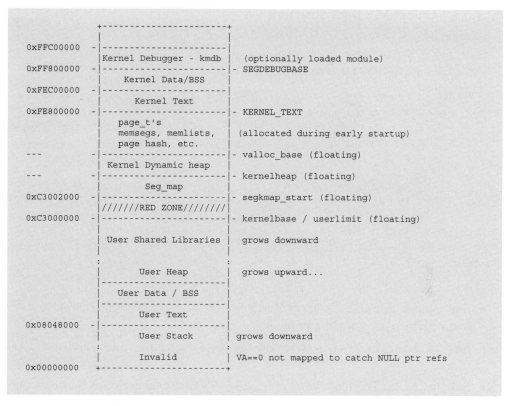

```
                  +-----------------------+
                  |                       |
  0xFFC00000   -  |-----------------------|
                  |Kernel Debugger - kmdb |   (optionally loaded module)
  0xFF800000   -  |-----------------------|-  SEGDEBUGBASE
                  |    Kernel Data/BSS     |
  0xFEC00000   -  |-----------------------|
                  |      Kernel Text       |
  0xFE800000   -  |-----------------------|-  KERNEL_TEXT
                  |    page_t's            |
                  |    memsegs, memlists,  |   (allocated during early startup)
                  |    page hash, etc.     |
    ---          -|-----------------------|-  valloc_base (floating)
                  |   Kernel Dynamic heap  |
    ---          -|-----------------------|-  kernelheap (floating)
                  |       Seg_map          |
  0xC3002000   -  |-----------------------|-  segkmap_start (floating)
                  |///////RED ZONE////////|
  0xC3000000   -  |-----------------------|-  kernelbase / userlimit (floating)
                  |                       |
                  |  User Shared Libraries |   grows downward
                  |                       |
                  :                       :
                  |      User Heap         |   grows upward...
                  |-----------------------|
                  |   User Data / BSS      |
                  |-----------------------|
                  |      User Text         |
  0x08048000   -  |-----------------------|
                  |      User Stack        |   grows downward
                  :                       :
                  |      Invalid           |   VA==0 not mapped to catch NULL ptr refs
  0x00000000      +-----------------------+
```

Figure 12.13 32-Bit Kernel's Address Space Layout

12.3.6 HAT Implementation

The x64 HAT layer has several major data structures:

- **struct hat (a.k.a. hat_t).** Contains information about each address space. These are arranged in a doubly linked list starting with the kernel address space's hat_t.

- **struct htable (htable_t).** Manages a page table (one per page table needed in an address space). These are stored in a hash table based in the hat_t.

- **struct hment (hment_t).** Tracks which physical memory pages are mapped by which page tables. These are in a linked list off the struct page.

12.3.6.1 `struct hat` Data Structure

```
/*
 * The hat struct exists for each address space.
 */
struct hat {
        kmutex_t          hat_mutex;
        kmutex_t          hat_switch_mutex;
        struct as         *hat_as;
        uint_t            hat_stats;
        pgcnt_t           hat_pages_mapped[MAX_PAGE_LEVEL + 1];
        cpuset_t          hat_cpus;
        uint16_t          hat_flags;
        htable_t          *hat_htable;    /* top-level htable */
        struct hat        *hat_next;
        struct hat        *hat_prev;
        uint_t            hat_num_hash;   /* number of htable hash buckets */
        htable_t          **hat_ht_hash;  /* htable hash buckets */
        htable_t          *hat_ht_cached; /* cached free htables */
        x86pte_t          hat_vlp_ptes[VLP_NUM_PTES];
};
typedef struct hat hat_t;
```

- **hat_pages_mapped.** An array that gives the number of pages currently mapped (by page size) in a process.

- **hat_htable.** The `htable_t` for the top-level page table in this address space.

- **hat_ht_hash.** The hash table of `htable_t`'s that belong to this address space.

- **hat_vlp_ptes.** Explained next.

The 64-bit kernel (and 32-bit PAE) creates page tables only for the bottom levels (0 and 1) of the page table tree for 32-bit user processes. The level-3 page table entries are instead stored in the `hat_vlp_ptes[]` in the `hat_t` and are copied to/from a per-cpu set of upper-level page tables whenever the process is running. This reduces memory consumption by two 4K pages for each 32-bit process. So in the above example, the `hat_vlp_ptes[]` values represent level-2 page table entries for a 32-bit process.

12.3.6.2 Page Tables and `struct htable`

For each page table needed, there is a `struct htable` to manage it. To find the `htables` being used to map an address, you can use the `::vatopfn` and `::pte` dcmds in `mdb`.

```
> ffffffff80aa8000::vatopfn
        level=0 htable=ffffffff8067f5e8 pte=800000007fc78763
        level=1 htable=ffffffff8067ec68 pte=7fc88027
        level=2 htable=ffffffff8067e290 pte=9697027
        level=3 htable=ffffffff8067f678 pte=2d2da992435c7878
Virtual ffffffff80aa8000 maps Physical 7fc78000
```

The ::pte command can decode a page table entry.

```
> 800000007fc78763::pte
PTE=800000007fc78763: noexec page=0x7fc78 noconsist nosync global write
```

The example shows that the kernel heap virtual address 0xffffffff80aa8000 is mapped to physical address 0x7fc78000 and that it's a global kernel writable mapping.

To go from a physical page to all its usage in the HAT, use the ::report_maps dcmd.

```
> 7fc78::report_maps
Pagetable for hat=ffffffff8012ff38 htable=ffffffff8067f438
hat=ffffffff8012ff38 maps addr=fffffe80bf800000
hat=ffffffff8012ff38 maps addr=ffffffff80aa8000
```

The example shows that the page 7fc78 is a page table and that 0xffffffff8067f438 is where the corresponding htable_t is. The page is also mapped by a mapping starting at virtual address 0xfffffe80bf800000 (the segkpm mapping to the page) and by an additional kernel mapping at virtual address 0xffffffff80aa8000. Let's look at the actual htable.

```
> ffffffff8067f438::print -t htable_t
{
    struct htable *ht_next = 0
    struct hat *ht_hat = 0xffffffff8012ff38
    uintptr_t ht_vaddr = 0xfffffe80bf800000
    level_t ht_level = 0
    uint16_t ht_flags = 0
    int16_t ht_busy = 0x1
    uint16_t ht_num_ptes = 0x200
    int16_t ht_valid_cnt = 0xe6
    uint32_t ht_lock_cnt = 0
    pfn_t ht_pfn = 0x7fc78
    struct htable *ht_prev = 0xffffffff8067e9e0
    struct htable *ht_parent = 0xffffffff8067f480
    struct htable *ht_shares = 0
}
```

- **ht_next.** Links htables in the hash table rooted in the `hat_t`.

- **ht_hat.** Identifies the `hat_t` that is using this htable.

- **ht_pfn.** Is the physical page number of the page table that goes with this htable.

- **ht_vaddr.** Is the virtual address that corresponds to the first entry of the page table.

- **ht_level.** Is the level (0, 1, 2, 3) of the page table.

- **ht_valid_cnt.** Number of entries in use in the page table.

- **ht_parent.** The `htable` at one level higher (`ht_level` + 1) whose page table has an entry for this htable.

The HAT does not normally maintain virtual kernel mappings to all page tables. Instead, it remembers only the page frame number (PFN) of the page tables and then either remaps them when needed in a window (32-bit kernel) or uses `seg_kpm` (64-bit kernel) to access them. When debugging, you can use the `::ptable` command to examine the contents of a page table when you know its PFN.

```
> 0x7fc78::ptable
htable=ffffffff8067f438
[   0]  va=fffffe80bf800000 PTE=800000006f3c8121: noexec page=0x6f3c8 global
[   4]  va=fffffe80bf804000 PTE=8000000070b5c121: noexec page=0x70b5c global
[   5]  va=fffffe80bf805000 PTE=800000007633d121: noexec page=0x7633d global
[   6]  va=fffffe80bf806000 PTE=800000007137e121: noexec page=0x7137e global
[   9]  va=fffffe80bf809000 PTE=800000006f871121: noexec page=0x6f871 global
[  10]  va=fffffe80bf80a000 PTE=800000006f852121: noexec page=0x6f852 global
[  12]  va=fffffe80bf80c000 PTE=800000006f874121: noexec page=0x6f874 global
[  14]  va=fffffe80bf80e000 PTE=800000006f896121: noexec page=0x6f896 global
[  16]  va=fffffe80bf810000 PTE=800000006f3f8121: noexec page=0x6f3f8 global
[  18]  va=fffffe80bf812000 PTE=800000006f3da121: noexec page=0x6f3da global
[  20]  va=fffffe80bf814000 PTE=800000006f33c121: noexec page=0x6f33c global
[  21]  va=fffffe80bf815000 PTE=800000006f35d121: noexec page=0x6f35d global
...
```

The example shows active page table entries by index, the VA mapped, the actual PTE, and its decoded meaning. These are all kernel heap addresses, so the global bit is set and they are marked with the NX (no execute) bit.

12.3.6.3 struct hment and struct Page

The HAT also maintains a reverse mapping which, given a page, can tell which and where address spaces have virtual mappings to a page. To save memory usage, the HAT tries to embed the mapping information directly into the page's `page_t` structure. Let's start by looking at page number 0x6f3c8.

```
> 6f3c8::page_num2pp
6f3c8 has page at fffffffffaee77d0
> fffffffffaee77d0::print -t page_t
{
    u_offset_t p_offset = 0
    struct vnode *p_vnode = 0xffffffff83227440
...
    uchar_t p_nrm = 0x2
    uchar_t p_embed = 0x1
    uchar_t p_index = 0
    uchar_t p_toxic = 0
    void *p_mapping = 0xffffffff8067f438
    pfn_t p_pagenum = 0x6f3c8
    uint_t p_share = 0
    uint_t p_sharepad = 0
    uint_t p_msresv_1 = 0
    uint_t p_mlentry = 0
    uint64_t p_msresv_2 = 0
}
```

- **p_embed.** Non-zero indicates a page that is mapped only once and that the mapping information is embedded in the page_t structure.

- **p_mapping.** Since p_embed is 1, the htable whose page table maps this page.

- **p_mlentry.** Index for the page table entry.

If there is more than one mapping to a page, then a list is used and these fields change their meaning.

```
> f7a41::page_num2pp
f7a41 has page at fffffffffb5d7e30
> fffffffffb5d7e30::print page_t
{
    p_offset = 0
    p_vnode = 0xffffffff833a8840
...
    p_nrm = 0x2
    p_embed = 0
    p_index = 0
    p_toxic = 0
    p_mapping = 0xffffffff83249a28
    p_pagenum = 0xf7a41
    p_share = 0x1
    p_sharepad = 0
    p_msresv_1 = 0
    p_mlentry = 0x1f0
    p_msresv_2 = 0
}
> 0xffffffff83249a28::print -t hment_t
{
    struct hment *hm_hashnext = 0
    struct hment *hm_next = 0
    struct hment *hm_prev = 0
    htable_t *hm_htable = 0xffffffff83246dc8
    uint16_t hm_entry = 0x1f0
    uint16_t hm_pad = 0x8324
    uint32_t hm_pad2 = 0xffffffff
}
```

In this case p_embed is 0, so p_mapping is interpreted as an hment_t pointer. The hment then gives the htable and the entry index in the htable's page table. If there are multiple mappings to this page, then the list pointers would be filled in. Since most memory in processes are not shared, mapping information is usually found directly in the page_t structures.

12.3.6.4 Physical Memory and DMA

The lists used to track free physical memory pages are broken up into four ranges (by address) that roughly track the sort of legacy DMA ranges needed in the past on the PC architecture:

- 0 to 16 Mbytes
- 0 to 2 Gbytes
- 2 Gbytes to 4 Gbytes
- More than 4 Gbytes

Memory allocations for devices with DMA range limitations are directed to the appropriate memory range. All other memory allocations go to the highest range with available memory. Once physical pages are allocated and mapped into the kernel for DMA, the I/O system tracks the memory, using power-of-two allocation bins (16 Mbytes, 32 Mbytes, 64 Mbytes, etc.) to speed up subsequent DMA allocate() and free() operations.

12.4 MDB Reference

Table 12.10 MDB Reference for HAT

dcmd or walker	Description
dcmd page_num2pp	Page frame number to page structure
dcmd sfmmu_vtop	Print virtual-to-physical mapping
dcmd tsbinfo	Show TSB information
dcmd whatis	Given an address, return information
walk sfmmu1_cache	Walk the sfmmu1_cache cache
walk sfmmu8_cache	Walk the sfmmu8_cache cache
walk sfmmu_tsb8k_cache	Walk the sfmmu_tsb8k_cache cache
walk sfmmu_tsb_cache	Walk the sfmmu_tsb_cache cache
walk sfmmu_tsbinfo_cache	Walk the sfmmu_tsbinfo_cache cache

continues

Table 12.10 MDB Reference for HAT (*continued*)

dcmd or walker	Description
walk sfmmuid_cache	Walk the sfmmuid_cache cache
walk ism_blk_cache	Walk the ism_blk_cache cache
walk ism_ment_cache	Walk the ism_ment_cache cache
walk HatHash	Walk the HatHash cache
walk hat_t	Walk the hat_t cache
walk hment_t	Walk the hment_t cache
walk htable_t	Walk the htable_t cache

Working with Multiple Page Sizes in Solaris

This chapter introduces a strategy for measuring the potential performance gain that could be yielded from an increase in page size. We begin by discussing a powerful Solaris tool, `trapstat`, for easily quantifying the potential gains of using a larger page size. We discuss "`trapstat(1M)`." on page 640. We then follow by discussing legacy methods to estimate the gain in Solaris 8 by use of the `cpustat` command.

13.1 Determining When to Use Large Pages

To determine whether we can improve application performance by using a larger page size, we need to determine the amount of time the microprocessor or operation spends servicing translation lookaside buffer (TLB) misses on behalf of a target application. TLB misses are typically accounted for in the context of the process running; for example, if a TLB miss occurs in a user-mode application, it will be counted as user time. Thus, an application might spend a large amount of time having TLB misses serviced for it but still report that it spends 100% of its time in user mode.

```
sol8# mpstat 1 3
CPU minf mjf xcal  intr ithr  csw icsw migr smtx  srw syscl  usr sys  wt idl
  0    2   0    1   234  134   91   46    0    0    0    25  100    0   0   0
  0    2   0    1   234  134   91   46    0    0    0    25  100    0   0   0
  0    2   0    1   234  134   91   46    0    0    0    25  100    0   0   0
.
```

13.2 Measuring Application Performance

Two different types of page-size observability tools are available in Solaris: those that describe the page sizes in use by the system or application, and those that help determine whether using large pages will benefit performance. The pmap(1M) and pagesize(1M) commands, getpagesize(3C), and meminfo(2) interfaces discover information about the system's ability to support different TLB page sizes. The trapstat(1M) and cpustat(1M) commands can approximate the amount of time that our target application spends waiting for the platform to service TLB misses.

We can use two methods to approximate the amount of time spent on servicing TLB misses: (1) we can observe the rate of TLB misses and then multiply rate of TLB misses by the cost of the TLB miss; or (2) if TLB misses are serviced by system software, we can directly measure the time spent in the TLB miss handlers. On Solaris 8, the cpustat(1M) command measures the rate of TLB misses, whereas Solaris 9 provides a new command, trapstat, which computes and displays the amount of time spent servicing TLB misses.

trapstat(1M).   The Solaris trapstat command provides information about processor exceptions on UltraSPARC platforms. Since TLB misses are serviced in software on UltraSPARC microprocessors, trapstat can also provide statistics about TLB misses.

Using the trapstat command, we can observe the number of TLB misses and the amount of time spent servicing TLB misses. The -t and -T options provide information about TLB misses. Again with trapstat, we can use the amount of time servicing TLB misses to approximate the potential gains we could make by using a larger page size or by moving to a platform that uses a microprocessor with a larger TLB.

The -t option provides first-level summary statistics. The time spent servicing TLB misses is summarized in the lower-right corner; in this case, 46.2% of the total execution time is spent servicing misses. Miss detail is provided for TLB misses incurred in the data portion of the address space and for the instruction portion of the address space. Data is also provided for user- and kernel-mode misses (we are primarily interested in the user-mode misses, since our application likely runs in user mode).

```
sol9# trapstat -t 1 111
cpu m| itlb-miss %tim itsb-miss %tim | dtlb-miss %tim dtsb-miss %tim |%tim
-----+--------------------------------+--------------------------------+----
  0 u|      1  0.0        0  0.0 |  2171237 45.7        0  0.0 |45.7
  0 k|      2  0.0        0  0.0 |     3751  0.1        7  0.0 | 0.1
=====+================================+================================+====
 ttl |      3  0.0        0  0.0 |  2192238 46.2        7  0.0 |46.2
```

For further details, use the -T option to provide a per-page-size breakdown. In this example, trapstat shows us that all of the misses occurred on 8-Kbyte pages.

```
sol9# trapstat -T 1 111
cpu m size| itlb-miss %tim itsb-miss %tim | dtlb-miss %tim dtsb-miss %tim |%tim
----------+------------------------------------+------------------------------------+----
  0 u  8k|       30  0.0        0  0.0  |  2170236 46.1        0  0.0 |46.1
  0 u 64k|        0  0.0        0  0.0  |        0  0.0        0  0.0 | 0.0
  0 u 512k|       0  0.0        0  0.0  |        0  0.0        0  0.0 | 0.0
  0 u  4m|        0  0.0        0  0.0  |        0  0.0        0  0.0 | 0.0
- - - - -+ - - - - - - - - - - - - -+ - - - - - - - - - - - - -+ - -
  0 k  8k|        1  0.0        0  0.0  |     4174  0.1       10  0.0 | 0.1
  0 k 64k|        0  0.0        0  0.0  |        0  0.0        0  0.0 | 0.0
  0 k 512k|       0  0.0        0  0.0  |        0  0.0        0  0.0 | 0.0
  0 k  4m|        0  0.0        0  0.0  |        0  0.0        0  0.0 | 0.0
==========+====================================+====================================+====
      ttl |       31  0.0        0  0.0  |  2174410 46.2       10  0.0 |46.2
```

We can conclude from this analysis that our application could potentially run almost twice as fast if we could eliminate the majority of the TLB misses. Our objective in using the mechanisms discussed below is to minimize the user-mode data TLB (dTLB) misses, by instructing the application to use larger pages for its data segments. Typically, data misses are incurred in the program's heap or stack segments. We can use the Solaris multiple-page-size support commands to direct the application to use 4-Mbyte pages for its heap, stack, or anonymous memory mappings.

cpustat(1M). The cpustat command programs and reads the hardware counters in the microprocessor. These counters measure hardware events within the processor itself. Typically, two counters and a larger number of events can be counted. The UltraSPARC III processors can count TLB miss events. Since Solaris 8 lacks trapstat, the CPU counters can estimate the amount of time spent servicing TLB misses.

For example, the following cpustat command instructs the system to measure the number of DTLB miss events and the number of microprocessor cycles on each processor.

```
sol8# cpustat -c pic0=Cycle_cnt,pic1=DTLB_miss 1
   time cpu event       pic0      pic1
  1.006   0  tick 663839993   3540016
  2.006   0  tick 651943834   3514443
  3.006   0  tick 630482518   3398061
  4.006   0  tick 634483028   3418046
  5.006   0  tick 651910256   3511458
  6.006   0  tick 651432039   3510201
  7.006   0  tick 651512695   3512047
  8.006   0  tick 613888365   3309406
  9.006   0  tick 650806115   3510292
```

By default, the `cpustat` command reports only counts representing the user-mode processes. This `cpustat` output shows us that on processor 0, a user-mode process consumes approximately 650 million cycles and that 3.5 million dTLB misses are serviced. An UltraSPARC TLB miss typically ranges from about 50 cycles (if the TLB entry being loaded is found in the microprocessor's cache) to about 300 cycles (if a memory load is required to fetch the new TLB entry). We can, therefore, approximate that between 175 million and 1050 million cycles are spent servicing TLB misses, per 1 second sample.

A quick check of the processor speed allows us to calculate the ratio of time spent servicing misses.

```
sol8# psrinfo -v
Status of processor 0 as of: 11/10/2002 20:14:09
  Processor has been on-line since 11/05/2002 20:59:17.
  The sparcv9 processor operates at 900 MHz,
       and has a sparcv9 floating point processor.
```

Our microprocessor is running at 900 MHz, providing 900 million cycles per second. Therefore, at least 175/900, or 19%, of the time, is spent servicing TLB misses. The actual number could be larger if a large fraction of the TLB misses require memory loads.

13.2.1 Determination Allocated Page Sizes

The `pmap` command allows us to query a target process about page-size information, and the `meminfo` system call provides a programmatic query to the operating system for information about the page sizes provided to it.

`pmap(1)`.   The `pmap` command displays the page sizes of memory mappings within the address space of a process. The `-xs` option directs `pmap` to show the page size for each mapping.

```
sol9# pmap -sx `pgrep testprog`
2909:   ./testprog
  Address   Kbytes      RSS     Anon  Locked Pgsz Mode    Mapped File
 00010000        8        8        -       -  8K r-x--  dev:277,83 ino:114875
 00020000        8        8        8       -  8K rwx--  dev:277,83 ino:114875
 00022000   131088   131088   131088       -  8K rwx--  [ heap ]
 FF280000      120      120        -       -  8K r-x--  libc.so.1
 FF29E000      136      128        -       -   - r-x--  libc.so.1
 FF2C0000       72       72        -       -  8K r-x--  libc.so.1
 FF2D2000      192      192        -       -   - r-x--  libc.so.1
 FF302000      112      112        -       -  8K r-x--  libc.so.1
 FF31E000       48       32        -       -   - r-x--  libc.so.1
 FF33A000       24       24       24       -  8K rwx--  libc.so.1
```

continues

```
FF340000        8        8        8        -    8K rwx--  libc.so.1
FF390000        8        8        -        -    8K r-x--  libc_psr.so.1
FF3A0000        8        8        -        -    8K r-x--  libdl.so.1
FF3B0000        8        8        8        -    8K rwx--    [ anon ]
FF3C0000      152      152        -        -    8K r-x--  ld.so.1
FF3F6000        8        8        8        -    8K rwx--  ld.so.1
FFBFA000       24       24       24        -    8K rwx--    [ stack ]
-------- ------- ------- ------- -------
total Kb 132024   132000   131168        -.
```

The `pmap` command shows us the MMU page size for each mapping. In this case, 8 Kbytes are used for all mappings. To demonstrate a larger page size, we can use the Solaris `ppgsz` command (we discuss `ppgsz` in more detail in a later section) to set the page size for the heap of our test program to 4 Mbytes.

```
sol9# ppgsz -o heap=4M ./testprog &
sol9# pmap -sx `pgrep testprog`
2953:    ./testprog
 Address  Kbytes     RSS    Anon Locked Pgsz Mode   Mapped File
00010000        8        8        -        -    8K r-x--  dev:277,83 ino:114875
00020000        8        8        8        -    8K rwx--  dev:277,83 ino:114875
00022000     3960     3960     3960        -    8K rwx--    [ heap ]
00400000   131072   131072   131072        -    4M rwx--    [ heap ]
FF280000      120      120        -        -    8K r-x--  libc.so.1
FF29E000      136      128        -        -     - r-x--  libc.so.1
FF2C0000       72       72        -        -    8K r-x--  libc.so.1
FF2D2000      192      192        -        -     - r-x--  libc.so.1
FF302000      112      112        -        -    8K r-x--  libc.so.1
FF31E000       48       32        -        -     - r-x--  libc.so.1
FF33A000       24       24       24        -    8K rwx--  libc.so.1
FF340000        8        8        8        -    8K rwx--  libc.so.1
FF390000        8        8        -        -    8K r-x--  libc_psr.so.1
FF3A0000        8        8        -        -    8K r-x--  libdl.so.1
FF3B0000        8        8        8        -    8K rwx--    [ anon ]
FF3C0000      152      152        -        -    8K r-x--  ld.so.1
FF3F6000        8        8        8        -    8K rwx--  ld.so.1
FFBFA000       24       24       24        -    8K rwx--    [ stack ]
-------- ------- ------- ------- -------
total Kb 135968   135944   135112        -
```

meminfo(2).   The `meminfo()` system call enables a program to inquire about the physical pages mapping its address space. This system call provides a programmatic way of determining the page sizes allocated within a process's address space. An array is filled with a description of each page that backs the mapping.

```
NAME
     meminfo - provide information about memory

SYNOPSIS
     #include <sys/types.h>
     #include <sys/mman.h>
```

continues

```
int meminfo(const uint64_t inaddr[], int addr_count, const
uint_t  info_req[],  int  info_count,  uint64_t  outdata[],
uint_t validity[]);
```

DESCRIPTION
    The meminfo() function provides information about virtual
    and physical memory particular to the calling process. The
    user or developer of performance utilities can use this
    information to analyze system memory allocations and develop
    a better understanding of the factors affecting application
    performance.

13.2.2 Discovery of Supported Page Sizes

The three commands that enable us to determine information about the page size supported by Solaris are described in this section.

pagesize(1M).   The pagesize command displays the base page size (default page size) used by the Solaris Operating System on the given microprocessor. The default is currently 8 Kbytes for all UltraSPARC platforms, and 4 Kbytes on x86/x64 platforms.

```
sol8# pagesize
8192
```

The pagesize command can also display the available page sizes on the given microprocessor in Solaris. In this example, we can see that four page sizes are available on our UltraSPARC processor.

```
sol9# pagesize -a
8192
65536
524288
4194304
```

getpagesize(3C).   The getpagesize() function returns the base page size in bytes.

getpagesizes(3C).   The getpagesizes() function reports the available page sizes on the given microprocessor.

```
NAME
     getpagesizes - get system supported page-sizes

SYNOPSIS
     #include <sys/mman.h>

     int getpagesizes(size_t pagesize[], int nelem);

DESCRIPTION
     The getpagesizes() function returns either the number of
     different page sizes supported by the system or the actual
     sizes themselves. When called with nelem as 0 and pagesize
     as NULL, getpagesizes() returns the number of supported page
     sizes. Otherwise, up to nelem page-sizes are retrieved and
     assigned to successive elements of pagesize[]. The return
     value is the number of page sizes retrieved and set in
     pagesize[].
```

13.3 Configuring for Multiple Page Sizes

Once we determine that our application warrants the use of large pages, we need to construct a strategy for determining what parts of our application to enhance to use large pages. For example, should we attempt to enable large pages for our target process's heap, stack, text, etc.? The trapstat utility gives us a little information about the types of our address space that incur the TLB misses.

The instruction TLB (iTLB) miss information is likely a result from the process's text and library text since instructions typically reside in these mappings. It is possible, however, for a program to execute code from other mappings; for example, the Java virtual machine compiles instructions on-the-fly into its heap and then executes from there. However, for the vast majority of applications, we can first guess that iTLB misses result from the text/library mappings.

Data TLB misses are likely to occur from the program's writable segments: its heap, stack, data mapping and read-only data within the text mapping.

The default page size (base page size) for the Solaris OS is 8 Kbytes on UltraSPARC and 4 Kbytes on Intel x86 microprocessors. Larger pages (4 Mbytes) are used by the Solaris kernel for its instruction and data sections; however, user applications requiring larger pages must explicitly request them.

The use of larger page sizes in Solaris 2.6 through Solaris 8 is only available through a special form of System V shared memory. To optimize database performance, we can use this form of shared memory—intimate shared memory (ISM). ISM is requested by the shmat(2) system call with the SHM_SHARE_MMU flag and is allocated as 4-Mbyte pages if possible. Databases such as Oracle, Informix, and Sybase request shared memory by using this flag and typically perform as much as 10%–20% better as a result of a reduced TLB miss rate.

Solaris 9 introduces a generic framework for allowing user applications to request larger page sizes. At the same time, ISM was also enhanced to take advantage of the other supported large page sizes (e.g., 64 Kbytes and 512 Kbytes). Unmodified applications can be directed to use larger page sizes by means of the ppgsz(1M) command and the libmpss.so library. Applications can also be customized to request larger page sizes by the memcntl(2) system call.

The Solaris 9 large-page infrastructure allows larger pages to be requested for the mappings of /dev/zero, that is, the heap, stack, and other anonymous mappings.

13.3.1 Enabling Large Pages

Solaris 9 provides a new framework: Multiple Page-Size Support (MPSS). This allows larger page sizes to be requested for user processes. The memcntl() system call specifies page-size advice for a given address range. A wrapper program, ppgsz, and an interposition library, libmpss.so, call memcntl() on behalf of the target process so that unmodified binaries can make use of larger page sizes.

13.3.2 Advising Page-Size Preferences with ppgsz(1M)

The ppgsz command is a wrapper that advises a preferred page size for a process's heap or stack of a target process. These page-size preferences are inherited across fork() but *not* across exec(). Thus, if the target program spawns (forks then execs) another program, page sizes will not be inherited. If inheritance of page sizes is required, the mpss.so library should be used instead.

For example, to start a target process with 4-Mbyte pages for its heap, we could use the ppgsz wrapper.

```
sol9# ppgsz -o heap=4M ./testprog &
sol9# pmap -sx `pgrep testprog`
2953:   ./testprog
 Address   Kbytes      RSS     Anon  Locked Pgsz Mode   Mapped File
00010000        8        8        -       -  8K r-x--  dev:277,83 ino:114875
00020000        8        8        8       -  8K rwx--  dev:277,83 ino:114875
00022000     3960     3960     3960       -  8K rwx--   [ heap ]
00400000   131072   131072   131072       -  4M rwx--   [ heap ]
FF280000      120      120        -       -  8K r-x--  libc.so.1
FF29E000      136      128        -       -   - r-x--  libc.so.1
FF2C0000       72       72        -       -  8K r-x--  libc.so.1
FF2D2000      192      192        -       -   - r-x--  libc.so.1
FF302000      112      112        -       -  8K r-x--  libc.so.1
FF31E000       48       32        -       -   - r-x--  libc.so.1
FF33A000       24       24       24       -  8K rwx--  libc.so.1
FF340000        8        8        8       -  8K rwx--  libc.so.1
FF390000        8        8        -       -  8K r-x--  libc_psr.so.1
FF3A0000        8        8        -       -  8K r-x--  libdl.so.1
FF3B0000        8        8        8       -  8K rwx--   [ anon ]
FF3C0000      152      152        -       -  8K r-x--  ld.so.1
FF3F6000        8        8        8       -  8K rwx--  ld.so.1
FFBFA000       24       24       24       -  8K rwx--   [ stack ]
-------- ------- ------- ------- -------
total Kb   135968   135944   135112       -
```

13.3.3 Interposing Shared Libraries with `libmpss.so`

The `mpss.so` shared object in `/usr/lib` provides a means by which the preferred stack or heap page size can be selectively configured for launched processes and their descendants. The library has an the advantage over the wrapper in that page sizes are inherited across `exec()`. To enable `mpss.so`, ensure that the following string is present in the environment (see `ld.so.1(1)`) along with one or more MPSS (multiple page-size support) environment variables:

```
sol9# LD_PRELOAD=$LD_PRELOAD:mpss.so.1
```

Once preloaded, the `mpss.so.1` shared object reads the following environment variables to determine preferred page-size requirements and processes for which these requirements are specific:

```
MPSSHEAP=size

MPSSSTACK=size
        MPSSHEAP and  MPSSSTACK  specify  the   preferred  page
        sizes for the heap and stack, respectively. The speci-
        fied  page  size(s)  are  applied  to   all   created
        processes.

MPSSCFGFILE=config-file
        config-file is a text file which contains one or  more
        mpss configuration entries of the form:

        exec-name:heap-size:stack-size
```

For example, the following commands enable 4-Mbyte pages for the heap of all subsequently started processes:

```
sol9# export LD_PRELOAD=$LD_PRELOAD:mpss.so.1
sol9# export MPSSHEAP=4M
sol9# ./testprog
```

You can use a configuration file to configure a mechanism to enable 4-Mbyte pages only for matching processes. For example, the following commands enable 4-Mbyte pages for just `testprog`:

```
sol9# cat >/usr/local/etc/mpss.cfg
testprog:4M:*

sol9# export LD_PRELOAD=$LD_PRELOAD:mpss.so.1
sol9# export MPSSCFGFILE=/usr/local/etc/mpss
```

See mpss.so.1(1) for all available configuration options.

13.3.4 Request Larger Page Sizes with the Compiler

The Sun Studio compilers provide options to cause the target application to request specific page sizes. The following options are supported for the compiler:

-xpagesize = n.   (SPARC) Sets the preferred page size for the stack and the heap. The n value must be one of the following: 8K, 64K, 512K, 4M, 32M, 256M, 2G, 16G, or default.

You must specify a valid page size for the Solaris Operating System on the target platform, as returned by getpagesize(3C). If you do not specify a valid page size, the request is silently ignored at runtime. The Solaris OS offers no guarantee that the page-size request will be honored. You can use pmap(1) or meminfo(2) to determine the page size of the target platform.

The -xpagesize option has no effect unless you use it at compile time and at link time. Note: This feature is not available on the Solaris 7 and Solaris 8 operating environments. A program compiled with this option will not link on the Solaris 7 and Solaris 8 operating environments.

If you specify -xpagesize=default, the Solaris OS sets the page size. -xpagesize without an argument is the equivalent to -xpagesize=default.

Compiling with this option has the same effect as setting the LD_PRELOAD environment variable to mpss.so.1 with the equivalent options, or running the Solaris 9 command ppgsz(1) with the equivalent options before running the program. See the Solaris 9 man pages for details.

This option is a macro for -xpagesize_heap and -xpagesize_stack. These two options accept the same arguments as -xpagesize: 8K, 64K, 512K, 4M, 32M, 256M, 2G, 16G, or default. You can set them both with the same value by specifying -xpagesize, or you can specify them individually with different values.

-xpagesize_heap = n.   (SPARC) Sets the page size in memory for the heap. n can be 8K, 64K, 512K, 4M, 32M, 256M, 2G, 16G, or default. You must specify a valid page size for the Solaris OS on the target platform, as returned by getpagesize(3C). If you do not specify a valid page size, the request is silently ignored at runtime.

You can use pmap(1) or meminfo(2) to determine page size at the target platform. If you specify -xpagesize_heap=default, the Solaris OS sets the page size. -xpagesize_heap without an argument is equivalent to -xpagesize_heap=default.

Compiling with this option has the same effect as setting the LD_PRELOAD environment variable to mpss.so.1 with the equivalent options, or running the Solaris 9 command ppgsz(1) with the equivalent options before running the program. See the Solaris 9 man pages for details.

Note: This feature is not available on the Solaris 7 and Solaris 8 operating environments. A program compiled with this option will not link on the Solaris 7 and Solaris 8 operating environments.

-xpagesize_stack = *n*.   (SPARC) Sets the page size in memory for the stack. *n* can be 8K, 64K, 512K, 4M, 32M, 256M, 2G, 16G, or default. You must specify a valid page size for the Solaris OS on the target platform, as returned by getpagesize(3C). If you do not specify a valid page size, the request is silently ignored at runtime. You can use pmap(1) or meminfo(2) to determine page size at the target platform.

If you specify -xpagesize_stack=default, the Solaris OS sets the page size. -xpagesize_stack without an argument is equivalent to -xpagesize_stack= default.

Compiling with this option has the same effect as setting the LD_PRELOAD environment variable to mpss.so.1 with the equivalent options, or running the Solaris 9 command ppgsz(1) with the equivalent options before running the program. See the Solaris 9 man pages for details.

Note: This feature is not available on the Solaris 7 and Solaris 8 operating environments. A program compiled with this option will not link on the Solaris 7 and Solaris 8 operating environments.

13.3.5 Interfaces to Request Larger Page Sizes

The memcntl(3C) interface has been enhanced to allow page-size requests to be made on behalf of a process. Thus, an application can automatically request larger page sizes when appropriate. Such an application wanting to request a larger page size should do so by using the existing memcntl() interface:

```
int memcntl(caddr_t addr, size_t len, int cmd, caddr_t arg,int attr, int mask);
```

With the cmd argument we can now specify a new control operation, MC_HAT_ ADVISE, for page-size operations. When the cmd argument is set to MC_HAT_ ADVISE, the caddr_t argument is interpreted as a pointer to a new structure, as shown below. Currently, only three commands are supported; each command sets a preferred page size. mha_flags must always be set to zero. It is reserved for future use. Only one command can be specified at a time.

```
struct memcntl mha{
        uint_t mha_cmd; /* command(s) */
        uint_t mha_flags; /* flags */
        size_t mha_pagesize;
};
```

If mha_cmd is set to MHA_MAPSIZE_VA, we apply the set preferred page-size operation to the address range (addr, addr + len). mha_pagesize must be a supported page size, as returned by getpagesizes(), or zero to let the system select the page size. The address and size of the range must be aligned to the new preferred page size. The access protections within new page-size regions contained in the range must be the same or the operation will fail. If there are holes in the address range or if the mapping is mapped with MAP_NORESERVE, the operation will fail. The address range can be contained inside a larger mapping or can span many mappings of varying sizes.

The memcntl() interface promotes or demotes the preferred page sizes for any MAP_PRIVATE /dev/zero mappings, provided that the constraints mentioned above are met. Two special objects in the user address space require special handling: the process's heap and the primary thread stack (not the stack for additional threads).

The heap consists of the last .bss adjacent to the brk area and the brk area itself. Figure 13.1 illustrates the mapping procedure.

For these two cases we have separate commands:

```
MHA_MAPSIZE_STACK   /* token for processes main stack */
MHA_MAPSIZE_BSSBRK /* token heap */
```

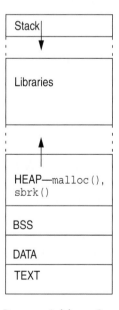

Figure 13.1 Process Address Space Mappings

When `MHA_MAPSIZE_STACK` and `MHA_MAPSIZE_BSSBRK` are used, `mha_pagesize` must be a supported page size, as returned by `getpagesizes(3C)`, or zero to let the system select the page size. The operation is then applied to the entire existing stack or heap mappings. The advice is then used for future page allocations. These commands for changing the preferred page size for stack or heap may first adjust the existing range in accordance with the new page size. This could involve creating new segments to pad out the base and length of the existing range to the new, preferred, page-size alignment.

Applications need to know what to align their memory requests on to attain maximum performance (e.g., when using `mmap()` for creating new mappings) and to avoid misaligned `mprotect()`, `munmap()`, and `mmap()` requests that could result in *page demotion* (when larger pages are broken up into smaller pages).

Most applications that use `mmap()` pass in NULL for its `addr` argument to let the OS manage its address space. If applications also want to use large pages with `memcntl()`, they should suggest to the OS that it specify, by means of a new flag, `MAP_ALIGN`, the minimum page-size alignment desired. If specified, `mmap()` interprets the `addr` argument only as the required minimum alignment and is free to find a hole in the user address space that satisfies the minimum alignment specified in the `addr` argument. The alignment must be a power of two multiple of `PAGESIZE`, or zero to let the system choose the alignment. If `MAP_ALIGN` is specified along with `MAP_FIXED`, the request will fail. If the alignment request cannot be satisfied, `mmap()` will also fail.

For reference, we provide the example below. This code fragment sets the page size for the program's heap to 4 Mbytes. Note the use of `memalign`, to align the request on a 4-Mbyte boundary. Since the heap starts on a boundary that is not 4-Mbyte-aligned, the first few megabytes of the heap may reside on 8-Kbyte pages. If the performance-sensitive data structures reside within this area, the program might not realize the full benefits of a larger page size. By allocating a 4-Mbyte aligned area, we increase the chance that the subsequent virtual addresses allocated will land on a large page.

```
#include <sys/types.h>
#include <sys/mman.h>
#include <stdlib.h>

#define MEGABYTE ((size_t)(1024 * 1024))
#define FOUR_MEGABYTE ((size_t)4 * MEGABYTE)

int
main(int argc, char *argv[])
{
        struct memcntl_mha mha;
        char *my_memory;
```

continues

```
/* Set pagesize to 4MB for heap */
mha.mha_cmd = MHA_MAPSIZE_BSSBRK;
mha.mha_flags = 0;
mha.mha_pagesize = FOUR_MEGABYTE;
memcntl(NULL, 0, MC_HAT_ADVISE, (char *)&mha, 0, 0);

/* Ensure user memory starts on first large page */
my_memory = (char *)memalign(FOUR_MEGABYTE, (size_t)100 * MEGABYTE);
```

13.3.6 CPU Specific Large Page Support

The TLB configurations are quite different across versions of UltraSPARC processors, but they share a few items in common. UltraSPARC I through IV support four page sizes: 8 Kbytes, 64 Kbytes, 512 Kbytes, and 4 Mbytes. In addition, there are separate TLBs for the instruction and data paths.

UltraSPARC I and II.   The UltraSPARC I and II microprocessors (143 MHz–480 MHz) have two TLBs, one for the instruction path and one for the data path. Each TLB is a 64-entry, fully associative TLB that supports all four page sizes. User applications can use any of the four page sizes.

750 MHz UltraSPARC III.   The 750 MHz UltraSPARC III microprocessor has four TLBs: two for instruction and two for data. The instruction TLBs are implemented as a 16-entry, fully associative TLB that supports all four page sizes and a larger 128-entry TLB that supports only 8-Kbyte entries. The data TLBs are implemented as a 16-entry, fully associative TLB that supports all four page sizes and a larger 512-entry, two-way set associative TLB that supports only 8-Kbyte entries.

The 16-entry DTLB has nine locked entries (locked by software for the Solaris kernel), leaving only seven slots for large page sizes. Thus, use of large pages is typically not beneficial on 750 MHz UltraSPARC III systems.

900 MHz+ UltraSPARC III.   The 900 MHz onwards UltraSPARC III microprocessors have five TLBs: two for instruction and three for data. The instruction TLBs are configured as a 16-entry, fully associative TLB that supports all four page sizes and a larger 128-entry TLB that supports only 8-Kbyte entries. The data TLBs are configured as a 16-entry, fully associative TLB that supports all four page sizes and two larger 512-entry, two-way set associative TLBs that support one page size per process. The increased size of the data TLBs on a 900 MHz UltraSPARC III provides a large TLB spread (2 Gbytes when 4-Mbyte pages are used) and typically increases performance significantly for large memory applications.

The large data TLBs are configured automatically in accordance with the most common page sizes in a process's address space. A process using one large page size in addition to the base page size (8 Kbytes) will have one of its large TLBs automatically programmed to enable the large page size when eight or more pages are using the larger page size within the process (it is assumed that the smaller TLB is available if there are fewer than eight pages).

Since the large TLBs support all four page sizes, large pages can be used effectively on UltraSPARC III. However, since the large TLBs can only be configured for one page size at a time per process, only two pages sizes should be used concurrently, where one of those pages sizes should be the system's base page size (8 Kbytes) for mappings not using large pages—for example. program text, libraries, etc,—leaving just one other larger page size available for the remainder of the mappings. The most common selections for page sizes are 8 Kbytes and 4 Mbytes, providing the greatest TLB spread for the large TLB.

x86.   The implementation of Solaris on x86 processors provides support for 4-Kbyte pages only.

AMD 64/x64.   The AMD Opteron processor supports both 4-Kbyte and 2-Mbyte page sizes.

PART FIVE

File Systems

14

File System Framework

From its inception, UNIX has been built around two fundamental entities: *processes* and *files*. In this chapter, we look at the implementation of files in Solaris and discuss the framework for file systems.

14.1 File System Framework

Solaris OS includes a framework, the *virtual file system framework*, under which multiple file system types are implemented. Earlier implementations of UNIX used a single file system type for all of the mounted file systems, typically, the UFS file system from BSD UNIX. The virtual file system framework was developed to allow Sun's distributed computing file system (NFS) to coexist with the UFS file system in SunOS 2.0; it became a standard part of System V in SVR4 and Solaris OS. We can categorize Solaris file systems into the following types:

- **Storage-based.** Regular file systems that provide facilities for persistent storage and management of data. The Solaris UFS and PC/DOS file systems are examples.

- **Network file systems.** File systems that provide files that are accessible in a local directory structure but are stored on a remote network server; for example, NFS.

- **Pseudo file systems.** File systems that present various abstractions as files in a file system. The /proc pseudo file system represents the address space of a process as a series of files.

657

The framework provides a single set of well-defined interfaces that are file system independent; the implementation details of each file system are hidden behind these interfaces. Two key objects represent these interfaces: the virtual file, or *vnode,* and the virtual file system, or *vfs* objects. The vnode interfaces implement file-related functions, and the vfs interfaces implement file system management functions. The vnode and vfs interfaces direct functions to specific file systems, depending on the type of file system being operated on. Figure 14.1 shows the file system layers. File-related functions are initiated through a system call or from another kernel subsystem and are directed to the appropriate file system by the vnode/vfs layer.

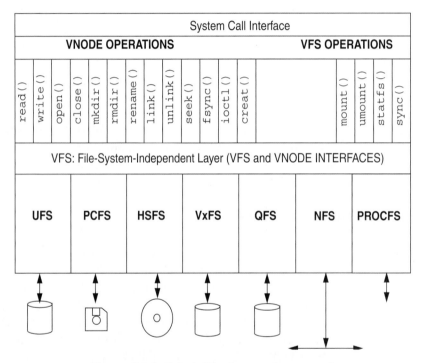

Figure 14.1 Solaris File System Framework

14.2 Process-Level File Abstractions

Within a process, a file is referenced through a *file descriptor.* An integer space of file descriptors per process is shared by multiple threads within each process. A file descriptor is a value in an integer space. It is assigned when a file is first opened and freed when a file is closed.

Each process has a list of active file descriptors, which are an index into a *per-process file table*. Each file table entry holds process-specific data including the current file's seek offset and has a reference to a systemwide virtual file node (vnode). The list of open file descriptors is kept inside a process's user area (struct user) in an `fi_list` array indexed by the file descriptor number. The `fi_list` is an array of `uf_entry_t` structures, each with its own lock and a pointer to the corresponding `file_t` file table entry.

Although multiple file table entries might reference the same file, there is a single vnode entry, as Figure 14.2 highlights. The `vnode` holds systemwide information about a file, including its type, size, and containing file system.

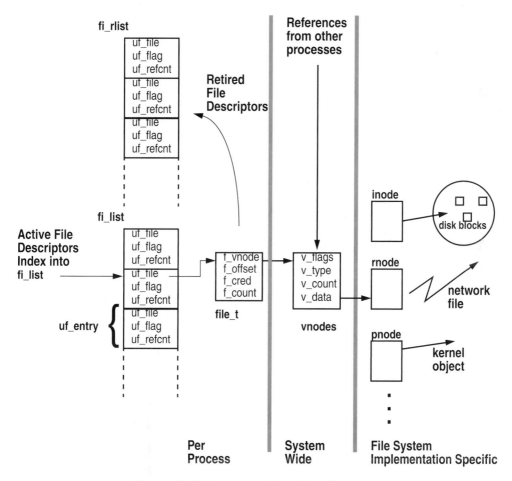

Figure 14.2 Structures Used for File Access

14.2.1 File Descriptors

A *file descriptor* is a non-negative integer that is returned from the system calls
open(), fcntl(), pipe(), or dup(). A process uses the file descriptor on other
system calls, such as read() and write(), that perform operations on open files.
Each file descriptor is represented by a uf_entry_t, shown below, and the file
descriptor is used as an index into an array of uf_entry_t entries.

```
/*
 * Entry in the per-process list of open files.
 * Note: only certain fields are copied in flist_grow() and flist_fork().
 * This is indicated in brackets in the structure member comments.
 */
typedef struct uf_entry {
        kmutex_t        uf_lock;        /* per-fd lock [never copied] */
        struct file     *uf_file;       /* file pointer [grow, fork] */
        struct fpollinfo *uf_fpollinfo; /* poll state [grow] */
        int             uf_refcnt;      /* LWPs accessing this file [grow] */
        int             uf_alloc;       /* right subtree allocs [grow, fork] */
        short           uf_flag;        /* fcntl F_GETFD flags [grow, fork] */
        short           uf_busy;        /* file is allocated [grow, fork] */
        kcondvar_t      uf_wanted_cv;   /* waiting for setf() [never copied] */
        kcondvar_t      uf_closing_cv;  /* waiting for close() [never copied] */
        struct portfd   *uf_portfd;     /* associated with port [grow] */
        /* Avoid false sharing - pad to coherency granularity (64 bytes) */
        char            uf_pad[64 - sizeof (kmutex_t) - 2 * sizeof (void*) -
                2 * sizeof (int) - 2 * sizeof (short) -
                2 * sizeof (kcondvar_t) - sizeof (struct portfd *)];
} uf_entry_t;
```
                                        See usr/src/uts/common/sys/user.h

The file descriptor list is anchored in the process's user area in the uf_info_t
structure pointed to by u_finfo.

```
typedef struct  user {
...
        uf_info_t       u_finfo;        /* open file information */
} user_t;

/*
 * Per-process file information.
 */
typedef struct uf_info {
        kmutex_t        fi_lock;        /* see below */
        kmutex_t        fi_pad;         /* unused -- remove in next release */
        int             fi_nfiles;      /* number of entries in fi_list[] */
        uf_entry_t *volatile fi_list;   /* current file list */
        uf_rlist_t      *fi_rlist;      /* retired file lists */
} uf_info_t;
```
                                        See usr/src/uts/common/sys/user.h

There are two lists of file descriptor entries in each process: an *active set* (fi_list) and a *retired set* (fi_rlist). The active set contains all the current file descriptor entries (open and closed), each of which points to a corresponding file_t file table entry. The retired set is used when the fi_list array is resized; as part of a lock-less find algorithm, once file_t entries are allocated, they are never unallocated, so pointers to file_t entries are always valid. In this manner, the algorithm need only lock the fi_list during resize, making the common case (find) fast and scalable.

14.2.2 The open Code Path

As an example, a common path through file descriptor and file allocation is through the open() system call. The open() system call returns a file descriptor to the process for a given path name. The open() system call is implemented by copen (common open), which first allocates a new file_t structure from the file_cache kernel allocator cache. The algorithm then looks for the next available file descriptor integer within the process's allocate fd integer space by using fd_find(), and reserves it. With an fd in hand, the lookup routine parses the "/"-separated components, calling the file-system-specific lookup function for each. After all path-name components are resolved, the vnode for the path is returned and linked into the file_t file table entry. The file-system-specific open function is called to increment the vnode reference count and do any other per-vnode open handling (typically very little else, since the majority of the open is done in lookup rather than the file systems' open() function. Once the file table handle is set up, it is linked into the process's file descriptor fi_list array and locked.

```
-> copen                    Common entry point from open(2)
  -> falloc                 Allocate a per-process file_t file table entry
    -> ufalloc_file         Allocate a file descriptor uf_entry
      -> fd_find            Find the next available fd integer
      <- fd_find
      -> fd_reserve         Reserve the fd integer
      <- fd_reserve
    <- ufalloc_file
  <- falloc
  -> fop_lookup             Look up the file name supplied in open()
    -> ufs_lookup           In this case, get UFS to do the hard work
      -> dnlc_lookup        Check in the DNLC
      <- dnlc_lookup
    <- ufs_lookup           Return a vnode to copen()
  <- fop_lookup
  -> fop_open               Call the file system specific open function
    -> ufs_open             Bump ref count in vnode, etc...
    <- ufs_open
  <- fop_open
  -> setf                   Lock the processes uf_entry for this file
  <- setf
<- copen                    All done
```

14.2.3 Allocating and Deallocating File Descriptors

One of the central functions is that of managing the file descriptor integer space. The fd_find(file_t *, int minfd) and fd_reserve() functions are the primary interface into the file descriptor integer space management code. The fd_find() function locates the next lowest available file descriptor number, starting with minfd, to support fcntl(fd, F_DUPFD, minfd). The fd_reserve() function either reserves or unreserves an entry by passing a 1 or –1 as an argument.

Beginning with Solaris 8, a significantly revised algorithm manages the integer space. The file descriptor integer space is a binary tree of per-process file entries (uf_entry) structures.

The algorithm is as follows. Keep all file descriptors in an infix binary tree in which each node records the number of descriptors allocated in its right subtree, including itself. Starting at minfd, ascend the tree until a non-fully allocated right subtree is found. Then descend that subtree in a binary search for the smallest fd. Finally, ascend the tree again to increment the allocation count of every subtree containing the newly allocated fd. Freeing an fd requires only the last step: Ascend the tree to decrement allocation counts. Each of these three steps (ascent to find non-full subtree, descent to find lowest fd, ascent to update allocation counts) is O(log n); thus the algorithm as a whole is O(log n).

We don't implement the fd tree by using the customary left/right/parent pointers, but instead take advantage of the glorious mathematics of full infix binary trees. For reference, here's an illustration of the logical structure of such a tree, rooted at 4 (binary 100), covering the range 1–7 (binary 001–111). Our canonical trees do not include fd 0; we deal with that later.

We make the following observations, all of which are easily proven by induction on the depth of the tree:

- **(T1).** The lowest-set bit (LSB) of any node is equal to its level in the tree. In our example, nodes 001, 011, 101, and 111 are at level 0; nodes 010 and 110 are at level 1; and node 100 is at level 2 (see Figure 14.3).

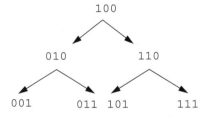

Figure 14.3 File Descriptor Integer Space as an *Infix* Binary Tree

- **(T2).** The child size (CSIZE) of node N—that is, the total number of right-branch descendants in a child of node N, including itself—is given by clearing all but the lowest-set bit of N. This follows immediately from (T1). Applying this rule to our example, we see that CSIZE(100) = 100, CSIZE(x10) = 10, and CSIZE(xx1) = 1.

- **(T3).** The nearest left ancestor (LPARENT) of node N—that is, the nearest ancestor containing node N in its right child—is given by clearing the LSB of N. For example, LPARENT(111) = 110 and LPARENT(110) = 100. Clearing the LSB of nodes 001, 010, or 100 yields zero, reflecting the fact that these are leftmost nodes. Note that this algorithm automatically skips generations as necessary. For example, the parent of node 101 is 110, which is a *right* ancestor (not what we want); but its grandparent is 100, which is a left ancestor. Clearing the LSB of 101 gets us to 100 directly, skipping right past the uninteresting generation (110).

  Note that since LPARENT clears the LSB, whereas CSIZE clears all *but* the LSB, we can express LPARENT() nicely in terms of CSIZE():

$$LPARENT(N) = N - CSIZE(N)$$

- **(T4).** The nearest right ancestor (RPARENT) of node N is given by

$$RPARENT(N) = N + CSIZE(N)$$

- **(T5).** For every interior node, the children differ from their parent by CSIZE(parent) / 2. In our example, CSIZE(100) / 2 = 2 = 10 binary, and indeed, the children of 100 are 100 ± 10 = 010 and 110.

Next, we need a few two's-complement math tricks. Suppose a number, N, has the following form:

$$N = xxxx10...0$$

That is, the binary representation of N consists of some string of bits, then a 1, then all 0's. This amounts to nothing more than saying that N has a lowest-set bit, which is true for any $N \neq 0$. If we look at N and $N - 1$ together, we see that we can combine them in useful ways:

$$N - 1 = xxxx01...1:$$

$$N \;\&\; (N - 1) = xxxx000000$$
$$N \mid (N - 1) = xxxx111111$$
$$N \;\hat{}\; (N - 1) = \;\;\;\; 111111$$

In particular, this suggests several easy ways to clear all but the LSB, which by (T2) is exactly what we need to determine CSIZE(N) = 10...0. We opt for this formulation:

$$(C1)\ CSIZE(N) = (N - 1) \wedge (N \mid (N - 1))$$

Similarly, we have an easy way to determine LPARENT(N), which requires that we clear the LSB of N:

$$(L1)\ LPARENT(N) = N\ \&\ (N - 1)$$

We note in the above relations that (N | (N – 1)) – N = CSIZE(N) – 1. When combined with (T4), this yields an easy way to compute RPARENT(N):

$$(R1)\ RPARENT(N) = (N \mid (N - 1)) + 1$$

Finally, to accommodate `fd` 0, we must adjust all of our results by ± 1 to move the `fd` range from [1, 2^n) to [0, 2^n – 1). This is straightforward, so there's no need to belabor the algebra; the revised relations become

$$(C1a)\ CSIZE(N) = N \wedge (N \mid (N + 1))$$
$$(L1a)\ LPARENT(N) = (N\ \&\ (N + 1)) - 1$$
$$(R1a)\ RPARENT(N) = N \mid (N + 1)$$

This completes the mathematical framework. We now have all the tools we need to implement `fd_find()` and `fd_reserve()`.

The `fd_find(fip, minfd)` function finds the smallest available file descriptor ≥ `minfd`. It does not actually allocate the descriptor; that's done by `fd_reserve()`. `fd_find()` proceeds in two steps:

1. Find the leftmost subtree that contains a descriptor ≥ `minfd`. We start at the right subtree rooted at `minfd`. If this subtree is not full—if `fip->fi_ list[minfd].uf_alloc != CSIZE(minfd)`—then step 1 is done. Otherwise, we know that all `fd`s in this subtree are taken, so we ascend to RPARENT(`minfd`) using (R1a). We repeat this process until we either find a candidate subtree or exceed `fip->fi_nfiles`. We use (C1a) to compute CSIZE().

2. Find the smallest `fd` in the subtree discovered by step 1. Starting at the root of this subtree, we descend to find the smallest available `fd`. Since the left children have the smaller `fd`s, we descend rightward only when the left child is full.

We begin by comparing the number of allocated `fd`s in the root to the number of allocated `fd`s in its right child; if they differ by exactly CSIZE(child), we know the left subtree is full, so we descend right; that is, the right child becomes the search root. Otherwise, we leave the root alone and start following the right child's left children. As fortune would have it, this is simple computationally: by (T5), the right child of fd is just fd + size, where size = CSIZE (fd) / 2. Applying (T5) again, we find that the right child's left child is fd + size – (size / 2) = fd + (size / 2); *its* left child is fd + (size / 2) – (size / 4) = fd + (size / 4), and so on. In general, fd's right child's leftmost nth descendant is fd + (size >> n). Thus, to follow the right child's left descendants, we just halve the size in each iteration of the search.

When we descend leftward, we must keep track of the number of fds that were allocated in all the right subtrees we rejected so that we know how many of the root fd's allocations are in the remaining (as yet unexplored) leftmost part of its right subtree. When we encounter a fully allocated left child—that is, when we find that fip->fi_list[fd].uf_alloc == ralloc + size—we descend right (as described earlier), resetting ralloc to zero.

The fd_reserve(fip, fd, incr) function either allocates or frees fd, depending on whether incr is 1 or –1. Starting at fd, fd_reserve() ascends the leftmost ancestors (see (T3)) and updates the allocation counts. At each step we use (L1a) to compute LPARENT(), the next left ancestor.

14.2.4 File Descriptor Limits

Each process has a hard and soft limit for the number of files it can have opened at any time; these limits are administered through the Resource Controls infrastructure by process.max-file-descriptor (see Section 7.5 for a description of Resource Controls). The limits are checked during falloc(). Limits can be viewed with the prctl command.

```
sol9$ prctl -n process.max-file-descriptor $$
process: 21471: -ksh
NAME       PRIVILEGE       VALUE    FLAG   ACTION              RECIPIENT
process.max-file-descriptor
           basic           256       -     deny                  21471
           privileged      65.5K     -     deny                    -
           system          2.15G    max    deny                    -
```

If no resource controls are set for the process, then the defaults are taken from system tuneables; rlim_fd_max is the hard limit, and rlim_fd_cur is the current limit (or soft limit). You can set these parameters systemwide by placing entries in the /etc/system file.

```
set rlim_fd_max=8192
set rlim_fd_cur=1024
```

14.2.5 File Structures

A kernel object cache segment is allocated to hold file structures, and they are simply allocated and linked to the process and vnode as files are created and opened.

We can see in Figure 14.2 that each process uses file descriptors to reference a file. The file descriptors ultimately link to the kernel file structure, defined as a file_t data type, shown below.

```
/*
 * fio locking:
 *    f_rwlock    protects f_vnode and f_cred
 *    f_tlock     protects the rest
 *
 *    The purpose of locking in this layer is to keep the kernel
 *    from panicking if, for example, a thread calls close() while
 *    another thread is doing a read().  It is up to higher levels
 *    to make sure 2 threads doing I/O to the same file don't
 *    screw each other up.
 */
/*
 * One file structure is allocated for each open/creat/pipe call.
 * Main use is to hold the read/write pointer associated with
 * each open file.
 */
typedef struct file {
        kmutex_t        f_tlock;        /* short term lock */
        ushort_t        f_flag;
        ushort_t        f_pad;          /* Explicit pad to 4 byte boundary */
        struct vnode    *f_vnode;       /* pointer to vnode structure */
        offset_t        f_offset;       /* read/write character pointer */
        struct cred     *f_cred;        /* credentials of user who opened it */
        struct f_audit_data     *f_audit_data;  /* file audit data */
        int             f_count;        /* reference count */
} file_t;
```
                                              See usr/src/uts/common/sys/file.h

The fields maintained in the file structure are, for the most part, self-explanatory. The f_tlock kernel mutex lock protects the various structure members. These include the f_count reference count, which lists how many file descriptors reference this structure, and the f_flag file flags.

Since files are allocated from a systemwide kernel allocator cache, you can use MDB's ::kmastat dcmd to look at how many files are opened systemwide. The sar command also shows the same information in its file-sz column.

This example shows 1049 opened files. The format of the sar output is a holdover from the early days of static tables, which is why it is displayed as 1049/1049. Originally, the value on the left represented the current number of occupied table slots, and the value on the right represented the maximum number of slots. Since file structure allocation is completely dynamic in nature, both values will always be the same.

```
sol8# mdb -k
> ::kmastat !grep file
cache                         buf    buf    buf    memory     alloc alloc
name                          size in use total   in use     succeed fail
--------------------------    ------ ------ ------ ---------- --------- -----
file_cache                    56     1049   1368   77824      9794701   0

# sar -v 3 333

SunOS ozone 5.10 Generic i86pc     07/13/2005

17:46:49  proc-sz     ov  inod-sz     ov  file-sz     ov  lock-sz
17:46:52  131/16362    0  8884/70554   0  1049/1049    0  0/0
17:46:55  131/16362    0  8884/70554   0  1049/1049    0  0/0
```

We can use MDB's ::pfiles dcmd to explore the linkage between a process and file table entries.

```
sol8# mdb -k
> 0t1119::pid2proc
ffffffff83135890
> ffffffff83135890::pfiles -fp
         FILE FD    FLAG            VNODE   OFFSET            CRED  CNT
ffffffff85ced5e8  0     1 ffffffff857c8580       0 ffffffff83838a40    1
ffffffff85582120  1     2 ffffffff857c8580       0 ffffffff83838a40    2
ffffffff85582120  2     2 ffffffff857c8580       0 ffffffff83838a40    2
ffffffff8362be00  3  2001 ffffffff836d1680       0 ffffffff83838c08    1
ffffffff830d3b28  4     2 ffffffff837822c0       0 ffffffff83838a40    1
ffffffff834aacf0  5     2 ffffffff83875a80      33 ffffffff83838a40    1
> ffffffff8362be00::print file_t
{
    f_tlock = {
        _opaque = [ 0 ]
    }
    f_flag = 0x2001
    f_pad = 0xbadd
    f_vnode = 0xffffffff836d1680
    f_offset = 0
    f_cred = 0xffffffff83838c08
    f_audit_data = 0
    f_count = 0x1
}
> 0xffffffff836d1680::vnode2path
/zones/gallery/root/var/run/name_service_door
```

For a specific process, we use the pfiles(1) command to create a list of all the files opened.

```
sol8$ pfiles 1119
1119:   /usr/lib/sendmail -Ac -q15m
  Current rlimit: 1024 file descriptors
   0: S_IFCHR mode:0666 dev:281,2 ino:16484 uid:0 gid:3 rdev:13,2
      O_RDONLY
      /zones/gallery/root/dev/null
```

continues

```
1: S_IFCHR mode:0666 dev:281,2 ino:16484 uid:0 gid:3 rdev:13,2
   O_WRONLY
   /zones/gallery/root/dev/null
2: S_IFCHR mode:0666 dev:281,2 ino:16484 uid:0 gid:3 rdev:13,2
   O_WRONLY
   /zones/gallery/root/dev/null
3: S_IFDOOR mode:0444 dev:279,0 ino:34 uid:0 gid:0 size:0
   O_RDONLY|O_LARGEFILE FD_CLOEXEC  door to nscd[762]
   /zones/gallery/root/var/run/name_service_door
4: S_IFCHR mode:0666 dev:281,2 ino:16486 uid:0 gid:3 rdev:21,0
   O_WRONLY FD_CLOEXEC
   /zones/gallery/root/dev/conslog
5: S_IFREG mode:0600 dev:102,198 ino:11239 uid:25 gid:25 size:33
   O_WRONLY
   /zones/gallery/root/var/spool/clientmqueue/sm-client.pid
```

In the preceding examples, the `pfiles` command is executed on PID 1119. The PID and process name are dumped, followed by a listing of the process's opened files. For each file, we see a listing of the file descriptor (the number to the left of the colon), the file type, file mode bits, the device from which the file originated, the inode number, file UID and GID, and the file size.

14.3 Solaris File System Framework

The `vnode/vfs` interfaces—the "top end" of the file system module—implement vnode and vfs objects. The "bottom end" of the file system uses other kernel interfaces to access, store, and cache the data they represent. Disk-based file systems interface to device drivers to provide persistent storage of their data. Network file systems access remote storage by using the networking subsystem to transmit and receive data. Pseudo file systems typically access local kernel functions and structures to gather the information they represent.

- **Loadable file system modules.** A dynamically loadable module type is provided for Solaris file systems. File system modules are dynamically loaded at the time each file system type is first mounted (except for the root file system, which is mounted explicitly at boot).
- **The vnode interface.** As discussed, this is a unified file-system-independent interface between the operating system and a file system implementation.
- **File system caching.** File systems that implement caching interface with the virtual memory system to map, unmap, and manage the memory used for caching. File systems use physical memory pages and the virtual memory system to cache files. The kernel's `seg_map` driver maps file system cache

into the kernel's address space when accessing the file system through the read() and write() system calls. (See Section 14.8.1.)

- **Path-name management.** Files are accessed by means of path names, which are assembled as a series of directory names and file names. The file system framework provides routines that resolve and manipulate path names by calling into the file system's lookup() function to convert paths into vnode pointers.

- **Directory name caching.** A central directory name lookup cache (DNLC) provides a mechanism to cache pathname-to-vnode mappings, so that the directory components need not be read from disk each time they are needed.

14.3.1 Evolution of the File System Framework

Solaris 10 introduces a new file system interface that significantly improves the portability of file systems. In prior releases of Solaris OS, the vnode and vfs structures were entirely visible to their consumers. A file system client would reference, manipulate, or update raw vfs and vnode structure members directly, which meant that file systems had operating system revision-specific assumptions compiled into them. Whenever the vfs or vnode structures changed in the Solaris kernel, file systems would need to be recompiled to match the changes. The new interface allows the vnode structures to change in many ways without breaking file system compatibility.

The new model replaces the old file system VOP macros with a new set of functions. The goals of the new interface are as follows:

- It separates the vnode from FS-dependent node so that changes in the vnode structure that affect its size do not affect the size of other data structures.

- It provides interfaces to access nonpublic vnode structure members.

- It delivers a flexible operation registration mechanism that provides appropriate defaults for unspecified operations and allows the developer to specify a corresponding default or error routine.

- It delivers a flexible mechanism to invoke vnode/vfs operations without requiring the client module to have knowledge of how the operations are stored.

- It provides a facility for creation, initialization, and destruction of vnodes.

- It provides accessor functions for file systems that require information on the following characteristics of a vnode: existence of locks, existence of cached data, read-only attribute.

The following major changes have been made to the file system interface as part of this project:

- The following related vnode fields are now private: v_filocks, v_shrlocks, v_nbllock, v_pages and v_cv.

- Support routines allow a vnode/vfs client to set a vnode's or vfs's operations, retrieve the operations, compare the operations vector to a given value, compare a specific operation in the operations vector to a given value. The related vnode field v_op and the related vfs field vfs_op should not be directly accessed by file systems.

- An accessor routine returns a pointer to the vfs, if any, which may be mounted on a given vnode. Another routine determines whether a given vnode is mounted on. The related vnode field v_vfsmountedhere is now private.

- An operation registration mechanism can fill in default operation values (if appropriate) for operations that are not explicitly specified by the file system.

- The operation registration mechanism enables developers to add new operations to a new (updated) version of Solaris OS without requiring existing file systems to support those new operations, provided that the new operations have system-defined defaults.

- The file system module loading mechanism is updated to enable these changes.

- Vnodes are no longer embedded in file system data structures (for example, inodes).

- The following functions have been added to support the separation of the vnode from the FS-dependent node: vn_alloc(), vn_free(), and vn_reinit().

- Certain fields in the vnode have been made "private" to satisfy the requirements of other projects. Also, the fields in the vnode have been rearranged to put the "public" structure members at the top and the private members at the bottom.

- File systems now register their vnode and vfs operations by providing an operation definition table that specifies operations by using name/value pairs.

- The VOP and VFSOP macros no longer directly dereference the vnode and vfs structures and their operations tables. They each call corresponding functions that perform that task.

- File system module loading no longer takes a vfs switch entry. Instead, it takes a vfsdef structure that is similar. The difference is that the vfsdef structure includes a version number but does not include a vfsops table.

The following accessor functions have been added to provide information about the state and characteristics of a vnode.

- **vn_is_readonly()**. Returns non-zero if the vnode is on a read-only file system.
- **vn_has_flocks()**. Returns non-zero if the vnode has active file locks.
- **vn_has_mandatory_locks()**. Returns non-zero if the vnode has mandatory locks.
- **vn_has_cached_data()**. Returns non-zero if the vnode has pages in the page cache.
- **vn_mountedvfs()**. Returns the vfs mounted on this vnode, if any.
- **vn_ismntpt()**. Returns true (non-zero) if this vnode is mounted on, zero otherwise.

New interfaces have been developed to register vnode and vfs operations.

- **vn_make_ops()**. Creates and builds the private vnodeops table.
- **vn_freevnodeops()**. Frees a vnodeops structure created by vn_make_ops().
- **vfs_setfsops()**. Builds a vfsops table and associates it with a vfs switch table entry.
- **vfs_freevfsops_by_type()**. Frees a vfsops structure created by vfs_makefsops().
- **vfs_makefsops()**. Creates and builds (dummy) vfsops structures.
- **vfs_freevfsops()**. Frees a vfsops structure created by vfs_makefsops().

The following support routines have been developed to set and provide information about the vnode's operations vector.

- **vn_setops()**. Sets the operations vector for this vnode.
- **vn_getops()**. Retrieves the operations vector for this vnode.
- **vn_matchops()**. Determines if the supplied operations vector matches the vnode's operations vector. Note that this is a "shallow" match. The pointer to the operations vector is compared, not each individual operation.
- **vn_matchopval()**. Determines if the supplied function exists for a particular operation in the vnode's operations vector.

The following support routines have been developed to set and provide information about the `vfs`'s operations vector.

- **vfs_setops().** Sets the operations vector for this `vfs`.
- **vfs_getops().** Retrieves the operations vector for this `vfs`.
- **vfs_matchops().** Determines if the supplied operations vector matches the `vfs`'s operations vector. Note that this is a "shallow" match. The pointer to the operations vector is compared, not each individual operation.
- **vfs_can_sync().** Determines if a `vfs` has an FS-supplied (nondefault, non-error) sync routine.

14.3.2 The Solaris File System Interface

The file system interface can be categorized into three major parts:

- A single systemwide, file system module-specific declaration
- A per-file system mount instance declaration
- A set of per-file operations with each file system mount instance

14.4 File System Modules

A file system is implemented as a dynamically loadable kernel module. Each file system declares the standard module _init, _info, and _fini entry points, which are used to install and remove the file system within the running kernel instance.

The primary descriptive entry for each file system is provided by a static declaration of a `vfsdef_t`, which includes the following:

- The version of the `vfs` interface used at module compile time (by specification of VFSDEF_VERSION).
- The name of the file system (a string).
- The global initialization function to be called when the file system module is loaded. Although a file system module is typically loaded on the first mount, a module can be loaded modload(1M) without mounting a file system.
- A set of options that can be set at mount time.

```
static mntopt_t tmpfs_options[] = {
        /* Option name           Cancel Opt      Arg       Flags           Data */
        { MNTOPT_XATTR,          xattr_cancel,   NULL,     MO_DEFAULT,     NULL},
        { MNTOPT_NOXATTR,        noxattr_cancel, NULL,     NULL,           NULL},
        { "size",                NULL,           "0",      MO_HASVALUE,    NULL}
};

static mntopts_t tmpfs_proto_opttbl = {
        sizeof (tmpfs_options) / sizeof (mntopt_t),
        tmpfs_options
};

static vfsdef_t vfw = {
        VFSDEF_VERSION,
        "tmpfs",
        tmpfsinit,
        VSW_HASPROTO,
        &tmpfs_proto_opttbl
};
```
                                              See usr/src/uts/common/fs/tmpfs/tmp_vfsops.c

14.4.1 Interfaces for Mount Options

The options template is used to accept and validate options at mount time. A standard set is defined in sys/vfs.h, but you can add your own by simply supplying a string (as tmpfs does for size).

The mntopts_t struct (usually called the mount options table) consists of a count of the number of options and an array of options structures of length count. Each file system should define a prototype mount options table that will be used by the vfs_initopttbl() function to initialize the working mount options table for each mount instance. The text below describes the initialization of the prototype mount options table. The vfs_initopttbl() function should be used to initialize working mount options tables from the prototype mount options table.

```
typedef struct mntopts {
        int             mo_count;       /* number of entries in table */
        mntopt_t        *mo_list;       /* list of mount options */
} mntopts_t;
```
                                              See usr/src/uts/common/sys/vfs.h

Each mount option contains fields to drive the parser and fields to accept the results of the parser's execution. Here is the structure that defines an individual option in the mount options table.

```
typedef struct mntopt {
        char    *mo_name;       /* option name */
        char    **mo_cancel;    /* list of options cancelled by this one */
        char    *mo_arg;        /* argument string for this option */
        int     mo_flags;       /* flags for this mount option */
        void    *mo_data;       /* file system specific data */
} mntopt_t;
```
                                              See usr/src/uts/common/sys/vfs.h

Each option must have a string that gives the name of the option. Additionally, if an option is one that invalidates other options, the `mo_cancel` field points to a NULL-terminated list of names of options to turn off if this option is recognized. If an option accepts an argument (that is, it is of the form `opt=arg`), then the `mo_arg` field should be initialized with the string that is the default for the argument (if it has a default value; otherwise NULL). During option parsing, the parser will then replace the string in the working mount options table with the string provided by the user if the option is recognized during option parsing. The following flags are recognized by or set by the parser during option parsing.

- **MO_NODISPLAY.** Option will not be listed in mounted file system table.
- **MO_HASVALUE.** Option is expected to have an argument (that is, of form `opt = arg`)
- **MO_IGNORE.** Option is ignored by the parser and will not be set even if seen in the options string. (Can be set manually with `vfs_setmntopt` function.)
- **MO_DEFAULT.** Option is set on by default and will show in `mnttab` even if not seen by parser in options string.

The `mo_data` field is for use by a file system to hold any option-specific data it may wish to make use of.

14.4.2 Module Initialization

A standard file system module will provide a module `_init` function and register an initialization function to be called back by the file system module-loader facility. The following example shows the initialization linkage between the module declaration and the file-system-specific initialization function.

```
static vfsdef_t vfw = {
        VFSDEF_VERSION,
        "tmpfs",
        tmpfsinit,
        VSW_HASPROTO,
        &tmpfs_proto_opttbl
};

/*
 * Module linkage information
 */
```

continues

```
static struct modlfs modlfs = {
        &mod_fsops, "filesystem for tmpfs", &vfw
};

static struct modlinkage modlinkage = {
        MODREV_1, &modlfs, NULL
};

int
_init()
{
        return (mod_install(&modlinkage));
}

/*
 * initialize global tmpfs locks and such
 * called when loading tmpfs module
 */
static int
tmpfsinit(int fstype, char *name)
{
...
}
```
                                    See usr/src/uts/common/fs/tmpfs/tmp_vfsops.c

The module is automatically loaded by the first invocation of mount(2) (typically from a mount command). Upon module load, the _init() function of the file system is called; this function completes its self-install with mod_install(), which subsequently calls the file system init function (tmpfsinit() in this example) defined in the vfsdef_t.

Note that file systems no longer need to create and install a vfs switch entry; this is done automatically by the module loading using the information supplied in the vfsdef_t.

14.5 The Virtual File System (vfs) Interface

The vfs layer provides an administrative interface into the file system to support commands like mount and umount in a file-system-independent manner. The interface achieves independence by means of a virtual file system (vfs) object. The vfs object represents an encapsulation of a file system's state and a set of methods for each of the file system administrative interfaces. Each file system type provides its own implementation of the object. Figure 14.4 illustrates the vfs object. A set of support functions provides access to the contents of the vfs structure; file systems should not directly modify the vfs object contents.

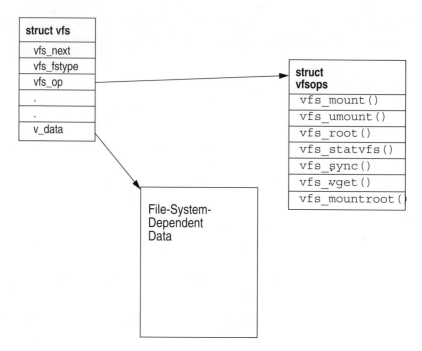

Figure 14.4 The vfs Object

14.5.1 `vfs` Methods

The methods within the file system implement operations on behalf of the common operating system code. For example, given a pointer to a `tmpfs`'s `vfs` object, the generic `VFS_MOUNT()` call will invoke the appropriate function in the underlying file system by calling the `tmpfs_mount()` method defined within that instance of the object.

```
#define VFS_MOUNT(vfsp, mvp, uap, cr) fsop_mount(vfsp, mvp, uap, cr)

int
fsop_mount(vfs_t *vfsp, vnode_t *mvp, struct mounta *uap, cred_t *cr)
{
        return (*(vfsp)->vfs_op->vfs_mount)(vfsp, mvp, uap, cr);
}
```

See usr/src/uts/common/sys/vfs.h

A file system declares its `vfs` methods through a call to `vfs_setfsops()`. A template provides allows a selection of methods to be defined, according to Table 14.1.

Table 14.1 Solaris 10 `vfs` Interface Methods from `sys/vfs.h`

Method	Description
VFS_MOUNT	Mounts a file system on the supplied `vnode`. The file-system-dependent part of mount includes these actions. • Determine if mount device is appropriate. • Prepare mount device (e.g., flush pages/blocks). • Read file-system-dependent data from mount device. • Sanity-check file-system-dependent data. • Create/initialize file-system-dependent kernel data structures. • Reconcile any transaction devices.
VFS_UNMOUNT	Unmounts the file system. The file-system-dependent part of unmount includes these actions. • Lock out new transactions and complete current transactions. • Flush data to mount device. • Close down any helper threads. • Tear down file-system-dependent kernel data structures.
VFS_ROOT	Finds the root `vnode` for a file system.
VFS_STATVFS	Queries statistics on a file system.
VFS_SYNC	Flushes the file system cache.
VFS_VGET	Finds a `vnode` that matches a unique file ID.
VFS_MOUNTROOT	Mounts the file system on the root directory.
VFS_FREEVFS	Calls back to free resources after last unmount. NFS appears to be the only one that needs this. All others default to `fs_freevfs()`, which is a no-op.
VFS_VNSTATE	Interface for `vnode` life cycle reporting.

A regular file system will define `mount`, `unmount`, `root`, `statvfs`, and `vget` methods. The `vfs` methods are defined in an `fs_operation_def_t` template, terminated by a NULL entry. The template is constructed from an array of `fs_operation_def_t` structures. The following example from the `tmpfs` implementation shows how the template is initialized and then instantiated with `vfs_setfsops()`. The call to `vfs_setfsops()` is typically done once per module initialization, systemwide.

```
static int
tmpfsinit(int fstype, char *name)
{
        static const fs_operation_def_t tmp_vfsops_template[] = {
                VFSNAME_MOUNT, tmp_mount,
                VFSNAME_UNMOUNT, tmp_unmount,
                VFSNAME_ROOT, tmp_root,
                VFSNAME_STATVFS, tmp_statvfs,
                VFSNAME_VGET, tmp_vget,
                NULL, NULL
        };
        int error;

        error = vfs_setfsops(fstype, tmp_vfsops_template, NULL);
...
}
```
                                        See usr/src/uts/common/fs/tmpfs/tmp_vfsops.c

A corresponding free of the `vfs` methods is required at module unload time and is typically located in the `_fini()` function of the module.

```
int
_fini()
{
        int error;

        error = mod_remove(&modlinkage);
        if (error)
                return (error);
        /*
         * Tear down the operations vectors
         */
        (void) vfs_freevfsops_by_type(tmpfsfstype);
        vn_freevnodeops(tmp_vnodeops);
        return (0);
}
```
                                        See usr/src/uts/common/fs/tmpfs/tmp_vfsops.c

The following routines are available in the `vfs` layer to manipulate the `vfs` object. They provide support for creating and modifying the FS methods (fsops),

```
/*
 * File systems use arrays of fs_operation_def structures to form
 * name/value pairs of operations.  These arrays get passed to:
 *
 *      - vn_make_ops() to create vnodeops
 *      - vfs_makefsops()/vfs_setfsops() to create vfsops.
 */
typedef struct fs_operation_def {
        char *name;                     /* name of operation (NULL at end) */
        fs_generic_func_p func;         /* function implementing operation */
} fs_operation_def_t;

int vfs_makefsops(const fs_operation_def_t *template, vfsops_t **actual);

Creates and builds (dummy) vfsops structures
```

continues

```
void vfs_setops(vfs_t *vfsp, vfsops_t *vfsops);
```

Sets the operations vector for this vfs

```
vfsops_t * vfs_getops(vfs_t *vfsp);
```

Retrieves the operations vector for this vfs

```
void vfs_freevfsops(vfsops_t *vfsops);
```

Frees a vfsops structure created by vfs_makefsops()

```
int vfs_freevfsops_by_type(int fstype);
```

For a vfsops structure created by vfs_setfsops(), use vfs_freevfsops_by_type()

```
int vfs_matchops(vfs_t *vfsp, vfsops_t *vfsops);
```

Determines if the supplied operations vector matches the vfs's operations vector. Note that this is a "shallow" match. The pointer to the operations vector is compared, not each individual operation.

See usr/src/uts/common/sys/vfs.h

14.5.2 vfs Support Functions

The following support functions are available for parsing option strings and filling in the necessary vfs structure fields. The file systems also need to parse the option strings to learn what options should be used in completing the mount request. The routines and data structures are all defined in the vfs.h header file.

It is expected that all the fields used by the file-system-specific mount code in the vfs structure are normally filled in and interrogated only during a mount system call. At mount time the vfs structure is private and not available to any other parts of the kernel. So during this time, locking of the fields used in mnttab/options is not necessary. If a file system wants to update or interrogate options at some later time, then it should be locked by the vfs_lock_wait()/vfs_unlock() functions. All memory allocated by the following routines is freed at umount time, so callers need not worry about memory leakage. Any arguments whose values are preserved in a structure after a call have been copied, so callers need not worry about retained references to any function arguments.

```
struct mntopts_t *vfs_opttblptr(struct vfs *vfsp);
```

Returns a pointer to the mount options table for the given vfs structure.

```
void vfs_initopttbl(const mntopts_t *proto, mntopts_t *tbl);
```

Initializes a mount options table from the prototype mount options table pointed to by the first argument. A file system should always initialize the mount options table in the vfs structure for the current mount but may use this routine to initialize other tables if desired. See the documentation below on how to construct a prototype mount options table. Note that the vfs_opttblptr() function described above should be used to access the vfs structures mount options table.

continues

void vfs_parsemntopts(mntopts_t *tbl, char *optionstr);

Parses the option string pointed to by the second argument, using the mount options table pointed to by the first argument. Any recognized options will be marked by this function as set in the pointed-to options table and any arguments found are recorded there as well. Normally file systems would call this with a pointer to the mount options table in the vfs structure for the mount currently being processed. The mount options table may be examined after the parse is completed, to see which options have been recognized, by using the vfs_optionisset() function documented below. Note that the parser will alter the option string during parsing, but will restore it before returning. Any options in the option string being parsed that are not recognized are silently ignored. Also if an option requires an arg but it is not supplied, the argument pointer is silently set to NULL. Since options are parsed from left to right, the last specification for any particular option in the option string is the one used. Similarly, if options that toggle each other on or off (i.e. are mutually exclusive), are in the same options string, the last one seen in left to right parsing determines the state of the affected option(s).

void vfs_clearmntopt(mntopts_t *tbl, const char *opt);

Clears the option whose name is passed in the second argument from the option table pointed to by the first argument, i.e., marks the option as not set and frees any argument that may be associated with the option. Used by file systems to unset options if so desired in a mount options table. Note that the only way to return options to their default state is to reinitialize the options table with vfs_initopttbl().

void vfs_setmntopt(mntopts_t *tbl, const char *opt, const char *arg, int flags);

Marks the option whose name is given by the second argument as set in the mount options table pointed to by the first argument. If the option takes an argument, the third parameter points to the string for the argument. The flags arg is provided to affect the behavior of the vfs_setmntopt function. It can cause it to override the MO_IGNORE flag if the particular option being set has this flag enabled. It can also be used to request toggling the MO_NODISPLAY bit for the option on or off. (see the documentation for mount option tables). Used by file systems to manually mark options as set in a mount options table. Possible flags to vfs_setmntopt:
VFS_DISPLAY 0x02 /* Turn off MO_NODISPLAY bit for option */
VFS_NODISPLAY 0x04 /* Turn on MO_NODISPLAY bit for option */

int vfs_optionisset(mntopts_t *tbl, const char *opt, char **argp);

Inquires if the option named by the second argument is marked as set in the mount options table pointed to by the first argument. Returns non-zero if the option was set. If the option has an argument string, the arg pointed to by the argp pointer is filled in with a pointer to the argument string for the option. The pointer is to the saved argument string and not to a copy. Users should not directly alter the pointed to string. If any change is desired to the argument string the caller should use the set/clearmntopt() functions.

int vfs_buildoptionstr(mntopts_t *tbl, char *buf, int len);

Builds a comma-separated, null-terminated string of the mount options that are set in the table passed in the first argument. The buffer passed in the second argument is filled in with the generated options string. If the length passed in the third argument would be exceeded, the function returns EOVERFLOW; otherwise, it returns zero on success. If an error is returned, the contents of the result buffer are undefined.

int vfs_setoptprivate(mntopts_t *tbl, const char *opt, void *arg);

Sets the private data field of the given option in the specified option table to the provided value. Returns zero on success, non-zero if the named option does not exist in the table. Note that option private data is not managed for the user. If the private data field is a pointer to allocated memory, then it should be freed by the file system code prior to returning from a umount call.

continues

```
int vfs_getoptprivate(mntopts_t *tbl, const char *opt, void **argp);
```

Fills in the pointer pointed to by the argp pointer with the value of the private data field of the given option in the specified table. Returns zero on success, non-zero if the named option does not exist in the table.

```
void vfs_setmntpoint(struct vfs *vfsp, char *mp);
```

Sets the vfs_mntpt field of the vfs structure to the given mount point. File systems call this if they want some value there other than what was passed by the mount system call.

```
int vfs_can_sync(vfs_t *vfsp);
```

Determines if a vfs has an FS-supplied (non default, non error) sync routine.

```
void vfs_setresource(struct vfs *vfsp, char *resource);
```

Sets the vfs_resource field of the vfs structure to the given resource. File systems call this if they want some value there other than what was passed by the mount system call.

See usr/src/uts/common/sys/vfs.h

14.5.3 The `mount` Method

The `mount` method is responsible for initializing a per-mount instance of a file system. It is typically invoked as a result of a user-initiated `mount` command.

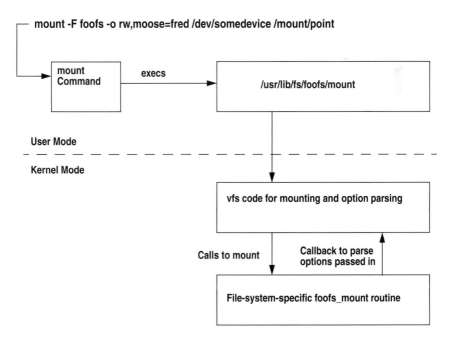

Figure 14.5 Mount Invocation

The tasks completed in the `mount` method will often include

- A security check, to ensure that the user has sufficient privileges to perform the requested mount. This is best done with a call to `secpolicy_fs_mount()`, with the Solaris Least Privilege framework.

- A check to see if the specified mount point is a directory.

- Initialization and allocation of per-file system mount structures and locks.

- Parsing of the options supplied into the mount call, with the assistance of the `vfs_option_*` support functions.

- Manufacture of a unique file system ID, with the help of `vfs_make_fsid()`. This is required to support NFS mount instances over the wire protocol using unique file system IDs.

- Creation or reading of the root inode for the file system.

An excerpt from the `tmpfs` implementation shows an example of the main functions within a file system mount method.

```
static int
tmp_mount(
        struct vfs *vfsp,
        struct vnode *mvp,
        struct mounta *uap,
        struct cred *cr)
{
        struct tmount *tm = NULL;
...

        if ((error = secpolicy_fs_mount(cr, mvp, vfsp)) != 0)
                return (error);

        if (mvp->v_type != VDIR)
                return (ENOTDIR);

        /* tmpfs doesn't support read-only mounts */
        if (vfs_optionisset(vfsp, MNTOPT_RO, NULL)) {
                error = EINVAL;
                goto out;
        }
...

        if (error = pn_get(uap->dir,
            (uap->flags & MS_SYSSPACE) ? UIO_SYSSPACE : UIO_USERSPACE, &dpn))
                goto out;

        if ((tm = tmp_memalloc(sizeof (struct tmount), 0)) == NULL) {
                pn_free(&dpn);
                error = ENOMEM;
                goto out;
        }
```

continues

```
...
        vfsp->vfs_data = (caddr_t)tm;
        vfsp->vfs_fstype = tmpfsfstype;
        vfsp->vfs_dev = tm->tm_dev;
        vfsp->vfs_bsize = PAGESIZE;
        vfsp->vfs_flag |= VFS_NOTRUNC;
        vfs_make_fsid(&vfsp->vfs_fsid, tm->tm_dev, tmpfsfstype);
...
        tm->tm_dev = makedevice(tmpfs_major, tmpfs_minor);
...
```

See usr/src/uts/common/fs/tmpfs/tmp_vfsops.c

14.5.4 The umount Method

The umount method is almost the reverse of mount. The tasks completed in the umount method will often include

- A security check, to ensure that the user has sufficient privileges to perform the requested mount. This is best done with a call to secpolicy_fs_mount(), with the Solaris Least Privilege framework.

- A check to see if the mount is a forced mount (to take special action, or reject the request if the file system doesn't support forcible unmounts and the reference count on the root node is >1).

- Freeing of per-file system mount structures and locks.

14.5.5 Root vnode Identification

The root method of the file system is a simple function used by the file system lookup functions when traversing across a mount point into a new file system. It simply returns a pointer to the root vnode in the supplied vnode pointer argument.

```
static int
tmp_root(struct vfs *vfsp, struct vnode **vpp)
{
        struct tmount *tm = (struct tmount *)VFSTOTM(vfsp);
        struct tmpnode *tp = tm->tm_rootnode;
        struct vnode *vp;

        ASSERT(tp);

        vp = TNTOV(tp);
        VN_HOLD(vp);
        *vpp = vp;
        return (0);
}
```

See usr/src/uts/common/fs/tmpfs/tmp_vfsops.c

14.5.6 `vfs` Information Available with `MDB`

The mounted list of `vfs` objects is linked as shown in Figure 14.6.

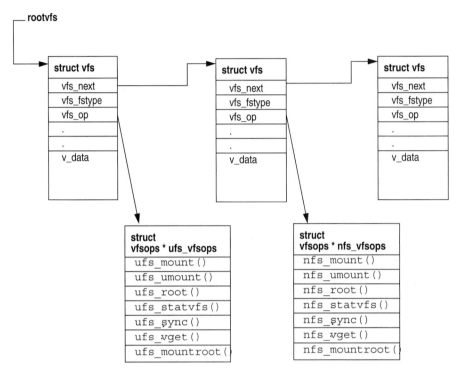

Figure 14.6 The Mounted `vfs` List

You can traverse the list with an `mdb` walker. Below is the output of such a traversal.

```
sol10# mdb -k
> ::walk vfs
ffffffffffbc7a7a0
ffffffffffbc7a860
> ::walk vfs |::fsinfo -v
                 VFSP FS               MOUNT
ffffffffffbc7a7a0 ufs                 /
                 R: /dev/dsk/c3d1s0
                 O: remount,rw,intr,largefiles,logging,noquota,xattr,nodfratime
ffffffffffbc7a860 devfs
/devices
                 R: /devices
ffffffff80129300 ctfs                 /system/contract
                 R: ctfs
ffffffff80129240 proc                 /proc
                 R: proc
```

You can also inspect a `vfs` object with `mdb`. An example is shown below.

```
sol10# mdb -k
> ::walk vfs
ffffffffffbc7a7a0
ffffffffffbc7a860
> ffffffffffbc7a7a0::print vfs_t
{
    vfs_next = devices
    vfs_prev = 0xffffffffba3ef0c0
    vfs_op = vfssw+0x138
    vfs_vnodecovered = 0
    vfs_flag = 0x420
    vfs_bsize = 0x2000
    vfs_fstype = 0x2
    vfs_fsid = {
        val = [ 0x19800c0, 0x2 ]
    }
    vfs_data = 0xffffffff8010ae00
    vfs_dev = 0x66000000c0
    vfs_bcount = 0
    vfs_list = 0
    vfs_hash = 0xffffffff816a8b40
    vfs_reflock = {
        _opaque = [ 0, 0 ]
    }
    vfs_count = 0x2
    vfs_mntopts = {
        mo_count = 0x20
        mo_list = 0xffffffff8133d580
    }
    vfs_resource = 0xffffffff8176dbb8
    vfs_mntpt = 0xffffffff81708590
    vfs_mtime = 2005 May 17 23:47:13
    vfs_femhead = 0
    vfs_zone = zone0
    vfs_zone_next = devices
    vfs_zone_prev = 0xffffffffba3ef0c0
}
```

14.6 The Vnode

A vnode is a file-system-independent representation of a file in the Solaris kernel. A vnode is said to be objectlike because it is an encapsulation of a file's state and the methods that can be used to perform operations on that file. A vnode represents a file within a file system; the vnode hides the implementation of the file system it resides in and exposes file-system-independent data and methods for that file to the rest of the kernel.

A vnode object contains three important items (see Figure 14.7).

- **File-system-independent data.** Information about the vnode, such as the type of vnode (file, directory, character device, etc.), flags that represent state, pointers to the file system that contains the vnode, and a reference count that keeps track of how many subsystems have references to the vnode.

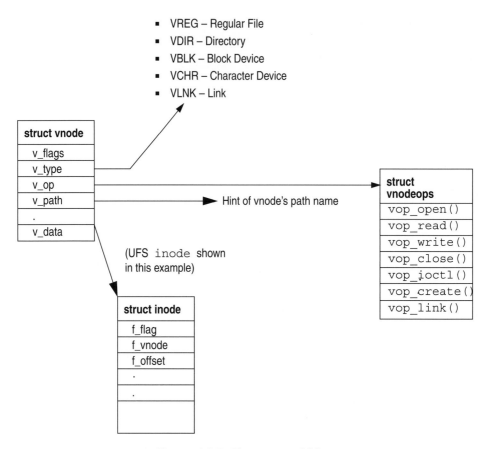

Figure 14.7 The vnode Object

- **Functions to implement file methods.** A structure of pointers to file-system-dependent functions to implement file functions such as open(), close(), read(), and write().
- **File-system-specific data.** Data that is used internally by each file system implementation: typically, the in-memory inode that represents the vnode on the underlying file system. UFS uses an inode, NFS uses an rnode, and tmpfs uses a tmpnode.

14.6.1 Object Interface

The kernel uses wrapper functions to call vnode functions. In that way, it can perform vnode operations (for example, read(), write(), open(), close()) without knowing what the underlying file system containing the vnode is. For example, to read from a file without knowing that it resides on a UFS file system, the kernel would simply call the file-system-independent function for `read()`, `VOP_READ()`, which would call the `vop_read()` method of the vnode, which in turn calls the UFS function, `ufs_read()`. A sample of a vnode wrapper function from `sys/vnode.h` is shown below.

```
#define VOP_READ(vp, uiop, iof, cr, ct) \
        fop_read(vp, uiop, iof, cr, ct)
int
fop_read(
        vnode_t *vp,
        uio_t *uiop,
        int ioflag,
        cred_t *cr,
        struct caller_context *ct)
{
        return (*(vp)->v_op->vop_read)(vp, uiop, ioflag, cr, ct);
}
                                        See usr/src/uts/common/sys/vnode.h
```

The vnode structure in Solaris OS can be found in `sys/vnode.h` and is shown below. It defines the basic interface elements and provides other information contained in the vnode.

```
typedef struct vnode {
        kmutex_t         v_lock;         /* protects vnode fields */
        uint_t           v_flag;         /* vnode flags (see below) */
        uint_t           v_count;        /* reference count */
        void             *v_data;        /* private data for fs */
        struct vfs       *v_vfsp;        /* ptr to containing VFS */
        struct stdata    *v_stream;      /* associated stream */
        enum vtype       v_type;         /* vnode type */
        dev_t            v_rdev;         /* device (VCHR, VBLK) */

        /* PRIVATE FIELDS BELOW - DO NOT USE */

        struct vfs       *v_vfsmountedhere; /* ptr to vfs mounted here */
        struct vnodeops  *v_op;          /* vnode operations */
        struct page      *v_pages;       /* vnode pages list */
        pgcnt_t          v_npages;       /* # pages on this vnode */
        pgcnt_t          v_msnpages;     /* # pages charged to v_mset */
        struct page      *v_scanfront;   /* scanner front hand */
        struct page      *v_scanback;    /* scanner back hand */
        struct filock    *v_filocks;     /* ptr to filock list */
        struct shrlocklist *v_shrlocks;  /* ptr to shrlock list */
        krwlock_t        v_nbllock;      /* sync for NBMAND locks */
        kcondvar_t       v_cv;           /* synchronize locking */
        void             *v_locality;    /* hook for locality info */
        struct fem_head  *v_femhead;     /* fs monitoring */
        char             *v_path;        /* cached path */
        uint_t           v_rdcnt;        /* open for read count (VREG only) */
        uint_t           v_wrcnt;        /* open for write count (VREG only) */
        u_longlong_t     v_mmap_read;    /* mmap read count */
        u_longlong_t     v_mmap_write;   /* mmap write count */
```

continues

```
            void           *v_mpssdata;    /* info for large page mappings */
            hrtime_t       v_scantime;     /* last time this vnode was scanned */
            ushort_t       v_mset;         /* memory set ID */
            uint_t         v_msflags;      /* memory set flags */
            struct vnode   *v_msnext;      /* list of vnodes on an mset */
            struct vnode   *v_msprev;      /* list of vnodes on an mset */
            krwlock_t      v_mslock;       /* protects v_mset */
    } vnode_t;
                                                See usr/src/uts/common/sys/vnode.h
```

14.6.2 vnode Types

Solaris OS has specific vnode types for files. The v_type field in the vnode structure indicates the type of vnode, as described in Table 14.2.

Table 14.2 Solaris 10 vnode Types from sys/vnode.h

Type	Description
VNON	No type
VREG	Regular file
VDIR	Directory
VBLK	Block device
VCHR	Character device
VLNK	Symbolic link
VFIFO	Named pipe
VDOOR	Doors interface
VPROC	procfs node
VSOCK	sockfs node (socket)
VPORT	Event port
VBAD	Bad vnode

14.6.3 vnode Method Registration

The vnode interface provides the set of file system object methods, some of which we saw in Figure 14.1. The file systems implement these methods to perform all file-system-specific file operations. Table 14.3 shows the vnode interface methods in Solaris OS.

File systems register their `vnode` and `vfs` operations by providing an operation definition table that specifies operations using name/value pairs. The definition is typically provided by a predefined template of type `fs_operation_def_t`, which is parsed by `vn_make_ops()`, as shown below. The definition is often set up in the file system initialization function.

```
/*
 * File systems use arrays of fs_operation_def structures to form
 * name/value pairs of operations.  These arrays get passed to:
 *
 *       - vn_make_ops() to create vnodeops
 *       - vfs_makefsops()/vfs_setfsops() to create vfsops.
 */
typedef struct fs_operation_def {
        char *name;                     /* name of operation (NULL at end) */
        fs_generic_func_p func;         /* function implementing operation */
} fs_operation_def_t;

int
vn_make_ops(
        const char *name,                       /* Name of file system */
        const fs_operation_def_t *templ,        /* Operation specification */
        vnodeops_t **actual);                   /* Return the vnodeops */

Creates and builds the private vnodeops table

void vn_freevnodeops(vnodeops_t *vnops);

Frees a vnodeops structure created by vn_make_ops()

void vn_setops(vnode_t *vp, vnodeops_t *vnodeops);

Sets the operations vector for this vnode

vnodeops_t * vn_getops(vnode_t *vp);

Retrieves the operations vector for this vnode

int vn_matchops(vnode_t *vp, vnodeops_t *vnodeops);

Determines if the supplied operations vector matches the vnode's operations vector.
Note that this is a "shallow" match. The pointer to the operations vector is compared,
not each individual operation. Returns non-zero (1) if the vnodeops matches that of the
vnode. Returns zero (0) if not.

int vn_matchopval(vnode_t *vp, char *vopname, fs_generic_func_p funcp)

Determines if the supplied function exists for a particular operation in the vnode's
operations vector

                                    See usr/src/uts/common/sys/vfs.h
```

The following example shows how the `tmpfs` file system sets up its `vnode` operations.

```
struct vnodeops *tmp_vnodeops;

const fs_operation_def_t tmp_vnodeops_template[] = {
        VOPNAME_OPEN, tmp_open,
        VOPNAME_CLOSE, tmp_close,
        VOPNAME_READ, tmp_read,
        VOPNAME_WRITE, tmp_write,
        VOPNAME_IOCTL, tmp_ioctl,
        VOPNAME_GETATTR, tmp_getattr,
        VOPNAME_SETATTR, tmp_setattr,
        VOPNAME_ACCESS, tmp_access,
                                    See usr/src/uts/common/fs/tmpfs/tmp_vnops.c


static int
tmpfsinit(int fstype, char *name)
{
...
        error = vn_make_ops(name, tmp_vnodeops_template, &tmp_vnodeops);
        if (error != 0) {
                (void) vfs_freevfsops_by_type(fstype);
                cmn_err(CE_WARN, "tmpfsinit: bad vnode ops template");
                return (error);
        }

...}

                                    See usr/src/uts/common/fs/tmpfs/tmp_vfsops.c
```

14.6.4 vnode Methods

The following section describes the method names that can be passed into vn_make_ops(), followed by the function prototypes for each method.

Table 14.3 Solaris 10 vnode Interface Methods from sys/vnode.h

Method	Description
VOP_ACCESS	Checks permissions
VOP_ADDMAP	Increments the map count
VOP_CLOSE	Closes the file
VOP_CMP	Compares two vnodes
VOP_CREATE	Creates the supplied path name
VOP_DELMAP	Decrements the map count
VOP_DISPOSE	Frees the given page from the vnode.
VOP_DUMP	Dumps data when the kernel is in a frozen state
VOP_DUMPCTL	Prepares the file system before and after a dump

continues

Table 14.3 Solaris 10 vnode Interface Methods from `sys/vnode.h` (*continued*)

Method	Description
VOP_FID	Gets unique file ID
VOP_FRLOCK	Locks files and records
VOP_FSYNC	Flushes out any dirty pages for the supplied vnode
VOP_GETATTR	Gets the attributes for the supplied vnode
VOP_GETPAGE	Gets pages for a vnode
VOP_GETSECATTR	Gets security access control list attributes
VOP_INACTIVE	Frees resources and releases the supplied vnode
VOP_IOCTL	Performs an I/O control on the supplied vnode
VOP_LINK	Creates a hard link to the supplied vnode
VOP_LOOKUP	Looks up the path name for the supplied vnode
VOP_MAP	Maps a range of pages into an address space
VOP_MKDIR	Makes a directory of the given name
VOP_VNEVENT	Support for File System Event Monitoring
VOP_OPEN	Opens a file referenced by the supplied vnode
VOP_PAGEIO	Supports page I/O for file system swap files
VOP_PATHCONF	Establishes file system parameters
VOP_POLL	Supports the `poll()` system call for file systems
VOP_PUTPAGE	Writes pages in a vnode
VOP_READ	Reads the range supplied for the given vnode
VOP_READDIR	Reads the contents of a directory
VOP_READLINK	Follows the symlink in the supplied vnode
VOP_REALVP	Gets the real vnode from the supplied vnode
VOP_REMOVE	Removes the file for the supplied vnode
VOP_RENAME	Renames the file to the new name
VOP_RMDIR	Removes a directory pointed to by the supplied vnode
VOP_RWLOCK	Holds the reader/writer lock for the supplied vnode
VOP_RWUNLOCK	Releases the reader/writer lock for the supplied vnode
VOP_SEEK	Checks seek bounds within the supplied vnode
VOP_SETATTR	Sets the attributes for the supplied vnode
VOP_SETFL	Sets file-system-dependent flags on the supplied vnode
VOP_SETSECATTR	Sets security access control list attributes

continues

Table 14.3 Solaris 10 vnode Interface Methods from `sys/vnode.h` (*continued*)

Method	Description
VOP_SHRLOCK	Supports NFS shared locks
VOP_SPACE	Frees space for the supplied vnode
VOP_SYMLINK	Creates a symbolic link between the two path names
VOP_WRITE	Writes the range supplied for the given vnode

```
extern int fop_access(vnode_t *vp, int mode, int flags, cred_t *cr);
```

Checks to see if the user (represented by the cred structure) has permission to do an operation. Mode is made up of some combination (bitwise OR) of VREAD, VWRITE, and VEXEC. These bits are shifted to describe owner, group, and "other" access.

```
extern int fop_addmap(vnode_t *vp, offset_t off, struct as *as, caddr_t addr,
                size_t len, uchar_t prot, uchar_t maxprot, uint_t flags,
                cred_t *cr);
```

Increments the map count.

```
extern int fop_close(vnode_t *vp, int flag, int count, offset_t off, cred_t *cr);
```

Closes the file given by the supplied vnode. When this is the last close, some file systems use vop_close() to initiate a writeback of outstanding dirty pages by checking the reference count in the vnode.

```
extern int fop_cmp(vnode_t *vp1, vnode_t *vp2);
```

Compares two vnodes. In almost all cases, this defaults to fs_cmp() which simply does a: return (vp1 == vp2);

NOTE: NFS/NFS3 and Cachefs have their own CMP routines, but they do exactly what fs_cmp() does. Procfs appears to be the only exception. It looks like it follows a chain.

```
extern int fop_create(vnode_t *dvp, char *name, vattr_t *vap, vcexcl_t excl, int mode,
                vnode_t **vp, cred_t *cr, int flag);
```

Creates a file with the supplied path name.

```
extern int fop_delmap(vnode_t *vp, offset_t off, struct as *as, caddr_t addr,
                size_t len, uint_t prot, uint_t maxprot, uint_t flags, cred_t *cr);
```

Decrements the map count.

```
extern void fop_dispose(vnode_t *vp, struct page *pp, int flag, int dn, cred_t *cr);
```

Frees the given page from the vnode.

```
extern int fop_dump(vnode_t *vp, caddr_t addr, int lbdn, int dblks);
```

Dumps data when the kernel is in a frozen state.

```
extern int fop_dumpctl(vnode_t *vp, int action, int *blkp);
```

Prepares the file system before and after a dump.

continues

```
extern int fop_fid(vnode_t *vp, struct fid *fidp);
```

Puts a unique (by node, file system, and host) vnode/xxx_node identifier into fidp. Used for NFS file-handles.

```
extern int fop_frlock(vnode_t *vp, int cmd, struct flock64 *bfp, int flag,
                      offset_t off, struct flk_callback *flk_cbp, cred_t *cr);
```

Does file and record locking for the supplied vnode. Most file systems either map this to fs_frlock() or do some special case checking and call fs_frlock() directly. As you might expect, fs_frlock() does all the dirty work.

```
extern int fop_fsync(vnode_t *vp, int syncflag, cred_t *cr);
```

Flushes out any dirty pages for the supplied vnode.

```
extern int fop_getattr(vnode_t *vp, vattr_t *vap, int flags, cred_t *cr);
```

Gets the attributes for the supplied vnode.

```
extern int fop_getpage(vnode_t *vp, offset_t off, size_t len, uint_t protp,
                       struct page **plarr, size_t plsz, struct seg *seg,
                       caddr_t addr, enum seg_rw rw, cred_t *cr);
```

Gets pages in the range offset and length for the vnode from the backing store of the file system. Does the real work of reading a vnode. This method is often called as a result of read(), which causes a page fault in seg_map, which calls vop_getpage.

```
extern int fop_getsecattr(vnode_t *vp, vsecattr_t *vsap, int flag, cred_t *cr);
```

Gets security access control list attributes.

```
extern void fop_inactive(vnode_t *vp, cred_t *cr);
```

Frees resources and releases the supplied vnode. The file system can choose to destroy the vnode or put it onto an inactive list, which is managed by the file system implementation.

```
extern int fop_ioctl(vnode_t *vp, int cmd, intptr_t arg, int flag, cred_t *cr,
                      int *rvalp);
```

Performs an I/O control on the supplied vnode.

```
extern int fop_link(vnode_t *targetvp, vnode_t *sourcevp, char *targetname, cred_t
*cr);
```

Creates a hard link to the supplied vnode.

```
extern int fop_lookup(vnode_t *dvp, char *name, vnode_t **vpp, int flags, vnode_t
*rdir,
                      cred_t *cr);
```

Looks up the name in the directory vnode dvp with the given dirname and returns the new vnode in vpp. The vop_lookup() does file-name translation for the open, stat system calls.

```
extern int fop_map(vnode_t *vp, offset_t off, struct as *as, caddr_t *addrp, size_t len,
                   uchar_t prot, uchar_t maxprot, uint_t flags, cred_t *cr);
```

Maps a range of pages into an address space by doing the appropriate checks and calling as_map().

continues

```
extern int fop_mkdir(vnode_t *dvp, char *name, vattr_t *vap, vnode_t **vpp, cred_t
*cr);
```

Makes a directory in the directory vnode (dvp) with the given name (dirname) and returns
the new vnode in vpp.

```
extern int fop_vnevent(vnode_t *vp, vnevent_t vnevent);
```

Interface for reporting file events. File systems need not implement this method.

```
extern int fop_open(vnode_t **vpp, int mode, cred_t *cr);
```

Opens a file referenced by the supplied vnode. The open() system call has already done
a vop_lookup() on the path name, which returned a vnode pointer and then calls to vop_
open(). This function typically does very little, since most of the real work was performed by vop_lookup(). Also called by file systems to open devices as well as by anything else that needs to open a file or device.

```
extern int fop_pageio(vnode_t *vp, struct page *pp, u_offset_t io_off, size_t io_len,
                      int flag, cred_t *cr);
```

Paged I/O support for file system swap files.

```
extern int fop_pathconf(vnode_t *vp, int cmd, ulong_t *valp, cred_t *cr);
```

Establishes file system parameters with the pathconf system call.

```
extern int fop_poll(vnode_t *vp, short events, int anyyet, short *reventsp,
                    struct pollhead **phpp);
```

File system support for the poll() system call.

```
extern int fop_putpage(vnode_t *vp, offset_t off, size_t len, int, cred_t *cr);
```

Writes pages in the range offset and length for the vnode to the backing store of the
file system. Does the real work of writing a vnode.

```
extern int fop_read(vnode_t *vp, uio_t *uiop, int ioflag, cred_t *cr,
                    caller_context_t *ct);
```

Reads the range supplied for the given vnode. vop_read() typically maps the requested
range of a file into kernel memory and then uses vop_getpage() to do the real work.

```
extern int fop_readdir(vnode_t *vp, uio_t *uiop, cred_t *cr, int *eofp);
```

Reads the contents of a directory.

```
extern int fop_readlink(vnode_t *vp, uio_t *uiop, cred_t *cr);
```

Follows the symlink in the supplied vnode.

```
extern int fop_realvp(vnode_t *vp, vnode_t **vpp);
```

Gets the real vnode from the supplied vnode.

```
extern int fop_remove(vnode_t *dvp, char *name, cred_t *cr);
```

Removes the file for the supplied vnode.

```
extern int fop_rename(vnode_t *sourcedvp, char *sourcename, vnode_t *targetdvp,
                      char *targetname, cred_t *cr);
```

Renames the file named (by sourcename) in the directory given by sourcedvp to the new
name (targetname) in the directory given by targetdvp.

continues

```
extern int fop_rmdir(vnode_t *dvp, char *name, vnode_t *vp, cred_t *cr);
```

Removes the name in the directory given by dvp.

```
extern int fop_rwlock(vnode_t *vp, int write_lock, caller_context_t *ct);
```

Holds the reader/writer lock for the supplied vnode. This method is called for each
vnode, with the rwflag set to 0 inside a read() system call and the rwflag set to 1
inside a write() system call. POSIX semantics require only one writer inside write() at
a time. Some file system implementations have options to ignore the writer lock inside
vop_rwlock().

```
extern void fop_rwunlock(vnode_t *vp, int write_lock, caller_context_t *ct);
```

Releases the reader/writer lock for the supplied vnode.

```
extern int fop_seek(vnode_t *vp, offset_t oldoff, offset_t *newoffp);
```

Checks the FS-dependent bounds of a potential seek.
NOTE: VOP_SEEK() doesn't do the seeking. Offsets are usually saved in the file_t structure and are passed down to VOP_READ/VOP_WRITE in the uiostructure.

```
extern int fop_setattr(vnode_t *vp, vattr_t *vap, int flags, cred_t *cr,
                       caller_context_t *cr);
```

Sets the file attributes for the supplied vnode.

```
extern int fop_setfl(vnode_t *vp, int oldflags, int newflags, cred_t *cr);
```

Sets the file system-dependent flags (typically for a socket) for the supplied vnode.

```
extern int fop_setsecattr(vnode_t *vp, vsecattr_t *vsap, int flag, cred_t *cr);
```

Sets security access control list attributes.

```
extern int fop_shrlock(vnode_t *vp, int cmd, struct shrlock *shr, int flag, cred_t *cr);
```

ONC shared lock support.

```
extern int fop_space(vnode_t vp*, int cmd, struct flock64 *bfp, int flag,
                     offset_t off, cred_t *cr, caller_context_t *ct);
```

Frees space for the supplied vnode.

```
extern int fop_symlink(vnode_t *vp, char *linkname, vattr_t *vap, char *target,
                       cred_t *cred);
```

Creates a symbolic link between the two path names.

```
extern int fop_write(vnode_t *vp, uio_t *uiop, int ioflag, cred_t *cr,
                     caller_context_t *ct);
```

Writes the range supplied for the given vnode. The write system call typically maps the
requested range of a file into kernel memory and then uses vop_putpage() to do the real
work.

See usr/src/uts/common/sys/vnode.h

14.6.5 Support Functions for Vnodes

Following is a list of the public functions available for obtaining information from within the private part of the vnode.

```
int vn_is_readonly(vnode_t *);

Is the vnode write protected?

int vn_is_opened(vnode_t *, v_mode_t);

Is the file open?

int vn_is_mapped(vnode_t *, v_mode_t);

Is the file mapped?

int vn_can_change_zones(vnode_t *vp);

Check if the vnode can change zones: used to check if a process can change zones. Mainly
used for NFS.

int vn_has_flocks(vnode_t *);

Do file/record locks exist for this vnode?

int vn_has_mandatory_locks(vnode_t *, int);

Does the vnode have mandatory locks in force for this mode?

int vn_has_cached_data(vnode_t *);

Does the vnode have cached data associated with it?

struct vfs *vn_mountedvfs(vnode_t *);

Returns the vfs mounted on this vnode if any

int vn_ismntpt(vnode_t *);

Returns true (non-zero) if this vnode is mounted on, zero otherwise
```

See usr/src/uts/common/sys/vnode.h

14.6.6 The Life Cycle of a Vnode

A vnode is an in-memory reference to a file. It is a transient structure that lives in memory when the kernel references a file within a file system.

A vnode is allocated by vn_alloc() when a first reference to an existing file is made or when a file is created. The two common places in a file system implementation are within the VOP_LOOKUP() method or within the VOP_CREAT() method.

When a file descriptor is opened to a file, the reference count for that vnode is incremented. The vnode is always in memory when the reference count is greater

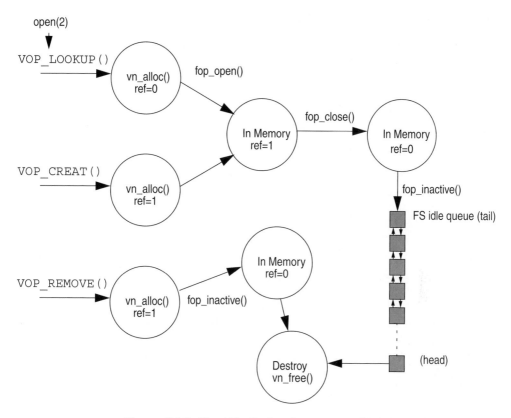

Figure 14.8 The Life Cycle of a vnode Object

than zero. The reference count may drop back to zero after the last file descriptor has been closed, at which point the file system framework calls the file system's VOP_INACTIVE() method.

Once a vnode's reference count becomes zero, it is a candidate for freeing. Most file systems won't free the vnode immediately, since to recreate it will likely require a disk I/O for a directory read or an over-the-wire operation. For example, the UFS keeps a list of inactive inodes on an "inactive list" (see Section 15.3.1). Only when certain conditions are met (for example, a resource shortage) is the vnode actually freed.

Of course, when a file is deleted, its corresponding in-memory vnode is freed. This is also performed by the VOP_INACTIVE() method for the file system: Typically, the VOP_INACTIVE() method checks to see if the link count for the vnode is zero and then frees it.

14.6.7 **vnode** Creation and Destruction

The allocation of a vnode must be done by a call to the appropriate support function. The functions for allocating, destroying, and reinitializing vnodes are shown below.

```
vnode_t *vn_alloc(int kmflag);

Allocate a vnode and initialize all of its structures.

void vn_free(vnode_t *vp);

Free the allocated vnode.

void vn_reinit(vnode_t *vp);

(Re)initializes a vnode.
                                    See usr/src/uts/common/sys/vnode.h
```

14.6.8 The **vnode** Reference Count

A vnode is created by the file system at the time a file is first opened or created and stays active until the file system decides the vnode is no longer needed. The vnode framework provides an infrastructure that keeps track of the number of references to a vnode. The kernel maintains the reference count by means of the VN_HOLD() and VN_RELE() macros, which increment and decrement the v_count field of the vnode. The vnode stays valid while its reference count is greater than zero, so a subsystem can rely on a vnode's contents staying valid by calling VN_HOLD() before it references a vnode's contents. It is important to distinguish a vnode reference from a lock; a lock ensures exclusive access to the data, and the reference count ensures persistence of the object.

When a vnode's reference count drops to zero, VN_RELE() invokes the VOP_INACTIVE() method for that file system. Every subsystem that references a vnode is required to call VN_HOLD() at the start of the reference and to call VN_RELE() at the end of each reference. Some file systems deconstruct a vnode when its reference count falls to zero; others hold on to the vnode for a while so that if it is required again, it is available in its constructed state. UFS, for example, holds on to the vnode for a while after the last release so that the virtual memory system can keep the inode and cache for a file, whereas PCFS frees the vnode and all of the cache associated with the vnode at the time VOP_INACTIVE() is called.

14.6.9 Interfaces for Paging **vnode** Cache

Solaris OS unifies file and memory management by using a vnode to represent the backing store for virtual memory (see Chapter 8). A page of memory represents a particular vnode and offset. The file system uses the memory relationship to implement caching for vnodes within a file system. To cache a vnode, the file system has the memory system create a page of physical memory that represents the vnode and offset.

The virtual memory system provides a set of functions for cache management and I/O for vnodes. These functions allow the file systems to cluster pages for I/O and handle the setup and checking required for synchronizing dirty pages with their backing store. The functions, described below, set up pages so that they can be passed to device driver block I/O handlers.

```
int pvn_getdirty(struct page *pp, int flags);
```

Queries whether a page is dirty. Returns 1 if the page should be written back (the iolock is held in this case), or 0 if the page has been dealt with or has been unlocked.

```
void pvn_plist_init(struct page *pp, struct page **pl, size_t plsz,
                    u_offset_t off, size_t io_len, enum seg_rw rw);
```

Releases the iolock on each page and downgrades the page lock to shared after new pages have been created or read.

```
void pvn_read_done(struct page *plist, int flags);
```

Unlocks the pages after read is complete. The function is normally called automatically by pageio_done() but may need to be called if an error was encountered during a read.

```
struct page *pvn_read_kluster(struct vnode *vp, u_offset_t off,
                              struct seg *seg, caddr_t addr, u_offset_t *offp,
                              size_t *lenp, u_offset_t vp_off, size_t vp_len,
                              int isra);
```

Finds the range of contiguous pages within the supplied address / length that fit within the provided vnode offset / length that do not already exist. Returns a list of newly created, exclusively locked pages ready for I/O. Checks that clustering is enabled by calling the segop_kluster() method for the given segment. On return from pvn_read_kluster, the caller typically zeroes any parts of the last page that are not going to be read from disk, sets up the read with pageio_setup for the returned offset and length, and then initiates the read with bdev_strategy().Once the read is complete, pvn_plist_init() can release the I/O lock on each page that was created.

```
void pvn_write_done(struct page *plist, int flags);
```

Unlocks the pages after write is complete. For asynchronous writes, the function is normally called automatically by pageio_done() when an asynchronous write completes. For synchronous writes, pvn_write_done() is called after pageio_done to unlock written pages. It may also need to be called if an error was encountered during a write.

```
struct page *pvn_write_kluster(struct vnode *vp, struct page *pp,
                               u_offset_t *offp, size_t *lenp, u_offset_t vp_off,
                               size_t vp_len, int flags);
```

Finds the contiguous range of dirty pages within the supplied offset and length. Returns a list of dirty locked pages ready to be written back. On return from pvn_write_kluster(), the caller typically sets up the write with pageio_setup for the returned offset and length, then initiates the write with bdev_strategy(). If the write is synchronous, then the caller should call pvn_write_done() to unlock the pages. If the write is asynchronous, then the io_done routine calls pvn_write_done when the write is complete.

continues

```
int pvn_vplist_dirty(struct vnode *vp, u_offset_t off,
                    int (*putapage)(vnode_t *, struct page *, u_offset_t *,
                    size_t *, int, cred_t *),
                    int flags, struct cred *cred);
```

Finds all dirty pages in the page cache for a given vnode that have an offset greater than the supplied offset and calls the supplied putapage() routine. pvn_vplist_dirty() is often used to synchronize all dirty pages for a vnode when vop_putpage is called with a zero length.

```
int pvn_getpages(int (*getpage)(vnode_t *, u_offset_t, size_t, uint_t *,
                        struct page *[], size_t, struct seg *,
                        caddr_t, enum seg_rw, cred_t *),
                    struct vnode *vp, u_offset_t off, size_t len,
                    uint_t *protp, struct page **pl, size_t plsz,
                    struct seg *seg, caddr_t addr, enum seg_rw rw,
                    struct cred *cred);
```

Handles common work of the VOP_GETPAGE routines when more than one page must be returned by calling a file-system-specific operation to do most of the work. Must be called with the vp already locked by the VOP_GETPAGE routine.

```
void pvn_io_done(struct page *plist);
```

Generic entry point used to release the "shared/exclusive" lock and the "p_iolock" on pages after i/o is complete.

```
void pvn_vpzero(struct vnode *vp, u_offset_t vplen, size_t zbytes);
```

Zeros-out zbytes worth of data. Caller should be aware that this routine may enter back into the fs layer (xxx_getpage). Locks that the xxx_getpage routine may need should not be held while calling this.

See usr/src/uts/common/sys/pvn.h

14.6.10 Block I/O on vnode Pages

The block I/O subsystem supports I/O initiation to and from vnode pages. It schedules I/O from the device drivers directly to and from a page without buffering the data in the buffer cache. These functions are typically used in the implementation of vop_getpage() and vop_putpage() to do the physical I/O on behalf of the file system. Three functions, shown below, initiate I/O between a physical page and a device.

```
struct buf *pageio_setup(struct page *, size_t, struct vnode *, int);
```

Sets up a block buffer for I/O on a page of memory so that it bypasses the block buffer cache by setting the B_PAGEIO flag and putting the page list on the b_pages field.

```
extern int bdev_strategy(struct buf *);
```

Initiates an I/O on a page, using the block I/O device.

```
void pageio_done(struct buf *);
```

Waits for the block device I/O to complete.

See usr/src/uts/common/sys/bio.h

14.6.11 vnode Information Obtainable with mdb

You can use mdb to traverse the vnode cache, inspect a vnode object, view the path name, and examine linkages between vnodes.

With the centralized vn_alloc(), a central vnode cache holds all the vnode structures. It is a regular kmem cache and can be traversed with mdb and the generic kmem cache walker.

```
sol10# mdb -k
> ::walk vn_cache
ffffffff80f24040
ffffffff80f24140
ffffffff80f24240
ffffffff8340d940
...
```

Similarly, you can inspect a vnode object.

```
sol10# mdb -k
> ::walk vn_cache
ffffffff80f24040
ffffffff80f24140
ffffffff80f24240
ffffffff8340d940
...
> ffffffff8340d940::print vnode_t
{
    v_lock = {
        _opaque = [ 0 ]
    }
    v_flag = 0x10000
    v_count = 0x2
    v_data = 0xffffffff8340e3d8
    v_vfsp = 0xffffffff816a8f00
    v_stream = 0
    v_type = 1 (VREG)
    v_rdev = 0xffffffffffffffff
    v_vfsmountedhere = 0
    v_op = 0xffffffff805fe300
    v_pages = 0
    v_npages = 0
    v_msnpages = 0
    v_scanfront = 0
    v_scanback = 0
    v_filocks = 0
    v_shrlocks = 0
    v_nbllock = {
        _opaque = [ 0 ]
    }
    v_cv = {
        _opaque = 0
    }
    v_locality = 0
    v_femhead = 0
    v_path = 0xffffffff8332d440 "/zones/gallery/root/var/svc/log/work-inetd:default.log"
```

continues

```
    v_rdcnt = 0
    v_wrcnt = 0x1
    v_mmap_read = 0
    v_mmap_write = 0
    v_mpssdata = 0
    v_scantime = 0
    v_mset = 0
    v_msflags = 0
    v_msnext = 0
    v_msprev = 0
    v_mslock = {
        _opaque = [ 0 ]
    }
}
```

With other `mdb` d-commands, you can view the `vnode`'s path name (a guess, cached during `vop_lookup`), the linkage between `vnodes`, which processes have them open, and vice versa.

```
> ffffffff8340d940::vnode2path
/zones/gallery/root/var/svc/log//network-inetd:default.log
> ffffffff8340d940::whereopen
file ffffffff832d4bd8
ffffffff83138930
> ffffffff83138930::ps
S    PID   PPID  PGID   SID   UID     FLAGS           ADDR NAME
R    845     1    845   845     0  0x42000400 ffffffff83138930 inetd
> ffffffff83138930::pfiles
FD   TYPE           VNODE INFO
  0  CHR  ffffffff857c8580 /zones/gallery/root/dev/null
  1  REG  ffffffff8340d940 /zones/gallery/root/var/svc/log//network-inetd:default.log
  2  REG  ffffffff8340d940 /zones/gallery/root/var/svc/log//network-inetd:default.log
  3  FIFO ffffffff83764940
  4  DOOR ffffffff836d1680 [door to 'nscd' (proc=ffffffff835ecd10)]
  5  DOOR ffffffff83776800 [door to 'svc.configd' (proc=ffffffff8313f928)]
  6  DOOR ffffffff83776900 [door to 'svc.configd' (proc=ffffffff8313f928)]
  7  FIFO ffffffff83764540
  8  CHR  ffffffff83776500 /zones/gallery/root/dev/sysevent
  9  CHR  ffffffff83776300 /zones/gallery/root/dev/sysevent
 10  DOOR ffffffff83776700 [door to 'inetd' (proc=ffffffff83138930)]
 11  REG  ffffffff833fcac0 /zones/gallery/root/system/contract/process/template
 12  SOCK ffffffff83215040 socket: AF_UNIX /var/run/.inetd.uds
 13  CHR  ffffffff837f1e40 /zones/gallery/root/dev/ticotsord
 14  CHR  ffffffff837b6b00 /zones/gallery/root/dev/ticotsord
 15  SOCK ffffffff85d106c0 socket: AF_INET6 :: 48155
 16  SOCK ffffffff85cdb000 socket: AF_INET6 :: 20224
 17  SOCK ffffffff83543440 socket: AF_INET6 :: 5376
 18  SOCK ffffffff8339de80 socket: AF_INET6 :: 258
 19  CHR  ffffffff85d27440 /zones/gallery/root/dev/ticlts
 20  CHR  ffffffff83606100 /zones/gallery/root/dev/udp
 21  CHR  ffffffff8349ba00 /zones/gallery/root/dev/ticlts
 22  CHR  ffffffff8332f680 /zones/gallery/root/dev/udp
 23  CHR  ffffffff83606600 /zones/gallery/root/dev/ticots
 24  CHR  ffffffff834b2d40 /zones/gallery/root/dev/ticotsord
 25  CHR  ffffffff8336db40 /zones/gallery/root/dev/tcp
 26  CHR  ffffffff83626540 /zones/gallery/root/dev/ticlts
 27  CHR  ffffffff834f1440 /zones/gallery/root/dev/udp
 28  CHR  ffffffff832d5940 /zones/gallery/root/dev/ticotsord
 29  CHR  ffffffff834e4b80 /zones/gallery/root/dev/ticotsord
```

continues

```
30 SOCK ffffffff83789580 socket: AF_INET 0.0.0.0 514
31 SOCK ffffffff835a6e80 socket: AF_INET6 :: 514
32 SOCK ffffffff834e4d80 socket: AF_INET6 :: 5888
33  CHR ffffffff85d10ec0 /zones/gallery/root/dev/ticotsord
34  CHR ffffffff83839900 /zones/gallery/root/dev/tcp
35 SOCK ffffffff838429c0 socket: AF_INET 0.0.0.0 11904
```

14.6.12 DTrace Probes in the vnode Layer

DTrace provides probes for file system activity through the vminfo provider and, optionally, through deeper tracing with the fbt provider. All the cpu_vminfo statistics are updated from pageio_setup() (see Section 14.6.10).

The vminfo provider probes correspond to the fields in the "vm" named kstat: a probe provided by vminfo fires immediately before the corresponding vm value is incremented. Table 14.4 lists the probes available from the VM provider; these are further described in Section 6.11 in *Solaris™ Performance and Tools*. A probe takes the following arguments.

arg0. The value by which the statistic is to be incremented. For most probes, this argument is always 1, but for some it may take other values; these probes are noted in Table 14.4.

arg1. A pointer to the current value of the statistic to be incremented. This value is a 64-bit quantity that is incremented by the value in arg0. Dereferencing this pointer allows consumers to determine the current count of the statistic corresponding to the probe.

For example, the following paging activity that is visible with vmstat indicates page-in from the file system (fpi).

```
sol8# vmstat -p 3
     memory              page             executable      anonymous        filesystem
   swap   free  re  mf  fr  de  sr  epi epo epf  api apo apf  fpi fpo fpf
 1512488 837792 160 20  12   0   0    0   0   0  8102   0   0   12  12  12
 1715812 985116  7  82   0   0   0    0   0   0  7501   0   0   45   0   0
 1715784 983984  0   2   0   0   0    0   0   0  1231   0   0   53   0   0
 1715780 987644  0   0   0   0   0    0   0   0  2451   0   0   33   0   0

sol10$ dtrace -n fspgin'{@[execname] = count()}'
dtrace: description 'fspgin' matched 1 probe
  svc.startd                                                1
  sshd                                                      2
  ssh                                                       3
  dtrace                                                    6
  vmstat                                                    8
  filebench                                                13
```

See Section 6.11 in *Solaris™ Performance and Tools* for examples of how to use dtrace for memory analysis.

Table 14.4 DTrace VM Provider Probes and Descriptions

Probe Name	Description
anonfree	Fires whenever an unmodified anonymous page is freed as part of paging activity. Anonymous pages are those that are not associated with a file; memory containing such pages include heap memory, stack memory, or memory obtained by explicitly mapping zero(7D).
anonpgin	Fires whenever an anonymous page is paged in from a swap device.
anonpgout	Fires whenever a modified anonymous page is paged out to a swap device.
as_fault	Fires whenever a fault is taken on a page and the fault is neither a protection fault nor a copy-on-write fault.
cow_fault	Fires whenever a copy-on-write fault is taken on a page. arg0 contains the number of pages that are created as a result of the copy-on-write.
dfree	Fires whenever a page is freed as a result of paging activity. Whenever dfree fires, exactly one of anonfree, execfree, or fsfree will also subsequently fire.
execfree	Fires whenever an unmodified executable page is freed as a result of paging activity.
execpgin	Fires whenever an executable page is paged in from the backing store.
execpgout	Fires whenever a modified executable page is paged out to the backing store. If it occurs at all, most paging of executable pages will occur in terms of execfree; execpgout can only fire if an executable page is modified in memory—an uncommon occurrence in most systems.
fsfree	Fires whenever an unmodified file system data page is freed as part of paging activity.
fspgin	Fires whenever a file system page is paged in from the backing store.
fspgout	Fires whenever a modified file system page is paged out to the backing store.
kernel_asflt	Fires whenever a page fault is taken by the kernel on a page in its own address space. Whenever kernel_asflt fires, it will be immediately preceded by a firing of the as_fault probe.
maj_fault	Fires whenever a page fault is taken that results in I/O from a backing store or swap device. Whenever maj_fault fires, it will be immediately preceded by a firing of the pgin probe.
pgfrec	Fires whenever a page is reclaimed off the free page list.

Below is an example of tracing a generic vnode layer with DTrace.

```
dtrace:::BEGIN
{
        printf("%-15s %-10s %51s %2s %8s %8s\n",
                "Event", "Device", "Path", "RW", "Size", "Offset");
        self->trace = 0;
        self->path = "";
}


fbt::fop_*:entry
/self->trace == 0/
{
        /* Get vp: fop_open has a pointer to vp */
        self->vpp = (vnode_t **)arg0;
        self->vp = (vnode_t *)arg0;
        self->vp = probefunc == "fop_open" ? (vnode_t *)*self->vpp : self->vp;

        /* And the containing vfs */
        self->vfsp = self->vp ? self->vp->v_vfsp : 0;

        /* And the paths for the vp and containing vfs */
        self->vfsvp = self->vfsp ? (struct vnode *)((vfs_t *)self->vfsp)->vfs_vnodecov-
ered : 0;
        self->vfspath = self->vfsvp ? stringof(self->vfsvp->v_path) : "unknown";

        /* Check if we should trace the root fs */
        ($1 == "/all" ||
         ($1 == "/" && self->vfsp && \
         (self->vfsp == `rootvfs))) ? self->trace = 1 : self->trace;

        /* Check if we should trace the fs */
        ($1 == "/all" || (self->vfspath == $1)) ? self->trace = 1 : self->trace;
}

/*
 * Trace the entry point to each fop
 *
 */
fbt::fop_*:entry
/self->trace/
{
        self->path = (self->vp != NULL && self->vp->v_path) ? stringof(self->vp->v_path)
: "unknown";
        self->len = 0;
        self->off = 0;

        /* Some fops has the len in arg2 */
        (probefunc == "fop_getpage" || \
         probefunc == "fop_putpage" || \
         probefunc == "fop_none") ? self->len = arg2 : 1;

        /* Some fops has the len in arg3 */
        (probefunc == "fop_pageio" || \
         probefunc == "fop_none") ? self->len = arg3 : 1;

        /* Some fops has the len in arg4 */
        (probefunc == "fop_addmap" || \
         probefunc == "fop_map" || \
         probefunc == "fop_delmap") ? self->len = arg4 : 1;
```

continues

```
        /* Some fops has the offset in arg1 */

        (probefunc == "fop_addmap" || \
         probefunc == "fop_map" || \
         probefunc == "fop_getpage" || \
         probefunc == "fop_putpage" || \
         probefunc == "fop_seek" || \
         probefunc == "fop_delmap") ? self->off = arg1 : 1;

        /* Some fops has the offset in arg3 */
        (probefunc == "fop_close" || \
         probefunc == "fop_pageio") ? self->off = arg3 : 1;

        /* Some fops has the offset in arg4 */
        probefunc == "fop_frlock" ? self->off = arg4 : 1;

        /* Some fops has the pathname in arg1 */
        self->path = (probefunc == "fop_create" || \
         probefunc == "fop_mkdir" || \
         probefunc == "fop_rmdir" || \
         probefunc == "fop_remove" || \
         probefunc == "fop_lookup") ?
                strjoin(self->path, strjoin("/", stringof(arg1))) : self->path;
        printf("%-15s %-10s %51s %2s %8d %8d\n",
                probefunc,
                "-", self->path, "-", self->len, self->off);
        self->type = probefunc;
}


fbt::fop_*:return
/self->trace == 1/
{
        self->trace = 0;
}


/* Capture any I/O within this fop */
io:::start
/self->trace/
{
        printf("%-15s %-10s %51s %2s %8d %8u\n",
                self->type, args[1]->dev_statname,
                self->path, args[0]->b_flags & B_READ ? "R" : "W",
                args[0]->b_bcount, args[2]->fi_offset);

}

sol10# ./voptrace.d /tmp
Event           Device                                       Path RW    Size    Offset
fop_putpage     -               /tmp/bin/i386/fastsu            -       4096      4096
fop_inactive    -               /tmp/bin/i386/fastsu            -          0         0
fop_putpage     -               /tmp/WEB-INF/lib/classes12.jar  -       4096    204800
fop_inactive    -               /tmp//WEB-INF/lib/classes12.jar -          0         0
fop_putpage     -               /tmp/s10_x86_sparc_pkg.tar.Z    -       4096   7655424
fop_inactive    -               /tmp/s10_x86_sparc_pkg.tar.Z    -          0         0
fop_putpage     -               /tmp/xanadu/WEB-INF/lib/classes12.jar -  4096    782336
fop_inactive    -               /tmp/xanadu/WEB-INF/lib/classes12.jar -     0         0
fop_putpage     -               /tmp/bin/amd64/filebench        -       4096     36864
```

14.7 File System I/O

Two distinct methods perform file system I/O:

- `read()`, `write()`, and related system calls
- Memory-mapping of a file into the process's address space

Both methods are implemented in a similar way: Pages of a file are mapped into an address space, and then paged I/O is performed on the pages within the mapped address space. Although it may be obvious that memory mapping is performed when we memory-map a file into a process's address space, it is less obvious that the `read()` and `write()` system calls also map a file before reading or writing it. The major differences between these two methods lie in where the file is mapped and who does the mapping; a process calls `mmap()` to map the file into its address space for memory mapped I/O, and the kernel maps the file into the kernel's address space for `read` and `write`. The two methods are contrasted in Figure 14.9.

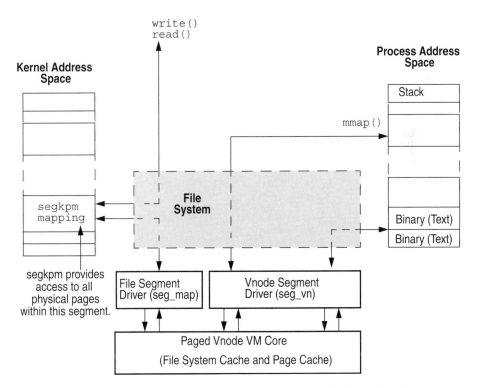

Figure 14.9 The `read()`/`write()` vs. `mmap()` Methods for File I/O

14.7.1 Memory Mapped I/O

A request to memory-map a file into an address space is handled by the file system vnode method vop_map() and the seg_vn memory segment driver (see Section 14.7.4). A process requests that a file be mapped into its address space. Once the mapping is established, the address space represented by the file appears as regular memory and the file system can perform I/O by simply accessing that memory.

Memory mapping of files hides the real work of reading and writing the file because the seg_vn memory segment driver quietly works with the file system to perform the I/Os without the need for process-initiated system calls. I/O is performed, in units of pages, upon reference to the pages mapped into the address space; reads are initiated by a memory access; writes are initiated as the VM system finds dirty pages in the mapped address space.

The system call mmap() calls the file system for the requested file with the vnode's vop_map() method. In turn, the file system calls the address space map function for the current address space, and the mapping is created. The protection flags passed into the mmap() system call are reduced to the subset allowed by the file permissions. If mandatory locking is set for the file, then mmap() returns an error.

Once the file mapping is created in the process's address space, file pages are read when a fault occurs in the address space. A fault occurs the first time a memory address within the mapped segment is accessed because at this point, no physical page of memory is at that location. The memory management unit causes a hardware trap for that memory segment; the memory segment calls its fault function to handle the I/O for that address. The segvn_fault() routine handles a fault for a file mapping in a process address space and then calls the file system to read in the page for the faulted address, as shown below.

```
segvn_fault (hat, seg, addr, len, type, rw) {

        for ( page = all pages in region ) {

                advise = lookup_advise (page);   /* Look up madvise settings for page */
                if (advise == MADV_SEQUENTIAL)
                        free_all_pages_up_to (page);

                /* Segvn will read at most 64k ahead */
                if ( len > PVN_GETPAGE_SZ)
                        len = PVN_GETPAGE_SZ;

                vp = segvp (seg);
                vpoff = segoff (seg);
```

continues

```
                    /* Read 64k at a time if the next page is not in memory,
                     * else just a page
                     */
                    if (hat_probe (addr+PAGESIZE)==TRUE)
                            len=PAGESIZE;

                    /* Ask the file system for the next 64k of pages if the next*/
                    VOP_GETPAGE(vp, vp_off, len,
                            &vpprot, plp, plsz, seg, addr + (vp_off - off), arw, cred)
            }
    }
                                                      See usr/src/uts/common/vm/seg_vn.c
```

For each page fault, seg_vn reads in an 8-Kbyte page at the fault location. In addition, seg_vn initiates a read-ahead of the next eight pages at each 64-Kbyte boundary. Memory mapped read-ahead uses the file system cluster size (used by the read() and write() system calls) unless the segment is mapped MA_SHARED or memory advice MADV_RANDOM is set.

Recall that you can provide paging advice to the pages within a memory mapped segment by using the madvise system call. The madvise system call and (as in the example) the advice information are used to decide when to free behind as the file is read.

Modified pages remain unwritten to disk until the fsflush daemon passes over the page, at which point they will be written out to disk. You can also use the memcntl() system call to initiate a synchronous or asynchronous write of pages.

14.7.2 `read()` and `write()` System Calls

The vnode's vop_read() and vop_write() methods implement reading and writing with the read() and write() system calls. As shown in Figure 14.10, the seg_map segment driver directly accesses a page by means of the seg_kpm mapping of the system's physical pages within the kernel's address space during the read() and write() system calls. The read and write file system calls copy data to or from the process during a system call to a portion of the file that is mapped into the kernel's address space by seg_kpm. The seg_map driver maintains a cache of addresses between the vnode/offset and the virtual address where the page is mapped.

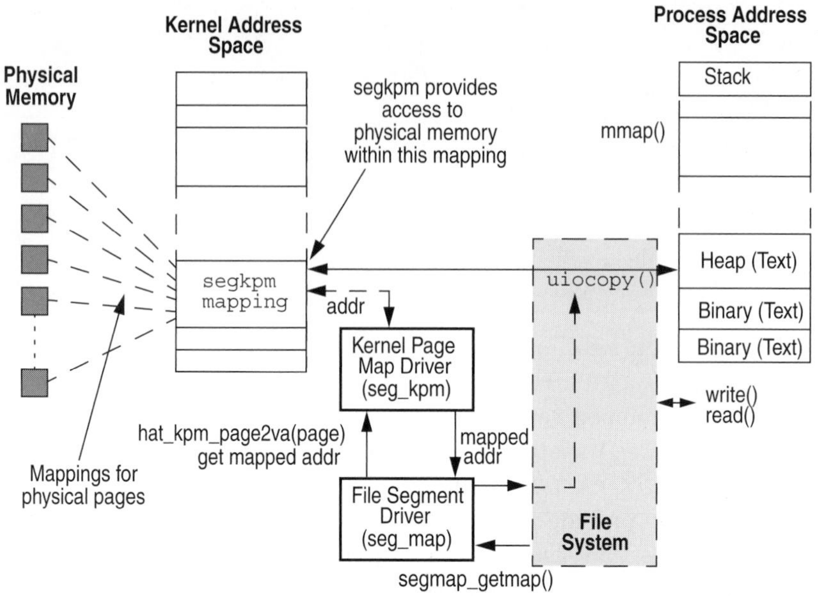

Figure 14.10 File System Data Movement with `seg_map/seg_kpm`

14.7.3 The `seg_kpm` Driver

The `seg_kpm` driver provides a fast mapping for physical pages within the kernel's address space. It is used by file systems to provide a virtual address when copying data to and from the user's address space for file system I/O. The use of this `seg_kpm` mapping facility is new for Solaris 10.

Since the available virtual address range in a 64-bit kernel is always larger than physical memory size, the entire physical memory can be mapped into the kernel. This eliminates the need to map/unmap pages every time they are accessed through `segmap`, significantly reducing code path and the need for TLB shoot-downs. In addition, `seg_kpm` can use large TLB mappings to minimize TLB miss overhead.

14.7.4 The `seg_map` Driver

The `seg_map` driver maintains the relationship between pieces of files into the kernel address space and is used only by the file systems. Every time a `read` or `write` system call occurs, the `seg_map` segment driver locates the virtual address space where the page of the file can be mapped. The system call can then copy the data to or from the user address space.

The `seg_map` segment provides a full set of segment driver interfaces (see Section 9.5); however, the file system directly uses a small subset of these inter-

faces without going through the generic segment interface. The subset handles the
bulk of the work that is done by the `seg_map` segment for file read and write operations. The functions used by the file systems are shown on page 714.

The `seg_map` segment driver divides the segment into block-sized slots that represent blocks in the files it maps. The `seg_map` block size for the Solaris kernel is
8,192 bytes. A 128-Mbyte `segkmap` segment would, for example, be divided into
128-MB/8-KB slots, or 16,384 slots. The `seg_map` segment driver maintains a hash
list of its page mappings so that it can easily locate existing blocks. The list is based
on file and offsets. One list entry exists for each slot in the `segkmap` segment. The
structure for each slot in a `seg_map` segment is defined in the `<vm/segmap.h>`
header file, shown below.

```
/*
 * Machine independent per instance kpm mapping structure
 */
struct kpme {
        struct kpme     *kpe_next;
        struct kpme     *kpe_prev;
        struct page     *kpe_page;     /* back pointer to (start) page */
};
```
                                                    See usr/src/uts/common/vm/kpm.h

```
/*
 * Each smap struct represents a MAXBSIZE sized mapping to the
 * <sm_vp, sm_off> given in the structure.  The location of the
 * the structure in the array gives the virtual address of the
 * mapping. Structure rearranged for 64bit sm_off.
 */
struct   smap {
        kmutex_t        sm_mtx;        /* protect non-list fields */
        struct   vnode  *sm_vp;        /* vnode pointer (if mapped) */
        struct   smap   *sm_hash;      /* hash pointer */
        struct   smap   *sm_next;      /* next pointer */
        struct   smap   *sm_prev;      /* previous pointer */
        u_offset_t      sm_off;        /* file offset for mapping */
        ushort_t        sm_bitmap;     /* bit map for locked translations */
        ushort_t        sm_refcnt;     /* reference count for uses */
        ushort_t        sm_flags;      /* smap flags */
        ushort_t        sm_free_ndx;   /* freelist */
#ifdef   SEGKPM_SUPPORT
        struct kpme     sm_kpme;       /* segkpm */
#endif
};
```
                                                    See usr/src/uts/common/vm/segmap.h

The key `smap` structures are

- **sm_vp.** The file (vnode) this slot represents (if slot not empty)

- **sm_hash, sm_next, sm_prev.** Hash list reference pointers

- **sm_off.** The file (vnode) offset for a block-sized chunk in this slot in the file

- **sm_bitmap.** Bitmap to maintain translation locking
- **sm_refcnt.** The number of references to this mapping caused by concurrent reads

The important fields in the smap structure are the file and offset fields, sm_vp and sm_off. These fields identify which page of a file is represented by each slot in the segment.

An example of the interaction between a file system read and segmap is shown in Figure 14.11.

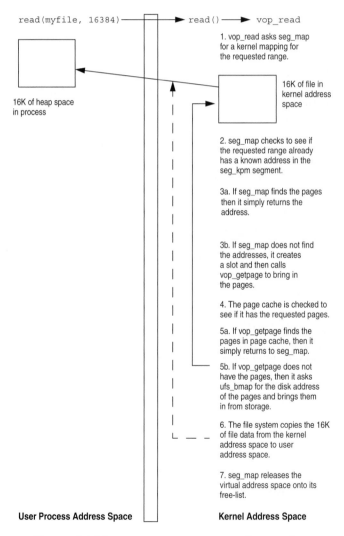

read(myfile, 16384) ──────► read() ──► vop_read

1. vop_read asks seg_map for a kernel mapping for the requested range.

16K of file in kernel address space

16K of heap space in process

2. seg_map checks to see if the requested range already has a known address in the seg_kpm segment.

3a. If seg_map finds the pages then it simply returns the address.

3b. If seg_map does not find the addresses, it creates a slot and then calls vop_getpage to bring in the pages.

4. The page cache is checked to see if it has the requested pages.

5a. If vop_getpage finds the pages in page cache, then it simply returns to seg_map.

5b. If vop_getpage does not have the pages, then it asks ufs_bmap for the disk address of the pages and brings them in from storage.

6. The file system copies the 16K of file data from the kernel address space to user address space.

7. seg_map releases the virtual address space onto its free-list.

User Process Address Space   **Kernel Address Space**

Figure 14.11 vop_read() segmap Interaction

A read system call invokes the file-system-dependent vop_read function. The vop_read method calls into the seg_map segment to locate a virtual address in the kernel address space via segkpm for the file and offset requested with the segmap_getmapflt() function. The seg_map driver determines whether it already has a slot for the page of the file at the given offset by looking into its hashed list of mapping slots. Once a slot is located or created, an address for the page is located, and segmap then calls back into the file system with vop_getpage() to soft-initiate a page fault to read in a page at the virtual address of the seg_map slot. While the segmap_getmapflt() routine is still running, the page fault is initiated by a call to segmap_fault(), which in turn calls back into the file system with vop_getpage().

The file system's vop_getpage() routine handles the task of bringing the requested range of the file (vnode, offset, and length) from disk into the virtual address and length passed into the vop_getpage() function.

Once the page is read by the file system, the requested range is copied back to the user by the uio_move() function. Then, the file system releases the slot associated with that block of the file with the segmap_release() function. At this point, the slot is not removed from the segment because we may need the same file and offset later (effectively caching the virtual address location); instead, it is added onto a seg_map free list so it can be reclaimed or reused later.

Writing is a similar process. Again, segmap_getmap() is called to retrieve or create a mapping for the file and offset, the I/O is done, and the segmap slot is released. An additional step is involved if the file is being extended or a new page is being created within a hole of a file. This additional step calls the segmap_pagecreate() function to create and lock the new pages, then calls segmap_pageunlock() to unlock the pages that were locked during the page_create().

The key segmap functions are shown below.

```
caddr_t segmap_getmapflt(struct seg *seg,
                         struct vnode *vp,
                         u_offset_t off,
                         size_t len,
                         int forcefault,
                         enum seg_rw rw);
```

Retrieves an address in the kernel's address space for a range of the file at the given offset and length. segmap_getmap allocates a MAXBSIZE big slot to map the vnode vp in the range <off, off + len). off doesn't need to be MAXBSIZE aligned. The return address is always MAXBSIZE aligned. If forcefault is nonzero and the MMU translations haven't yet been created, segmap_getmap will call segmap_fault(..., F_INVAL, rw) to create them.

```
int segmap_release(struct seg *seg, caddr_t addr, uint_t flags);
```

Releases the mapping for a given file at a given address.

continues

```
int segmap_pagecreate(struct seg *seg, caddr_t addr, size_t len, int softlock);
```

Creates new page(s) of memory and slots in the seg_map segment for a given file. Used
for extending files or writing to holes during a write. This function creates pages
(without using VOP_GETPAGE) and loads up translations to them. If softlock is TRUE, then
set things up so that it looks like a call to segmap_fault with F_SOFTLOCK.   Returns 1
if a page is created by calling page_create_va(), or 0 otherwise.

All fields in the generic segment (struct seg) are considered to be read-only for "segmap" even though the kernel address space (kas) may not be locked; hence, no lock is
needed to access them.

```
void segmap_pageunlock(struct seg *seg, caddr_t addr, size_t len, enum seg_rw rw);
```

Unlocks pages in the segment that was locked during segmap_pagecreate().

See usr/src/uts/common/vm/segmap.h

We can observe the seg_map slot activity with the kstat statistics that are col-
lected for the seg_map segment driver. These statistics are visible with the kstat
command, as shown below.

```
sol10$ kstat -n segmap
module: unix                              instance: 0
name:   segmap                            class:     vm
        crtime                            42.268896913
        fault                             352197
        faulta                            0
        free                              1123987
        free_dirty                        50836
        free_notfree                      2073
        get_nofree                        0
        get_nomtx                         0
        get_reclaim                       5644590
        get_reuse                         1356990
        get_unused                        0
        get_use                           386
        getmap                            7005644
        pagecreate                        1375991
        rel_abort                         0
        rel_async                         291640
        rel_dontneed                      291640
        rel_free                          7054
        rel_write                         304570
        release                           6694020
        snaptime                          1177936.33212098
        stolen                            0
```

Table 14.5 describes the segmap statistics.

Table 14.5 Statistics from the `seg_map` Segment Driver

Field Name	Description
`fault`	The number of times `segmap_fault` was called, usually as a result of a `read` or `write` system call.
`faulta`	The number of times the `segmap_faulta` function was called. It is called to initiate asynchronous paged I/O on a file.
`getmap`	The number of times the `segmap_getmap` function was called. It is called by the `read` and `write` system calls each time a `read` or `write` call is started. It sets up a slot in the `seg_map` segment for the requested range on the file.
`get_use`	The number of times a valid mapping was found in `seg_map`, which was also already referenced by another user.
`get_reclaim`	The number of times a valid mapping was found in `seg_map`, which was otherwise unused.
`get_reuse`	The number of times `getmap` deleted the mapping in a non-empty slot and created a new mapping for the file and offset requested.
`get_unused`	Not used—always zero.
`get_nofree`	The number of times a request for a slot was made and none was available on the internal free list of slots. This number is usually zero because each slot is put on the free list when `release` is called at the end of each I/O. Hence, ample free slots are usually available.
`rel_async`	The slot was released with a delayed I/O on it.
`rel_write`	The slot was released as a result of a write system call.
`rel_free`	The slot was released, and the VM system was told that the page may be needed again but to free it and retain its file/offset information. These pages are placed on the cache list tail so that they are not the first to be reused.
`rel_abort`	The slot was released and asked to be removed from the `seg_map` segment as a result of a failed aborted write.
`rel_dontneed`	The slot was released, and the VM system was told to free the page because it won't be needed again. These pages are placed on the cache list head so they will be reused first.
`released`	The slot was released and the release was not affected by `rel_abort`, `rel_async`, or `rel_write`.
`pagecreate`	Pages were created in the `segmap_pagecreate` function.

continues

Table 14.5 Statistics from the `seg_map` Segment Driver *(continued)*

Field Name	Description
`free_notfree`	An attempt was made to free a page which was still mapped
`free_dirty`	Pages that were dirty were freed from `segmap`.
`free`	Pages that were clean were freed from `segmap`.
`stolen`	A `smap` slot was taken during a `getmap`.
`get_nomtx`	This field is not used.

14.7.5 Interaction between segmap and segkpm

The following three examples show the code flow through the file system into `segmap` for three important cases:

1. The requested vnode/offset has a cached slot in `seg_map`, and the physical page is in the page cache.

2. The requested vnode/offset does not have a cached slot in `seg_map`, but the physical page is in the page cache.

3. The requested vnode/offset is not in either.

```
Hit in page cache and segmap:
-> ufs_read                    read() Entry point into UFS
  -> segmap_getmapflt          Locate the segmap slot for the vnode/off
    -> hat_kpm_page2va         Identify the virtual address for the vnode/off
    <- hat_kpm_page2va
  <- segmap_getmapflt
  -> uiomove                   Copy the data from the segkpm address to userland
  <- uiomove
  -> segmap_release            Release the segmap slot
    -> hat_kpm_vaddr2page      Locate the page by looking up its address
    <- hat_kpm_vaddr2page
    -> segmap_smapadd          Add the segmap slot to the reuse pool
    <- segmap_smapadd
  <- segmap_release
<- ufs_read

                                               See examples/segkpm.d
```

```
Hit in page cache, miss in segmap:
-> ufs_read                    read() Entry point into UFS
  -> segmap_getmapflt          Locate the segmap slot for the vnode/off
    -> get_free_smp            Find a segmap slot that can be reused
      -> grab_smp              Flush out the old segmap slot identity
        -> segmap_hashout
        <- segmap_hashout
        -> hat_kpm_page2va     Identify the virtual address for the vnode/off
        <- hat_kpm_page2va
```

continues

```
        <- grab_smp
        -> segmap_pagefree        Put the page back on the cachelist
        <- segmap_pagefree
      <- get_free_smp
      -> segmap_hashin            Set up the segmap slot for the new vnode/off
      <- segmap_hashin
      -> segkpm_create_va         Create a virtual address for this vnode/off
      <- segkpm_create_va
      -> ufs_getpage              Find the page already in the page-cache
      <- ufs_getpage
      -> hat_kpm_mapin            Reuse a mapping for the page in segkpm
      <- hat_kpm_mapin
    <- segmap_getmapflt
    -> uiomove                    Copy the data from the segkpm address to userland
    <- uiomove
    -> segmap_release             Add the segmap slot to the reuse pool
      -> hat_kpm_vaddr2page
      <- hat_kpm_vaddr2page
      -> segmap_smapadd
      <- segmap_smapadd
    <- segmap_release
<- ufs_read
```

See examples/segkpm.d

Miss in page cache, miss in segmap:
```
-> ufs_read                       read() Entry point into UFS
  -> segmap_getmapflt             Locate the segmap slot for the vnode/off
    -> get_free_smp               Find a segmap slot that can be reused
      -> grab_smp                 Flush out the old segmap slot identity
        -> segmap_hashout
        <- segmap_hashout
        -> hat_kpm_page2va        Identify the virtual address for the vnode/off
        <- hat_kpm_page2va
        -> hat_kpm_mapout         Unmap the old slot's page(s)
        <- hat_kpm_mapout
      <- grab_smp
      -> segmap_pagefree
      <- segmap_pagefree
    <- get_free_smp
    -> segmap_hashin              Set up the segmap slot for the new vnode/off
    <- segmap_hashin
    -> segkpm_create_va           Create a virtual address for this vnode/off
    <- segkpm_create_va
    -> ufs_getpage                Call the file system getpage() to read in the page
      -> bdev_strategy             Initiate the physical read
      <- bdev_strategy
    <- ufs_getpage
    -> hat_kpm_mapin              Create a mapping for the page in segkpm
      -> sfmmu_kpm_mapin
        -> sfmmu_kpm_getvaddr
        <- sfmmu_kpm_getvaddr
      <- sfmmu_kpm_mapin
      -> sfmmu_kpme_lookup
      <- sfmmu_kpme_lookup
      -> sfmmu_kpme_add
      <- sfmmu_kpme_add
    <- hat_kpm_mapin
  <- segmap_getmapflt
  -> uiomove                      Copy the data from the segkpm address to userland
  <- uiomove
  -> segmap_release               Add the segmap slot to the reuse pool
```

continues

```
      -> get_smap_kpm
        -> hat_kpm_vaddr2page
        <- hat_kpm_vaddr2page
      <- get_smap_kpm
        -> segmap_smapadd
        <- segmap_smapadd
    <- segmap_release
  <- ufs_read
```
See examples/segkpm.d

14.8 File Systems and Memory Allocation

File system caching has been implemented as an integrated part of the Solaris virtual memory system since as far back as SunOS 4.0. This has the great advantage of dynamically using available memory as a file system cache. While this integration has many positive advantages (like being able to speed up some I/O-intensive applications by as much as 500 times), there were some historic side effects: Applications with a lot of file system I/O could swamp the memory system with demand for memory allocations, pressuring the memory system so much that memory pages were aggressively stolen from important applications. Typical symptoms of this condition were that everything seemed to "slow down" when file I/O was occurring and that the system reported it was constantly out of memory. In Solaris 2.6 and 7, the paging algorithms were updated to steal only file system pages unless there was a real memory shortage, as part of the feature named "priority paging." This meant that although there was still significant pressure from file I/O and high "scan rates," applications didn't get paged out or suffer from the pressure. A healthy Solaris 7 system still reported it was out of memory, but performed well.

14.8.1 Solaris 8—Cyclic Page Cache

Starting with Solaris 8, we significantly enhanced the architecture to solve the problem more effectively. We changed the file system cache so that it steals memory from itself, rather than from other parts of the system. Hence, a system with a large amount of file I/O will remain in a healthy virtual memory state—with large amounts of visible free memory and, since the page scanner doesn't need to run, with no aggressive scan rates. Since the page scanner isn't constantly required to free up large amounts of memory, it no longer limits file-system-related I/O throughput. Other benefits of the enhancement are that applications that need to allocate a large amount of memory can do so by efficiently consuming it directly from the file system cache. For example, starting Oracle with a 50-Gbyte SGA now takes less than a minute, compared to the 20–30 minutes with the prior implementation.

14.8.2 The Old Allocation Algorithm

To keep this explanation relatively simple, let's briefly look at what used to happen with Solaris 7, even with priority paging.

The file system consumes memory from the free lists every time a new page is read from disk (or wherever) into the file system. The more pages read, the more pages depleted from the system's free list (the central place where memory is kept for reuse). Eventually (sometimes rather quickly), the free memory pool is depleted. At this point, if there is enough pressure, further requests for new memory pages are blocked until the free memory pool is replenished by the page scanner. The page scanner scans inefficiently through all of memory, looking for pages it can free, and slowly refills the free list, but only by enough to satisfy the immediate request. Processes resume for a short time, and then stop as they again run short on memory. The page scanner is a bottleneck in the whole memory life cycle.

In Figure 14.12, we can see the file system's cache mechanism (segmap) consuming memory from the free list until the list is depleted. After those pages are

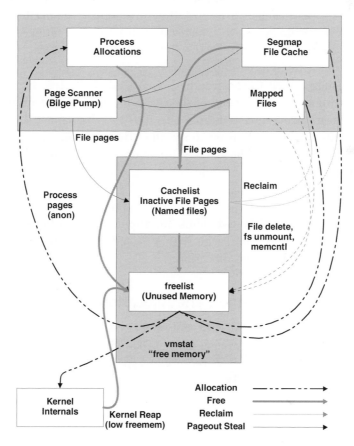

Figure 14.12 Life Cycle of Physical Memory

used, they are kept around, but they are only immediately accessible by the file system cache in the direct reuse case; that is, if a file system cache hit occurs, then they can be "reclaimed" into segmap to avoid a subsequent physical I/O. However, if the file system cache needs a new page, there is no easy way of finding these pages; rather, the page scanner is used to stumble across them. The page scanner effectively "bilges out" the system, blindly looking for new pages to refill the free list. The page scanner has to fill the free list at the same rate at which the file system is reading new pages—and thus is a single point of constraint in the whole design.

14.8.3 The New Allocation Algorithm

The new algorithm uses a central list to place the inactive file cache (that which isn't immediately mapped anywhere), so that it can easily be used to satisfy new memory requests. This is a very subtle change, but one with significant demonstrable effects. First, the file system cache now appears as a single age-ordered FIFO: Recently read pages are placed at the tail of the list, and new pages are consumed from the head. While on the list, the pages remain as valid cached portions of the file, so if a read cache hit occurs, they are simply removed from wherever they are on the list. This means that pages that are accessed often (cache hit often) are frequently moved to the tail of the list, and only the oldest and least used pages migrate to the head as candidates for freeing.

The cache list is linked to the free list, such that if the free list is exhausted, then pages are taken from the head of the cache list and their contents discarded. New page requests are requested from the free list, but since this list is often empty, allocations occur mostly from the head of the cache list, consuming the oldest file system cache pages. The page scanner doesn't need to get involved, thus eliminating the paging bottleneck and the need to run the scanner at high rates (and hence, not wasting CPU either).

If an application process requests a large amount of memory, it too can take from the cache list via the free list. Thus, an application can take a large amount of memory from the file system cache without needing to start the page scanner, resulting in substantially faster allocation.

14.8.4 Putting It All Together: The Allocation Cycle

The most significant central pool physical memory is the free list. Physical memory is placed on the free list in page-size chunks when the system is first booted and then consumed as required. Three major types of allocations occur from the free list, as shown in Figure 14.12.

Anonymous/Process Allocations. Anonymous memory, the most common form of allocation from the free list, is used for most of a process's memory allocation, including heap and stack. Anonymous memory also fulfills shared memory mappings allocations. A small amount of anonymous memory is also used in the kernel for items such as thread stacks. Anonymous memory is pageable and is returned to the free list when it is unmapped or if it is stolen by the page scanner daemon.

File System Page Cache. The page cache caches file data for file systems. The file system page cache grows on demand to consume available physical memory as a file cache and caches file data in page-size chunks. Pages are consumed from the free list as files are read into memory. The pages then reside in one of three places: on the `segmap` cache, in a process's address space to which they are mapped, or on the cache list.

The cache list is the heart of the page cache. All unmapped file pages reside on the cache list. Working in conjunction with the cache list are mapped files and the segmap cache.

Think of the `segmap` file cache as the fast first-level file system read/write cache. `segmap` is a cache that holds file data read and written through the read and write system calls. Memory is allocated from the free list to satisfy a read of a new file page, which then resides in the `segmap` file cache. File pages are eventually moved from the `segmap` cache to the cache list to make room for more pages in the `segmap` cache.

The cachelist is typically 12% of the physical memory size on SPARC systems. The `segmap` cache works in conjunction with the system cache list to cache file data. When files are accessed—through the read and write system calls—up to 12% of the physical memory file data resides in the `segmap` cache and the remainder is on the cache list.

Memory mapped files also allocate memory from the free list and remain allocated in memory for the duration of the mapping or unless a global memory shortage occurs. When a file is unmapped (explicitly or with `madvise`), file pages are returned to the cache list.

The cache list operates as part of the free list. When the free list is depleted, allocations are made from the oldest pages in the cache list. This allows the file system page cache to grow to consume all available memory and to dynamically shrink as memory is required for other purposes.

Kernel Allocations. The kernel uses memory to manage information about internal system state, for example, memory that holds the list of processes in the system. The kernel allocates memory from the free list for these purposes with its own allocators: `vmem` and `slab`. However, unlike process and file allocations, the kernel seldom returns memory to the free list; memory is allocated and freed between kernel subsystems and the kernel allocators. Memory is consumed from the free list only when the total kernel allocation grows.

Memory allocated to the kernel is mostly nonpageable and so cannot be managed by the system page scanner daemon. Memory is returned to the system free list proactively by the kernel's allocators when a global memory shortage occurs. See Chapter 11.

14.9 Path-Name Management

All but a few of the vnode methods operate on vnode pointers rather than on path names. Before calling file system vnode methods, the vnode framework first converts path names and file descriptors into vnode references. File descriptors may be directly translated into vnodes for the files they referenced, whereas path names must be converted into vnodes by a lookup of the path-name components and a reference to the underlying file. The file-system-independent lookuppn() function converts path names to vnodes. An additional wrapper, lookupname(), converts path names from user-mode system calls.

14.9.1 The lookuppn() Method

Given a path name, the lookuppn() method attempts to return a pointer to the vnode the path represents. If the vnode is already available, then a new reference to the vnode is established. If no vnode is available, one is created. The lookuppn() function decomposes the components of the path name, separating them by "/" and ".", and calls the file-system-specific vop_lookup() method (see below) for each component of the path name.

If the path name begins with a "/", path-name traversal starts at the user's root directory. Otherwise, it starts at the vnode pointed to by the user's current directory. lookuppn() traverses the path one component at a time, using the vop_lookup() vnode method.

If a directory vnode has v_vfsmountedhere set, then it is a mount point. If lookuppn() encounters a mount point while going down the file system tree, then it follows the vnode's v_vfsmountedhere pointer to the mounted file system and calls the vfs_root() method to obtain the root vnode for the file system. Path-name traversal then continues from this point.

If lookuppn() encounters a root vnode (VROOT flag in v_flag set) when following "..", then lookuppn() follows the vfs_vnodecovered pointer in the vnode's associated vfs to obtain the covered vnode.

If lookuppn() encounters a symbolic link, then it calls the vn_readlink() vnode method to obtain the symbolic link. If the symbolic link begins with a "/", the path-name traversal is restarted from the root directory; otherwise, the traversal continues from the last directory. The caller of lookuppn() specifies whether the last component of the path name is to be followed if it is a symbolic link.

This procedure continues until the path name is exhausted or an error occurs. When lookuppn() completes, it returns a vnode representing the desired file.

14.9.2 The vop_lookup() Method

The vop_lookup() method searches a directory for a path-name component matching the supplied path name. The vop_lookup() method accepts a directory vnode and a string path-name component as an argument and returns a vnode pointer to the vnode representing the file. If the file cannot be located, then ENOENT is returned.

Many regular file systems will first check the directory name lookup cache, and if an entry is found there, the entry is returned. If the entry is not found in the directory name cache, then a real lookup of the file is performed.

14.9.3 The vop_readdir() Method

The vop_readdir() method reads chunks of the directory into a uio structure. Each chunk can contain as many entries as will fit within the size supplied by the uio structure. The uio_resid structure member shows the size of the getdents request in bytes, which is divided by the size of the directory entry made by the vop_readdir() method to calculate how many directory entries to return.

Directories are read from disk with the buffered kernel file functions fbread and fbwrite. These functions, described below, are provided as part of the generic file system infrastructure.

```
/*
 * A struct fbuf is used to get a mapping to part of a file using the
 * segkmap facilities.  After you get a mapping, you can fbrelse() it
 * (giving a seg code to pass back to segmap_release), you can fbwrite()
 * it (causes a synchronous write back using the file mapping information),
 * or you can fbiwrite it (causing indirect synchronous write back to
 * the block number given without using the file mapping information).
 */

struct fbuf {
        caddr_t  fb_addr;
        uint_t   fb_count;
};
```

continues

```
extern int fbread(struct vnode *, offset_t, uint_t, enum seg_rw, struct fbuf **);
```

Returns a pointer to locked kernel virtual address for the given <vp, off> for len
bytes. The read may not cross a boundary of MAXBSIZE (8192) bytes.

```
extern void fbzero(struct vnode *, offset_t, uint_t, struct fbuf **);
```

Similar to fbread(), but calls segmap_pagecreate(), not segmap_fault(), so that SOFT-
LOCK can create the pages without using VOP_GETPAGE(). Then, fbzero() zeroes up to the
length rounded to a page boundary.

```
extern int fbwrite(struct fbuf *);
```

Direct write.

```
extern int fbiwrite(struct fbuf *, struct vnode *, daddr_t bn, int bsize);
```

Writes directly and invalidates pages.

```
extern int fbdwrite(struct fbuf *);
```

Delayed write.

```
extern void fbrelse(struct fbuf *, enum seg_rw);
```

Releases fbp.

See usr/src/uts/common/sys/fbuf.h

14.9.4 Path-Name Traversal Functions

Several path-name manipulation functions assist with decomposition of path
names. The path-name functions use a path-name structure, shown below, to pass
around path-name components.

```
/*
 * Pathname structure.
 * System calls that operate on path names gather the path name
 * from the system call into this structure and reduce it by
 * peeling off translated components.  If a symbolic link is
 * encountered the new path name to be translated is also
 * assembled in this structure.
 *
 * By convention pn_buf is not changed once it's been set to point
 * to the underlying storage; routines which manipulate the path name
 * do so by changing pn_path and pn_pathlen.  pn_pathlen is redundant
 * since the path name is null-terminated, but is provided to make
 * some computations faster.
 */
typedef struct pathname {
        char    *pn_buf;                        /* underlying storage */
        char    *pn_path;                       /* remaining pathname */
        size_t  pn_pathlen;                     /* remaining length */
        size_t  pn_bufsize;                     /* total size of pn_buf */
} pathname_t;
```

See usr/src/uts/common/sys/pathname.h

The path-name functions are shown below.

---

void pn_alloc(struct pathname *pnp);

Allocates a new path-name buffer.Structure is typically an automatic variable in calling routine for convenience.May sleep in the call to kmem_alloc() and so must not be
called from interrupt level.

int pn_get(char *str, enum uio_seg seg, struct pathname *pnp);

Copies path-name string from user and mounts arguments into a struct path name.

int pn_set(struct pathname *pnp, char *path);

Sets a path name to the supplied string.

int pn_insert(struct pathname *pnp, struct pathname *sympnp, size_t complen);

Combines two argument path names by putting the second argument before the first in the
first's buffer. This isn't very general; it is designed specifically for symbolic link
processing. This function copies the symlink in-place in the path name. This is to
ensure that vnode path caching remains correct. At the point where this is called (from
lookuppnvp), we have called pn_getcomponent(), found it is a symlink, and are now
replacing the contents. The complen parameter indicates how much of the path name to
replace. If the symlink is an absolute path, then we overwrite the entire contents of
the pathname.

int pn_getsymlink(vnode_t *vp, struct pathname *pnp, cred_t *crp);

Follows a symbolic link for a path name.

int pn_getcomponent(struct pathname *pnp, char *component);

Extracts the next delimited path-name component.

void pn_setlast(struct pathname *pnp);

Sets pn_path to the last component in the path name, updating pn_pathlen. If pathname
is empty or degenerate, leaves pn_path pointing at NULL char.The path name is explicitly
null-terminated so that any trailing slashes are effectively removed.

void pn_skipslash(struct pathname *pnp);

Skips over consecutive slashes in the path name.

int pn_fixslash(struct pathname *pnp);

Eliminates any trailing slashes in the path name.

int pn_addslash(struct pathname *pnp);

Add sa slash to the end of the path name, if it will fit.Return ENAMETOOLONG if it
won't.

void pn_free(struct pathname *pnp);

Frees a struct path name.

See usr/src/uts/common/sys/pathname.h

14.10 The Directory Name Lookup Cache

The directory name lookup cache (DNLC) is based on BSD 4.2 code. It was ported to Solaris 2.0 and threaded and has undergone some significant revisions. Most of the enhancements to the DNLC have been performance and threading, but a few visible changes are noteworthy. Table 14.6 summarizes the important changes to the DNLC.

Table 14.6 Solaris DNLC Changes

Year	OS Rev	Comment
1984	BSD 4.2	14-character name maximum
1990	Solaris 2.0	31-character name maximum
1994	Solaris 2.4	Performance (new locking/search algorithm)
1998	Solaris 7	Variable name length
2001	Solaris 8	Directory caching and negative entry caching

14.10.1 DNLC Operation

Each time we open a file, we call the open() system call with a path name. That path name must be translated to a vnode by the process of reading the directory and finding the corresponding name that matches the requested name. To prevent us from having to reread the directory every time we translate the path name, we cache the containing directory vnode/file-name name and the corresponding vnode mappings in the directory name lookup cache. The cache is managed as an LRU cache, so that most frequently used directory entries are kept in the cache.

The Solaris DNLC replaces the original SVR4 DNLC algorithm. It yielded a significant improvement in scalability. The Solaris 2.4 DNLC algorithm removed LRU list lock contention by eliminating the LRU list completely. In addition, the list takes into account the number of references to a vnode and whether the vnode has any pages in the page cache. This design allows the DNLC to cache the most relevant vnodes, rather than just the most frequently looked-up vnodes.

Figure 14.13 illustrates the Solaris DNLC.

The lookup algorithm uses a rotor pointing to a hash chain; the rotor switches chains for each invocation of dnlc_enter() that needs a new entry. The algorithm starts at the end of the chain and takes the first entry that has a vnode reference count of 1 or no pages in the page cache. In addition, during lookup, entries are moved to the front of the chain so that each chain is sorted in LRU order.

The DNLC was enhanced to use the kernel memory allocator to allocate a variable length string for the name; this change removed the 31-character limit. In the

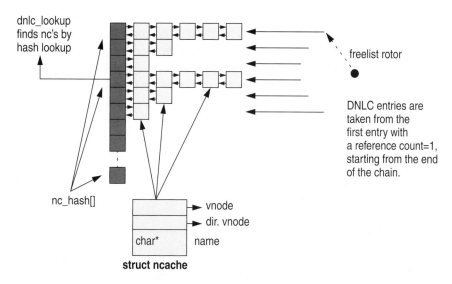

Figure 14.13 Solaris DNLC

Solaris 7 DNLC structure, shown in Figure 14.13, note that the name field has changed from a static structure to a pointer.

The number of entries in the DNLC is controlled by the ncsize parameter, which is initialized to 4 * (max_nprocs + maxusers) + 320 at system boot.

Most of the DNLC work is done with two functions: dnlc_enter() and dnlc_lookup(). When a file system wants to look up the name of a file, it first checks the DNLC with the dnlc_lookup() function, which queries the DNLC for an entry that matches the specified file name and directory vnode. If no entry is found, dnlc_lookup fails and the file system reads the directory from disk. When the file name is found, it is entered into the DNLC with the dnlc_enter() function. The DNLC stores entries on a hashed list (nc_hash[]) by file name and directory vnode pointer. Once the correct nc_hash chain is identified, the chain is searched linearly until the correct entry is found.

The original BSD DNLC had 8 nc_hash entries, which was increased to 64 in SunOS 4.x. Solaris 2.0 sized the nc_hash list at boot, attempting to make the average length of each chain no more than 4 entries. It used the total DNLC size, ncsize, divided by the average length to establish the number of nc_hash entries. Solaris 2.3 had the average length of the chain dropped to 2 in an attempt to increase DNLC performance; however, other problems, related to the LRU list locking and described below, adversely affected performance.

Each entry in the DNLC is also linked to an LRU list, in order of last use. When a new entry is added into the DNLC, the algorithm replaces the oldest entry from the LRU list with the new file name and directory vnode. Each time a lookup is done, the DNLC also takes the entry from the LRU and places it at the end of the list so that it won't be reused immediately. The DNLC uses the LRU list to attempt to keep most-used references in the cache. Although the DNLC list had been made short, the LRU list still caused contention because it required that a single lock be held around the entire chain.

14.10.2 Primary DNLC Support Functions

The primary DNLC support functions are summarized below.

```
void    dnlc_enter(vnode_t *dvp, char *name, vnode_t *vp, cred_t *cr);
```

Enters a new ncache entry into the DNLC for the given name and directory vnode pointer. If an entry already exists for the name and directory pointer, the function returns with no action.

```
void    dnlc_update(vnode_t *dvp, char *name, vnode_t *vp, cred_t *cr);
```

Enters a new ncache entry into the DNLC for the given name and directory vnode pointer. If an entry already exists for the name and directory pointer but the vnode is different, then the entry is overwritten. Otherwise, the function returns with no action.

```
vnode_t *dnlc_lookup(vnode_t *dvp, char *name, cred_t *cr);
```

Locates an ncache entry that matches the supplied name and directory vnode pointer. Returns a pointer to the vnode for that entry or returns NULL.

```
void    dnlc_purge(void);
```

Called by the vfs framework when an umountall() is called.

```
void    dnlc_purge_vp(vnode_t *vp);
```

Purges all entries matching the vnode supplied.

```
int     dnlc_purge_vfsp(vfs_t *vfs, int);
```

Purges all entries matching the vfs supplied.

```
void    dnlc_remove(vnode_t *vp, char *name);
```

Removes the entry matching the supplied name and directory vnode pointer.

```
int     dnlc_fs_purge1(struct vnodeops *vop);
```

Purge 1 entry from the dnlc that is part of the file system(s) represented by 'vop'. The purpose of this routine is to allow users of the dnlc to free a vnode that is being held by the dnlc.If we find a vnode that we release which will result in freeing the underlying vnode (count was 1), return 1, 0 if no appropriate vnodes found.

See usr/src/uts/common/sys/dnlc.h

14.10.3 DNLC Negative Cache

The DNLC has support for negative caching. Some applications repeatedly test for the existence or nonexistence of a file (for example, a lock file or a results file). In addition, many shell PATH variables list directories that don't exist. For these applications, caching the fact that the file doesn't exist (negative caching) is a performance boost.

The DNLC negative cache follows the NFS negative-cache solution. It defines a negative cache vnode that is initialized with the reference count set to 1 so that VOP_INACTIVE() never gets called on it.

```
vnode_t negative_cache_vnode;

#define DNLC_NO_VNODE &negative_cache_vnode
```

See usr/src/uts/common/sys/dnlc.h

File systems were updated in Solaris 8 to use negative caching so that each dnlc_lookup() checks for a DNLC_NO_VNODE return. Negative cache entries will be added when directory lookups fail, and will be invalidated by dnlc_update() when a real file of that name is added.

14.10.4 DNLC Directory Cache

The directory cache adds a new set of interfaces to the DNLC to cache entire directories. The directory cache eliminates performance bottlenecks for directories with tens of thousands of files. This helps performance when the file name repeatedly changes and when new files are created. It removes the need to search the entire directory to find out if the file name already exists. It turns out that mail and news spool directories see this scenario all the time.

The DNLC structure is shown below.

```
/*
 * This structure describes the elements in the cache of recent
 * names looked up.
 *
 * Note namlen is a uchar_t to conserve space
 * and alignment padding. The max length of any
 * pathname component is defined as MAXNAMELEN
 * which is 256 (including the terminating null).
 * So provided this doesn't change, we don't include the null,
 * we always use bcmp to compare strings, and we don't start
 * storing full names, then we are ok. The space savings are worth it.
 */
```

continues

```
typedef struct ncache {
        struct ncache *hash_next;        /* hash chain, MUST BE FIRST */
        struct ncache *hash_prev;
        struct vnode *vp;                /* vnode the name refers to */
        struct vnode *dp;                /* vnode of parent of name */
        int hash;                        /* hash signature */
        uchar_t namlen;                  /* length of name */
        char name[1];                    /* segment name - null terminated */
} ncache_t;
```
                                               See usr/src/uts/common/sys/dnlc.h

File systems must provide a structure for use only by the DNLC directory caching code for each directory.

```
typedef struct dcanchor {
        void *dca_dircache;        /* opaque directory cache handle */
        kmutex_t dca_lock;         /* protects the pointer and cache */
} dcanchor_t;
```

All file systems have an in-memory *xx*node (for example, inode in `ufs`) that could contain such a structure. Following is an example of how a file system would use the directory cache interfaces.

```
fs_lookup(dir, name)
{
        Return entry if in regular dnlc
        dcap = dir->dcap;
        switch dnlc_dir_lookup(dcap, name, &handle)
        case DFOUND:
                use handle to get and return vnode
                break
        case DNOENT:
                return ENOENT
        }
        caching = 0;
        if want to cache directory {
                switch dnlc_dir_start(dcap, num_dir_entries)
                case DNOMEM:
                case DTOOBIG:
                        mark directory as non cache-able
                        break;
                case
                        caching = 1;
        }
        while not end of directory {
                if entry && caching
                        handle = ino and offset;
                        dnlc_dir_add_entry(dcap, entry_name, handle)
                if free space && caching
                        handle = offset;
                        dnlc_dir_add_space(dcap, length. handle)
                if entry matches
                        get vnode
```

continues

```
            if various errors
                    if caching
                            dnlc_dir_purge(dcap)
                    return error

    }
    if caching
            dnlc_dir_complete(dcap)
    return vnode or ENOENT
}
```

The following set of new `dnlc` interfaces will be provided to cache complete directory contents (both entries and free space).

Status returns from the directory cache interfaces

```
#define DOK          0       /* operation successful */
#define DNOCACHE     1       /* there is no cache */
#define DFOUND       2       /* entry found */
#define DNOENT       3       /* no entry found */
#define DTOOBIG      4       /* exceeds tunable dnlc_dir_max_size */
#define DNOMEM       5       /* no memory */
```

Interfaces for building and adding to the directory cache

int dnlc_dir_start(dcanchor_t *dcap, uint_t num_entries);

Requests that a directory be cached. This must be called initially to enable caching on a directory. After a successful call, directory entries and free space can be added (see below) until the directory is marked complete. num_entries is an estimate of the current number of directory entries. The request is rejected with DNOCACHE if num_entries falls below the tunable dnlc_dir_min_size (see below), and rejected with DTOOBIG if it's above dnlc_dir_max_size.

Returns DOK, DNOCACHE, DTOOBIG, DNOMEM (see below)

int dnlc_dir_add_entry(dcanchor_t *dcap, char *name, uint64_t handle);

Adds an entry (name and handle) into the partial or complete cache. Handle is a file-system-specific quantity that is returned on calls to dnlc_dir_lookup() - see below. Handle for ufs holds the inumber and a directory entry offset.

Returns DOK, DNOCACHE, DTOOBIG

int dnlc_dir_add_space(dcanchor_t *dcap, uint_t len, uint64_t handle);

Add free space (length and file-system-specific handle) into the partial or complete cache. Handle for ufs holds the directory entry offset

Returns DOK, DNOCACHE, DTOOBIG

void dnlc_dir_complete(dcanchor_t *dcap);

Indicates the previously partial cache is now complete

void dnlc_dir_purge(dcanchor_t *dcap);

Deletes the partial or complete cache

continues

```
Interface for reading the directory cache

int dnlc_dir_lookup(dcanchor_t *dcap, char *name, uint64_t *handlep);

Looks up a file in the cache. Handlep must be non-null, and will be set to point to the
file-system-supplied handle

Returns DFOUND, DNOENT, DNOCACHE

Interfaces for amending the cache

int dnlc_dir_update(dcanchor_t *dcap, char *name, uint64_t handle);

Update the handle for the given entry

Returns DFOUND, DNOENT, DNOCACHE

int dnlc_dir_rem_entry(dcanchor_t *dcap, char *name, uint64_t *handlep);

Remove an entry

Returns the handle if handlep non-null and DFOUND, DNOENT, DNOCACHE

int dnlc_dir_rem_space_by_len(dcanchor_t *dcap, uint_t len, uint64_t *handlep);

Find and remove a space entry with at least the given length and
Returns the handle, and DFOUND, DNOENT, DNOCACHE

int dnlc_dir_rem_space_by_handle(dcanchor_t *dcap, uint64_t handle);

Find and removes the free space with the given handle

Returns DFOUND, DNOENT, DNOCACHE

Interfaces for initializing and finishing with the directory cache anchor

void dnlc_dir_init(dcanchor_t *dcap);

Initializes the anchor. This macro clears the dca_dircache field and does a mutex_init
on the lock

void dnlc_dir_fini(dcanchor_t *dcap);

Called to indicate the anchor is no longer used. This macro asserts there's no cache and
mutex_destroys the lock.
```

Additional notes on the directory cache interface are as follows:

- Because of memory shortages, directory caches can be purged at any time. If the last directory cache is purged because of a memory shortage, then the directory cache is marked internally as "no memory." Future returns will all be DNOCACHE until the next dnlc_start_dir(), which will return DNOMEM once. This memory shortage may only be transient. It's up to the file system to handle this condition, but an attempt to immediately rebuild the cache will very likely lead to the same shortage of memory and to thrashing.

- It's file system policy as to when and what size directories to cache.

- Directory caches are purged according to LRU basis when a plea to release memory comes from the kmem system. A kmem_cache is used for one data structure, and on the reclaim callback, the LRU directory cache is released. Directory caches are also purged on failure to get additional memory. Otherwise, directories are cached as much as memory allows.

14.10.5 DNLC Housekeeping Thread

The DNLC maintains a task queue. The dnlc_reduce_cache() activates the task queue when there are ncsize name cache entries, and it reduces the size to dnlc_nentries_low_water, which is by default one hundredth less than (or 99% of) ncsize. If dnlc_nentries hits dnlc_max_nentries (twice ncsize), then this means that dnlc_reduce_cache() is failing to keep up. In this case, we refuse to add new entries to the dnlc until the task queue catches up.

14.10.6 DNLC Statistics

Below is an example of DNLC statistics obtained with the kstat command.

```
sol10$ kstat -n dnlcstats
module: unix                             instance: 0
name:   dnlcstats                        class:     misc
        crtime                           70.644144966
        dir_add_abort                    0
        dir_add_max                      0
        dir_add_no_memory                0
        dir_cached_current               0
        dir_cached_total                 269
        dir_entries_cached_current       0
        dir_fini_purge                   0
        dir_hits                         131992
        dir_misses                       1312735
        dir_reclaim_any                  23
        dir_reclaim_last                 4
        dir_remove_entry_fail            0
        dir_remove_space_fail            0
        dir_start_no_memory              0
        dir_update_fail                  0
        double_enters                    310146
        enters                           22732358
        hits                             384680010
        misses                           2390823
        negative_cache_hits              6048394
        pick_free                        0
        pick_heuristic                   15613169
        pick_last                        632544
        purge_all                        0
        purge_fs1                        0
        purge_total_entries              5369737
        purge_vfs                        27052
        purge_vp                         3009
        snaptime                         4408540.56846945
```

14.11 The File System Flush Daemon

The `fsflush` process writes modified pages to disk at regular intervals. The `fsflush` process scans through physical memory looking for dirty pages. When it finds one, it initiates a `write` (or `putpage`) operation on that page.

The `fsflush` process is launched by default every second and looks for pages that have been modified (the modified bit is set in the `page` structure) more than 30 seconds ago. If a page has been modified, then a page-out is scheduled for that page, but without the free flag so that the page remains in memory. The `fsflush` daemon flushes both data pages and inodes by default. Table 14.7 describes the parameters that affect the behavior of `fsflush`.

Table 14.7 Parameters That Affect `fsflush`

Parameter	Description	Min	Solaris 10 Default
`tune_t_fsflushr`	This specifies the number of seconds between `fsflush` scans.	1	1
`autoup`	Pages older than `autoup` in seconds are written to disk.	1	30
`doiflush`	By default, `fsflush` flushes both inode and data pages. Set to 0 to suppress inode updates.	0	1
`dopageflush`	This is set to 0 to suppress page flushes.	0	1

14.12 File System Conversion to Solaris 10

If you are porting a file system source to Solaris 10, you can follow these steps to convert an older file system to the new Solaris 10 APIs.

1. Vnodes must be separated from FS-specific nodes (for example, inodes). Previously, most file systems embedded the vnode in the FS-specific node. The node should now have a pointer to the vnode. vnodes are allocated by the file system with `vn_alloc()` and freed with `vn_free()`. If the file system recycles vnodes (by means of a node cache), then vnodes can be reinitialized with `vn_reinit()`.

   Note: Make sure the `VTO{node}()` and `{node}TOV()` routines and the corresponding FS-node macros are updated.

2. Change all references to the "private" vnode fields to use accessors. The only "public" fields are listed below.

```
kmutex_t        v_lock;        /* protects vnode fields */
uint_t          v_flag;        /* vnode flags (see below) */
uint_t          v_count;       /* reference count */
caddr_t         v_data;        /* private data for fs */
struct vfs      *v_vfsp;       /* ptr to containing VFS */
struct stdata   *v_stream;     /* associated stream */
enum vtype      v_type;        /* vnode type */
dev_t           v_rdev;        /* device (VCHR, VBLK) */
```

Otherwise, information about the vnode can be accessed, as shown below.

```
For:                    Use:

v_vfsmountedhere        vn_ismntpt() or vn_mountedvfs()
v_op                    vn_setops(), vn_getops(), vn_matchops(),
                        vn_matchopval()
v_pages                 vn_has_cached_data()
v_filocks               vn_has_flocks(), vn_has_mandatory_locks()
```

3. The only significant change to the vfs structure is that the vfs_op field should not be used directly. Any references or accesses to that field *must* go through one of the following: vfs_setops(),vfs_getops(), vfs_matchops(),vfs_can_sync().

4. Create an FS definition structure (vfsdef_t). This is similar to, but replaces, the vfssw table entry.

5. Create the operation definition tables for vnode and vfs operations.

6. Update (or create) the FS initialization routine (called at module-loader time) to create the vfsops and vnodeops structures. You do this by calling vn_make_ops() and either vfs_setfsops() (or vfs_makefsops()), using the "operations definition table" (created above).

7. Update the following vnode operation routines (if applicable):

Add a pointer to the caller_context structure to the argument list for the following FS-specific routines: *xxx*_read(), *xxx*_write(), *xxx*_space(), *xxx*_setattr(), *xxx*_rwlock(), *xxx*_rwunlock().

Add a pointer to the cred structure to the argument list for the following FS-specific routine: *xxx*_shrlock().

Important note: Because the compilers don't yet support "designated initializers," the compiler cannot strongly type-check the file-system-specific vnode/vfs operations through the registration system. It's important that any changes to the argument list be done very carefully.

8. vnode life cycle: When a vnode is created (fully initialized, after locks are
    dropped but before anyone can get to it), call vn_exists(vnode *vp). This
    notifies anyone with registered interest on this file system that a new vnode
    has been created. If just the vnode is to be torn down (still fully functional,
    but before any locks are taken), call vn_invalid(vnode_t *vp) so that
    anyone with registered interest can be notified that this vnode is about to
    go away.

14.13 MDB Reference

Table 14.8 File System MDB Reference

dcmd or walker	Description
dcmd dnlc	Print DNLC contents
dcmd fsinfo	Print mounted filesystems
dcmd inode	Display summarized inode_t
dcmd inode_cache	Search/display inodes from inode cache
dcmd vnode2path	Vnode address to pathname
dcmd vnode2smap	Translate vnode to smap
dcmd whereopen	Given a vnode, dumps procs which have it open
walk dnlc_space_cache	Walk the dnlc_space_cache cache
walk vfs	Walk file system list
walk vn_cache	Walk the vn_cache cache

15

The UFS File System

Updated by Frank Batschulat, Shawn Debnath, Sarah Jelinek,
Dworkin Muller, and Karen Rochford

The UFS file system is the general-purpose, disk-based file system that is shipped with Solaris today and has been the default file system since early versions of SunOS 4.x. For over 20 years, UFS has undergone extensive changes to keep pace with the performance, security, and reliability requirements of today's modern enterprise applications.

15.1 UFS Development History

The original version of UFS is derived from the Berkeley Fast File System (FFS) work from BSD UNIX, architected by Marshall Kirk McKusick and Bill Joy in the mid 1980s. The Berkeley FFS was the second major file system available for UNIX and was a leap forward from the original System V file system. The System V file system was lightweight and simple but had significant shortcomings: poor performance, unreliability, and lack of functionality.

During the development of Sun OS 2.0, a file-system-independent interface was introduced to support concurrent, different file systems within an operating system instance. This interface, today known as the vnode/vfs interface, is the mechanism that all file systems use to interface with the file-related system calls. (The vnode/vfs architecture is discussed further in Section 14.6.) UFS was modified so that it could be used within this new vnode/vfs framework and since has been the focus of much of the file system development effort in Solaris.

A second major overhaul for UFS came about at the time of SunOS 4.0, when the virtual memory (VM) system was redeveloped to use the vnode as the core of virtual memory operations. The new VM system implemented the concept of virtual file caching—a departure from the traditional physical file cache (known as the "buffer cache" in previous versions of UNIX). The old buffer cache was layered under the file systems and was responsible for caching physical blocks from the file system to the storage device. The new model is layered above the file systems and allows the VM system to act as a cache for files rather than blocks. The new system caches page-sized pieces of files, whereby the file and a particular offset are cached as pages of memory. From this point forward, the buffer cache was used only for file system metadata, and the VM system implemented the file system caching. The introduction of the virtual file caching affected file systems in many ways and required significant changes to the vnode interface. At that point, UFS was substantially modified to support the new vnode and VM interfaces.

The third major change to UFS came about in Solaris 2.4 in the year 1994 with the introduction of file system metadata logging in an effort to provide better reliability and faster reboot times after a system crash or outage. The first versions of logging were introduced with the unbundled Online: DiskSuite 3.0 software package, the precursor to Solstice DiskSuite (SDS) product and the Solaris Volume Manager (SVM) as it is known today. Solaris 7 saw the integration of logging into UFS, and after six years of development, Solaris 10 shipped with logging turned on by default. Table 15.1 summarizes the major UFS development milestones.

Table 15.1 UNIX File System Evolution

1984	SunOS 1.0	FFS from 4.2 BSD.
1985	SunOS 2.0	UFS rearchitected to support vnodes/vfs.
1988	SunOS 4.0	UFS integrated with new VM virtual file cache.
1991	SunOS 4.1	I/O clustering added to allow extentlike performance.
1992	SunOS 4.1	1TB file system and ability to grow UFS file systems with Online: Disk Suite 1.0.
1992	Solaris 2.0	1TB file system support included in base Solaris.
1994	Solaris 2.4	Metadata logging option with Online: DiskSuite 3.0.
1995	Solaris 2.5	Access Control Lists.
1995	Solaris 2.6	Large file support allows 1TB files. Direct I/O uncached access added.
1998	Solaris 7	Metadata logging integrated into base Solaris UFS.
2002	Solaris 9	File System Snapshots Extended Attributes
2003	Solaris 9 Update 4	Multi-terabyte UFS support was added.
2004	Solaris 10 and Solaris 9 Update 7	Logging on by default in UFS.

15.2 UFS On-Disk Format

UFS is built around the concept of a disk's geometry, which is described as the number of sectors in a track, the location of the head, and the number of tracks. UFS uses a hybrid block allocation strategy that allocates full blocks or smaller parts of the block called fragments. A block is a set of contigous fragments starting on a particular boundary. This boundary is determined by the size of a fragment and the number of fragments that constitute a block. For example, fragment 32 and block 32 both relate to the same physical location on disk. Although the next fragment on disk is 33 followed by 34, 35, 36, 37 and so on, the next block is at 40, which begins on fragment 40. This is true in the case of 8-Kbyte block size and 1-Kbyte fragment size, where 8 fragments constitutes a file system block.

15.2.1 On-Disk UFS Inodes

In UFS, all information pertaining to a file is stored in a special file index node called the inode (except for the name of the file, which is stored in the directory). There are two types of inodes: in-core and on-disk. The on-disk inodes, as the name implies, reside on disk, whereas the in-core inode is created only when a particular file is opened for reading or writing.

The on-disk inode is represented by `struct icommon`. It occupies exactly 128 bytes on disk and can also be found embedded in the in-core inode structure, as shown in Figure 15.1.

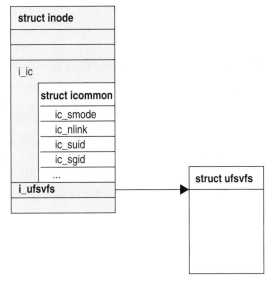

Figure 15.1 Embedded On-Disk in In-Core Inode

The structure of icommon looks like this.

```
struct  icommon {
        o_mode_t ic_smode;      /*  0: mode and type of file */
        short   ic_nlink;       /*  2: number of links to file */
        o_uid_t ic_suid;        /*  4: owner's user id */
        o_gid_t ic_sgid;        /*  6: owner's group id */
        u_offset_t ic_lsize;    /*  8: number of bytes in file */
#ifdef _KERNEL
        struct timeval32 ic_atime;      /* 16: time last accessed */
        struct timeval32 ic_mtime;      /* 24: time last modified */
        struct timeval32 ic_ctime;      /* 32: last time inode changed */
#else
        time32_t ic_atime;      /* 16: time last accessed */
        int32_t ic_atspare;
        time32_t ic_mtime;      /* 24: time last modified */
        int32_t ic_mtspare;
        time32_t ic_ctime;      /* 32: last time inode changed */
        int32_t ic_ctspare;
#endif
        daddr32_t       ic_db[NDADDR];  /* 40: disk block addresses */
        daddr32_t       ic_ib[NIADDR];  /* 88: indirect blocks */
        int32_t ic_flags;       /* 100: cflags */
        int32_t ic_blocks;      /* 104: 512 byte blocks actually held */
        int32_t ic_gen;         /* 108: generation number */
        int32_t ic_shadow;      /* 112: shadow inode */
        uid_t   ic_uid;         /* 116: long EFT version of uid */
        gid_t   ic_gid;         /* 120: long EFT version of gid */
        uint32_t ic_oeftflag;   /* 124: extended attr directory ino, 0 = none */
};
```

See usr/src/uts/common/sys/fs/ufs_inode.h

Most of the fields are self-explaining, but a couple of them need a bit of help:

- **ic_smode.** Indicates the type of inode. There are primarily four main types of inode: zero, special node (IFCHR, IFBLK, IFIFO, IFSOCK), symbolic link (IFLNK), a directory (IFDIR), a file (IFREG), or an extended metadata inode (IFSHAD, IFATTRDIR). Type zero indicates that the inode is not in use and ic_nlink should be zero, unless logging's reclaim_needed flag is set. With the special nodes, no data blocks are associated. They are used for character and block devices, pipes and sockets. The type file indicates where this inode is a directory, a regular file, a shadow inode, or an extended attribute directory.

- **ic_nlink.** Refers to the number of links to a file, that is, the number of names in the namespace that correspond to a specific file identifier. A regular file will have link count of 1 because only one name in the namespace corresponds to that particular file identifier. A directory link count has the value

2 by default: one is the name of the directory itself, and the other is the "."
entry within the directory. Any subdirectory within a directory causes the
link count to be incremented by 1 because of the ".." entry. The limit is 32,767
and hence, the limit for the number of subdirectories is 32,765 and also the
total number of links. The ".." entry counts against the parent directory only.

- **ic_db.** Is an array that holds 12 pointers to data blocks. These are called the
  direct blocks. On a system with block size of 8192 bytes or 8 Kbytes, these can
  accommodate up to 98,304 bytes or 96 Kbytes. If the file consists entirely of
  direct blocks, then the last block for the file (not the last ic_db entry) may
  contain fragments. Note that if the file size exceeds the capacity of the ic_db
  array, then the block list for the file must consist entirely of full-sized file system blocks.

- **ic_ib.** Is a small array of only three pointers but allows a file to be up to one
  terabyte. How does this work? Well, the first entry in ic_ib points to a block
  that stores 2048 block addresses. A file with a single indirect block can accommodate up to 8192 * (12 + 2048) bytes or 16 Mbytes. If more storage is required,
  another level of indirection is added and the second indirect block is used.

  The second entry in ic_ib points to 2048 block addresses, and each of
  those 2048 entries points to another block containing 2048 entries that finally
  point to the data blocks. With two levels of indirection, a file can accommodate up to 8192 * 12 + 2048 + (2048 * 2048) bytes, or 32 Gbytes. A third level
  of indirection permits the file to be 8192 * 12 + 2048 + (2048 * 2048) + (2048 *
  2048 * 2048) = 70,403,120,791,552 bytes long or—yes, you guessed it—64 Tbytes!
  However, since all addresses must be addressable as fragments, that is, a
  31-bit count, the maximum is 2TB (2^{31} * 1KB). Multi-terrabyte UFS
  (MTBUFS) enables 16TB filesystem sizes by enforcing the minimum frag
  size to be 8K, which gives you 2^{31} * 2^{10} * 8k, or 16 TB.

  Figure 15.2 illustrates the layout.

- **ic_shadow.** If non-zero, contains the number of an inode providing shadow
  metadata (usually, this data would be ACLs).

- **ic_oeftflag.** If non-zero, contains the number of an inode of type
  IFATTRDIR, which is a directory containing extended attribute files.

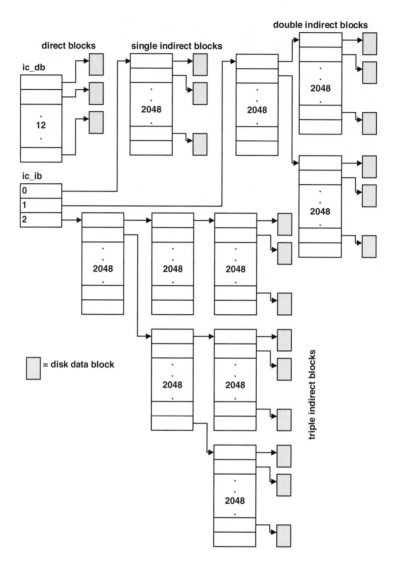

Figure 15.2 UFS Block Layout

15.2.2 UFS Directories

The file name information and hierarchy information that constitute the directory structure of UFS are stored in directories. Each directory stores a list of file names and the inode number for each file; this information (stored in `struct direct`) allows the directory structure to relate file names to real disk files.

The directory itself is stored in a file as a series of chunks, which are groups of the directory entries. Earlier file systems like the System V file system had a fixed directory record length, which meant that a lot of space would be wasted if provision was made for long file names. In the UFS, each directory entry can be of variable length, thus providing a mechanism for long file names without a lot of wasted space. UFS file names can be up to 255 characters long.

The group of directory chunks that constitute a directory is stored as a special type of file. The notion of a directory as a type of file allows UFS to implement a hierarchical directory structure: Directories can contain files that are directories. For example, the root directory has a name, "/", and an inode number, 2, which holds a chunk of directory entries holding a number of files and directories. One of these directory entries, named etc, is another directory containing more files and directories. For traversal up and down the file system, the chdir system call opens the directory file in question and then sets the current working directory to point to the new directory file. Figure 15.3 illustrates the directory hierarchy.

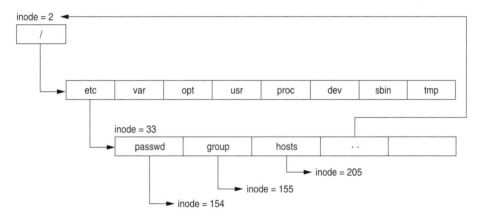

Figure 15.3 UNIX Directory Hierarchy

Each directory contains two special files. The file named "." is a link to the directory itself; the file named ".." is a link to the parent directory. Thus, a change of directory to .. leads to the parent directory.

Now let's switch gears and see what the on-disk structures for directories look like.

The contents of a directory are broken up into DIRBLKSIZ chunks, also known as dirblks. Each of these contains one or more direct structures. DIRBLKSIZ was chosen to be the same as the size of a disk sector so that modifications to directory entries could be done atomically on the assumption that a sector write either completes successfully or fails (which can no longer be guaranteed with the advancement of cached hard drives).

Each directory entry is stored in a structure called `direct` that contains the inode number (`d_ino`), the length of the entry (`d_reclen`), the length of the name (`d_namelen`), and a null-terminated string for the name itself (`d_name`).

```
#define DIRBLKSIZ        DEV_BSIZE
#define MAXNAMLEN        255

struct   direct {
         uint32_t         d_ino;          /* inode number of entry */
         ushort_t         d_reclen;       /* length of this record */
         ushort_t         d_namlen;       /* length of string in d_name */
         char     d_name[MAXNAMLEN + 1];  /* name must be no longer than this */
};
```

See usr/src/uts/common/sys/fs/ufs_fsdir.h

`d_reclen` includes the space consumed by all the fields in a directory entry, including `d_name`'s trailing null character. This facilitates directory entry deletion because when an entry is deleted, if it is not the first entry in the current directory, the entry before it is grown to include the deleted one, that is, `d_reclen` is incremented to account for the size of the next entry. The procedure is relatively inexpensive and helps keep internal fragmentation down. Figure 15.4 illustrates the concept of directory deletion.

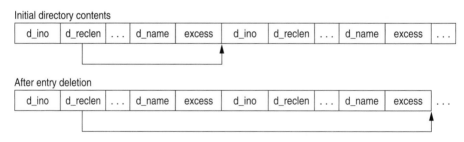

Figure 15.4 Deletion of a Directory Entry

15.2.3 UFS Hard Links

There is one inode for each file on disk; however, with hard links, each file can have multiple file names. With hard links, file names in multiple directories point to the same on-disk inode. The inode reference count field reflects the number of hard links to the inode. Figure 15.5 illustrates inode 1423 describing a file; two separate directory entries with different names both point to the same inode number. Note that the reference count, `refcnt`, has been incremented to 2.

inode = 1423

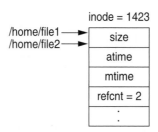

/home/file1 ⟶
/home/file2 ⟶

| size |
| atime |
| mtime |
| refcnt = 2 |
| . |

Figure 15.5 UFS Links

15.2.4 Shadow Inodes

UFS allows storage of additional per-inode data through the use of shadow inodes. The implementation of a shadow inode is generic enough to permit storage of any arbitrary data. All that is needed are a tag to identify the data and functions to convert the appropriate data structures from on-disk to in-core, and vice versa. As of this writing (2005), only two data types are defined: FSD_ACL for identification of ACLs and FSD_DFACL for default ACLs. Only one shadow inode is permitted per inode today, and as a result both ACLs and default ACLs are stored in the same shadow inode.

```
typedef struct ufs_fsd {
        int     fsd_type;              /* type of data */
        int     fsd_size;             /* size in bytes of ufs_fsd and data */
        char    fsd_data[1];          /* data */
} ufs_fsd_t;

                                   See usr/src/uts/common/sys/fs/ufs_acl.h
```

The way a shadow inode is laid out on disk is quite simple (see Figure 15.6). All the entries for the shadow inode contain one header that includes the type of data and the length of the whole record, data + header. Entries are then simply concatenated and stored to disk as a separate inode with the inode's ic_smode set to ISHAD. The parent's ic_shadow is then updated to point to this shadow inode.

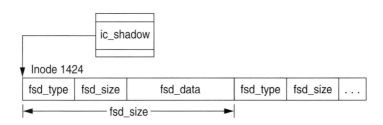

Figure 15.6 On-Disk Shadow Inode Layout

15.2.5 The Boot Block

Figure 15.7 illustrates the UFS layout discussed in this section. At the start of the file system is the boot block. This is a spare sector reserved for the boot program when UFS is used as a root file system. At boot time, the boot firmware loads the first sector from the boot device and then starts executing code residing in that block. The firmware boot is file system independent, which means that the boot firmware has no knowledge about the file system. We rely on code in the file system boot block to mount the root file system. When the system starts, the UFS boot block is loaded and executed, which, in turn, mounts the UFS root file system. The boot program then passes control to a larger kernel loader, in /platform/ sun4[mud]/ufsboot, to load the UNIX kernel.

The boot program is loaded onto the first sector of the file system at install time with the installboot(1M) command. The 512-byte install boot image resides in /usr/platform/sun4[mud]/lib/fs/ufs/bootblk in the platform-dependent directories.

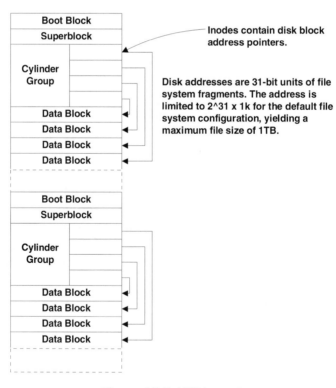

Figure 15.7 UFS Layout

15.2.6 The Superblock

The superblock contains all the information about the geometry and layout of the file system and is critical to the file system state. As a safety precaution, the superblock is replicated across the file system with each cylinder group so that the file system is not crippled if the superblock becomes corrupted. It is initially created by mkfs and updated by tunefs and mkfs (in case a file system is grown). The primary superblock starts at an offset of 8192 bytes into the partition slice and occupies one file system block (usually 8192 bytes, but can be 4096 bytes on x86 architectures). The superblock contains a variety of information, including the location of each cylinder group and a summary list of available free blocks. The major information in the superblock that identifies the file system geometry is listed below.

- **fs_sblkno.** Address of superblock in file system; defaults to block number 16.
- **fs_cblkno.** Offset of the first cylinder block in the file system.
- **fs_iblkno.** Offset of the first inode blocks in the file system.
- **fs_dblkno.** Offset of the first data blocks after the first cylinder group.
- **fs_cgoffset.** Cylinder group offset in the cylinder.
- **fs_cgmask.** Mask to obtain physical starting fragment number of the cylinder group.
- **fs_time.** Last time written.
- **fs_size.** Number of blocks in the file system.
- **fs_dsize.** Number of data blocks the in file system.
- **fs_ncg.** Number of cylinder groups.
- **fs_cpg.** Number of cylinders in a cylinder group.
- **fs_ipg.** Number of inodes in a cylinder group.
- **fs_fpg.** Number of fragments (including metadata) in a cylinder group.
- **fs_bsize.** Size of basic blocks in the file system.
- **fs_fsize.** Size of fragmented blocks in the file system.
- **fs_frag.** Number of fragments in a block in the file system.
- **fs_magic.** A magic number to validate the superblock.

The file system configuration parameters also reside in the superblock. The file system parameters include some of the following, which are configured at the time the file system is constructed. You can tune the parameters later with the tunefs command.

- **fs_minfree.** Minimum percentage of free blocks.

- **fs_rotdelay.** Number of milliseconds of rotational delay between sequential blocks. The rotational delay was used to implement block interleaving when the operating system could not keep up with reading contiguous blocks. Since this is no longer an issue, fs_rotdelay defaults to zero.
- **fs_rps.** Disk revolutions per second.
- **fs_maxcontig.** Maximum number of contiguous blocks, controls the number of read-ahead blocks.
- **fs_maxbpg.** Maximum number of data blocks per cylinder group.
- **fs_optim.** Optimization preference, space, or time.

And here are the significant logging related fields in the superblock:

- **fs_rolled.** Determines whether any data in the log still needs to be rolled back to the file system.
- **fs_si.** Indicates whether logging summary information is up to date or whether it needs to be recalculated from cylinder groups.
- **fs_clean.** Is set to FS_LOG for logging file system.
- **fs_logbno.** Is the disk block number of logging metadata.
- **fs_reclaim:** Is set to indicate if the reclaim thread is running or needs to be run.

See struct fs in usr/src/uts/common/sys/fs/ufs_fs.h for the complete superblock structure definition

15.2.7 The Cylinder Group

The cylinder group is made up of several logically distinct parts. At logical offset zero into the cylinder group is a backup copy of the file system's superblock. Following that, we have the cylinder group structure, the blktot array (indicating how many full blocks are available), the blks array (representing the full-sized blocks that are free in each rotational position), inode bitmap (marking which inodes are in use), and finally, the bitmap of which fragments are free. Next in the layout is the array of inodes whose size varies according to the number of inodes in a cylinder group (on-disk inode size is restricted to 128 bytes). And finally, the rest of the cylinder group is filled by the data blocks.

Figure 15.8 illustrates the layout.

| fs superblock | struct cg + bitmaps | inodes | data blocks ... |

Figure 15.8 Logical Layout of a Cylinder Group

The last cylinder group in a file system may be incomplete because the number of cylinders in a disk drive is usually not exactly rounded up to the cylinder groups. In this case, we simply reduce the number of data blocks available in the last cylinder group; however, the metadata portion of the cylinder group stays the same throughout the file system. The cg_ncyl and cg_nblk fields of the cylinder group structure guide us to the size so that we don't accidentally go out of bounds.

```
/*
 * Cylinder group block for a file system.
 *
 * Writable fields in the cylinder group are protected by the associated
 * super block lock fs->fs_lock.
 */
#define CG_MAGIC          0x090255
struct  cg {
        uint32_t cg_link;                   /* NOT USED linked list of cyl groups */
        int32_t cg_magic;                   /* magic number */
        time32_t cg_time;                   /* time last written */
        int32_t cg_cgx;                     /* we are the cgx'th cylinder group */
        short    cg_ncyl;                   /* number of cyl's this cg */
        short    cg_niblk;                  /* number of inode blocks this cg */
        int32_t cg_ndblk;                   /* number of data blocks this cg */
        struct   csum cg_cs;                /* cylinder summary information */
        int32_t cg_rotor;                   /* position of last used block */
        int32_t cg_frotor;                  /* position of last used frag */
        int32_t cg_irotor;                  /* position of last used inode */
        int32_t cg_frsum[MAXFRAG];          /* counts of available frags */
        int32_t cg_btotoff;                 /* (int32_t)block totals per cylinder */
        int32_t cg_boff;                    /* (short) free block positions */
        int32_t cg_iusedoff;                /* (char) used inode map */
        int32_t cg_freeoff;                 /* (uchar_t) free block map */
        int32_t cg_nextfreeoff;             /* (uchar_t) next available space */
        int32_t cg_sparecon[16];            /* reserved for future use */
        uchar_t cg_space[1];                /* space for cylinder group maps */
/* actually longer */
};
```

See usr/src/uts/common/sys/fs/ufs_fs.h

15.2.8 Summary of UFS Architecture

Figure 15.9 puts it all together.

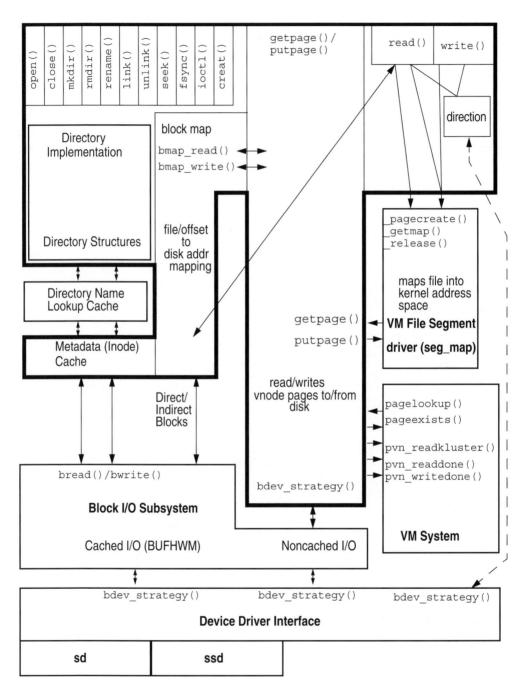

Figure 15.9 The UFS File System

15.3 The UFS Inode

The *inode* (Index Node) is UFS's internal descriptor for a file. Each file system has two forms of an inode: the on-disk inode and the in-core (in-memory) inode. The on-disk inode resides on the physical medium and represents the on-disk format and layout of the file.

15.3.1 In-Core UFS Inodes

The in-core inode, as you may have guessed, resides in memory and contains the file-system-dependent information, free-list pointers, hash anchors, kernel locks (covered in UFS locking below), and inode state.

```
typedef struct inode {
        struct  inode *i_chain[2];      /* must be first */
        struct inode *i_freef;  /* free list forward - must be before i_ic */
        struct inode *i_freeb;  /* free list back - must be before i_ic */
        struct  icommon i_ic;   /* Must be here */
        struct  vnode *i_vnode; /* vnode associated with this inode */
        struct  vnode *i_devvp; /* vnode for block I/O */
        dev_t   i_dev;          /* device where inode resides */
        ino_t   i_number;       /* i number, 1-to-1 with device address */
        off_t   i_diroff;       /* offset in dir, where we found last entry */
                                /* just a hint - no locking needed */
        struct ufsvfs *i_ufsvfs; /* incore fs associated with inode */
        struct  dquot *i_dquot; /* quota structure controlling this file */
        krwlock_t i_rwlock;     /* serializes write/setattr requests */
        krwlock_t i_contents;   /* protects (most of) inode contents */
        kmutex_t i_tlock;       /* protects time fields, i_flag */
        offset_t i_nextr;       /*                                        */
                                /* next byte read offset (read-ahead)     */
                                /*   No lock required                     */
                                /*                                        */
        uint_t  i_flag;         /* inode flags */
        uint_t  i_seq;          /* modification sequence number */
        boolean_t i_cachedir;   /* Cache this directory on next lookup */
                                /* - no locking needed   */
        long    i_mapcnt;       /* mappings to file pages */
        int     *i_map;         /* block list for the corresponding file */
        dev_t   i_rdev;         /* INCORE rdev from i_oldrdev by ufs_iget */
        size_t  i_delaylen;     /* delayed writes, units=bytes */
        offset_t i_delayoff;    /* where we started delaying */
        offset_t i_nextrio;     /* where to start the next clust */
        long    i_writes;       /* number of outstanding bytes in write q */
        kcondvar_t i_wrcv;      /* sleep/wakeup for write throttle */
        offset_t i_doff;        /* dinode byte offset in file system */
        si_t *i_ufs_acl;        /* pointer to acl entry */
        dcanchor_t i_danchor;   /* directory cache anchor */
        kthread_t *i_writer;    /* thread which is in window in wrip() */
} inode_t;
```

See usr/src/uts/common/sys/fs/ufs_inode.h

New with Solaris 10, an inode sequence number was added to the in-core `inode` structure to support NFSv3 and NFSv4 detection of atomic changes to the inode. Two caveats with this new value: `i_seq` must be updated if `i_ctime` and `i_mtime` are changed; the value of `i_seq` is only guaranteed to be persistent while the inode is active.

15.3.2 Inode Cache

When the last reference to a vnode is released, the `vop_inactive()` routine for the file system is called. (See vnode reference counts in Section 14.6.8.) UFS uses `vop_inactive()` to free the inode when it is no longer required. If we were to destroy each vnode when the last reference to a vnode is relinquished, we would throw away all the data relating to that vnode, including all the file pages cached in the page cache. This practice could mean that if a file is closed and then reopened, none of the file data that was cached would be available after the second open and would need to be reread from disk. To remedy the situation, UFS caches all unused inodes in its global cache.

The UFS inode cache contains an entry for every open inode in the system. It also attempts to keep as many closed inodes as possible so that inactive inodes/ vnodes and associated pages are around in memory for possible reuse. This is a global cache and not a per-file system cache, and that unfortunately leads to several performance issues.

The inode cache consists of several disconnected queues or chains, and each queue is linked with the inode's `i_forw` and `i_backw` pointers (see Figure 15.10). Starting with Solaris 10, hashing of inode entries is done with the inode number (because of recent `devfs` changes) rather than with the inode number and the device number (Solaris 9 and earlier). These queues are managed according to least recently used (LRU) scheme.

An inode free list is also maintained within the cache which is built upon the `i_freef` and `i_freeb` pointers. These enable the free list to span several hash chains. If an inode is not on the free list, then the `i_freef` and `i_freeb` values point back to the inode itself.

Inodes on the free list can be part of two separate queues:

- **Idle queue.** Holds the idle or unreferenced inodes (where the `v_count` equals 1, t and the `i_nlink` is greater than 0). This queue is managed by the global file system idle thread, which frees entries, starting at the head. When new entries are added, `ufs_inactive()` adds an inode to the head if the inode has no associated pages; otherwise, the inode is added to the tail. This ensures that pages are retained longer in memory for possible reuse—the frees are done starting at the head.

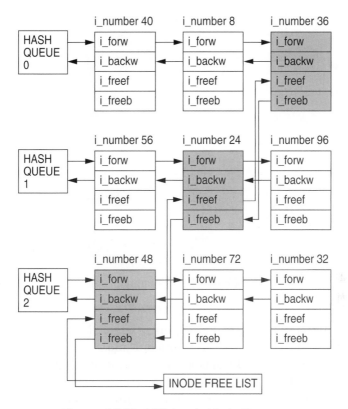

Figure 15.10 UFS Inode Hash Queues

Starting with Solaris 10, the idle queue architecture was reorganized into two separate hash queues: `ufs_useful_iq` and `ufs_junk_iq`. If an inode has pages associated with it (`vn_has_cached_data(vnode)`) or is a fast symbolic link (`i_flag` and `IFASTSYMLNK`), then it is attached to the useful idle queue. All other inodes are attached to the junk idle queue instead. These queues are not used for searching but only for grouping geographically local inodes for faster updates and fewer disk seeks upon reuse. Entries from the junk idle queue are destroyed first when `ufs_idle_free()` is invoked by the UFS idle thread so that cached pages pertaining to entries in the `ufs_useful_iq` idle queue stay in memory longer.

The idle thread is adjusted to run when there are 25% of `ufs_ninode` entries on the idle queue. When it runs, it gives back half of the idle queue until the queue falls below the low water mark of `ufs_q->uq_lowat`. Inodes on the junk queue get destroyed first. Figure 15.11 illustrates the process.

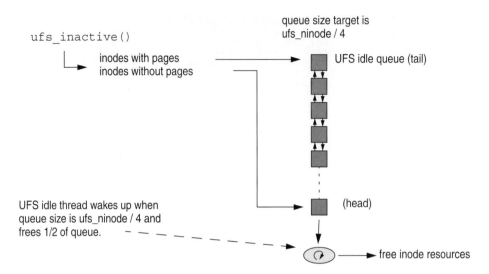

Figure 15.11 UFS Idle Queue

- **Delete queue.** Is active if UFS logging is enabled and consists of inodes that
  are unlinked or deleted (v_count equals 1 and i_nlink is less than or equal
  to 0). This queue is a performance enhancer for file systems with logging
  turned on and observing heavy deletion activity. The delete queue is handled
  by the per-file system delete thread, which queues the inodes to be deleted by
  the ufs_delete() thread. This significantly boosts response times for
  removal of large amounts of data. If logging is not enabled, ufs_delete()
  is called immediately. ufs_delete() calls VN_RELE() after it has finished
  processing, which causes the inode to once again be processed by ufs_
  inactive, which this time puts it on the idle queue. While on the delete
  queue, the inode's i_freef and i_freeb point to the inode itself since the
  inodes are not free yet.

15.3.3 Block Allocation

The UFS file system is block based where each file is represented by a set of fixed
sized units of disk space, indexed by a tree of *physical-meta-data* blocks.

15.3.3.1 Layout Policy

UFS uses block sizes of 4 and 8 Kbytes, which provides significantly higher performance than the 512-byte blocks used in the System V file system. The downside of
larger blocks was that when partially allocated blocks were created, several kilo-

bytes of disk space for each partly filled file system block was wasted. To overcome this disadvantage, UFS uses the notion of file system fragments. Fragments allow a single block to be broken up into 2, 4, or 8 fragments when necessary (4 Kbytes, 2 Kbytes or 1 Kbyte, respectively).

UFS block allocation tries to prevent excessive disk seeking by attempting to co-locate inodes within a directory and by attempting to co-locate a file's inode and its data blocks. When possible, all the inodes in a directory are allocated in the same cylinder group. This scheme helps reduce disk seeking when directories are traversed; for example, executing a simple ls -l of a directory will access all the inodes in that directory. If all the inodes reside in the same cylinder group, most of the data are cached after the first few files are accessed. A directory is placed in a cylinder group different from that of its parent.

Blocks are allocated to a file sequentially, starting with the first 96 Kbytes (the first 12 direct blocks), skipping to the next cylinder group and allocating blocks up to the limit set by the file system parameter maxbpg (maximum-blocks-per-cylinder-group). After that, blocks are allocated from the next available cylinder group.

By default, on a file system greater than 1 Gbyte, the algorithm allocates 96 Kbytes in the first cylinder group, 16 Mbytes in the next available cylinder group, 16 Mbytes from the next, and so on. The maximum cylinder group size is 54 Mbytes, and the allocation algorithm allows only one-third of that space to be allocated to each section of a single file when it is extended. The maxbpg parameter is set to 2,048 8-Kbyte blocks by default at the time the file system is created. It is also tunable but can only be tuned downward since the maximum cylinder group size is 16-Mybte allocation per cylinder group.

Selection of a new cylinder group for the next segment of a file is governed by a rotor and free-space algorithm. A per-file-system allocation rotor points to one of the cylinder groups; each time new disk space is allocated, it starts with the cylinder group pointed to by the rotor. If the cylinder group has less than average free space, then it is skipped and the next cylinder group is tried. This algorithm makes the file system attempt to balance the allocation across the cylinder groups.

Figure 15.12 shows the default allocation that is used if a file is created on a large UFS. The first 96 Kbytes of file 1 are allocated from the first cylinder group. Then, allocation skips to the second cylinder group and another 16 Mbytes of file 1 are allocated, and so on. When another file is created, we can see that it consumes the holes in the allocated blocks alongside file 1. There is room for a third file to do the same.

The actual on-disk layout will not be quite as simple as the example shown but does reflect the allocation policies discussed. We can use an add-on tool, filestat, to view the on-disk layout of a file, as shown below.

```
sol8# /usr/local/bin/filestat testfile
Inodes per cyl group:    128
Inodes per block:        64
Cylinder Group no:       0
Cylinder Group blk:      64
File System Block Size:  8192
Block Size:              512
Number of 512b Blocks:   262288

Start Block     End Block      Length (512 byte Blocks)
-----------     -----------    -----------------------------
        144 ->  335            192
        400 ->  33167          32768
     110800 ->  143567         32768
     221264 ->  221343         80
     221216 ->  221263         48
     221456 ->  254095         32640
     331856 ->  331999         144
     331808 ->  331855         48
     332112 ->  364687         32576
     442448 ->  442655         208
     442400 ->  442447         48
     442768 ->  475279         32512
```

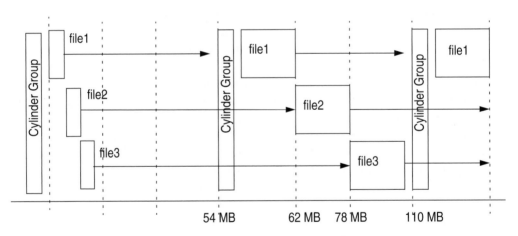

Figure 15.12 Default File Allocation in 16-Mbyte Groups

The filestat output shows that the first segment of the file occupies 192 (512-byte) blocks, followed by the next 16 Mbytes, which start in a different cylinder group. This particular file system was not empty when the file was created, which is why the next cylinder group chosen is a long way from the first.

We can observe the file system parameters of an existing file system with the fstyp command. The fstyp command simply dumps the superblock information for the file, revealing all the cylinder group and allocation information. The following example shows the output for a 4-Gbyte file system with default parameters.

We can see that the file system has 8,247,421 blocks and has 167 cylinder groups spaced evenly at 6,272 (51-Mbyte) intervals. The maximum blocks to allocate for each group is set to the default of 2,048 8-Kbyte, 16 Mbytes.

```
sol8# fstyp -v /dev/vx/dsk/homevol |more
ufs
magic    11954     format  dynamic time    Sat Mar  6 18:19:59 1999
sblkno   16        cblkno  24      iblkno  32       dblkno   800
sbsize   2048      cgsize  8192    cgoffset 32      cgmask   0xffffffe0
ncg      167       size    8378368 blocks  8247421
bsize    8192      shift   13      mask    0xffffe000
fsize    1024      shift   10      mask    0xfffffc00
frag     8         shift   3       fsbtodb 1
minfree 1%         maxbpg  2048    optim   time
maxcontig 32       rotdelay 0ms    rps     120
csaddr   800       cssize  3072    shift   9        mask     0xffffffe00
ntrak    32        nsect   64      spc     2048     ncyl     8182
cpg      49        bpg     6272    fpg     50176    ipg      6144
nindir   2048      inopb   64      nspf    2
nbfree   176719    ndir    10241   nifree  956753   nffree   21495
cgrotor  152       fmod    0       ronly   0        logbno   0
```

The UFS-specific version of the fstyp command dumps the superblock of a UFS file system, as shown below.

```
sol8# fstyp -v /dev/vx/dsk/homevol |more
ufs
magic    11954     format  dynamic time    Sat Mar  6 18:19:59 1999
sblkno   16        cblkno  24      iblkno  32       dblkno   800
sbsize   2048      cgsize  8192    cgoffset 32      cgmask   0xffffffe0
ncg      167       size    8378368 blocks  8247421
bsize    8192      shift   13      mask    0xffffe000
fsize    1024      shift   10      mask    0xfffffc00
frag     8         shift   3       fsbtodb 1
minfree 1%         maxbpg  2048    optim   time
maxcontig 32       rotdelay 0ms    rps     120
csaddr   800       cssize  3072    shift   9        mask     0xffffffe00
ntrak    32        nsect   64      spc     2048     ncyl     8182
cpg      49        bpg     6272    fpg     50176    ipg      6144
nindir   2048      inopb   64      nspf    2
nbfree   176719    ndir    10241   nifree  956753   nffree   21495
cgrotor  152       fmod    0       ronly   0        logbno   0
fs_reclaim is not set
file system state is valid, fsclean is 0
blocks available in each rotational position
cylinder number 0:
      position 0:      0     4     8    12    16    20    24    28    32    36    40    44
                      48    52    56    60    64    68    72    76    80    84    88    92
                      96   100   104   108   112   116   120   124
      position 2:      1     5     9    13    17    21    25    29    33    37    41    45
                      49    53    57    61    65    69    73    77    81    85    89    93
                      97   101   105   109   113   117   121   125
      position 4:      2     6    10    14    18    22    26    30    34    38    42    46
                      50    54    58    62    66    70    74    78    82    86    90    94
                      98   102   106   110   114   118   122   126
      position 6:      3     7    11    15    19    23    27    31    35    39    43    47
                      51    55    59    63    67    71    75    79    83    87    91    95
                      99   103   107   111   115   119   123   127
```

continues

```
cs[].cs_(nbfree,ndir,nifree,nffree):
          (23,26,5708,102) (142,26,5724,244) (87,20,5725,132) (390,69,5737,80)
          (72,87,5815,148) (3,87,5761,110) (267,87,5784,4) (0,66,5434,4)
          (217,46,5606,94) (537,87,5789,70) (0,87,5901,68) (0,87,5752,20)
   .
   .
cylinders in last group 48
blocks in last group 6144


cg 0:
magic    90255    tell    6000     time    Sat Feb 27 22:53:11 1999
cgx      0        ncyl    49       niblk   6144    ndblk   50176
nbfree   23       ndir    26       nifree  5708    nffree  102
rotor    1224     irotor  144      frotor  1224
frsum    7        7       3        1       1       0       9
sum of frsum: 102
iused:   0-143, 145-436
free:    1224-1295, 1304-1311, 1328-1343, 4054-4055, 4126-4127, 4446-4447, 4455, 4637-
4638,
```

15.3.3.2 Mapping Files to Disk Blocks

At the heart of a disk-based file system are the block map algorithms, which implement the on-disk file system format. These algorithms map UFS file and offsets pairs into disk addresses on the underlying storage. For UFS, two main functions—bmap_read() and bmap_write()—implement the on-disk format. Calling these functions has the following results:

- bmap_read() *queries* the file system as to which physical disk sector a file block resides on; that is, requests a lookup of the direct/indirect blocks that contain the disk address(es) of the required blocks.

- bmap_write() *allocates*, with the aid of helper functions, new disk blocks when extending or allocating blocks for a file.

The bmap_read() function reads file system block addresses. It accepts an inode and offset as input arguments, and a pointer to a disk address and contiguity length as output arguments.

```
int
bmap_read(struct inode *ip, u_offset_t off, daddr_t *dap, int *lenp)
```

See usr/src/uts/common/fs/ufs/ufs_bmap.c

The file system uses the bmap_read() algorithm to locate the physical blocks for the file being read. The bmap_read() function searches through the direct, indirect, and double-indirect blocks of the inode to locate the disk address of the disk blocks that map to the supplied offset. The function also searches forward from the offset, looking for disk blocks that continue to map contiguous portions of the inode, and returns the length of the contiguous segment (in blocks) in the length pointer argument. The length and the file system block clustering parameters are used within the file system as bounds for clustering contiguous blocks to provide better performance by reading larger parts of a file from disk at a time. See `ufs_getpage_ra()`, defined in `usr/src/uts/common/fs/ufs_vnops.c`, for more information on read-aheads.

```
int
bmap_write(struct inode *ip, u_offset_t off, int size,
           int alloc_only, struct cred *cr);
```

See usr/src/uts/common/fs/ufs/ufs_bmap.c

The `bmap_write()` function allocates file space in the file system when a file is extended or a file with holes has blocks written for the first time and is responsible for storing the allocated block information in the inode. `bmap_write()` traverses the block free lists, using the rotor algorithm (discussed in Section 15.3.3), and updates the local, direct, and indirect blocks in the inode for the file being extended. `bmap_write` calls several helper functions to facilitate the allocation of blocks.

```
daddr_t blkpref(struct inode *ip, daddr_t lbn, int indx, daddr32_t *bap)
```

Guides bmap_write in selecting the next desired block in the file. Sets the policy as described in Section 15.3.3.1.

```
int realloccg(struct inode *ip, daddr_t bprev, daddr_t bpref, int osize, int nsize,
       daddr_t *bnp, cred_t *cr)
```

Re-allocates a fragment to a bigger size. The number and size of the old block size is specified and the allocator attempts to extend the original block. Failing that, the regular block allocator is called to obtain an appropriate block.

```
int alloc(struct inode *ip, daddr_t bpref, int size, daddr_t *bnp, cred_t *cr)
```

Allocates a block in the file system. The size of the block is specified which is a multiple of (fs_fsize <= fs_bsize). If a preference (usually obtained from blkpref()) is specified, the allocator will try to allocate the requested block. If that fails, a rotationally optimal block in the same cylinder is found. Failing that a block in the same cylinder group is searched for. And in case that fails, the allocator quadratically rehashes into other cylinder groups (see hashalloc() in uts/common/fs/ufs/ufs_alloc.c) to locate an available block. If no preference is given, a block in the same cylinder is found, and failing that the allocator quadratically searches other cylinder groups for one.

See uts/common/fs/ufs/ufs_alloc.c

```
static void ufs_undo_allocation(inode_t *ip,
                       int block_count,
                       struct ufs_allocated_block table[],
                       int inode_sector_adjust)
```

In the case of an error, bmap_write() will call ufs_undo_allocation to free any blocks which were used during the allocation process.

See uts/common/fs/ufs/ufs_bmap.c

15.3.3.3 Reading and Writing UFS Blocks

A file system read calls `bmap_read()` to find the location of the underlying physical blocks for the file being read. UFS then calls the device driver's strategy routine for the device containing the file system to initiate the read operation by calling `bdev_strategy()`.

A file system write operation that extends a file first calls `bmap_write()` to allocate the new blocks and then calls `bmap_read()` to obtain the block location for the write. UFS then calls the device driver's strategy routine, by means of `bdev_strategy()`, to initiate the file write.

15.3.3.4 Buffering Block Metadata

The block map functions access metadata (single, double and triple indirect blocks) on the device media through the buffer cache, using the `bread_common()` and `bwrite_common()` buffered block I/O kernel functions. The block I/O functions read and write device blocks in 512-byte chunks, and they cache physical disk blocks in the block buffer cache (note: this cache is different from the page cache, used for file data). The UFS file system requires 1 Mbyte of metadata for every 2 Gbytes of file space. This relationship can be used as a rule to calculate the size of the block buffer cache, set by the `bufhwm` kernel parameter.

15.3.4 Methods to Read and Write UFS Files

Files can be read or written in two ways: by the `read()` or `write()` system calls or by mapped file I/O. The `read()` and `write()` system calls call the file system's `ufs_read()` and `ufs_write()` method. These methods map files into the kernel's address space and then use the file system's `ufs_getpage()` and `ufs_putpage()` methods to transfer data to and from the physical media.

15.3.4.1 `ufs_read()`

An example of the steps taken by a UFS read system call is shown in Figure 15.13. A read system call invokes the file-system-dependent read function, which turns the read request into a series of `vop_getpage()` calls by mapping the file into the kernel's address space with the `seg_kpm` driver (through the `seg_map` driver), as described in Section 14.7.

The `ufs_read` method calls into the `seg_map` driver to locate a virtual address in the kernel address space for the file and offset requested with the `segmap_getmapflt()` function. The `seg_map` driver determines whether it already has a mapping for the requested offset by looking into its hashed list of mapping slots. Once a slot is located or created, an address for the page is located. `segmap` then calls back into the file system with `ufs_getpage()` to soft-initiate a page fault to

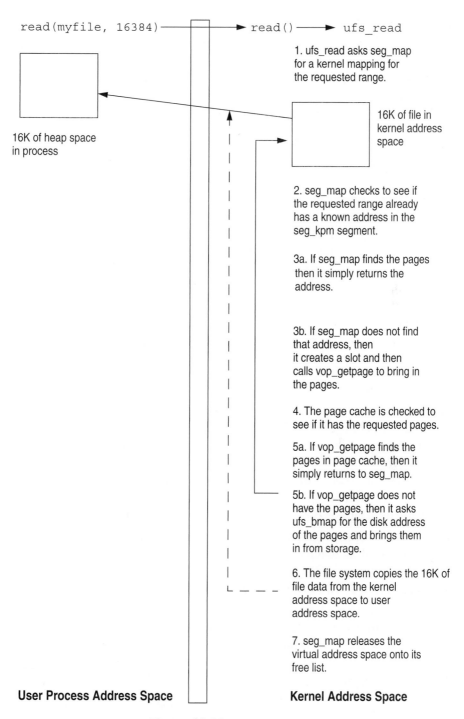

read(myfile, 16384) ────────▶ read() ────▶ ufs_read

1. ufs_read asks seg_map
for a kernel mapping for
the requested range.

16K of file in
kernel address
space

16K of heap space
in process

2. seg_map checks to see if
the requested range already
has a known address in the
seg_kpm segment.

3a. If seg_map finds the pages
then it simply returns the
address.

3b. If seg_map does not find
that address, then
it creates a slot and then
calls vop_getpage to bring in
the pages.

4. The page cache is checked to
see if it has the requested pages.

5a. If vop_getpage finds the
pages in page cache, then it
simply returns to seg_map.

5b. If vop_getpage does not
have the pages, then it asks
ufs_bmap for the disk address
of the pages and brings them
in from storage.

6. The file system copies the 16K of
file data from the kernel
address space to user
address space.

7. seg_map releases the
virtual address space onto its
free list.

User Process Address Space   **Kernel Address Space**

Figure 15.13 ufs_read()

read in the page at the virtual address of the seg_map slot. The page fault is initiated while we are still in the segmap_getmap() routine, by a call to segmap_fault(). That function in turn calls back into the file system with ufs_getpage(), which calls out file system's _getpage(). If not, then a slot is created and ufs_getpage() is called to read in the pages.

The ufs_getpage() routine brings the requested range of the file (vnode, off-set, and length) from disk into the virtual address, and the length is passed into the ufs_getpage() function. The ufs_getpage() function locates the file's blocks (through the block map functions discussed in Section 15.3.3.2) and reads them by calling the underlying device's strategy routine.

Once the page is read by the file system, the requested range is copied back to the user by the uiomove() function. The file system then releases the slot associated with that block of the file by using the segmap_release() function. At this point, the slot is not removed from the segment, because we may need the same file and offset later (effectively caching the virtual address location); instead, it is added to a seg_map free list so that it can be reclaimed or reused later.

15.3.4.2 ufs_write()

Writing to the file system is performed similarly, although it is more complex because of some of the file system write performance enhancements, such as delayed writes and write clustering. Writing to the file system follows the steps shown in Figure 15.14.

The write system call calls the file-system-independent write, which in our example calls ufs_write(). UFS breaks the write into 8-Kbyte chunks and then processes each chunk. For each 8-Kbyte chunk, the following steps are performed.

1. UFS asks the segmap driver for an 8-Kbyte mapping of the file in the kernel's virtual address space. The page for the file and offset is mapped here so that the data can be copied in and then written out with paged I/O.

2. If the file is being extended or a new page is being created within a hole of a file, then a call is made to the segmap_pagecreate function to create and lock the new pages. Next, a call is made segmap_pageunlock() to unlock the pages that were locked during the page_create.

3. If the write is to a whole file system block, then a new zeroed page is created with segmap_pagecreate(). In the case of a partial block write, the block must first be read in so that the partial block contents can be replaced.

4. The new page is returned, locked, to UFS. The buffer that is passed into the write system call is copied from user address space into kernel address space.

5. The ufs_write throttle first checks to see if too many bytes are outstanding for this file as a result of previous delayed writes. If more than the kernel

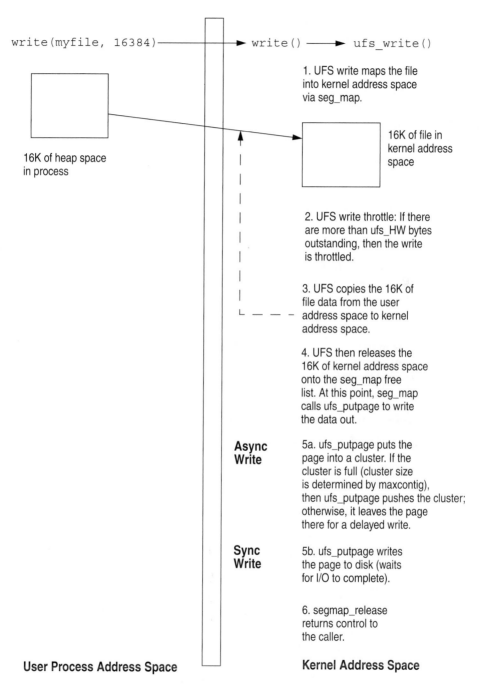

write(myfile, 16384) ────────── write() ──────► ufs_write()

1. UFS write maps the file
into kernel address space
via seg_map.

16K of file in
kernel address
space

16K of heap space
in process

2. UFS write throttle: If there
are more than ufs_HW bytes
outstanding, then the write
is throttled.

3. UFS copies the 16K of
file data from the user
address space to kernel
address space.

4. UFS then releases the
16K of kernel address space
onto the seg_map free
list. At this point, seg_map
calls ufs_putpage to write
the data out.

Async Write

5a. ufs_putpage puts the
page into a cluster. If the
cluster is full (cluster size
is determined by maxcontig),
then ufs_putpage pushes the cluster;
otherwise, it leaves the page
there for a delayed write.

Sync Write

5b. ufs_putpage writes
the page to disk (waits
for I/O to complete).

6. segmap_release
returns control to
the caller.

User Process Address Space   **Kernel Address Space**

Figure 15.14 ufs_write()

parameter `ufs_HW` bytes are outstanding, the write is put to sleep until the amount of outstanding bytes drops below the kernel parameter `ufs_LW`.

The file system calls the `seg_map` driver to map in the portion of the file we are going to write. The data is copied from the process's user address space into the kernel address space allocated by `seg_map`, and `seg_map` is then called to release the address space containing the dirty pages to be written. This is when the real work of write starts, because `seg_map` calls `ufs_putpage()` when it realizes there are dirty pages in the address space it is releasing.

15.4 Access Control in UFS

The traditional UNIX File System provides a simple file access scheme based on users, groups, and world, whereby each file is assigned an owner and a UNIX group, and then is assigned a bitmap of permissions for user, group, and world, as illustrated in Figure 15.15.

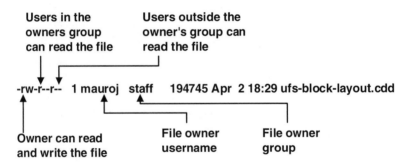

Figure 15.15 Traditional File Access Scheme

This scheme is flexible when file access permissions align with users and groups of users, but it does not provide a mechanism to assign access to lists of users that do not coincide with a UNIX group. For example, if we want to give read access to file 1 to Mark and Chuck, and then read access to file 2 to Chuck and Barb, then we would need to create two UNIX groups, and Chuck would need to switch groups with the `chgrp` command to gain access to either file.

To overcome this drawback, some operating systems use an access control list (ACL), whereby lists of users with different permissions can be assigned to a file. Solaris introduced the notion of access control lists in the B1 secure version, known as Trusted Solaris, in 1993. Trusted Solaris ACLs were later integrated with the commercial Solaris version in 1995 with Solaris 2.5.

With Solaris ACLs, administrators can assign a list of UNIX user IDs and groups to a file by using the `setfacl` command and can review the ACLs by using the `getfacl` command, as shown below.

```
# setfacl -m user:jon:rw- memtool.c
# getfacl memtool.c

# file: memtool.c
# owner: rmc
# group: staff
user::r--
user:jon:rw-            #effective:r--
group::r--              #effective:r--
mask:r--
other:r--

# ls -l memtool.c
-r--r--r--+  1 rmc        staff          638 Mar 30 11:32 memtool.c
```

For example, we can assign access to a file for a specific user by using the `setfacl` command. Note that the UNIX permissions on the file now contain a +, signifying that an access control list is assigned to this file.

Multiple users and groups can be assigned to a file, offering a flexible mechanism for assigning access rights. ACLs can be assigned to directories as well. Note that unlike the case with some other operating systems, access control lists are not inherited from a parent, so a new directory created under a directory with an ACL will not have an ACL assigned by default.

ACLs are divided into three parts: on-disk, in-core, and user level. On-disk format is used to represent the ACL data that is stored in the file's shadow inode, in-core structure is used by UFS internally, and the user-level format is used by the system to present data to the requester.

The `ufs_acl` structure defines an ACL entry that is encapsulated in the `ufs_fsd` structure and then stored on disk in a shadow inode. Refer to Section 15.2.4 for more information on shadow inode storage.

```
/*
 * On-disk UFS ACL structure
 */
typedef struct ufs_acl {
        union {
                uint32_t        acl_next;       /* Pad for old structure */
                ushort_t        acl_tag;        /* Entry type */
        } acl_un;
        o_mode_t        acl_perm;       /* Permission bits */
        uid_t           acl_who;        /* User or group ID */
} ufs_acl_t;

                                        See usr/src/uts/common/sys/fs/ufs_acl.h
```

The in-core format consists of the `ufs_ic_acl` structure and the in-core ACL mask (`ufs_aclmask`) structure.

```
/*
 * In-core UFS ACL structure
 */
typedef struct ufs_ic_acl {
        struct ufs_ic_acl    *acl_ic_next;    /* Next ACL for this inode */
        o_mode_t             acl_ic_perm;     /* Permission bits */
        uid_t                acl_ic_who;      /* User or group ID */
} ufs_ic_acl_t;

/*
 * In-core ACL mask
 */
typedef struct ufs_aclmask {
        short         acl_ismask;      /* Is mask defined? */
        o_mode_t      acl_maskbits;    /* Permission mask */
} ufs_aclmask_t;
                              See usr/src/uts/common/sys/fs/ufs_acl.h
```

When ACL data is exchanged to and from the application, a `struct acl` relays the permission bits, user or group ID, and the type of ACL.

```
typedef struct acl {
        int           a_type;     /* the type of ACL entry */
        uid_t         a_id;       /* the entry in -uid or gid */
        o_mode_t      a_perm;     /* the permission field */
} aclent_t;
                              See usr/src/uuts/common/sys/acl.h
```

The following routines are available in UFS to manipulate ACLs.

```
static int
ufs_setsecattr(struct vnode *vp, vsecattr_t *vsap, int flag, struct cred *cr)
```

Used primarily for updates to ACLs. The structure vsecattr is converted to ufs_acl for in-core storage of ACLs. All file mode changes are updated via this routine.

```
static int
ufs_getsecattr(struct vnode *vp, vsecattr_t *vsap, int flag, struct cred *cr)
```

If ACL data is present, it is converted to vsecattr. Otherwise a new entry is created from the mode bits and returned.

```
int
ufs_acl_access(struct inode *ip, int mode, cred_t *cr)
```

Checks the inode's ACLs to see if access of type mode is allowed.

```
int
ufs_acl_get(struct inode *ip, vsecattr_t *vsap, int flag, cred_t *cr)
```

Called by ufs_getsecattr() to obtain ACL information.

continues

```
int
ufs_acl_set(struct inode *ip, vsecattr_t *vsap, int flag, cred_t *cr)

Called by ufs_setsecattr() to set the inode's ACL information.

si_t *
ufs_acl_cp(si_t *sp)

Copies ACL information from one shadow inode into a new created shadow inode.

int
ufs_acl_setattr(struct inode *ip, struct vattr *vap, cred_t *cr)

Sets the inode's ACL attributes.

usr/src/uuts/common/fs/ufs/ufs_acl.c
```

15.5 Extended Attributes in UFS

In Solaris 9, a new interface was added to UFS for the storage of attributes. Rather than ACLs, which added a shadow inode to each file for permission storage; extended attributes adds a directory inode to each file (see `struct icommon`). This directory is not part of the regular file system name space, rather it is in its own dimension and is attached to ours via a worm-hole of function calls, such as `openat(2)` and `attropen(3C)`.

An excellent discussion of extended attributes can be found in `fsattr(5)`. This interface exists to support any extra attributes desired for files - this may be to support files from other file systems that require the storing of non-UFS attributes. Other uses will be discovered over time.

The following demonstration should get to the point quickly. Here we create an innocuous file, `tardis.txt`, and copy (yes, copy) several other files into its extended attribute name space, purely as a demonstration.

```
$ date > tardis.txt
$ ls -l tardis.txt
-rw-r--r--   1 user1    other          29 Apr  3 10:46 tardis.txt

$ runat tardis.txt cp /etc/motd /etc/group /usr/bin/ksh .
$ runat tardis.txt ls -l
total 352
-rw-r--r--   1 user1    other         286 Apr  3 10:47 group
-r-xr-xr-x   1 user1    other      171396 Apr  3 10:47 ksh
-rw-r--r--   1 user1    other          55 Apr  3 10:47 motd

$ ls -l tardis.txt
-rw-r--r--   1 user1    other          29 Apr  3 10:46 tardis.txt
$ ls -@ tardis.txt
-rw-r--r--@  1 user1    other          29 Apr  3 10:46 tardis.txt
$
$ du -ks tardis.txt
184      tardis.txt
```

The `runat tardis.txt ls -l` command is listing the contents of the extended attribute name space associated with tardis.txt, which now contains a copy of three files. Note that the final `ls -l tardis.txt` doesn't show any difference unless the `-@` option is used (displaying "@" in the same place where files with ACLs display "+"). The `-@` option is new to `ls(1)`, `cp(1)`, `tar(1)` and `cpio(1)`. The `find(1)` command has a `-xattr` option to find files that have extended attributes. The demonstration also shows that `du` is extended attribute aware.

Copying the `ksh` file was deliberate, as it allows us to journey to another world:

```
$ runat tardis.txt ./ksh
cannot access parent directories
$ ls -la
total 33136
drwxr-xr-x   2 user1    other          180 Apr  3 10:47 .
-rw-r--r--   1 user1    other     16777245 Apr  3 10:52 ..
-rw-r--r--   1 user1    other          286 Apr  3 10:47 group
-r-xr-xr-x   1 user1    other       171396 Apr  3 10:47 ksh
-rw-r--r--   1 user1    other           55 Apr  3 10:47 motd
$ pwd
cannot access parent directories
$ cd ..
./ksh: ..: not a directory
$ exit
```

Those security minded readers may imagine many entertaining abuses of extended attributes at this point. The can be turned off if needed, in Solaris 10 a `-noxattr` UFS mount option was added.

15.6 Locking in UFS

UFS uses two basic types of locks: `kmutex_t` and `krwlock_t`. The workings of these synchronization primitives is covered in Chapter 17. UFS locks can be divided into eight categories:

- Inode locks
- Queue locks
- ACL locks
- VNODE locks
- VFS locks
- VOP_RWLOCK
- ufs_iuniqtime_lock
- Logging locks

15.6.1 UFS Lock Descriptions

Tables 15.2 through 15.9 describe the UFS locks in more detail.

Table 15.2 Inode Locks

Name	Type	Description
i_rwlock	krwlock_t	• Serializes write requests. Allows reads to proceed in parallel. Serializes directory reads and updates. • Does not protect inode fields. • Indirectly protects block lists since it serializes allocations/deallocations in UFS. • Must be taken before starting UFS logging transactions if operating on a file; otherwise, taken after starting logging transaction.
i_contents	krwlock_t	• Protects most fields in the inode. • When held as a writer, protects all the fields protected by the i_tlock.
i_tlock	kmutex_t	• When held with the i_contents reader lock, protects the following inode fields: i_utime, i_ctime, i_mtime, i_flag, i_delayoff, i_delaylen, i_nextrio, i_writes, i_writer, i_mapcnt. • Also used as mutex for write throttling in UFS. • i_contents and i_tlock held together allows parallelism in updates.
i_hlock	kmutex_t	• Inode hash lock.

Table 15.3 Inode Queue Locks

Name	Type	Description
ufs_scan_lock	kmutex_t	• Synchronizes ufs_scan_inodes threads • ufs_update(), ufs_sync(), ufs_scan_inodes(). • Needed because of global inode list.
ufs_q->uq_mutex	krwlock_t	• Protects the two inode idle queues ufs_junk_iq and ufs_useful_iq.

continues

Table 15.3 Inode Queue Locks (*continued*)

Name	Type	Description
ufs_hlock	kmutex_t	• Used by the hlock thread. For more information, see man `lockfs`(1M), hardlock section.
ih_lock	kmutex_t	• Protects the inode hash. The inode hash is global, per system, not per file system.

Table 15.4 Quota Queue Locks

Name	Type	Description
dq_cachelock	kmutex_t	• Protects the quota cache list. Prerequisite before taking the `dquot.dq_lock`.
dq_freelock	kmutex_t	• Protects the free quota list.
dq_rwlock	krwlock_t	• Protects the entire quota subsystem. • Taken as writer when the quota subsystem is initialized. Taken as reader when we do not want entire quota subsystem to be quiesced. • As writer, allows updates to quota-related fields in the `ufsvfs` structure. Also protects the `dquot` file as writer to allow quota updates. • As reader, allows reads from the quota-related fields in the `ufsvfs` structure.
dqout.dq_lock	kmutex_t	• Gives exclusive access to `dquot` struct.

Table 15.5 VNODE Locks

Name	Type	Description
v_lock	kmutex_t	• Protects the `vnode` fields. Also used by VN_HOLD/VN_RELE.

Table 15.6 ACL Locks

Name	Type	Description
s_lock	krwlock_t	• Protects the in-core shadow inode structure.

Table 15.7 VFS Locks

Name	Type	Description
vfs_lock	kmutex_t	• Locks contents of file system and cylinder groups. Also protects fields of the vfs_dio.
vfs_dqrwlock	krwlock_t	• Manages quota subsystem quiescence. • If held as writer, UFS quota subsystem may be experiencing changes in quotas, enabling/disabling of quotas, setting new quota limits. • Protects d_quot structure. This structure keeps track of all the enabled quotas per file system. • **Important note:** UFS shadow inodes that are used to hold ACL data and extended attribute directories are not counted against user quotas. Thus, this lock is not held for updates to these. • Reader held for this lock indicates to quota subsystem that major changes should not be occurring during that time. • Held when the i_contents writer lock is held, as described above, signifying that changes are occurring that affect user quotas. • Since UFS quotas can be enabled/disabled on the fly, this lock must be taken in all appropriate situations. It is not sufficient to check if the UFS quota subsystem is enabled before taking the lock.
ufsvfs_mutex	kmutex_t	• Protects access to the list that links all UFS file system instances. • Updates lists as a part of the mount operation. • Allows synchronization of all UFS file systems.

Table 15.8 `VOP_RWLOCK` or `ufs_rwlock`

Name	Type	Description
`ufs_rwlock()`	function	• Prevents concurrent reads and writes to a file. • Used by NFS when calling a `VOP_READDIR`, to prevent directory contents from changing. • NFS uses this lock to get attributes before and after a read or write to disable another operation from modifying the file.

Table 15.9 Logging Locks

Name	Type	Description
`mtm_lock`	kmutex_t	• Protects `mtm_taskq_sync_count` (keeps track of the number of pending `top_issue_sync` requests) field in `mt_map_t`.
`mtm_mutex`	kmutex_t	• Protects all the fields in the `mt_map_t` structure except `mtm_mapext` and `mtm_refcnt`.
`mtm_rwlock`	krwlock_t	• Protects `agenext_mapentry` field.
`un_log_mutex`	kmutex_t	• Allows one write to the log at a time. Part of `ml_unit_t` structure (in-core log data structure).
`un_state_mutex`	kmutex_t	• Allows one log state update at a time.

15.6.2 Inode Lock Ordering

Now that we are all familiar with the several different types of locks available in UFS, let us put them in order as if we were to work on an inode. Lock ordering is critical, and any mistake will more than likely cause the system to deadlock, and may end up panicking it!

Figure 15.16 give us a quick overview of lock ordering specific to the inode.

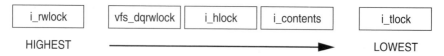

Figure 15.16 Inode Lock Ordering Precedence

15.6.3 UFS Lockfs Protocol

Along with basic inode locking, UFS also provides a mechanism to quiesce a file system for file system locking and for the forced unmounting of a file system. All VOPs (vnode operations) in UFS are required to follow the UFS lock protocol with `ufs_lockfs_begin()` and `ufs_lockfs_end()`, although the following functions purposely do not adhere to the tradition:

- `ufs_close`
- `ufs_putpage`
- `ufs_inactive`
- `ufs_addmap`
- `ufs_delmap`
- `ufs_rwlock`
- `ufs_rwunlock`
- `ufs_poll`

The basic principle here is that UFS supports various file system lock states (see list below) and each vnode operation must initiate the protocol by calling `ufs_lockfs_begin()` with an appropriate lock mask (a lock that this operation might grab while it is being processed) and end the protocol by calling `ufs_lockfs_end` before it returns. This way, UFS knows exactly how many vnode operations are in progress for the given file system by incrementing and decrementing the `ul_vnops_cnt` variable in the file-system-dependent `ulockfs` structure. If the file system is hard-locked, the thread gets an `EIO` error. If the file system is error-locked, then the thread is blocked.

Here are the file system locks and their actions.

- **Write lock.** Suspends writes that would modify the file system. Access times are not kept while a file system is write-locked.
- **Name lock.** Suspends accesses that could change or remove existing directories entries.
- **Delete lock.** Suspends access that could remove directory entries.
- **Hard lock.** Returns an error upon every access to the locked file system and cannot be unlocked. Hard-locked file systems can be unmounted. Hard lock supports forcible unmount.
- **Error lock.** Blocks all local access to the file system and returns `EWOULDBLOCK` on all remote access. File systems are error-locked by UFS upon detection of

internal inconsistency. They can only be unlocked after successful repair by
fsck, which is usually done automatically. Error-locked file systems can be
unmounted. Once the file system becomes clean, it can be upgraded to a
hard lock.

- **Soft lock.** Quiesces a file system.

- **Unlock.** Awakens suspended accesses, releases existing locks, and flushes
  the file system.

While a vnode operation is being executed in UFS, a call can be made to another
vnode function on the same UFS or a different UFS. This is called recursive VOP.
The per-file system vnode operation counter is not incremented or decremented
during recursive calls.

Here is the basic ordering to initiate and complete the lock protocol when operating on an inode in UFS.

```
1) Acquire i_rwlock (from the vnode layer in most cases).
2) Begin the UFS lock protocol by calling ufs_lockfs_begin().
3) Open UFS logging transactions if necessary now.
4) Acquire inode and quota locks (vfs_dqrwlock, i_contents, i_tlock, ...).
5) [work on inode]
6) Drop inode and quota locks (i_tlock, i_contents, vfs_dqrwlock, ...).
7) Close logging transactions.
8) End the UFS lock protocol by calling ufs_lockfs_end().
9) Release i_rwlock.
```

When working with directories, you need to make one minor change. i_rwlock
is acquired after the logging transaction is initialized, and i_rwlock is released
before the transaction is ended. Here are the steps.

```
1) Begin the UFS lock protocol by calling ufs_lockfs_begin().
2) Open UFS logging transactions if necessary now.
3) Acquire i_rwlock.
4) Acquire inode and quota locks (vfs_dqrwlock, i_contents, i_tlock, ...).
5) [work on inode]
6) Drop inode and quota locks (i_tlock, i_contents, vfs_dqrwlock, ...).
7) Release i_rwlock.
8) Close logging transactions.
9) End the UFS lock protocol by calling ufs_lockfs_end().
```

15.7 Logging

Important criteria for commercial systems are reliability and availability, both of which may be compromised if the file system does not provide the required level of robustness. We have become familiar with the term *journaling* to mean just one thing, but, in fact, file system logging can be implemented in several ways. The three most common forms of journaling are

- **Metadata logging.** Logs only file system structure changes
- **File and metadata logging.** Logs all changes to the file system
- **Log-structured file system.** Is an entire file system implemented as a log

The most common form of file system logging is metadata logging, and this is what UFS implements. When a file system makes changes to its on-disk structure, it uses several disconnected synchronous writes to make the changes. If an outage occurs halfway through an operation, the state of the file system is unknown, and the whole file system must be checked for consistency. For example, if the file is being extended the free block bitmap must be updated to mark the newly allocated block as no longer free. The inode block list must also be updated to indicate that the allocated block is owned by the file. If an outage occurs after the block is allocated, but before the inode is updated, file system inconsistency occurs.

A metadata logging file system such as UFS has an on-disk, cyclic, append-only log area that it can use to record the state of each disk transaction. Before any on-disk structures are changed, an intent-to-change record is written to the log. The directory structure is then updated, and when complete, the log entry is marked complete. Since every change to the file system structure is in the log, we can check the consistency of the file system by looking in the log, and we need not do a full file system scan. At mount time, if an intent-to-change entry is found but not marked complete the changes will not be applied to the file system. Figure 15.17 illustrates how metadata logging works.

Logging was first introduced in UFS in Solaris 2.4; it has come a long way since then, to being turned on by default in Solaris 10. Enabling logging turns the file system into a transaction-based file system. Either the entire transaction is applied or it is completely discarded. Logging is on by default in Solaris 10; however, it can be manually turned on by mount(1M) -o logging (using the _FIOLOGENABLE ioctl). Logging is not compatible with Solaris Logical Volume Manager (SVM) translogging, and attempt to turn on logging on a UFS file system that resides on an SVM will fail.

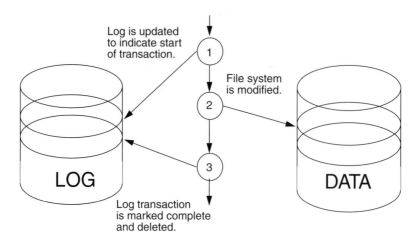

Figure 15.17 File System Metadata Logging

15.7.1 On-Disk Log Data Structures

The on-disk log is allocated from contiguous blocks where possible, and are only allocated as full sized file system blocks, no fragments are allowed. The initial pool of blocks is allocated when logging is first enabled on a file system, and blocks are not freed until logging is disabled. UFS uses these blocks for its own metadata and for times when it needs to store file system changes that have not yet been applied to the file system. This space on the file system is known as the "on disk" log, or log for short. It requires approximately 1 Mbyte per 1 Gbyte of file system space. The default minimum size for the log is 1 Mbyte, and the default maximum log size is 64 Mybtes. Figure 15.18 illustrates the on-disk log layout.

The file system superblock contains the block number where the main on-disk logging structure (extent_block_t) resides. This is defined by the extent_block structure. Note that the extent_block structure and all the accompanying extent structures fit within a file system block.

```
typedef struct extent_block {
        uint32_t        type;           /* Set to LUFS_EXTENTS to identify */
                                        /*   structure on disk. */
        int32_t         chksum;         /* Checksum over entire block. */
        uint32_t        nextents;       /* Size of extents array. */
        uint32_t        nbytes;         /* # bytes mapped by extent_block. */
        uint32_t        nextbno;        /* blkno of next extent_block. */
        extent_t        extents[1];
} extent_block_t;

                                        See usr/src/uts/common/sys/fs/ufs_log.h
```

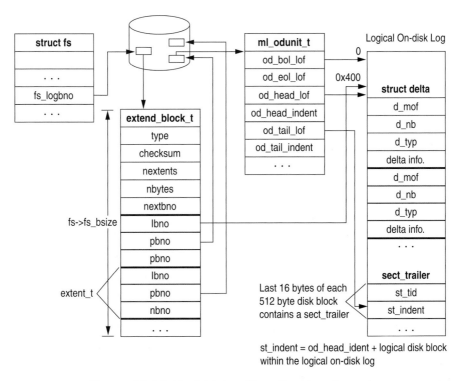

Figure 15.18 On-Disk Log Data Structure Layout

The `extent_block` structure describes logging metadata and is the main data structure used to find the on-disk log. It is followed by a series of extents that contain the physical block number for on-disk logging segments. The number of extents present for the file system is described by the `nextents` field in the `extent_block` structure.

```
typedef struct extent {
        uint32_t        lbno;    /* Logical block # within the space */
        uint32_t        pbno;    /* Physical block number of extent. */
                                 /* in disk blocks for non-MTB ufs */
                                 /* in frags for MTB ufs */
        uint32_t        nbno;    /* # blocks in this extent */
} extent_t;
```

                                    See usr/src/uts/common/sys/fs/ufs_log.h

Only the first extent structure is allowed to contain a `ml_odunit` structure (simplified: metadata logging on-disk unit structure).

```
typedef struct ml_odunit {
        uint32_t        od_version;     /* version number */
        uint32_t        od_badlog;      /* is the log okay? */
        uint32_t        od_unused1;

        /*
         * Important constants
         */
        uint32_t        od_maxtransfer; /* max transfer in bytes */
        uint32_t        od_devbsize;    /* device bsize */
        int32_t         od_bol_lof;     /* byte offset to begin of log */
        int32_t         od_eol_lof;     /* byte offset to end of log */

        /*
         * The disk space is split into state and circular log
         */
        uint32_t        od_requestsize; /* size requested by user */
        uint32_t        od_statesize;   /* size of state area in bytes */
        uint32_t        od_logsize;     /* size of log area in bytes */
        int32_t         od_statebno;    /* first block of state area */
        int32_t         od_unused2;

        /*
         * Head and tail of log
         */
        int32_t         od_head_lof;    /* byte offset of head */
        uint32_t        od_head_ident;  /* head sector id # */
        int32_t         od_tail_lof;    /* byte offset of tail */
        uint32_t        od_tail_ident;  /* tail sector id # */
        uint32_t        od_chksum;      /* checksum to verify ondisk contents */

        /*
         * Used for error recovery
         */
        uint32_t        od_head_tid;    /* used for logscan; set at sethead */

        /*
         * Debug bits
         */
        int32_t         od_debug;

        /*
         * Misc
         */
        struct timeval  od_timestamp;   /* time of last state change */
} ml_odunit_t;
```

See usr/src/uts/common/sys/fs/ufs_log.h

The values in the `ml_odunit_t` structure represent the location, usage and state of the on-disk log. The contents in the on-disk log consist of delta structures, which define the changes, followed by the actual changes themselves. Each 512 byte disk block of the on-disk log will contain a `sect_trailer` at the end of the block. This `sect_trailer` is used to identify the disk block as containing valid deltas. The `*_lof` fields reference the byte offset in the logical on-disk layout and not the physical on-the-disk contents.

```
struct delta {
        int64_t         d_mof;   /* byte offset on device to start writing */
                                 /*    delta */
        int32_t         d_nb;    /* # bytes in the delta */
        delta_t         d_typ;   /* Type of delta.  Defined in ufs_trans.h */
};
```

See usr/src/uts/common/sys/fs/ufs_log.h

```
typedef struct sect_trailer {
        uint32_t        st_tid;        /* transaction id */
        uint32_t        st_ident;      /* unique sector id */
} sect_trailer_t;
```

See usr/src/uts/common/sys/fs/ufs_log.h

15.7.2 In-Core Log Data Structures

Figure 15.19 illustrates the data structures for in-core logging.

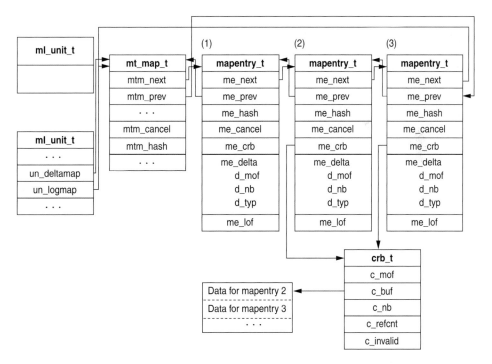

Figure 15.19 In-Core Log Data Structure Layout

ml_unit_t is the main in-core logging structure. There is only one per file system, and it contains all logging information or pointers to all logging data structures for the file system. The un_ondisk field contains an in-memory replica of the on-disk ml_odunit structure.

```
typedef struct ml_unit {
        struct ml_unit  *un_next;       /* next incore log */
        int             un_flags;       /* Incore state */
        buf_t           *un_bp;         /* contains memory for un_ondisk */
        struct ufsvfs   *un_ufsvfs;     /* backpointer to ufsvfs */
        dev_t           un_dev;         /* for convenience */
        ic_extent_block_t *un_ebp;      /* block of extents */
        size_t          un_nbeb;        /* # bytes used by *un_ebp */
        struct mt_map   *un_deltamap;   /* deltamap */
        struct mt_map   *un_logmap;     /* logmap includes moby trans stuff */
        struct mt_map   *un_matamap;    /* optional - matamap */

        /*
         * Used for managing transactions
         */
        uint32_t        un_maxresv;     /* maximum reservable space */
        uint32_t        un_resv;        /* reserved byte count for this trans */
        uint32_t        un_resv_wantin; /* reserved byte count for next trans */

        /*
         * Used during logscan
         */
        uint32_t        un_tid;

        /*
         * Read/Write Buffers
         */
        cirbuf_t        un_rdbuf;       /* read buffer space */
        cirbuf_t        un_wrbuf;       /* write buffer space */

        /*
         * Ondisk state
         */
        ml_odunit_t     un_ondisk;      /* ondisk log information */

        /*
         * locks
         */
        kmutex_t        un_log_mutex;   /* allows one log write at a time */
        kmutex_t        un_state_mutex; /* only 1 state update at a time */
} ml_unit_t;

                                        See usr/src/uts/common/sys/fs/ufs_log.h
```

mt_map_t tracks all the deltas for the file system. At least three mt_map_t structures are defined:

- **deltamap.** Tracks all deltas for currently active transactions. When a file system transaction completes, all deltas from the delta map are written to the log map and all the entries are then removed from the delta map.

- **logmap.** Tracks all committed deltas from completed transactions, not yet applied to the file system.
- **matamap.** Is the debug map for delta verification.

See `usr/src/uts/common/sys/fs/ufs_log.h` for the definition of `mt_map` structure

```
struct mapentry {
        /*
         * doubly linked list of all mapentries in map -- MUST BE FIRST
         */
        mapentry_t      *me_next;
        mapentry_t      *me_prev;

        mapentry_t      *me_hash;
        mapentry_t      *me_agenext;
        mapentry_t      *me_cancel;
        crb_t           *me_crb;
        int             (*me_func)();
        ulong_t         me_arg;
        ulong_t         me_age;
        struct delta    me_delta;
        uint32_t        me_tid;
        off_t           me_lof;
        ushort_t        me_flags;
};
```

See usr/src/uts/common/sys/fs/ufs_log.h

The `mapentry` structure defines changes to filesystem metadata. All existing mapentries for a given `mt_map` are linked into the `mt_amp` at the `mtm_next` and `mtm_prev` fields. The `mtm_hash` field of the `mt_map` is a hash list of all the mapentries, hashed according to the master byte offset of the delta on the file system and the `MAPBLOCKSIZE`. For example, the `MTM_HASH` macro determines the hash list in which a mapentry for the offset `mof` (where `mtm_nhash` is the total number of hash lists for the map). The default size used for `MAPBLOCKSIZE` is 8192 bytes, the hash size for the delta map is 512 bytes, and the hash size for the log map is 2048 bytes.

```
#define MAP_INDEX(mof, mtm) \
        (((mof) >> MAPBLOCKSHIFT) & (mtm->mtm_nhash-1))
#define MAP_HASH(mof, mtm) \
        ((mtm)->mtm_hash + MAP_INDEX((mof), (mtm)))
```

See usr/src/uts/common/sys/fs/ufs_log.h

A canceled `mapentry` with the `ME_CANCEL` bit set in the `me_flags` field is a special type of `mapentry`. This type of `mapentry` is basically a place holder for free blocks and fragments. It can also represent an old `mapentry` that is no longer valid due to a new `mapentry` for the same offset. Freed blocks and fragments are not eligible for reallocation until all deltas have been written to the on-disk log. Any attempt to allocate a block or fragment in which a corresponding canceled `mapentry` exists in the logmap, results in the allocation of a different block or fragment.

```
typedef struct crb {
        int64_t         c_mof;          /* master file offset of buffer */
        caddr_t         c_buf;          /* pointer to cached roll buffer */
        uint32_t        c_nb;           /* size of buffer */
        ushort_t        c_refcnt;       /* reference count on crb */
        uchar_t         c_invalid;      /* crb should not be used */
} crb_t;
```

See sys/fs/ufs_log.h

The `crb_t`, or cache roll buffer, caches blocks that exist within the same disk-block. It is merely a performance enhancement when information is rolled back to the file system. It helps reduce reads and writes that can occur while writing completed transactions deltas to the file system. It also acts as a performance enhancement on read hits of deltas.

UFS logging maintains private buf_t structures used for reading and writing of the on-disk log. These `buf_t` structures are managed through `cirbuf_t` structures. Each file system will have 2 `cirbuf_t` structures. One is used to manage log reads, and one to manage log writes.

```
typedef struct cirbuf {
        buf_t           *cb_bp;         /* buf's with space in circular buf */
        buf_t           *cb_dirty;      /* filling this buffer for log write */
        buf_t           *cb_free;       /* free bufs list */
        caddr_t         cb_va;          /* address of circular buffer */
        size_t          cb_nb;          /* size of circular buffer */
        krwlock_t       cb_rwlock;      /* r/w lock to protect list mgmt. */
} cirbuf_t;
```

See sys/fs/ufs_log.h

15.7.3 Summary Information

Summary information is critical to maintaining the state of the file system. Summary information includes counts of directories, free blocks, free fragments, and free inodes. These bits of information exist in each cylinder group and are valid only for that respective cylinder group. All cylinder group summary information is totaled; these numbers are kept in the `fs_cstotal` field of the superblock. A copy of all the cylinder group's summary information is also kept in a buffer pointed to from the file system superblock's `fs_csp` field. Also kept on disk for redundancy is a copy of the `fs_csp` buffer, whose block address is stored in the `fs_csaddr` field of the file system superblock.

All cylinder group information can be determined from reading the cylinder groups, as opposed to reading them from `fs_csaddr` blocks on disk. Hence, updates to `fs_csaddr` are logged only for large file systems (in which the total number of cylinder groups exceeds `ufs_ncg_log`, which defaults to 10,000). If a file system isn't logging deltas to the `fs_csaddr` area, then the `ufsvfs->vfs_nolog_si` is set to 1 and instead marks the `fs_csaddr` area as bad by setting the superblock's `fs_si` field to `FS_SI_BAD`. However, these changes are brought up to date when an unmount or a log roll takes place.

15.7.4 Transactions

A transaction is defined as a file system operation that modifies file system metatdata. A group of these file system transactions is known as a moby transaction.

Logging transactions are divided into two types:

- **Synchronous file system transactions** are those that are committed and written to the log as soon as the file system transaction ends.

- **Asynchronous file system transactions** are those for which the file system transactions are committed and written to the on-disk log after closure of the moby transaction. In this case the file system transaction may complete, but the metadata that it modified is not written to the log and not considered commited until the moby transaction has been completed.

So what exactly are committed transactions? Well, they are transactions whose deltas (unit changes to the file system) have been moved from the delta map to the log map and written to the on-disk log.

There are four steps involved in logging metadata changes of a file system transaction:

1. Reserve space in the log.
2. Begin a file system transaction.
3. Enter deltas in the delta map for all the metadata changes.
4. End the file system transaction.

15.7.4.1 Reserving Space in the Log

A file system transaction that is to log metadata changes should first reserve space
in the log. This prevents hangs if the on-disk log is full. A file system transaction
that is part of the current moby transaction can not complete if there isn't enough
log space to log the deltas. Log space can not be reclaimed until the current moby
transation completes and is committed. And the current moby transaction can't
complete until all file system transaction in the current moby transaction complete. Thus reserving space in the log must be done by the file system transaction
when it enters the current moby transation. If there is not enough log space available, the file system transaction will wait until sufficient log space becomes available, before enteering the the current moby transaction.

The amount of space reserved in the log for write and truncation vary, depending on the size of the operation. The macro TRANS_WRITE_RESV estimates how
much log space is needed for the operation.

```
#define TRANS_WRITE_RESV(ip, uiop, ulp, resvp, residp)  \
        if ((TRANS_ISTRANS(ip->i_ufsvfs) != NULL) && (ulp != NULL))  \
                ufs_trans_write_resv(ip, uiop, resvp, residp);
                                                        See sys/fs/ufs_trans.h
```

All other file system transactions have a constant transaction size, and UFS has
predefined macros for these operations:

```
/*
 * size calculations
 */
#define TOP_CREATE_SIZE(IP)        \
        (ACLSIZE(IP) + SIZECG(IP) + DIRSIZE(IP) + INODESIZE)
#define TOP_REMOVE_SIZE(IP)        \
        DIRSIZE(IP)  + SIZECG(IP) + INODESIZE + SIZESB
#define TOP_LINK_SIZE(IP)          \
        DIRSIZE(IP) + INODESIZE
#define TOP_RENAME_SIZE(IP)        \
        DIRSIZE(IP) + DIRSIZE(IP) + SIZECG(IP)
#define TOP_MKDIR_SIZE(IP)         \
        DIRSIZE(IP) + INODESIZE + DIRSIZE(IP) + INODESIZE + FRAGSIZE(IP) + \
             SIZECG(IP) + ACLSIZE(IP)
#define TOP_SYMLINK_SIZE(IP)       \
        DIRSIZE((IP)) + INODESIZE + INODESIZE + SIZECG(IP)
#define TOP_GETPAGE_SIZE(IP)       \
        ALLOCSIZE + ALLOCSIZE + ALLOCSIZE + INODESIZE + SIZECG(IP)
#define TOP_SYNCIP_SIZE            INODESIZE
#define TOP_READ_SIZE             INODESIZE
#define TOP_RMDIR_SIZE            (SIZESB + (INODESIZE * 2) + SIZEDIR)
#define TOP_SETQUOTA_SIZE(FS)     ((FS)->fs_bsize << 2)
#define TOP_QUOTA_SIZE            (QUOTASIZE)
#define TOP_SETSECATTR_SIZE(IP)   (MAXACLSIZE)
#define TOP_IUPDAT_SIZE(IP)       INODESIZE + SIZECG(IP)
#define TOP_SBUPDATE_SIZE         (SIZESB)
```

continues

```
#define TOP_SBWRITE_SIZE          (SIZESB)
#define TOP_PUTPAGE_SIZE(IP)      (INODESIZE + SIZECG(IP))
#define TOP_SETATTR_SIZE(IP)      (SIZECG(IP) + INODESIZE + QUOTASIZE + \
                ACLSIZE(IP))
#define TOP_IFREE_SIZE(IP)        (SIZECG(IP) + INODESIZE + QUOTASIZE)
#define TOP_MOUNT_SIZE            (SIZESB)
#define TOP_COMMIT_SIZE           (0)
sys/fs/ufs_trans.h
```

15.7.4.2 Starting Transactions

Starting a transaction simply means that the transaction has successfully entered the current moby transaction. As a result, once started, the moby will not end until all active file system transactions have completed. A moby transaction can accommodate both synchronous and asynchronous transactions. Most file system transactions in UFS are asynchronous; however, a synchronous transaction occurs if any of the following are true:

- If the file system is mounted `syncdir`
- If a `fsync()` system call is executed
- If `DSYNC` or `O_SYNC` open modes are set on reads and writes
- If `RSYNC` is set on reads
- During an unmount of a file system

A transaction can be started with one of the following macros:

- `TRANS_BEGIN_ASYNC`—Enters a file system transaction into the current moby transaction. Once the file system transaction ends, the moby transaction may still be active and hence the changes the file system transaction has made have not yet been committed.

```
#define TRANS_BEGIN_ASYNC(ufsvfsp, vid, vsize)\
{\
        if (TRANS_ISTRANS(ufsvfsp))\
                (void) top_begin_async(ufsvfsp, vid, vsize, 0); \
}
                                                      See sys/fs/ufs_trans.h
```

- **TRANS_BEGIN_SYNC.** Enters a file system transaction into the current moby transaction with the requirement that the completion of the file system transaction forces a completion and commitment of the moby transaction. All file system transactions that have occurred within the moby transaction are also considered as committed.

```
#define TRANS_BEGIN_SYNC(ufsvfsp, vid, vsize, error)\
{\
        if (TRANS_ISTRANS(ufsvfsp)) { \
                error = 0; \
                top_begin_sync(ufsvfsp, vid, vsize, &error); \
        } \
}
```

See sys/fs/ufs_trans.h

- **TRANS_BEGIN_CSYNC.** Does a TRANS_BEGIN_SYNC if the mount option syncdir is set; otherwise, does a TRANS_BEGIN_ASYNC.
- **TRANS_TRY_BEGIN_ASYNC and TRANS_TRY_BEGIN_CSYNC.** Try to enter the file system transaction into the moby transaction. If the result would cause the thread to block, then do not block and return EWOULDBLOCK instead. This macro is used in cases where the calling thread must not block.

```
#define TRANS_TRY_BEGIN_ASYNC(ufsvfsp, vid, vsize, err)\
{\
        if (TRANS_ISTRANS(ufsvfsp))\
                err = top_begin_async(ufsvfsp, vid, vsize, 1); \
        else\
                err = 0; \
}

#define TRANS_TRY_BEGIN_CSYNC(ufsvfsp, issync, vid, vsize, error)\
{\
        if (TRANS_ISTRANS(ufsvfsp)) {\
                if (ufsvfsp->vfs_syncdir) {\
                        ASSERT(vsize); \
                        top_begin_sync(ufsvfsp, vid, vsize, &error); \
                        ASSERT(error == 0); \
                        issync = 1; \
                } else {\
                        error = top_begin_async(ufsvfsp, vid, vsize, 1); \
                        issync = 0; \
                }\
        }\
}
```

See usr/src/uts/common/sys/fs/ufs_trans.h

15.7.4.3 Ending the Transaction

Once all metadata changes have been completed, the transaction must be ended. This is accomplished by calling one of the following macros:

- **TRANS_END_CSYNC.** Calls TRANS_END_ASYNC or TRANS_END_SYNC, depending on which type of file system transaction was initially started.
- **TRANS_END_ASYNC.** Ends an asynchronous file system transaction. If, at this point, the log is getting full, (the number of mapentries in the logmap is greater than the global variable logmap_maxnme_async) committed deltas

in the log will be applied to the file system and removed from the log. This is known as "rolling the log" and is done in by a seperate thread.

```
#define TRANS_END_ASYNC(ufsvfsp, vid, vsize)\
{\
        if (TRANS_ISTRANS(ufsvfsp))\
                top_end_async(ufsvfsp, vid, vsize); \
}
                                    See usr/src/uts/common/sys/fs/ufs_trans.h
```

- **TRANS_END_SYNC.** Closes and commits the current moby transaction, and writes all deltas to the on-disk log. A new moby transaction is then started.

```
#define TRANS_END_SYNC(ufsvfsp, error, vid, vsize)\
{\
        if (TRANS_ISTRANS(ufsvfsp))\
                top_end_sync(ufsvfsp, &error, vid, vsize); \
}
                                    See usr/src/uts/common/sys/fs/ufs_trans.h
```

15.7.5 Rolling the Log

Occasionally, the data in the log needs to be written back to the file system, a procedure called log rolling. Log rolling occurs for the following reasons:

- To update the on-disk file system with committed metadata deltas
- To free space in the log for new deltas
- To roll the entire log to disk at unmount
- To partially roll the on-disk log when it is getting full
- To completely roll the log with the _FIOFFS ioctl (file system flush)
- To partially roll the log every 5 seconds when no new deltas exist in the log
- To roll some deltas when the log map is getting full (that is, when logmap has more than logmap_maxnme mapentries, by default, 1536)

The actual rolling of the log is handled by the log roll thread, which executes the trans_roll() function found in usr/src/uts/common/fs/lufs_thread.c. The trans_roll() function preallocates a number of rollbuf_t structures (based on LUFS_DEFAULT_NUM_ROLL_BUF = 16, LUFS_DEFAULT_MIN_ROLL_BUFS = 4, LUFS_DEFAULT_MAX_ROLL_BUFS = 64) to handle rolling deltas from the log to the file system.

```
typedef uint16_t rbsecmap_t;
typedef struct rollbuf {
        buf_t rb_bh;                  /* roll buffer header */
        struct rollbuf *rb_next; /* link for mof ordered roll bufs */
        crb_t *rb_crb;                /* cached roll buffer to roll */
        mapentry_t *rb_age;          /* age list */
        rbsecmap_t rb_secmap;        /* sector map */
} rollbuf_t;
```
                                               See usr/src/uts/common/sys/fs/ufs_log.h

Along with allocating memory for the `rollbuf_t` structures, `trans_roll` also allocates `MAPBLOCKSIZE * lufs_num_roll_bufs` bytes to be used by `rollbuf_t`'s `buf_t` structure stored in `rb_bh`. These `rollbuf_t`'s are populated according to information found in the rollable mapentries of the logmap. All rollable mapentries will be rolled starting from the logmap's `un_head_lof` offset, and continuing until an unrollable mapentry is found. Once a rollable mapentry is found, all other rollable mapentries within the same `MAPBLOCKSIZE` segment on the file system device are located and mapped by the same rollbuf structure.

If all mapentries mapped by a rollbuf have the same cache roll buffer (crb), then this `crb` maps the on-disk block and buffer containing the deltas for the rollbuf's `buf_t`. Otherwise, the rollbuf's `buf_t` uses `MAPBLOCKSIZE` bytes of kernel memory allocated by the `trans_roll` thread to do the transfer. The `buf_t` reads the `MAPBLOCKSIZE` bytes on the file system device into the `rollbuf` buffer. The deltas defined by each mapentry overlap the old data read into the `rollbuf` buffer. This buffer is then writen to the file system device.

If the rollbufs contain holes, these rollbufs may have to issue more than one write to disk to complete writing the deltas. To asynchronously write these deltas, the rollbuf's `buf_t` structure is cloned for each additional write required for the given rollbuf. These cloned `buf_t` structures are linked into the rollbuf's `buf_t` structure at the `b_list` field. All writes defined by the rollbuf's `buf_t` structures and any clone `buf_t` structures are issued asynchronously.

The `trans_roll()` thread waits for all these writes to complete. If any fail, a warning is printed to the console and the log is marked as `LDL_ERROR` in the `logmap->un_flags` field. If the roll completes successfully, all corresponding mapentries are completely removed from the log map. The head of the log map is then adjusted to reflect this change, as illustrated in Figure 15.20.

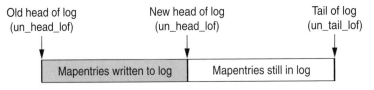

Figure 15.20 Adjustment of Head of Log Map

15.7.6 Redirecting Reads and Writes to the Log

When the UFS module is loaded, the global variable bio_lufs_strategy is set to point to the lufs_strategy() function. As a result, bread_common() and bwrite_common() functions redirect reads and writes to the bio_lufs_strategy (if it exists and if logging is enabled). lufs_strategy() then determines if the I/O request is a read or a write and dispatches to either lufs_read_strategy() or lufs_write_strategy(). These functions are responsible for resolving the read/write request from and to the log. In some instances in UFS, the functions lufs_read_strategy() and lufs_write_strategy() are called directly, bypassing the bio_lufs_strategy() code path.

15.7.6.1 lufs_read_strategy() Behavior

The lufs_read_strategy() function is called for reading metadata in the log. Mapentries already in the log map that correspond to the requested byte range are linked in the me_agenext list and have the ME_AGE bit set to indicate that they are in use. If the bytes being read are not defined in a logmap mapentry, the data is read from the file system as normal. Otherwise, lufs_read_strategy() then calls ldl_read() to read the data from the log.

The function ldl_read() can get the requested data from a variety of sources:

- A cache roll buffer
- The write buffer originally used to write this data to the log (mlunit->un_wrbuf)
- The buffer previously used to read this data from the log (mlunit->un_rdbuf)
- The on-disk log itself

15.7.6.2 lufs_write_strategy() Behavior

The lufs_write_strategy() function writes deltas defined by mapentries from the delta map to the log map if any exist. It does so by calling logmap_add() or logmap_add_buf(). logmap_add_buf() is used when crb buffers are being used, otherwise logmap_add() is used. These function in turn call ldl_write() to actually write the data to log.

The function ldl_write() always writes data into the the memory buffer of the buf_t contained in the write cirbuf_t structure. Hence, requested writes may or may not always actually be written to the physical on-disk log. Writes to the physical on-disk log occur when the log rolls the tail around back to the head, the write buf_t buffer is full, or a commit record is written.

15.7.7 Failure Recovery

An important aspect of file system logging is the ability to recover gracefully after an abnormal operating system halt. When the operating system is restarted and the file system remounted, the logging implementation will complete any outstanding operations by replaying the commited log transactions. The on-disk log is read and any commited deltas found are populated into the logmap as committed logmap mapentries. The roll thread will then write these to the file system and remove the mapentries from the logmap. All uncommitted deltas found in the ondisk log will be discarded.

15.7.7.1 Reclaim Thread

A system panic can leave inodes in a partially deleted state. This panic can be caused by an interrupted delete thread (refer to Section 15.3.2 for more information on the delete thread) in which `ufs_delete()` never finished processing the inode. The sole purpose of the UFS reclaim thread (`ufs_thread_reclaim()` in `usr/src/uts/common/fs/ufs/ufs_thread.c`) is to clean up the inodes left in this state. This thread is started if the superblock's `fs_reclaim` field has either `FS_RECLAIM` or `FS_RECLAIMING` flags set, indicating that freed inodes exist or that the reclaim thread was previously running.

The reclaim thread reads each on-disk inode from the file system device, checking for inodes whose `i_nlink` is zero and `i_mode` isn't zero. This situation signifies that `ufs_delete()` never finished processing these inodes. The thread simply calls `VN_RELE()` for every inode in the file system. If the node was partially deleted, the `VN_RELE()` forces the inode to go through `ufs_inactive()`, which in turn queues the inode in the `vfs_delete` queue to be processed later by the delete thread.

15.8 MDB Reference

Table 15.10 UFS MDB Reference

`dcmd or walker`	Description
`dcmd acl`	Given an inode, display its in core acl's
`dcmd cg`	Display a summarized cylinder group structure
`dcmd inode`	Display summarized inode_t

continues

Table 15.10 UFS MDB Reference (*continued*)

dcmd or walker	Description
dcmd inode_cache	Search/display inodes from inode cache
dcmd mapentry	Dumps ufslog mapentry
dcmd mapstats	Dumps ufslog stats
walk acl	Given an inode, walk chains of in core acl's
walk cg	Walk cg's in bio buffer cache
walk inode_cache	Walk inode cache
walk_ufslogmap	Walk the log map
walk ufs_inode_cache	Walk the ufs_inode_cache cache

PART SIX

Platform Specifics

16

Support for NUMA and CMT Hardware

Contributions by Bart Smaalders, Eric Saxe, and Jonathan Chew

Sun historically built symmetric multiprocessor (SMP) machines in which all of memory was seen as a single pool, equidistant in terms of latency from the set of independent, identical CPUs. Thus, the memory hierarchy from the core of the CPU through the various on- and off-chip caches, buses, etc., to main memory was identical for all the CPUs in the machine. In addition, any components that were shared were shared by all the CPUs in the same manner.

Newer systems depart from this relatively straightforward architecture in two fundamental ways. The first type are machines in which some memory is closer to some CPUs than others. These are known as NonUniform Memory Access (NUMA) machines. The second type are machines in which some of the CPUs share various processor components and caches. This is referred to here as chip multithreading (CMT).

The Memory Placement Optimization (MPO) feature and CMT optimizations allow Solaris OS to support hardware with asymmetric memory hierarchies, such as cache coherent NUMA (ccNUMA) systems and systems with chip-level multi-threading and multiprocessing. Solaris runs on both NUMA and CMT machines and can further optimize performance by being locality aware (that is, Solaris knows which CPUs and memory are close to each other) and CMT aware (Solaris is aware of which logical CPUs share caches, data paths, and other processor facilities).

16.1 Memory Hierarchy Designs

In this section we take a closer look at NUMA and CMT: what they are and why we need them.

16.1.1 What Is NUMA?

Typically, NUMA machines are made up of a number of nodes, each with CPUs, memory, and (possibly) I/O devices that use a small, fast local bus and special hardware to connect the buses of the various nodes. All the nodes are interconnected such that they can share one physical address space and can access the memory in all the other nodes. However, it takes longer to access the memory in a remote node than in the local one. There may also be varying degrees of remote latency. (That is, some memory will be close, some farther away, and some farther away still.) A node may physically be a board, a machine consisting of multiple boards, or even a single processor with local memory.

Among the factors affecting just how much longer a remote access takes are the speed of the interconnect, the topology of how the nodes are connected, whether the memory location is currently in cache (and which cache it's in), and whether any cache coherency must be maintained. For example, incurring a remote read miss on Starcat is about 1.5 to 3 times slower than a local miss, depending on these factors.

The Starcat and AMD Opteron hypertransport based machines are examples of these systems.

16.1.1.1 Why NUMA?

Building an SMP with a large number of fast CPUs is a hard problem. The physical size of the backplane required to allow connection of all the CPUs, I/O devices, etc., tends to limit the speed at which the backplane can operate, while at the same time the increasing number and speed of the CPUs places a constant upward pressure on the desired backplane speed (and thus capacity).

Various techniques have been employed to work around these issues. For example, plugging cards in from both sides (centerplane), using a crossbar switch rather than a traditional bus (basically making the bus more parallel), and increasing the width of the bus. However, over the long term it is likely that if SMP machines are to continue to grow in overall capacity, another approach is needed. NUMA offers a solution to this problem by allowing the computer to scale beyond a single SMP.

NUMA is a design trade-off, however. NUMA designs, while allowing for larger systems can introduce prohibitively large memory latencies, which in turn can impact performance. Because the amount of memory latency experienced by a given thread may vary depending on where the thread is running and which memory it is accessing, application performance on NUMA systems can be nondeterministic. This can be especially problematic for programmers who predicate their application's performance on the assumption that multiple parallel threads of execution will complete a given task in a constant amount of time (as is common in barrier synchronization).

Programmers concerned with extracting the highest possible performance from the entire machine will need to tune their applications to reflect the processor-memory-I/O topology. However, our experience so far with the adoption of new Solaris APIs has shown that ISVs would rather have their software work well without any changes. They do not want to optimize their code for a particular platform, because their code would be less portable and their testing and maintenance costs would increase. To address that concern, Solaris OS introduces a set of optional APIs that allow the ISV to advise any intentional relationship between threads and memory—advice that is completely portable to any specific machine topology. If ISVs are unable or unwilling to modify their application to use the optional APIs, the Solaris kernel will, by default, employ a default set of policies and optimizations to enhance the application's performance while reducing the performance variability the application would otherwise experience.

16.1.1.2 What Is Cache Coherent NUMA?

Cache coherent NUMA (ccNUMA) is a fairly common flavor of NUMA among the computer vendors, including Sun, who make NUMA machines today. In ccNUMA machines, hardware keeps the memory cache lines coherent across all the nodes in the machine. This approach is much faster than the alternatives of ensuring the coherency with software or disabling the caching of remote memory altogether. The MPO enhancements in Solaris are found only with ccNUMA machines.

16.1.2 What Is CMT?

Chip multithreading (CMT) refers to the family of processor technologies that allow a given physical processor to simultaneously execute multiple threads of execution. Several techniques presently exist for implementing CMT.

The first is chip multiprocessing (CMP), wherein multiple processing cores are implemented in a single physical processor package. UltraSPARC IV is Sun's first CMP, incorporating two UltraSPARC III+ cores per chip. Each UltraSPARC IV appears to the operating system as two logical processors (one per core).

Another technique is vertical multithreading (VT), wherein a single processor core may multiplex multiple threads of execution across its pipeline. Rather than stalling the pipeline when waiting for a memory request, the core can simply switch to another thread. Because this multiplexing is managed by the hardware, each VT core appears to the operating system as multiple logical CPUs upon which threads may be scheduled to run. Sun's UltraSPARC T1 (Niagara) is an example of a vertically threaded CMP processor, incorporating 8 cores with 4 threads per core. Each UltraSPARC T1 chip therefore presents to the OS 32 logical CPUs.

Like vertical threading, simultaneous multithreading (SMT) allows a single processor core to execute multiple threads, but SMT differs from VT in that the core can process instructions from multiple instruction streams simultaneously.

P4/Xeon is an example of an SMT processor.

16.1.2.1 Why CMT?

Chip multithreading represents a divergence from the traditional set of techniques used to increase the performance of a given processor architecture.

As the gap between processor and memory speeds widens, trying to increase performance by ramping up the processor clock speed begins to have diminishing returns because the time spent by the processor stalled waiting for memory will tend to dominate. CMT attacks this problem by allowing useful work from other instruction streams to fill what would otherwise be a stalled pipeline.

The design of CMT focuses therefore not on executing a single instruction stream as quickly as possible (stalling along the way) but rather on increasing the aggregate amount of work done by the processor in a given unit of time (throughput), a goal fulfilled by multiple threads running in parallel. In VT and SMT, we achieve this parallelism by filling pipeline stalls with instructions from other streams. In CMP, we achieve additional parallelism by adding more processing cores (each with the capability of running one or more threads) to the chip.

16.1.2.2 CMT and Solaris

Without CMT support, the kernel would see and treat each logical CPU presented by the chip no differently than it would any other CPU. It is important for the kernel to consider, however, the various sharing relationships that exist among a CMT chip's logical CPUs. Some CPUs may share a pipeline for example, while others may share caches or perhaps a data path to cache or memory. The performance of a thread running on a given logical CPU can therefore be impacted (for better or worse) by threads running elsewhere on the core or chip.

CMT support in Solaris allows the dispatcher to be aware of the sharing relationships that exist among a given chip's logical CPUs. To reduce contention over shared processor resources and to improve bandwidth, the dispatcher load-balances running threads across the system's physical processors and cores. Where caches are shared among multiple logical CPUs, threads are given an affinity for the set of

CPUs sharing a cache such that if the thread must migrate, it should try to next run on another CPU sharing that same cache.

Without CMT awareness, the dispatcher could, for example, schedule multiple memory-bandwidth-hungry threads to run on CPUs all sharing the same memory controller, when it would have been far better to load-balance the threads across the physical processors such that each thread has dedicated use of a memory controller and need not contend.

16.2 Memory Placement Optimization Framework

Three concepts enable the Solaris kernel to perform well on NUMA machines:

- Locality awareness
- Balancing
- Dynamic topology support

For an application to run well on a NUMA machine, it is beneficial for all the required resources—CPU, cache, memory, and perhaps I/O—to be co-located. Co-location helps minimize memory latencies by keeping most or all of the memory accesses local and avoiding the higher remote memory latencies. To enable co-location, the MPO Solaris kernel is locality aware; that is, it knows which hardware resources reside on which nodes, so it can try to allocate the resources needed by the application closer together for optimal performance.

Furthermore, the kernel provides an interface to allow an application to be more aware of machine topology or even to control, if the application developer so chooses, how its resources are allocated.

While locality awareness is important, the resources on the machine may become overloaded with too many threads trying to use the resources in too few nodes. The kernel will try to balance this load across the whole machine in this case so that no one node is much more loaded than any other node. The MPO framework also takes into account any changes in the hardware configuration of the machine during runtime, to refresh the information that the kernel has to keep for locality awareness.

To make optimal decisions on scheduling and resource allocation, the kernel is aware of the latency topology of the hardware. The kernel uses a simpler representation of the latency topology and may or may not mirror the physical topology exactly.

16.2.1 Latency Model

The latency model consists of one or more locality groups (lgroups). See Figure 16.1. Conceptually, each locality group is made up of all the hardware resources in a machine that are "close" to a defined reference point, for some value of close. It usually consists of the following:

- One or more CPUs
- Zero or more pages of physical memory and any devices that the platform chooses to associate with this locality group

Using this model, we can represent the latency behavior of AMD Opteron, Starcat, and other NUMA machines. A simple example is that of a Starcat system: Each board contains set of processors that are close to the local memory on the

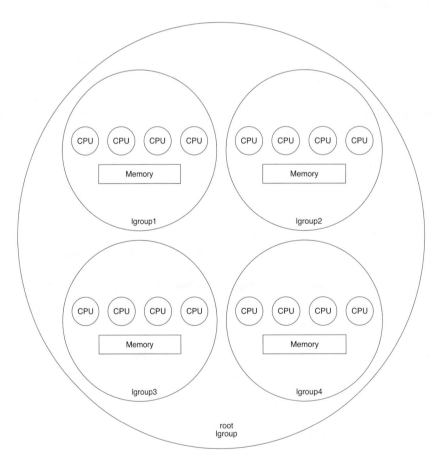

Figure 16.1 Lgroups and Hierarchies

board and less close to the memory on a remote board. In this case, a simple flat descriptions of lgroups—one per board—is sufficient.

16.2.2 More Complex Models

In the case of more complex systems, more than two levels of latency may be present, for example, as in a four-processor AMD Opteron system. The CPUs and memory are connected in a ring topology as shown in Figure 16.2.

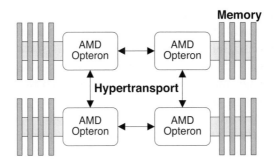

Figure 16.2 4-Way Hypertransport Ring

In this example, three levels of memory latency exist: local to the processor, one hop away, and two hops away. Eight processors are typically connected in a ladder configuration as shown in Figure 16.3.

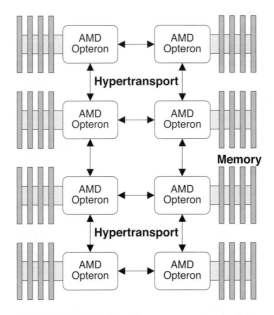

Figure 16.3 8-Way Hypertransport Ladder

The kernel creates and organizes lgroups into a hierarchy that can be quickly consulted and traversed to find the resources are closest, farther away, farther away still, etc.

16.3 Initial Thread Placement

A home lgroup is chosen for each thread upon creation. This home lgroup minimizes the frequency with which a thread moves from one board to another. The thread will have an affinity for that lgroup and tend to run and allocate its memory there to achieve good locality. The home lgroup is chosen based on the number of threads in the process, the lgroups that the process is spread across, and the size and relative load of each lgroup.

An thread's home lgroup can change in two ways. The most obvious way an thread's home lgroup can change is if all the processors in its home lgroup are removed from the system, either through off-lining or by a dynamic reconfiguration operation. The other way that an thread's home lgroup can change is when that thread is bound to a processor in a different lgroup. In that case, the new processor's lgroup becomes the thread's new home. Even if the thread is subsequently unbound, it will retain this new home lgroup.

16.4 Scheduling

The dispatcher will always try to run the thread on its home lgroup if possible. If all the CPUs in the home lgroup are busy and running higher priority threads, the dispatcher will try to find the nearest CPU that is not busy. Even if a thread runs on a remote lgroup (an lgroup other than its home), its home lgroup will remain unchanged. The next time the thread is scheduled, the thread will try to return to its home lgroup if a CPU is available.

Dispatching a thread to its home locality group as often as possible is a critical component in improving performance through locality, along with locality aware memory allocation. Locality-aware scheduling reduces the number of internode cache-to-cache transfers. Avoiding remote cache transfers shortens the ramp-up time should a thread be migrated from one CPU's run queue to another. This sort of CPU migration occurs frequently in transaction-processing workloads, which run with thousands of threads that frequently sleep waiting on I/O.

Note that scheduling affinity is not done for real-time threads, since the implementation is POSIX conformant. Hence, jobs should be placed into timeshare (TS), interactive (IA), fixed priority (FX), or fair share (FSS) scheduling classes in order to benefit from MPO.

See Chapter 3 for more information on the dispatcher's implementation of locality group awareness.

16.5 Memory Allocation

In Solaris, memory allocation is a two-step process. The first step assigns virtual memory. This step occurs when an application calls brk() to extend its heap or when the application maps in a file. The second step assigns physical memory to back the virtual memory. The assignment of physical memory does not occur until the application first tries to read or write to the new virtual address. At that point, the kernel will select a physical memory page and create a mapping from the application's virtual address to this physical page.

The key to delivering the best performance on systems with sizable memory locality differences is to ensure that physical memory is allocated close to the threads that are expected to access it. This allows for both lower latency and higher bandwidth. Obviously, when a process allocates memory, the kernel cannot predict with certainty how that memory will be used. However, the kernel can make several different assumptions that hold in many cases.

The simplest policy that one can adopt when allocating memory for locality awareness is "first touch." This simply means that memory is allocated from the home lgroup of the thread that first tries to access that memory. This approach assumes that whichever thread first accesses the memory is likely to be the thread that will access that memory most frequently in the future. This assumption obviously holds for single-threaded applications, but it also holds for many multithreaded applications. First touch is the default memory allocation policy used for private memory. Note that memory is allocated from the thread's home lgroup, even if the thread is running remote from its home at the time the memory is allocated. This behavior reflects an assumption that the thread will primarily be scheduled to run on its home lgroup.

Shared memory (for example, Intimate Shared Memory (ISM), MAP_SHARED memory-mapped files, etc.) is, by definition, likely to be accessed by multiple threads. Assuming that some significant number of those threads will be running in different lgroups, the kernel allocates shared memory by using the default random memory placement policy. This policy optimizes for bandwidth while trying to minimize average latency for the threads accessing it throughout the server. It spreads the memory across as many memory banks as possible, distributing the load across many memory controllers and bus interfaces, thereby preventing any single component from becoming a performance-limiting hot spot. In addition, random placement improves the reproducibility of performance measurements by ensuring that the relative locality of threads and memory remains roughly constant across multiple runs of an application.

16.6 Lgroup Implementation

A data structure called an lgroup represents a locality group. The lgroup contains information about itself and its resources. Each lgroup contains

- A unique ID that identifies this lgroup
- A pointer to the parent lgroup
- A pointer to a list of child lgroups
- A pointer to chips present in this lgroup
- A pointer to sets of memory groups in this lgroup
- A platform handle used between the common and platform-specific parts of Solaris to identify this lgroup and the hardware resources that are inside it

```
/*
 * lgroup structure
 *
 * Visible to generic code and contains the lgroup ID, CPUs in this lgroup,
 * and a platform handle used to identify this lgroup to the lgroup platform
 * support code
 */
typedef struct lgrp {

        lgrp_id_t        lgrp_id;        /* which lgroup */
        int              lgrp_latency;
        lgrp_handle_t    lgrp_plathand;  /* handle for platform calls */
        struct lgrp      *lgrp_parent;   /* parent lgroup */
        uint_t           lgrp_reserved1; /* filler */
        uint_t           lgrp_childcnt;  /* number of children lgroups */
        klgrpset_t       lgrp_children;  /* children lgroups */
        klgrpset_t       lgrp_leaves;    /* (direct descendant) leaf lgroups */


        /*
         * set of lgroups containing a given type of resource
         * at this level of locality
         */
        klgrpset_t       lgrp_set[LGRP_RSRC_COUNT];

        mnodeset_t       lgrp_mnodes;    /* set of memory nodes in this lgroup */
        uint_t           lgrp_nmnodes;   /* number of memnodes */
        uint_t           lgrp_reserved2; /* filler */

        struct cpu       *lgrp_cpu;      /* pointer to a cpu may be null */
        uint_t           lgrp_cpucnt;    /* number of cpus in this lgrp  */
        uint_t           lgrp_chipcnt;
        struct chip      *lgrp_chips;    /* pointer to chips in this lgrp */
        kstat_t          *lgrp_kstat;    /* per-lgrp kstats */
} lgrp_t;
```

The lgroup platform handle enables the separation of the lgroup implementation into common (platform-independent) and platform-specific components. This separation fosters a clean interface between the two components, makes the implementation more portable, and allows the common part to focus on scheduling, virtual memory, APIs, etc., while the platform-specific part can deal with the hardware resources. The handles are managed and maintained by the platform code, so the platform can implement them as it chooses and decide what CPUs, memory, etc., to associate with each one (and consequently each corresponding lgroup).

For some machines, proper expression of the latency topology will require that some lgroups have no CPUs or no memory. Our implementation deals with this by letting the platform-specific code decide how to implement this and whether the CPUs or memory should be in their own lgroup or associated with another lgroup.

The data structure is defined below.

16.6.1 Parameters Affecting MPO

Most of the locality-related optimizations introduced with MPO rely on some fairly simple heuristics to provide good performance for most applications. Some applications that do not behave as expected may possibly experience performance problems with this new functionality. In case of any such issues, the values of the MPO internal system variables can help explain the system behavior, and the controlling APIs described in the next section can help provide a solution.

Important. The description of the MPO system variables is provided here solely to explain the MPO implementation. Changes to these variables are not supported, and customers experiencing any problems may be required to change the variables back to their default values for proper diagnostics.

Users should keep in mind that these variables are all internal kernel variables and do not constitute a formal interface. Although the commands and variables below are implemented in current releases of Solaris, these variables may change or disappear over time. In addition, since these are internal variables, there may be no error detection should they be changed to unexpected values. Their default values have been carefully chosen to work well together.

`lgrp_mem_default_policy`. This variable reflects the default memory allocation policy used by the kernel. This variable is an integer, and its value should correspond to one of the policies listed in `<sys/lgrp.h>`. On Sun Fire 3800–6800 servers, this value is LGRP_MEM_POLICY_NEXT, starting with the Solaris 9, signifying that memory allocation will default to first touch. On Sun Fire 12K and 15K servers, this value is

- LGRP_MEM_POLICY_RANDOM in the Solaris 9 9/02 OS, meaning that 1 defaults to random allocation
- LGRP_MEM_POLICY_NEXT starting with the Solaris 9 12/02 OS, meaning that 1 defaults to first touch allocation. However, on Sun Fire 12K and 15K servers

without the hardware prerequisite installed, all processors and memory will be placed in a single lgroup, essentially disabling the MPO feature.

lgrp_shm_random_thresh.   As described above, large shared memory regions are allocated randomly rather than by first touch. This variable controls how large a region can be before we switch to random allocation. The default is 8 Mbytes, which is large enough to allow communication buffers such as those used by MPI programs to be local to one of the ends of the communication pipe; yet it is small enough that memory regions which are likely to become hot spots will be spread across the system's memory controllers.

This variable is an unsigned 64-bit integer; it can be modified at runtime with a kernel debugger or through /etc/system.

lgrp_mem_pset_aware.   If a process is running within a user processor set (see psrset(1M)), this variable determines whether randomly placed memory for the process is selected from among all the lgroups in the system or only from those lgroups that are spanned by the processors in the processor set. This value defaults to zero, signifying that the kernel will select memory from all the lgroups in the system. This default is appropriate for systems in which processor sets are not used or are only used to isolate applications from operating system threads. If processor sets are used to isolate applications from one another, then setting this value to 1 will likely lead to more reproducible performance.

lgrp_expand_proc_thresh.   This variable controls how quickly a process's threads will spread across multiple lgroups. If the lowest load among all the lgroups across which the process is spread exceeds this threshold, that suggests that our current lgroups are all approaching or exceeding their capacity. Thus, we will consider placing the next thread on a new lgroup.

This value reflects the fraction of an lgroup's capacity that is being used. To allow the kernel to evaluate loads by using only integer arithmetic, we make this value an unsigned 32-bit integer that is set to INT16_MAX times some fractional capacity.

On Sun Fire 12K and 15K servers, this value defaults to (INT16_MAX*3)/4, meaning that we will not consider spreading a process to a new lgroup until each of its existing lgroups is at least 75% loaded. On Sun Fire 3800–6800 servers, this value defaults to (INT16_MAX/4), meaning that we will consider spreading to a new lgroup if our existing lgroups are at least 25% loaded. The different values arise from the differences in architecture between the two servers. On Sun Fire 12K and 15K servers, the remote latency is significantly higher than the remote latency on Sun Fire 3800–6800 servers, and, conversely, the available bandwidth is much greater. Thus, these values reflect an attempt to manage load to minimize an application's latency on a Sun Fire 12K/15K server and maximize an application's bandwidth on Sun Fire 3800–6800 servers.

lgrp_privm_random_thresh.   As described above, by default, private memory is always allocated by first touch. This variable makes it possible to allocate large private memory regions by using random placement rather than first touch. By default, this value is ULONG_MAX.

This variable is an unsigned 64-bit integer; it can be safely modified at runtime with a kernel debugger or through /etc/system.

lgrp_expand_proc_diff.   Once we have decided to spread a process out to a new lgroup, there is no point in spreading it to a new lgroup that is just as loaded as the lgroups we are already running on. This variable uses the same capacity units as lgrp_expand_proc_thresh, and it specifies how much lower the load must be on a new lgroup before we will assign a new thread to that lgroup. On both Sun Fire 3800–6800 and 12K/15K servers, this value defaults to (INT16_MAX/4), or a 25% difference in load.

lgrp_loadavg_tolerance.   As with system load, an lgroup's load is calculated with a decaying average function; this tends to be more useful than the "instantaneous" load measurement, which can fluctuate widely and quickly. Thus, the load value for an lgroup is really only a constantly changing estimate. When this value is actually used to decide which lgroup a new thread should be placed on, lgrp_loadavg_tolerance is used as a "fudge factor." If the current estimated loads on two lgroups are within lgrp_loadavg_tolerance of each other, we treat those lgroups as being identically loaded and choose randomly between them. The value is specified with the same units as the other load variables. The default value is 0x10000, which leads to good performance results for a variety of database and mixed workloads. Our tests have shown that HPC workloads frequently benefit from a lower value, such as 0x1000.

16.7 MPO APIs

Several new APIs added to Solaris OS will help developers explore ways in which MPO technology can optimize an application's performance.

16.7.1 Informational

It is not always easy to identify potential memory-locality-related problems simply by studying an algorithm in isolation. Furthermore, the use of autoparallelizing compilers can introduce memory locality problems that do not exist in the serial algorithm. The APIs in this section allow an application to dynamically determine how its threads and virtual memory have been assigned to processors and physical memory by the kernel. The following is a high-level description of each of the new APIs. The full details of each can be found in the man pages starting with the Solaris 9 OS.

getcpuid(3C).   This routine returns the cpuid on which the calling thread was running when it executed the call. Unless a thread is bound to a CPU, the kernel is free to schedule it on any CPU in the system (but following lgroup policies). Hence, there is no guarantee that a thread will still be running on this CPU.

lgroup_home(3C).   This routine returns the ID of the home lgroup of the calling thread. A thread's home lgroup is a much less transitory value than the current CPU ID. Once a thread is assigned a home lgroup, that lgroup will not change unless the thread is explicitly bound to a CPU in a different lgroup or unless all the CPUs in the lgroup are taken offline. Note that this permanence may not continue to be true in future releases of the Solaris. It is possible that in the future, threads will eventually migrate from one lgroup to another in response to system utilization and migration policies.

meminfo(2).   The meminfo(2) system call allows us to query the operating system about both virtual and physical memory assigned to the calling process. Given a virtual address in the calling process's address space, this call can return the physical address, the lgroup to which that physical address belongs, and the size of the page. Given a physical address, the call can return the lgroup in which the memory exists.

This call is useful for diagnostic and verification purposes. Knowing where a range of memory is physically stored can help explain why accesses to that memory take longer than expected. This information can then be used to determine where, or if, calls to madvise(3C) (see next section) might allow the kernel to make better decisions about where memory should be allocated. Once calls to madvise(3C) have been added, the meminfo(2) call can be used to verify that the kernel has made the expected changes in its behavior.

16.7.1.1 MPO Advice APIs

The goal of MPO technology in the kernel is to deliver good performance on servers with memory locality properties without making any changes to the applications. However, some applications could achieve better performance by improving the kernel's default placement policies.

For example, an application in which one thread allocates and initializes a large dataset from private memory will likely have all of its memory located on a single lgroup. If the application then spawns many new threads to access that data, a significant number of those threads are likely to be running on remote lgroups. Rather than making extensive modifications to an application, we can use the madvise(3C) API, which provides a relatively easy method for improving such an application's performance. While madvise(3C) is easy to use, using its MADV_ ACCESS flags has some overhead. Consequently, we obtain optimal performance by simply having each thread initialize its own data for this example. This means that, for some applications, it may be the case that optimal performance may require that the application be restructured so that each thread initializes and uses a limited portion of the full dataset.

madvise(3C). This routine allows an application to provide the kernel with hints about how it expects a range of memory to be used. Specifically, it allows an application to indicate whether a range of memory will be used by many threads (MADV_ACCESS_MANY) or by the next thread that touches it (MADV_ACCESS_ LWP).

The MADV_ACCESS_MANY hint may be used by an application that creates and initializes a large data structure in private memory and then creates multiple threads that will all access that data structure. This behavior is typical of many autoparallelized applications. Since the data structure is created while the application has only a single thread, by default the kernel will attempt to allocate it all on a single Uniboard. This hint will prompt the kernel to allocate the data structure according to a random placement policy, which offers higher bandwidth to all the application's threads.

The MADV_ACCESS_LWP hint is most useful when an application changes how it expects a range of memory to be used. If after this hint is received, the next thread to touch a page in the specified range is in a different lgroup from the memory, then the kernel may migrate the page to that thread's lgroup. This can be useful for applications that have multiple phases, each with distinctly different memory usage patterns. It can also be used for applications that allocate a large ISM segment in order to get large pages but that do not intend to share those pages with other threads. Note that migrating memory can be time consuming, so use MADV_ ACCESS_LWP and MADV_ACCESS_MANY with discretion.

madv.so.1. madv.so.1 is a shared object that is superimposed on memory allocation system calls to allow the user to apply the hints described above without modifying the source code of the application. This functionality is less precise than that offered by the madvise() interface, since a user cannot choose to apply the advisement to specific address ranges, but only to the whole heap, just ISM or Dynamic ISM (DISM) segments, just private segments, and so on. This functionality is most useful for rapid prototyping and for tuning applications for which the source code is not available.

16.7.1.2 Explicit Lgroup APIs

The lgroup APIs export the lgroup abstraction for applications to use for observability and performance tuning. A new library, called `liblgrp`, contains the new APIs. Applications can use the APIs to perform the following tasks:

- Traverse the group hierarchy
- Discover the contents and characteristics of a given lgroup
- Affect the thread and memory placement on lgroups

16.7.2 Verifying the Interface Version

The `lgrp_version(3LGRP)` function must be used to verify the presence of a supported lgroup interface before the lgroup API is used. The `lgrp_version()` function has the following syntax:

```
#include <sys/lgrp_user.h>

int lgrp_version(const int version);
```

The `lgrp_version()` function takes a version number for the lgroup interface as an argument and returns the lgroup interface version that the system supports. When the current implementation of the lgroup API supports the version number in the version argument, the `lgrp_version()` function returns that version number. Otherwise, the `lgrp_version()` function returns LGRP_VER_NONE.

```
#include <sys/lgrp_user.h>
if (lgrp_version(LGRP_VER_CURRENT) != LGRP_VER_CURRENT) {
    fprintf(stderr, "Built with unsupported lgroup interface %d\n",
        LGRP_VER_CURRENT);
    exit (1);
}
```

16.7.3 Initialization of the Locality Group Interface

Applications must call `lgrp_init(3LGRP)` in order to use the APIs for traversing the lgroup hierarchy and to discover the contents of the lgroup hierarchy. The call to `lgrp_init()` gives the application a consistent snapshot of the lgroup hierarchy. The application developer can specify whether the snapshot contains only the resources that are available to the calling thread specifically or the resources that are available to the operating system in general. The `lgrp_init()` function returns a cookie that is used for the following tasks:

- Navigating the lgroup hierarchy
- Determining the contents of an lgroup
- Determining whether the snapshot is current

lgrp_init(). The lgrp_init() function initializes the lgroup inter-face and takes a snapshot of the lgroup hierarchy.

lgrp_fini(). The lgrp_fini(3LGRP) function ends the use of a given cookie and frees the corresponding lgroup hierarchy snapshot.

16.8 Locality Group Hierarchy

The lgroup hierarchy is a directed acyclic graph that is similar to a tree, except that a node might have more than one parent. The root lgroup represents the whole machine. The root lgroup is the lgroup with the highest latency value in the system. Each of the child lgroups contains a subset of the hardware in the root lgroup. Each child lgroup is bounded by a lower latency value. Locality groups that are closer to the root have more resources and a higher latency. Locality groups that are closer to the leaves have fewer resources and a lower latency.

The following APIs enable the calling thread to navigate the lgroup hierarchy.

lgrp_cookie_stale(). The lgrp_cookie_stale(3LGRP) function determines whether the snapshot of the lgroup hierarchy represented by the given cookie is current.

lgrp_view(). The lgrp_view(3LGRP) function determines the view with which a given lgroup hierarchy snapshot was taken.

lgrp_nlgrps(). The lgrp_nlgrps(3LGRP) function returns the number of locality groups in the system. If a system has only one locality group, memory placement optimizations have no effect.

lgrp_root(). The lgrp_root(3LGRP) function returns the root lgroup ID.

lgrp_parents(). The lgrp_parents(3LGRP) function takes a cookie that represents a snapshot of the lgroup hierarchy and returns the number of parent lgroups for the specified lgroup.

lgrp_children(). The lgrp_children(3LGRP) function takes a cookie that represents the calling thread's snapshot of the lgroup hierarchy and returns the number of child lgroups for the specified lgroup.

lgrp_cpus().   The lgrp_cpus(3LGRP) function takes a cookie that represents a snapshot of the lgroup hierarchy and returns the number of CPUs in a given lgroup.

lgrp_mem_size().   The lgrp_mem_size(3LGRP) function takes a cookie that represents a snapshot of the lgroup hierarchy and returns the size of installed or free memory in the given lgroup. The lgrp_mem_size() function reports memory sizes in bytes.

16.8.1 Locality Group Characteristics

The following API retrieves information about the characteristics of a given lgroup.

lgrp_latency().   The lgrp_latency(3LGRP) function returns the latency between a CPU in one lgroup to the memory in another lgroup.

16.8.2 Locality Groups and Thread and Memory Placement

The locality group APIs used to discover and affect thread and memory placement with respect to lgroups are as follows:

lgrp_home().   The lgrp_home(3LGRP) function discovers thread placement.

meminfo(2).   The meminfo(2) system call discovers memory placement.

madvise(3C).   The MADV_ACCESS flags to the madvise(3C) function affect memory allocation among lgroups.

lgrp_affinity_set(3LGRP).   The lgrp_affinity_set(3LGRP) function can affect thread and memory placement by setting a thread's affinity for a given lgroup.

In addition, the following applies:

- The affinities of an lgroup may specify an order of preference for lgroups from which to allocate resources.
- The kernel needs information about the likely pattern of an application's memory use in order to allocate memory resources efficiently.
- The madvise() function and its shared object analogue madv.so.1 provide this information to the kernel.
- A running process can gather memory usage information about itself by using the meminfo() system call.

16.9 MPO Statistics

The exports kstats from the "lgrp" module of the MPO framework are shown in Table 16.1.

Table 16.1 MPO Lgroup Statistics

Statistic	Description
lwp migrations	# migrations away from this lgrp
alloc fail	# times alloc fails for chosen lgrp
pages migrated from	# pages migrated from this lgrp
pages migrated to	# pages migrated to this lgrp
pages failed to migrate to	# pages failed to migrate to this lgrp
pages failed to migrate from	# pages failed to migrate from this lgrp
pages marked for migration	# pages marked to migrate from this lgrp
pages failed to mark	# pages marked to migrate from this lgrp
default policy	# of times default policy applied
next-touch policy	# of times next touch policy applied
random policy	# of times random policy applied
span process policy	# of times random proc policy applied
span psrset policy	# of times random pset policy applied
round robin policy	# of times round robin policy applied

The statistics can be accessed through the kstat interfaces.

```
sol9# kstat lgrp
module: lgrp                         instance: 1
name:   lgrp1                        class:    misc
        alloc fail                   278218728
        cpus                         4
        crtime                       291.87058224
        default policy               0
        load average                 72495
        lwp migrations               0
        next-touch policy            689363494
        pages avail                  2097152
        pages failed to mark         0
        pages failed to migrate from 0
        pages failed to migrate to   0
        pages free                   1778727
        pages installed              2097152
        pages marked for migration   0
        pages migrated from          0
```

continues

```
pages migrated to           0
random policy               12575460
round robin policy          0
snaptime                    678923.87893152
span process policy         0
span psrset policy          0
```

16.10 MDB Reference

Table 16.2 Lgroup MDB Reference

dcmd or walker	Description
dcmd lgrp	Display an lgrp
walk lgrp_cpulist	Given an lgrp, walk cpus
walk lgrptbl	Walk the lgrp table

Locking and
Synchronization

In this chapter, we continue our discussion of core kernel facilities, with an examination of the synchronization objects implemented in the Solaris kernel.

17.1 Synchronization

Solaris runs on a variety of different hardware platforms, including multiprocessor systems based on both the SPARC and Intel processors. Several multiprocessor architectures in existence today offer various trade-offs in performance and engineering complexity in both hardware and software. The current multiprocessor architecture that Solaris supports is the symmetric multiprocessor (SMP) and shared memory architecture, which implements a single kernel shared by all processors and a single memory address space. To support such an architecture, the kernel must synchronize access to critical data to maintain data integrity, coherency, and state. The kernel synchronizes access by defining a lock for a particular kernel data structure or variable and requiring that code reading or writing the data must first acquire the appropriate lock. The holder of the lock is required to release the lock once the data operation has been completed.

The synchronization primitives and associated interfaces are used by virtually all kernel subsystems: device drivers, the dispatcher, process and thread support code, file systems, etc. Insight into what the synchronization objects are and how they are implemented is key to understanding one of the core strengths of the

Solaris kernel—scalable performance on multiprocessor systems. An equally important component to the scalability equation is the avoidance of locks altogether whenever possible. The use of synchronization locks in the kernel is constantly being scrutinized as part of the development process in kernel engineering, with an eye to minimizing the number of locks required without compromising data integrity.

Several alternative methods of building parallel multiprocessor systems have emerged in the industry over the years. So, in the interest of conveying the issues surrounding the implementation, we need to put things in context. First, we take a brief look at the different parallel systems architectures that are commercially available today, and then we turn to the specifics of support for multiprocessor architectures by the Solaris kernel.

17.2 Parallel Systems Architectures

Multiprocessor (MP) systems from Sun (SPARC-processor-based), as well as several x86/x64-based MP platforms, are implemented as symmetric multiprocessor (SMP) systems. Symmetric multiprocessor describes a system in which a peer-to-peer relationship exists among all the processors (CPUs) on the system. A master processor, defined as the only CPU on the system that can execute operating system code and field interrupts, does *not* exist. All processors are equal. The SMP acronym can also be extended to mean Shared Memory Multiprocessor, which defines an architecture in which all the processors in the system share a uniform view of the system's physical address space and the operating system's virtual address space. That is, all processors share a single image of the operating system kernel. Sun's multiprocessor systems meet the criteria for both definitions.

Alternative MP architectures alter the kernel's view of addressable memory in different ways. Massively parallel processor (MPP) systems are built on nodes that contain a relatively small number of processors, some local memory, and I/O. Each node contains its own copy of the operating system; thus, each node addresses its own physical and virtual address space. The address space of one node is not visible to the other nodes on the system. The nodes are connected by a high-speed, low-latency interconnect, and node-to-node communication is done through an optimized message passing interface. MPP architectures require a new programming model to achieve parallelism across nodes.

The shared memory model does not work since the system's total address space is not visible across nodes, so memory pages cannot be shared by threads running on different nodes. Thus, an API that provides an interface into the message passing path in the kernel must be used by code that needs to scale across the various nodes in the system.

Other issues arise from the nonuniform nature of the architecture with respect to I/O processing since the I/O controllers on each node are not easily made visible to all the nodes on the system. Some MPP platforms attempt to provide the illusion of a uniform I/O space across all the nodes by using kernel software, but the nonuniformity of the access times to nonlocal I/O devices still exists.

NUMA and ccNUMA (nonuniform memory access and cache coherent NUMA) architectures attempt to address the programming model issue inherent in MPP systems. From a hardware architecture point of view, NUMA systems resemble MPPs—small nodes with few processors, a node-to-node interconnect, local memory, and I/O on each node. Note: It is not required that NUMA/ccNUMA or MPP systems implement small nodes (nodes with four or fewer processors). Many implementations are built that way, but there is no architectural restriction on the node size.

On NUMA/ccNUMA systems, the operating system software provides a single system image, where each node has a view of the entire system's memory address space. In this way, the shared memory model is preserved. However, the nonuniform nature of speed of memory access (latency) is a factor in the performance and potential scalability of the platform. When a thread executing on a processor node on a NUMA or ccNUMA system incurs a page fault (references an unmapped memory address), the latency involved in resolving the page fault varies according to whether the physical memory page is on the same node of the executing thread or on a node somewhere across the interconnect. The latency variance can be substantial. As the level of memory page sharing increases across threads executing on different nodes, a potentially higher volume of page faults needs to be resolved from a nonlocal memory segment. This problem adversely affects performance and scalability.

The three different parallel architectures can be summarized as follows:

- **SMP.** Symmetric multiprocessor with a shared memory model; single kernel image
- **MPP.** Message-based model; multiple kernel images
- **NUMA/ccNUMA.** Shared memory model; single kernel image

Figure 17.1 illustrates the different architectures.

The challenge in building an operating system that provides scalable performance when multiple processors are sharing a single image of the kernel and when every processor can run kernel code, handle interrupts, etc., is to synchronize access to critical data and state information. Scalable performance, or scalability, generally refers to accomplishment of an increasing amount of work as more hardware resources are added to the system. If more processors are added to a multiprocessor system, an incremental increase in work is expected, assuming sufficient resources in other areas of the system (memory, I/O, network).

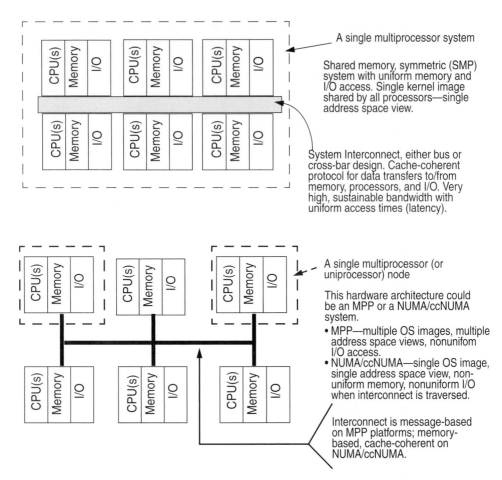

Figure 17.1 Parallel Systems Architectures

To achieve scalable performance, the system must be able to concurrently support multiple processors executing operating system code. Whether that execution is in device drivers, interrupt handlers, the threads dispatcher, file system code, virtual memory code, etc., is, to a degree, load dependent. Concurrency is key to scalability.

The preceding discussion on parallel architectures only scratched the surface of a very complex topic. Entire texts discuss parallel architectures exclusively; you should refer to them for additional information. See, for example, [13], [25], and [27].

The difficulty is maintaining data integrity of data structures, kernel variables, data links (pointers), and state information in the kernel. We cannot, for example, allow threads running on multiple processors to manipulate pointers to the same data structure on the same linked list all at the same time. We should prevent one processor from reading a bit of critical state information (for example, is a processor online?) while a thread executing on another processor is changing the same state data (for example, in the process of bringing online a processor that is still in a state transition).

To solve the problem of data integrity on such systems, the kernel implements locking mechanisms. It requires that all operating system code be aware of the number and type of locks that exist in the kernel and comply with the locking hierarchy and rules for acquiring locks before writing or reading kernel data. It is worth noting that the architectural issues of building a scalable kernel are not very different from those of developing a multithreaded application to run on a shared memory system. Multithreaded applications must also synchronize access to shared data, using the same basic locking primitives and techniques that are used in the kernel. Other synchronization problems, such as dealing with interrupts and trap events, exist in kernel code and make the problem significantly more complex for operating systems development, but the fundamental problems are the same.

17.3 Hardware Considerations for Locks and Synchronization

Hardware-specific considerations must enter into the implementation of lock primitives on a system. The first consideration has to do with the processor's instruction set and the availability of machine instructions suitable for locking code. The second deals with the visibility of a lock's state when it is examined by executing kernel threads.

To understand how these considerations apply to lock primitives, keep in mind that a lock is a piece of data at a specific location in the system's memory. In its simplest form, a lock is a single byte location in RAM. A lock that is *set*, or *held* (has been acquired), is represented by all the bits in the lock byte being 1's (lock value 0xFF). A lock that is available (not being held) is the same byte with all 0's (lock value 0x00). This explanation may seem quite rudimentary, but is crucial to understanding the text that follows.

Most modern processors shipping today provide some form of byte-level *test-and-set* instruction that is guaranteed to be *atomic* in nature. The instruction sequence is often described as read-modify-write; that is, the referenced memory location (the memory address of the lock) is read, modified, and written back in one atomic operation. In RISC processors (such as the UltraSPARC T1 processor), reads are *load* operations and writes are *store* operations. An atomic operation is required for consistency. An instruction that has atomic properties means that no other store operation is allowed between the load and store of the executing instruction. Mutex and RW lock operations must be atomic, such that when the instruction execution to get the lock is complete, we either have the lock or have the information we need to determine that the lock is already being held.

Consider what could happen without an instruction that has atomic properties. A thread executing on one processor could issue a load (read) of the lock and while it is doing a test operation to determine if the lock is held or not, another thread executing on another processor issues a lock call to get the same lock at the same time. If the lock is not held, both threads would assume the lock is available and would issue a store to hold the lock. Obviously, more than one thread cannot own the same lock at the same time, but that would be the result of such a sequence of events. Atomic instructions prevent such things from happening.

SPARC processors implement memory access instructions that provide atomic test-and-set semantics for mutual exclusion primitives, as well as instructions that can force a particular ordering of memory operations (more on the latter feature in a moment). UltraSPARC processors (the SPARC V9 instruction set) provide three memory access instructions that guarantee atomic behavior: ldstub (load and store unsigned byte), cas (compare and swap), and swap (swap byte locations). These instructions differ slightly in their behavior and the size of the datum they operate on.

Figure 17.2 illustrates the ldstub and cas instructions. The swap instruction (not shown) simply swaps a 32-bit value between a hardware register and a memory location, similar to what cas does if the compare phase of the instruction sequence is equal.

The implementation of locking code with the assembly language test-and-set style of instructions requires a subsequent test instruction on the lock value, which is retrieved with either a cas or ldstub instruction.

For example, the ldstub instruction retrieves the byte value (the lock) from memory and stores it in the specified hardware register. Locking code must test the value of the register to determine if the lock was held or available when the ldstub executed. If the register value is all 1's, the lock was held, so the code must branch off and deal with that condition. If the register value is all 0's, the lock was not held and the code can progress as being the current lock holder. Note that in both cases, the lock value in memory is set to all 1's, by virtue of the behavior of the ldstub instruction (store 0xFF at designated address). If the lock was already held, the value simply didn't change. If the lock was 0 (available), it will now reflect that the lock is held (all 1's). The code that releases a lock sets the lock value to all 0's, indicating the lock is no longer being held.

The Solaris lock code uses assembly language instructions when the lock code is entered. The basic design is such that the entry point to acquire a lock enters an assembly language routine, which uses either ldstub or cas to grab the lock. The assembly code is designed to deal with the simple case, meaning that the desired

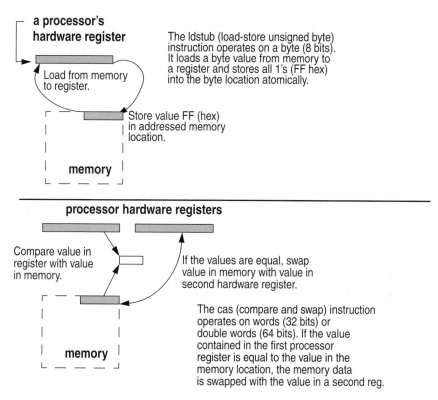

Figure 17.2 Atomic Instructions for Locks on SPARC Systems

lock is available. If the lock is being held, a C language code path is entered to deal with this situation. We describe what happens in detail in the next few sections that discuss specific lock types.

The second hardware consideration referred to earlier has to do with the visibility of the lock state to the running processors when the lock value is changed. It is critically important on multiprocessor systems that all processors have a consistent view of data in memory, especially in the implementation of synchronization primitives—mutex locks and reader/writer (RW) locks. In other words, if a thread acquires a lock, any processor that executes a load instruction (read) of that memory location must retrieve the data following the last store (write) that was issued. The most recent state of the lock must be globally visible to all processors on the system.

Modern processors implement hardware buffering to provide optimal performance. In addition to the hardware caches, processors also use load and store buffers to hold data being read from (load) or written to (store) memory in order to keep the instruction pipeline running and not have the processor stall waiting for data or a data write-to-memory cycle. The data hierarchy is illustrated in Figure 17.3.

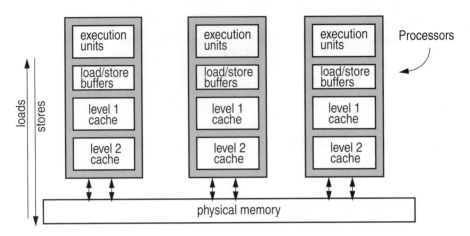

Figure 17.3 Hardware Data Hierarchy

The illustration in Figure 17.3 does not depict a specific processor; it is a generic representation of the various levels of data flow in a typical modern high-end microprocessor. It shows the flow of data to and from physical memory from a processor's main execution units (integer units, floating point units, etc.).

The sizes of the load/store buffers vary across processor implementations, but they are typically several words in size. The load and store buffers on each processor are visible only to the processor they reside on, so a load issued by a processor that issued the store fetches the data from the store buffer if it is still there. However, it is theoretically possible for other processors that issue a load for that data to read their hardware cache or main memory before the store buffer in the store-issuing processor was flushed. Note that the store buffer we are referring to here is *not* the same thing as a level 1 or level 2 hardware instruction and data cache. Caches are beyond the store buffer; the store buffer is closer to the execution units of the processor. Physical memory and hardware caches are kept consistent on SMP platforms by a hardware bus protocol. Also, many caches are implemented as *write-through* caches (as is the case with the level 1 cache in Sun UltraSPARC), so data written to cache causes memory to be updated.

The implementation of a store buffer is part of the *memory model* implemented by the hardware. The memory model defines the constraints that can be imposed on the order of memory operations (loads and stores) by the system. Many processors implement a *sequential consistency* model, where loads and stores to memory are executed in the same order in which they were issued by the processor. This model has advantages in terms of memory consistency, but there are performance trade-offs with such a model because the hardware cannot optimize cache and memory operations for speed. The SPARC architecture specification [47] provides for building SPARC-based processors that support multiple memory models, the choice being left up to the implementors as to which memory models they wish to support. All current SPARC processors implement a Total Store Ordering (TSO) model, which requires compliance with the following rules for loads and stores:

- Loads (reads from memory) are blocking and are ordered with respect to other loads.

- Stores (writes to memory) are ordered with respect to other stores. Stores cannot bypass earlier loads.

- Atomic load-stores (ldstub and cas instructions) are ordered with respect to loads.

The TSO model is not quite as strict as the sequential consistency model but not as relaxed as two additional memory models defined by the SPARC architecture. SPARC-based processors also support Relaxed Memory Order (RMO) and Partial Store Order (PSO), but these are not currently supported by the kernel and not implemented by any Sun systems shipping today.

A final consideration in data visibility applies also to the memory model and concerns instruction ordering. The execution unit in modern processors can reorder the incoming instruction stream for processing through the execution units. The goals again are performance and creation of a sequence of instructions that will keep the processor pipeline full.

The hardware considerations described in this section are summarized in Table 17.1, along with the solution or implementation detail that applies to the particular issue.

The issues of consistent memory views in the face of a processor's load and store buffers, relaxed memory models, and atomic test-and-set capability for locks are addressed at the processor instruction-set level. The mutex lock and RW lock primitives implemented in the Solaris kernel use the ldstub and cas instructions for

Table 17.1 Hardware Considerations and Solutions for Locks

Consideration	Solution
Need for an atomic test-and-set instruction for locking primitives.	Use of native machine instructions. ldstub and cas on SPARC, cmpxchgl (compare/exchange long) on x86.
Data global visibility issue because of the use of hardware load and store buffers and instruction reordering, as defined by the memory model.	Use of memory barrier instructions.

lock testing and acquisition on UltraSPARC-based systems and use the cmpxchgl
(compare/exchange long) instruction on x86. The lock primitive routines are part of
the architecture-dependent segment of the kernel code.

SPARC processors provide various forms of *memory barrier (membar)* instructions, which, depending on options that are set in the instruction, impose specific
constraints on the ordering of memory access operations (loads and stores) relative to the sequence with which they were issued. To ensure a consistent memory
view when a mutex or RW lock operation has been issued, the Solaris kernel issues
the appropriate membar instruction after the lock bits have changed.

As we move from the strongest consistency model (sequential consistency) to the
weakest model (RMO), we can build a system with potentially better performance.
We can optimize memory operations by playing with the ordering of memory
access instructions that enable designers to minimize access latency and to maximize interconnect bandwidth. The trade-off is consistency, since the more relaxed
models provide fewer and fewer constraints on the system to issue memory access
operations in the same order in which the instruction stream issued them. So, processor architectures provide memory barrier controls that kernel developers can
use to address the consistency issues as necessary, with some level of control on
which consistency level is required to meet the system requirements. The types of
membar instructions available, the options they support, and how they fit into the
different memory models described would make for a highly technical and lengthy
chapter on its own. Readers interested in this topic should read [4] and [27].

17.4 Introduction to Synchronization Objects

The Solaris kernel implements several types of synchronization objects. Locks provide mutual exclusion semantics for synchronized access to shared data. Locks
come in several forms and are the primary focus of this chapter. The most commonly used lock in the Solaris kernel is the mutual exclusion, or *mutex* lock, which
provides exclusive read and write access to data. Also implemented are *reader/
writer* (RW) locks, for situations in which multiple readers are allowable but only
one writer is allowed at a time. Kernel *semaphores* are also employed in some
areas of the kernel, where access to a finite number of resources must be managed. A special type of mutex lock, called a *dispatcher lock*, is used by the kernel
dispatcher when synchronization requires access protection through a locking
mechanism, as well as protection from interrupts.

Condition variables, which are not a type of lock, are used for thread synchronization and are an integral part of the kernel sleep/wakeup facility. Condition variables are introduced here and covered in detail in Chapter 3.

The actual number of locks that exist in a running system at any time is dynamic and scales with the size of the system. Several hundred locks are defined in the kernel source code, but a lock count based on static source code is not accurate because locks are created dynamically during normal system activity—when kernel threads and processes are created, file systems are mounted, files are created and opened, network connections are made, etc. Many of the locks are embedded in the kernel data structures that provide the abstractions (processes, files) provided by the kernel, and thus the number of kernel locks will scale up linearly as resources are created dynamically.

This design speaks to one of the core strengths of the Solaris kernel: scalability and scaling synchronization primitives dynamically with the size of the kernel. Dynamic lock creation has several advantages over static allocations. First, the kernel is not wasting time and space managing a large pool of unused locks when running on a smaller system, such as a desktop or workgroup server. On a large system, a sufficient number of locks is available to sustain concurrency for scalable performance. It is possible to have literally thousands of locks in existence on a large, busy system.

17.4.1 Synchronization Process

When an executing kernel thread attempts to acquire a lock, it will encounter one of two possible lock states: free (available) or not free (owned, held). A requesting thread gets ownership of an available lock when the lock-specific get lock function is invoked. If the lock is not available, the thread most likely needs to block and wait for it to come available, although, as we will see shortly, the code does not always block (sleep), waiting for a lock. For those situations in which a thread will sleep while waiting for a lock, the kernel implements a sleep queue facility, known as *turnstiles*, for managing threads blocking on locks.

When a kernel thread has completed the operation on the shared data protected by the lock, it must release the lock. When a thread releases a lock, the code must deal with one of two possible conditions: threads are waiting for the lock (such threads are termed *waiters*), or there are no waiters. With no waiters, the lock can simply be released. With waiters, the code has several options. It can release the lock and wake up the blocking threads. In that case, the first thread to execute acquires the lock. Alternatively, the code could select a thread from the turnstile (sleep queue), based on priority or sleep time, and wake up only that thread. Finally, the code could select which thread should get the lock next, and the lock owner could hand the lock off to the selected thread. As we will see in the following sections, no one solution is suitable for all situations, and the Solaris kernel uses all three methods, depending on the lock type. Figure 17.4 provides the big picture.

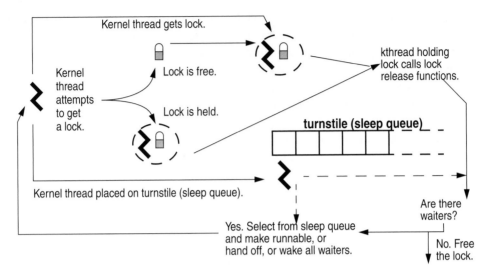

Figure 17.4 Solaris Locks—The Big Picture

Figure 17.4 provides a generic representation of the execution flow. Later we will see the results of a considerable amount of engineering effort that has gone into the lock code: improved efficiency and speed with short code paths, optimizations for the hot path (frequently hit code path) with well-tuned assembly code, and the best algorithms for lock release as determined by extensive analysis.

17.4.2 Synchronization Object Operations Vector

Each of the synchronization objects discussed in this section—mutex locks, reader/writer locks, and semaphores—defines an operations vector that is linked to kernel threads that are blocking on the object. Specifically, the object's operations vector is a data structure that exports a subset of object functions required for kthreads sleeping on the lock. The generic structure is defined as follows:

```
/*
 * The following data structure is used to map
 * synchronization object type numbers to the
 * synchronization object's sleep queue number
 * or the synch. object's owner function.
 */
typedef struct _sobj_ops {
        int             sobj_type;
        kthread_t       *(*sobj_owner)();
        void            (*sobj_unsleep)(kthread_t *);
        void            (*sobj_change_pri)(kthread_t *, pri_t, pri_t *);
} sobj_ops_t;
```

See sys/sobject.h

The structure shown above provides for the object type declaration. For each synchronization object type, a type-specific structure is defined: `mutex_sobj_ops` for mutex locks, `rw_sobj_ops` for reader/writer locks, and `sema_sobj_ops` for semaphores.

The structure also provides three functions that may be called on behalf of a kthread sleeping on a synchronization object:

- An *owner* function, which returns the ID of the kernel thread that owns the object.
- An *unsleep* function, which transitions a kernel thread from a sleep state.
- A *change_pri* function, which changes the priority of a kernel thread, used for priority inheritance. (See Section 17.7.)

We will see how references to the lock's operations structure are implemented as we move through specifics on lock implementations in the following sections.

It is useful to note at this point that our examination of Solaris kernel locks offers a good example of some of the design trade-offs involved in kernel software engineering. Building the various software components that make up the Solaris kernel is a series of design decisions, when performance needs are measured against complexity. In areas of the kernel where optimal performance is a top priority, simplicity might be sacrificed in favor of performance. The locking facilities in the Solaris kernel are an area where such trade-offs are made—much of the lock code is written in assembly language, for speed, rather than in the C language; the latter is easier to code with and maintain but is potentially slower. In some cases, when the code path is not performance critical, a simpler design will be favored over cryptic assembly code or complexity in the algorithms. The behavior of a particular design is examined through exhaustive testing, to ensure that the best possible design decisions were made.

17.5 Mutex Locks

Mutual exclusion, or *mutex* locks, are the most common type of synchronization primitive used in the kernel. Mutex locks serialize access to critical data, when a kernel thread must acquire the mutex specific to the data region being protected before it can read or write the data. The thread is the lock *owner* while it is holding the lock, and the thread must release the lock when it has finished working in the protected region so other threads can acquire the lock for access to the protected data.

17.5.1 Overview

If a thread attempts to acquire a mutex lock that is being held, it can basically do one of two things: it can *spin* or it can *block*. Spinning means the thread enters a tight loop, attempting to acquire the lock in each pass through the loop. The term *spin lock* is often used to describe this type of mutex. Blocking means the thread is placed on a sleep queue while the lock is being held and the kernel sends a wakeup to the thread when the lock is released. There are pros and cons to both approaches.

The spin approach has the benefit of not incurring the overhead of context switching, required when a thread is put to sleep and also has the advantage of a relatively fast acquisition when the lock is released, since there is no context-switch operation. It has the downside of consuming CPU cycles while the thread is in the spin loop—the CPU is executing a kernel thread (the thread in the spin loop) but not really doing any useful work.

The blocking approach has the advantage of freeing the processor to execute other threads while the lock is being held; it has the disadvantage of requiring context switching to get the waiting thread off the processor and a new runnable thread onto the processor. There's also a little more lock acquisition latency, since a wakeup and context switch are required before the blocking thread can become the owner of the lock it was waiting for.

In addition to the issue of what to do if a requested lock is being held, the question of lock granularity needs to be resolved. Let's take a simple example. The kernel maintains a process table, which is a linked list of process structures, one for each of the processes running on the system. A simple table-level mutex could be implemented, such that if a thread needs to manipulate a process structure, it must first acquire the process table mutex. This level of locking is very coarse. It has the advantages of simplicity and minimal lock overhead. It has the obvious disadvantage of potentially poor scalability, since only one thread at a time can manipulate objects on the process table. Such a lock is likely to have a great deal of contention (become a *hot* lock).

The alternative is to implement a finer level of granularity: a lock-per-process table entry versus one table-level lock. With a lock on each process table entry, multiple threads can be manipulating different process structures at the same time, providing concurrency. The disadvantages are that such an implementation is more complex, increases the chances of deadlock situations, and necessitates more overhead because there are more locks to manage.

In general, the Solaris kernel implements relatively fine-grained locking whenever possible, largely due to the dynamic nature of scaling locks with kernel structures as needed.

The kernel implements two types of mutex locks: *spin locks* and *adaptive locks*. Spin locks, as we discussed, spin in a tight loop if a desired lock is being held when a thread attempts to acquire the lock. Adaptive locks are the most common type of lock used and are designed to dynamically either spin or block when a lock is being held, depending on the state of the holder. We already discussed the trade-offs of spinning versus blocking. Implementing a locking scheme that only does one or the other can severely impact scalability and performance. It is much better to use an adaptive locking scheme, which is precisely what we do.

The mechanics of adaptive locks are straightforward. When a thread attempts to acquire a lock and the lock is being held, the kernel examines the state of the thread that is holding the lock. If the lock holder (owner) is running on a processor, the thread attempting to get the lock will spin. If the thread holding the lock is not running, the thread attempting to get the lock will block. This policy works quite well because the code is such that mutex hold times are very short (by design, the goal is to minimize the amount of code to be executed while a lock is held). So, if a thread is holding a lock and running, the lock will likely be released very soon, probably in less time than it takes to context-switch off and on again, so it's worth spinning.

On the other hand, if a lock holder is not running, then we know that minimally one context switch is involved before the holder will release the lock (getting the holder back on a processor to run), and it makes sense to simply block and free up the processor to do something else. The kernel will place the blocking thread on a turnstile (sleep queue) designed specifically for synchronization primitives and will wake the thread when the lock is released by the holder. (See Section 17.7.)

The other distinction between adaptive locks and spin locks has to do with interrupts, the dispatcher, and context switching. The kernel dispatcher is the code that selects threads for scheduling and does context switches. It runs at an elevated Priority Interrupt Level (PIL) to block interrupts (the dispatcher runs at priority level 11 on SPARC systems). High-level interrupts (interrupt levels 11–15 on SPARC systems) can interrupt the dispatcher. High-level interrupt handlers are not allowed to do anything that could require a context switch or to enter the dispatcher (we discuss this further in Section 3.4). Adaptive locks can block, and blocking means context switching, so only spin locks can be used in high-level interrupt handlers. Also, spin locks can raise the interrupt level of the processor when the lock is acquired.

```
struct kernel_data {
        kmutex_t klock;
        char *forw_ptr;
        char *back_ptr;
        uint64_t data1;
        uint64_t data2;
} kdata;
```

continues

```
void function()
        .
        mutex_init(&kdata.klock);
        .
        mutex_enter(&kdata.klock);
        klock.data1 = 1;
        mutex_exit(&kdata.klock);
```

The preceding block of pseudocode illustrates the general mechanics of mutex locks. A lock is declared in the code; in this case, it is embedded in the data structure that it is designed to protect. Once declared, the lock is initialized with the kernel `mutex_init()` function. Any subsequent reference to the `kdata` structure requires that the `klock` mutex be acquired with `mutex_enter()`. Once the work is done, the lock is released with `mutex_exit()`. The lock type, spin or adaptive, is determined in the `mutex_init()` code by the kernel. Assuming an adaptive mutex in this example, any kernel threads that make a `mutex_enter()` call on `klock` will either block or spin, depending on the state of the kernel thread that owns `klock` when the `mutex_enter()` is called.

17.5.2 Solaris Mutex Lock Implementation

The kernel defines different data structures for the two types of mutex locks, adaptive and spin, as shown below.

```
/*
 * Public interface to mutual exclusion locks.  See mutex(9F) for details.
 *
 * The basic mutex type is MUTEX_ADAPTIVE, which is expected to be used
 * in almost all of the kernel.  MUTEX_SPIN provides interrupt blocking
 * and must be used in interrupt handlers above LOCK_LEVEL.  The iblock
 * cookie argument to mutex_init() encodes the interrupt level to block.
 * The iblock cookie must be NULL for adaptive locks.
 *
 * MUTEX_DEFAULT is the type usually specified (except in drivers) to
 * mutex_init().  It is identical to MUTEX_ADAPTIVE.
 *
 * MUTEX_DRIVER is always used by drivers.  mutex_init() converts this to
 * either MUTEX_ADAPTIVE or MUTEX_SPIN depending on the iblock cookie.
 *
 * Mutex statistics can be gathered on the fly, without rebooting or
 * recompiling the kernel, via the lockstat driver (lockstat(7D)).
 */
typedef enum {
        MUTEX_ADAPTIVE = 0,     /* spin if owner is running, otherwise block */
        MUTEX_SPIN = 1,         /* block interrupts and spin */
        MUTEX_DRIVER = 4,       /* driver (DDI) mutex */
        MUTEX_DEFAULT = 6       /* kernel default mutex */
} kmutex_type_t;
```

continues

```
typedef struct mutex {
#ifdef _LP64
        void    *_opaque[1];
#else
        void    *_opaque[2];
#endif
} kmutex_t;
```
See sys/mutex.h

The 128-bit mutex object is used for each type of lock, as shown in Figure 17.5.

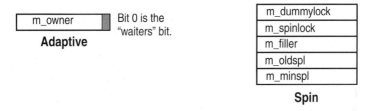

Figure 17.5 Solaris 10 Adaptive and Spin Mutex

In Figure 17.5, the m_owner field in the adaptive lock, which holds the address of the kernel thread that owns the lock (the kthread pointer), plays a double role, in that it also serves as the actual lock; successful lock acquisition for a thread means it has its kthread pointer set in the m_owner field of the target lock. If threads attempt to get the lock while it is held (waiters), the low-order bit (bit 0) of m_owner is set to reflect that case. Because kthread pointers values are always word aligned, they do not require bit 0, allowing this work.

```
/*
 * mutex_enter() assumes that the mutex is adaptive and tries to grab the
 * lock by doing a atomic compare and exchange on the first word of the mutex.
 * If the compare and exchange fails, it means that either (1) the lock is a
 * spin lock, or (2) the lock is adaptive but already held.
 * mutex_vector_enter() distinguishes these cases by looking at the mutex
 * type, which is encoded in the low-order bits of the owner field.
 */
typedef union mutex_impl {
        /*
         * Adaptive mutex.
         */
        struct adaptive_mutex {
                uintptr_t _m_owner;     /* 0-3/0-7 owner and waiters bit */
#ifndef _LP64
                uintptr_t _m_filler;    /* 4-7 unused */
#endif
        } m_adaptive;
```

continues

```
    /*
     * Spin Mutex.
     */
    struct spin_mutex {
            lock_t  m_dummylock;    /* 0    dummy lock (always set) */
            lock_t  m_spinlock;     /* 1    real lock */
            ushort_t m_filler;      /* 2-3  unused */
            ushort_t m_oldspl;      /* 4-5  old pil value */
            ushort_t m_minspl;      /* 6-7  min pil val if lock held */
    } m_spin;

} mutex_impl_t;
```
See sys/mutex_impl.h

The spin mutex, as we pointed out earlier, is used at high interrupt levels, where context switching is not allowed. Spin locks block interrupts while in the spin loop, so the kernel needs to maintain the priority level the processor was running at before entering the spin loop, which raises the processor's priority level. (Elevating the priority level is how interrupts are blocked.) The m_minspl field stores the priority level of the interrupt handler when the lock is initialized, and m_oldspl is set to the priority level the processor was running at when the lock code is called. The m_spinlock fields are the actual mutex lock bits.

Each kernel module and subsystem implementing one or more mutex locks calls into a common set of mutex functions. All locks must first be initialized by the mutex_init() function, whereby the lock type is determined on the basis of an argument passed in the mutex_init() call. The most common type passed into mutex_init() is MUTEX_DEFAULT, which results in the init code determining what type of lock, adaptive or spin, should be used. It is possible for a caller of mutex_init() to be specific about a lock type (for example, MUTEX_SPIN).

If the init code is called from a device driver or any kernel module that registers and generates interrupts, then an *interrupt block cookie* is added to the argument list. An interrupt block cookie is an abstraction used by device drivers when they set their interrupt vector and parameters. The mutex_init() code checks the argument list for an interrupt block cookie. If mutex_init() is being called from a device driver to initialize a mutex to be used in a high-level interrupt handler, the lock type is set to spin. Otherwise, an adaptive lock is initialized. The test is the interrupt level in the passed interrupt block; levels above LOCK_LEVEL (10 on SPARC systems) are considered high-level interrupts and thus require spin locks. The init code clears most of the fields in the mutex lock structure as appropriate for the lock type. The m_dummylock field in spin locks is set to all 1's (0xFF). We'll see why in a minute.

The primary mutex functions called, aside from mutex_init() (which is only called once for each lock at initialization time), are mutex_enter() to get a lock and mutex_exit() to release it. mutex_enter() assumes an available, adaptive lock. If the lock is held or is a spin lock, mutex_vector_enter() is entered to reconcile what should happen. This is a performance optimization. `mutex_enter()` is implemented in assembly code, and because the entry point is designed for the simple case (adaptive lock, not held), the amount of code that gets executed to acquire a lock when those conditions are true is minimal. Also, there are significantly more adaptive mutex locks than spin locks in the kernel, making the quick test case effective most of the time. The test for a lock held or spin lock is very fast. Here is where the `m_dummylock` field comes into play: `mutex_enter()` executes a compare-and-swap instruction on the first byte of the mutex, testing for a zero value. On a spin lock, the `m_dummylock` field is tested because of its positioning in the data structure and the endianness of SPARC processors. Since `m_dummylock` is always set (it is set to all 1's in `mutex_init()`), the test will fail for spin locks. The test will also fail for a held adaptive lock since such a lock will have a nonzero value in the byte field being tested. That is, the `m_owner` field will have a kthread pointer value for a held, adaptive lock.

If the lock is an adaptive mutex and is not being held, the caller of `mutex_enter()` gets ownership of the lock. If the two conditions are not true, that is, either the lock is held or the lock is a spin lock, the code enters the `mutex_vector_enter()` function to sort things out. The `mutex_vector_enter()` code first tests the lock type. For spin locks, the `m_oldspl` field is set, based on the current Priority Interrupt Level (PIL) of the processor, and the lock is tested. If it's not being held, the lock is set (`m_spinlock`) and the code returns to the caller. A held lock forces the caller into a spin loop, where a loop counter is incremented (for statistical purposes; the `lockstat(1M)` data), and the code checks whether the lock is still held in each pass through the loop. Once the lock is released, the code breaks out of the loop, grabs the lock, and returns to the caller.

Adaptive locks require a little more work. When the code enters the adaptive code path (in `mutex_vector_enter()`), it increments the `cpu_sysinfo.mutex_adenters` (adaptive lock enters) field, as is reflected in the `smtx` column in `mpstat(1M)`. `mutex_vector_enter()` then tests again to determine if the lock is owned (held), since the lock may have been released in the time interval between the call to `mutex_enter()` and the current point in the `mutex_vector_enter()` code. If the adaptive lock is not being held, `mutex_vector_enter()` attempts to acquire the lock. If successful, the code returns.

If the lock is held, `mutex_vector_enter()` determines whether or not the lock owner is running by looping through the CPU structures and testing the lock `m_owner` against the `cpu_thread` field of the CPU structure. (`cpu_thread` contains the kernel thread address of the thread currently executing on the CPU.) A match indicates the holder is running, which means the adaptive lock will spin. No match means the owner is not running, in which case the caller must block. In the blocking case, the kernel turnstile code is entered to locate or acquire a turnstile, in preparation for placement of the kernel thread on a sleep queue associated with the turnstile.

The turnstile placement happens in two phases. After `mutex_vector_enter()` determines that the lock holder is not running, it makes a turnstile call to look up the turnstile, sets the `waiters` bit in the lock, and retests to see if the owner is running. If yes, the code releases the turnstile and enters the adaptive lock spin loop, which attempts to acquire the lock. Otherwise, the code places the kernel thread on a turnstile (sleep queue) and changes the thread's state to sleep. That effectively concludes the sequence of events in `mutex_vector_enter()`.

Dropping out of `mutex_vector_enter()`, either the caller ended up with the lock it was attempting to acquire or the calling thread is on a turnstile sleep queue associated with the lock. In either case, the `lockstat(1M)` data is updated, reflecting the lock type, spin time, or sleep time as the last bit of work done in `mutex_vector_enter()`.

`lockstat(1M)` is a kernel lock statistics command that was introduced in Solaris 2.6. It provides detailed information on kernel mutex and reader/writer locks.

The algorithm described in the previous paragraphs is summarized in pseudocode below.

```
mutex_vector_enter()
        if (lock is a spin lock)
                lock_set_spl() /* enter spin-lock specific code path */
        increment cpu_sysinfo.ademters.
spin_loop:
        if (lock is not owned)
                mutex_trylock() /* try to acquire the lock */
                if (lock acquired)
                        goto bottom
                else
                        continue /* lock being held */
        if (lock owner is running on a processor)
                goto spin_loop
        else
                lookup turnstile for the lock
                set waiters bit
                if (lock owner is running on a processor)
                        drop turnstile
                        goto spin_loop
                else
                        block /* the sleep queue associated with the turnstile */

bottom:
        update lockstat statistics
```

When a thread has finished working in a lock-protected data area, it calls the `mutex_exit()` code to release the lock. The entry point is implemented in assembly language and handles the simple case of freeing an adaptive lock with no waiters. With no threads waiting for the lock, it's a simple matter of clearing the lock fields (m_owner) and returning. The C language function `mutex_vector_exit()` is entered from `mutex_exit()` for anything but the simple case.

In the case of a spin lock, the lock field is cleared and the processor is returned to the PIL level it was running at before entering the lock code. For adaptive locks, a waiter must be selected from the turnstile (if there is more than one waiter), have its state changed from sleeping to runnable, and be placed on a dispatch queue so it can execute and get the lock. If the thread releasing the lock was the beneficiary of priority inheritance, meaning that it had its priority improved when a calling thread with a better priority was not able to get the lock, then the thread releasing the lock will have its priority reset to what it was before the inheritance. Priority inheritance is discussed in Section 17.7.

When an adaptive lock is released, the code clears the `waiters` bit in `m_owner` and calls the turnstile function to wake up *all* the waiters. Readers familiar with sleep/wakeup mechanisms of operating systems have likely heard of a particular behavior known as the *"thundering herd problem,"* a situation in which many threads that have been blocking for the same resource are all woken up at the same time and make a mad dash for the resource (a mutex in this case)—like a herd of large, four-legged beasts running toward the same object. System behavior tends to go from a relatively small run queue to a large run queue (all the threads have been woken up and made runnable) and high CPU utilization until a thread gets the resource, at which point a bunch of threads are sleeping again, the run queue normalizes, and CPU utilization flattens out. This is a generic behavior that can occur on any operating system.

The wakeup mechanism used when `mutex_vector_exit()` is called may seem like an open invitation to thundering herds, but in practice it turns out not to be a problem. The main reason is that the blocking case for threads waiting for a mutex is rare; most of the time the threads will spin. If a blocking situation does arise, it typically does not reach a point where very many threads are blocked on the mutex—one of the characteristics of the thundering herd problem is resource contention resulting in a lot of sleeping threads. The kernel code segments that implement mutex locks are, by design, short and fast, so locks are not held for long. Code that requires longer lock-hold times uses a reader/writer write lock, which provides mutual exclusion semantics with a selective wakeup algorithm. There are, of course, other reasons for choosing reader/writer locks over mutex locks, the most obvious being to allow multiple readers to see the protected data.

17.6 Reader/Writer Locks

Reader/writer (RW) locks provide mutual exclusion semantics on write locks. Only one thread at a time is allowed to own the write lock, but there is concurrent access for readers. These locks are designed for scenarios in which it is acceptable to have multiple threads reading the data at the same time, but only one writer.

While a writer is holding the lock, no readers are allowed. Also, because of the wakeup mechanism, a writer lock is a better solution for kernel code segments that require relatively long hold times, as we will see shortly.

The basic mechanics of RW locks are similar to mutexes, in that RW locks have an initialization function (rw_init()), an entry function to acquire the lock (rw_enter()), and an exit function to release the lock (rw_exit()). The entry and exit points are optimized in assembly code to deal with the simple cases, and they call into C language functions if anything beyond the simplest case must be dealt with. As with mutex locks, the simple case is that the requested lock is available on an entry (acquire) call and no threads are waiting for the lock on the exit (release) call.

17.6.1 Solaris Reader/Writer Locks

Reader/writer locks are implemented as a single-word data structure in the kernel, either 32 bits or 64 bits wide, depending on the data model of the running kernel, as depicted in Figure 17.6.

```
typedef struct rwlock_impl {
        uintptr_t        rw_wwwh;        /* waiters, write wanted, hold count */
} rwlock_impl_t;

#endif  /* _ASM */

#define RW_HAS_WAITERS         1
#define RW_WRITE_WANTED        2
#define RW_WRITE_LOCKED        4
#define RW_READ_LOCK           8
#define RW_WRITE_LOCK(thread)  ((uintptr_t)(thread) | RW_WRITE_LOCKED)
#define RW_HOLD_COUNT          (-RW_READ_LOCK)
#define RW_HOLD_COUNT_SHIFT    3               /* log2(RW_READ_LOCK) */
#define RW_READ_COUNT          RW_HOLD_COUNT
#define RW_OWNER               RW_HOLD_COUNT
#define RW_LOCKED              RW_HOLD_COUNT
#define RW_WRITE_CLAIMED       (RW_WRITE_LOCKED | RW_WRITE_WANTED)
#define RW_DOUBLE_LOCK         (RW_WRITE_LOCK(0) | RW_READ_LOCK)

                                                    See sys/rwlock.h
```

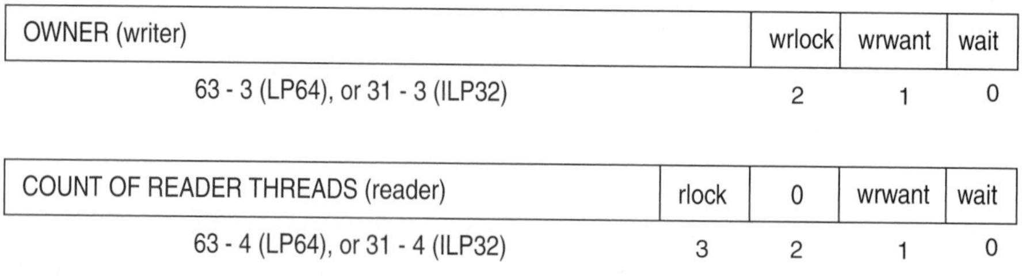

OWNER (writer)		wrlock	wrwant	wait
63 - 3 (LP64), or 31 - 3 (ILP32)		2	1	0

COUNT OF READER THREADS (reader)	rlock	0	wrwant	wait
63 - 4 (LP64), or 31 - 4 (ILP32)	3	2	1	0

Figure 17.6 Reader/Writer Lock

There are two states for the reader writer lock, depending on whether the lock is held by a writer, as indicated by bit 2, `wrlock`. Bit 2, `wrlock`, is the actual write lock, and it determines the meaning of the high-order bits. If the write lock is held (bit 2 set), then the upper bits contain a pointer to the kernel thread holding the write lock. If bit 2 is clear, then the upper bits contain a count of the number of threads holding the lock as a read lock.

The Solaris 10 RW lock defines bit 0, the `wait` bit, set to signify that threads are waiting for the lock. The `wrwant` bit (write wanted, bit 1) indicates that at least one thread is waiting for a write lock. The simple cases for lock acquisition through `rw_enter()` are the circumstances listed below:

- The write lock is wanted and is available.

- The read lock is wanted, the write lock is not held, and no threads are waiting for the write lock (`wrwant` is clear).

The acquisition of the write lock results in bit 2 getting set and the kernel thread pointer getting loaded in the upper bits. For a reader, the hold count (upper bits) is incremented. Conditions where the write lock is being held, causing a lock request to fail, or where a thread is waiting for a write lock, causing a read lock request to fail, result in a call to the `rw_enter_sleep()` function.

Important to note is that the `rw_enter()` code sets a flag in the kernel thread used by the dispatcher code when establishing a kernel thread's priority before preemption or changing state to sleep. We cover this in more detail in the paragraph beginning "It is in the dispatcher queue insertion code" on page 262. Briefly, the kernel thread structure contains a t_kpri_req (kernel priority request) field that is checked in the dispatcher code when a thread is about to be preempted (forced off the processor on which it is executing because a higher-priority thread becomes runnable) or when the thread is about to have its state changed to sleep. If the t_kpri_req flag is set, the dispatcher assigns a kernel priority to the thread, such that when the thread resumes execution, it will run before threads in scheduling classes of lower priority (timeshare and interactive class threads). More succinctly, the priority of a thread holding a write lock is set to a better priority to minimize the hold time of the lock.

Getting back to the `rw_enter()` flow: If the code falls through the simple case, we need to set up the kernel thread requesting the RW lock to block.

1. `rw_enter_sleep()` establishes whether the calling thread is requesting a read or write lock and does another test to see if the lock is available. If it is, the caller gets the lock, the `lockstat(1M)` statistics are updated, and the code returns. If the lock is not available, then the turnstile code is called to look up a turnstile in preparation for putting the calling thread to sleep.

2. With a turnstile now available, another test is made on the lock availability. (On today's fast processors, and especially multiprocessor systems, it's quite possible that the thread holding the lock finished what it was doing and the lock became available.) Assuming the lock is still held, the thread is set to a sleep state and placed on a turnstile.

3. The RW lock structure will have the `wait` bit set for a reader waiting (forced to block because a writer has the lock) or the `wrwant` bit set to signify that a thread wanting the write lock is blocking.

4. The `cpu_sysinfo` structure for the processor maintains two counters for failures to get a read lock or write lock on the first pass: `rw_rdfails` and `rw_wrfails`. The appropriate counter is incremented just prior to the turnstile call; this action places the thread on a turnstile sleep queue. The `mpstat(1M)` command sums the counters and displays the fails-per-second in the *srw* column of its output.

The acquisition of a RW lock and subsequent behavior if the lock is held are straightforward and similar in many ways to what happens in the mutex case. Things get interesting when a thread calls `rw_exit()` to release a lock it is holding—there are several potential solutions to the problem of determining which thread gets the lock next. A wakeup is issued on all threads that are sleeping, waiting for the mutex, and we know from empirical data that this solution works well for reasons previously discussed. With RW locks, we're dealing with potentially longer hold times, which could result in more sleepers, a desire to give writers priority over readers (it's typically best to not have a reader read data that's about to be changed by a pending writer), and the potential for the priority inversion problem described in Section 17.7.

For `rw_exit()`, which is called by the lock holder when it is ready to release the lock, the simple case is that there are no waiters. In this case, the `wrlock` bit is cleared if the holder was a writer, or the hold count field is decremented to reflect one less reader. The more complex case of the system having waiters when the lock is released is dealt with in the following manner:

1. The kernel does a direct transfer of ownership of the lock to one or more of the threads waiting for the lock when the lock is released, either to the next writer or to a group of readers if more than one reader is blocking and no writers are blocking.

   This situation is very different from the case of the mutex implementation, for which the wakeup is issued and a thread must obtain lock ownership in the usual fashion. Here, a thread or threads wake up owning the lock they were blocking on.

The algorithm used to figure out who gets the lock next addresses several requirements that provide for generally balanced system performance. The kernel needs to minimize the possibility of starvation (a thread never getting the resource it needs to continue executing) while allowing writers to take precedence whenever possible.

2. `rw_exit_wakeup()` retests for the simple case and drops the lock if there are no waiters (clear `wrlock` or decrement the hold count).

3. When waiters are present, the code grabs the turnstile (sleep queue) associated with the lock and saves the pointer to the kernel thread of the next write waiter that was on the turnstile's sleep queue (if one exists).

    The turnstile sleep queues are organized as a FIFO (first in, first out) queue, so the queue management (turnstile code) makes sure that the thread that was waiting the longest (the first in) is the thread that is selected as the next writer (first out). Thus, part of the fairness policy we want to enforce is covered.

The remaining bits of the algorithm go as follows:

4. If a writer is releasing the write lock and there are waiting readers and writers, readers of the same or higher priority than the highest-priority blocked writer are granted the read lock.

5. The readers are handed ownership, and then woken up by the `turnstile_wakeup()` kernel function,

    These readers also inherit the priority of the writer that released the lock if the reader thread is of a lower priority (inheritance is done on a per-reader thread basis when more than one thread is being woken up). Lock ownership handoff is a relatively simple operation. For read locks, there is no notion of a lock owner, so it's a matter of setting the hold count in the lock to reflect the number of readers coming off the turnstile, then issuing the wakeup of each reader.

6. An exiting reader always grants the lock to a waiting writer, even if there are higher-priority readers blocked.

7. It is possible for a reader freeing the lock to have waiting readers, although it may not be intuitive, given the multiple reader design of the lock. If a reader is holding the lock and a writer comes along, the `wrwant` bit is set to signify that a writer is waiting for the lock. With `wrwant` set, subsequent readers cannot get the lock—we want the holding readers to finish so the writer can get the lock. Therefore, it is possible for a reader to execute `rw_exit_wakeup()` with waiting writers and readers.

The "let's favor writers but be fair to readers" policy described above was first implemented in Solaris 2.6.

17.7 Turnstiles and Priority Inheritance

A turnstile is a data abstraction that encapsulates sleep queues and priority inheritance information associated with mutex locks and reader/writer locks. The mutex and RW lock code use a turnstile when a kernel thread needs to block on a requested lock. The sleep queues implemented for other resource waits do not provide an elegant method of dealing with the priority inversion problem through priority inheritance. Turnstiles were created to address that problem.

Priority inversion describes a scenario in which a higher-priority thread is unable to run because a lower-priority thread is holding a resource it needs, such as a lock. The Solaris kernel addresses the priority inversion problem in its turnstile implementation, providing a *priority inheritance* mechanism, where the higher-priority thread can *will* its priority to the lower-priority thread holding the resource it requires. The beneficiary of the inheritance, the thread holding the resource, will now have a higher scheduling priority and thus get scheduled to run sooner so it can finish its work and release the resource, at which point the original priority is returned to the thread.

In this section, we assume you have some level of knowledge of kernel thread priorities, which are covered in Section 3.7. Because turnstiles and priority inheritance are an integral part of the implementation of mutex and RW locks, we thought it best to discuss them here rather than later. For this discussion, it is important to be aware of these points:

- The Solaris kernel assigns a global priority to kernel threads, based on the scheduling class they belong to.
- Kernel threads in the timeshare and interactive scheduling classes will have their priorities adjusted over time, based on three things: the amount of time the threads spend running on a processor, sleep time (blocking), and the case when they are preempted. Threads in the real-time class are fixed priority; the priorities are never changed regardless of runtime or sleep time unless explicitly changed through programming interfaces or commands.

The Solaris kernel implements sleep queues for the placement of kernel threads blocking on (waiting for) a resource or event. For most resource waits, such as those for a disk or network I/O, sleep queues, in conjunction with condition variables, manage the systemwide queue of sleeping threads. These sleep queues are covered in Section 3.10. This set of sleep queues is separate and distinct from turnstile sleep queues.

17.7.1 Turnstiles Implementation

Figure 17.7 illustrates the Solaris 10 turnstiles. Turnstiles are maintained in a systemwide hash table, `turnstile_table[]`, which is an array of `turnstile_chain` structures; each entry in the array (each `turnstile_chain` structure) is the beginning of a linked list of turnstiles. The array is indexed via a hash function on the address of the synchronization object (the mutex or reader/writer lock), so locks that hash to the same array location will have a turnstile on the same linked list. The `turnstile_table[]` array is statically initialized at boot time.

```
typedef struct turnstile_chain {
        turnstile_t    *tc_first;     /* first turnstile on hash chain */
        disp_lock_t    tc_lock;       /* lock for this hash chain */
} turnstile_chain_t;

turnstile_chain_t       turnstile_table[2 * TURNSTILE_HASH_SIZE];
                                                  See common/os/turnstile.c
```

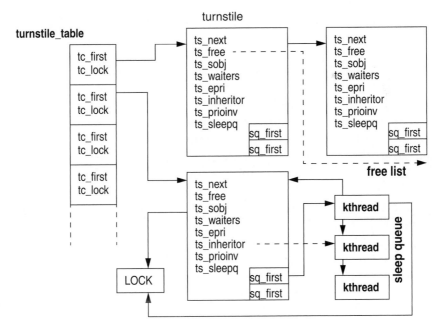

Figure 17.7 Turnstiles

Each entry in the chain has its own lock, `tc_lock`, so chains can be traversed concurrently. The turnstile itself has a different lock; each chain has an active list (`ts_next`) and a free list (`ts_free`). There are also a count of threads waiting on the sync object (`waiters`), a pointer to the synchronization object (`ts_sobj`), a thread pointer linking to a kernel thread that had a priority boost through priority inheritance, and the sleep queues. Each turnstile has two sleep queues, one for readers and one for writers (threads blocking on a read/write lock are maintained on separate sleep queues). The priority inheritance data is integrated into the turnstile.

```
#define TS_WRITER_Q     0       /* writer sleepq (exclusive access to sobj) */
#define TS_READER_Q     1       /* reader sleepq (shared access to sobj) */
#define TS_NUM_Q        2       /* number of sleep queues per turnstile */

typedef struct turnstile turnstile_t;
struct _sobj_ops;

struct turnstile {
        turnstile_t     *ts_next;       /* next on hash chain */
        turnstile_t     *ts_free;       /* next on freelist */
        void            *ts_sobj;       /* s-object threads are blocking on */
        int             ts_waiters;     /* number of blocked threads */
        pri_t           ts_epri;        /* max priority of blocked threads */
        struct _kthread *ts_inheritor;  /* thread inheriting priority */
        turnstile_t     *ts_prioinv;    /* next in inheritor's t_prioinv list */
        sleepq_t        ts_sleepq[TS_NUM_Q]; /* read/write sleep queues */
};
```

See sys/turnstile.h

Every kernel thread is *born* with an attached turnstile. That is, when a kernel thread is created (by the kernel `thread_create()` routine), a turnstile is allocated for the kthread and linked to kthread's `t_ts` pointer. A kthread can block on only one lock at a time, so one turnstile is sufficient.

We know from the previous sections on mutex and RW locks that a turnstile is required if a thread needs to block on a synchronization object. It calls `turnstile_lookup()` to look up the turnstile for the synchronization object in the `turnstile_table[]`. Since we index the array by hashing on the address of the lock, if a turnstile already exists (there are already waiters), then we get the correct turnstile. If no kthreads are currently waiting for the lock, `turnstile_lookup()` simply returns a null value. If the blocking code must be called (recall from the previous sections that subsequent tests are made on lock availability before it is determined that the kthread must block), then `turnstile_block()` is entered to place the kernel thread on a sleep queue associated with the turnstile for the lock.

Kernel threads *lend* their attached turnstile to the lock when a kthread becomes the first to block (the lock acquisition attempt fails, and there are no waiters). The thread's turnstile is added to the appropriate turnstile chain, based on the result of a hashing function on the address of the lock. The lock now has a turnstile, so subsequent threads that block on the same lock will donate their turnstiles to the free list on the chain (the `ts_free` link off the active turnstile).

In `turnstile_block()`, the pointers are set up as determined by the return from `turnstile_lookup()`. If the turnstile pointer is null, we link up to the turnstile pointed to by the kernel thread's `t_ts` pointer. If the pointer returned from the lookup is not null, there's already at least one kthread waiting on the lock, so the code sets up the pointer links appropriately and places the kthread's turnstile on the free list.

The thread is then put into a sleep state through the scheduling-class-specific sleep routine (for example, `ts_sleep()`). The `ts_waiters` field in the turnstile is incremented, the threads `t_wchan` is set to the address of the lock, and `t_sobj_ops` in the thread is set to the address of the lock's operations vectors: the `owner`, `unsleep`, and `change_priority` functions. The kernel `sleepq_insert()` function actually places the thread on the sleep queue associated with the turnstile.

The code does the priority inversion check (now called out of the `turnstile_block()` code), builds the priority inversion links and applies the necessary priority changes. The priority inheritance rules apply; that is, if the priority of the lock holder is less (worse) than the priority of the requesting thread, the requesting thread's priority is "willed" to the holder. The holder's `t_epri` field is set to the new priority, and the inheritor pointer in the turnstile is linked to the kernel thread. All the threads on the blocking chain are potential inheritors, based on their priority relative to the calling thread.

At this point, the dispatcher is entered through a call to `swtch()`, and another kernel thread is removed from a dispatch queue and context-switched onto a processor.

The wakeup mechanics are initiated as previously described, where a call to the lock exit routine results in a `turnstile_wakeup()` call if threads are blocking on the lock. `turnstile_wakeup()` does essentially the reverse of `turnstile_block()`; threads that inherited a better priority have that priority waived, and the thread is removed from the sleep queue and given a turnstile from the chain's free list. Recall that a thread donated its turnstile to the free list if it was not the first thread placed on the blocking chain for the lock; coming off the turnstile, threads get a turnstile back. Once the thread is unlinked from the sleep queue, the scheduling class wakeup code is entered, and the thread is put back on a processor's dispatch queue.

17.8 Kernel Semaphores

Semaphores provide a method of synchronizing access to a sharable resource by multiple processes or threads. A semaphore can be used as a binary lock for exclusive access or as a counter, allowing for concurrent access by multiple threads to a finite number of shared resources.

In the counter implementation, the semaphore value is initialized to the number of shared resources (these semaphores are sometimes referred to as counting semaphores). Each time a process needs a resource, the semaphore value is decremented to indicate there is one less of the resource. When the process is finished with the resource, the semaphore value is incremented. A 0 semaphore value tells the calling process that no resources are currently available, and the calling process blocks until another process finishes using the resource and frees it. These functions are historically referred to as semaphore P and V operations—the P operation attempts to acquire the semaphore, and the V operation releases it.

The Solaris kernel uses semaphores where appropriate, when the constraints for atomicity on lock acquisition are not as stringent as they are in the areas where mutex and RW locks are used. Also, the counting functionality that semaphores provide makes them a good fit for things like the allocation and deallocation of a fixed amount of a resource.

The kernel semaphore structure maintains a sleep queue for the semaphore and a count field that reflects the value of the semaphore, shown in Figure 17.8. The figure illustrates the look of a kernel semaphore for all Solaris releases covered in this book.

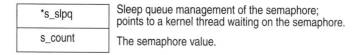

Figure 17.8 Kernel Semaphore

Kernel functions for semaphores include an initialization routine (sema_init()), a destroy function (sema_destroy()), the traditional P and V operations (sema_p() and sema_v()), and a test function (test for semaphore held, sema_held()). There are a few other support functions, as well as some variations on the sema_p() function, which we discuss later.

The init function simply sets the count value in the semaphore, based on the value passed as an argument to the sema_init() routine. The s_slpq pointer is set to NULL, and the semaphore is initialized. The sema_destroy() function is used when the semaphore is an integral part of a resource that is dynamically created and destroyed as the resource gets used and subsequently released. For example, the bio (block I/O) subsystem in the kernel, which manages buf structures for page I/O support through the file system, uses semaphores on a per-buf structure basis. Each buffer has two semaphores, which are initialized when a buffer is allocated by sema_init(). Once the I/O is completed and the buffer is released, sema_destroy() is called as part of the buffer release code. (sema_destroy() just nulls the s_slpq pointer.)

Kernel threads that must access a resource controlled by a semaphore call the sema_p() function, which requires that the semaphore count value be greater than 0 in order to return success. If the count is 0, then the semaphore is not available and the calling thread must block. If the count is greater than 0, then the count is decremented in the semaphore and the code returns to the caller. Otherwise, a sleep queue is located from the systemwide array of sleep queues, the thread state is changed to sleep, and the thread is placed on the sleep queue. Note that turnstiles are not used for semaphores—turnstiles are an implementation of sleep queues specifically for mutex and RW locks. Kernel threads blocked on anything other than mutexes and RW locks are placed on sleep queues.

Sleep queues are discussed in more detail in Section 3.10. Briefly though, sleep queues are organized as a linked list of kernel threads, and each linked list is rooted in an array referenced through a sleepq_head kernel pointer. Figure 17.9 illustrates how sleep queues are organized.

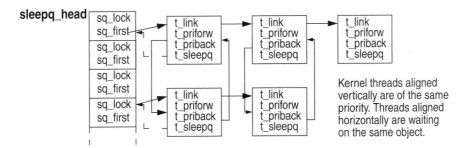

Figure 17.9 Sleep Queues

A hashing function indexes the sleepq_head array, hashing on the address of the object. A singly linked list that establishes the beginning of the doubly linked sublists of kthreads at the same priority is in ascending order based on priority. The sublist is implemented with a t_priforw (forward pointer) and t_priback (previous pointer) in the kernel thread. Also, a t_sleepq pointer points back to the array entry in `sleepq_head`, identifying which sleep queue the thread is on and providing a quick method to determine if a thread is on a sleep queue at all; if the thread's `t_sleepq` pointer is `NULL`, then the thread is not on a sleep queue.

Inside the `sema_p()` function, if we have a semaphore count value of 0, the semaphore is not available and the calling kernel thread needs to be placed on a sleep queue. A sleep queue is located through a hash function into the `sleep_head` array, which hashes on the address of the object the thread is blocking, in this case, the address of the semaphore. The code also grabs the sleep queue lock, `sq_lock` (see Figure 17.9), to block any further inserts or removals from the sleep queue until the insertion of the current kernel thread has been completed (that's what locks are for!).

The scheduling-class-specific sleep function is called to set the thread wakeup priority and to change the thread state from `ONPROC` (running on a processor) to `SLEEP`. The kernel thread's `t_wchan` (wait channel) pointer is set to the address of the semaphore it's blocking on, and the thread's `t_sobj_ops` pointer is set to reference the `sema_sobj_ops` structure. The thread is now in a sleep state on a sleep queue.

A semaphore is released by the `sema_v()` function, which has the exact opposite effect of `sema_p()` and behaves very much like the lock release functions we've examined up to this point. The semaphore value is incremented, and if any threads are sleeping on the semaphore, the one that has been sitting on the sleep queue longest will be woken up. Semaphore wakeups always involve waking one waiter at a time.

Semaphores are used in relatively few areas of the operating system: the buffer I/O (`bio`) module, the dynamically loadable kernel module code, and a couple of device drivers.

17.9 DTrace Lockstat Provider

The lockstat provider makes available probes that can be used to discern lock contention statistics or to understand virtually any aspect of locking behavior. The `lockstat(1M)` command is actually a DTrace consumer that uses the lockstat provider to gather its raw data.

17.9.1 Overview

The lockstat provider makes available two kinds of probes: content-event probes and hold-event probes.

Contention-event probes correspond to contention on a synchronization primitive; they fire when a thread is forced to wait for a resource to become available. Solaris is generally optimized for the noncontention case, so prolonged contention is not expected. These probes should be used to understand those cases where contention does arise. Because contention is relatively rare, enabling contention-event probes generally doesn't substantially affect performance.

Hold-event probes correspond to acquiring, releasing, or otherwise manipulating a synchronization primitive. These probes can be used to answer arbitrary questions about the way synchronization primitives are manipulated. Because Solaris acquires and releases synchronization primitives very often (on the order of millions of times per second per CPU on a busy system), enabling hold-event probes has a much higher probe effect than does enabling contention-event probes. While the probe effect induced by enabling them can be substantial, it is not pathological; they may still be enabled with confidence on production systems.

The lockstat provider makes available probes that correspond to the different synchronization primitives in Solaris; these primitives and the probes that correspond to them are discussed in the remainder of this chapter.

17.9.2 Adaptive Lock Probes

Adaptive locks enforce mutual exclusion to a critical section and can be acquired in most contexts in the kernel. Because adaptive locks have few context restrictions, they comprise the vast majority of synchronization primitives in the Solaris kernel. These locks are adaptive in their behavior with respect to contention. When a thread attempts to acquire a held adaptive lock, it will determine if the owning thread is currently running on a CPU. If the owner is running on another CPU, the acquiring thread will spin. If the owner is not running, the acquiring thread will block.

The four lockstat probes pertaining to adaptive locks are in Table 17.2. For each probe, arg0 contains a pointer to the kmutex_t structure that represents the adaptive lock.

Table 17.2 Adaptive Lock Probes

Probe Name	Description
adaptive-acquire	Hold-event probe that fires immediately after an adaptive lock is acquired.
adaptive-block	Contention-event probe that fires after a thread that has blocked on a held adaptive mutex has reawakened and has acquired the mutex. If both probes are enabled, adaptive-block fires before adaptive-acquire. At most one of adaptive-block and adaptive-spin fire for a single lock acquisition. arg1 for adaptive-block contains the sleep time in nanoseconds.

continues

Table 17.2 Adaptive Lock Probes (*continued*)

Probe Name	Description
adaptive-spin	Contention-event probe that fires after a thread that has spun on a held adaptive mutex has successfully acquired the mutex. If both are enabled, adaptive-spin fires before adaptive-acquire. At most one of adaptive-spin and adaptive-block fire for a single lock acquisition. arg1 for adaptive-spin contains the spin count: the number of iterations that were taken through the spin loop before the lock was acquired. The spin count has little meaning on its own but can be used to compare spin times.
adaptive-release	Hold-event probe that fires immediately after an adaptive lock is released.

17.9.3 Spin Lock Probes

Threads cannot block in some contexts in the kernel, such as high-level interrupt context and any context manipulating dispatcher state. In these contexts, this restriction prevents the use of adaptive locks. Spin locks are instead used to effect mutual exclusion to critical sections in these contexts. As the name implies, the behavior of these locks in the presence of contention is to spin until the lock is released by the owning thread. The three probes pertaining to spin locks are in Table 17.3.

Table 17.3 Spin Lock Probes

Probe Name	Description
spin-acquire	Hold-event probe that fires immediately after a spin lock is acquired.
spin-spin	Contention-event probe that fires after a thread that has spun on a held spin lock has successfully acquired the spin lock. If both are enabled, spin-spin fires before spin-acquire. arg1 for spin-spin contains the spin count: the number of iterations that were taken through the spin loop before the lock was acquired. The spin count has little meaning on its own but can be used to compare spin times.
spin-release	Hold-event probe that fires immediately after a spin lock is released.

Adaptive locks are much more common than spin locks. The following script displays totals for both lock types to provide data to support this observation.

```
lockstat:::adaptive-acquire
/execname == "date"/
{
        @locks["adaptive"] = count();
}

lockstat:::spin-acquire
/execname == "date"/
{
        @locks["spin"] = count();
}
```

Run this script in one window, and a date(1) command in another. When you terminate the DTrace script, you will see output similar to the following example.

```
# dtrace -s ./whatlock.d
dtrace: script './whatlock.d' matched 5 probes
^C
spin                                                        26
adaptive                                                  2981
```

As this output indicates, over 99 percent of the locks acquired in running the date command are adaptive locks. It may be surprising that so many locks are acquired in doing something as simple as a date. The large number of locks is a natural artifact of the fine-grained locking required of an extremely scalable system like the Solaris kernel.

17.9.4 Thread Locks

A thread lock is a special kind of spin lock that locks a thread for purposes of changing thread state. Thread lock hold events are available as spin lock hold-event probes (that is, spin-acquire and spin-release), but contention events have their own probe specific to thread locks. The thread lock hold-event probe is described in Table 17.4.

17.9.5 Readers/Writer Lock Probes

Readers/writer locks enforce a policy of allowing multiple readers or a single writer—but not both—to be in a critical section. These locks are typically used for structures that are searched more frequently than they are modified and for which

Table 17.4 Thread Lock Probes

Probe Name	Description
`thread-spin`	Contention-event probe that fires after a thread has spun on a thread lock. Like other contention-event probes, if both the contention-event probe and the hold-event probe are enabled, `thread-spin` fires before `spin-acquire`. Unlike other contention-event probes, however, `thread-spin` fires *before* the lock is actually acquired. As a result, multiple `thread-spin` probe firings may correspond to a single `spin-acquire` probe firing.

there is substantial time in the critical section. If critical section times are short, readers/writer locks will implicitly serialize over the shared memory used to implement the lock, giving them no advantage over adaptive locks. See `rwlock(9F)` for more details on readers/writer locks.

The probes pertaining to readers/writer locks are in Table 17.5. For each probe, `arg0` contains a pointer to the `krwlock_t` structure that represents the adaptive lock.

Table 17.5 Readers/Writer Lock Probes

Probe Name	Description
`rw-acquire`	Hold-event probe that fires immediately after a readers/writer lock is acquired. `arg1` contains the constant `RW_READER` if the lock was acquired as a reader, and `RW_WRITER` if the lock was acquired as a writer.
`rw-block`	Contention-event probe that fires after a thread that has blocked on a held readers/writer lock has reawakened and has acquired the lock. `arg1` contains the length of time (in nanoseconds) that the current thread had to sleep to acquire the lock. `arg2` contains the constant `RW_READER` if the lock was acquired as a reader, and `RW_WRITER` if the lock was acquired as a writer. `arg3` and `arg4` contain more information on the reason for blocking. `arg3` is nonzero if and only if the lock was held as a writer when the current thread blocked. `arg4` contains the readers count when the current thread blocked. If both the `rw-block` and `rw-acquire` probes are enabled, `rw-block` fires *before* `rw-acquire`.

continues

Table 17.5 Readers/Writer Lock Probes (*continued*)

Probe Name	Description
`rw-upgrade`	Hold-event probe that fires after a thread has successfully upgraded a readers/writer lock from a reader to a writer. Upgrades do not have an associated contention event because they are only possible through a nonblocking interface, `rw_tryupgrade(TRYUPGRADE.9F)`.
`rw-downgrade`	Hold-event probe that fires after a thread had downgraded its ownership of a readers/writer lock from writer to reader. Downgrades do not have an associated contention event because they always succeed without contention.
`rw-release`	Hold-event probe that fires immediately after a readers/writer lock is released. `arg1` contains the constant `RW_READER` if the released lock was held as a reader, and `RW_WRITER` if the released lock was held as a writer. Due to upgrades and downgrades, the lock may *not* have been released as it was acquired.

PART SEVEN

Networking

Networking

The Solaris Network Stack

Contributed by Sunay Tripathi

Network hardware and software have been an integral part of Sun technology from the very beginning, going back to 1982 when Sun introduced the Sun-1 workstation running Sun's earliest implementation of SunOS. The Sun-1 operating system included a built-in Ethernet port and a fully functional TCP/IP software stack. In the 24 years since the Sun-1 workstation, work has continued on network hardware and software, keeping pace with the industry and the increasing demands of network-centric applications and workloads.

Several years ago, the blueprints for a new network software architecture began to take shape, designed to address the changing dynamics of network-centric computing and to leverage the technology of the hardware platforms (network cards, I/O buses, multiprocessors, etc.) running volume applications and services.

Solaris 10 incorporates several significant changes in the network software stack. In this chapter, we look at the implementation in earlier Solaris releases and describe the new software stack in Solaris 10.

18.1 STREAMS and the Network Stack

The networking stack of the Solaris 1.x release was a variant of the BSD UNIX implementation and was similar to the BSD Reno implementation. The BSD stack worked fine for the low-end machines, but Solaris was required to meet the demands of data-center enterprise installations as well as desktops and low-end systems. Thus, the Solaris code base was migrated to the AT&T SVR4 architecture, which became the Solaris 2.X product (Sun OS 5.X system).

With the Solaris 2.X release, the networking stack went through a makeover and transitioned from a BSD-style stack to a STREAMS-based stack, which aligned with the SVR4 architecture. The STREAMS framework provided an easy message passing interface, making it relatively simple to create a message flow by which STREAMS modules interact with other STREAMS modules. The kernel STREAMS framework includes a perimeters facility for managing thread concurrency in STREAMS modules, thereby guaranteeing exclusive access to STREAMS queues. Using the STREAMS inner- and outer-perimeter feature, the module writer could provide mutual exclusion without making the implementation complex.

The demand on systems providing network services changed with the expansion of the World Wide Web (WWW) and the increase in volume and processing power of client systems (for example, personal computers). A salient example is connection setup and teardown. In early implementations, the cost of setting up a STREAMS device was high, but the number of connection setups per second was not an important consideration, and connections were usually long-lived. With the Internet explosion, large numbers of short-lived connections are common, and require an implementation that can do fast connection setup and teardown. This is just one of several areas addressed in Solaris 10.

The networking stack in Solaris 10 went through further transitions by which the core pieces (that is, socket layer, TCP, UDP, IP, and device driver) use an IP classifier and serialization queue to improve the connection setup time and scalability and to reduce packet processing cost. STREAMS modules are still used to provide the flexibility that ISVs need to implement additional functionality.

18.1.1 The STREAMS Model

STREAMS[1] allows users to create modules to provide standard data communications services and then manipulate the modules on a stream. The modules are precompiled and can be dynamically interconnected to form a stream from the application level without any explicit linking to other modules in the stream.

The fundamental STREAMS unit is the stream. A stream is a full-duplex bidirectional data-transfer path between a process in user space and a STREAMS driver in kernel space. A stream has three parts: a stream head, zero or more modules, and a driver.

---

1. The capitalized word "STREAMS" refers to the STREAMS programming model and facilities. The word "stream" refers to an instance of a full-duplex path using the model and facilities between a user application and a driver.

An application creates a stream by opening a STREAMS device driver and optionally inserting one or more STREAMS modules between the stream head and device driver. This string of STREAMS modules (see Figure 18.1) creates a bidirectional flow in which data moves between the STREAMS driver and modules in the kernel space and an application in user space. A stream head is the end of the stream nearest the user process. It is the interface between the stream and the user process. When a STREAMS device is first opened, the stream consists of only a stream head and a STREAMS driver.

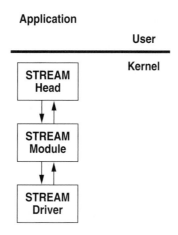

Figure 18.1 STREAMS Example

A STREAMS module is a defined set of kernel-level routines and data structures. A STREAMS device driver is a character device driver that implements the STREAMS interface. A STREAMS device driver exists below the stream head and any modules. It can act on an external I/O device, or it can be an internal software driver, called a pseudo device driver. The driver transfers data between the kernel and the device.

Data on a stream is passed in the form of messages. Messages are the means by which all I/O is done under STREAMS. Each stream head, STREAMS module, and driver has a read side and a write side. When messages go from one module's read side to the next module's read side, they are said to be traveling upstream. Messages passing from one module's write side to the next module's write side are said to be traveling downstream.

Each stream head, STREAMS driver, and STREAMS module has its own pair of queues, one queue for the read side and one queue for the write side. Messages are ordered into queues, generally on a first-in, first-out basis (FIFO), according to priorities associated with them (see Figure 18.2).

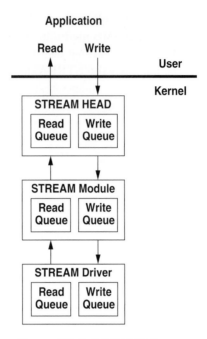

Figure 18.2 STREAMS Queues

The stream head or STREAMS device driver uses the putnext() routine and passes the pointer to the read side or the write side and the message block. STREAMS determines the next element (driver, module, or head as appropriate) and calls the read or write procedure registered at the STREAMS creation time with the correct queue and message block.

To communicate with a STREAMS device, an application uses the read(2), write(2), getmsg(2), getpmsg(2), putmsg(2), putpmsg(2), and ioctl(2) system calls to transmit or receive data on a stream.

The data written by the application is converted into a STREAMS message, which is made up of one or more message blocks, referenced by a pointer to a msgb structure. The b_next and b_prev pointers in the msgb structure are used to link messages together on a queue. The b_cont pointer links message blocks together when a message consists of more than one block. Each msgb structure also includes a pointer to a datab structure, the data block that contains pointers to the actual data of the message, and the message type.

The STREAMS modules, device driver, and stream head communicate with each other, passing the STREAMS messages with the putnext(9F) or put(9E) routine.

STREAMS also allows a module or device driver to describe the concurrency model for itself. It can choose to be fully multithreaded, in which case the burden of protecting its data structures from multiple threads is the responsibility of the module. Modules can also choose the perimeter protection model that ensures that the STREAMS framework allows only one thread inside the module at any time. In-between options are available, whereby modules can specify that processing is single-threaded during setup and teardown of the stream but multithreaded during the data exchange.

18.1.2 Network Stack as STREAMS Module

STREAMS provided an excellent framework to implement the networking stack. Each protocol layer was implemented as a STREAMS module, and the network driver was implemented as a STREAMS device driver. The incoming packets were converted into STREAMS messages by the network device drivers and sent upstream to be processed by the various protocol layers (IP, TCP, UDP, etc.). Similarly, data sent by the application (by writing to an open socket) was converted by the stream head into a message and sent downstream to be processed by various protocol layers that were put together when the stream was constructed.

When an application opens a socket for communication, the domain and type argument determine what kind of stream is created. For example, an AF_INET domain and SOCK_STREAM type means that the application intends to establish a TCP stream to a remote endpoint. The stream created by opening such a socket would consist of a stream head, a TCP STREAMS module, and IP as the device driver. The socket domain and type to the STREAMS driver mapping is controlled by the /etc/sock2path file.

IP was implemented both as a STREAMS module and STREAMS device driver for multiplexing reasons. To the application, IP appeared as a device driver but it was also inserted as a module on top of each network device driver (see Figure 18.3). Each module and device driver is the instance of same code with common data structures, which help IP direct a packet received by a device driver to the correct application stream by means of an IP client table. Similarly, data sent by the application needs to be sent through the correct device driver instance. An Internet route entry (ire) data structure maintained by IP stores the mapping between a destination and the network interface device driver.

Creating the TCP stream for outbound connections is simple enough. The application initiates the process by opening a socket that creates the stream, and all subsequent operations (for example, connect) are processed on that stream. The incoming connection case is more complex since the stream to handle this connection doesn't yet exist.

Incoming SYN packets are sent to TCP through one of the listener TCP streams. TCP creates a new TCP data structure (often referred to as "eager TCP") for this incoming connection. The three-way handshake for connection setup is completed

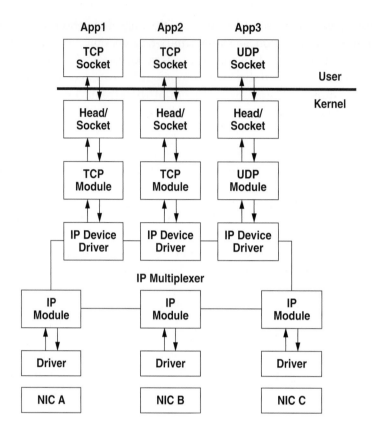

Figure 18.3 TCP/IP Stack as STREAMS Modules

on the listener TCP stream. Once done, TCP sends a "connection indication" to the application. Once the application "accepts" the connection, a new stream for this connection is created, the eager-TCP instance is transferred from the listener to this stream, and an appropriate entry is made in the IP client table. Since a remote endpoint can continue to send packets after the three-way handshake is completed, the packets can be sent to TCP by means of the listener stream or the correct IP client, which may be in the process of being created.

So the TCP receive-side code had to deal with significant complexity in setting up an incoming connection. This also limited the ability of the Solaris STREAMS-based stack to accept a large number of incoming TCP connections, since all the incoming packets for a particular listener were serialized at the listener instance and required opening a stream with IP as device and autopushing TCP as a module.

TCP and UDP also maintain a global stream to IP. This allows IP to pass incoming packets for which it can't find the correct IP client to the correct module on basis of protocol alone.

While this implementation of TCP/IP as STREAMS modules served us well for many years, work began in the early days of Solaris 10 development to build a new, more efficient implementation that significantly reduced the use of STREAMS.

18.1.2.1 Key Data Structures

The key data structures and the protection mechanism used to manage synchronized access include the following:

- **TCP structures.** TCP maintains the connection state in a connection-specific `tcp_t` data structure. This contains local and remote IP addresses, TCP port information, send/receive sequence numbers and round-trip time among other important members. Access is restricted to one thread at a time so there is no need to hold a lock while accessing these members.

  Because of this model, a unique TCP stream is created per connection, and STREAMS offers the serialized access to TCP module in the stream. TCP stores `tcp_t` data structures as a STREAMS queue private instance at connection creation time; the instance is passed to TCP when called by STREAMS while passing messages to TCP. TCP also maintains a connection hash table computed on the local and remote IP address and TCP ports. Each connection-specific `tcp_t` is also inserted in the TCP connections hash table and is used to find the connection instance for messages received on the TCP global stream or listener stream where its not possible to determine the `tcp_t` from the queue itself.

- **UDP structures.** UDP maintains per UDP stream information similar to TCP in a `udp_t` structure. This structure is also stored as the read-side and write-side queue private member. Most of the work of connecting UDP is similar to the TCP module.

  UDP also deals with applications sending datagrams to multiple remote destinations on the same local socket by sending them to IP and letting IP multiplex them to the correct Network Interface Card (NIC).

- **IP structures.** IP has two main data structures: `ipc_t` and `ill_t`.

  `ipc_t` is the structure for IP as a device. The `ipc_t` structure includes the stream-specific information to send the incoming packets to the correct TCP or UDP client stream.

  `ill_t` is the structure, unique to each physical NIC, for IP as a module inserted on each network device driver. The `ill_t` structure contains the physical NIC-specific information and pointers to each `ipif_t` structure, which represents each logical NIC on top of the physical NIC.

  IP also maintains hash tables for connected TCP clients, TCP listener clients, UDP clients, and other protocol streams. An `ipc_t` is inserted in these tables with a hash value computed on IP address and port information. The routing table is also maintained by IP. Routes are cached in the form of an Internet route entry (`ire_t`) data structure. The `ire_t` structure contains a pointer to an outbound NIC queue through which the destination is reachable.

18.1.2.2 IP as a Multiplexer

IP is by far the most important component of the network stack. Its job is to multiplex the incoming packets to the correct IP client stream and send the outbound packets to the correct NIC. When an NIC receives a packet, it sends the packet upstream to IP acting as a module. IP looks at the protocol type and, for anything other than TCP and UDP, passes the packet to the correct protocol stream.

For TCP and UDP, it tries to find an `ipc_t` in the connected hash table or the listener hash table and uses the pointer to the upstream queue stored in `ipc_t` to pass the packet up the correct stream.

The outbound multiplexing is done by means of the `ire_t`. When upstream modules want to send packets out, IP uses the `ire_t` to determine which outbound NIC it should use.

18.1.3 Issues with STREAMS-Based Stacks

The STREAMS-based stack served pretty well until the days of the Web. When the number of connections was small and more long-lived (NFS, ftp, etc.), the cost of setting up a new stream was amortized over the life of the connection. With the explosion of the Web and faster machines, even the long-lived connection became short-lived, and a typical server had to deal with a large number of incoming connections at any given time.

During the same period, servers became larger, multiprocessor-based systems with larger memory capacity. The cost of switching processing from one CPU to another became high as the mid-to-high-end machines became more nonuniform in their memory access. Since STREAMS by design had no CPU affinity, packets for particular connections moved around to different CPUs. It was apparent that Solaris needed to move away from the STREAMS architecture.

18.2 Solaris 10 Stack: Design Goals

The Solaris 10 release was a landmark release for Sun. After a decade and a half of a STREAMS-based network stack, Solaris 10 OS switched to a new architecture (internally named FireEngine) which provided better connection affinity to CPUs, greatly reducing the connection setup cost and the cost of per-packet processing. It still retained the STREAMS flexibility in allowing third-party STREAMS modules to be inserted into the stack if necessary.

The Solaris 10 networking architecture encompasses six key design points:

- **Scalability.** As the number of CPUs in a machine continues to grow, scalability becomes really important, not only for Sun's SPARC-based multiprocessor systems but also for recent offerings based on the AMD Opteron processor, which are available as multicore and multiprocessor systems. The simple BSD-style stack is no longer adequate, and more connection affinity to CPUs is needed to scale the stack with a number of CPUs and NICs.

- **Packet processing cost.** A typical server does more than a gigabit per second of network traffic at 1500-byte packets. Things are already moving toward 10 gigabit per second and trunks of high-bandwidth NICs. The size of the maximum transfer unit (MTU) is still restricted to 1500 bytes, so the per-packet processing cost plays an important role in deciding how much compute power is used for network processing.

- **Connection setup cost.** The number of connections a server has to handle continues to grow as more and more devices are connected to Internet. Furthermore, the short-lived connections dominate more and more, and as a result, the connection setup cost plays a major role as a design point for a new networking architecture. This applies to most TCP, SCTP, and connected UDP environments.

- **Latency issues.** Now that Solaris running on commodity hardware is widely used in database clusters and high-performance throughput computing (HPTC) environments, the per-packet latency plays an increasingly important role.

- **Observability.** Apart from performance and scalability, users need more observability to determine the root cause of problems. Also, with the amount of data flowing through the stack, any observability mechanism needs to keep up with the data flow and not induce performance problems.

- **Out-of-the-box performance.** The Solaris 10 stack departs from the long-standing approach of tuning the stack according to the workload. Instead, the design is based on an understanding of the flow of packets through the stack and the automatic application of the most suitable policies. Predictability and repeatability for a particular workload are maintained.

18.3 Solaris 10 Network Stack Framework

The pre-Solaris 10 stack used the STREAMS perimeter facility and kernel adaptive mutexes for multithreading. TCP used a STREAMS QPAIR perimeter, UDP used a STREAMS QPAIR with the `PUTSHARED` attribute, and IP a PERMOD perimeter with `PUTSHARED`. Various TCP, UDP, and IP global data structures were protected by mutexes. The stack was executed by userland threads executing various system calls, the network device driver read-side interrupt or device driver worker thread, and by STREAMS framework worker threads. The then current perimeter provided a per-module, per-protocol stack layer, or horizontal perimeter. This could, and often did, lead to a packet being processed on more than one CPU and by more than one thread, leading to excessive context switching and poor CPU data locality. The problem was compounded by the various places at which packets could be queued under load and by the various threads that finally processed the packet.

The FireEngine approach is to merge all protocol layers into one STREAMS module that is fully multithreaded. Inside the merged module, instead of using per data structure locks, FireEngine uses a per-CPU synchronization mechanism called *vertical perimeter*. The vertical perimeter is implemented by a serialization queue abstraction called *squeue*. Each squeue is bound to a CPU, and each connection is in turn bound to an squeue, thereby providing any synchronization and mutual exclusion needed for the connection-specific data structures.

The connection (or context) lookup for inbound packets is done outside the perimeter by an IP connection classifier as soon as the packet reaches IP. The classification provides the basis by which the connection structure is identified. Since the lookup happens outside the perimeter, we can bind a connection to an instance of the vertical perimeter or squeue when the connection is initialized and processes all packets for that connection on the squeue it is bound to, maintaining better cache locality. More details about the vertical perimeter and classifier are given in later sections.

The classifier also becomes the database for storing a sequence of function calls necessary for all inbound and outbound packets. This facilitates a change in the Solaris networking stacks, from the current message passing interface to a BSD-style function call interface. The string of functions created on the fly (event list) for processing a packet for a connection provides the basis for an eventual new framework in which other modules, including third-party, high-performance modules, can participate in the framework.

18.3.1 Vertical Perimeter

An squeue guarantees that only a single thread can process a given connection at any given time, thus serializing access to the TCP connection structure by multiple threads (both from the read and write side) in the merged TCP/IP module. It is similar to the STREAMS QPAIR perimeter, but instead of just protecting a module instance, it protects the whole connection state from IP to sockfs (the socket file system—the implementation of sockets in Solaris introduced in the Solaris 8 release).

Vertical perimeters or squeues by themselves just provide packet serialization and mutual exclusion for the data structures, but by creating per CPU perimeters and binding a connection to the instance attached to the CPU processing interrupts, we can guarantee much better data locality. We could have chosen between creating a per-connection perimeter or a per-CPU perimeter, that is, an instance for each connection or each CPU. However, the overhead involved with a per-connection perimeter and thread contention gives lower performance, so we opted for a per-CPU instance.

For the per-CPU instance, we had the choice of queuing a connection structure for processing or instead just queuing the packet itself and storing the connection structure pointer in the packet. The former approach leads to some interesting starvation scenarios when packets for a connection keep arriving at a steady rate, and managing the potential starvation issue came at a high overhead (performance) cost. Queuing the packets lets us protect the ordering and is much simpler, and this is the approach we have taken for FireEngine.

As mentioned before, each connection instance is assigned to a single squeue and is thus processed only within the vertical perimeter. An squeue is processed by a single thread at a time, so all data structures used to process a given connection from within the perimeter can be accessed without additional locking. This approach improves the CPU and thread context data locality of access of the connection metadata, the packet metadata, and the packet payload data. In addition, it lets us remove per-device-driver worker thread schemes, which are problematic in solving a systemwide resource issue. With that removal, we can implement additional strategic algorithms to best handle a given network interface according to the network interface throughput and the system throughput. For example, fanning-out per-connection packet processing to a group of CPUs is now possible. The thread entering an squeue may either process the packet right away or queue it for later processing by another thread or worker thread. The choice depends on the squeue entry point and the state of the squeue. The immediate processing is possible only when no other thread has entered the same squeue. The squeue is represented by the following abstraction.

```
struct squeue_s {
        /* Keep the most used members 64bytes cache aligned */
        kmutex_t        sq_lock;        /* lock before using any member */
        uint32_t        sq_state;       /* state flags and message count */
        int             sq_count;       /* # of mblocks in squeue */
        mblk_t          *sq_first;      /* first mblk chain or NULL */
        mblk_t          *sq_last;       /* last mblk chain or NULL */
        clock_t         sq_awaken;      /* time async thread was awakened */
        kthread_t       *sq_run;        /* Current thread processing sq */
        void            *sq_rx_ring;
        clock_t         sq_avg_drain_time; /* Avg time to drain a pkt */
```

continues

```
        processorid_t   sq_bind;         /* processor to bind to */
        kcondvar_t      sq_async;        /* async thread blocks on */
        clock_t         sq_wait;         /* lbolts to wait after a fill() */
        uintptr_t       sq_private[SQPRIVATE_MAX];
        timeout_id_t    sq_tid;          /* timer id of pending timeout() */
        kthread_t       *sq_worker;      /* kernel thread id */
        char            sq_name[SQ_NAMELEN + 1];
...
};
```

                                       See usr/src/uts/common/sys/squeue_impl.h

It is important to note that the squeues are created on the basis of per-hardware execution pipelines, that is, cores, hyperthreads, and the like. The stack processing of the serialization queue (and the hardware execution pipeline) is limited to one thread at a time, but this actually improves performance because the new stack ensures that there are no waits for any resources such as memory or locks inside the vertical perimeter. Allowing more than one kernel thread to timeshare execution pipelines incurs more overhead than allowing only one thread to run uninterrupted.

FireEngine provides three models for flexible squeue processing:

- **Queuing model.** The queue is strictly FIFO (first in, first out) for both the read and write side, which ensures that any particular connection does not suffer or is not starved. A read-side or write-side thread queues packets at the end of the chain. The thread can then be allowed to process the packet or to signal the worker thread according to the processing model.

- **Processing model.** After enqueueing its packet, the enqueuing thread returns if another thread is already processing the squeue, and the packet is drained later according to the drain model. If the squeue is not being processed and no packets are queued, the thread can mark the squeue as being processed (represented by sq_flag) and processes the packet. Once the thread has processed the packet, it removes the "processing in progress" flag and frees the squeue for future processing.

- **Drain model.** A thread that successfully processed its own packet can also drain any packets that were queued while it was processing the request. In addition, if the squeue is not being processed but packets are already queued, then instead of queuing its packet and leaving, the thread can drain the queue and then process its own packets. The worker thread is always allowed to drain the entire queue. Choosing the correct drain model is quite complicated. The choices show below can be independently applied to the read thread and the write thread.

  - Always queue.

  - Process your own packet if you can.

  - Time-bounded process and drain.

Typically, draining by an interrupt thread should always be time-bounded "process and drain," whereas the write thread can choose between "process your own" and time-bounded "process and drain." For Solaris 10, the write thread behavior is tunable and defaults to "process your own," whereas the read side is fixed to time-bounded "process and drain."

Signaling the worker thread is another option worth exploring. If the packet arrival rate is low and a thread is forced to queue its packet, then, when there is work to be done, the worker thread should be allowed to run as soon as the entering thread finishes processing the squeue. On the other hand, if the packet arrival rate is high, it may be desirable to delay waking up the worker thread and hope that an interrupt will shortly arrive to complete the drain. Waking up the worker thread immediately when the packet arrival rate is high creates unnecessary contention between the worker and interrupt threads.

The default for Solaris 10 is delayed wakeup of the worker thread. Initial experiments on available servers showed that the best results were obtained by waking up the worker thread after a 10 ms delay.

Placing a request on the squeue requires a per-squeue lock to protect the state of the queue; this doesn't introduce scalability problems, because the lock is distributed among CPUs and is only held for a short period of time. We also utilize optimizations that allow avoiding context switches while still preserving the single-threaded semantics of squeue processing. We create an instance of an squeue per CPU in the system and bind the worker thread to that CPU. Each connection is then bound to a specific squeue and thus to a specific CPU as well.

The binding of an squeue to a CPU can be changed, but the binding of a connection to an squeue never changes because of the squeue protection semantics. In the merged TCP/IP case, the vertical perimeter protects the TCP state for each connection. The squeue instance used by each connection is chosen either at the "open," "bind," or "connect" time for outbound connections or at "eager connection creation time" for inbound connections.

The choice of the squeue instance depends on the relative speeds of the CPUs and the NICs in the system. There are two cases:

- **The CPU is faster than the NIC.** The incoming connections are assigned to the "squeue instance" of the interrupted CPU. For the outbound case, connections are assigned to the squeue instance of the CPU the application is running on.
- **The NIC is faster than the CPU.** A single CPU is not capable of handling the NIC. The connections are randomly bounded on all available squeues.

For Solaris 10, the system administrator determines whether the NIC should be faster or slower than the CPU by tuning the global variable `ip_squeue_fanout`.

The default is *no fan-out*; that is, assign the incoming connection to the squeue attached to the interrupted CPU. To take a CPU offline, the worker thread bound to this CPU removes its binding and restores it when the CPU comes back online. This allows dynamic reconfiguration functionality to work correctly. When packets for a connection are arriving on multiple NICs (and thus interrupting multiple CPUs), they are always processed on the squeue on which the connection was originally established. In Solaris 10, the vertical perimeter is provided only for TCP-based connections. The interface to the vertical perimeter is done at the TCP and IP layer after a determination that the perimeter is a TCP connection. Solaris 10 updates will introduce the general vertical perimeter for any use.

The function prototypes for the squeue interfaces are listed below.

```
extern void squeue_init(void);
extern squeue_t *squeue_create(char *, processorid_t, clock_t, pri_t);
extern void squeue_bind(squeue_t *, processorid_t);
extern void squeue_unbind(squeue_t *);
extern void squeue_enter_chain(squeue_t *, mblk_t *, mblk_t *,
    uint32_t, uint8_t);
extern void squeue_enter(squeue_t *, mblk_t *, sqproc_t, void *, uint8_t);
extern void squeue_enter_nodrain(squeue_t *, mblk_t *, sqproc_t, void *,
    uint8_t);
extern void squeue_fill(squeue_t *, mblk_t *, sqproc_t, void *, uint8_t);
extern uintptr_t *squeue_getprivate(squeue_t *, sqprivate_t);
extern processorid_t squeue_binding(squeue_t *);
```

See usr/src/uts/common/sys/squeue.h

`squeue_create()` instantiates a new squeue and uses `squeue_bind()` and `squeue_unbind()` to bind and unbind itself from a particular CPU. Once created, the squeues are never destroyed. The `squeue_enter()` function accesses the squeue, and the entering thread processes and drains the squeue according to the models previously discussed. `squeue_fill()` just queues a packet on the squeue to be processed by a worker thread or by other threads.

18.3.2 IP Classifier

The IP connection fan-out mechanism consists of three hash tables: a five-tuple hash table (protocol, remote and local IP addresses, and remote and local ports) to keep fully qualified TCP (ESTABLISHED) connections; a three-tuple lookup consisting of protocol, local address, and local port to keep the listeners; and a single-tuple lookup for protocol listeners. As part of the lookup, a connection structure (a superset of all connection information) is returned. This connection structure is called conn_t. A few of the key structure members are shown below.

```
struct conn_s {
        kmutex_t          conn_lock;
        uint32_t          conn_ref;              /* Reference counter */
        uint_t            conn_state_flags;      /* IP state flags */
        ire_t             *conn_ire_cache;       /* outbound ire cache */
        uint32_t          conn_flags;            /* Conn Flags */
...
        tcp_t             *conn_tcp;             /* Pointer to the tcp struct */
        squeue_t          *conn_sqp;             /* Squeue for processing */
        edesc_rpf         conn_recv;             /* Pointer to recv routine */
        void              *conn_pad1;
...
        queue_t           *conn_rq;              /* Read queue */
        queue_t           *conn_wq;              /* Write queue */
        dev_t             conn_dev;              /* Minor number */

        cred_t            *conn_cred;            /* Credentials */
...
        connf_t           *conn_fanout;         /* Hash bucket we're part of */
...
};
```

See usr/src/uts/common/inet/ipclassifier.h

The interesting member to note is the pointer to the squeue or vertical perimeter. The lookup is done outside the perimeter and the packet is processed or queued on the squeue to which the connection is attached. Also, conn_recv and conn_send point to the read-side and write-side functions. The read-side function can be tcp_input() if the packet is meant for TCP.

The connection fan-out mechanism supports wildcard listeners, that is, INADDR ANY. Currently, the connected and bind tables are primarily for TCP and UDP only. A listener entry is made during a listen() call. The entry is made into the connected table after the three-way handshake is complete for TCP.

For reference, the IPClassifier interfaces are listed below.

```
conn_t      *ipcl_conn_create(uint32_t type, int sleep);
void        ipcl_conn_destroy(conn_t *connp);
int         ipcl_proto_insert(conn_t *connp, uint8_t protocol);
int         ipcl_proto_insert_v6(conn_t *connp, uint8_t protocol);
conn_t      *ipcl_proto_classify(uint8_t protocol);
int         *ipcl_bind_insert(conn_t *connp, uint8_t protocol, ipaddr_t src, uint16_
t lport);
int         *ipcl_bind_insert_v6(conn_t *connp, uint8_t protocol, const in6_addr_t *
src, uint16_t lport);
int         *ipcl_conn_insert(conn_t *connp, uint8_t protocol, ipaddr_t src, ipaddr_
t dst, uint32_t ports);
int         *ipcl_conn_insert_v6(conn_t *connp, uint8_t protocol, in6_addr_t *src,
in6_addr_t *dst, uint32_t ports);
void        ipcl_hash_remove(conn_t *connp);
conn_t      *ipcl_classify_v4(mblk_t *mp);
conn_t      *ipcl_classify_v6(mblk_t *mp);
conn_t      *ipcl_classify(mblk_t *mp);
```

See usr/src/uts/common/inet/ipclassifier.h

18.3.3 Synchronization Mechanism

Since the stack is fully multithreaded (barring the per-CPU serialization enforced by the vertical perimeter), it uses a reference-based scheme to ensure that connection instances are available when needed. The reference count is implemented in the `conn_t` structure through the `conn_ref` field and is protected by `conn_lock`. The prime purpose of the lock is not to protect the bulk of the `conn_t` structure but to protect just the reference count. Each time some entity references the data structure (stores a pointer to the data structure for later processing), it increments the reference count by calling the `CONN_INC_REF` macro. This macro acquires the `conn_lock`, increments `conn_ref`, and then drops the `conn_lock`. Each time the entity drops the reference to the connection instance, it drops its reference by means of the `CONN_DEC_REF` macro.

An established TCP connection is guaranteed to have three references on it. Each protocol layer has a reference on the instance (one each for TCP and IP), and the classifier itself has a reference since it is an established connection. Each time a packet arrives for the connection and the classifier looks up the connection instance, an extra reference is placed. That reference is dropped when the protocol layer finishes processing that packet. Similarly, any timers running on the connection instance have a reference to ensure that the instance is around whenever the timer fires. The memory associated with the connection instance is freed once the last reference is dropped.

18.4 TCP as an Implementation of the New Framework

Solaris 10 provides the same view for TCP as in previous releases; that is, TCP appears as a clone device but is actually a composite, with the TCP and IP code merged into a single D_MP STREAMS module.

The merged TCP/IP module's STREAMS entry points for open and close are the same as IP's entry points: *ip_open()* and *ip_close()*. Based on the major number passed during an open, IP decides whether the open corresponds to a TCP open or an IP open. The put and service STREAMS entry points for TCP are *tcp_wput()*, *tcp_wsrv()*, and *tcp_rsrv()*. The *tcp_wput()* entry point simply serves as a wrapper routine and enables sockfs and other modules from the top to talk to TCP by using STREAMS. Note that *tcp_rput()* is missing, because IP calls TCP functions directly. IP STREAMS entry points remain unchanged from earlier Solaris releases.

The operational part of TCP is fully protected by the vertical perimeter, which entered through the squeue primitives, as illustrated in Figure 18.4.

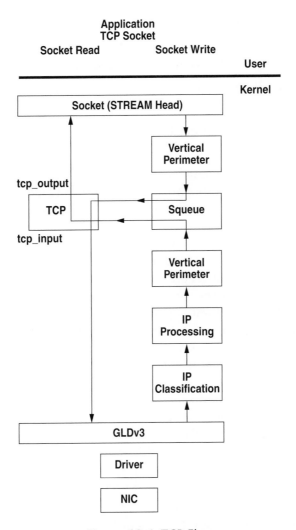

Figure 18.4 TCP Flow

Packets flowing from the top enter TCP through the wrapper function $tcp\_wput()$, which then tries to execute the real TCP output processing function $tcp\_output()$ after entering the corresponding vertical perimeter. Similarly, packets coming from the bottom try to execute the real TCP input processing function $tcp\_input()$ after entering the vertical perimeter. There are multiple entry points into TCP through the vertical perimeter:

- **$tcp\_input()$.** All inbound data packets and control messages
- **$tcp\_output()$.** All outbound data packets and control messages

- **tcp_close_output ()**. On user close
- **tcp_timewait_output ()**. timewait expiry
- **tcp_rsrv_input ()**. Flow control relief on read side
- **tcp_timer ()**. All tcp timers

18.4.1 The Interface between TCP and IP

FireEngine changes the interface between TCP and IP from the existing STREAMS-based message passing interface to an interface based on a function calls, both in the control and data paths. On the outbound side, TCP passes a fully prepared packet directly to IP by calling ip_output () while inside the vertical perimeter.

Similarly, control messages are also passed directly as function arguments. ip_bind_v{4, 6}() receives a bind message as an argument, performs the required action, and returns a result message pointer to the caller. TCP directly calls ip_bind_v{4, 6}() in the connect(), bind(), and listen() paths. IP still retains all its STREAMS entry points, but TCP (/dev/tcp) becomes a real device driver, that is, it cannot be pushed over other device drivers.

The basic protocol processing code is unchanged. Let's look at common socket calls and see how they interact with the framework.

- **socket ()**. A socket open of TCP (or /dev/tcp) eventually calls into ip_open (). The open then calls into the IP connection classifier and allocates the per-TCP endpoint control block already integrated with the conn_t structure. It chooses the squeue for this connection. In the case of an internal open (that is, by sockfs for an acceptor stream), almost nothing is done, and we delay doing useful work until accept time.

- **bind ()**. tcp_bind () eventually needs to talk to IP to determine whether the address passed in is valid. FireEngine TCP prepares this request as usual in the form of a TPI message. However, this messages is directly passed as a function argument to ip_bind_v{4, 6} (), which returns the result as another message. The use of messages as parameters is helpful in leveraging the existing code with minimal change. The port hash table used by TCP to validate binds still remains in TCP since the classifier has no use for it.

- **connect ()**. The changes in tcp_connect () are similar to those in tcp_bind (). The full bind () request is prepared as a TPI message and passed as a function argument to ip_bind_v{4, 6} (). IP calls into the classifier and inserts the connection in the connected hash table. The conn_ hash table in TCP is no longer used.

- **listen().** This path is part of `tcp_bind()`. The `tcp_bind()` function prepares a local bind TPI message and passes it as a function argument to `ip_bind_v{4, 6}()`. IP calls the classifier and inserts the connection in the bind hash table. The listen hash table of TCP does not exist any more.

- **accept().** The pre-Solaris 10 `accept()` implementation did the bulk of the connection setup processing in the listener context. The three-way handshake was completed in the listener's perimeter, and the connection indication was sent up the listener's stream. The messages necessary to perform the accept were sent down the listener stream, and the listener was single-threaded from the point of sending the T_CONN_RES message to TCP until sockfs received the acknowledgment. If the connection arrival rate was high, the ability of the pre-Solaris 10 stack to accept new connections deteriorated significantly. Furthermore, some additional TCP overhead contributed to slower accept rates: When sockfs opened an acceptor stream to TCP to accept a new connection, TCP was not aware that the data structures necessary for the new connection had already been allocated. So it allocated new structures and initialized them, but later, as part of the accept processing, these were freed.

  Another major problem with the pre-Solaris 10 design was that packets for a newly created connection arrived on the listener's perimeter. This requires a check for every incoming packet, and packets landing on the wrong perimeter had to be sent to their correct perimeter, causing additional delay. The FireEngine model establishes an eager connection (an incoming connection is called *eager* until `accept()` completes) in its own perimeter as soon as a SYN packet arrives, thus ensuring that packets always land on the correct connection. As a result, the TCP global queues are completely eliminated. The connection indication is still sent to the listener on the listener's stream, but the accept happens on the newly created acceptor stream. Thus, data structures need not be allocated for this stream, and the acknowledgment can be sent on the acceptor stream. As a result, sockfs need not become single-threaded at any time during the accept processing.

  The new model was carefully implemented because the new incoming connection (eager) exists only because there is a listener for it, and both eager and listener can disappear at any time during accept processing as a result of the eager receiving a reset or listener closing. The eager starts out by placing a reference on the listener so that the eager reference to the listener is always valid, even though the listener might close. When a connection indication needs to be sent after the three-way handshake is completed, the eager places a reference on itself so that it can close on receiving a reset, but any reference to it is still valid. The eager sends a pointer to itself as part of the connection indication message, which is sent through the listener's stream after checking that the listener has not closed. When the T_CONN_RES message comes down the newly created acceptor stream, we again enter the eager's perimeter and check that the eager has not closed because of receiving a reset before completing the accept processing. For applications based on TLI or XTI, the T_CONN_RES message is still handled on the listener's stream, and the acknowledgment is sent back on listener's stream, so there is no change in behavior.

- **close().** Close processing in TCP now does not have to wait until the reference count drops to zero, since references to the closing queue and references to TCP are now decoupled. close() can return as soon as all references to the closing queue are gone. In most cases, the TCP data structures can continue to stay around as a detached TCP. The release of the last reference to the TCP frees the TCP data structure. A user-initiated close closes only the stream. The underlying TCP structures may continue to stay around. The TCP then goes through the FIN/ACK exchange with the peer after all user data is transferred and enters the TIME_WAIT state, where it stays around for a certain duration. This kind of TCP is called a detached TCP. These detached TCPs also need protection to prevent outbound and inbound processing from occurring at the same time on a given detached TCP.

- **datapath.** TCP does not need to call IP to transmit the outbound packet in the most common case if it can access the IRE. With a merged TCP/IP we have the advantage of being able to access the cached IRE for a connection, and TCP can execute putnext() on the data directly to the link layer driver on the basis of information in the IRE. This is exactly what FireEngine does.

18.4.2 TCP Loopback

TCP Fusion is a nonprotocol data path for loopback TCP connections in Solaris 10. The fusion of two local TCP endpoints occurs when the connection is established. By default, all loopback TCP connections are fused. You can change this behavior by setting the systemwide tunable do_tcp_fusion to 0. For fusion to be successful, various conditions on both endpoints need to be met:

- They must share a common squeue.
- They must be TCP, and not raw sockets.
- They must not require protocol-level processing; that is, IPsec or IPQoS policy is not present for the connection.

If the fusion fails, we fall back to the regular TCP data path; if it succeeds, both endpoints use `tcp_fuse_output()` as the transmit path. `tcp_fuse_output()` queues application data directly onto the peer's receive queue; no protocol processing is involved. After queueing the data, the sender can either push—by calling `putnext()`—the data up the receiver's read queue. Or the sender can simply return and let the receiver retrieve the queued data through the synchronous STREAMS entry point. The latter path is taken if synchronous STREAMS is enabled. It is automatically disabled if sockfs no longer resides directly on top of the TCP module because a module was inserted or removed.

Locking in TCP Fusion is handled by the squeue and the mutex `tcp_fuse_lock`. One of the requirements for fusion to succeed is that both endpoints must be using the same squeue. This ensures that neither side can disappear while the other side is still sending data. By itself, the squeue is not sufficient for guaranteeing safe access when synchronous STREAMS is enabled. The reason is that `tcp_fuse_rrw()` doesn't enter the squeue, and its access to the `tcp_rcv_list` and other fusion-related fields needs to be synchronized with the sender. `tcp_fuse_lock` is used for this purpose.

Rate limit for small writes flow control for TCP Fusion in synchronous stream mode is achieved by checking the size of receive buffer and the number of data blocks, both set to different limits. This is different from regular STREAMS flow control, wherein cumulative size check dominates data block count check. Each queuing triggers notifications sent to the receiving process; a buildup of data blocks indicates a slow receiver, and the sender should be blocked or informed at the earliest moment instead of further wasting system resources. In effect, this is equivalent to limiting the number of outstanding segments in flight.

The minimum number of allowable queued data blocks defaults to 8 and is changeable with the systemwide tunable `tcp_fusion_burst_min` to either a higher value or to 0 (the latter disables the burst check).

18.5 UDP

Apart from the framework improvements, the Solaris 10 product contained additional changes in the UDP packet flow through the stack. The internal code name for the project was Yosemite. Before the Solaris 10 release, the UDP processing cost was evenly divided between per-packet processing cost and per-byte processing cost. The packet processing cost was generally due to STREAMS, the stream head processing, and packet drops in the stack and driver. The per-byte processing cost was due to lack of hardware checksum and unoptimized code branches throughout the network stack.

18.5.1 UDP Packet Drop within the Stack

Although UDP is supposed to be unreliable, local area networks (LANs) have become quite reliable, and applications tend to assume that there will be no packet loss in a LAN environment. This assumption was largely true, but the pre-Solaris 10 stack was not very effective in dealing with UDP overload and tended to drop packets within the stack itself.

With inbound flow, packets were dropped at more than one layer throughout the receive path. For UDP, the most common and obvious place was at the IP layer, which lacked the resources needed to queue the packets. Another important area of packet drops was at the network adapter layer. This type of drop was fairly common when the machine was dealing with a high rate of incoming packets.

The UDP sockfs extension (`sockudp`) is an alternative path to `socktpi` used for handling socket-based UDP applications. It provides a more direct channel between the application and the network stack by eliminating the stream head and TPI message-passing interface. This channel allows direct data and function access throughout the socket and transport layers. That way, the stack becomes more efficient and, coupled with UDP hardware checksum offload (even for fragmented UDP), ensures that UDP packets are rarely dropped within the stack.

18.5.2 UDP Module

In Solaris 10, a fully-multithreaded UDP module runs under the same protection domain as IP. Solaris 10 more tightly integrates transport (UDP) with the layers above and below it, allowing `socktpi` to make direct calls to UDP. Similarly UDP can also make direct calls to the data link layer. With the latest generic LAN driver (GLDv3, see Section 18.8), the data link layer can also directly call to the transport. In addition, utility functions can be called directly instead of from a message-based interface.

UDP needs exclusive operations on endpoints when executing functions that modify the endpoint state. The `udp_rput_other()` function deals with packets with IP options, and when processing these packets, ends up having to update the endpoint's option-related state. The `udp_wput_other()` function deals with control operations from the top, such as `connect()`, which need to update the endpoint state. In the STREAMS world this synchronization was achieved by means of shared inner-perimeter entry points and with `qwriter_inner()` to gain exclusive access to the endpoint.

The Solaris 10 model uses an internal, STREAMS-independent perimeter to achieve the above synchronization and is described below.

- **udp_enter()**. Enter the UDP endpoint perimeter.

- **udp_become_writer().** Become exclusive on the UDP endpoint. Specifies a function that will be called exclusively either immediately or later when the perimeter is available exclusively.
- **udp_exit().** Exit the UDP endpoint perimeter.

Entering UDP from the top or from the bottom must be done with udp_enter(). As in the general cases, no locks may be held across these perimeters. When the exclusive mode is no longer required, udp_exit() must be called to exit from the perimeter. To support this, the new UDP model employs two modes of operation: UDP MT HOT mode and UDP SQUEUE mode.

In the UDP MT HOT mode, multiple threads may enter a UDP endpoint concurrently. This mode is used for sending or receiving normal data and is similar to the putshared() STREAMS entry points. Control operations and other special cases call udp_become_writer() to become exclusive to an endpoint, and this results in a transition to the UDP SQUEUE mode. An squeue, by definition, serializes access to the conn_t structure. When no more messages are pending on the squeue for the UDP connection, the endpoint reverts to MT HOT mode. When not all of the MT threads of an endpoint have finished, messages are queued in the endpoint and the UDP is in one of two transient modes: UDP MT QUEUED or UDP QUEUED SQUEUE mode.

While in stable modes, UDP keeps track of the number of threads operating on the endpoint. The udp_reader_count variable represents the number of threads entering the endpoint as readers while it is in UDP MT HOT mode. Transitioning to UDP SQUEUE happens when there is only a single reader, that is, when the counter drops to 1. Likewise, udp_squeue_count represents the number of threads operating on the endpoint's squeue while it is in UDP SQUEUE mode. The mode transitions to UDP MT HOT after the last thread exits the endpoint.

Though UDP and IP are running in the same protection domain, they are still separate STREAMS modules. Therefore, STREAMS plumbing is kept unchanged, and a UDP module instance is always pushed above IP. Although this behavior causes an extra open and close for every UDP endpoint, it provides backward compatibility for some applications that rely on such plumbing geometry to do certain things, for example, issuing I POP on the stream to obtain direct access to IP9.

The actual UDP processing is done within the IP instance. The UDP module instance possesses no state about the endpoint and merely acts as a dummy module, whose presence keeps the STREAMS plumbing appearance unchanged.

Solaris 10 permits two plumbing modes:

- **Normal.** IP is opened first, and UDP is later pushed directly on top. This is the default action that occurs when a UDP socket or device is opened.
- **SNMP.** UDP is pushed on top of a module other than IP. When this happens, UDP supports only SNMP semantics.

These modes imply that we don't support any intermediate module between IP and UDP. But in fact, no Solaris release has ever supported such a scenario, because the interlayer communication semantics between IP and transport modules are private.

18.5.3 UDP and Socket Interaction

A significant event that takes place during the `socket()` system call is the plumbing of modules associated with the socket's address family and protocol type. A TCP or UDP socket will most likely result in sockfs residing directly on top of the corresponding transport module. Before the Solaris 10 release, the socket layer used STREAMS primitives to communicate with the UDP module. Solaris 10 OS allows for a functionally callable interface, which eliminates the need to use T UNITDATA REQ messages for metadata during each transmit from sockfs to UDP. Instead, data and its ancillary information (that is, remote socket address) is provided directly to an alternative UDP entry point, thereby avoiding the extra allocation cost.

Transport modules, being directly beneath sockfs, can use synchronous STREAMS. This enables the transport layer to buffer incoming data for later retrieval (through synchronous STREAMS) when a read operation is issued, thereby shortening the receive processing time.

18.6 Synchronous STREAMS

Synchronous STREAMS extends the traditional STREAMS interface for message passing and processing. It was originally added as part of the combined copy and checksum effort. It offers a way for the entry point of the module or driver to be called synchronously with respect to a user I/O request. In traditional STREAMS, the stream head is the synchronous barrier for such requests. Synchronous STREAMS provides a mechanism to move this barrier from the stream head to a module below.

18.6.1 TCP Synchronous STREAMS

The TCP implementation of synchronous STREAMS before the Solaris 10 release was complicated by several factors. A major factor was the combined checksum and copyin/copyout operations. In Solaris 10, TCP does not depend on checksum during copyin/copyout, so the mechanism was greatly simplified for use with loopback TCP and UDP on the read side. The synchronous STREAMS entry points are called during requests such as `read(2)` or `recv(3SOCKET)`. Instead of sending the data upstream with `putnext(9F)`, these modules queue the data in their internal receive queues and enable the send thread to return sooner. This avoids a call `strrput()` to queue the data at the stream head from within the send thread context, thus allowing better dynamics. In turn, the amount of time taken to queue and signal/poll-notify the receiving application is reduced, so the send thread returns faster to do further work; things are less serialized than before.

Each time data arrives, the transport module schedules the application to retrieve it. If the application is currently blocked (sleeping) during a read operation, it is unblocked so that it can resume execution. Unblocking is achieved by a call to `STR WAKEUP SET()` on the stream. Likewise, when no more data is available for the application, the transport module calls `STR WAKEUP CLEAR()` to block the application again during the next read attempt. Any new data that arrives before then will override this state and cause subsequent read operations to proceed.

An application can also be blocked in `poll(2)` until a read event occurs, or it may be waiting for a SIGPOLL or SIGIO signal if the socket used is nonblocking. Because of this, the transport module delivers the event notification or signals the application each time it receives data. It does this by calling `STR SENDSIG()` on the corresponding stream.

As part of the read operation, the transport module delivers data to the application by returning it from its read-side synchronous STREAMS entry point. In the case of loopback TCP, the synchronous STREAMS read entry point returns the entire content (byte stream) of its receive queue to the stream head. Any remaining data is requeued at the stream head, awaiting the next read. For UDP, the read entry point returns only one message (datagram) at a time.

18.6.2 STREAMS Fallback

By default, direct transmission and read-side synchronous STREAMS optimizations are enabled for all UDP and loopback TCP sockets when sockfs is directly above the corresponding transport module. Several cases require these features to be disabled. When such a case occurs, message exchange between sockfs and the transport module must then be done through `putnext(9F)`. The cases are described as follows.

- **Intermediate module.** A module is configured to be autopushed at open time on top of the transport module by `autopush(1M)` or is I PUSH'd on a socket by `ioctl(2)`.

- **Stream conversion.** The imaginary sockmod module is I_POP'd from a socket, causing it to be converted from a socket endpoint to a device stream. (Note that I INSERT or I REMOVE ioctl is not permitted on a socket endpoint, and therefore a fallback is not required to handle it.)

If a fallback is required, sockfs notifies the transport module that direct mode is disabled. The notification is sent down by the sockfs module in the form of an ioctl message, which indicates to the transport module that `putnext(9F)` must now be used to deliver data upstream. This scheme enables data to flow through the intermediate module and provides compatibility with device stream semantics.

18.7 IP

As mentioned before, all the transport layers have been merged in the IP module, which is fully multithreaded and acts as a pseudo device driver as well a STREAMS module. The key change in IP was the removal of IP client functionality and the multiplexing of the inbound packet stream. The new IP classifier (which is still part of the IP module) classifies the inbound packets to the correct connection instance. The IP module is still responsible for network layer protocol processing and plumbing and managing the network interfaces.

Let's quickly look at how plumbing of network interfaces, multipathing, and multicast works in the new stack. The table below describes the data types referenced in the following section, some of which have been discussed earlier in the chapter, but are included here for completeness. The structure definitions can be found in `usr/src/uts/common/inet/ip.h`.

Table 18.1 Network Interface Structure Types and Names

Name/Type	Description
`ill` / `ill_t`	The structure associated with a physical NIC interface
`ipif` / `ipif_t`	The logical interface, associated with an `ill`
`ire` / `ire_t`	Internet route entry. Contains the information to get the packet to its correct destination, including the correct physical interface
`ilg` / `ilg_t`	Maintains the state of multicast addresses associated with a socket (and network communication endpoint)
`ilm` / `ilm_t`	Maintains the state of multicast addresses associated with a physical interface (NIC)

18.7.1 Plumbing NICs

Plumbing is a long sequence of operations involving message exchanges between IP, Address Resolution Protocol (ARP), and device drivers. Set `ioctl()` calls are typically involved in plumbing operations. A natural model is to serialize these ioctls. For example, plumbing of hme0 and qfe0 can go on in parallel without any interference, but various set ioctls on hme0 will all be serialized.

Another possibility is to refine even further and serialize operations for the virtual interface (ipif) rather than the physical interface (ill). This will be beneficial only if many ipifs are hosted on an interface and if the operations on different ipifs don't interfere with one another. Another possibility is to completely multithread all ioctls with standard Solaris multithreading techniques, but this is needlessly complex and does not add much value. It is hard to hold locks across the entire plumbing sequence, which involves waits and message exchanges with drivers or other modules.

Not much is gained in performance or functionality by simultaneously allowing multiple set ioctls on an ipif at the same time, since these are purely nonrepetitive control operations. Broadcast ires are created for each ill rather than for each ipif. Hence, trying to start more than one ipif simultaneously on an ill involves extra complexity in the broadcast ire creation logic. On the other hand, serializing plumbing operations for each ill lends itself easily to the existing IP code base. During the course of plumbing, IP exchanges messages with the device driver and ARP. The messages received from the underlying device driver are also handled exclusively in IP. This is convenient since we can't hold standard mutex locks across the putnext() in trying to provide mutual exclusion between the write-side and read-side activities. Instead of the all-exclusive PERMOD syncq, this effect can be easily achieved by a per-ill serialization queue.

18.7.2 IP Network Multipathing

IP network multipathing (IPMP) operations are all driven around the notion of an IPMP group. Failover and failback operations operate between two ills, usually part of the same IPMP group. The ipifs and ilms are moved between the ills. This move involves shutting down the source ill and could involve starting up the destination ill. Shutting down or starting up ills affects broadcast ires. Broadcast ires need to be grouped as an IPMP group to suppress duplicate broadcast packets that are received. Thus, broadcast ire manipulation affects all members of the IPMP group. Setting IFF_FAILED or IFF_STANDBY causes evaluation of all ills in the IPMP group and causes regrouping of broadcast ires. Thus, serializing IPMP operations for each IPMP group lends itself easily to the existing code base. An IPMP group includes both the IPv4 and IPv6 ills.

18.7.3 Multicast

Multicast joins operate on both the ilg and ilm structures. Multiple threads operating on an Interprocess Communication (IPC) socket, trying to do multicast joins, need to synchronize when operating on the ilg. Multiple threads (potentially operating on different socket endpoints) trying to do multicast joins could eventually end up trying to manipulate the `ilm` simultaneously and need to synchronize on the access to the `ilm`. Both are amenable to standard Solaris mutlithreading techniques. Considering all the above—plumbing, IPMP, and multicast—the common denominator is to serialize all the exclusive operations for each IPMP group. If IPMP is not enabled, then serialize on a physical interface. For example, `hme0 v4` and `hme0 v6 ills` taken together share a physical interface NIC. In the above, multicast has a potentially higher degree of multithreading. But it has to coexist with other exclusive operations. For example, we don't want a thread to create or delete an `ilm` when a failover operation is already trying to move `ilms` between two `ills`. So the lowest common denominator is to serialize multicast joins for the physical interface or for each IPMP group.

18.8 Solaris Device Driver Framework

Let's quickly look at how network device drivers were implemented before Solaris 10 and why they needed to change with the new Solaris 10 stack.

18.8.1 GLDv2 and DLPI Drivers (Solaris 9 and Prior)

Before the Solaris 10 release, the network stack depends on Data-Link Provider Interface (DLPI1) providers, which are normally implemented in one of two ways. Figure 18.5 illustrates two stacks: one based on a monolithic DLPI driver and one based on a driver utilizing the generic LAN driver (GLDv2) module.

The GLDv2 module essentially behaves like a library. The client still talks to the driver instance bound to the device, but the DLPI protocol processing is handled by a call into the GLDv2 module, which then calls back into the driver to access the

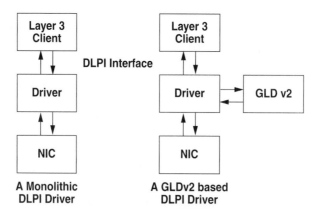

Figure 18.5 GLDv2 and DLPI Stacks

hardware. Using the GLD module has a clear advantage in that the driver writer need not reimplement large amounts of mostly generic DLPI protocol processing. Layer 2 (Data-Link) features such as 802.1q virtual LANs (VLANs) can also be implemented centrally in the GLD module, where they can be leveraged by all drivers. The architecture still poses a problem, though, with respect to implementing features such as 802.3ad link aggregation (a.k.a. trunking) where the one-to-one correspondence between network interface and device is broken.

Both GLDv2 and monolithic drivers depend on DLPI messages and communicate with upper layers through the STREAMS framework. This mechanism was relatively ineffective for link aggregation or 10-Gbit NICs. With the new stack, we needed a better mechanism that could ensure data locality and allow the stack to control the device drivers at much finer granularity to deal with interrupts.

18.8.2 A New Architecture: GLDv3

The Solaris 10 release introduced a new device driver framework called GLDv3 (internal name project Nemo) along with the new stack. Most of the major device drivers were ported to this framework, and all future and 10-Gbit device drivers will be based on this framework. This framework also provided a STREAMS-based DLPI layer for backward compatibility (to allow external, non-IP modules to continue to work).

The GLDv3 architecture virtualizes layer 2 of the network stack. There is no longer a one-to-one correspondence between network interfaces and devices. Figure 18.6

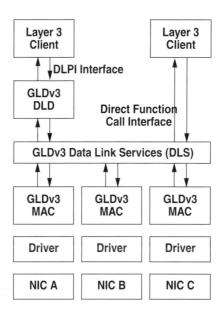

Figure 18.6 GLDv3 Architecture

shows multiple devices registered with a MAC Services (MAC) module. It also
shows two clients: one traditional client that communicates through DLPI to a
data-link driver (DLD) and a kernel-based client that simply makes direct function calls into the Data-Link Services (DLS) module.

18.8.2.1 GLDv3 Drivers

GLDv3 drivers are similar to GLD drivers. The driver must be linked with a dependency on the misc/mac and misc/dld kernel modules. It must call `mac_register()`
with a pointer to an instance of the following structure to register with the MAC
module.

```
typedef struct mac {
        const char      *m_ident;      /* MAC_IDENT */
        mac_ext_t       *m_extp;
        mac_impl_t      *m_impl;        /* MAC private data */
        void            *m_driver;      /* Driver private data */
        dev_info_t      *m_dip;
        uint_t          m_port;
        mac_info_t      m_info;
        mac_stat_t      m_stat;
        mac_start_t     m_start;
        mac_stop_t      m_stop;
        mac_promisc_t   m_promisc;
        mac_multicst_t  m_multicst;
        mac_unicst_t    m_unicst;
        mac_resources_t m_resources;
        mac_ioctl_t     m_ioctl;
        mac_tx_t        m_tx;
} mac_t;
```
                                              See usr/src/uts/common/sys/mac.h

This structure must persist for the lifetime of the registration, that is, it cannot be
deallocated until after `mac_unregister()` is called. A GLDv3 driver `_init(9E)`
entry point is also required to call `mac_init_ops()` before calling `mod_
install(9F)`, and they are required to call `mac_fini_ops()` after calling `mod_
remove(9F)` from `_fini(9E)`.

The following are important members of the `mac_t` structure:

- **m_impl.** This field is used by the MAC module to point to its private data. It
  must not be read or modified by a driver.
- **m_driver.** This field should be set by the driver to point to its private data.
  This value is supplied as the first argument to the driver entry points.
- **m_dip.** This field must be set to the `dev_info_t` pointer of the driver
  instance calling `mac_register()`.

Key MAC layer functions include the following:

- **m_stat().** Entry point that retrieves a value for one of the statistics defined in the mac_stat_t enumeration (below). All values are stored and returned in 64-bit unsigned integers. Values are not requested for statistics that the driver has not explicitly declared to be supported.

- **m_start().** Entry point that brings the device out of the reset/quiesced state it was in when the interface was registered. No packets are submitted by the MAC module for transmission, and no packets are submitted by the driver for reception before this call is made. If this function succeeds, then zero is returned. If it fails, then an appropriate errno value is returned.

- **m_stop().** Entry point that stops the device and puts it in a reset/quiesced state such that the interface can be unregistered. No packets are submitted by the MAC for transmission once this call has been made, and no packets are submitted by the driver for reception once it has completed.

- **m_promisc().** Entry point that sets the promiscuity of the device. If the second argument is B_TRUE, then the device receives all packets on the media. If it is set to B_FALSE, then only packets destined for the device's unicast address and the media broadcast address are received.

- **m_multicst().** Entry point that adds and removes addresses to and from the set of multicast addresses for which the device will receive packets. If the second argument is B_TRUE, then the address pointed to by the third argument is added to the set. If the second argument is B_FALSE, then the address pointed to by the third argument is removed.

- **m_unicst().** Entry point that sets a new device unicast address. Once this call is made, then only packets with the new address and the media broadcast address are received unless the device is in promiscuous mode.

- **m_resources().** Entry point that requests that the driver register its individual receive resources or RX rings.

- **m_tx().** Entry point that submits packets for transmission by the device. The second argument points to one or more packets contained in mblk_t structures. Fragments of the same packet are linked by the b_cont field. Separate packets are linked by the b_next field in the leading fragment. Packets are scheduled for transmission in the order in which they appear in the chain. Any remaining chain of packets that cannot be scheduled is returned. If m_tx() returns packets that cannot be scheduled, the driver must call mac_tx_update() when resources become available. If all packets are scheduled for transmission, then NULL is returned.

- **m_info.** An embedded structure defined as follows:

```
typedef struct mac_info_s {
        uint_t          mi_media;
        uint_t          mi_sdu_min;
        uint_t          mi_sdu_max;
        uint32_t        mi_cksum;
        uint32_t        mi_poll;
        uint_t          mi_addr_length;
        uint8_t         mi_unicst_addr[MAXADDRLEN];
        uint8_t         mi_brdcst_addr[MAXADDRLEN];
        boolean_t       mi_stat[MAC_NSTAT];
} mac_info_t;
```
                                        See usr/src/uts/common/sys/mac.h

Where:

- `mi_media` is set to the media type.

- `mi_sdu_min` is the minimum payload size.

- `mi_sdu_max` is the maximum payload size.

- `mi_cksum` details the device checksum capabilities flag.

- `mi_poll` details if the driver supports polling.

- `mi_addr_length` is set to the length of the addresses used by the media.

- `mi_unicst_addr` is set with the unicast address of the device at the point at which `mac_register()` is called.

- `mi_brdcst_addr` is set to the broadcast address of the media.

- `mi_stat` is an array of boolean values, defined in the `mac.h` header file.

The macros `MAC_MIB_SET()`, `MAC_ETHER_SET()`, and `MAC_MII_SET()` set all the values in each of the three groups respectively to `B_TRUE`.

18.8.2.2 MAC Services Module

The driver support functions of the interfaces described in this section are intended to be used by GLDv3 driver developers.

```
typedef void (*mac_blank_t)(void *, time_t, uint_t);
typedef mblk_t *(*mac_poll_t)(void *, unit_t);
typedef enum {
      MAC_RX_FIFO = 1
} mac_resource_type_t;

typedef struct mac_rx_fifo_s {
        mac_resource_type_t     mrf_type;       /* MAC_RX_FIFO */
        mac_blank_t             mrf_blank;
        void                    *mrf_arg;
        time_t                  mrf_normal_blank_time;
        uint_t                  mrf_normal_pkt_count;
} mac_rx_fifo_t;
```

continues

```
typedef struct mac_txinfo_s {
        mac_tx_t                    mt_fn;
        void                        *mt_arg;
} mac_txinfo_t;

typedef union mac_resource_u {
        mac_resource_type_t         mr_type;
        mac_rx_fifo_t               mr_fifo;
} mac_resource_t;

typedef mac_resource_handle_t   (*mac_resource_add_t)(void *, mac_resource_t *);
usr/src/uts/common/sys/mac.h
```

The mac_resource_add() function should be called from the m_resources()
entry point to register individual receive resources (commonly, ring buffers of DMA
descriptors) with the MAC module. The returned mac_resource_handle_t value
should then be supplied in calls to mac_rx(). The second argument to mac_
resource_add() specifies the resource being added. Resources are specified by
the mac_resource_t structure. Currently, only resources of type MAC_RX_FIFO
are supported. MAC_RX_FIFO resources are described by the mac_rx_fifo_t
structure.

The upper layers use the mac_blank() function to control the interrupt rate of
the device. The first argument is the device context that is to be used as the first
argument to the poll_blank() function.

The fields mrf_normal_blank_time and mrf_normal_pkt_cnt specify the
default interrupt interval and packet count threshold, respectively. These parameters can be the second and third arguments to mac_blank() when the upper layer
wants the driver to revert to the default interrupt rate.

The interrupt rate is controlled by the upper layer by a call to poll_blank()
with different arguments. The interrupt rate can be increased or decreased: the
upper layer passes a multiple of these values to the last two arguments of mac_
blank(). Setting these values to zero disables the interrupts, and the NIC is
deemed to be in polling mode.

mac_poll() is the driver-supplied function used by upper layers to retrieve a
chain of packets (up to max count, specified by the second argument) from the RX
ring corresponding to the earlier supplied mrf_arg during mac_resource_add()
(supplied as first argument to mac_poll()).

The function mac_resource_update() is invoked by the driver when available resources have changed.

The function mac_rx() function delivers a chain of packets, contained in mblk_
t structures, for reception. The b_cont field links fragments of the same packet.
The b_next field of the leading fragment links separate packets. If the packet
chain was received by a registered resource, then the appropriate mac_resource_
handle_t value should be supplied as the second argument to the function. The

protocol stack uses this value as a hint when trying to load-spread across multiple CPUs. It is assumed that packets belonging to the same flow are always received by the same resource. If the resource is unknown or is unregistered, then NULL should be passed as the second argument.

18.8.2.3 Data-Link Services Module

The Data-Link Services (DLS) module provides the Data-Link Services interface analogous to DLPI. The DLS interface is a kernel-level functional interface, as opposed to the STREAMS message-based interface specified by DLPI. This module provides the interfaces necessary for the upper layer to create and destroy a data link service. It also provides the interfaces necessary to plumb and unplumb the NIC. The plumbing and unplumbing of an NIC for GLDv3-based device drivers is unchanged from the older GLDv2 or monolithic DLPI device drivers. The major changes are in data paths that allow direct calls, packet chains, and much finer-grained control over an NIC.

18.8.2.4 Data-Link Driver

The Data-Link Driver (DLD) provides a DLPI by using interfaces from the DLS and MAC modules. The driver is configured by ioctls passed to a control node. These ioctls create and destroy separate DLPI provider nodes. This module deals with DLPI messages necessary to plumb and unplumb the NIC and affords backward compatibility for the data path through STREAMS for non-GLDv3-aware clients.

18.8.3 GLDv3 Link Aggregation Architecture

The GLDv3 framework supports link aggregation as defined by IEEE 802.3ad. The key principles governing the design of this facility are these:

- Allow GLDv3 MAC drivers to be aggregated without code change.
- Preserve the performance of nonaggregated devices.
- Keep overhead due to aggregation to a minimum. That is, the performance of aggregated devices should be the cumulative line rate for each member.
- Support both manual configuration and the Link Aggregation Control Protocol (LACP).

GLDv3 link aggregation is implemented by means of a pseudo-driver called aggr. It registers virtual ports corresponding to link aggregation groups with the GLDv3 MAC layer. It uses the client interface provided by the MAC layer to control and communicate with aggregated MAC ports as illustrated in Figure 18.7. It also exports a pseudo aggr device driver that the dladm(1M) command uses to configure and control the link-aggregated interface. Once a MAC port is configured to be part of a link aggregation group, it cannot be simultaneously accessed by other MAC clients such as the DLS layer. The exclusive access is enforced by the MAC layer. The implementation of LACP is implemented by the aggr driver, which has access to individual MAC ports or links.

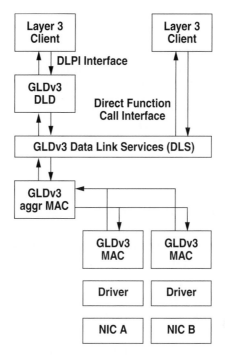

Figure 18.7 GLDv3 Link Aggregation Architecture

The GLDv3 aggr driver acts as a normal MAC module to the upper layer and appears as a standard NIC interface which, once created with dladm(1M), can be configured and managed by the ifconfig(1M) command. The aggr module registers each MAC port that is part of the aggregation with the upper layer by using the mac_resource_add() function, such that the data paths and interrupts from each MAC port can be independently managed by the upper layers (see Section 18.9.2).

In short, the aggregated interface is managed as a single interface with possibly one IP address, and the data paths are managed as individual NICs by unique CPUs and squeues. This management scheme gives aggregation capability to Solaris 10 with near zero overhead and linear scalability with respect to the number of MAC ports that are part of the aggregation group.

18.8.4 Checksum Offload

Solaris 10 improved the hardware checksum offload capability further to improve overall performance for most applications. A 16-bit, one's complement, checksum offload framework has existed in Solaris for some time. It was originally added as a requirement for Zero Copy TCP/IP in the Solaris 2.6 release but was only recently extended to handle other protocols. Solaris 10 defines two classes of checksum offload:

- **Full.** Complete checksum calculation in the hardware, including pseudo-header checksum computation for TCP and UDP packets. The hardware is assumed to be able to parse protocol headers.
- **Partial.** Dumb one's complement checksum based on start, end, and stuff offsets describing the span of the checksummed data and the location of the transport checksum field, with no pseudo-header calculation ability in the hardware.

Adding support for nonfragmented IPV4 cases (unicast or multicast) is trivial for both transmit and receive since most modern network adapters support either class of checksum offload with minor differences in the interface. The IPV6 cases are not as straightforward, because very few full-checksum network adapters can handle checksum calculation for TCP/UDP packets over IPV64.

The fragmented IP cases have similar constraints. On transmit, checksumming applies to the unfragmented datagram. An adapter that is to support checksum offload must be able to buffer all the IP fragments (or perform the fragmentation in hardware) before finally calculating the checksum and sending the fragments over the wire; until then, checksum offloading for outbound IP fragments cannot be done. On the other hand, the receive fragment reassembly case is more flexible since most full-checksum (and all partial-checksum) network adapters can compute and provide the checksum value to the network stack. During the fragment reassembly stage, the network stack can derive the checksum status of the unfragmented datagram by combining all the values.

Things are simplified by not offloading the checksum when the IP option is present. For partial-checksum offload, certain adapters limit the start offset to a width sufficient for simple IP packets. When the length of protocol headers exceeds such a limit (because certain options are present), the start offset wraps around, causing an incorrect calculation. For full-checksum offload, none of the capable adapters correctly handle the IPV4 source routing option.

When transmit checksum offload takes place, the network stack associates eligible packets with ancillary information needed by the driver to offload the checksum computation to hardware.

In the inbound case, the driver has full control over the packets that become associated with hardware-calculated checksum values. Once a driver advertises its capability through DL CAPAB HCKSUM, the network stack accepts full- or partial-checksum information for IPV4 and IPV6 packets. This process happens for both nonfragmented and fragmented payloads.

Fragmented packets first need to be reassembled because checksum validation happens for fully reassembled datagrams. During reassembly, the network stack combines the hardware-calculated checksum value of each fragment.

18.9 Interrupt Model and NIC Speeds

Any discussion about networking in a modern operating system is incomplete without talking about the way in which the stack deals with incoming packets (receive) and about the interrupts resulting from them.

18.9.1 Solaris 9 and Earlier Releases

When the 100-Mbit speed was common, the bulk of inbound packet processing was done in the interrupt context. In a typical server doing heavy transmit, writes from an application queue data in the TCP transmit queue and the data is actually sent out when incoming ACKs open the congestion window (known as ACK-driven transmit). The ACKs themselves are processed by the interrupt thread, which also checks that the congestion window has opened and transmits any queued data. On a 100-Mbit Ethernet, this approach had two advantages: it provided extra cache locality to the data structures (since packets for a particular connection land on the same CPU and are processed on the same CPU) and there was no thread-switching overhead, resulting in better performance.

When the 1-Gbit NICs arrived in the Solaris 8 time frame, processor speeds lagged the NIC and were no longer capable of driving the NIC; the time spent processing network interrupts began to starve other system activities. This also resulted in some pathological cases in which the interrupted CPU would become 100% busy while other CPUs were mostly idle and the system became live-locked.

To get around this problem, the 1-Gbit NICs in the Solaris 8 and 9 releases adhered to a worker thread model, in which they used one or more worker threads to spread the work across several CPUs instead of sending the packet to IP in interrupt context. To avoid excessive D-cache misses with packets for the same connections landing on different CPUs, the driver did a simple hash computation on source IP address to assign a packet to a particular worker thread. It helped the scalability, but single CPU performance degraded because of the extra context switching involved: computation of an additional hash and the worker threads themselves migrating across CPUs.

The device driver became increasingly complex and burdened with decisions better left for the higher layers. The device driver had no good means of figuring out how many worker threads it should use to spread out the load. Worker threads based on number of CPUs on the system created chaos when multiple NICs became active on the same system with the same policy. The arrival of 10-Gbit NICs made matters worse because the packet size on the Internet was still 1500 bytes, resulting in potentially 80,000 packets per second at line rate and leaving the processor about 12 μsec to process each packet while doing useful work.

18.9.2 Dynamic Switch between Interrupt vs. Polling Mode

The popularity of 10-Gbit NICs is increasing in the data center because, apart from throughput, 10-Gbit NICs simplify the data center wiring and offer better latencies. To handle the interrupt load from a 10-Gbit NIC, the NIC vendors use interrupt coalescing schemes, by which they interrupt the CPU according to either n number of packets received or t time elapsed. This scheme was employed by several 1-Gbit NICs as well. It suffers from the fact that under lower load, when interrupts are firing based on time t elapsing, the latencies are poor, and under higher load, the system suddenly goes through an interrupt storm or longer interrupt processing time, resulting in application threads getting pinned by interrupts.

The problem is not as acute with 1-Gbit NICs (with current processor speed of 1 GHz and more), but performance still suffers. The NIC interrupts the CPU on the basis of its local policies, preempting the current thread and causing unnecessary context switches, lock contention, thread migration, etc. In most cases, the packet delivered can't be immediately processed because the squeue is busy, resulting in packets queuing on the squeue.

The Solaris 10 stack simplified device driver writing once again by unburdening the device driver from handling interrupt frequency and load spreading. The new GLDv3 framework allows the device to be tied to an squeue of the interrupted CPU. The squeue controls the interrupt frequency or switches the device into a polling mode.

As discussed earlier, the squeue is a common FIFO for both inbound and outbound packets, and only one thread is allowed to process it at any given time. As such, the per-CPU backlog is easy to figure out. If packets are queued, the squeue can switch the NIC associated with it from interrupt to polling mode, as illustrated in Figure 18.8. The NIC stops interrupting the CPU, and the squeue moveg packets from the NIC to the squeue from time to time. The move is done for the entire chain instead of the usual interrupt per packet. The NIC is essentially in polling mode at this point.

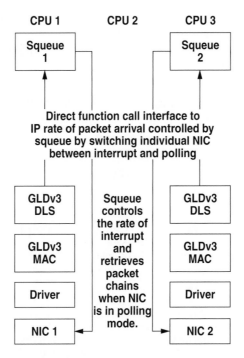

Figure 18.8 NIC Mode Switching

If the squeue finds that it has no packets to process and the NIC also has nothing queued in the ring buffer, it switches the NIC back to interrupt mode and the squeue worker thread goes back to sleep. As long as the NIC's interrupt can process its packet without queuing on the squeue, the NIC continues to be in interrupt mode. In other words, as long as the interarrival rate of packets is more than the processing time, the NIC continues to be in interrupt mode and the packets are processed in the interrupt context.

This scheme creates a powerful mechanism for processing incoming packets without putting the complexity in the device driver. The overall system performance improves significantly because interrupts are not clashing with system and application threads, lock contention, and the like.

The scheme also significantly boosts performance and helps improve latency because the system can cope with incoming packets and switch to throughput mode when a backlog builds. Since the system does this in milliseconds, it can deal with bursts very effectively.

18.9.3 Interrupt Load Spreading

The ability of a GLDv3-based device driver to dynamically switch between interrupt and polling mode helps boost both 1-Gbit and 10-Gbit NIC performance. It also ensures that a system will never suffer from the interrupt live-lock problem. But this mechanism by itself doesn't spread the load to multiple CPUs when they are available. For that purpose, GLDv3 provides a soft ring facility that is controlled by IP. Basically, IP asks the GLDv3 device driver to create n number of soft rings, each of which has its own worker threads to deliver the packets to IP. The soft ring worker threads are bound to same squeue (CPU) that owns the soft ring. The NIC still interrupts the CPU as needed, but very early, the packets are sent to one of the soft rings according to load spreading policies (hash of src IP address, for example). The ring is controlled by some squeue that either pulls the packet chain from the ring (the poll mode) or lets the ring send the packet up (the interrupt mode), as illustrated in Figure 18.9.

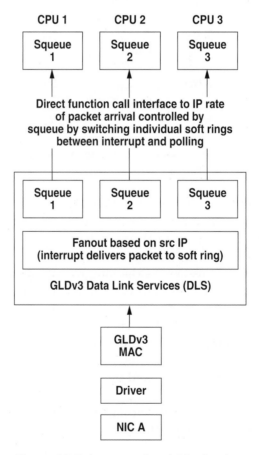

Figure 18.9 Interrupt Load Distribution

The stack accounts for hardware features such as multiple core processors or hardware hyperthreading, and hyperthreading for multiple cores. The soft rings are controlled by squeues of hardware strands on the same core if possible, giving better cache affinity.

18.10 Summary

Networking in the Solaris 10 product underwent significant change to facilitate the loading characteristics of the Internet age and to effectively use modern network interfaces. The changes involved work up and down the network stack, with the new implementation of the TCP/IP layer (FireEngine), a new UDP layer (Yosemite), and a new Generic Lan Driver (GLD) layer (GLDv3, or Nemo).

18.11 MDB Reference

Table 18.2 Networking MDB Reference

Module	`dcmd` or `walker`	Description
genunix		
	`walk ip_minor_1`	Walk the ip_minor_1 cache
	`walk ip_minor_arena_1`	Walk the ip_minor_arena_1 cache
	`walk ipcl_conn_cache`	Walk the ipcl_conn_cache cache
	`walk ipcl_tcpconn_cache`	Walk the ipcl_tcpconn_cache cache
	`walk ipp_action`	Walk the ipp_action cache
	`walk ipp_mod`	Walk the ipp_mod cache
	`walk ipp_packet`	Walk the ipp_packet cache
	`walk ipsec_actions`	Walk the ipsec_actions cache
	`walk ipsec_info`	Walk the ipsec_info cache
	`walk ipsec_policy`	Walk the ipsec_policy cache
	`walk ipsec_selectors`	Walk the ipsec_selectors cache
	`walk sctp_assoc`	Walk the sctp_assoc cache
	`walk sctp_conn_cache`	Walk the sctp_conn_cache cache
	`walk sctp_faddr_cache`	Walk the sctp_faddr_cache cache
	`walk sctp_ftsn_set_cache`	Walk the sctp_ftsn_set_cache cache

continues

Table 18.2 Networking MDB Reference (*continued*)

Module	dcmd or walker	Description
	walk sctp_set_cache	Walk the sctp_set_cache cache
	walk sctpsock	Walk the sctpsock cache
	walk tcp_iphc_cache	Walk the tcp_iphc_cache cache
	walk tcp_sack_info_cache	Walk the tcp_sack_info_cache cache
	walk tcp_timercache	Walk the tcp_timercache cache
	walk udp_cache	Walk the udp_cache cache
ip		
	dcmd illif	Display or filter IP Lower Level InterFace structures
	dcmd ip6hdr	Display an IPv6 header
	dcmd iphdr	Display an IPv4 header
	dcmd ire	Display Internet Route Entry structures
	dcmd sctphdr	Display an SCTP header
	dcmd squeue	Print core squeue_t info
	dcmd tcphdr	Display a TCP header
	dcmd udphdr	Display an UDP header
	walk illif	Walk list of ill interface types
	walk ire	Walk active ire_t structures
nca		
	dcmd nca_conn	Print core NCA nca_conn_t info
	dcmd nca_io2	Print core NCA io2_t info
	dcmd nca_node	Print core NCA node_t info
	dcmd nca_tcpconn	Print TCP NCA nca_conn_t info
	dcmd nca_timer	Print core NCA timer info
	walk nca_conn_bind	Walk the NCA connection bind chain
	walk nca_conn_hash	Walk the NCA connection hash chain
	walk nca_conn_miss	Walk the NCA connection miss chain
	walk nca_conn_tw	Walk the NCA connection TIME_WAIT chain
	walk nca_connf	Walk the NCA connection fanout
	walk nca_cpu	Walk the NCA CPU table

continues

Table 18.2 Networking MDB Reference (*continued*)

Module	`dcmd` or `walker`	Description
	walk nca_ctag_hash	Walk the NCA ctag node hash table
	walk nca_file_hash	Walk the NCA file node hash table
	walk nca_node_chunk	Walk the NCA node chunk chain
	walk nca_node_ctag	Walk the NCA node ctag chain
	walk nca_node_file	Walk the NCA node file chain
	walk nca_node_hash	Walk the NCA node hash chain
	walk nca_node_plru	Walk the NCA node physical LRU chain
	walk nca_node_vlru	Walk the NCA node virtual LRU chain
	walk nca_timer	Walk the NCA timer table
	walk nca_uri_hash	Walk the NCA URI node hash table
	walk nca_vnode_hash	Walk the NCA vnode node hash table
sctp		
	dcmd sctp	Display sctp control structure
	dcmd sctp_faddr	Display a faddr
	dcmd sctp_instr	Display instr
	dcmd sctp_istr_msgs	Display msg list on an instream
	dcmd sctp_mdata_chunk	Display a data chunk in an mblk
	dcmd sctp_reass_list	Display reass list
	dcmd sctp_set	Display a SCTP set
	dcmd sctp_uo_reass_list	Display un-ordered reass list
	dcmd sctp_xmit_list	Display sctp xmit lists
	walk sctp_bind_fanout	Walk the sctp bind fanout
	walk sctp_conn_fanout	Walk the sctp conn fanout
	walk sctp_listen_fanout	Walk the sctp listen fanout
	walk sctp_walk_faddr	Walk the peer address list of a given sctp_t
	walk sctp_walk_ill	Walk the sctp_g_ills list
	walk sctp_walk_ipif	Walk the sctp_g_ipif list
	walk sctp_walk_saddr	Walk the local address list of a given sctp_t
	walk sctps	Walk the full chain of sctps

continues

Table 18.2 Networking MDB Reference (*continued*)

Module	dcmd or walker	Description
sppp		
	dcmd sppa	Display PPP attachment state structures
	dcmd sppp	Display PPP stream state structures
	dcmd tuncl	Display sppptun client stream state structures
	dcmd tunll	Display sppptun lower stream state structures
	walk sppa	Walk active sppa_t structures
	walk sppp	Walk active spppstr_t structures
	walk tuncl	Walk active tuncl_t structures
	walk tunll	Walk active tunll_t structures

PART EIGHT

Kernel Services

Clocks and Timers

In this chapter, we discuss the central facilities related to time and time-based events scheduling.

19.1 The System Clock Thread

The Solaris clock thread performs routine processing as a lock-level client of the cyclic subsystem (Section 19.4). For example, it triggers the dispatcher to recalculate thread priorities at regular intervals, and also initiates callout queue processing. Figure 19.1 shows the interaction between the system timing interfaces and subsystems.

The kernel installs a cyclic to call the clock thread at regular intervals, by default 100 times per second. With each clock interrupt, a handler is entered. It performs the following functions:

- Sets available kernel anon space (anon_free) value, for tracking and reporting.
- Sets free memory (freemem) value, for tracking and reporting.
- Adjusts the time-of-day clock for possible jitter.
- Calculates system dispatch (run queue) queue size.
- Does clock-tick processing for the thread running on the CPU (except the CPU running the clock interrupt thread) and threads that are exiting. Note

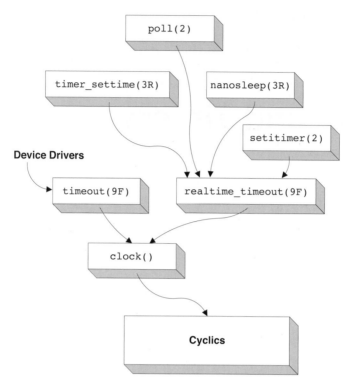

Figure 19.1 Clock and Timer Interactions

that kernel threads that do not have an associated LWP—that is, kernel service threads that are an integral part of the operating system—are not subject to tick processing.

- Updates the lbolt counter. lbolt counts the number of clock ticks since boot.
- Processes the kernel callout table (described in Section 19.2).
- Wakes up any threads waiting for the kernel cage resize.
- If on a one-second interval, calculates kernel swap parameters (free, reserved, and allocated swap) and adjusts systemwide run queue size and swap queue size.

Once the clock interrupt handling is completed, the clock interrupt thread is context-switched off the processor, and the thread that was executing when the interrupt occurred resumes.

19.1.1 Thread Tick Processing

Tick processing is done for each kernel thread (if that thread is not an interrupt handler or an operating system kernel thread) running on a CPU. The kernel determines whether it is necessary to do tick processing for a thread by comparing the thread's t_lbolt with lbolt.

```
if ((!thread_away) && (lbolt - t->t_lbolt != 0)) {
        t->t_lbolt = lbolt;
        clock_tick(t);
}
```

The clock_tick() code is passed the kernel thread ID and invokes the scheduling-class-specific clock-tick function, that is, ts_tick() for timeshare and interactive class threads and rt_tick() for real-time class threads. These functions are discussed in "Real-Time Tick Processing." on page 229. Briefly, the functions determine if the thread has used up its time quantum, and they take the thread off the processor if it has. Back in the clock_tick() function, the following actions are performed:

- The user or system time values in the process and the LWP are incremented, depending on the mode the thread is in (system or user). Note that if a thread is executing in short bursts between clock samples, not all CPU time will be accounted for. User-based tools have been updated to avoid using these tick-based user or system times; instead they will now source microstate accounting data.

- The per-thread interval timers are tested (profiling and virtual timer, enabled with the setitimer(2) system call), and the appropriate signal—SIGPROF or SIGVTALRM—is sent if either timer has expired.

- The per-process CPU resource control limits are checked (maximum CPU seconds the process or project can consume).

- The process memory usage is updated in the uarea u_mem, which reflects the total address space size of the process.

The update completes the clock-tick processing for the thread.

19.1.2 DTrace Providers for Tick Processing

Some DTrace static probes are part of the `sched` provider.

```
# dtrace -l -n 'sched:::' |grep tick
  2870       sched          genunix                            clock_tick tick
 12666       sched              TS                               ts_tick schedctl-nopreempt
 30273       sched              FX                               fx_tick schedctl-nopreempt
```

The `sched` tick probe fires as a part of clock-tick-based accounting. In clock-tick-based accounting, CPU accounting is performed by examination of the threads and processes running when a fixed-interval interrupt fires. The `lwpsinfo_t` that corresponds to the thread that is being assigned CPU time is pointed to by `args[0]`. The `psinfo_t` that corresponds to the process that contains the thread is pointed to by `args[1]`.

```
typedef struct psinfo {
        int       pr_nlwp;              /* number of active lwps in the process */
        pid_t     pr_pid;              /* unique process id */
        pid_t     pr_ppid;             /* process id of parent */
        pid_t     pr_pgid;             /* pid of process group leader */
        pid_t     pr_sid;              /* session id */
        uid_t     pr_uid;              /* real user id */
        uid_t     pr_euid;             /* effective user id */
        gid_t     pr_gid;              /* real group id */
        gid_t     pr_egid;             /* effective group id */
        uintptr_t pr_addr;             /* address of process */
        dev_t     pr_ttydev;           /* controlling tty device (or PRNODEV) */
        timestruc_t pr_start;          /* process start time, from the epoch */
        char      pr_fname[PRFNSZ];    /* name of execed file */
        char      pr_psargs[PRARGSZ];  /* initial characters of arg list */
        int       pr_argc;             /* initial argument count */
        uintptr_t pr_argv;             /* address of initial argument vector */
        uintptr_t pr_envp;             /* address of initial environment vector */
        char      pr_dmodel;           /* data model of the process */
        taskid_t  pr_taskid;           /* task id */
        projid_t  pr_projid;           /* project id */
        poolid_t  pr_poolid;           /* pool id */
        zoneid_t  pr_zoneid;           /* zone id */
} psinfo_t;
```

19.2 Callouts and Callout Tables

The Solaris kernel provides a callout facility for general-purpose, time-based event scheduling. A system callout table is initialized at boot time, and kernel routines can place functions on the callout table through the `timeout(9F)` interface. A callout table entry includes a function pointer, optional argument, and clock-tick value. With each clock interrupt, the tick value is tested and the function is executed when the time interval expires. The kernel interface, timeout (9F), is part of the device driver interface (DDI) specification and is commonly used by device drivers. Other kernel facilities, such as the page fsflush daemon, which sleeps at regular intervals, make use of callouts as well.

The kernel callout table is laid out as shown in Figure 19.2.

At boot time, the callout_table array is initialized with pointers to callout_table structures; the structures are also created at boot time. There are 16 callout tables—8 for each of the two callout types, *normal* and *real-time*. Normal callouts are those callout entries created with a timeout (9F) call. The kernel also

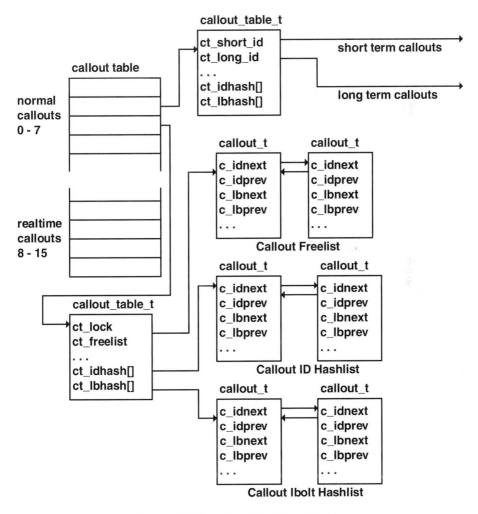

Figure 19.2 Solaris 10 Callout Tables

supports real-time callouts, created with the internal `realtime_timeout()` function. Real-time callouts are handled more expediently than are normal callouts through a soft interrupt mechanism, whereas normal callouts are subject to scheduling latency. Once the callout mechanism has executed the function placed on the callout queue, the callout entry is removed.

Each callout entry has a unique callout ID, `c_xid`, the extended callout ID. The callout ID contains the table ID, indicating which callout table the callout belongs to, a bit indicating whether this is a short-term or long-term callout, and a running counter.

The callout ID name space is partitioned into two pieces for short-term and long-term callouts. (A long-term callout is defined as a callout with a tick counter greater than 16,384, a value derived through testing and monitoring of real production systems.) This partitioning prevents collisions on the callout ID, which can result from the high volume of `timeout(9f)` calls typically generated by a running system. It's possible to run out of unique callout IDs, so IDs can be recycled. For short-term callouts, ID recycling is not a problem; a particular callout will likely have been removed from the callout table before its ID gets reused. A long-term callout could collide with a new callout entry reusing its ID.

High-volume, short-term callout traffic is handled on a callout table with short-term callouts, and the relatively few long-term callouts are maintained on their own callout table. The callout table maintains a `ct_short_id` and `ct_long_id`, to determine if a callout table is supporting long-term or short-term callout entries.

The short and long IDs are set to an initial value at boot time in each callout table structure, with short IDs ranging from 0x10000000 to 0x1000000f and long IDs ranging from 0x30000000 to 0x3000000f. The other callout table structure fields set at boot time are the `ct_type` field (eight each of normal or real-time) and the `ct_runtime` and `ct_curtime`, both set to the current `lbolt` value when the initialization occurs.

The callout entries, each represented by a callout structure, are linked to a callout table through the `ct_idhash[]` and `ct_lbhash[]` arrays, where each array element is either null or a pointer to a callout structure. The callout entries are stored on each array; one hashes on the callout ID, the other hashes on the `lbolt` value. At initialization, the kernel also creates two callout threads with each callout table. The callout threads are signaled through a condition variable when the `callout_schedule()` function executes (called from the clock handler) if functions with expired timers need to execute.

As we alluded to, the insertion and removal of callout table entries by the `timeout(9F)` function is a regular and frequent occurrence on a running Solaris system. The algorithm for placing an entry on the callout queue goes as follows (the `timeout(9F)` flow):

1. `timeout (function_pointer, argument_pointer, time value (delta))` enters `timeout_common()`, with all the arguments passed to `timeout(9F)` along with an index into the `callout_table` array. The index derivation is based on the CPU `cpu_seqid` (sequential ID) field and on the callout type, where normal callouts are placed on tables indexed between array locations 0 through 7 (real-time callouts, 8 through 15).

   Basically, the algorithm causes callout entries to cycle through indexes 8 through 15 as CPU IDs increment; the same CPU will reference the same index location every time.

2. `timeout_common()` grabs a callout structure from the `ct_freelist` if one is available, or the kernel memory allocator allocates a new one.

3. The `c_func` and `c_arg` fields are set in the callout structure, and the `c_runtime` field is set to the sum of the current `lbolt` value and the passed timer value.

4. `timeout_common()` establishes the ID in the callout table structure, setting either the `ct_short_id` or `ct_long_id` (if the timer is larger than 16,384, it's a long ID).

   We saw earlier that the ID fields are initialized at boot time. As callout entries are added, the algorithm essentially counts up until it wraps around and starts over again. This process leads to the reuse problem we just discussed, which is why we have short-term and long-term IDs.

5. The `c_xid` in the callout structure is set to the same ID value as the callout table ID.

6. A callout entry (callout structure) is inserted into the callout table by adding the entry to both the `ct_idhash[]` and `ct_lbhash[]` arrays in the callout table.

7. The algorithm derives the array index by hashing on the ID for `ct_idhash[]` placement and hashing on the `c_runtime` value set in the callout structure for the entry for `ct_lbhash[]`. If the array index already has a pointer, the algorithm links the callout structure by means of the `next` and `prev` pointers.

The callout entry is now established on the callout table, and `timeout(9F)` returns the ID to the calling function. The sequence of events for `realtime_timeout()` is the same.

The work done when `callout_schedule()` is called from the clock interrupt handler essentially happens through multiple loops. The outer loop hits all the callout *tables*, and the inner loop hits the callout *entries* in the table.

1. A local function variable set to the current `lbolt` value is used for entry to the inner loop, and the callout entries' `c_runtime` values determine whether the callouts are due for execution.

2. If the callout is not due or is already running, the code moves on to the next entry. Otherwise, it's time for the function in the callout entry to run.

3. For normal callout types, a condition variable signal function is set to wake up one of the callout threads to execute the function. For real-time callouts, the kernel `softcall()` function is invoked to generate a soft interrupt, which interrupts a processor, resulting in the function executing without going through the dispatcher.

4. Once the callout table is processed in the inner loop, the outer loop moves the code on to the next callout table. A mutex lock (`ct_lock`) is acquired in the inner loop to prevent another processor from processing the same callout table at the same time. The mutex is released when the inner loop through the callout table is completed.

5. The callout threads created at initialization (two per callout table) then loop, waiting for the `ct_threadpool` condition variable. They're signaled through the condition variable when a normal callout entry is due to execute (as above), at which point they call the `callout_execute()` function. `callout_execute()` is also invoked through the `softcall()` interrupt function to run a function placed on a callout table by `realtime_timeout()`.

   To reiterate, a normal callout can be exposed to some additional latency for the callout threads to be scheduled once they are signaled by the condition variable. The `softcall()` method will force a processor into the `callout_execute()` function sooner through the interrupt facility.

6. `callout_execute()` loops again through the callout table, testing the conditions for function execution. It's possible that another processor took care of things in the interim between function calls and lock releases, so the kernel tests the time values and running flag for the entries in the table before actually executing the function.

7. Assuming that it is time to run, `callout_execute()` sets the CALLOUT_EXECUTING flag in the callout entry's c_xid field, and the function is invoked.

8. The callout entry is then removed from the callout table, the callout structure is placed on the free list (`ct_freelist`), and a condition variable is broadcasted if any threads are sleeping on the c_done condition variable. This condition variable is part of the callout entry and provides a method of generating a notification that a function placed on the callout table has executed.

The kernel also provides an `untimeout(9F)` interface, which removes a callout. `untimeout(9F)` is passed the ID (which was returned from `timeout(9F)` when the function was placed on the callout table). The entry is located by means of the `ct_idhash[]` array and removed, with the callout structure being added to the free list. Callout entries added by `realtime_timeout(9F)` can also be removed with `untimeout(9F)`. There is no separate function for the removal of real-time callouts.

You can examine the callout table on a running system with the callout dcmd in mdb.

```
# mdb -k
Loading modules: [ unix krtld genunix specfs dtrace ufs ip sctp usba s1394 fcp fctl nca
lofs zpool random nfs audiosup sppp crypto logindmux ptm fcip md cpc ipc ]
> ::callout
FUNCTION                ARGUMENT        ID                      TIME
setrun                  ffffffff8357a820 3fffffff27126120        3458ec80  (T+798)
setrun                  ffffffff816d2dc0 3fffffff27120340        3458e9a5  (T+67)
setrun                  ffffffff8337f7a0 3fffffff27120350        3458e9a1  (T+63)
setrun                  ffffffff83530100 3fffffff27120380        3458eb1b  (T+441)
setrun                  ffffffff832cd280 3fffffff27120390        3458e976  (T+20)
setrun                  ffffffff8172cf00 3fffffff271203a0        3458ef4b  (T+1513)
setrun                  ffffffff8358b200 3fffffff271203b0        3458eaf9  (T+407)
setrun                  ffffffff83634060 3fffffff27120420        3458eef0  (T+1422)
```

Some of the kernel functions that you will consistently find on the callout table of a running Solaris system include the following:

- **polltime.** A real-time callout. Set from the `poll(2)` system call and based on the poll interval. `polltime()` wakes up a thread waiting on a poll event.

- **realitexpire.** A real-time callout. Used in the real-time interval timer support when a timer is set. Callout ticks are derived from timer value. `realitexpire()` generates the SIGALRM to the process.

- **setrun.** A real-time callout. Placed on the callout queue by sleep/wakeup code (condition variables) to force a thread wakeup when the sleep event has a timeout value; for example, an `aiowait(2)` call can specify a maximum tick count to wait for the I/O to complete. `aiowait(2)` with a timeout specificity uses a timed condition variable, which in turn places a `setrun()` event on the callout queue to force a thread wakeup if the time expires before the I/O has completed.

- **schedpaging.** A normal callout. Part of the page-out subsystem in the VM system, used to manage the page-out rate.

- **mi_timer_fire.** A normal callout. Part of the STREAMS-based TCP/IP protocol support. `mi_timer_fire()` generates regular message block processing through a STREAMS queue.

- **sigalarm2proc.** A normal callout. The alarm(2) system call places sigalarm2proc on the callout queue to generate a SIGALRM when the timer expires.

- **ts_update.** A normal callout. Checks a list of timeshare and interactive class threads and updates their priority as needed.

- **seg_pupdate.** A normal callout. Used by the address space segment reclaim thread to find page-locked pages that have not been used in a while and reclaim them.

- **kmem_update.** A normal callout. Performs low-level kernel memory allocator management.

This is by no means a complete list of all the kernel functions placed on the callout queue, and of course you will typically see several of the same functions on the callout queue at the same time, with different IDs and timeout values.

19.3 System Time Facilities

19.3.1 High-Resolution Timer

The kernel also maintains a high-resolution timer for nanosecond-level timing functions. On UltraSPARC-based systems, the hardware TICK register is used; it is incremented with every processor clock tick, that is, every 2.5 nanoseconds on a 400 MHz processor. An internal gethrestime() (get high-resolution time) function is used in a few areas of the kernel where fine-grained time is needed, such as the support for real-time interval timers (the setitimer(2) system call with the ITIMER_REAL flag). A gethrtime(3C) interface provides programs with nanosecond-level granularity for timing. The gethrtime(3C) function has an optimized code path to read the TICK register and return a normalized (converted to nanoseconds) value to the calling program.

19.3.2 Time-of-Day Clock

All computer systems—from desktop PCs to high-end multiprocessor systems—have a clock circuit of some sort. SPARC-based systems include clock circuitry in the EEPROM area of the hardware (for example, the Mostek 48T59 clock chip is used on UltraSPARC-based systems). This time-of-day (TOD) clock chip is addressable by the kernel as part of the firmware address space and has a hardware register specification; a kernel interface to the TOD hardware is implemented as a TOD device driver.

The chip itself implements several registers, readable and writable by the kernel through the device driver, that provide multiple counters for the numeric components that make up the date and time (for example, minute-of-the-hour, hour-of-the-day, day-of-the-week, month-of-the-year).

Figure 19.3 illustrates the hardware and software hierarchy for the TOD. Each component of a day and time value is stored as a separate counter value in the clock chip, and each counter increments the next logical value when it reaches its top value; for example, seconds count values 0–59, then increment minutes and restart at 0. Executing the date(1) command to set the date calls the stime(2) system call, which in turn calls the tod_set() device driver interface that sets the values in the TOD clock hardware.

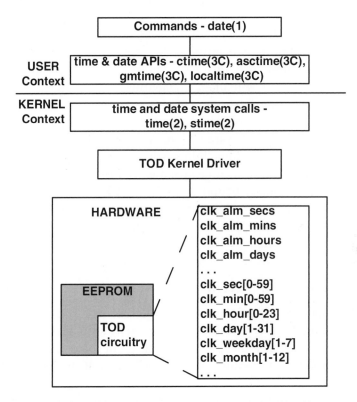

Figure 19.3 Example Time-of-Day Clock Stack

To comply with industry-standard interfaces (system calls and library routines), the kernel provides functions for converting the date values read from the clock hardware to the UNIX convention of the number of seconds since the epoch, and vice-versa.

19.4 The Cyclic Subsystem

Historically, most computer architectures have specified interval-based timer parts (for example, the SPARCstation counter/timer; the Intel i8254). While these parts deal in relative (that is, not absolute) time values, they are typically used by the operating system to implement the abstraction of absolute time. As a result, these parts cannot typically be reprogrammed without introducing error in the system's notion of time.

Starting in about 1994, chip architectures began specifying high-resolution timestamp registers. As of this writing (2006), all major chip families (UltraSPARC, PentiumPro, MIPS, PowerPC, Alpha) have high-resolution timestamp registers, and two (UltraSPARC and MIPS) have added the capacity to interrupt according to timestamp values. These timestamp-compare registers present a time-based interrupt source that can be reprogrammed arbitrarily often without introducing error. Given the low cost of implementing such a timestamp-compare register (and the tangible benefit of eliminating discrete timer parts), it is reasonable to expect that future chip architectures will adopt this feature.

The cyclic subsystem takes advantage of chip architectures with the capacity to interrupt on the basis of absolute, high-resolution time values. The cyclic subsystem is a low-level kernel subsystem that provides arbitrarily high resolution, per-CPU interval timers (to avoid colliding with existing terms, we dub such an interval timer a "cyclic"). Cyclics can be specified to fire at high, lock, or low interrupt level and can be optionally bound to a CPU or CPU partition. A cyclic's CPU or CPU partition binding can be changed dynamically; the cyclic will be "juggled" to a CPU that satisfies the new binding. Alternatively, a cyclic can be specified to be "omnipresent," denoting firing on all online CPUs.

19.4.1 Cyclic Subsystem Interface Overview

The cyclic subsystem has interfaces with the kernel at-large, with other kernel subsystems (for example, the processor management subsystem, the checkpoint-resume subsystem) and with the platform (the cyclic back end). Each of these interfaces is synopsized here and is described in full in Section 19.4.4 and Section 19.4.6.

Figure 19.4 displays the cyclic subsystem's interfaces to other kernel components. The arrows denote a "calls" relationship, with the large arrow indicating the cyclic subsystem's consumer interface.

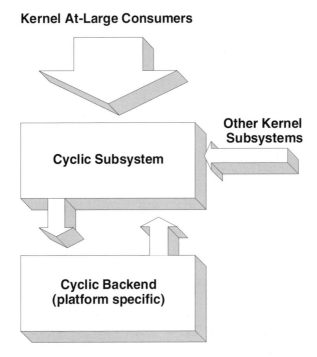

Figure 19.4 Cyclic Subsystem Overview

19.4.2 Cyclic Subsystem Implementation Overview

The cyclic subsystem minimizes interference between cyclics on different CPUs. Thus, all the cyclic subsystem's data structures hang off of a per-CPU structure, `cyc_cpu`.

Each `cyc_cpu` has a power-of-2 sized array of cyclic structures (the `cyp_cyclics` member of the `cyc_cpu` structure). If `cyclic_add()` is called and the `cyp_cyclics` array has no free slot, the size of the array is doubled. The array will never shrink. Cyclics are referred to by their index in the `cyp_cyclics` array, which is of type `cyc_index_t`.

The cyclics are kept sorted by expiration time in the `cyc_cpu`'s heap. The heap is keyed by cyclic expiration time, with parents expiring earlier than their children.

19.4.2.1 Heap Management

The heap is managed primarily by `cyclic_fire()`. Upon entry, `cyclic_fire()` compares the root cyclic's expiration time to the current time. If the expiration time is in the past, `cyclic_expire()` is called on the root cyclic. Upon return from `cyclic_expire()`, the cyclic's new expiration time is derived by adding its interval to its old expiration time, and a downheap operation is performed. After the downheap, `cyclic_fire()` examines the (potentially changed) root cyclic, repeating the `cyclic_expire()`/add interval/`cyclic_downheap()` sequence until the root cyclic has an expiration time in the future. This expiration time (guaranteed to be the earliest in the heap) is then communicated to the back end by `cyb_reprogram()`. Optimal back ends will next call `cyclic_fire()` shortly after the root cyclic's expiration time.

To allow efficient, deterministic downheap operations, we implement the heap as an array (the `cyp_heap` member of the `cyc_cpu` structure), with each element containing an index into the CPU's `cyp_cyclics` array.

The heap is laid out in the array according to the following:

1. The root of the heap is always in the 0th element of the heap array.

2. The left and right children of the *n*th element are element

$$(((n + 1) << 1) - 1) \text{ and element } ((n + 1) << 1), \text{ respectively.}$$

This layout is standard (see, for example, Cormen's "Algorithms"); the proof that these constraints correctly lay out a heap (or indeed, any binary tree) is trivial and left to the reader. To see the heap by example, assume our cyclics array has the following members (at time *t*), as shown in Table 19.1.

Table 19.1 Cyclic Array Example

	cy_handler	cy_level	cy_expire
0	clock()	LOCK	t+10000000
1	deadman()	HIGH	t+1000000000
2	clock_highres_fire()	LOW	t+100
3	clock_highres_fire()	LOW	t+1000
4	clock_highres_fire()	LOW	t+500
5	(free)	—	—
6	(free)	—	—
7	(free)	----	----

The heap array could be

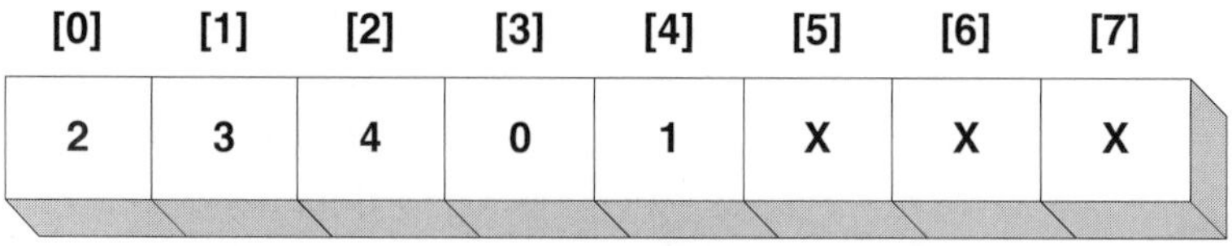

[0]	[1]	[2]	[3]	[4]	[5]	[6]	[7]
2	3	4	0	1	X	X	X

Figure 19.5 Cyclic Array Example, Starting

Graphically, this array corresponds to the graph shown in Figure 19.6.

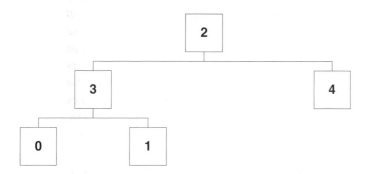

Figure 19.6 Cyclic Graph for Figure 19.5

Note that the heap is laid out by layer. All nodes at a given depth are stored in consecutive elements of the array. Moreover, layers of consecutive depths are in adjacent element ranges. This property guarantees high locality of reference during downheap operations. Specifically, we are guaranteed that we can downheap to a depth of

$$lg\ (cache\_line\_size\ /\ sizeof\ (cyc\_index\_t))$$

nodes with at most one cache miss. On UltraSPARC (64 byte e-cache line size), this corresponds to a depth of four nodes. Thus, if fewer than 16 cyclics are in the heap, downheaps on UltraSPARC miss at most once in the e-cache.

Downheaps are required to compare siblings as they proceed down the heap. For downheaps proceeding beyond the one-cache-miss depth, every access to a left child could potentially miss in the cache. However, if we assume

$$(cache\_line\_size\ /\ sizeof\ (cyc\_index\_t)) > 2$$

then all siblings are guaranteed to be on the same cache line. Thus, the miss on the left child will guarantee a hit on the right child; downheaps will incur at most one cache miss per layer beyond the one-cache-miss depth. The total number of cache misses for heap management during a downheap operation is thus bounded by

$$lg\ (n)\ -\ lg\ (cache\_line\_size\ /\ sizeof\ (cyc\_index\_t))$$

Traditional pointer-based heaps are implemented without regard to locality. Downheaps can thus incur two cache misses per layer (one for each child), but at most one cache miss at the root. This yields a bound of

$$2 * lg\ (n) - 1$$

on the total cache misses.

This difference may seem theoretically trivial (the difference is, after all, constant), but can become substantial in practice—especially for caches with very large cache lines and high miss penalties (for example, TLBs).

Heaps must always be full, balanced trees. Heap management must therefore track the next point-of-insertion into the heap. In pointer-based heaps, recomputing this point takes $O(lg\ (n))$. Given the layout of the array-based implementation, however, the next point-of-insertion is always

$$heap[number\_of\_elements]$$

We exploit this property by implementing the free-list in the unused heap elements. Heap insertion, therefore, consists only of filling in the cyclic at *cyp_cyclics[cyp_heap[number_of_elements]]*, incrementing the number of elements, and performing an upheap. Heap deletion consists of decrementing the number of elements, swapping the to-be-deleted element with the element at *cyp_heap[number_of_elements]*, and downheaping.

Figure 19.7 fills in more details in our earlier example.

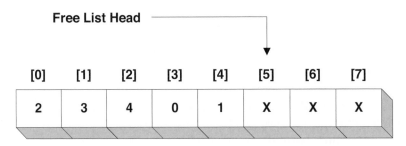

Figure 19.7 More Details Added to Cyclic Array Example

To insert into this heap, we would just need to fill in the cyclic at *cyp_cyclics[5]*, bump the number of elements (from 5 to 6), and perform an upheap.

If we wanted to remove, say, *cyp_cyclics[3]*, we would first scan for it in the cyp_heap, and discover it at *cyp_heap[1]*. We would then decrement the number of elements (from 5 to 4), swap *cyp_heap[1]* with *cyp_heap[4]*, and perform a downheap from *cyp_heap[1]*. The linear scan is required because the cyclic does not keep a back-pointer into the heap. This makes heap manipulation (for example, downheaps) faster at the expense of removal operations.

19.4.2.2 Expiry Processing

As alluded to above, `cyclic_expire()` is called by `cyclic_fire()` at CY_HIGH_LEVEL to expire a cyclic. Cyclic subsystem consumers are guaranteed that for an arbitrary time t in the future, their cyclic handler will have been called *(t - cyt_ when) / cyt_interval* times. Thus, there must be a one-to-one mapping between a cyclic's expiration at CY_HIGH_LEVEL and its execution at the desired level (CY_HIGH_LEVEL, CY_LOCK_LEVEL, or CY_LOW_LEVEL).

For CY_HIGH_LEVEL cyclics, this is trivial; cyclic_expire() simply needs to call the handler.

For CY_LOCK_LEVEL and CY_LOW_LEVEL cyclics, however, there exists a potential disconnect: If the CPU is at an interrupt level less than CY_HIGH_LEVEL but greater than the level of a cyclic for a period of time longer than twice the cyclic's interval, the cyclic will be expired twice before it can be handled.

To maintain the one-to-one mapping, we track the difference between the number of times a cyclic has been expired and the number of times it has been handled in a "pending count" (the cy_pend field of the cyclic structure). cyclic_expire() thus increments the cy_pend count for the expired cyclic and posts a soft interrupt at the desired level. In the cyclic subsystem's soft interrupt handler, cyclic_softint(), we repeatedly call the cyclic handler and decrement cy_pend until we have decremented cy_pend to zero.

19.4.2.3 The Producer/Consumer Buffer

To avoid a linear scan of the cyclics array at the soft interrupt level, cyclic_softint() must be able to quickly determine which cyclics have a non-zero cy_pend count. We thus introduce a per-soft-interrupt-level producer/consumer buffer shared with CY_HIGH_LEVEL. These buffers are encapsulated in the cyc_pcbuffer structure and, like cyp_heap, are implemented as cyc_index_t arrays (the cypc_buf member of the cyc_pcbuffer structure).

The producer (cyclic_expire() running at CY_HIGH_LEVEL) enqueues a cyclic by storing the cyclic's index to cypc_buf[cypc_prodndx] and incrementing cypc_prodndx. The consumer (cyclic_softint() running at either CY_LOCK_LEVEL or CY_LOW_LEVEL) dequeues a cyclic by loading from cypc_buf[cypc_consndx] and bumping cypc_consndx. The buffer is empty when *cypc_prodndx == cypc_consndx*.

To bound the size of the producer/consumer buffer, cyclic_expire() only enqueues a cyclic if its cy_pend was zero (if the cyclic's cy_pend is non-zero, cyclic_expire() only bumps cy_pend). Symmetrically, cyclic_softint() only consumes a cyclic after it has decremented the cy_pend count to zero.

Returning to our example, Figure 19.8 shows what the CY_LOW_LEVEL producer/consumer buffer might look like.

In particular, note that clock()'s cy_pend is 1 but that it is *not* in this producer/consumer buffer; it would be enqueued in the CY_LOCK_LEVEL producer/consumer buffer.

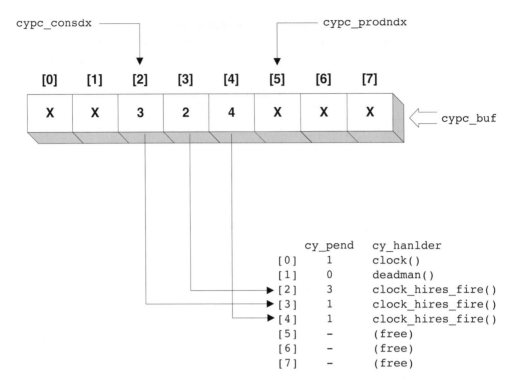

Figure 19.8 Cyclic Array Example with Producer/Consumer Buffer

19.4.2.4 Locking

Traditionally, access to per-CPU data structures shared between interrupt levels is serialized by manipulation of the programmable interrupt level: Readers and writers are required to raise their interrupt level to that of the highest-level writer.

The producer/consumer buffers are shared between `cyclic_fire()`/`cyclic_expire()`, which execute at `CY_HIGH_LEVEL`, and `cyclic_softint()`, which executes at one of `CY_LOCK_LEVEL` or `CY_LOW_LEVEL`. So forcing `cyclic_softint()` to raise the programmable interrupt level is undesirable. Aside from the additional latency incurred by manipulating the interrupt level in the hot `cy_pend` processing path, raising the interrupt level would create the potential for soft-level `cy_pend` processing to delay `CY_HIGH_LEVEL` firing and expiry processing. `CY_LOCK/LOW_LEVEL` cyclics could thereby induce jitter in `CY_HIGH_LEVEL` cyclics.

To minimize jitter, then, we would like the `cyclic_fire()`/`cyclic_expire()` and `cyclic_softint()` code paths to be lock free.

For `cyclic_fire()`/`cyclic_expire()`, lock-free execution is straightforward. Because these routines execute at a higher interrupt level than `cyclic_` `softint()`, their actions on the producer/consumer buffer appear atomic. In particular, the increment of `cy_pend` appears to occur atomically with the increment of `cypc_prodndx`.

For `cyclic_softint()`, however, lock-free execution requires more delicacy. When `cyclic_softint()` discovers a cyclic in the producer/consumer buffer, it calls the cyclic's handler and attempts to atomically decrement the `cy_pend` count with a compare-and-swap operation.

- If the compare-and-swap operation succeeds, `cyclic_softint()` behaves conditionally, depending on the value it atomically wrote to `cy_pend`.

- If the `cy_pend` was decremented to 0, the cyclic has been consumed; `cyclic_softint()` increments the `cypc_consndx` and checks for more enqueued work.

If the count was decremented to a non-zero value, more work must be done on the cyclic; `cyclic_softint()` calls the cyclic handler and repeats the atomic decrement process.

If the compare-and-swap operation fails, `cyclic_softint()` recognizes that `cyclic_expire()` has intervened and bumped the `cy_pend` count. (Resizes and removals complicate this, however—see the sections on their operation, below.) `cyclic_softint()` thus reloads `cy_pend` and reattempts the atomic decrement.

Recall that we bound the size of the producer/consumer buffer by having `cyclic_expire()` enqueue the specified cyclic only if its `cy_pend` count is zero; thus we ensure that each cyclic is enqueued at most once. This leads to a critical constraint on `cyclic_softint()`, however. After the compare-and-swap operation that successfully decrements `cy_pend` to zero, `cyclic_softint()` must *not* reexamine the consumed cyclic. In part to obey this constraint, `cyclic_softint()` calls the cyclic handler before decrementing `cy_pend`.

19.4.2.5 Resizing

All the discussion thus far has assumed a static number of cyclics. Obviously, static limitations are not practical; we need the capacity to resize our data structures dynamically.

We resize our data structures lazily, and only on a per-CPU basis. The size of the data structures always doubles and never shrinks. We serialize adds (and thus resizes) on `cpu_lock`; we never need to deal with concurrent resizes. Resizes should be rare; they may induce jitter on the CPU being resized, but should not affect cyclic operation on other CPUs. Pending cyclics may not be dropped during a resize operation.

Three key `cyc_cpu` data structures need to be resized: the cyclics array, the heap array, and the producer/consumer buffers. Resizing the first two is relatively straightforward:

1. The new, larger arrays are allocated in `cyclic_expand()` (called from `cyclic_add()`).
2. `cyclic_expand()` cross-calls `cyclic_expand_xcall()` on the CPU undergoing the resize.
3. `cyclic_expand_xcall()` raises the interrupt level to `CY_HIGH_LEVEL`.
4. The contents of the old arrays are copied into the new arrays.
5. `bzero()` is executed on the old cyclics array.
6. The pointers are updated.

The producer/consumer buffer is dicier: `cyclic_expand_xcall()` may have interrupted `cyclic_softint()` in the middle of consumption. To resize the producer/consumer buffer, we implement up to two buffers per soft interrupt level: a hard buffer (the buffer being produced into by `cyclic_expire()`) and a soft buffer (the buffer from which `cyclic_softint()` is consuming). During normal operation, the hard buffer and soft buffer point to the same underlying producer/consumer buffer.

During a resize, however, `cyclic_expand_xcall()` changes the hard buffer to point to the new, larger producer/consumer buffer; all future `cyclic_expire()` functions will produce into the new buffer. `cyclic_expand_xcall()` then posts a `CY_LOCK_LEVEL` soft interrupt, landing in `cyclic_softint()`.

As under normal operation, `cyclic_softint()` consumes cyclics from its soft buffer. After the soft buffer is drained, however, `cyclic_softint()` will see that the hard buffer has changed. At that time, `cyclic_softint()` changes its soft buffer to point to the hard buffer, and repeats the producer/consumer buffer draining procedure.

After the new buffer is drained, `cyclic_softint()` determines whether both soft levels have seen their new producer/consumer buffer. If both have, `cyclic_softint()` posts on the semaphore `cyp_modify_wait`. If not, a soft interrupt is generated for the remaining level.

`cyclic_expand()` blocks on the `cyp_modify_wait` semaphore (a semaphore is used instead of a condition variable because of the race between the `sema_p()` in `cyclic_expand()` and the `sema_v()` in `cyclic_softint()`). In that way, `cyclic_expand()` recognizes when the resize operation is complete, and all the old buffers (the heap, the cyclics array and the producer/ consumer buffers) can be freed.

A final caveat on resizing: We described step (5) in the `cyclic_expand_xcall()` procedure without providing any motivation. This step addresses the problem of a `cyclic_softint()` attempting to decrement a `cy_pend` count while interrupted by a `cyclic_expand_xcall()`. Because `cyclic_softint()` has already called the handler by the time `cy_pend` is decremented, we want to ensure that it doesn't decrement a `cy_pend` count in the old cyclics array. By zeroing the old cyclics array in `cyclic_expand_xcall()`, we are zeroing out every `cy_pend` count. When `cyclic_softint()` attempts to compare-and-swap on the `cy_pend` count, it fails and recognizes that the count has been zeroed. `cyclic_softint()` updates its stale copy of the `cyp_cyclics` pointer, rereads the `cy_pend` count from the new cyclics array, and reattempts the compare-and-swap.

19.4.2.6 Removals

Cyclic removals should be rare. To simplify the implementation (and to allow optimization for the `cyclic_fire()`/`cyclic_expire()`/`cyclic_softint()` path), we force removals and adds to serialize on `cpu_lock`.

Cyclic removal is complicated by a guarantee made to the consumer of the cyclic subsystem: After `cyclic_remove()` returns, the cyclic handler has returned and will never again be called.

Here is the procedure for cyclic removal:

1. `cyclic_remove()` calls `cyclic_remove_xcall()` on the CPU undergoing the removal.
2. `cyclic_remove_xcall()` raises the interrupt level to `CY_HIGH_LEVEL`.
3. The current expiration time for the removed cyclic is recorded.
4. If the `cy_pend` count on the removed cyclic is non-zero, it is copied into `cyp_rpend` and subsequently zeroed.
5. The cyclic is removed from the heap.
6. If the root of the heap has changed, the back end is reprogrammed.
7. If the `cy_pend` count was non-zero, `cyclic_remove()` blocks on the `cyp_modify_wait` semaphore.

The motivation for step (3) is explained in Section 19.4.2.7.

The `cy_pend` count is decremented in `cyclic_softint()` after the cyclic handler returns. Thus, if we find a `cy_pend` count of zero in step (4), we know that `cyclic_remove()` doesn't need to block.

If the cy_pend count is non-zero, however, we must block in cyclic_remove() until cyclic_softint() has finished calling the cyclic handler. To let cyclic_softint() know that this cyclic has been removed, we zero the cy_pend count. This causes cyclic_softint()'s compare-and-swap to fail. cyclic_softint() then recognizes that the zero cy_pend count is zero, either because cyclic_softint() has been caught during a resize (see Section 19.4.2.5) or because the cyclic has been removed. In the latter case, it calls cyclic_remove_pend() to call the cyclic handler *cyp_rpend – 1* times, and posts on cyp_modify_wait.

19.4.2.7 Juggling

At first glance, cyclic juggling seems to be a difficult problem. The subsystem must guarantee that a cyclic doesn't execute simultaneously on different CPUs, while also ensuring that a cyclic fires exactly once per interval. We solve this problem by leveraging a property of the platform: gethrtime() is required to increase in lock-step across multiple CPUs. Therefore, to juggle a cyclic, we remove it from its CPU, recording its expiration time in the remove cross-call (step (3) in Section 19.4.2.6). We then add the cyclic to the new CPU, explicitly setting its expiration time to the time recorded in the removal. This leverages the existing cyclic expiry processing, which will compensate for any time lost while juggling.

19.4.3 Clients of the Cyclic Subsystem

Clients of the cyclic subsystem include the following:

- clock() is now a lock-level cyclic.
- Profiling is a high-level cyclic (so we now have MP i86 pc profiling!)
- Deadman is a high-level cyclic (we now have deadman on all platforms!)
- Panic/dump timeouts now run out of deadman cyclic.
- The POSIX high-resolution timer (a timer created with timer_create() using CLOCK_HIGHRES) is implemented on top of a low-level cylic. When the client application that uses the high-resolution timer is bound to a process that has interrupts disabled, the timers exhibit low latency and very low jitter (Figure 19.9).

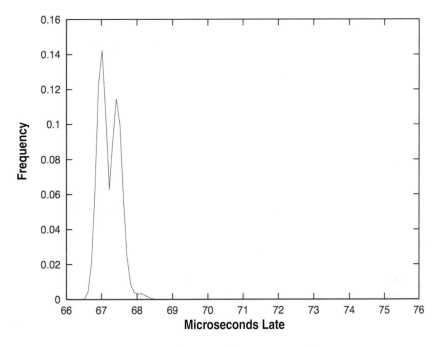

Figure 19.9 Cyclic Jitter Example

19.4.4 Cyclic Kernel At-Large Interfaces

The cyclic interfaces for the kernel at-large are described in Table 19.2.

Table 19.2 Solaris 10 Cyclic Kernel At-Large Interfaces

Interface	Description
cyclic_add()	Creates a cyclic
cyclic_add_omni()	Creates an omnipresent cyclic
cyclic_remove()	Removes a cyclic
cyclic_bind()	Changes a cyclic's CPU or partition binding

19.4.5 Cyclic Kernel Inter-Subsystem Interfaces

The cyclic interfaces between subsystems are described in Table 19.3.

Table 19.3 Solaris 10 Cyclic Inter-Subsystem Interfaces

Interface	Description
cyclic_juggle()	Juggles cyclics away from a CPU
cyclic_offline()	Offlines cyclic operation on a CPU
cyclic_online()	Reenables operation on an offlined CPU
cyclic_move_in()	Notifies subsystem of change in CPU partition
cyclic_move_out()	Notifies subsystem of change in CPU partition
cyclic_suspend()	Suspends the cyclic subsystem on all CPUs
cyclic_resume()	Resumes the cyclic subsystem on all CPUs

19.4.6 Cyclic Backend Interfaces

The cyclic backend interfaces are described in Table 19.4.

Table 19.4 Solaris 10 Cyclic Backend Interfaces

Interface	Description
cyclic_init()	Initializes the cyclic subsystem
cyclic_fire()	CY_HIGH_LEVEL interrupt entry point
cyclic_softint()	CY_LOCK/LOW_LEVEL soft interrupt entry point

The interfaces supplied by the back end (through the cyc_backend structure) are documented in detail in <sys/cyclic_impl.h> and in the next section.

19.4.7 Cyclic Subsystem Backend-Supplied Interfaces

The design, implementation and interfaces of the cyclic subsystem are covered in detail in block comments in the implementation. This comment covers the interface from the cyclic subsystem into the cyclic back end. The back end is specified by a structure of function pointers defined in Table 19.5.

Table 19.5 Solaris 10 Cyclic-Supplied Backend Interfaces

Method	Description
cyb_configure()	Configures the back end on the specified CPU
cyb_unconfigure()	Unconfigures the back end
cyb_enable()	Enables the CY_HIGH_LEVEL interrupt source
cyb_disable()	Disables the CY_HIGH_LEVEL interrupt source
cyb_reprogram()	Reprograms the CY_HIGH_LEVEL interrupt source
cyb_softint()	Generates a soft interrupt
cyb_set_level()	Sets the programmable interrupt level
cyb_restore_level()	Restores the programmable interrupt level
cyb_xcall()	Cross-calls to the specified CPU
cyb_suspend()	Suspends the back end
cyb_resume()	Resumes the back end

Task Queues

Contributions by Alexander Kolbasov

I n this chapter, we discuss task queues in Solaris.

20.1 Overview of Task Queues

It is common for you, the kernel programmer, to postpone the processing of some tasks and delegate their execution to another kernel thread. There may be several reasons for doing this:

- You have a task that isn't time-critical, but a current code path that is.
- You have a task that may require grabbing locks that a thread already holds.
- You have a task that needs to block (for example, to wait for memory), but you have a thread that cannot block in its current context.
- You have a code path that can't complete because of a specific condition but also can't sleep or fail. In this case, the task is immediately queued and then is executed after the condition disappears.
- You just want to launch multiple tasks in parallel.

In all these cases, you need, in essence, to execute a piece of code (task) in a different context, where context usually means another kernel thread with a different set of locks held and, possibly, a different priority.

Until introduction of task queues in Solaris 8 there was no generic OS facility for such in-kernel context change. Every subsystem used its own ad hoc mechanisms, usually utilizing "worker threads" together with a list of jobs to give them. The task queues interface abstracts common code out of these mechanisms and substitutes a simple way of scheduling asynchronous tasks.

A task queue consists of a list of tasks, with one or more threads to service the list. If a task queue has a single service thread, all tasks are guaranteed to execute in the order in which they were dispatched. Otherwise, they can be executed in any order. Note that since tasks are placed on a list, execution of one task should not depend on the execution of another task lest deadlock should occur. A task queue (taskq) created with a single servicing thread guarantees that all tasks are serviced in the order in which they are scheduled.

20.2 Dynamic Task Queues

Dynamic task queues first appeared in Solaris 9, as the first major revision to their introduction in Solaris 8.

20.2.1 Why a *Dynamic* Task Queue?

Suppose that two friends, Bob and Alice, are standing in a cafeteria line with Alice standing behind Bob. When the cashier checks Bob's tray, it turns out that Bob doesn't have enough money, so he wants to borrow from Alice. But Alice is not sure whether she has enough cash until she knows the cost of her lunch. This is a typical deadlock situation—neither Bob nor Alice can make any forward progress because of waiting for the other. The same kind of deadlock may occur if two tasks A and B are placed on a queue that is served by a single thread and a resource dependency exists between A and B. One way to prevent such a deadlock is to guarantee that A and B are processed by two different threads; that way, when A stalls for B, the thread processing A will block until B makes enough progress to release the needed resource to B.

Dynamic task queues provide exactly such a deadlock-free way of scheduling potentially dependent tasks on the same queues. They guarantee that every task is processed by a separate thread. Since the number of tasks that can be scheduled at the same time is not known in advance, dynamic task queues maintain a dynamic thread pool that grows when the workload increases and shrinks when the workload dies off.

Dynamic task queues cannot (yet) be used through the DDI interfaces. Some kernel subsystems use the internal taskq calls directly to create and use dynamic task queues. The system also maintains one shared dynamic task queue, called system_taskq. You use it by specifying system_taskq as the taskq argument to the taskq_dispatch() function. We recommend that you also add TQ_NOSLEEP | TQ_NOQUEUE to the flags when using system_taskq.

20.2.2 Problems Addressed by Dynamic Task Queues

- **SMP scalability.** In the prior implementation, each task queue uses a single list of entries and a single lock to protect it, so on a multiple-CPU SMP system, this behavior may become a performance bottleneck, especially for some "hot" (frequently accessed) task queue.

- **Thread usage.** In many cases, programmers have no knowledge of how many worker threads they need to process task queues, so they usually choose some random number that seems reasonable, for example, number of processors. The number of worker threads servicing a task queue never changes during its lifetime and cannot adapt to a real task queue workload. Since all subsystems use their own private task queues, each with its own set of threads, the total thread pool may become very unbalanced—some threads will sleep most of the time while others will be busy most of the time.

- **Processing latency.** A sequential taskq executes its tasks one by one, which means that the time between task dispatch and execution will be no less than the total time to process all preceding tasks in the list. This property may lead to a high processing latency and makes it more difficult to guarantee processing latency within certain boundaries (since both maximum number of tasks on the queue and individual processing time for each task need to be bound). What is worse, if some task sleeps or blocks, waiting for a resource, it blocks all tasks behind it. This cumulative behavior is very bad for latency-sensible applications. A dynamic taskq suffers the same problem when number of dispatched tasks is greater than the number of servicing threads.

- **Ordering constraints.** Programmers should be careful to avoid dispatching dependent tasks on the same task queue. If some task depends on another one scheduled later, it may block forever because of a deadlock. This is especially a problem for a sequential task queue, but it can also happen for a dynamic one.

- **Blocking tasks.** This is a more general issue than the previous one. Any blocking task or task that takes a very long time to complete potentially blocks or delays some or all tasks dispatched after it.

- **Priority dispatching.** All worker threads have the same fixed priority specified at taskq creation, but there are no facilities to allow certain tasks to be scheduled with different priorities.

20.2.3 Task Pool Model

The design requirements for the new dynamic task queues specify that task queues should do the following:

1. Provide bounded scheduling latency.
2. Allow scheduling of dependent tasks in the same task queue.
3. Support a pool of threads that dynamically reflects system workload.
4. Scale well for any number of processors in the system, which means that it should not grab any global locks or write global data.
5. Allow scheduling of individual tasks with specified priorities.
6. Allow scheduling of tasks with different priorities.
7. Limit the total amount of servicing threads to prevent a task queue from exhausting system resources.
8. Be compatible with current uses of task queues.

Dependency and bounded latencies requirements 1 and 2 imply that execution of a task should not depend on execution of another one (unless some implicit dependencies are imposed by tasks themselves); this requirement can only be met if each of these tasks is processed by an independent thread. This immediately implies that the number of threads servicing a task queue should be at least the same as the number of pending tasks in this task queue and that each task should be assigned its own thread. This is the most important design decision that we made, and you can see that it logically follows the requirements. One interesting implication is that individual tasks can sleep without affecting execution of other tasks.

Obviously, we don't need to have more worker threads than pending tasks, so the number of pending jobs may also provide an upper boundary on the number of worker threads. But we do not use this requirement as a constraint, and we allow more threads. Being able to quickly use these extra threads for any new scheduled tasks more than compensates for the minor inefficiency stemming from these extra resources. Still, for efficiency we would like to keep extra threads to a minimum, so we set a hard limit for the maximum number of created threads.

The model with a worker thread assigned to each pending task also satisfies dynamic configuration requirement 3 since the total number of worker threads is based on the existing system workload (as defined by the number of outstanding tasks) and not by some arbitrary static decisions.

An interesting consequence of this design and the upper boundary requirement 6 is that if the threads' hard limit is set to M, we should not allow more than M outstanding tasks, and that means that a dispatch operation may fail even on a system with plenty of memory. This, in turn, means that users of task queues should be prepared to deal with dispatch fails and, possibly, provide backup mechanisms to schedule their tasks. We cannot do it transparently from users because of the ordering requirement 2, since a task queue has no knowledge of any ordering constraints. But programmers do have such knowledge, so if they want to schedule a task with no execution dependencies from other tasks, they can advise the dispatch operation that a task can safely be queued in a sequential task queue. In all other cases, the dispatch operation has no choice other than to fail and let the user decide the best backup method, for example, revert to using sequential task queues.

We use the term *task pool* to refer to the dynamic set of pending tasks, each of which has an assigned servicing thread. We chose this name to distinguish the dynamic set from the *task queue* since the former no longer operates like a queue.

The compatibility requirement means that the taskq_dispatch() function should work as expected for both standard task queues and the new task pool model. Since we also need to introduce priority dispatching (requirement 7), we extend our taskq API with a new function, taskq_pridispatch(), which includes an extra "priority" argument.

20.2.4 Interface Changes to Support Dynamic Task Queues

- **taskq_create().** For the new task pool model we use the existing API with some changes. First of all, we introduce a new taskq creation flag, TASKQ_ DYNAMIC, which creates a taskq with a new semantics. The taskq created with this flag consists of a regular sequential task queue with a single worker thread (we call it "backing queue") and a set of data structures needed to implement a dynamic pool. All servicing threads needed to process a task pool are created dynamically when tasks are dispatched. The TASKQ_DYNAMIC flag changes the meaning of the arguments passed to taskq_create(). With this flag set, nthreads means the maximum number of worker threads servicing the task pool (not counting a single task queue thread). The minalloc and maxalloc arguments are used in the usual way for the backing task queue. The TASKQ_DYNAMIC flag cannot be used in conjunction with TASKQ_ CPR_SAFE, and TASKQ_PREPOPULATE flag prepopulates the backing task queue in the usual way.

- **taskq_dispatch().** The return type for the taskq_dispatch() function is changed from int to an opaque type taskqid_t.

```
typedef void *taskqid_t;

taskqid_t taskq_dispatch(taskq_t *taskq, task_func_t f, void *a, uint_t flags);
```

This function returns NULL when the dispatch failed and some non-NULL value when the task was dispatched. The purpose of this extension is to allow cancellation of task queues in the future. The new set of dispatching flags is defined as follows:

TQ_NOQUEUEL: Do not queue a task if it can't be dispatched because available resources are lacking and return NULL. If this flag is not set and the task pool is exhausted, the task may be scheduled in a backing task queue. This flag should always be used when a task queue is used for tasks that may depend on each other for completion. Queuing dependent tasks may create deadlocks, as discussed earlier.

TQ_SLEEP: Do not wait for resources; may return NULL.

TQ_NOSLEEP: May block waiting for resources. May still fail for dynamic task queues if TQ_NOQUEUE is also specified.

- **taskq_wait() and taskq_lock().** We also decided to avoid supporting functions taskq_wait and taskq_lock for dynamic task queues. Support for such operations requires implementation to access some global (per-taskq) locks that we need to avoid for processor scalability. Instead, the following new functions are introduced to provide the functionality achieved by taskq_lock() in a more abstract way.

- **taskq_suspend(tq).** Suspends any new dispatched tasks from being executed.

- **taskq_suspended(tq).** Returns 1 if the task is in the suspended state, and 0 otherwise.

- **taskq_resume(tq).** Resumes execution of tasks in the task queue.

- **taskq_member(tq, thread).** Returns 1 if the thread is executing in the task queue context, and 0 otherwise. It is intended for ASSERTions checking that some piece of code is executed only by a task queue mechanism.

20.3 Task Queues Kernel Programming Interfaces

Kernel users should use the documented DDI interface for all taskq operations. These interfaces are defined in the usr/src/uts/common/sys/sunddi.h header file. The exported interface consists of the following functions.

```
taskq_t *taskq_create(const char *name, int nthreads, pri_t pri, int minalloc,
                      int maxalloc, int flags);
```

Creates a task queue with nthreads worker threads at priority pri and returns the pointer to the opaque taskq_t type. The minalloc and maxalloc arguments describe the behavior of the task entries cache. The flags may be any combination of the following - TASKQ_PREPOPULATE: Prepopulate task entries cache with minalloc entries.TASKQ_CPR_SAFE: Task queue uses special CPR protocol. This flag is only used by special system task queues and is not intended for general use. Since taskqs are queues, tasks are guaranteed to be executed in the order they are scheduled if nthreads equals one. Otherwise, task execution order is not predictable.

Specifying a flag of TASKQ_DYNAMIC creates a taskq with dynamic semantics. The taskq created using this flag consists of a regular sequential task queue with a single worker thread (we call it "backing queue") and a set of data structures needed to implement a dynamic pool. All servicing threads needed to process a task pool are created dynamically when tasks are dispatched. The TASKQ_DYNAMIC flag changes the meaning of the arguments, passed to taskq_create(). With this flag set, nthreads means the maximum number of worker threads, servicing task pool (not counting a single task queue thread). The minalloc and maxalloc arguments are used in the usual way for the backing task queue. The TASKQ_DYNAMIC flag can not be used together with TASKQ_CPR_SAFE, and TASKQ_PREPOPU-LATE flag prepopulates the backing task queue in the usual way.

```
void taskq_destroy(taskq_t *tq);
```

Waits for any scheduled tasks to complete, then destroys the taskq.

```
int taskq_dispatch(taskq_t *tq, task_func_t f, void *a, int flags);
```

Dispatches the task specified by function f and argument a to taskq tq. It returns 1 on success and 0 on failure.

Flags can be one of:

> TQ_NOQUEUE: Do not enqueue a task if it can't be dispatched due to lack of available resources and return NULL. If this flag is not set and the task pool is exhausted, the task may be scheduled in backing task queue. This flag should always be used when a task queue is used for tasks that may depend on each other for completion. Enqueueing dependent tasks may create deadlocks.
> TQ_SLEEP: Do not wait for resources; may return NULL.
> TQ_NOSLEEP: May block waiting for resources. May still fail for dynamic task queues if TQ_NOQUEUE is also specified.

```
void taskq_wait(taskq_t *tq);
```

Waits for all previously scheduled tasks to complete.

```
krwlock_t *taskq_lock(taskq_t *tq);
```

Returns a pointer to the task queue's thread lock, which is always held as RW_READER by taskq threads while executing tasks. There are two intended uses for this:

1. To ASSERT that a given function is called in taskq context only, and
2. To allow the caller to suspend all task execution temporarily by grabbing the lock as RW_WRITER.

See usr/src/uts/common/sys/sunddi.h

20.4 Device Driver Interface for Task Queues

Device driver or file system developers should use the documented DDI for all taskq operations. These interfaces are defined in the usr/src/uts/common/sys/ sunddi.h header file. The exported interface consists of the following functions.

```
ddi_taskq_t *ddi_taskq_create(dev_info_t *dip, const char *name, int nthreads,
                              pri_t pri, uint_t flags);
```

Creates a new taskq object with specified number of threads servicing it. All threads will run with a single specified priority. The priority may have a special value TASKQ_ DEFAULTPRI meaning that the priority will be chosen by the system. dip is a pointer to the dev_info_t structure (Some subsystems do not have a dip pointer and may pass NULL instead). name is a descriptive string. The priority of threads servicing the task queue can be specified by pri (drivers and modules should specify TASKQ_DEFAULTPRI). flags should be always zero in this release.

```
int ddi_taskq_dispatch(ddi_taskq_t *taskq, void (* func)(void *), void *arg,
                       uint_t dflags);
```

Schedules a task for a specified taskq, as returned by ddi_taskq_create(). A task is just a pair {f, a} where f is a function, accepting a single pointer argument and a is its argument value. Additional flags specify whether dispatch may or may not sleep waiting for resources. Once the task is dispatched it will be scheduled asynchronously at some later time and there is no way to cancel a task that is dispatched but has not been executed yet. All the tasks are executed with a fixed priority specified at the time of taskq creation.

Flags controlling the dispatch behavior are specified by flags: DDI_SLEEP, allow sleeping/blocking) until memory is available; or DDI_NOSLEEP, return DDI_FAILURE immediately if memory is not available.

```
void ddi_taskq_wait(ddi_taskq_t *taskq);
```

Blocks the taskq from any new dispatches and waits for all previously scheduled tasks to complete, then unblocks the taskq. This function does not stop any new task dispatches. Its single argument is the taskq to wait for.

```
void ddi_taskq_suspend(ddi_taskq_t *taskq);
```

Suspends all task execution until ddi_taskq_resume() is called. Although ddi_taskq_suspend() attempts to suspend pending tasks, there are no guarantees that they will be suspended. The only guarantee is that all tasks dispatched after ddi_taskq_suspend() will not be executed. Because it will trigger a deadlock, the function should never be called by a task executing on a taskq. Its single argument is the taskq to suspend.

```
boolean_t ddi_taskq_suspended(ddi_taskq_t *taskq);
```

Returns B_TRUE if taskq is suspended, and B_FALSE otherwise. It is intended to ASSERT that the task queue is suspended. Its single argument is the taskq to check.

```
void ddi_taskq_resume(ddi_taskq_t *taskq);
```

Resumes taskq execution. Its single argument is the taskq to resume.

See usr/src/uts/common/sys/sunddi.h

Each taskq is implemented as a list of tasks protected by a per-taskq lock. One or more worker threads execute tasks one by one by calling f(a) and then sleep, waiting for new entries. A taskq created with a single servicing thread has an important property: It guarantees that all its tasks are executed in the order they are scheduled. We call such a task queue a *sequential taskq*. When a task queue is created with several servicing threads, task execution order is not predictable; we call such task queue a *dynamic taskq*.

Task queues keep a cache of structures needed to schedule a task, and programmers can prepopulate this cache to guarantee that dispatch operation will succeed without waiting for memory.

20.5 Task Queue Observability

20.5.1 Kstat Counters

Every taskq created in the system keeps a set of associated kstat counters. Try running the following command on your system.

```
sol9$ kstat -c taskq
module: unix                         instance: 0
name:    ata_nexus_enum_tq           class:     taskq
         crtime                      53.877907833
         executed                    0
         maxtasks                    0
         nactive                     1
         nalloc                      0
         priority                    60
         snaptime                    258059.249256749
         tasks                       0
         threads                     1
         totaltime                   0

module: unix                         instance: 0
name:    callout_taskq               class:     taskq
         crtime                      0
         executed                    13956358
         maxtasks                    4
         nactive                     4
         nalloc                      0
         priority                    99
         snaptime                    258059.24981709
         tasks                       13956358
         threads                     2
         totaltime                   120247890619
...
```

The kstat information above includes

- Name of the taskq and its instance number
- Number of scheduled and executed tasks
- Number of kernel threads processing the taskq and their priority
- Total time (in nanoseconds) spent processing all the tasks

You can use the power of the `kstat` command to observe how some counter
increases over time.

```
sol9$ kstat -p unix:0:callout_taskq:tasks 1 5
unix:0:callout_taskq:tasks        13994642

unix:0:callout_taskq:tasks        13994711

unix:0:callout_taskq:tasks        13994784

unix:0:callout_taskq:tasks        13994855

unix:0:callout_taskq:tasks        13994926

...
```

20.5.2 DTrace SDT Probes

The taskq implementation also provides several useful SDT probes. The probes
described below have two arguments: the taskq pointer and the pointer to the
taskq_ent_t structure, which can extract the function and the argument from
the D script.

- `taskq-enqueue` probe fires whenever a task is queued on the taskq.
- `taskq-exec-start` probe fires just before the task is about to be executed.
- `taskq-exec-end` probe fires immediately after the task is executed.

Developers can use these probes to collect precise timing information about individual task queues and individual tasks being executed through them. For example, the following script prints the functions that were scheduled through task
queues every 10 seconds.

```
#!/usr/sbin/dtrace -qs

sdt:genunix::taskq-enqueue
{
  this->tq  = (taskq_t *)arg0;
  this->tqe = (taskq_ent_t *) arg1;
  @[this->tq->tq_name,
    this->tq->tq_instance,
    this->tqe->tqent_func] = count();
}

tick-10s
{
  printa ("%s(%d): %a called %@d times\n", @);
  trunc(@);
}
```

Running this on a desktop produced the following output.

```
callout_taskq(1): genunix`callout_execute called 51 times
callout_taskq(0): genunix`callout_execute called 701 times
kmem_taskq(0): genunix`kmem_update_timeout called 1 times
kmem_taskq(0): genunix`kmem_hash_rescale called 4 times
callout_taskq(1): genunix`callout_execute called 40 times
USB_hid_81_pipehndl_tq_1(14): usba`hcdi_cb_thread called 256 times
callout_taskq(0): genunix`callout_execute called 702 times
kmem_taskq(0): genunix`kmem_update_timeout called 1 times
kmem_taskq(0): genunix`kmem_hash_rescale called 4 times
callout_taskq(1): genunix`callout_execute called 28 times
USB_hid_81_pipehndl_tq_1(14): usba`hcdi_cb_thread called 228 times
callout_taskq(0): genunix`callout_execute called 706 times
callout_taskq(1): genunix`callout_execute called 24 times
USB_hid_81_pipehndl_tq_1(14): usba`hcdi_cb_thread called 141 times
callout_taskq(0): genunix`callout_execute called 708 times
```

20.6 Task Queue Implementation Notes

20.6.1 Use of Kmem Caches

The kmem subsystem (see Section 11.2) affords a convenient building block for task queues. A special kmem cache manages threads instead of memory. Threads are created in the cache constructor and destroyed in the cache destructor. The cache entries themselves hold the thread pointer and some information needed for internal housekeeping (flags, locks, and condition variables). Threads execute scheduled tasks and then call kmem_cache_free for their own entries. The kmem subsystem uses distributed locks internally, so the whole thing scales well over many CPUs.

This model is elegant, efficient, and simple (the whole design fit on a standard restaurant paper napkin, and the implementation took one evening), but it had a serious problem: There is no way to control the total number of allocated entries. Cache size is controlled by memory pressure and may grow quite a lot before memory pressure starts destroying free entries. This may sometimes create huge number of idle threads that waste system resources. And thus a new model appeared.

20.6.2 Use of Vmem Arenas

To address the problem of limiting the total number of threads created, we use a close sibling of kmem caches—*vmem arenas*—which allocates just integer numbers. A task pool with maximum of N threads then becomes an array of N entries, and each entry is allocated by index by the integer covering interval $(0, N]$ of the vmem arena. The vmem subsystem provides a needed scalability if the arena is backed by a kmem cache; in that case, the vmem subsystem uses this kmem cache internally for all allocations.

When a task is scheduled, we use vmem_alloc() to allocate an index in the array. Use of vmem_alloc() is close to the use of kmem caches in the previous model—it is scalable and guarantees that nothing can access the allocated array entry until we free the array. vmem_alloc() also tends to allocate entries that were freed recently.

The allocated control structure may have a running thread assigned to it. In this case, we simply wake up the thread, which executes the task and then goes back to sleep. If there is no thread, we create one. When the thread executes a job, it sleeps for some time, waiting for a new task to arrive. If it does not get a new job for a while, it wakes up and destroys itself. Such a strategy allows us to keep just enough working threads to handle the current workload.

Unfortunately, it turned out that vmem arenas backed by kmem caches have interesting implementation properties that make them difficult to use:

- Arena size should be large enough to accommodate the kmem subsystem entries, which are allocated in full per-CPU slabs.

- The recently freed entry is not allocated by the next vmem_alloc(), and the total number of used entries tends to be high, increasing number of idle threads.

- The allocator behavior again depends on the memory pressure.

To address this problem we need to drop the use of backing kmem caches and use vmem arenas directly. Then we need to address the scalability issue somehow. And so another new model appeared.

20.6.3 Hashed Vmem Arenas

Usual vmem arenas use a single per-arena lock to protect internal state. To avoid lock and resource contention on multiple-CPU systems, we introduced an array of vmem arenas, each controlling its own array of task entries. If we have M arenas each of size N, then the maximum number of allocated entries is M × N. A good choice for M is the number of CPUs in the system, but we could use any number because it doesn't matter which arena we actually use for each allocation. When we can't allocate an entry from a specific arena, we try others until some arena has free entries or until no arenas left.

This model has all the nice properties we need, but it has some drawbacks also:

- The whole set of M × N entries is allocated permanently and independently of actual system load, and much of that space may be unused. On modern hardware, the potential number of CPUs can be quite high (it can reach 512 on some platforms), and we usually need several dozen entries in each bucket. With a typical entry size around 64 bytes, the whole table may consume several megabytes of precious kernel memory.

- Use of vmem arenas looks like overkill when all we need is a simple FIFO-type allocator that returns recently used entries first. A simple list of free entries seems sufficient for that purpose.

So, in the next cycle we get rid of vmem arenas and static per-bucket arrays and introduce a list of free entries. And that is how task pools are currently implemented.

20.6.4 Cached List of Entries

To keep the implementation scalable, we continue to use a per-CPU hash of entry buckets. Each bucket has a list of free entries that were used recently. Each entry has a thread servicing it. When a task is scheduled, we first try to find an idle entry in the free list. If the free list is empty, we go to the next bucket and so on. If a free entry is found, we just put task information there and wake up a sleeping thread. If there are no free entries, we create a new one in the original bucket and populate it with a thread. When a thread sleeps long enough waiting for a new job, it wakes up, removes itself from the free list, and destroys itself. All thread synchronization uses per-bucket locks and condition variables, and no global locks are used.

There is one problem, though. The `thread_create()` call may sleep waiting for memory so we cannot use it in `NOSLEEP` dispatches. So in this case, instead of allocating an entry with a thread, we schedule a background job by using a backing task queue, which allocates an entry and creates a new servicing thread. The original dispatch operation fails, but the next one is likely to use the newly created entry. This means that even on a system with plenty of memory, the `taskq_dispatch()` call may fail during warmup period.

When the system is low on memory, all SLEEP allocations begin blocking waiting for memory, so we do not create new entries and new threads when we detect that memory is low—memory shortage may actually limit the number of created threads. Under rare circumstances it is possible that all existing threads in the pool will die from inactivity and no new threads will be created because of the memory shortage. In this case, all dispatch operations will fail and all dispatches will revert to their backup versions (which will probably be some variation of single-threaded task queues).

Such behavior has an interesting property: It slows down task execution and increases latencies when the system is low on memory. It may well be a good property under such severe circumstances.

Currently, there are no provisions for changing the priority of the servicing thread needed to support priority dispatching correctly. In the future, however, adding them should be easy since we know the exact state of the servicing thread at the dispatch time and we can properly update its priority. At present, there is no kernel API to change priority of the running thread, but we can easily implement priority scheduling once such an API comes into existence.

20.6.5 Problems with Task Pool Implementation

Various problems still attend the current implementation and could impact its performance under heavy load.

Although initial bucket hashing is done with the CPU number, actual threads are not bound to any CPU and may migrate from one CPU to another, so it is quite possible that the task will be scheduled on one CPU and executed on another one. This behavior increases system cache pollution and may be especially harmful on nonsymmetric architectures like ccNUMA. Binding threads to CPUs might solve this problem but could have other bad impacts on the system:

- Each dispatch-execution cycle has a context switch from a dispatching thread to an executing thread. Regular task queues may have fewer context switches since the servicing thread may execute several task before it goes to sleep.

- We may create more threads than there are spare CPUs on the system, so these extra threads will have no CPUs to execute them. Ideally, we would like to know the state of each CPU and create new threads only when some CPUs are idle.

Overall, our experiments with this implementation show that we do achieve significant benefits on multiple-CPU systems without hurting performance on the smaller systems.

20.6.6 Use of Dynamic Task Pools in STREAMS

The original motivation for designing and implementing the new dynamic task queue extensions came from our attempts to develop a good replacement for the current background-job scheduling in the Solaris STREAMS subsystem. You can get a good idea of the STREAMS scheduler from, but here's a quick summary.

Solaris STREAMS has five different queues for background job processing.

- Background queue scheduling (STREAMS scheduler), which calls module and driver service procedures; the entries are placed in the queue by the `qenable()` function, usually called from `putq()`.

- Background syncq scheduling through `sqenable()` function.
- Background scheduling of `qwriter(9F)` callbacks, entered through `queue_writer()` function.
- Asynchronous freeing of memory obtained through `esballoc()`.
- Handling of bufcalls that are used when the system is low on memory.

The queue scheduling turns out to be the hottest task queue. It is heavily used throughout networking code and its implementation is extremely inefficient, so we focused on fixing just queue scheduling. The prototype results showed that we could achieve significant performance gains by distributing the locks and optimizing the scheduler. So the next logical step was to design a generic task scheduler that can meet high-stress networking demands and that can replace most of the STREAMS ad hoc scheduling implementations.

As a result, we reimplemented all the above schedulers, except bufcalls, to take advantage of the task queues. It turned out that the code became cleaner, simpler, and more efficient.

kmdb Implementation

Contributed by Matthew Simmons

This chapter broadly explains the implementation of the kernel modular debugging infrastructure.

21.1 Introduction

The best way to understand kmdb is by first understanding how mdb does things. We begin with an overview of the portions of mdb that are relevant to our later discussion of kmdb. For more information about mdb and its operation, consult the Modular Debugger AnswerBook. Having set the stage, we next discuss the major design goals behind kmdb. With those goals in mind, we return to the list of components we discussed from an mdb perspective, analyzing them this time from the point of view of kmdb, showing how their implementation fulfills kmdb's design goals. Finally, we embark on a whirlwind tour of some of the lower-level components of kmdb that weren't described in earlier sections.

21.1.1 MDB Components

In this section, we review the parts of MDB that are particularly relevant for our later discussion of kmdb, focusing on how those components are implemented in mdb. That is, we concentrate only on those components whose implementation changes significantly in kmdb. The design of MDB is sufficiently modular that we

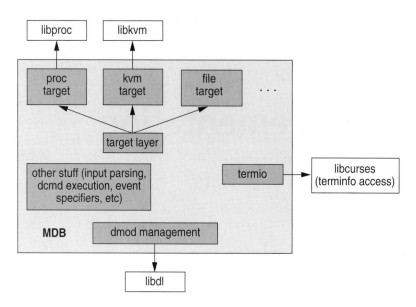

Figure 21.1 MDB Components

could replace the components requiring change without disrupting the remainder of the debugger. The components described are shown in Figure 21.1.

21.1.1.1 The Target Layer

The MDB answerbook describes targets as follows:

> *The target is the program being inspected by the debugger. [...] Each target exports a standard set of properties, including one or more address spaces, one or more symbol tables, a set of load objects, and a set of threads.*

Targets are implemented by means of an ops vector, with each target implementing a subset of the functions in the vector. In-situ targets, such as the user process or `proc`, implement virtually all operations. Targets that debug entities whose execution cannot be controlled, such as the kvm target used for crash dump analysis, implement a smaller subset of the operations. As with many other parts of MDB, the targets are modular and are designed to be easily replaceable depending on the requirements of the debugging environment.

Figure 21.1 shows three of the targets used by MDB. The first is the `proc` target, which is used for the debugging and control of user processes as well as the analysis of user core dumps. The `proc` target is implemented on top of `libproc`, which provides the primitives used for process control. The interfaces provided by libproc simplify the implementation of the proc target by hiding the differences between in-situ and postmortem debugging (one is done with a live process, whereas the other uses a corefile). The target itself is largely concerned with mapping the requests of the debugger to the interfaces exposed by libproc.

Also shown in Figure 21.1 is the kvm target, which is used for both live and postmortem kernel debugging. Like the proc target, the kvm target uses a support library (libkvm) to abstract the differences between live and postmortem debugging. While the capabilities of the kvm and proc targets are largely the same when used for postmortem debugging, they differ when the subjects are live. The proc target fully controls process execution, whereas the kvm target allows only the inspection and alteration of kernel state. Allowing the debugger to control the execution of the kernel that is responsible for running the debugger would be difficult at best. Consequently, most debugging done with the kvm target is of the postmortem variety.

The third target shown in Figure 21.1 is used for the "debugging" of raw files. This allows the data-presentation abilities of MDB to be brought to bear upon flat (usually binary) files. This target lays the foundation for the eventual replacement of something like fsdb, the filesystem debugger.

21.1.1.2 Debugger Module Management

Today's kernels are made up of a great many modules, each implementing a different subsystem and each requiring different tools for analysis and debugging. The same can be said for modern, large-scale user processes, which can incorporate tens or even hundreds of shared libraries and subsystems. A modern modular debugger should, therefore, allow for the augmentation of its basic tool set as needed. MDB allows subsystem-specific debugging facilities to be provided through shared objects known as debugger modules, or dmods. Each dmod provides debugging commands (also known as dcmds) and walkers (iterators) that debug a given subsystem. These modules interface with MDB through the module API layer and use well-defined interfaces for data retrieval and analysis. This is enforced by the fact that, in the case of both major targets (kvm and proc), the debugger runs in a separate address space from the entity being analyzed. The dcmds are therefore forced to use the module API to access the target. While some dmods link with other support libraries to reduce the duplication of code, most dmods stand alone, consuming only the header files from the subsystems they support.

While the core debugger uses its own code for the management of debugger modules and their metadata, it relies upon a system library, libdl, for the mechanics of module unloading and unloading. It is libdl, for example, that knows how to load the dmod into memory, and it is libdl that knows how to integrate that dmod into the debugger's address space.

21.1.1.3 Terminal I/O

MDB was designed with an eye toward the eventual implementation of something like kmdb and thus performs most terminal interaction directly. Having built up a list of terminal attributes, MDB handles cursor and character manipulation directly. The MDB subsystem that performs terminal I/O is known as termio.

While termio handles a great deal itself, there is one aspect of terminal management that is provided by a support library. MDB uses libcurses to retrieve the list of terminal attributes for the current terminal from the terminfo database. The current terminal type is retrieved from the environment variable TERM.

21.1.1.4 Other Stuff

MDB is a large program, with many more subsystems than are described here. One of the benefits arising from the modular design of the debugger is that these other subsystems don't need to change even when used in an environment as radically different as kmdb is from MDB. For example, MDB implements its own routines for the management of ELF symbol tables. ELF being ELF regardless of source, the same subsystem can be used, as is, in both MDB and kmdb. A description of the MDB subsystems unaffected by kmdb is beyond the scope of this document.

21.1.2 Major kmdb Design Decisions

In this section we explore the rationale behind the major design decisions.

21.1.2.1 The Kernel/Debugger Interface (KDI)

When we implement an in-situ kernel debugger, we must determine the extent to which the debugger will be intermingled with the kernel being debugged. Should the debugger call kernel functions to accomplish its duties, or should the debugger be entirely self-contained? The legacy Solaris in-situ kernel debugger, kadb, hewed to the latter philosophy to a significant extent. The kadb module was as self-contained as possible, to the point where it contained copies of certain low-level kernel routines. That said, there were some kernel routines to which kadb needed access. During debugger startup, it would search for a number of functions by name, saving pointers to them for later use.

There are a number of problems with kadb's approach. First of all, by duplicating low-level kernel code in the debugger, we introduce duplication. Furthermore, this duplication, due to the layout of the Solaris source code, results in the copies being significantly separated. It's hard enough to maintain code rife with duplication when the duplicates are co-located. Maintaining duplicates located in wildly disparate locations is next to impossible. During initial analysis of kadb as part of the kmdb project, we discovered several duplicated functions in kadb that had not kept up with hardware-specific changes to the versions in the kernel. The second problem concerns the means by which kadb gained access to the kernel functions it did use. Searching for those functions by name is dangerous because it leaves the debugger vulnerable to changes in the kernel. A change in the signature of a kernel function used by kadb, for example, would not be caught until kadb failed while trying to use said function.

To some extent, the nature of a kernel debugger requires duplication. The kernel debugger cannot, for example, hold locks, and therefore requires lock-free versions of any kernel code that it must call. The lock-free version of a function may not be safe when used in a running kernel context and therefore must be kept separate from the normal version. Rather than placing that duplicate copy within the debugger itself, we decided to co-locate the duplicate with the original. This reduces the chances of code rot, since an engineer changing the normal version is much more likely to notice the debugger-specific version sitting right next to it.

Access to kernel functionality was formalized through an interface known as the KDI, or Kernel/Debugger Interface. The KDI is an ops vector through which all kernel function calls must pass. Each function called by the debugger has a member in this vector. Whereas an assessment of kernel functionality used by kadb required a search for symbol lookup routines and their consumers, a similar assessment in kmdb simply requires the review of the single ops vector. Furthermore, our use of an ops vector allowed us to use the compiler to monitor the evolution of kernel functions used by kmdb. Any change to a KDI function significant enough to change the function signature will be caught by the compiler during the initialization of the KDI ops vector. Furthermore, the initialization of said vector is easily visible to code analysis tools such as cscope, allowing engineers to quickly determine whether kmdb is a consumer of a given function. With kadb, such a check would require a check of the symbol lookup routines, something that is not automatically done by the code analysis tools used today.

21.1.2.2 Implementation as a Kernel Module

kadb was implemented as a stand-alone module. In Solaris, this means that the kadb module was an executable, directly loadable by the boot loader. It had no static dependencies on other modules, thus leading to the symbol lookup problems discussed above. When the use of kadb was requested, the boot process ran something like this:

1. Boot loader loads kadb.
2. kadb initializes.
3. kadb loads normal stand-alone, UNIX.
4. kadb loads the UNIX interpreter, krtld.
5. kadb passes control to krtld.

6. krtld loads the UNIX dependencies (genunix, CPU module, platform
   module, etc.).

7. krtld transfers control to UNIX.

   While this allowed the debugger to take early control of the system (it could
debug from the first instruction in krtld), that ability came with some significant
penalties. The decision to load a 32-bit or 64-bit kernel being made after kadb had
loaded and initialized, kadb had to be prepared to debug either variety. The need
for kadb to execute prior to the loading of UNIX itself meant that it could not use
any functions located in the kernel until the kernel was loaded. While some essential functions were dynamically located later, the result of this restriction was the
location of many low-level kernel functions in the debugger itself. A further penalty comes in the form of increased debugger complexity. kadb's need to load UNIX
and krtld requires that it know how to process ELF files and how to load modules into the address space. The boot loader already needs to know how to do that,
as does krtld. With kadb as a stand-alone module, the number of separate copies
of ELF-processing and module-loading code goes up to three.

   The remaining limitations have to do with the timing of the decision to load
kadb. As stated above, kadb was a stand-alone module and as such could only be
loaded at boot. Moreover, an administrator was required to decide, before rebooting, whether to load kadb. Once loaded, it could not be unloaded. While the inability to unload the debugger isn't a major limitation, the inability to dynamically
load it, is. Not knowing whether kadb would be needed during the life of a given
system boot, administrators would be faced with an unfortunate choice. On the one
hand, they could always load kadb at boot. This kept it always ready for use, but
at the cost of the wiring down of a chunk of kernel address space. This could be
avoided, of course, by making the other choice—not loading the debugger at boot.
Administrators then ran the risk of not having the debugger around when they
needed it.

   The implementation of kmdb as a normal kernel module solves all of these problems, with only a minor activation-time penalty compared to kadb. When kmdb is
loaded at boot, the boot process looks something like this:

1. Boot loader loads UNIX.

2. Boot loader loads the UNIX interpreter, krtld.

3. Boot loader passes control to krtld.

4. krtld loads the UNIX dependencies (genunix, CPU module, platform
   module, etc.).

5. krtld loads kmdb.

6. krtld transfers control to UNIX.

As shown above, kmdb loads after the primary kernel modules have been selected and loaded. kmdb can therefore assume that it will be running with the same bit width as that of the underlying kernel. That is, a 32-bit kmdb will never have to deal with a 64-bit kernel, and vice versa.

By loading after the primaries, kmdb can have static symbol dependencies on the other primary kernel modules. It is this ability that allows the KDI to exist. Even better, kmdb can rely on krtld's selection of the proper CPU and platform modules for this machine. Rather than having to carry around several processor-specific implementations of the same function (or compiling one module for each of four platform types, as kadb did), kmdb can, using the KDI, simply use the proper implementation of a given function from the proper module. When a new platform-specific KDI function is implemented, the developer implements it in a platform-specific way in each platform module. krtld selects the proper platform module on boot, and kmdb automatically ends up using the proper version for the host machine.

Last but certainly not least, the implementation of kmdb as a normal kernel module allows it to be dynamically loaded and unloaded. It can still be loaded at boot, but it can also be loaded on-demand by the administrator. If dynamically loaded, it can also be unloaded when no longer needed. This can be a consolation to wary administrators who would otherwise object to the running of a kernel debugger on certain types of machines.

The only disadvantage of the use of a normal kernel module versus a stand-alone one is the loss of the ability to debug the early stages of krtld. In practice, this has not turned out to be a problem, because the early stages of krtld are fairly straightforward and stable.

Every attempt has been made to minimize the effects of the two load types (boot and runtime). Obviously initialization differs in some respects, a number of common kernel subsystems simply won't be available during the initialization of boot-loaded kmdb. Largely, though, these differences are dealt with under the covers and are not visible to the user.

21.1.3 The Structure of kmdb

We can best understand the inner workings of kmdb by first reviewing the debugger's external structure. kmdb's external structure is dictated, to some extent, by the environments in which it will be used. Those requirements are

- The debugger must be loadable at boot.
- The debugger must be loadable at runtime.
- The debugger must restrict its contact with the running kernel to a set of operations defined in advance.

To satisfy the first two requirements, kmdb exists as two separate kernel modules. The first, misc/kmdbmod, contains the meat of the debugger; it is the module loaded by krtld when kmdb is loaded at boot. The second module, drv/kmdb, exists solely to gather property values from the device tree and to present an ioctl-based interface to controlling userland programs such as mdb(1). When kmdb is to be loaded at runtime, mdb opens /dev/kmdb and uses the ioctl interface to command it to activate. The opening of /dev/kmdb causes drv/kmdb to load. drv/kmdb has a dependency on misc/kmdbmod, which gets loaded as well. Upon receipt of the appropriate ioctl, drv/kmdb calls into misc/kmdbmod, and the debugger is initialized.

If the debugger was loaded at boot, only misc/kmdbmod will be loaded. The module loading subsystem is not fully initialized at that point. Userland does not exist yet, and given that drv/kmdb exists only to convey ioctl requests from userland to misc/kmdbmod, there is no need to force drv/kmdb to load until an attempt is made to open /dev/kmdb. When someone does attempt to control the debugger through ioctls to /dev/kmdb, drv/kmdb is loaded. It then sends commands to misc/kmdbmod as in the runtime case above.

We now focus our attention more closely on misc/kmdbmod, which itself is composed of two parts. The first, referred to as the debugger, contains the core debugger functionality, as well as the primary subsystems needed to allow the core to control the kernel. The second, referred to as the controller, interacts with the running kernel.

The debugger interacts with the outside world only through a set of well-defined interfaces. One of these is the KDI; the other is composed of a set of functions passed during initialization by the controller. Aside from these interactions, the debugger must, by nature, function as a fully self-contained entity. Put in compilation terms, the debugger, which is built separately from the controller, must not have any unresolved symbols at link time. It is the debugger, and only the debugger, that is active when kmdb has control of the machine.

Behind the scenes, as it were, the controller works to ensure that the debugger's runtime needs are met. The debugger has a limited set of direct interactions with the kernel. And it can only be active when the world has stopped. Those two facts necessarily limit the sorts of things the debugger can do. For example, it can neither perform the early stages of kmdb initialization nor load or unload kernel modules.

The former takes place before debugger initialization starts and is taken care of by the controller. A memory region, known as Oz, is allocated and is set aside for use by the debugger. Other initialization tasks performed by the controller include the creation of trap tables or IDTs, as appropriate, after which control is passed to the debugger for the completion of initialization.

Kernel module loading and unloading, which is discussed in more detail below, is a task that must be performed by the running kernel. The debugger must rely on the controller to perform these sorts of tasks for it.

In the text that follows, we use the words driver, debugger, and controller to refer to the components we've just discussed. These three components are indicated in Figure 21.2 by regions surrounded by dotted lines. When we discuss the entire entity, we refer to it as kmdb. References to the core debugger refer to the set of shaded boxes labeled MDB. One unfortunate note: The term "controller" is a relatively recent invention. In many instances, the source code refers to the driver when it means the controller. This doesn't cause nearly as many issues as one might imagine because of the minor role played by the entity we refer to as the driver.

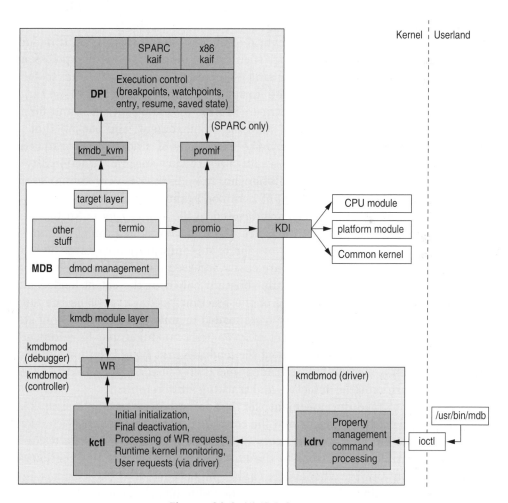

Figure 21.2 KMDB Structure

21.1.4 MDB Components and Their Implementation in kmdb

We now use our earlier discussion of mdb to motivate our review of the major subsystems used by kmdb. Recall that the three subsystems discussed were the target layer, module management, and terminal management (termio). The implementation of kmdb is largely the story of the replacement of support libraries with subsystems designed to work in kmdb's unique environment. Figure 21.2 shows how these replacement subsystems relate to the core debugger.

21.1.4.1 The Target Layer

The target layer itself is unchanged in kmdb. What changes is the target implementation itself. Gone are the proc, kvm, and file targets, replaced with a single target called kmdb_kvm. We continue to call it kmdb_kvm to avoid confusion with the kvm target used by mdb.

kmdb_kvm can be thought of as a hybrid of the proc and kvm targets. It includes the execution control aspects of proc, such as the ability to set breakpoints and watchpoints, as well as support for single-stepping, continuation, and so forth. This functionality is coupled with the kernel-oriented aspects of the kvm target. The kmdb_kvm target is common between SPARC and x86 machines and for the most part handles the bits of kernel analysis, management, and control that are generic to the two architectures. With the exceptions of stack trace construction and the display of saved registers, all architecture-specific functionality is abstracted into the DPI. The DPI's relationship to kmdb_kvm is very similar to that of libkvm to the kvm target or to that of libproc to the proc target.

A significant portion of kmdb_kvm is devoted to the monitoring of kernel state. As an example, target implementations are required to provide symbol lookup routines for use by the core debugger. Provision of this information requires access to kernel module symbol tables, which are easily accessed by kmdb_kvm. What is not so simple, however, is dealing with the constant churn in the set of loaded modules. Whenever kmdb regains control of the machine, kmdb_kvm scans the entire module list, looking for modules that have loaded or unloaded. The tracking state (symbol table references, and so forth) of kmdb_kvm modules that have unloaded is destroyed, while new state is created for modules that have been loaded. Challenges arise when a module has unloaded and then reloaded since kmdb last had control. This churn must be detected, and tracking state rebuilt.

The tracking of module movement, for lack of a better term, illustrates the interaction between the debugger and the controller. While the debugger could certainly rescan the entire list upon every entry, that approach would be wasteful. Instead, the controller subscribes to the kernel's module change notification service and bumps a counter whenever a change has occurred. kmdb_kvm can, upon reentry, check the value of that counter. If the value has changed since kmdb_kvm last saw it, a module list rescan is necessary.

While this interaction with the controller results in a useful optimization for module state management, it becomes crucial for the management of deferred breakpoints. Deferred breakpoints are breakpoints requested for modules that haven't yet loaded. The user's expectation is that the breakpoint will activate when the named module loads. The debugger is responsible for the creation, deletion, enabling, disabling, activation, and deactivation of breakpoints. The user creates the breakpoint by using the breakpoint command (::bp). This being a deferred breakpoint for a module that hasn't been loaded, the debugger leaves the breakpoint in a disabled state. When that module has loaded, the breakpoint is enabled. Enabled breakpoints are activated by the debugger when the world is resumed. The activation is what makes the breakpoint actually happen. In kmdb_kvm, the DPI installs a breakpoint instruction at the specified virtual address. The key design question: How do we detect the loading of the requested module?

The simplest, cleanest, and slowest approach would be to have kmdb_kvm place an internal breakpoint on the kernel's module loading routine. Whenever a module is loaded, the debugger would activate, would check the identity of the loaded module, and would decide whether to enable the breakpoint. Debugger entry isn't cheap. All CPUs must be stopped, and their state must be saved. This particular stop would happen after a module load, so we would need to rescan the module list. All in all, this is something that we really don't want to have to do every time a module is loaded or unloaded.

If we involve the controller, we can eliminate the unnecessary debugger activations, entering the debugger only when a module named in a deferred breakpoint is loaded or unloaded. How do we do this? We bend the boundaries between the debugger and controller slightly, exposing the list of deferred breakpoints to code that runs when the world is turning. Tie this into the controller's registration with the kernel's module change notification service, and we end up entering the debugger only when a change has occurred in a module named in a deferred breakpoint. We use a quasi-lock-free data structure to allow access to the deferred breakpoint list both from within the debugger (when the world is stopped) and within the module change check (when the world is running).

Like the proc and kvm targets, kmdb_kvm is also home to dcmds that could not be implemented elsewhere. Implemented in the target, they have access to everything the target does and can thus do things that dcmds implemented in dmods could only dream of doing. As implied above, kmdb_kvm (as well as kvm and proc) implement dcmds that provide stack tracing and register access.

21.1.4.2 Debugger Module Management

As discussed earlier, mdb uses libdl for the management of dmods, which are implemented as shared objects. The implementation of kmdb is similar, but without libdl. Nor does the debugger have the way to actually load or unload modules. Other than that, kmdb and mdb are the same.

We decompose module management into two pieces: the requesting of module loads and unloads, and the implementation of a libdl replacement atop the results of the loading and unloading.

21.1.4.3 Module Loads and Unloads: The Work Request Queue (WR)

kmdb implements debugger modules as kernel modules. While we engage in some sleight of hand to keep the dmods off the kernel's main module list, the mechanics of loading and unloading dmods is largely the same as that used for "normal" kernel modules. The primary difference is in the means by which a load or unload is requested. Recall that the debugger, which will receive the load or unload request from the user, can only run when the world is stopped. Also note that the loading or unloading of a kernel module is a process that uses many different kernel subsystems. The kernel runtime linker (krtld), the disk driver, VM system, file system, and many others come into play. Use of these subsystems of course entails the use of locks, threads, and various other things that are anathema to the debugger.

To load a dmod, the debugger must therefore ask the controller to do it. The controller runs when the world is turning and is more than capable of loading and unloading kernel modules. The only thing we need is a channel for communication between the two. That channel is provided by the Work Request Queue, or WR. The WR consists of two queues: one for messages from the debugger to the controller and one for messages from the controller to the debugger. The rough sequence of events for a module load is as follows:

1. User requests a dmod load with ::load.
2. The kmdb module layer receives the request and passes it to the WR debugger → controller queue.
3. The world is resumed.
4. The controller receives the request.
5. The controller loads the module.
6. The controller returns the requests to the debugger as a (successful) reply on the controller → debugger queue.
7. The controller initiates a debugger reentry.
8. The debugger receives the reply and makes the contents of the dmod available to the debugger core.

A few details bear mentioning. The debugger can be activated at any time—even in the midst of the controller's processing of a load request. The controller must keep this in mind when checking and manipulating the WR queues. The queues themselves are lock-free and have very strict rules regarding the methods used to access them. For example, the controller may only add to the end of the controller → debugger queue. It sets the next pointer on its request and updates the tail pointer for the queue. Even though the queue is doubly linked, there's no easy way for the controller, which may be interrupted at any time by the debugger, to set the prev pointer. Accordingly, the debugger's first action upon preparing to process the controller → debugger queue is to traverse it, from tail to head, building the `prev` pointers. The debugger doesn't have to worry about being interrupted by the controller and can thus take its time. Similar rules are in place for the debugger → controller queue.

Every request must be tracked and sent back as a reply at some point. Even fire-and-forget requests, such as those establishing new module search paths, must be returned as replies, even if those replies don't come until the debugger is unloaded. To see why this is necessary, consider the source of the memory underlying the requests. Requests from the debugger are allocated from debugger memory by the debugger's allocator and can thus only be freed by the debugger. Requests initiated by the controller (for example, an automatic dmod load triggered by the loading of the corresponding kernel module) are allocated by the controller from kernel memory and can thus be freed only by the kernel. Replies therefore serve a dual purpose—they provide status to the requester and also return the request to the requester for freeing.

We'd like to minimize the impact of the debugger on the running system to the extent practicable and so don't want the controller to poll for updates to the WR queues. Instead, we want the debugger to tell the controller when work is available for processing. This isn't as simple as it may seem. In the real world, we would use semaphores or condition variables to signal the availability of work. To use kernel synchronization objects, the debugger would need to call into the kernel to release them. The kernel is most definitely not prepared for a `cv_broadcast()` call with every CPU stuck in the debugger. Unpleasantness would ensue. The lightest-weight way to communicate with the controller is to post a soft interrupt, the implementation of which is essentially the setting of a bit in the kernel's `cpu_t` structure. When the world has resumed, normal Normal interrupt processing will encounter this bit and will call the soft interrupt handler registered by the controller. That handler bangs on a semaphore, which triggers the controller's WR processing. Note that these problems apply only for communications from the debugger to the controller. The debugger can simply poll for messages sent in the opposite direction. Since the debugger is activated relatively infrequently, the occasional check of a message-waiting bit doesn't impose a burden. When users request a debugger activation, the last thing on their mind is whether the debugger is wasting a few cycles to check for messages.

`libdl` supplies a synchronous loading and unloading interface to mdb, thus considerably simplifying its management of dmods. kmdb has no such luxury. As the reader might surmise from the preceding discussion, kmdb's loading and unloading of dmods is decidedly asynchronous. Every attempt is made to preserve the user's illusion of a blocking load, but the asynchronous nature occasionally pokes its head into the open. A breakpoint encountered before the completion of the load, for example, causes an early debugger reentry. The user is told that a load or an unload is still pending and is told how to allow it to complete.

21.1.4.4 `libdl` Wrapper

MDB's dmod management code uses the `libdl` interfaces for manipulating dmods. `dlopen()` loads modules, `dlclose()` unloads them, and `dlsym()` looks up symbols. The debugger implements its own versions of these functions (using the same function signatures) to support the illusion of `libdl`. Underneath, the debugger's symbol table facilities are retargeted to implement `dlsym()`'s searches of dmod symbol tables.

21.1.4.5 Terminal I/O

To implement terminal I/O handling, we need three things: access to the terminal type, the ability to manipulate that terminal, and routines for actually sending I/O to and from that terminal. The second of these can be further subdivided into the retrieval of terminal characteristics and the use of that knowledge to manipulate the terminal. mdb implements the most difficult of these—the routines that actually manipulate the terminal according to the gathered characteristics. mdb handles the tracking of cursor position, in-line editing, and the implementation of a parser and knows how to use the individual terminal attributes (echo this to make the cursor move right, echo that to enable bold, etc.) to accomplish those tasks.

Left to mdb and kmdb are terminal type determination, attribute retrieval, and I/O to the terminal itself. For mdb, this is relatively straightforward. The terminal type can be gathered from the environment, attributes can be retrieved from the terminfo database with `libcurses`, and I/O accomplished with stdin, stdout, and stderr.

kmdb, as is its wont, has a more difficult time of things. There is no environment from which to gather the current terminal type. There's no easy access to the terminfo database. Completing the trifecta, the I/O methods vary with the type of platform, progress of the boot process, and phase of the moon. As a bonus, kmdb's termio implementation handles interrupt (^C) processing. We discuss each in turn. While the preceding sections had happy endings, in that pleasing solutions were found for the enumerated problems, the reader is warned that there are no happy endings in terminal management. Tales of wading through terminal types, to say nothing of the terminfo/termcap databases, are generally suitable only for frightening small children and always end in woe and the gnashing of teeth.

21.1.4.6 Retrieving the Terminal Type

At first glance, gaining access to the terminal type would seem straightforward. Sadly, no. kmdb can be loaded at boot or at runtime. It can be used on a locally attached console/framebuffer, or it can be used through a serial console. If loaded at runtime, the invocation could be made from a console login, or it could be made from an rsh (or telnet or ...) session. Boot-loaded kmdb on a serial console is the worst because we have no information regarding the type of terminal attached to the other end of the serial connection. We end up assuming the worst, which is a 80 × 24 VT100. Boot-loaded kmdb on a machine with a locally attached console or framebuffer is easier because we know the terminal type and terminal dimensions for SPARC and x86 consoles. Also easy is a runtime-loaded kmdb from a console login. Assuming that the user set the terminal type correctly, we can use the value of the TERM environment variable. But unfortunately we can't trust $TERM to be set correctly, so we ignore $TERM if the console is locally attached. We end up with a pile of heuristics, which generally come up with the right answer. If they don't, they can always be overridden.

21.1.4.7 Terminal Attributes

After considering the mess that is access to $TERM, retrieval of terminfo data is almost trivial. We don't want to compile in a copy of the terminfo database, and we can't rely on the ability to gain access to it while the debugger is running. We compromise by hard-coding a selection of terminal types into the debugger. The build process extracts the attributes for each selected terminal from the terminfo database and compiles them into the debugger. Terminal type selection in kmdb is thus limited to the types selected during the build. It turns out, though, that the vast majority of common terminal types can be covered by a set of 15 terminal types.

21.1.4.8 Console I/O

Access to the terminal entails the reading of input, the writing of output, and the retrieval of hardware parameters (terminal size and so forth), generally through an ioctl-based interface. MDB's modular I/O subsystem makes our job somewhat easier. Each I/O module provides an ops vector, exposing interfaces for reading, writing, ioctls, and so forth. kmdb has its own I/O module, called promio. promio acts as a front end for promif, which we discuss in a moment. For the most part, promio is a pass-through, with the exception of the ioctl function. promio interprets the ioctls sent from termio and invokes the appropriate promif functions to gather the necessary information. In addition to the aforementioned terminal size ioctl (TIOCGWINSZ), promio's ioctl handler is prepared to deal with requests to get (TCGETS) and set (TCSETSW) hardware parameters. The parameters of interest to kmdb are largely concerned with echoing and newlines.

`promif` interfaces the debugger with the system's OpenBoot PROM (OBP). While x86 systems don't have PROMs, Solaris (and thus `kmdb`) try very hard to pretend that they do. For the most part, this means functions called `prom_something()` are named to mimic their SPARC counterparts. Whereas the SPARC versions jump into OBP, the x86 versions do whatever is necessary to implement the same functionality without a PROM. `promif` exposes two classes of interface: those that deal with console (terminal) I/O, and those that are merely wrappers around PROM routines. We cover the former group here.

Both SPARC and x86 systems get help from the boot loader (OBP on SPARC) for console I/O during the initial stages of boot. SPARC systems without USB keyboards can use OBP for console I/O even after boot. x86 systems and SPARC systems with USB keyboards use a kernel subsystem known as polled I/O. Exposed to `kmdb` through the KDI, polled I/O is a method for interacting directly with the I/O hardware, be it a serial driver, the USB stack, or something completely different without blocking. Rather than waiting for interrupts, as can be done while the world is turning, the polled I/O subsystem is designed to poll I/O devices until input is available or output has been sent. The bottom line is that the method used for console I/O changes during the boot process. The portion of `promif` dedicated to console I/O hides this complexity from consumers, exposing only routines for reading and writing bytes. Consumers need not concern themselves with where those bytes come from or go to.

21.1.4.9 Interrupt (^C) Management

Given that `kmdb` console I/O is synchronous, there is no easy way for an interrupt (^C) from a user to get to the core debugger. In userland, the kernel detects interrupts asynchronously, generates a signal, and inflicts it upon the process. There is no parallel in `kmdb`. The debugger doesn't know about pending interrupts until it reads the interrupt character from the keyboard. With a simplistic I/O implementation, reading only when we need to, a user would never be able to interrupt anything.

`promif` works around this limitation by implementing a read-ahead buffer. That buffer is drained when the debugger needs input from the user. It is filled whenever input is available by a nonblocking reader. Attempts are made to fill the buffer whenever input is requested, when data is to be output, or when an attempt is made to read or write the kernel's address space. If an interrupt character is discovered during a buffer fill, control passes to the interrupt-handling routine, which halts the command that was executing. Debugger commands that aren't constantly writing to the console, reading from the kernel, or writing to the kernel are very rare (and probably of questionable utility). In practice, this means that a buffer fill attempt will be made soon after the user presses ^C. As a future enhancement, we could, barring the implementation of an asynchronous interrupt-delivery mechanism, expand the number of fill points. In practice, though, this doesn't seem like it would be necessary.

21.1.5 Conclusion

A significant portion of the design and implementation of kmdb was spent filling in the gaping holes left when mdb was separated from its supporting libraries. Certainly, we didn't realize how much is provided by those supporting libraries until we attempted to take them away. These gaps were filled by replacement subsystems whose operations were complicated by the restrictive environment in which kmdb operates. The balance of kmdb's implementation was spent in the development of the KDI functions and in the implementation of the DPI, more on which below. The DPI provides the low-level code that allows the remainder of kmdb to be largely architecture neutral.

21.1.6 Remaining Components

In this section, we cover some remaining discussion items related to the implementation of kmdb.

21.1.6.1 The Debugger/PROM Interface (DPI)

The DPI has a somewhat sordid history, the twists and turns of which have influenced the way it appears today.

kadb on x86, having no PROM, did everything itself. The SPARC version on the other hand, depended on a great many services provided by OBP. OBP provided trap handling for the debugger. It also took care of debugger entry, the saving of a portion of processor state, among other things.

kmdb was initially planned to be released in conjunction with an enhanced OBP. This new OBP would accord more sophisticated debugging facilities, thus freeing kmdb from having to deal with many low-level, hardware-specific details. For example, the new OBP would manage software breakpoints itself. It would capture and park processors during debugger execution. It would also manage watchpoints.

Recognizing that not all systems would have this new OBP, we initially designed kmdb with a pluggable interface that would allow for its use on systems with both types of OBP. That interface is called the Debugger/PROM interface, or DPI. SPARC would have one module for the old-style OBP interface, which we called the kadb-style interface (or kaif). SPARC would have a second module for the new-style OBP interface, the name for which has been buried in the sands of time. The debugger would choose between the two modules according to an assessment of OBP features. x86 systems would have a single module, also called kaif.

Some time into the implementation of kmdb (well after the terms DPI and kaif had cemented themselves throughout the source code), the plans for the new-style OBP were dropped. This turned out to be for the best, the reasons for which are beyond the scope of this document. As a result, modern-day kmdb has one module for each architecture. The intervening layer, the DPI, is not strictly necessary. It may not have been invented had it not been for our earlier plans to accommodate multiple styles of OBP interaction. It remains, though, and serves as a useful repository for some functionality common to the two `kaif` implementations.

The bulk of the `kaif` module is devoted to the performance of the following five tasks:

1. Coordination of debugger entry
2. Manipulation of processor state
3. Source analysis for execution control
4. Management of breakpoints and watchpoints
5. Trap handling

21.1.6.2 Coordination of Debugger Entry

`kmdb` is single threaded and establishes a master-slave relationship between the CPUs on the machine. The first CPU to encounter an event that triggers debugger entry, such as a breakpoint, watchpoint, or deliberate entry, becomes the master. The master then cross-traps the remaining CPUs, causing them to enter the debugger as slaves. Slaves spin in busy loops until the world is resumed or until one of them switches places with the master. If multiple CPUs encounter debugger entry events at the same time and thus race for debugger entry, only one will win. The first to grab the master lock wins, with the remainder becoming slaves.

21.1.6.3 Manipulation of Processor State

When processors enter the debugger, they save their register state into per-processor save areas. This state is then exposed to the user of the debugger. The `kaif` module coordinates the saving of this state and also implements the search routines that allow for its retrieval.

21.1.6.4 Source Analysis for Execution Control

MDB supports a number of execution control primitives. In addition to breakpoints and watchpoints, which we discuss shortly, it provides for single-step, step-over, step-out, and continue. Single-step halts execution at the next instruction. Step-over is similar, except that it does not step into subroutines. That is, it steps to the next instruction in the current routine. Step-out steps to the next instruction in the calling routine. Continue resumes system execution on all processors (single-step resumes execution only on the processor being stepped).

Single-step is implemented directly by the `kaif` module. On x86, this entails the setting of `EFLAGS.TF`. On SPARC, we set breakpoints at the next possible execution points. If the next instruction is a branch, for example, we may have to set two breakpoints to cover both possible results of the branch.

Step-over and step are implemented independently of single-step. For step-over, MDB calls into the target, which calls into the DPI and `kaif`, asking whether the next instruction requires special processing. If the next instruction is a call, `kaif` returns with the address of the instruction after the call. MDB places a breakpoint at that location and uses continue to "step" over the call. If the next instruction is not a call, the `kaif` module so indicates, and MDB uses normal single-step. When the user requests a step-out, MDB requests, through the target and the DPI, that the `kaif` module locate the next instruction in the calling function.

Whereas single-step releases a single processor to execute a single instruction, continue releases all processors and fully resumes the world. Continue also posts the soft interrupt to the controller if necessary, in support of debugger module management.

21.1.6.5 Management of Breakpoints and Watchpoints

Both SPARC and x86 rely on software breakpoints. That is, a specific instruction (`int $3` on x86, and `ta 0x7e` on SPARC) is written at a given location. When control reaches that location, the debugger is entered. Breakpoints are activated by installation of one of these instructions and are deactivated by restoration of the original instruction.

Watchpoints are implemented by hardware on both platforms. Space on processors being at a premium and watchpoints being relatively rarely used (though oh-so-helpful), processors don't provide many of them and impose restrictions on the ones they do. SPARC, for example, has two watchpoints—one physical and one virtual. SPARC watchpoint sizes are restricted to 8 bytes or any non-zero power of 256. x86 implements four watchpoints, even allowing watchpoints on individual I/O port numbers, but imposes restrictions on their size and access type. Hardware activates watchpoints by writing to the appropriate hardware registers and deactivates them by clearing those registers. The `kaif` ensures that the target activates only the supported number of watchpoints. It also checks to make sure that the watchpoints requested meet the hardware limitations. No attempt is made to synthesize more flexible watchpoints.

21.1.6.6 Trap Handling

On SPARC, `kmdb` has drastically reduced its dependency upon OBP as the project has progressed. This is somewhat ironic in light of our earlier attempts to increase that dependency. Whereas `kadb` allowed OBP to handle traps and to coordinate entrance into the debugger, `kmdb` has its own trap table, handles its own debugger entry, and even handles its own MMU misses.

kmdb also installs its own trap table on x86, although the trap table there is called an IDT. Not having ever had an OBP upon which to become dependent, Solaris x86 in-situ debuggers have always handled their own traps and debugger entry.

When kmdb gains control of the machine, it switches to its trap table. When the world resumes, the trap table used prior to debugger entry is restored. While kmdb is running, traps that are immediately resolvable by the handler (MMU misses to valid addresses, for example) are handled and control is returned to the execution stream that caused the trap. Traps that are not resolvable by the handler cause a debugger reentry. In some cases, such as when an access is being made to the kernel's address space, the debugger takes precautions against traps resulting from those accesses. Reentry caused by such a trap would cause control to be transferred back to the code that initiated the access, with a return code set indicating that an error occurred. Unexpected traps are signs that something has gone wrong and are grounds for entry into a debugger fault state. The stack trace leading up to the access is displayed, and the user is offered the option to induce a crash dump.

APPENDICES

Kernel Virtual Address Maps

In this appendix, we illustrate the allocation- and location-specific information for the segments that constitute the Solaris 10 kernel address space.

The kernel address space is represented by the address space pointed to by the system object, kas. The segment drivers manage the manipulation of the segments within the kernel address space. Figure A.1 illustrates the architecture.

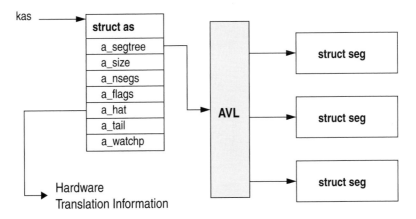

Figure A.1 Kernel Address Space and Segments

You can look at the kernel address space with the as seg walker and D command, using the kernel address space pointer. The seg walker will show the kernel address space segments and the `::seg` D Command will show detail for each of the segments.

```
sol9 # mdb -k
> kas ::walk seg |::seg
            SEG              BASE              SIZE          DATA OPS
        1841258          1000000           8f2000              0 segkmem_ops
        1835878           18f2000           40e000              0 segkmem_ops
        18358c8          70000000         10000000              0 segkmem_ops
        1843410          edd00000          2300000              0 segkmem_ops
        18355d0       2a100000000          1ec20000    300000c8090 segkp_ops
        18357e8       2a750000000           1cbc000    30000451f40 segmap_ops
        1835618       30000000000        1fff8000000              0 segkmem_ops
        18455f8       50000000000       20000000000              0 segkmem_ops
        18389f0       70000000000           3da000              0 segkmem_ops
        1838a38 fffffa0000000000       40000000000    30000464760 segkpm_ops
```

For more detail, you can then use the `::print` D command to print a list of the kernel memory segments structures.

```
> kas ::walk seg |::print "struct seg"
{
    s_base = scb
    s_size = 0x8f2000
    s_szc = 0
    s_flags = 0
    s_as = kas
    s_tree = {
        avl_child = [ 0, 0 ]
        avl_pcb = 0x1835899
    }
    s_ops = segkmem_ops
    s_data = 0
}
{
    s_base = 0x18f2000
    s_size = 0x40e000
    s_szc = 0
    s_flags = 0
    s_as = kas
    s_tree = {
        avl_child = [ ktextseg+0x20, kvseg32+0x20 ]
        avl_pcb = 0x1843431
    }
    s_ops = segkmem_ops
    s_data = 0
}
...
```

The next figures illustrate Solaris 10 address space, as follows:

- Figure A.2 Solaris 10 sun4u 64-Bit Kernel Address Space
- Figure A.3 Solaris 10 amd64 64-Bit Kernel Address Space
- Figure A.4 Solaris 10 x86 32-Bit Kernel Address Space

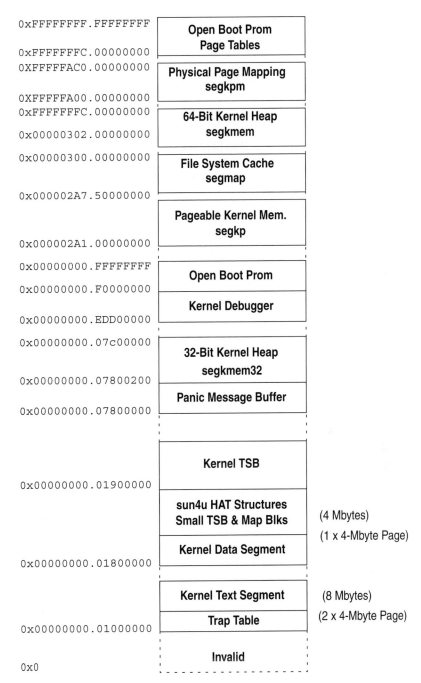

0xFFFFFFFF.FFFFFFFF	Open Boot Prom Page Tables
0xFFFFFFFC.00000000	
0XFFFFFAC0.00000000	Physical Page Mapping segkpm
0XFFFFFA00.00000000	
0xFFFFFFFC.00000000	64-Bit Kernel Heap segkmem
0x00000302.00000000	
0x00000300.00000000	File System Cache segmap
0x000002A7.50000000	
	Pageable Kernel Mem. segkp
0x000002A1.00000000	
0x00000000.FFFFFFFF	Open Boot Prom
0x00000000.F0000000	
	Kernel Debugger
0x00000000.EDD00000	
0x00000000.07c00000	32-Bit Kernel Heap segkmem32
0x00000000.07800200	
	Panic Message Buffer
0x00000000.07800000	
	Kernel TSB
0x00000000.01900000	
	sun4u HAT Structures Small TSB & Map Blks — (4 Mbytes) (1 x 4-Mbyte Page)
	Kernel Data Segment
0x00000000.01800000	
	Kernel Text Segment — (8 Mbytes)
	Trap Table — (2 x 4-Mbyte Page)
0x00000000.01000000	
	Invalid
0x0	

Figure A.2 Solaris 10 sun4u 64-Bit Kernel Address Space

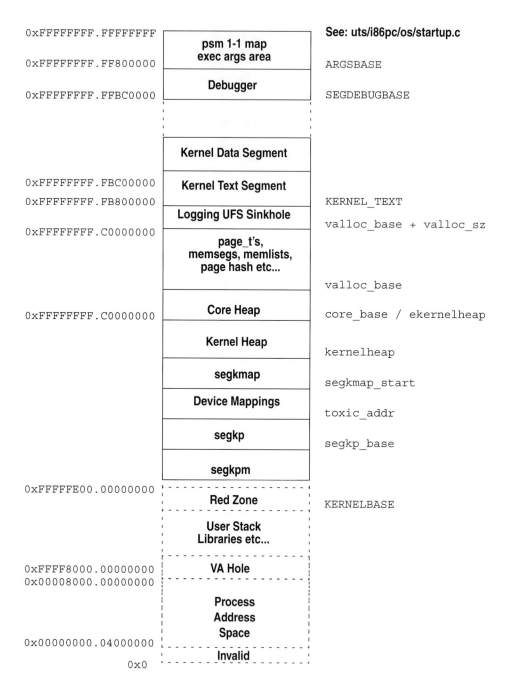

Figure A.3 Solaris 10 amd64 64-Bit Kernel Address Space

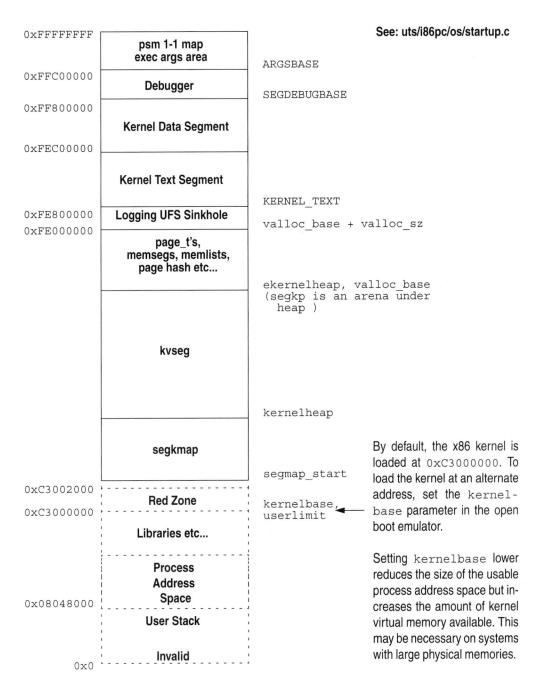

See: uts/i86pc/os/startup.c

0xFFFFFFFF	psm 1-1 map / exec args area — ARGSBASE
0xFFC00000	Debugger — SEGDEBUGBASE
0xFF800000	Kernel Data Segment
0xFEC00000	Kernel Text Segment
0xFE800000	Logging UFS Sinkhole — KERNEL_TEXT / valloc_base + valloc_sz
0xFE000000	page_t's, memsegs, memlists, page hash etc...
	kvseg — ekernelheap, valloc_base (segkp is an arena under heap)
	kernelheap
	segkmap
0xC3002000	segmap_start
0xC3000000	Red Zone — kernelbase, userlimit
	Libraries etc...
0x08048000	Process Address Space
	User Stack
0x0	Invalid

By default, the x86 kernel is loaded at 0xC3000000. To load the kernel at an alternate address, set the kernel-base parameter in the open boot emulator.

Setting kernelbase lower reduces the size of the usable process address space but increases the amount of kernel virtual memory available. This may be necessary on systems with large physical memories.

Figure A.4 Solaris 10 x86 32-Bit Kernel Address Space

Adding a System Call to Solaris

Contributed by Eric Schrock

In this appendix, we provide an example of how to add a system call to Solaris.

B.1 Setting Kernel Parameters

For the purposes of this appendix, we will assume that it's a simple system call that lives in the generic kernel code, and we'll put the code into an existing file to avoid having to deal with Makefiles. The goal is to print an arbitrary message to the console whenever the system call is issued.

B.1.1 Picking a Syscall Number

Before writing any real code, we first have to pick a number that will represent our system call. The main source of documentation here is syscall.h, which describes all the available system call numbers, as well as which ones are reserved. The maximum number of syscalls is currently 256 (NSYSCALL), which doesn't leave much space for new ones. This could theoretically be extended—I believe the hard limit is in the size of sysset_t, whose 16 integers must be able to represent a complete bitmask of all system calls. This puts our actual limit at 16*32, or 512, system calls. But for the purposes of this example, we'll pick system call number 56, which is currently unused. For my own amusement, we'll name our system call 'schrock.' So first we add the following line to `syscall.h`.

```
#define SYS_uadmin      55
#define SYS_schrock     56
#define SYS_utssys      57
```

See usr/src/uts/common/sys/syscall.h

B.1.2 Writing the Syscall Handler

Next, we have to actually add the function that will get called when we invoke the system call. What we should really do is add a new file `schrock.c` to `usr/src/uts/common/syscall.c`, but instead, we'll just use code from getpid.c.

```
#include <sys/cmn_err.h>

int
schrock(void *arg)
{
        char    buf[1024];
        size_t  len;

        if (copyinstr(arg, buf, sizeof (buf), &len) != 0)
                return (set_errno(EFAULT));

        cmn_err(CE_WARN, "%s", buf);

        return (0);
}
```

Note that declaring a buffer of 1024 bytes on the stack is a very bad thing to do in the kernel. We have limited stack space, and a stack overflow will result in a panic. We also don't check that the length of the string was less than our scratch space. But this will suffice for illustrative purposes. The `cmn_err()` function is the simplest way to display messages from the kernel.

B.1.3 Adding an Entry to the Syscall Table

We need to place an entry in the system call table. This table lives in `sysent.c`, and makes heavy use of macros to simplify the source. Our system call takes a single argument and returns an integer, so we'll need to use the `SYSENT_CI` macro. We need to add a prototype for our syscall, and add an entry to the sysent and `sysent32` tables.

```
int     rename();
void    rexit();
int     schrock();
int     semsys();
int     setgid();
```

continues

```
/* ... */
          /* 54 */ SYSENT_CI("ioctl",              ioctl,       3),
          /* 55 */ SYSENT_CI("uadmin",             uadmin,      3),
          /* 56 */ SYSENT_CI("schrock",            schrock,     1),
          /* 57 */ IF_LP64(
                   SYSENT_2CI("utssys",            utssys64,    4),
                   SYSENT_2CI("utssys",            utssys32,    4)),

/* ... */
          /* 54 */ SYSENT_CI("ioctl",              ioctl,       3),
          /* 55 */ SYSENT_CI("uadmin",             uadmin,      3),
          /* 56 */ SYSENT_CI("schrock",            schrock,     1),
          /* 57 */ SYSENT_2CI("utssys",            utssys32,    4),
```

See usr/src/uts/common/os/sysent.c

B.1.4 Updating `/etc/name_to_sysnum`

At this point, we could write a program to invoke our system call, but the point here is to illustrate everything that needs to be done to integrate a system call, so we can't ignore the little things. One of these little things is /etc/name_to_sysnum, which provides a mapping between system call names and numbers, and is used by dtrace(1M), truss(1), and friends. Of course, there is one version for x86 and one for SPARC, so you will have to add the following lines to both the Intel and SPARC versions.

```
ioctl              54
uadmin             55
schrock            56
utssys             57
fdsync             58
```

See /etc/name_to_sysnum

B.1.5 Updating `truss(1)`

Truss does fancy decoding of system call arguments. In order to do this, we need to maintain a table in truss that describes the type of each argument for every syscall. This table is found in systable.c. Since our syscall takes a single string, we add the following entry:

```
{"ioctl",       3, DEC, NOV, DEC, IOC, IOA},           /* 54 */
{"uadmin",      3, DEC, NOV, DEC, DEC, DEC},           /* 55 */
{"schrock",     1, DEC, NOV, STG},                     /* 56 */
{"utssys",      4, DEC, NOV, HEX, DEC, UTS, HEX},      /* 57 */
{"fdsync",      2, DEC, NOV, DEC, FFG},                /* 58 */
```

See usr/src/cmd/truss/systable.c

Don't worry too much about the different constants. But be sure to read up on the truss source code if you're adding a complicated system call.

B.1.6 Updating `proc_names.c`

This is the file that gets missed the most often when adding a new syscall. Libproc uses the table in proc_names.c to translate between system call numbers and names. Why it doesn't make use of /etc/name_to_sysnum is anybody's guess, but for now you have to update the systable array in this file:

```
        "ioctl",                /* 54 */
        "uadmin",               /* 55 */
        "schrock",              /* 56 */
        "utssys",               /* 57 */
        "fdsync",               /* 58 */
                          See usr/src/lib/libproc/common/proc_names.c
```

B.1.7 Putting It All Together

Finally, everything is in place. We can test our system call with a simple program:

```
#include <sys/syscall.h>

int
main(int argc, char **argv)
{
        syscall(SYS_schrock, "OpenSolaris Rules!");
        return (0);
}
```

If we run this on our system, we'll see the following output on the console:

```
June 14 13:42:21 halcyon genunix: WARNING: OpenSolaris Rules!
```

Because we did all the extra work, we can actually observe the behavior using `truss(1)`, `mdb(1)`, or `dtrace(1M)`.

A Sample Procfs Utility

C.1 Microstate Accounting Using /proc

```
$ msacct ls -1R
.:
total 3012
drwxrwxrwx   9 jmauro    tech         2560 Oct 22 13:02 2.X
[a LOT of output snipped]

*** Usage Counters ***
        Minor Faults:.................0
        Major Faults:.................0
        Swaps:........................0
        Input Blocks:.................0
        Output Blocks:................0
        STREAMS Messages Sent:........0
        STREAMS Messages Received:....0
        Signals:......................0
        Voluntary Context Switches:...1684
        Involuntary Context Switches:.25
        System Calls:.................3693
        Read/Write Characters:........53305
*** State Times ***
        Total Elapsed Time:...........11.065
        Total User Time:..............0.403
        Total System Time:............0.429
        Other System Trap Time:.......0.000
        Text Page Fault Sleep Time....0.000
        Data Page Fault Sleep Time....0.000
        Kernel Page Fault Sleep Time..0.000
        User Lock Wait Sleep Time.....0.000
        All Other Sleep Time..........10.201
        Time Waiting for a CPU........0.038
        Stopped Time..................0.000
```

C.2 Source Code for `msacct`

```
/*
 * Run a command and print all field resource
 * usage and microstat accounting fields when process terminates.
 *
 * Borrowed largely from ptime.c
 * (Thanks Roger Faulkner and Mike Shapiro)
 *
 * Usage: msacct command
 *
 */

#include <sys/types.h>
#include <sys/time.h>
#include <procfs.h>
#include <stdio.h>
#include <stdlib.h>
#include <unistd.h>
#include <fcntl.h>
#include <string.h>
#include <errno.h>
#include <math.h>
#include <wait.h>
#include <signal.h>

static          int        look(pid_t);
static          void        hr_min_sec(char *, long);
static          void        prtime(char *, timestruc_t *);
static          int        perr(const char *);

static          void        tsadd(timestruc_t *result, timestruc_t *a, timestruc_t *b);
static          void        tssub(timestruc_t *result, timestruc_t *a, timestruc_t *b);

static          char        *command;
static          char        procname[64];

main(int argc, char **argv)
{
        pid_t pid;
        struct siginfo info;
        int status;

        if ((command = strrchr(argv[0], ,Äô/‚Äô)) != NULL)
                command++;
        else
                command = argv[0];

        if (argc <= 1) {
                (void) fprintf(stderr,
                        "usage:%s command [ args ... ]\n", command);
                (void) fprintf(stderr,
                        "  (time a command using microstate accounting)\n");
                return (1);
        }

        switch (pid = fork()) {
        case -1:
                (void) fprintf(stderr, "%s: cannot fork\n", command);
                return (2);
        case 0:
                /* newly created child process */

                (void) execvp(argv[1], &argv[1]);
```

```
                        (void) fprintf(stderr, "%s: exec failed\n", command);
                        if (errno == ENOENT)
                                _exit(127);
                        else
                                _exit(126);
                }

        (void) sprintf("%d", procname, (int)pid);          /* for perr() */
        (void) signal(SIGINT, SIG_IGN);
        (void) signal(SIGQUIT, SIG_IGN);
        (void) waitid(P_PID, pid, &info, WEXITED | WNOWAIT);

        (void) look(pid);

        (void) waitpid(pid, &status, 0);

        if (WIFEXITED(status))
                return (WEXITSTATUS(status));
        else
                return ((status & ~WCOREFLG) | 0200);
}

static int
look(pid_t pid)
{
        char pathname[100];
        int rval = 0;
        int fd;
        prusage_t prusage;
        timestruc_t real, user, sys;
        prusage_t *pup = &prusage;

        (void) sprintf(pathname, "/proc/%d/usage", (int)pid);
        if ((fd = open(pathname, O_RDONLY)) < 0)
                return (perr("open usage"));

        if (read(fd, &prusage, sizeof (prusage)) != sizeof (prusage))
                rval = perr("read usage");
        else {
                real = pup->pr_term;
                tssub(&real, &real, &pup->pr_create);
                user = pup->pr_utime;
                sys = pup->pr_stime;
                tsadd(&sys, &sys, &pup->pr_ttime);
                (void) fprintf(stderr, "\n");
                printf("*** Usage Counters *** \n");
                printf("Minor Faults:................%ld\n", pup->pr_minf);
                printf("Major Faults:................%ld\n", pup->pr_majf);
                printf("Swaps:.......................%ld\n", pup->pr_nswap);
                printf("Input Blocks:................%ld\n", pup->pr_inblk);
                printf("Output Blocks:...............%ld\n", pup->pr_oublk);
                printf("STREAMS Messages Sent:.......%ld\n", pup->pr_msnd);
                printf("STREAMS Messages Received:...%ld\n", pup->pr_mrcv);
                printf("Signals:.....................%ld\n", pup->pr_sigs);
                printf("Voluntary Context Switches:..%ld\n", pup->pr_vctx);
                printf("Involuntary Context Switches:.%ld\n", pup->pr_ictx);
                printf("System Calls:................%ld\n", pup->pr_sysc);
                printf("Read/Write Characters:.......%ld\n", pup->pr_ioch);
                printf("*** State Times *** \n");
                prtime("Total Elapsed Time:..........", &real);
                prtime("Total User Time:.............", &user);
                prtime("Total System Time:...........", &sys);
                prtime("Other System Trap Time:......", &pup->pr_ttime);
                prtime("Text Page Fault Sleep Time....", &pup->pr_tftime);
                prtime("Data Page Fault Sleep Time....", &pup->pr_dftime);
                prtime("Kernel Page Fault Sleep Time..", &pup->pr_kftime);
```

```
                prtime("User Lock Wait Sleep Time.....", &pup->pr_ltime);
                prtime("All Other Sleep Time..........", &pup->pr_slptime);
                prtime("Time Waiting for a CPU........", &pup->pr_wtime);
                prtime("Stopped Time..................", &pup->pr_stoptime);
        }

        (void) close(fd);
        return (rval);
}

static void
hr_min_sec(char *buf, long sec)
{
        if (sec >= 3600)
                (void) sprintf(buf, "%ld:%.2ld:%.2ld",
                        sec / 3600, (sec % 3600) / 60, sec % 60);
        else if (sec >= 60)
                (void) sprintf(buf, "%ld:%.2ld",
                        sec / 60, sec % 60);
        else {
                (void) sprintf(buf, "%ld", sec);
        }
}

static void
prtime(char *name, timestruc_t *ts)
{
        char buf[32];

        hr_min_sec(buf, ts->tv_sec);
        (void) fprintf(stderr, "%s%s.%.3u\n",
                name, buf, (u_int)ts->tv_nsec/1000000);
}

static int
perr(const char *s)
{
        if (s)
                (void) fprintf(stderr, "%s: ", procname);
        else
                s = procname;
        perror(s);
        return (1);
}

static void
tsadd(timestruc_t *result, timestruc_t *a, timestruc_t *b)
{
        result->tv_sec = a->tv_sec + b->tv_sec;
        if ((result->tv_nsec = a->tv_nsec + b->tv_nsec) >= 1000000000) {
                result->tv_nsec -= 1000000000;
                result->tv_sec += 1;
        }
}

static void
tssub(timestruc_t *result, timestruc_t *a, timestruc_t *b)
{
        result->tv_sec = a->tv_sec - b->tv_sec;
        if ((result->tv_nsec = a->tv_nsec - b->tv_nsec) < 0) {
                result->tv_nsec += 1000000000;
                result->tv_sec -= 1;
        }
}
```

Bibliography

1. Bach, M. J., *The Design of the UNIX Operating System*, Prentice Hall, 1986.

2. Bonwick, J., *The Slab Allocator: An Object-Caching Kernel Memory Allocator.* Sun Microsystems, Inc. White paper.

3. Bourne, S. R., *The UNIX System*, Addison-Wesley, 1983.

4. Catanzaro, B., *Multiprocessor System Architectures*, Prentice Hall, 1994.

5. Cockcroft, A., *Sun Performance and Tuning—Java and the Internet,* 2nd Edition, Sun Microsystems Press/Prentice Hall, 1998.

6. Cockcroft, A., *CPU Time Measurement Errors*, Computer Measurement Group Paper 2038, 1998.

7. Cypress Semiconductor, *The CY7C601 SPARC RISC Users Guide*, Ross Technology, 1990.

8. Drake, C. and Brown, K., *Panic! UNIX System Crash Dump Analysis*, Prentice Hall, 1995.

9. Eykholt, J. R., et al., *Beyond Multiprocessing—Multithreading the SunOS Kernel*, Summer '92 USENIX Conference Proceedings.

10. Gingell, R. A., Moran, J. P., Shannon, W. A., *Virtual Memory Architecture in SunOS*, Proceedings of the Summer 1987 USENIX Conference.

11. Goodheart, B., Cox, J., *The Magic Garden Explained—The Internals of UNIX System V Release 4*, Prentice Hall, 1994.

12. Hoffman, F. "Crash Dump Analysis for x86/x64," http://www.genunix.org, 2005.

13. Hwang, K., Xu, Z., *Scalable Parallel Computing*, McGraw-Hill, 1998.

14. Intel Corp., *The Intel Architecture Software Programmers Manual, Volumes 1, 2 and 3*, Intel Part Numbers 243190, 24319102, and 24319202, 1993.

15. Johnstone, Mark S. and Wilson, Paul R. *The Memory Fragmentation Problem: Solved?* ISMM'98 Proceedings of the ACM SIGPLAN International Symposium on Memory Management, pp. 26-36. Available at ftp://ftp.dcs.gla.ac.uk/pub/drastic/gc/wilson.ps.

16. Kleiman, S. R., *Vnodes: An Architecture for Multiple File System Types in Sun UNIX*, Proceedings of Summer 1986 Usenix Conference.

17. Kleiman, S., Shah, D., Smaalders, B., *Programming with Threads*, Prentice Hall, SunSoft Press, 1996.

18. Knuth, D., *The Art of Computer Programming: Fundamental Algorithms*, Addison Wesley, 1973.

19. Leffler, S. J., McKusick, M. K., Karels, M. J., Quarterman, J. S., *The Design and Implementation of the 4.3BSD UNIX Operating System*, Addison-Wesley, 1989.

20. Lewis, B., Berg, D. J., *Threads Primer. A Guide to Multithreaded Programming*, SunSoft Press/Prentice Hall, 1996.

21. Lewis, B., Berg, D. J., *Multithreaded Programming with Pthreads*. Sun Microsystems Press/Prentice Hall. 1998

22. McKusick, M. K., Bostic, K., Karels, M. J., Quarterman, J. S., *The Design and Implementation of the 4.4 BSD Operating System*, Addison-Wesley, 1996.

23. McKusick, M. K., Joy, W., Leffler, S., Fabry, R., *A Fast File System for UNIX*, ACM Transactions on Computer Systems, 2(3):181–197, August 1984.

24. Moran, J. P., *SunOS Virtual Memory Implementation*, Proceedings of 1988 EUUG Conference.

25. Pfister, G., *In Search of Clusters*, Prentice Hall, 1998.

26. Rosenthal, David S., *Evolving the Vnode Interface*, Proceedings of Summer 1990 USENIX Conference.

27. Schimmel, C., *UNIX Systems for Modern Architectures*, Addison-Wesley, 1994.

28. Seltzer, M., Bostic, K., McKusick, M., Staelin, C. *An Implementation of a Log-Structured File System for UNIX*, Proceedings of the Usenix Winter Conference, January 1993.

29. Shah, D. K., Zolnowsky, J., *Evolving the UNIX Signal Model for Lightweight Threads*, Sun Proprietary/Confidential Internal Use Only, White paper, SunSoft TechConf '96.

30. Snyder, P., *tmpfs: A Virtual Memory File System*, Sun Microsystems White paper.

31. SPARC International, *System V Application Binary Interface—SPARC Version 9 Processor Supplement*, 1997.

32. Sun Microsystems, *Writing Device Drivers—Part Number 805-3024-10*, Sun Microsystems, 1998

33. Sun Microsystems, *STREAMS Programming Guide—Part Number 805-4038-10*, Sun Microsystems, 1998

34. Sun Microsystems, *UltraSPARC Microprocessor Users Manual—Part Number 802-7220*, Sun Microsystems, 1995.

35. Stevens, W. R., *Advanced Programming in the UNIX Environment*, Addison-Wesley, 1992.

36. Stevens, W. R., *UNIX Network Programming, Volume 2. Interprocess Communication, Second Edition*. Addison-Wesley, 1998.

37. Swain, P., Softway. Personal communication.

38. Talluri, M., *Use of Superpages and subblOcking in the Address Translation Hierarchy*, Thesis for the doctorate of computer science, University of Wisconsin, 1995.

39. Tanenbaum, A. *Operating Systems: Design and Implementation*. Prentice Hall, 1987.

40. Taylor, R., Veritas Software. Personal communication.

41. Tucker, A., *Scheduler Activations*, PSARC 1996/021, Sun Internal Proprietary Document. March, 1996.

42. Tucker, A., *Scheduler Activations in Solaris*, SunSoft TechConf '96. Sun Proprietary/Confidential—Internal Use Only Document.

43. Tucker, A., Private Communication.

44. UNIX Software Operation, *System V Application Binary Interface—UNIX System V*. Prentice Hall/UNIX Press. 1990.

45. Vahalia, U., *UNIX Internals—The New Frontiers*, Prentice Hall, 1996.

46. Van der Linden, P., *Expert C Programming—Deep C Secrets*, SunSoft Press/Prentice Hall, 1994.

47. Weaver, D., Germond, T. (editors), *The SPARC Architecture Manual, Version 9*, Prentice Hall, 1994.

48. Weinstock, C. B. and Wulf, W. A., *QuickFit: An Efficient Algorithm for Heap Storage Allocation*. ACM SIGPLAN Notices, v.23, no. 10, pp. 141–144 (1988).

49. Wilson, P. R, Johnstone, M. S., Neely, M., Boles D., *Dynamic Storage Allocation: A Survey and Critical Review. Proceedings of the International Workshop on MemoryManagement*, September 1995. Available at `http://citeseer.nj.nec.com/wilson95dynamic.html`.

50. Wong, B., *Configuration and Capacity Planning on Sun Solaris Servers*, Sun Microsystems Press/Prentice Hall, 1996.

51. Zaks, R., *Programming the Z80*, Sybex Computer Books, 1982.

Index

solaris™

TEN MOVES AHEAD

1. APPLICATIONS CAN RUN UP TO 30 TIMES FASTER

2. ACCESS TO OPENSOLARIS™ AND OVER 1,600 PATENTS

3. IP INDEMNIFICATION

4. REAL TIME APPLICATION DEBUGGING WITH SOLARIS™ DYNAMIC TRACING

5. AUTOMATED WORKLOAD MANAGEMENT WITH SOLARIS CONTAINERS

6. AUTOMATED AVAILABILITY SERVICES WITH PREDICTIVE SELF-HEALING

7. WORLD'S MOST ADVANCED SECURITY FEATURES— BUILT IN

8. SAME OS ON MORE THAN 360 SPARC® AMD OPTERON,™ AND INTEL SYSTEMS

9. ACCESS TO 85% OF FORTUNE 500 IT ORGANIZATIONS, RUNNING THE SOLARIS OS

10. APPLICATIONS GUARANTEED FROM RELEASE TO RELEASE, PLATFORM TO PLATFORM*

MOVE AHEAD TODAY AT:
SUN.COM/SOLARIS10

Sun
microsystems
The Network is the Computer

FOR MORE INFORMATION ON SUN MICROSYSTEMS PRESS, VISIT WWW.SUN.COM/BOOKS

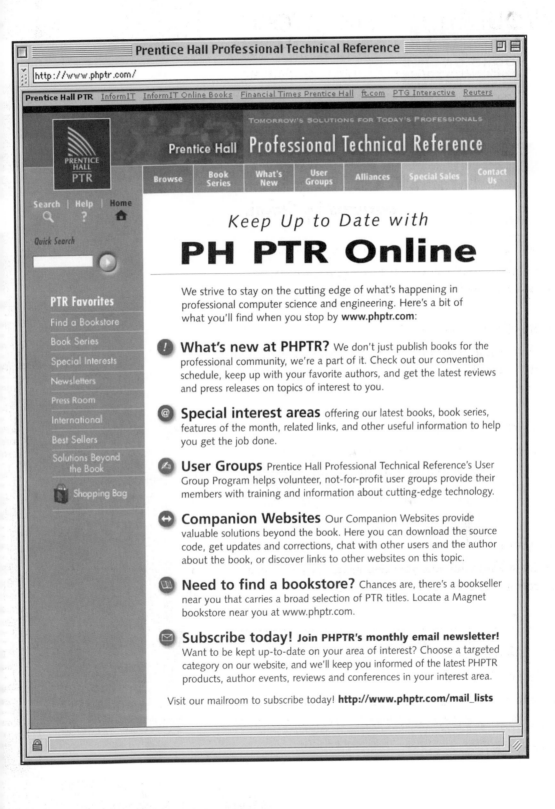